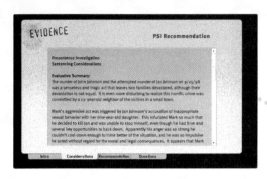

Listen

"Listen" icons explore additional key concepts with audio notes that help clarify important concepts that often cause confusion for students.

Evidence

"Evidence" icons provide resources, such as illustrations and synopses from popular movies, to reinforce and expand concepts in the text.

Visualize

"Visualize" icons in the E-Book provide additional notes and information on key topics in the text through the use of maps, graphs, and diagrams.

Assessments and Individualized Study Plan

MyCrimeLab provides students with multiple assessment opportunities within each chapter. This integrated quizzing and testing program, combined with the students' individualized study plan, helps students focus their efforts where they're needed most. The five assessment features are Pre-Test, Post-Test, Practice, Exam, and Individualized Study Plan.

Homework

Homework links take students to homework assignments. Each assignment is based on the media in the textbook. The Homework feature is a great way to integrate technology into the classroom. Homework assignments include: watching video clips, reading "In the News" articles, and more!

Research Navigator™

Research Navigator™ is the easiest way to start a research assignment. This comprehensive research tool gives users access to four exclusive databases of authoritative and reliable source material. Databases include: EBSCO's Content Select, *The New York Times, Financial Times,* and Link Library.

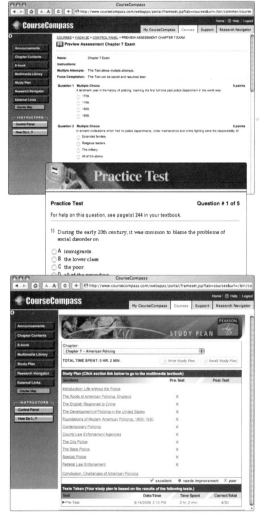

Screen content is representative.

 VISUALIZE WATCH LISTEN EVIDENCE PRE-TEST PRACTICE POST-TEST EXAM INVESTIGATE

One place. **Everything** your students need to succeed.

www.mycrimelab.com

Juvenile Delinquency

Frank Schmalleger

Emeritus, University of North Carolina

Clemens Bartollas

University of Northern Iowa

PEARSON

Boston ■ New York ■ San Francisco

Mexico City ■ Montreal ■ Toronto ■ London ■ Madrid ■ Munich ■ Paris

Hong Kong ■ Singapore ■ Tokyo ■ Cape Town ■ Sydney

To our beautiful daughters, Kristin Bartollas Polatty and
Nicole Schmalleger Solano

Series Editor: David E. Repetto
Editorial Assistant: Jack Cashman
Senior Marketing Manager: Kelly May
Senior Production Administrator: Donna Simons
Composition Buyer: Linda Cox
Manufacturing Buyer: Debbie Rossi
Cover Administrator and Designer: Joel Gendron
Editorial Production Service: Publishers' Design and Production Services, Inc.
Electronic Composition: Publishers' Design and Production Services, Inc.
Interior Design: Carol Somberg
Photo Research: Katharine S. Cebik

For related titles and support materials, visit our online catalog at
www.ablongman.com.

Library of Congress Cataloging-in-Publication Data
Schmalleger, Frank.
    Juvenile delinquency / Frank Schmalleger, Clemens Bartollas
        p.   cm.
    "Frank Schmalleger and Clemens Bartollas . . . together . . . coauthor this new and
substantially updated version of Bartollas's well-known text, *Juvenile Delinquency*"—
Preface.
    Includes bibliographical references and index.
    ISBN 0-205-51524-X
    1. Juvenile delinquency—United States. I. Bartollas, Clemens. II. Title.

HV9104.S32275 2008
364.360973—dc22   2006052706

Instructor's Annotated Edition ISBN 0-205-52562-8

Photo credits appear on page 613, which constitutes an extension of the copyright page.

Printed in the United States of America

10   9   8   7   6   5   4   3   RRD-OH   11   10   09

Contents

CHAPTER 2

CHAPTER 4

CHAPTER 5

CHAPTER 6

part THREE

Environmental Influences on Delinquency   210

CHAPTER 7

CHAPTER 8

CHAPTER 9

Gangs and Delinquency   322

CHAPTER 11

part FOUR

Preventing and Controlling Delinquency 404

CHAPTER 12

CHAPTER 14

CHAPTER 15

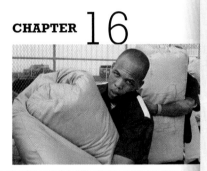

Preface

In late 2006, the nation's police chiefs, mayors, and other government officials met in Washington, D.C., to participate in a National Violent Crime Summit. Although violent crime had been dropping for almost a decade, officials at the meeting talked about new FBI statistics that may presage the end of that decline and a resurgence in some forms of violence—especially violent crime by juveniles. The central topic of concern was "a growing trend of teenagers shooting robbery victims even if they surrender their valuables."* Cincinnati Police Chief Thomas Streicher gave voice to what many others already knew: "There's almost a different code on the streets, that it's not a robbery unless you shoot somebody."

Juvenile delinquency—crimes committed by young people—constitutes, by recent estimates, nearly one-third of the property crimes and one-sixth of all crimes against persons in the United States. Not only does the relativity high incidence of juvenile crime make the study of juvenile delinquency vital to any understanding of American society today, but special kinds of violent offenses—such as gang killings tied to perceived slights or imagined signs of "disrespect"—are on the upswing. Los Angeles police chief William Bratton, one of the attendees at the Washington summit, told meeting participants, "Crime is coming back, and it has a new and troubling element—a youthful population that is largely disassociated from the mainstream of America."

Frank Schmalleger and Clemens Bartollas, who were classmates and friends at The Ohio State University during their Ph.D. studies, have joined together to coauthor this new and substantially updated version of Bartollas's well-known text, *Juvenile Delinquency*, which was published in seven editions.

The authors believe that students and instructors alike will find the following features especially helpful in understanding delinquency today, and in preparing society to deal with it:

- A strong sociological focus throughout the text. The root causes of delinquency, along with the environments in which it either flourishes or is discouraged—including family, school, peers, and community—receive major emphasis.
- A theme of delinquency across the life course, which is one of the most promising and exciting perspectives in the study of delinquency. This theme helps students understand how delinquent behavior originates and then either continues and evolves into adult criminality or terminates.
- Special attention to desistance, which dovetails with the examination of behavior across the life course. Some individuals persist in antisocial behavior throughout life, whereas others make the decision to end their involvement in antisocial behavior and to become law-abiding citizens. This book helps identify what young people in given circumstances are likely to do.
- A series of interviews with significant spokespersons representing various theoretical perspectives in the study of juvenile delinquency. These boxed interviews, called *Voices Across the Profession*, highlight the cumulative knowledge of such insightful crime and delinquency scholars as Albert K. Cohen, Donald R. Cressey, Karen Heimer, John H. Laub, Travis Hirschi, David Matza, Terrie E. Moffitt, and Richard Quinney.
- An emphasis on the important roles that gender, race, social class, and place of residence play in the formative adolescent years. Specifically, Chapter 7 examines gender and delinquency, while race and ethnicity receive attention in Chapter 13.

---

*Richard Willing, "Violent Crime on the Rise, Summit Participants Say," *USA Today*, August 31, 2006, p. 5A.

- Discussion of gangs and gang activity. Gangs, an increasingly important aspect of juvenile offending, are given special coverage, with significant discussion of groups such as *Mara Salvatrucha,* or MS-13.
- Substantial policy-oriented analyses. In the midst of national soul-searching about what to do with serious and repeat juvenile offenders, nearly every chapter of this text offers policy recommendations on prevention and suggests possible treatment interventions.

Organization of the Text

This text is divided into four parts: The Nature and Extent of Delinquency, The Causes of Delinquency, Environmental Influences on Delinquency, and Preventing and Controlling Delinquency.

- Part One explores how delinquent behavior affects the larger society and reports on the measurement of the nature and extent of delinquency by examining the available statistical tools.
- Part Two looks at four types of explanations for delinquent behavior: (1) individual causes, ranging from free will to biological and psychological positivism; (2) social structural factors; (3) social process factors; and (4) social reaction theories.
- Part Three examines the relationship between delinquency and gender; problems in the family, such as child neglect and abuse; experiences in the school; peer and gang delinquency; and drug abuse.
- Part Four looks at primary, secondary, and tertiary prevention of delinquency and programs aimed at delinquency control. It also includes an overview of the juvenile justice process encompassing police–juvenile relations, the juvenile court, community-based corrections, and institutions for juveniles.

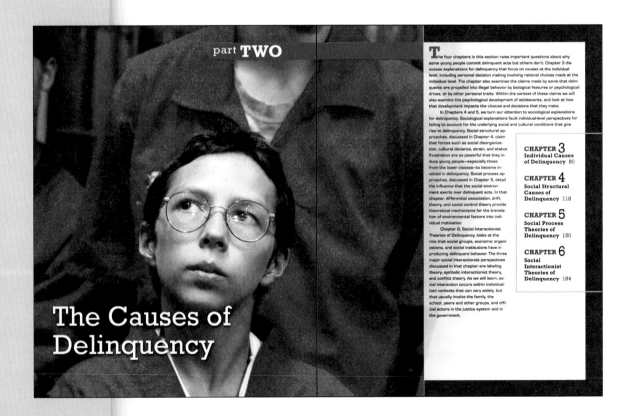

part **TWO**

The four chapters in this section raise important questions about why some young people commit delinquent acts but others don't. Chapter 3 discusses explanations for delinquency that focus on causes at the individual level, including personal decision making involving rational choices made at the individual level. The chapter also examines the claims made by some that delinquents are propelled into illegal behavior by biological features or psychological drives, or by other personal traits. Within the context of these claims we will also examine the psychological development of adolescents, and look at how that development impacts the choices and decisions that they make.

In Chapters 4 and 5, we turn our attention to sociological explanations for delinquency. Sociological explanations fault individual-level perspectives for failing to account for the underlying social and cultural conditions that give rise to delinquency. Social structural approaches, discussed in Chapter 4, claim that forces such as social disorganization, cultural deviance, strain, and status frustration are so powerful that they induce young people—especially those from the lower classes—to become involved in delinquency. Social process approaches, discussed in Chapter 5, detail the influence that the social environment exerts over delinquent acts. In that chapter, differential association, drift theory, and social control theory provide theoretical mechanisms for the translation of environmental factors into individual motivation.

Chapter 6, Social Interactionist Theories of Delinquency, looks at the role that social groups, economic organizations, and social institutions have in producing delinquent behavior. The three major social interactionist perspectives discussed in that chapter are labeling theory, symbolic interactionist theory, and conflict theory. As we will learn, social interaction occurs within individualized contexts that can vary widely, but that usually involve the family, the school, peers and other groups, and official actors in the justice system and in the government.

CHAPTER **3**
Individual Causes of Delinquency 80

CHAPTER **4**
Social Structural Causes of Delinquency 118

CHAPTER **5**
Social Process Theories of Delinquency 150

CHAPTER **6**
Social Interactionist Theories of Delinquency 184

The Causes of Delinquency

Special Features

This text contains a number of special features that students should find especially helpful in understanding juvenile delinquency, including its causes, consequences, deterrence, prevention, and treatment. These features are:

- **Two types of news story boxes.** Real-life, up-to-the-minute news stories from such respectable sources as *USA Today*, the *New York Times*, *Science News*, and the international media focusing on both national and transnational events related to juvenile delinquency are found in every chapter of the text. Two types of boxes, *Delinquency in America* and *Delinquency International*, provide insights into events shaping social policy toward delinquency both at home and abroad. The text includes stories describing how disruptive youths grow into violent behavior, how sparing the rod might actually improve the child, how American cities today are dealing with crime by juveniles, how programs for minority youths are making a difference, and how concern in England, Japan, and Russia is focused on reducing delinquency.

- **Interview boxes.** The *Voices Across the Profession* boxes, found in many of the text's chapters, include interviews with experts in understanding juvenile behavior and delinquency. Notable contributors to our contemporary understanding of delinquency, such as John H. Laub, Terrie E. Moffitt, Albert K. Cohen, Donald R. Cressey, Karen Heimer, Richard Quinney, and Meda Chesney-Lind, are interviewed on topics as diverse as life-course theory, gangs, adolescent self-image, and delinquency prevention and control.

- **Four types of thematic boxes.** This book builds on three exciting themes, each represented by boxes found in the text: delinquency across the life course, social context, and social policy. Life-course theory, which is also called life-course criminology or the life-course perspective, is detailed in a series of *Across the Life Course* boxes. The social context of delinquency, which refers to the settings and situations in which young people find themselves, is brought to life through our series of *Social World of the Delinquent* boxes. Social policy concerns are illustrated in boxes titled *Focus on Social Policy* and *Juvenile Law*.

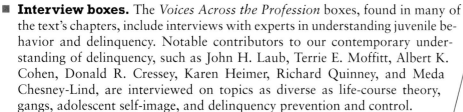

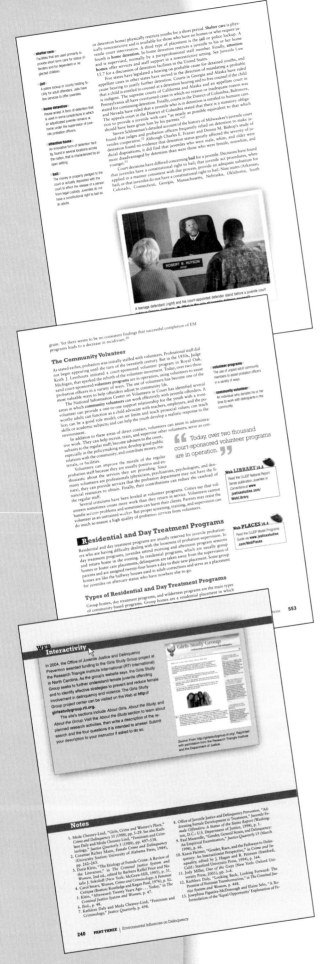

■ **Marginal glossary terms and a comprehensive end-of-book glossary.** Key terms and their definitions are found throughout the book in the margins, and a comprehensive end-of-book glossary makes it easy for students to learn the terminology used by professionals who work with delinquents. The Glossary incorporates selected terms adapted from the FBI's *Uniform Crime Reporting Handbook*, the *Juvenile Court Statistics* report series, and the Census of Juveniles in Residential Placement. The National Center for Juvenile Justice's *State Juvenile Justice Profiles* was also influential in determining the content of selected definitions.

■ **Web features.** An outstanding assortment of Web-based resources complement the text and are found in the margin or at the end of chapters for ease of access. Included here are *Web Library* and *Web Places* features. Web Library items consist of documents found on the Web that are available as supplements to the discussions in the text. Web Library documents include publications from the Office of Juvenile Justice and Delinquency Prevention (OJJDP), the National Institute of Justice (NIJ), the federal Office of Community Oriented Policing Services (COPS), and the National Institute on Drug Abuse (NIDA), as well as articles from some of the field's most notable journals. Web Places consist of websites of special relevance to the study of juvenile delinquency, and include sites such as the Office of Juvenile Justice and Delinquency Prevention, the Child Trends Databank, the Child Welfare Information Gateway of the U.S. Department of Health and Human Services, the National Youth Gang Center, the American Bar Association, the National Library of Medicine, and the Centers for Disease Control and Prevention.

■ **Web interactivity exercises.** *Web Interactivities* are informative Web-based, end-of-chapter assignments that ask students to use some the field's premier Internet resources to complete tasks that can be submitted to their instructors. Web interactivity sites include ChildStats.gov, the National Center for Juvenile Justice, the Project on Human Development in Chicago Neighborhoods, the Girls Study Group at North Carolina's Research Triangle Institute, the National Criminal Justice Reference Service, Homeboy Industries, and the National Council of Juvenile and Family Court Judges.

Supplements

A carefully designed supplements package supports the aims of *Juvenile Delinquency* and provides both students and instructors with a wealth of support materials to ensure success in teaching and in learning. Most student supplements are available free when packaged with the textbook so that students can benefit from them without incurring additional cost.

Instructor Resources

- **Instructor's Annotated Edition.** This special version of the text for instructors illustrates important aspects of the text and provides various teaching tools within the context of the text.
- **Instructor's Manual and Test Bank.** Each chapter in the Instructor's Manual contains Learning Objectives, Chapter Summaries, Lecture Outlines, Key Terms, and Classroom Activities and Assignments. Each chapter in the Test Bank includes a multitude of true/false, multiple-choice, short-answer, and essay questions.
- **TestGen EQ Computerized Testing Program.** This computerized version of the Test Bank is available with Tamarack's easy-to-use TestGen software, which lets you prepare both print and online tests. It provides full editing capability for Windows and Macintosh.
- **Blackboard and WebCT Test Item Files.** Both of these popular online learning platforms are available for use with the text.
- **PowerPoint™ Lecture Presentations.** This complete set of chapter-by-chapter PowerPoint presentations contains approximately twenty slides per chapter, specific to the text, to reinforce the text's central ideas.

Student Resources

- **Study Guide.** The Study Guide offers students a traditional format in which they can test their understanding of key material presented in the text through practice questions, key-concept review, and other tools.
- **MyCrimeLab—www.mycrimelab.com.** This interactive and instructive multimedia resource can be used as a supplement to the traditional lecture course, or to completely administer an online course. MyCrimeLab features a text-specific e-book with multimedia and assessment icons in the margins. These icons launch to exciting resources such as animations, video clips, audio explanations, and more. MyCrimeLab also features a unique assessment program including pre- and posttests, along with an Individualized Study Plan that helps students achieve success. Geared to meet the teaching and learning needs of every professor and student, MyCrimeLab is a valuable tool for any classroom setting.
- **Themes of the Times.** Approximately thirty current articles from *The New York Times* have been specially selected for their relevance to the topics covered in the text.
- **Research Navigator.** This handy reference guide covers the basics of Internet research for juvenile delinquency students. The guide includes access to an online database of thousands of academic journal and periodical articles as well as to *The New York Times*.

A Special Supplement: *Voices of Delinquency*

Voices of Delinquency, also available through Allyn & Bacon, is an additional resource for students interested in learning about the life experiences of delinquent youths. The real-life stories it contains range from those told by children who quickly turned their delinquent behavior around during their adolescent years and then lived exemplary lives as adults, to those related by delinquents who committed serious crimes such as murder and who are now serving life in prison. These fascinating and sometimes very sad stories reveal how the theoretical explanations in this textbook apply to the actual life experiences of delinquents.

Acknowledgments

Many individuals have made invaluable contributions to this text. Foremost we would like to thank our wives, Harmonie Star-Schmalleger and Linda Dippolid Bartollas. We are grateful to the many criminologists who consented to be interviewed, and who so graciously share their insights with our readers. Reviewers who participated in the preparation of this edition, and whose efforts we applaud, include Bonnie Black, Mesa Community College; Ruth X. Liu, San Diego State University; Jerome L. Neapolitan, Tennessee Technological University; and Theodore P. Skolnicki, Niagra Community College.

We are especially grateful to Gordon Armstrong for the care he took in polishing the final manuscript and in developing the PowerPoint presentations that accompany this book. A special thank-you goes to acquisitions editor David Repetto; senior production administrator Donna Simons; development editor Jennifer Jacobson; production manager Sue Brown; photo researcher Kate Cebik; project manager Lynda Griffiths; designer Carol Somberg; permissions editor Renee Nicholls; marketing manager Kelly May; marketing assistant Debbie Makucin; and Allyn & Bacon's point man, Jack Cashman, who fielded many issues and concerns as production unfolded. We also thank Betty Heine, Jerome VanDaele, and Jake Lancaster for their assistance in the office, and we very much appreciate the efforts of our supplements author, Thomas McAninch.

about the
Authors

Frank Schmalleger, Ph.D., is Distinguished Professor Emeritus at the University of North Carolina at Pembroke. He holds an undergraduate degree from the University of Notre Dame and both the master's (1970) and doctoral (1974) degrees, with special emphasis in sociology, from The Ohio State University. From 1976 to 1994, he taught criminology and criminal justice courses at the University of North Carolina at Pembroke. For the last sixteen of those years, he chaired the university's Department of Sociology, Social Work, and Criminal Justice. The university named him Distinguished Professor in 1991.

Dr. Schmalleger has taught in the online graduate program of the New School for Social Research, helping to build the world's first electronic classrooms in support of distance learning through computer telecommunications. As an adjunct professor with Webster University in St. Louis, Missouri, Dr. Schmalleger helped develop the university's graduate programs in both administration of justice and security administration and loss prevention. He taught courses in those curricula for more than a decade. A strong advocate of Web-based instruction, Dr. Schmalleger is also the creator of numerous award-winning websites.

Dr. Schmalleger is the author of numerous articles and more than thirty books, including the widely used *Criminal Justice: A Brief Introduction* (Prentice Hall, 2008), *Criminology Today* (Prentice Hall, 2006), *Criminal Law Today* (Prentice Hall, 2006), and *Corrections in the Twenty-First Century* (with John Smykla; McGraw-Hill, 2009). He is also founding editor of the journal *Criminal Justice Studies*, and has served as imprint adviser for Greenwood Publishing Group's criminal justice reference series. Visit the author's website at www.schmalleger.com.

Clemens Bartollas, Ph.D., is Professor of Sociology at the University of Northern Iowa. He holds a B.A. from Davis and Elkins College, a B.D. from Princeton Theological Seminary, an S.T.M. from San Francisco Theological Seminary, and a Ph.D. in sociology, with a special emphasis in criminology, from The Ohio State University. He taught at Pembroke State University from 1973 to 1975, Sangamon State University from 1975 to 1980, and at the University of Northern Iowa from 1981 to the present. He has received a number of honors at the University of Northern Iowa, including Distinguished Scholar, the Donald McKay Research Award, and the Regents' Award for Faculty Excellence. Dr. Bartollas, like his coauthor, is also the author of numerous articles and more than thirty books, including previous editions of *Juvenile Delinquency* (Allyn & Bacon, 2006), *Juvenile Justice in America* (with Stuart J. Miller, Prentice Hall, 2005), and *Women and the Criminal Justice System* (with Katherine Stuart van Wormer, Allyn & Bacon, 2007).

part ONE

The Nature
and Extent of
Delinquency

The study of juvenile delinquency is vitally important today, just as it was in the 1930s when sociologist Clifford R. Shaw first began using case studies to explore this exciting field. Later, Henry D. McKay, with colleagues at the University of Chicago, helped Shaw develop what became known as the Chicago Area Projects. In the Area Projects, which thrived throughout Chicago for fifty years, local neighborhoods took responsibility for the problems of youths, including juvenile crime.

Contemporary studies examine delinquency from the same three perspectives that brought focus to the work of Shaw and McKay. The first perspective reminds us that the study of delinquency is about delinquents—young people who frequently have disruptive home lives, struggle through school, become involved with troubled peers, and make poor decisions along the way. The second perspective focuses on such factors as the extent and scope of delinquency, the causes of delinquency, and how delinquency can be controlled. Finally, we magnify our approach to delinquency through the lens of social policy. The social policy perspective is concerned with how we can prevent and control delinquent behavior.

Our first chapter examines delinquency from within the larger framework of adolescence. Adolescents have differing life experiences, and some encounter more of life's problems than others. As we will see, those who experience more problems are more likely to engage in negative behaviors, including delinquency. In the first chapter, both delinquent and status offenses are defined, and attention is given to how the behavior of status offenders differs from that of delinquents. The chapter then turns to how delinquents have been perceived and handled in the United States, from colonial times to the present.

Our second chapter focuses on four subjects. The first is the extent and measurement of delinquent behavior. The chapter asks questions such as: How can delinquent behavior be measured? What do various methods of measurement contribute to our understanding of delinquency? How pervasive is delinquency? The chapter's second focus is on how delinquency varies by gender, race, ethnicity, and social class. The descriptive dimensions of delinquent behavior receive attention next, including age of onset, the escalation of offenses, the specialization of offenses, and chronic offending. Finally, Chapter 2 expands the concept of *delinquency through the life course*—one of the central themes of this text first introduced at the end of Chapter 1.

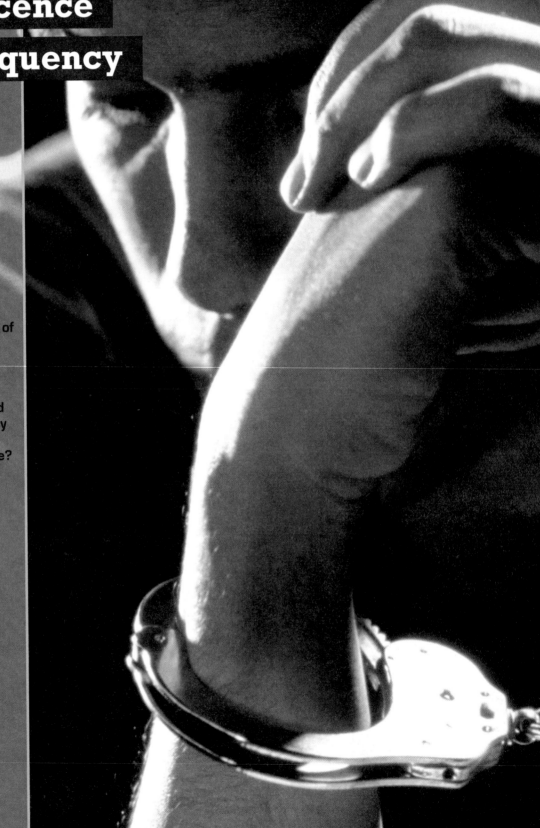

1

Adolescence and Delinquency

> " The future promise of any nation can be directly measured by the present prospects of its youth. "
>
> —President John F. Kennedy, February 14, 1963

CHAPTER Objectives

AFTER READING THIS CHAPTER, YOU SHOULD BE ABLE TO ANSWER THE FOLLOWING QUESTIONS:

- What does it mean to be an adolescent in American society today?

- Are adolescents treated the same now as in the past?

- What problem behaviors characterize adolescence?

- How can delinquency be defined?

- What is a status offense?

- How have delinquents been handled throughout history?

- What are the major themes of this text?

3

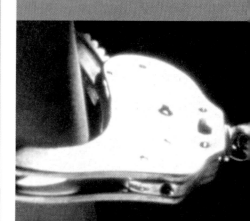

Introduction

Seniors at Winslow Township High School in New Jersey can leave early if they have afternoon jobs, use their own transportation, and finish required classes in the morning. They typically gather in the parking lot in front of the school to engage in a bit of socializing before leaving the school grounds.

In 2006, however, as Easter vacation approached, the tenor in the parking lot was clearly different. "Look up there," said one senior, who asked to be identified only as James, pointing to two police cruisers parked at the front entrance to the school. "That is what it is all about now. That is what we will leave as our legacy at Winslow High."

Four male students had been arrested in early April after several students reported rumors of a Columbine-like plot about to be hatched at the school. The four suspects were arraigned on a variety of charges, including alleged violations of the federal anti-terrorism law enacted after the infamous attacks of September 11, 2001.

Some people in town have preferred not to discuss the arrests. School board members and school administrators declined to talk to the news media. Others in the community, though, have expressed emotions ranging from outrage to deep concern.

"I heard one girl say that she never missed school before this thing, and she became too scared to go to school for several days afterward," said Tammy Wall, owner of the Cedar Brook Deli on State Route 73, about a mile south of the high school. "Something has to be done. You can't have kids live in fear of going to school."

Winslow's mayor, Sue Ann Metzner, has a tremble in her voice whenever she talks about the potential massacre. "I think this has been a great wake-up call from the community," Metzner said, "These problems don't happen in isolation."

The police say that 25 students, teachers, and other community members were on a hit list, and that the boys who were arrested had been repeatedly teased for wearing Goth-style clothing.

Adapted from Robert Strauss, "In Winslow, the Specter of Columbine," *New York Times*, April 23, 2006. Copyright © 2006 by The New York Times Co. Reprinted with permission.

In this illustration a serious incident appears to have been prevented. Communities, however, are increasingly finding themselves having to react to juvenile offenses that might have been prevented by effective proactive measures. People are most concerned about violent crime. The victims of violent juveniles are often those youths' parents, peers, or teachers—the people the violent youths perceive to be the causes of their problems. Consequently, even though homicides committed by juveniles are near a twenty-year low, they still garner a lot of media attention. A few recent news bites, for example, include the following: "17-year-old [in Newark, New Jersey] accused of fatally stabbing his mother and father in their home;"[1] "In Baltimore, Rickey Prince, a 17-year-old who witnessed a gang murder and agreed to testify against the killer, was shot in the back of the head a few days after a prosecutor read Mr. Prince's name aloud in a packed courtroom;"[2] and "9-year-old girl accused of stabbing her 11-year-old friend to death in a tussle over a ball."[3]

Adolescence is a term that refers to the life interval between childhood and adulthood. The term has been used in the last few decades to mark a new stage of human growth and development, but there is no agreed-on way to pinpoint this period chronologically or to restrict it within physiological boundaries. For purposes of dis-

adolescence

The life interval between childhood and adulthood; usually the period between the ages of twelve and eighteen years.

cussion in this chapter, however, adolescence is considered to be the years between ages twelve and eighteen. Within this transitional period, youngsters experience many biological changes and develop new attitudes, values, and skills that they will carry into their young adult years.

Delinquency and other problem behaviors increase during the adolescent years for several reasons. These years bring increasing freedom from parental scrutiny, and with this freedom comes more opportunities to be involved in socially unacceptable behavior. Teenagers develop new, often expensive tastes for such things as sound systems, clothing, automobiles, and alcohol, yet legitimate means for satisfying these desires are often not available. The lengthening of adolescence in U.S. culture has further expanded the crises and struggles of this life period, thereby increasing the chance of problems with the law, at school, and in the home. In addition, there is often a mismatch between adolescents' needs and the opportunities provided them by their social environment.[4] Finally, in some cases, the unmet needs and frustrations of early childhood fester into socially unacceptable behavior in later years.

The Changing Treatment of Adolescents

Adolescence, as a term describing a particular stage of human growth and development, evolved out of the modern notion of childhood. The concept of childhood, as reflected in today's child-centered culture, is a relatively recent phenomenon.[5] Much of recorded history reveals abuse and indifference to be the fate of many children. Lloyd de Mause, an American social thinker known for his work in the field of psychohistory, depicts childhood historically as a time when children were "killed, abandoned, beaten, terrorized, and sexually abused"; he prefaces this statement by saying, "The history of childhood is a nightmare from which we have only recently begun to awaken."[6]

The end of child labor was one of the watersheds in the development of modern adolescence. Throughout history, children have worked, but until the Industrial Revolution their work was usually done within or around the house, often outdoors. As work moved from the home to the factory, children were considered a source of cheap labor. It was not unusual for them to work in the worst of conditions for sixteen hours a day, six days a week.[7] Until the child labor laws were actually enforced, children as young as ages four and five worked in mines, mills, and factories. But with advancing technology and mechanization, children and adolescents were no longer needed in the labor market, and by 1914, every state but one had passed laws prohibiting the employment in industry of children under a certain age, generally fourteen.

Another important stage in the development of modern adolescence was compulsory public schooling. As Chapter 9 discusses, nineteenth-century U.S. schools were violent and chaotic places in which teachers attempted to maintain control over unmotivated and unruly children, sometimes using brutal disciplinary methods. The Progressive education movement arose partly because of the dissatisfaction of some elements of society with the schools. The influence of John Dewey and other Progressive educators encouraged individualism and personal growth in the classroom. Compulsory education laws also evolved from early-twentieth-century social and religious views, which held that adolescents should be kept in school because they needed guidance and control.

Web **LIBRARY** 1.1

Read the National Institute of Justice (NIJ) publication *A Century of Juvenile Justice* at **www.justicestudies.com/ WebLibrary**.

A further stage in the development of modern adolescence was the development in the twentieth century of the belief that raising children had less to do with conquering their spirits than with training and socializing them. Parents in the United States, especially since the 1940s, have emphasized a helping relationship, attempting to meet their children's expanding needs in a democratic and supportive environment.[8]

An additional stage in this development took place in the 1960s and 1970s when special legal protections for juveniles were granted, highlighting the perception of adolescents as needing special attention, guidance, and support.[9] Psychologist Eric H. Erickson has observed, "Childhood . . . is the model of all oppression and enslavement, a kind of inner colonization, which forces grown-ups to accept inner repression and self-restriction."[10] A chief reason for the repression of childhood, according to Erickson and others, is the lack of rights given to young people. The children's rights movement, which encompasses a spectrum of approaches, became popular in the 1970s as a means to compensate for young people's lack of rights. Consensus also increased on what is thought necessary for an adolescent to achieve responsible adulthood, including:

- The search for self-identity
- The search for a personal set of values
- The acquisition of competencies necessary for adulthood, such as problem solving and decision making
- The acquisition of skills necessary for social interaction
- The attainment of emotional independence from parents
- The ability to negotiate between the need for personal achievement and the need for peer acceptance
- The need to experiment with a wide variety of behaviors, attitudes, and activities[11]

In sum, the concept of adolescence centers on a set of beliefs that emerged during the late nineteenth and twentieth centuries. These beliefs have had the result of removing young people from the employment world and the mainstream of society. This process of lengthening childhood and delaying adult responsibilities was strongly influenced not only by humanitarian considerations but also by major economic, social, and political forces in society.

▌Youths at Risk

juvenile
A youth at or below the upper age of juvenile court jurisdiction in a particular state.

The population of children in the United States is increasing and becoming more racially and ethnically diverse. In 2003, there were approximately 73 million children, ages newborn to seventeen, in the United States. This represented 25 percent of the population, which was down from a peak of 36 percent at the end of the baby boom in 1964.[12] The **juvenile** population, according to the U.S. Census Bureau estimate, will increase 14 percent between 2000 and 2025; by 2050 the juvenile population will be 36 percent larger than it was in 2000.[13] In 2003, 60 percent of this nation's children were white, 16 percent were African American, and 4 percent were Asian. The proportion of Hispanic children has increased faster than the other racial and ethic groups, as it has grown from 9 percent of the population of children in 1980 to 19 percent in 2003.[14]

Noted youth researcher Nanette J. Davis says that this population of children, increasing in number and diversity, is experiencing a crisis that, according to Davis, ranges from "the personal to the global, from the specific to the general, and from the material to the symbolic levels."[15] She adds that an important feature of this crisis is that much of it is invisible. Invisible crises lurk beneath the surface of many adults' everyday lives, and they may choose not to see them. Yet youths caught in crises are involved in such "structural" arrangements as the discrimination and humiliations of racism, the hazards and deprivations of poverty, the culture of violence, and the ever-present temptation of drugs and alcohol. The consequences of these crises are burgeoning youth gangs, rising homelessness among young persons, dropout rates of 50 percent in inner-city schools, widespread experimentation with various forms of dangerous drugs, and increasing numbers of youths sentenced to adult prisons.[16]

> The population of children in the United States is increasing and becoming more racially and ethnically diverse.

Davis rejects the notion that it is the youths who are the problem. Instead, she argues that the sources of the problems are within society. She hypothesizes that American institutions are contributing in major ways to this youth crisis, suggesting

Two-year-old Emily Sayler pushes a cart at the donations-supported foodbank in McArthur, Ohio. Poverty increases the risk of illness and delinquency among children, and decreases the likelihood that they will receive quality education or find suitable employment later in life.

■ **What other risk factors increase with lower income levels?**

Web **PLACES** 1.1

Visit the Office of Juvenile Justice and Delinquency Prevention's (OJJDP) website via **www .justicestudies.com/ WebPlaces**.

that U.S. cultural arrangements "have made life more difficult, often impossible, much less welcoming, and certainly far less nurturing for those growing up today."[17]

The Children's Defense Fund (CDF) has argued for the past thirty years that children, especially poor and minority children and children with disabilities, are in grave crisis. This nonprofit organization seeks to educate the nation about the needs of children and to encourage preventive investment before youngsters become sick, get into trouble, drop out of school, or suffer family breakdown.[18] See Focus on Social Policy 1.1, which shows how poverty is related to the crises of so many children in our society.

In a press release on July 1, 2004, the Children's Defense Fund further charged that it is "morally and economically indefensible" that the plight of African American children is what it is in the United States. The CDF says that:

■ African American children are more likely than white children to be sick because they are more inclined to be poor. They are more likely than white children to lack a regular source of health care, to have unmet or delayed medical care, and to have had no dental visits in the past two years. In addition, they are more than five times as likely as white children to be forced to rely on hospital emergency rooms for basic health care.

■ Two out of five African American babies today are born into poverty and face a losing struggle with poverty throughout childhood. African American families are more than twice as likely as whites to live in overcrowded housing. African American fathers are twice as likely as white fathers to be unemployed, and when African American men find work, they bring home $162 a week less than white men.

■ An African American preschool child is three times as inclined as a white child to depend solely on a mother's earnings.

■ An African American mother is more likely to go out to work sooner, to work longer hours, and to make less money than a white mother. An African American child is seven times more likely than a white child to be on welfare.

■ An African American child is only half as likely as a white child to grow up with parents who graduated from college.

FOCUS ON
Social Policy 1.1

Poverty and U.S. Children, 2005

The first chapter of the Children's Defense Fund's publication, examines how poverty affects some children in the United States.

> Poverty kills. It also maims and stunts the growth and eclipses the dreams of hundreds of millions of children around the world. . . . A childhood spent in poverty can have negative impacts on an individual's entire life. Children living in families that are poor are more likely than children living in other families to be exposed to inadequate education, inadequate or absent health-care, hazardous housing, and poor nutrition. These multiple barriers associated with poverty build upon one another and unjustly deprive children of the opportunity to reach their full potential as parents, employees, and citizens. Children who grow up in poverty are more likely to become teen parents and, as adults, to earn less, to be unemployed more frequently, and to raise their own children in poverty. . . .

This worsening reality not only hurts children and families; it dims our prospects as a nation. Impressive progress was made between 1992 and 2000, when close to 4 million children were lifted out of poverty. Since 2000 this positive trend has sharply reversed, and more than 1.4 million additional children have fallen into poverty. If poverty had continued to decline between 2000 and 2004 at the same annual rate as it did between 1992 and 2000, the likelihood of a child being poor in America would have been reduced by an additional 13.7 percent. This means that, instead of nearly one and a half million children falling into poverty over four years, 1.4 million more children would have escaped it.

Two Incomes and Still Too Little

Tabitha and her husband are raising three sons, ages 8, 6, and 20 months, near Columbus, Ohio. They are both employed; Tabitha works at check-out at Value City, while her husband works at Subway. Both earn the federal minimum wage, $5.15 an hour, for monthly earnings of $1,785. Still, their annual earnings of $21,424 leave them below the poverty line of $22,543 for a family with two parents and three children. . . .

Far too many poor and minority children are without protection. Single mothers struggle with two and three jobs just to provide the basics of clothing, food, and shelter for their children. Parents face enormous odds in affording or providing the

measures that will protect their children from delinquency, while cash-strapped schools, communities, and states are unable to provide adequate funding for quality after-school programs. Unemployment in high-poverty urban areas gives way to a proliferation of drug trafficking, firearms, and gang violence among youths and young adults. Children desperate for a sense of belonging will find it wherever it is available. When the doors to churches and community programs are all too closed, they find it on the streets. With little or no protection against the risks, children are left to fend for themselves.

The result? An accumulation of disadvantages, from birth onward, that puts these children at great risk of entering the juvenile justice system or adult criminal justice system. They are pulled into a "cradle to prison pipeline" that diminishes their chances for college and meaningful work and makes it much more likely that they will follow a trajectory to prison or even premature death. Children with needs or problems that go unaddressed because of unjust economic policies and priorities, as well as failures in the health-care, early childhood, education, and child welfare systems, find that there is one child-serving system that always remains open to them: the juvenile justice system. Here in the richest nation on earth, we ignore and neglect the needs of our most vulnerable children until they have done something that lands them in trouble with the law. Then we snap to attention, readily handing children over to a penal system that all too often makes matters even worse.

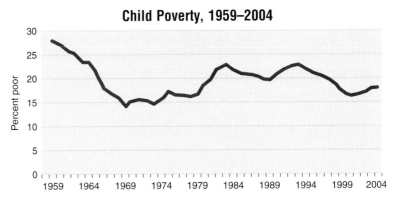

Child Poverty, 1959–2004

Source: U.S. Department of Commerce, Bureau of the Census.

> ■ Why is the issue of poverty so closely related to the general problem of youth crisis and the particular problem of juvenile delinquency? Why did the poor do better in the 1990s than they have in the early years of the twenty-first century? What do you believe society needs to do about the issue of poor children who seem to be getting poorer?

- One out of every three African American children attends a school with 90 percent enrollment of minorities. An African American child is more than twice as likely as a white child to be suspended, expelled, and given corporal punishment. An African American child is more likely than a white child to drop out of school, more than twice as likely to be behind grade level or to be labeled mentally retarded, but is only one-half as likely to be labeled gifted. Whites are almost 3.5 times more inclined than African Americans to take advanced placement exams. The longer an African American child is in school, the further he or she falls behind.
- An African American youth is twice as likely as a white youth to be unemployed. An African American college graduate has a greater chance of being unemployed than a white high school graduate.[19]

High-Risk Behaviors

Researchers have identified several important insights into adolescence and problem behaviors. First, high-risk youths often experience multiple difficulties. They are frequently socialized in economically stressed families and communities, more often than not have histories of physical abuse and sexual victimization, typically have educational and vocational skill deficits, and are prone to become involved in alcohol and other drug abuse and forms of delinquency.[20] The more of these problem behaviors that are present, the more likely it is that a youth will become involved in socially undesirable behaviors.[21] Second, adolescent problem behaviors—especially delinquent acts such as drug and alcohol abuse, failing in or dropping out of school, and unprotected sex—are interrelated. An involvement in one problem behavior is generally indicative of some participation in other socially undesirable behaviors. Finally, a common factor may underlie all problem behaviors. The pursuit of this general tendency is generating considerable excitement among those interested in adolescent research.[22]

The Program of Research on the Causes and Correlates of Delinquency (Causes and Correlates Program, which is described in more detail in Chapter 2) comprised three coordinated longitudinal projects: the Denver Youth Survey, the Pittsburgh Youth Study, and the Rochester Youth Development study. These three projects examined the co-occurrence or overlaps of delinquent behavior with drug use, problems in school, and mental health problems. Across all three study sites, the prevalence of persistent problem behaviors was usually consistent. Twenty to thirty percent of males were serious delinquents, 7 to 22 percent had school problems, 14 to 17 percent used drugs, and 7 to 14 percent had mental health problems (see Figure 1.1).[23]

John E. Donovan and Richard Jessor not only corroborated the interrelationships among high-risk behaviors in a study on adolescent drinking but also suggested that a common factor of "unconventionality" underlies all of these behaviors. This factor of unconventionality is measured by lower religiosity, tolerance of deviance, approval of drug abuse, peer approval of deviant behavior, more liberal views, and poor school performance.[24]

Travis Hirschi explains the relationship between drug abuse and delinquency by suggesting that the two are not merely influenced by the same factors but "are manifestations of the same thing." This "thing" is criminality, which Hirschi defines as "the tendency or propensity of the individual to seek short-term, immediate pleasure," which provides "money without work, sex without courtship, revenge without court delays."[25] In their 1990 publication *A General Theory of Crime*, Michael R. Gottfredson and Travis Hirschi define lack of self-control as the common factor underlying problem behaviors.[26]

Yet researchers tend to be dubious about accepting this "generality of deviance hypothesis." Helene Raskin White suggests that several factors challenge the acceptability of a total generality of deviance hypothesis.[27] She states that "the low correlations among problem behaviors indicate that the majority of the variance in one behavior is not shared with the others.[28] Various problem behaviors," according to

Web PLACES 1.2

Visit the Youth Risk Behavior Surveillance System (YRBSS) website, part of the Centers for Disease Control and Prevention, via **www.justicestudies.com/WebPlaces**.

Web LIBRARY 1.2

Read Chapter 1 of the Office of Juvenile Justice and Delinquency Prevention (OJJDP) publication *Juvenile Offenders and Victims: 2006 National Report* at **www.justicestudies.com/WebLibrary**.

Web LIBRARY 1.3

Read the OJJDP publication *Risk Factors for Delinquency: An Overview* at **www.justicestudies.com/WebLibrary**.

FIGURE 1.1

Prevalence of Persistent Problem Behaviors among Young Males

Serious Delinquency
- 24%
- 30%
- 20%

Drug Use
- 14%
- 15%
- 17%

School Problems
- 7%
- 8%
- 22%

Mental Health Problems
- 7%
- 8%
- 14%

Legend:
- ■ Denver
- ■ Pittsburgh
- ■ Rochester

Percentage (0, 10, 20, 30, 40)

Source: David Huizinga, Rolf Loeber, Terence P. Thornberry, and Lynn Cothern, *Co-Occurrence of Delinquency and Other Problem Behaviors* (Washington, D.C.: Office of Juvenile Justice and Delinquency Prevention, 2000), p. 3. Reprinted with permission from the U.S. Department of Justice.

juvenile delinquency

An act committed by a minor that violates the penal code of the government with authority over the area in which the act occurs.

White, "follow different developmental paths, for example, delinquency peaks between ages 15 and 17 and then declines, whereas polydrug use increases through adolescence into young adulthood."[29] White's longitudinal study of males and females also revealed that the constellation of problems varied by gender and that the associations among problem behavior over time were unstable.[30] Moreover, White reports that the "data indicate that problem behaviors do not cluster together in one homogeneous group of adolescents and the degree of overlap among problems is often low."[31] Finally, she claims that "there are several independent influences on each behavior."[32]

Of the twenty-five million adolescents (ages twelve through seventeen) in the United States in 2003, approximately one in four was at high risk of engaging in multiple problem behaviors. These behaviors, particularly committing delinquent acts and abusing drugs and alcohol, quickly bring adolescents to the attention of the juvenile justice system. This means that over six million adolescents living primarily in disadvantaged neighborhoods are in dire need of assistance. Although minority adolescents have higher prevalence rates, the majority of these youths with multiple problems are white and male. Another six million youngsters, making up 25 percent, practice risky behavior but to a lesser degree and, consequently, are less likely to experience negative consequences. It is estimated that nearly thirteen million, or half the adolescent population, are not currently involved in high-risk behaviors.[33]

Delinquency is one of the problem behaviors with which all but low-risk adolescents become involved from time to time (see Chapter 2). *Delinquency* is a legal term initially used in 1899 when Illinois passed the first law on juvenile delinquent behavior. **Juvenile delinquency** is typically defined

Teenage girls smoking marijuana. According to the Program of Research on the Causes and Correlates of Delinquency, drug use and other problem behaviors correlate with other forms of delinquency. ■ **What factors are likely to account for the relationship?**

as an act committed by a minor that violates the penal code of the government with authority over the area in which the act occurs. The age at which an individual is considered a minor varies among states, but it is sixteen or seventeen and younger in most states.

Some evidence indicates that delinquency in U.S. society is changing. Beginning in the late 1980s and extending even more throughout the 1990s, adolescents participated widely in street gangs, some of which provided a base for trafficking narcotics; had rising rates of murder from 1989 through 1993; were more likely to own and use firearms than ever before; and were becoming increasingly involved in various forms of hate crimes. These trends are continuing in the first decade of the twenty-first century.

Yet the average American delinquent is far more likely to shoplift, commit petty theft, use marijuana, violate liquor laws, or destroy property than to commit a violent or serious crime. In 2005, juveniles between the ages of ten and seventeen were arrested for 307,784 property crimes, compared with 69,840 arrests for violent crimes. In other words, juveniles were arrested for committing four and one-half times more property crimes than violent crimes.[34]

Besides committing the same crimes as adults, juveniles also are arrested for truancy, incorrigibility, curfew violations, and runaway behavior. Such offenses are called **status offenses,** because they would not be defined as criminal if adults committed them. (Status offenses are discussed in more detail on the next page.) The legal separation between status offenders and delinquents is important because of the large number of arrests each year for acts such as truancy, disobeying parents, and running away from home. The FBI's *Crime in the United States 2005 (CUS 2005)* data (see Chapter 2) reveals that three times as many youths were arrested for committing status offenses as for violent crimes. This ratio between status offenses and violent crimes would be even greater if *CUS 2005* included truancy and incorrigibility, two of the most common status offenses.[35]

status offense

A nondelinquent/noncriminal offense; an offense that is illegal for underage persons but not for adults. Status offenses include curfew violations, incorrigibility, running away, truancy, and underage drinking.

Juvenile Court Codes and Definitions of Delinquency

Juvenile court codes, which exist in every state, specify the conditions under which the state can legitimately intervene in a juvenile's life. State juvenile codes, as part of the *parens patriae* philosophy of the juvenile court, were enacted to eliminate the arbitrary nature of juvenile justice beyond the rights afforded juveniles by the U.S. Constitution and to deal with youths more leniently because they were seen as not fully responsible for their behavior. The *In re Poff* (1955) decision aptly expresses the logic of this argument:

> The original Juvenile Court Act enacted in the District of Columbia . . . was devised to afford the juvenile protections in addition to those he already possessed under the Federal Constitution. Before this legislative enactment, the juvenile was subject to the same punishment for an offense as an adult. It follows logically that in the absence of such legislation the juvenile would be entitled to the same constitutional guarantees and safeguards as an adult. If this is true, then the only possible reason for the Juvenile Court Act was to afford the juvenile safeguards in addition to those he already possessed. The legislative intent was to enlarge and not diminish those protections.[36]

Juvenile court codes usually specify that the court has jurisdiction in relation to three categories of juvenile behavior: delinquency, dependency, and neglect. First, the courts may intervene when a youth has been accused of committing an act that would be a misdemeanor or felony if committed by an adult. Second, the courts may intervene when a juvenile commits certain status offenses. Third, the courts may intervene in cases involving dependency and neglect. If a court determines that a child is being deprived of needed support and supervision, it may decide to remove the child from the home for his or her own protection.

Juvenile Law 1.1

Definitions of Delinquency

- Violates any law or ordinance
- Violates juvenile court order
- Associates with criminal or immoral persons
- Engages in any calling, occupation, or exhibition punishable by law
- Frequents taverns or uses alcohol
- Wanders the streets in the nighttime
- Grows up in idleness or breaks curfew
- Enters or visits a house of ill repute
- Is habitually truant
- Is habitually disobedient or refuses to obey reasonable and proper (lawful) orders of parents, guardians, or custodians

- Engages in incorrigibility or ungovernability
- Absents himself or herself from home without permission
- Persists in violating rules and regulations of school
- Endangers welfare, morals, and/or health of self or others
- Uses vile, obscene, or vulgar language (in a public place)
- Smokes cigarettes (around a public place)
- Engages in dissolute or immoral life or conduct
- Wanders about railroad yards or tracks
- Jumps a train or enters a train without authority
- Loiters, sleeps in alleys
- Begs or receives alms (or is in the street for that purpose)

■ **These definitions are taken from various state codes. Which of these definitions is most surprising to you? Are these definitions especially favorable or unfavorable to any particular economic, racial, or ethnic group? Explain your response.**

An examination of the various juvenile court codes, or statutes, shows the diverse definitions of delinquent behavior that have developed. Some statutes define a "delinquent youth" as a young person who has committed a crime or violated probation; others define a "delinquent child" in terms of such behaviors as "associating with immoral or vicious persons" (West Virginia) or "engaging in indecent or immoral conduct" (Connecticut).[37] A particular juvenile, then, could be considered a delinquent under some juvenile codes and not under others. Juvenile Law 1.1 lists behaviors that have been defined as delinquent.

Some controversy surrounds the issue of how long juveniles should remain under the jurisdiction of the juvenile court. The age at which a youthful offender is no longer treated as a juvenile ranges from sixteen to eighteen. In thirty-seven states and the District of Columbia, persons under eighteen years of age charged with a law violation are considered juveniles. In ten states, the upper limit of juvenile court jurisdiction is sixteen years, and in three states, the upper limit is fifteen years. (See Figure 1.2 for the upper age of juvenile court jurisdiction.)[38]

What Is a Status Offense?

In various jurisdictions, status offenders are known as MINS (minors in need of supervision), CHINS (children in need of supervision), JINS (juveniles in need of supervision), CHINA (children in need of assistance), PINS (persons in need of supervision), CHIPS (children in need of protection and services), or members of FINS (families in need of supervision). They also may be termed *predelinquent, incorrigible, beyond control, ungovernable,* or *wayward.* What these terms and acronyms have in common is that they view the status offender as being in need of supervision or assistance.

status offender

A juvenile who commits a minor act that is considered illegal only because he or she is underage.

There are three important questions about **status offenders:** Why do they behave the way they do? Do status offenders differ in offense behavior from delinquents? How should society respond to their behavior?

FIGURE 1.2

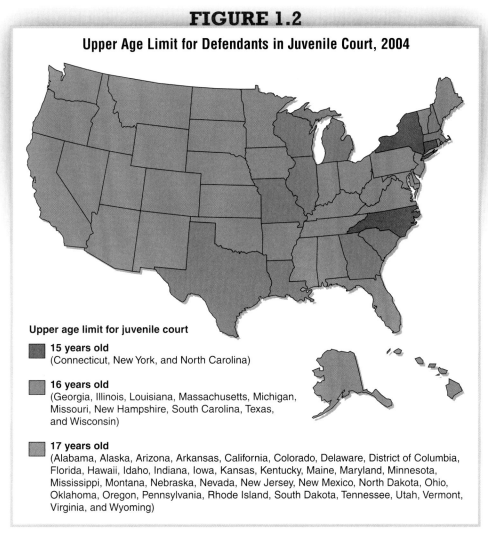

Upper Age Limit for Defendants in Juvenile Court, 2004

Upper age limit for juvenile court

■ **15 years old**
(Connecticut, New York, and North Carolina)

□ **16 years old**
(Georgia, Illinois, Louisiana, Massachusetts, Michigan, Missouri, New Hampshire, South Carolina, Texas, and Wisconsin)

□ **17 years old**
(Alabama, Alaska, Arizona, Arkansas, California, Colorado, Delaware, District of Columbia, Florida, Hawaii, Idaho, Indiana, Iowa, Kansas, Kentucky, Maine, Maryland, Minnesota, Mississippi, Montana, Nebraska, Nevada, New Jersey, New Mexico, North Dakota, Ohio, Oklahoma, Oregon, Pennsylvania, Rhode Island, South Dakota, Tennessee, Utah, Vermont, Virginia, and Wyoming)

Source: Howard N. Snyder and Melissa Sickmund, *Juvenile Offenders and Victims: 2006 National Report* (Washington, D.C.: Office of Juvenile Justice and Delinquency Prevention, March 2006), p. 103. Reprinted with permission from the U.S. Department of Justice.

Explanations for Status Offense Behavior

In an effort to determine and explain the behavior of status offenders, the authors interviewed probation officers, juvenile judges, teachers in public schools, and institutional staff. Interviewees shared a number of insights about status offenders, including descriptions of how they view the problems they are having, the nature of parental conflicts, and the difficulties they have in school. One caveat should be mentioned: These observations are generalizations and may not apply to all offenders.[39]

Generally speaking, status offenders, many of whom come from single-parent homes, place the blame for their problems on parental figures in the home. They believe that fulfilling their need for a warm, accepting, and loving relationship with their parents is not possible. They want to be loved by a parent who may not have the capacity to provide that love. Although their needs for sustenance and shelter may have been met, some have been physically or sexually abused. At the least, they feel rejected and neglected. They become resentful and angry with their parents, who may have problems in expressing physical affection, setting reasonable and consistent limits, and showing acceptance to their children. Many of these parents were abused as children, have limited parenting skills, or evince immature behaviors themselves.

The parents, in turn, often view status offenders as defiant, demanding, and obnoxious. Parents usually believe that they have no control over their children, who

DELINQUENCY in America 1.1

Rise in Income Improves Children's Behavior

The notion that poverty and mental illness are intertwined is nothing new, as past research has demonstrated time and time again. But finding evidence that one begets the other has often proved difficult.

Now new research that coincided with the opening of an Indian casino may have come a step closer to identifying a link by suggesting that lifting children out of poverty can diminish some psychiatric symptoms, though others seem unaffected.

A study published in last week's issue of *The Journal of the American Medical Association* looked at children before and after their families rose above the poverty level. Rates of deviant and aggressive behaviors, the study noted, declined as incomes rose.

"This comes closer to pointing to a causal relationship than we can usually get," said Dr. E. Jane Costello, a psychiatric epidemiologist at Duke who was the lead author. "Moving families out of poverty led to a reduction in children's behavioral symptoms."

The study took place over eight years in rural North Carolina and tracked 1,420 children ages 9 to 13, 25 percent of them from a Cherokee reservation. Tests for psychiatric symptoms were given at the start of the study and repeated each year.

When the study began, 68 percent of the children were from families living below the federally defined poverty line. On average, the poorer children exhibited more behaviors associated with psychiatric problems than those who did not live in poverty. But midway through the study, the opening of a local casino offered researchers a chance to analyze the effects of quick rises in income.

Just over 14 percent of the American Indian children rose above the poverty level when the casino started distributing a percentage of its profits to tribal families. The payment, given to people over age 18 and put into a trust fund for those younger, has increased slightly each year, reaching about $6,000 per person by 2001.

"This is unique because it's a situation where everybody got the extra money," Dr. Costello said. "You can't take a bunch of babies and randomly assign them to grow up in comfort or poverty. So this is about as close to a natural experiment as you can get."

When the researchers conducted their tests soon after, they noticed that the rate of psychiatric symptoms among the chil-

dren who had risen from poverty was dropping. As time went on, the children were less inclined to stubbornness, temper tantrums, stealing, bullying and vandalism—all symptoms of conduct and oppositional defiant disorders.

After four years, the rate of such behaviors had dropped to the same levels found among children whose families had never been poor. Children whose families broke the poverty threshold had a 40 percent decrease in behavioral symptoms. But the payments had no effect on children whose families had been unable to rise from poverty or on the children whose families had not been poor to begin with.

The researchers also found that symptoms of anxiety and depression, although more common in poor children, remained the same despite moving out of poverty.

The deciding factor appeared to be the amount of time parents had to supervise their children. Parents who moved out of poverty reported having more time to spend with their children. In the other groups, the amount of time the parents had on their hands was not much different.

"What this shows very nicely is that an economic shift can allow for more time and better parenting," said Dr. Nancy Adler, professor of medical psychology at the University of California at San Francisco.

In children, acting out is often a result of frustration that can stem from feeling ignored or not getting enough validation from the parents, said Dr. Arline Geronimus, a professor of public health at the University of Michigan.

As a result, behaviors associated with frustration would be the first to change when parents had more attention to devote to their children. "Anxiety and depression, on the other hand, are a little more extreme and might not be as susceptible to change," Dr. Geronimus added.

Recent research suggests that anxiety disorders and depression run in families and probably reflect a mix of genetic and environmental causes.

The study highlights the role that adult supervision may have on mental health in children, but another factor, Dr. Geronimus said, may be the psychological benefits that the casino payments produce.

The Indian families were much more likely to be poor than their non-Indian

neighbors at the start of the study. After the payments, though, a higher proportion of Indian families moved out of poverty.

"There's the possibility that this improved the general outlook of the families—that the whole community has more than before," Dr. Geronimus said. "In addition to the material resources, there might have been some psychological benefits."

Those psychological benefits may also be a byproduct of the jobs that the casino has generated, said James Sanders, director of an adolescent drug and alcohol treatment center on the reservation.

"The jobs give people the chance to pull themselves up by their bootstraps and get out of poverty," said Mr. Sanders, whose son took part in the study. "That carries over into less juvenile crime, less domestic violence and an overall better living experience for the families."

But one question that lingers is why the economic change had a significant effect on only a small proportion of the children. All of the families that received the payment were given the same amount of money, but only 14 percent moved out of poverty while 53 percent remained poor.

The answer could be related to the number of siblings in each family. A $6,000 payment could be a huge help to a poor family with one child, for example, "but that money might not go as far for a family with multiple children," Dr. Adler said.

In 2002, the average poverty threshold for a family of three was $14,348.

Though some questions remain, the study ultimately suggests that poverty puts stress on families, which can increase the likelihood that children will develop behavioral problems. That, said Dr. Geronimus, speaks to the notion that welfare policy is heading in the wrong direction.

"Parents on welfare are increasingly required to work more and more hours while spending less time with their families," she said. "These findings suggest the opposite: parents value having more time to spend with their kids, not less, and their kids respond favorably to that."

Source: Anahad O'Connor, "Rise in Income Improves Children's Behavior," *The New York Times*, October 21, 2003. Copyright © 2003 by The New York Times Co. Reprinted with permission.

will not accept restrictions or limitations on their behavior. A power struggle results. The struggle often climaxes in verbal altercations, and physical violence can erupt when the child strikes or pushes the parent. As a result, parents call the police to intervene with their abusive or unmanageable children. Sometimes a parent asks police to act because the youngster stays out very late, associates with older youth or delinquent friends, or responds to the parent with rage.

School officials and teachers tend to view status offenders, some of whom have had conflicts with teachers since kindergarten, as resistant to authority. Besides refusing to accept the limits placed on their behavior, status offenders also tend to be disruptive, disrespectful, belligerent, emotionally withdrawn or explosive, and unfocused or unconcerned. Many are psychologically tested and are found to be hyperactive or to have attention deficit disorder. They are then prescribed varying doses of medication, typically Imipramine or Ritalin, to help them focus and control their emotional difficulties.

While acknowledging these psychological explanations, some theorists argue that society's response to status offenders, especially female status offenders, is a major contributing factor in defining who belongs to this legal status. Society believes that young males should behave in a certain way, typically granting leniency for the right of "boys to be boys." Society's expectations for young females, however, are still based on the notion that "Sugar and spice and everything nice, that's what little girls are made of." University of Hawaii Women's Studies Professor Meda Chesney-Lind and Lisa J. Pasko found during their examination of the judicial handling of female status offenders that the juvenile justice system discriminates against girls because of the fear of sexual activity.[40] According to Chesney-Lind and Pasko, a double standard exists between male and female adolescents because society believes it must protect adolescent girls from the potential consequences of sexual activity. The labeling of female adolescents continues when they are victims of violence and sexual abuse at home. If they run away from these abusive environments, they are regarded as runaways and processed as status offenders. Their cycle of victimization continues as they are forced to engage in panhandling, petty theft, and sometimes prostitution to survive.[41]

Offense Behavior of Status Offenders and Delinquents

Charles W. Thomas challenges the notion that status offenders are merely incorrigible youths with family problems. In a randomly selected sample of 2,589 juveniles who appeared before one of two juvenile courts in Virginia, Thomas found that many juveniles who appeared in court for charges involving status offenses had previously appeared for more serious charges and that those juveniles whose first appearance involved a status offense were more likely to be returned to court than were those who had first been charged with a misdemeanor or felony. Thomas contends, based on these data, that status offenders not only differ very little in offense behavior from delinquent offenders but they also tend to progress from status to delinquent offenses.[42]

Maynard L. Erickson found that those who commit only status offenses represent a very small proportion of all youths who come into contact with the juvenile justice system. Most adolescents who are brought to court for status offense behavior, he adds, are mixed offenders who have, at one time or another, been involved in misdemeanors and felonies as well as status offenses.[43]

Researchers have generally agreed, however, that the majority of status offenders do differ in offense behavior from delinquents. For example, Solomon Kobrin, Frank R. Hellum, and John W. Peterson, evaluating data from a national study of status offenders, identified three groups of such offenders: the "heavies," who were predominantly serious delinquent offenders; the "lightweights," who committed misdemeanors as well as status offenses; and the "conforming youths," who occasionally became involved in status offenses. The meaning of "status offenses," according to this study, differed for each group. For heavies, a status offense was likely to be an incidental event. For lightweights, the pattern was one of minor and intermittent

Web PLACES 1.3

Visit the Child Trends Databank, with the latest national trends and research on over 100 key indicators of child and youth well-being, via **www.justicestudies.com/ WebPlaces**.

Status offenses involve acts that are illegal only because of a person's age, such as smoking, drinking, or running away from home. Very few youths who commit only status offenses come into contact with the juvenile justice system. ■ **Should status offenders be treated more harshly?**

delinquent acts as well as status offenses. Conforming youths were likely to restrict themselves to multiple status offenses, perhaps as an outburst of rebellion against adult authority.[44]

This national study further found that most youths who received a citation for a status offense had no official record of a prior offense of any kind. These youths were principally between the ages of thirteen and sixteen, equally distributed between males and females, and more likely to be white than nonwhite. Significantly, of those with no prior status or delinquent offenses, 83.1 percent remained free of subsequent offenses of any kind.[45]

J. G. Weis and associates found that juveniles "who began their offender careers engaging in status offenses only" (or in petty illegal behavior) were not likely to graduate into more serious crime.[46] Joseph H. Rankin and L. Edward Wells, whose longitudinal study followed more than 2,000 adolescent males, also found little evidence of escalation; indeed, about two-thirds remained status offenders or never committed another offense.[47] Moreover, Thomas Kelley's analysis of the offense patterns of status offenders who appeared before a large urban court drew the following conclusions: (1) Status offenders are less prone to recidivism than are delinquent offenders, (2) their offense careers are not as long, and (3) the process of referring status offenders to the juvenile court appears to result in more serious delinquent acts.[48]

Randall G. Shelden, John A. Horvath, and Sharon Tracy's data from a longitudinal study of juvenile court referrals further revealed that the majority of youths whose first referral was a status offense did not become serious delinquents. Yet, according to these researchers, significant differences existed between male and female status offenders and among those referred for various status offenses. Male status offenders' behavior was much more likely to escalate than females'; and those who were referred to the court for violations of liquor laws, truancy, and curfew were much more likely to commit more serious offenses than were runaways and incorrigibles.[49]

In sum, although the studies generally concluded that status offenders differ in offense behavior from delinquents and that status offenders are not likely to escalate to more serious behaviors, one-third of the status offenders in Kobrin and colleagues' study had committed delinquent offenses and continued to commit such offenses.[50] Furthermore, Shelden and colleagues found that gender and types of status offense behavior affected the likelihood of escalation into serious forms of delinquent behavior.[51]

Social Control and the Status Offender

The handling of status offenders, one of the most controversial issues in juvenile justice, has focused on two questions: First, should status offenders be institutionalized with delinquents? And second, should the juvenile court retain jurisdiction over status offenders?

In the 1970s, the policy of confining status offenders with delinquents came under increased criticism. One disturbing finding was that before their dispositional hearing, status offenders were more likely to be detained or treated more harshly than delinquents.[52] Studies of juvenile institutionalization also show that status offenders stayed longer in training schools than did delinquents, were vulnerable to victimization in these settings, and found institutionalization with delinquents to be a destructive experience.[53]

The passage of the **Juvenile Justice and Delinquency Prevention Act of 1974** and its various modifications gave the criminal justice system the impetus to deinstitu-

Juvenile Justice and Delinquency Prevention Act of 1974
A federal law that established a juvenile justice office within the Law Enforcement Assistance Administration to provide funds for the prevention and control of youth crime.

tionalize status offenders (no longer to confine them in secure detention facilities or secure correctional facilities with delinquents). This act also limits the placement of juveniles in adult jail facilities.[54] The effectiveness of this federal mandate is seen in the fact that in 1975, 143,000 status offense cases involved detention, but in 2003, only 1,250 status offenders were in secure detention.[55]

The **Deinstitutionalization of Status Offenders Project (DSO)**, funded by the Office of Juvenile Justice and Delinquency Prevention (OJJDP), evaluated the effects of deinstitutionalization at eight local sites. Overall, the evaluations revealed that these programs did reduce the number of white status offenders held in secure detention but that the detention of African American status offenders actually increased after the DSO project was implemented. There also was little evidence that the recidivism rate was reduced by the deinstitutionalization of status offenders.[56]

Nearly every state is currently participating in the DSO mandate. Annual state monitoring reports show that the vast majority of states are in compliance with the requirements, either reporting no violations or meeting *de minimis* or other compliance criteria.[57] However, the chronic status offender presents a stumbling block to some states' compliance with the DSO mandate. Chronic status offenders who are runaways and those who have emotional and behavioral problems are typically the least amenable to community-based intervention strategies. As a result, some juvenile judges and juvenile justice officials view losing the option to hold these youth as losing the opportunity to help them.[58]

Juvenile court personnel have the option of labeling youngsters downward as dependent or neglected youths, upward as delinquent youths, or laterally into private mental health facilities.[59] Thus, even in states that strongly support deinstitutionalization, the juvenile court still can institutionalize status offenders by redefining them as delinquents or as requiring mental health services. A truant may be charged with a minor delinquent offense and be institutionalized in a private facility, or a court may require school attendance as a condition of probation and then define further truancy as a delinquent offense.[60] This permits the "invisible" institutionalization of status offenders in either private or public institutions.

The juvenile court's jurisdiction over status offenders, an equally volatile issue, faces several challenges. Critics argue that the status offender statutes' lack of clarity often makes these laws blatantly discriminatory, especially in regard to gender. It is further argued that governmental bodies have no legitimate interest, or right to intercede, in many of the behaviors categorized as status offenses. Other critics contend that the juvenile court's intervention promotes rather than inhibits status offense behaviors. Many insist that status offenders represent a special class that must be treated differently from delinquents.[61]

According to Barry Feld, one of the nation's leading scholars of juvenile justice and Centennial Professor of Law at the University of Minnesota Law School, juvenile court judges frequently challenge the movement to strip courts of jurisdiction over status offenders (which is called "divestiture"). They charge that status offenders will have no one to provide for or protect them if they are removed from the court's jurisdiction. This argument is reinforced every time a status offender is victimized or commits a serious crime. For example, following a murder of a runaway girl in 1993, the Washington state legislature reinstated police and court authority to hold status offenders in secure facilities for up to five days.[62]

Several states, including Maine, New York, and Washington, have decriminalized status offenses, thus removing them from the juvenile court's jurisdiction. However, the status offense legislation in Maine and Washington was partly repealed to give the juvenile courts a degree of jurisdiction, especially over abandoned, runaway, or seriously endangered children.[63]

The most broad-based movement to strip the juvenile court of jurisdiction over status offenders has taken place in New York State, heralded by the passage of the 1985 PINS Adjustment Services Act. A central goal of this legislation was to displace the family court as the institution of first choice for minor family-related matters. The PINS legislation also has constructed an innovative system of its own that operates as formally as the family court. Children whose families are receptive are referred to the Designated Assessment Service (DAS), which in turn refers these youths to a community-based agency for long-term services. As long as youths are responsive to the rehabilitative programs designed for them, legal proceedings are suspended.[64]

The Handling of Juvenile Delinquents

Many sociological interpretations of delinquency lack a sense of history. Ahistorical approaches to understanding delinquency have a serious shortcoming, because the history of how law-violating juveniles have been dealt with is important in understanding how delinquent youths are handled today. The philosopher George Santayana reminds us that "those who cannot remember the past are condemned to repeat it."[65]

The history of social responses to juvenile delinquency in the United States can be divided into seven periods: the colonial, houses of refuge, juvenile court, and juvenile rights periods; the reform agenda of the late 1970s; social control and juvenile crime in the 1980s; and contemporary delinquency and U.S. society.

The Colonial Period (1636–1823)

The history of juvenile justice in the United States actually began in the colonial period. The colonists saw the family as the source and primary means of social control of children. In colonial times the law was uncomplicated, and the family was the cornerstone of the community.[66] Town fathers, magistrates, sheriffs, and watchmen were the only law enforcement officials, and the only penal institutions were jails for prisoners awaiting trial or punishment.

> " In colonial times the law was uncomplicated, and the family was the cornerstone of the community. "

Juvenile lawbreakers did not face a battery of police, probation, or parole officers, nor would the juvenile justice system try to rehabilitate them. Young offenders were sent back to their families for punishment. If they were still recalcitrant after harsh whippings and other forms of discipline, they could be returned to community officials for more punishment, such as public whippings, dunkings, the stocks—or, in more serious cases, expulsion from the community or even capital punishment.

The Houses of Refuge Period (1824–1898)

In the nineteenth century, reformers became disillusioned with the family and looked for a substitute that would provide an orderly, disciplined environment similar to that of the "ideal" Puritan family.[67] **Houses of refuge** were proposed as the solution; there, discipline was to be administered firmly and harshly. These facilities were intended to protect wayward children from "weak and criminal parents," "the manifold temptations of the streets," and "the peculiar weakness of [the children's] moral nature."[68] Houses of refuge reflected a new direction in juvenile justice, for no longer were parents and family the first line of control for children. The family's authority had been superseded by that of the state, and wayward children were placed in facilities presumably better equipped to reform them.

Houses of refuge flourished for the first half of the nineteenth century; but by the middle of the century, reformers were beginning to suspect that these juvenile institutions were not as effective as had been hoped. Some had grown unwieldy in size; discipline, care, and order had disappeared from most. Reformers also were aware that many youth were being confined in institutions—jails and prisons—that were filthy, dangerous, degrading, and ill equipped to manage juveniles effectively. A change was in order, and reformers proposed the juvenile court as a way to provide for more humane care of law-violating youths.

Children playing in the stocks at Colonial Williamsburg, Virginia. Throughout much of history, children were treated the same as adults for purposes of the law, and those who committed crimes were severely punished. ■ **Why are children treated differently today?**

The Juvenile Court Period (1899–1966)

First created in Cook County, Illinois, the juvenile court was a new court for children based on the legal concept of *parens patriae*. This medieval English doctrine sanctioned the right of the Crown to intervene in natural family relations whenever a child's welfare was threatened. The concept was explained by the committee of the Chicago Bar Association that created the new court:

> The fundamental idea of the juvenile court law is that the state must step in and exercise guardianship over a child found under such adverse social or individual conditions as to encourage the development of crime. . . . The juvenile court law proposes a plan whereby he may be treated, not as a criminal, or legally charged with crime, but as a ward of the state, to receive practically the care, custody, and discipline that are accorded the neglected and dependent child, and which, as the act states, "shall approximate as nearly as may be that which should be given by its parents."[69]

Proponents of the juvenile court promised that it would be flexible enough to give individual attention to the specific problems of wayward children. These reformers believed that once the causes of deviance were identified accurately, specific problems could be treated and cured; thus, juveniles would be kept out of jails and prisons, thereby avoiding corruption by adult criminals.

The juvenile court period did not see radical change in the philosophy of juvenile justice, because the family continued to be subservient to the state and children still could be institutionalized. What differed was the viewpoint that children were not altogether responsible for their behavior. They were seen as victims of a variety of factors, including poverty, the ills of city life, and inadequate families, schools, and neighborhoods. No longer regarded as criminals, youthful violators were defined as children in need of care, protection, moral guidance, and discipline. Accordingly, the juvenile court was established as another official agency to aid in controlling wayward children. Juvenile delinquents would continue to be under the control of the state until they were either rehabilitated or too old to remain under the jurisdiction of juvenile authorities.

parens patriae

A medieval English doctrine that sanctioned the right of the Crown to intervene in natural family relations whenever a child's welfare was threatened. The philosophy of the juvenile court is based on this legal concept.

Society extended its control over the young in several other ways. Police departments established juvenile bureaus. The notion of treating juveniles for their specific problems was evidenced by the implementation in the first part of the twentieth century of both probation and parole (aftercare) agencies. Commitment to a training or industrial school, a carryover from the nineteenth century, was reserved for those whose needs became secondary to the protection of society.

The Juvenile Rights Period (1967–1975)

Mounting criticism of the juvenile court culminated in the 1960s, when the court was widely accused of dispensing capricious and arbitrary justice. The U.S. Supreme Court responded to this criticism with a series of decisions that changed the course of juvenile justice: *Kent v. United States,* 1966; *In re Gault,* 1967; *In re Winship,* 1970; *McKeiver v. Pennsylvania,* 1971; and *Breed v. Jones,* 1975.[70] The *In re Gault* decision, a landmark case, stated that juveniles have the right to due process safeguards in proceedings in which a finding of delinquency could lead to confinement; that juveniles have rights to notice of charges, counsel, confrontation, and cross-examination; and that juveniles are privileged against self-incrimination. The intent of the Court decisions was to ensure that children would have due process rights in the juvenile justice system.[71]

Reformers also believed that inconsiderate treatment by the police, five-minute hearings in juvenile courts, and degrading and sometimes brutal treatment in training schools fostered rather than reduced juvenile crime. Lower-level federal courts responded to the curbstone justice dispensed by police and the repressive justice administered in training schools by handing down numerous decisions that brought more due process rights to juveniles at the time they were arrested and taken into custody and more humane conditions during their time of confinement.

Community-based programs received an enthusiastic response in the late 1960s and early 1970s as more and more states began a process of deinstitutionalization under which only hard-core delinquents were sent to long-term training schools. Enthusiasm for community-based corrections was so widespread in the early 1970s that many observers believed that training schools would soon become extinct.

The children's rights movement also gathered momentum during the 1960s. Interest groups began to examine children's special needs, and in the 1970s, the rights of children were litigated in the courts. The decade saw progress in the areas of custody in divorce cases, guardianship for foster children, protection of privacy rights, independent access to medical care, and legislation on child abuse.

The Reform Agenda of the Late 1970s

The reform agenda of the mid- to late 1970s emphasized reducing the use of juvenile correctional institutions, diverting minor offenders and status offenders from the juvenile justice system, and reforming the juvenile justice system. The major purpose of the reform agenda was to divert the handling of status offenses from a criminal to a noncriminal setting. Status offenders were accorded such an emphasis because of the mandate of the federal Juvenile Justice and Delinquency Prevention Act of 1974, discussed earlier. The principal objectives of this act were to promote the deinstitutionalization of status offenders as dependent, neglected, and abused children; to encourage the elimination of the practice of jailing juveniles; and to encourage the development of "community-based alternatives to juvenile detention and correctional facilities."[72]

> The major purpose of the reform agenda was to divert the handling of status offenses from a criminal to a noncriminal setting.

However, noted gang researchers Lloyd Ohlin, Ira M. Schwartz and others argue that proponents of this liberal agenda blundered by paying too little attention to the problem of serious juvenile crime. At a time when public concern about serious juvenile crime was running high, the federal government was emphasizing a very different agenda.[73] Less than 10 percent of the nearly $120 million in discretionary funds given out by the Office of Juvenile Justice and Delinquency Prevention between 1975 and 1980, for example, targeted the population of violent and serious juvenile offenders.[74] At that time, Ohlin predicted that the failure to address violent youth crime and repeat offenders would prove to be "the Achilles' heel of the reform process."[75] The failure of the reformers of the 1970s to provide meaningful programs and policies aimed at youthful offenders who committed serious crimes contributed to the wave of "get tough" legislation that was to later sweep across the United States.[76]

Web PLACES 1.4

Visit the U.S. Department of Health and Human Services (HHS) Child Welfare Information Gateway via **www.justicestudies.com/ WebPlaces**. This online portal connects visitors to information and resources targeted to the safety, permanency, and well-being of children and families.

Social Control and Juvenile Crime in the 1980s

By the 1980s, the public had been alerted by the media to the chilling realities of youth crime and wanted something done to curb the serious problem of juvenile delinquency. Ronald Reagan was in the White House, and the hard-liners' formerly muted criticisms suddenly became public policy. The new federal agenda attacked the Juvenile Justice and Delinquency Prevention Act as being "anti-family" and called for cracking down on juvenile law violators. Alfred S. Regnery, administrator in the Office of Juvenile Justice and Delinquency Prevention, communicated this new federal perspective in a speech delivered on December 2, 1984:

> In essence, we have changed the outlook of the office from emphasizing the lesser offender and the nonoffender to one emphasizing the serious juvenile offender. We have placed less emphasis on juvenile crime as a social problem and more emphasis on crime as a justice problem. In essence, the office now reflects the general philosophy of President Reagan and his administration rather than that of President Carter and his administration.[77]

In 1984, the National Advisory Committee for Juvenile Justice and Delinquency Prevention (NAC) said that "the time has come for a major departure from the existing philosophy and activity of the federal government in the juvenile justice field."[78] The NAC recommended that the "federal effort in the area of juvenile delinquency should focus primarily on the serious, violent, or chronic offender."[79] The committee also recommended that federal initiatives be limited to research, carefully designed and evaluated demonstration projects, "dissemination of information," and providing "training and technical assistance."[80] It rejected basic components of the Juvenile Justice and Delinquency Prevention Act, such as the continued provision of grants to accomplish deinstitutionalization of status offenders and the removal of juveniles from jail. [81]

Several factors led to this reassessment of the soft-line, or least restrictive, approach to minor offenders and status offenders. Young people seemed to be out of control. Drug and alcohol abuse were viewed as serious problems, teenage pregnancy had reached epidemic proportions, and teenage suicide was increasing at an alarming rate.[82] Additionally, the spirit of the times was about "getting tough." Nationwide, politicians assured their constituencies that the answer to youth problems was to crack down at all levels. Furthermore, "tough love" and other such movements evidenced a growing acceptance of the notion that parents must be stricter with their children. Finally, the Reagan administration made a concerted effort to show that the soft-line approach had had disastrous consequences in children's lives. Government-sponsored studies, for example, showed that increasing numbers of middle-class runaway girls had ended up as prostitutes.

The major thrusts of the Reagan administration's crime control policies for juveniles, then, were to get tough on serious and violent juvenile crime and to undermine the reform efforts of the 1970s. This federal mandate encouraged the development of five trends: (1) preventive detention; (2) the transfer of violent juveniles to adult court; (3) mandatory and determinate sentencing for violent juveniles; (4) increased confinement of juveniles; and (5) enforcement of the death penalty for juveniles who commit brutal murders.[83] These trends are described and evaluated later in this text.

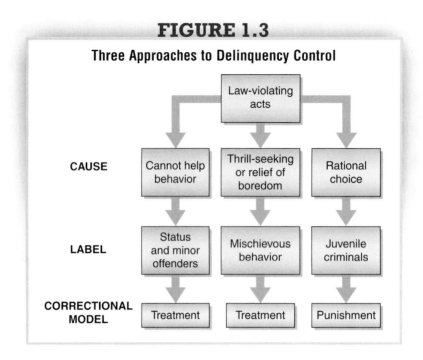

FIGURE 1.3

Three Approaches to Delinquency Control

Law-violating acts

CAUSE

| Cannot help behavior | Thrill-seeking or relief of boredom | Rational choice |

LABEL

| Status and minor offenders | Mischievous behavior | Juvenile criminals |

CORRECTIONAL MODEL

| Treatment | Treatment | Punishment |

Even though the federal government and the public favored a more punishment-oriented response to juvenile delinquency, the juvenile court continued throughout the 1980s to have three approaches to juvenile lawbreakers (see Figure 1.3). On one end of the spectrum, the court applied the *parens patriae* doctrine to status offenders and minor offenders. As in the past, these youths were presumed to need treatment rather than punishment, because their offenses were seen as caused by internal psychological or biological conditions or by sociological factors in their environment.

On the other end of the spectrum, juveniles who committed serious crimes or continued to break the law were presumed to deserve punishment rather than treatment, on the grounds that such youngsters possessed free will and knew what they were doing. That is, the court viewed serious delinquents' crimes as purposeful activities resulting from rational decisions in which youths weighed the pros and cons and performed the acts that promised the greatest potential gains.[84] Their behavior was seen as being bad rather than sick and as arising from a rational decision-making process. In other words, youths in this group were to be treated by the juvenile justice system more like adults than juveniles.

Between these two groups fell youths who saw crime as a form of play and committed delinquent acts because they enjoyed the thrill of getting away with illegal behavior or because they wanted to relieve their boredom. Although criminologists usually conclude that the crimes these juveniles commit represent purposeful activity, the court in the 1980s did not consider the youths in this middle group to be as bad as the serious delinquents. It was reasoned that even though these youths might be exercising free will, their behavior was mischievous rather than delinquent. The juvenile court today commonly continues to excuse such mischievous behavior.

Contemporary Delinquency and U.S. Society

Several interrelated social trends emerged in the 1980s, influenced delinquency in U.S. society in rather dramatic ways in the 1990s, and continue to the present. In the mid-1980s crack cocaine became widely available in urban areas. There was soon a large demand for this drug—some even referred to it as a crack epidemic—and this led to the recruitment of young people into the market to sell crack. By 1988 and 1989, the crack epidemic became a major impetus for the development and spread of drug-trafficking street gangs across the nation. Indeed, by the end of the decade, street gangs were found in nearly every city and in many smaller communities across the nation. One of the consequences of this illegal marketplace was that young people used guns to protect themselves from being robbed of the "valuable goods" they were carrying. Significantly, by the early 1990s, the use of guns had spread from individuals involved in drug transactions to larger numbers of young people. The availability and use of guns, the spread of the drug market, and the skyrocketing growth of street gangs all contributed to a dramatic rise in murder rates among young people.[85] Finally, beginning in the 1980s and continuing in the 1990s, young people became increasingly involved in various forms of hate crimes.

This changing nature of delinquency, as well as increased media coverage of violent juveniles who carry weapons and are typically involved in gangs, began to harden public attitudes toward the juvenile delinquent. The resulting "get tough" attitude toward the violent juvenile led to a number of juvenile justice initiatives in the 1990s that went beyond those implemented in the 1980s. The urgency with which states responded is seen in the fact that in the 1990s, nearly every state enacted legislation changing the way juvenile delinquents were handled.[86] This legislation led to nine state initiatives in juvenile justice that continue in force today: (1) curfews, (2) parental responsibility laws, (3) combating street gangs, (4) the movement toward graduated sanctions, (5) juvenile boot camps, (6) youths and guns, (7) juvenile proceedings and records, (8) juvenile transfer to criminal court, and (9) expanded sentencing authority.

Curfew Curfews have reemerged as a popular means to control delinquent behavior. Most curfews restrict minors to their homes between 11 P.M. and 6 A.M., with some jurisdictions allowing later hours on weekends and during the summer months. States with curfew ordinances include Minnesota, Ohio, and Tennessee.[87] One survey found that of the 200 largest cities in the United States, 60 percent enacted a new curfew statute or revised an existing law between 1990 and 1995. By 1995, more than three-quarters of these cities had a curfew ordinance in effect.[88] Juvenile arrests for curfew and loitering violations increased 113 percent between 1990 and 1999. In 1999, 28 percent of curfew arrests involved juveniles under age fifteen, and 30 percent involved females.[89] The constitutionality of juvenile curfews has been litigated in several states, but the current trend is for courts to uphold juvenile curfews as long as ordinances make exception for legitimate activities.[90]

Parental Responsibility Laws In 1995, Susan and Anthony Provenzino of St. Clair Shores, Michigan, were each fined $100 and ordered to pay an additional $1,000 in court fees because they were convicted of violating the local parental accountability ordinance. This case brought national attention to a growing trend at both local and state levels: the effort to combat youth crime by making parents criminally responsible for the delinquent behavior of their children. Of course, parents have been civilly responsible for their children's actions for a long time. What is new is the body of law that now makes parents criminally liable for their children's actions.[91] More than forty jurisdictions have mandated some type of parental responsibility provision above and beyond parents' civil liability for their children's actions.[92]

Combating Street Gangs In the mid- and late 1990s, some communities developed gang prevention and control strategies incorporating grassroots community involvement and providing services to gang youths. More typically, however, approaches to gang control involved repressive methods. The word *combating*, aptly portrays anti-gang measures such as harsher penalties for gang leaders convicted of drug dealing; increased penalties for gang-related violence, such as drive-by shootings; and enhanced penalties for any criminal act committed by a gang member.[93]

Movement Toward Graduated Sanctions Through graduated, or accountability-based, sanctions, states are endeavoring to ensure that youths who are adjudicated delinquent receive an appropriate disposition by the juvenile court. Underlying the philosophy of graduated sanctions is "the notion of providing swift

Anthony and Susan Provenzino, shown here, were convicted of violating a parental responsibility ordinance when their sixteen-year-old son was charged with breaking and entering and possession of marijuana. Such laws make parents liable for the actions of their dependent children. ■ **Do you agree with the idea of holding parents responsible for the behavior of their underage children?**

and appropriate punishment to youthful offenders based on the gravity of their offense and an assessment of the potential risk for reoffending, coupled with appropriate treatment to reduce the risk of reoffending."[94]

Juvenile Boot Camps   First started in Georgia in 1983, adult boot camps soon spread across the United States. Indeed, more than seventy adult boot camp programs are now operating in thirty states. It did not take long for the prevailing "get tough" climate to prompt the use of boot camps in juvenile justice as well. As of 1999, ten states had implemented about 50 boot camps for juveniles, which housed a total of about 4,500 juvenile offenders.[95]

Youths and Guns   In the midst of a continuing debate over gun control in the United States, there is consensus about the need to maintain and strengthen current laws restricting the possession, storage, licensing, and transfer of guns to juveniles and to enact new laws regarding juveniles who bring guns to school.[96] School shootings in recent years have added urgency to the public's desire to get guns out of the hands of juveniles.

Juvenile Proceedings and Records   Not only is the public concerned about juvenile crime, but government agencies, school officials, and victims also want more information about juvenile offenders. An increasing number of states are responding to this need by broadening access to juvenile records, allowing public access to and victim participation in juvenile proceedings, altering expungement laws for juvenile records, and fingerprinting and photographing youthful offenders.[97]

Juvenile Transfer to Criminal Court   In the 1990s, many states expanded the legislation passed in the 1980s allowing for prosecution of juveniles in adult court. This trend has increased to permit transfer of younger offenders for a larger number of offenses. The three mechanisms used to transfer juvenile offenders to adult court are judicial waiver, statutory exclusion, and direct file. The extensiveness of this movement of juvenile transfer is evident in the fact that in 1995, seventeen states expanded or amended their waiver sanctions.[98]

Expanded Sentencing Authority   Several states have created blended sentencing structures for cases involving repeat and serious juvenile delinquents. A mechanism for holding juveniles accountable for their offenses, this expanded sentencing authority allows criminal and juvenile courts to impose either juvenile or adult sentences, or at times both.[99]

In sum, a review of history reveals that juveniles constitute the only age group required to obey special laws; that juveniles receive less punishment than adults who commit the same offenses; that contemporary juveniles are viewed (accurately or not) as committing more frequent and serious offenses than juveniles in the past; and that juvenile justice policies are consistently blamed for the high rates of juvenile crime because the public views these policies as either too lenient or too harsh.[100]

▊Themes in the Study of Delinquency

Before concluding this introductory chapter, it is important to discuss some themes that flow through this text. The first theme focuses on the *social context* in which youngsters grow up and by which they are influenced. An appreciation for social context provides one critical component in understanding delinquent behavior. The second theme, *delinquency across the life course*, examines risk factors that contribute to delinquent behavior, and how such behavior affects subsequent life experiences. *Social policy* concerns form our third theme—one that asks what can be done to improve the quality of young people's lives, and one that provides ideas for effectively preventing and controlling youth crime.

Focus on Social Context

A focus on social context harks back to the 1930s Chicago school of sociology and has a long history in American scholarship.[101] In his writings, Andrew Abbott, a contemporary professor of sociology at the University of Chicago, notes the Chicago school's emphasis on context in understanding social life when he says:

> [According to the Chicago school], one cannot understand social life without understanding the arrangements of particular social actors in particular social times and places. . . .
>
> No social fact makes any sense abstracted from its context in social (and often geographic) space and social time.[102]

Applying the notion of social context to the study of juvenile delinquency helps us to understand that definitions of delinquency, the portrayal of delinquent events, the reform and punishment of delinquents, and policy decisions about delinquency, all take place within a social setting shaped by historical, legal, sociocultural, economic, and political contexts.

The *historical context* defines how juvenile delinquents were handled in the past and influences how they are perceived and handled in the present. A study of history also enables us to perceive previous cycles of juvenile justice and to understand the emergence and the eventual decline of the philosophies undergirding these cycles.[103]

The *legal context* establishes the definition of delinquent behavior and status offense behavior. It is within this context that the roles and jurisdictions of the juvenile courts are determined. This context also determines the legal basis of juvenile court decisions and the constitutional procedure for dealing with youths in trouble.

The *sociocultural context* shapes the relationship between the delinquent and societal institutions, including the family, the school, and the church or synagogue. Sociocultural research investigates the extent to which peer groups, neighborhoods, urbanization, and industrialization contribute to delinquent behavior. Sociocultural forces also shape society's norms and values, including its attitudes toward youth crime.

The *economic context* sets the conditions under which delinquents live and determines the extent to which economic factors contribute to delinquent behavior. This context cannot be ignored in U.S. society, because so many attitudes and behaviors are influenced by success goals and the means people employ to achieve them. The economic context gains in importance in fiscally hard times, as high unemployment and tight budgets affect all institutions in society, including those for youth.

Finally, the *political context* influences local and national policy decisions that deal with youth crime. It is in this context that decisions are made to toughen or soften the approach to juvenile crime. Political factors have a direct impact on juvenile justice agencies; the mood of reform may begin in the wider society, but it is in the political context that the philosophy of reform is designed and the procedures for reform are implemented.

Some studies of delinquency use contextual analysis to understand how much the interrelationships of various contexts affect the interpretation and handling of delinquency. Interest in doing contextual analysis in examinations of delinquency increased during the 1980s and 1990s. We will describe some of these studies later in this text.

Young Killers at Heart of Capital Punishment Fight in Japan

(Tokyo) After a juvenile received a life sentence in 2000 for the murder and attempted rape of Yayoi Motomura, 23, and the murder of her 11-month-old daughter, Yuka, the killer wrote a letter to a friend that placed him at the center of Japan's capital punishment debate.

"I've always been able to hurt others, run away and win. I won. Evil gets the first and last laugh," he wrote in the note, which his friend revealed to the media.

Describing the murders he committed on April 14, 1999, at the age of 18, the killer, who cannot be named because he was a minor at the time, said: "A dog saw a cute dog. (Then) it just did it right there."

His flippant attitude at the time and during his trial outraged Yayoi's husband, Hiroshi, and prosecutors, who appealed the life sentence, demanding the death penalty.

But the appellate court upheld the Yamaguchi District Court's sentence, and the case is now before the Supreme Court. The court took receipt of the defense statement Thursday in which lawyers claimed the defendant did not intend to kill, but was only trying to silence their screams and panicked.

The court is expected to rule on the lower court sentence in the next few months.

At issue is whether the death penalty should apply in the case of one young murderer. But people on both sides of the death penalty debate believe the future of capital punishment in Japan is at stake.

Strong Public Sentiment

The Supreme Court began hearing defense arguments in March—an unusual move for the highest court, which usually makes rulings based only on papers submitted by the two sides.

The decision to invite oral arguments fueled speculation that the Supreme Court was considering overturning the lower court decision and sending the case back to the lower court. If that happens, the high court might well reverse its earlier sentence and opt for capital punishment.

The defendant replaced his first attorney with Yoshihiro Yasuda, a well-known human rights lawyer and death penalty opponent. He also wrote to the victim's husband in April.

Hiroshi Motomura said he has no interest in reading it. "He did not write to me once in the past seven years to apologize, explain or make sense of what happened," said Motomura, who suspects the letter is only a defense tactic aimed at showing contrition. "But it does show he is finally ready to take this trial seriously."

The possibility that someone could be hanged for a double-murder the accused committed as a minor has alarmed death penalty foes.

Hiroshi Motomura, whose wife and infant child were murdered by a minor, speaks to reporters at the Japanese Supreme Court in Tokyo.
■ What issues were at stake in the case?

The public is increasingly sympathetic to victims and their families in such crimes, according to opinion polls by the Cabinet Office, which point to an 80 percent support rate for capital punishment.

"More victims of crime are speaking out, and the public is taking a harder line against juvenile criminals," said Kenji Hirose, a former judge and professor of law at Rikkyo University in Tokyo.

"Sentences for taking a human life have, for the most part, been lighter in Japan than those overseas," he said, noting among judges, it was a rule of thumb that a murderer should spend about 10 years in prison for each life taken.

When the Hiroshima High Court upheld the defendant's life sentence in 2002, the court said there was a possibility the accused could learn to live a useful life.

Delinquency Across the Life Course

life-course perspective
A sociological framework suggesting that four key factors determine the shape of the life course: location in time and place, linked lives, human agency, and timing of lives.

human agency
The active role juveniles take in their lives; the fact that juveniles are not merely subject to social and structural constraints but also make choices and decisions based on the alternatives that they see before them.

The **life-course perspective**, a relatively new but extremely promising theoretical orientation, represents a major change in how we think about and study lives.[104] Until recently, sociological research largely neglected life histories and individual life trajectories. However, the many publications of Glen H. Elder Jr. and his colleagues have done much to stimulate the use of life-course theory as an appropriate research base in the study of individuals and groups.[105] Drawing on the increased numbers of longitudinal studies that examine the lives of young children, and that follow these cohorts sometimes for decades, many researchers are using the life-course perspective in the study of delinquent behavior.[106]

The increased attention given to the life course in both sociology and delinquency studies has been accompanied by a dramatic resurgence of interest in **human agency.** The term *human agency,* or *agency,* recognizes the important fact that juveniles, like people everywhere, are influenced by social opportunities and structural constraints, and that they make choices and decisions based on the alternatives that they perceive. Life-course theory relates individuals to a broad social context, and recognizes that within the constraints of their social world, individuals purposely plan and make

The court also mentioned his troubled childhood, during which his mother committed suicide, as a reason for clemency.

It is still possible the defendant, now 25, may reform, said Koichi Kikuta, a law professor at Meiji University in Tokyo.

"I suspect the (Supreme) court is being influenced by the growing tendency among the public to support crime victims," Kikuta said.

"The previous court decisions cited the possibility that the defendant could be rehabilitated. I think handing down a harsher penalty in response to public sentiment is unjust."

Motomura, who has been vocal in his criticism of the killer, joined with other crime victims in an effort to expand their rights at a time when they were given little access to trials of the accused offenders.

In April 2005, a law to allow the victimized to play a greater role during trials took effect. And the government now grants them greater access to information on investigations and trials.

Effective Deterrent?

Death sentences can be handed down to people aged 18 and older, but the Juvenile Law states that life imprisonment should be meted out when sentencing someone who was under 20 when the crime was committed.

Since the end of the World War II, there have been eight exceptions made to this rule, where people who were under 20 at the time of their crimes have been sentenced to death.

They include the Aug. 1, 1995, hanging of Norio Nagayama, who was originally sentenced to life for murdering four people when he was 19. The Supreme Court in 1983 overturned that sentence and ruled he should be executed.

"The Nagayama case became the standard—if you're a minor and kill four people, you could face death, but with fewer victims, you could avoid it," Motomura said. "That is precisely why the perpetrator assumed he would not be put to death, but he is wrong."

Those like Motomura who are pushing for harsher juvenile sentences argue they will deter crime.

"An 18-year-old should be aware of the consequences of killing another person," said Yoshikazu Otsuka, a lawyer based in Urawa, Saitama Prefecture.

Capital punishment maintains order in society and, he figured, prevents lynching of perpetrators by victims' families.

But attorney Yasuda disagrees: "Capital punishment is cruel, brutal and senseless. Will putting this man to death bring the victims back? No. Will crime go down if we put this man to death? No."

But beyond the usual arguments, the case spotlights how much weight Japan gives to both victims and perpetrators.

Motomura visited Napoleon Beazley, a 30-year-old on death row in Texas in January 2002.

Beazley, a star student, was given a lethal injection four months later on May 28 for shooting a 63-year-old man in a carjacking at age 17.

Beazley told Motomura that he only realized the full weight of the suffering he caused the victim's family when he saw his mother collapse in tears when his sentence was handed down.

Motomura went away convinced that the death penalty was necessary to make people realize what they had done.

But Beazley's conclusion differed from Motomura's. His last words were a passionate plea to give death-row inmates a second chance.

"Give those men a chance to do what's right. Give them a chance to undo their wrongs. A lot of them want to fix the mess they started, but don't know how. The problem is not in that people aren't willing to help them find out, but in the system telling them it won't matter anyway," he said. "No one wins tonight. No one gets closure. No one walks away victorious."

Source: Mayumi Negishi and Kaho Shimizu, "Young Killers at Heart of Capital Punishment Fight," *The Japan Times,* May 20, 2006. http://search .japantimes.co.jp/cgi-bin/nn20060520f2 .html. Reprinted with permission from *The Japan Times.*

choices from among the options they believe are available to them. Those decisions largely determine their life course.[107]

Giele and Elder identified four key factors that determine the shape of the life course: (1) location in time and place (cultural background), (2) linked lives (social integration), (3) human agency (individual goal orientation), and (4) timing of lives (strategic adaptation). First, individual location affects personal experience and therefore can be understood as being socially and individually patterned in ways that carry through time. Second, all levels of social action (cultural, social, institutional, psychological, and sociobiological) interact and mutually influence one another—not only as parts of the individual's whole but also as the result of contact with other individuals sharing similar experiences. Some individuals will show discontinuity and disruption, whereas others will show a harmonious interweaving of individual attainments with social and cultural expectations. Third, in order to meet their needs, individuals make decisions and organize their lives around goals: to be economically secure, to find satisfaction, to avoid pain. Fourth, to accomplish their goals, individuals both respond to the timing of external events and undertake actions and engage in events and behavior in order to use the available resources.[108] As diagrammed in

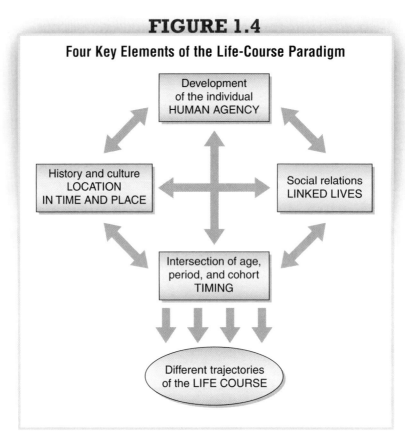

FIGURE 1.4

Four Key Elements of the Life-Course Paradigm

Source: Janet Z. Giele and Glen H. Elder Jr., "Life Course Research: Development of a Field," in *Methods of Life Course Research: Qualitative and Quantitative Approaches*, edited by Janet Z. Giele and Glen H. Elder Jr., p. 9. Copyright © 1998 by Sage Publications. Reprinted by permission of Sage Publications, Inc.

Figure 1.4, the first three elements come together through the funnel of the fourth—timing.

On November 16, 2005, John H. Laub delivered the Sutherland Award Address at the Annual Meeting of the American Society of Criminology in Toronto, Ontario. In his speech, Laub identified the five principles of what he, along with collaborator Robert Sampson, call *Life-Course Criminology*. Laub asserts "that these [principles] can provide the basis of a paradigm on the causes and dynamics of crime for the field. In turn, this body of knowledge can be referred to as the core, that is, the soul of criminology."[109]

The first principle, then, is that *crime is more likely to occur when an individual's ties to society are attenuated.* . . .

The second principle . . . is that *delinquency and other forms of antisocial behavior in childhood are strongly related to troublesome adult behaviors including crime as well as other problem behaviors in a variety of life domains.* . . .

The third principle . . . is that *social ties embedded in adult transitions explain variation in crime unaccounted for by childhood propensities. The adult life course matters.* . . .

The fourth principle . . . is that *human agency is vitally important to understanding patterns of stability and change in criminal behavior over the life course. Individuals, whether criminal actors or not, make choices and are active participants in the construction of their lives.*

The fifth principle . . . is that *a dual policy focus emphasizing prevention and reform should be the central feature of criminal justice practices* (italics in the original).[110]

Studies of delinquency across the life course are described in many chapters in this text. The *Voices of Delinquency* supplement, which is available with this text, records the trajectories of individuals across their life course. A few stories describe

Web PLACES 1.5

View the OJJDP PowerPoint presentation "Juvenile Population Characteristics" at **www** **.justicestudies.com/** **WebPlaces**.

how individuals made decisions that have resulted in their being on death row or being sentenced to prison for the remainder of their lives. Other stories are stirring and even inspiring accounts of how individuals used life's turning points to desist from crime and to change their own futures.

Policy-Oriented Analysis

There is much to be discouraged about in the approach to handling juveniles in general and of law-violating juveniles in particular in this society. Far too many children are involved in delinquent behaviors and go on to adult crime. The Children's Defense Fund's *State of America's Children 2005* is quick to remind us of the cost of letting vast numbers of young people grow up without realizing their potential:

> To stay on the path to successful adulthood, children need significant support and protection, including: strong families; early development and education; quality health and mental health care; good schools; healthy communities; constructive peer relationships; after-school and summer programs; and positive role models. Parents, community and faith leaders, service providers, policy makers and others must meet our children's needs for support and guide them in navigating the risks of childhood. It is our job to protect our children.[111]

The pressing and exciting challenge for all of us is to design recommendations that provide helpful directions for dealing more effectively with adolescents in general and with delinquents in particular.

CHAPTER Summary

This chapter has placed delinquent behavior within the wider context of adolescent problem behaviors and has emphasized the following points:

- Those adolescents most likely to become delinquents are high-risk youths who are involved in multiple problem behaviors.

- Characteristic problem behaviors include school failure and dropout, teenage pregnancy and fatherhood, and drug use and other forms of delinquency.

- About one in every four adolescents is at high risk of engaging in multiple problem behaviors.

- The history of responses to juvenile misbehavior displays a pattern in which society has taken authority away from the family and given it to juvenile authorities—while simultaneously growing dissatisfied with the official handling of juvenile crime.

- The legal context for dealing with delinquency stems from the early philosophy of *parens patriae* and provides for the juvenile court to become a substitute parent for wayward children. Historically, the task of the juvenile court has been to reconcile the best interests of the child with the adequate protection of society.

- Although they sometimes commit the same crimes as adults, juveniles may also be apprehended for status offenses—for behaviors that would not be defined as criminal if adults engaged in them.

- Delinquency in the United States occurs within a social framework that has become increasingly child centered. The least restrictive approach to youth problems, however, has traditionally been reserved for middle- and upper-class youths. Realistically speaking, lower-class youths who violate the law frequently receive more punitive sanctions from the juvenile court.

- Although the public is child centered, there is a growing concern about serious juvenile crime, and a "get tough" attitude has come to characterize recent public awareness.

- Policymakers are presently focused on the serious and repeat juvenile criminal, and both the public and legislators want to make certain that these offenders are held accountable.

- One theme of this text is *delinquency across the life course,* which is also called life-course theory, life-course criminology, or the life-course perspective.

- Another of our book's themes focuses on the *various social contexts* in which young people find themselves and considers how these contexts influence the likelihood of delinquent behavior.

- A third text theme is related to *social policy,* which is the process of proposing and enacting means by which youngsters in our society can realize their potential and lead productive and satisfying lives while ensuring safety and security for all.

1. How has the role of the family changed throughout the history of juvenile justice in the United States?
2. Define the concept of *parens patriae*. Why is it important in the history of juvenile delinquency?
3. What are the three categories in which the juvenile court has jurisdiction over youths?
4. What are some of the factors that make juvenile delinquency a serious problem in U.S. society?
5. How have the juvenile justice initiatives of the 1990s affected how delinquents are handled?

WEB
Interactivity

Visit **www.childstats.gov** to read the Federal Interagency Forum on Child and Family Statistics publication *America's Children in Brief: Key National Indicators of Well-Being, 2006.*

The report includes detailed information on the well-being of children and families throughout the United States.

The first section, "Population and Family Characteristics," describes the context in which children live (including things such as changes in children's family settings and living arrangements). The sections that follow highlight indicators of child well-being in four key areas: economic security, health, behavior and social environment, and education. Among other things, the data in the 2006 report show that adolescent birthrates continued to decline to the lowest ever recorded, immunization rates were at record highs, more young children were being read to daily by a family member, average mathematics scores of fourth- and eighth-graders reached an all-time high, and teen smoking was at its lowest level since data collection began.

The data also show, however, that the proportion of births to unmarried women continues to rise, and that the rate of infants born with low or very low birthweight continues to increase.

For this assignment you should visit the Forum's website, view the report's findings, and then answer this question: Which of the findings contained in *America's Children in Brief: Key National Indicators of Well-Being, 2006* seem especially relevant to issues of crime and delinquency, and why?

Source: From www.childstats.gov. Reprinted with permission from the Federal Interagency Forum on Child and Family Statistics.

Notes

1. Ronald Smothers, "Newark Teenager Is Ordered Held in Fatal Shooting of His Parents," *New York Times,* June 19, 2003.
2. Fox Butterfield, "Guns and Jeers Used by Gangs to Buy Silence," *New York Times,* January 16, 2005.
3. Michael Wilson, "A 9-Year-Old Suspect in Court: 'Traumatized,' Her Lawyer Says," *New York Times,* June 3, 2005.
4. Jacquelynne S. Eccles, Carol Midgley, Allan Wigfield, Christy Miller Buchanan, David Reuman, Constance Flanagan, and

Douglas MacIver, "Development during Adolescence: The Impact of Stage–Environment Fit on Young Adolescents' Experiences in Schools and in Families," *American Psychologist* (February 1993), p. 90.

5. The concept of childhood is usually identified as beginning in the early decades of the twentieth century. For a good discussion of the social construction of adolescence, see Barry C. Feld, *Bad Kids: Race and the Transformation of the Juvenile Court* (New York: Oxford Press, 1999), pp. 19–31.

6. Lloyd de Mause, ed., *The History of Childhood* (New York: Psycho-History Press), 1974, p. 1.

7. George Henry Payne, *The Child in Human Progress* (New York: G. P. Putnam, 1969), p. 324.

8. Gerald R. Adams and Thomas Gullotta, *Adolescent Life Experiences* (Monterey, Calif.: Brooks/Cole Publishing, 1983), p. 6.

9. Ibid., pp. 7–8.

10. Eric H. Erikson and Huey P. Newton, *In Search of Common Ground* (New York: W. W. Norton, 1973), p. 52.

11. Joy G. Dryfoos, *Adolescents at Risk: Prevalence and Prevention* (New York: Oxford University Press, 1990), p. 25.

12. Federal Intragency Forum on Child and Family Statistics, *America's Children: Key National Indictators of Well-Being, 2005* (Washington, D.C.: U.S. Government Printing Office, 2005), p. vii.

13. Howard N. Snyder and Melissa Sickmund, *Juvenile Offenders and Victims: 2006 National Report* (Washington, D.C.: National Center for Juvenile Justice and Office of Justice Programs, 2006), p 2.

14. Federal Intragency Forum on Child and Family Statistics, *America's Children: Key National Indicators of Well-Being, 2005*, p. vii.

15. Nanette J. Davis, *Youth Crisis: Growing Up in the High-Risk Society* (Westport, Conn.: Praeger, 1999), p. 3.

16. Ibid., pp. 4–5.

17. Ibid., p. iii.

18. Children's Defense Fund's Mission Statement at www.childrensdefense.org.

19. Children's Defense Fund press release, July 1, 2004. See www.childrensdefense.org press release.

20. Richard Dembo, Linda Williams, Jeffrey Fagan, and James Schmeidler, "Development and Assessment of a Classification of High-Risk Youths," *Journal of Drug Issues* 24 (1994), p. 26.

21. Marc Le Blanc, "Family Dynamics, Adolescent Delinquency and Adult Criminality." Paper presented at the Society for Life History Research Conference, Keystone, Colorado (November 1990).

22. Richard Jessor and S. L. Jessor, *Problem Behavior and Psychosocial Development: A Longitudinal Study of Youth* (New York: Academic Press, 1977). See also Richard Jessor, John E. Donovan, and Francis M. Costa, *Beyond Adolescence: Problem Behavior and Young Adult Development* (New York: Cambridge University Press, 1991).

23. David Huizinga, Rolf Loeber, Terence P. Thornberry, and Lynn Cothern, *Co-Occurrence of Delinquency and Other Problem Behaviors* (Washington, D.C.: Office of Juvenile Justice and Delinquency Prevention, 2000), p. 1. For an examination of the prevalence and patterns of co-occurring mental health problem symptoms, substance use, and delinquent conduct in a sample of multiple-problem and detained youth, see Cathryn C. Potter and Jeffrey M. Jenson, "Cluster Profiles of Multiple Problem Youth: Mental Health Problem Symptoms, Substance Use, and Delinquent Conduct," *Criminal Justice and Behavior* 30 (April 2003), pp. 230–250.

24. John E. Donovan and Richard Jessor, "Structure of Problem Behavior in Adolescence and Young Adulthood," *Journal of Consulting and Clinical Psychology* 53 (1985), pp. 890–904. See also D. Wayne Osgood, Lloyd D. Johnston, Patrick M. O'Malley, and Jerald G. Bachman, "The Generality of Deviance in Late Adolescence and Early Adulthood," *American Sociological Review* 53 (1988), pp. 81–93.

25. Travis Hirschi, "A Brief Commentary on Akers' 'Delinquent Behavior, Drugs and Alcohol: What Is the Relationship,' " *Today's Delinquent* 3 (1984), pp. 49–52.

26. Michael R. Gottfredson and Travis Hirschi, *A General Theory of Crime* (Stanford, Calif.: Stanford University Press, 1990), pp. 90–91.

27. Helene Raskin White, "Early Problem Behavior and Later Drug Problems," *Journal of Research in Crime and Delinquency* 29 (November 1992), p. 414.

28. For this position, see also D. Wayne Osgood, "Covariation among Adolescent Problem Behaviors." Paper presented at the Annual Meeting of the American Society of Criminology, Baltimore, Md. (November 1990); and Helene R. White, "The Drug Use–Delinquency Connection in Adolescence," in *Drugs, Crime and the Criminal Justice System*, edited by Ralph Weisheit (Cincinnati, Ohio: Anderson, 1990), pp. 215–256.

29. See also Delbert S. Elliott, David Huizinga, and Scott Menard, *Multiple Problem Youth: Delinquency, Substance Use and Mental Health Problems* (New York: Springer-Verlag, 1989).

30. White, "Early Problem Behavior and Later Drug Problems," p. 412.

31. Ibid. See also Jeffrey Fagan, Joseph G. Weis, Y.-T. Cheng, and John K. Watters, *Drug and Alcohol Use, Violent Delinquency and Social Bonding: Implications for Theory and Intervention* (San Francisco: URSA Institute, 1987).

32. See also Delbert S. Elliott et al., *Multiple Problem Youth;* and Denise B. Kandel, Ora Simcha-Fagan, and Mark Davies, "Risk Factors for Delinquency and Illicit Drug Use from Adolescence to Young Adulthood," *Journal of Drug Issues* 16 (1986), pp. 67–90.

33. Dryfoos, *Adolescents at Risk,* pp. 245–246.

34. Federal Bureau of Investigation, *Crime in the United States 2005.* www.fbi.gov/ucr/05cius/index.html.

35. Ibid.

36. *In re Poff,* 135 F. Supp. 224 (C.C.C. 1955).

37. Barry Krisberg and James Austin, *The Children of Ishmael: Critical Perspectives on Juvenile Justice* (Palo Alto, Calif.: Mayfield Publishing, 1978), p. 60.

38. Carol J. DeFrances, *Juveniles Prosecuted in State Criminal Courts* (Washington, D.C.: Office of Juvenile Justice and Delinquency Prevention, U.S. Department of Justice, 1997), p. 1.

39. These interviews were conducted in two phases: as part of the juvenile victimization study in the 1970s and the follow-up of this study in 1989. In addition, Linda Dippold Bartollas interviewed parents, probation officers, juvenile court judges,

and public school teachers in Illinois, Iowa, and Minnesota during the late 1980s and 1990s.

40. Meda Chesney-Lind and Lisa J. Pasko, *The Female Offender: Girls, Women, and Crime,* 2nd ed. (Thousand Oaks, Calif.: Sage, 2004), pp. 60–61.

41. See Chesney-Lind on the feminist theory of delinquency in Chapter 7.

42. Charles W. Thomas, "Are Status Offenders Really So Different?" *Crime and Delinquency* 22 (1976), pp. 438–455.

43. Maynard L. Erickson, "Some Empirical Questions Concerning the Current Revolution in Juvenile Justice," in *The Future of Childhood and Juvenile Justice,* edited by LaMar Empey (Charlottesville: University of Virginia Press, 1979).

44. Solomon Kobrin, Frank R. Hellum, and John W. Peterson, "Offense Patterns of Status Offenders," in *Critical Issues in Juvenile Delinquency,* edited by David Shichor and Delos H. Kelley (Lexington, Mass.: Heath, 1980), p. 211.

45. Ibid., pp. 230–231.

46. J. G. Weis, Karleen Sakumoto, John Sederstrom, and Carol Zeiss, *Jurisdiction and the Elusive Status Offender: A Comparison of Involvement in Delinquent Behavior and Status Offenses* (Washington, D.C.: U.S. Government Printing Office, 1980), p. 96.

47. Joseph H. Rankin and L. Edward Wells, "From Status to Delinquent Offense Escalation," *Journal of Criminal Justice* 13 (1985), pp. 171–180.

48. Thomas Kelley, "Status Offenders Can Be Different: A Comparative Study of Delinquent Careers," *Crime and Delinquency* 29 (1983), pp. 365–380.

49. Randall G. Shelden, John A. Horvath, and Sharon Tracy, "Do Status Offenders Get Worse? Some Clarifications on the Question of Escalation," *Crime and Delinquency* 35 (April 1989), pp. 214–215.

50. Solomon Kobrin et al., "Offense Patterns of Status Offenders," p. 213.

51. Shelden et al., "Do Status Offenders Get Worse? Some Clarifications on the Question of Escalation," p. 215.

52. See Chris E. Marshall, Ineke Haen Marshall, and Charles W. Thomas, "The Implementation of Formal Procedures in Juvenile Court Processing of Status Offenders," *Journal of Criminal Justice* 11 (1983), pp. 195–211.

53. See Clemens Bartollas, Stuart J. Miller, and Simon Dinitz, *Juvenile Victimization: The Institutional Paradox* (New York: Halsted Press, 1976).

54. U.S. Congress, Senate, Committee on the Judiciary Subcommittee to Investigate Juvenile Delinquency, 1973, *The Juvenile Justice and Delinquency Prevention Act—S.3148 and S.821.* 92d Cong., 2d sess.; 93d Cong., 1st sess.

55. See State Juvenile Justice Profiles website at http://ojjdp.ncjrs.org/ojstatbb/dat.html.

56. M. A. Bortner, Mary Sutherland, and Russ Winn, "Race and the Impact of Juvenile Institutionalization," *Crime and Delinquency* 31 (1985), pp. 35–46; and Anne L. Schneider, *The Impact of Deinstitutionalization on Recidivism and Secure Confinement of Status Offenders* (Washington, D.C.: U.S. Department of Justice, 1985).

57. Howard N. Snyder and Melissa Sickmund, *Juvenile Offenders and Victims: 1999 National Report* (Washington, D.C.: Office of Juvenile Justice and Delinquency Prevention, 1999), p. 88.

58. Gwen A. Holden and Robert A. Kapler, "Deinstitutionalizing Status Offenders: A Record of Progress," *Juvenile Justice* 2 (Fall/Winter, 1995), p. 8.

59. Feld, *Bad Kids,* p. 178.

60. Thomas J. Bernard, *The Cycle of Juvenile Justice* (New York: Oxford University Press, 1992), p. 28.

61. Thomas, "Are Status Offenders Really So Different?" pp. 440–442.

62. Feld, *Bad Kids,* p. 178.

63. Ibid., p. 179.

64. Martin Rouse, "The Diversion of Status Offenders, Criminalization, and the New York Family Court." Revised paper presented at the Annual Meeting of the American Society of Criminology, Reno, Nevada (November 1989), pp. 1, 2, 10–11.

65. George Santayana, *The Life of Reason* (London: Constable, 1905), p. 284.

66. David J. Rothman, *The Discovery of the Asylum* (Boston: Little, Brown, 1971), pp. 46–53.

67. Ibid., pp. 225–227.

68. Bradford Kinney Peirce, *A Half Century with Juvenile Delinquents* (Montclair, N.J.: Patterson Smith, 1969 [1869]), p. 41.

69. Roscoe Pound, "The Juvenile Court and the Law," *National Probation and Parole Association Yearbook* 1 (1944), p. 4.

70. *Kent v. United States,* 383 U.S. 541, 86 S. Ct. 1045, 16 L. Ed. 2d 84 (1966); *In re Gault,* 387 U.S. 1, 18 L. Ed. 368 (1970); *McKeiver v. Pennsylvania,* 403 U.S. 528, 535 (1971); *In re Barbara Burrus,* 275 N.C. 517, 169 S.E. 2d 879 (1969); and *Breed v. Jones,* 421 U.S. 519, 95 S. Ct. 1779 (1975).

71. *In re Gault.*

72. U.S. Congress, *The Juvenile Justice and Delinquency Prevention Act.*

73. Ira M. Schwartz, *(In)justice for Juveniles: Rethinking the Best Interests of the Child* (Lexington, Mass.: Lexington Books, 1989), p. 118.

74. National Advisory Committee for Juvenile Justice and Delinquency Prevention, *Serious Juvenile Crime: A Redirected Federal Effort* (Washington, D.C.: U.S. Department of Justice, 1984), p. 18.

75. R. B. Coates, A. D. Miller, and L. E. Ohlin, *Diversity in a Youth Correctional System: Handling Delinquents in Massachusetts* (Cambridge, Mass.: Ballinger Publishing, 1978), p. 190.

76. Barry Krisberg et al., "The Watershed of Juvenile Justice Reform," *Crime and Delinquency* 32 (January 1986), p. 30.

77. Alfred S. Regnery, "A Federal Perspective on Juvenile Justice Reform," *Crime and Delinquency* 32 (January 1986), p. 40. For an extensive examination of crime control in the 1980s, see Ted Gest, *Crime and Politics: Big Government's Erratic Campaign for Law and Order:* (New York: Oxford, 2001), pp. 41–62.

78. National Advisory Committee for Juvenile Justice and Delinquency Prevention (NAC), *Serious Juvenile Crime: A Redirected Federal Effort,* p. 9.

79. Ibid., pp. 9, 11.

80. Ibid., p. 11.

81. Krisberg et al., "Watershed of Juvenile Justice Reform," p. 7.

82. Schwartz, *(In)justice for Juveniles,* p. 132.

83. Krisberg et al., "Watershed of Juvenile Justice Reform," p. 9; Barry C. Feld, "Legislative Policies toward the Serious Juvenile Offender," *Crime and Delinquency* 27 (October 1981), p. 500.

84. Edward Cimler and Lee Roy Bearch, "Factors Involved in Juvenile Decisions about Crime," *Criminal Justice and Behavior* 8 (September 1981), pp. 275–286.

85. For the development of these trends, see the interview with Alfred Blumstein in *Law Enforcement News* 21 (April 30, 1995), pp. 1–2 and 11–12.

86. National Criminal Justice Association, *Juvenile Justice Reform Initiatives in the States: 1994–1996* (Washington, D.C.: Office of Juvenile Justice and Delinquency Prevention, 1997), p. 9.

87. David McDowall, Colin Loftin, and Brian Wiersema, "The Impact of Youth Curfew Laws on Juvenile Crime Rates," *Crime and Delinquency* 46 (January 2000), p. 76.

88. U.S. Conference of Mayors, *A Status Report on Youth Curfews in America's Cities: A 347-City Survey,* www.usmayors.org/uscm/news/publications/curfew.htm.

89. Howard N. Snyder, *Juvenile Arrests 1999: Juvenile Justice Bulletin* (Washington, D.C. Office of Juvenile Justice and Delinquency Prevention, 2000), p. 1.

90. National Criminal Justice Association, *Juvenile Justice Reform Initiatives in the States,* p. 13.

91. Ibid., p. 18.

92. Susan Pollet, "Responses to Juvenile Crime Consider the Extent of Parents' Responsibility for Children's Acts," *New York State Bar Journal* (July–August, 2004), pp. 26–30.

93. National Criminal Justice Association, *Juvenile Justice Reform Initiatives in the States,* p. 24.

94. Ibid., p. 27.

95. Doris Layton MacKenzie, David B. Wilson, Gaylene Styve Armstrong, and Angela R. Gover, "The Impact of Boot Camps and Traditional Institutions on Juvenile Residents: Perceptions, Adjustment, and Change," *Journal of Research in Crime and Delinquency* 38 (August 2000), pp. 279–313.

96. National Criminal Justice Association, *Juvenile Justice Reform Initiatives in the States,* p. 33.

97. Ibid., p. 36.

98. Donna Lyons, "National Conference of State Legislatures, State Legislature Report," *Juvenile Crime and Justice State Enactments* 9 (November 1995), pp. 13–14.

99. National Criminal Justice Association, *Juvenile Justice Reform Initiatives in the States,* p. 46.

100. Bernard, *The Cycle of Juvenile Justice,* pp. 21–22.

101. Andrew Abbott, "Of Time and Space: The Contemporary Relevance of the Chicago School," *Social Forces* 75 (1997), pp. 1149–1182. Quoted in James F. Short Jr., "The Level of Explanation Problem Revisited—The American Society of Criminology 1997 Presidential Address," *Criminology* 36 (1998), p. 6.

102. Abbott, "Of Time and Space," p. 1152.

103. Bernard, *The Cycle of Juvenile Justice,* p. 64.

104. Glen H. Elder Jr., Monica Kirkpatrick Johnson, and Robert Crosnoe, "The Emergence and Development of Life Course Theory," in *Handbook of the Life Course,* edited by Jeylan T. Mortimer and Michael J. Shanahan (New York: Kluwer Academic/Plenum Publishers, 2003), p. 3.

105. See G. H. Elder Jr., *Children of the Great Depression: Social Change in Life Experience, 25th Anniversary Edition* (Boulder, Co.: Westview Press, 1999); G. H. Elder Jr. and E. D. Conger, *Children of the Land: Adversity and Success in Rural America* (Chicago: University of Chicago Press, 2000); and Elder, "Time, Human Agency, and Social Change," pp. 4–15.

106. The two most influential studies of the life course of the many that are cited in this text are Robert J. Sampson and John H. Laub, *Crime in the Making: Pathways and Turning Points through Life* (Cambridge, Mass.: Harvard University Press, 1993); and John H. Laub and Robert J. Sampson, *Shared Beginnings, Divergent Lives: Delinquent Boys to Age 70* (Cambridge, Mass.: Harvard University Press, 2003).

107. Glen H. Elder, Jr., "Time, Human Agency, and Social Change: Perspectives on the Life Course," *Social Psychology Quarterly* 57 (1994), p. 6. For an excellent review of agency, see Mustafas Emirbayer and Ann Mische, "What Is Agency?" *American Journal of Sociology* 103 (January 1998), pp. 962–1023.

108. Janet Z. Giele and Glen H. Elder Jr., "Life Course Research: Development of a Field," in *Methods of Life Course Research: Qualitative and Quantitative Approaches,* edited by Janet Z. Giele and Glen H. Elder Jr. (Thousand Oaks, Calif.: Sage Publications, 1998), pp. 9–10.

109. John H. Laub, "Edwin H. Sutherland and the Michael-Adler Report: Searching for the Soul of Criminology Seventy Years Later," *Criminology* 44 (May 2006), p. 241.

110. Ibid., pp. 242–246. Reprinted with permission from the American Society of Criminology.

111. Children's Defense Fund, *The State of America's Children 2005,* p. 164.

2

The Measurement and Nature of Delinquency

> " Most juvenile crime does not come to the attention of the juvenile justice system. "
>
> —Juvenile Offenders and Victims: 2006 National Report

CHAPTER Objectives

AFTER READING THIS CHAPTER, YOU SHOULD BE ABLE TO ANSWER THE FOLLOWING QUESTIONS:

- What do official and unofficial statistics tell us about the extent of juvenile delinquency?

- Is juvenile violent crime increasing in the United States?

- How do such social factors as gender, racial and ethnic background, and social class relate to delinquency?

- What other dimensions of offending appear to be important in delinquent behavior?

- Why do the majority of juvenile offenders exit from delinquent activity by the end of their adolescent years?

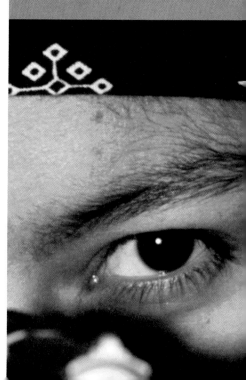

An 11-year-old New Brunswick, N.J., boy who admitted luring a 3-year-old boy from a library and beating him to death with a baseball bat was sentenced in December 2003 to spend 18 years in the custody of New Jersey's juvenile-justice system.

Under a plea bargain, the boy admitted kidnapping and murdering Amir Beeks of Woodbridge, N.J., on March 26, 2003. He was sentenced in a closed hearing after the slain child's adoptive mother read a letter that she said described the crime as a "senseless, horrible beating" of a normal, happy 3-year-old.

The mother, Rosalyn Singleton, 38, said she grieved that her son would never know the milestones and happy occasions of childhood—the first day of kindergarten, the loss of a first tooth, or Christmas and holidays with family.

Ms. Singleton also denounced the 11-year-old and his father for what she said was their failure to show remorse during the sentencing hearing before Judge Roger W. Daley.

Law enforcement authorities said the older boy lured the younger one from a library, walked with him to the backyard, bludgeoned him with a bat, and placed him, mortally injured, in a nearby culvert. The attack occurred in a plastic, log-cabin-style child's playhouse near the library.

The boy, whom neighbors described as lonely and hostile, became one of the youngest detainees in the custody of New Jersey's Juvenile Justice Commission. He will be under detention or parole supervision for 24 years, until he is age 35.

Adapted from Robert Hanley, "Boy Sentenced to 18 years for Murder of a 3-Year-old," *New York Times*, December 13, 2003. Copyright © 2003 by The New York Times Co. Reprinted with permission.

Sensational crimes like the murder of little Amir Beeks have fueled public concern over juvenile crime. Some of the questions that we will address in the pages that follow include: Is juvenile crime more serious today than it was in the past? Is it increasing or decreasing? What do we know about violent and chronic delinquents? Is a major juvenile crime wave about to engulf our society? Are there more juvenile "monsters" now than there were before, or have the media merely sensationalized the violent acts of a few?

To determine answers to these questions, it will be necessary to examine the extent of delinquent behavior, the social factors related to delinquency, the dimensions of delinquent behavior, and the various ways that are used today to measure delinquency.

Uniform Crime Reporting Program data, juvenile court statistics, cohort studies, self-report studies, and victimization surveys are the major sources of data that researchers use to measure the extent and nature of delinquent behavior. Knowledge of both the prevalence and the incidence of delinquency is necessary if we are to understand the extent of youth crime. The term **prevalence of delinquency** has to do with the proportion of members of a cohort or specific age category who have committed delinquent acts by a certain age;[1] **incidence of delinquency** refers to the frequency of offending, or to the number of delinquent events.

prevalence of delinquency
The percentage of the juvenile population who are involved in delinquent behavior.

incidence of delinquency
The frequency with which delinquent behavior takes place.

Measuring Delinquency

New York, Massachusetts, and Maine were the first states to collect crime statistics; for the most part, record keeping by states and localities during the early years of U.S. history was haphazard or nonexistent. Federal record keeping was authorized in 1870 when Congress created the Department of Justice. Initially the states and local police establishments largely ignored the task of record keeping (either because of indifference or because of fear of federal control), but this tendency began to reverse in the early part of the twentieth century when the International Association of Chiefs of Police formed a committee on uniform crime reports. In 1930, the attorney general designated the Federal Bureau of Investigation to serve as the national clearinghouse for data collected by the Uniform Crime Reports program. Beginning with the 2005 data set (posted in 2006), the UCR Program no longer publishes a printed copy of annual crime data. Instead, it is electronically posted to the FBI's website under the title *Crime in the United States (CUS) XXXX,* where *XXXX* indicates the respective year.

An examination of the *CUS 2005* indicates that juveniles are arrested for the same kinds of offenses as adults, as well as for status offenses (see Chapter 1). For example, although both adults and juveniles are arrested for such serious offenses as murder and aggravated assault and for such less serious offenses as simple assault and carrying weapons, only juveniles can be taken into custody for running away, violating curfew, or truancy from school.

The crimes for which the FBI collects information are divided into two classes, Part I and Part II offenses. Part I offenses, also known as **index offenses,** are subdivided further into crimes against the person, such as murder, rape, robbery, and aggravated assault, and crimes against property, such as burglary, larceny, auto theft, and arson. Juveniles who are arrested for the violent Part I offenses are more likely to be held for trial as adults, whereas those arrested for less serious offenses usually are processed by juvenile authorities. The exceptions to this general rule are those juveniles who have lengthy records of crime, including violent offenses, and those who are held over for trial in adult courts because they are believed to be threats to society.

Each month, police departments across the United States report to the FBI the number of offenses that come to their attention and the number of offenses that the police are able to clear by arrest. **Clearance by arrest** indicates that a person was arrested because he or she confessed to an offense or was implicated by witnesses or by other criminal evidence. These monthly reports are summarized in year-end reports, which constitute our major official source of information about crime in the United States. The data are subdivided into many different statistical categories, including the backgrounds of alleged offenders and the types of crimes for which they are arrested.

In response to law enforcement's need for more flexible, in-depth data, the UCR Program formulated the National Incident-Based Reporting System (NIBRS), which presents comprehensive, detailed information about crime incidents. One advantage of NIBRS is that, unlike the UCR, it reports all offenses committed during a crime event, not just the most serious offense. Although more law enforcement agencies are participating, the data still are not pervasive enough to make generalizations about crime in the United States.

Crime in the United States 2005 data pose numerous problems. One of the most serious complaints is that the police can report only crimes that come to their attention. Many crimes are hidden or are not reported to the police; therefore, the Uniform Crime Reporting program vastly underestimates the actual amount of crime in the United States. Some critics also charge that because the police arrest only juveniles who commit serious property and personal crimes and ignore most of the other offenses committed by young people, these statistics tell us more about official police policy and practice than about the amount of youth crime. Moreover, youthful offenders may be easier to detect in the act of committing a crime than older offenders, with a resulting inflation of the rates for youths. Finally, there is the issue that local police departments often manipulate the statistics that are reported to the FBI. The intent may be to make the problem appear worse or better depending on the reporting agency's agenda.

Uniform Crime Reporting Program
The Federal Bureau of Investigation's program for compiling annual data about crime committed in the United States.

index offenses
The most serious offenses reported in the FBI's Uniform Crime Reporting Program, including murder and non-negligent manslaughter, forcible rape, robbery, aggravated assault, burglary, larceny–theft, motor vehicle theft, and arson.

clearance by arrest
The solution of a crime by arrest of a perpetrator who has confessed or who has been implicated by witnesses or evidence. Clearances can also occur by exceptional means, as when a suspected perpetrator dies prior to arrest.

Crime by Age Groups

The Uniform Crime Reporting Program examines the extent of juvenile crime; compares youth crime to adult crime; considers gender and racial variations in youth crime; and presents urban, suburban, and rural differences in youth crime. The chief findings of the *Crime in the United States 2005*[2] data as they relate to juveniles are:

1. Youth crime is widespread in U.S. society. For example, the *CUS 2005* data revealed 1,582,068 juveniles under age eighteen were arrested in that year. While juveniles between the ages of ten and seventeen constituted about 25 percent of the U.S. population, youths in this age group were arrested for 15.8 percent of the violent crimes and 25.9 percent of property crimes.
2. The percentages of total arrests involving juveniles are highest in curfew breaking, loitering, running away, arson, vandalism, motor vehicle theft, burglary, and larceny–theft.
3. Juveniles are arrested for serious property offenses as well as violent offenses. As Figure 2.1 indicates, juveniles were arrested for 26 percent of all burglaries, 25 percent of robberies, 23 percent of weapon offenses, 9 percent of murders, and 13.6 percent of aggravated assaults in 2005.

FIGURE 2.1

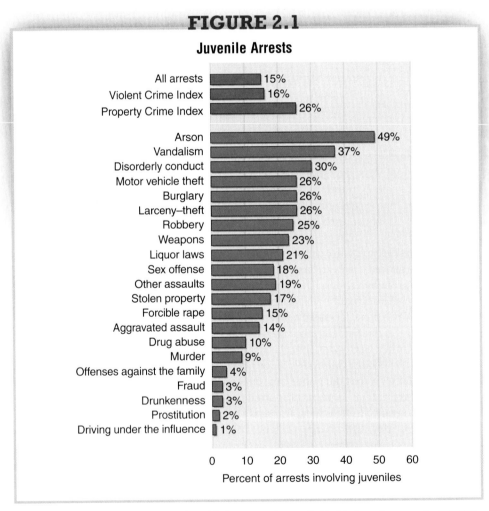

Note: Running away from home and curfew violations are not presented in this figure because, by definition, only juveniles can be arrested for these offenses.

Source: Data from *Crime in the United States 2005* (www.fbi.gov/ucr/05cius.htm).

Amnesty Program Takes Aim at UK's "Knife Culture"

LONDON — Hundreds of teens in black-and-blue uniforms poured out of the doors of the London Academy last week at the end of another school day.

They rushed past the three security guards in bright yellow jackets and the balloons, flags, banners and soccer memorabilia propped at the front gate in a memorial to the high school's star athlete, Kiyan Prince.

Kiyan, 15, was stabbed May 18, just yards from the front gate of the affluent north London school. The teen's death and the stabbing murder of a young policewoman earlier this month have compelled authorities to get tough on what Prime Minister Tony Blair last week called Britain's "knife culture."

In its latest and broadest attempt to get knives off the streets and especially out of the hands of young people, the government Thursday announced a nationwide knife amnesty program. Police hope to collect 30,000 knives that will be turned in at police stations, churches, supermarkets and schools around the country. Home Secretary Charles Clark told the BBC a coinciding public-awareness campaign's message "is simple: Carrying knives on the streets will not be tolerated."

Stabbings are the most common form of murder in Britain, where firearms—except certain shotguns and sporting rifles—are outlawed. Most police officers in Britain do not carry firearms.

Of the 839 homicides in England and Wales in the 12 months ending Nov. 28 [2005]—the most recent period for which Home Office figures are available—29% involved sharp instruments including knives, blades and swords. Firearms account for just 9% of murders in Britain. The murder rate in Britain is 15 per million people.

The U.S. murder rate is 55 per million, according to the FBI. Of those, 70% of murders were committed with firearms; just 14% involved knives or cutting instruments.

In London alone, there were 12,589 knife-related crimes last year. Police say the people most likely to carry knives are males ages 15 to 18.

A poll released this month by the Police Federation found that 30% of officers had been threatened by a knife-wielding suspect while on duty.

It is illegal for anyone under 16 to buy a knife, a fact that is posted anywhere knives are sold—from independent cutlery shops to department store housewares departments. The Home Office defines a knife as any article with a blade or a point. Folding pocket knives with blades less than 3 inches long are exempt from the . . . amnesty and crackdown.

Carrying a blade in school is punishable by up to four years imprisonment, but that penalty is rarely handed out. Instead, most first-time offenders are expelled or receive other punishments that don't involve prison time, says the Victims Of Crime Trust, a support group for people whose family or friends have been murdered.

A 16-year-old boy has been charged in the death of Kiyan.

London Academy Principal Phil Hearne said in a Press Association interview that there is a "real issue" of knives in the community. But he noted, "It's our first encounter with knives as a school community."

Kiyan's murder was the latest—but not the last—of several recent fatal stabbing attacks: Police constable Nisha Patel-Nasri, 29, was stabbed and killed earlier this month while investigating a suspicious noise outside her London home. Mental health worker Ashleigh Ewing, 22, was found stabbed to death May 19 [2006] at the home of one of her patients.

[Recently], Thomas Grant, 19, a St. Andrews University student, was stabbed to death on a train. The attack came despite the launch last month by British Transport Police of a program that uses metal detectors to identify and arrest pas-

A message of condolence left outside the London Academy following the murder of 15-year-old Kiyan Prince at the school on May 18, 2006. Kiyan was fatally stabbed outside the school as pupils were going home. His death led to increased calls to combat Britain's "knife culture," and to get knives off of English streets. ■ **How does Britain's knife culture compare to what some have called America's "gun culture"?**

sengers carrying knives or other weapons on trains.

The House of Lords is considering a crime-reduction bill that would raise the minimum age to buy a knife from 16 to 18, give teachers the power to physically search students and mandate jail time for possessing a knife without cause.

In the meantime, officials hope setting up collection bins across the country during the amnesty will raise awareness and help reduce knife attacks.

Norman Brennan, director of the Victims of Crime Trust, calls the amnesty program, "no more than a public relations exercise." The victims' rights advocacy group proposes tougher penalties, including a mandatory five-year prison sentence for anyone possessing a knife.

"It's difficult to discuss the issue of knife crime without discussing the bigger picture of finding solutions to deal with the knife-carrying culture," says Frances Lawrence, an anti-knife activist. Her husband, Philip, a high school principal, was stabbed to death in 1995 while trying to protect a pupil outside his London school.

Source: César G. Soriano, "Amnesty Program Takes Aim at UK's 'Knife Culture'," *USA Today*, May 31, 2006, p. 5A. Copyright © 2006 by *USA Today*. Reprinted with permission.

4. Juvenile murder rates increased substantially between 1987 and 1993. In the peak year of 1993, there were about 3,800 juvenile arrests for murder. Between 1993 and 2003, however, juvenile arrests for murder declined; the number of arrests in 2005 (929) was about one-fourth of the 1993 figure.

5. The 465,700 juvenile females arrested in 2005 represented 29 percent of all juvenile arrests that year.

6. Juveniles were involved in 10.3 percent of all drug arrests in 2005. Juvenile males were arrested for 117,197 drug abuse violations; juvenile females were arrested for 23,838 drug abuse violations.

Youth Crime Trends

Crime in the Unites States 2005 data provide one indicator of the rise and fall of youth crime. According to these official statistics, between 1971 and 2005 the percentage of Part I arrests involving juveniles under the age of eighteen declined from 45 percent to 16.3 percent. In those years the percentage of violent arrests declined from 22 percent to 15.7 percent, and the percentage of property crimes declined from 51 to 26 percent.[3]

> " The most pressing question concerning youth crime is where youth crime trends are headed. "

The most pressing question concerning youth crime is where youth crime trends are headed. Back in 1995, Alfred Blumstein expressed pessimism about the trends in youth crime. The bad news, Blumstein said, "makes for a grim, chilling picture. Between 1995 and 2010, this population cohort will grow by some 30 percent, and many of them will have grown up in poverty to single mothers."[4]

Blumstein noted that the crime rate had changed dramatically in 1985 with the introduction of crack cocaine, especially in urban areas. This "gave rise to a large demand for crack, and the recruitment of lots of people, particularly young people, into the market to sell crack."[5] Young people soon began carrying guns, Blumstein added,

> to protect themselves because they were carrying lots of valuable stuff; they were in no position to call the police if somebody set upon them. The more kids started carrying guns, the more the incentive for the other kids to start carrying.
>
> This gave rise to an escalating arms race out in the streets among the kids. Kids are not very good at resolving disputes verbally, as most middle-class folks are. When you look in school yards, we're always seeing pushing and shoving. When the guns are around, that pushing and shoving and fighting escalate into shooting. That's really contributed to what has been the most dramatic growth of homicide by young people of young people.[6]

Blumstein argued that a long-term decline in the rates of homicide by young people depended on both getting guns out of the hands of the young and addressing the fact that an increasing number of youths are being socialized in high-risk settings.

In 1996, James Alan Fox also forsaw a grim picture concerning increased juvenile violence. He stated that "there are now 39 million children in the country who are under the age of ten, more children than we've had for decades."[7] The critical problem, according to Fox, was that millions of these children were at high risk, lived in poverty, lacked full-time

A back alley handgun purchase. Studies show that violent crimes committed by juveniles are directly linked to the availability of handguns. ■ **How might the availability of handguns be better controlled?**

supervision at home, and that "by the year 2005, the number of teens, ages 14–17, will increase by 20 percent, with a larger increase among blacks in this age group (26 percent)."[8] Fox projected that "even if the per-capita rate of teen homicide remains the same, the number of 14–17 year-olds who will commit murder should increase to nearly 5,000 annually because of changing demographics."[9]

Similarly, in 1995, John J. DiIulio Jr. commented that the United States was "sitting on a demographic crime bomb."[10] By the year 2000, DiIulio predicted, there would be an additional 500,000 youngsters between 14 and 17. He contended that this "large population of seven-to-10-year old boys now growing up fatherless, Godless, and jobless, and surrounded by deviant, delinquent, and criminal adults, will give rise to a new and more vicious group of predatory street criminals than the nation has ever known."[11] He added that "we must therefore be prepared to contain the explosion's force and limit its damage."[12]

In a book published in 1996, William Bennett, John DiIulio Jr., and John Walters further argued that a new generation of juvenile criminals was emerging that would be far worse than in the past. In referring to this new generation of juvenile criminals as "superpredators," they stated that "today's bad boys are far worse than yesteryear's, and tomorrow's will be even worse than today's."[13] The result, as they saw it, was that "America is now home to thicker ranks of juvenile 'superpredators'—radically impulsive, brutally remorseless youngsters, including ever more preteenage boys who murder, assault, rob, burglarize, deal deadly drugs, join gun-toting gangs, and create serious communal disorders."[14] The underlying cause of the superpredator phenomenon, they asserted, was "moral poverty—children growing up without love, care, and guidance from responsible adults."[15]

In the midst of these predictions of a violent juvenile crime wave, Franklin E. Zimring as well as Philip J. Cook and John Laub represented dissenting voices. In 1996, Zimring argued that "using demographic statistics to project how many kids are going to commit homicide [has] extremely limited utility."[16] He added that "the overall incidence of homicide, which is variable and cyclical, is still a much better predictor of future violence than assumptions based on demographic shifts."[17]

Cook and Laub's 1998 explanation for why youth gun violence had peaked in 1993 and had rapidly declined since then represented another dissenting voice.[18] They proposed that a change in context could help explain the reduced rate of juvenile homicides between 1993 and 1997. This changing context, especially a more limited availability of guns, according to Cook and Laub, would continue to depress rather than to escalate youth homicide in the immediate future.[19] (See Focus on Social Policy 2.1.)

FOCUS ON
Social Policy 2.1

Guns, Juveniles, and the Life Course

There is common agreement that the national epidemic of youth violence, which began in the mid-1980s and peaked in the 1990s, was as deadly as it was because more guns were carried and used than ever before. Homicide death rates of males aged thirteen to seventeen tripled, primarily because of gun assaults.

There is general agreement on the following findings:

- Youths who carried guns were more likely to live in communities that had high prevalence of gun ownership.
- Youths who lived in communities with high rates of violence were more likely to carry guns than were those who lived in communities with low rates of violence.
- Youths who carried guns were significantly more likely to engage in serious assaults and robberies than were those who did not carry guns.
- Youths who sold large amounts of drugs at every age were more likely to carry guns than were those who did not sell drugs.

- Youths who were dealing large quantities of drugs and money that could be stolen were more likely to carry guns because they believed that gun carrying was necessary to protect themselves and their investment.
- Youths who were heavy drug users were also more likely to carry guns because they believed that buying drugs from armed dealers made it necessary for them to be armed themselves.
- Youths who were members of gangs had a higher probability of carrying a hidden gun than were those who were not members of gangs.
- Youths who were chronic offenders and were involved in gangs played some part in most youth homicides, both as offenders and victims.

■ **Why would juveniles who are involved in neither gangs nor drugs carry guns? Other than for protection, how is gang membership related to carrying guns?**

Sources: Alan J. Lizotte, Marvin D. Krohn, James C. Howell, Kimberly Tobin, and Gregory J. Howard, "Factors Influencing Gun Carrying among Young Urban Males over the Adolescent–Young Adult Life Course," *Criminology* 38 (2000), pp. 811–834; Philip J. Cook and Jens Ludwig, "Does Gun Prevalence Affect Teen Gun Carrying after All?," *Criminology* 42 (2004), pp. 27–54; and Anthony A. Braga, "Serious Youth Gun Offenders and the Epidemic of Youth Violence in Boston," *Journal of Quantitative Criminology* 19 (March 2003), pp. 33–54.

In a 1998 publication Alfred Blumstein and Richard Rosenfeld abandoned somewhat Blumstein's earlier gloomy prophecies about the prospects of a juvenile crime wave. They agreed that the reduction in arrests of juveniles for homicides could be attributed in large part to the reduced use of handguns by young people. But Blumstein and his colleague warned, "No one can be certain when the next upturn in homicide [with juveniles] will occur, but the present reductions cannot continue indefinitely."[20]

In recent years, the early support for a violent juvenile crime wave, especially from such recognized scholars as Blumstein, Fox, and DiIulio, has given way to the realization that youth homicide rates have been declining since 1993 and that the reduced use of handguns by minority youth in large cities has been a chief contributor to this decline. As we will see in Chapter 4, however, the decades-long decrease in juvenile crime now may be at an end—partly because of the upsurge in the numbers of young people in the United States.

Juvenile Court Statistics

juvenile court statistics

Data about youths who appear before the juvenile court, compiled annually by the National Center for Juvenile Justice.

Most information about the number of children appearing before the juvenile court each year comes from the publication, *Juvenile Court Statistics*. In 1926, the Juvenile Court Statistics Project was inaugurated by the Children's Bureau of the Department of Labor. One of the most important objectives of compiling **juvenile court statistics** was "to furnish an index of the general nature and extent of the problems brought before the juvenile court."[21]

The reporting procedures, content, and project objectives of the annual reports of juvenile court statistics have been modified since the project was implemented. Initial reports included analyses of trends in delinquency based on factors such as gender, race, home conditions, reasons for referral, place of detention care, and disposition. Then, in 1952, the amount of information requested from jurisdictions was limited to a summary account of delinquency, dependency, neglect, traffic cases, and cases involving special proceedings. In 1967, responsibility for collecting the *Juvenile Court Statistics* was shifted from the Department of Health, Education and Welfare to the Law Enforcement Assistance Administration (LEAA). Under a grant awarded by LEAA in 1975, the National Center for Juvenile Justice was given the responsibility for maintaining the series, and today works in conjunction with OJJDP.

The *Juvenile Court Statistics*, like the *Crime in the United States* data, have some serious limitations. First, the usual time lag in these statistics lessens their usefulness. Second, the cases reported make up only a small percentage of the total number of juvenile offenses. Third, the data collected by the Office of Juvenile Justice and Delinquency Prevention represent only an estimate of juvenile crimes that come to the attention of the juvenile court. Still, these national statistics, as well as statistics of local juvenile courts, provide a means by which researchers can examine the characteristics of referred juveniles and the emerging trends in juvenile justice.

> " The *Juvenile Court Statistics,* like *Crime in the United States* data, have some serious limitations. "

The number of children appearing before the juvenile court significantly increased from 1960 until the early 1980s when it began to level off. It then started to rise again and continued to rise until the late 1980s when it began to level off again. In 2002, juvenile courts in the United States handled over 1.6 million delinquency cases. Data shown in Figure 2.2 indicate that 41 percent of these cases were property cases; 23 percent were person offenses; 24 percent were public order offenses; and 12 percent were drug offenses. The largest percentage of person offenses consisted of simple assaults, followed by aggravated assaults and then robberies; larceny–theft made up the largest number of property offenses, followed by burglary and vandalism. Obstruction of justice and disorderly conduct comprised the largest percentages of public order offenses.[22]

Juvenile Court Statistics 2002 describes what happens to the cases brought into the system. For example, 58 percent of the delinquency cases were petitioned; that

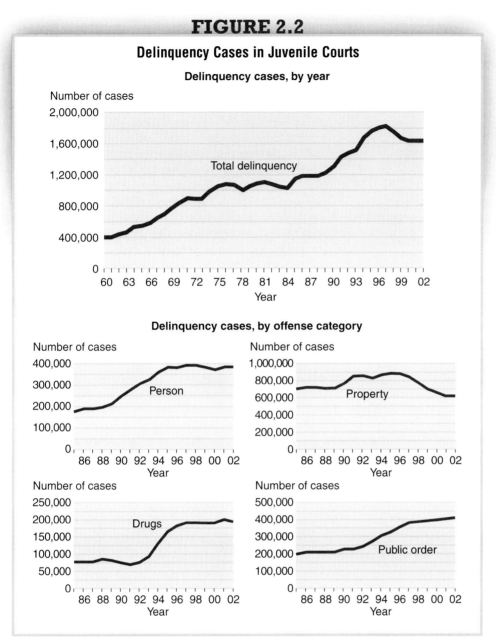

FIGURE 2.2

Delinquency Cases in Juvenile Courts

Delinquency cases, by year

Number of cases

Total delinquency

Delinquency cases, by offense category

Number of cases

Person

Number of cases

Property

Number of cases

Drugs

Number of cases

Public order

Source: Howard W. Snyder and Melissa Sickmund, *Juvenile Offenders and Victims: 2006 National Report* (Washington, D.C.: National Center for Juvenile Justice and Office of Justice Programs, 2006), p. 158.

is, these youths came into the juvenile court as a result of the filing of a petition or complaint requesting the court to declare the youths as delinquents or dependents, or to transfer the youths to an adult court. In terms of nonpetitioned delinquency cases, 42 percent of the total were informally handled cases in which authorized court personnel screened a case prior to the filing of a formal petition and decided not to prosecute the offender.[23]

Cohort Studies

Juvenile delinquency has been studied from a wide variety of perspectives and with an equally wide variety of research methods. The longitudinal method has recently gained popularity, and the **cohort study** is a specific example of the longitudinal method. In the cohort study, researchers follow a group of people who have something

cohort study
Research that usually includes all individuals who were born in a specific year in a particular city or county and follows them through part or all of their lives.

in common—they were born in the same year, graduated from high school in the same year, or were first arrested in the same year—over a period of time.

Delinquency cohort studies usually include all people born in a particular year in a city or county and follow this group, or cohort, through part or all of their lives. Although this procedure is extremely costly, it permits researchers to determine, through a year-by-year search of police files and community records, interviews, and self-report studies, which individuals in a cohort were arrested and which were not. Investigators can identify offenders early, follow them throughout their lives, and compare them with nonoffenders, thereby giving a picture of their criminal careers and how they progressed.

> " Cohort studies, like all forms of criminal statistics, have their share of problems. One major difficulty is that their findings cannot be generalized with certainty beyond the individuals in the cohort. "

Cohort studies, like all forms of criminal statistics, have their share of problems. One major difficulty is that their findings cannot be generalized with certainty beyond the individuals in the cohort. Such studies also are very expensive and time consuming. Keeping track of a **cohort** of youths even up to age thirty-five is next to impossible: Names and addresses change, some people die, and others simply drop out of sight. The same holds true for researchers and their assistants. Finally, to provide a true picture of the national crime rate would require that a sample be taken each year in every area of the country. Still, even with these drawbacks, cohort studies remain an accepted and useful addition to other official and nonofficial statistics in illuminating the problem of delinquency and crime.

Table 2.1 compares the findings of four cohort studies based on official data and conducted in Philadelphia; London, England; Racine, Wisconsin; and Columbus, Ohio. The four studies have been useful in filling out the picture of youth crime and have agreed far more than they disagreed. The most significant findings on which the cohort studies agree are that socioeconomically lower-class minority males committed the most serious offenses, that a few offenders committed the majority of serious property and violent offenses, and that punishments by the juvenile justice system tended to encourage rather than discourage future criminality. There was also general agreement that males committed more offenses and more serious offenses than did females, that youth crimes progressed from less serious to more serious, and that the probability of becoming an adult offender increased for individuals with a record of juvenile delinquency.[24]

cohort
A generational group as defined in demographics, in statistics, or for the purpose of social research.

Self-Reports and Official Statistics Compared

In the late 1950s and 1960s, the use of delinquency studies that relied on official statistics on incarcerated populations declined, whereas self-report surveys using community or school samples rapidly increased.[25] Like other forms of measurements, **self-report studies** have shortcomings, but criminologists generally consider them to be helpful tools in efforts to measure and understand delinquent behavior. The main justifications for self-report surveys are that a large proportion of youthful offenders are never arrested and that a large amount of **hidden delinquency** is not contained in official arrest statistics.

New national interview data that became available in the 1980s and 1990s have led to improved self-report studies. The National Youth Survey (NYS) involves a probability sample of seven birth cohorts in a panel design. The sample of 1,725 adolescents aged eleven to seventeen was selected to be a representative sample of U.S. youths born in the years 1959 through 1965. This youth panel has been interviewed nine times: in the calendar years 1977–1981 (waves 1 to 5); in 1984 (wave 6); in 1987 (wave 7); in 1990 (wave 8); and in 1993 (wave 9).[26]

Another study, the 1997 National Longitudinal Survey of Youth, consists of a nationally representative sample of 9,000 youths who were between the ages of twelve

self-report studies
Studies of juvenile crime based on surveys in which youths report on their own delinquent acts.

hidden delinquency
Unobserved or unreported delinquency.

TABLE 2.1

Comparison of Four Cohort Studies

	PHILADELPHIA COHORTS	LONDON COHORT	RACINE COHORTS	COLUMBUS COHORT
Sample	Males born in 1945 and males and females born in 1958	Males born between 1951 and 1954	Males and females born in 1942, 1949, and 1955	Males and females born between 1956 and 1960
Delinquent population	32.6 percent in first cohort and 34.9 percent in second cohort	About one-third of the cohort	90 percent of males and 65 to 70 percent of females in each cohort	1,138 youths born during these years committed a violent offense
Gender	Females not as delinquent	N.A.	White females had least involvement with the police	Males outnumbered females by almost 6 to 1
Race	Nonwhites committed more serious crimes and were more likely to be recidivists	N.A.	African American males had more police contacts and committed more serious crimes	African Americans were more likely to commit violent offenses than were whites
Chronic offenders	6.3 percent of first cohort and 7.5 percent of males in second cohort	6 percent; 23 boys of the 396 had 6 or more convictions	N.A.	Nearly one-third of the violent offenders were arrested 5 or more times
Patterns of delinquent behavior	Reasonably constant	Chronics exhibited high and stable recidivism rates through 6th involvement of 72 percent	Declining seriousness and discontinuation after teenage period	Did not progress from less to more serious crimes
Impact of intervention by justice system	Profitable if early in a delinquent career	Early discrimination and treatment of persisters can help prevent adult criminality	Increase in seriousness and involvement following sanctions	Length of time outside an institution between arrests reduced after each commitment

and sixteen at year-end 1996. The survey asked youths to report whether they had engaged in a variety of deviant and delinquent behaviors. This survey has the strength of being able to assess which delinquent behaviors cluster together. Analysis of the first round revealed connections between drug use or sale and other problem behaviors, such as belonging to a gang, consuming alcohol, or carrying a handgun. Round 6 of this sample became available in 2003.[27]

The logic of self-report studies is based on the fundamental assumption of survey research, "If you want to know something, ask."[28] Researchers have gone to juveniles themselves and asked them to admit to any illegal acts they have committed. However, self-report studies have been criticized for three reasons: Their research designs have often been deficient, resulting in the drawing of false inferences; the

> " The logic of self-report studies is based on the fundamental assumption of survey research, 'If you want to know something, ask.' "

varied nature of social settings in which the studies have been undertaken makes it difficult for investigators to test hypotheses; and the studies' reliability and validity are questionable.[29]

Reliability and Validity of Self-Report Studies

The most serious questions about self-report studies relate to their validity and their reliability. In terms of **validity,** how can researchers be certain that juveniles are telling the truth when they fill out self-report questionnaires? James F. Short Jr. and F. Ivan Nye argue that items can be built into questionnaires to "catch the random respondent, the over-conformist, and the individual who is out to impress the researcher with his devilishness, the truth notwithstanding."[30] Yet Michael J. Hindelang and his colleagues contend that self-report studies are likely to underestimate the illegal behavior of the seriously delinquent youth, because the juvenile who has committed frequent offenses is less likely to answer questions truthfully than is the youth who is less delinquent.[31] Stephen A. Cernkovich and his colleagues, who surveyed both a youth sample in the community and an institutional sample, add that "institutionalized youth are not only more delinquent than the 'average kid' in the general youth population, but also considerably more delinquent than the *most delinquent* youth identified in the typical self-report survey."[32]

Reliability gauges the consistency of a questionnaire or an interview—that is, the degree to which administration of a questionnaire or an interview will elicit the same answers from the same juveniles when they are questioned two or more times. After analyzing the reliability of self-report studies, Hindelang and colleagues concluded that "reliability measures are impressive, and the majority of studies produce validity coefficients in the moderate to strong range."[33]

Findings of Self-Report Studies

In the 1940s, Austin L. Porterfield conducted the first study of hidden delinquency: He asked several hundred college students whether they had ever engaged in delinquent acts.[34] Although all of the students reported that they had engaged in delinquent acts, few of them had been brought to police or court attention. But it was Short and Nye in the late 1950s who pioneered the first self-report study of a delinquent population.[35] After their first study of a training school population, they conducted a self-report study that surveyed members of three Washington communities, students in three midwestern towns, and delinquents in training schools in Washington state.[36] In their findings from these two studies, as well as in other published papers, Short and Nye concluded that delinquency was widespread throughout the adolescent population, that the seriousness and frequency of delinquent behavior were major factors determining the actions taken against juvenile lawbreakers, and that no relationship could be found between delinquency and social class.[37]

Self-report studies also commonly agree that almost every youth commits some act of delinquency. In 1987, David Huizinga and Delbert S. Elliott, using information from the National Youth Survey, *Uniform Crime Reports,* and other sources, concluded that only 24 percent of juveniles who committed offenses for which they could have been arrested were in fact arrested.[38] Franklyn W. Dunford and Elliott's 1984 analysis of self-report data from a national youth panel wave and seven birth cohorts of youths aged eleven to seventeen also had found that arrest data reflected only a small fraction of the delinquent activity occurring in U.S. society.[39] Of course, offenders who commit violent or predatory crimes are more likely than minor offenders to be arrested and referred to the juvenile court. Yet Dunford and Elliott found that of 242 self-reported career offenders, 207, or 86 percent, had no record of arrest during a three-year period when they were involved in frequent and serious delinquent offenses.[40] (Table 2.2 is an example of a self-report questionnaire form.)

Self-report studies conducted in the early 1990s in several locations, as part of the Program of Research on the Causes and Correlates of Delinquency, showed that

TABLE 2.2

Example of a Self-Report Questionnaire

Please indicate how often you have done each of the following in the last 12 months.

Remember: Your answers are private so you can answer honestly.

During the last 12 months, how many times did you:

1. Break into a place to do something illegal?   _____
2. Take something from a store on purpose without paying for it (shoplifting)?   _____
3. Steal something worth more than $100 (not counting shoplifting)?   _____
4. Steal something worth less than $100 (not counting shoplifting)?   _____
5. Beat up or hurt someone on purpose?   _____
6. Get into any fistfights or brawls (not counting the times you beat up or hurt someone on purpose)?   _____
7. Ruin, break, or damage someone else's property on purpose?   _____
8. Take a car without the owner's permission?   _____
9. Take money or something by threatening someone with a weapon (gun, knife, etc.)?   _____
10. Take money or something by threatening someone without a weapon?   _____

Source: Excerpted from a high school survey used in research by M. L. Erickson, J. P. Gibbs, and G. F. Jensen as part of a National Institutes of Mental Health study titled "Community Tolerance and Measures of Delinquency."

a surprisingly large proportion of juveniles committed violent acts.[41] By the time they were tenth- or eleventh-graders, 58 percent of the Rochester, New York, youths and 54 percent of the Denver juveniles reported that they had been involved in a violent crime at some time in their lives. Chronic violent offenders, constituting 14 percent of the sample in Denver and 15 percent in Rochester, accounted for 82 percent of the violent offenses in Denver and 75 percent of the violent offenses in Rochester. According to these self-report studies, a large proportion of those who became involved in violent behavior at an early age later became chronic violent offenders. In Denver, chronic violent offenders reported a total of 4,134 violent crimes, an average of 33.6 per person. In Rochester, chronic violent offenders reported 5,164 violent acts, an average of 51.7 per person.[42] See Exhibit 2.3 for more extensive findings from these longitudinal self-report studies.

The desire to uncover the true rate of delinquency and the recognition that official statistics on juvenile delinquency have serious limitations have led to a growing reliance on the use of self-report studies. These studies reveal the following:

1. Considerable undetected delinquency takes place, and police apprehension is low—probably less than 10 percent.
2. Juveniles in both the middle- and lower-classes are involved in considerable illegal behavior.
3. Not all hidden delinquency involves minor offenses; a significant number of serious crimes are committed each year by juveniles who elude apprehension by the police.
4. Socioeconomically lower-class youths appear to commit more frequent delinquent acts, especially in their early years, and are more likely to be chronic offenders than are youths in the socioeconomic middle-class.
5. African Americans are more likely than whites to be arrested, convicted, and institutionalized, even though both groups commit offenses of similar seriousness.

Exhibit 2.1

Highlights from the Denver, Pittsburgh, and Rochester Youth Surveys

Denver

The Denver longitudinal self-report study followed 1,527 boys and girls from high-risk neighborhoods in Denver who were seven, nine, eleven, thirteen, and fifteen years old in 1987. In exploring the changes in the nature of delinquency and drug use from the 1970s to the 1990s, the Denver study's findings were as follows:

- Overall, there was little change in the prevalence rates of delinquency, including serious delinquency and serious violence. However, the prevalence rate of gang fights among males doubled (from 8 percent to 16 percent).
- The level of injury from violent offenses increased substantially.
- The prevalence of drug use decreased substantially: alcohol, from 80 percent to 50 percent; marijuana, from 41 percent to 18 percent; and other drug use, from 19 percent to 4 percent.
- The relationship between drug use and delinquency changed, in that a smaller percentage (from 48 percent to 17 percent) of serious delinquents were using hard drugs other than marijuana, and a greater percentage (from 27 percent to 48 percent) of hard drug users were serious offenders.
- More than half (53 percent) of the youth in the study ages eleven through fifteen in 1987 were arrested over the next five years.

Pittsburgh

The Pittsburgh study, a longitudinal study of 1,517 inner-city boys, followed three samples of boys for more than a decade to advance knowledge about how and why boys become involved in delinquency and other problem behaviors. Its chief findings were as follows:

- There were no differences between African American and white boys at age six; but differences gradually developed, the prevalence of serious delinquency at age sixteen reaching 27 percent for African American boys and 19 percent for white boys.
- As prevalence increased, so did the average frequency of serious offending, which rose more rapidly for African American boys than for white boys.

- The onset of offending among boys involved in serious delinquency occurred by age fifteen, when 51 percent of African American boys and 28 percent of white boys had committed serious delinquent acts.
- The boys generally developed disruptive and delinquent behavior in an orderly, progressive fashion, with less serious problem behaviors preceding more serious problem behaviors.
- The researchers identified three groups of developmental pathways.

Rochester

The Rochester study, a longitudinal study of 1,000 urban adolescents, investigated the causes and consequences of adolescent delinquency and drug use by following a sample of high-risk urban adolescents from their early teenage years through their early adult years. Its chief findings were as follows:

- Attachment and involvement were both significantly related to delinquency. Children who were more attached to and involved with their parents were less involved in delinquency.
- The relationship between family process factors and delinquency was bidirectional—poor parenting increased the probability of delinquent behavior, and delinquent behavior further weakened the relationship between parent and child.
- The impact of family variables appeared to fade as adolescents became older and more independent from their parents. Weak school commitment and poor school performance were associated with increased involvement in delinquency and drug use.
- Association with delinquent peers was strongly and consistently related to delinquency, in part because peers provided positive reinforcement for delinquency. There was a strong relationship between gang membership and delinquent behavior, particularly serious and violent delinquency.

■ **What do the findings of these three studies have in common? How do they differ?**

Sources: Katharine Browning, Terence P. Thornberry, and Pamela K. Porter, "Highlights of Findings from the Rochester Youth Development Study," *OJJDP Fact Sheet* (Washington, D.C.: Office of Juvenile Justice and Delinquency Prevention, 1999); Katharine Browning and Rolf Loeber, "Highlights from the Pittsburgh Youth Study," *OJJDP Fact Sheet* (Washington, D.C.: Office of Juvenile Justice and Delinquency Prevention, 1999); and Katharine Browning and David Huizinga, "Highlights from the Denver Youth Survey," *OJJDP Fact Sheet* (Washington D.C.: Office of Juvenile Justice and Delinquency Prevention, 1999).

6. Females commit more delinquent acts than official statistics indicate, but males still appear to commit more delinquent acts and to perpetrate more serious crimes than do females.

7. Alcohol and marijuana are the most widely used drugs among adolescents, but other drug use has decreased in recent years.

Youth Crime Trends

The use of national samples enables self-report studies to shed more light on youth crime trends. For example, the Monitoring the Future study, an annual national survey of high school seniors conducted by the University of Michigan's Institute for Social Research, tracked large samples over twenty-two years (1975–1996). The study showed that some offenses increased during this period but others did not. Overall crime trends, especially in the population of seventeen- to twenty-three-year-olds, failed to indicate any increased tendency toward criminality.[43]

Self-report studies have been particularly useful in helping researchers estimate the prevalence and incidence of drug use among adolescents in the United States. They reveal how drug use among adolescents reached epidemic proportions in the late 1960s and into the 1970s, appeared to peak sometime around 1979, and decreased into the 1990s and early years of the twenty-first century. As revealed in the Centers for Disease Control and Prevention survey, the percentage of students who reported marijuana use was 47.2 percent in 1999, 42.4 percent in 2001, and 40.2 percent in 2003.[44] (See Chapter 11 for a more extensive discussion of drug use among adolescents.)

▮Victimization Surveys

In 1972, the Census Bureau began conducting **victimization studies** to determine as accurately as possible the extent of crime in the United States. New data were needed because the *Uniform Crime Reports* measured only the number of arrests that police made, not the actual numbers of crimes committed. The volume of "hidden crime" has long been known to be substantial, and it exists because people often simply fail to report victimizations to the police. The National Crime Victimization Surveys (NCVS) were created to address this issue and to give policymakers a better idea of just how much crime actually occurs.

Initial NCVS surveys involved three different procedures. The largest component of the program was the National Crime Panel, which oversaw the interviewing of a national sample of approximately 125,000 people in 60,000 households every six months for up to three and one-half years. Data from these individuals were used to estimate the national frequency of the crimes found in the FBI's Crime Index (except for murder, which is almost always reported to or discovered by the police). The Census Bureau also interviewed the owners, managers, and clerks of 42,000 businesses selected randomly to provide an estimate of business robbery and burglary rates. This portion of the survey ended in 1976. Finally, the Census Bureau conducted victimization surveys in twenty-six major cities. Housing units in the central area of each city were randomly selected, and each member in the household aged twelve or older was questioned about his or her experiences, if any, as a victim of crime.[45]

The Bureau of Justice Statistics (BJS) took over the responsibility for conducting crime victimization surveys in the 1990s, and the NCVS was completely redesigned in 1993. The redesign came about following criticisms that the survey seemed unable to effectively gather information about certain crimes such as sexual assault and domestic violence. Moreover, by 1993, the survey's designers realized that public attitudes toward victims had changed, and those changes permitted more direct questioning about sexual assaults. In addition, enhanced survey methodology improved the ability of those being interviewed to recall events. As a result of the redesign, victims quickly began reporting more types of criminal incidents, including

victimization studies
Ongoing surveys of crime victims in the United States conducted by the Bureau of Justice Statistics to determine the extent of crime.

A child abuse victim. Children are at risk for many kinds of violent victimization, some at the hands of their peers and some at the hands of their caregivers. ■ **Why do juveniles experience such high rates of violent victimization?**

undetected victimizations, to interviewers. Under the redesigned survey, for example, victims are now more likely to report aggravated and simple assault, nonrape sexual assault, and unwanted or coerced sexual contacts that involve a threat or an attempt to harm.[46]

The 2005 National Crime Victimization Survey was administered to a random sample of 134,000 residents in 77,200 households across the United States, and collected data from household residents twelve years of age or older. Data were used to assess the prevalence of all crimes—whether or not they had been reported to the police.[47]

Findings from the 2005 NCVS show that persons twelve years or older suffered nearly 23 million criminal victimizations per year, of which 18 million were property crimes, 5.2 million were violent crimes, and approximately 13.6 million were crimes of theft.[48] Overall, the number of victimizations discovered was much higher than the number of offenses reported to the police. See Figure 2.3 for changes in reported property and violent crime victimization rates since 1973.

Data from the NCVS show that juveniles are highly overrepresented in comparison to other age groups in the population of those victimized. Juveniles between the ages of sixteen and nineteen experience the highest victimization rate of any age group for all violent crimes. Youths between ages twelve and fifteen have the next highest rate, with rates dropping with the victim's increasing age. Data also show that adolescents are more likely than adults to commit violent crimes against peers and to report knowing their assailants. Crimes against adolescents are also less likely to be reported to the police than crimes against adults.[49]

Within the adolescent population, males are more likely than females to become victims of most violent crimes, but females are much more likely to be victims of rape and sexual assault (see Figure 2.4). The survey also shows that African Americans are several times more likely than whites to be victims of violence overall—including rape, sexual assault, aggravated assault, and robbery. Finally, the NCVS shows that persons aged sixteen to nineteen experienced overall violence, rape, sexual assault, and assault at rates at least slightly higher than rates for individuals in other age categories.[50]

FIGURE 2.3

Crime Rates 1973–2004

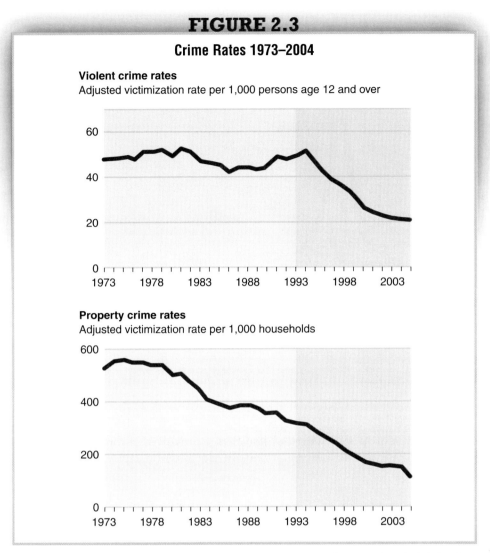

Violent crime rates
Adjusted victimization rate per 1,000 persons age 12 and over

Property crime rates
Adjusted victimization rate per 1,000 households

Note: Violent crimes include rape, robbery, aggravated and simple assault. Property crimes include burglary, theft, and motor vehicle theft. The National Crime Victimization Survey redesign was implemented in 1993; the area with the lighter shading is before the redesign and the darker area after the redesign. The data before 1993 are adjusted to make them consistent with later years.
Source: Bureau of Justice Statistics, *Criminal Victimization, 2005* (Washington, DC.: BJS 2006).

Although victimization surveys have not been used as widely in analyzing delinquency as have the *Uniform Crime Reports, Juvenile Court Statistics,* cohort studies, and self-report studies, they add significantly to what is known about crime in the United States. Some of the principal findings of victimization surveys are:

1. Much more crime is committed than is recorded, and the discrepancy between the number of people who say they have been victimized and the number of crimes known to the police varies with the type of offense.
2. The rank order of serious offenses reported by victims, with the exception of vehicle theft, is identical to that of the *Uniform Crime Reports.*
3. The probability of being victimized varies with the kind of crime and with where people live. The centers of cities are more probable sites of violent crimes.
4. Juveniles are more likely to commit crimes, especially property offenses, than any other age group; juveniles also are more likely to be victimized than any other age group.
5. African Americans are overrepresented both as perpetrators and as victims of serious personal crimes. Official arrest data indicate that a somewhat greater

Web PLACES 2.1

View the OJJDP PowerPoint presentation "Juvenile Victims" at **www.justicestudies.com/ WebPlaces.**

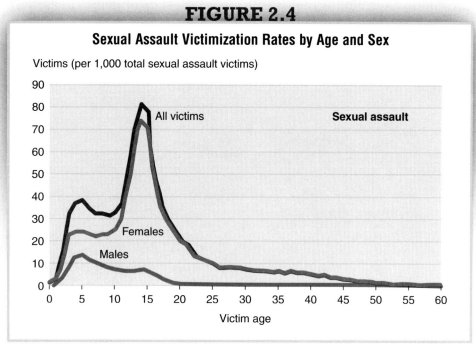

FIGURE 2.4

Sexual Assault Victimization Rates by Age and Sex

Victims (per 1,000 total sexual assault victims)

Sexual assault

All victims

Females

Males

Victim age

Source: Office of Juvenile Justice and Delinquency Prevention, *Juvenile Offenders and Victims: 2006 National Report* (Washington, D.C.: OJJDP, 2006), p. 31.

proportion of African American offenders are involved in forcible rape, aggravated assault, and simple assault than the victimization data indicate.[51]

Social Factors Related to Delinquency

The first half of this chapter has examined the extent of delinquency in the United States; the second half will focus on the nature of youth crime, another important topic in understanding delinquency. The social factors related to delinquent behavior, the dimensions of delinquent behavior, and delinquency across the life course are highly significant features in describing the nature of delinquency.

An examination of gender, racial and ethnic relations, and social class reveals much about the social factors affecting delinquency in U.S. society. The importance of gender in delinquency is examined in Chapter 7; the relationship of social class and delinquency is considered in Chapter 4; and the disproportionate handling of racial and ethnic groups is a major juvenile justice concern addressed throughout Chapters 13 through 16. Here, we'll focus on the measurement of these social factors.

Gender and Delinquent Behavior

Official arrest statistics, victimization data, and self-report studies show that adolescent females are involved in less frequent and less serious delinquent acts than are adolescent males. *Crime in the United States 2005* data documented that male/female arrest ratios were five to one for drug violations, more than five to one for violent crimes, and more than three to one for property crimes. The gender ratios were much closer for some offenses, averaging about two to one for larceny–theft and embezzlement. The overall ratio between adolescent male and female arrests in 2005 was about three to one (females accounted for almost 30 percent of the total arrests.)[52] See Figure 2.5 for trends in arrest rates by gender.

Adolescent males are far more likely to be arrested for possession of stolen property, vandalism, weapons offenses, and assaults. In contrast, adolescent females are

FIGURE 2.5

Arrest Trends by Gender

Arrest trends by gender, males/females aged 10–17 (per 100,000)

(Line graph showing arrest trends from 1980 to 2005. The y-axis shows values from 0 to 16,000 in increments of 2,000. The x-axis shows years: 1980, 1983, 1986, 1989, 1992, 1995, 1998, 2001, 2005. The "Males" line starts around 12,000, dips, rises to about 14,000 around 1994-1997, then declines to about 9,500 by 2005. The "Females" line starts around 3,500, rises to about 5,000 around 1995-1997, then declines to about 3,500 by 2005.)

Source: Howard Snyder, *Juvenile Arrests 2001* (Washington, D.C.: Office of Juvenile Justice and Delinquency Prevention, 2003, updated); FBI, *Crime in the United States, 2005* (Washington, D.C.: FBI, 2006).

more likely to be arrested for running away from home and prostitution; indeed, arrests for running away from home account for nearly one-fifth of all female arrests.[53]

Longitudinal research adds that males are arrested for more serious charges than are females. In Cohort II of the Philadelphia study, the ratio for male/female arrests was almost nine to one for index crimes and fourteen to one for violent offenses.[54] Furthermore, males are more likely than females to begin their careers at an early age and to extend their delinquent careers into their adult lives.[55]

A homeless girl on the sidewalk in the Soho District of Manhattan holding a sign that reads: "Traveling, Broke, Hungry." Self-reports seem to show that female delinquency is more prevalent and more similar to male delinquency than official statistics suggest. ■ **What kinds of delinquency are most likely to characterize girls?**

Self-report studies indicate, however, that female delinquency is more prevalent and more similar to male delinquency than official arrest statistics suggest.[56] For example, in the early 1990s, David C. Rowe, Alexander T. Vazsonyi, and Daniel J. Flannery found that the correlates of delinquency were similar for both adolescent males and females. In examining whether such variables as impulsivity, rebelliousness, and deceitfulness could explain the gender differences in delinquency, they found that the mean differences in delinquent behavior between boys and girls arise largely because boys are exposed more to criminogenic factors than are girls.[57]

Victimization data reveal that adolescent females are more likely to be victims than are adolescent males, and that their victimization is shaped by their gender, race, and social class.[58] Meda Chesney-Lind has argued that many adolescent females become victimized by "multiple marginality," in that their gender, race, and class place them at the economic periphery of society.[59] (See Chapter 7 for a more extensive development of this thesis.) Gender differences in child abuse are particularly pronounced. Data from the federal Child Welfare Information Gateway (formerly the National Clearinghouse on Child Abuse and Neglect) show that the rate of sexual abuse is significantly higher for girls (1.7 per 1,000) than for boys (0.4 per 1,000).[60]

Racial/Ethnic Background and Delinquent Behavior

Studies based on official statistics have reported that African Americans are overrepresented in arrest, conviction, and incarceration relative to their population base. In contrast, most studies using self-report measures have found that African Americans are more likely to be adjudicated delinquent, but are not significantly worse than whites in their prevalence or frequency of offending.[61] See Figure 2.6 for arrest rates by race.

> " African Americans are overrepresented in arrest, conviction, and incarceration relative to their population base. "

Early self-report studies revealed less relationship between race and crime than have more recent studies. In the 1960s, William J. Chambliss and Richard H. Nagasawa, in comparing questionnaire responses of high school boys in a high-delinquency area with official records obtained from the juvenile court, found that the arrest rate for African Americans was substantially higher than that for whites. But when the investigators examined the students' self-reported delinquent behavior, they found little difference in involvement between African Americans and whites.[62] Also in the 1960s, Leroy C. Gould's self-report data on all seventh-grade boys in two junior high schools in Seattle found that race was strongly related to official delinquency but not to self-reported delinquent activity.[63] And Travis Hirschi also found that the differences in offense behavior between African Americans and whites were much less in self-report accounts.[64] Huizinga and Elliott's 1987 examination of the National Youth Survey concluded that "there are few if any substantial and consistent differences between the delinquency involvement of different racial groups."[65] The researchers suggest that differences in official responses to offenders, rather than differences in delinquent behavior, explain the differentials in arrest, conviction, and incarceration figures.[66]

Two national studies published in the 1970s found that whites and African Americans reported involvement in seventeen delinquent behaviors with similar frequencies; but when the seriousness of delinquency was tallied, investigators found that the seriousness of self-reported delinquency was slightly greater for African American males than for white males.[67] Furthermore, when Suzanne S. Ageton and Elliott analyzed the ratio of African Americans to whites for the total number of offenses, they found that it was nearly two to one. They concluded that this difference was due primarily to the greater involvement of African Americans in serious property offenses, and especially to the involvement of a large number of multiple, or chronic, African American offenders.[68]

Race also affects the relationship between gender and delinquent behavior: Official statistics document that African American females violate the law more fre-

Web PLACES 2.2

View the OJJDP PowerPoint presentation "Juvenile Offenders" at **www.justicestudies.com/ WebPlaces.**

Web LIBRARY 2.1

Read the OJJDP publication *Disproportionate Minority Confinement: Year 2002 Update* at **www.justicestudies.com/ WebLibrary.**

FIGURE 2.6

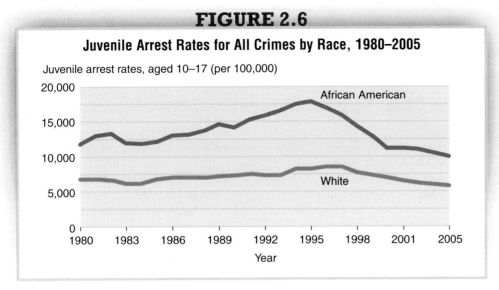

Juvenile Arrest Rates for All Crimes by Race, 1980–2005

Juvenile arrest rates, aged 10–17 (per 100,000)

African American

White

Source: FBI, *Crime in the United States 2005.* www.fbi.gov/ucr/05cius/index.html.

quently and seriously than do white females. In an analysis published in 1981, self-report studies indicated that African American females were much more likely than white females to admit committing the theft of $50 or more or the offenses of auto theft, aggravated assault, and robbery, whereas both groups were about equally involved in burglary. African American females had a higher rate of involvement than white males for robbery, and the two were about equal for aggravated assault.[69]

In the 1970s, Gary Jensen and Raymond Eve's study in Richmond, California, found that for two major property offenses, theft of $50 or more and auto theft, African American females were twice as likely as white females to admit to the theft of $50 or more, but both groups were equally likely to admit to auto theft.[70] Cernkovich and Giordano discovered that the acts predominately committed by African American females were attacking someone with fists, using a weapon to attack someone, engaging in gang fights, extortion, and carrying a weapon. The acts committed mostly by white females included disobeying or defying parents, drinking alcohol, using drugs, driving while intoxicated (DWI), property destruction (under $10), and disturbing the peace.[71]

Thomas L. McNulty and Paul E. Bellair, using data from the National Longitudinal Survey of Adolescent Health, compared involvement in serious violence among African Americans, Asians, Hispanics, Native Americans, and whites. The results from this analysis published in 2003 indicated that African American, Hispanic, and Native American adolescents were involved in significantly higher, and Asians in significantly lower, levels of serious violence than were whites. The researchers explained the statistical differences between whites and minority groups by variation in community disadvantage (for African Americans), situational variables (for Asians), involvement in gangs (Hispanics), and social bonds (for Native Americans). They further found that differences in violent behavior among African Americans, Hispanics, and Native Americans were not significant.[72]

A 2005 article by University of Miami professor Joanne M. Kaufman also called for research that considers the importance of community context. Using the Add Health data collected at the University of North Carolina, Kaufmann found that both macro- and microcontexts are important in understanding why African Americans and Latinos tend to be over-represented as violent offenders. According to Kaufman, the combination of neighborhood context, social class, and social psychological processes can explain most of the relationship between race and violence and ethnicity and violence.[73]

Furthermore, race affects the rates of victimization of females. African American females, regardless of age, are more likely than white females to be victimized by violent crime. In fact, the victimization rate for violent offenses of twelve- to fifteen-year-old African American females is equal to the rate for white males. For crimes of theft, adolescent white females report more property victimization than either African American adolescent males or females and are victimized at a rate nearly equivalent to that of adolescent white males.[74]

Social Class and Delinquent Behavior

Web LIBRARY 2.2

View the OJJDP *Statistical Briefing Book* (*SBB*) at **www.justicestudies .com/WebLibrary.**

Decades of debate still have not produced consensus on the true relationship between social class and delinquency. Common sense tells us if a child comes from a neighborhood where crime prevails, from a poverty-stricken family in which the parent is unable to provide basic needs, or from an environment where friends are involved in and arrested for delinquent acts, there is not much hope that the child will avoid delinquent activity. Consistent with this reasoning, we know that juvenile arrest rates are highest in economically deprived and socially disorganized communities. Yet the empirical reality is that available research data still do not consistently support a relationship between social class and delinquency.

One of the most startling findings of self-report studies published in the 1950s and 1960s was that middle- and upper-class juveniles were as delinquent as their lower-class peers.[75] In 1972, J. R. Williams and Martin Gold, in their national study of thirteen- to sixteen-year-old boys and girls, forcefully made this point: "In no case is the relationship between social status and delinquent behavior strong."[76] Travis Hirschi's 1969 survey of 4,000 junior and senior high school students in Richmond, California, showed little association existed between self-reported delinquencies and income, education, and occupation, except that the sons of professionals and executives committed fewer delinquent acts.[77] In 1980, Richard Johnson, in redefining social class as underclass and earning class, concluded: "The data provide no firm evidence that social class, no matter how it is measured, is a salient factor in generating delinquent involvement."[78] Charles Tittle, Wayne Villemez, and Douglas Smith's 1978 review of thirty-five studies examining the relationship between class and crime concluded that very little support existed for the contention that delinquency is basically a lower-class phenomenon.[79]

Critics charge that self-report studies overload their questionnaires with trivial offenses. Thus, when middle- and upper-class youths record their participation in such offenses as swearing or curfew violations, they are found to be as delinquent as lower-class youth. Ageton and Elliott's national study (1978) found that a different pattern emerged when juveniles were asked how many times they had violated the law during the previous year. They found that the average number of delinquent acts reported by lower-class youngsters exceeded the numbers reported by working-class or middle-class youths. The average number of crimes against persons reported by lower-class juveniles was one and one-half times greater than that reported by the working-class group and nearly four times greater than that reported by the middle-class group. The average number of reported crimes against property was also slightly higher for lower-class than for working-class or middle-class youth.[80]

Elliott and Huizinga applied to a national probability sample of adolescents a new self-report measure deemed to be more representative of the full range of official acts for which juveniles could be arrested. In 1983, these researchers reported class differences in how widespread youth crime was in society (prevalence) and in the frequency of delinquent acts for serious offenses (incidence). Their study also revealed class differences in the incidence of nonserious offenses. Class differences, according to these researchers, were more pervasive and stronger according to an incidence as opposed to a prevalence measure.[81]

Margaret Farnworth and her colleagues, in examining the first four waves of data from the Rochester Youth Development Study (RYDS), found that the "strongest and most consistent class-crime associations are found between measures of continuing underclass status and sustained involvement in street crimes."[82] Their 1994 article also explored the possibility that "inadequate measurement may explain past findings indicating no relationship between class and delinquency."[83]

Social Class and Delinquency

The middle-class youth interviewed for this feature was never arrested or referred to juvenile court, even though she was involved in both status offenses and delinquent behaviors. The interview originally took place in 1995 and was updated in 2003.

I was a real mess as a teenager. I got into the party crowd in high school. My mother is a doctor, and I ran around with lawyers' and doctors' kids. We were looked upon as rich kids. But I had such low self-esteem at the time that I would do just about anything to make friends.

Fourteen was a big turning point for me. I had my first beer, my first cigarette, had sex for the first time, and started to do drugs. I would sleep with guys just to make myself feel like I was liked. We would get high before school or skip classes and get high. It started out with marijuana, but by my junior year I started to do acid. We drank a lot. We got drunk every weekend and sometimes during the week. A lot of people I hung out with did cocaine, but I pretty much stayed away from it.

I never got into the crime thing. I think the reason for this was I was a good student. I went to a Catholic school, made good grades, and didn't have to put any effort into it. I did

run away from home my junior year and stayed with an abusive boyfriend for a week. I almost got kicked out of school for that.

I came from the classic dysfunctional family. My father is an alcoholic. He controlled every aspect of my life. My father is incapable of loving anyone but himself. The turning point for me was when my parents divorced my senior year in high school.

I got rid of my abusive boyfriend. I started to grow up and realize that I am not totally worthless. Now, I am a senior in college. It has been two years since I've done drugs. I have a boyfriend who loves me and wants to marry me. I've learned so much by everything I've been through. It makes me appreciate what I have and what I am now.

I am now working with kids a lot like I was. The only difference is that I never got involved with the system, and these kids have been arrested, referred to the juvenile court, and sent to this residential facility.

■ **Why might social class make a difference in how the juvenile justice system handles law-violating youths? Are you surprised that this young person, who regularly came to school intoxicated and high on drugs, who smoked marijuana, who ran away from home, and who was sexually active throughout her adolescent years, was never brought before the juvenile justice system for formal handling? Why or why not?**

Bradley R. Wright and his colleagues, in research published in 1999, found that socioeconomic status (SES) has both a negative and a positive indirect effect on delinquency but that these negative and positive effects coexist and cancel each other out. As a result, these investigators conclude that there are many causal links between socioeconomic status and delinquency but little overall correlation.[84]

There are those who argue that membership in certain social classes influences the reporting of delinquent behavior. This position holds that middle-class youngsters, especially those who are white and whose parents possess substantial financial resources or hold valued social positions, are more likely to be diverted from formal handling by the justice system than are lower-class youths. See Social World of the Delinquent 2.1 for more information.

Dimensions of Delinquent Behavior

Delinquent behavior can be described along a number of dimensions. The most significant dimensions of delinquent behavior include (1) age of onset, (2) escalation of offenses, (3) specialization of offenses, and (4) the tendency toward chronic offending. This section examines each of these dimensions in detail.

Age of Onset

Several studies have found that the **age of onset** is one of the best predictors of the length and intensity of delinquent careers.[85] Marvin E. Wolfgang, Terence P.

age of onset
The age at which a child begins to commit delinquent acts; an important dimension of delinquency.

Web LIBRARY 2.3

Read Chapter 2 of the OJJDP publication *Juvenile Offenders and Victims: 2006 National Report* at **www.justicestudies.com/ WebLibrary.**

Thornberry, and Robert M. Figlio followed a 10 percent sample of Cohort I of the Philadelphia study to the age of thirty and found that those who began their criminal careers at age ten or younger were arrested an average of seven times. Those who began their careers at ages eleven or twelve, however, were arrested an average of ten times—the highest average number for any age-of-onset category. For those who began their careers after the age of thirteen, the average number of offenses tended to decline uniformly as their age of onset increased.[86]

Patrick H. Tolan, in a reanalysis of three waves of the National Youth Survey data, categorized youths aged eleven to thirteen in the first wave into three onset groups: early onset (thirteen or before), late onset (after thirteen), and no onset. He concluded that early-onset delinquents tend to engage in more delinquent behavior, exhibit more serious offenses, are more likely to persist in their offending behavior, and are more likely to have more arrests.[87]

Blumstein, David P. Farrington, and Soumyo Moitra also showed that one of the factors predicting those who became chronic offenders was offending at an early age.[88] Farrington found that those who were first convicted at the earliest ages (ten to twelve) offended consistently at a higher rate and for a longer period than did those first convicted at later ages.[89]

Ronald L. Simons and his colleagues examined four waves of data on 177 adolescent boys and found that early and late starters had different paths to delinquent behavior. For early starters the quality of parenting predicted oppositional/defiant behavior, but for late starters the quality of parenting predicted affiliation with deviant peers, which in turn was associated with involvement with the justice system.[90]

The previously mentioned Program of Research on the Causes and Correlates of Delinquency is an especially significant research effort comprised of three coordinated longitudinal projects: the Denver Youth Survey, directed by David Huizinga at the University of Colorado; the Pittsburgh Youth Study, directed by Rolf Loeber, Magda Stouthamer-Loeber, and David Farrington at the University of Pittsburgh; and the Rochester Youth Development Study, directed by Terence P. Thornberry at the University at Albany, State University of New York. Initiated in 1986 by the Office of Juvenile Justice and Delinquency Prevention, the Causes and Correlates projects

Bullying behavior on a Texas playground. Some studies have found that the age of onset is one of the best predictors of the length and intensity of delinquent careers. ■ **How might the findings of those studies help in delinquency prevention efforts?**

are designed to improve the understanding of serious delinquency, violence, and drug use by examining how youths develop within the context of family, school, peers, and community.

The Causes and Correlates program represents an important milestone in criminological research because it constitutes the largest shared-measurement approach ever undertaken in delinquency research. The three research teams work together to ensure that certain core measures are identical across all sites, including self-reported delinquency and drug use; community and neighborhood characteristics; youth, family, and peer variables; and arrest and judicial processing histories.

The studies have yielded important insights into serious, violent, and chronic juvenile careers. In the Rochester study, for example, 39 percent of the youths who initiated the commission of violent offenses at age nine or younger became chronic violent offenders during their adolescent years. Of those who began committing violent offenses between ages ten and twelve, 30 percent became violent offenders.[91] The Denver findings were even more striking: Of those who began committing violent behavior at age nine or younger, 62 percent became chronic violent offenders.[92]

R. Loeber, D. P. Farrington, and D. Petechuk's 2003 study revealed that the average age of onset for self-reported serious delinquency was 11.9 years, while the first court contact for an index offense took place at an average age of 14.5 years.[93] Moffitt and colleagues' 2001 study further contended that "investigations that rely on official data to study crime careers will ascertain age of onset approximately 3–5 years after it has happened."[94]

Escalation of Offenses

The findings on **escalation of offenses,** or the increase in the frequency and severity of an individual's delinquent offenses, are more mixed than those on age of onset. Official studies of delinquency have generally found that the incidence of arrest accelerates at age thirteen and peaks at about age seventeen, but this pattern is not so clearly evident in self-report studies.

Jay R. Williams and Martin Gold's self-report study found that older juveniles were more frequently and seriously delinquent than were younger ones.[95] Yet in their national study, Ageton and Elliott found that the incidence of some offenses, such as assault and robbery, increased with age, whereas that of others peaked between ages thirteen and fifteen.[96] Elliott and Huizinga, combining data from three cohorts, provide information not only about the prevalence of different kinds of offending at each age but also about the percentage of individuals initiating and terminating their involvement in criminal activity. They concluded that initiation peaked at thirteen to fifteen, prevalence at sixteen to seventeen, and termination at eighteen to nineteen.[97]

Wolfgang, Figlio, and Sellin's findings from Philadelphia's Cohort I revealed that the average seriousness of offenses was reasonably constant during the juvenile years but then increased during the young adult years.[98] In the follow-up to age thirty of Cohort I, Wolfgang, Thornberry, and Figlio concluded that "for both the whites and nonwhites, the average number of offenses committed at each age is relatively constant from ages 10 to 30."[99] Pamela Tontodonato's examination of the data from Cohort II found that offenders who had three arrests by the age of fifteen had higher transition rates to additional arrests than did juveniles who accumulated arrests more slowly. Juveniles who were members of minorities, Tontodonato found, showed a higher rate of movement to injury and theft offenses than did whites.[100] In contrast, in the older two of Lyle W. Shannon's Racine cohorts, the average seriousness of offenses decreased steadily with age.[101] Furthermore, Katherine T. Van Dusen and Sarnoff A. Mednick found in their replication of the Philadelphia cohort study in Copenhagen that the average seriousness of offenses decreased with age, reaching a minimum level at age seventeen to eighteen, and then increased again.[102]

Rolf Loeber and colleagues' longitudinal study on the development of antisocial and prosocial behavior in 1,517 adolescent males in Pittsburgh found numerous correlates of escalation in offending among the three samples. The across-age effects were

Web LIBRARY 2.4

Read the OJJDP Fact Sheet *Highlights of Findings from the Rochester Youth Development Study* at **www.justicestudies.com/WebLibrary.**

Web PLACES 2.3

Visit the OJJDP-sponsored Program of Research on the Causes and Correlates of Delinquency via **www.justicestudies.com/WebPlaces.**

escalation of offenses

An increase in the frequency and severity of an individual's offenses; an important dimension of delinquency.

Web LIBRARY 2.5

Read Chapter 3 of the OJJDP publication *Juvenile Offenders and Victims: 2006 National Report* at **www.justicestudies.com/WebLibrary.**

low educational achievement and low school motivation. The age-specific effects were physical aggression, untrustworthiness, unaccountability, truancy, negative attitude toward school, school suspension, positive attitude to problem behavior, single parenthood, and negative caretaker–child relation.[103] Using data from two community samples of boys, Loeber and colleagues identified three developmental pathways to a delinquent career:

1. An early "authority conflict" pathway, which consists of a sequence of stubborn behavior, defiance, and authority avoidance;
2. A "covert" pathway, which consists of minor covert behaviors, property offenses, and moderate to serious forms of delinquent behavior; and
3. An "overt" pathway, which consists of fighting, aggression, and violence.[104]

They found that these pathways are interconnected; that is, youths may embark on two or three paths simultaneously. An implication of this research is that the youths' problem behavior may escalate as youths become involved in more than one developmental pathway. See Figure 2.7 for a diagrammatic representation of these three pathways to boys' disruptive behavior and delinquency.[105]

Terrie Moffitt and her colleagues have differentiated the small group of early-onset, persistent offenders from the much larger category of "adolescence-limited" delinquent males. These researchers found that these two groups differ both in age-related profiles of offending and in patterns of early risk. For persistent offenders,

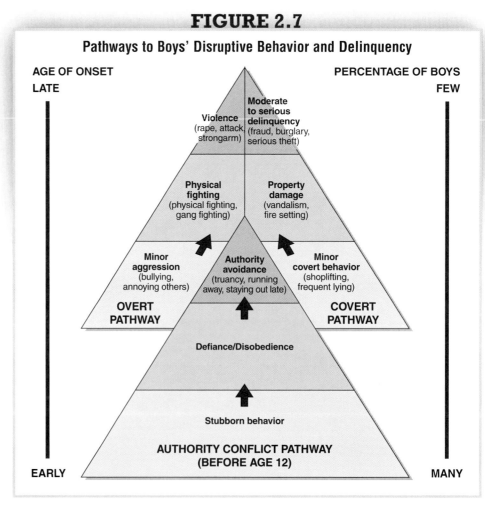

FIGURE 2.7

Pathways to Boys' Disruptive Behavior and Delinquency

Source: Barbara Tatem Kelley, Rolf Loeber, Kate Keenan, and Mary DeLamatre, *Developmental Pathways in Boys' Disruptive and Delinquent Behavior* (Washington, D.C.: Office of Juvenile Justice and Delinquency Prevention, 1997), p. 9. Reprinted with permission from the U.S. Department of Justice.

risks center on individual vulnerabilities that were evident early in childhood. In contrast, later-onset, adolescence-limited groups are characterized by more marginal levels of psychosocial and individual risks. Their adolescent difficulties are perceived to be prompted by frustrations associated with an adolescent maturity gap and by copying the behavior of deviant peers. (See Chapter 3 for more discussion of Moffitt's theory.)[106]

Barbara Maughan and her colleagues, in their longitudinal study of aggressive and nonaggressive conduct problems in the Great Mountain Study of Youth, identified three developmental trajectories: stable low problem levels, stable high problem levels, and declining levels of conduct problems for both aggressive and nonaggressive behaviors. Boys were overrepresented in the stable high trajectory class on the aggressive trajectory, but the researchers found that the overlap between aggressive and nonaggressive trajectory classes was quite limited. In addition, the study found strong associations between the risks of police contact and arrest in early adolescence and the aggressive and nonaggressive trajectory classes.[107]

Using data from the Seattle social development project, Todd I. Herrenkohl and colleagues examined whether socialization processes in the social development model (see Chapter 5) predict violence in late adolescence (age eighteen) for childhood initiators of violence (ages ten to eleven) and adolescent initiators of violence (ages twelve to sixteen). The investigators followed a group of children who were in the fifth grade in 1985 and found "that during adolescence, socialization pathways leading to violence at age 18 were similar for those who initiated violence in childhood and those who initiated violence in adolescence." They concluded that the same preventive interventions might be effective for individuals in both groups.[108]

Specialization of Offenses

The findings on **specialization,** or repeated involvement in one type of offense, reach a greater consensus than those on escalation. Farrington and colleagues, in examining juvenile court statistics, found "a small but significant degree of specialization in offending superimposed on a great deal of versatility."[109] Specialization was identified among nearly 20 percent of the offenders, and the most specialized offenses were running away, burglary, motor vehicle theft, drinking liquor, incorrigibility, violating curfew, truancy, and using drugs. Farrington and colleagues further reported that the degree of specialization tended to increase with successive referrals as more versatile offenders dropped out. Moreover, they concluded that more serious offenses such as robbery, aggravated assault, and motor vehicle theft tended to escalate in frequency with the number of referrals—whereas less serious offenses, such as running away and being truant, tended to decrease.[110]

Wolfgang and colleagues' Cohort I study (Philadelphia) showed no specialization from one age to the next and showed no specialization from one arrest to the next. But the probability of an index offense being followed by no offense declined steadily with age (from ten to sixteen).[111] Donna Martin Hamparian and her colleagues also reported no specialization among the violent offenders in Columbus. In fact, nonviolent offenses constituted nearly 70 percent of their delinquent behaviors.[112]

Susan K. Datesman and Michael Aickin, in examining a sample of status offenders who had been referred to the family court in Delaware during a three-year period, found that specialization was much more typical of status offenders. The majority of status offenders, regardless of gender and race, were referred to court within the same offense category 50 to 70 percent of the time. Females, particularly white females, specialized in official offense behavior to a greater extent than did males; 35.2 percent of the white females were referred to court for the same offense, a sizable proportion of them for running away. The findings of this study further suggest that no evidence exists of escalation in seriousness of offense as the offense career lengthens.[113]

Paul Mazerolle and his colleagues, in using data from the second Philadelphia Birth Cohort study, examined the interaction between gender and age at onset of offending and asked how these factors relate to specialization. They found that offenders

specialization

Repeated involvement of a juvenile in one type of delinquency during the course of his or her offending.

Web LIBRARY 2.6

Read the Bureau of Justice Statistics (BJS) publication *Juvenile Victimization and Offending* at **www.justicestudies.com/ WebLibrary.**

Members of a Chicago street gang. A small number of chronic youthful offenders account for a disproportionate share of all juvenile offenses. ■ **What kinds of prevention programs might successfully target chronic offenders?**

who initiated earlier in the life course demonstrated more versatility in their offending patterns and that delinquents who began offending at a later age tended to be more specialized. Early-onset females tended more toward offending diversity than early-onset males, whereas among late-onset groups males tended more toward offending diversity than females.[114]

Glenn Deanne, David Armstrong, and Richard Felson used data from the National Longitudinal Study of Adolescent Health in their 2005 examination of delinquency and violence, and dispelled the belief that there is a great deal of versatility in offending. Instead, they found that violent offenders are more likely to engage in additional violent offenses, and that nonviolent offenders are more likely to continue nonviolent offense patterns.[115]

Chronic Offending

Chronic offending is drawing increased attention for several reasons. Some believe that **chronic youthful offenders** constitute a majority of the active offenders. The finding that a small number of chronic juvenile offenders account for a disproportionate share of all crimes also helps to account for this increased attention. Furthermore, it is commonly believed that these young offenders are treated much more leniently than are their older counterparts.[116] To understand chronic youthful offenders, researchers examine their social backgrounds and analyze potential predictors of chronic offending.

Social Backgrounds   The cohort studies consistently report that chronic offenders are more frequently involved in violence than are other juvenile offenders. They also are more likely than other youthful offenders to use crack cocaine or other hard-core drugs or to traffic drugs to other juveniles at school and in the neighborhood.[117] Furthermore, they generally assume leadership roles in drug-trafficking gangs and, as they become adults, are more likely to continue their gang involvement. Finally, they frequently are involved in gang assaults and drive-by shootings.[118]

The vast majority of chronic offenders are identified by most cohort studies as coming from the ever-growing minority underclass that finds itself permanently

chronic youthful offender

A juvenile who engages repeatedly in delinquent behavior. The Philadelphia cohort studies defined chronic offenders as youths who had committed five or more delinquent offenses. Other studies use this term to refer to a youth involved in serious and repetitive offenses.

trapped. These youths are marginal to the social order and perceive crime as representing the best option they have. With no stake in the system, they are not easily amenable to measures designed to rehabilitate them by making them employable or to deter them from delinquent or criminal conduct. Contributing to the hopelessness among African American males is the realization that they are several times more likely to be victims of homicides than any other demographic group and that they finish last in nearly every socioeconomic category, from the high school dropout rate to unemployment. Indeed, a 1997 study found that half (49.9 percent) of African American men ages eighteen to thirty-five in the District of Columbia were under criminal justice supervision.[119]

Predictions of Chronic Offending   One of the most important but controversial issues is whether chronic juvenile offending can be predicted. Blumstein and colleagues identified three population groups in their study: a group of "innocents" never involved with law enforcement, a group of "amateurs" with a relatively low recidivism probability, and a group of "persisters" with a relatively high recidivism probability. The investigators found that seven factors distinguished the chronics, or persisters, from other convicted offenders: (1) conviction for crime before age thirteen; (2) low family income; (3) "troublesome" rating by teachers and peers at ages eight to ten; (4) poor public school performance by age ten; (5) psychomotor clumsiness; (6) low nonverbal IQ; and (7) convicted sibling.[120]

Farrington and J. David Hawkins's examination of the Cambridge Study in Delinquent Development found that persistence in crime between ages twenty-one and thirty-two was predicted "by low paternal involvement with the boy in leisure activities, a low degree of commitment to school and low verbal IQ at ages eight to ten years," and by heavy drinking and unemployment during the adolescent years.[121] Kimberly L. Kempf's analysis of Cohort II (Philadelphia study) found that "delinquents who became adult offenders by the age of twenty-six were somewhat more likely than other delinquents to have had more seriously offensive adolescent careers."[122]

A more alarming approach is the popular assumption that childhood factors, some of which are crime related, can be used to predict chronic delinquency and adult criminality and that intervention is justified based on these predicted factors. Peter Greenwood—and Paul Tracy, Marvin Wolfgang, and Robert Figlio as well as Alfred Blumstein, David Farrington, and Soumyo Moitra—claimed that a group of chronic offenders who are responsible for a disproportionate share of crime can be identified.[123] Although Greenwood argues that he has developed a calculus that can predict who adult chronic offenders will be and can produce estimates of crime reduction that would be achieved through their imprisonment,[124] this selective incapacitation policy has been soundly dismissed by a host of researchers.[125]

Lila Kazemian and David P. Farrington's 2006 longitudinal study of a sample of British males and their fathers examined *residual career length* (i.e., the average remaining number of years in criminal careers until the last offense) and *residual number of offenses* (i.e., the average remaining number of offenses in criminal careers). They concluded that official records make it difficult to accurately predict criminal career outcomes.[126]

In sum, the research literature gives us extensive documentation of the lower-class and deprived backgrounds of chronic offenders, of their sociopathic attitudes, and of the seriousness and violence of their offending. What is debatable, however, is whether it is possible to predict the continuation of chronic offending.

Delinquency Across the Life Course

One question we might ask is whether delinquency ends with adolescence, or if offending behavior tends to continue throughout life. For some individuals, delinquency is strictly confined to their adolescent years. (See Voices Across the

Web **PLACES** 2.4

View the OJJDP PowerPoint presentation "Law Enforcement and Juvenile Crime" at **www .justicestudies.com/ WebPlaces.**

Web **LIBRARY** 2.7

Read Chapter 5 of the OJJDP publication *Juvenile Offenders and Victims: 2006 National Report* at **www.justicestudies.com/ WebLibrary.**

Profession 2.1 for insight into how a majority of the individuals exit from delinquency by the end of their adolescent years). Other individuals, however, transition from delinquency during adolescence to crime during their adult years.

Developmental and life-course criminology (DLC) is particularly concerned with documenting and explaining within-individual changes in offending across the life course. This paradigm has greatly advanced knowledge about the measurement of criminal career features such as onset, continuation, and desistance. One of the reasons DLC became important during the 1990s was the enormous volume of longitudinal research on offending that was published during this decade.[127] Especially important contributions were the three self-report youth surveys in Denver, Pittsburgh, and Rochester (refer to Exhibit 2.1).[128] Other important longitudinal projects were the Dunedin study in New Zealand,[129] the Seattle Social Development project,[130] the Montreal Longitudinal–Experimental Study,[131] and the further analyses by Robert J. Sampson and Laub (1993 and 2003) of the Gluecks' classic longitudinal study of 1,000 men.[132]

One of the first longitudinal studies was the follow-up of the first and second Philadelphia cohorts (refer to Table 2.1). Wolfgang, Thornberry, and Figlio, in a follow-up to age thirty of a 10 percent sample of Cohort I, selected a random sample of 975 subjects. They were able to locate and interview 567 of these subjects when the subjects were twenty-six to thirty years of age. For the 567 members of the follow-up sample, the probability of being arrested by age thirty was 0.47, an increase over the 0.35 probability observed up to age eighteen. Significantly, for the subjects who were members of minorities, the probability of ever being arrested before age thirty was 0.69, compared with 0.38 for the white subjects.[133]

Wolfgang and colleagues identified three groups in this follow-up study: offenders only during their juvenile years, offenders only during their adult years, and persistent offenders during both periods. Of 459 offenders, 170 (37 percent) were juvenile delinquents only; 111 (24.2 percent) were adult offenders only; and 178 (38.8 percent) were persistent offenders. A comparison of the frequency of violations showed that the juvenile and adult offenders committed an average of slightly more than 2 offenses. The persistent offenders, however, committed an average of 8.9 offenses; furthermore, the offenses became more serious as their careers developed, and the offenses committed during adulthood were much more serious than those committed during the juvenile years.[134]

Hamparian and colleagues expanded the analysis of a cohort of violent juvenile offenders and followed them into early adulthood, the period ending when the offenders were in their mid-twenties. Tracking the adult criminal involvement of 1,222 persons who had been arrested for at least one violent or assaultive offense as juveniles, the investigators found that almost 60 percent of them were arrested at least once as a young adult for a felony offense, that the first adult arrest generally took place before age twenty, and that there was a clear continuity between juvenile and adult criminal careers.[135]

Katherine S. Ratcliff and Lee N. Robins, using data on a cohort of 233 African American males who grew up in St. Louis, studied the relationship between childhood and adult criminal behavior and concluded that (1) serious antisocial behavior in adults rarely takes place without high levels of childhood antisocial behavior—70 percent of highly antisocial adults were highly antisocial children; (2) only about half of very antisocial children become antisocial adults; and (3) the number of antisocial behaviors in childhood is the best indicator of severe antisocial behavior in adults. They also found that having an antisocial father is the best predictor of severe antisocial behavior in adulthood among mildly antisocial children; that being placed away from both parents and having few childhood years with parents of both sexes in the home are predictors of antisocial behavior in adulthood; and that being subjected to severe poverty in childhood is a predictor of severe antisocial behavior in adulthood.[136]

Michael Gottfredson and Travis Hirschi's *A General Theory of Crime* concluded that "competent research regularly shows that the best predictor of crime is prior criminal behavior."[137] James Q. Wilson and Richard Herrnstein also observed that "the offender offends not just because of immediate needs and circumstances but also because of enduring personal characteristics, some of whose traces can be found in his behavior from early childhood on. . . ."[138] Both of these works draw on a vast literature that shows a positive association between delinquency and adult criminality and such factors as poor parental supervision, parental rejection, parental criminality, delinquent sibling, and low IQ.[139]

Daniel S. Nagin and Raymond Paternoster, in examining the relationship between delinquency and adult criminality, suggest two interpretations of this relationship. The first is that "prior participation has a genuine behavioral impact on the individual. Prior participation may, for example, reduce inhibitions against engaging in delinquent activity."[140] Nagin and Paternoster refer to such an effect as "state dependence." Another explanation is that individuals have different propensities to delinquency and that each person's innate "propensity is persistent over time." This second explanation is similar to the findings of Gottfredson and Hirschi and of Wilson and Herrnstein.[141] Nagin and Paternoster, in using a three-wave panel set, found that the positive association between past and future delinquency is due to a state-dependence influence.[142]

> " Competent research regularly shows that the best predictor of crime is prior criminal behavior. "

Sampson and Laub sought to explain both the continuity of delinquency into adult criminality and noncriminality, or change, in adulthood for those who were delinquent as children. Their basic thesis was threefold:

1. Structural context mediated by informal family and school social control explains delinquency in childhood and adolescence.
2. In turn, there is continuity in antisocial behavior from childhood through adulthood in a variety of life domains.
3. Informal social bonds in adulthood to family and employment explain changes in criminality over the life span despite early childhood propensities.[143]

Using life-history data drawn from the Gluecks' longitudinal study, Laub and Sampson found that although adult crime is connected to childhood behavior, both incremental and abrupt changes still take place through changes in adult social bonds. The emergence of strong bonds to work and family among adults deflects early, established behavior trajectories. Laub and Sampson also argue that the events that trigger the formation of strong adult bonds to work and family commonly occur by chance or luck.[144]

The concept of a **turning point** in the life course is one of the fascinating contributions of Laub and Sampson's research. A turning point involves a gradual or dramatic change and may lead to "a modification, reshaping, or transition from one state, condition, or phase to another."[145] In seeking to unravel the mechanisms that operate at key turning points to redirect a risk trajectory to a more adaptive path, Laub and Sampson found that stable employment and a good marriage, or changing roles and environments, can lead to investment of social capital or relations among persons.[146] "Social capital," according to James S. Coleman, "is productive, making possible the achievements of certain ends that in its absence would not be possible."[147] (See Chapter 4 for a discussion of the development of social capital theory.)

turning point
A gradual or dramatic change in the trajectory of an individual's life course.

More recently, Raymond Paternoster, Robert Brame, and David Farrington, using data from the Cambridge Study in Delinquent Development, investigated the relationship between adolescent and adult involvement in criminal behavior. In opposition to Sampson and Laub, Paternoster and colleagues found that adult offending "is not systematically related to events and experiences after adolescence." They argue that variation in adult offending is consistent with a random process and, accordingly, that it is impossible to conclude that relatively simple explanations, such

Adult Antipsychotics Can Worsen Troubles

Evan Kitchens, a cheerful fourth-grader who loves basketball and idolizes his 16-year-old brother, had been hospitalized for mental illness by the time he was 8.

The boy from Bandera, Texas, was aggressive and hyperactive and had been diagnosed with a variety of other ailments, including obsessive-compulsive disorder and an autism spectrum disorder.

A couple of years ago, Evan was taking five psychiatric drugs, says his mother, Mary Kitchens. Two were so-called atypical antipsychotics, a group of relatively new drugs approved by the Food and Drug Administration for treating adults with schizophrenia or bipolar disorder.

"Evan was a walking zombie on all those drugs," Kitchens says. At the harrowing nadir two years ago, she wondered whether her son would survive, let alone live a normal life.

Evan shook with severe body tremors and hardly talked. He had crossed eyes, a dangerously low white blood cell count and a thyroid disorder, all symptoms that emerged after he started the atypical antipsychotic drugs, Kitchens says. Now, he has been weaned from the drugs and takes medicine only for attention-deficit disorder, she says. And he is mentally healthier than he has ever been.

These six new antipsychotic drugs—Clozaril, Risperdal, Zyprexa, Seroquel, Abilify and Geodon—are not approved for children, but doctors can prescribe them to kids "off label." And prescribing atypical antipsychotics for aggressive children such as Evan is leading the field in a growing pediatric business, according to a new analysis of a federal survey by Vanderbilt Medical School researchers.

Outpatient prescriptions for children ages 2 to 18 jumped about five-fold—from just under half a million to about 2.5 million—from 1995 to 2002, the survey shows.

At the same time, reports of deaths and dangerous side effects potentially linked to the drugs are increasing. A *USA TODAY* analysis of Food and Drug Administration data shows at least 45 deaths of children from 2000 to 2004 where an atypical was considered the "primary suspect." More than 1,300 cases reported bad side effects, including some that can be life threatening, such as convulsions and a low white blood cell count.

Many children today have been diagnosed as hyperactive, autistic, or suffering from behavioral problems such as Attention Deficit Disorder — resulting in an increased use of psychotropic medications.
■ **What are the dangers associated with the overuse of such medications?**

Non-Drug Treatments

Treating children's disruptive behavior with pills is a complicated issue and the subject of debate among experts.

"In my experience, and that of many psychiatrists, antipsychotics are often overused for aggression in young patients," says Ronald Pies, a clinical professor at Tufts University and author of *Handbook of Essential Psychopharmacology.*

That doesn't mean it's necessarily wrong to give the pills, he adds.

Nobody disputes that the lives of schizophrenic or severely manic children might be saved by antipsychotics. But many non-drug treatments can help to keep aggressive, disruptive children off the atypicals, says John March, chief of child and adolescent psychiatry at Duke University School of Medicine.

So much hinges on whether safer treatments can work for a child.

Kids who show up on antipsychotics for aggression often can be weaned off if there are family changes, says behavioral pediatrician Lawrence Diller of Walnut Creek, Calif. For instance, adolescents may lash out angrily if their parents are fighting or discipline is inconsistent, Diller says. In a divorce, the child sometimes ends up with the less effective parent.

Last year, Diller saw an 8-year-old boy on four psychiatric drugs, including an atypical. He lived with his mother, "a highly anxious, incompetent parent." When he went to live with his father, his symptoms virtually disappeared, and he didn't need any drugs, Diller says.

Child psychiatrist George Stewart says he has seen dozens of aggressive children weaned off the atypical antipsychotic drugs in his consulting work and as medical director of a residential treatment facility in Concord, Calif. Too often, he says, doctors give the drugs without considering family conditions or life experiences that cause aggressive behavior, which can be changed with intensive counseling. Three examples he offers:

- A boy younger than 3 was treated with two antipsychotics at a therapeutic preschool for kids with severe behavior problems. Stewart got a full family history, discovering his teen mother had a series of abusive boyfriends. "He was acting out due to that, but nobody took the time to find out what was going on at home," says Stewart, who worked with the mom to improve conditions. "She settled down."

The child was taken off atypicals and is doing fine.

- A 12-year-old boy with out-of-control rage—"we're talking smearing poop all over the 'quiet room'"—was treated at Stewart's center. Intensive therapy identified the sources of his rage and taught the boy how to cope. He returned home, off all meds.
- A teen girl seemed to be intractably violent. "She was trying to stab pencils in people's eyes," Stewart says. It turned out she had been raped and experienced

other severe trauma. She was weaned off antipsychotics and counseled. Now in her late teens, she's living independently and doing well with no psychiatric drugs.

One of the most disturbing, potentially dangerous trends linked to atypicals is called "polypharmacy": routinely giving kids several psychiatric drugs, says child psychiatrist Joseph Penn of Bradley Hospital and Brown University School of Medicine in Providence. "We know very little about the interaction of these drugs, the effects they could be having on kids," he says.

The benefits of prescribing multiple drugs may outweigh risks in some cases, but Penn says he is appalled at how many times he has seen the mega-powerful atypicals prescribed to children suffering from insomnia when they're taking other medicines.

"I've seen hundreds of cases," he says, "and often parents don't seem to have been told about the many less risky prescription and non-prescription options out there."

Sometimes medical conditions or drugs for attention-deficit hyperactivity disorder cause the insomnia. Rather than attacking causes, doctors add an atypical to the mix, he says.

More Research Needed

There has been little carefully controlled, long-term research on children taking most psychiatric drugs, including the atypical antipsychotics. The FDA is trying to get more pediatric research on the atypicals, says Thomas Laughren, the agency's director of the psychiatry products division.

The FDA has asked five pharmaceutical companies that make the drugs to test them in children with schizophrenia and bipolar disorder, the uses they're approved for in adults. Under law, they can get a six-month extension on their patents for doing these studies.

Also, the drug companies are doing their own pediatric studies on children with disorders as diverse as ADHD, autism, conduct disorder and Tourette's syndrome.

Janssen LP has applied to the FDA for approval to use its atypical antipsychotic, Risperdal, in the treatment of symptoms of autism, says Ramy Mahmoud, vice president of medical affairs for Janssen. The National Institute of Mental Health also is conducting pediatric studies, but the research is primarily funded and supervised by pharmaceutical companies.

Even if the companies win approval, it won't guarantee safety or effectiveness of the drugs in children, says David Graham of the FDA Office of Drug Safety, who emphasizes he doesn't speak for the agency. "You basically know the drug isn't cyanide. You don't know much else," says Graham, who was the whistle-blower in the 2004 Vioxx heart disease scandal. Industry-funded trials are four to five times more likely than independent studies to show effectiveness for a drug, he says.

According to a research review published in February, 90% of drug-company-funded studies come up with findings that support the company's drug.

In head-to-head research testing more than one atypical antipsychotic drug, the outcomes are contradictory, coming down on the side of whichever company is paying for the research. (The research included studies of Risperdal, Zyprexa, Clozaril and Geodon, but none on Seroquel or Abilify.)

"It appears that whichever company sponsors the trial produces the better antipsychotic drug," writes lead author Stephan Heres of the Technical University of Munich in the *American Journal of Psychiatry*.

And the short-term, smaller studies required of companies rarely detect any but the most glaring problems, Graham says.

"The American public is operating under the illusion that a drug is safe just because it's approved by the FDA," says Jeffrey Lieberman, chairman of psychiatry at the Columbia College of Physicians and Surgeons in New York. Studies lasting a few weeks to a few months, with a couple of thousand patients total, won't reveal all that's wrong with a drug, he says.

Laughren agrees that "it's very difficult to answer every question we'd like to answer with these studies, because obviously they're not huge. Sometimes bad things that happen are going to be discovered only when a drug is used more widely."

He says he, too, shares concern about the antipsychotics prescribed for children without proof of safety or effectiveness. Much more pediatric information on the atypicals will be available within five years, he says.

Recommended Changes

Others favor fundamental changes to get the needed facts about drug safety. Lieberman thinks one solution would be for the FDA to be given a new legal authority: the right to require drug com-

panies seeking to gain approval of a drug to contribute to a collective pool at the National Institutes of Health. The NIH could supervise larger safety and effectiveness studies of medicines after they're on the market.

A national electronic medical records database that would capture all bad side effects of drugs, and require ages and diagnoses, could do a lot to protect children from careless prescribing and reveal the effects of antipsychotics, Duke's March says.

"We know so little about what's happening to all the kids who are getting these powerful antipsychotics," he says.

March also thinks more private insurers ought to insist that aggressive children with short fuses try non-drug therapies proven to help before doctors jump in with antipsychotics. These pills can seem like an appealing "quick fix," he says, so they're popular.

For foster children with mental health problems, medication is a mainstay, says Ira Burnim, legal director at the Bazelon Center for Mental Health Law, an advocacy group for those with mental disabilities. There's proof that the most effective care is "wraparound," he says, meaning that caseworkers touch base regularly with a child's school, doctor, foster and perhaps birth families, in addition to ensuring therapy or medication as needed.

"Now they're medicating many kids instead of giving them the services they need. But there's very little time spent with psychiatrists and not much attention paid to side effects from these heavy drugs," Burnim says.

States vary in how much wraparound care they provide for foster kids, "but a typical pattern is patches here and there," Burnim says. "They rely heavily on medications like the antipsychotics. This costs more than wraparound in the long run, and it's less safe for the kids."

March considers the widespread use of antipsychotics on children without proof of safety or effectiveness "a very large experiment." Many kids are getting the short end of the stick, he says. "We're not even gathering good data on the outcome of the experiment. It's the worst of all possible worlds."

as employment and marriage, can explain complex life-course decisions. They propose that much further study is needed to clarify the relationship between adolescent delinquent acts and adult criminal behaviors.[148]

Desistance from Crime

The age of **desistance**, or the termination of delinquent behavior, is a recent consideration of researchers. One of the problems of establishing desistance is the difficulty of distinguishing between a gap in a delinquent career and true termination. There are bound to be crime-free intervals in the course of delinquent careers. Long-term follow-up is clearly required to establish the age of termination.[149] To explain change in offending over time, or desistance, theorists have proposed several explanations, which we'll consider by category.

Maturation and Aging Accounts for Desistance   The maturation process appears to be involved in desistance, as youths or adults become aware either of the desirability of pursuing a conventional lifestyle or of the undesirability of continuing with unlawful activities. Sheldon and Eleanor Glueck drew this conclusion during their follow-up of juvenile delinquent careers: "With the passing of the years there was . . . both a decline in criminality and a decrease in the seriousness of the offenses of those who continued to commit crimes."[150] James Q. Wilson and Herrnstein contend that the relatively minor gains from crime lose their power to reinforce deviant behavior as juveniles mature and develop increasing ties to conventional society. Another aspect of this maturation process, according to Wilson and Herrnstein, is the individual's ability to delay gratification and forgo the immediate gains that delinquent or criminal acts bring.[151]

Developmental Accounts for Desistance   There have been several developmental explanations of desistance. One explanation is that identity changes account for reduction in or cessation of crime. Edward Mulvey and John LaRosa, focusing on the period from age seventeen to twenty—the period they call the time of "natural" recovery—found that desistance was linked to a cognitive process taking place in the late teens when delinquents realized that they were "going nowhere" and that they had better make changes in their lives if they were going to be successful as adults.[152]

Shadd Maruna, in examining how English ex-offenders reformed and rebuilt their lives, found that the life stories of desisting ex-offenders were characterized by the offenders' taking on a self-identity narrative, or "redemptive script." This redemptive script allowed "the person to rewrite a shameful past into a necessary prelude to a productive and worthy life.[153] Peggy C. Giordano and colleagues, in a longitudinal study of serious female offenders, found that desistance took place when there were cognitive shifts in these offenders. Cognitive transformation provided desisters "with a detailed plan of action or a fairly elaborate *cognitive blueprint* for proceeding as a changed individual.[154]

Another developmental explanation is offered by W. R. Gove, who argued that explanations of desistance must incorporate biological, psychological, and sociological variables. After reviewing six sociological themes of deviance, Gove concluded that biological and psychological factors appear to play major roles in the cessation of deviant behavior, because the peak and decline in individuals' physical strength, psychological drive, energy, and need for stimulation maps well the peak and decline of deviant behavior.[155]

A third and more influential developmental account of persistence in and desistance from crime is offered by Terrie Moffitt. Life-course persistent offenders start early in childhood, when neuropsychological deficits in conjunction with disrupted attachment relationships and academic failure drive long-term antisocial behavior.

Moffitt does not believe that these offenders desist from crime. In contrast, the delinquent behavior of adolescence-limited offenders is situational; as a result, virtually all of these offenders desist from antisocial behavior over time. They have more prosocial skills, stronger attachments, and more academic achievement than their life-course persistent counterparts. Moffitt sums up her position by saying that "the age of desistance from criminal offending will be a function of age of onset of antisocial behavior, mastery of conventional prosocial skills, and the number and severity of 'snares' encountered during the foray into delinquency. Snares are consequences of crime, such as incarceration or injury," that can hamper the development of conventional behavior.[156]

Web LIBRARY 2.8

Read the OJJDP Fact Sheet *Causes and Correlates of Delinquency Program* at **www.justicestudies .com/WebLibrary**.

Rational Choice Accounts for Desistance   The main idea of the rational choice framework is that the decision to give up or continue with crime is based on a person's conscious reappraisal of the costs and benefits of criminal activity. Proponents of this theory see persisters and desisters as "reasoned decisionmakers."[157] Offenders' increased fear of punishment with aging is one of the important components of their decision to desist. For example, Barry Glassner and colleagues studied youths in a medium-size city in New York State and reported that many youths curtailed involvement in delinquent activities at age sixteen because they feared being jailed if they were apprehended as adults.[158] David Farrington also noted that the severity of the adult penal system appeared to be a deterrent with the population he studied.[159]

Social Learning Accounts for Desistance   Ronald Akers contends that social learning accounts incorporate all of the major elements of the rational choice and deterrence frameworks, including moral reasoning. According to the social learning framework, the basic variables explaining initiation into crime are essentially the same factors that account for the desistance from crime. In other words, as an integrative framework to explain desistance, social learning presents an account of desistance that is, for the most part, the account of initiation in reverse.[160] In two publications Mark Warr supported the social learning account of desistance. In the first he argued that differential association accounted for the decline in crime with age.[161] In the second he contended that changing peer relations accounted for the association between marital status and desistance from crime. The transition to marriage was followed by "a dramatic decline in time spent with friends" and "reduced exposure to delinquent peers."[162]

A Life-Course Account for Desistance   The major objective of the life-course perspective, whose framework was discussed in Chapter 1, is to link social history and social structure. In *Crime in the Making* Sampson and Laub developed an age-graded theory of informal social control to explain childhood problem behavior, adolescent delinquency, and crime in adulthood.[163]

In 2003, John H. Laub and Robert J. Sampson published *Shared Beginnings, Divergent Lives,* which promises to be a classic study of life-course and developmental criminology. They argue that the data from the Gluecks' original study support the notion that explanations of desistance from crime and of persistence in crime are two sides of the coin. From their analysis of offender narratives and life histories, Laub and Sampson conclude that "offenders desist as a result of individual actions (choice) in conjunction with situational contexts and structural influences linked to key institutions that help sustain desistance." They perceive desistance as a process, rather than an event—a process that operates simultaneously at different levels (individual, situational, and community) and across different contextual environments (especially family, work, and military service).[164]

A central element in the desistance process, according to Laub and Sampson, is any change that "knifes off" individual offenders from their environment and at the same time offers them a new script for the future. A new "structured role stability"

Voices
Across the Profession 2.1

Interview with John H. Laub

Question: Psychologist Anne Colby has concluded that "the establishment of [the life-course] approach, which is widely shared internationally as well as across disciplines, is one of the most important achievements of social science in the second half of the twentieth century." How much do you believe the life-course approach will impact the study of juvenile delinquency/criminology in the twenty-first century?

Laub: I think that the life-course approach will greatly influence the study of juvenile delinquency and criminology in the twenty-first century. First, from a theoretical perspective, the importance of studying the unfolding of individual lives across the entire life course is becoming more prominent in criminology and the social sciences at large. It is well recognized now that crime does not just happen, but needs to be understood in a larger developmental and life-course framework. Secondly, and perhaps more practically, there are a number of longitudinal studies whose subjects are coming of age and entering adulthood. Thus, the challenge will be to assess how the diversity of life-course experiences across various groups (e.g., race/ethnicity, gender, socioeconomic status, and place) will affect the stability and change in criminal offending and deviance over the life course.

Question: Your concept that "adult life course matters" is certainly corrective to the deterministic message of "the child is father to the man," especially the antisocial child, found in so many studies. But does the persistent, chronic, or whatever this offender may be called have a different process of desistance from the other offenders?

Laub: In our analysis of the Glueck delinquents from age seven to seventy, we found that while all offenders eventually desisted from crime, some do so at different ages or at different rates. Thus, the age–crime curve is *not* invariant across all offenders. At the same time, we found no support for the idea of a life-course persistent offender; namely, someone whose rate of offending does not decline with age. In our study, we found that all offenders undergo a similar process of the desistance, albeit at different times in the life course. Desistance results from strong social ties to family (typically the result of marriage), military service, or stable employment. Moreover, we see strong evidence that persistent offending and desistance from crime can be understood through a common theoretical lens; namely, a revised age-graded general theory of informal social control that emphasizes social ties, routine activities, and human agency.

Question: What best explains the behavior of those who zigzag back and forth between criminal behavior and noncriminal behavior?

Laub: Drawing on Dan Glaser's notion of zigzag offending, we find that this idea captures the true nature of criminal offending. Even the most persistent offender does not offend each minute of the day, and those that desist from crime may well relapse and commit minor crimes. In our work we see the propensity to offend as the result of a variety of individual, situational, and community factors. Offenders cease offending when they experience structural turning points (for example, marriage) that lead to a strengthening of their social support systems *in conjunction with* a resolve to change their life. They are thus better positioned situationally to respond to the monitoring and control and the love and social support around them.

Question: When I first read Matza, I was intrigued by his notion of "will." Interestingly, this concept of will or human agency until recently has been largely ignored by criminological studies. With the various contributions of life-course theorists (Clausen, "planful competence"; Maruna, "redemptive scripts"; Giordano et al., "cognitions of human agency," etc.), human agency is increasingly found in criminological publications. This human construction appears to be changing the perception of the delinquent from a reactor to a redactor. Do you believe this will have a long-term effect on delinquency and criminology research?

can emerge across various life domains (for example, work, marriage, and/or community). The men desisting in this study shared a daily routine that provided structure and meaningful activity. Laub and Sampson add that although there are multiple pathways to desistance, they found what seem to be important general processes or mechanisms consistent with the idea of informal social control. The major turning points implicated in this study's desistance process included marriage/spouses, employment, reform school, the military, and neighborhood change. All of these turning points involve, to varying degrees, "(1) New situations that knife off the past from

Laub: As David Matza said almost forty years ago, the missing element in traditional social control theory is human agency [1964, p. 183]; motivation has always been its weakest link. I think that our work underscores the point that individuals actively create their own life course as it is being shaped by larger structural forces. Perhaps the concept that best captures this idea is "situated choice." It is important then to reconcile the idea of choice or will with a structuralist notion of turning points, and that is one of the challenges for future research.

In crucial ways, criminal persistence is more than a weakening of social bonds, and desistance is more than the presence of a social bond, as one might be led to conclude (mistakenly) from our earlier work, *Crime in the Making* [Sampson and Laub, 1993]. At a metatheoretical level, our long-term follow-up data direct us to insist that a focus purely on institutional, or structural, turning points and opportunities is incomplete, for such opportunities are mediated by perceptions and human decision making. Even if below the surface of active consciousness, as in the concept of desistance by default, actions to desist are in fundamental sense willed by the offender, bringing a richer meaning to the notion of commitment. Further supporting this idea is that the men who desisted from crime, and even those who persisted, accepted responsibility for their actions and freely admitted getting into trouble. They did not, for the most part, offer excuses. Tough times due to the Great Depression, uncaring parents, poor schools, discrimination based on ethnicity and class, and the like, were not invoked to explain their criminal pasts.

Question: By the way, how can human agency (choice, decision making, planning, resourcefulness, resilience, etc.) ever be measured or calibrated?

Laub: There is no easy answer to this question. In our book *Shared Beginnings, Divergent Lives,* our effort was to reposition human agency as a central element in understanding crime and deviance over the life- course. We did not develop an explicit theory of human agency replete with testable causal hypotheses. This will be a first-order challenge for future work in life-course criminology. One strategy might be to unpack agency and begin to articulate the key elements—planfulness, self-efficacy, time orientation, etc. Regardless, in the end, I think some combination of quantitative and qualitative data are needed to measure agency in its fullest sense of the term.

Question: One of the damning things, as my in-service students like to remind me, is that the explanations of delinquent behavior do not work in the real world. The process model found in *Shared Beginnings, Divergent Lives* seems to present a much more multidimensional (and I think accurate) understanding of human behavior. How do you think the criminological community will respond to this process model?

Laub: The criminological research community has been very receptive to what you call "the process model," because it does add the complexity that is evident in the "real world." However, at the same time, there are elements of the model that seem out of control of policymakers—for example, marriage, human agency, and aging. However, objections to the model on this basis are short-sighted. Our theory provides a framework to understand continuity and change in offending over the life course. Also, our work reminds policymakers of the difficulty of predicting adult outcomes based solely on childhood characteristics. We found that while childhood prognoses are modestly accurate in predicting level differences, they simply do not yield distinct groupings that are valid prospectively for troubled kids. Not only is prediction clearly poor at the individual level; our data reveal the tenuous basis for the sorts of distinct groupings that dominate theoretical discussion (e.g., "superpredator"; "life-course persistent offender"). These groupings wither when placed under the microscope of long-term observation.

> ■ Why is the life course an important topic in the study of delinquency? What is your evaluation of Laub and Sampson's presentation of desistance? Why would their model be considered a process one?

Source: Reprinted with permission from John H. Laub. John H. Laub is professor of criminology at the University of Maryland. He and Robert J. Sampson have authored the award-winning *Crime in the Making: Pathways and Turning Points through Life, Shared Beginnings, Divergent Lives,* and many other publications.[165]

the present. (2) New situations that provide both supervision and monitoring as well as new opportunities of social support and growth. (3) New situations that change and structure routine activities. (4) New situations that provide the opportunity for identity transformation."[166] In sum, offenders "choose to desist in response to structurally induced turning points that serve as the catalyst for sustaining long-term behavior change.[167] See Voices Across the Profession 2.1 for an interview with John H. Laub. In this interview, Laub answers questions about life-course theory which Robert Sampson and he refer to as the "soul of criminology."[168]

Official and unofficial statistics reveal much of significance about youth crime in U.S. society today:

- Juveniles under the age of eighteen commit a disproportionate number of property and violent offenses.

- Juveniles today are committing more violent crimes than their counterparts did in the past. But juvenile rates of homicide have been decreasing since 1994.

- Juveniles are carrying far more guns than in the past. The good news is that law enforcement efforts in large urban areas in the mid- to late 1990s have had some success in reducing juveniles' use of guns.

- Most youths are involved in delinquent behavior at some point, but more than 90 percent of delinquent acts go unreported.

- Lower-class youths are involved in more frequent and more serious offenses than are middle-class youths. Indeed, serious long-lasting youth crime is primarily found among the lower classes.

- Nonwhites commit more frequent and more serious offenses than do whites.

- Males commit more frequent and more serious offenses than do females.

- Urban youths commit more frequent and more serious offenses than do suburban or rural youths.

- A small group of youthful offenders, primarily lower-class minority males, commits half or more of all serious offenses in urban areas.

- Developmental and life-course criminology has offered several explanations for the process of desistance from delinquent or criminal behavior.

- In the midst of the continuity of childhood antisocial behavior, some young adults experience turning points, or changes, usually related to such matters as stable jobs or a satisfying marriage or family life.

- Interventions by the juvenile justice system sometimes make youths' behavior worse rather than better.

- Evidence exists that at least some youthful offenders progress to increasingly serious forms of delinquent behavior and crime.

- Young people who begin offending early tend to have long delinquent careers.

- The juvenile crime wave predicted in the 1990s is probably unlikely to materialize anytime soon.

1. What do the *Crime in the United States* data generally show about official delinquency in U.S. society?
2. What problems do the official *Crime in the United States* data present to researchers?
3. What do juvenile court statistics show about juvenile delinquency in U.S. society?
4. Identify the various studies that were discussed in this chapter. What do their findings reveal about the nature and extent of youth crime?

5. The youthful chronic offender is a concern to the public and its policymakers. What do we know about these youths?
6. Discuss the various dimensions of delinquent behavior. What do we know about each dimension?
7. What is the importance of the concept of the "turning point"?

WEB
Interactivity

View the OJJDP PowerPoint presentation "Juvenile Offenders" by going to **www.justicestudies.com/WebPlaces** and clicking on Web Places 2-2.

Compare the data provided in the OJJDP presentation with the material in Chapter 2 of this textbook. What similar materials are presented? What additional materials does the PowerPoint presentation contain? How does the PowerPoint presentation add to this chapter? Write down your answers to these questions and submit them to your instructor if asked to do so.

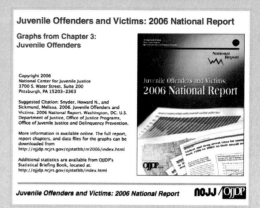

Source: From http://ojjdp.ncjrs.org/ojstatbb/nr2006/ downloads/chapter3.ppt. Reprinted with permission from the U.S. Department of Justice.

Notes

1. Donald J. Shoemaker, *Theories of Delinquency: An Examination of Explanations of Delinquent Behavior,* 5th ed. (New York: Oxford University Press, 2005), p. 53.
2. Federal Bureau of Investigation, *Crime in the United States 2005.* Online at www.fbi.gov/ucr/05cius/index.html.
3. Ibid., p. 244.
4. Marie Simonetti Rosen, "A LEN Interview with Professor Alfred Blumstein," *Law Enforcement News* 21 (John Jay College of Criminal Justice, New York City) (April 30, 1995), p. 10. Reprinted with permission.
5. Ibid.
6. Ibid.
7. James Alan Fox, *Trends in Juvenile Violence: A Report to the United States Attorney General on Current and Future Rates of Juvenile Offending.* Prepared for the Bureau of Justice Statistics (March 1996), executive summary, p. 19.
8. Ibid.
9. Ibid.
10. John J. DiIulio Jr., "Arresting Ideas: Tougher Law Enforcement Is Driving Down Urban Crime," *Policy Review* (Fall 1995), p. 15.
11. Ibid.
12. Ibid.
13. William J. Bennett, John J. DiIulio Jr., and John P. Walters, *Body Count: Moral Poverty and How to Win America's War against Crime and Drugs* (New York: Simon and Schuster, 1996).
14. Cited in Philip J. Cook, "The Epidemic of Youth Gun Violence," *Perspectives on Crime and Justice: 1997–1998* (Washington, D.C.: The National Institute of Justice, 1998), pp. 110–111.
15. Ibid., p. 111.
16. Franklin E. Zimring, Presentation at National Criminal Justice Association Annual Meeting (May 30, 1996).
17. Franklin E. Zimring, "Crying Wolf over Teen Demons," *L. A. Times,* August 19, 1996, p. A17.
18. Philip J. Cook and John Laub, "The Unprecedented Epidemic in Youth Violence," in *Crime and Justice,* edited by Mark H. Moore and Michael Tonry (Chicago: University of Chicago Press, 1998), pp. 101–138.
19. Cook, "The Epidemic of Youth Gun Violence," p. 111.
20. Alfred Blumstein and Richard Rosenfeld, "Assessing the Recent Ups and Downs in U.S. Homicide Rates," *National Institute of Justice Journal* 237 (October 1998), pp. 10–11.
21. I. R. Perlman, "Juvenile Court Statistics," *Juvenile Court Judges Journal* 16 (1965), pp. 1–3.
22. A Stahl, T. Finnegan, and W. Kang, *Easy Access to Juvenile Court Statistics, 1985–2002.* Online at http://ojjdp.ncjs.org/ org/ojsdtabb/exajcs.
23. Ibid.
24. For the Philadelphia cohort study, see Marvin E. Wolfgang, Robert M. Figlio, and Thorsten Sellin, *Delinquency in a Birth Cohort* (Chicago: University of Chicago Press, 1972). For the London, England, cohort, see Alfred Blumstein, David P. Farrington, and Soumyo Moitra, "Delinquency Careers: Innocents, Amateurs, and Persisters," in *Crime and Justice: An Annual Review* 6, edited by Michael Tonry and Norval Morris (Chicago: University of Chicago Press, 1985), pp. 187–220. For the Racine, Wisconsin, cohort, see Lyle W. Shannon, *Assessing the Relationships of Adult Criminal Careers to Juvenile Careers: A Summary* (Washington, D.C.: U.S. Government Printing Office, 1982). For the Columbus

cohort, see Donna Martin Hamparian et al., *The Violent Few: A Study of Dangerous Juveniles* (Lexington, Mass.: Lexington Books, 1980).

25. Stephen A. Cernkovich, Peggy C. Giordano, and Meredith D. Pugh, "Chronic Offenders: The Missing Cases in Self-Report Delinquency," *Journal of Criminal Law and Criminology* 76 (1985), p. 705.

26. Cynthia Jakob-Chien provided this information on the National Youth Survey.

27. Charles Puzzanchera, Anne L. Stahl, Terrence A. Finnegan, Nancy Tierney, and Howard N. Snyder, *Juvenile Court Statistics, 1999* (Pittsburgh, Pa.: National Center for Juvenile Justice, 2003), p. 58.

28. Michael J. Hindelang, Travis Hirschi, and Joseph G. Weis, *Measuring Delinquency* (Beverly Hills, Calif.: Sage, 1981), p. 22.

29. Ibid., p. 86.

30. James F. Short Jr. and F. Ivan Nye, "Reported Behavior as a Criterion of Deviant Behavior," *Social Problems* 5 (Winter 1957–1958), p. 211.

31. Hindelang et al., *Measuring Delinquency*, p. 295.

32. Cernkovich et al., "Chronic Offenders," p. 706. For other efforts to include frequent and serious offenders, see Ross Matsueda, Rosemary Gartner, Irving Piliavin, and Michael Polakowski, "The Prestige of Criminal and Conventional Occupations: A Subcultural Model of Criminal Activity," *American Sociological Review* 57 (1992), pp. 752–770; and James Inciardi, Ruth Horowitz, and Anne Pottieger, *Street Kids, Street Drugs, Street Crime: An Examination of Drug Use and Serious Delinquency in Miami* (Belmont, Calif.: Wadsworth Publishing, 1993).

33. Hindelang et al., *Measuring Delinquency*, p. 126. For the reliability of self-report studies, see also David H. Huizinga and Delbert S. Elliot, *A Longitudinal Study of Drug Use and Delinquency in a National Sample of Youth: An Assessment of Causal Order* (A Report of the National Youth Survey, Boulder, Colo.: Behavioral Research Institute, 1981); and Beatrice A. Rouse, Nicholas J. Kozel, and Louise G. Richards, eds., *Self-Report Methods of Estimating Drug Use: Meeting Current Challenges to Validity*, NIDA Research Monograph 57 (Rockville, Md.: National Institute on Drug Abuse, 1985).

34. Austin L. Porterfield, "Delinquency and Its Outcome in Court and College," *American Journal of Sociology* 49 (November 1943), pp. 199–208.

35. James F. Short Jr., "A Report on the Incidence of Criminal Behavior, Arrests, and Convictions in Selected Groups," *Research Studies of the State College of Washington* 22 (June 1954), 110–118.

36. James F. Short Jr. and F. Ivan Nye, "Extent of Unrecorded Juvenile Delinquency: Tentative Conclusions," *Journal of Criminal Law, Criminology and Police Science* 49 (November–December 1958), pp. 296–302.

37. Short and Nye, "Reported Behavior as a Criterion of Deviant Behavior," pp. 207–213.

38. David H. Huizinga and Delbert S. Elliott, "Juvenile Offenders: Prevalence, Offender Incidence, and Arrest Rates by Race," *Crime and Delinquency* 33 (April 1987), pp. 208, 210.

39. Franklyn W. Dunford and Delbert S. Elliott, "Identifying Career Offenders Using Self-Reported Data," *Journal of Research in Crime and Delinquency* 21 (February 1984), pp. 57–82.

40. Ibid.

41. David H. Huizinga, Rolf Loeber, and Terence P. Thornberry, *Urban Delinquency and Substance Abuse: Initial Findings* (Washington, D.C.: U.S. Department of Justice, Office of Juvenile Justice and Delinquency Prevention, 1994).

42. Cited in *Guide for Implementing the Comprehensive Strategy for Serious, Violent, and Chronic Juvenile Offenders* (Washington, D.C.: Office of Juvenile Justice and Delinquency Prevention, 1995), p. 3.

43. Jerald G. Bachman and Patrick M. O'Malley, *A Continuing Study of American Youth (12th-Grade Survey, 1996)* (Ann Arbor, Mich.: Institute for Social Research, 1998).

44. Centers for Disease Control and Prevention, *Youth Risk Behavior Surveillance—United States* (Washington, D.C.: Centers for Disease Control and Prevention, 2004), Table 11.2.

45. Shannon M. Catalano, *Criminal Victimization, 2005* (Washington, D.C.: Bureau of Justice Statistics, 2006).

46. See Summary Page of National Crime Victimization Survey, 2005.

47. Catalano, *Criminal Victimization, 2005.*

48. Ibid.

49. Ibid.

50. Ibid.

51. Ibid.

52. FBI, *Crime in the United States 2005.*

53. Snyder, "Juvenile Arrests 1999."

54. Peter E. Tracy, Marvin E. Wolfgang, and Robert M. Figlio, *Delinquency in Two Birth Cohorts: Executive Summary* (Washington, D.C.: U.S. Department of Justice, 1985).

55. Meda Chesney-Lind and Randall G. Shelden, *Girls, Delinquency, and Juvenile Justice,* 3rd ed. (Belmont, Calif.: Wadsworth/Thompson, 2004), p. 24.

56. For a review of these studies, see Chesney-Lind and Shelden, *Girls,* pp. 19–23.

57. David C. Rowe, Alexander T. Vazsonyi, and Daniel J. Flannery, "Sex Differences in Crime: Do Means and Within-Sex Variation Have Similar Causes," *Journal of Research in Crime and Delinquency* 32 (February 1995), pp. 84–100.

58. Chesney-Lind and Shelden, *Girls,* p. 24.

59. Meda Chesney-Lind and Lisa Pasko, *The Female Offender: Girls, Women, and Crime* (Thousand Oaks, Calif.: Sage Publications, 2004), p. 4.

60. Cited in Chesney-Lind and Shelden, *Girls,* p. 145.

61. David P. Farrington, Rolf Loeber, Magda Stouthamer-Loeber, Welmoet B. Van Kammen, and Laura Schmidt, "Self-Reported Delinquency and a Combined Delinquency Seriousness Scale Based on Boys, Mothers, and Teachers: Concurrent and Predict Validity for African Americans and Caucasians," *Criminology* 34 (November 1996), p. 495.

62. William J. Chambliss and Richard H. Nagasawa, "On the Validity of Official Statistics: A Comparative Study of White, Black and Japanese High-School Boys," *Journal of Research in Crime and Delinquency* (January 1969), pp. 71–77.

63. Leroy C. Gould, "Who Defines Delinquency: A Comparison of Self-Reported and Officially Reported Indices of Delinquency for Three Racial Groups," *Social Problems* (Winter 1969), pp. 325–336.

64. Travis Hirschi, *Causes of Delinquency* (Berkeley: University of California Press, 1969), Table 14.

65. Huizinga and Elliott, "Juvenile Offenders," p. 215.

66. Ibid., p. 219.

67. Jay R. Williams and Martin Gold, "From Delinquent Behavior to Official Delinquency," *Social Problems* 20 (1972); and Martin Gold and David J. Reimer, "Changing Patterns of Delinquent Behavior among Americans 13 through 16 Years Old: 1967–1972," *Crime and Delinquency Literature* 7 (1975), pp. 483–517.

68. Suzanne S. Ageton and Delbert S. Elliott, *The Incidence of Delinquent Behavior in a National Probability Sample of Adolescents* (Boulder, Colo.: Behavioral Research Institute, 1978).

69. Michael J. Hindelang et al., *Measuring Delinquency.*

70. Gary Jensen and Raymond Eve, "Sex Differences in Delinquency," *Criminology* 13 (1976), pp. 427–448.

71. Steven A. Cernkovich and Peggy Giordano, "A Comparative Analysis of Male and Female Delinquency," *Sociological Quarterly* 20 (1979), pp. 131–145.

72. Thomas L. McNulty and Paul E. Bellair, "Explaining Racial and Ethnic Differences in Serious Adolescent Violent Behavior," *Criminology* 41 (August 2003), pp. 709–746.

73. Joanne M. Kaufman, "Explaining the Race/Ethnicity-Violence Relationship: Neighborhood Context and Psychological Processes," *Justice Quarterly* 22 (June 2005), p. 247.

74. Chesney-Lind and Shelden, *Girls,* pp. 24–25.

75. F. I. Nye, *Family Relationships and Delinquent Behavior* (New York: John Wiley and Sons, 1958); Short and Nye, "Extent of Unrecorded Juvenile Delinquency," pp. 296–302; Robert A. Dentler and Lawrence J. Monroe, "Social Correlates of Early Adolescent Theft," *American Sociological Review* 26 (October 1961), pp. 733–743; Ronald L. Akers, "Socio-Economic Status and Delinquent Behavior: A Retest," *Journal of Research in Crime and Delinquency* (January 1964), pp. 38–46; W. L. Slocum and C. L. Stone, "Family Culture Patterns and Delinquent-Type Behavior," *Journal of Marriage and Family Living* 25 (1963), pp. 202–208; LaMar T. Empey and Maynard L. Erickson, "Hidden Delinquency and Social Status," *Social Forces* 44 (June 1966), pp. 546–554; Travis Hirschi, *Causes of Delinquency;* Williams and Gold, "From Delinquent Behavior to Official Delinquency"; D. H. Kelly and W. T. Pink, "School Commitment, Youth Rebellion, and Delinquency," *Criminology* 10 (1973), pp. 473–485.

76. Williams and Gold, "From Delinquent Behavior to Official Delinquency," p. 217.

77. Hirschi, *Causes of Delinquency,* p. 75.

78. Richard E. Johnson, "Social Class and Delinquent Behavior: A New Test," *Criminology* 18 (May 1980), p. 91.

79. Charles Tittle, Wayne Villemez, and Douglas Smith, "The Myth of Social Class and Criminality: An Empirical Assessment of the Empirical Evidence," *American Sociological Review* 43 (1978), pp. 643–656.

80. Ageton and Elliott, *The Incidence of Delinquent Behavior.*

81. Elliott and Huizinga, "Social Class and Delinquent Behavior in a National Youth Panel," *Criminology* 21 (May 1983), pp. 149–177. For a discussion about whether different definitions of class are likely to produce different results on social class and delinquency, see Margaret Farnworth, Terence P. Thornberry, Alan J. Lizotte, and Marvin D. Krohn, "Social Background and the Early Onset of Delinquency: Exploring the Utility of Various Indicators of Social Class Background" (Albany, N. Y.: Rochester Youth Development Study, June 1990).

82. Margaret Farnworth, Terence P. Thornberry, Marvin D. Krohn, and Alan J. Lizotte, "Measurement in the Study of Class and Delinquency: Integrating Theory and Research," *Journal of Research in Crime and Delinquency* 31 (1994), p. 32.

83. Ibid.

84. Bradley R. Entner Wright, Avshalom Caspi, Terrie Moffitt, Richard A. Miech, and Phil A. Silva, "Reconsidering the Relationship between SES and Delinquency: Causation but Not Correlation," *Criminology* 37 (February 1999), pp. 175, 190.

85. Lila Kazemian and David P. Farrington, "Comparing the Validity of Prospective, Retrospective, and Official Onset for Different Offending Categories," *Journal of Quantitative Criminology* 21 (June 2005), p. 128.

86. Marvin E. Wolfgang, Terence P. Thornberry, and Robert M. Figlio, *From Boy to Man, from Delinquency to Crime* (Chicago: University of Chicago Press, 1987), pp. 37, 39.

87. Patrick H. Tolan, "Age of Onset and Delinquency Patterns, Legal Status, and Chronicity of Offending." Paper presented at the Annual Meeting of the American Society of Criminology, Montreal, Canada (November 1987), p. 44.

88. Alfred Blumstein, David P. Farrington, and Soumyo Moitra, "Delinquency Careers, Innocents, Desisters, and Persisters," in *Crime and Justice: An Annual Review* 6, edited by Michael Tonry and Norval Morris (Chicago: University of Chicago Press, 1985).

89. David P. Farrington, "Offending from 10 to 25 Years of Age," in *Prospective Studies of Crime and Delinquency,* edited by K. T. Van Dusen and S. A. Mednick (Boston: Kluwer-Nijhoff, 1983).

90. Ronald L. Simons, Chyi-In Wu, Rand D. Conger, and Frederick O. Lorenz, "Two Routes to Delinquency: Differences between Early and Late Starters in the Impact of Parenting and Deviant Peers," *Criminology* 32 (1994), p. 247.

91. Cited in Barry Krisberg, *Guide for Implementing the Comprehensive Strategy for Serious, Violent, and Chronic Juvenile Offenders* (Washington, D.C.: Office of Juvenile Justice and Delinquency Prevention, 1995), pp. 3–4.

92. Ibid., p. 4. For a comparison of prospective self-report, retrospective self-report, and official records in terms of onset of minor and serious forms of delinquency, see Kazemian and Farrington, "Comparing the Validity of Prospective, Retrospective, and Official Onset for Different Offending Categories," pp. 127–147.

93. R. Loeber, D. P. Farrington, and D. Petechuk, *Child Delinquency: Early Intervention and Prevention,* Child Development Bulletin Series (Washington, D.C.: Office of Juvenile Justice and Delinquency Prevention, 2003).

94. T. Moffitt, A. Caspi, M. Rutter, and P. A. Silva, *Sex Differences in Antisocial Behavior.* (Cambridge, England: Cambridge University Press, 2001), p. 83.

95. Williams and Gold, "From Delinquent Behavior to Official Delinquency," p. 215.

96. Ageton and Elliott, *The Incidence of Delinquent Behavior in a National Probability Sample of Adolescents.*

97. Elliott and Huizinga, "Social Class and Delinquent Behavior in a National Youth Panel," pp. 149–177.

98. Marvin E. Wolfgang, Robert M. Figlio, and Thorsten Sellin, *Delinquency in a Birth Cohort* (Chicago: University of Chicago Press, 1972).

99. Wolfgang et al., *From Boy to Man,* p. 41.

100. Pamela Tontodonato, "Explaining Rate Changes in Delinquent Arrest Transitions Using Event History Analysis," *Criminology* 26 (1988), p. 454.

101. Lyle W. Shannon, *Assessing the Relationships of Adult Criminal Careers to Juvenile Careers: A Summary* (Washington, D.C.: U.S. Government Printing Office, 1982), p. v.

102. Cited in Farrington, "Age and Crime," p. 224.

103. Rolf Loeber, Magda Stouthamer-Loeber, Welmoet Van Kammen, and David P. Farrington, "Initiation, Escalation and Desistance in Juvenile Offending and Their Correlates," *Journal of Criminal Law and Criminology* 82 (1991), p. 37.

104. Rolf Loeber, Phen Wung, Kate Keenan, Bruce Giroux, Magda Stouthamer-Loeber, and Welmoet B. Van Kammen, "Developmental Pathways in Disruptive Child Behavior," *Development and Psychopathology* 5 (Winter–Spring, 1993), pp. 103–133.

105. See Barbara Tatem Kelley, Rolf Loeber, Kate Keenan, and Mary DeLamatre, *Developmental Pathways in Boys' Disruptive and Delinquent Behavior* (Washington, D.C.: Office of Juvenile Justice and Delinquency Prevention, 1997).

106. T. E. Moffitt, "Adolescent-Limited and Life-Course Persistent Antisocial Behavior: A Developmental Taxonomy," *Psychological Review* 100 (1993), pp. 674–701. For one of the studies that is highly supportive of Moffitt's taxonomy of offending behavior, see Paul Mazerolle, Robert Brame, Ray Paternoster, Alex Piquero, and Charles Dean, "Onset Age, Persistence, and Offending Versatility: Comparisons across Gender," *Criminology* 38 (November 2000), pp. 1143–1172.

107. Barbara Maughan, Andrew Pickles, Richard Rowe, E. Jane Costello, and Adrian Angold, "Developmental Trajectories of Aggressive and Nonaggressive Conduct Problems," *Journal of Quantitative Criminology* 16 (2000), p. 199.

108. Todd I. Herrenkohl, Bu Huang, Rick Kosterman, J. David Hawkins, Richard F. Catalano, and Brian H. Smith, "A Comparison of Social Development Processes Leading to Violent Behavior in Late Adolescence for Childhood Initiators and Adolescent Initiators of Violence," *Journal of Research in Crime and Delinquency* 38 (February 2001), p. 45.

109. David P. Farrington, Howard N. Snyder, and Terrence A. Finnegan, "Specialization in Juvenile Court Careers," *Criminology* 26 (August 1988), p. 461.

110. Ibid.

111. Wolfgang et al., *Delinquency in a Birth Cohort*.

112. Hamparian et al., *The Young Criminal Years of the Violent Few*.

113. Susan K. Datesman and Michael Aickin, "Offense Specialization and Escalation among Status Offenders," *Journal of Criminal Law and Criminology* 75 (1984), pp. 1260–1273.

114. Mazerolle et al., "Onset, Age, Persistence, and Offending Versatility," pp. 1143–1172.

115. Glenn Deanne, David P. Armstrong, and Richard B. Felson, "An Examination of Offense Specialization Using Marginal Logit Models," *Criminology* 43 (November 2005), pp. 955–988.

116. Peter Greenwood, "Differences in Criminal Behavior and Court Responses among Juvenile and Young Adult Defendants," in *Crime and Justice: An Annual Review,* edited by Michael Tonry and Norval Morris (Chicago: University of Chicago Press, 1986), p. 153.

117. For an investigation of gang involvement in crack cocaine sales, see Malcolm W. Klein, Cheryl L. Maxson, and Lea C. Cunningham, " 'Crack,' Street Gangs, and Violence," *Criminology* 29 (1991), pp. 623–650.

118. Information derived from interviews and interactions with these youths in 1990–1991.

119. Eric Lotke, "Hobbling a Generation: Young African American Men in Washington, D.C.'s Criminal Justice System—Five Years Later," *Crime and Delinquency* 44 (1998), p. 355.

120. Blumstein, Farrington, and Moitra, "Delinquency Careers: Innocents, Amateurs, and Persisters."

121. David P. Farrington and J. David Hawkins, "Predicting Participation, Early Onset and Later Persistence in Officially Recorded Offending," *Criminal Behaviour and Mental Health* 1 (1991), p. 1.

122. Kimberly L. Kempf, "Crime Severity and Criminal Career Progression," *Journal of Criminal Law and Criminology* (1988), p. 537.

123. Peter Greenwood, *Selective Incapacitation* (Santa Monica, Calif.: Rand, 1982); Tracy, Wolfgang, and Figlio, *Delinquency in Two Birth Cohorts;* and Blumstein, Farrington, and Moitra, "Delinquent Careers."

124. Greenwood, *Selective Incapacitation.*

125. See Scott H. Decker and Barbara Salert, "Predicting the Career Criminal: An Empirical Test of the Greenwood Scale," *Journal of Criminal Law and Criminology* 77 (1986), p. 219.

126. Lila Kazemian and David P. Farrington, "Exploring Residual Career Length and Residual Number of Offenses for Two Generations of Repeat Offenders," *Journal of Research in Crime and Delinquency* 47 (February 2006), pp. 89–113.

127. David P. Farrington, "Developmental and Life-Course Criminology: Key Theoretical and Empirical Issues: The 2002 Sutherland Award Address," *Criminology* 41 (February 2003), pp. 221–222.

128. David Huizinga, Anne Wylie Weiher, Rachele Espiritu, and Finn Esbensen, "Delinquency and Crime: Some Highlights from the Denver Youth Survey," in *Taking Stock of Delinquency: An Overview of Findings from Contemporary Longitudinal Studies,* edited by Terence P. Thornberry and Marvin D. Krohn (New York: Kluwer/Plenum, 2003); Rolf Loeber, David P. Farrington, Magda Stouthamer-Loeber, Terrie E. Moffitt, Avshalom Caspi, Helene Raskin White, Evelyn H. Wei, and Jennifer M. Beyers, "The Development of Male Offending: Key Findings from Fourteen Years of the Pittsburgh Youth Studies," in *Taking Stock of Delinquency,* edited by Thornberry and Krohn; and Terence P. Thornberry, Alan J. Lizotte, Marvin D. Krohn, Carolyn A. Smith, and Pamela K. Porter, "Causes and Consequences of Delinquency: Findings from the Rochester Youth Development Study," in *Taking Stock of Delinquency,* edited by Thornberry and Krohn.

129. Terrie E. Moffitt, Avshalom Caspi, Michael Rutter, and Phil A. Silva, *Sex Differences in Antisocial Behavior: Conduct Disorder, Delinquency, and Violence in the Dunedin Longitudinal Study* (Cambridge, England: Cambridge University Press, 2001).

130. J. David Hawkins, Brian H. Smith, Karl G. Hill, Rick Kosterman, Richard F. Catalano, and Robert D. Abbott, "Understanding and Preventing Crime and Violence: Findings from the Seattle Social Development Project," in

Taking Stock of Delinquency, edited by Thornberry and Krohn.

131. Richard E. Tremblay, Frank Vitaro, Daniel Nagin, Linda Pagani, and Jean R. Seguin, "The Montreal Longitudinal and Experimental Study: Rediscovering the Power of Description," in *Taking Stock of Delinquency,* edited by Thornberry and Krohn.

132. Robert J. Sampson and John H. Laub, *Crime in the Making: Pathways and Turning Points through Life* (Cambridge, Mass.: Harvard University Press, 1993); and John H. Laub and Robert J. Sampson, *Shared Beginnings, Divergent Lives: Delinquent Boys to Age 70* (Cambridge, Mass.: Harvard University Press, 2003).

133. Wolfgang et al., *From Boy to Man,* p. 20.

134. Ibid., p. 21.

135. Hamparian et al., *The Young Criminal Years of the Violent Few,* pp. 3, 12.

136. Katherine S. Ratcliff and Lee N. Robins, "Risk Factors in the Continuation of Childhood Antisocial Behaviors into Adulthood," *International Journal of Mental Health* 7 (1979), pp. 96–116.

137. Michael Gottfredson and Travis Hirschi, *A General Theory of Crime* (Palo Alto, Calif.: Stanford University Press, 1990), p. 107.

138. James Q. Wilson and Richard Herrnstein, *Crime and Human Nature* (New York: Simon and Schuster, 1985), p. 209.

139. Daniel S. Nagin and Raymond Paternoster, "On the Relationship of Past to Future Participation in Delinquency," *Criminology* 29 (May 1991), p. 165.

140. Ibid., p. 163.

141. Ibid., p. 163.

142. Ibid., p. 163.

143. Sampson and Laub, *Crime in the Making,* p. 7. For further support of life-course theory, see Ronald L. Simons, Christine Johnson, Rand D. Conger, and Glen Elder Jr., "A Test of Latent Trait versus Life-Course Perspectives on the Stability of Adolescent Antisocial Behavior," *Criminology* 36 (May 1998), pp. 217–243.

144. John H. Laub and Robert J. Sampson, "Turning Points in the Life Course: Why Change Matters to the Study of Crime," *Criminology* 31 (August 1993), pp. 301–320.

145. Ibid., p. 309.

146. Ibid., p. 310.

147. James S. Coleman, "Social Capital in the Creation of Human Capital," *American Journal of Sociology* 94 (1988), p. 98.

148. Raymond Paternoster, Robert Brame, and David P. Farrington, "On the Relationship between Adolecsent and Adult Conviction Frequencies," *Journal of Quantitative Criminology* 17 (2001), pp. 201, 222.

149. Farrington, "Age and Crime," pp. 221–222. This chapter's section on desistance and crime is adapted in part from Robert J. Sampson and John H. Laub, "Understanding Desistance from Crime," in *Crime and Justice* 28, edited by Michael Tonry (Chicago: University of Chicago Press, 2001).

150. Sheldon Glueck and Eleanor Glueck, *Juvenile Delinquents Grown Up* (New York: Commonwealth Fund, 1940), p. 89.

151. Wilson and Herrnstein, *Crime and Human Nature,* pp. 126–147.

152. Edward Mulvey and John LaRosa, "Delinquency Cessation and Adolescent Development: Preliminary Data," *American Journal of Orthopsychiatry* 56 (1986), pp. 212–214.

153. Shadd Maruna, *Making Good: How Ex-Convicts Reform and Rebuild Their Lives* (Washington, D.C.: American Psychological Association, 2001), pp. 86–88.

154. Peggy C. Giordano, Stephen A. Cernkovich, and Jennifer L. Rudolph, "Gender, Crime, and Desistance: Toward a Theory of Cognitive Transformation," *American Journal of Sociology* 107 (January 2002), p. 1055.

155. W. R. Gove, "The Effect of Age and Gender on Deviant Behavior: A Biopsychosocial Perspective," In *Gender and the Life Course,* edited by A. S. Rossi (New York: Aldine, 1985).

156. Terrie E. Moffitt, "Natural History of Delinquency," in *Cross-National Longitudinal Research on Human Development and Criminal Behavior,* edited by G. M. Weitekamp and B. J. Kerner (Netherlands: Dordrecht, 1994), p. 45.

157. See D. B. Cornish and R. V. Clark, *The Reasoning Criminal: Rational Choice Perspectives on Offending* (New York: Springer Verlag, 1986).

158. Barry Glassner, Margret Ksander, and Bruce Berg, "A Note on the Deterrent Effect of Juvenile vs. Adult Jurisdiction," *Social Problems* 31 (December 1983), p. 221.

159. Farrington, "Age and Crime," p. 224.

160. Ronald L. Akers, *Social Learning and Social Structure: A General Theory of Crime and Deviance* (Boston: Northeastern University Press, 1998).

161. Mark Warr, "Age, Peers, and Delinquency," *Criminology* 31 (1993), pp. 17–40.

162. Mark Warr, "Life Course Transitions and Desistance from Crime," *Criminology* 36 (1998), pp. 183–216.

163. Sampson and Laub, *Crime in the Making.*

164. Summary of *Shared Beginnings, Divergent Lives* found in Sampson and Laub,"A General Age-Graded Theory of Crime: Lessons Learned and the Future of Life-Course Criminology," in *Advances in Criminological Theory: Testing Integrated Developmental/Life Course Theories of Offending 13,* edited by David Farrington (New Brunswick, N.J.: Transaction, 2004), p. 10.

165. This interview took place in August 2004.

166. Ibid., p. 11. For another study that found incarceration to be negatively associated with marriage and employment, see Beth M. Huebner, "The Effect of Incarceration on Marriage and Work Over the Life Course," *Justice Quarterly* 22 (September 2005), pp. 281–303.

167. Ibid., p. 11.

168. John H. Laub, "Edwin H. Sutherland and the Michael-Adler Report: Searching for the Soul of Criminology Seventy Years Later," *Criminology* 44 (May 2006), p. 241.

part TWO

The Causes of Delinquency

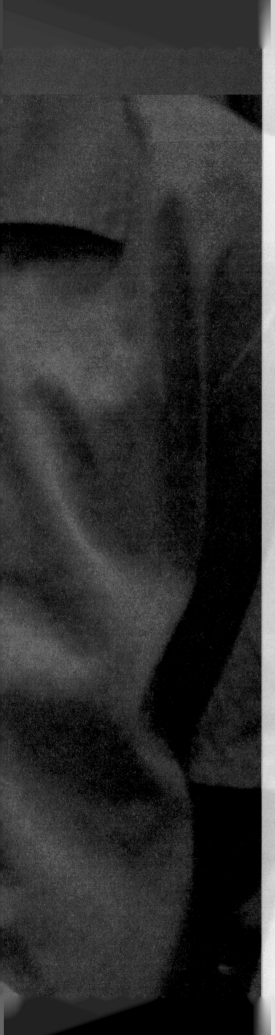

The four chapters in this section raise important questions about why some young people commit delinquent acts but others don't. Chapter 3 discusses explanations for delinquency that focus on causes at the individual level, including personal decision making involving rational choices made at the individual level. The chapter also examines the claims made by some that delinquents are propelled into illegal behavior by biological features or psychological drives, or by other personal traits. Within the context of these claims we will also examine the psychological development of adolescents, and look at how that development impacts the choices and decisions that they make.

In Chapters 4 and 5, we turn our attention to sociological explanations for delinquency. Sociological explanations fault individual-level perspectives for failing to account for the underlying social and cultural conditions that give rise to delinquency. Social structural approaches, discussed in Chapter 4, claim that forces such as social disorganization, cultural deviance, strain, and status frustration are so powerful that they induce young people—especially those from the lower classes—to become involved in delinquency. Social process approaches, discussed in Chapter 5, detail the influence that the social environment exerts over delinquent acts. In that chapter, differential association, drift theory, and social control theory provide theoretical mechanisms for the translation of environmental factors into individual motivation.

Chapter 6, Social Interactionist Theories of Delinquency, looks at the role that social groups, economic organizations, and social institutions have in producing delinquent behavior. The three major social interactionist perspectives discussed in that chapter are labeling theory, symbolic interactionist theory, and conflict theory. As we will learn, social interaction occurs within individualized contexts that can vary widely, but that usually involve the family, the school, peers and other groups, and official actors in the justice system and in the government.

3

Individual
Causes of Delinquency

> " America's best hope for reducing crime is to reduce juvenile delinquency and youth crime. "
>
> —President's Commission on Law Enforcement and Administration of Justice, 1967

CHAPTER Objectives

AFTER READING THIS CHAPTER, YOU SHOULD BE ABLE TO ANSWER THE FOLLOWING QUESTIONS:

- What role does free will have in the classical school's understanding of criminal or delinquent behavior?

- What are the main forms of positivism? How does each form explain delinquent behavior?

- How does rational choice theory differ from positivism?

- What type of delinquencies are more likely to be brought about by biological factors?

- Which type of delinquents are more likely to be held responsible for their actions?

When a Trenton, New Jersey, newborn was found crying at the bottom of an air shaft in September, 2005, the baby's teenage mother was charged with trying to kill the child.

But after the decomposing body of a second infant was found in the same place, authorities began unraveling a gruesome story: The teenager soon told them that her own father had fathered both babies.

The mother, a high school junior, was accused by police officers of throwing her newborn son into the air shaft from the third-story window of her apartment. The boy survived, landing on a trash pile at the bottom of the shaft, and residents called police after hearing his cries.

That's when investigators made an even more gruesome discovery: the remains of an infant girl believed to have died more than a year earlier. Hudson County prosecutor Gaetano T. Gregory, said investigators would have to wait for DNA test results before determining the baby's paternity, but he said they believe the girl's account.

The young mother was charged with attempted murder and aggravated assault. Homicide charges were added a day later. The names of the girl and her father were withheld because the girl is considered the victim of a sex crime.

Prosecutors said the girl, who was undergoing a psychiatric evaluation, would be tried in juvenile court on the murder charge because she was not 18 when the death took place.

The father was charged with aggravated sexual assault, endangering the welfare of a child and child abuse. If convicted, he could face 10 to 20 years in prison.

Adapted from "Two Infants Found in Trash, and a Darker Tale Unfolds," *New York Times*, September 17, 2005. Reprinted with permission from the Associated Press.

In this chapter we will seek to explain the kind of behavior described by this opening story. Why did this young mother try to kill her children? Individual perspectives on juvenile delinquency, which form the bulk of this chapter, would explain her behavior in several different ways.

One answer might be that her behavior was rational. As we shall see, some authors suggest that much delinquency is caused not by factors beyond the offender's control, but by "the conscious thought processes that give purpose to and justify conduct, and the underlying cognitive mechanisms by which information about the world is selected, attended to, and processed."[1]

A second answer might be that she could not help herself. Caught up in an abusive relationship with her father, she may have been strongly influenced by psychological factors or inherent biological traits that led her to murder. This kind of deterministic view—that delinquents cannot stop themselves from committing socially unacceptable behavior because of some inborn overpowering influences—builds on a perspective known as **positivism**, a major theoretical position in criminology.

A third explanation discussed in this chapter highlights the significance of developmental theories. A developmental approach might suggest that the young mother did not have the opportunity to learn how to avoid abuse nor how to act legally and morally. She may have felt that taking care of her children was an impossibility in her situation. In the midst of constant sexual abuse, the effects of her

positivism
The view that, just as laws operate in the medical, biological, and physical sciences, laws govern human behavior, and that these laws can be understood and used.

life circumstances and her lack of moral development placed her on a trajectory with tragic consequences.

The Classical School and Delinquency

The association between criminal behavior and the rationality of crime has roots in the eighteenth-century classical school of criminology. This school's founders were Charles de Secondat, Baron de Montesquieu; Cesare Bonesana, Marquis of Beccaria; and Jeremy Bentham. These thinkers viewed humans as rational creatures who are willing to surrender enough liberty to the state so that society can establish rules and sanctions for the preservation of the social order.[2]

- *Montesquieu:* The debate on the classical school was begun by its advocate, the French aristocrat Montesquieu, who was primarily concerned with government's proper role in the punishment of criminals. In his 1747 book, *On the Spirit of the Laws,* he argued that "the severity of punishment is fitter for despotic governments whose principle is terror, than for a monarchy or a republic whose strength is honor and virtue. In moderate governments the love of one's country, shame and the fear of blame, are restraining motives, capable of preventing a great multitude of crimes."[3] Montesquieu added that under a moderate and lenient government, "the greatest punishment of a bad action is conviction. The civil laws have therefore a softer way of correcting, and do not require so much force and severity."[4] His book was a literary success; twenty-two editions were published in less than two years. But many readers of this time, used to the ghastly punishments inflicted in England and France, considered Montesquieu's ideas of moderation of punishment nothing less than sedition.

> " The association between criminal behavior and the rationality of crime has roots in the eighteenth-century classical school of criminology. "

- *Beccaria:* In 1764, Cesare Bonesana, Marquis of Beccaria, an Italian who was then only twenty-six years old and just out of law school, published a slim volume entitled *On Crime and Punishments.* This essay, which appeared anonymously because Beccaria feared reprisals if its authorship were known, was read avidly and translated into all the languages of Europe.[5] Beccaria based the legitimacy of criminal sanctions on the **social contract.** The authority for making laws rested with the legislator, who should have only one view in sight: "the greatest happiness of the greatest number." Beccaria saw punishment as a necessary evil and suggested that "it should be public, immediate, and necessary; the least possible in the case given; proportioned to the crime; and determined by the laws."[6] He then defined the purpose and consequences of punishment as being "to deter persons from the commission of crime and not to provide social revenge. Not severity, but certainty and swiftness in punishment best secure this result."[7]

> **social contract**
> An unstated or explicit agreement between a people and their government as to the rights and obligations of each.

- *Jeremy Bentham:* In 1780, the Englishman Jeremy Bentham published *An Introduction to the Principles of Morals and Legislation,* which further developed the philosophy of the classical school. Believing that a rational person would do what was necessary to achieve the most pleasure and the least pain, Bentham contended that punishment would deter criminal behavior, provided it was made appropriate to the crime. He stated that punishment has four objectives: (1) to prevent all offenses if possible; (2) to persuade a person who has decided to offend to commit a less rather than a more serious offense; (3) "to dispose [a person who has resolved on a particular offense] to do no more mischief than is necessary to his purpose"; and (4) to prevent crime at as cheap a cost to society as possible.[8]

The following are the basic theoretical constructs of the classical school of criminology:

High school students in Mission Viejo, California, fill out applications at a community college recruiting fair. Rational choice approaches to explaining delinquency claim that juvenile offenders are active, rational decision makers who respond to the incentives and deterrents they encounter. ■ **What implications might rational choice theory have for delinquency prevention and control?**

■ Human beings were looked on as rational creatures who, being free to choose their actions, could be held responsible for their behavior. This doctrine of **free will** was substituted for the widely accepted concept of theological determinism, which saw humans as predestined to certain actions.

■ Punishment was justified because of its practical usefulness, or utility. No longer was punishment acceptable for purposes of vengeful retaliation or as expiation on the basis of superstitious theories of guilt and repayment. According to **utilitarianism** the aim of punishment was the protection of society, and the dominant theme was deterrence.

■ The classical school saw the human being as a creature governed by a **felicific calculus**—an orientation toward obtaining a favorable balance of pleasure and pain.

■ There should be a rational scale of punishment that would be painful enough to deter the criminal from further offenses and to prevent others from following his or her example of crime.

■ Sanctions should be proclaimed in advance of their use; these sanctions should be proportionate to the offense and should outweigh the rewards of crime.

■ Equal justice should be offered to everyone.

■ Individuals should be judged by the law solely for their acts, not for their beliefs.

According to the principles of the classical school, then, juveniles who commit serious crimes or continue to break the law are presumed to deserve punishment rather than treatment, because they possess free will and know what they are doing. Proponents of the classical school view delinquencies as purposeful activity resulting from rational decisions in which offenders weigh the pros and cons and perform the acts that promise the greatest potential gains.[9] For an examination of the complexity of determining when delinquent behavior is rational, see Social World of the Delinquent 3.1.

free will

The ability to make rational choices among possible actions and to select one over the others.

utilitarianism

A doctrine that holds that the useful is the good, and that the aim of social or political action should be the greatest good for the greatest number.

felicific calculus

A method for determining the sum total of pleasure and pain produced by an act. Also the assumption that human beings strive to obtain a favorable balance of pleasure and pain.

The Rationality of Crime

In the 1970s and 1980s, workers in a variety of academic disciplines, including the sociology of deviance, criminology, economics, and cognitive psychology, began to view crime as the outcome of rational choices and decisions.[10] The ecological tradition in criminology and the economic theory of markets, especially, have applied the notion of rational choice to crime.

Ecological researchers have inferred from the distribution of particular crimes that offenders make rational choices. For example, findings from several studies have revealed that homes on the borderline of affluent districts are at most risk of burglary. Paul J. Brantingham and Patricia L. Brantingham suggested that burglars preying on such districts select the nearest of the suitable targets because escape is easier and they prefer to operate where they feel least conspicuous.[11]

Economic analysis of criminal behavior argues that criminals, like noncriminals, are active, rational decision makers who respond to incentives and deterrents. In economic models of criminal decision making, crime is assumed to involve rational calculation and is viewed essentially as an economic transaction or a question of occupational choice.[12] Ernest van den Haag, who is acknowledged as one of the leading spokespersons for this position, puts it this way:

The Sad World of Billy

John Conrad tells the sad story of Billy, one of the many stories of juveniles whose lives ended early:

A seventeen-year-old whom I shall call Billy was one of a fairly large family of Appalachian antecedents living on the margins of the economy. His parents had been more often on welfare than not. Poor managers, they had been unable to provide their children with more than subsistence. Love and harmony were rarely manifest in a home chiefly remarkable for violence. Billy recalled having been beaten with electric cords, straps, belts, sticks, broom handles, and boards from early childhood. This type of discipline went on until one day, when he was fourteen, his mother came at him in a fury, armed with a plank with which she was going to beat him. He knocked her out. From that time on he was mostly on his own.

School had been an arena of defeat. He had great difficulty in reading and was eventually found to be dyslexic—neurologically impaired so that letters did not arrive in his brain in intelligible order for words to be made out of them. He learned to think of himself as a dummy, the word that other kids applied to him. School records noted that by the time he was nine, he had taken to sniffing glue, which certainly did not improve his nervous system. When he was fourteen, he dropped out, perhaps because of his unrelieved scholastic failures, perhaps because of his assault on his mother.

He took to hanging around, sometimes in the company of an uncle fourteen years older who introduced him to homosexual practices. It was not long before he was earning $20 a trick as a prostitute. A large portion of his earnings was spent on various uppers and downers and marijuana. He does not seem to have used "heavy stuff."

One of his customers was the old man who was to become a victim on the Fourth of July weekend last summer. Billy and his uncle spent the holiday at the old man's apartment. They drank heavily and smoked pot. As they became more and more drunk, conviviality turned into acrimony. They ran out of beer, and the old man told Billy to go out and get some more, calling him a dummy and a punk as he issued the order. The police account [relates] that, in a rage, Billy attacked him with his fists, knocked him flat, and then stomped him until the old man succumbed. The pathologist's report showed that the alcoholic content of [the old man's] blood was so high that death would have been imminent anyway.

Billy stood condemned of the most serious of crimes, the murder of another human being. His background and personal situation inspired no confidence at all in his ability to change. To argue that he was not dangerous was to dismiss the horrible affair on the Fourth of July, a record of violent family relations, and a life without adult control for the previous three years.

The public defender was concerned whether Billy, a slight youngster with chestnut blond hair, could survive in prison. He had scored well above average on an IQ test but spoke haltingly and seemed painfully childish. He intended, if he got out of his trouble, to go to Florida and find work as a deep-sea fisherman. His dreams of a fisherman's life were never realized. The juvenile court decided to transfer Billy over for trial in the adult court. Three weeks later, Billy hanged himself with a sheet in his cell.

■ **Why do you believe Billy committed the crime he did? When did he start to go wrong? If your mother had attacked you with a large board when you were adolescent, what would you have done? How rational was the murder he committed?**

Source: John P. Conrad, "The Hoodlum in the Helpless Society," unpublished paper.

If you or I committed a crime, we might be irrational, because we stand a great deal to lose and relatively little to gain. But most of the people who commit crime have very little to lose and a lot to gain. They know that the chances of being punished are very small, so crime for them is perfectly rational.

. . . Currently crime pays. Crime pays for adults. It pays even more for juveniles. Juveniles will take things seriously only when crime stops paying. Hard-core juvenile offenders know that the chances of being punished are very small, so crime for them is perfectly rational. We must make crime irrational. It is not the criminal who is irrational; it is society. . . .

My position is based more on incentives and disincentives than on the rationality of behavior. Whether a person is a juvenile or an adult, I think you can have disincentives for certain types of behavior and incentives for other types of behavior. Obviously, the purpose of the criminal law is to give disincentives strong enough to discourage criminal and delinquent behavior.[13]

Rational Choice Theory

Rational choice theory, borrowed primarily from the utility model in economics, is one of the hottest topics today in criminology, sociology, political science, and law.[14] Rational choice theory in its pure form can be seen, at least in part, as an extension of the deterrence doctrine found in the classical school, which includes incentives as well as disincentives and focuses on individuals' rational calculations of payoffs and costs before delinquent and criminal acts are committed.[15]

Philip J. Cook, using a market perspective, has developed what he calls **criminal opportunity theory.** He claims that "criminals tend to be somewhat selective in choosing a crime target and are most attracted to targets that appear to offer a high payoff with little effort or risk of legal consequence."[16] He sees the interaction between potential offenders (who respond to the net payoff of crime) and potential victims (who take actions to modify the payoff of crime) as akin to the interaction between buyers and sellers in a marketplace. Thus, criminal opportunity theory emphasizes individual choice guided by the perceived costs and benefits of criminal activity.[17]

Lawrence E. Cohen and Marcus Felson, guided by ecological concepts and the presumed rationality of offenders, developed a **routine activities approach** for analyzing crime rate trends and cycles. This approach links the dramatic increase in crime rates since 1960 to changes in the routine activity structure of U.S. society and to a corresponding increase in target suitability and decrease in the presence of "guardians" such as neighbors, friends, and family. The decline of the daytime presence of adult caretakers in homes and neighborhoods is partly the result of a trend toward increased female participation in the labor force. Cohen and Felson believe that the volume and distribution of predatory crime are related to the interaction of three variables relating to the routine activities of U.S. life: the availability of suitable targets, the absence of capable guardians, and the presence of motivated offenders.[18]

Steven F. Messner and Kenneth Tardiff used the routine activity approach to help interpret patterns of homicides in Manhattan and found that the approach did indeed provide a useful framework for interpreting the social ecology involved in urban homicides. They found that people's lifestyles affected patterns of victimization. For example, people who were victimized by strangers tended to go out more often, whereas those who preferred to stay at home were more likely to be victimized by someone they knew.[19]

D. Wayne Osgood and colleagues, in analyzing within-individual changes in routine activities and deviance across five waves of data from a national sample, extended routine activity's situational analysis of crime to a broad range of deviant behaviors.[20] They found that "unstructured socializing with peers in the absence of authority figures presents opportunities for deviance. In the presence of peers," they added, "deviant acts will be easier and more rewarding; the absence of authority figures reduces the potential for social control responses to deviance; and the lack of structure leaves time available for deviant behavior."[21]

Ronald L. Akers's examination of rational choice theory led him to conclude that a key issue is whether the rational choice perspective proposes a purely "rational man" theory of criminal behavior. He questions: Does rational choice theory argue for a direct resurrection of classical criminology, in which each person approaches the commission or noncommission of a crime with a highly rational calculus? Is rational choice theory essentially free of all constraining elements? Does it propose that each individual chooses, with full free will and knowledge, to commit or not to commit a crime, taking into account a carefully reasoned set of costs and benefits?[22]

Akers answers these questions by saying that current rational choice models emphasize "limitations and constraints on rationality through lack of information, structural constraints, values, and other 'non-rational' influences. Indeed," Akers adds, "the rational choice models in the literature . . . paint a picture of partial rationality"

criminal opportunity theory

A theory claiming that criminals tend to be attracted to targets that offer a high payoff with little risk of legal consequences.

routine activities approach

The contention that crime rate trends and cycles are related to the nature of everyday patterns of social interaction that characterize the society in which they occur.

Web LIBRARY 3.1

Read the Wikipedia article on rational choice theory at **www .justicestudies.com/ WebLibrary.**

with all kinds of situational and cognitive constraints and all kinds of positivistic and deterministic notions of causes.[23]1

Derek B. Cornish and Ronald V. Clarke's *The Reasoning Criminal* is probably the most frequently cited source on rational choice and crime. Yet in both the preface and the introductory essay, Cornish and Clarke say that the starting assumption of their model is that

> offenders seek to benefit themselves by their criminal behavior; that this involves the making of decisions and choices, however rudimentary on occasion these processes might be; and that these processes exhibit a measure of rationality, albeit constrained by limits of time and ability and the availability of relevant information."[24]

They perceive offenders as "reasoning decision makers" based on the assumption that criminals or delinquents "exercise some degree of planning and foresight."[25]

Raymond Paternoster also presents what he labels a "deterrence/rational choice model" to examine a youth's decision to participate in, continue with, or desist from delinquent acts. Rational choice, according to Paternoster, recognizes that there are "choice-structuring" variables and that choices do not require complete information or rational analytic methods.[26]

In sum, rational choice theory in criminology has recently moved away from the strictly rational, reasoning model of behavior to a more limited and confined role for rational thought. Rational choice theory does not even assume that all or even most delinquent or criminal acts result from clear, planned, well-informed, and calculated choices.[27] It can still be argued, of course, that the rational choice model places more emphasis on rationality and free will than do other theories of delinquent behavior.[28] We consider the question of whether delinquency is rational behavior in the next section.

Is Delinquent Behavior Rational?

An analysis of delinquent behavior leads to the conclusion that antisocial behavior often appears purposeful and rational. Some youthful offenders clearly engage in delinquent behavior because of the low cost or risk of such behavior. The low risk comes from the *parens patriae* philosophy, which is based on the presumption of innocence for the very young as well as of reduced responsibility for youths up to midadolescence. In early adolescence, therefore, the potential costs of all but the most serious forms of delinquent behavior are relatively slight.[29]

Juveniles also are protected from punishment by the existence of enormous probation caseloads in large cities, the confidentiality of juvenile court records, and the increased costs of long-term training schools. Youths on probation, then, can sometimes repeatedly violate the law and suffer no real consequences. According to a delinquent testifying before the New York State Select Committee at a hearing on assault and robbery against the elderly:

> If you're 15 and under you won't go to jail. . . . That's why when we do a "Rush and Crib"—which means you rush the victim and push him or her into their apartment, you let the youngest member do any beatings. See, we know if they arrest him, he'll be back on the street in no time.[30]

In addition, Timothy Brezina contends that much of delinquency can be interpreted as a form of problem-solving behavior in response to the pressures of adolescence. In others words, delinquent conduct is frequently undertaken by youthful offenders as a reasonably effective means of short-term coping. Finding themselves struggling with issues of perceived control, seeking positive evaluation of self, and facing the negative impact of others who punish, sanction, or reject them, delinquents address these problems by deriving short-term pleasures from delinquent involvements.[31]

Conversely, offenders also may decide on rational grounds that the risks of continued delinquent behavior are not justified by the rewards. Howard J. Parker found that many in a group of adolescents gave up shoplifting and the opportunistic theft of car radios when increased police activity resulted in some group members' being apprehended and placed in custody.[32] W. Gordon West's study of the careers of young thieves provides similar evidence of the rational nature of their decisions to desist.[33]

Even more to the point, most persistent offenders appear to desist from crime as they reach their late teens or early twenties. They claim that continued criminality is incompatible with the demands of holding a full-time job or settling down to marriage and a family.[34] Desistance from crime, or maturing out of crime, as was previously mentioned, is a process of deciding that the benefits of crime are less than the advantages of continuing to commit crime.

Yet there are important qualifications in assuming too much rationality in delinquent behavior. Rationality theory is based on the notion that delinquent behavior is planned. Planning has to do with formulating a scheme or a procedure for doing something before doing it or having an intention of acting. It has to do with assessing the possible alternative courses of actions available, choosing a particular course, and constructing a complex set of acts to achieve the intended results.[35] Michael Hindelang's study did reveal that planning was most evident when events were serious and profit oriented.[36] But many studies of delinquency have reported that most delinquent behavior is not planned; spur-of-the-moment decision making most frequently characterizes juvenile wrongdoing.[37]

> " Rationality theory is based on the notion that delinquent behavior is planned. "

The concept of rationality also assumes that individuals have free will and are not controlled by their emotions. But many youngsters do not appear to have such control. Youths who are mentally ill or who engage in obsessive–compulsive acts, such as compulsive arsonists, kleptomaniacs, or sex offenders, seem to be held in bondage by their emotions.

Furthermore, in examining the actual process of rational choice, it is apparent that there are degrees of freedom for all juveniles and that with juveniles rationality

Confined in a Los Angeles County correctional facility, this youth contemplates his future.
■ **What might he be thinking?**

is contextually oriented. The notion of degrees of freedom suggests, then, that delinquents "are neither wholly free nor completely constrained but fall somewhere between."[38] The contextual nature of rationality further suggests that in most situations delinquents do have some control over their acts, but that in some situations they may have little or no control.

Robert Agnew's examination of hard and soft determinism led him to conclude that freedom of choice varies from one individual to another. It is dependent on factors—such as biological, psychological, or social nature—that exist previous to the choice process itself. For example, one individual may be forced to choose between two different alternatives, but another may have six different alternatives. The latter, Agnew suggests, has more freedom of choice.[39] For an examination of the relationship between rationality and human agency in juvenile offending, see Across the Life Course 3.1.

Positivism and Delinquency

This section examines perspectives such as biological and psychological positivism to see how they might enhance our understanding of why delinquent behavior occurs. Instead of viewing delinquency as a logical selection from among an available set of alternative behaviors, as rational choice theorists do, this section suggests that delinquents are affected by biological or psychological factors that impair their decision-making abilities.

According to many philosophers of natural law, human behavior is merely one facet of a universe that is part of a natural order, but human beings can study behavior and discover how natural laws operate. Two positions diverge at this point. One view states that because a natural order with its own laws exists, changing human behavior is impossible. The other view is that the laws that govern human behavior can be understood and used: The causes of human behavior, once discovered, can be modified to eliminate or ameliorate many of society's problems. This second position is the one most scientists accept. The concept, as it applies to juvenile justice, is called positivism.

Positivism became the dominant philosophical perspective of juvenile justice at the time the juvenile court was established in the last year of the nineteenth century. During the **Progressive Era** (the period from about 1890 to 1920), the wave of optimism that swept through U.S. society led to the acceptance of positivism. The doctrines of the emerging social sciences assured reformers that through positivism their problems could be solved. The initial step was to gather all the facts of the case. Equipped with these data, reformers were then expected to analyze the issues in scientific fashion and discover the right solutions.[40]

Armed with these principles, reformers set out to deal with the problem of delinquency, confident that they knew how to find its cause. Progressives looked first to environmental factors, pinpointing poverty as the major cause of delinquency. Some progressives were attracted also to the doctrine of eugenics and believed that biological limitations drove youthful offenders to delinquency. But eventually the psychological origins of delinquency came to be more widely accepted than either the environmental or biological origins.[41]

The positivist approach to youth crime is based on three basic assumptions.[42] First, the character and personal backgrounds of individuals explain delinquent behavior. Positivism, relegating the law and its administration to a secondary role, looks for the cause of deviancy in the actor.

Second, the existence of scientific **determinism** is a critical assumption of positivism. Delinquency, like any other phenomenon, is seen as determined by prior causes; it does not just happen. Because of this deterministic position, positivism rejects the view that the individual exercises freedom, possesses reason, and is capable of choice.

Third, the delinquent is seen as fundamentally different from the nondelinquent. The task then is to identify the factors that have made the delinquent a different kind of person. In attempting to explain this difference, positivism has concluded that wayward youths are driven into crime by something in their physical makeup, by aberrant psychological impulses, or by the meanness and harshness of their social environment.[43]

Early Theories of Biological Positivism

The belief in a biological explanation for criminality has a long history. For example, the study of physiognomy, which attempts to discern inner qualities through outward appearance, was developed by the ancient Greeks. Indeed, a physiognomist charged that Socrates' face reflected a brutal nature.[44]

The attention given to **biological positivism** in the United States may be divided into two periods. The first period was characterized by the nature–nurture debate during the latter part of the nineteenth century and the early twentieth century. Cesare

Lombroso's theory of physical anomalies, genealogical studies, and theories of human somatotypes, or body types, represent early approaches relating crime and delinquency to biological factors.

Lombroso and Biological Positivism

Cesare Lombroso, frequently regarded as the founder of biological positivism, is best known for his theory of the atavistic criminal. According to Lombroso, the **born criminal** was atavistic—a reversion to an earlier evolutionary form or level; that is, the characteristics of primitive men periodically reappeared in certain individuals.[45] Lombroso claimed that he discovered the secret of criminal behavior when he was examining the skull of the notorious criminal Vihella:

> This was not merely an idea, but a flash of inspiration. At the sight of that skull, I seemed to see all of a sudden, lighted up as a vast plain under a flaming sky, the problem of the nature of the criminal—an atavistic being who reproduces in his person the ferocious instincts of primitive humanity and the inferior animals. Thus were explained anatomically the enormous jaws, high cheek bones, prominent superciliary arches, solitary lines in the palms, extreme size of the orbits, handle-shaped or sensile ears found in criminals, savages, and apes, insensibility to pain, extremely acute sight, tattooing, excessive idleness, love of orgies, and the irresistible craving for evil for its own sake, the desire not only to extinguish life in the victim, but to mutilate the corpse, tear its flesh, and drink its blood.[46]

Initially Lombroso insisted that all criminals or delinquents were born criminals, but a study of several thousand criminals led him to modify his theory. In 1897, by the time of the fifth edition of his book *L'Uomo Delinquente*, he had reduced his estimate of the percentage of born criminals to 40 percent. He eventually concluded that environment was more responsible for crime than was atavism. He also identified a continuum of "criminaloids"—individuals who fell between atavistic and other types of criminals.[47]

Lombroso's theory of the atavistic criminal has not stood the test of scientific investigation. Enrico Ferri, one of Lombroso's students, found that 63 percent of Italian soldiers showed some of the same physical signs of "degeneration".[48] Furthermore, Charles Goring, after studying 3,000 English convicts as well as students and sailors who served as controls, concluded that his results did not confirm Lombroso's assertions concerning the atavistic, or biologically inferior, criminal.[49]

Yet Lombroso did make two significant contributions to the study of juvenile delinquency. He provided the impetus for criminologists to study the individual offender rather than the crimes committed by the person. His manner of studying the criminal, which involved control groups and a desire to have his theories tested impartially, also influenced the development of the scientific method.

Genealogical Studies and Delinquency

In 1877, Richard Dugdale did a detailed genealogical study of the Jukes family, covering some 1,200 individuals and spanning nearly a century. He documented an extensive pattern of "pauperism, prostitution, exhaustion, disease, fornication, and illegitimacy."[50] In 1913, Henry H. Goddard conducted another now well-known genealogical study at a training school in New Jersey for "feebleminded" boys and girls. On investigating the family history of one of the wards, Deborah Kallikak, Goddard discovered that she was a descendant of a brief union between a Revolutionary War soldier and a feebleminded girl. He was able to locate 484 descendants of this union, of whom 143 were feebleminded and several were alcoholics and prostitutes. Impressed by these findings, Goddard concluded that "bad stock" was the cause of feeblemindedness and that such persons should not be permitted to reproduce.[51] See Social World of the Delinquent 3.2 for a twentieth-century examination of how violent behavior in a family appeared to be passed from one generation to the next.

Henry Goddard's recommendations received little support, but his finding that at least half of all juvenile delinquents were mentally defective sparked intense debate

Willie Bosket and His Family

Fox Butterfield's fascinating 1995 book *All God's Children* chronicles several generations of an African American family, the Boskets—a story of violence seemingly passed as an inheritance from one generation to the next.

With the assistance of Willie Bosket, who had received a life sentence for murder, Butterfield was able to trace violence in the Bosket family back to Willie's father, grandfather, great-grandfather, and great-great-grandfather. Each generation of Bosket males seemed to repeat the violent patterns of past generations. Both Willie's father, Butch, and Willie himself felt that they had inherited genes that influenced them to explode in violence time after time.

This book is far more than a narrative of a violent family, as tragic as the history of the Bosket family is. The book depicts the origin and growth of violence in the United States, a violence that grew out of a culture that flourished in the antebel-

lum rural South. This tradition was shaped by whites long before it was adopted and recast by some blacks in reaction to their plight.

The importance of this book also is related to the fact that Willie Bosket was labeled as a juvenile delinquent at an early age. Indeed, at the age of twenty-six, when Bosket defended himself in court for stabbing a prison guard in the visiting room of a state prison in New York, he charged that his violent behavior was a direct result of his having been labeled as a delinquent at an early age and having been institutionalized in juvenile and adult institutions since the age of nine.

■ **What do you think of the assumption that a "bad seed," or tendency toward criminality or delinquency, can exist in a family from generation to generation? What would be the difference between the "heritability" of such a tendency (with the Boskets it would be violent behavior) and the heritability of physical appearance, personality traits, or mental acuity?**

Source: Fox Butterfield, *All God's Children: The Bosket Family and the American Tradition of Violence* (New York: Avon Books, 1995).

---

for more than a decade.[52] William Healy and Augusta Bronner were supporters of the correlation between low intelligence and delinquent behavior. In 1926, they tested a group of delinquents in Chicago and Boston and concluded that delinquents were five to ten times more likely to be mentally deficient than were nondelinquents.[53] But the findings of John Slawson and Edwin Sutherland discouraged future investigations of the correlation between intelligence and delinquency. Slawson, studying 1,543 delinquent boys in New York City, found that delinquents were about normal in mechanical aptitude and nonverbal intelligence and lower in abstract verbal intelligence. Slawson also found no relationships among the number of arrests, the types of offenses, and IQ.[54] Edwin Sutherland, evaluating IQ studies of delinquents and criminals, concluded that the lower IQs of offenders were related more to testing methods and scoring than to the offenders' actual mental abilities.[55]

Body Type Theories

Ernst Kretscher, a German, first developed the theory that there are two body types, the schizothyme and the cyclothyme. Schizothymes are strong and muscular, and according to Kretscher they are more likely to be delinquent than are cyclothymes, who are soft-skinned and lack muscle.[56]

William Sheldon, author of *Varieties of Delinquent Youth*, was the first U.S. researcher to examine the relationship between body type and delinquent behavior. Sheldon described three body types: *endomorphic* (soft, round, and fat); *mesomorphic* (bony, muscular, and athletic); and *ectomorphic* (tall, thin, and fragile). Sheldon postulated that these somatotypes had temperamental correlates. He investigated with great thoroughness 200 delinquent boys whose ages ranged from fifteen to twenty-four years. He found that the delinquents were more likely to be mesomorphic and

Twin brothers sharing a pizza at the Twins Days Festival in Twinsburg, Ohio. Genealogical studies seems to say that a predilection for various types of behavior, including delinquency, might have at least a partial genetic basis. ■ **What implications might such theories have for controlling delinquency?**

less likely to be ectomorphic. The temperamental correlations with mesomorphy pertained to such characteristics as social assertiveness, lesser submissiveness to authority, and less-inhibited motor responses.[57]

Sheldon's work came under intense criticism soon after its publication. He was criticized for numerous flaws in his research, including sampling defects and lack of reliability in the assignment of youths to the three groups. Critics also charged that Sheldon's use of photographs was too subjective to inspire confidence in its accuracy. But perhaps most damaging was that Sheldon's definition of delinquency—which he vaguely defined as "disappointingness"—made its measurement nearly impossible.

Sheldon Glueck and Eleanor Glueck's *Physique and Delinquency* was the result of comprehensive research into persistent delinquency. They studied the causes of delinquency through a comparison of 500 persistent delinquents and 500 nondelinquents. Their comparison indicated marked and significant differences in the somatotypes of the two groups—60.1 percent of the delinquents were mesomorphic as compared to 30.7 percent of the nondelinquents. "Among the delinquents, mesomorphy is far and away the most dominant component," they found, "with ectomorphic, endomorphic, and balanced types about equally represented but in relatively minor strength."[58]

Juan B. Cortes and Florence M. Gatti drew on body type theory to develop a biopsychosocial theory of delinquency. Yet they criticized the Gluecks' study on the grounds that all the delinquents the Gluecks studied were committed to correctional institutions; accordingly, they argued, the results might apply to institutionalized delinquents but not necessarily to delinquents in general. Cortes and Gatti also questioned the reliability of the methods the Gluecks used to estimate the somatotype. Furthermore, the age of the 500 delinquents ranged from nine to seventeen years, with an average age of fourteen years and six months; the problem with somatotyping youths this age is the general acceleration of growth and morphological changes of the teenage growth spurt.[59]

Sociobiology: Contemporary Biological Positivism

Sociobiology stresses the interaction between the biological factors within an individual and the influence of the particular environment. Supporters of this form of biological positivism claim that what produces delinquent behavior, like other behaviors, is a combination of genetic traits and social conditions. Recent advances in experimental behavior genetics, human population genetics, knowledge of the biochemistry of the nervous system, experimental and clinical endocrinology and neurophysiology, and other related areas have led to more sophisticated knowledge of the way in which the environment and human genetics interact to affect the growth, development, and functioning of the human organism.[60]

Sociological research has examined environment and genetics through twin and adoption studies; it has also addressed intelligence; neuropsychological, behavioral, and learning disabilities; and biochemical factors in delinquency. Let's look at each of these areas of investigation.

Twins and Adoption

The role of genetic influences on behavior has been suggested by numerous twin and adoption studies.[61] These studies were supported early on by research done in Denmark and other European countries, but more recently they have found support among researchers in the United States.

Twin Studies.　The comparison of identical twins (MZ—monozygotic) with same-sex nonidentical or fraternal twins (DZ—dizygotic) provides the most comprehensive data for exploring genetic influences on human variation. Identical twins develop from a single fertilized egg that divides into two embryos; hence, their genes are the same. Fraternal twins develop from two separate eggs that were both fertilized during the act of conception; hence, about half their genes are the same. Early in the twentieth century, researchers reasoned that by studying twins they could accurately determine hereditary influences on behavior. They could do this by comparing concordance rates of behavior (rates of agreement in behavior outcomes among pairs of individuals) of identical and fraternal twins. If heredity influenced behavior more than environment, identical twins should have higher concordance rates than fraternal twins.[62]

Karl O. Christiansen and S. A. Mednick reported on a sample of 3,586 twin pairs from Denmark between 1870 and 1920. The subset used by these researchers included almost all the twins born between 1881 and 1910 in a certain region of Denmark. Criminal justice statistics turned up 926 offenses for the 7,172 twins, coming from 799 twin pairs. The probability of finding a criminal twin when the other twin was a criminal was .5 for MZ twins and .21 for DZ (same-sex) twins. Although the concordance rates (i.e., frequency of both twins showing the same trait) in this study were lower than in earlier surveys, they were still significant and indicated a genetic contribution to criminal behavior.[63]

> " Sociobiology stresses the interaction between the biological factors within an individual and the influence of the particular environment. "

Thomas Bouchard Jr. examined three large data sets to assess the heritability of five basic personality traits: extroversion, neuroticism, agreeableness, conscientiousness, and openness.[64] He found that a common environment explained very little of the variance in these traits but that genetic inheritance explained 51 percent of the variance in the early twin studies and 42 percent and 46 percent in two later studies. According to Bouchard, the conclusion is straightforward: "The similarity we see in the personality between biological relatives is almost entirely genetic in origin."[65]

In another publication Robert Plomin, Michael Owen, and Peter McGuffin summarized the findings on medical disorders, behavioral disorders, and various abilities in identical and nonidentical twins. They concluded that a strong genetic component appears to be present with a wide range of disorders and abilities, but that a wide variation in the importance of genetics also seems to be evident among the disorders and abilities considered.[66]

Russell Barkley's study of twins provides strong support for a genetic influence on brain structure and functioning, particularly as it relates to self-control.[67] Paul Thompson and colleagues, with the use of complex imaging, analyzed brain structural differences in a sample of monozygotic and dizygotic twins. Their results suggested a genetic foundation for brain growth and functioning, which seemed to produce similar outcomes in cases involving monozygotic twins.[68] Other imaging studies have found the presence of genetic heritability in the brain structure of twins through the seventh and eighth decades of life.[69]

In addition, M. J. H. Rietveld and colleagues' 2003 study of 3,853 twin pairs found that shared environment, which is usually conceived of as family environment, had little effect on a child's level of overactivity.[70] This study of twins, drawn from the Netherlands Twin Registry, suggests that attention problems are due more to genetic factors than to environmental influences. The study adds weight to the literature supporting a significant role for genetic factors as determinants of human behavior.[71]

Adoption Studies. The largest systematic adoption study of criminality examined all nonfamilial adoptions in Denmark from 1924 to 1947. This sample included 14,427 male and female adoptees and their biological and adoptive parents. After exclusions—because criminal records or other kinds of demographic information were missing—the analysis involved no fewer than 10,000 parents in the four parental categories (i.e., biological/adoptive, mother/father) and more than 13,000 adoptees. The parents were counted as criminal if either the mother or father had a criminal conviction. Of adopted boys who had neither adoptive nor biological criminal parents, 13.5 percent had at least one conviction. The percentage rose slightly to 14.7 if adoptive (but not biological) parents were criminal; and if biological (but not adoptive) parents were criminal, 20 percent of the boys had at least one conviction. Boys with both adoptive and biological criminal parents had the highest proportion, 24.5 percent. Christiansen concluded that criminality of the biological parents is more important than that of the adoptive parents, a finding that suggests genetic transmission of some factor or factors associated with crime.[72]

In sum, the evidence of these and other studies of twins and adoptions is impressive. However, the twin method does have a number of weaknesses. The differences in MZ and DZ twin similarity tell us about genetic involvement only to the extent that the MZ–DZ difference is not related to environmental differences. Also, the small number of twin pairs makes adequate statistical comparisons difficult. Further, it is not always easy to determine if twins are monozygotic or dizygotic. And, finally, official definitions of crime and delinquency, with all their limitations, are exclusively used.[73]

Web **LIBRARY** 3.3

Read the NIJ-sponsored report, *Problem Behaviors in Maltreated Children and Youth: Influential Child, Peer, and Caregiver Characteristics*, at **www .justicestudies.com/ WebLibrary.**

Intelligence

With the growing acceptance of sociobiology in the 1960s and 1970s, researchers again turned their attention to intelligence as a possible factor in delinquent behavior. D. J. West and D. P. Farrington, in conducting a longitudinal study of 411 English boys, found that those who later became criminals typically had lower IQs than those who did not. The authors concluded that intelligence is a meaningful predictive factor for future delinquency.[74] Lis Kirkegaard-Sorensen and Sarnoff A. Mednick also conducted a longitudinal study on the value of adolescent intelligence test scores for the prediction of later criminality. They found that adolescents who later committed criminal acts had lower tested intelligence scores than their more law-abiding peers.[75] Robert A. Gordon, in comparing delinquency prevalence rates and delinquency incidence rates, concluded that minority juvenile males had higher arrest rates and court appearance rates than white males or females, regardless of any specific geographical location, rural or urban. He proposed that differences in IQ might provide the strongest explanation of these persistent differences in unlawful behavior.[76] In another paper Gordon stated that lower "IQ was always more successful in accounting for the black–white differences [in crime] than income, education, or occupational status."[77]

Travis Hirschi and Michael Hindelang reexamined three research studies—Hirschi's 1969 data from California, Marvin Wolfgang and associates' Philadelphia data, and Joseph Weis's data from the state of Washington—and found that "the weight of evidence is that IQ is more important than race and social class" for predicting delinquency. These researchers also rejected the contention that IQ tests are race and class biased in that they favor middle-class whites and are therefore invalid means of comparing lower- and middle-class youths. They concluded that low IQ affects school performance, resulting in an increased likelihood of delinquent behavior.[78] James Q. Wilson and Richard J. Herrnstein further contended that there is an inverse relationship between intelligence and certain types of adult criminality.[79]

Sociologists thought that the IQ issue was dead in the mid 1930s, when research consistently challenged the relationship between IQ and delinquency, but later studies resurrected the issue. Unquestionably, whatever the correlation between IQ and delinquency, the association is strengthened by other environmental factors, such as school performance.[80]

Neuropsychological Factors

Some neuropsychological factors appear to be more directly related to delinquent behavior than others. Studies by Hans Eysenck on the **autonomic nervous system** have received wide attention. Eysenck's theory of the autonomic nervous system, like body type theory, has its origins in the earlier attempts to understand the relationship between constitutional factors and delinquency. But his sociobiological theory goes one step farther in noting the interaction of both biological and environmental factors. Eysenck contends that some children are more difficult to condition morally than others because of the inherited sensitivity of their autonomic nervous systems. He argues that individuals range from those in whom it is easy to excite conditioned reflexes and whose reflexes are difficult to inhibit to those whose reflexes are difficult to condition and easy to extinguish. Yet the moral conditioning of the child also depends on the quality of the conditioning the child receives within the family.[81]

Individuals whose autonomic nervous systems are more difficult to condition tend to be extroverts rather than introverts. Extroverts are much more likely, according to Eysenck, to welcome involvement in delinquent behavior. He sees extroverts as people who crave excitement, take chances, act on the spur of the moment, and frequently are impulsive. He also believes that extroverts tend to be aggressive and to lose their tempers quickly, are unable to keep their feelings under control, and are not always reliable.[82] Although Eysenck's theory has come under extensive criticism, especially his research techniques, other research on the organic sources of behavioral disorders appears to be much more promising.[83] For example, Diana H. Fishbein and Robert W. Thatcher argue that electroencephalographic (EEG) abnormalities have been significantly correlated with individuals who are at risk for antisocial and aggressive behavior.[84] R. R. Monroe found abnormal EEGs in 41 percent of aggressive recidivists, whereas the general population has an incidence of 10 to 15 percent.[85] W. W. Surwillo claimed that abnormal EEGs are found in 48 to 70 percent of aggressive psychopaths.[86]

Fishbein and Thatcher report that computerized electroencephalographic equipment can now measure the adequacy of neural processing. They contend that an examination of EEG measures provides the hope of early detection and intervention for children with abnormal EEGs before behavioral problems develop. The dynamic interaction among physiology, biochemistry, environment, and behavior, then, can be identified by factors that have negative effects on brain development and functioning.[87]

autonomic nervous system

The system of nerves that govern reflexes, glands, the iris of the eye, and activities of interior organs that are not subject to voluntary control.

Web LIBRARY 3.4

Read the OJJDP Research Overview, *Juvenile Firesetting*, at **www.justicestudies.com/WebLibrary.**

Numerous studies have found that violent criminal offenders may have neuropsychological impairments.[88] An underlying contention of these studies, according to Elizabeth Kandel and Sarnoff A. Mednick, is that developmental deficits, in turn, may "predispose affected children to aggressive or violent behavior."[89] There is some evidence that pregnancy and birth complications may result in fetal brain damage, predisposing a child to impulsive and aggressive behavior.[90] For example, Kandel and Mednick's study of a Danish birth cohort found that "delivery events predicted adult violent offending, especially in high-risk subjects and recidivistically violent offenders."[91]

In Focus on Social Policy 3.1, see how a disruptive child becomes violent.

Brain Functioning and Temperament

A child's temperament is hard to define but can more easily be identified by the behaviors associated with it. Activity and emotionality are two of these behaviors. The term *activity* in this context refers to gross motor movements, such as the movement of arms and legs, crawling, or walking. Children who exhibit an inordinate amount of movement compared with peers are sometimes labeled "hyperactive" or said to have **attention deficit hyperactivity disorder (ADHD)**. **Emotionality** ranges from very little reaction to intense emotional reactions that are out of control.

Some research suggests that temperament, including tendencies toward aggression, has a biological basis. ■ **What implications might such theories have for controlling or preventing delinquency?**

The hyperactive child remains a temperamental mystery. This child's three behaviors are inattention (the child is easily distracted and does not want to listen), impulsivity (shifts quickly from one activity to another), and excessive motor activity (cannot sit still, runs about, is talkative, and noisy). Educators note that ADHD children have difficulty staying on task, sustaining academic achievement in the school setting, remaining cognitively organized, and maintaining control over their behavior.[92]

ADHD is the most common neurobehavioral disorder of children; the condition affects between 5 and 10 percent of the children in the United States.[93] A 1999 study indicated that two-thirds of children with ADHD have at least one other condition, such as depression, anxiety, or learning disabilities.[94] There is also evidence that ADHD children have other problem behaviors, in addition to those in school—and that these problem behaviors increase the likelihood that such youngsters will become involved in delinquent acts and perhaps even go on to adult crime.[95] Table 3.1 covers ADHD in detail.

attention deficit hyperactivity disorder (ADHD)

A cognitive disorder of childhood that can include inattention, distractibility, excessive activity, restlessness, noisiness, impulsiveness, and so on.

emotionality

An aspect of temperament; it can range from a near absence of emotional response to intense, out-of-control emotional reactions.

Learning Disabilities (LD)

Some evidence points to a link between learning disabilities and delinquent behavior. Research on **learning disabilities** (LD) had its origin in 1948, when scientists labeled an organic disorder in children a "hyperkinetic impulse."[96] A learning disability is different from other types of disabilities because it does not disfigure or leave visible signs that would invite others to be understanding or offer support. It is a disorder that affects people's "ability to either interpret what they see and hear or to link information from different parts of the brain. These limitations can show up in many ways—as specific difficulties with spoken and written language, coordination, self-control, or attention. Such difficulties extend to schoolwork and can impede learning to read or write or to do math."[97]

A learning disability can be a lifelong condition that affects many parts of an individual's life: school or work, family life, daily routines, and even friendships and

learning disabilities (LD)

Disorders in one or more of the basic psychological processes involved in understanding or using spoken or written language.

FOCUS ON
Social Policy 3.1

Violent Development

Henry was headed for serious trouble. The 15-year-old provoked an endless series of fights at school and frequently bullied girls. Teachers regularly suspended him for his classroom disruptions. Older students taunted Henry in the hallways by calling him a sexual pervert or jeered him for having been held back in kindergarten. At home, his father browbeat and denigrated the boy, while his mother cried and muttered about how sick Henry had become.

Henry liked violent video games. He downloaded information from a Web site on how to make pipe bombs and drew pictures of gory deaths of people who mistreated him. The boy openly expressed jealousy of the attention lavished on the youths in Columbine, Colo., who in 1999 fatally shot 12 of their classmates and a teacher and then committed suicide.

In 2001, Henry's life took a fortunate turn. At his high school principal's insistence, he and his parents sought psychotherapy from Stuart W. Twemlow of the Menninger Clinic in Houston. In individual and family sessions, psychiatrist Twemlow zeroed in on the boy's fury at his parents and his tendency at school to view himself as a passive victim who needed to strike back at evil tormentors.

Henry's feelings of rage abated as he grasped that his father struggled with his own deep-seated problems. Henry began taking martial arts training, as suggested by Twemlow, and attending a new school that had a healthier social environment. His grades improved. He started dating.

Henry's story highlights a theme that is attracting scientific attention: Like all children, chronic troublemakers and hellraisers respond to a shifting mix of social and biological influences as they grow. Some developmental roads are relentlessly toward brutality and tragedy. Others, like Henry's, plunge into a dark place before heading into the light of adjustment.

Developmentally minded researchers are now beginning to map out violence-prone paths in hopes of creating better family and school interventions. New evidence indicates that a gene variant inherited by some people influences brain development in ways that foster impulsive violence, but only in combination with environmental hardships. Other studies explore how family and peer interactions build on a child's makeup to promote delinquency. Separate work examines ways to counteract the malign effect of bullying rituals and other types of coercion in schools.

"Violence is such a complicated issue," Twemlow says, "There's always a set of preconditions to violent behavior and never just one cause."

Signature Brains

Andreas Meyer-Lindenberg says that he knows what a genetic risk for impulsive violence looks like in the brain. Ironically, he and his colleagues at the National Institute of Mental Health in Bethesda, Md., traced a portrait of rash aggression in the brains of placid people free of emotional problems, brain disorders, substance abuse, and arrest records.

Meyer-Lindenberg, a neuroscientist, directed studies of 142 white adults who had inherited one of two common versions of a gene that triggers production of an enzyme called monoamine oxidase A (MAOA). That enzyme controls the supply of an important brain chemical. One of the gene variants yields weak MAOA activity in the brain, resulting in elevated concentrations of serotonin. Too much of that chemical messenger upsets the regulations of emotions and impulses.

The other gene variant sparks intense MAOA activity, leading to serotonin concentrations at the low end of the normal range.

Several teams have already reported that children who endure severe abuse and also possess the weak-MAOA gene variant commit violent and delinquent acts later in life far more often than do abused kids who carry the strong-MAOA gene variant.

> ■ Even if a person has a genetic preposition to violence, do you believe that there are more stories of adolescents like Henry who can be helped by such people as Dr. Twemlow? What actually set Henry off on a different developmental path?

play. Some people have many overlapping learning disabilities, while others may have a single, isolated learning problem that has little impact on other areas of their lives. Learning disabilities can be divided into three broad categories:

- Developmental speech and language disorders
- Academic skills disorders
- "Other," a catch-all catergory including certain coordination disorders and learning handicaps not covered by the other classifications[98]

TABLE 3.1

Attention Deficit/Hyperactivity Disorder (AD/HD)

AD/HD symptoms typically arise in early childhood, unless they are associated with some type of brain injury later in life. Criteria for the three primary subtypes are as follows:

In AD/HD predominantly inattentive type, the child:

- Fails to give close attention to details or makes careless mistakes.
- Has difficulty sustaining attention.
- Does not appear to listen.
- Struggles to follow through on instructions.
- Has difficulty with organization.
- Avoids or dislikes tasks requiring sustained mental effort.
- Loses things.
- Is easily distracted.
- Is forgetful in daily activities.

In AD/HD predominantly hyperactive/impulsive type, the child:

- Fidgets with hands or feet or squirms in chair.
- Has difficulty remaining seated.
- Runs about or climbs excessively.
- Has difficulty engaging in activities quietly.
- Acts as if driven by a motor.
- Talks excessively.
- Blurts out answers before questions have been completed.
- Has difficulty waiting or taking turns.
- Interrupts or intrudes upon others.

In AD/HD combined type, the child:

- Meets criteria for both inattentive and hyperactive/impulsive types.

Youngsters with AD/HD frequently experience a two- to four-year developmental delay that makes them seem less mature and responsible than their peers. Adolescents with AD/HD present a special challenge. During these years school makes demands on them; in addition, they face typical adolescent issues such as the need to discover their identity, deal with peer pressure, resist illegal drugs, establish independence, and cope with their emerging sexuality.

Diagnosis

Because everyone shows signs of AD/HD behaviors at one time or another, the guidelines for determining whether a person has AD/HD are very specific. To be diagnosed with this behavioral disorder, a child or teenager must exhibit six of the nine characteristics in either or both of the categories listed above, and the symptoms must be more frequent or more severe than in other children the same age.

Multimodal Treatment

Persons with AD/HD who do not receive treatment or who receive inadequate treatment may face serious consequences, among them low self-esteem, social and academic failure, career underachievement, and a higher risk for antisocial and delinquent behavior and perhaps adult criminality. Treatment plans should be tailored to meet the specific needs of each individual and family and often entail medical, educational, behavioral, and psychological intervention. This comprehensive approach is called "multimodal treatment" and includes:

- Parent training
- Behavioral intervention strategies
- An appropriate educational program
- Education regarding AD/HD
- Individual and family counseling
- Medication, when required

Source: Adapted from *The Disorder Named AD/HD,* web posted at www.help4adhd.org/en/about/what/WWK1.

The most common types of LD are dyslexia, aphasia, and hyperkinesis. Dyslexia is expressed in reading problems, particularly the inability to interpret written symbols. Aphasia consists of speech difficulties, often resulting from both auditory and visual deficiencies. Hyperkinesis, frequently equated with hyperactivity, is excessive muscular movement.[99] The dominant explanations for the cause of LD lie in organic or neurological disorders, including birth injury or anything contributing to premature birth, infant or childhood disease, a head injury, or lack of proper health care or nutrition.[100]

The possibility of a link between learning disabilities and delinquency has been the subject of considerable debate; but the research findings are mixed.[101] Although the link between LD and delinquency is questionable, however, the fact is that youngsters with LD frequently do fail in school, and officials of the justice system seem to be influenced by this school failure to process them through the juvenile justice system.

Biochemical Factors

Research has shown that some delinquent behavior can be attributed to **orthomolecular imbalances** in the body or to brain toxicity. (The term *orthomolecular* refers to "correct chemical balances in the body.") Biochemists suggest that when normal functioning is affected by diet, pollutants, and/or genetic deficiencies such as allergies, abnormal deficits or excesses in molecular brain concentrations of certain substances can lead to various mental and behavioral problems including delinquency.[102]

For example, there has been some interest in recent years in investigating the relationship between inadequate diet and delinquent behavior. Stephen Schoenthaler and his associates have conducted several tests in which they have consistently found a significant association between adolescents' diets and aggresive or delinquent behavior.[103]

Additionally, several studies have found that the presence of lead in a person's system can lead to increased delinquent behavior. Lead in extreme amounts can be fatal, but in smaller amounts it will cause negative behavior.[104] For example, Paul Stretesky and Michael Lynch examined lead concentrations in air across the United States and found that the areas with the highest amounts of lead reported the highest level of homicidal behaviors.[105]

In sum, there is some support for the idea that chemical imbalances in the body, resulting from faulty nutrition, allergies, and lead, are related to delinquent behavior. At best, however, the link is very weak. Although faulty diet and vitamin deficiencies may affect how a juvenile feels, it does not necessarily follow that the adolescent will become involved in delinquent behavior.

◼P︎sychological Positivism

Psychological factors have long been popular in the positivist approach to the causes of juvenile delinquency. Psychological positivism differs from both classical and contemporary biological positivism because its focus is more on the emotional makeup of the personality than on the biological nature of the individual. At first, psychoanalytic (Freudian) theory was widely used with delinquents, but more recently other behavioral and humanistic schools of psychology have been applied to the problems of youth crime.

Psychoanalytic Explanations

Sigmund Freud, in developing **psychoanalytic theory**, contributed three insights that have shaped the handling of juvenile delinquents: (1) The personality is made up

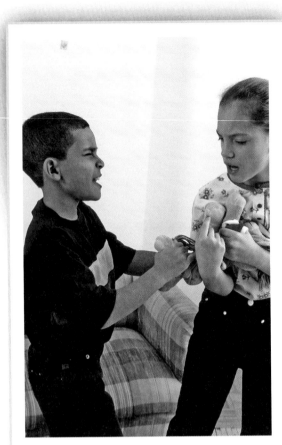

Fighting is characteristic of children who have ADHD.
◼ **What is likely to happen to such children as they grow up?**

orthomolecular imbalances
Chemical imbalances in the body, resulting from poor nutrition, allergies, and exposure to lead and certain other substances, which are said to lead to delinquency.

psychoanalytic theory
Sigmund Freud's insights, which have helped shape the handling of juvenile delinquents. They include these axioms: (1) the personality is made up of three components—id, ego, and superego; (2) all normal children pass through three psychosexual stages of development—oral, anal, and phallic; and (3) a person's personality traits are developed in early childhood.

of three components; (2) all normal children pass through three psychosexual stages of development; and (3) a person's personality traits are developed in early childhood.

Freud's theory of the personality involves the id, the ego, and the superego. The id has to do with a person's raw instincts and primitive drives; it wants immediate gratification of its needs and therefore tends to be primitive and savage. The ego and superego, the other two components, have the express purpose of controlling the primitive drives of the id. The ego mediates between the id and superego and is important in the socialization of the child. The superego, or the conscience, internalizes the rules of society. Thus, as a child develops, he or she learns to distinguish socially acceptable behavior from socially unacceptable behavior.[106]

Freud identified the oral, anal, and phallic stages as the life stages that shape personality development. The oral stage is experienced by the newborn infant. Pleasure is experienced in this stage through eating, sucking, and chewing. In the anal stage, which takes place between one and three years of age, urinary and bowel movements replace sucking as the basic source of pleasure for the child. During the phallic stage, which takes place in normal children between the ages three to six, the child receives pleasure from the genitals. Each stage brings increased social demands on the child and affects the way in which he or she deals with basic, innate drives. The sexual and aggressive drives, in particular, create tensions that a child must learn to resolve in socially acceptable ways.[107]

Freud also argued that by age five, all the essential ingredients of a child's adult personality are determined. What a child has experienced emotionally by the age of five affects that child for the rest of his or her life. Emotional traumas experienced in childhood are likely to cause lifelong psychological problems.[108] Delinquency across the life course, according to this position, is continually affected by what a person has experienced as a young child.

Freud's followers have identified four ways in which emotional problems that develop in childhood might lead to delinquent behavior.[109] First, delinquent behavior is related to neurotic development in the personality. Freud established a relationship between desire and behavior; that is, everything is integrated in the subconscious drives of the organism. A youth may feel guilty about a socially unacceptable desire and, as a result, seek out self-defeating behaviors.

Second, Freudians attribute delinquent behavior to a defective superego. A person who fails to develop a normally functioning superego can be unable to feel guilt, to learn from experience, or to feel affection toward others.[110] Such individuals, sometimes called sociopathic or psychopathic, may constantly express aggressive and antisocial behavior toward others.

Third, violent delinquent behavior sometimes can result if a child with an overdeveloped superego represses all negative emotional feelings throughout childhood to the degree that these repressed feelings explode in a violent act in adolescence. So-called model adolescents occasionally become involved in violent crimes toward parents and neighbors, sometimes horribly mutilating their victims.[111]

Fourth, delinquent involvements can be related to a search for compensatory gratification. According to Freud, individuals who are deprived at an early age of development later seek the gratification they missed. An adolescent may become an alcoholic to satisfy an oral craving or may become sadistic because of poor toilet training received during the anal period.

Many workers have taken the insights of psychoanalysis and applied them to the situations of delinquents. William Healy's particular adaptation of psychoanalytic theory focused on mental conflicts that originated in unsatisfactory family relationships. Healy pioneered the establishment of psychiatric child guidance clinics in several U.S. cities under the auspices of the Commonwealth Fund Program for the Prevention of Delinquency. Although Healy specified that such mental conflicts originated in the child's family relationships, he also realized the importance of the community in modifying delinquent behavior.[112]

Web LIBRARY 3.5

Read the Greater Boston Physicians for Social Responsibility publication, *In Harm's Way: Toxic Threats to Child Development*, at **www .justicestudies.com/ WebLibrary.**

Web LIBRARY 3.6

Read the article *The Juvenile Psychopath: Fads, Fictions, and Facts* at **www.justicestudies .com/WebLibrary.**

August Aichhorn, another proponent of psychoanalytic theory, also worked extensively with youths in trouble. Aichhorn thought that delinquents had considerable hatred toward their parents because of the conflictual nature of the family relationship and that they transferred this hatred to other authority figures. He believed that institutionalized delinquents, exposed to the love and acceptance of a therapeutic relationship, would learn to trust one adult figure and, in turn, to respond more appropriately to other adults.[113]

Kate Friedlander provided another psychoanalytic approach to treating delinquents. She focused on the development of antisocial characteristics in the personality, such as selfishness, impulsiveness, and irresponsibility, which she defined as the results of disturbed ego development in early childhood. According to Friedlander, delinquency is an alternative way to fulfill desires the youth is unwilling to express directly.[114]

Sensation Seeking and Delinquency

Sensation seeking is a much different approach to psychological positivism. Derived from optimal arousal theory, sensation seeking can be defined as "an individual's need for varied, novel and complex sensations and experiences and the willingness to take physical and social risks for the sake of such experience."[115] Ideas about sensation seeking assume that organisms are driven or motivated to obtain an optimal level of arousal.[116] Could this desire for excitement be a factor in delinquency?

Several observers have noted that delinquency is an enjoyable activity. Frederick Thrasher thought that a "sport motive" was more important in stealing than a desire for material gain.[117] Henry McKay, Paul Tappan, and Albert Cohen described delinquency as a form of play.[118] J. J. Tobias found that middle- and upper-middle-class offenders mention boredom as a major reason for engaging in delinquent acts and that they usually discount the need for money as a contributing factor.[119] M. J. Hindelang found that delinquents are more pleasure seeking than are nondelinquents.[120]

Researchers in the 1980s and 1990s gave frequent attention to the relationship between sensation seeking and crime. Helene Raskin White, Erich W. Labouvie, and Marsha E. Bates found that both male and female delinquents have higher rates of sensation seeking and lower rates of inhibited behavior than nondelinquents.[121] Also, ethnographic studies of criminals found that sensation seeking was an important factor in explaining their criminality.[122] For example, Walter R. Gove and colleagues found from their study of inmates in a medium-security prison that inmates most frequently cited sensation seeking as an important motive for the crimes of shoplifting, burglary, robbery, assault, and rape. When inmates were asked how they felt when committing a crime, "being on a high" was most frequently reported, especially with violent crimes.[123] According to this study, inmates conceptualized "being on a high" as being "powerful, pumped up, living on the edge, on a 'high' or rush, intensely alive, and able to do anything."[124]

Jack Katz's controversial book *Seduction of Crime* conjectures that when individuals commit a crime, they become involved in "an emotional process—seductions and compulsions that have special dynamics." It is this "magical" and "transformative" experience that makes crime "sensible," even "sensually compelling." For example, Katz states that for many adolescents, shoplifting and vandalism offer "the attractions of a thrilling melodrama," because "quite apart from what is taken, they may regard 'getting away with it' as a thrilling demonstration of personal competence, especially if it is accomplished under the eyes of adults."[125]

Katz is arguing that instead of approaching criminal or delinquent behavior from the traditional focus on background factors, we need to give more consideration to the foreground or situational factors that directly precipitate antisocial acts and reflect crimes' sensuality. According to Katz, offenders' immediate social environment and experiences encourage them to construct crimes as sensually compelling.[126]

Personality and Crime

Trait-based personality models offer another set of perspectives on the sources of criminal behavior.[127] Traits are essential personal characteristics of individuals that are relevant to a wide variety of behavioral domains, including delinquency and criminality.[128]

Glueck and Glueck's study *Unraveling Juvenile Delinquency* examined a sample of 500 juvenile offenders and 500 nonoffenders in an effort to discover significant distinctions in the personality traits of the two groups. The Gluecks found that the delinquents were more defiant, ambivalent about authority, extroverted, fearful of failure, resentful, hostile, suspicious, and defensive than the nondelinquents. The Rorschach test (which is used to determine personality structure through subjects' interpretations of ink blots) was used as the basis of the Gluecks' assessment.[129]

J. J. Conger and W. C. Miller, in a longitudinal study of male delinquents using all the boys entering the tenth grade in Denver, Colorado, public schools in 1956, found that by the age of fifteen, delinquents could be differentiated from nondelinquents either by the standard personality tests or by teacher evaluations. Delinquents, on the average, were characterized as emotionally unstable, impulsive, suspicious, hostile, given to petty expressions of irritation, egocentric, and typically more unhappy, worried, and dissatisfied than their nondelinquent counterparts.[130]

Eysenck found that crime could be associated with extreme individual values on the personality factors of extroversion, neuroticism, and psychoticism.[131] Marvin Zuckerman contended that offenders are high on a factor he calls "P-ImpUSS," which is characterized by lack of responsibility, impulsivity, and aggressiveness.[132] In addition, C. Robert Cloninger contended that individuals high in novelty seeking and low in harm avoidance and reward dependence are likely to be delinquents today and criminals tomorrow.[133]

Avshalom Caspi and his colleagues examined the personality traits of youthful offenders in New Zealand and Pittsburgh and found that "the personality correlates of delinquency were robust in different nations, in different age cohorts, across gender, and across race."[134] The investigators added that "greater delinquent participation was associated with a personality configuration characterized by high Negative Emotionality and weak Constraint."[135] They concluded that "negative emotions may be translated more readily into antisocial acts when Negative Emotionality (the tendency to experience aversive affective states) is accompanied by weak Constraint (difficulty in impulse control)."[136]

Joshua D. Miller and Donald Lynam, in their meta-analysis of the basic models of personality, identified certain traits that are more characteristic of antisocial personalities. These traits are hostility, self-centeredness, spitefulness, jealousy, and indifference to others. Antisocial individuals also typically lack ambition, perseverance, and motivation; hold nontraditional and unconventional values and beliefs (e.g., are low in conscientiousness); and have difficulty controlling their impulses.[137]

The Psychopath

The hard-core juvenile delinquent often is a **psychopath or sociopath:** a person with a conduct disorder, a personality disorder, or an antisocial personality, to mention a few characterizations. The claim is made that the psychopath or sociopath is the unwanted, rejected child who grows up but remains an undomesticated "child" and never develops trust in or loyalty to other adults.[138] Hervey Cleckley gave the most complete clinical description of this type of personality. He indicated that the psychopath is charming and of good intelligence; is not delusional or irrational; is unreliable; is insecure and cannot be trusted; lacks shame and remorse; will commit all

Web PLACES 3.1

Visit the Society for Research in Psychopathology via **www .justicestudies.com/ WebPlaces.**

kinds of misdeeds for astonishingly small stakes, and sometimes for no reason at all; has poor judgment; never learns from experience; will repeat over and over again patterns of self-defeating behavior; has no real capacity for love; lacks insight; does not respond to consideration, kindness, or trust; and shows a consistent inability to make or follow any sort of life plan.[139]

The continuity between childhood symptoms of emotional problems and adult behavior emerged in L. N. Robins's thirty-year follow-up of 526 white children who were patients in a St. Louis, Missouri, guidance clinic in the 1920s. Robins was looking for clues of the adult "antisocial personality" or "sociopathy."[140] Excluding cases involving organic brain damage, schizophrenia, mental retardation, or symptoms that appeared only after heavy drug or alcohol use, she found that the adult sociopath is almost invariably an antisocial child grown up. In fact, she found no case of adult sociopathy without antisocial behavior before the age of eighteen. More than 50 percent of the sociopathic males showed an onset of symptoms before the age of eight.[141]

Linda Mealey argues that there are two kinds of sociopaths: primary sociopaths and secondary sociopaths. *Primary sociopaths* have inherited traits that predispose them to illegal behavior; that is, they have a genotype that predisposes them to antisocial behavior. *Secondary sociopaths*, in contrast, are constitutionally normal but are influenced by such environmental factors as poor parenting. Thus, she argues that one type of sociopathic behavior has a genetic basis and the other is environmentally induced.[142]

Reinforcement Theory

Web PLACES 3.2

View the antisocial personality disorder treatment material available from the National Library of Medicine's website via **www .justicestudies.com/ WebPlaces.**

reinforcement theory

A perspective that holds that behavior is governed by its consequences, especially rewards and punishments that follow from it.

James Q. Wilson and Richard Herrnstein's *Crime and Human Nature* combines biosocial factors and psychological research with rational choice theory to redevelop reinforcement theory.[143] Wilson and Herrnstein consider potential causes of crime and of noncrime within the context of **reinforcement theory;** that is, the theory that behavior is governed by its consequent rewards and punishments, as reflected in the history of the individual.

The rewards of crime, according to Wilson and Herrnstein, are found in the form of material gain, revenge against an enemy, peer approval, and sexual gratification. The consequences of crime include pangs of conscience, disapproval of peers, revenge by the victim, and, most important, the possibility of punishment. The rewards of crime tend to be more immediate, whereas the rewards of noncrime generally are realized in the future. Wilson and Herrnstein are able to show how gender, age, intelligence, families, schools, communities, labor markets, mass media, and drugs, as well as variations across time, culture, and race, greatly influence the propensity to commit criminal behavior, especially violent offenses.[144]

Wilson and Herrnstein's theory does have serious flaws. Most important, according to Edgar Z. Friedenberg, is that their theory shows a disdain for the social context in which crime occurs. What Wilson and Herrnstein do, in effect, is factor society out of their consideration of crime. Instead of examining criminal behavior as part of complex social mechanisms and attempting to understand the connection, they typically reason that no conclusion is possible from the available data, and therefore that no programs for reducing criminality among groups perceived as major sources of crime are worth their costs.[145]

In sum, psychologists present an abundance of qualitative evidence that delinquents are psychologically different. But it is difficult to substantiate on paper-and-pencil tests that personality differences actually exist between delinquents and nondelinquents.[146] What appears to be a reasonable position is that most delinquents have psychological traits within the normal adolescent range but that some delinquents do have acute emotional problems. Table 3.2 summarizes the biological, sociobiological, and psychological theories of delinquency.

" Psychologists present an abundance of qualitative evidence that delinquents are psychologically different. "

TABLE 3.2

Summary of Biological, Sociobiological, and Psychological Theories of Crime

THEORY	PROPONENTS	CAUSES OF CRIME IDENTIFIED	SUPPORTING RESEARCH
Atavistic, or born, criminal	Lombroso	The atavistic criminal is a reversion to an earlier evolutionary form.	Weak
Genealogical studies	Dugdale Goddard	Criminal tendencies are inherited.	Weak
Body type	Sheldon Glueck and Glueck Cortes and Gatti	Mesomorphic body type correlates with criminality.	Weak
Genetic factors	Christiansen Mednick	Twins and adoption studies show a genetic influence on criminal tendencies.	Moderately strong
Intelligence	Hirschi Hindelang	IQ is a meaningful factor in criminal behavior when combined with environmental factors.	Moderately strong
Autonomic nervous system	Eysenck	Insensitivity of the autonomic nervous system, as well as faulty conditioning by parents, may cause delinquent behavior.	Weak
Psychoanalytic theory	Freud	Unconconscious motivations resulting from early childhood experiences lead to criminality.	Weak
Psychopathic or sociopathic personality	Cleckley	Inner emptiness as well as biological limitations cause criminal tendencies.	Moderately strong
Reinforcement theory	Wilson and Herrnstein	Several key constitutional and psychological factors cause crime.	Weak

Developmental Theories of Delinquency

The effort to understand why individuals commit unlawful behavior began in earnest in the eighteenth century with the classical school of criminology. It continued throughout the twentieth century, where positivism took various forms: biological, psychological, and sociological. The twentieth century also saw renewed interest in the rational nature of criminal and delinquent behaviors. In the closing decades of the twentieth century, longitudinal, or developmental, studies of delinquency—in which measurements of study subjects and groups were made over time—were undertaken in Canada, England, New Zealand, and the United States.[147]

These developmental studies found that delinquency has a beginning, continues for some youths into adulthood, and ends for most at some point during their lives.

Developmental studies uncovered multiple dimensions to delinquency, and underscored the importance of an integrative approach to understanding human behavior. Multicausal understandings of delinquency recognize the role played by society, individual psychology, biology (neurology and genetics), and the social pressures and opportunities facing young people. Still, developmental perspectives usually acknowledge that the adolescent retains human agency, or the ability to make decisions, at least to some degree. Thus, the final piece in understanding individual-level causes of delinquent behavior is recognition of the interrelationships among neurological, psychological, and sociological factors across the life course.

This section, which concludes this chapter, presents three well-known longitudinal studies of offending: (1) the New Zealand Developmental Study of Terrie Moffitt and colleagues, (2) the Montreal Longitudinal Study of Richard E. Tremblay and colleagues, and (3) the Cambridge Study in Delinquent Development led by David P. Farrington. The Rochester Youth Development Study, the Denver Youth Survey, the Pittsburgh Youth Study, and the Seattle Social Development Project are other important longitudinal studies of delinquent behavior that are described elsewhere in this text. The three studies discussed here, like most longitudinal studies in the field of delinquency, concerned themselves with accurately predicting antisocial behavior.

Moffitt's Trajectories of Offending

Terrie E. Moffitt, Donald R. Lynam, and Phil A. Silva, in their examination of the neuropsychological status of several hundred New Zealander males between the ages of thirteen and eighteen, found that poor neuropsychological scores "were associated with early onset of delinquency," but were "unrelated to delinquency that began in adolescence."[148] Moffitt's developmental theory views the emergence of delinquency as proceeding along two developmental paths. On one path, children develop a life-long tendency toward delinquency and crime at an age as early as three. They may begin to bite and hit at age four, shoplift and be truant at age ten, sell drugs and steal cars at age sixteen, rob and rape at age twenty-two, and commit fraud and child abuse at age thirty.[149] These "life-course-persistent" (LCP) offenders, according to Moffitt, are likely to continue to engage in illegal activity throughout their lives, regardless of the social conditions and personal situations they experience. During childhood, they may also exhibit such neuropsychological problems as attention deficit disorders or hyperactivity and learning problems in school.[150]

Moffitt also identified a second path, wherein the delinquents start offending during their adolescent years and then begin to desist from delinquent behavior around their eighteenth birthday. Moffitt refers to these youthful offenders as "adolescent-limited" (AL) delinquents, and it is this limited form of delinquency that characterizes most children who become involved in illegal activity.

The early and persistent problems that characterize members of the LCP group are not found with the AL delinquents Yet the frequency of offending and even the violence of offending among members of the AL group during their adolescent years may be as high as in LCP delinquents. Moffitt notes that AL antisocial behavior is learned from peers and sustained through peer-based rewards and reinforcements. Adolescent-limited delinquents continue in delinquent acts as long as such behaviors appear profitable or rewarding to them, but they will abandon those forms of behavior when prosocial activities become more rewarding.[151] See Voices Across the Profession 3.1, an interview with Terrie E. Moffitt, for further insight into Moffitt's perspective.

Moffitt also examined gender differences in the Dunedin Longitudinal Study (see Chapter 7 for a more detailed description of this study), looking closely at life-course differences between males and females. The study measured alcohol and drug use, family adversity, cognitive deficits, self-discipline, hyperactivity, undercontrolled temperament, and rejection by peers. Study authors found extreme overrepresentation in male LCP delinquents, which they attributed to neurodevelopmental factors associated with the onset of male adolescence. In the AL group, which the researchers said could be "best understood as a social phenomenon originating in the context of social relationships," they found much more similar rates of offending between genders. Behaviors of males and females "are particularly alike when alcohol and drugs are involved, near the time of female puberty, and when females are yoked with males in intimate relationships."[152]

Tremblay's Trajectories of Offending

The Montreal Longitudinal-Experimental Study (MLES) began in 1984. Its original aim was to study the development of antisocial behavior from kindergarten to high school with a major focus on the role of parent–child interactions. The study initially assessed all kindergarten boys in 53 schools located in poor socioeconomic areas in Montreal in an effort to identify the most disruptive boys. The study also examined parent–child social interactions of a subset of approximately 80 of these boys through high school. Study authors believed that disruptive kindergarten boys from low socioeconomic environments in large urban areas would be more at risk of frequent and serious delinquent behavior later in life when compared to population samples of other young males and females. It was hoped that comparisons of the two groups would provide cues to the causes of delinquency in the high-risk group, and that the results would also provide indicators of effective preventive interventions using parent–child interaction.[153]

Mother and teacher ratings and self-reported delinquency were the main instruments used to assess behavioral problems under the MLES. Behavior ratings were obtained annually from mothers and from classroom peers at ages ten, eleven, and twelve. A psychiatric interview was conducted with the boys and their mothers when the boys were fifteen years old. Direct observations of social interactions were made at home, at school, and in laboratory situations from ages seven to fifteen. Psychophysiological and neuropsychological tests, as well as various biological assessments, were made on boys in the study group until they reached the age of twenty.[154]

The study produced the following key findings:

- Higher levels of disruptive behavior during kindergarten effectively predicted higher levels of delinquency before entry into high school.
- Physical aggression during kindergarten is the best behavioral predictor of later delinquency.
- No significant group of boys started to show chronic problems of physical aggression, opposition, or hyperactivity after their kindergarten year.
- Hyperactivity and anxiety significantly predicted the age of onset of cigarette smoking, drinking to excess, and using drugs up to fifteen years of age. Boys who had a high score on hyperactivity and a low score on anxiety were more likely to use substances at an early age.
- Boys exhibiting high levels of aggression and fighting between five and twelve years of age had generally lower heart rates at eleven and twelve years of age than other boys, controlling for pubertal status, body size, and level of family adversity.
- Family poverty predicted academic failure at age sixteen. Family poverty also predicted delinquency, but only more serious forms of adolescent antisocial behavior.
- Not being in an age-appropriate classroom at age sixteen was associated with delinquency.
- Less parental monitoring was associated with an increased risk of self-reported extreme delinquency.
- Deviant friends led to more delinquency, irrespective of boys' disruptiveness.
- Assessment of the boys up to seventeen years of age revealed that parent-training interventions had long-term beneficial influences on many boys' development.[155]

Realizing that the potential for later antisocial behavior could be identified as early as kindergarten, Tremblay and his colleagues decided to investigate the earliest age of delinquency onset with new longitudinal studies beginning at birth and even extending to pregnancy. The initial results indicated "that children initiate oppositional behavior, taking things away from others, and physical aggression as soon as they have the motor coordination and the opportunity to do so."[156]

The Cambridge Study of Delinquent Development

This Cambridge study is a forty-year longitudinal survey that followed the development of antisocial behavior in 411 South London boys who were mostly born in 1953. The study was begun in 1961, with Donald West as its director during the first twenty years. For the last twenty years, David P. Farrington served as director.[157] The study aimed to measure as many factors as possible that might contribute to the development of delinquency.

Participants in the study were interviewed from ages eight to forty-six. They were also periodically interviewed and tested in their schools, in their homes, and at the researchers' offices. Interviews with parents were also conducted by psychiatric social workers about once a year until each boy was in his last year of compulsory education. In addition, teachers completed questionnaires, and a variety of other behavioral and health information was collected.[158]

Voices
Across the Profession 3.1

Interview with Terrie E. Moffitt

Question: What do you feel are the best features of developmental theory as you and colleagues have developed it?

Moffitt: We proposed that people who engage in delinquent and offending behavior should be viewed as falling into two main patterns, life-course-persistent and adolescence-limited. I think one of the main advantages of this two-group approach is that it accounts for the known "big facts" about antisocial behavior's relations with age, sex, and social class. The two-group approach also explains why some correlates of antisocial behavior appear, disappear, and reappear across the life course. For example, low social class, reading difficulties, and genetic risk are all strong correlates of antisocial behavior during childhood and adulthood, but not during adolescence. Conversely, peer influences on antisocial behavior are strong during adolescence, but not during childhood and

adulthood. If two different kinds of people take part in antisocial behavior at different developmental stages, that would explain these curious "disappearing" findings. Finally, the two-group approach focuses attention on different intervention plans needed to prevent early-onset versus late-onset delinquency.

Question: Do you see any areas that need to be expanded or reformulated?

Moffitt: One aspect that clearly needs to be expanded is the number of offender groups. The original theory proposed only two, life-course-persistent and adolescence-limited. But subsequently researchers have tested for the correct number of groups needed to account for the delinquent activity in representative samples. From this work a third group of offenders has emerged: the "low-level chronics." In my own longitudinal study this group was highly aggressive in childhood, but then was only minimally in-

volved in delinquency during adolescence. As adults, the group emerged as steady low-level chronic offenders. They are very unusual males, because they are socially isolated, have many fears and phobias, lack friendships or female partners, and have low intelligence and low-status jobs, or no jobs. David Farrington's London longitudinal study finds the same low-level chronic offenders who are poorly functioning social isolates. We need to know more about them.

Question: How did you come to be involved in the formulation of this theory?

Moffitt: I was taught an important lesson by the birth cohort of 1,000 young New Zealanders we followed as they grew up. In the 1980s, when the cohort were children, my students and I found there were not many antisocial study members, but their antisocial behavior had many strong correlates, such as difficult temperament, harsh parenting, and low IQ. We published lots of papers about this. When we recontacted the cohort in the 1990s at age fifteen to collect more data from them, we found many more study members had taken up antisocial behavior. We were pleased about that because

The study's chief findings are as follows:

- Forty percent of the males in the study group were convicted of criminal offenses up to age forty, compared to a national prevalence of convictions for same-aged males born in England and Wales of 31 percent.
- The prevalence of offending increased up to age seventeen and then decreased.
- The peak age of increase in the prevalence of offending was fourteen.
- Up to age forty, the mean age of first conviction was 18.6, and the mean age of last conviction was 25.7. Hence, criminal careers lasted an average of 7.1 years.
- Persistence in offending was seen, in that significant continuity of offending took place from one age range to another.
- Little specialization was evident in offending.
- Most juvenile and young adult offenses resulting in convictions were committed with others, but the incidence of co-offending declined steadily with age.
- The most important risk factors of later offending were (1) antisocial behavior during childhood, including troublesomeness, dishonesty, and aggressiveness; (2) hyperactivity-impulsivity; (3) low intelligence; (4) poor school achievement; (5) family criminality; (6) family poverty; and (7) poor parenting.[159]

we now had more delinquents to study. However, we found that all the former correlates of antisocial behavior had suddenly dropped to non-significance. What a surprise! Because we had nothing to publish, we had to find an explanation for these disappearing findings! This motivated me to brainstorm about why more participants in delinquency would be associated with disappearing correlates of delinquency. While thinking about this puzzle, I remembered my own experience of school. In my primary school, there were some really bad kids that my good-student friends and I were afraid of, but by junior high school, many of us began to hang out with those bad kids and got into a fair amount of serious trouble ourselves. After high school, my good-student friends and I have moved on to be more successful. I wondered if this small-town story applied to young people more widely, and apparently it does.

Question: Have you been encouraged or discouraged by the response that the theory has received?

Moffitt: I am delighted that so many people have found this simple two-

group theory worthy of their attention, and I am even overwhelmed by this. This taxonomy of childhood versus adolescent onset antisocial behavior is codified in the American Psychiatric Association's guidelines for diagnosing conduct disorders (DSM-IV, 1994), and has been invoked in the National Institute of Mental Health Factsheet on Child and Adolescent Violence (2000) and the Surgeon General's report on Youth Violence (2001). The original paper that proposed the two prototypes and their different etiologies appeared about ten years ago (Moffitt, 1993), and in the seven years since it has been cited by readers more than 600 times in their own papers, which is a high compliment. Several research teams in nine countries have tested hypotheses put forward from the theory. Most of the research teams have reported findings that are consistent with the theory, but some have pointed to important issues that need to be resolved. For example, a Baltimore study found that the theory fit young African American men better than young white men, but a California study found the theory did not fit African American men at all. Obviously, this

needs more work! It is exciting that the theory is stimulating so much research activity and debate, and I'm pleased that it can make this contribution. Most criminologists now think about human development, and this is quite gratifying to me.

> ■ **What new insights about developmental theory are found in this interview? What does it mean to think in terms of human development? How do you evaluate Moffitt and colleagues' developmental theory?**

Source: Reprinted with permission from Terrie E. Moffitt. Terrie E. Moffitt is professor of psychology at the University of Wisconsin. She does life-span longitudinal research with large samples in field settings. Her research topics include (1) natural history of antisocial behavior from childhood to adulthood, (2) etiology of conduct disorder, juvenile delinquency, and antisocial personality disorder, (3) interactionist approaches to psychopathology, (4) longitudinal research methodology, (5) neuropsychological assessment, and (6) neurobehavioral disorders.[160]

Study: Spare the Rod, Improve the Child

A recent report is the second major study within two weeks to condemn the practice of spanking children. But other experts raise questions and continue to debate the controversial discipline technique used in many American homes.

The latest study, presented at a Denver conference, gives an optimistic assessment of the effects of not spanking youngsters.

Children who are not spanked tend to be better behaved and do better in school, grow up to have better marriages, earn more money and live better lives, according to Murray Straus of the Family Research Laboratory at the University of New Hampshire. Straus summed up 50 years of research on the effectiveness and side effects of spanking. That mass of research indicates agreement among professionals on two things, he said in a statement released prior to the conference:

- Spanking is not the most effective method of discipline. "Although spanking works, it does not work better than other methods of correcting and teaching kids."
- Spanking has harmful side effects. It increases "the chance that a child will become rebellious or depressed." These side effects may take years to show up, he says.

"Lots of people are worried that if parents never spanked, the result would be kids running wild, higher rates of delinquency, and when they grow up, more crime," he says. "Actually, what the research shows is just the opposite."

Toddlers and young children who are not spanked tend to have faster mental development, do better in school and have a better chance of graduating from college, he says. They also hit other children less and grow up to be parents who tend not to spank.

The earlier comprehensive report also was critical of spanking but found that it changes behavior. The child complies with the parent's wishes, said a study in the July issue of the *Psychological Bulletin* from the American Psychological Association. But the researcher also found 10 negatives linked with spanking that outweigh the fact the child stops misbehaving, including increased aggression and antisocial behavior. The practice also does not teach a child right from wrong.

Not all children who are spanked turn out to be aggressive or delinquent, wrote Elizabeth Thompson Gershoff, a researcher and psychologist at Columbia University. Many factors can moderate the punishment, such as how well the parent and child get along. Studying the effects of spanking is difficult because parents differ in how often they spank, how vigorously they do it, how emotionally aroused they are when they

"Spare the rod and spoil the child" is an American adage. Most child care professionals today, however, condemn the use of corporal punishment in child rearing. ■ **Are there more effective techniques for disciplining children than spanking?**

spank, and how accurately they report such factors.

Gershoff evaluated 88 studies done over 62 years on corporal punishment by parents.

Experts differ on even the definition of spanking, but they worry that any suggestion that it might be acceptable in the mildest of forms might lead to child abuse.

Gershoff's analysis in the bulletin was accompanied by commentary from other psychologists. One team wrote that mild to moderate spanking can be effective and used safely by parents who know not to cross the line to child abuse.

Source: Karen S. Peterson, "Study: Spare the Rod, Improve the Child," *USA Today,* July 8, 2002. Copyright © 2002 by *USA Today.* Reprinted with permission.

The Cambridge study appears to show that delinquent acts that lead to convictions are components of a larger syndrome of relatively persistent antisocial behavior. Farrington observed a high degree of delinquent continuity between ages eighteen and thirty-two and proposed that behavioral stability can be found mostly in the individual rather than in the environment. Study authors noted "that there are individual differences between people in some general underlying theoretical construct which might be termed 'antisocial tendency,' which is relatively stable from childhood to adulthood."[161]

CHAPTER Summary

This chapter examines individual-level explanations for delinquency, including personal decision making and the behavioral impact of rational choices made by young people. This chapter also points out that:

- Policymakers in growing numbers are concluding that increasing the "cost" of crime to the perpetrator is the best way to reduce serious youth crime in the United States.

- To justify punishing juveniles, theorists have turned to classical school principles or to the principles of rational choice theory, which build on classical thought. Both perspectives assert that individuals have free will and should be held responsible for their behavior.

- Biological and psychological positivism point to biological and psychological factors within the individual as the most significant determinants of delinquency.

- Biological and psychological factors may be very elusive, such as an autonomic nervous system that is difficult to condition or an inadequately developed superego, or they may be more easily discerned, such as inappropriate interpersonal relationships.

- Both early biological and psychological positivism theories have developed into more refined explanations of delinquent behavior. Early biological positivism has largely been replaced by sociobiology, and psychoanalysis has been replaced by developmental models that give greater weight to the interactions between the individual and the environment.

- Children who have attention deficit hyperactivity disorder (ADHD) and learning disorders (LD) tend to have problems in school and, in turn, they tend to become involved with peers who demonstrate higher rates of delinquency.

- According to developmental perspectives, human behavior progresses along certain paths and its outcomes are relatively predictable.

- Terrie Moffitt identified "adolescent-limited" or "life-course" paths, in which young people either temporarily experiment with delinquency or engage in persistent crime violation.

- Richard Tremblay and colleagues' Montréal Longitudinal-Experimental Study found that antisocial behavior was at its peak during the kindergarten years and that physical aggression during the kindergarten year is the best behavior predictor of later delinquency.

- In the Cambridge Study in Delinquent Development, David P. Farrington found that the types of acts that lead to convictions tend to be components of a larger pattern of antisocial behavior.

CRITICAL THINKING Questions

1. Why do you think the juvenile court and policymakers have been so quick to apply the concept of free will to violent juvenile criminals?
2. What are the basic flaws in the courts' use of punishment to deter youth crime in the United States?
3. A rational choice theorist who studied the case of "Billy" would conclude that it was unfortunate that this young man had such a toxic and deprived family life but that this background did not take away his ability to make responsible decisions for his life. According to the concept of the rationality of crime, Billy freely chose to kill the old man, and therefore he deserves to be punished for the murder. In your opinion, was Billy's decision rational? How much freedom did he have, and how much punishment did he deserve?
4. Describe the sociopath or psychopath. Why are sociopaths so difficult to treat?

Visit the Annie E. Casey Foundation on the Web at **www.aecf.org** and access the Foundation's *Kids Count Data Book* (**www.aecf .org/kidscount/sld/databook.jsp**). As the website says, the *Data Book* provides national and state-by-state reports on the well-being of America's children. Its purpose is to promote discussion on ways to secure better futures for all U.S. children. The *Data Book* ranks states on ten key indicators and provides information on child health, education, and family economic conditions. In the *Data Book,* writers explore how early childhood development prepares children for success in school and life, and how to support family-based child care providers.

Source: From www.aecf.org/kidscount/sld/databook.jsp. Reprinted with permission from KIDS COUNT, a project of the Annie E. Casey Foundation.

Access the *Data Book's* section on population and family characteristics and view the child population by household type. Which states have the largest percentages of mother-only households (i.e., 30 percent or greater)? Which have the largest percentages of married-couples households (i.e., 70 percent or greater)? Which have the largest percentages of father-only households (i.e., 8 percent or greater)? What do you think accounts for these differences between the states?

Next, click on the "poverty" *Data Book* selection and then on "Children in Extreme Poverty" to see extreme poverty levels by state. Which states have the highest levels of children living in extreme poverty? Which have the lowest? What accounts for these differences?

Submit your answers to these questions to your instructor if asked to do so.

Notes

1. Ronald V. Clarke and Derek B. Cornish, "Modeling Offenders' Decisions: A Framework for Research and Policy," in *Crime and Justice* 6, edited by Michael Tonry and Norval Morris (Chicago: University of Chicago Press, 1985), p. 147.
2. Montesquieu, *On the Spirit of the Laws,* trans. Thomas Nugent, ed. David W. Carithers (Berkeley: University of California Press, 1977); originally published as *L'Esprit des Lois* (1747); Cesare Bonesana Beccaria, *On Crimes and Punishments,* trans. H. Paolucci (1764; reprint ed., Indianapolis: Bobbs-Merrill, 1963); Jeremy Bentham, *An Introduction to the Principles of Morals and Legislation* (1823; reprint ed., New York: Hafner Publishing, 1948).
3. Montesquieu, *On the Spirit of the Laws,* p. 158.
4. Ibid.
5. Beccaria, *On Crimes and Punishments.*
6. Ysabel Rennie, *The Search for Criminal Man: A Conceptual History of the Dangerous Offender* (Lexington, Mass.: Lexington Books, 1978), p. 15.
7. Beccaria, *On Crimes and Punishments,* p. 179.
8. Rennie, *The Search for Criminal Man,* p. 22.
9. Edward Cimler and Lee Roy Bearch, "Factors Involved in Juvenile Decisions about Crime," *Criminal Justice and Behavior* 8 (September 1981), pp. 275–286.
10. Anne Campbell, *Girl Delinquents* (New York: St. Martin's Press, 1981), p. 149.
11. Paul J. Brantingham and Patricia L. Brantingham, "The Spatial Patterning of Burglary," *Howard Journal of Penology and Crime Prevention* 14 (1975), pp. 11–24.

12. Clarke and Cornish, "Modeling Offenders' Decisions," p. 156.

13. Interviewed in 1983.

14. Derek B. Cornish and Ronald V. Clarke, eds., *The Reasoning Criminal: Rational Choice Perspectives on Offending* (New York: Springer, 1986); Kirk R. Williams and Richard Hawkins, "The Meaning of Arrest for Wife Assault," *Criminology* 27 (1989), pp. 163–181; Irving Piliavin, Craig Thornton, Rosemary Gartner, and Ross L. Matsueda, "Crime, Deterrence, and Rational Choice," *American Sociological Review* 51 (1986), pp. 101–119; Raymond Paternoster, "Decisions to Participate in and Desist from Four Types of Common Delinquency: Deterrence and the Rational Choice Perspective," *Law and Society Review* 23 (1989), pp. 7–40; Raymond Paternoster, "Absolute and Restrictive Deterrence in a Panel of Youth: Explaining the Onset, Persistence/Desistance, and Frequency of Delinquent Offending," *Social Problems* 36 (1989), pp. 289–309; Marcus Felson, "Predatory and Dispute-Related Violence: A Social-Interactionist Approach," in *Routine Activity and Rational Choice: Advances in Criminological Theory,* Vol. 5, edited by R. V. Clarke and M. Felson (New Brunswick, N.J.: Transaction Books, 1993); Marcus Felson, *Crime and Everyday Life: Insight and Implications for Society* (Thousand Oaks, Calif.: Pine Forge Press, 1994).

15. Ronald L. Akers, "Rational Choice, Deterrence, and Social learning Theory in Criminology: The Path Not Taken," *Journal of Criminal Law and Criminology* 81 (Fall 1990), pp. 653–676.

16. Philip J. Cook, "The Demand and Supply of Criminal Opportunities," in *Crime and Justice* 7, edited by Michael Tonry and Norval Morris (Chicago: University of Chicago Press, 1986), p. 2.

17. Ibid, pp. 2–3.

18. Lawrence E. Cohen and Marcus Felson, "Social Change and Crime Rate Trends: A Routine Activity Approach," *American Sociological Review* (August 1979), pp. 588–609. For more recent expressions of the routine activity approach, see Felson, *Crime and Everyday Life.*

19. Steven F. Messner and Kenneth Tardiff, "The Social Ecology of Urban Homicides: An Application of the 'Routine Activities' Approach," *Criminology* 23 (1985), pp. 241–267.

20. D. Wayne Osgood, Janet K. Wilson, Patrick M. O'Malley, Jerald G. Bachman, and Lloyd D. Johnson, "Routine Activities and Individual Deviant Behavior," *American Sociological Review* 61 (1996), p. 635.

21. Ibid.

22. Akers, "Rational Choice, Deterrence, and Social Learning Theory in Criminology," p. 661.

23. Ibid., pp. 661–662.

24. Cornish and Clarke, *The Reasoning Criminal,* pp. 1–2.

25. Ibid., p. 13.

26. Paternoster, "Absolute and Restrictive Deterrence in a Panel of Youth" and "Decisions to Participate in and Desist from Four Types of Common Delinquency."

27. Akers, "Deterrence, Rational Choice, and Social Learning Theory," p. 12.

28. Akers, however, questions this in his paper, "Deterrence, Rational Choice, and Social Learning Theory," p. 11.

29. David F. Greenberg, "Delinquency and the Age Structure of Society," *Contemporary Crisis* 1 (1977), p. 209.

30. Ibid., p. 210.

31. Timothy Brezina, "Delinquent Problem-Solving: An Interpretive Framework," *Journal of Research in Crime and Delinquency* (2000), pp. 3–30.

32. Howard J. Parker, *View from the Boys: A Sociology of Down-Town Adolescents* (Newton Abbot, England: David and Charles, 1974).

33. W. Gordon West, "The Short-Term Careers of Serious Thieves," *Canadian Journal of Criminology* 20 (1978), pp. 169–190.

34. D. F. Greenberg, "Delinquency and the Age Structure of Society," pp. 189–223; Gordon B. Trasler, "Delinquency, Recidivism, and Desistance," *British Journal of Criminology* 19 (1979), pp. 314–322.

35. Gove, "Why We Do What We Do," p. 370.

36. Michael J. Hindelang, *Situational Influences on the Delinquent Act* (Rockville, Md.: National Institutes of Mental Health, 1972).

37. Marvin E. Wolfgang, Terence P. Thornberry, and Robert M. Figlio, *From Boy to Man: From Delinquency to Crime* (Chicago: University of Chicago Press, 1987), p. 125. See also James F. Short Jr., and Fred L. Strodtbeck, *Group Process and Gang Delinquency* (Chicago: University of Chicago Press, 1965), pp. 248–265; and Charles W. Thomas and Donna M. Bishop, "The Effect of Formal and Informal Sanctions on Delinquency: A Longitudinal Comparison of Labeling and Deterrence Theories," *Journal of Criminal Law and Criminology* 75 (1984), p. 1244.

38. David Matza, *Delinquency and Drift,* p. 27. See also Silvan S. Tomkins, *Affect, Imagery, Consciousness: The Positive Affects* (New York: Springer, 1962), pp. 108–109.

39. Robert Agnew, "Determinism, Indeterminism, and Crime: An Empirical Exploration," *Criminology* 33 (1995), pp. 87–88.

40. This section on the Progressive Era and the influence of positivism is based on David J. Rothman, *Conscience and Convenience: The Asylum and Its Alternatives in Progressive America* (Boston: Little, Brown, 1980), p. 32.

41. Ibid., pp. 43–60.

42. David Matza, *Delinquency and Drift* (New York: Wiley, 1964), p. 5.

43. Donald C. Gibbons, "Differential Treatment of Delinquents and Interpersonal Maturity Level: A Critique," *Social Services Review* 44 (1970), p. 68.

44. James Q. Wilson and Richard J. Herrnstein, *Crime and Human Nature* (New York: Simon and Schuster, 1985), p. 71.

45. Ian Taylor, Paul Walton, and Jock Young, *The New Criminology: For a Social Theory of Deviance* (New York: Harper and Row, 1973), pp. 41–42.

46. Cesare Lombroso, introduction, in Gina Lombroso-Ferrero, *Criminal Man According to Classification of Cesare Lombroso* (Montclair, NJ: Patterson Smith, 1972).

47. Gina Lombroso-Ferrero, *Criminal Man* (New York: Putnam, 1911), p. xiv.

48. M. F. A. Montagu, "The Biologist Looks at Crime," *Annals of the American Academy of Political and Social Science* 217 (1941), pp. 46–57.

49. Charles Goring, *The English Convict: A Statistical Study* (Montclair, N.J.: Patterson Smith, 1972).

50. Saleem A. Shah and Loren H. Roth, "Biological and Psychophysiological Factors in Criminality," in *Handbook of*

Criminology, edited by Daniel Glaser (Chicago: Rand McNally, 1974), p. 107.

51. Henry H. Goddard, *Efficiency and Levels of Intelligence* (Princeton: Princeton University Press, 1920).

52. Ibid.

53. William Healy and Augusta Bronner, *Delinquency and Criminals: Their Making and Unmaking* (New York: Macmillan, 1926).

54. John Slawson, *The Delinquent Boys* (Boston: Budget Press, 1926).

55. Edwin Sutherland, "Mental Deficiency and Crime," in *Social Attitudes,* edited by Kimball Young (New York: Henry Holt, 1973).

56. William Sheldon, *Varieties of Delinquent Youth* (New York: Harper and Row, 1949).

57. Ibid.

58. Sheldon Glueck and Eleanor Glueck, *Physique and Delinquency* (New York: Harper and Row, 1956), p. 9.

59. Juan B. Cortes with Florence M. Gatti, *Delinquency and Crime: A Biopsychosocial Approach: Empirical, Theoretical, and Practical Aspects of Criminal Behavior* (New York: Seminar Press, 1972), pp. 18–19.

60. Shah and Roth, "Biological and Psychophysiological Factors in Criminality," p. 101.

61. Karl O. Christiansen, "A Preliminary Study of Criminality among Twins," in *Biosocial Bases of Criminal Behavior,* edited by S. A. Mednick and K. O. Christiansen (New York: Gardner, 1977) pp. 89–108; D. R. Cloninger et al., "Predisposition to Petty Criminality: II. Cross-Fostering Analysis of Gene–Environment Interaction," *Archives of General Psychiatry* 39 (November 1982), pp. 1242–1247; R. Crowe, "An Adoptive Study of Psychopathy: Preliminary Results from Arrest Records and Psychiatric Hospital Records," in *Genetic Research in Psychiatry,* edited by R. Fieve et al. (Baltimore: Johns Hopkins University Press, 1975); William F. Gabrielli and Sarnoff A. Mednick, "Urban Environment, Genetics, and Crime," *Criminology* 22 (November 1984), pp. 645–652; S. Sigvardsson et al., "Predisposition to Petty Criminality in Swedish Adoptees: III. Sex Differences and Validation of Male Typology," *Archives of General Psychiatry* 39 (November 1982), pp. 1248–1253.

62. Donald J. Shoemaker, *Theories of Delinquency: An Examination of Explanations of Delinquent Behavior,* 5th ed. New York: Oxford University Press, 2005), p. 29.

63. Christiansen, "A Preliminary Study of Criminality among Twins," pp. 89–108.

64. Thomas Bouchard, Jr., "Genes, Environment, and Personality," *Science* 264 (1994), pp. 1700–1701.

65. Ibid., p. 1701.

66. Robert Plomin, Michael Owen, and Peter McGuffin, "The Genetic Basis of Complex Behaviors," *Science* 264 (1994), pp. 1733–1739.

67. Russell A. Barkley, *ADHD and the Nature of Self-Control* (New York: Guilford Press, 1997). See also Dr. Russell Barkley on AD/HD: excerpts from his lecture in San Francisco, Calif., on June 17, 2000.

68. Paul Thompson, Tyrone D. Cannon, Katherine L. Narr et al., "Genetic Influences on Brain Structure," *Neuroscience* 4 (2001), pp. 1–6.

69. Adolf Pfefferbaum, Edith V. Sullivan, Gary E. Swan, and Dorit Carmelli, "Brain Structure in Men Remains Highly Heritable in the Seventh and Eighth Decades of Life," *Neurobiology of Aging* 21 (2000), pp. 63–74.

70. M. J. H. Rietveld, J. J. Hudziak, M. Bartels, C. E. M. van Beijsterveldt, and D. I. Boomsma, "Heritability of Attention Problems in Children: Cross-Sectional Results from a Study of Twins, Age 3 to 12," *Neuropsychiatric Genetics* 1176 (2003), pp. 102–113.

71. The above discussion on recent studies of twins is based on John Paul Wright and Kevin M. Beaver, "Do Parents Matter in Creating Self-Control in Their Children? A Genetically Informed Test of Gottfredson and Hirschi's Theory of Low Self-Control," *Criminology* 43 (November 2005), pp. 116–1197.

72. Christiansen, "A Preliminary Study of Criminality among Twins," pp. 89–108.

73. Edwin H. Sutherland and Donald R. Cressey, *Criminology,* 10th ed. (New York: Lippincott, 1978).

74. D. J. West and D. P. Farrington, *Who Becomes Delinquent?* (London: Heinemann, 1973).

75. Lis Kirkegaard-Sorensen and Sarnoff A. Mednick, "A Prospective Study of Predictors of Criminality: Intelligence," in *Biosocial Basis of Criminal Behavior,* edited by Sarnoff A. Mednick and Karl O. Christiansen (New York: Gardner Press, 1977).

76. Robert A. Gordon, "Prevalence: The Rare Datum in Delinquency Measurement and Its Implications for the Theory of Delinquency," in *The Juvenile Justice System,* edited by Malcolm Klein (Beverly Hills, Calif.: Sage, 1976), pp. 201–284.

77. Robert A. Gordon, "IQ—Commensurability of Black–White Differences in Crime and Delinquency." Paper presented at the Annual Meeting of the American Psychological Association (Washington, D.C.: August 1986), p. 1.

78. Travis Hirschi and Michael Hindelang, "Intelligence and Delinquency: A Revisionist Review," *American Sociological Review* 42 (1977), pp. 471–486.

79. James Q. Wilson and Richard J. Herrnstein, *Crime and Human Nature,* pp. 166–167.

80. For a study that supported the school performance model over the IQ/LD connection, see David A. Ward and Charles R. Tittle, "IQ and Delinquency: A Test of Two Competing Explanations," *Journal of Quantitative Criminology* 10 (1994), pp. 189–200.

81. Hans Eysenck, "The Technology of Consent," *New Scientist* 26 (June 1969), p. 689.

82. Hans Eysenck, *Fact and Fiction in Psychology* (Harmondsworth, England: Penguin, 1965), pp. 260–261.

83. See Diana H. Fishbein, "Biological Perspectives in Criminology," *Criminology* 28 (1990), p. 27–72.

84. Diana H. Fishbein and Robert W. Thatcher, "New Diagnostic Methods in Criminology: Assessing Organic Sources of Behavioral Disorders," *Journal of Research in Crime and Delinquency* 23 (August 1986), pp. 240–241.

85. R. R. Monroe, *Brain Dysfunction in Aggressive Criminals* (Lexington, Mass.: D.C. Heath, 1987).

86. W. W. Surwillo, "The Electroencephalogram and Childhood Aggression," *Aggressive Behavior* 6 (1980), pp. 9–18.

87. Fishbein and Thatcher, "New Diagnostic Methods in Criminology," pp. 252–259.

88. F. A. Elliott, "Neurological Aspects of Antisocial Behavior," in *The Psychopath,* edited by W. H. Reid (New York:

Bruner/Mazel, 1978); V. E. Krynicki, "Cerebral Dysfunction in Repetitively Assaultive Adolescents," *Journal of Nervous and Mental Disease* 166 (1978), pp. 59–67; F. Spellacy, "Neuropsychological Differences between Violent and Nonviolent Adolescents," *Journal of Clinical Psychology* 33 (1977), pp. 966–969; F. Spellacy, "Neuropsychological Discrimination between Violent and Nonviolent Men," *Journal of Clinical Psychology* 34 (1978), pp. 49–52.

89. Elizabeth Kandel and Sarnoff A. Mednick, "Perinatal Complications Predict Violent Offending," *Criminology* 29 (1991), p. 519.

90. S. Litt, "Perinatal Complications and Criminality." In *Proceedings,* 80th Annual Convention of the American Psychological Association in Washington, D.C. (1972); D. Mungas, "An Empirical Analysis of Specific Syndromes of Violent Behavior," *Journal of Nervous and Mental Disease* 17 (1983), pp. 354–361.

91. Kandel and Mednick, "Perinatal Complications Predict Violent Offending," p. 519.

92. Curt R. Bartol and Anne M. Bartol, *Delinquency and Justice: A Psychosocial Approach,* 2nd ed. (Upper Saddle River, N.J.: Prentice-Hall, 1998), p. 89.

93. Attention Deficit Disorder (ADD) webpage, www.dg58 .dupage.kl2il.usx/counselors/add.htm, accessed July 15, 2004.

94. MTA Cooperative Group, "A 14-Month Randomized Clinical Trail of Treatment Strategies for Attention Deficit Hyperactivity Disorder," *Archives of General Psychiatry* 56 (1999), p. 12.

95. Karen Stern, "A Treatment Study of Children with Attention Deficit Hyperactivity Disorder," *OJJDP Fact Sheet* #20 (May 2001).

96. Karen V. Unger, "Learning Disability and Juvenile Delinquency," *Journal of Juvenile and Family Courts* 29 (1978), pp. 25–30.

97. Sharyn Neuwirth, *Learning Disabilities* (Washington, D.C.: National Institute of Mental Health, 1993), p. 3.

98. Ibid.

99. Donald Shoemaker, *Theories of Delinquency,* 5th ed. (New York: Oxford, 2005), pp. 35–36.

100. Shah and Roth, "Biological and Psychophysiological Factors in Delinquency."

101. Among the research supporting the link between LD and delinquency is A. Berman, "Delinquents Are Disabled: An Innovative Approach to the Prevention and Treatment of Juvenile Delinquency." Final report on the Neuropsychology Diagnostic Laboratory at the Rhode Island Training School, December 1974. One of the studies that do not show this link is Paul K. Broader et al., "Further Observations on the Link between Learning Disabilities and Juvenile Delinquency," *Journal of Educational Psychology* 73 (1981), p. 838.

102. Abraham Hoffer was one of the early pioneers in this area. See Abraham Hoffer, "The Relation of Crime to Nutrition," *Humanist in Canada* 8 (1975), pp. 3–9.

103. S. Schoenthaler and I. Bier, "The Effect of Vitamin–Mineral Supplementation on Juvenile Delinquency among American Schoolchildren: A Randomized Double-Blind Placebo-Controlled Trial," *The Journal of Alternative and Complementary Medicine: Research on Paradigm, Practice and Policy* 6 (2000), pp. 7–18.

104. Herbert Needleman, Julie Riess, Michael Tobin, Gretchen Biesecker, and Joel Greenhouse, "Bone Lead Level and Delinquent Behavior," *Journal of Medical Association* 275 (1996), pp. 363–369.

105. Paul Stretesky and Michael Lynch, "The Relationship between Lead Exposure and Homicide," *Archives of Pediatric Adolescent Medicine* 155 (2001), pp. 579–582.

106. Sigmund Freud, *An Outline of Psychoanalysis,* translated by James Strachey (1940; reprint, New York: W. W. Norton, 1963).

107. Ibid.

108. Ibid.

109. LaMar T. Empey, *American Delinquency: Its Meaning and Construction* (Homewood, Ill.: Dorsey Press, 1982), pp. 172–173.

110. Hervey Cleckley, *The Mask of Sanity,* 3rd ed. (St. Louis: Mosby, 1955), pp. 382–417.

111. See Kathleen M. Heide, "Parents Who Get Killed and the Children Who Kill Them," *Journal of Interpersonal Violence* 8 (December 1993), pp. 531–544.

112. William Healy, *Twenty-Five Years of Child Guidance,* Studies from the Institute of Juvenile Research, Series C. no. 256 (Chicago: Illinois Department of Public Welfare, 1934), pp. 14–15.

113. August Aichhorn, *Wayward Youth* (New York: Viking Press, 1963).

114. Kate Friedlander, *The Psychoanalytic Approach to Juvenile Delinquency* (London: Routledge and Kegan Paul, 1947).

115. Marvin Zuckerman, *Sensation Seeking Beyond the Optimal Level of Arousal* (Hillsdale, N.J.: Lawrence Erlbaum, 1979), p. 10.

116. Ibid.

117. Frederick Thrasher, *The Gang* (Chicago: University of Chicago Press, 1936).

118. Henry D. McKay, "The Neighborhood and Child Conduct," *Annals of the American Academy of Political and Social Science* 261 (1949), pp. 32–41; P. Tappan, *Juvenile Delinquency* (New York: McGraw-Hill, 1949), and A. Cohen, "The Delinquent Subculture," in *The Sociology of Crime and Delinquency,* 2nd ed., edited by M. Wolfgang, L. Savitz, and N. Johnston (New York: Wiley, 1970).

119. J. J. Tobias, "The Affluent Suburban Male Delinquent," *Crime and Delinquency* 16 (1970), pp. 273–279.

120. M. J. Hindelang, "The Relationship of Self-Reported Delinquency to Scales of the CPI and MMPI," *Journal of Criminal Law, Criminology and Police Science* 63 (1972), pp. 75–81.

121. Helene Raskin White, Erich W. Labouvie, and Marsha E. Bates, "The Relationship between Sensation Seeking and Delinquency: A Longitudinal Analysis," *Journal of Research in Crime and Delinquency* 22 (August 1985), pp. 195–211.

122. Paul F. Cromwell, James N. Olson, and D'Aunn Wester Avary, *Breaking and Entering: An Ethnographic Analysis of Burglary* (Newbury Park, Calif.: Sage, 1991); and Jack Katz, *Seductions of Crime: Moral and Sensual Attractions in Doing Evil* (New York: Basic Books, 1988).

123. Walter R. Gove, "Why We Do What We Do: A Biopsychosocial Theory of Human Motivation," *Social Forces* 73 (1994), pp. 374–375.

124. Ibid., p. 388.

125. Katz, *Seductions of Crime,* p. 9.

126. Bill McCarthy, "Not Just 'For the Thrill of It': An Instrumentalist Elaboration of Katz's Explanation of Sneaky Thrill Property Crimes," *Criminology* 33 (November 1995), p. 519. For other studies that have identified the importance of sensual experience, see S. Lyng, "Edgework: A Social Psychological Analysis of Voluntary Risk Taking," *American Journal of Sociology* 95 (1990), pp. 851–856; and William J. Miller, "Edgework: A Model for Understanding Juvenile Delinquency." A paper presented at the Academy of Criminal Justice Sciences Annual Meeting in Albuquerque, New Mexico (March 1998).

127. Avshalom Caspi, Terrie E. Moffitt, Phil A. Silva, Magda Stouthamer-Loeber, Robert F. Krueger, and Pamela S. Schmutte, "Are Some People Crime-Prone? Replications of the Personality–Crime Relationships across Countries, Genders, Races, and Methods," *Criminology* 32 (1994), p. 165. See also Douglas T. Kenrick and David C. Funder, "Profiting from Controversy: Lessons from the Person–Situation Debate," *American Psychologist* 43 (1988), pp. 23–34.

128. Caspi et al., "Are Some People Crime-Prone?" p. 165.

129. Sheldon Glueck and Eleanor Glueck, *Unraveling Juvenile Delinquency* (Cambridge: Harvard University Press for the Commonwealth Fund, 1950).

130. J. J. Conger and W. C. Miller, *Personality, Social Class, and Delinquency* (New York: Wiley, 1966).

131. The following studies on personality and crime are found in Caspi et al., "Are Some People Crime-Prone?" pp. 164–165; Hans J. Eysenck, *Crime and Personality* (London: Routledge and Kegan Paul, 1977).

132. Marvin Zuckerman, "Personality in the Third Dimension: A Psychobiological Approach," *Personality and Individual Differences* 10 (1989), pp. 391–418.

133. C. Robert Cloninger, "A Systematic Method for Clinical Description and Classification of Personality Variants," *Archives of General Psychiatry* 44 (1987), pp. 573–588.

134. Caspi et al., "Are Some People Crime-Prone?" p. 163.

135. Ibid.

136. Ibid.

137. Joshua D. Miller and Donald Lynam, "Structural Models of Personality and Their Relation to Antisocial Behavior: A Meta-Analytic Review," *Criminology* 39 (2001), p. 780.

138. Richard L. Jenkins, "Delinquency and a Treatment Philosophy," in *Crime, Law and Corrections,* edited by Ralph Slovenko (Springfield, Ill.: Charles C. Thomas, 1966), pp. 135–136.

139. Cleckley, *The Mask of Sanity,* pp. 382–417.

140. L. N. Robins, *Deviant Children Grown Up: A Sociological and Psychiatric Study of Sociopathic Personality* (Baltimore: Williams and Wilkins, 1966), p. 256.

141. L. N. Robins et al., "The Adult Psychiatric Status of Black Schoolboys," *Archives of General Psychiatry* 24 (1971), pp. 338–345.

142. Linda Mealey, "The Sociobiology of Sociopathy: An Integrated Evolutionary Model," *Behavioral and Brain Sciences* 18 (1995), pp. 523–540.

143. Wilson and Herrnstein, *Crime and Human Nature.*

144. Ibid.

145. Edgar Z. Friedenberg, "Solving Crime," *Readings: A Journal of Reviews* (March 1986), p. 21.

146. For a study that concluded it was impossible to determine significant differences between criminal and noncriminal personalities, see Karl Schuessler and Donald Cressey, "Personality Characteristics of Criminals," *American Journal of Sociology* 55 (1955), pp. 476–484. For an investigation that found statistical differences in 81 percent of the studies, see Gordon Waldo and Simon Dinitz, "Personality Attributes of the Criminal: An Analysis of Research Studies 1950–1965," *Journal of Research in Crime and Delinquency* 4 (1967), pp. 185–201. The latter study does warn that these studies are full of methodological weaknesses. For a study that replicated Waldo and Dinitz's study and found that between the years 1966 and 1975, 80 percent of personality tests showed significant differences between criminals and noncriminals, see David J. Tennenbaum, "Personality and Criminality: A Summary and Implications of the Literature," *Journal of Criminal Justice* 5 (1977), pp. 225–235.

147. See citations for these studies in Chapter 2.

148. Terrie E. Moffitt, Donald R. Lynam, and Phil A. Silva, "Neuropsychological Tests Predicted Persistent Male Delinquency," *Criminology* 32 (May 1994), p. 277.

149. Terrie E. Moffitt, "Adolescent-Limited and Life-Course-Persistent Antisocial Behavior: A Developmental Taxonomy," *Psychological Review* 100 (1993), p. 679.

150. Terrie E. Moffitt, "The Neuropsychology of Conduct Disorder," *Development and Psychopathology* 5 (1993); and Terrie E. Moffitt, Avshalom Caspi, N. Dickson, Phil A. Silva, and W. Stanton, "Childhood-Onset versus Adolescent-Onset Antisocial Conduct Problems in Males: Natural History from Ages 3 to 18," *Development and Psychopathology* 8 (1996), pp. 399–424.

151. Ibid. For research that tested Moffitt's model of adolescence-limited delinquency, see Alex R. Piquero and Timothy Brezina, "Testing Moffitt's Account of Adolescence-Limited Delinquency," *Criminology* 39 (May 2001), pp. 353–410. These researchers found from their data from the Youth-in-Transition survey that adolescence-limited delinquency is characterized by rebellious delinquency rather than aggressive delinquency. Andrea G. Donker, Wilma H. Smeenk, Peter H. van der Laan, and Frank C. Verhulat, using data from the South-Holland Study, found support for Moffitt's prediction on the stability of longitudinal antisocial behavior. See Donker, Smeenk, van der Laan, and Verhulst, "Individual Stability of Antisocial Behavior from Childhood to Adulthood: Testing the Stability Postulate of Moffitt's Developmental Theory," *Criminology* 41 (August 2003), pp. 593–609.

152. Terrie E. Moffitt, Avshalom Caspi, Michael Rutter, and Phil A. Silva, *Sex Differences in Antisocial Behavior* (Cambridge, England: Cambridge University Press, 2001).

153. Richard E. Tremblay, Frank Vitaro, Daniel Nagin, et al., "The Montreal Longitudinal and Experimental Study: Rediscovering the Power of Descriptions," in *Taking Stock of Delinquency: An Overview of Findings from Contemporary Longitudinal Studies,* edited by Terence P. Thornberry and Marvin D. Krohn (New York: Kluwer Academic/Plenum Publishers, 2003), pp. 205–206.

154. Ibid., p. 209.

155. Ibid., pp. 210–223.

156. Ibid., p. 243.

157. David P. Farrington, "Key Results from the First Forty Years

of the Cambridge Study in Delinquent Development," in *Taking Stock of Delinquency,* p. 137.

158. Ibid., p. 139.

159. Ibid., pp. 142–150.

160. This interview took place in February 2002.

161. Ibid., p. 174.

4

Social Structural Causes of Delinquency

> "When we speak of a delinquent subculture, we speak of a way of life that has somehow become traditional among certain groups in American society."

—Albert K. Cohen, *Delinquent Boys*

CHAPTER Objectives

AFTER READING THIS CHAPTER, YOU SHOULD BE ABLE TO ANSWER THE FOLLOWING QUESTIONS:

- How is cultural deviance theory related to lower-class delinquency?

- What is the relationship between socially disorganized communities and delinquent behavior?

- How does strain propel juveniles into delinquent behavior?

- What delinquent behavior explains homelessness among youth?

119

On April 14, 2006, the Manhattan District Attorney's office announced that four Harlem teenagers accused of killing a New York University student by chasing him into a car's path during a robbery attempt would be tried as juveniles rather than adults.

The teenagers—two are thirteen and two are fifteen—were initially arraigned as adults on second-degree murder charges in the death of the student, Broderick J. Hehman, age twenty. But prosecutors found that there was not enough evidence to support the underlying theory of "depraved indifference" to life that a second-degree murder charge requires.

Prosecutors did persuade the grand jury to charge the boys with seven lesser charges—including felony murder, manslaughter and attempted robbery.

Had they been tried as adults and convicted of second-degree murder, the boys would have faced sentences of up to life in prison. Assistant District Attorney Joel J. Seidemann, described the crime in Harlem—in which Mr. Hehman was struck by a Mercedes-Benz on 125th Street near Park Avenue—as particularly heinous. He also defended the prosecution's initial attempt to seek to have the juveniles tried as adults. He said the boys held Hehman in a bearhug, punched the side of his head and tried to rob him. Hehman broke free, and the boys chased him into the street.

Seidemann said the boys stood on the corner and laughed while watching as Mr. Hehman was hit by the car, then flew into the air and smashed headfirst into the windshield, shattering it.

"They didn't call for an ambulance," Mr. Seidermann said of the attackers. "They didn't call for help. Rather, they stood on the street corner and laughed as he lay in the road."

Hehman, who lived on the Upper East Side, was a junior majoring in urban studies at New York University. He was walking to a friend's apartment to play video games when he was attacked.

Adapted from Anemona Hartocollis, "4 Harlem Boys Will Be Tried as Juveniles," *New York Times*, April 15, 2006. Copyright © 2006 by The New York Times Co. Reprinted with permission.

social structure

The relatively stable formal and informal arrangements that characterize a society, including its economic arrangements, social institutions, and its values and norms.

Chapters 4 through 6 examine sociological explanations for delinquency. This chapter looks closely at features of the social environment, termed **social structure**, that influence young people, causing some of them to commit delinquent acts.

The term *social structure* can have a variety of meanings. As used by sociologists, it can refer to entities or groups in relation to each other, to relatively enduring patterns of behavior and relationship within social systems, or to social institutions and norms embedded in social systems in such a way that they shape the behavior of actors within those systems.

Many of the social structural elements that we'll examine in this chapter could be found in the lives of the four youngsters in this chapter's opening story. They came from socially disorganized surroundings and, as lower-class youths, were part of a peer culture that had little stake in conventional values. Indeed, the pressure they felt to have more money, combined with their lack of ability to legitimately acquire it, was probably the determining factor in their attempt at robbery.

According to social structural theorists, explanations that focus on the individual fail to grasp the underlying social and cultural conditions that give rise to delinquent behavior. These theorists believe that the overall crime picture reflects conditions requiring collective social solutions. They urge that social reform, not individual counseling, be given the highest priority in efforts to reduce crime.

Elijah Anderson and the Code of the Street

Elijah Anderson's *Code of the Streets* grew out of the ethnographic work Anderson did in two urban communities in Philadelphia. The author focuses on the theme of interpersonal violence between and among inner-city youths. He asks why so many inner-city youths are inclined to commit aggression and violence toward one another—and he answers the question by suggesting that in economically depressed and crime- and drug-ridden pockets of the city, the rule of civil law has been severely weakened and has been replaced by a "code of the street."

This code of the street has at its base a set of informal rules, or prescriptions for behavior, that are organized around a desperate search for respect. In this context youth understand respect as being treated "right" or being granted their "props" (or proper due). In the street culture, especially among young people, respect is hard won, can easily be lost, and so must be constantly guarded. Respect may be viewed as a form of social capital that is very valuable, especially when other forms of capital have been denied or are unavailable.

Respect and identity have come to be expressed in the concept of "manhood." Manhood on the street implies physicality and a certain ruthlessness. Manhood and respect both require a sense of control or being in charge. To gain respect is to manifest nerve. To avoid being bothered, both decent and delinquent youths must communicate through behavior, words, and gestures that "if you mess with me, there will be a severe physical penalty—coming from me. I'm man enough to make you pay."

This code of the street, contends Anderson, is found in an environment of persistent poverty and deprivation that includes alienation from society's institutions, notably that of criminal justice. The code emerges when the influence of the police ends and youth feel that they must take on personal responsibility for their own safety, resulting in a kind of "people's law" based on "street justice."

■ **Do you believe that this code of the street is found in other urban settings? What is the relationship between social disorganization, poverty, and such a code? Is there anything that can be done to reduce the effects of the code on social relations, especially violence, in urban settings?**

The causes of delinquency, as suggested by social structural theorists, include the social and cultural environment in which adolescents grow up and/or the subcultural groups in which they choose to become involved. See Social World of the Delinquent 4.1 for a look at Elijah Anderson's *Code of the Streets*, an influential book tracing the relationship between the structural breakdown of the community and the disorders of crime and drug use.[1]

Social structural theorists typically use official statistics as proof of their claim that forces such as social disorganization, cultural deviance, status frustration, and social mobility are so powerful that they induce lower-class youths to become involved in delinquent behavior. This chapter will examine several of these perspectives.

■ Social Disorganization Theory

Social disorganization can be defined "as the inability of a community structure to realize the common values of its residents and maintain effective social control."[2] **Social disorganization theory** suggests that macrosocial forces (e.g., migration, segregation, structural transformation of the economy, and housing discrimination) interact with community-level factors (concentrated poverty, family disruption, residential turnover) to impede social organization. This sociological viewpoint focuses attention on the structural characteristics and mediating processes of community social organization that help explain crime, while also recognizing the larger historical, political, and social forces that shape local communities.[3]

The intellectual antecedents of social disorganization theory can be traced to the work of Emile Durkheim; William I. Thomas and Florian Znaniecki; Robert E. Park,

social disorganization theory
An approach which posits that juvenile delinquency results when social control among the traditional primary groups, such as the family and the neighborhood, breaks down because of social disarray within the community.

Ernest W. Burgess, and Roderick D. McKenzie; S. P. Breckinridge and Edith Abbott; and Frederick M. Thrasher. In Durkheim's view, anomie, or "normlessness," resulted from society's failure to provide adequate regulation of its members' attitudes and behaviors. Loss of regulation was particularly likely when society and its members experienced rapid change and laws did not keep pace.[4] To Thomas and Znaniecki, social disorganization reflected the influences of an urban, industrial setting on the ability of immigrant subcultures, especially parents, to socialize and effectively control their children.[5] From Park, Burgess, and McKenzie came the idea of the ecological processes of invasion, dominance, and succession in the development of the city.[6] Breckinridge and Abbott contributed the idea of plotting "delinquency maps."[7] Thrasher viewed the gang as a substitute socializing institution whose function was to provide order (social organization) where there was none (social disorganization).[8]

Shaw and McKay

Social disorganization theory was developed by Clifford R. Shaw and Henry D. McKay during the first half of the twentieth century. Shaw and McKay were farm boys who came to Chicago to undertake graduate work in sociology at the University of Chicago. Both were born and brought up in rural areas of the Midwest: Shaw was from an Indiana crossroads that barely constituted a town, and McKay hailed from the prairie regions of South Dakota.[9] The rural settings from which they came made Shaw and McKay acutely aware of the importance of community life in which "people were brought together by certain ties of long acquaintance and friendship" and "by certain common beliefs and interests."[10] In such communities people would join together "to meet a crisis or disaster when the occasion arose."[11]

> " Social disorganization theory was developed by Clifford R. Shaw and Henry D. McKay during the first half of the twentieth century. "

Jon Snodgrass suggests that perhaps the glaring contrast between the order of their home communities and the disorder of Chicago during the early decades of the twentieth century so intrigued Shaw and McKay that they spent their careers examining the effects of social disorganization on delinquency. Snodgrass adds that Shaw's method of delinquency prevention was "actually an effort to create numerous replicas of his agrarian home community in the urban environs of Chicago."[12]

Shaw and McKay extended social disorganization theory by focusing specifically on the social characteristics of the community as a cause of delinquency.[13] Their pioneering investigations established that delinquency varied in inverse proportion to the distance from the center of the city, that it varied inversely with socioeconomic status, and that delinquency rates in a residential area persisted regardless of changes in racial and ethnic composition of the area.[14]

Social Disorganization and the Community Shaw and McKay viewed juvenile delinquency as resulting from the breakdown of social control among the traditional primary groups, such as the family and the neighborhood, because of the social disorganization of the community. Rapid industrialization, urbanization, and immigration processes contributed to the disorganization of the community. Delinquent behavior, then, became an alternative mode of socialization through which youths who were part of disorganized communities were attracted to deviant lifestyles.[15] The delinquent values and traditions, replacing traditional ones, were passed from one generation to the next.

Shaw and McKay turned to ecology to show this relationship between social disorganization and delinquency. Park and Burgess had earlier used the concept of ecology in explaining the growth of cities. Burgess, for example, suggested that cities do not merely grow at their edges, but rather have a tendency to expand radially from their centers in patterns of concentric circles, each moving gradually outward.[16] Figure 4.1 is a diagram of the growth zones as Burgess envisioned them.

A former Hispanic gang member in a wheelchair counsels teens at a Los Angeles school.
■ **How might the social environment of a community contribute to delinquency?**

In 1929, Shaw reported that marked variations in rates of school truancy, juvenile delinquency, and adult criminality existed among different areas in Chicago. These rates varied inversely with the distance from the center of the city; that is, the nearer a given locality was to the center of the city, the higher its rates of delinquency and crime. Shaw also found that areas of concentrated crime maintained their high rates over a long period, even when the composition of the population changed markedly.[17] In a study Shaw and McKay performed for the National Commission on Law Observance and Enforcement, they reported that this basic ecological finding was true for several other cities also.[18]

In 1942, Shaw and McKay published their classic work *Juvenile Delinquency and Urban Areas*, which developed these ecological insights in greater scope and depth.[19] What Shaw and McKay had done was to study males brought into the Cook County Juvenile Court on delinquency charges from 1900 to 1906, 1917 to 1923, and 1927 to 1933. They discovered that over this thirty-three-year period, the vast majority of the delinquent boys came either from an area adjacent to the central business and industrial areas or from neighborhoods along two forks of the Chicago River. Then, applying Burgess's concentric zone

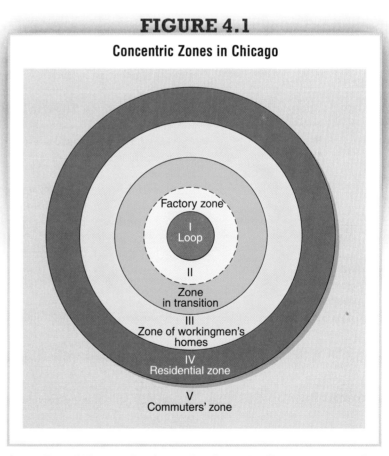

FIGURE 4.1

Concentric Zones in Chicago

I Loop
Factory zone
II
Zone in transition
III
Zone of workingmen's homes
IV
Residential zone
V
Commuters' zone

Source: Ernest W. Burgess, "The Growth of the City," in *The City,* edited by Robert E. Park, Ernest W. Burgess, and Roderick D. McKenzie (Chicago: University of Chicago Press, 1928), p. 51. Reprinted by permission.

hypothesis of urban growth, they constructed a series of concentric circles, like the circles on a target, with the bull's-eye in the central city. Measuring delinquency rates by zone and by areas within the zones, they found that in all three periods the highest rates of delinquency were in Zone I (the central city), the next highest in Zone II (next to the central city), and so forth, in progressive steps outward to the lowest in Zone V. Significantly, although the delinquency rates changed from one period to the next, the relationship among the different zones remained constant, even though in some neighborhoods the ethnic compositions of the population had changed totally. During the first decade of the century, the largest portion of the population was German or Irish, but thirty years later it was Polish and Italian.[20]

In analyzing the official data, Shaw and McKay found that several patterns of events were related to high rates of delinquency. First, landlords allowed residential buildings to deteriorate in anticipation of the expansion of industry. Second, as a result of the anticipated displacement of residential dwellings by industry, the population began to decrease. Third, the percentage of families in the area that received financial aid from the United Charities and the Jewish Charities increased. Fourth, lower-class African Americans and foreign-born individuals were attracted to these inner-city areas.[21]

Opportunity Structure and Delinquency   Shaw and McKay eventually refocused their analysis from the influence of social disorganization of the community to the importance of economics on high rates of delinquency. They found that the economic and occupational structure of the larger society was more influential in the rise of delinquent behavior than was the social life of the local community. They concluded that the reason members of lower-class groups remained in the inner-city community was less a reflection of their newness of arrival and their lack of acculturation to American institutions than a function of their class position in society.[22]

The consequence of this **differential opportunity structure** led to a conflict of values in local communities; some residents embraced illegitimate standards of behavior, whereas others maintained allegiance to conventional values. Delinquent groups were characterized by their own distinctive standards, and Shaw and McKay became increasingly involved in examining the process through which delinquents came to learn and to pass on these standards.[23]

Cultural Transmission Theories   Shaw and McKay also elaborated on social disorganization theory in arguing that delinquent behavior became an alternative mode of socialization through which youths who were part of disorganized communities were attracted to deviant lifestyles.[24] This line of thought became known as the cultural deviance component of social disorganization theory.

Shaw and McKay further contended that the delinquent values and traditions that replaced traditional social standards were not the property of any one ethnic or racial group but were culturally transmitted from one generation to the next.[25] As evidence in support of this **cultural transmission theory**, these researchers found that certain inner-city areas continued to have the highest delinquency rates in Chicago, despite shifts of nearly all of these areas' populations.

Shaw and McKay assumed that juvenile and adult gangs in these areas accounted for the transmission of this tradition of delinquency. Figure 4.2 diagrams the theoretical constructs of Shaw and McKay's social disorganization theory.

Evaluation of Shaw and McKay's Disorganization Theory   Few studies in the area of delinquency have been as influential in the development of research, theory, and social action as those of social disorganization theory. Let's survey the reasons why social disorganization theory has been so influential in the development of criminological theory.

- First, Shaw and McKay's studies addressed the problem of crime in terms of multiple levels of analysis. They shifted attention away from individual characteris-

differential opportunity structure

Differences in economic and occupational opportunities open to members of different socioeconomic classes.

cultural transmission theory

An approach which holds that areas of concentrated crime maintain their high rates over a long period, even when the composition of the population changes rapidly, because delinquent "values" become cultural norms and are passed from one generation to the next.

FIGURE 4.2

Shaw and McKay's Social Disorganization Theory

Socially disorganized neighborhood → Failure of informal social controls → Increased gang activity → Cultural transmission of delinquent traditions → Increased delinquent activity

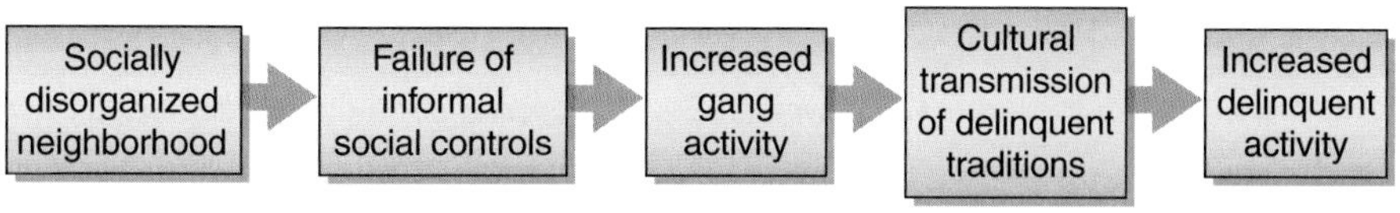

tics of delinquents and nondelinquents and toward group traditions in delinquency and the influence of the larger community. Thus, Shaw and McKay provided a theoretical framework bridging sociological and social psychological explanations.[26]

■ The fact that Shaw and McKay's model incorporates specific images of the delinquent at each stage of social change permits such bridging. Shaw and McKay viewed delinquents as "disaffiliated" in the social disorganization stage, for delinquents were part of disorganized communities and as such were alienated from the values and norms of the larger society. They saw delinquents in the functionalist stage as "frustrated social climbers," primarily because these youths were poor and longed for the cultural goals that could be achieved only through illegitimate means. Shaw and McKay described delinquents in the third, or interactionist, stage as "aggrieved citizens." Delinquents were faced with cultural groups in their own communities that provided social acceptance but also involved them in socially unacceptable behavior. To gain acceptance among peers, then, meant courting rejection by the larger society and punishment by its social control agencies.[27]

■ Shaw and McKay's social disorganization theory also contributed to a rediscovery of the importance of macrolevels and the community in studies of delinquency. This rediscovery has led to the conclusion that an adequate understanding of the causes of illegal behavior requires an examination of the social structure, the individual, and other social contexts (such as primary groups) that mediate between the individual and that structure.[28] In several studies contextual analysis has examined the effects of community structure on individual behavior and the interaction of community and individual/familial characteristics.[29] See Focus on Social Policy 4.1 regarding "collective efficacy" and the Project on Human Development in Chicago Neighborhoods.

> Few studies in the area of delinquency have been as influential as those of social disorganization theory.

■ Shaw and McKay further contributed important insights on gang formation. They saw the delinquent gang as a normal response to slum conditions and the social deprivations of local environments. Shaw and McKay regarded delinquent behavior as an understandable choice given the lack of legitimate opportunity for lower-class families in the inner city.

■ Moreover, Shaw and McKay's theory also has influenced research on how people and institutions adapt to their environment.[30] In the 1980s and 1990s, several studies examined the relationship between ecological change and crime and delinquency rates in Cleveland and San Diego,[31] Baltimore,[32] and Racine, Wisconsin.[33]

■ Finally, recent examination of the social disorganization perspective has opened up exciting new avenues of research inquiry that to some extent have gone beyond Shaw and McKay's original work. One area that has received extensive examination concerns effects of neighborhood contexts on motivational processes that lead to the commission of illegal behavior.[34] Other areas of research include an expansion of social disorganization theory to include cultural

FOCUS ON
Social Policy 4.1

Project on Human Development in Chicago Neighborhoods

Robert J. Sampson and colleagues developed the concept of "collective efficacy" as characteristics of a community that they felt would work together to prevent and control crime. A community is high on collective efficacy to the extent that residents have mutual trust, share values, and have a disposition to intervene for the public good. Sampson and colleagues contended that the most important influence on a neighborhood's crime is neighbors' willingness to act, when necessary or needed, for one another's benefit, and especially for the benefit of one another's children. Several studies have found that collective efficacy does function to mediate much of the effect of such community structure variables as high prevalence of poverty, unemployment, single-parent families, and racial/ethnic heterogeneity.

The Project on Human Development in Chicago Neighborhoods, directed by Felton Earls and other researchers from the Harvard School of Public Health, including Sampson, has two main goals: to develop a coordinated approach to the study of human development and to enrich policy planning with new prevention, treatment, and rehabilitation strategies. The hopeful end result will be to enrich the understanding of collective efficacy in community life and to be helpful in how more communities can attain such collective efficacy.

This large-scale, interdisciplinary study of the complex influences exerted on human development is one in which the National Institute of Justice has so far spent over $18 million; the MacArthur foundation has spent another $23.6 million on the project. Jerome Travis, director of the National Institute of Justice from 1994 to 2000, noted, "It is far and away the most important research insight in the last decade. I think it will shape policy for the next generation."

The city of Chicago was selected as the research site because of its diversity in race, ethnicity, and social class. Data were collected in three waves: 1994 to 1997, 1997 to 1999, and 2000 to 2001. Researchers collapsed 847 census tracts into 347 neighborhood clusters (NC) based on seven groupings of racial/ethnic composition and three levels of socioeconomic status. The NCs were designed to be ecologically meaningful, composed of contiguous census tracts, and based on both geographic boundaries and knowledge of Chicago neighborhoods. Each NC was composed of around 8,000 people.

Data collection was conducted based on four separate components that focused on a variety of individual and community characteristics.

- *Community Survey:* The dynamic structure of the local community, neighborhood organizational and political structures, cultural values, informal and formal social control, and social cohesion were measured.

- *Systematic Social Observation:* A standardized approach for directly observing the physical, social, and economic characteristics of neighborhoods, one block at a time, was applied to 80 of the 343 NCs (i.e., over 23,000 blocks). These observations were coded to assess neighborhood characteristics such as land use, housing, litter, graffiti, and social interactions.

- *Longitudinal Cohort Study:* An accelerated longitudinal design with seven cohorts were separated by three-year intervals. These randomly selected cohorts of children, adolescents, young adults, and their primary caregivers were followed over a period of seven years to study changes in their personal characteristics and the circumstances of their lives.

- *Infant Assessment Unit:* As part of the Longitudinal Cohort Study, 412 infants from the birth cohort and their primary caregivers were studied during Wave 1 (1994 to 1997) to examine the effects of prenatal and postnatal conditions on their growth and health, cognitive abilities, and motor skills.

As the immense data gathered by this project are analyzed in the years to come, it is hoped that they will provide resources and directions for policymakers not only in Chicago but also for other urban areas to develop more of what Sampson and colleagues call "collective efficacy."

■ **Interestingly, this concept of "collective efficacy" is what Shaw had in mind when he developed the Chicago Area Projects in the early 1930s. Do you believe it is possible to develop the characteristics of collective efficacy in contemporary Chicago neighborhoods? How can the data from this project be helpful in this process of renewal in other urban neighborhoods across the nation?**

Sources: From www.icpsr.umich.edu/PHDCN. Reprinted with permission from the Inter-university Consortium for Political and Social Research. For more information on collective efficacy, see Robert J. Sampson, "The Embeddedness of Child and Adolescent Development: A Community-Level Perspective on Urban Violence," in Joan McCord, ed., *Childhood Violence in the Inner City* (New York: Cambridge, 1997); Robert J. Sampson, Jeffrey Morenoff, and Felton Earls, "Beyond Social Capital: Spatial Dynamics of Collective Efficacy for Children," *American Sociological Review* 64 (1999), pp. 663–660; and Robert J. Sampson, Stephen W. Raudenbush, and Felton Earls, "Neighborhoods and Violent Crime: A Multilevel Study of Collective Efficacy," *Science* 277 (1997), pp. 918–924.

According to sociologist Albert Cohen, the destruction of property is a consequence of reaction formation, in which lower-class youths respond to the strain of being held to the standards of middle-class culture. ■ **What about middle-class youths who commit such acts? Does Cohen's theory hold true for them, or can their acts be attributed to other factors?**

disorganization;[35] the means by which routine activity theory and social disorganization theory can be integrated;[36] and the relationships among neighborhood disorder, religiosity, and drug use.[37]

On the negative side, however, Robert J. Burisk Jr. has evaluated social disorganization theory and summarizes the main criticisms of this perspective as follows:

■ Critics generally argue that the aggregate nature of group or neighborhood findings does not allow us to make predictions concerning individual behavior.
■ Shaw and McKay's analysis of delinquent behavior was based on official statistics, and (as Chapter 2 emphasized) official rates of delinquency tend to distort the extent and nature of delinquent behavior.
■ The lack of conceptual clarity in this perspective has led to confusion and rejection. For example, critics charge that classic social disorganization theories have often used delinquency rates as "both an example of disorganization and something caused by disorganization."[38]
■ Critics also assert that Shaw and McKay assumed stable ecological structures that no longer exist in urban settings.
■ The failure to take seriously the importance of power in community organization appears to many to be insensitive to the current realities of political and social life.[39]

Social disorganization theory lost much of its vitality as a prominent criminological theory in the late 1960s and through the 1970s, because theory and research in that period focused primarily on individual rather than group and community characteristics.[40] Despite the criticisms it received, however, social disorganization theory experienced "a quiet, but significant revival" in the 1980s and later.[41] As the reemergence of interest in social disorganization theory shows, the work of Shaw and McKay has had an enduring impact on the study of delinquency in the United States.

Cities Grapple with Crime by Kids

MINNEAPOLIS — Barely 15, the skinny youth from the city's troubled North Side already had a long rap sheet.

His juvenile court record included citations for 19 offenses, dating back three years. Last Thursday, police pulled up beside him with a warrant to arrest him again: He allegedly had violated the terms of his probation from a robbery citation last month by cutting off a leg bracelet that allowed Hennepin County authorities to monitor his whereabouts.

After a chase on foot through a crowded city park, "Killer," one of several aliases the youth uses, was back in handcuffs. "I am a maniac!" he screamed, declaring his affiliation with a local gang. "I am a maniac!"

The fugitive, whose name was not released by police because he is a juvenile, was among eight frequent-offender youths pursued last week by a team of officers from the Minneapolis Police Department, the county Probation Department and the U.S. Marshals Service.

The team was formed last month as part of a crackdown on violent young offenders who represent an increasing problem at a time when crime rates are ticking upward.

Rise in Crime

After nearly a decade in which violent-crime rates fell or were stable throughout the USA, the FBI reported last month that there was a 2.5% rise last year in violent crimes, which include homicides, rapes, robberies and aggravated assaults.

Here and in cities across the nation—including Washington, Milwaukee and Boston—police are linking the increase to a growing problem: Crime by kids as young as 10, many of whom have been recruited by gangs.

Budget cuts may be factor   The reasons for rising crime among juveniles are complex.

Tight local budgets and reduced federal funding for police, along with new anti-terrorism duties, have stretched police departments and led to cuts in community programs for youths. Historically low crime rates in recent years often have been linked to a booming economy. Now, with the economy slowing, officials in several cities are tying poverty and financial uncertainty to rising crime, particularly among juveniles.

Milwaukee Mayor Tom Barrett says 41% of the children in his city are in households in which the annual income is below the federal poverty line, about $20,000 for a family of four. "A lot of young people have no hope in their lives," Barrett says, and many "think nothing of carrying a gun."

"We have a lot of young people involved in robbery," Milwaukee Deputy Police Chief Brian O'Keefe says. "Some are 10 and 11. A lot of the kids we see never know anything but violence."

Many officials, including Boston police Superintendent Paul Joyce, say the release of thousands of felons who were imprisoned during drug crackdowns in the 1990s also has become a significant factor in boosting juvenile crime.

Joyce says just-released gang members, seeking to stake out turf without getting arrested again, have recruited juveniles to carry weapons for them or make drug deliveries. Earlier this year, Joyce says, Boston police found a 13-year-old boy with a handgun, standing with a 23-year-old gang member.

"The young kids don't think about the consequences of their actions," Joyce says.

"We have videotapes of young children working as mules for gang members," says Tom Cochran, executive director of the U.S. Conference of Mayors. The group has hosted two summits during the past year to discuss the gang problem and plans to examine juvenile violence when it meets in September.

Juveniles "are carrying the guns and the drugs for the gang leaders so [the leaders] can avoid prosecution," Cochran says. "This is a major problem."

In Minneapolis, police began looking for "Killer" early last week, after he removed the leg bracelet. Keeping the bracelet on was a condition of the youth's probation, Hennepin County probation officer Mick Sandin says. The group that rounded up the fugitive youths represents an effort to reduce a backlog of 500 juvenile arrest warrants that grew after budget cuts forced the closure of the police department's Juvenile Division in 2001. The division was re-established in May.

"Before now, the pursuit of juveniles had not been a high priority," says police Lt. Bryan Schafer, who heads the Juvenile Division. "That created a perception that nothing much happens to juveniles" who commit crimes. "So [adult gang members] began sending the kids

A Minneapolis police officer and a U.S. Marshall take a juvenile suspect into custody. Recent FBI data seem to show a rise in violent crime among juveniles, especially those living in urban environments. ■ **What might explain the increase?**

out to carry their guns, because they knew nothing would happen to them. We think we're changing that perception."

Since the fugitive-hunting team began work, many parents and family members of juvenile suspects have been reluctant to provide information to police, says police Sgt. Ron Stenerson, who leads the team.

That wasn't the case with "Killer," however. A concerned family member provided the tip that led to his capture by telling police they should search a park near his home.

Sandin spotted the youth at the park. When Stenerson called his name, the teenager turned toward the officers and then sprinted away. After running about 50 yards, he was hauled down by Deputy U.S. Marshal Justin Payton, who's training for a triathlon.

Witnesses told investigators that the youth had tossed a gun into some tall grass before he was chased, police Lt. Bryan Schafer says. Police found a loaded .38-caliber gun, and are investigating whether it belonged to the youth.

Proliferation of guns   Minneapolis Mayor R. T. Rybak, noting that the number of juveniles suspected in violent crimes jumped by 18% from 2004 to 2005, says a "shocking proliferation" of guns is partly to blame.

Rybak has recruited local businesses to fill gaps in community programs for young people, from evening recreation events to summer job placements and college tuition assistance. He says the key is "winning back" kids who have drifted into delinquency.

"The issue of hopelessness is what we are addressing."

Source: Kevin Johnson, "Cities Grapple with Crime by Kids," *USA Today,* July 13, 2006, p. 3A. Copyright © 2006 by *USA Today.* Reprinted with permission.

Cultural Deviance Theory and Delinquency

Social disorganization theory focused on the structural breakups of urban communities, but the next theory, **cultural deviance theory,** turns to the delinquent values that are found in some lower-class cultures. Cultural deviance theory is generally defined as viewing delinquent and criminal behavior as an expression of conformity to cultural values and norms that are in opposition to those of the larger society. According to Ruth Rosner Kornhauser, the necessary and sufficient cause of delinquency in cultural deviance models "is socialization to subcultural values condoning as right conduct what the controlling legal system defines as crime."[42]

Miller's Lower-Class Culture and Delinquent Values

In his version of cultural deviance theory, anthropologist Walter B. Miller argued that the motivation to become involved in delinquent behavior is endemic to lower-class culture:

> The cultural system which exerts the most direct influence on [delinquent] behavior is that of the lower-class community itself—a long-established, distinctively patterned tradition with an integrity of its own—rather than a so-called "delinquent subculture" which has arisen through conflict with middle-class culture and is oriented to the deliberate violation of middle-class norms.[43]

Web PLACES 4.1

Visit the Project on Human Development in Chicago Neighborhoods's (PHDCN) website via **www.justicestudies .com/WebPlaces**.

Focal Concerns of Lower-Class Culture   Miller argued that a set of **focal concerns of the lower class** characterizes this socioeconomic group. These concerns command widespread attention and a high degree of emotional involvement. They are trouble, toughness, smartness, excitement, fate, and autonomy.[44]

- *Trouble:* Miller contended that staying out of trouble represents a major challenge for lower-class citizens and that personal status is therefore often determined in terms of this law-abiding/non–law-abiding dimension. But which of the two qualities an individual values depends largely on the individual and his or her circumstances. A person may make an overt commitment to abiding by the law while giving a covert commitment to breaking the law. Miller adds that membership in adolescent gangs may be contingent on a commitment to the law-violating alternative.
- *Toughness:* Physical prowess, as demonstrated by strength and endurance, is valued in lower-class culture: In the eyes of lower-class boys, the tough guy who is hard, fearless, undemonstrative, and a good fighter is the ideal man. Miller contended that the intense concern over toughness is directly related to the fact that a significant proportion of lower-class males are reared in matriarchal households; he found a nearly obsessive concern with masculinity in these youths.
- *Smartness:* The capacity to outsmart, outfox, outwit, con, dupe, and "take" others is valued in lower-class culture; in addition, a man also must be able to avoid being outwitted, "taken," or duped himself. Smartness also is necessary if people are to achieve material goods and personal status without physical effort.
- *Excitement:* The search for excitement or a thrill is another of the focal concerns of lower-class life. The widespread use of alcohol by both genders and gambling of all kinds spring from this quest for excitement. Going out on the town is the most vivid expression of searching for a thrill—but, of course, pursuits of this nature frequently lead to trouble. In between periods of excitement, lower-class life is characterized by long periods of inaction or passivity.
- *Fate:* Lower-class individuals, according to Miller, often feel that their lives are subject to a set of forces over which they have little control; they may accept the

> " Walter B. Miller argued that the motivation to become involved in delinquent behavior is endemic to lower-class culture. "

concept of destiny and sense that their lives are guided by strong spiritual forces. They believe that good luck can rescue them from lower-class life; this belief in fate, in fact, encourages the lower-class person to gamble.

■ *Autonomy:* The desire for personal independence is an important concern, partly because the lower-class individual feels controlled so much of the time. A consequence of this desire for autonomy is an inability to deal with controlled environments such as those found in schools or correctional facilities.

Miller is contending that the lower class has a distinctive culture of its own. Its focal concerns, or values, make lower-class boys more likely to become involved in delinquent behavior. These boys want to demonstrate that they are tough and are able to outwit the cops. They look at the pursuit of crime as a thrill. Yet they are likely to believe that if an individual is going to get caught, there is nothing he or she can do about it. Crime, then, permits lower-class youths to show personal independence from the controls placed on them. Crime also provides an avenue through which youths hope to gain material goods and personal status with a minimum of physical effort.

Membership in One-Sex Peer Group   The all-male peer group, according to Miller, is a significant structural form in the lower-class community. This group is a reaction to female-dominated homes. Often the male parent is absent from the household; is present only occasionally; or, when present, is only minimally involved in the support and rearing of children. The male-oriented peer group, then, represents the first real opportunity for lower-class boys to learn the essential aspects of the male role in the context of peers facing similar problems of sex-role identification. The desire to prove their masculinity, Miller reasoned, is what attracts lower-class boys to these one-sex peer groups. Miller saw delinquent behavior as the lower-class boy's attempt to prove that he is grown up and no longer tied to his mother's apron strings. Delinquent offenses are motivated primarily by the desire to achieve ends, status, or qualities valued within the youth's most significant cultural milieu.[45] See Figure 4.3 for the theoretical constructs of Miller's theory.

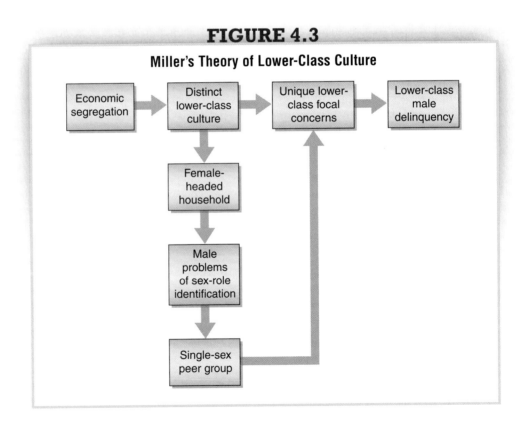

FIGURE 4.3

Miller's Theory of Lower-Class Culture

Economic segregation → Distinct lower-class culture → Unique lower-class focal concerns → Lower-class male delinquency

Distinct lower-class culture → Female-headed household → Male problems of sex-role identification → Single-sex peer group → Unique lower-class focal concerns

Evaluation of Miller's Thesis   Miller's theory appears most plausible when applied to the behavior of lower-class gang delinquents. These gang cultures appear to establish their own values and norms, distinct from the values and norms of the larger culture. In addition, Marvin E. Wolfgang and Franco Ferracuti argue that a subculture of violence among young males in the lower social classes legitimates the use of violence in various social situations.[46]

Miller's contention that the lower classes have distinctive values has been widely criticized, however. Some critics argue that the evidence shows that lower-class youths hold to the same values as those of the larger culture. For example, Travis Hirschi has found little disagreement among youngsters from different classes concerning their attachment to the social bond.[47] As discussed later in this chapter, Albert K. Cohen as well as Richard A. Cloward and Lloyd E. Ohlin have claimed that lower-class youths have internalized middle-class values and that their delinquent acts in fact reflect these middle-class values.[48]

Strain and Delinquency

Strain theory proposes that delinquency results from the frustration individuals feel when they are unable to achieve the goals they desire. Merton, Cohen, and Cloward and Ohlin all have contributed variations of strain theory.

Merton's Theory of *Anomie*

Robert K. Merton has made an important contribution to our understanding of how deviant behavior is produced by different social structures. According to Merton,

> Socially deviant behavior is just as much a product of social structure as conformist behavior. . . . Our primary aim is to discover how some social structures exert a definite pressure upon certain persons in the society to engage in nonconforming rather than conforming behavior.[49]

In *Social Theory and Social Structure,* Merton considered two elements of social and cultural systems. The first is the set of "**culturally defined goals,** purposes, and interests held out as legitimate objectives for all or for diversely located members of the society." These are the goals that people feel are worth striving for; they may be considered cultural goals. A second important aspect "defines, regulates, and controls the acceptable means of reaching out for these goals." Although a specific goal may be attained by a variety of means, the culture does not sanction all of these means. The acceptable method is referred to as the **institutionalized means.** Merton contended that the two elements must be reasonably well integrated if a culture is to be stable and run smoothly. If individuals believe that a particular goal is important, they should have a legitimate means to attain it. When a culture lacks such integration, then a state of normlessness, or *anomie,* occurs. Merton further asserted that contemporary U.S. culture seemed to "approximate the polar type in which great emphasis upon certain success-goals occurs without equivalent emphasis upon institutional means."[50] For example, the lower classes are asked to orient their behavior toward the prospect of accumulating wealth, but they are largely denied the means to do so legitimately. The opposition of the cultural emphasis and the social structure creates intense pressure for deviation.

Merton developed a typology of the modes of adaptation that individuals may use when confronted with *anomie.* Table 4.1 lists five types of individual adaptation: a plus (+) signifies acceptance, a minus (−) signifies rejection, and a plus-or-minus (±) signifies a rejection of the prevailing values and a substitution of new ones. Merton's theory uses these modes of adaptation to explain how deviant behavior in general is produced by the social structure, but they can also be applied specifically to juvenile lawbreaking.[51]

TABLE 4.1

Merton's Theory of *Anomie*

MODES OF ADAPTATION	CULTURAL GOAL	INSTITUTIONAL MEANS
1. Conformity	+	+
2. Innovation	+	−
3. Ritualism	−	+
4. Retreatism	−	−
5. Rebellion	±	±

Source: This material appears in Robert K. Merton, "Social Structure and Anomie," *American Sociological Review* 3 (1938), p. 676.

Conformity   If a society is well integrated and therefore *anomie* is absent, conformity both to cultural goals and to institutionalized means will be the most common adaptation. Conforming juveniles accept the cultural goals of society as well as the institutional means of attaining them; they work hard in legitimate ways to become a success.

Innovation   When adolescents accept the cultural goal but reject the institutional means of attaining it, they may pursue other paths that frequently are not legitimate in terms of cultural values. Merton expressed the opinion that innovation resulting in deviant behavior is especially likely to occur in a society that offers success as a goal for all but at the same time withholds from a segment of the population the legitimate means of attaining that goal. For example, lower-class youths who have accepted the cultural goal of wealth are likely to steal if they are denied legitimate opportunities to achieve the goal they have internalized.[52] Unable to "make it" in socially acceptable ways, they tend to pursue the wealth goal in law-violating ways.

Ritualism   Although they may have abandoned the cultural goals, some juveniles will continue to abide by the acceptable means for attaining them. Ritualism consists of "individually seeking a private escape from the dangers and frustrations . . . inherent in the competition for major cultural goals by abandoning these goals and clinging all the more closely to the safe routines and institutional norms."[53] For example, some youngsters, while keeping their behavior within the confines of the law, stop trying to achieve in school. They go through the motions of attending classes and studying but abandon the goal of success.

Whereas innovation is a mode of adaptation typical of the lower class, ritualism is encountered more frequently in the lower middle class, because parents of lower-middle-class children exert continuous pressure on them to abide by the moral mandates of society.

Retreatism   When individuals have rejected both the goals of the culture and the institutionalized means of attaining them, they have, in effect, retreated from their society. Drug addicts have divorced themselves from the cultural goal of success and must break the law to obtain and use their drugs. Yet even though they have none of the rewards held out by society, these socially disinherited persons face few of the frustrations involved in continuing to seek those rewards.

Web LIBRARY 4.1

Read the NIJ publication *National Evaluation of the "I Have a Dream" Program* at **www.justicestudies.com/WebLibrary**.

Rebellion   Rebellion consists of rejecting the values and institutions of one's culture and substituting for them a new set of values and institutions. The rebellious juvenile, for example, may commit himself or herself to some ideology or movement promising a new social order with a "closer correspondence between merit, effort, and reward."[54]

Merton argued that his theory of *anomie* was "designed to account for some, not all, forms of deviant behavior customarily described as criminal or delinquent."[55] Thus, instead of attempting to explain all the behaviors prohibited by criminal law, Merton focused attention on the pressure or strain resulting from the discrepancy between culturally induced goals and the opportunities inherent in the social structure.[56] See Figure 4.4 for the theoretical constructs of Merton's theory.

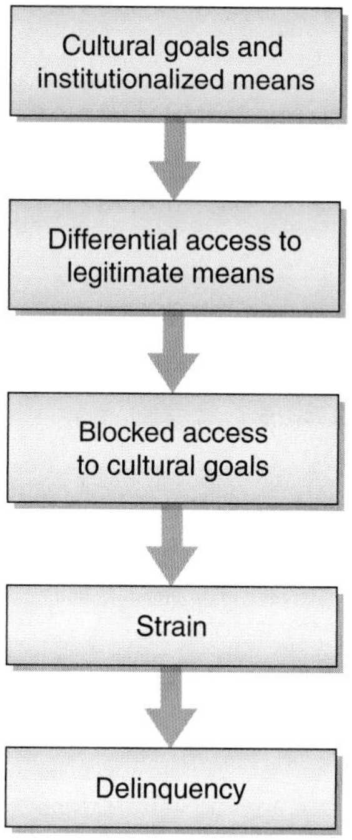

Evaluation of Merton's Theory One of the main emphases of Merton's theory—an emphasis that has been largely ignored—is that it is "a theory of societal *anomie,* not of individually felt strain."[57] Velmer S. Burton Jr. and Francis T. Cullen state that Merton's theoretical purpose is fundamentally sociological: to explain rates of deviance or crime across the social structure, rather than to explain why individuals feel the pressure to engage in wayward activities. Here, they note, Merton is "true to his Durkheimian roots and portrays crime as rooted in the breakdown of normative control."[58]

In a testing of cross-national data sets, Jukka Savolainen finds supports for the institutional anomie theory. This study indicated that the demonstrable effects of economic inequality on the level of lethal violence are limited to nations characterized by weak collective institutions of social protection.[59] Scott Menard developed a rigorous test of Merton's anomie theory for a national sample of adolescents (National Youth Survey) in their early, middle, and late adolescence.[60] He found that such a test explained 17 to 23 percent of the variance in the frequency of minor delinquency, 8 to 14 percent of index offending, 14 to 30 percent of marijuana use, and 2 to 18 percent of polydrug use. He concluded that "the predictive power of strain theory in general and of Merton's anomie theory in particular" has been seriously underestimated.[61]

In sum, Merton's revision of anomie theory has been called "the most influential single formulation in the sociology of deviance in the last 25 years and . . . possibly the most frequently quoted single paper in modern sociology."[62] This theory's influence on the later theoretical contributions of Albert K. Cohen and Richard A. Cloward and Lloyd D. Ohlin demonstrates its importance to delinquency theory.[63]

FIGURE 4.4

Merton's Strain Theory

Cultural goals and institutionalized means

↓

Differential access to legitimate means

↓

Blocked access to cultural goals

↓

Strain

↓

Delinquency

" One of the main emphases of Merton's theory is that it is 'a theory of societal *anomie,* not of individually felt strain.' "

Strain Theory and the Individual Level of Analysis

Strain theory, described below, dominated criminology in the 1960s before labeling theory gained acceptance in the late 1960s and early 1970s. A major reason for the wide acceptance of strain theory in that decade was that its central thesis of **blocked opportunity** resonated with Americans' growing concern over equal opportunity and with liberals' fear that injustice has serious costs. Strain theory also "did not require a broad rejection of the social order."[64]

Strain theory met increased criticism in the 1970s. Many commentators at the time argued that strain theory had little empirical support and ought to be abandoned as a causal explanation of crime.[65] Strain theory survived those attacks, though it now plays a more limited role in explaining crime/delinquency.[66] In the 1980s, Thomas J. Bernard defended strain theory as not having been tested adequately.[67]

Margaret Farnworth and Michael J. Leiber's 1989 analysis of a self-report study of 1,614 delinquents revealed that the appropriate operationalization of strain theory is to measure the disjunction between economic aspirations and educational expectations.[68] "Strain" will result, these researchers suggested, "when a person is

blocked opportunity
Limited or nonexistent chances of success; according to strain theory, a key factor in delinquency.

strongly committed to making a lot of money, but views college as beyond attainment."[69] Farnworth and Leiber further stated that "strain is a better predictor of delinquency than financial goals alone when commitment is operationalized in a way that is consistent with a strain perspective."[70] They contended that the failure of strain theory in empirical studies had more to do with inappropriate operationalization than with the empirical invalidity of the theory's basic postulates.[71]

Robert Agnew's revised strain theory of delinquency points to another source of frustration and strain: the blockage of pain-avoidance behavior.[72] Agnew argued that when juveniles are compelled to remain in painful or aversive environments, such as family and school, the ensuing frustration is likely to lead to escape attempts or anger-based delinquent behavior. His examination of data from the Youth in Transition survey revealed that a juvenile's location in aversive environments in the school and family "has a direct effect on delinquency and an indirect effect through anger."[73]

General Strain Theory (GST)   Agnew also developed a "general strain theory of crime and delinquency" that distinguishes three different sources of strain: "failure to achieve positively valued goals," "the removal of positively valued stimuli from the individual," and "the presentation of negative stimuli." Agnew's GST then presents guidelines, or a strategy, for measuring strain and explores under what conditions strain is likely to result in "nondelinquent and delinquent coping."[74] Timothy Brezina built on Agnew's GST by exploring the ways in which delinquency may enable adolescents to cope with strain. Brezina found that "delinquency enables adolescents to minimize the negative emotional consequences of strain," and that delinquency thus becomes an adaptive response to aversive environments.[75]

Raymond Paternoster and Paul Mazerolle conducted a comprehensive test of GST with a longitudinal sample of adolescents and found that several dimensions of strain are positively related to a wide range of delinquent involvements. "Strain," according to Paternoster and Mazerolle's findings, "has both a direct effect on delinquency and indirect effects by weakening the inhibitions of the social bond and increasing one's involvement with delinquent peers."[76] Paternoster and Mazerolle concluded that "general strain theory makes an important contribution to delinquency theory."[77]

Lisa M. Broidy's test of GST included measures of negative emotions, including anger, and legitimate coping mechanisms. She found that strain, negative emotions, and legitimate coping all are related, but not always in the expected direction. The nature of the links among these three variables and criminal/delinquent outcomes are shaped by the types of strain and negative affect that individuals experience.[78]

Stephen W. Baron studied a population of homeless youths to find out how ten specific forms of strain may lead to criminal behavior, either as main effects or when interacting with other variables. His findings are consistent with the findings of general strain theory, especially his finding that anger is a strong predictor of crime. However, some differences do exist in the types of interactions that predict property offenses and more general forms of crime and those that predict violent offending.[79]

In sum, after a period of neglect, individual-level strain theory has experienced a revival, primarily through the work of Robert Agnew, especially his general strain theory.[80] Subsequent studies examining the effects of strain have contributed to the revival of the individual-level strain theory.

Cohen's Theory of Delinquent Subcultures

Albert K. Cohen's thesis in his 1955 book *Delinquent Boys: The Culture of the Gang* stated that lower-class youths are actually internalizing the goals of middle-class culture, but that they experience **status frustration**, or strain, because they are unable to attain them. This strain explains their membership in delinquent gangs and their nonutilitarian, malicious, and negativistic behavior.[81]

The Delinquent Subculture   The social structure in American society, Cohen claimed, has an immense hold on citizens; even twelve- or thirteen-year-old children

Web LIBRARY 4.2

Read the article *Robert Agnew's Strain Theory Approach* at **www .justicestudies.com/ WebLibrary**.

status frustration

The stress that individuals experience when they cannot attain their goals because of their socioeconomic class.

know about the class system.[82] This class system defines the middle-class values and norms children are expected to aspire to and to achieve:

> These norms are, in effect, a tempered version of the Protestant ethic which has played such an important part in the shaping of American character and American society. In brief summary, this middle-class ethic prescribes an obligation to strive, by dint of rational, ascetic, self-disciplined, and independent activity, to achieve in worldly affairs. A not irrebuttable but common corollary is the presumption that "success" is itself a sign of the exercise of these moral qualities.[83]

Status at school especially is measured by these middle-class standards. First, the teacher is hired to foster the development of middle-class personalities. Second, the teacher is likely to be a middle-class person who values ambition and achievement and quickly recognizes and rewards these virtues in others. Third, Cohen pointed out, the educational system itself favors "quiet, cooperative, 'well-behaved' pupils" who make the teacher's job easier. It greets with disapproval the "lusty, irrepressible, boisterous youngsters who are destructive of order, routine, and predictability in the classroom."[84]

A pivotal assumption in Cohen's theory is that lower-class males internalize middle-class norms and values but then are unable to attain middle-class goals. Status frustration occurs, and the mechanism of **reaction formation** is used to handle it. On the one hand, according to Cohen, the delinquent claims that the middle-class standards do not matter; but on the other hand, he directs irrational, malicious, unaccountable hostility toward the norms of the respectable middle-class society.[85]

The delinquent subculture offers the lower-class male the status he does not receive from the larger culture. But, of course, the status offered by the delinquent subculture is status only in the eyes of his fellow delinquents. According to this theory, the same middle-class value system in America is instrumental in generating both respectability and delinquency.[86]

Cohen added that the delinquent subculture is nonutilitarian: Delinquents commit crimes "for the hell of it," without intending to gain or profit from their crimes. Cohen also claimed that malice is evident in the crimes of the delinquent subculture, that delinquents often display an enjoyment in the discomfort of others and a delight in the defiance of taboos. Further, the delinquent's conduct is right by the standards of the subculture precisely because it is wrong by the norms of the larger culture.[87] Moreover, the delinquent subculture demonstrates versatility in its delinquent behaviors; members of this subculture do not specialize, as do many adult criminal gangs and "solitary" delinquents. The delinquent subculture is characterized by "short-run hedonism." Its members have little interest in planning activities, setting long-term goals, budgeting time, or gaining knowledge and skills that require practice, deliberation, and study. Instead, gang members hang around the corner waiting for something to turn up. A further characteristic of this subculture is its emphasis on group autonomy, which makes gang members intolerant of any restraint except the informal pressures of the gang itself.[88] See Figure 4.5 for the theoretical constructs of Cohen's theory.

Cohen, along with James F. Short Jr., refined the original theory a few years later in defining five adaptations of the delinquent subculture. (See Voices Across the Profession 4.1 for a 1983 update of Cohen's theory.) The five adaptations are:[89]

1. *Parent Male Subculture:* The negativistic subculture identified in *Delinquent Boys.*
2. *Conflict-Oriented Subculture:* A large gang culture that becomes involved in collective violence.

An Hispanic gang member at a southern California beach during spring break. ■ **How might Cohen's notion of status frustration explain youth gang membership and delinquency?**

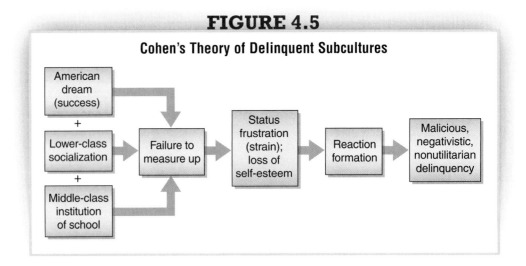

FIGURE 4.5

Cohen's Theory of Delinquent Subcultures

American dream (success) + Lower-class socialization + Middle-class institution of school → Failure to measure up → Status frustration (strain); loss of self-esteem → Reaction formation → Malicious, negativistic, nonutilitarian delinquency

3. *Drug-Addict Subculture:* Groups of adolescents whose lives revolve around the trafficking and use of narcotics.
4. *Semiprofessional Theft:* Youths who rob or steal for monetary gain.
5. *Middle-Class Subculture:* Delinquent groups that develop because of the strain of living in middle-class environments.[90]

Evaluation of Cohen's Theory Cohen's *Delinquent Boys* made a seminal contribution to the delinquency literature. James S. Short Jr. and Fred L. Strodtbeck used it to develop their research design to study youth gangs.[91] Cloward and Ohlin's later subcultural theory profited from Cohen's earlier discussion.[92] Cohen's theory is important because it views delinquency as a process of interaction between the delinquent youths and others rather than as the abrupt and sudden product of strain or anomie, as proposed by Merton's theory. Cohen contended that delinquency arises during a continuous interaction process whereby changes in the self result from the activities of others.[93]

Nevertheless, numerous criticisms have been leveled at Cohen's theory. Travis Hirschi questioned the feasibility of using status frustration as the motivational energy to account for delinquency, because most delinquent boys eventually become law abiding, even though their lower-class status does not change.[94] David Matza challenged Cohen's radical distinction between the delinquent and the conventional actor. Matza, who sees the values of the delinquent as largely in harmony with those of the larger culture, rejected the oppositional viewpoint between delinquent and conventional values.[95] David Greenberg argued that the choice of target may be more rational than Cohen allows; rather than engaging only in nonutilitarian activities, Greenberg contends, some delinquent youths can be seen as committing crime for rational purposes such as profit or gain.[96] Finally, Cohen does not offer any empirical evidence to support his theory, and the vagueness of such concepts as reaction formation and lower-class internalization of middle-class values makes it difficult to test his theory.

In sum, not only Cohen's theory but also the critiques and controversies surrounding this theory have done much to spark the development of delinquency theory. Much of the delinquency research since the publication of *Delinquent Boys* has built on Cohen's findings.

Cloward and Ohlin's Opportunity Theory

Richard A. Cloward and Lloyd E. Ohlin sought to integrate the theoretical contributions of Merton and Cohen with the ideas of Edwin H. Sutherland (see Chapter 5). Although Merton argued that lower-class youths strive for monetary success and Cohen contended that they strive for status, Cloward and Ohlin conceptualized suc-

Interview with Albert K. Cohen

Question: Let's begin with the thesis that you expressed in *Delinquent Boys* thirty years ago. Would you express it any differently today?

Cohen: I don't know what form it would take, except that it would be different. It has been subject to a lot of criticisms, and I have developed some of my own reservations about it, which have not necessarily been embodied in the public criticism in the literature. It obviously would have to be rethought.

But I think in certain respects my own thinking has not been altered—the notion that most delinquent activity, like most human activity, consists of actions that people do more or less together, or that are at least oriented to other people, is still true. The motivation to engage in those activities always is to some extent the function of a person's relationships to other people, and one's participation in those activities is in some sense instrumental to the promotion of satisfying relationships with others. This, I think, is the fundamental premise of the whole book; it's a basic premise, I think, to the whole idea of sociology.

What has bothered me most in the years since the publication of that book is not so much the declining influence or acceptance of some of the ideas specific to that particular interpretation of delin-

quency, but rather the decline of this general perspective on human conduct as applied to delinquency. I think it is a safe generalization that, in the past fifteen years or so, the literature is coming to focus more and more on the nature, the character, and the individual circumstances of persons. Thus, rather than seeing the delinquent act as something that occurs in an interactive situation and is the product of an interaction, the delinquent's actions are interpreted through that person's personality and background.

Delinquency needs to be perceived and treated as events performed in the company of others or oriented to others, guided somehow by the norms, expectations, and beliefs that are derived from and are sustained by one's communication with other people. The delinquent act is an event in a matrix of interaction, and in that matrix there are a number of people. One of the persons will be the person to whom the act will be accredited. Amongst all the people there is one person whom we point the finger at and we say, "That's the person who did it!" But if you are trying to explain the action or the event, you don't explain it by saying, "This person did it," and then look at that person and try to find out what's special about that person, because the event was a product

of the whole context in which it was embedded. What was going on at the time will include all the contributions by all the participants.

I think there is a very fundamental kind of linkage between the sociological and the psychological level. But having answered the psychological question, you are still left with the sociological question. I think *Delinquent Boys* was in a way quintessentially sociological. That doesn't make it superior to Hirschi or other studies of delinquency. The sociological question is not any more legitimate than the psychological question. But this book was addressed to the sociological question. By this I mean, it looked at certain kinds of events, in this case delinquency. It located these events in a certain space, and that space was within the social system. It raised such questions as: What's going on in this society? Where does it happen? On what scale? And why?

■ What does Cohen see as the fundamental distinction between his theory and other delinquency theories focusing on youths' personalities and backgrounds? Does Cohen's sociological theory of explaining delinquency make more or less sense to you than the theories found in Chapter 3?

Source: Albert K. Cohen, professor emeritus of sociology at the University of Connecticut, is the author of the classic study *Delinquent Boys: The Culture of the Gang*. He is also the author of *Deviance and Control* and edited the *Sutherland Papers* and *Prison Violence*.[97]

---

cess and status as separate strivings that can operate independently of each other. In their **opportunity theory** Cloward and Ohlin portrayed delinquents who seek an increase in status as striving for membership in the middle class, whereas other delinquent youths try to improve their economic post without changing their class position.[98]

Cloward and Ohlin proposed four basic categories of delinquent youths, Types I through IV. Contesting Cohen's argument, they claimed that boys of Type I and Type II, who are striving to increase their status and whose values are consistent with those of the middle class, do not constitute the major group of delinquents. They also argued that Type IV youths, who may incur criticism from middle-class authorities for

opportunity theory
A perspective which holds that gang members turn to delinquency because of a sense of injustice about the lack of legitimate opportunities open to them.

their "lack of ambition," usually avoid trouble with the law because they tend to avoid middle-class institutions and authorities as much as possible.[99]

Cloward and Ohlin contended that the most serious delinquents are Type III youths, who are oriented toward conspicuous consumption. Of the four groups, Type III youths experience the greatest conflict with middle-class values, since they "are looked down upon both for what they do want (i.e., the middle-class style of life) and for what they do not want (i.e., 'crass materialism')."[100] Cloward and Ohlin use Merton's theory to explain the particular form of delinquency that Type III youths commit. They assume that these youths have no legitimate opportunities to improve their economic position and therefore that they will become involved in one of three specialized gang subcultures: "criminal," "conflict," and "retreatist."[101]

The Criminal Subculture   The criminal subculture is primarily based on criminal values. Within this subculture illegal acts such as extortion, fraud, and theft are accepted as means to achieve economic success. This subculture provides the socialization by which new members learn to admire and respect older criminals and to adopt their lifestyles and behaviors. As new members master the techniques and orientations of the criminal world through criminal episodes, they become hostile and distrust representatives of the larger society, whom they regard as "suckers" to be exploited whenever possible.[102]

The Conflict Subculture   Violence is the key ingredient in the conflict subculture, whose members pursue status, or "rep," through force or threats of force. Warrior youth gangs exemplify this subculture. The "bopper," the basic role model, fights with weapons to win respect from other gangs and to demand deference from the adult world. The bopper's role expectation is to show great courage in the face of personal danger and always to defend his personal integrity and the honor of the gang.[103]

A reputation for toughness, the primary goal of fighting gangs, ensures respect from peers and fear from adults and provides a means of gaining access to the scarce resources for pleasure and opportunity in underprivileged areas. Relationships with the adult world are typically weak, because gang members are unable to find appropriate adult role models who offer a structure of opportunity leading to adult success.[104]

The Retreatist Subculture   The consumption of drugs is the basic activity of the retreatist subculture. Feeling shut out from conventional roles in the family or occupational world, members of this subculture have withdrawn into an arena where the ultimate goal is the "kick." The "kick" may mean alcohol, marijuana, hard drugs, sexual experiences, hot music, or any combination of these; whatever is chosen, retreatists are seeking an intense awareness of living and a sense of pleasure that is "out of this world."[105]

The retreatist subculture generates a new order of goals and criteria of achievement. But instead of attempting to impose their system of values on the world of the "straights," retreatists are content merely to strive for status and deference within their own subculture.[106]

Cloward and Ohlin noted that although these subcultures exhibit essentially different orientations, the lines between them may become blurred. For example, a subculture primarily involved with conflict may on occasion become involved in systematic theft. Members of a criminal subculture may sometimes become involved in conflict with a rival gang.[107] Figure 4.6 shows the main theoretical constructs of Cloward and Ohlin's theory.

> " The consumption of drugs is the basic activity of the retreatist subculture. "

Evaluation of Cloward and Ohlin's Theory   Cloward and Ohlin's opportunity theory is important because of the impact it has had on the development of public policy and criminological theory.[108] The research of James B. Short Jr. and his

FIGURE 4.6

Cloward and Ohlin's Opportunity Theory

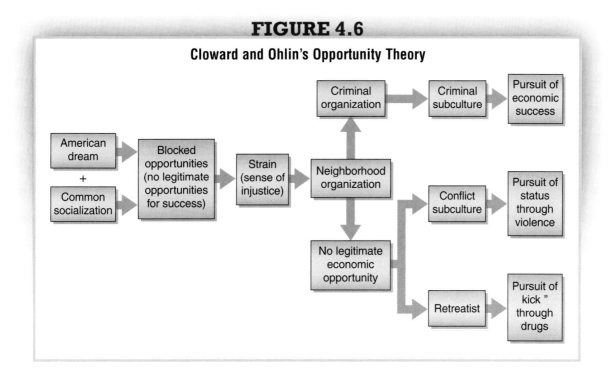

associates offered mixed support for Cloward and Ohlin's opportunity theory,[109] although several studies of gang delinquents have failed to find evidence of the particular kind of thought processes suggested by Cloward and Ohlin.[110]

However, the findings of several studies disagree sharply with the assumptions of Cloward and Ohlin's opportunity theory.[111] It has been criticized because it portrays gang delinquents as talented youth who have a sense of injustice about the lack of legitimate opportunities available to them. In reality, many studies have found that gang delinquents have limited social and intellectual abilities.[112] In 1978, Ruth Kornhauser, having reviewed the empirical research on the aspirations and expectations of delinquents, claimed that the research showed that delinquency was consistently associated with both low expectations and low aspirations; delinquents might not expect to get much, but they did not want much either. Thus, Kornhauser challenged the strain aspect of opportunity theory.[113]

In sum, strain theory explains that juveniles are "pushed" into delinquency as a result of a lack of access to opportunities for the realization of a set of success goals. In other words, those who are denied legitimate achievement of their success goals often turn to delinquency as a means of reaching desired goals or of striking back at an unfair system.[114] The role of blocked opportunity, whether found in Merton or Cloward and Ohlin, has received considerable attention in the sociological analysis of male delinquency. Table 4.2 compares the structural and cultural theories of delinquency.

Social Stratification and Delinquency

Social structure explanations of delinquency relate delinquent behavior to the structural and cultural characteristics of youth in the United States. As we've seen, social structure theorists suggest that a youth may become delinquent because he or she lives in a disorganized community, because he or she is unable to achieve middle-class standards, because he or she becomes part of a delinquent subculture due to status frustration, or because of the lower-class values held by the subculture to which he or she belongs.

TABLE 4.2

Summary of Social Structure and Cultural Theories of Crime

THEORY	CAUSE OF CRIME IDENTIFIED IN THE THEORY	SUPPORTING RESEARCH
CULTURAL DEVIANCE THEORIES *Shaw and McKay*	Delinquent behavior becomes an alternative mode of socialization through which youths who are part of disorganized communities are attracted to delinquent values and traditions.	Moderate
Miller	Lower-class culture has a distinctive culture of its own, and its focal concerns, or values, make lower-class boys more likely to become involved in delinquent behavior.	Weak
Wolfgang and Ferracuti	Subcultures of violence exist among lower-class males and legitimize the use of violence.	Weak
STRAIN THEORIES *Merton*	Social structure exerts pressure on individuals who cannot attain the cultural goal of success, leading them to engage in nonconforming behavior.	Moderate
Cohen	Lower-class boys are unable to attain the goals of middle-class culture, and therefore they become involved in nonutilitarian, malicious, and negative behavior.	Weak
OPPORTUNITY THEORY *Cloward and Ohlin*	Lower-class boys seek out illegitimate means to attain middle-class success goals if they are unable to attain them through legitimate means, usually through one of three specialized gang contexts.	Moderate

These theories ultimately rest on the importance of class as a significant variable in the explanation of delinquent behavior. But, as previously indicated, self-report studies frequently show that delinquent behavior is widespread through all social classes.[115] Charles Tittle and his associates, for example, declare that the relationship between social class and delinquency is a myth.[116]

However, Delbert S. Elliott and David Huizinga's national sample revealed that, among males, class differences are found in the prevalence and incidence of all serious offenses and in the incidence of nonserious and total offenses. Among females, the only significant and persistent class differences involved felony assault and public disorder offenses.[117] A survey by John Braithwaite also found that research tends to support higher offense rates among lower-class juveniles. Braithwaite added that studies not reporting those higher rates are particularly susceptible to methodological criticism. He concluded: "The sociological study of crime does not need to 'shift away from class-based theories' as Tittle et al. [advocate]. What we require are class-based theories which explain why certain types of crimes are perpetuated disproportionately by the powerless, while other forms of crime are almost exclusively the prerogative of the powerful."[118]

social capital theory

A perspective which holds that lower-class youths may become delinquent because they lack "social capital," or resources that reside in the social structure, including norms, networks, and relationships.

Social capital theory, developed by James S. Coleman in the late 1980s, suggests that one of the reasons lower-class individuals have higher rates of crime and delinquency is that they lack social capital. Coleman defines social capital as "the resources that reside in the social structure itself—norms, social networks and interpersonal relationships that contribute to a child's growth."[119]

In a subsequent paper, Coleman adds that "just as physical capital is created by making changes in materials so as to form tools and facilitate production, human capital is created by changing persons so as to give them skills and capabilities that make them able to act in new ways."[120] An important consideration is how parents use the

A graffiti "artist" at work. How does social capital theory explain delinquency? ■ **What is social capital?**

social capital of the family to create the capabilities and skills that become the human capital of their children.

Coleman explains that the social capital needed to create human capital includes more than the family:

> Beyond the family, social capital in the community exists in the interest, and even the intrusiveness, of one adult in the activities of someone else's child. Sometimes that interest takes the form of enforcing norms imposed by parents or by the community; sometimes it takes the form of lending a sympathetic ear to problems not discussable with parents; sometimes volunteer youth group leadership, or participation in other youth-related activities.[121]

Coleman goes on to suggest how social capital found in effective, functioning, intact nuclear and extended families, as well as in well-integrated neighborhoods and communities, can achieve more effective crime control in the United States.[122] For example, he notes that "effective norms that inhibit crime in a city make it possible for women to walk freely outside at night and for old people to leave their homes without fear."[123]

Bill McCarthy and John Hagan, combining insights from Coleman's work on social capital, Sutherland's theory of differential association (see Chapter 5), and Mark Granovetter's research on embeddedness, suggest that "embeddedness in networks of deviant associations provides access to tutelage relationships that facilitate the acquisition of criminal skills and attitudes, assets that we call 'criminal capital.' "[124] In testing this hypothesis with a sample of homeless youth who were involved in drug selling, theft, and prostitution, McCarthy and Hagan found that embeddedness in criminal networks does enhance exposure to tutelage relationships, resulting in increased rates of delinquency.[125]

Hagan and McCarthy's prizewinning book, *Mean Streets: Youth Crime and Homelessness,* addressed the issue of the lack of social capital in the lives of homeless youths. Using observational, survey, and interview data gathered in Toronto and Vancouver, the authors documented the family and school histories, living conditions, and criminal experiences of youth who were living on the streets. The homeless population they studied was about two-thirds male and one-third female, and the males

Two young women snorting cocaine in a back street. Some theorists suggest that lower-class youths turn to delinquency because they are unable to attain their goals legitimately.
■ **How can the lack of opportunity faced by many lower-class youths be effectively addressed?**

were a little older than the females (18.1 versus 17.1 years old). Between a quarter and a third came from families that experienced frequent unemployment. Less than a third of these youths lived with both biological parents at the time they left home. Most had experienced physical abuse (87 percent) and neglect. Also common was parental use of alcohol and drugs.[126] One youth told why he left home at sixteen:

> My parents threw me out. . . . They're drug addicts. Hash, weed, coke, crack—everything. I didn't want to leave but they just threw me out. I had a huge fight with my dad. We'd fight 'cause I'd go, "quit drugs," and he would go "no." . . . I'd go, "quit drinking." He'd say "no." So we just argued about that most of the time. And one day he goes, "I think its about time you leave, get on your own." So I just left.[127]

Explanations of Delinquency Across the Life Course

Three important structural explanations of delinquency across the life course point to the consequences of the reduced social capital that lower-class children have, the importance of disorganized communities in affecting the decisions of lower-class children, and the relationship between structure and human agency in the process of desistance from crime.

Reduced Social Capital

Lower-class youngsters often lack access to social capital—to the norms, networks, and supportive relationships they need if they are to realize their potential. They may be forced to struggle to meet their basic survival needs. Economic deprivation is first felt at home, and it is this deprivation that drives many youths to the streets.[128] Not surprisingly, the father frequently leaves, and the mother is gone much of the time simply trying to make ends meet. G. Roger Jarjoura, Ruth A. Triplett, and Gregory P. Brinker, using fourteen years of longitudinal data for a national sample of younger adolescents, found that the exposure to poverty and the timing of such exposure are indeed related to an increased likelihood of delinquent involvement.[129]

Lower-class youngsters further encounter the difficulty of coping in constructive ways when they are not able to meet the success goals of society. This inability usually becomes evident at school. Both lower- and middle-class youths may respond to lack of success with disruptive behavior, truancy, and crime. The inability to find a job or to compete in the marketplace further encourages these adolescents to pursue illegitimate means. Robert Gillespie's survey of fifty-seven studies shows considerable support for a relationship between unemployment and property crime. Gillespie found the relationship most evident in studies that use such variables as class, crime, and delinquency in a methodologically sophisticated manner.[130] Stephen W. Baron and Timothy F. Hartnagel's study of 200 homeless male street youths found that lengthy unemployment and lack of income, as well as anger, increase the youths' criminal activities.[131] However, Steven F. Messner and his colleagues, using national data for 1967 through 1998, found that child poverty is positively related to arrest rates, but that changing unemployment yields a negative effect on youth offending.[132]

Disorganized Communities

In addition, lower-class children must deal with the impact of disorganized communities on their attitudes and worldview. In order to adapt to a disorganized community, adolescents may learn to accept cultural patterns that are conducive to delinquent behavior. For youths who experience economic deprivation at home, the streets offer the promise of attaining goods and services that their parents could never afford. In these disorganized communities youth gangs typically are well established; in many communities youngsters may feel required to join a gang for safety. Disorganized communities also offer drugs of every type, frequent contact with adult criminals, and ongoing exposure to violence. Mary E. Pattillo's study of an African American middle-class neighborhood in Chicago found that the neighborhood was closer to high-poverty and high-crime areas than were white middle-class neighborhoods and, as a result, had more problems with gang members and drug dealers.[133]

Thomas J. Bernard's article, "Angry Aggression among the 'Truly Disadvantaged,'" explained the high levels of anger and aggression among members of the underclass.[134] Bernard theorized that three social factors—urban environments, low social position, and racial and ethnic discrimination—increase the likelihood that the "truly disadvantaged" will react in frequent or intense physiological arousal. In Bernard's model, social isolation (a fourth social factor) concentrates the effects of the first three factors through multiple feedback loops. The end result, according to Bernard's theory, is a "peak" of angry aggression that is comparable to learned helplessness.[135]

This theory begins at an individual level and considers the physiological and cognitive bases of angry aggression in the context of a person's biological and psychological characteristics. Then an aggregate-level theory addresses the distribution of crime rates among social groups in circumstances such as those in which the "truly disadvantaged" live. The individual-level theory predicts that individuals who live under such circumstances will demonstrate high levels of angry aggression even if they have normal biological and psychological characteristics. The third level of theory construction considers individuals' abnormal biological and psychological characteristics that, the theory predicts, will intensify and increase the degree of angry aggression. Existing research, according to Bernard, has found that each of these theoretical postulates is associated with increased rates of violence and delinquency.[136]

Thus, research evidence appears to support a relationship between social class, disorganization of the community, and delinquency. The type of informal community controls found in the Chicago Area Projects during the 1930s and 1940s perhaps offers one of the most hopeful means to reduce the rates of delinquency in high-crime areas (see Chapter 12 for more description of the Chicago Area Projects). In their innovative work on neighborhoods and crime, Robert Sampson and colleagues developed the notion of "collective efficacy," which relates to informal social control and cohesion, or mutual trust, found among neighborhoods that effectively control youth crime.[137] This collective efficacy characterized the most effective of the Chicago Area Projects' communities and is found in present-day low-crime urban communities. The task of policymakers is to provide the structure or framework from which neighborhood solidarity and grass-roots community organization can arise.

Human Agency and Social Structure

There has been an intense interest among sociological theorists in the relationship between agency and structure. Margaret Archer has contended that "the problem of structure and agency has rightly come to be seen as the basic issue in modern social theory."[138] In 1964, George Homans had called for a move to "bring men [sic] in" and to return to an action theory grounded firmly in the instrumental, calculating, and purposive orientations of individuals.[139] In 1990, Coleman's major work, *Foundations of Social Theory*, linked purposive action at the micro level to interdependence at the macro level, showing that action is a complex social and interactive phenomenon.[140]

The theories presented in this chapter disclose how U.S. society imposes structural and cultural values on individuals without much concern for how individuals choose to respond to the influence of the sociocultural context and to the economic factors in their immediate environment. These theories leave two basic questions unanswered: What explains the fact that many youths in the same cultural setting do not become delinquent? And why is it that many culturally deprived youths who do become delinquent desist from delinquent behavior at the end of their teenage years, even when their social and economic situations remain the same?

John H. Laub and Robert J. Sampson, in their follow-up of the delinquent boys from the Gluecks' sample to the age of seventy, emphasized the importance of human agency in the desistance process. They viewed the men who desisted as "acting players" who accepted responsibility for what they had done. They concluded that desistance takes place "as a result of individual actions (choice) in conjunction with situational contexts and structural influences linked to important institutions that help sustain desistance."[141]

In the Laub and Sampson study, work and employment, as well as the structured role stability that came from marriage and family, provided the desisters with the context in which they could choose to forge a new identity and from which they could receive support and encouragement. Those offenders who persisted were the individuals whose lives were characterized by failure to maintain regular employment, by a tendency to abuse alcohol, and by inability to receive the support of marriage and family. They seemed to be unable to rise above the lower-class background of their childhood and, in fact, continued much of the defiance that they had expressed in their younger years. Not surprisingly, their lives were characterized by ongoing contact with the criminal justice system and imprisonment.[142]

CHAPTER
Summary

This chapter describes social structural theories of delinquency. *Social structure* refers to the relatively stable formal and informal arrangements that characterize a society—including its economic arrangements, social institutions, and values and norms. Social structure theories propose that the structured arrangements within society can lead to delinquency, whereas structural and cultural

disorder may result in high rates of crime and unsafe and disruptive living conditions. Among the best known social structural approaches are the following:

- Clifford R. Shaw and Henry D. McKay, members of the Chicago School of Sociology, demonstrated the importance of social ecology, specifically the locations where young people live. The closer they live to the inner city, the researchers said, the more likely young people are to become involved in delinquency.

■ Explanations for delinquency in inner-city areas go beyond social disorganization, however. It is well known, for example, that cultural traditions characteristic of the inner city pass criminogenic norms and values from one generation to the next.

■ Walter B. Miller contends that lower-class youths do not aspire to middle-class values because they have their own lower-class values, or focal concerns, which encourage involvement in delinquent behavior.

■ Robert K. Merton's anomie theory says that the social structure of a society influences the behavior that occurs in that society because of the way in which it structures opportunities.

■ Merton notes that young people who are caught up in anomie, or normlessness, feel the strain that such conditions produce, and are more likely to become deviant or delinquent than those who are not.

■ Albert K. Cohen's theory of reaction formation contends that lower-class youths aspire to middle-class values but that their inability to attain those values causes them to invert the values and become involved in negativistic, malicious, and nonutilitarian behaviors.

■ Richard A. Cloward and Lloyd D. Ohlin argue that youthful lower-class gang members aspire to middle-class values but become involved in illegitimate pursuits because they are unable to attain their goals legitimately.

■ All of the theories discussed in this chapter see delinquency as a response to inequalities built into the very structure of society.

CRITICAL THINKING
Questions

1. According to Shaw and McKay, what are the relationships among ecology, social disorganization, and transmission of deviant culture?
2. Which of the theories in this chapter impressed you as being most logical? Why?
3. Should poverty exclude a youngster from responsibility for delinquent behavior? Why or why not?

4. Do you believe that lower-class youngsters aspire to middle-class values? Or do they have their own values?
5. How important does poverty appear to be as a root cause of delinquency?
6. What structural explanations of delinquency are most likely to explain middle-class delinquency?

WEB
Interactivity

Visit the Project on Human Development in Chicago Neighborhoods' website at **www.icpsr.umich.edu/PHDCN** to learn about the project.

As the website says, the Project on Human Development in Chicago Neighborhoods (PHDCN) is a large-scale, interdisciplinary study of how families, schools, and neighborhoods affect child and adolescent development. The project was designed to advance the understanding of the developmental pathways of both positive and negative human social behaviors. Project managers examine the causes and pathways of juvenile delinquency, adult crime, substance abuse, and violence. The project also provides a detailed look at the environments in which these social behaviors occur by collecting substantial amounts of information about Chicago, including its people, institutions, and resources.

Describe the data-gathering methods used by the project and summarize some of its findings. (*Hint:* Visit the project's Methods and Publications pages on the Web). Submit your description and summary to your instructor if asked to do so.

Source: From www.icpsr.umich.edu/PHDCN. Reprinted with permission from the Inter-university Consortium for Political and Social Research.

1. For an article that lent support to Anderson's "code of the street" thesis, see Eric A. Stewart and Ronald L. Simons, "Structure and Culture in African American Adolescent Violence: a Partial Test of the 'Code of the Street' Thesis," *Justice Quarterly* 23 (March 2006), p. 1.

2. Robert J. Sampson and W. B. Groves, "Community Structure and Crime: Testing Social-Disorganization Theory," *American Journal of Sociology* 94 (1989), pp. 774–802.

3. Robert J. Sampson and William Julius Wilson, "Toward a Theory of Race, Crime, and Urban Equality," in *Crime and Inequality,* edited by John Hagan and Ruth D. Peterson (Stanford, California: Stanford University Press, 1995), p. 49.

4. See Emile Durkheim, *Suicide,* translated by John A. Spaulding and George Simpson (New York: Free Press of Glencoe, 1893).

5. William I. Thomas and Florian Znaniecki, *The Polish Peasant in Europe and America,* 5 volumes (New York: Knopf, 1927). For an excellent review of Thomas and Znaniecki's work, see Randall Collins and Michael Makowsky, *The Discovery of Society,* 4th ed. (New York: Random House, 1989), pp. 189–190.

6. Robert E. Park, Ernest W. Burgess, and Roderick D. McKenzie, eds., *The City* (Chicago: University of Chicago Press, 1967 [1925]).

7. S. P. Breckinridge and Edith Abbott, *The Delinquent Child and the Home* (New York: Arno Press, 1970).

8. Frederick M. Thrasher, *The Gang: A Study of 1,313 Gangs in Chicago* (Chicago: University of Chicago Press, 1927).

9. Jon Snodgrass, "Clifford R. Shaw and Henry D. McKay, Chicago Criminologists," *British Journal of Criminology* 16 (January 1976), pp. 1–19.

10. Clifford R. Shaw, *The Natural History of Delinquent Careers* (Chicago: University of Chicago Press, 1931), pp. 69–70.

11. Ibid.

12. Jon Snodgrass, *The American Criminological Tradition: Portraits of the Men and Ideology in a Discipline.* Ph.D. dissertation, University of Pennsylvania, 1972.

13. There is a cultural deviance component to Shaw and McKay's perspective, but Ruth Rosner Kornhauser claims it is an unnecessary aspect of their social disorganization theory. See Ruth Rosner Kornhauser, *Social Sources of Delinquency: An Appraisal of Analytic Models* (Chicago: University of Chicago Press, 1978), p. 79.

14. Albert J. Reiss Jr., "Settling the Frontiers of a Pioneer in American Criminology: Henry McKay," in *Delinquency, Crime and Society,* edited by James F. Short Jr. (Chicago: University of Chicago Press, 1976), p. 79.

15. Harold Finestone, *Victims of Change: Juvenile Delinquents in American Society* (Westport, Conn.: Greenwood Press, 1976), p. 90.

16. George B. Vold and Thomas J. Bernard, *Theoretical Criminology,* 3rd ed. (New York: Oxford University Press, 1986), p. 163.

17. Clifford R. Shaw, *Delinquency Areas* (Chicago: University of Chicago Press, 1929), pp. 198–203.

18. Clifford R. Shaw and Henry D. McKay, *Social Factors in Juvenile Delinquency; Report on the Causes of Crime,* Vol. II (Washington, D.C.: National Commission on Law Observance and Enforcement, 1931), p. 60.

19. Clifford R. Shaw and Henry D. McKay, *Juvenile Delinquency and Urban Areas* (Chicago: University of Chicago Press, 1942).

20. Ysabel Rennie, *The Search for Criminal Man* (Lexington, Mass.: Lexington Books, 1978), p. 129.

21. Finestone, *Victims of Change,* pp. 83–84.

22. Ibid., p. 92.

23. Ibid., p. 99.

24. Ibid., p. 90.

25. Shaw and McKay, *Juvenile Delinquency and Urban Areas,* pp. 38–39.

26. John Laub, *Criminology in the Making: An Oral History* (Boston: Northeastern University Press, 1983), p. 10.

27. James F. Short Jr., introduction to *Delinquency, Crime and Society,* edited by James F. Short Jr. (Chicago: University of Chicago Press, 1976), p. 3.

28. Robert J. Bursik Jr., "Social Disorganization and Theories of Crime and Delinquency: Problems and Prospects," *Criminology* 26 (November 1988), p. 522. See also Justice W. Patchin, Beth M. Huebner, John D. McCluskey, Sean P. Varano, and Timothy S. Bynum, "Exposure to Community Violence and Childhood Delinquency," *Crime and Delinquency* 52 (April 2006), pp. 307–332; and Amie L. Nielsen, Matthew T. Lee, and Ramiro Martinez Jr., "Integrating Race, Place and Motive in Social Disorganization Theory: Lessons from a Comparison of Black and Latino Homicide Types in Two Immigrant Destination Cities," *Criminology* 43 (August 2005), pp. 837–871.

29. Ora Simcha-Fagan and Joseph E. Schwartz, "Neighborhood and Delinquency: An Assessment of Contextual Effects," *Criminology* 24 (1986), pp. 667–704; Sampson and Groves, "Community Structure and Crime," pp. 704, 774–802. For an article that examines how neighborhood factors influence rates of delinquency among African American youths, see Faith Peeples and Rolf Loeber, "Do Individual Factors and Neighborhood Context Explain Ethnic Differences in Juvenile Delinquency?" *Journal of Quantitative Criminology* 10 (1994), pp. 141–157. Also Robert J. Sampson, "Linking Time and Place: Dynamic Contextualism and the Future of Criminological Inquiry," *Journal of Research in Crime and Delinquency* 30 (November 1993), pp. 426, 435; and Robert J. Sampson and Stephen W. Raudenbush, *National Institute of Justice Research in Brief,* "Disorder in Urban Neighborhoods— Does It Lead to Crime?" (Washington, D.C.: U.S. Department of Justice, 2001), p. 2.

30. Bursik, "Social Disorganization and Theories of Crime and Delinquency," pp. 519–551; James M. Byrne and Robert J. Sampson, eds., *The Social Ecology of Crime* (New York: Springer-Verlag, 1986); Reiss and Tonry, *Communities and Crime;* Stark, "Deviant Places," pp. 893–909.

31. Dennis W. Roncek, "High Schools and Crime: A Replication," *Sociological Quarterly* 26 (1985), pp. 491–505; Dennis W. Roncek and Antoinette LoBosco, "The Effect of High Schools on Crime in Their Neighborhoods," *Social Science Quarterly* 64 (1983), pp. 598–613.

32. Jeanette Covington and Ralph B. Taylor, "Neighborhood Revitalization and Property Crime." Paper presented at the Annual Meeting of the American Sociological Association in Atlanta (1988).

33. Lyle W. Shannon, *The Relationship of Juvenile Delinquency and Adult Crime to the Changing Ecological Structure of the City.* Executive Report submitted to the National Institute of Justice, 1982; Lyle W. Shannon, *The Development of Serious Criminal Careers and the Delinquent Neighborhood.* Executive Report submitted to the National Institute of Justice and Delinquency Prevention, 1984; Janet L. Heitgerd and Robert J. Bursik Jr., "Extracommunity Dynamics and the Ecology of Delinquency," *American Journal of Sociology* 92 (January 1987), pp. 775–787; Paul E. Bellair, "Social Interaction and Community Crime: Examining the Importance of Neighbor Networks," *Criminology* 35 (1997), pp. 677–703; Fred E. Markowitz, Paul E. Bellair, Allen E. Liska, and Jianhong Liu, "Extending Social Disorganization Theory: Modeling the Relationships between Cohesion, Disorder, and Fear," *Criminology* 39 (2001), p. 293; and D. Wayne Osgood and Jeff M. Chambers, "Social Disorganization outside the Metropolis: An Analysis of Rural Youth Violence," *Criminology* 38 (February 2000), p. 81.

34. Bursik Jr., "Social Disorganization and Theories of Crime and Delinquency: Problems and Prospects." See also Charis E. Kubrin and Eric A. Stewart, "Predicting Who Reoffends: The Neglected Role of Neighborhood Context in Recidivism Studies," *Criminology* 44 (February 1, 2006), p. 165.

35. Barbara D. Warner, "The Role of Attenuated Culture in Social Disorganization Theory," *Criminology* 41 (February 2003), pp. 73–97.

36. William R. Smith, Sharon Glave Frazee, and Elizabeth L. Davison, "Furthering the Integration of Routine Activity and Social Disorganization Theories: Small Units of Analysis and the Study of Street Robbery as a Diffusion Process," *Criminology* 38 (May 2000), pp. 489–521.

37. Sung Joon Jang and Bryon R. Johnson, "Neighborhood Disorder, Individual Religiosity, and Adolescent Use of Illicit Drugs: A Test of Multilevel Hypotheses," *Criminology* (February 2001), pp. 109–141. For an examination of the relationship between neighborhood context and race/ethnicity–violence, see Joanne M. Kaufman, "Explaining the Race/Ethnicity-Violence Relationship: Neighborhood Context and Social Psychological Processes," *Justice Quarterly* 22 (June 2005), pp. 224–251.

38. Stephen J. Pfohl, *Images of Deviance and Social Control* (New York: McGraw Hill, 1985), p. 167.

39. Bursik, "Social Disorganization and Theories of Crime and Delinquency," pp. 521–538.

40. Rodney Stark, "Deviant Places: A Theory of the Ecology of Crime," *Criminology* 25 (1987), p. 894.

41. Robert J. Bursik Jr., "Ecological Stability and the Dynamics of Delinquency," in *Communities and Crime,* Vol. 8, edited by Albert J. Reiss Jr., and Michael Tonry (Chicago: University of Chicago Press, 1986), p. 36.

42. Kornhauser, *Social Sources of Delinquency,* p. 25. For a review of the decline of cultural deviance theory, see J. Mitchell Miller, Albert K. Cohen, and Kevin M. Bryant, "On the Demise and Morrow of Subculture Theories of Crime and Delinquency," *Journal of Crime and Justice* 20 (1997), pp. 167–178.

43. Walter B. Miller, "Lower-Class Culture as a Generation Milieu of Gang Delinquency," *Journal of Social Issues* 14 (1958), pp. 9–10.

44. Ibid., pp. 11–14.

45. Ibid., pp. 14–16.

46. Marvin E. Wolfgang and Franco Ferracuti, *The Subculture of Violence* (London: Tavistock, 1957). For a study that challenges the black subculture of violence thesis, see Liqun Cao, Anthony Adams, and Vickie J. Jensen, "A Test of the Black Subculture of Violence Thesis: A Research Note," *Criminology* 35 (May 1997), pp. 367–379.

47. Travis Hirschi, *Causes of Delinquency* (Berkeley: University of California Press, 1969).

48. Richard A. Cloward and Lloyd E. Ohlin, *Delinquency and Opportunity: A Theory of Delinquent Boys: The Culture of the Gang* (Glencoe, Ill.: Free Press, 1955).

49. This section's analysis of social structure and anomie is based on Robert K. Merton, *Social Theory and Social Structure,* 2nd ed. (New York: Free Press, 1957), pp. 131–132.

50. Morton Deutsch and Robert M. Krauss, *Theories in Social Psychology* (New York: Basic Books, 1965), p. 198.

51. Merton, *Social Theory and Social Structure,* pp. 139–152.

52. Cloward and Ohlin, *Delinquency and Opportunity.*

53. Merton, *Social Theory and Social Structure,* p. 151.

54. Ibid., p. 155.

55. Ibid.

56. For Merton's recent thoughts about the emergence and present status of strain theory, see Robert K. Merton, "Opportunity Structure: The Emergence, Diffusion, and Differentiation of a Sociological Concept, 1930s–1950s," in *The Legacy of Anomie Theory: Advances in Criminological Theory,* Vol. 6, edited by Freda Adler and William S. Laufer (New Brunswick, N.J.: Transaction Publishers, 1995), pp. 3–78.

57. Velmer S. Burton Jr. and Francis T. Cullen, "The Empirical Status of Strain Theory," *Journal of Crime and Justice* 15 (1992), p. 5.

58. Ibid.

59. Jukka Savolainen, "Inequality, Welfare State, and Homicide: Further Support for the Institutional Anomie Theory," *Criminology* 38 (November 2000), p. 1021.

60. Scott Menard, "A Developmental Test of Mertonian Anomie Theory," *Journal of Research in Crime and Delinquency* 32 (May 1995), pp. 136–166.

61. Ibid., p. 169.

62. Marshall B. Clinard, "The Theoretical Implications of Anomie and Deviant Behavior," in *Anomie and Deviant Behavior,* edited by Marshall B. Clinard (New York: Free Press, 1964), p. 10.

63. Albert K. Cohen, *Delinquent Boys: The Culture of the Gang* (Glencoe, Ill.: Free Press, 1955); and Cloward and Ohlin, *Delinquency and Opportunity.*

64. Burton and Cullen, "The Empirical Status of Strain Theory," pp. 2–3.

65. Travis Hirschi, *Causes of Crime* (Berkeley: University of California Press, 1969); and Ruth Kornhauser, *Social Sources of Delinquency.*

66. Robert Agnew, "Foundations for a General Strain Theory of Crime and Delinquency," *Criminology* 30 (February 1992), p. 47.

67. Thomas J. Bernard, "Control Criticisms of Strain Theory: An Assessment of Theoretical and Empirical Adequacy,"

Journal of Research in Crime and Delinquency 21 (1984), pp. 353–372; Thomas J. Bernard, "Testing Structural Strain Theories," *Journal of Research in Crime and Delinquency* 24 (1987), pp. 262–280.

68. Margaret Farnworth and Michael J. Leiber, "Strain Theory Revisited: Economic Goals, Educational Means, and Delinquency," *American Sociological Association* 54 (1989), pp. 259–279.

69. Ibid., p. 264.

70. Ibid., p. 272.

71. Ibid.

72. Agnew, "A Revised Strain Theory of Delinquency," pp. 151–167.

73. Ibid., p. 151.

74. Agnew, "Foundations for a General Theory of Crime and Delinquency," pp. 47–87. See also Robert Agnew, "Building on the Foundation for a General Strain Theory." Paper presented to the Annual Meeting of the American Society of Criminology in Washington, D.C. (November 1998); and John P. Hoffman and Alan S. Miller, "A Latent Variable Analysis of General Strain Theory," *Journal of Quantitative Criminology* 14 (1998), pp. 83–110.

75. Timothy Brezina, "Adapting to Strain: An Examination of Delinquent Coping Responses," *Criminology* 34 (1996), p. 39.

76. Raymond Paternoster and Paul Mazerolle, "General Strain Theory and Delinquency: A Replication and Extension," *Journal of Research in Crime and Delinquency* 31 (August 1994), p. 235.

77. Ibid.

78. Lisa M. Broidy, "A Test of General Strain Theory," *Criminology* 39 (February 2001), pp. 9–10. For another test of general strain theory, see John P. Hoffmann and Alan S. Miller, "A Latent Variable Analysis of General Strain Theory," *Journal of Quantitative Criminology* 14 (1998), pp. 83–110.

79. Stephen W. Baron, "General Strain, Street Youth and Crime: A Test for Agnew's Revised Theory," *Criminology* (May 2004), pp. 457–483.

80. Agnew, "Foundations for a General Theory of Crime and Delinquency," pp. 47–87. See also Agnew, "Building on the Foundation for a General Strain Theory," and Hoffman and Miller, "A Latent Variable Analysis of General Strain Theory," pp. 83–110.

81. Cohen, *Delinquent Boys*, 25.

82. Ibid., p. 82.

83. Ibid., p. 87.

84. Ibid., pp. 113–114.

85. Ibid., p. 133.

86. Ibid., p. 137.

87. Ibid., p. 28.

88. Ibid., pp. 26–31.

89. Albert Cohen and James F. Short, "Research on Delinquent Subcultures," *Journal of Social Issues* 14 (1958), pp. 25–31.

90. Ibid.

91. James F. Short Jr. and Fred L. Strodtbeck, *Group Process and Gang Delinquency* (Chicago: University of Chicago Press, 1965).

92. Cloward and Ohlin, *Delinquency and Opportunity*.

93. Albert K. Cohen, "The Sociology of the Deviant Act: Anomie Theory and Beyond," *American Sociological Review* 30 (1965), p. 9.

94. Hirschi, *Causes of Delinquency*.

95. David Matza, *Delinquency and Drift* (New York: Wiley, 1964).

96. David F. Greenberg, "Delinquency and the Age Structure of Society," *Contemporary Crises* 1 (1977), p. 199.

97. This interview took place in November 1983.

98. Vold and Bernard, *Theoretical Criminology*, p. 196.

99. Cloward and Ohlin, *Delinquency and Opportunity*.

100. Vold and Bernard, *Theoretical Criminology*, p. 197.

101. Cloward and Ohlin, *Delinquency and Opportunity*, p. 97.

102. Ibid., p. 20.

103. Ibid., p. 23.

104. Ibid., p. 24.

105. Ibid., p. 25.

106. Ibid., pp. 25–26.

107. Ibid., p. 27.

108. Delbert S. Elliott and Harwin L. Voss, *Delinquency and Dropout* (Lexington, Mass.: Lexington Books, 1974).

109. James F. Short Jr., Ramon Rivera, and Ray Tennyson, "Perceived Opportunities, Gang Membership and Delinquency," *American Sociological Review* 30 (1965), p. 56–57.

110. Hagan, *Modern Criminology*, 196.

111. Gwynn Nettler, *Explaining Crime*, 3d ed. (New York: McGraw-Hill, 1984), pp. 212–218.

112. Ibid., pp. 228–230.

113. Kornhauser, *Social Sources of Delinquency*, pp. 139–180.

114. Merton, "Social Structure and Anomie," and Cloward and Ohlin, *Delinquency and Opportunity*.

115. See Chapter 2 for the findings of these self-report studies.

116. Charles R. Tittle, Wayne J. Villemez, and Douglas A. Smith, "The Myth of Social Class and Criminality: An Empirical Assessment of the Empirical Evidence," *American Sociological Review* 43 (October 1978), pp. 643–656. See also Joseph Weis, "Social Class and Crime," in *Positive Criminology*, edited by Michael Gottfredson and Travis Hirschi (Newbury Park, Calif.: Sage, 1987); and Gary Jensen and Kevin Thompson, "What's Class Got to Do with It? A Further Examination of Power–Control Theory," *American Journal of Sociology* 95 (1990), pp. 1009–1023.

117. Delbert S. Elliott and David Huizinga, "Social Class and Delinquent Behavior in a National Youth Panel," *Criminology* 21 (May 1983), p. 49.

118. John Braithwaite, "The Myth of Social Class and Criminality Reconsidered," *American Sociological Review* 46 (February 1981), p. 49.

119. James S. Coleman, "Social Capital in the Development of Human Capital: The Ambiguous Position of Private Schools." Paper presented at the Annual Conference of the National Association of Independent Schools in New York (February 25–26, 1988), pp. 1, 5.

120. James Coleman, *Foundations of Social Theory* (Cambridge: Harvard University Press, 1990), p. 304.

121. Coleman, "Social Capital in the Development of Human Capital," pp. 7–8. For an examination of social capital among twelve- to fourteen-year-old African American males, see Joseph B. Richardson, "Social Capital and Delinquency among Young African American Males." Paper presented to the Annual Meeting of the American Society of Criminology in Washington, D.C. (November 1998).

122. John Hagan, *Crime and Disrepute* (Thousand Oaks, Calif.: Pine Forge Press, 1994), pp. 68–69.

123. Coleman, *Foundations of Social Theory*, p. 310.
124. Bill McCarthy and John Hagan, "Getting into Street Crimes: The Structure and Process of Criminal Embeddedness," *Social Science Research* 24 (1995), p. 63.
125. Ibid.
126. John Hagan and Bill McCarthy, *Mean Streets: Youth Crime and Homelessness* (Cambridge, England: Cambridge University Press, 1997), pp. 23–25.
127. Ibid., p. 25.
128. For articles that examine children's poverty, see Greg J. Duncan, "Has Children's Poverty Become More Persistent?" *American Sociological Review* 56 (August 1991), pp. 538–550; and David J. Eggebeen and Daniel T. Lichter, "Race, Family Structure, and Changing Poverty among American Children," *American Sociological Review* 56 (December 1991), pp. 801–817.
129. G. Roger Jarjoura, Ruth A. Triplett, and Gregory P. Brinker, "Growing Up Poor: Examining the Link between Persistent Poverty and Delinquency," *Journal of Quantitative Criminology* 18 (June 2002), pp. 159–187.
130. Robert Gillespie, "Economic Factors in Crime and Delinquency: A Critical Review of the Empirical Evidence," *Hearings, Subcommittee on Crime of the Committee of the Judiciary, House of Representatives*, 95th Congress, serial 47 (Washington, D.C.: U.S. Government Printing Office, 1978), pp. 601–625.
131. Stephen W. Baron and Timothy F. Hartnagel, "Attributions, Affect, and Crime: Street Youths' Reactions to Unemployment," *Criminology* 35 (August 1997), p. 409. However, another study challenges this relationship between employment and reduced rates of delinquency: see Matthew Ploeger, "Youth Employment and Delinquency: Reconsidering a Problematic Relationship," *Criminology* 35 (November 1997), pp. 659–675.
132. Steven F. Messner, Lawrence E. Raffalovich, and Richard McMillan, "Economic Deprivation and Changes in Homicide Arrest Rates for White and Black Youths, 1967–1998: A National Time-Series Analysis," *Criminology* 39 (August 2001), 591.
133. Mary E. Pattillo, "Sweet Mothers and Gangbangers: Managing Crime in a Black Middle-Class Neighborhood," *Social Forces* (March 1998), pp. 747–774.
134. Thomas J. Bernard, "Angry Aggression among the 'Truly Disadvantaged,' " *Criminology* 28 (1990), pp. 73–96. See also William Julius Wilson, *The Truly Disadvantaged* (Chicago: University of Chicago Press, 1987).
135. Ibid., p. 74.
136. Ibid.
137. Robert J. Sampson, Jeffrey D. Morenoff, and Felton Earls, "Beyond Social Capital: Spatial Dynamics of Collective Efficacy for Children," *American Sociological Review* 64 (1999), 633–660.
138. Margaret S. Archer, *Culture and Agency: The Place of Culture in Social Theory* (Cambridge, England: Cambridge University Press, 1988), p. ix.
139. George C. Homans, "Bringing Men Back In," *American Sociological Review* 29 (1964), pp. 809–818.
140. Coleman, *Foundations of Social Theory*.
141. John H. Laub and Robert J. Sampson, *Shared Beginnings. Divergent Lives: Delinquent Boys to Age 70* (Cambridge, Mass.: Harvard University Press, 2003), p. 145.
142. Ibid. See Chapters 6 and 7.

5

Social Process Theories of Delinquency

> " The theory I advocate sees in the delinquent a person relatively free of the intimate attachments, the aspirations, and the moral beliefs that bind people to a life within the law. "
>
> —Travis Hirschi, *Causes of Delinquency*

CHAPTER Objectives

AFTER READING THIS CHAPTER, YOU SHOULD BE ABLE TO ANSWER THE FOLLOWING QUESTIONS:

- Do delinquents learn crime from others?

- Why is it that some young people routinely go from delinquent to non-delinquent acts and then back to delinquent behavior?

- What control mechanisms insulate teenagers from delinquent behavior?

- What role does a teen's self-concept play in delinquency?

- Does considering more than one theory increase our ability to explain delinquency?

The story of the Bogle family illustrates how criminal behavior can be passed from one generation to the next. Dale Vincent Bogle came to Oregon's fertile Willamette Valley from Texas as a migrant worker in 1961. He had already served time in prison and quickly gained a reputation as a wife beater. He also taught his children to steal.

Rooster, as Bogle was known, had three sons. By the time, they were 10 years old the boys were breaking into liquor stores and stealing tractor-trailer trucks. The girls turned to petty crimes to support drug habits.

In time, everyone went to jail or to state prison, as did many of Rooster's brothers and their families. By official count, 28 in the Bogle clan have been arrested and convicted, including several of Rooster's grandchildren. Rooster died in 1998 of natural causes.

"Rooster raised us to be outlaws," said Tracey Bogle, the youngest of Rooster's children. "There is a domino effect in a family like ours," Tracey said, "What you're raised with, you grow to become. You don't escape."

Tracey Bogle, now 29, is serving a 15-year sentence at the Snake River Correctional Institution in the high desert of eastern Oregon near the Idaho border for kidnapping, rape, assault, robbery and burglary. He committed the crimes with one of his older brothers, Robert Zane Bogle. Their oldest brother, Tony, is serving a life term in Arizona for murder. Their mother was released from Klamath County jail only recently.

For all their criminal activity, the Bogle clan is merely one example of a phenomenon that prison officials, the police and criminal justice experts have long observed, that crime often runs in families.

Justice Department figures show that 47 percent of inmates in state prisons have a parent or other close relative who has also been incarcerated. Similarly, the link between generations is so powerful that half of all juveniles who are in custody today have a father, mother, or other close relative who has been in jail or prison.

Adapted from Fox Butterfield, "Father Steals Best: Crime in an American Family," New York Times, August 21, 2002. Copyright © 2002 by The New York Times Co. Reprinted with permission.

social process theories

Theoretical approaches to delinquency that examine the interactions between individuals and their environments, especially those that might influence them to become involved in delinquent behavior.

Social process theories of delinquency, which provide the focus of this chapter, examine the interaction between individuals and their environments for clues to the root causes of delinquency. Differential association, drift, and social control theories became popular in the 1960s because they provided a theoretical mechanism for understanding aspects of the social environment as a determinant of individual behavior. Differential association theory examines how delinquents learn crime from others. Drift theory proposes that any examination of the process of becoming deviant must take seriously both the internal components of the individual and the influence of the external environment. Social control theory provides an explanation for why some young people violate the law while others resist pressures to become delinquent. In addition to discussing these three social process perspectives, this chapter also describes and evaluates four integrated theories and considers process theories within a life-course perspective.

Differential Association Theory

Edwin H. Sutherland's formulation of **differential association theory** proposed that delinquents learn crime from others. His basic premise was that delinquency, like any other form of behavior, is a product of social interaction. In developing the theory of differential association, Sutherland contended that individuals are constantly being changed as they take on the expectations and points of view of the people with whom they interact in small, intimate groups.[1] Sutherland began with the notion that criminal behavior is to be expected of individuals who have internalized a preponderance of definitions that are favorable to law violations.[2] In 1939, he first developed the theory in his text *Principles of Criminology*, and he continued to revise it until its final form appeared in 1945. Exhibit 5.1 provides a look at the development of Sutherland's theory of differential association.

Propositions of Differential Association

Sutherland's theory of differential association is outlined in these nine propositions:

1. Criminal behavior, like other behavior, is learned from others. That is, delinquent behavior is not an inherited trait but rather an acquired one.
2. Criminal behavior is learned through a youth's active involvement with others in a process of communication. This process includes both verbal and nonverbal communication.
3. The principal learning of criminal behavior occurs within intimate personal groups. The meanings that are derived from these intimate relationships are far more influential for adolescents than is any other form of communication, such as movies and newspapers.
4. When criminal behavior is learned, the learning includes techniques of committing the crime, which are sometimes very simple, and the specific direction of motives, drives, rationalizations, and attitudes. For example, a youth may learn how to hot-wire a car from a delinquent companion with whom he is involved; he also acquires from the other boy the attitudes or mind-set that will enable him to set aside the moral bounds of the law.
5. The specific direction of motives and drives is learned from definitions of legal codes as favorable and unfavorable. Adolescents come into contact both with people who define the legal codes as rules to be observed and with those whose

differential association theory
The view that delinquency is learned from others, and that delinquent behavior is to be expected of individuals who have internalized a preponderance of definitions that are favorable to law violations.

Web LIBRARY 5.1

Read the NIJ-sponsored research publication *Trajectories of Violent Offending and Risk Status in Adolescence and Early Adulthood* at **www.justicestudies.com/ WebLibrary**.

Exhibit 5.1

Edwin H. Sutherland's Background

Edwin H. Sutherland had much in common with Clifford R. Shaw and Henry D. McKay (see Chapter 4). All were born before the turn of the century and hailed from small midwestern towns. They all did their graduate work at the University of Chicago during the early decades of the twentieth century. They knew one another personally and frequently responded to each other's work.

McKay and Sutherland, especially, were very good friends. They corresponded regularly and got together each year during the summer. Their friendship was not surprising because the two men were so alike in ancestry, geography, demeanor,

and character. It was McKay who first identified the theory of differential association in the second edition of Sutherland's 1934 criminology textbook.

In a conversation with Sutherland in 1935, McKay referred to the "Sutherland theory." Sutherland sheepishly inquired what the "Sutherland theory" was. McKay responded that he should read pages 51 and 52 of his own criminology text. Sutherland quickly located the pages and was surprised to find the statement "The conflict of cultures is the fundamental principle in explanations of crime." In helping Sutherland discover his own theory in his own book, McKay actually stimulated the evolution of differential association theory.

Source: Derived from Jon Snodgrass, *The American Criminological Tradition: Portraits of the Men and Ideology in a Discipline.* Ph.D. dissertation, The University of Pennsylvania, 1972.

Web LIBRARY 5.2

Read the article *Social Learning and Structural Factors in Adolescent Substance Use* at **www.justicestudies.com/ WebLibrary**.

definitions of reality favor the violation of the legal codes. This creates culture conflict; the next proposition explains how this conflict is resolved.

6. A person becomes delinquent because of an excess of definitions that are favorable to violation of law over definitions that are unfavorable to violation of law. This proposition expresses the basic principle of differential association. A person becomes delinquent, then, because he or she has more involvement with delinquent peers, groups, or events than with nondelinquent peers, groups, or events. Both an excess of contacts with delinquent definitions and isolation from antidelinquent patterns are important.

7. Differential associations may vary in frequency, duration, priority, and intensity. The impact that delinquent peers or groups have on a young person depends on the frequency of the social contacts, the time period over which the contacts take place, the age at which a person experiences these contacts, and the intensity of these social interactions.

8. The process of learning criminal behavior by association with criminal and anticriminal patterns involves all the mechanisms that are involved in any other learning. The learning of delinquent behavior is not restricted to mere imitation of others' behavior.

9. Although criminal behavior is an expression of general needs and values, it is not explained by those general needs and values, because noncriminal behavior is an expression of the same needs and values. The motives for delinquent behavior are different from those for conventional behavior because they are based on an excess of delinquent definitions learned from others.[3]

These nine propositions of differential association theory consist of three interrelated concepts—normative (culture) conflict, differential association, and differential social organization. The interrelated concepts operate at two levels of the explanation: the society or group and the individual.[4]

Sutherland assumes that delinquents must be taught antisocial behavior. Those who do not engage in socially unacceptable behavior have been socialized or enculturated to conventional values, but those who become involved in delinquent behavior do so because they have been taught other values. Sutherland developed a quantitative metaphor, in which conventional and criminal value systems are composed of elementary units called "definitions." Each unit can be weighted by the modalities of frequency, priority, duration, and intensity of contact. Thus, delinquency or criminality is determined by the algebraic sum of these weighted units.[5] Figure 5.1 depicts Sutherland's explanation of differential association. Donald R. Cressey, who was the spokesperson for differential association theory after Sutherland's death, explains this theory in Voices Across the Profession 5.1.

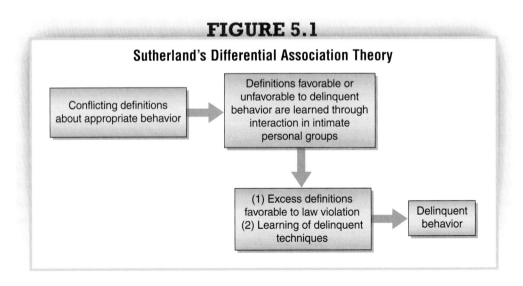

FIGURE 5.1

Sutherland's Differential Association Theory

Conflicting definitions about appropriate behavior → Definitions favorable or unfavorable to delinquent behavior are learned through interaction in intimate personal groups → (1) Excess definitions favorable to law violation (2) Learning of delinquent techniques → Delinquent behavior

Across the Profession 5.1

Interview with Donald R. Cressey

Question: What do you feel are the best features of differential association theory, and do you see any areas that need to be reformulated?

Cressey: The strongest characteristic of differential association theory is its orientation to the scientific method and thus to empiricism. This means that its users do not assume that human behavior is prompted by deeply hidden "pushers," whether they be biological, psychological, or social. On the contrary, the theory is based on an assumption that every social scientist used to make, namely, that human events are as natural as physical and biological events. Put more specifically, down deep under differential association theory is an assumption that humans come into the world as complex but unprogrammed computers. Then, during the course of their lives, they get programmed to behave in certain ways. The programming is not systematic or consistent, as it is when a technician programs a real computer. Still, various rules for behavior are fed into us, and we behave accordingly. No behavior that has not been programmed into a person will ever show up in the person's actions. Nowadays a lot of people object to that scientific assumption. They want the human to be more dignified and majestic than other animals, so they give us a soul, a psyche, a mind, or a will. But because such pushers are not observable or measurable, differential association theory assumes that we must look elsewhere for explanations of why people behave as they do.

So starting with the assumption, all the differential association theory says is that if people are programmed to behave in a certain way, they will act that way. If

you are programmed to know only that "honesty is the best policy," then you will be honest. If you are programmed to know only that it is all right to steal, then you will steal. But the matter is not so simple because, starting when we are at our mothers' knees, we are programmed in both ways. What the theory says, then, is that whether you will steal or not depends on the *ratio* of these two kinds of behavior patterns that have been put into the computer which is you.

Now that's a great oversimplification of what differential association theory says about human learning. If you start to explore the process seriously and in detail, it gets very complicated in a hurry. The biggest problem I see with the theory is the idea that the effects of behavior patterns—whether favorable to crime or unfavorable to it—are cumulative. It isn't that behavior patterns are not observable.

At least hypothetically, one can measure the ratio of the two kinds of behavior patterns a person has learned. But no one has shown how behavior patterns presented at one time in a person's life link up with behavior patterns presented at a later time, if indeed they do.

The strength of differential association is that it makes good sense of the so-called "factors" that are correlated with high crime and delinquency rates. Indeed, the theory makes better sense of the sex ratio, the age ratio, and the social class ratio in crime and delinquency than does any other theory. Consider poverty. Street crimes are clearly associated with poverty, and a popular theory is that poverty causes crime and delinquency. But if you think about the relationship for a moment, it will dawn on you that poverty doesn't

grab people by the shoulders, kick them in the butt, and make them commit crime. Girls living in ghetto areas are in equal poverty with boys, but their delinquency rates are much lower than the rates for boys. So something else is at work. The "something else" that accounts for the differences in the rates is associated with the behavior patterns unfavorable or favorable to delinquent behavior.

Differential association theory is often misinterpreted. Some think it refers to association with delinquents or criminals, but it doesn't. It refers to association with criminal *behavior patterns,* which often are presented by mothers, fathers, and others who are not criminals. The idea that differential association is a theory about criminality in general also is an error. The error stems from the way the theory is presented, but if you think about it for a while, it's clear that differential association is really a theory about specific kinds of crime. For example, if you have an excess of associations favorable to shoplifting sweaters from local department stores, as teenaged girls are likely to do, that doesn't mean you have an excess of associations favorable to burglary, robbery, or stealing hubcaps. People don't become criminals in general. They are programmed to believe that committing only some kinds of crime is "really" bad, indecent, immoral, or otherwise unacceptable.

■ **Does differential association theory make sense to you? What types of delinquency do you think it most applies to? Which ones appear to be explained least by this learning theory?**

Source: The late Donald R. Cressey was acknowledged as one of the top criminologists in the United States. He was the author of books such as *Other People's Money* and *Theft of the Nation* and coauthor of the classic text *Criminology* (with Edwin H. Sutherland) and of such books as *Social Problems* and *Justice by Consent.*[6]

Evaluation of Differential Association Theory

Sutherland's differential association theory represented a watershed in criminology. Criminology was under heavy criticism before this theory was developed, because it lacked a general theoretical perspective to integrate findings and guide research.[7] In addition to providing this theoretical perspective, differential association theory offers the following strengths:

■ Some support for the differential association theory can be found in the research.[8]

■ It is difficult to reject the argument that juveniles learn crime from others. Needless to say, juveniles learn their basic values, norms, skills, and self-perceptions from others; accordingly, the idea that they also learn criminal behavior patterns from significant others seems irrefutable. The proposition that youngsters learn from people whose definitions are favorable to law violations appears to fit our understanding of juveniles and of their extreme vulnerability to the influence of the group.

■ Differential association theory also has appeal in that it is seen as positive. It does not reduce delinquency to psychological and biological models, which postulate that personal inadequacies cannot be penetrated by outside influence. Instead, Sutherland sees individuals as changeable and as subject to the opinions and values of others. The chief task in delinquency prevention, then, is to strive for change in the small groups in which adolescents are involved rather than attempting to change an entire society.

differential identification theory

A modification of differential association theory that applies the interactionist concept of the self, allows for choice, and stresses the importance of motives.

■ Differential association theory has had an enduring impact on the study of juvenile delinquency, as is apparent in the attempts to revise this theory. Melvin DeFleur and Richard Quinney argued that the theory could be formally tightened if it were based on the concepts of symbolic interaction and attitude formation.[9] Daniel Glaser's modification of differential association theory, which is called **differential identification theory**, applied the interactionist concept of the self: "A person pursues criminal behavior to the extent that he identifies himself with real or imaginary persons from whose perspective his criminal behavior seems acceptable."[10] Glaser's revision allowed for human choice and stressed the importance of motives existing in the wider culture independent of direct intimate association. Robert J. Burgess Jr. and Ronald L. Akers's differential reinforcement theory proposed a step-by-step restatement of differential association according to such ideas as reinforcement and punishment (operant conditioning). This reformulation, now known as social learning theory, contended that criminal or delinquent behavior is learned primarily "in those groups which comprise the individual's major source of reinforcements."[11] Marvin D. Krohn's network approach to delinquent behavior incorporates some of the elements of differential association theory. Krohn's term *network analysis* refers to sets of groups or organizations linked by the web of social relationships. Krohn suggests that the most important concept in accounting for delinquency is multiplexity. If members of a social network participate jointly in a number of activities, they are likely to influence the behavior of actors within the network.[12]

Criticisms of differential association theory can be grouped into four areas.

■ Ruth Kornhauser's reduction of differential association to a cultural deviance perspective has been widely accepted in the field.[13] This criticism has influenced many researchers either to reject differential association theory outright in favor of a social control theory or to place it with a version of integrated theory (see later sections of this chapter).

■ The terms of differential association theory are so vague that it is nearly impossible to test the theory empirically.[14] For example, how can an excess of definitions toward criminality be measured statistically?[15] How can frequency, duration, priority, and intensity be studied? How can the learning process be more clearly specified?[16] What defines an intimate personal group? Exactly what techniques, motives, and rationalizations do youngsters learn from others?

In the movie *Mean Girls*, this Wannabe is hoping for acceptance from the Queen Bees.
■ **How might the concept of differential association explain the interaction depicted here?**

■ Differential association theory has been accused of failing to deal with several critical questions relating to the process of learning crime from others. For example, why is it that one youth succumbs to delinquent definitions but another does not? Why do youths who are exposed to delinquent definitions still engage in conforming behavior most of the time? How did the first "teacher" learn delinquent techniques and definitions to pass on? Why do most youths desist from delinquent behavior at the age of seventeen or eighteen? Why do youths frequently continue delinquent behavior even after the removal of the antisocial stimuli (delinquent peers)? Finally, what is the effect of punishment on delinquents?

■ Critics point out that differential association theory has no room for human purpose and meaning, because it ultimately reduces the individual to an object that merely reacts to the bombardment of external forces and cannot reject the material being presented.[17] According to the theory, then, the delinquent is a passive vessel into which various definitions are poured, and the resultant mixture is something over which the youth has no control.[18]

On balance, although differential association theory has been subjected to sharp attack over the years, it remains one of the best known and most enduring theories of delinquent behavior. In 1988, Ross L. Matsueda offered a favorable analysis of differential association theory, proposing that research be done to specify "the concrete elements of the theory's abstract principles" and especially to identify "the content of definitions favorable to crime."[19]

Drift Theory and Delinquency

The process of becoming a delinquent, David Matza says in *Delinquency and Drift* (1964), begins when a juvenile neutralizes himself or herself from the moral bounds of the law and "drifts" into delinquency. Drift, according to Matza, means that "the delinquent transiently exists in limbo between convention and crime, responding in turn to the demands of each, flirting now with one, now the other, but postponing commitment, evading decision. Thus he drifts between criminal and conventional action."[20]

Matza's concepts of drift and differential association have many assumptions in common, but Matza's **drift theory** does place far greater importance than differential association theory on the exercise of juveniles' choices and on the sense of injustice that juveniles feel about the discriminatory treatment they have received.

Having established that the delinquent is one who drifts back and forth between convention and deviancy, Matza then examines the process by which legal norms are neutralized. But fundamental to his analysis is the contention that delinquent youths remain integrated into the wider society and that a violation of legal norms does not mean surrendering allegiance to them:[21]

> There are millions of occasions during which a delinquency may be committed. Except for occasions covered by surveillance, virtually every moment experienced offers an opportunity for offense. Yet delinquency fails to occur during all but a tiny proportion of these moments. During most of the subcultural delinquent's life he is distracted and restrained by convention from the commission of offenses. Episodically, he is released from the moral bind of conventional order. This temporary though recurrent release from the bind of convention has been taken for compulsion or commitment. It is, instead, almost the opposite. During release the delinquent is not constrained to commit an offense; rather, he is free to drift into delinquency. Under the condition of widely available extenuating circumstances, the subcultural delinquent may choose to commit delinquencies.[22]

Delinquency, then, becomes permissible when responsibility is neutralized. According to a well-known article by Gresham M. Sykes and Matza, **neutralization theory** provides a means of understanding how delinquents insulate themselves from responsibility for wrongdoing. Sykes and Matza claim that there are five techniques of neutralization, or justifications, of delinquent behavior that precede delinquent behavior and make such behavior possible by defining it as acceptable.[23]

- ■ Denial of responsibility ("I didn't mean it.")
- ■ Denial of injury ("I didn't hurt anyone.")
- ■ Denial of the victim ("They had it coming to them.")
- ■ Condemnation of the condemners ("Everyone is picking on me.")
- ■ Appeal to higher loyalties ("I didn't do it for myself.")[24]

A teenager argues with his mother. ■ **What parental role might drift theory posit in the prevention of delinquency?**

The sense of responsibility, then, is the immediate condition of drift. But other conditions of drift include the sense of injustice, the primacy of custom, and the assertion of tort. Matza claims that subcultural delinquents are filled with a sense of injustice because they depend on a memory file that collects examples of inconsistency. The primacy of custom relates to the male delinquent's observation of the virtues of his subculture; these virtues stress the "traditional precepts of manliness, celebrating as they do the heroic themes of honor, valor, and loyalty." In the group setting, the delinquent must demonstrate valor and loyalty when faced with dare, challenge, and insult. The assertion of tort, which has to do with a private transaction between the accused and the victim, occurs when the subcultural delinquent considers a harmful wrong to be a tort instead of a crime. Subcultural delinquents frequently believe that the justice process cannot be invoked unless the victim is willing to file a complaint.[25]

Matza concludes that "the breaking of the moral bind to law arising from neutralization and resulting in drift does not assure the commission of a delinquent act."[26] The missing element that provides "the thrust or impetus by which the delinquent act is realized is *will*."[27] The will is activated both on mundane occasions and in extraordinary situations.[28] But the subcultural delinquent is not likely to have the will to repeat an old offense if he or she has failed in the past: "Few persons—clowns and fools are among them—like to engage in activities they do badly."[29] Desperation, reasons Matza, also can activate one's will to commit infractions. Matza sees desperation intertwined with the mood of fatalism; that is, because the delinquent feels pushed around, he or she needs to make something happen to restore the mood of humanism. Crime then enables the subcultural delinquent to see himself or herself as cause rather than as effect.[30]

Matza developed the drift theory to account for the majority of adolescents who, from time to time, engage in delinquent behavior. But in his 1969 book, *Becoming Deviant*, he introduces the concepts of will, commitment, and conversion. Using nonempirical terms that are traditionally reserved for the theologian or the philosopher, Matza suggests that delinquents' will must be captured by deviant influences before they are committed to a delinquent way of life. In **commitment to delinquency**, delinquents permit their will to be captured, and a type of conversion experience happens. The former nondelinquent becomes a different kind of person and is willing to stand up for this new way of life.[31] Figure 5.2 presents Matza's explanation of delinquent behavior.

commitment to delinquency
A term for the attachment that a delinquent juvenile has to a deviant identity and values.

Evaluation of Drift Theory

Drift theory has been largely ignored in recent analyses of delinquency, which is unfortunate because it does have several strengths:

- Drift theory builds on the assumption that delinquent behavior is a learning process that takes place in interactions with others. The theory examines how group influence can encourage youths to release themselves from the moral binds of the law.
- Drift theory can also help account for the fact that the majority of adolescents commit occasional delinquent acts but then go on to accept roles as law-abiding adults. Matza's explanation for the fact that delinquency declines as adolescents approach adulthood is that many teenage delinquents were not committed to delinquent norms in the first place.
- Additionally, drift theory helps us understand the situational aspects of delinquent behavior. Matza views the delinquent as a youth who is pressured to engage in delinquent behavior by a specific situational context and by the norms of that context. Matza rightly contends that youths are influenced by group processes to commit behaviors that they might not otherwise commit.
- In *Delinquency and Drift*, Matza challenges the notion that delinquents are "constrained" (compelled) to engage in delinquency. He contends that hard determinism predicts far too much delinquency and that a **soft determinism** much more accurately explains delinquent behavior.[32] This argument for soft determinism,

soft determinism
The view that delinquents are neither wholly free nor wholly constrained in their choice of actions.

FIGURE 5.2

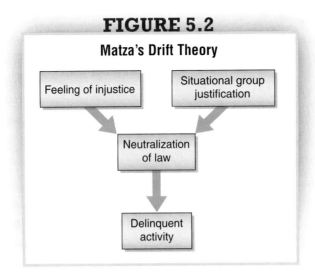

Matza's Drift Theory

first found in drift theory, is similar to later versions of soft determinism or in-determinism found in control theory,[33] rational choice theory,[34] social learning theory,[35] and conflict theory.[36]

- Another important conjecture of drift theory is that the attitudes of delinquents and nondelinquents toward unlawful behaviors are basically the same. There are mixed findings in the literature concerning this conjecture.[37]

- John Hagan integrated drift with social control theory and a life-course concep-tualization to study cultural stratification. He found that "adolescents adrift from parental and educational control are more likely than those with more controls to develop mild or more seriously deviant subcultural preferences" and that "among males with working-class origins, identification with the subculture of delinquency has a negative effect on trajectories of early adult status attain-ment."[38]

- The basic constructs of drift theory have been examined more extensively in Sykes and Matza's work on delinquents' techniques of self-justification or rationaliza-tion, better known as neutralization theory. John E. Hamlin suggests that neu-tralization theory has come to occupy a central place in delinquency theory because it has contributed to two broad traditions: learning theory and control theory.[39] Akers's learning theory implies that delinquents must neutralize moral prescriptions before committing unlawful acts.[40] Control theory also utilizes the assumptions of neutralization theory.[41] Robert Agnew's analysis of data from the second and third waves of the National Youth Survey revealed that neutraliza-tion is more likely to accompany violent behaviors than nonviolent behaviors.[42] Walter C. Reckless and Shlomo Shoham developed another theory of neutral-ization that they called *norm erosion*, which is a process of "give" in moral and ethical resistance.[43]

In sum, even though Matza's drift theory has received less attention than neu-tralization theory, it still is one of the most useful expressions of the dynamics of why individuals become involved in delinquent behavior. Sykes and Matza's neutraliza-tion theory has been more influential in the development of delinquency theory, but it appears to apply to some delinquent behaviors more than others. In Voices Across the Profession 5.2, David Matza expands on some of his thoughts on drift and neu-tralization theories.

Social Control and Delinquent Behavior

Differential association and drift theories are both learning theories of crime, but con-trol theory is focused more on an internal mechanism that helps youngsters avoid

Interview with David Matza

Question: Has your thinking changed concerning the process of becoming a delinquent since you wrote *Delinquency and Drift?*

Matza: Not too much, but some. I would now place more emphasis on racial oppression and the class correlates of racial oppression. The underlying social and political basis for the sense of injustice is left too implicit in *Delinquency and Drift.* Partly that was because the usual theories in the early sixties were based on class injustice and such theories were not very firmly based in fact, as I tried to point out in sections of the book and in *Becoming Deviant.* In my opinion, the thesis of racial injustice is based much more securely in the known facts of American history and social structure and very accurately reflected in the composition of prison and juvenile correctional populations.

Question: Are you as convinced that most subcultural delinquents adhere to societal norms as you were when you wrote *Delinquency and Drift?*

Matza: I am not as convinced, yet I still believe that even in rebellion against a morality whose application is unjust, a belief in the truth of an uncorrupted morality is asserted. When Frederick Douglass asserted that to be free, the slave was compelled to break most, if not all, of the rules of the oppressor, he was not by that statement breaking with the idea of society or with the belief in morality. Increasingly, I have come to think that what we call juvenile delinquency is, in part, the behavior of the youthful section of what traditionally has been termed the dangerous classes. The nineteenth-century ideas of the dangerous classes are today lodged in the writings of Edward Banfield. Without understanding the oppressive context of social life among oppressed populations, the dangerous behav-

ior of youth is likely to be misconceived as deriving from biological factors, a tendency which is once again rampant in criminology and sociology thanks to ideologues like Banfield and his followers.

Question: Commitment to delinquency is one concept in your publications which has been widely debated. What is your reaction to this concept today?

Matza: I still do not think that very many youngsters are committed to delinquency. I am not sure how fruitful the debate is since "commitment" is a very slippery term. Commitment to an institution is a much firmer basis for subsequent juvenile delinquency than anything so intangible as an attitudinal commitment.

Question: In a 1971 interview, you indicated that *Delinquency and Drift* is a "confused jumbling of conservative, liberal, and radical views" and that "*Becoming Deviant* is sort of liberal and radical, maybe a little conservative too." What did you mean by these comments?

Matza: I meant to imply that I was quite disappointed if not angry at the way criminal justice systems were already beginning to twist much of the writings of the sixties toward their punitive and correctional ends. I guess I thought and still think that if my writing was unclear enough to appeal to conservatives, I must have been pretty confused. I was being critical of myself and perhaps others of similar perspective for having presented material so easily absorbed by an establishment which, between 1970 and 1984, abandoned and then turned against improving or at least reforming the penal system. I also meant that I was not very happy about my work, that a deeper formulation of the phenomenon would eliminate some of the philosophical ambiguity.

Question: Interest and research in the attributes, motivations, and socialization of youthful offenders have largely waned today. Instead, theorists are discussing the neoclassical revival; biosociological focus; radical, or critical, criminology; and the labeling perspective. What is your reaction to this current emphasis? Does this take us farther away from the real delinquent?

Matza: I think the emphasis is intellectually and scientifically repressive, taking us very far from the actual person caught breaking the rules. My reaction is to continue being critical of such tendencies in my classroom teaching and perhaps awaiting the opportunity to propose more realistic theories of practice when the population finally realizes the conservative fringe has led absolutely nowhere with regard to the problems of poverty, injustice, and crime. Even talking about crime to students over the past fifteen years has been difficult. Under the conservative mentality the study of crime is not really possible, not in any deep scientific or intellectual sense.

Question: What other thoughts about the prevention and control of delinquency in American society would you like to add?

Matza: Delinquency cannot be controlled when government is hostile to poor and working people. Delinquency can only be prevented by a just and peaceful social order.

> ■ Do you agree with Matza that "delinquency can only be prevented by a just and peaceful social order"? What new direction does Matza seem to be taking his theory of delinquency and drift?

David Matza is professor emeritus of sociology at the University of California, Berkeley. He is the author of *Delinquency and Drift* and *Becoming Deviant* and coauthor of "Techniques of Neutralization."[44]

control theory

Any of several theoretical approaches that maintain that human beings must be held in check, or somehow be controlled, if delinquent tendencies are to be repressed.

delinquent behavior. The core ideas of **control theory** have a long history, going back at least to the nineteenth century. Control theorists agree on one especially significant point: Human beings must be held in check, or somehow controlled, if delinquent tendencies are to be repressed. Control theorists also generally agree that delinquency is the result of a deficiency in something. Juveniles commit delinquency because some controlling force is absent or defective.[45]

Early versions of control theory include Albert J. Reiss Jr.'s theory of personal and social controls and F. Ivan Nye's family-focused theory of social control. Reiss described how the weak egos of delinquents lacked the personal controls to produce conforming behavior.[46] Nye added that the problem for the theorist was not to find an explanation for delinquent behavior; rather, it was to explain why delinquent behavior is not more common.[47] Walter C. Reckless's containment theory and Travis Hirschi's social control theory are the most developed examples of control theory, and we'll examine them next.

Containment Theory

containment theory

A theoretical perspective that strong inner containment and reinforcing external containment provide insulation against delinquent and criminal behavior.

Reckless developed **containment theory** in the 1950s and 1960s to explain crime and delinquency. Containment theory, which can explain both conforming behavior and deviancy, has two reinforcing elements: an inner control system and an outer control system. The assumption is that strong inner containment and reinforcing external containment provide insulation against deviant behavior. But Reckless noted that containment theory does not explain the entire spectrum of delinquent behavior. It does not account for delinquency that emerges from strong inner pushes, such as compulsions, anxieties, and personality disorders, or from organic impairments, such as brain damage.[48]

Elements of Containment Theory   Reckless defines the ingredients of inner containment as self-components, such as self-control, positive self-concept, well-developed superego, ego strength, high frustration tolerance, high resistance to diversions, high sense of responsibility, ability to find substitute satisfactions, goal orientations, and tension-reducing rationalizations.

Outer containment, or external regulators, represents the structural buffers in the person's immediate social world or environment that are able to hold him or her within bounds. External controls consist of such items as the presentation of a consistent moral front to the person; institutional reinforcement of his or her norms, goals, and expectations; effective supervision and discipline; provision for a reasonable scope of activity, including limits and responsibilities; and opportunity for acceptance, identity, and belongingness.

Internal pushes consist of the drives, motives, frustrations, restlessness, disappointments, rebellion, hostility, and feelings of inferiority that encourage a person to become involved in socially unacceptable behavior. Environmental pressures are those associated with poverty or deprivation, conflict and discord, external restraint, minority group status, and limited access to success in an opportunity structure. Finally, the pulls of the environment consist of distractions, attractions, temptations, patterns of deviancy, carriers of delinquent patterns, and criminogenic advertising and propaganda in the society.

Relationship of Containment and Delinquency   If a youth has a weak outer containment, the external pressures and pulls need to be handled by the inner control system. If the youth's outer buffer is relatively strong and effective, his or her inner defense does not have to play such a critical role. Similarly, if the youth's inner controls are not equal to the ordinary pushes, an effective outer defense may help to hold him or her within socially acceptable behavior. But if the inner defenses are in good working order, the outer structure does not have to come to the rescue. Juveniles who have both strong external and internal containment, then, are much less likely to become delinquent than those who have only either strong external containment

Web LIBRARY 5.3

Read the OJJDP publication *Causes and Correlates: Findings and Implications* at **www .justicestudies.com/ WebLibrary**.

or strong internal containment. Youths who have both weak external and internal controls are the most prone to delinquent behavior, although weak internal controls appear to result in delinquent behavior more often than do weak external controls.

Web LIBRARY 5.4

Read the testimony of John Wilson, Acting Administrator of the Office of Juvenile Justice and Delinquency Prevention, before the U.S. House of Representatives, Committee on the Judiciary on October 2, 2000, at **www.justicestudies.com/ WebLibrary**.

The Self-Concept as Insulation Against Delinquency   Containment theory involves both outer and inner containment, but inner containment, or self-concept, has received far more attention than has outer containment. Reckless, Simon Dinitz, and their students spent over a decade investigating the effects of self-concept on delinquent behavior. The subjects for this study were sixth-grade boys living in the area of Columbus, Ohio, that had the highest white delinquency rate. Teachers were asked to nominate those boys who, in their point of view, were insulated against delinquency. In the second phase of the study, teachers in the same area schools were asked to nominate sixth-grade boys who appeared to be heading toward delinquency. Both the "good boy" group and the "bad boy" group were given the same battery of psychological tests; the mothers of both groups were interviewed.[49]

Reckless and Dinitz concluded from these studies that one of the preconditions of law-abiding conduct is a good self-concept. This insulation against delinquency may be viewed as an ongoing process reflecting an internalization of nondelinquent values and conformity to the expectations of significant others—parents, teachers, and peers. Thus, a good self-concept, the product of favorable socialization, steers youths away from delinquency by acting as an inner buffer or containment against delinquency.

> " One of the preconditions of law-abiding conduct is a good self-concept. "

In the 1960s, Reckless and Dinitz undertook a four-year intervention project that involved seventh-grade boys in all of the Columbus junior high schools and was designed to improve the self-concept of potential delinquents. But the follow-up data indicated that the special classes had no appreciable impact.[50]

Several studies have found that a positive self-concept does help insulate adolescents from delinquent behavior.[51] Other studies have found little relationship between positive self-esteem and reduced rates of delinquency.[52] Still other researchers have argued that people behave in a fashion designed to maximize their self-esteem and therefore youngsters adopt deviant reference groups for the purpose of enhancing self-esteem.[53] Delinquent behavior then becomes a coping strategy to defend against negative self-evaluation.[54]

The major flaw of inner containment, or self-concept, theory is the difficulty of defining self-concept in such a way that researchers can be certain they are accurately measuring the key variables of this concept.[55] M. Schwartz and S. S. Tangri proposed that a poor self-concept might have other outcomes besides vulnerability to delinquency. They further disputed the adequacy of Reckless and Dinitz's measures of self-concept and questioned the effects of labeling on the subsequent behavior of both the "good" and "bad" boys.[56]

Social Control Theory

Travis Hirschi is the theorist most closely identified with **social control theory**, or *bonding theory*. In *Causes of Delinquency*, Hirschi linked delinquent behavior to the quality of the bond an individual maintains with society, stating that "delinquent acts result when an individual's bond to society is weak or broken."[57] Hirschi is indebted to Emile Durkheim for recognition of the importance of the social bond to society and accepts the view of Thomas Hobbes, Puritan theologians, and Sigmund Freud that humans are basically antisocial and sinful. In Hirschi's words, "We are all animals and thus all naturally capable of committing criminal acts."[58] Hence, he argues that humans' basic impulses motivate them to become involved in crime and delinquency unless there is reason for them to refrain from such behavior. Instead of the standard question, "Why do they do it?" Hirschi asserts that the most important question becomes, "Why don't they do it?"[59]

social control theory
A perspective that delinquent acts result when a juvenile's bond to society is weak or broken.

Cyberdelinquents: Bot Herders and Cybercrooks

SEATTLE — At the height of his powers, Jeanson James Ancheta felt unstoppable.

From his home in Downey, Calif., the then-19-year-old high school dropout controlled thousands of compromised PCs, or "bots," that helped him earn enough cash in 2004 and 2005 to drive a souped-up 1993 BMW and spend $600 a week on new clothes and car parts.

He once bragged to a protégé that hacking Internet-connected PCs was "easy, like slicing cheese," court records show.

But Ancheta got caught. In the first case of its kind, he pleaded guilty in January 2006 to federal charges of hijacking hundreds of thousands of computers and selling access to others to spread spam and launch Web attacks.

In separate cases, federal authorities last August also assisted in the arrest of Farid Essebar, 18, of Morocco, and last month indicted Christopher Maxwell, 19, of Vacaville, Calif., on suspicion of similar activities.

The arrests underscore an ominous shift in the struggle to keep the Internet secure: Cybercrime undergirded by networks of bots—PCs infected with malicious software that allows them to be controlled by an attacker—is soaring.

Without you realizing it, attackers are secretly trying to penetrate your PC to tap small bits of computing power to do evil things. They've already compromised some 47 million PCs sitting in living rooms, in bedrooms, even on the desk in your office.

Bot networks have become so ubiquitous that they've also given rise to a new breed of low-level bot masters, typified by Ancheta, Essebar and Maxwell.

Tim Cranton, director of Microsoft's Internet Safety Enforcement Team, calls bot networks "the tool of choice for those intent on using the Internet to carry out crimes."

Budding cyberthieves use basic programs and generally stick to quick-cash schemes. Brazen and inexperienced, they can inadvertently cause chaos: Essebar is facing prosecution in Morocco on charges of releasing the Zotob worm that crippled systems in banks and media companies around the world; Maxwell awaits a May 15 trial for allegedly spreading bots that disrupted operations at Seattle's Northwest Hospital.

More elite bot herders, who partner with crime groups to supply computer power for data theft and other cyber-fraud, have proved to be highly elusive. But the neophytes tend to be sloppy about hiding their tracks. The investigations leading to the arrests of Ancheta, Essebar and Maxwell have given authorities their most detailed look yet at how bots enable cybercrime.

Estimating the number of bots is difficult, but top researchers who participate in meetings of high-tech's Messaging Anti-Abuse Working Group often use a 7% infection rate as a discussion point. That means as many as 47 million of the 681 million PCs connected to the Internet worldwide may be under the control of a bot network.

Security giant McAfee detected 28,000 distinct bot networks active last year, more than triple the amount in 2004. And a February survey of 123 tech executives, conducted by security firm nCircle, pegged annual losses to U.S. businesses because of computer-related crimes at $197 billion.

Law enforcement officials say the ground floor is populated by perhaps hundreds of bot herders, most of them young men. Mostly, they assemble networks of compromised PCs to make quick cash by spreading adware—those pop-up advertisements for banking, dating, porn and gambling websites that clutter the Internet. They get paid for installing adware on each PC they infect.

"The low-level guys . . . can inflict a lot of collateral damage," says Steve Martinez, deputy assistant director of the FBI's Cyber Division.

Ancheta and his attorney declined to be interviewed, and efforts to reach Essebar with help from the FBI were unsuccessful. Steven Bauer, Maxwell's attorney, said his client was a "fairly small player" who began spreading bots "almost as a youthful prank."

The stories of these three young men, pieced together from court records and interviews with regulators, security experts and independent investigators, illustrate the mind-set of the growing fraternity of hackers and cyberthieves born after 1985. They also provide a glimpse of Cybercrime Inc.'s most versatile and profitable tool.

Ancheta: Trading Candy

School records show that Ancheta transferred out of Downey High School, in a suburb near Los Angeles, in December 2001 and later attended an alternative program for students with academic or behavioral problems. Eventually, he earned a high school equivalency certificate. Ancheta worked at an Internet cafe and expressed an interest in joining the military reserves, his aunt, Sharon Gregorio, told the Associated Press.

Instead, in June 2004, court records show, he discovered rxbot, a potent—but quite common—computer worm, malicious computer code designed to spread widely across the Internet.

Ancheta likely gravitated to it because it is easy to customize, says Nicholas Albright, founder of Shadowserver.org, a watchdog group. Novices often start by tweaking worms and trading bots. "I see high school kids doing it all the time," says Albright. "They trade bot nets like candy."

Ancheta proved more enterprising than most. He infected thousands of PCs and started a business—#botz4sale—on a private Internet chat area. From June to September 2004, he made about $3,000 on more than 30 sales of up to 10,000 bots at a time, according to court records.

By late 2004, he started a new venture, court records show. He signed up with two Internet marketing companies, LoudCash of Bellevue, Wash., and GammaCash Entertainment of Montreal, to distribute ads on commission.

But instead of setting up a website and asking visitors for permission to install ads—a common, legal practice—he used his bots to install adware on vulnerable Internet-connected PCs, court records show. Typically, payment for each piece of adware installed ranges from 20 cents to 70 cents.

Working at home, Ancheta nurtured his growing bot empire during a workday that usually began shortly after 1 p.m. and stretched non-stop until 5 a.m., a source with direct knowledge of the case says. He hired an assistant, an admiring juvenile from Boca Raton, Fla., nicknamed SoBe, court records show. Chatting via AOL's free instant-messaging service, Ancheta taught him how to spread PC infections and manage adware installations.

Checks ranging as high as $7,996 began rolling in from the two marketing firms. In six months, Ancheta and his helper pulled in nearly $60,000, court records show.

During one online chat with SoBe about installing adware, Ancheta, who awaits sentencing May 1, advised his helper: "It's immoral, but the money makes it right."

Sean Sundwall, a spokesman for Bellevue, Wash.-based 180solutions, LoudCash's parent company, said Ancheta distributed its adware in only a small number of incidents listed in the indictment. GammaCash had no comment.

Maxwell: Infecting a Hospital

At about the same time—in early 2005—Christopher Maxwell and two co-conspirators were allegedly hitting their stride running a similar operation. From his parents' home in Vacaville, Calif., Maxwell, then an 18-year-old community college student, conspired with two minors in other states to spread bots and install adware, earning $100,000 from July 2004 to July 2005, according to a federal indictment.

They ran into a problem in January 2005 when a copy of the bot they were using inadvertently found its way onto a vulnerable PC at Seattle's Northwest Hospital. Once inside the hospital's network, it swiftly infected 150 of the hospital's 1,100 PCs and would have compromised many more. But the simultaneous scanning of 150 PCs looking for other machines to infect overwhelmed the local network, according to an account in court records.

Computers in the intensive care unit shut down. Lab tests and administrative tasks were interrupted, forcing the hospital into manual procedures.

Over the next few months, special agent David Farquhar, a member of the FBI's Northwest Cyber Crime Task Force, traced the infection to a NetZero Internet account using a phone number at Maxwell's parents' home, leading to Maxwell's indictment on Feb. 9. He pleaded not guilty.

Essebar: Birth of a Worm

As authorities closed in on Ancheta and Maxwell last summer, 18-year-old Farid Essebar was allegedly just getting started in the bots marketplace. The FBI says the skinny, Russian-born resident of Morocco operated under the nickname Diabl0 (pronounced Diablo but spelled with a zero). Diabl0 began attracting notice as one of many copycat hackers tweaking the ubiquitous Mytob

e-mail worm. E-mail worms compromise a PC in much the same way as a bot, but the victim must help, by clicking on an e-mail attachment to start the infection.

Diabl0 created a very distinctive version of Mytob designed to lower the security settings on infected PCs, install adware and report back to Diabl0 for more instructions. Last June, David Taylor, an information security specialist at the University of Pennsylvania, spotted Diabl0 on the Internet as he was about to issue such instructions. Taylor engaged the hacker in a text chat.

Diabl0 boasted about using Mytob to get paid for installing adware. "I really thought that he was immature," Taylor recalls. "He was asking me what did I think about his new bot, with all these smiley faces. Maybe he didn't realize what he was doing was so bad."

In early August, Diabl0 capitalized on a golden opportunity when Microsoft issued its monthly set of patches for newly discovered security holes in Windows. As usual, independent researchers immediately began to analyze the patches as part of a process to develop better security tools. Cybercrooks closely monitor the public websites where results of this kind of research get posted.

Diabl0 latched onto one of the test tools and turned it into a self-propagating worm, dubbed Zotob, says Charles Renert, director of research at security firm Determina. Much like Mytob, Zotob prepared the infected PC to receive adware. But Zotob did one better: It could sweep across the Internet, infecting PCs with no user action required.

Diabl0 designed Zotob to quietly seek out certain Windows computer servers equipped with the latest compilation of upgrades, called a service pack. But he failed to account for thousands of Windows servers still running outdated service packs, says Peter Allor, director of intelligence at Internet Security Systems.

By the start of the next workweek, Zotob variants began snaking into older servers at the Canadian bank CIBC, and at ABC News, *The New York Times* and CNN. The servers began rebooting repeatedly, disrupting business and drawing serious attention to the new worm. "Zotob had a quality-assurance problem," says Allor. Diabl0 had neglected to ensure Zotob would run smoothly on servers running the earlier service packs, he says.

A victim of a computer hacker displays his frustration. ■ **Why does computer crime seem to attract so many techno-savvy youngsters?**

Within two weeks, Microsoft's Internet Safety Enforcement Team, a group of 65 investigators, paralegals and lawyers, identified Essebar as Diabl0 and pinpointed his base of operations. Microsoft's team also flushed out a suspected accomplice, Atilla Ekici, 21, nicknamed Coder.

Microsoft alerted the FBI, which led to the Aug. 25 arrests by local authorities of Essebar in Morocco and Ekici in Turkey.

The FBI holds evidence that Ekici paid Essebar with stolen credit card numbers to create the Mytob variants and Zotob, Louis Reigel, assistant director of the FBI's Cyber Division told reporters.

While Ancheta operated as a sole proprietor, and Maxwell was part of a three-man shop, Essebar and Ekici functioned more like freelancers, says Allor. They appeared to be part of a loose "confederation of folks who have unique abilities," says Allor.

"They come together with others who have unique abilities, and from time to time they switch off who they work with."

Despite their notoriety, Essebar, Ancheta and Maxwell represent mere flickers in the Internet underworld. More elite hackers collaborating with organized crime groups take pains to cover their tracks—and rarely get caught.

"Those toward the lower levels of this strata are the ones that tend to get noticed and arrested pretty quickly," says Martin Overton, a security specialist at IBM.

Source: Byron Acohido and Jon Swartz, "Cybercrime Inc.—Malicious-Software Spreaders Get Sneakier, More Prevalent," *USA Today,* April 23, 2006, pp. 1B & 3B. Copyright © 2006 by *USA Today.* Reprinted with permission.

A father helps his children with school work. According to social control theorists, a child's attachment to and respect for his or her parents is the most important variable in preventing delinquency. ■ **What might rank second? Third?**

commitment to the social bond
The attachment that a juvenile has to conventional institutions and activities.

Hirschi theorized that individuals who are most tightly bonded to social groups such as the family, the school, and peers are less likely to commit delinquent acts.[60] Commitment to the social bond, according to Hirschi, is made up of four main elements: attachment, commitment, involvement, and belief.

Attachment   An individual's attachment to conventional others is the first element of the social bond. Sensitivity toward others, argues Hirschi, relates to the ability to internalize norms and to develop a conscience.[61] Attachment to others also includes the ties of affection and respect children have to parents, teachers, and friends. The stronger the attachment to others, the more likely that an individual will take this into consideration when and if he or she is tempted to commit a delinquent act.[62] Attachment to parents is the most important variable insulating a child against delinquent behavior. Even if a family is broken by divorce or desertion, the child needs to maintain attachment to one or both parents. "If the child is alienated from the parent," Hirschi asserted, "he will not develop an adequate conscience or superego."[63]

Commitment   The second element of the social bond is commitment to conventional activities and values. An individual is committed to the degree that he or she is willing to invest time, energy, and self in attaining conventional goals such as education, property, or reputation. When a committed individual considers the cost of delinquent behavior, he or she uses common sense and thinks of the risk of losing the investment already made in conventional behavior.[64] Hirschi contended that if juveniles are committed to these conventional values and activities, they develop a stake in conformity and will refrain from delinquent behavior.

Involvement   Involvement also protects an individual from delinquent behavior. Because any individual's time and energy are limited, involvement in conventional activities leaves no time for delinquent behavior. "The person involved in conventional activities is tied to appointments, deadlines, working hours, plans, and the like," reasoned Hirschi, "so the opportunity to commit deviant acts rarely arises. To the extent that he is engrossed in conventional activities, he cannot even think about deviant acts, let alone act out his inclinations."[65]

Belief   The fourth element of the social bond is belief. Delinquency results from the absence of effective beliefs that forbid socially unacceptable behavior.[66] Such beliefs, for example, include respect for the law and for the social norms of society. This respect for the values of the law and legal system develops through intimate relations with other people, especially parents. Hirschi portrayed a causal chain "from attachment to parents, through concern for the approval of persons in positions of authority, to belief that the rules of society are binding on one's conduct."[67]

Empirical Validation of the Theory   Travis Hirschi tested his theory by administering a self-report survey to 4,077 junior high and high school students in Contra Costa County, California. He also used school records and police records to analyze the data he received on the questionnaires. His analysis of the data yielded data on the basic elements of the social bond.

Hirschi analyzed attachment of respondents in the sample to parents, to the school, and to peers. The greater the attachment to parents, he found, the less likely the child was to become involved in delinquent behavior. But more than the fact of communication with the parents, the quality or the intimacy of the communication was the critical factor. The more love and respect found in the relationship with parents, the more likely that the child would recall the parents when and if a situation of potential delinquency arose.[68]

Hirschi also found that in terms of attachment to the school, students with little academic competence and those who performed poorly were more likely to become involved in delinquent behavior. Significantly, he found that students with weak affectional ties to parents tended to have little concern for the opinions of teachers and to dislike school.[69]

The attachment to peers, Hirschi added, did not imply lack of attachment to parents. The respondents who were most closely attached to and respectful of their friends were least likely to have committed delinquent acts. Somewhat surprisingly, delinquents were less dependent on peers than nondelinquents. Hirschi theorized from his data "that the boy's stake in conformity affects his choice of friends rather than the other way around."[70]

In terms of commitment, Hirschi found that if a boy claimed the *right* to smoke, drink, date, and drive a car, he was more likely to become involved in delinquency. The automobile, like the cigarette and bottle of beer, indicated that the boy had put away childish things. Also, the more a boy was committed to academic achievement, the less likely he was to become involved in delinquent acts. Hirschi further reported that the higher the occupational expectations of boys, the less likely it was that they would become involved in delinquent behavior.[71]

Hirschi found that the more a boy was involved in school and leisure activities, the less likely he was to become involved in delinquency. In other words, the more that boys in the sample felt that they had nothing to do, the more likely they were to become involved in delinquent acts. Hirschi theorized that lack of involvement and commitment to school releases a young person from a primary source of time structuring.[72]

Moreover, he found that the less boys believed they should obey the law, the less likely they were to obey it. He added that delinquents were relatively free of concern for the morality of their actions and therefore they were relatively amoral and differed significantly in values from nondelinquents. Additionally, the data in this study failed to show much difference between lower- and middle-class young people in terms of values.[73] In Voices Across the Profession 5.3, Hirschi expresses some further thoughts about social control theory. Figure 5.3 depicts the main constructs of Hirschi's theory.

Evaluation of Social Control Theory

Social control theory has received wide support.[74] This theory of the causes of delinquent behavior has several strengths:

Interview with Travis Hirschi

Question: If you were to rewrite *Causes of Delinquency,* would you reformulate control theory in any way?

Hirschi: Control theory as I stated it can't really be understood unless one takes into account the fact that it was attached to a particular method of research. When I was working on the theory, I knew that my data were going to be survey data; therefore, I knew I was going to have mainly the perceptions, attitudes, and values of individuals as reported by them. So I knew the theory had to be stated from the perspective of individuals committing or not committing delinquent acts. Had I data on other people, or on the structure of the community, I would have stated the theory in a quite different way. There are lots of control theories, but the major differences among them stem from differences in the vantage point of the theorists, not from differences in their understanding of the theory.

For example, I was aware at the time I wrote my theory that it was well within the social disorganization tradition. I knew that, but you have to remember the status of social disorganization as a concept in the middle 1960s when I was writing. I felt I was swimming against the current in stating a social control theory at the individual level. Had I tried to sell social disorganiza-

tion at the same time, I would have been in deep trouble. So I shied away from that tradition. As a result, I did not give social disorganization its due. I went back to Durkheim and Hobbes and ignored an entire American tradition that was directly relevant to what I was saying. But I was aware of it and took comfort in it. I said the same things the social disorganization people had said, but since they had fallen into disfavor I had to disassociate myself from them. Further, as Ruth Kornhauser so acutely points out, social disorganization theories had been associated with the cultural tradition. That was the tradition I was working hardest against; so in that sense, I would have compromised my own position or I would have introduced a lot of debate I didn't want to get into had I dealt explicitly with social disorganization theory. Now, with people like Kornhauser on my side, and social disorganization back in vogue, I would emphasize my roots in this illustrious tradition.

Question: Can control theory be expanded? What would be the main propositions and underpinnings of this expanded control theory?

Hirschi: Jack Gibbs mentioned the other day that, traditionally, the problem with so-

cial control as a concept is that it tends to expand until it becomes synonymous with sociology, and then it dies. It dies because then there is nothing unique or distinct about it. This danger is present even when the concept is limited initially to delinquency. I enjoy papers that apply my theory to areas other than delinquency, such as Watergate and white-collar crime, but I recognize the risk. Because of it, generality is not something I would move toward. Instead, I would try to focus on the theory's image of criminality and ask how far that might take us. I think I've generally worked with a too restrictive image of delinquency. I did this because I thought the field had made a mistake by bringing things into delinquency that were not delinquency. If, for example, smoking and drinking are part of delinquency, they cannot be causes of delinquency. I thought that was a mistake because I wanted to use those kinds of behaviors as independent variables. I now believe that smoking and drinking are delinquency.

■ **Do you believe that adolescents' smoking is delinquent behavior? What are other control theories?**

Source: Travis Hirschi is professor emeritus of sociology at the University of Arizona. He is the author of *Causes of Delinquency* and most recently is coauthor of *A General Theory of Crime.*[75]

- Social control theory is amenable to empirical examination. Unlike other theorists discussed in this unit, Hirschi was able to test his theory with a population of adolescents. The basic theoretical constructs of control theory—concepts such as *attachment to parents, involvement in school,* and *commitment to conventional activities*—are clearly defined and measurable.
- Social control theory has provided valuable insights into delinquent behavior. For example, the importance of the intrafamily relationship has been substantiated. The relationship between the school and delinquency is another important area that social control theory addresses. Especially valid is the proposition that attachments and commitments to societal institutions (the social bond) are associated with low rates of delinquency.
- Researchers are increasingly using this theory to develop integrated explanations of delinquent behavior.

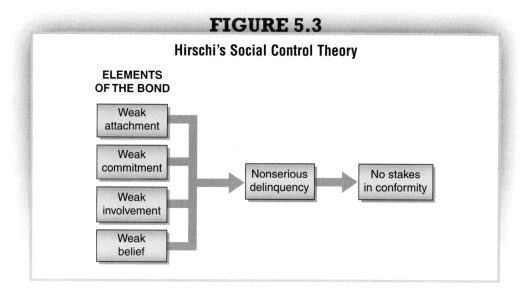

FIGURE 5.3

Hirschi's Social Control Theory

ELEMENTS OF THE BOND

Weak attachment

Weak commitment

Weak involvement

Weak belief

→ Nonserious delinquency → No stakes in conformity

In sum, although social control theory cannot explain all acts of delinquency, it still has more empirical support today than any other explanation of delinquency. However, even if Hirschi's theory adequately explains delinquency in juveniles who are involved only in relatively trivial offenses, whether its findings apply as well to serious delinquents can be earnestly questioned. Social control theory also fails to describe the chain of events that weaken the social bond, and it divides delinquents into either socialized or unsocialized youths.[76] As important as this theory is, greater attention must be given to the operational definitions of the elements of the social bond before the theoretical merits of social control theory can be fully ascertained.[77] Social process theories, including Hirschi's theory of social control, are summarized in Table 5.1.

Integrated Theories of Delinquency

The theoretical development of integrated explanations for delinquency has been one of the most highly praised concepts in criminology.[78] Theory integration generally

TABLE 5.1

Summary of Social Process Theories of Crime

THEORY	PROPONENTS	CAUSE OF CRIME IDENTIFIED IN THE THEORY	SUPPORTING RESEARCH
Differential association	Edwin Sutherland	Criminal behavior is to be expected in individuals who have internalized a preponderance of definitions favorable to law violations.	Moderate
Drift	David Matza	Juveniles neutralize themselves from the moral bounds of the law and drift into delinquent behavior.	Moderate
Containment	Walter Reckless	Strong inner containment and reinforcing external containment provide insulation against criminal behavior.	Moderate
Social control	Travis Hirschi	Criminal acts result when an individual's bond to society is weak or broken.	Strong

TABLE 5.2

Hirschi's Typology of Propositional Integration

Three Types of Forms	
Side-by-side or parallel integration	The dividing of the subject matter into types or forms; most common ex-offender typologies.
End-to-end or sequential integration	Independent variables of some theories are used to become the dependent variables of the integrated theory; most widely used.
Up-and-down or deductive integration	The process of consolidating into one formulation the ideas of two or more theories; infrequently used.

implies the combination of two or more existing theories on the basis of their perceived commonalities. According to Steven Messner, Marvin Krohn, and Allen Liska, the two main types of theoretical integration are propositional and conceptual. They also suggest that a "middle range," including both conceptual and propositional integration, might be useful.[79] The overarching purpose of theoretical integration is the development of a new theory that improves on the constituent theories from which the reformulated theory is derived. The ultimate goal of theory integration, then, is the advancement of our understanding of crime and delinquency.[80]

Hirschi has developed a typology that is a useful means of summarizing propositional integration,[81] and identified three types or forms that theoretical integration may take: side-by-side or parallel integration, end-to-end or sequential integration, and up-and-down or deductive integration.[82] *Side-by-side integration* refers to the dividing of the subject matter into constituent types or forms; the most common expression of side-by-side integration is offender typologies. *End-to-end integration,* perhaps the most widely used today, refers to placing causal variables in a temporal order so that the independent variables of some theories are used to become the dependent variables of the integrated theory. The process of integrating macro-level causes with micro-level causes is another common use of the end-to-end approach.[83] For example, as Mark Colvin and John Pauly argue, the macro-level of social class is linked to delinquency indirectly through the micro-level factor of parenting.[84] *Up-and-down integration* is the process of consolidating into one formulation the ideas of two or more theories by identifying a more abstract or general perspective from which at least parts of the theories can be deduced. This strategy is not frequently used because of the difficulty in compromising different assumptions.[85] See Table 5.2.

Issues and Concerns of Integrated Theory

Attempts to combine theoretical explanations of delinquency into a coherent sequence of connecting events and outcomes give rise to several issues and concerns:

- Because the specific form of delinquent behavior to be explained may vary from one theory to another, variations will likely be present in the power and utility of the integrated theory.[86]
- When theoretical expressions of delinquency are mixed, the question of which factors to use as a representation of theories used in the model becomes an issue. Differential association theory illustrates this second issue. It is divided into nine propositions and even further subcategories. The question becomes: Which proposition or propositions should be used as representative of differential association theory?[87]
- In regard to synthesis efforts, an issue sometimes arises as to the generalizability of the theory to all segments of the population. For example, most theories of delinquency focus on lower-class adolescent males, but these theories may or may

not apply to lower-class adolescent females or to middle- or upper-class adolescent males and females.[88]

■ Another concern is the fact that included theories may have different basic assumptions with respect to motivations, attitudes, and specific factors contributing to delinquency. Interdisciplinary theories, especially, offer opposing views on the feelings and attitudes of delinquents; and it is not uncommon for structural or process sociological theories to have widely divergent views on delinquents' attitudes, motivations, and effects of stimuli.[89]

Despite these daunting challenges, several integrated theories for delinquent behavior have been developed.[90] Four of the most important are Michael R. Gottfredson and Hirschi's general theory of crime, Delbert S. Elliott's integrated social process theory, Terence P. Thornberry's interactional theory, and J. David Hawkins and Joseph G. Weis's social development theory.[91]

Gottfredson and Hirschi's General Theory of Crime

Researchers are interested in the possibility that a common factor underlies all problem behavior. As discussed in Chapter 1, Donovan and Jessor's adolescent drinking study substantiated connections between and among high-risk behaviors and led them to propose that these behaviors share a common trait they termed "unconventionality." Liberal views, inferior academic performance, toleration or approval of deviant behavior, a disinclination to participate in church activities, and outright approval of drug abuse are measures of this unconventionality.[92]

Drug abuse and delinquency, Hirschi suggests, are symptoms of criminality.[93] His definition of criminality[94] describes the individual's commitment to instant gratification or profit without conformance to such conventional demands as earning one's money ("I'll just take what I need"); establishing normal sexual relationships ("I'll just take what I want"); or resolving conflicts through the courts ("I'll just impose my own form of justice").

In *A General Theory of Crime,* Gottfredson and Hirschi defined lack of self-control as the common factor underlying problem behaviors.[95]

> People who lack self-control will tend to be impulsive, insensitive, physical (as opposed to mental), risk-taking, short-sighted, and nonverbal, and they will tend therefore to engage in criminal and analogous acts [which include smoking, drinking, using drugs, gambling, having children out of wedlock, and engaging in illicit sex]. Since these traits can be identified prior to the age of responsibility for crime, since there is considerable tendency for these traits to come together in the same people, and since the traits tend to persist through life, it seems reasonable to consider them as comprising a stable construct useful in the explanation of crime.[96]

Thus, self-control is the degree to which an individual is "vulnerable to the temptations of the moment."[97] The other pivotal construct in this theory of crime is crime opportunity, which is a function of the structural or situational circumstances encountered by the individual. In combination, these two constructs are intended to capture the simultaneous influence of external and internal restraints on behavior.[98]

Gottfredson and Hirschi propose that only their theory of self-control explains the facts revolving around the stability of differences in individuals' propensity to crime. Self-control accounts for all variations by culture, gender, age, and circumstances and "explains all crime, at all times, and, for that matter, many forms of behavior that are not sanctioned by the state."[99] Individuals with high self-control are "substantially less likely at all periods of life to engage in criminal acts."

Ineffective or incomplete socialization, according to Gottfredson and Hirschi, causes low self-control. Parents are able to socialize their children into self-control by being attached to them, by supervising them closely, by recognizing their lack of self-control, and by punishing

Web LIBRARY 5.5

Read the OJJDP Fact Sheet, *Highlights of Findings from the Denver Youth Survey,* at **www .justicestudies.com/ WebLibrary**.

❝ Ineffective or incomplete socialization . . . causes low self-control. ❞

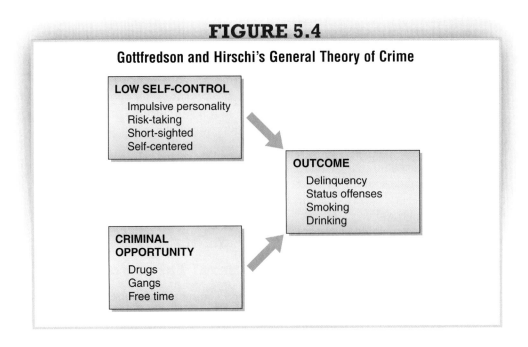

FIGURE 5.4
Gottfredson and Hirschi's General Theory of Crime

LOW SELF-CONTROL

Impulsive personality
Risk-taking
Short-sighted
Self-centered

OUTCOME

Delinquency
Status offenses
Smoking
Drinking

CRIMINAL OPPORTUNITY

Drugs
Gangs
Free time

deviant acts. Once self-control is formed in childhood, they add, it remains relatively stable throughout life.[100] See Figure 5.4.

Evaluation of General Theory More than two dozen studies have been conducted on general theory, and the vast majority have been largely favorable.[101] Indeed, *A General Theory of Crime* ranked second in citations of all criminal and criminal justice books in the 1990s.[102] It has been found that self-control is related to self-reported crime among a variety of population groups.[103] In addition, Gottfredson and Hirschi's theory of self-control is part of a trend of thought that pushes the causes of crime and delinquency farther back in the life course into the family. The emphasis on early childhood socialization as the cause of crime, of course, departs from the emphasis on more proximate causes of crime found in rational choice theory and in most sociological theories.[104] The focus on a unidimensional trait also departs from the movement toward multidimensional integrated theories of crime.[105] Criticisms of general theory have focused largely on its lack of conceptual clarity.[106] Nevertheless, in spite of these criticisms, general theory will likely continue to spark continued interest and research.

Elliott's Integrated Social Process Theory

Delbert S. Elliott and colleagues offer "an explanatory model that expands and synthesizes traditional strain, social control, and social learning perspectives into a single paradigm that accounts for delinquent behavior and drug use."[107] They argue that all three theories are flawed in explaining delinquent behavior. Strain theory is able to account for some initial delinquent acts but does not adequately explain why some juveniles enter into delinquent careers while others avoid them. Control theory is unable to explain prolonged involvement in delinquent behavior in light of there being no reward for this behavior, and learning theories portray the delinquent as passive and susceptible to influence when confronted with delinquency-producing reinforcements.[108]

Integrating the strongest features of these theories into a single theoretical model, Elliott and colleagues contended that the experience of living in socially disorganized areas leads youths to develop weak bonds with conventional groups, activities, and norms. High levels of strain, as well as weak bonds with conventional groups, lead some youths to seek out delinquent peer groups. These antisocial peer groups provide both positive reinforcement for delinquent behavior and role models for this behavior. Consequently, Elliott and colleagues theorize, there is a high probability of

A gathering of Drug Free Youth at Parrot Jungle in Miami, Florida. ■ **What does the general theory of crime say leads to low self-control among young people?**

involvement in delinquent behavior when bonding to delinquent groups is combined with weak bonding to conventional groups.[109]

The model was tested on a national probability sample of more than 1,700 U.S. eleven- to seventeen-year-olds, who were interviewed three times between 1977 and 1979. Elliott and colleagues found that their integrated theory was generally supported, with the major exception that some youths reported developing both strong bonds to delinquent peers and acceptance of the values of conventional society. Their interpretation of this finding was that youths living in a disorganized area may not have conventional groups that they can join.[110]

Elliott and colleagues did not attempt to integrate this theoretical perspective at the macrosociological level. Instead, the integration occurs at an individual level as it provides an explanation for how youngsters become involved in delinquent acts. Although the model initially was conceived to explain the causes of delinquent behavior, it was developed more fully and used to explain drug-using behavior as well.[111] See Figure 5.5.

Evaluation of Integrated Social Process Theory This theory represents a pure type of integrated theory. It can be argued that general theory and interactional theory are not fully integrated theories but rather are elaborations of established theories. In contrast, there is no question that integrated social process theory is an integrated theory.

Examinations of this theory have generally been positive. Yet some question has been raised about its application to various types of delinquent behaviors. Questions have even been raised about its power and utility with different types of drug activity. For example, integrated social process theory explained 59 percent of the variation in marijuana use but only 29 to 34 percent of the distribution of hard drug use.[112]

Thornberry's Interactional Theory

In Terence P. Thornberry's interactional theory of delinquency the initial impetus toward delinquency comes from a weakening of the person's bond to conventional society, represented by attachment to parents, commitment to school, and belief in conventional values. Associations with delinquent peers and delinquent values make

FIGURE 5.5

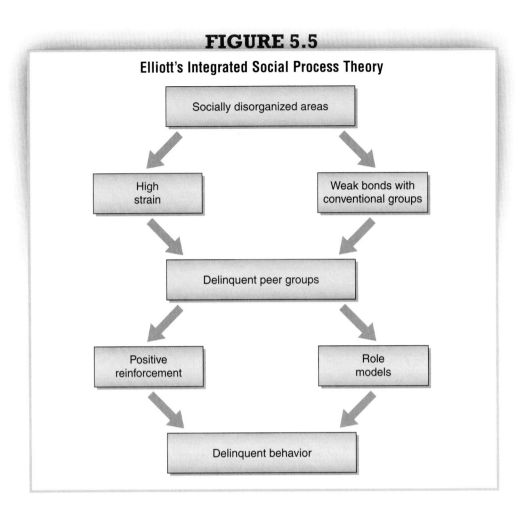

Elliott's Integrated Social Process Theory

up the social setting in which delinquency, especially prolonged serious delinquency, is learned and reinforced. These two variables, along with delinquent behavior itself, form a mutually reinforcing causal loop that leads toward increasing delinquency involvement over time.[113]

Moreover, this interactive process develops over the person's life cycle. During early adolescence the family is the most influential factor in bonding the youngster to conventional society and reducing delinquency. But as the youth matures and moves through middle adolescence, the world of friends, school, and youth culture becomes the dominant influence over behavior. Finally, as the person enters adulthood, commitment to conventional activities, and to family especially, offers new avenues to reshape the person's bond to society and involvement with delinquent behavior.[114]

Finally, interactional theory holds that these process variables are systematically related to the youngster's position in the social structure. Class, minority-group status, and the social disorganization of the community all affect the initial values of the interactive variables as well as the behavioral trajectories. It is argued that youths from the most socially disadvantaged backgrounds begin the process least bonded to conventional society and most exposed to the world of delinquency. The nature of the process increases the chances that they will continue on to a career of serious criminal involvement; on the other hand, youths from middle-class families enter a trajectory that is oriented toward conformity and away from delinquency.[115] See Figure 5.6.

Evaluation of Interactional Theory Thornberry's theory views delinquency as the result of events that occur in a developmental fashion. Interactional theory does not see delinquency as the end product; instead, the theory suggests that delinquency leads to the formation of delinquent values, which then contribute to disconnections in social bonds, more attachments to antisocial peers, and further involvement in delinquent behavior.[116]

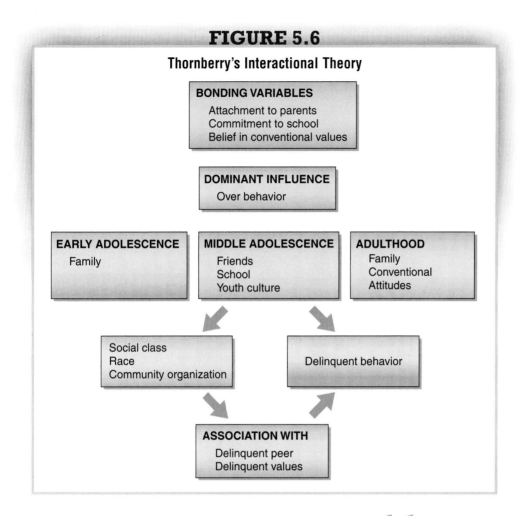

FIGURE 5.6
Thornberry's Interactional Theory

BONDING VARIABLES
Attachment to parents
Commitment to school
Belief in conventional values

DOMINANT INFLUENCE
Over behavior

EARLY ADOLESCENCE
Family

MIDDLE ADOLESCENCE
Friends
School
Youth culture

ADULTHOOD
Family
Conventional
Attitudes

Social class
Race
Community organization

Delinquent behavior

ASSOCIATION WITH
Delinquent peer
Delinquent values

Interactional theory has several positive features that should assure its continued examination. Thornberry and colleagues offer support for interactional theory in the Rochester Youth Development Study. Studies that use an interactional framework are becoming more commonly used among delinquency researchers; in addition, such studies are being increasingly used in interdisciplinary research. Furthermore, the interactional approach is consistent with the social settings in which individuals live and interact with others.[117] The most significant limitations of interactional theory are that it fails to address the presence of middle-class delinquency and that it basically ignores racial and gender issues.[118]

> " Interactional theory does not see delinquency as the end product. "

Hawkins and Weis's Social Development Model

In terms of developing a new strategy, Joseph G. Weis and J. David Hawkins's **social development model** offers an integrated approach to delinquency prevention that could have long-range consequences for dealing with youth crime in American society.[119]

The social development model is based on the integration of social control theory and cultural learning theory. According to social control theory, the weakening, absence, or breakdown of social controls leads to delinquency.[120] Cultural learning, or cultural deviance, theory emphasizes the role of peers and the community in the rise of delinquency. In disorganized communities, then, youths are at greater risk of delinquency.[121]

Social control theory focuses on the individual characteristics that lead to delinquent behavior and the impact of the major socializing institutions on delinquency, whereas

social development model
A perspective based on the integration of social control and cultural learning theories which proposes that the development of attachments to parents will lead to attachments to school and a commitment to education as well as a belief in and commitment to conventional behavior and the law.

FIGURE 5.7

Hawkins and Weis's Social Development Model

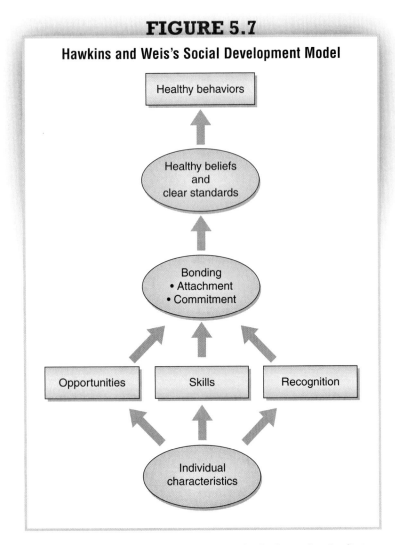

Source: James C. Howell, ed. *Guide for Implementing the Comprehensive Strategy for Serious, Violent, and Chronic Juvenile Offenders* (Washington, D.C.: Office of Juvenile Justice and Delinquency Prevention, 1995), p. 23. Reprinted with permission from the U.S. Department of Justice.

cultural learning theory examines the role of the community context in the process of learning criminal and delinquent attitudes and behaviors. Social control theory posits that youths become delinquent because of inadequate social controls; cultural learning theory adds that juveniles become socialized to delinquency in disorganized communities.

The social development model proposes that the development of attachments to parents will lead to attachments to school and a commitment to education, as well as a belief in and commitment to conventional behavior and the law. Learning theory describes the process by which these bonds develop. If juveniles are given adequate opportunities for involvement in legitimate activities and are able to acquire the necessary skills with a consistent reward structure, they will develop the bonds of attachment, commitment, and belief. Figure 5.7 presents a diagram of the social development model.

Bu Huang and colleagues examined the ability of the social development model to predict violent behavior at age eighteen. Using construct measures at ages ten, thirteen, fourteen, and sixteen, they found that the social development model adequately predicts the likelihood of violence at age eighteen and is able to mediate much of the effect of prior violence.[122] Yet a disorganized community with high rates of delinquency and crime reduces the potential of delinquency prevention, because the socializing institutions are weakened by higher rates of family disorganization, inadequate educational facilities, few material and social resources, and less respect for the law. Consequently, youths who are not receiving adequate support and direction from their families and who are not experiencing success in school are most vulnerable to delinquency.[123]

Evaluation of the Social Development Model   As a sound foundation for delinquency prevention, the social development model has linked families, schools, and peer groups as appropriate objects for intervention, depending on the child's developmental stage. Interventions aimed at increasing the likelihood of social bonding to the family are appropriate from early childhood through early adolescence. Interventions that seek to increase the likelihood of social bonding to school are appropriate throughout the years of school attendance and are especially important as juveniles approach and enter adolescence.[124] Thus, the social development model offers communities an empirically grounded basis for designing, implementing, and assessing delinquency prevention programs.

■ Social Process and Delinquency Across the Life Course

The theories in this chapter focus on process. Delinquency, like other processes, starts at a particular point and either continues or ceases. Crime continuation or desistance involves several ongoing processes: lack of competence in adolescence, cumulative disadvantage, and turning points and/or the establishment of a new identity.

A young man accepts a job from an employer. ■ **How does the social development model explain positive achievement? How does it explain delinquency?**

Lack of Competence in Adolescence

John Claussen's classic study of children of the Great Depression followed the study members of the Berkeley longitudinal studies for nearly fifty years—from childhood through the later years of the participants' lives. Claussen found that competence and social influence at the end of adolescence gave shape to the evolving life course.[125] Claussen defined what he called "planful competence" as comprising the dimensions of self-confidence, dependability, and intellectual investment. He found that a youth who demonstrated planful competence was "equipped with an ability to evaluate accurately personal efforts as well as the intentions and responses of others, with an informed knowledge of self, others, and options, and with the self-discipline to pursue chosen goals."[126]

Early competence in study participants, according to Claussen, meant fewer crises in every decade up to their fifties. Highly competent men were more likely to find the right job and to remain in this rewarding line of work. Highly competent women were more likely to find the right husband and to feel rewarded in family life. Choice and selection were both involved: A choice of attractive options and an ability to be selective permitted the most competent to take advantage of their opportunities. In contrast, Claussen concluded that adolescents who lacked planful competence had different trajectories or pathways. They made choices that led to job difficulties, marital breakup, and personal difficulties with the law and with figures in authority.[127]

Cumulative Disadvantage

Most juvenile delinquents' lives are not characterized by the kind of planful competence that leads to one successful experience after the other throughout the life course. Instead delinquent youths deal with personal deficits that lead to a series of cumulative disadvantages. For example, Thornberry and Marvin Krohn's examination of the Rochester data revealed that individuals who begin antisocial behavior early have individual deficits (i.e., negative temperamental qualities) that both contribute to and are adversely affected by parental deficits (explosive physical disciplinary styles and low affective ties). Over time, these researchers contend, parents and children will develop a coercive interaction; the result will be children who express persistent patterns of oppositional and aggressive behavior.[128]

The disorders in these adolescents' lives make delinquent behavior, drug use, and gang involvement more attractive. Involvement in various forms of delinquency then makes young people more likely to drop out of school; to become pregnant or impregnate someone else; to be unemployed into their adult years; and to be arrested, convicted, and sentenced in the juvenile and later the adult system. Thus, distracted from conventional pathways, they become more involved in antisocial behaviors, which can continue from adolescence into adulthood.[129]

What this concept of cumulative disadvantage suggests is that each negative event in an offender's life tends to limit the positive options available to the individual and becomes a disadvantage in living a crime-free life. Incarceration, especially, leads to cumulative disadvantage in other areas. Thus, arrest and incarceration may spark failure in school, unemployment, and weak community bonds, which in turns increase adult crime.[130]

Turning Points

Web PLACES 5.1

Learn about serious violent juvenile offenders **www.justicestudies .com/WebPlaces**.

As discussed in Chapter 2, Robert J. Sampson and John H. Laub explored the concept of a "turning point" in *Crime in the Making: Pathways and Turning Points through Life*[131] and further developed the idea in *Shared Beginnings, Divergent Lives*.[132] Sampson and Laub's social control explanation emphasizes the gradual buildup of investments that accrue in the presence of social bonds of attachment. They found five turning points in the desistance process: marriage/spouses, employment, reform school, the military, and neighborhood change. These are "structurally induced turning points that serve as the catalyst for sustaining long-term behavioral change."[133]

Another view of the turning point emerges in the research that Shadd Maruna conducted on English ex-offenders. Maruna contends that ex-offenders desist from crime when they develop a coherent and prosocial identity for themselves. Accordingly, they need a coherent and credible self-story to explain to themselves and to others how their past could have led to their new identity. Maruna refers to this self-story as a "redemptive script" and describes how interviewees used such scripts to link their past lives to positive outcomes.[134]

Web PLACES 5.2

Visit the National Youth Violence Prevention Resource Center's website via **www.justicestudies .com/WebPlaces**.

Peggy C. Giordano and colleagues developed a theory of cognitive transformation to explain desistance in their follow-up of a sample of serious adolescent female delinquents. These researchers found that four types of cognitive transformation take place as an integral part of the desistance process: (1) There is a shift in the actor's openness to change; (2) the individual is exposed to a hook or set of hooks for change; (3) the individual begins to envision and fashion an appealing and conventional "replacement self"; and (4) a transformation takes place in the way the actor views the former deviant behavior or lifestyle. These various cognitive transformations or shifts not only influence receptivity to one or more hooks of change, but also inspire and direct behavior.[135]

In sum, desistance requires that a combination of positive attitudes, prosocial behaviors, and reinforcing transitions in marriage, family, and employment replace the negative patterns found in delinquency, criminality, and drug involvement. These processes not only require human agency but also are gradual, perhaps even unknown to the offender at the time.

CHAPTER
Summary

Each of the social process theories discussed in this chapter contributes to our understanding of how adolescents become delinquent. Among the perspectives discussed are the following:

- Differential association theory suggests that individuals learn from their association with small groups; if they are involved in antisocial groups, they are more likely to accept and internalize antisocial conduct norms and behavioral definitions.

- Social control approaches, including bonding theory, maintain that the more strongly adolescents are attached to positive social bonds, the more likely it is that they will refrain from delinquent behavior.

- Containment theory states that positive experiences in the home, in the school, and in the community will lead to the development of positive self-concepts, thereby insulating individuals from delinquency.

- Process theories, such as those discussed in this chapter, are also helpful in understanding the continuation of, or desistance from, delinquency across the life course. The process of bonding to significant others, drifting in and out of delinquent behavior, and self-concept development are key ideas in these theories.

- Theories of delinquency and drift, as well as other social control theories, emphasize the decision-making process at the individual level.

- Gottfredson and Hirschi's general theory of crime defines the lack of self-control as the common element underlying problem behaviors.

- Theory integration usually implies the combination of two or more existing theories on the basis of their perceived commonalities.

- Elliott's integrated social process theory contends that the experience of living in socially disorganized areas leads young people to develop weak social bonds with conventional groups, activities, and norms. High levels of strain, as well as weak bonds, lead some youths to seek out delinquent peer groups.

- Thornberry's interactional theory suggests that delinquency leads to the formation of delinquent values, which then contribute to the disintegration of conventional bonds and greater attachment to antisocial peers.

- Criticisms of social process theories center on their level of analysis—which is the individual delinquent and the personal decision-making process. Critics point out that these theories fail to place sufficient emphasis on the impact of larger political and economic systems on adolescents and their development.

CRITICAL THINKING
Questions

1. Why is differential association theory called a "learning" theory?
2. Self-concept, according to containment theory, is vitally important in affecting behavior. Do you agree?
3. Matza and Hirschi proposed different interpretations of the degree to which delinquents identify with the norms and values of society. Define the position of each theorist and explain which position you find more credible.
4. Which of the four integrated theories make the most sense to you? What are the advantages of integrated theory? What are its disadvantages?
5. Does Matza's drift theory seem to be present in the lives of delinquents? What forces seem to set in motion the drift toward delinquency?
6. Matza also talked about commitment to delinquency. What does that term mean?

WEB
Interactivity

Visit Wikipedia, the Free Encyclopedia, on the Internet at **http://en.wikipedia.org**, and read the article that it contains on differential association. (You can search for the article using the phrase "differential association"— with the quotation marks—or you can go there directly by typing in this URL: **http://en .wikipedia.org/wiki/Differential_association**.)

Follow the links within the article to see what Wikipedia authors have to say about Edwin Sutherland, criminology, and criminals. Summarize what you've learned and submit it to your instructor if asked to do so.

Because Wikipedia is an open resource, users are permitted to post new articles and to revise existing ones. You and your instructor might decide to expand the existing article on differential association. If you were to supplement the article, what might you add?

Source: From http://en.wikipedia.org/wiki/Main_Page. For copyright information, please see the full license on page 614.

Notes

1. For this symbolic interactionist perspective, see Charles H. Cooley, *Human Nature and the Social Order* (1902; reprint ed. New York: Schocken Books, 1964); George H. Mead, *Mind, Self and Society* (Chicago: University of Chicago Press, 1934.)

2. Edwin H. Sutherland, "A Statement of the Theory," in *The Sutherland Papers*, edited by Albert Cohen, Alfred Lindesmith, and Karl Schuessler (Bloomington: Indiana University Press, 1956), p. 9.

3. Edwin H. Sutherland, *Principles of Criminology* (Philadelphia: J. B. Lippincott, 1947).

4. Ross L. Matsueda, "The Current State of Differential Association Theory," *Crime and Delinquency* 34 (July 1988), p. 280.

5. Harold Finestone, *Victims of Change: Juvenile Delinquents in American Society* (Westport, Conn.: Greenwood Press, 1976), p. 157.

6. This interview took place in November 1983.

7. Matsueda, "The Current State of Differential Association Theory," pp. 277–278.

8. Craig Reinarman and Jeffrey Fagan, "Social Organization and Differential Association: A Research Note from a Longitudinal Study of Violent Juvenile Offenders," *Crime and Delinquency* 34 (July 1988), p. 307; Ross L. Matsueda, "Testing Control Theory and Differential Association: A Causal Modeling Approach," *American Sociological Association* 47 (1982), pp. 489–504; Ross L. Matsueda and Karen Heimer, "Race, Family Structure, and Delinquency," *American Sociological Review* 52 (1987), pp. 826–840. See also Raymond Paternoster and Ruth Triplett, "Disaggregating Self-Reported Delinquency and Its Implications for Theory," *Criminology* 25 (1987), pp. 591–620; Richard E. Johnson, Anastasios C. Marcos, and Stephen J. Bahr, "The Role of Peers in the Complex Etiology of Adolescent Drug Use," *Criminology* 25 (1987), pp. 323–340; and Delbert S. Elliott, David Huizinga, and Suzanne S. Ageton, *Explaining Delinquency and Drug Use* (Beverly Hills, Calif.: Sage, 1985).

9. Melvin DeFleur and Richard Quinney, "A Reformulation of Sutherland's Differential Association Theory and a Strategy for Empirical Verification," *Journal of Research in Crime and Delinquency* 3 (January 1966), pp. 1–11; Daniel Glaser, "Criminality Theory and Behavioral Images," *American Journal of Sociology* 61 (1956), pp. 433–444.

10. Daniel Glaser, "Differential Association and Criminological Prediction," *Social Problems* 8 (1960), pp. 6–14.

11. Robert J. Burgess Jr. and Ronald L. Akers, "A Differential Association–Reinforcement Theory of Criminal Behavior," *Social Problems* 14 (1966), pp. 128–147. See also Ronald L. Akers, *Deviant Behavior: A Social Learning Approach*, 3rd ed. (Belmont, Calif.: Wadsworth, 1985), p. 41.

12. Marvin D. Krohn et al., "Social Learning Theory and Adolescent Cigarette Smoking: A Longitudinal Study," *Social Problems* 32 (June 1985), pp. 455–474.

13. Ruth R. Kornhauser, *Social Sources of Delinquency* (Chicago: University of Chicago Press, 1978).

14. For those who see little value in a theory such as differential association that cannot be tested, see Jack P. Gibbs, "The State of Criminology Theory," *Criminology* 25 (1987), pp. 821–840; Sheldon Glueck, "Theory and Fact in Criminology," *British Journal of Criminology* 7 (1956), pp. 92–109; and Travis Hirschi, *Causes of Delinquency* (Berkeley: University of California Press, 1969). For a defense of the testability of differential association theory, see James D. Orcutt, "Differential Association and Marijuana Use: A Closer Look at Sutherland (with a Little Help from Becker)," *Criminology* 25 (1987), pp. 341–358.

15. Ronald L. Akers, "Is Differential Association/Social Learning Cultural Deviance Theory?" *Criminology* 34 (1996), p. 230.

16. Ibid.

17. Steven Box, *Deviance, Reality and Society* (New York: Holt, Rinehart and Winston, 1971), p. 21.

18. C. R. Jeffery, "An Integrated Theory of Crime and Criminal Behavior," *Journal of Criminal Law, Criminology and Police Science* 49 (1959), pp. 533–552.

19. Matsueda, "The Current State of Differential Association Theory," p. 295.

20. David Matza, *Delinquency and Drift* (New York: Wiley, 1964), p. 28.

21. Ibid., p. 49.

22. Ibid., p. 69.

23. Gresham M. Sykes and David Matza, "Techniques of Neutralization: A Theory of Delinquency," *American Sociological Review* 22 (December 1957), pp. 664–666.

24. Ibid.

25. Matza, *Delinquency and Drift*, p. 156.

26. Ibid., p. 181.

27. Ibid.

28. Ibid., p. 184.

29. Ibid., p. 185.

30. Ibid., pp. 188–189.

31. David Matza, *Becoming Deviant* (Englewood Cliffs, N.J.: Prentice-Hall, 1969).

32. Matza, *Delinquency and Drift*. See also Robert Agnew, "Determinism, Interdeterminism, and Crime: An Empirical Exploration," *Criminology* 33 (February 1995), p. 83.

33. Travis Hirschi, "On the Compatibility of Rational Choice and Social Control Theories of Crime," in *The Reasoning Criminal*, edited by Derek B. Cornish and Ronald V. Clarke (New York: Springer-Verlag, 1986); Michael R. Gottfredson and Travis Hirschi, eds., *Positive Criminology* (Newbury Park, Calif.: Sage, 1987); Michael R. Gottfredson and Travis Hirschi, *A General Theory of Crime* (Palo Alto, Calif.: Stanford University Press, 1990).

34. See John S. Goldkamp, "Rational Choice and Determinism," in *Positive Criminology*.

35. Ronald L. Akers, "Rational Choice, Deterrence, and Social Learning in Criminology: The Path Not Taken," *Journal of Criminal Law and Criminology* 81 (1990), p. 666.

36. Ian Taylor, Paul Walton, and Jock Young, *The New Criminology* (New York: Harper and Row, 1973).

37. Robert Regoli and Eric Poole, "The Commitment of Delinquents to Their Misdeeds: A Reexamination," *Journal of Criminal Justice* 6 (1978), pp. 261–269; Michael J. Hindelang, "The Commitment of Delinquents to Their Misdeeds: Do Delinquents Drift?" *Social Problems* 17 (1970), pp. 50–59; and Michael J. Hindelang, "Moral Evaluation of Illegal Behaviors," *Social Problems* 21 (1974), pp. 370–385.

38. John Hagan, "Destiny and Drift: Subcultural Preferences, Status Attainments, and the Risks and Rewards of Youth," *American Sociological Review* 56 (1991), p. 567.

39. John E. Hamlin, "The Misplaced Role of Rational Choice in Neutralization Theory," *Criminology* 26 (1988), p. 426.

40. Ronald L. Akers, *Deviance Behavior: A Social Learning Approach,* 2nd ed. (Belmont, Calif.: Wadsworth, 1977).

41. Hirschi, *Causes of Delinquency,* pp. 207–208.

42. Robert Agnew and Ardith A. R. Peters, "The Techniques of Neutralization: An Analysis of Predisposing and Situational Factors," *Criminal Justice and Behavior* 13 (1986), pp. 81–97; Roy L. Austin, "Commitment, Neutralization, and Delinquency," in *Juvenile Delinquency: Little Brother Grows Up,* edited by Theodore N. Ferdinand (Beverly Hills, Calif.: Sage, 1977); William W. Minor, "Techniques of Neutralization: A Reconceptualization and Empirical Examination," *Journal of Research in Crime and Delinquency* 18 (1981), pp. 295–318; and Quint C. Thurman, Craig St. John, and Lisa Riggs, "Neutralization and Tax Evasion: How Effective Would a Moral Appeal Be in Improving Compliance to Tax Laws?" *Law and Policy* 6 (1984), pp. 309–327.

43. Walter C. Reckless and Shlomo Shoham, "Norm Containment Theory as Applied to Delinquency and Crime," *Excerpta Criminologica* 3 (November–December 1963), pp. 637–644.

44. This interview took place in April 1984 and is used with permission.

45. Donald J. Shoemaker, *Theories of Delinquency: An Examination of Explanations of Delinquent Behavior,* 5th ed. (New York: Oxford University Press, 2005), p. 167.

46. Albert J. Reiss Jr., "Delinquency as the Failure of Personal and Social Controls," *American Sociological Review* 16 (1951), pp. 196–207.

47. F. Ivan Nye, *Family Relationships and Delinquent Behavior* (New York: John Wiley, 1958), p. 5.

48. The principles of containment theory draw on Walter C. Reckless, "A New Theory of Delinquency and Crime," *Federal Probation* 24 (December 1961), pp. 42–46.

49. Simon Dinitz and Betty A. Pfau-Vicent, "Self-Concept and Juvenile Delinquency: An Update," *Youth and Society* 14 (December 1982), pp. 133–158.

50. Walter C. Reckless and Simon Dinitz, *The Prevention of Juvenile Delinquency: An Experiment* (Columbus: Ohio State University Press, 1972).

51. E. D. Lively, Simon Dinitz, and Walter C. Reckless, "Self-Concept as a Prediction of Juvenile Delinquency," *American Jounrnal of Orthopsychiatry* 32 (1962), pp. 159–168; Gary F. Jensen, "Inner Containment and Delinquency," *Criminology* 64 (1973), pp. 464–470; and Franco Ferracuti, Simon Dinitz, and E. Acosta de Brenes, *Delinquents and Nondelinquents in the Puerto Rican Slum Culture* (Columbus: Ohio State University Press, 1975).

52. Timothy J. Owens, "Two Dimensions of Self-Esteem: Reciprocal Effects of Positive Self-Worth and Self-Deprecations on Adolescent Problems," *American Sociological Review* 59 (1994), pp. 391, 405; L. Edward Wells and Joseph H. Rankin, "Self-Concept as a Mediating Factor in Delinquency," *Social Psychology Quarterly* 46 (1983), p. 19; John D. McCarthy and Dean R. Hoge, "The Dynamics of Self-Esteem and Delinquency," *American Journal of Sociology* 90 (1984), p. 396; and W. E. Thompson and R. A. Dodder, "Juvenile Delinquency Explained? A Test of Containment Theory," *Youth and Society* 15 (December 1983), pp. 171–194.

53. Florence R. Rosenberg and Morris Rosenberg, "Self-Esteem and Delinquency," *Journal of Youth and Adolescence* 7 (1978), p. 280.

54. H. B. Kaplan, *Deviant Behavior in Defense of Self* (New York: Academic Press, 1980); and Rosenberg and Rosenberg, "Self-Esteem and Delinquency," p. 289. See also Morris Rosenberg, Carmi Schooler, and Carrie Schoenbach, "Self-Esteem and Adolescent Problems," *American Sociological Review* 54 (1989), pp. 1004–1018.

55. Dinitz and Pfau-Vicent, "Self-Concept and Juvenile Delinquency," p. 155.

56. Michael Schwartz and Sandra S. Tangri, "A Note on 'Self-Concept as an Insulator against Delinquency'," *American Sociological Review* 30 (1965), pp. 922–926.

57. Hirschi, *Causes of Delinquency,* p. 16.

58. Ibid., p. 31.

59. Ibid., p. 34.

60. Ibid., pp. 16–34.

61. Ibid., p. 18.

62. Ibid., p. 83.

63. Ibid., p. 86.

64. Ibid., p. 20.

65. Ibid., p. 22.

66. Ibid., p. 198.

67. Ibid., p. 200.

68. Ibid., p. 108.

69. Ibid., pp. 110–134.

70. Ibid., pp. 135–161.

71. Ibid., pp. 162–185.

72. Ibid., pp. 187–196.

73. Ibid., pp. 197–224.

74. Barbara J. Costello and Paul R. Vowell, "Testing Control Theory and Differential Association: A Reanalysis of the Richmond Youth Project Data," *Criminology* 37 (November 1999), p. 815; and Charles R. Tittle, *Control Balance: Toward a General Theory of Deviance* (Boulder, Colo: Westview, 1995). For a recent attempt to test Tittle's control balance theory, see Alex R. Piquero and Matthew Hickman, "An Empirical Test of Tittle's Control Balance Theory," *Criminology* 37 (May 1999), pp. 319–341. See also Steven A. Cernkovich, "Evaluating Two Models of Delinquency Causation: Structural Theory and Control Theory," *Criminology* 25 (1987), pp. 335–352; Raymond A. Eve, "A Study of the Efficacy and Interactions of Several Theories for Explaining Rebelliousness among High School Students," *Journal of Criminal Law and Criminology* 69 (1978), pp. 115–125; Marvin D. Krohn and James L. Massey, "Social Control and Delinquent Behavior: An Examination of the Elements of the Social Bond," *Sociological Quarterly* 21 (August 1980), p. 542; Elliott et al., *Explaining Delinquency and Drug Use;* Joseph H. Rankin, "Investigating the Interrelations among Social Control Variables and Conformity," *Journal of Criminal Law and Criminology* 67 (1977), pp. 470–480; Robert Agnew, "Social Control Theory and Delinquency: A Longitudinal Test," *Criminology* 23 (1985), pp. 47–61; Randy L. LaGrange and Helene Raskin White, "Age Differences in Delinquency: A Test of Theory," *Criminology* 23 (1985), pp. 19–45; Kimberly Kempf Leonard and Scott H. Decker, "Theory of Social Control: Does It Apply to the Very Young," *Journal of Criminal Justice* 22 (1994), p. 89;

Robert L. Gardner and Donald J. Shoemaker, "Social Bonding and Delinquency: A Comparative Analysis," *The Sociological Quarterly* 39 (1989), p. 481; and Eric A. Stewart, "School Social Bonds, Social Climate, and School Misbehavior: A Multilevel Analysis," *Justice Quarterly* 20 (September 2003), pp. 575–604.

75. This interview took place in 1984.

76. Shoemaker, *Theories of Delinquency*, p. 197.

77. Leonard and Decker, "Theory of Social Control," p. 89.

78. Among the growing number of works citing the advantages of integrated theory are Richard Johnson, *Juvenile Delinquency and Its Origins: An Integrated Theoretical Approach* (New York: Cambridge University Press, 1979); Elliot et al., *Explaining Delinquency and Drug Use*; Steven Messner, Marvin Krohn, and Allen Liska, eds., *Theoretical Integration in the Study of Deviance and Crime: Problems and Prospects* (Albany: State University of New York at Albany Press, 1989); and John Hagan and Bill McCarthy, *Mean Streets: Youth Crime and Homelessness* (New York: Cambridge University Press, 1997).

79. Messner, Krohn, and Liska, *Theoretical Integration in the Study of Deviance and Crime*. Cited in Thomas J. Bernard and Jeffrey B. Snipes, "Theoretical Integration in Criminology," in *Crime and Justice: A Review of Research*, Vol. 20, edited by Michael Tonry (Chicago and London: The University of Chicago Press, p. 306.)

80. Margaret Farnworth, "Theory Integration Versus Model Building," in *Theoretical Integration in the Study of Deviance and Crime*, p. 93.

81. Barnard and Snipes, "Theoretical Integration in Criminology," p. 307.

82. Travis Hirschi, "Separate and Equal Is Better," *Journal of Research in Crime and Delinquency* 16 (January 1979), pp. 34–37.

83. Ibid.

84. Mark Colvin and John Pauly, "A Critique of Criminology: Toward an Integrated Structural–Marxist Theory of Delinquency Production," *American Journal of Sociology* 89 (November 1983), pp. 513–551.

85. Hirshi, "Separate and Equal Is Better," pp. 34–37.

86. Shoemaker, *Theories of Delinquency*, pp. 278–279.

87. Ibid., pp. 279–280.

88. Ibid., p. 280.

89. Ibid., p. 281.

90. For other integrated theories, see James Q. Wilson and Richard J. Herrnstein, *Crime and Human Nature* (New York: Simon and Schuster, 1985), which is discussed in Chapter 3; Robert J. Sampson and John H. Laub, *Crime in the Making: Pathways and Turning Points through Life* (Cambridge, Mass.: Harvard University Press, 1993), which is discussed in Chapter 2; Colvin and Pauly, "A Critique of Criminology," pp. 513–551, which is discussed in Chapter 6; John Hagan, A. R. Gillis, and John Simpson, "The Class Structure of Gender and Delinquency: Toward a Power-Control Theory of Common Delinquent Behavior," *American Journal of Sociology* 90 (1985), pp. 1151–1178, which is discussed in Chapter 6; and John Hagan and Bill McCarthy, *Mean Streets: Youth Crime and Homelessness*, which is discussed in Chapter 4.

91. Michael R. Gottfredson and Travis Hirschi, *A General Theory of Crime* (Palo Alto, Calif.: Stanford University Press, 1990); Elliot et al., *Explaining Delinquency and Drug Use*;

Delbert S. Elliot, Suzanne S. Ageton, and Rachelle J. Canter, "An Integrated Theoretical Perspective on Delinquent Behavior," *Journal of Research in Crime and Delinquency* 16 (1979), pp. 3–27; Terence P. Thornberry, "Toward an Interactional Theory of Delinquency," *Criminology* 25 (1987), pp. 862–891; Terence P. Thornberry, Alan J. Lizotte, Marvin D. Krohn, Margaret Farnworth, and Sung Joon Jang, "Testing Interactional Theory: An Examination of Reciprocal Causal Relationships among Family, School, and Delinquency," *Journal of Criminal Law and Criminology* 82 (1991), pp. 3–35; and J. David Hawkins and Joseph G. Weis, "The Social Development Model: An Integrated Approach to Delinquency Prevention," *Journal of Primary Prevention* 6 (Winter 1985), pp. 77–78.

92. John E. Donovan and Richard Jessor, "Structure of Problem Behavior in Adolescence and Young Adulthood," *Journal of Consulting and Clinical Psychology* 53 (1985), pp. 89–904. See also D. Wayne Osgood, Lloyd D. Johnston, Patrick M. O'Malley, and Jerald G. Bachman, "The Generality of Deviance in Late Adolescence and Early Childhood,"*American Sociological Review* 53 (1988), pp. 81–93.

93. Travis Hirschi, "A Brief Commentary on Akers' 'Delinquent Behavior, Drugs and Alcohol: What Is the Relationship?'," *Today's Delinquent* 3 (1984), pp. 49–52.

94. Ibid.

95. Gottfredson and Hirschi, *A General Theory of Crime*.

96. Ibid., pp. 90–91.

97. Ibid., p. 87.

98. Douglas Longshore, Susan Turner, and Judith A. Stein, "Self-Control in a Criminal Sample: An Examination of Construct Validity," *Criminology* 34 (1996), p. 209.

99. Gottfredson and Hirschi, *A General Theory of Crime*, p. 117.

100. Ibid.

101. Dennis Giever, "Empirical Testing of Gottfredson and Hirschi's General Theory of Crime." Paper presented to the Annual Meeting of the American Society of Criminology in San Diego, California (November 1995), p. 15. See also Charles R. Tittle, David A. Ward, and Harold G. Grasmick, "Capacity for Self-Control and Individuals' Interest in Exercising Self-Control," *Journal of Quantitative Criminology* 20 (June 2004), p. 143.

102. Travis C. Pratt and Francis T. Cullen, "The Empirical Status of Gottfredson and Hirschi's General Theory of Crime: A Meta-Analysis," *Criminology* 38 (August 2000), p. 931.

103. For a review of these studies, see T. David Evans, Francis T. Cullen, Velmer S. Burton Jr., R. Gregory Dunaway, and Michael L. Benson, "The Social Consequences of Self-Control: Testing the General Theory of Crime," *Criminology* (1997), pp. 476–477. See also Teresa C. LaGrange and Robert A. Silverman, "Low Self-Control and Opportunity: Testing the General Theory of Crime as an Explanation for Gender Differences in Delinquency," *Criminology* 37 (February 1999), p. 41; Raymond Paternoster and Robert Brame, "On the Association among Self-Control, Crime, and Analogous Behaviors," *Criminology* 38 (August 2000), p. 971; David Brownfield and Marie Soreson, "Self-Control and Juvenile Delinquency: Theoretical Issues and an Empirical Assessment of Selected Elements of a General Theory of Crime," *Deviant Behavior* 4 (1993), pp. 243–264; Alex Piquero and Stephen Tibbetts, "Specifying the Direct and Indirect Effects of Low Self-Control and Situational Factors

in Decision Making: Toward a More Complete Model of Rational Offending," *Justice Quarterly* 13 (1996), pp. 481–510; Dennis M. Giever, Dana C. Lynskey, and Danette S. Monnet, "Gottfredson and Hirschi's General Theory of Crime and Youth Gangs: An Empirical Test on a Sample of Middle-School Students," unpublished paper sent to author, 1998; and Carter Hay, "Parenting, Self-Control, and Delinquency: A Test of Self-Control Theory," *Criminology* 39 (August 2001), p. 726.

104. Harold G. Grasmick, Charles R. Tittle, Robert J. Bursik Jr., and Bruce J. Arneklev, "Testing the Core Empirical Implications of Gottfredson and Hirschi's General Theory of Crime," *Journal of Research in Crime and Delinquency* 30 (February 1993), p. 5.

105. For other criticisms of this general theory of crime, see Ronald L. Akers, "Self-Control as a General Theory of Crime," *Journal of Quantitative Criminology* 7 (1991), pp. 291–211; Michael L. Benson and Elizabeth Moore, "Are White-Collar and Common Offenders the Same? An Empirical and Theoretical Critique of a Recently Proposed General Theory of Crime," *Journal of Research in Crime and Delinquency* 29 (August 1992), pp. 251–272; Bruce J. Arneklev, Harold G. Grasmick, Charles R. Tittle, and Robert J. Bursik Jr., "Low Self-Control and Imprudent Behavior," *Journal of Quantitative Criminology* 9 (1993), pp. 225–247; Susan L. Miller and Cynthia Burack, "A Critique of Gottfredson and Hirschi's General Theory of Crime: Selective (In)Attention to Gender and Power Positions," *Women and Criminal Justice* 4 (1993), pp. 115–133; and Michael Polakowski, "Linking Self- and Social Control with Deviance: Illuminating the Structure Underlying a General Theory of Crime and Its Relation to Deviant Activity," *Journal of Quantitative Criminology* 10 (1994), pp. 41–78.

106. Shoemaker, *Theories of Delinquency*, p. 277.

107. Elliott et al., "An Integrated Theoretical Perspective on Delinquent Behavior," p. 11.

108. Ibid., p. 3–27.

109. Ibid.

110. Elliott et al., *Explaining Delinquency and Drug Use*.

111. Ibid. For an extension of this model, see Cynthia Chien, "Testing the Effect of the Key Theoretical Variable of Theories of Strain, Social Control and Social Learning on Types of Delinquency." Paper presented to the Annual Meeting of the American Society of Criminology, Baltimore, Maryland (November 1990).

112. Shoemaker, *Theories of Delinquency*, p. 286.

113. Thornberry, "Toward an Interactional Theory of Delinquency," p. 886. See also Terence P. Thornberry, "Reflections on the Advantages and Disadvantages of Theoretical Integration," in *Theoretical Integration in the Study of Deviance and Crime: Problems and Prospects* (Albany: State University of New York Press, 1989), pp. 51–60.

114. Thornberry, "Toward an Interactional Theory of Delinquency," p. 886.

115. Ibid.

116. This evaluation of interactional theory is largely derived from Shoemaker, *Theories of Delinquency*, p. 288.

117. Thornberry et al., "Testing Interactional Theory," pp. 19–25.

118. Terence P. Thornberry, Alan J. Lizotte, Marvin D. Krohn, Margaret Farnworth, and Sung Joon Jang, "Delinquency Peers, Beliefs, and Delinquent Behavior: A Longitudinal Test of Interactional Theory," *Theoretical Integration in the Study of Deviance and Crime*, p. 74.

119. J. David Hawkins and Joseph G. Weis, "The Social Development Model: An Integrated Approach to Delinquency Prevention," *Journal of Primary Prevention* 6 (Winter 1985), pp. 77–78.

120. Hirschi, *Causes of Delinquency*.

121. Clifford R. Shaw, *Delinquent Areas* (Chicago: University of Chicago Press, 1929); Clifford Shaw and Henry D. McKay, *Juvenile Delinquency in Urban Areas* (Chicago: University of Chicago Press, 1942).

122. Bu Huang, Rick Kosterman, Richard F. Catalano, J. David Hawkins, and Robert D. Abbott, "Modeling Mediation in the Etiology of Violent Behavior in Adolescence: A Test of the Social Development Model," *Criminology* 39 (February 2001), p. 75.

123. See Shaw, *Delinquent Areas*, and Shaw and McKay, *Juvenile Delinquency in Urban Areas*.

124. Hawkins et al., *Typology of Cause-Focused Strategies*.

125. John A. Clausen, *American Lives: Looking Back at the Children of the Great Depression* (New York: The Free Press, 1993), p. 1.

126. Ibid., p. viii.

127. Ibid., pp. 519–521.

128. Marvin D. Krohn, Terence P. Thornberry, Craig Rivera, and Marc Le Blanc, "Later Delinquency Careers," in *Child Development*, edited by Rolf Loeber and David P. Farrington (Thousand Oaks, Calif.: Sage Publishers, 2001), pp. 72–73.

129. Terence P. Thornberry, Marvin D. Krohn, Alan J. Lizotte, Carolyn A. Smith, and Kimberly Tobin, *Gangs and Delinquency in Developmental Perspective* (Cambridge, England: Cambridge University Press, 2003), pp. 164–165.

130. John H. Laub and Robert J. Sampson, *Shared Beginnings, Divergent Lives: Delinquent Boys to Age 70* (Cambridge, Mass.: Harvard University Press, 2003), p. 291. See also Robert J. Sampson and John H. Laub, "A Life-Course Theory of Cumulative Disadvantage and the Stability of Delinquency," in *Developmental Theories of Crime and Delinquency*, edited by Terence P. Thornberry (New Brunswick, N.J.: Transaction Publishers, 1997), pp. 133–161.

131. Sampson and Laub, *Crime in the Making*, p. 240.

132. Laub and Sampson, *Shared Beginnings, Divergent Lives;* see especially Chapters 3 and 6.

133. Ibid., p. 149.

134. Shadd Maruna, *Making Good: How Ex-Convicts Reform and Rebuild Their Lives* (Washington, D.C.: American Psychological Association, 2001), pp. 9–10, 85–108.

135. Peggy C. Giordano, Stephen A. Cernkovich, and Jennifer L. Rudolph, "Gender, Crime, and Delinquency: Toward a Theory of Cognitive Transformation," *American Journal of Sociology* 107 (January 2002), pp. 1000–1003.

6

Social Interactionist Theories of Delinquency

> We worry about what a child will become tomorrow, yet we forget that he is someone today. "

—Stacia Tauscher, National Center for Juvenile Justice, Annual Report, 2003

CHAPTER Objectives

AFTER READING THIS CHAPTER, YOU SHOULD BE ABLE TO ANSWER THE FOLLOWING QUESTIONS:

- How important is the concept of labeling as a cause of future behavior?

- What kinds of youngsters become more determined to succeed because they have been labeled?

- Does peer evaluation affect some young people more than others?

- How does social class affect the system's response to a troublesome youth?

During what was supposed to be a simple breaking and entering involving a small boatyard in Kennebunkport, Maine, in 2002, two intruders, Patrick V., 14, and his accomplice, Christopher Conley, 19, spotted what they thought were video surveillance cameras. The boys panicked and set fire to the building in an effort to destroy evidence of their entry. The building as well as several boats and boat motors were totally destroyed.

As it happened, one of the burned engines belonged to former President George H. W. Bush, whose summer house is seven miles from the site of the break-in.

Within days of the fire, Secret Service and other federal agents came to Patrick's house and told his mother that her son and his friend had "blown up the president's boat," and that it might have been "a terrorist act." The incident, said the agents, raised national security concerns.

Patrick soon found himself in a highly unusual situation. Instead of appearing before a Maine judge in local juvenile court, he was turned over to federal authorities. His case was heard in federal district court, where a federal judge ordered him to spend 30 months in the Cresson Secure Treatment Center—a maximum security juvenile facility in Pennsylvania.

Because Patrick is a juvenile, his court records are sealed. Federal officials, however, told reporters for the *New York Times* that Patrick's case came under federal jurisdiction because "arson is a crime of violence" and because the boatyard was engaged in interstate commerce.

There are so few juveniles in federal custody that the U.S. government doesn't even have its own juvenile prison. Instead, it contracts with states, like Pennsylvania, for the housing of serious juvenile offenders.

In 2004, a federal appeals court reopened Patrick's case to determine whether a more appropriate facility could be located closer to his home in Maine, but the length of his original sentence was not questioned.[1] Patrick's parents say that their son had no previous involvement in delinquency, but that the government overreacted to what began as a minor incident because property owned by a former President was destroyed in the resulting fire.

Adapted from Fox Butterfield, "A Federal Case for a Teenager: Family Sees Tie to Ex-President," *New York Times*, December 23, 2003, and Fox Butterfield, "New Look at Boy's Sentence in Boatyard Fire," *New York Times*, March 29, 2004. Copyright © 2003 and 2004 by The New York Times Co. Reprinted with permission.

social interactionist theories
Theoretical perspectives that derive their explanatory power from the give and take that continuously occurs between social groups, or between individuals and society.

labeling theory
The view that society creates the delinquent by labeling those who are apprehended as "different" from other youths, when in reality they are different primarily because they have been "tagged" with a deviant label.

This chapter discusses labeling theory, symbolic interactionist theory, and conflict theory. Labeling theory describes the creation and enforcement of society's rules and explains the important role those rules play in determining the nature and extent of delinquency. Symbolic interactionist theory considers the process by which deviant or delinquent behavior is influenced by reference groups and peers. Conflict theory sees delinquency as a by-product of the conflict that results when groups or classes with differing interests interact with one another.

These three perspectives are termed **social interactionist theories** of delinquency because they derive their explanatory power from the give and take that continuously occurs between social groups and between individuals and society.

Labeling Theory

During the 1960s and 1970s, the labeling perspective was one of the most influential approaches to understanding crime and delinquency.[2] **Labeling theory** or the la-

A young woman mentors a girls' softball team. ■ **How can mentoring programs help young people avoid the potential negative consequences of labeling?**

beling perspective, sometimes called the *interactional theory of deviance* or the *social reaction perspective,* is based on the premise that society creates deviants by labeling those who are apprehended as different from other individuals, when in reality they are different only because they have been tagged with a deviant label. Accordingly, labeling theorists focus on the processes by which individuals become involved in deviant behavior and stress the part played by social audiences and their responses to the norm violations of individuals.

The view that formal and informal social reactions to criminality can influence criminals' subsequent attitudes and behaviors has been recognized for some time. Frank Tannenbaum, Edwin M. Lemert, and Howard Becker, three of the chief proponents of the labeling perspective, focus on the process by which formal social control agents change the self-concept of individuals through these agents' reactions to their behavior. Recent work in labeling theory is also discussed in this section.

Frank Tannenbaum: The Dramatization of Evil

Frederick M. Thrasher's 1927 study of juvenile gangs in Chicago was one of the first to suggest that the consequences of official labels of delinquency were potentially negative.[3] In 1938, Tannenbaum developed the earliest formulation of labeling theory in his book *Crime and the Community*. Tannenbaum examined the process whereby a juvenile came to the attention of the authorities and was labeled as different from other juveniles. Tannenbaum theorized that this process produced a change in both how those individuals were then handled by the justice system and how they came to view themselves:

The process of making the criminal, therefore, is a process of tagging, defining, identifying, segregating, describing, emphasizing, making conscious and self-conscious; it becomes a way of stimulating, suggesting, emphasizing, and evoking the very traits that are complained of.[4]

Tannenbaum called this process the *dramatization of evil*. He wrote that the process of tagging a juvenile resulted in the youth's becoming involved with other delinquents and that these associations represented an attempt to escape the society that was responsible for negative labeling. The delinquent then became involved in a deviant career, and regardless of the efforts of individuals in the community and justice system to change his or her "evil" behavior, the negative behavior became increasingly hardened and resistant to positive values. Tannenbaum proposed that the less the evil is dramatized, the less likely youths are to become involved in deviant careers.[5]

Edwin Lemert: Primary and Secondary Deviation

The social reaction theory developed by Edwin H. Lemert provided a distinct alternative to the social disorganization theory of Shaw and McKay, the differential association notion of Edwin H. Sutherland, and the social structural approach of Merton. Lemert focused attention on the interaction between social control agents and rule violators and on how certain behaviors came to be labeled *criminal, delinquent*, or *deviant*.[6]

Lemert's concept of primary and secondary deviation is regarded as one of the most important theoretical constructs of the labeling perspective. According to Lemert, **primary deviation** consists of the individual's behavior, and **secondary deviation** is society's response to that behavior. The social reaction to the deviant, Lemert charged, could be interpreted as forcing a change in status or role; that is, society's reaction to the deviant resulted in a transformation in the individual's identity.[7] The social reaction to the deviant, whether a disapproving glance or a full-blown stigmatization, is critical in understanding the progressive commitment of a person to a deviant mode of life.

Lemert observed this **process of becoming deviant** as having the following stages:

> The sequence of interaction leading to secondary deviation is roughly as follows: (1) primary deviation; (2) social penalties; (3) further primary deviation; (4) stronger penalties and rejection; (5) further deviation, perhaps with hostilities and resentment beginning to focus upon those doing the penalizing; (6) crisis reached in the tolerance quotient, expressed in formal action by the community stigmatizing of the deviant; (7) strengthening of the deviant conduct as a reaction to the stigmatizing and penalties; (8) ultimate acceptance of deviant social status and efforts at adjustment on the basis of the associated role.[8]

The social reaction to deviance is expressed in this process of interaction. *Social reaction* is a general term that summarizes both the moral indignation of others toward deviance and the action directed toward its control. This concept also encompasses a social organizational perspective. As an organizational response, the concept of social reaction refers to the capacity of control agents to impose such constraints on the behavior of the deviant as are reflected in terms such as *treat, correct*, and *punish*.[9]

Howard Becker: Deviant Careers

Howard Becker, another major labeling theorist, conceptualized the relationship between the rules of society and the process of being labeled as an outsider:

> Social groups create deviance by making the rules whose infraction constitutes deviance, and by applying those rules to particular people and labeling them as outsiders. From this point of view, deviance is not a quality of the act the person commits, but rather a consequence of the application by others of rules and sanctions to an "offender." The deviant is one to whom that label has successfully been applied; deviant behavior is behavior that people so label.[10]

primary deviation
According to labeling theory, the initial act of deviance that causes a person to be labeled a deviant.

secondary deviation
According to labeling theory, deviance that is a consequence of societal reaction to an initial delinquent act.

process of becoming deviant
In labeling theory, the concept that the process of acquiring a delinquent identity takes place in a number of steps.

FIGURE 6.1

General Assumptions of Labeling Theory

Variety of causes or influences → Initial or primary deviation → Official label of delinquent/deviant → Delinquent/deviant self-image → Continued involvement in delinquency or deviance

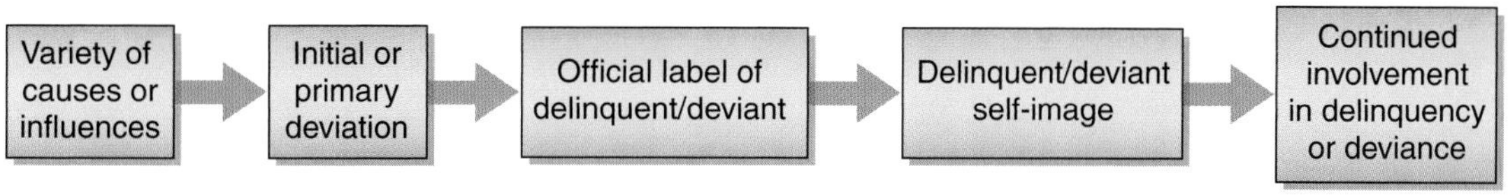

Becker argued that once a person is caught and labeled, that person becomes an outsider and gains a new social status, with consequences for both the person's self-image and his or her public identity. The individual is now regarded as a different kind of person.[11] Although the sequence of events that leads to the imposition of the label of "deviant" is presented from the perspective of social interaction, the analytical framework shifts to that of social structure once the label is imposed. In other words, before a person is labeled, he or she participates in a process of social interaction, but once labeling has occurred the individual is assigned a status within a social structure.[12] For the relationship among the theoretical constructs of labeling theory, see Figure 6.1.

Web PLACES 6.1

Learn about labeling theory from CrimeTheory.com via **www.justicestudies.com/WebPlaces**.

The Juvenile Justice Process and Labeling

There is a long history of arguments that the labeling found in the formal processing of youths through the juvenile justice system is what influences the secondary response of continued delinquent acts. Edwin Schur contended that most delinquent acts are insignificant and benign and therefore punishment is not needed. But when youths are arrested and brought before the juvenile court, they are stereotyped as different. Having acquired this label, they receive greater attention from authorities, and they are likely to be processed more deeply in the justice system because of this increased attention. Delinquency laws are actually counterproductive, Schur stated, because they produce more delinquency than they deter. In 1973, Schur went so far as to argue for a policy of **radical nonintervention,** which simply means "Leave the kids alone whenever possible."[13]

More recently, several studies have suggested that under certain circumstances, "official punishment appears to increase the likelihood of subsequent deviance as suggested by labeling theory."[14] Francis Palamara, Francis T. Cullen, and Joanne C. Gersten found that the formal reaction to delinquency affects the likelihood of subsequent delinquent behavior but that these effects are related to the types of reaction and the types of deviance.[15] Anthony Matarazzo, Peter J. Carrington, and Robert D. Hiscott investigated the relationship between prior and current youth court disposition and found support for labeling theory; their findings indicated that prior juvenile court dispositions exerted a significant impact on current disposition, even with the control of relevant variables.[16] See Social World of the Delinquent 6.1.

radical nonintervention
A policy toward delinquents which advises that authorities should "leave the kids alone whenever possible."

New Developments in Labeling Theory

The early versions of labeling theory came under serious attack for theoretical flaws and lack of support.[17] Critics of this perspective charged that "labeling theorists had grossly exaggerated the role of labeling by suggesting that it is the only factor responsible for persistent deviance and by implying that it always increases the likelihood of subsequent rule breaking."[18] Assailed by these and other criticisms, the theory was under serious challenge by 1980 and, as Raymond Paternoster and Leeann Iovanni observe, was "pronounced dead by 1985."[19] Yet the labeling perspective later enjoyed a resurgence because of its more sophisticated application.[20]

"Kansas Charley"

In 1892, the people of Cheyenne, Wyoming, prepared themselves for the hanging of a seventeen-year-old orphan from New York City, Charley Miller. "Kansas Charley," as he called himself and accordingly was called by everyone else, had a short, pitiful, and emotionally barren life. Among those who cared for him while he spent his last eighteen months in the Laramie County Jail, he evoked feelings of compassion. It was hard not to be touched by the combination of Charley's early deprivations, his adolescent voice, his small frame, and his emotional difficulties. Chronic bedwetting that lasted throughout his life was a sign of Charley's mental distress.

However, the crime he committed evoked no compassion from anyone. At fifteen, while traveling the country looking for work and adventure, he had killed two boys in a Union Pacific boxcar. The horror of this homicide drew widespread public attention and provoked heated debate about what was wrong with the perpetrator as well as with American society. In a Wyoming courtroom the prosecutor, Frank Taggart, took advantage of the way "Kansas Charley" had been demonized by the press and successfully convinced the jury of his bad-boy image. A short but well-publicized trial sentenced Charley to death for his crime. Charley Miller's execution was widely reported. His picture was published on the front page of the *Chicago Daily Tribune,* the *New York World,* the *Rocky Mountain News* (Denver), and the *San Francisco Chronicle.* Up until he faced the end of a rope, "Kansas Charley" relished the reputation that the press and public had created for him.

■ **How does the social construction of labels serve the various constituencies—the press, the public, the criminal justice system, and even the offender? There was stiff opposition to the execution of "Kansas Charley." Why do you think those who favored the death penalty for an adolescent prevailed?**

Source: Joan Jacobs Brumberg, *Kansas Charley: The Story of a Nineteenth-Century Boy Murderer* (New York: Viking Press, 2003), pp. 1, 237.

Recent Applications of Labeling Theory   Ruth Ann Triplett and G. Roger Jarjoura developed "new avenues for exploring the effects of labeling."[21] They separated labeling into formal and informal labeling. Formal labels, the emphasis of early labeling theorists, are the reactions by official agents of the justice system to illegal behaviors. In contrast, an informal label is "an attempt to characterize a person as a given 'type' . . . by persons who are not acting as official social control agents, and in social situations that are not formal social control 'ceremonies.' "[22] In other words, informal labels are those given by parents, neighbors, and friends. For example, John Braithwaite examined shaming in the family; his study showed that families use shaming, or reintegrative shaming, to bring an offender back into line with their beliefs.[23]

Triplett and Jarjoura also divided labels into subjective and objective labels. An audience's reaction to an actor is an objective label, whereas the actor's interpretation of that reaction is a subjective label. Although the importance of subjective labels has always been emphasized in symbolic interactionism, one of the important roots of labeling theory, it has remained largely unexplored in labeling theory and research.[24] Triplett, using the four waves of Elliott's National Youth Survey, concluded that the informal labels of significant others (parents) affect delinquent behavior both directly and indirectly for whites but that informal or subjective labels of significant others have no consistent direct or indirect effect on delinquent behavior for nonwhites.[25]

Moreover, Triplett and Jarjoura separated labels into exclusive and inclusive social reactions. J. D. Orcutt refers to these two types of reactions in his research on small-group reactions to deviance:

Inclusive reactions [are] those attempts at social control which are premised on the assumption that the rule-breaker is and will continue to be an ordinary member of the community. . . . This form of social reaction attempts to control rule-infractions by bringing the present or future behavior of the rule-breaker into conformity with the rules without excluding him from it. Exclusive reactions are those attempts at social control which operate to reject the rule-breaker from the group and revoke his privileges and status as an ordinary member.[26]

Robert J. Sampson and John H. Laub claim that labeling is one factor leading to "cumulative disadvantage" in future life chances (see Chapter 5), which increases the likelihood of a person's involvement in criminal acts during adulthood. This life-course approach views public labeling as a transitional event pushing young people on a trajectory of structural disadvantage and involvement in deviance and crime.[27] John Gunnar Bernburg and Marvin D. Krohn, in their analysis of data from the Rochester Youth Development Study, find support for this cumulative disadvantage position: Official intervention decreases the odds that those labeled will graduate from high school, and educational attainment has a direct effect on employment. Hence, official intervention during adolescence influences involvement in crime in early adulthood by helping to block the life chances afforded by education and employment.[28]

Evaluation of Labeling Theory

The labeling perspective has consistently received mixed responses, but it does have several strengths:

- Labeling theory provides an explanation for why youths who become involved in the juvenile justice process frequently continue delinquent acts until the end of their adolescent years.
- Labeling theory emphasizes the importance of rule making and power in the creation of deviance. Consideration of the broader contexts of the labeling process lifts the focus of delinquency from the behavior of an individual actor to the interactions of an actor and his or her immediate and broader influences.
- As part of a larger symbolic interactionist perspective, labeling theory points out that individuals do take on the roles and self-concepts that are expected of them; this means that they can indeed become victims of self-fulfilling prophecies.
- The more sophisticated applications of labeling theory developed since the early 1990s have moved this explanation of delinquent behavior from a unidimensional focus to a perspective that examines more contingencies of labeling effects, including both direct and indirect effects of labeling.

The labeling perspective has been criticized, however, because it fails to answer several critical questions raised by the assumptions it makes: Are the conceptions that we have of one another correct? Whose label really counts? When is a personal identity changed, and by whose stigmatizing effort? Does a bad name cause bad action? Is social response to crime generated more by the fact of the crime or by the legally irrelevant social characteristics of the offender? If official labels are so important, why do so many youths mature out of delinquency during their later adolescent years?[29]

In sum, delinquency is clearly related to factors other than official labels. It is extremely questionable to ascribe too much significance to the influence of the labeling process on adolescents' subsequent identities and behavior.[30] Nevertheless, the resurgence of labeling theory in the late 1980s and 1990s does prove that it remains alive and well. The theoretical refinements in labeling theory (i.e., formal and informal labels, subjective and objective labels, and exclusive and inclusive social reactions) promise to offer fruitful avenues for examining delinquency in the future.

Symbolic Interactionist Theory

The **symbolic interactionist theory** of delinquency was developed by Ross L. Matsueda and Karen Heimer.[31] This theory sees the social order as a dynamic process that is the ever-evolving product of an ongoing system of social interaction and communi-

symbolic interactionist theory
A perspective in social psychology that analyzes the process of interaction among human beings at the symbolic level, and that has influenced the development of several social process theories of delinquent behavior.

cation.[32] It proposes to explain delinquent behavior in terms of self-development mediated by language—which is the central medium through which symbolic interaction occurs.[33] Of central importance is the process by which shared meanings, behavioral expectations, and reflected appraisals are built up through interaction and applied to behavior.[34] This interactionist perspective, according to Heimer, also has the "potential for illuminating the dynamic relationship among gender inequality, racial inequality, and law violation."[35]

The intellectual roots of symbolic interactionism lie in the tradition of Scottish moral philosophers (e.g., Smith and Hume), and in the tradition of American pragmatists (e.g., Dewey, James, Cooley, and G. H. Mead). By the mid-twentieth century, symbolic interactionism had achieved a dominant position among sociological theories through the scholars who collectively became known as the Chicago school of sociology. For symbolic interactionism, individuals, groups, social systems, and situations constitute an ongoing social process, mutually influencing one another and merging imperceptibly in the web of daily interactions. The work of George Herbert Mead was especially influential in the development of this theoretical tradition. Mead's analysis of the social act is the basis of most versions of contemporary symbolic interactionism.[36]

Role-Taking and Delinquency

Matsueda and Heimer build on the social act as the unit of analysis. They begin with the immediate situation of delinquent behavior, which is made up of a social interaction between two or more individuals.[37] The situation can influence delinquency in two ways: First, the specific situation that juveniles encounter may present opportunities for delinquent behavior; and, second, and more importantly, the immediate situation influences delinquent behavior through its effects on the content and direction of social interaction.[38]

In analyzing social interaction, symbolic interactionists define the unit of analysis as the transaction that takes place in interaction between two or more individu-

Students having lunch in the cafeteria of Oswego High School in New York. ■ **How do modes of dress, hairstyle, and so on, signify a person's understanding of who he or she is? How do such understandings relate to social roles?**

als.[39] The important mechanism by which interactants influence each other is role-taking, which Mead viewed as the key to social control.[40] According to Matsueda, role-taking consists of

projecting oneself into the role of other persons and appraising, from their standpoint, the situation, oneself in the situation, and possible lines of action. With regard to delinquency, individuals confronted with delinquent behavior as a possible line of action take each other's roles through verbal and nonverbal communication, fitting their lines of action together into joint delinquent behavior.[41]

The transaction is built up through this process of reciprocal role-taking, in which one person initiates a lawful or unlawful action and a second takes the role of the other and responds. The first person then reacts to the response, which continues until a jointly developed goal is reached, a new goal is substituted, or the transaction is ended. Through such reciprocal role-taking, individual lines of action are coordinated and concerted action is taken toward achieving the goal. This means that the initiated delinquent act of one juvenile might elicit a negative response from another juvenile, perhaps contributing to the group's searching for another, more suitable alternative. (See Figure 6.2 for a model of reflected appraisals and behavior.) Matsueda goes on to suggest that "Whether or not a goal is achieved using unlawful means is determined by each individual's contribution to the direction of the transaction; those contributions, in turn, are determined by the individual's prior life experience or biography."[42]

This process by which role-taking can lead to delinquent behavior, according to Matsueda, can be illustrated by several classic studies of delinquency. Scott Briar and Irving Piliavin's study found that gang youth who are committed to nonconventional lines of action are often incited into delinquent behavior by "situationally induced motives," which are verbal motives presented by other youth. Free from considering how conventional others would react, they can take the role of each other, presenting delinquent motives and adopting delinquent behavior.[43] James F. Short Jr. and Fred L. Strodtbeck noted that a youth's willingness to join a gang fight frequently revolved around the risk of losing status with the gang. In taking the role of the group and considering the group's negative reactions, these gang youth would join in for fear of losing status.[44] Donald Gibbons's study of delinquent boys further found that one result of group interaction was the emergence of novel shades of norms and values that influenced the direction of joint behavior.[45]

Matsueda concludes that this discussion of role-taking implies four features of a theory of the self and delinquent behavior. First, the self is formed by how an

Web **LIBRARY** 6.1

Read the OJJDP publication *Report of the Comprehensive Strategy Task Force on Serious, Violent and Chronic Juvenile Offenders— Part 1* at **www.justicestudies .com/WebLibrary**.

FIGURE 6.2

Alternative Models of Reflected Appraisals

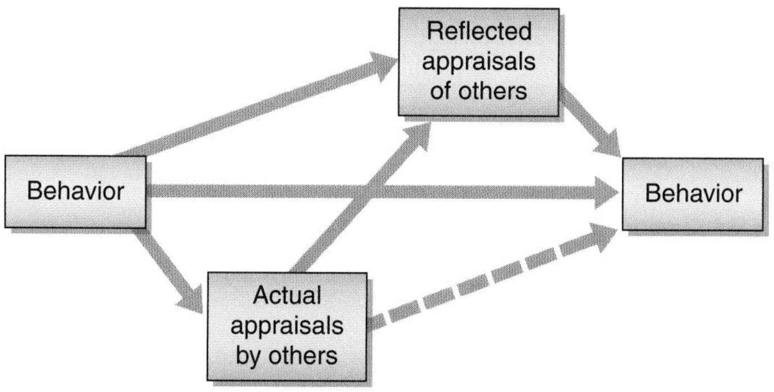

Source: Ross L. Matsueda, "Reflected Appraisals, Parental Labeling, and Delinquency: Specifying a Symbolic Interactionist Theory," *American Journal of Sociology* 97 (May 1992), p. 1585. Reprinted by permission of the University of Chicago Press.

individual perceives that others view him or her and thus is rooted in symbolic interaction. Second, the self is an object that "arises partly endogenously within situations, and partly exogenously from prior situational self being carried over from previous experience." Third, the self as an object becomes a process that has been determined by the self at a previous point in time and by prior resolutions of problematic situations. Fourth, delinquent behavior takes place partly because of the formation of habits and partly because the stable perception of oneself is shaped by the standpoint of others.[46]

Using classic symbolic interactionist theory, Matsueda talks about the self as a consistent "me" that is relatively stable across situations. This self, which is called "a looking-glass self" by Charles H. Cooley[47] or the "self as an object" by George H. Mead,[48] is a process that consists of three components: how others actually see us (others' actual appraisals); how we perceive the way others see us (reflected appraisals); and how we see ourselves (self-appraisals)."[49] One's self, then, is made up in part by a "reflected appraisal" of how significant others appraise or evaluate one.[50]

Matsueda used a sample from the National Youth Survey to test his theory. His findings supported a symbolic interactionist conceptualization of reflected appraisals and delinquency in a number of ways. Juveniles' reflected appraisals of themselves from the standpoint of parents, friends, and teachers "coalesced into a consensual self, rather than remaining compartmentalized as distinct selves."[51] This remained true whether the reflected appraisals were found in rule violators or socialized youths. In agreement with labeling theory, parental labels of youths as rule violators were more likely among nonwhites, urban dwellers, and delinquents. Delinquent youths' "appraisals of themselves are also strongly influenced by their parents' independent appraisals of them."[52] Moreover, prior delinquent behavior, both directly and indirectly, reflected appraisals of self. In addition, reflected appraisals as a rule violator exerted a large effect on delinquent behavior and mediated much of the effect of parental appraisals as a rule violator on delinquent behavior. Finally, age, race, and urban residence exerted significant effects on delinquency, most of which worked indirectly through prior delinquency and in part through the rule-violator reflected appraisal.[53]

Interactionist Perspectives on Gender, Race, and Delinquency   Heimer argues that "structural conflict gives rise to gender and race differences in motivations to break the law."[54] From the vantage point of the interactionist perspective, then, racial and gender inequality are consequential for law violation because they restrict the positions of minorities and females and therefore constrain communication networks and power needed to influence others.[55] She goes on to say:

> Hence, these forms of structural inequality influence definitions of situations because they partially determine the significant others and reference groups considered in the role-taking process. Through shaping definitions of situations, gender and racial inequality contribute to the patterning of crime and delinquency. Thus, consistent with the tradition of differerential association in criminology, an interactionist theory of delinquency argues that there will be differences across groups in definitions of situations and the law to the extent that communication networks vary.[56]

"'Structural conflict gives rise to gender and race differences in motivations to break the law.'"

Evaluation of Symbolic Interactionist Theory

Voices Across the Profession 6.1, which is an interview with Karen Heimer, provides some interesting insights about symbolic interactionist theory and delinquency. The approach has several strengths:

- It builds on symbolic interactionist theory, a great tradition in American sociology. This tradition has identified the locus of social control in the process of taking the role of the other and of linking with the broader social organization through role commitments, generalized others, and reference groups.[57]

Interview with Karen Heimer

Question: What do you feel are the best features of symbolic interactionist theory?

Heimer: One of the strengths of symbolic interactionist approaches is that they locate the individual within the social situation. These approaches share an emphasis on the general idea that people come to know the world around them and themselves through taking the perspectives of others. Consistent with some other interactionist theories of crime, differential social control theory focuses on how the *role-taking process* can lead to delinquency or crime. More specifically, differential social control posits that the following five key elements of interactions are consequential for law violation: (1) identities or reflected appraisals of self; (2) anticipated reactions to law violation from significant others (including family and peers); (3) definitions of the law and morality; (4) influence of delinquent peers; and (5) habitual or scripted responses to opportunities to break the law. All of these influence law violation through role-taking in situations. I think that an important strength of differential social control theory, therefore, is the specification of the mechanisms through which situations affect delinquency and crime. We have attempted to elaborate the theory to show how the link between changes over the life course and offending might be better understood, how gender differences in delinquency emerge, and how delinquency and depression are linked.

Question: Do you see any areas that need to be expanded or reformulated?

Heimer: There are several areas of the theory that need further refinement and elaboration. For example, there likely are dimensions of role-taking in situations other than those we have identified that are important for crime and delinquency. I hope that future research will uncover some of these. In addition, I would like to see research on the theory attempt to further elaborate the ways in which social structural circumstances constrain or facilitate interactions that lead to law violations. In our published work to date, we have shown how disadvantaged social circumstances increase the chances that individuals will associate with delinquent youths and criminal adults, and thereby become more likely to see themselves as deviant, perceive that others would not strongly disapprove of law violations, and adopt delinquent attitudes and beliefs. But the ways in which social structures can influence role-taking are certainly more complex and diverse. I would like to see this part of the theory elaborated more fully in future work. Finally, I think that our recent work on an interactionist view of the connections between delinquency and depression opens the door to exploring how a variety of "deviant" outcomes might be linked via similar role-taking mechanisms.

Question: How did you come to be involved in the formulation of the theory?

Heimer: My early education in graduate school was in sociological social psychology. When I began my graduate work in sociology, I took a course on sociological so-cial psychology in which I learned about the richness of theory and research on symbolic interactionism. So my interest in working on a symbolic interactionist approach to crime and delinquency can be traced to my early intellectual history.

Question: Have you been encouraged or discouraged by the response that the theory has received?

Heimer: I am very pleased that the differential social control perspective has come to gain recognition within criminology. I hope that future work will chart new territory by elaborating and extending the theory, especially along the lines of the areas that I mention above. I think that the theory has much promise for integrating a variety of theoretical approaches to crime and delinquency, as we argued in our 1994 paper. I also think that attention to the ways that social interactions lead to law violation is essential for understanding law violation more fully. For these reasons, I think that the theory offers a fruitful avenue for future work.

> ■ Why is it important to locate the delinquent within the social situation? What are other ways that social structure can influence role-taking with adolescents? Why do you think Karen Heimer refers to this theory as "the differential social control perspective"?

Source: Karen Heimer is associate professor of sociology at the University of Iowa. She is interested in developing and testing theories of juvenile delinquency and violence, with an emphasis on gender and racial disparities. Reprinted with permission.[58]

■ Symbolic interactionist theory and delinquency build on and add to the insights of labeling theory. At a time in which labeling is being reformulated and is emerging in a more sophisticated form, the insights that Matsueda, Heimer, and their colleagues provide in relating symbolic interactionism and delinquency promise to further enrich labeling's contributions to our understanding of delinquency.

Web LIBRARY 6.2

Read the OJJDP publication *Report of the Comprehensive Strategy Task Force on Serious, Violent and Chronic Juvenile Offenders—Part 2* at **www.justicestudies .com/WebLibrary**.

■ The symbolic interactionist theory of delinquent behavior is insightful about how both law-abiding and delinquent youths form their conceptions of themselves and about how these perceptions influence their decision making.
■ This theory contributes helpful insights about the influence of delinquent peers and the group context in youths' self-appraisals.

An evaluation of symbolic interactionist theory, of course, is limited by the fact that it has been tested by Matsueda, Heimer, and colleagues in only a few settings.[59] At this point it is uncertain how much delinquency it explains, even among group delinquents. Indeed, many of the criticisms aimed at labeling theory apply also to this theory. Nevertheless, symbolic interactionist theory is still a promising attempt to explain delinquent behavior.

Conflict Theory

conflict theory

A perspective which holds that delinquency can be explained by socioeconomic class, by power and authority relationships, and by group and cultural differences.

Conflict theory sees social control as the end result of the differential distribution of economic and political power in any society. Conflict theorists view laws as tools created by the powerful for their own benefit.[60]

The development of the conflict model is indebted to the concept of "dialectics." This concept, like that of order, can be traced back to the philosophers of ancient Greece. In antiquity the term *dialectics* referred to the art of conducting a dispute or bringing out the truth by disclosing and resolving contradictions in the arguments of opponents.[61]

Georg F. Hegel used this concept of dialectical thinking to explain human progress and social change. A prevailing idea, or "thesis," according to Hegel, would eventually be challenged by an opposing idea, or "antithesis." The resultant conflict usually would result in the merging of the two, or "synthesis." The synthesis gradually would be accepted as the thesis, but then would be challenged by a new antithesis and so forth throughout history.[62] Karl Marx, rather than applying the method to ideas as Hegel did, applied the concept to the material world. Marx's theory became one of dialectical materialism, as he contended that the conflict was one of competing economic systems, in which the weak must ward off exploitation by the strong or powerful in society.[63]

Georg Simmel, a twentieth-century conflict theorist, argued that unity and discord are inextricably intertwined and together act as an integrative force in society. Simmel added that "there probably exists no social unity in which convergent and divergent currents among its members are not inseparably interwoven."[64] Simmel's notion of dialectics thus acknowledged the existence of tendencies for order and disorder.

More recently, Ralf Dahrendorf contended that functionalists misrepresented reality by being overconcerned with order and consensus. Dahrendorf argued that functionalists present a description of a utopian society—a society that never has existed and probably never will. Dahrendorf proposed that social researchers would be wise to opt for the conflict model because of its more realistic view that society is held together by constraint rather than consensus, not by universal agreement but by the coercion of some people by others.[65]

Richard Quinney has argued that criminal law is a social control instrument of the state "organized to serve the interests of the dominant economic class, the capitalist ruling class."[66] William Bonger earlier made this same point: "In every society which is divided into a ruling class and a class ruled, penal law has been principally constituted according to the will of the former."[67]

A more humane social order is the vision of some radical criminologists.[68] The goals of this ideal society are reduced inequality, reduced reliance on formal institutions of justice, and reduced materialism. The social relations of this social order are committed to developing self-reliance, self-realization, and mutual aid.[69] This peaceful society can be attained by using compromise and negotiation on a community level to defuse violent social structures. Communities must organize themselves in such a way as to prevent crime and to help victims without punishing offenders when crime does occur.[70]

Dimensions of Conflict Criminology

A great deal of variation exists among the ideas of conflict criminologists. Some theories emphasize the importance of socioeconomic class, some focus primarily on power and authority relationships, and others emphasize group and cultural conflict.

Socioeconomic Class and Radical Criminology   Even though Marx wrote very little on the subject of crime as the term is used today, he inspired a new school of criminology that emerged in the early 1970s. This school is variously described as Marxist, critical, Socialist, left-wing, new, or **radical criminology**. Marx was concerned both with deriving a theory of how societies change over time and with discovering how to go about changing society. This joining of theory and practice is called "praxis."[71]

Marx saw the history of all societies as the history of class struggles, and crime as a result of these class struggles.[72] He wrote in the *Communist Manifesto:*

> Freeman and slave, patrician and plebian, lord and serf, guildmaster and journeyman, in a word, oppressor and oppressed, stood in constant opposition to one another, carried on an uninterrupted, now hidden, now open fight, a reconstruction of society at large, or in the common ruin of the contending classes.[73]

Emerging with each historical period, according to Marx's theory, is a new class-based system of ranking. Marx contended that with **capitalism**, "society as a whole is more and more and more splitting up into two great classes directly facing each other—bourgeoisie [capitalist class] and proletariat [working class]."[74] The relations between the bourgeoisie and the proletariat become increasingly strained as the bourgeoisie comes to control more and more of the society's wealth and the proletariat is increasingly pauperized. In this relationship between the oppressive bourgeoisie and the pauperized proletariat lie the seeds of the demise of capitalism.[75]

In the Marxist perspective, the state and the law itself are ultimately tools of the ownership class and reflect mainly the economic interests of that class. Capitalism produces egocentric, greedy, and predatory human behavior. The ownership class is guilty of the worst crime: the brutal exploitation of the working class. Revolution is a means to counter this violence and is generally both necessary and morally justifiable. Conventional crime is caused by extreme poverty and economic disenfranchisement, products of the dehumanizing and demoralizing capitalist system.[76] See Voices Across the Profession 6.2 for an interview with Quinney, one of many writers who have applied the Marxist perspective to the study of crime.

radical criminology
A perspective which holds that the causes of crime are rooted in social conditions that empower the wealthy and the politically well organized but disenfranchise the less fortunate.

capitalism
An economic system in which private individuals or corporations own and control capital (wealth and the means of production) and in which competitive free markets control prices, production, and the distribution of goods.

> " Marx saw the history of all societies as the history of class struggles and crime as a result of these class struggles. "

Power and Authority Relationships   A second important dimension of conflict criminology is the focus on power and authority relationships. Max Weber, Ralf Dahrendorf, Austin T. Turk, and John Hagan have made contributions to this body of scholarship.

Weber's theory, like the Marxist perspective, contains a theory of social stratification that has been applied to the study of crime. Although Weber recognized the importance of the economic context in the analysis of social stratification, he did not believe that such a unidimensional approach could explain satisfactorily the phenomenon of social stratification. He added power and prestige to the Marxist emphasis on property and held these three variables responsible for the development of hierarchies in society. Weber also proposed that property differences led to the de-

Interview with Richard Quinney

Question: Why is social justice lacking in American society?

Quinney: Justice in a capitalist society is limited to the overall needs of a continuing capitalist system. Justice is largely limited to "criminal justice," a punitive model that does not deal with the inadequacies of the system. Social justice, on the other hand, would serve the needs of all people, including their economic well-being. The goal of social justice can be attempted in our capitalist society, but true social justice can be achieved only in a socialist society. The struggle for social justice is a struggle for the transformation of our present society in the United States.

Question: What are the chief contradictions of capitalism and how do they contribute to the extent and nature of crime in American society?

Quinney: There are many contradictions in capitalism. The basic contradiction is between the goal of progress and a better society, on the one hand, and the reality of the inability of capitalism to ever attain this goal because of the inherent class structure of capitalism. The capitalist class owns and controls the means of production and distribution and, as such, assures that a subordinate class of workers and consumers will be dominated politically and economically—to assure the continuation of the capitalist system. Classes outside of the capitalist class commit crimes out of need, frustration, and brutalization. Members of the capitalist class commit crimes out of greed and power. The rates of crime under capitalism can never be substantially reduced. Capitalism generates its own crime and rates of crime.

Question: Why is the capitalist state oppressive and coercive?

Quinney: The capitalist state exists to perpetuate capitalist economics and the social relations of capitalism. It is the policy and enforcement arm of capitalist society. Thus, the actions carried out by the branches of the state are of a control nature, including the activities associated with dispensing education, welfare, and criminal justice. The state must also provide benefits for those who suffer and fail under capitalist economics, but even these services have a control function, attempting to assure the continuation of the capitalist system.

Question: How does the early Quinney differ from the Quinney of today? Or how has your approach to the crime problem changed?

Quinney: I have moved through the various epistemologies and ontologies in the social sciences. After applying one, I have found that another is necessary for incorporating what was excluded from the former, and so on. Also, I have tried to keep my work informed by the latest developments in the philosophy of science. In addition, I have always been a part of the progressive movements of the time. My work is thus an integral part of the social and intellectual changes that are taking place in the larger society, outside of criminology and sociology. One other factor has affected my work in recent years: the search for meaning in my life and in the world.

Question: What direction do you anticipate the new criminology or the critical criminology will take?

Quinney: This is the time to substantiate the critical Marxist perspective through studies of specific aspects of crime. We know generally the causes of crime. Further work is in large part a political matter—showing others through the ac- cepted means of research. In the long run, however, our interests must go beyond the narrow confines of criminology and sociology. The theoretical, empirical, political, and spiritual issues are larger than the issue of crime.

Question: Critical or new criminology theorists have written much less about delinquency than criminality in American society. What more needs to be contributed by Marxists in this area?

Quinney: Our society emphasizes youth and the youth culture while at the same time increasingly excluding youth from gainful and meaningful employment. Youth are being relegated to the consumption sector—without the economic means for consumption. Education—including college—has traditionally provided a place for youth that are not essential to a capitalist society. But with the widening of the economic gap between classes, will education be an outlet and opportunity for the majority of adolescents and young adults? We are approaching a structural crisis (and personal crises) that will require a solution beyond what is possible in a capitalist society. Our challenge is to understand the changes that are taking place around us and to have the courage to be a part of the struggle that is necessary.

> ■ Where do you find yourself in agreement with Quinney? Where are you in disagreement? How can what he said be applied to understanding delinquency in the United States?

Richard Quinney received his Ph.D. from the University of Wisconsin, and he is emeritus professor of sociology at Northern Illinois University. *The Social Reality of Crime; Criminology, Class, State, and Crime; Providence: The Reconstruction of Social and Moral Order;* and *Social Existence* are some of the books that have brought Dr. Quinney's analyses of crime and social problems to the attention of readers throughout the world.[77]

velopment of classes, power differences to the creation of political parties and development of classes, and prestige differences to the development of status groups.[78] Further, Weber discussed the concept of "life chances" and argued that they were differentially related to social class. From this perspective, criminality exists in all societies and is the result of the political struggle among different groups attempting to promote or enhance their own life chances.[79]

Both Dahrendorf and Turk have extended the Weberian tradition in the field of criminology by emphasizing the relationships between authorities and their subjects. Dahrendorf contended that power is the critical variable explaining crime. He argues that although Marx built his theory on only one form of power, property ownership, a more useful perspective could be constructed by incorporating broader conceptions of power.[80]

Turk, constructing his analysis from the work of both Weber and Dahrendorf, argued that the social order of society is based on the relationships of conflict and domination between authorities and subjects.[81] Focusing on power and authority relationships, this perspective of conflict theory examines the relationships between the legal authorities who create, interpret, and enforce right–wrong standards for individuals in the political collectivity and those who accept or resist but do not make such legal decisions. Turk also made the point that conflicts between authorities and subjects take place over a wide range of social and cultural norms.[82]

John Hagan and associates viewed the relationship between gender and nonserious delinquency as linked to power and control.[83] Using the data collected in Toronto, Ontario, they suggested that the presence of power among fathers and the greater control of girls explain why boys more often than girls are delinquent. Unlike Hirschi's control theory, Hagan and colleagues' **power-control thesis** based the measurement of class on the authority that parents have in their positions at work. Furthermore, these researchers assumed that the authority of parents at work translates into conditions of dominance in the household and in the degree of their parental control over youth.

Robert M. Regoli and John D. Hewitt's **theory of differential oppression** contends that in the United States authority is unjustly used against children, who must "adapt to adults' conceptions of what 'good children' are." Children experience oppression, in this view, because they exist in a social world in which adults look on them as inferior and in which they lack social power relative to adults. Oppression takes place when adults use their power to prevent children from attaining access to valued resources or to prevent them from developing a sense of self as a subject rather than an object. Accordingly, children must submit to the power and authority of adults, and when children react negatively or fail to conform to these pressures, a process begins that results in delinquent acts.[84]

The theory of differential oppression is organized around four principles:

1. Because children lack power on account of their age, size, and lack of resources, they are easy targets for adult oppression.
2. Adult oppression of children occurs in multiple social contexts and falls on a continuum ranging from benign neglect to malignant abuse.
3. Oppression leads to adaptive reactions by children. The oppression of children produces at least four adaptations: passive acceptance, exercise of illegitimate coercive power, manipulation of peers, and retaliation.
4. Children's adaptations to oppression create and reinforce adults' view of children as inferior subordinate beings and as troublemakers. This view enables adults to justify their role as oppressors and further reinforces children's powerlessness.[85]

Regoli and Hewitt recognize that the oppression of children falls along a continuum and that some children are oppressed to a greater degree than others. The very basis of their theory hinges on the belief that children who are reared in highly oppressive family conditions are more likely to become delinquent than those who are not raised in such aversive environments.[86]

power-control thesis
The view that the relationship between gender and delinquency is linked to issues of power and control.

theory of differential oppression
The view that, in the United States, authority is unjustly used against children, who must adapt to adults' ideas of what constitutes "good children."

DELINQUENCY International 6.1

Juvenile Crime Rises in Russia

MOSCOW—More minors are breaking the law, and their crimes are growing crueler, Interior Minister Rashid Nurgaliyev told Duma deputies on Wednesday.

Nurgaliyev said that last year, 150,000 youths under 16 committed crimes, including 1,200 murders, 3,300 assaults and 18,000 robberies. The number of girls who broke the law increased to 13,000, he said, without providing comparative figures.

"All serious crimes are committed, as a rule, in a group, and are noticeable for their high level of cruelty," he said. "This dangerous tendency has in no way changed for the better in the past few years."

Many minors committed crimes to obtain money to gamble, he said.

Nurgaliyev said 6,000 teenagers had criminal records connected to extremist activities and most of them lived near the cities of Moscow, St. Petersburg, Rostov, Samara, Voronezh, Murmansk and Nizhny Novgorod.

Nurgaliyev called for stiffer penalties for those convicted of promoting extremist ideas among minors.

Extremism has drawn the attention of leading government officials. "You can easily find cassettes, documents and Internet sites that spread extremist ideas," he said.

The interior minister also said that about 100,000 minors were alcoholics or drug users and urged deputies to pass legislation to limit the sale of alcohol to minors.

Last year, he said, police registered 175,000 crimes against minors, and 3,000 children went missing.

Some 24,000 runaways were detained, and 11,000 were sent home. About 2,500 of the runaways came from former Soviet republics, he said.

The Duma is to consider legislation on May 26 to improve cooperation with other former Soviet republics in dealing with runaways.

Russian street kids Anastasia, age fourteen, Natasha, age eleven, and Masha, age fourteen, hang out in St. Petersburg, Russia. They are among the 16,000 "working" street kids in Russia's second largest city who are caught up in juvenile prostitution and drugs. ■ **How does delinquency in Russia differ from its American counterpart?**

Source: Francesca Mereu, "Top Cop: Juvenile Crime Up," *The St. Petersburg Times* (Russia), May 19, 2006. Web posted at www.sptimes.ru/index.php?action_id=2&story_id=17614.

Graffiti-covered row houses in East Baltimore. According to the Marxist perspective, the very nature of capitalist society increases urban blight and contributes to the exploitation of lower-class youths, leading to an increased likelihood of crime. ■ **Is this perspective valid? If so, how might capitalist societies lower their crime rates?**

Group and Cultural Conflict   Another dimension of conflict criminology is **culture conflict theory,** which focuses on group conflict. Thorsten Sellin and George B. Vold advocated this approach to the study of crime. Sellin argued that to understand the cause of crime, it is necessary to understand the concept of **conduct norms.**[87] This concept refers to the rules of a group concerning the ways its members should act under particular conditions. The violation of these rules arouses a group reaction.[88] Each individual is a member of many groups (family group, work group, play group, political group, religious group, and so on), and each group has its own particular conduct norms.[89] According to Sellin:

> The more complex a culture becomes, the more likely it is that the number of normative groups which affect a person will be large, [and] the greater is the chance that the norms of these groups will fail to agree, no matter how much they may overlap as a result of a common acceptance of certain norms.[90]

Sellin noted that an individual experiences a conflict of norms "when more or less divergent rules of conduct govern the specific life situation in which a person may find himself."[91] The act of violating conduct norms is "abnormal behavior," and crime represents a particular kind of abnormal behavior distinguished by the fact that crime is a violation of the conduct norms defined by criminal law.[92] Regarding criminal law, Sellin wrote:

> The criminal law may be regarded as in part a body of rules, which prohibit specific forms of conduct and indicate punishments for violations. The character of these rules . . . depends upon the character and interests of those groups in the population which influence legislation. In some states these groups may comprise the majority, in others a minority, but the social values which receive the protection of criminal law are ultimately those which are treasured by the dominant interest groups.[93]

Sellin also has developed a theory of "primary and secondary culture conflict." Primary culture conflict occurs when an individual or group comes into contact with an individual or group from another culture and the conduct norms of the two cultures are not compatible. Secondary culture conflict refers to the conflict arising whenever society has diverging subcultures with conduct norms.[94]

Vold, like Sellin and in the tradition of Simmel, analyzed the dimension of group conflict. He viewed society "as a congeries [an aggregation] of groups held together in a shifting, but dynamic equilibrium of opposing group interests and efforts."[95] Vold formulated a theory of group conflict and applied it to particular types of crimes, but he did not attempt to explain all types of criminal behavior. He stated that group members are constantly engaged in defending and promoting their group's status. As groups move into each other's territory or sphere of influence and begin to compete in those areas, intergroup conflict is inevitable. The outcome of a group conflict results in a winner and a loser, unless a compromise is reached— but compromises never take place when one group is decidedly weaker than the other. Like Simmel, Vold believed that group loyalty develops and intensifies during group conflict.[96]

In sum, conflict criminologists can be divided into three basic groups: those emphasizing socioeconomic class, those emphasizing power and authority relationships, and those emphasizing group and cultural conflict. Those who emphasize socioeconomic class call themselves radical, Marxist, critical, humanist, or new criminologists and do not identify with the other two groups. Some significant differences do exist between radical criminologists and the other two groups. The non-Marxist conflict criminologists emphasize a plurality of interests and power and do not put a single emphasis on capitalism as do the Marxist conflict criminologists. Nor do the non-Marxist conflict criminologists reject the legal order as such or the use of legal definitions of crime.[97] Table 6.1 compares the three groups of conflict criminologists.

culture conflict theory
A perspective that delinquency or crime arises because individuals are members of a subculture that has conduct norms that are in conflict with those of the wider society.

conduct norms
The rules of a group governing the ways its members should act under particular conditions; the violation of these rules arouses a group reaction.

Web LIBRARY 6.3

Learn about OJJDP's Juvenile Mentoring Program (JUMP) at **www.justicestudies.com/ WebLibrary**.

TABLE 6.1

Comparisons of Conflict Perspectives

PERSPECTIVE	LEGAL DEFINITIONS	LEGAL ORDER	PURPOSE OF CONFLICT	CAPITALISM
Socioeconomic Class (Marxist)	Rejection	Rejection	Revolution	Rejection
Power and Authority Relationships	Acceptance	Acceptance	Reform	Acceptance
Group and Cultural Conflict	Acceptance	Acceptance	Reform	Acceptance

Radical Criminology

The theoretical contributions of criminologists working within the Marxist perspective diverge from mainstream liberal assumptions, ideology, and practice. Their theoretical position is radical in the sense that the implied policy would dramatically alter the way crime is defined, criminals are treated, and theories are formulated and tested—and quite possibly would alter even the sociopolitical–economic structure of the United States. Marxist criminologists themselves differ in their interpretation of crime, as Exhibit 6.1 indicates.

Marxist criminology sees little to be gained from efforts to understand the causes of delinquent behavior, believing that we need to examine how the political economy and social structure create conditions conducive to feelings among youth of powerlessness and alienation. Marxist criminologists further contend that the dominant classes create definitions of crime to oppress the subordinate classes, that the economic system exploits lower-class youths, and that social justice is lacking for lower-class youths.

Alienation and Powerlessness Among Youth In *The Children of Ishmael,* Barry Krisberg and James Austin noted that youths in a capitalist society generally are seen as a group of people who are in a sense expected to remain in a holding pattern until they can take their places in the workforce.[98] They added that "young people form a subservient class, alienated, powerless, and prone to economic manipulation."[99]

> *Marxist criminology sees little to be gained from efforts to understand the causes of delinquent behavior.*

Young people, according to Krisberg and Austin, also are excluded from full participation in society's political institutions. They lack organized lobbies, have limited voting power, and hold few positions of authority. Moreover, adolescents are subjected to controlling forces by the state; and, as with any other subordinate group in society, their rights, privileges, and identities are defined by the powerful arm of the state.[100]

David F. Greenberg stated, "The exclusion of young people from adult work and leisure activities forces adolescents into virtually exclusive association with one another, cutting them off from alternative sources of validation for the self."[101] Greenberg claimed that the long-term consequences of increased age segregation created by changing patterns of work and education have increased the vulnerability of youths to the expectations and evaluations of their peers.[102]

Quinney has stated that "violent gang activity may become a collective response of adolescents in slums to the problems of living in such areas of the city."[103] S. Balkan and colleagues noted that street gang activity is most frequently found in those social settings where poverty, unemployment, drugs, violence, and police encounters are commonplace. In such social contexts, gangs become the source of both juvenile and adult members' most meaningful social relationships—and the source of protection where "life on the streets" has made survival an issue.[104]

In short, Marxist criminologists have concluded that a lengthening of the time before youths assume adult roles and are given adult responsibilities has contributed to powerlessness and alienation among youths and has been a major factor leading to delinquent behavior. Lower-class youths, especially minority youngsters, are the most powerless and alienated.

Definitions of Delinquency   Marxist criminologists argue that certain acts are termed *delinquent* because it is in the interest of the ruling class to so define them.[105] Marxist criminologists see the law as an oppressive force that is used to promote and stabilize existing socioeconomic relations. The law maintains order, but it is an order imposed on the powerless by the powerful.[106] Anthony M. Platt's *The Child Savers,* which describes the role played by wealthy "child-saving" reformers in the nineteenth century, explains how dominant classes create definitions of crime to control the subordinate classes:

> The juvenile court system was part of a general movement directed towards developing specialized labor market and industrial discipline under corporate capitalism by creating new programs of adjudication and control for "delinquent," "dependent," and "neglected" youth. This in turn was related to augmenting the family and enforcing compulsory education in order to guarantee the proper reproduction of the labor force.[107]

The contention is that because delinquents are unsocialized children who are in danger of producing not only more crime but more children like themselves, it has been necessary to find legal means to discipline them. Otherwise, they would be unprepared to supply labor for the alienating work of capitalism.[108] Definitions of delinquency, then, are enforced on the children of the "dangerous classes" as a means of forcing them to conform to alienating work roles.

Economic Exploitation of Youths   Marxist criminologists charge that the "haves" exploit the "have-nots," with the result that the children of the have-nots become a marginal class. Krisberg's study of twenty-two gang members in Philadelphia

instrumental Marxists
A group whose members view the entire apparatus of crime control as a tool or instrument of the ruling class.

structural Marxists
A group which argues that the form taken by the legal system in a society can work to reinforce capitalist social relations.

critical criminologists
Social scientific thinkers who combine Marxist theory with the insights of later theorists, such as Sigmund Freud.

A teenager works a part-time job. Youths who don't have jobs are more likely to find other ways to provide for what they want.

■ **What "other ways" might they choose?**

revealed that the harsh realities of ghetto existence fostered a psychology of survival as a functional adaptation to an uncompromising social situation or environment.[109] Indeed, the gang members perceived "survival" in Spencerian terms as they had to extend themselves in every possible way to meet their needs. One gang leader put it this way: "Survival, man, is survival of the fittest. You do unto others before they do unto you, only do it to them first."[110]

Herman Schwendinger and Julia Siegel Schwendinger also stated that capitalism produces a marginal class of people who are superfluous from an economic standpoint.[111] They went so far as to say that "the historical facts are incontrovertible: capitalism ripped apart the ancient regime and introduced criminality among youth in all stations of life."[112]

The Schwendingers further argued that socialization agents within the social system, such as the school, tend to reinvent within each new generation the same class system: "The children of families that *have* more *get* more, because the public educational system converts human beings into potential commodities."[113] The schools tend to be geared toward rewarding and assisting those youths who exhibit early indications of achieving the greatest potential success in institutions of higher learning and later in the job market. Yet this selection is made at the expense of those who do not exhibit such potential in their early encounters with the educational system.[114]

The Schwendingers went on to develop **instrumental theory,** which states that the most important variable in identifying delinquency potential for teenagers is their relative status position among other adolescents. Delinquency, then, is conceptualized as linked to adolescents' social networks. The three prominent social networks are "socialites," "greasers," and "intellectuals." Those youths with economically deprived backgrounds are typically identified as "greasers" and are more likely to participate in theft, burglaries, and even violence. Middle-class youths who are identified as "socialites" are more likely to become involved in such behaviors as truancy, shoplifting, and vandalism. Youths identified as "intellectuals," regardless of their class position, are the least likely to become involved in illegal behaviors.[115]

Greenberg discussed juvenile theft in terms of structural obstacles to legitimate sources of funds. He pointed out that the persistent decline in teenage employment, especially among African American teenagers, has left adolescents less and less capable of financing an increasingly costly social life, the importance of which is enhanced as the age segregation of society grows. According to Greenberg, adolescent theft therefore occurs as a response to the disjunction between the desire to participate in social activities with peers and the absence of legitimate means to finance this participation.[116]

In sum, according to these studies, the structural conditions of capitalistic society lead to the exploitation of lower-class youths. This exploitation creates a marginal role for these juveniles and influences their pursuing illegitimate means to satisfy their desires.

Social Injustice Radical and other conflict-oriented criminologists argue that **social injustice** prevails in American society for three reasons. First, poor and disadvantaged youths tend to be disproportionately represented in the juvenile justice system, although research indicates that actual acts of delinquent behavior are uniformly distributed throughout the social spectrum.[117] Second, female status offenders are subjected to sexist treatment in the juvenile system.[118] Third, racism is present and minorities are dealt with more harshly than are whites.[119]

William J. Chambliss analyzed this issue of social justice in his study entitled "The Saints and the Roughnecks." He studied two groups of boys, one consisting of eight upper-middle-class boys (the Saints) and the second consisting of six lower-class boys (the Roughnecks). He found the Saints to be continually occupied with truancy, drinking, wild driving, petty theft, and vandalism. The parents of the Saints, as well as the community at large, tended to see the Saints as being essentially "good" boys who only occasionally engaged in "sowing a few wild oats." In contrast, the Roughnecks were "constantly in trouble with the police and community even though their rate of delinquency was about equal with that of the Saints."[120]

Radical criminologists also contend that the juvenile justice system is racist, because minorities are treated more punitively than whites. At the time of arrest, minority youths are more likely to be referred to the juvenile court than are whites. Once referred to the court, they are less likely than whites to be diverted to nonjudicial agencies. Furthermore, minority youths are more likely than whites to be found delinquent during the adjudication stage of the juvenile court proceedings; and during the disposition stage, they are more likely to be sent to training school than are whites.[121]

In short, most radical criminologists believe that the formal juvenile justice system, as well as the informal justice system, administers different sorts of justice to the children of the "haves" than to the children of the "have-nots," to boys who commit delinquent offenses than to girls who commit "moral" offenses, and to white youths than to nonwhite youths.

Alienation and Delinquency

Mark Colvin and John Pauly developed an integrated, structural theory of delinquency, the purpose of which was to provide "a comprehensive theoretical approach to understanding the social production of serious patterned delinquent behavior." Using the empirical findings of others to support their model, Colvin and Pauly contended that the power relations to which most lower-class workers are subjected are coercive.[122]

They argued that the parents' experience of coerciveness in the workplace contributes to the development of coercive family control structures, which lead to alienated children. The coercive social milieu in which many people work reduces their capacity as parents to deal with their own children in anything other than a repressive fashion, frequently by using physical punishments—and this punishment hinders the development of positive bonds between children and their parents.[123]

The situation is exacerbated because juveniles with alienated parental bonds, say Colvin and Pauly, are more likely to be placed in coercive school settings. Their alienation from both family and school encourages such juveniles to become involved with alienated peers, who form peer groups. These peer groups create two contrasting paths to delinquent involvement. In the first path, peer group coerciveness interacts with youngsters' earlier experiences of alienation to propel them into serious, patterned, violent delinquent behavior. In the second path, the experience of rewards from illegitimate sources builds a lasting attraction to serious and patterned delinquent behavior.[124]

Evaluation of Conflict Theory

Conflict criminology's critiques of the social order do contribute two important pieces to the puzzle of why juveniles commit delinquent acts. First, the various conflict criminology perspectives call attention to the macrostructural flaws that contribute to high rates of juvenile delinquency. Second, radical humanism, also rooted in the structural inequalities of the social order, emphasizes the dignity of the person and is quick to identify instances where children experience oppression in the United States.[125]

CHAPTER Summary

This chapter focuses on labeling theory, symbolic interactionist theory, and conflict approaches to delinquency. Some important points to remember are these:

- Reactions to deviance and crime play an important role in the creation of offender social identities.

- Reactions to deviance and crime occur within a social context, although it is one that may vary from the family to the group, to school settings, to official labeling by the justice system, and even to society's political decision-making mechanisms.

- In individual experience, social reaction occurs during the process of everyday interaction, and that process frequently involves the application of labels to what is perceived as unacceptable behavior.

- Societal responses to deviant behavior may result in the application of negative labels to individuals who engage in such behavior, and those labels may limit future possibilities for positive personal accomplishment.

- Radical criminologists relate delinquency to alienation and powerlessness among youths, especially lower-class youths; to the dominant class's creation of definitions of crime to control subordinate classes; and to what they see as economic exploitation of the lower classes.

CRITICAL THINKING Questions

1. What is the labeling perspective's explanation for why adolescents become delinquent? Do you agree with this interpretation?
2. Were you ever labeled when you were a young child or juvenile? What influence did it have on your subsequent attitudes and behavior?
3. Can you identify any groups beyond young children among which official labels may be more likely to influence subsequent attitudes and behavior?
4. How is symbolic interactionist theory of delinquency an extension of, but different from, labeling theory?
5. Illustrate the application of symbolic interactionist theory to decision making in youth gangs or in adolescent peer groups. How did such reference group norms affect your decision making and behavior as an adolescent?
6. What are the various dimensions of conflict theory? How do they differ?
7. What are the explanations of delinquency according to Marxist theory? Evaluate each of these explanations.
8. As an adolescent, did you feel powerless and out of control? If so, how did you respond to these feelings?

WEB Interactivity

Visit the Office of Juvenile Justice and Delinquency Prevention's Statistical Briefing Book (SBB) on the Web at **http://ojjdp.ncjrs .org/ojstatbb**. The SBB makes it easy to find basic statistical information on juvenile offending, the victimization of juveniles, and involvement of youths in the juvenile justice system. Write a one- or two-paragraph description of the site, describing the types and sources of information available there, the data analysis tools provided for visitors, the nature of the site's glossary, and an overview of related links available. Submit your description to your instructor if asked to do so.

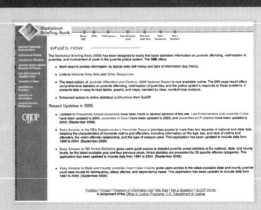

Source: From http://ojjdp.ncjs.org/ojstatbb/. Reprinted with permission from the U.S. Department of Justice.

Notes

1. Fox Butterfield, "New Look at Boy's Sentence in Boatyard Fire," *New York Times*, March 29, 2004.
2. Lening Zhang and Steven F. Messner, "The Severity of Official Punishment for Delinquency and Change in Interpersonal Relations in Chinese Society," *Journal of Research in Crime and Delinquency* 31 (November 1994), p. 417.
3. Frederick M. Thrasher, *The Gang* (Chicago: University of Chicago Press, 1927).
4. Frank Tannenbaum, *Crime and the Community* (New York: Columbia University Press, 1938), pp. 19–20.
5. Ibid.
6. Edwin M. Lemert, *Social Pathology* (New York: McGraw-Hill, 1951).
7. Harold Finestone, *Victims of Change: Juvenile Delinquents in American Society* (Westport, Conn.: Greenwood Press, 1976), p. 198.
8. Ibid. For discussion concerning the complexity of this process of moving from primary to secondary, see Daniel L. Dotter and Julian B. Roebuck, "The Labeling Approach Re-Examined: Interactionism and the Components of Deviance," *Deviant Behavior* 9 (1988), pp. 19–32.
9. Finestone, *Victims of Change*, pp. 192, 198.
10. Howard S. Becker, *Outsiders* (New York: Free Press, 1963), pp. 8–9.
11. Ibid., pp. 31–32.
12. Finestone, *Victims of Change*, p. 208.
13. Edwin Schur, *Radical Nonintervention* (Englewood Cliffs, N.J.: Prentice-Hall, 1973), p. 155.
14. Zhang and Messner, "The Severity of Official Punishment for Delinquency and Change in Interpersonal Relations in Chinese Society," p. 418.
15. Francis Polymeria, Francis T. Cullen, and Joanne C. Gersten, "The Effects of Police and Mental Health Intervention on Juvenile Delinquency: Specifying Contingencies in the Impact of Formal Reaction," *Journal of Health and Social Behavior* 27 (1986), pp. 90–105.
16. Anthony Matarazzo, Peter J. Carrington, and Robert D. Hiscott, "The Effect of Prior Youth Court Dispositions on Current Disposition: An Application of Societal-Reaction Theory," *Theory of Quantitative Criminology* 17 (2001), p. 169.
17. Jack P. Gibbs, "Conceptions of Deviant Behavior: The Old and the New," *Pacific Sociological Review* 9 (1966), pp. 9–14; Walter R. Gove, "Labeling and Mental Illness: A Critique," in *The Labeling of Deviance: Evaluating a Perspective*, 2nd ed., edited by Walter R. Gove (Beverly Hills, Calif.: Sage, 1980); John Hagan, "Extra-Legal Attitudes and Criminal Sanctioning: An Assessment and a Sociological Viewpoint," *Law and Society Review* 8 (1974), pp. 357–383; Travis Hirschi, "Labeling Theory and Juvenile Delinquency: An Assessment of the Evidence," in *The Labeling of Deviance: Evaluating a Perspective*, 2nd ed., edited by Walter R. Gove (Beverly Hills, Calif.: Sage, 1980), pp. 271–293; Charles R. Tittle, "Deterrence of Labeling?" *Social Forces* 53 (1975), pp. 399–410; Charles F. Wellford, "Labeling Theory and Criminology: An Assessment," *Social Problems* 22 (1975), pp. 332–345.
18. Zhang and Messner, "The Severity of Official Punishment for Delinquency and Change in Interpersonal Relations in Chinese Society," p. 419. See also Tittle, "Deterrence of Labeling?" and Gove, "Labeling and Mental Illness."
19. Raymond Paternoster and Leeann Iovanni, "The Labeling Perspective and Delinquency: An Elaboration of the Theory and an Assessment of the Evidence," *Justice Quarterly* 6 (1989), p. 359.
20. Zhang and Messner, "The Severity of Official Punishment for Delinquency and Change in Interpersonal Relations in Chinese Society," p. 418.
21. Ruth A. Triplett and G. Roger Jarjoura, "Theoretical and Empirical Specification of a Model of Informal Labeling," *Journal of Quantitative Criminology* 10 (1994), p. 243.
22. Raymond Paternoster and Ruth A. Triplett, "Disaggregating Self-Reported Delinquency and Its Implications for Theory," *Criminology* 26 (1988), p. 6. See also Lening Zhang, "Informal Reactions and Delinquency," *Criminal Justice and Behavior* 24 (March 1997), pp. 129–150.
23. John Braithwaite, *Crime, Shame and Reintegration* (Cambridge, England: Cambridge University Press, 1989). See also Toni Makkai and John Braithwaite, "Reintegrative Shaming and Compliance with Regulatory Standards," *Criminology* 32 (August 1994), pp. 361–385.
24. Triplett and Jarjoura, "Theoretical and Empirical Specification of a Model of Informal Labeling," p. 244.
25. Ruth Ann Triplett, *Labeling and Differential Association: The Effects on Delinquent Behavior*, Ph.D. dissertation, University of Maryland, 1990, pp. 74–84. For a model of informal labeling, see Triplett and Jarjoura, "Theoretical and Empirical Specialization of a Model of Informal Labeling," pp. 241–276.
26. J. D. Orcutt, "Societal Reaction and the Response to Deviation in Small Groups," *Social Forces* 52 (1973), pp. 259–267.
27. Robert J. Sampson and John H. Laub, "A Life-Course Theory of Cumulative Disadvantage and the Stability of Delinquency," in *Developmental Theories of Crime and Delinquency*, edited by Terence P. Thornberry (New Brunswick, N.J.: Transaction, 1997), p. 138.
28. Jon Gunnar Bernburg and Marvin D. Krohn, "Labeling, Life Chances, and Adult Crime: The Direct and Indirect Effects of Official Intervention in Adolescence on Crime in Early Adulthood," *Criminology* 41 (November 2003), pp. 1287–1313.
29. G. Nettler, *Explaining Crime*, 3rd ed. (New York: McGraw-Hill, 1984), p. 268.
30. Donald J. Shoemaker, *Theories of Delinquency: An Examination of Explanations of Delinquency Behavior*, 5th ed. (New York: Oxford University Press, 2005), p. 222.
31. Ross L. Matsueda, "Reflected Appraisals, Parental Labeling, and Delinquency: Specifying a Symbolic Interactional Theory," *American Journal of Sociology* 97 (1992), pp. 1577–1611; Karen Heimer and Ross L. Matsueda, "Role-Taking, Role Commitment, and Delinquency: A Theory of Differential Social Control," *American Sociological Review* 59 (1994), pp. 365–390; Karen Heimer, "Gender, Race, and the Pathways to Delinquency," in *Crime and Inequality*, edited by John Hagan and Ruth D. Peterson (Stanford, Calif.: Stanford University Press, 1995), pp. 140–173; Karen

Heimer and Ross L. Matsueda, "A Symbolic Interactionist Theory of Motivation and Deviance: Interpreting Psychological Research," in *Motivation and Delinquency*, Volume 44 of the Nebraska Symposium on Motivation, edited by D. Wayne Osgood (Lincoln and London: University of Nebraska Press, 1997), pp. 223–276; and Ross L. Matsueda and Karen Heimer, "A Symbolic Interactionist Theory of Role-Transitions, Role Commitments, and Delinquency," in *Advances in Criminological Theory*, edited by T. P. Thornberry 7 (New Brunswick, N.J.: Transaction Press, 1997), pp. 163–213.

32. Matsueda, "Reflected Appraisals, Parental Labeling, and Delinquency," p. 1580.

33. Ibid. p. 1577.

34. Ibid.

35. Heimer, "Gender, Race, and Delinquency," p. 141.

36. Matsueda and Heimer, "A Symbolic Interactionist Theory of Role-Transitions, Role Commitments, and Delinquency," p. 234.

37. Ibid.

38. Ibid.

39. The following discussion is based on ibid., pp. 1580–1581.

40. George H. Mead, *Mind, Self and Society* (Chicago: University of Chicago Press, 1934).

41. Matsueda, "Reflected Appraisals, Parental Labeling, and Delinquency," p. 1580. See also Mead, *Mind, Self and Society* and Herbert Blumer, *Symbolic Interactionism: Perspective and Method* (Englewood Cliffs, N.J.: Prentice-Hall, 1969).

42. Matsueda, "Reflected Appraisals, Parental Labeling, and Delinquency," p. 1581.

43. Scott Briar and Irving Piliavin, "Delinquency, Situational Inducements, and Commitment to Conformity," *Social Problems* 13 (1965), p. 35–45.

44. James F. Short Jr. and Fred L. Strodtbeck, *Group Process and Gang Delinquency* (Chicago: University of Chicago Press, 1965).

45. Donald Gibbons, "Observations on the Study of Crime Causation," *American Journal of Sociology* 77 (1971), pp. 262–278.

46. Matsueda, "Reflected Appraisals, Parental Labeling, and Delinquency," p. 1583.

47. Charles H. Cooley, *Human Nature and the Social Order*, rev. ed. (New York: Scribners, 1922).

48. Mead, *Mind, Self, and Society*.

49. Matsueda, "Reflected Appraisals, Parental Labeling, and Delinquency," p. 1584.

50. Ibid.

51. Ibid., p. 1602.

52. Ibid.

53. Ibid., pp. 1602–1603.

54. Heimer, "Gender, Race, and Delinquency," p. 145.

55. Ibid., p. 146.

56. Ibid.

57. Heimer and Matsueda, "Role-Taking, Role Commitment, and Delinquency," p. 365.

58. This interview took place in February 2002.

59. Bartusch and Matsueda, "Gender, Reflected Appraisals, and Labeling," pp. 145–177; Heimer, "Gender, Interaction, and Delinquency," pp. 39–61; Heimer, "Gender, Race, and the Pathways to Delinquency," pp. 140–173; and Stacy De Coster and Karen Heimer, "The Relationship between Law Violation and Depression: An Interactionist Analysis," *Criminology* 39 (November 2001), pp. 799–836.

60. David Shicor, "The New Criminology: Some Critical Issues," *The British Journal of* Criminology 20 (1980), p. 3.

61. Viktor Afanasyer, *Marxist Philosophy* (Moscow: Foreign Language Publishing House, n.d.), p. 14.

62. This interpretation of Hegel's "thesis–antithesis–synthesis" paradigm is frequently questioned. See Ron E. Roberts and Robert Marsh Kloss, *Social Movements: Between the Balcony and the Barricade,* 2nd ed. (St. Louis: C.V. Mosby, 1979), p. 16.

63. Stephen Spitzer, "Toward a Marxian Theory of Deviance," *Social Problems* 22 (1975), p. 638.

64. Georg Simmel, *Conflict,* translated by Kurt H. Wolf (Glencoe, Ill.: Free Press, 1955), pp. 15–30.

65. Ralf Dahrendorf, "Out of Utopia: Toward a Reorientation of Sociological Analysis," in *Sociological Theory: A Book of Readings,* edited by Lewis A. Coser and Bernard Rosenberg (New York: Macmillan, 1975), p. 198.

66. Richard Quinney, *Critique of Legal Order: Crime Control in Capitalist Society* (Boston: Little, Brown, 1974), p. 16.

67. William Bonger, *Criminality and Economic Conditions,* abridged ed. (Bloomington: Indiana University Press, 1969), p. 24.

68. See Larry Tifft and Dennis Sullivan, *Crime, Criminology, and Anarchism: The Struggle to Be Human* (Sanday, Orkney Islands, Scotland: Cienfuegos Press, 1980); Raymond J. Michalowski, *Order, Law, and Crime: An Introduction to Criminology* (New York: Random House, 1985); and Harold E. Pepinsky, "A Sociology of Justice," *Annual Review of Sociology* 12 (1986), pp. 93–108.

69. Tifft and Sullivan, *Crime, Criminology, and Anarchism,* p. 172, and Michalowski, *Order, Law, and Crime,* pp. 406–411.

70. Pepinsky, "A Sociology of Justice," pp. 102–105.

71. Jonathan H. Turner, *The Structure of Sociological Theory* (Homewood, Ill.: Dorsey Press, 1978), p. 124.

72. Karl Marx and Frederick Engels, *The Communist Manifesto* (1848; reprint ed., New York: International Publishers, 1979), p. 9.

73. Ibid.

74. Ibid.

75. Ibid., pp. 9–21.

76. David O. Friedrichs, "Radical Criminology in the United States: An Interpretative Understanding," in *Radical Criminology,* p. 38.

77. This interview took place in February 1984 and is used with permission.

78. Max Weber, "Class, Status, Party," in *Class, Status and Power,* edited by Richard Bendix and S. M. Lipset (New York: Macmillan, 1953), pp. 63–75.

79. Ibid.

80. Ralf Dahrendorf, *Class and Class Conflict in Industrial Society* (Palo Alto, Calif.: Stanford University Press, 1959).

81. A. T. Turk, "Class, Conflict, and Criminalization," *Sociological Focus* 10 (August 1977), pp. 209–220.

82. Ian Taylor, Paul Walton, and Jock Young, *The New Criminology: For a Social Theory of Deviance* (Boston: Routledge and Kegan Paul, 1973), p. 241.

83. John Hagan, A. R. Gillis, and John Simpson, "The Class Structure of Gender and Delinquency: Toward a Power-Control Theory of Common Delinquent Behavior," *American*

Journal of Sociology 90 (1985) pp. 1151–1178; John Hagan, John Simpson, and A. R. Gillis, "The Sexual Stratification of Social Control: A Gender-Based Perspective on Crime and Delinquency," *British Journal of Sociology* 30 (1979), pp. 25–38; John Hagan, John Simpson, and A. R. Gillis, "Class in the Household: A Power-Control Theory of Gender and Delinquency," *American Journal of Sociology* 92 (January 1987), pp. 788–816; John Hagan, A. R. Gillis, and John Simpson, "Clarifying and Extending Power-Control Theory," *American Journal of Sociology* 95 (1990), pp. 1024–1037; and John Hagan, *Structural Criminology* (New Brunswick, N.J.: Rutgers University Press, 1989).

84. Robert M. Regoli and John D. Hewitt, *Delinquency in Society,* 5th ed. (New York: McGraw-Hill, 2003), p. 199.

85. Beverly Kingston, Robert Regoli, and John D. Hewitt, "The Theory of Differential Oppression: A Developmental–Ecological Explanation of Adolescent Problem Behavior," *Critical Criminology* 11 (2003), p. 239.

86. Regoli and Hewitt, *Delinquency in Society*, pp. 199–200.

87. In *Social Sources of Delinquency,* Ruth Rosner Kornhauser includes the discussion of Sellin under cultural deviance theory.

88. Thorsten Sellin, *Culture, Conflict, and Crime* (New York: Social Science Research Council, 1938), p. 28.

89. Ibid., p. 29.

90. Ibid.

91. Ibid.

92. Ibid., pp. 32, 57.

93. Ibid., p. 21.

94. Ibid., pp. 104–105.

95. George B. Vold, *Theoretical Criminology,* 2nd ed., prepared by Thomas J. Bernard (New York: Oxford University Press, 1979), p. 283. For a more up-to-date analysis of Vold, see Thomas J. Bernard and Jeffrey B. Snipes, *Theoretical Criminology,* 4th ed. (New York: Oxford University Press, 1998), pp. 236–238.

96. Ibid.

97. Friedrichs, "Radical Criminology in the United States," p. 39.

98. Barry Krisberg and James Austin, eds., *Children of Ishmael: Critical Perspectives on Juvenile Justice* (Palo Alto, Calif.: Mayfield Publishing, 1978), p. 219.

99. Ibid., p. 1.

100. Ibid., pp. 1–2.

101. David F. Greenberg, "Delinquency and the Age Structure of Society," *Contemporary Crisis* 1 (1977), p. 196.

102. Ibid.

103. Richard Quinney, *Criminology,* 2nd ed. (Boston: Little, Brown, 1979), p. 227.

104. Sheila Balkan, Ronald J. Berger, and Janet Schmidt, *Crime and Deviance in America: A Critical Approach* (Belmont, Calif.: Wadsworth, 1980).

105. W. J. Chambliss, "Toward a Political Economy of Crime," *Theory and Society* 2 (Summer 1975), p. 152.

106. J. R. Hepburn, "Social Control and the Legal Order: Legitimate Repression in a Capitalist State," *Contemporary Crisis* 1 (1977), p. 77.

107. Anthony M. Platt, "The Triumph of Benevolence: The Origins of the Juvenile Justice System in the United States," in *Criminal Justice in America,* edited by Richard Quinney (Boston: Little, Brown, 1974), p. 377.

108. LaMar T. Empey, *American Delinquency: Its Meaning and Construction* (Homewood, Ill.: Dorsey Press, 1982), p. 430.

109. Barry Krisberg, "Gang Youth and Hustling: The Psychology of Survival," in Krisberg and Austin, *Children of Ishmael,* p. 244.

110. Ibid.

111. Herman Schwendinger and Julia S. Schwendinger, "Marginal Youth and Social Policy," *Social Problems* 24 (December 1976), pp. 84–91.

112. Herman Schwendinger and Julia Siegel Schwendinger, *Adolescent Subcultures and Delinquency* (New York: Praeger Publishers, 1985), p. 3.

113. Schwendinger and Schwendinger, "Marginal Youth and Social Policy," pp. 84–91.

114. Ibid.

115. Ibid.

116. Greenberg, "Delinquency and the Age Structure of Society," pp. 196–197.

117. Krisberg and Austin, *Children of Ishmael,* p. 53.

118. See the discussion in Chapter 7.

119. See Chapter 13 for discussions of racism in the justice system.

120. William J. Chambliss, "The Saints and the Roughnecks," *Society* 11 (1973), pp. 341–355.

121. Terence P. Thornberry, "Race, Socioeconomic Status, and Sentencing in the Juvenile Justice System," *Journal of Criminal Law and Criminology* 64 (1973), pp. 90–98; Charles W. Thomas and Anthony W. Fitch, *An Inquiry into the Association between Respondents' Personal Characteristics and Juvenile Court Dispositions* (Williamsburg, Va.: Metropolitan Criminal Justice Center, College of William and Mary, 1975); and Rosemary C. Sarri and Robert D. Vinter, "Justice for Whom? Varieties of Juvenile Correctional Approaches," in *The Juvenile Justice System,* edited by M. W. Klein (Beverly Hills, Calif.: Sage, 1976).

122. Mark Colvin and John Pauly, "A Critique of Criminology: Toward an Integrated Structural–Marxist Theory of Delinquency Production," *American Journal of Sociology* 89 (November 1983), pp. 513–551.

123. Ibid. p. 543.

124. Ibid.

125. For a review of radical humanism, see Kevin Anderson, "Humanism and Anti-Humanism in Radical Criminological Theory," in *Perspectives on Social Problems* 3 (1991), pp. 19–38; and Kevin Anderson, "Radical Criminology and the Overcoming of Alienation: Perspectives from Marxian and Gandhian Humanism," in *Criminology as Peacemaking,* edited by Harold E. Pepinsky and Richard Quinney (Bloomington: Indiana University Press, 1991), pp. 14–29.

part THREE

Environmental Influences on Delinquency

Traditional approaches to delinquency have been preoccupied with explaining why males commit delinquent acts. In contrast to those perspectives, the first chapter in this section examines the world of the female delinquent. Various feminist perspectives are explored and issues of gender, class, race, and ethnicity are examined to assess the influences they exert on the problem of female delinquency in American society today.

Chapters 8 and 9 deal with two of the most significant delinquency-related topics in the literature today. Chapter 8 asks how family relations affect the nature and extent of delinquent behavior. It examines the all-too-frequent abusive treatment of young people within the family. Chapter 9 explores the school as an arena in which conventional success or failure and adaptation to peer pressures can affect the likelihood of delinquent behavior. Violence, drug use, and other crimes that take place at school are also discussed.

Chapters 10 and 11 turn to two areas in which participation by adolescents tends to result in high rates of delinquency: gangs and drugs use. Gangs, long a problem in our nation's cities, are quickly expanding into other parts of the country and can now be found in small cities and towns. Drug use includes the consumption and abuse of alcoholic beverages, the diversion of pharmacological substances for nonmedical purposes, and the illicit consumption of controlled substances. As these chapters will show, the good news is that both the number of gangs and gang membership have been decreasing since the late 1990s, and the rate of drug use among at least certain categories of juveniles is considerably lower than it was in the late 1970s. The bad news, however, is that both gang participation and drug use continue to result in dangerous and often deadly forms of behavior—affecting young people, their families, schools, and the rest of society.

7

Gender and Delinquency

KEY
Terms

chivalry factor, p. 222
feminist theory of delinquency,
    p. 231
gender, p. 217
gender roles, p. 217
masculinity hypothesis, p. 226
peer group influence, p. 226
sex-role socialization, p. 225

" There has been growing concern that while most juvenile arrests have been decreasing, the number of female juvenile arrests in some offense categories (such as drug and alcohol violations) continues to rise. "

—Girls Study Group (Research Triangle Institute)

CHAPTER
Objectives

AFTER READING THIS CHAPTER, YOU SHOULD BE ABLE TO ANSWER THE FOLLOWING QUESTIONS:

- How is gender important in an understanding of delinquency?

- How are the categories of gender, class, and race helpful in understanding the issues faced by female

delinquents and status offenders?

- What strides toward gender equality have been made in the past few years? What led to these changes?

213

Noemi and her sister were arrested for "armed" robbery in July 2001, after they tried to rob a woman on a Los Angeles sidewalk with a screwdriver. Noemi was sixteen years old at the time. Two months earlier, California voters had approved Proposition 21, a popular initiative aimed at curbing serious juvenile crime. As a result of the new law, Noemi was taken directly to adult court. There, prosecutors offered her a deal: spend three to five years in a California Youth Authority (CYA) institution (California's network of youth prisons), or spend a year in the local county jail and receive a "strike" under the state's three-strikes law designed to put habitual offenders away for life. Noemi chose the year in jail, not realizing that much of that year would be spent in solitary confinement—a measure intended to keep her separate from adult inmates and away from their influence.

With only one or two young girls in Los Angeles County's Twin Towers jail facility, jail administrators were in a bind—keeping Noemi safe, as was required by California law, meant keeping her in her cell and segregating her from the jail's other inmates. California law requires that youths be separated by sight and sound from adult inmates while incarcerated in adult facilities. Unfortunately, adult facilities are not equipped with the staff, programming, or resources necessary to address the unique needs of youths.

Even while isolated, however, Noemi was not entirely free from contact with adult inmates. "They say they housed me there to keep me away from the adults, but they would leave my slot open. People could see me and talk to me. One time this lady reached in and touched me."

Adapted from *No Turning Back: Promising Approaches to Reducing Racial and Ethnic Disparities Affecting Youth of Color in the Justice System* (Washington, D.C.: Building Blocks for Youth Initiative, 2005), pp. 61–62. Reprinted with permission from the Center for Children's Law and Policy.

Until recently, the study of delinquency has largely been the study of *male* delinquency. Meda Chesney-Lind, a professor at the University of Hawaii at Manoa, and one of the country's most respected experts on female delinquency, says that the study of delinquency is gender biased and that delinquency theories are preoccupied with the delinquency of males. Consequently, she argues, the study of offending and of the juvenile justice process is shaped by male experiences and male understandings of the social world.[1] Former University of Illinois at Chicago criminologist, Coramae Richey Mann, charged that all of the major theorists writing in the area of crime and delinquency—including Edwin H. Sutherland, Albert K. Cohen, Richard A. Cloward and Lloyd E. Ohlin, David Matza, and Travis Hirschi—were lacking in the development of a female perspective.[2] Dorie Klein, an early writer on the topic, further noted that "the criminality of women has long been a neglected subject area of criminology." She added that "female criminality has often ended up as a footnote to works on men that purport to be works on criminality in general."[3]

Carol Smart and Klein were two of the first criminologists to suggest that a feminist criminology should be formulated because of the neglect of the feminist perspective in classical delinquency theories.[4] Klein's 1973 article ended in a call for "a new kind of research on women and crime—one that has feminist roots and a radical orientation. . . ."[5] In a 1995 update, Klein noted that the feminist critique of subjects such as women, crime, and justice "has exploded in volume and advanced light-years in depth, and interest. . . ."[6] Kathleen Daly and Meda Chesney-Lind defined a feminist perspective as one "in which women's experiences and ways of knowing are brought to the fore, not suppressed."[7] In Exhibit 7.1, Jody Miller and Christopher W. Mullins highlight key features that distinguish feminist theories from other theoretical perspectives in criminology.

Feminist criminologists agree on gender-based differences in adolescents' experiences, developmental rates, and the scope and motivation of male and female patterns of offending.[8] There is also general agreement that female adolescents enjoy greater social support and are more controlled than are males. Further, a review of available data show that females are less disposed to crime than males and have fewer opportunities for certain types of crimes.[9] And researchers commonly accept that high self-esteem has the effect of discouraging favorable risk-taking definitions among female adolescents while encouraging risk-taking definitions in males.[10]

There is disagreement, however, in how to address the male-oriented approach to delinquency, thought by many to be both persistent and dominant. One approach focuses on the question of generalizability. When samples include both males and females, researchers who emphasize cross-gender similarities routinely test whether given theoretical constructs account for the offending of both males and females. They also tend to pay little attention to how gender itself might intersect with other factors to create different meanings in the lives of boys and girls. Supporters of this gender-neutral position have examined such subjects as the family, social bonding, social learning, delinquent peer relationships, and, to a lesser degree, deterrence and strain.[11]

Some feminist theorists question the need for separate discussion of female delinquency, arguing that little evidence to date suggests that separate theories are needed to account for male and female delinquency. They also claim that latent structural analysis shows that female delinquency tends to operate through the same factors as male delinquency. They add that empirical studies generally reveal that much more variation exists within each gender than between the sexes.[12] Thus, many feminist theorists would recommend that the subject of female delinquency should be presented in textbooks as part of "a seamless whole rather than as a separate chapter."[13]

In contrast, other feminist theorists argue that new theoretical efforts are needed to understand female delinquency and women's involvement in adult crime. Sociologist Eileen Leonard, for example, questioned whether anomie, labeling,

---

Exhibit 7.1

Key Features Distinguishing Feminist Theories from Other Perspectives

- Feminist scholarship is grounded in the inquiry into the meaning and nature of gender relations.
- Feminist perspectives cut across a broad range of questions within criminology and criminal justice. Feminist research has particularly emphasized juvenile/criminal justice processing, including incarceration and violence against women and girls.
- Feminist criminologists grapple with what has been referred to as an "intellectual double shift." Feminist scholars face the challenge not only of examining the impact of gender and gender inequality in "real life" but also of deconstructing intertwined ideologies about gender guiding social practices.
- Feminist criminology is best suited to the development of theories of the "middle range." These middle-range the-

ories seek to explore how broader structural forces are realized within both organizational contexts and the micro-level interactions of social actors within a specific area. With the starting recognition that society and social life are patterned on the basis of gender, feminist criminology recognizes that gender order is complex and shifting.

■ Why is it important to consider the feminists' perspective in approaching an examination of female delinquency in the United States? How would this approach be different from approaching the subject of female delinquency in the ways it has traditionally been approached?

Source: Adapted from Jody Miller and Christopher W. Mullins, "Taking Stock: The Status of Feminist Theories in Criminology," in F. Cullen et al., *The Status of Criminological Theory: Advances in Criminological Theory*, Vol. 15. Edited by F. Adler and W. Laufer. New Brunswick, NJ: Transaction Publishers. Copyright © 2006 by Transaction Publishers. Reprinted by permission of the publisher.

differential association, subculture, and Marxist theories can be used to explain the crime patterns of women. She concluded that these traditional theories do not work and that they are basically flawed.[14] Chesney-Lind's application of male-oriented theories to female delinquency has argued that existing delinquency theories are inadequate to explain female delinquency. She suggested that there is a need for a feminist model of delinquency because a patriarchal context has shaped the explanations and handling of female delinquents and status offenders. She argues that the sexual and physical victimizations of adolescent females at home, and the relationship between these experiences and their crimes, has been systematically ignored.[15]

Leonard is one who has argued that new theoretical efforts to understand women's crime must include an analysis of the links among gender, race, class, and culture.[16] After accusing some feminists of ignoring racial, class, ethnic, religious, and cultural differences among women, Elizabeth V. Spelman concluded that it is only through an examination of such factors that oppression against women can be more clearly grasped and understood.[17] Chesney-Lind further extended this argument when she said that adolescent females and women are victims of "multiple marginality" because their gender, class, and race have placed them at the economic periphery of society. The labeling of a girl as delinquent takes place in a world, Chesney-Lind charged, "where gender still shapes the lives of young people in very powerful ways. Gender, then, matters in girls' lives and the way gender works varies by the community and the culture into which the girl is born."[18]

In the face of these two divergent positions—one seeking to explain away gender gaps and to be gender neutral, the other focusing on the importance of gender in understanding delinquency and crime—Darrell Steffensmeier and Emilie Allen have attempted to put the two approaches together. They contend that there "is no need for gender-specific theories," although they acknowledge that "qualitative studies reveal major gender differences in the context and nature of offending."[19] These researchers go on to develop a "middle road position,"[20] which has not received much acceptance or support in the literature.

Peggy C. Giordano and colleagues' sample from the Ohio Serious Offender Study led them to conclude "that the either/or dichotomy suggested by the contrast between traditional and feminist frameworks is neither necessary nor helpful to the theory-building process."[21] They suggest that the Ohio study "indicates that the basic tenets of these seemingly opposing viewpoints are not in themselves fundamentally incompatible, and the results require a more integrated approach." They found that this was particularly true when the focus is on the small subgroup of girls with serious delinquent histories.[22]

Giordano and colleagues' follow-up of their study of this subgroup of serious female offenders suggests that a comprehensive examination of their actions requires that we enlist the help of both classic explanations of delinquency and contemporary perspectives that emphasize uniquely gendered processes. Within the life histories of these girls there is ample evidence of both types of social dynamics. Frequent themes within the narrative include disadvantaged neighborhood, economic marginality, and an "excess of definitions favorable to the violation of law." At the same time, parents' criminal involvement and/or severe alcohol and drug problems can be identified early on, and continue throughout the women's childhood and adolescent years. The adult follow-up further supports the idea that some processes associated with continued crime or desistance seem to be "generic" (that is, they have a good fit with both women's and men's life experiences), whereas others appear to be more heavily gender specific.[23]

■ Gender Ratio in Offending

Important questions relate to the vastly different rates of criminal offending by gender: Why are females less likely than males to be involved in most crime? Conversely, why are males more crime-prone than females? What explains these gender differences in rates of offending?[24] The gender ratio of crime issue leads to inquiry into the factors that block or limit girls' or women's involvement in crime. It can be argued that this inquiry "reflects an androcentric [male-centered] perspective that makes men's behavior the norm from which women appear to deviate through their limited offending."[25]

Some feminist theorists propose treating gender as a key element of social organization rather than as an individual trait. This approach permits a more complex examination of the gender gap. Data on crime trends, for example, reveal that a gender gap is more persistent for some offenses than others, fluctuates over time, and varies by class, race/ethnicity, and age.[26] Approaches that merely address the gender gap miss the opportunity to examine how causal factors differently shape men's and women's offending across important social dimensions. Miller and Mullins illustrate this point by noting evidence of a link between "underclass" conditions and African American women's offending—a link that fails to have explanatory power for women's offending in other social contexts.[27]

Karen Heimer and colleagues examine the "economic marginalization thesis," which proposes "that the gender gap in crime decreases and females account for a greater proportion of crime when women's economic well-being declines."[28] "Not only are women more likely to live in poverty than men," they add, "but also the gender gap in poverty rates for women in the most crime-prone group continues to increase."[29] They conclude that continued economic oppression, instead of enhanced economic opportunities for women, may be the root cause of the narrowing of the gender gap in crime that has taken place over the past four decades.[30]

The most promising avenues for exploring the complexities of the gender ratio of offending are found in a conceptual scheme offered by Daly, and consist of these three areas of inquiry:

- *Gendered Pathways:* What trajectories propel females and males into offending? What social contexts and factors facilitate entrance to and desistance from offending, and how are they gendered?
- *Gendered Crime:* What are the ways in which street life, sex and drug markets, criminal opportunities, informal economics, and crime groups are structured by gender and other social features? What observed variation occurs in the sequencing and contexts of women's and men's lawbreaking?
- *Gendered Lives:* How does gender affect the daily lives of females and males? How does gender structure identities and courses of action? How do these experiences intersect with lawbreaking?[31]

Gender and Delinquency

To a large degree, understandings of **gender** and gender-based roles are acquired through socialization. Children are socialized into preexisting gender arrangements and construct understandings of themselves and of how they relate to others in terms of those frameworks. As Berkeley professor Barrie Thorne noted in her well-known book, *Gender Play:*

> Parents dress infant girls in pink and boys in blue, give them gender-differentiated names and toys, and expect them to act differently. Teachers frequently give boys more classroom attention than girls. Children pick up the gender stereotypes that pervade books, songs, advertisement, television programs, and movies. And peer groups, steeped in cultural ideas about what it is to be a girl or a boy, also perpetuate gender-typed play and interaction. In short, if boys and girls are different, they are not born but *made* that way.[32]

Although there has been a recent resurgence in recognizing the importance of biology in determining sex-linked behavior, children in today's society continue to be effectively socialized into **gender roles.** Thorne reminds her readers that children have an active role in society, and that the social construction of gender—an active and ongoing process in their lives—is most visible in play. When she observed children in

gender
The personal traits, social positions, and values and beliefs that members of a society attach to being male or female.

gender roles
Societal definitions of what constitutes masculine and feminine behavior.

middle school, she could identify the gender separation and integration that took place within classrooms, in the lunchroom, and on the playground. Children's active role in constructing gender could be seen as they formed lines, chose seats, gossiped, teased, and sought access to or avoided particular activities. Thorne particularly found extensive self-separation by gender on the playground, where adults have little control.[33]

In addition to the social construction of gender roles, there appears to be considerable evidence that girls develop differently than boys. Marty Beyer, a clinical psychologist who has examined adolescent males and females across the nation since 1980, states that research "has identified different vulnerabilities and protective factors in girls." Girls have a greater tendency to internalize and experience higher rates of anxiety, depression, withdrawal, and eating disorders.[34]

Girls also are more focused on relationships than boys, Beyer notes. This focus on connection with others "makes it difficult for them to resolve the conflict between being selfish and selfless." Girls' failure to receive sufficient nurturing and success within the family may restrict their ability to feel lovable and capable, and in turn may hinder their identity development. Girls have more negative body images during adolescence than boys and tend to dislike themselves more than boys do. Early puberty and the simultaneous occurrence of physical development and transition to middle or high school are especially stressful for girls.[35]

Delinquent girls' problems in school and family are correlated with depression, Beyer finds. Delinquent girls have more frequently been sexually molested than boys and thus are more likely to develop post-traumatic stress disorder in response to the experience. Much of the behavior of delinquent girls, Beyer continues, occurs because of immature thinking. In common with delinquent boys, delinquent girls react inappropriately to perceived threat, fail to anticipate or plan, make poor choices, and minimize danger.[36]

Many studies have pointed out the importance of gender in delinquent behaviors.[37] Gang studies confirm the pressures that young men and women experience in terms of appropriate displays of gender.[38] Gang experiences, for example, can be stigmatizing for girls, because gang participation violates traditional roles for females but not for males.[39] In a study of St. Louis gangs, Jody Miller and Scott H. Decker worked with young women and highlighted the significance of gender in shaping and limit-

A young woman looks at herself in the mirror of a cosmetics case on the streets of New York City's East Village. ■ **What gender differences does American delinquency display?**

218 **PART THREE** | Environmental Influences on Delinquency

ing their involvement in violence and in shaping their victimization risks in gangs.[40] In addition, studies of adolescent gender reveal that boys report frequent sexual activity and early sexual intercourse more than girls, and that patterns of male domination and female subordination are increasingly apparent during the adolescent years.[41]

Stephanie J. Funk's study on the need for separate risk assessment instruments for male and female delinquents found that varied assessments are helpful in identifying the risk for reoffending. Funk observed that the importance of social relationships for adolescent females increased their risk for delinquency in two ways. First, disruptions in family, community, and school relations affected females more negatively than males. Consequently, both potential and actual disruptions of relationships put females at risk for delinquency. Also, the importance of connection introduced a greater risk for delinquency when the others in those relationships engage in delinquent or criminal behaviors.[42]

According to Joanne Belknap and Kristi Holsinger, "The most significantly and potentially useful criminological research in recent years has been the recognition of girls' and women's pathways to offending."[43] To address these pathways, the National Council on Crime and Delinquency (NCCD) conducted a 1998 multidimensional study of girls in the California juvenile justice system.[44]

The first step along females' pathways into the juvenile justice system is victimization. The ages at which interviewed adolescent girls reportedly were most likely to be beaten, raped, stabbed, or shot were thirteen and fourteen.[45] A large proportion of girls first enter the juvenile justice system as runaways, who frequently are attempting to escape abuse at home.[46]

Certain abuses follow adolescent females into the juvenile justice system. Specific forms of abuse reportedly experienced by juvenile females include the consistent use of foul and demanding language by staff; inappropriate touching, pushing, and hitting by staff; placement in isolation for trivial reasons; and the withholding of clean clothing. Some girls were strip-searched in the presence of male officers.[47]

The majority of adolescent females' most serious charges fell into the assault category, but an examination of case files of these females revealed that most assault charges were the result of nonserious mutual combat situations with parents. The aggression, in many cases, was initiated by the adults.[48]

The disparate treatment of minorities appeared to be an important factor in the processing of adolescent females' cases. In the NCCD study, as well as nationally, two-thirds of females in the juvenile justice system are minorities, primarily African American and Hispanic.[49]

Another problem is that female offenders represented one of the least-serviced juvenile justice populations. There are only a few effective gender-specific programs nationally. The continuum of programs and services that are required to reduce females' entry into the juvenile justice system must be responsive both to gender and age and to developmental age.

Optimum environments for at-risk females of this age would be intensive family-based programs tailored to the needs of adolescent females.[50] Another possibility that has merit is a community-based all-girls school setting anchoring such services as family counseling, substance-abuse prevention, specialized educational services (e.g., learning disabilities assessment), and mentoring services. A further gender-specific strategy is offering programs that provide the opportunity for the development of positive relationships between female offenders and their children.[51]

Web PLACES 7.1

Visit the Center on Juvenile and Criminal Justice and learn about girls in the criminal justice system via **www.justicestudies .com/WebPlaces**.

Explanations of Female Delinquency

This section considers the important question of whether juvenile females commit delinquent acts for reasons different from those of males. Early explanations of female delinquency focused on biological and psychological factors. These explanations viewed adolescent females as having certain biological characteristics or psychological tendencies that made them more receptive to delinquency. However, there is general agreement that the hopelessly flawed biological and psychological explanations of delinquency view troublesome adolescent females in our patriarchal society through the lens of sexism. More recent explanations of female delinquency have placed much greater emphasis on sociological factors.

Criminologists, as previously discussed, come to vastly different conclusions concerning the question of whether female juveniles commit delinquent acts for reasons different from those of young males. Some criminologists challenge whether gender-specific explanations are needed, because they claim that existing sociological theories can account for both males' and females' delinquency.[52] Still others argue for gender-specific explanations because, they say, traditional sociological theories of delinquent behavior fail to adequately explain the experience of being female. Gender-specific theories are found later in this chapter.

Biological and Constitutional Explanations

In *The Female Offender,* initially published in 1903, Cesare Lombroso dealt with crime as atavism, or the survival of "primitive" traits in female offenders.[53] First, he argued that women are more primitive, or lower on the evolutionary scale, because they are less intelligent and have fewer variations in their mental capacities than men: "Even the female criminal is monotonous and uniform compared with her male companion, just as in general women are inferior to men."[54] Second, Lombroso contended that women are unable to feel pain and, therefore, are insensitive to the pain of others and lack moral refinement.[55] He stated:

> Women have many traits in common with children; that their moral sense is deficient; that they are revengeful, jealous. . . . In ordinary cases these defects are neutralized by piety, maternity, want of passion, sexual coldness, weakness, and an undeveloped intelligence.[56]

Third, Lombroso argued, women are characterized by a passive and conservative approach to life. Although he admitted that women's traditional sex roles in the family bind them to a more home-centered life, he insisted that women's passivity can be directly traced to the "immobility of the ovule compared with the zoosperm."[57]

Lombroso contended that because most women are born with "feminine" characteristics, their innate physiological limitations protect them from crime and predispose them to live unimaginative, dull, and conforming lives. But women criminals, he argued, have inherited male characteristics, such as excessive body hair, moles, wrinkles, crow's feet, and abnormal craniums.[58] He added that the female criminal, being doubly exceptional as a woman and as a criminal, is likely to be more vicious than the male criminal.[59]

> " Lombroso contended that because most women are born with 'feminine' characteristics, their innate physiological limitations protect them from crime. "

Later in the twentieth century, with the biosocial revival in criminology, biological or physiological explanations for delinquency regained some popularity. In a 1968 study, J. Cowie and colleagues presented data on an English approved school (training school) sample that emphasize genetic factors as the major cause of delinquency.[60] These researchers even proposed that these genetic factors might be specific enough to determine the types of crimes each sex will commit.[61] T. C. N. Gibbens also reported a high rate of sex chromosomal abnormalities in delinquent girls.[62] Furthermore, Cowie and colleagues noted the above-average weight of their institutional sample and suggested that physical overdevelopment tends to draw a girl's attention to sex earlier in life, resulting in sexual promiscuity.[63] In addition, they claimed that menstruation is a distressing reminder to females that they can never be males and that this distress makes them increasingly prone to delinquent acts.[64]

In sum, the viewpoints of Lombroso and other supporters of biological explanations for female delinquency can be regarded as merely a foolish testimony to the historical chauvinism of males. Unfortunately, the study of female criminality has not

Web LIBRARY 7.1

Read the OJJDP publication *Juvenile Female Offenders: A Status of the States Report* at **www.justicestudies.com/ WebLibrary**.

yet fully recovered from the idea "that the cause of a socially generated phenomenon might be reduced to a genetically transmitted biological unit."[65]

Psychological Explanations

The claimed "innate nature" of women is the basis of much of the writing on female delinquency.[66] W. I. Thomas, Sigmund Freud, Otto Pollak, Gisela Konopka, and others addressed this "innate" female nature and its relationship to deviant behavior.

Thomas's works marked a transition from physiological explanations to more sophisticated theories embracing physiological, psychological, and social structural factors. In *Sex and Society,* he suggested that there are basic biological differences between the sexes. Maleness, according to Thomas, is "katabolic," from the animal force that involves a destructive release of energy and allows the possibility of creative work through this outward flow, but femaleness is "anabolic"—motionless, lethargic, and conservative.[67] Thomas's underlying assumptions are physiological ones, for he credits men with higher amounts of sexual energy that lead them to pursue women for sexual pleasure. In contrast, he says that women possess maternal feelings devoid of sexuality and so exchange sex for domesticity.[68]

In his 1923 work, *The Unadjusted Girl,* Thomas dealt with female delinquency as a "normal" response under certain social conditions.[69] He argued that a girl is driven by four wishes or ambitions: the desires for new experiences, for security, for response, and for recognition. He assumed that the delinquent girl's problem is not criminality but immorality, and he confined himself almost exclusively to a discussion of prostitution. According to Thomas, the major cause of prostitution rests in the girl's need for love, and a secondary factor is her wish for recognition or ambition. Thomas maintained that it is not sexual desire that motivates delinquent girls, because they are no more passionate than nondelinquent girls, but that they are using male desire for sex to achieve their own ultimate needs.[70] He added:

> The beginning of delinquency in girls is usually an impulse to get amusement, adventure, pretty clothes, favorable notice, distinction, freedom in the larger world. . . . The girls have usually become "wild" before the development of sexual desire, and their casual sex relations do usually awaken sexual feelings. Their sex is used as a condition of the realization of other wishes. It is their capital.[71]

The sad commentary on the state of psychological theory regarding female delinquency is that until recent decades the psychoanalytic writings of Sigmund Freud have represented the most pervasive theoretical position.[72] The structure of the personality and the psychosexual stages of development of the child are the two major concepts from which theories based on Freud's work have evolved.

Freud developed the concept of "penis envy"—long-since abandoned. He said that at an unconscious level, a girl assumes she has lost her penis as punishment and, therefore, feels traumatized and grows up envious and revengeful. A woman becomes a mother to replace the "lost penis" with a baby. The delinquent girl, in the Freudian perspective, is one who is attempting to be a man. Her drive to accomplishment is the expression of her longing for a penis.[73]

The Freudian orientation is not limited to penis envy in its explanation of female delinquency, because it suggests that at any stage of psychosexual development, faulty mechanisms, fixations, and other problems may occur. Freud also claimed that women are inferior because they are concerned with personal matters and have little social sense. Women, according to Freud, have weaker social interests than men and less capacity for the sublimation of their interests.[74]

Peter Bols was one of the researchers who focused on the sexual aspect of Freudian psychoanalytic theory. For example, Bols directly stated that "in the girl, it seems, delinquency is an overt sexual act, or to be more correct, a sexual acting out."[75] In a later work, Bols developed three constellations of female delinquency. Those in the first constellation view delinquency as a defense against regression, a denial of the need for a nurturing mother, and an attempt to avoid homosexual surrender. The delinquent female included in the second constellation sexually acts out as a revenge against the mother, who deserves this hostility because she has degraded the girl's oedipal father. Those in the third constellation are female delinquents who attempt through sexual misconduct to restore a sense of reality to their lives. They have become emotionally alienated from their families, which have detrimentally affected their egos. Bols saw female delinquency as much more destructive and irreversible in its consequences than male delinquency.[76]

Herbert H. Herskovitz, another researcher who was influenced by the psychoanalytic tradition, stated that "the predominant expression of delinquency among females in our society is promiscuous sexual behavior."[77] The promiscuous adolescent female is psychologically maladjusted for several Freudian-based reasons: penis envy, a conscious desire for the father, and a need to be wanted and loved.[78]

Pollak's *The Criminality of Women* (1950) advanced the theory that women are more criminal than is usually believed, but that their crimes largely go unreported or are hidden. Pollak credited the nature of women themselves for the traditionally low official rates of female crime, because women are inherently deceitful and, therefore, act as instigators rather than perpetrators of criminal activity. The roles played by women are a factor in hidden crimes as well, because their roles as domestics, nurses, teachers, and housewives enable them to commit undetectable crimes. The **chivalry factor** is further advanced as a root cause of hidden crime; that is, the tendency of police and the court to forgive a girl for the same act for which they would convict a boy.[79]

Pollak also suggested two factors that influence adolescent females to become juvenile delinquents. First, he said, early physical development and sexual maturity allow a female more opportunities to engage in immoral or delinquent behavior. Second, a female's home life, especially if she has criminal parents or grows up in a broken home, may cause her to seek outside substitutes for that poor home life. She is likely to seek the company of other maladjusted females, and they will eventually become involved in a life of petty crimes.[80]

Konopka's study of delinquent females linked a poor home life with a deep sense of loneliness and low self-esteem. Her conception of delinquency relied heavily on the notion of individual pathology, as she concluded that only a female who is "sick" can become delinquent.[81] Konopka identified four key factors contributing to female delinquency: (1) a uniquely dramatic biological onset of puberty, (2) a complex identification process because of a girl's competitiveness with her mother, (3) the changing cultural position of females and the resultant uncertainty and loneliness, and (4) the hostile picture that the world presents to some young females.[82]

The idea of psychological impairment, or trait, of delinquent females has received support from a number of other writers. Clyde Vedder and Dora Somerville's *The Delinquent Girl* suggested that the delinquent behavior of girls usually indicates a problem of adjustment to family and social pressure.[83] Ruth Morris, in a study conducted in Flint, Michigan, added that delinquent girls experience rational problems more frequently than do nondelinquent girls.[84] Mary Riege asserted that delinquent girls evince excessive loneliness, low self-esteem, estrangement from adults, and low capacity for friendship.[85] Emmy E. Werner and Ruth S. Smith further found in their longitudinal study that "emotional instability" and the "need for long-term mental health services in the early elementary grades" were the best predictors of delinquency in girls.[86] Finally, William Wattenberg and Frank Saunders's Detroit study found a pattern of broken or disrupted homes connected with female delinquency.[87]

Psychological causes of female delinquency have been particularly applied to explaining the behaviors of female status offenders. It has been argued that female status offenders tend to place the blame for their problems on their parents. They often feel that their need for a warm, accepting, and meaningful relationship with parental figures is not being fulfilled, so they see themselves as rejected and neglected. Female status offenders frequently reject the limits placed on their behavior both in and outside the home. A juvenile probation officer describes the difficulty of dealing with female status offenders:

chivalry factor
The idea that the justice system tends to treat adolescent females and women more leniently because of their gender.

Status offenders are basically out of control and may have some emotional problems. I think they're tougher to work with than delinquents. It's easier to define what you can do with a delinquent. If you do this, you tell the delinquent, then this is what's going to happen. But with the status offender, you have no control over them; no one really does. They have been out of control for a long time, and you're not going to get them back into control unless you take some strict measures. And the [juvenile] code is not very helpful at all.[88]

The relationship between psychological impairment and delinquency in some adolescent females has also been widely acknowledged. The female adolescent, for example, who has experienced sexual abuse at home may become involved in such destructive behavior as prostitution because of her poor self-esteem. A sixteen-year-old adolescent female who drowned two children in a bathroom while babysitting one evening was found to possess intense hostility toward her mother. A social worker in a youth shelter describes how guilt can lead to psychological impairment:

> A lot of these girls feel they've done something wrong and that it was their fault. They don't feel they are good for anything else. Some of their anger toward self is expressed in drug and alcohol abuse, mutilating self, running away, and getting themselves in situations where they will be abused again. These girls tend to be very hard toward women because their anger is toward their mother, and very soft and flirtatious with men.[89]

In sum, psychological studies of female delinquency shifted in the 1950s from the psychoanalytical to the familial–social type. Considerable research continues to perpetuate the notion that personal maladjustment characterizes the female delinquent: She has a psychological problem, is unable to perform her proper sex role adequately, or suffers from the ill effects of a bad home life.[90] This means that the legacy of sexism continues to thrive in psychological explanations as it did in biological explanations of female delinquency. This sexual ideology can be seen in the assumptions about the inherent nature of females in the works of Lombroso, Thomas, Pollak, and Freud. It can also be seen in the crime categories in which girls and women are placed. If girls and women are violent, they are defined as "masculine" and suffering from atavism, penis envy, or chromosomal deficiencies. If they conform, they are accused of manipulation, sexual maladjustment, and promiscuity.[91] However, as Chapter 3 noted, both advances in the neurological sciences and the work done in developmental psychology reflect a much greater understanding of why both male and female delinquents become involved in crime.

Sociological Explanations

Beginning in the late 1970s, numerous studies have proceeded from the assumption that sociological processes traditionally related to males could also affect the delinquent involvement of females. General agreement exists among and between feminists and nonfeminists that literature approaching female delinquency from a sociological perspective appears to offer more promise than that which includes biological or psychological causes. Researchers have focused on sociological factors such as blocked opportunity, the women's liberation movement, social bonding, masculinity, power control, and peer group influence, among others.

Blocked Opportunity Theory   The role of blocked or limited opportunity has received considerable attention in the sociological analysis of male delinquency (see Chapter 4). The usefulness of such variables in studying female delinquency has been largely ignored. This is because males are seen as being concerned with achieving short- and long-term status and economic success, whereas juvenile females are viewed as possessing no such aspirations, instead being satisfied to occupy a role dependent on males.[92]

Susan Datesman and colleagues found that perception of limited opportunity was more strongly related to female delinquency than it was to male delinquency. Both African American and white female delinquents regarded their opportunities less positively than did the male delinquents in their sample. Status offenders also perceived

Web LIBRARY 7.2

Read the OJJDP publication *Guiding Principles for Promising Female Programming: An Inventory of Best Practices* at **www .justicestudies.com/ WebLibrary**.

their opportunties as being less favorable than did nondelinquents.[93] Jeffery O. Segrave and Douglas N. Hastad's self-report sample of 891 male and 885 female high school students also found that perception of limited opportunities was more strongly related to delinquency among adolescent females than among adolescent males.[94] Furthermore, Stephen A. Cernkovich and Peggy C. Giordano's self-report sample of 1,335 male and female high school students showed that, in general, perception of blocked opportunity was more predictive of delinquency than any other variable. The effect of this perception differed according to the racial background of the juvenile. For many minority males and females, blocked opportunity had no effect whatsoever on subsequent delinquency involvement, but for white males and females, it was a strong predictor of delinquency.[95]

Lisa Broidy and Robert Agnew's theoretical essay based on general strain theory (GST) hypothesizes that gender differences in crime at all ages are explained by gender-distinctive types of strain that in turn lead to different emotional and behavioral responses. Broidy and Agnew conceptualize gender as consisting of life experiences and conditions (including skills and personal characteristics).[96]

John P. Hoffman and S. Susan Su used Agnew's general strain model to assess the sex-specific effects of stressful life events on delinquency and drug use. Using two waves of data from the eleven- to seventeen-year-old adolescents who participated in the High Risk Youth Study, these researchers found that there were few important sex differences. Stressful life events tend to have a similar, short-term impact on delinquency and drug use among both males and females.[97]

Paul Mazerolle reported that general strain theory offered a useful framework for assessing similarities and differences in the risks and processes leading females and males to delinquent behavior. He found that the effect of GST did not differ between males and females at significant levels of measurement. But in focusing on crime-specific effects for violent and property-related delinquency, he did find "some evidence of gender differences in the effects of negative life events and experiences on subsequent delinquency."[98]

Overall, although strain theory has been applied solely to male delinquents, the Datesman, Segrave and Hastad, and Giordano and Cernkovich studies show that the perception of blocked opportunity may be even more strongly related to female involvement in delinquency than to male involvement. Giordano and Cernkovich also suggest that the racial background of the juvenile may be more important than the gender in determining the effect of blocked opportunity.

The Women's Movement Freda Adler argued in 1975 that a rise in crime among adult women and juvenile females was clearly linked to opportunity. The adolescent girl, according to Adler, faced the plight that she was instilled with almost boundless ambition but had no opportunities for the achievement of her desired goals. The end result was that adult and juvenile females imitated males in both goal desire and adoption of male roles to achieve them. Accordingly, in the 1970s, juvenile females were abandoning the traditional three offenses—incorrigibility, running away, and promiscuity—and were becoming involved instead in more aggressive and violent acts.[99] Adler contended that the rise in official rates of female crime reflected the changes brought about by the liberation of women—a social movement that was well underway at the time. The rise in female delinquency, she suggested, was directly related to females becoming more competitive with males and more aggressive and "masculine" in general.

> " Adler contended that the rise in official rates of female crime reflected the changes brought about by the liberation of women. "

Three criticisms have been leveled against Adler's assumption that the increase in female crime figures can be traced to increasing equality for women. First, Laura Crites points out that female offenders most often come from minority groups. They are frequently unemployed and usually are responsible for their own support and often for that of their children. In addition, their employment potential is limited in that over half have not graduated from high school and their work experience has generally been in low-wage, low-status occupations. Crites reasons that the psychological independence and expanded economic opportunities gained through the expansion of women's rights are almost meaningless for this group, members of which are caught up in a struggle for economic, emotional, and physical survival.[100]

Second, Steffensmeier asserts that the women's movement and changing sex roles have had no impact on levels of female crime, because "the changes we observed began prior to the late 1960s when the movement could be expected to have its greatest impact on levels of property crime."[101] That is, the movement can be shown to have had little impact because official female crime rates have gradually increased; they did not rise dramatically at the time when interest in the movement sharply increased.

Third, Joseph G. Weis claimed that the national arrest data and self-reports of delinquent behavior show that the new female criminal is more a social invention than an empirical reality, and that the criminality of women is not greatly increased when seen it terms of absolute numbers.[102]

Giordano and Cernkovich add that Steffensmeier and Adler both tend to see liberation in terms of an individually held set of attitudes and behaviors.[103] They argue, however, that the concept of sex roles must be understood as multidimensional, partly because important differences exist between an offender's attitudes about women in general and her attitudes about herself in particular. These researchers further challenged the causal influence of the sex-role attitudes of the women's movement because no systematic differences in attitudes are present between more and less delinquent girls.[104]

In sum, Adler's view that there is a direct relationship between the women's movement and the rise of female criminality appears to attribute to female criminals and delinquents a set of motivations and attitudes that are remote from their everyday lives.[105] Giordano and Cernkovich are likely correct in their appraisal that female sex roles are multidimensional and require a more sophisticated analysis than one based on an individual's attitudes and behaviors.

Social Control Theory   As discussed in Chapter 5, Hirschi's social control theory says that delinquency results when a juvenile's bond to the existing social order is weakened or broken.[106] Proponents of social control theory contend that females are less involved in delinquency than males because **sex-role socialization** results in greater ties to the social bond for females than for males. In addition, adolescent females may have less opportunity to engage in delinquent behavior because in general they are more closely supervised by parents. Adolescent females are also more dependent on others, whereas adolescent males are encouraged to be more independent and achievement oriented. Consequently, differences in **sex-role socialization** supposedly promote a greater allegiance to the social bond among females, and this allegiance insulates them from delinquency more than it does males.[107]

Bobbi Jo Anderson and colleagues found from a survey of adolescent males and females confined in the Wyoming boys' and girls' schools that there were no differences in males' and females' levels of attachment when parents and attitude toward school were controlled. Yet some gender differences were found in the effects of the various attachments on the severity of delinquency. Although attachment to parents reduced the severity of males' delinquency, attachment to peers and schools reduced the severity of females' delinquency.[108]

Furthermore, sex-role socialization results in greater belief in the legitimacy of social rules by girls than by boys, claim social control theorists. Austin T. Turk, analyzing the greater involvement of boys than girls in officially recorded crime, concluded that females are more likely to abide by legal norms than are males, because parents restrict their activity more than males.[109] Gary F. Jensen and Raymond Eve, using the same data that Hirschi used in the development of control theory, found that they did

sex-role socialization
The process by which boys and girls internalize their culture's norms, sanctions, and expectations for members of their gender.

provide Hirschi's social control perspective with some empirical support but that significant differences still remained between male and female delinquency.[110]

In sum, lack of commitment to the social bond appears to influence the development of delinquency in both males and females. Some evidence does suggest that socialization practices cause adolescent females to have stronger commitments to the social bond than do males, with the result that females require a greater "push" to become involved in delinquent acts. Yet much more research is needed on the relationship between social control and female delinquency.

General Theory of Crime   Teresa C. LaGrange and Robert A. Silverman tested Gottfredson and Hirschi's general theory of crime (see Chapter 5) as an explanation of gender differences in delinquency. Their results indicated that females, compared with males, reported more self-control and less access to delinquency. These differences, in turn, reduced the effect of gender in and of itself as a predictor of delinquency. But their analysis did reveal notable differences in the effects of self-control on delinquency across the sexes—for example, a positive relation between risk taking and general delinquency for females but not for males.[111]

Differential Association Theory   Karen Heimer and Stacy De Coster, in a study on the relation between violent delinquency and gender, tested the explanatory power of differential association theory (see Chapter 6)—which they reformulated to incorporate gender, using feminist theory and gender studies. Heimer and De Coster's study emphasized process, particularly the ways in which gender is linked to delinquency through "interplay" among structural and cultural influences. The data revealed that emotional bonds to families were negatively related to the learning of violent definitions for girls, but not for boys; coercive parental discipline and aggressive friends were positively related to the learning of violent definitions for boys, but not for girls; and patriarchal beliefs about gender inhibited female violence without having any effect on male violence.[112]

masculinity hypothesis
The idea that as girls become more boylike and acquire more "masculine" traits, they become more delinquent.

Masculinity Hypothesis   Several studies of female delinquents have proposed a **masculinity hypothesis**. Adler contended that as females become more malelike and acquire more "masculine" traits, they become more delinquent.[113] Francis Cullen and coworkers found that the more male and female adolescents possessed "male" personality traits, the more likely they were to become involved in delinquency, but that the relationship between masculinity and delinquency was stronger for males than for females.[114] William E. Thornton and Jennifer James found a moderate degree of association between masculine self-expectations and delinquency but concluded that males were still more likely to be delinquent than were females, regardless of their degree of masculinity.[115]

Stephen Norland and Neal Shover's examination of gender roles and delinquency, however, found that "when sex . . . and degree of social support for delinquency were held constant, males and females who hold [sic] more traditionally masculine expectations for themselves were no more likely to be highly delinquent than were their counterparts who hold [sic] less traditionally masculine expectations."[116] Giordano and Cernkovich also found no strong correlations between nontraditional sex-role attitudes and female delinquency.[117]

In sum, any indicator of female delinquency appears to be more complex than the notion that as females become more like males, they become more delinquent. Perhaps if it is applied in conjunction with another sociological explanation, the masculinity hypothesis will offer a better explanation of the relationship between sex differences and delinquency.[118]

peer group influence
The impact of the values and behaviors of fellow age-group members on teenagers' involvement in delinquency.

Peer Group Influence   The importance of **peer group influence** on male delinquency has been widely documented. Indeed, a frequently reported finding in the literature is that male delinquency is more influenced than female delinquency by delinquent peer groups or delinquent associates.[119]

Giordano and Cernkovich, pioneering the investigation of the importance of the peer group for delinquent females, argued that peer associations must be given a central role in any understanding of changing patterns of female delinquency involvement. In terms of the social context in which female delinquency took place, these researchers found that a female was most likely to commit a delinquent act when she was in a mixed-sex group. The second highest number of delinquent acts were committed by a female who was alone, then with a group of females, with one other female, with a group of males, and finally with one male. Significantly, the majority of delinquent acts occurred in mixed-sex contexts with males who were regarded simply as friends.[120] Females, Giordano and Cernkovich reasoned, appear to learn delinquent modes of behavior from males, but this does not mean that a boyfriend simply uses a female as an "accomplice" or in some other passive role while he commits a crime. These researchers also noted that other females are the most important reference group of delinquent females and that African American females are more likely to commit delinquent acts with a group of females than alone.[121]

Daniel P. Mears, Matthew Ploeger, and Mark Warr, building on Sutherland's theory of differential association and Carol Gilligan's theory of moral development, theorized that females and males are differentially affected by exposure to delinquent peers. Using data from the National Youth Survey, they found support for this hypothesis in that "moral evaluations act as a barrier to reduce or counteract the influence of delinquent peers among females, thereby producing large observed sex differences in delinquent behavior."[122]

In sum, although some evidence indicates that delinquent females learn delinquent modes of behavior from others, much more research is clearly needed. For example, in what particular ways does association with males influence delinquent behavior? What other interacting variables, along with friendship, increase the degree of delinquency involvement among females?

Power-Control Theory   John Hagan and colleagues, as discussed in Chapter 6, proposed a power-control theory to explain female delinquency.[123] Using a class-based framework and data collected in Toronto, Ontario, they contended that as mothers gain power relative to their husbands, usually by employment outside the home, daughters and sons alike are encouraged to be more open to risk taking. Parents in egalitarian families, then, redistribute their control efforts so that daughters are subjected to controls more like those imposed on sons.

In contrast, daughters in patriarchal families are taught by their parents to avoid risks.[124] Hagan and colleagues concluded that "patriarchal families will be characterized by large gender differences in common delinquent behavior while egalitarian families will be characterized by smaller gender differences in delinquency."[125] Power-control theory thus concludes that when daughters are freed from patriarchal family relations, they more frequently become delinquent.[126]

In evaluating power-control theory, Simon I. Singer and Murray Levine contended that it is unclear in what ways work relationships produce more egalitarian home environments. The balanced class categories of egalitarian households may still reflect unbalanced work situations; the husband and wife may both be managers, but the husband is likely to earn a higher income and to have more authority at work.[127] Chesney-Lind, in an even more stinging criticism, stated that power-control theory is a variation on the earlier liberation hypothesis, but now it is the mother's liberation that causes a daughter's crime.[128]

Labeling and an Interactionist Theory of Delinquency   Dawn Jeglum Bartusch and Ross L. Matsueda, in assessing whether an interactionist model can account for the gender gap in delinquency, used data from the National Youth Survey. Based on the symbolic interactionist model of delinquency discussed in Chapter 6, they argued that "delinquency is determined in part by the self as conceived by symbolic interactionists, which in turn is determined by a process of labeling by significant others."[129] They did find some gender interactions. Parental labeling and

A teenage prostitute solicits a man near MacArthur Park in Los Angeles. Although the reasons offered for turning to prostitution may differ for white and African American juveniles, some feminist theorists contend that the fundamental reason is the same: the social and economic inequities of a patriarchal, capitalist system. ■ **Do you agree?**

reflecting appraisals had a larger effect on male delinquency, and parents were more likely to falsely accuse male delinquents.[130]

Heimer reported that delinquency for both females and males occurred through a process of role-taking, in which youth considered the perspectives of significant others. Among both boys and girls, attitudes favoring deviance encouraged delinquency. She also found that "girls' misbehavior can be controlled by inculcating values and attitudes, whereas more direct controls may be necessary to control boys' deviance."[131]

Evaluating Explanations of Female Delinquency

Gender is one of the strongest correlates of delinquent behavior.[132] The discussion of female delinquency readily leads to the conclusion that biological explanations are the less predictive factors. Assumptions of sexual inferiority appear to be tied more to the historical context of male chauvinism than to the reality of female delinquency. Personal maladjustment hypotheses may have some predictive ability in determining the frequency of delinquency in girls, but these variables have been overemphasized in the past. Some feminists are satisfied with the conclusions of sociological studies that males and females are differentially exposed or affected by the same criminogenic associations.[133] Strain theory, general theory, social control theory, power-control theory, and labeling and symbolic interactionist theory all have received some support.[134] Other feminists, as the next two sections of this chapter will show, contend that the unique experiences of females require gender-specific theories.

Types of Feminist Theories

Seen historically, there have been seven expressions of feminist theory: liberal feminism, phenomenological feminism, socialist feminism, Marxist feminism, radical feminism, third-wave feminism, and postmodern feminism. Some of these approaches have focused squarely on juvenile delinquency, whereas others have been less concerned with law violations by adolescents. Chesney-Lind's radical feminist theory of delinquency, for example, which is discussed in this chapter, is one of the most exciting efforts to explain delinquent behavior in adolescent females.[135]

Liberal Feminism

Liberal feminism, or egalitarianism, calls for equality of opportunity and enhanced freedom of choice for women. Liberal feminism theorists do not believe that the system is inherently unequal or that discrimination is systematic. They hold that affirmative action, the Equal Rights Amendment, and other opportunity laws or policies provide evidence that men and women can work together to "androgynize" gender roles (blend male and female traits and characteristics) and eliminate discriminatory policies and practices.[136]

Alison M. Jaggar and Paula Rothenberg trace liberal feminism to the eighteenth- and nineteenth-century social ideals of liberty and equality.[137] Liberal feminists contend that a major reason for the discrimination against women and female adolescents is gender-role socialization. Conventional family patterns, as Hagan and other theorists in this chapter have noted, structure masculine and feminine identities.[138]

Josephina Figueira-McDonough's formulation of feminist opportunity theory contended that similar levels of strain (arising from high success aspirations and low legitimate opportunities) lead to similar delinquency patterns by both genders, provided that both are equal in their knowledge of and access to illegitimate means.[139] Adler argued in *Sisters in Crime* that both adult women and adolescent females are imitating males in the desire for the same goals and adopting male roles to achieve them. Because of this merging of gender roles, the adolescent female, as well as her older counterpart, engages in more violent crime.[140]

In 1972, Congress passed the Equal Rights Amendment (ERA). During the campaign for state ratification, many women were drawn to feminist causes, and liberal feminists were introduced to the political mainstream. Liberal feminists argued that the physiological differences between men and women were not a sufficient basis for the continued inequality of opportunity that women, as a group, experienced. The National Organization for Women (NOW) was formed and began promoting what came to be called liberal feminism or egalitarianism.[141]

Liberal feminism grew into a social reform movement that sought to bring about change within the existing social order. By the end of the 1970s, NOW had broadened its stance to include social issues such as lesbian and gay rights, homemakers' rights, the threat of nuclear energy and proliferation, and legal and economic equality for all people. The ERA, however, failed to be ratified—ushering in a conservative backlash during which rights previously won by feminists and other social rights advocates, were challenged.[142]

Phenomenological Feminism

Phenomenological feminist theory pays more attention to the regulator than the regulated. That is, phenomenological feminists examine matters such as whether adolescent females receive the benefits of chivalrous treatment, why adolescent females have received discriminatory treatment by the juvenile justice system, and how juvenile laws penalize females.

The assumption that adult female offenders are protected by the old norms of chivalry and receive more lenient treatment by the justice system is frequently accepted in adult corrections. But if this is true for adult female offenders, strong evidence exists that it is not so for adolescent females.

Although many of the writers on female delinquency in the twentieth century claimed that adolescent females are protected more than adolescent males because they receive the benefits of chivalrous treatment, Steven Schlossman and Stephanie Wallach showed that females have been treated more harshly than males from the time of the founding of the juvenile court at the turn of the century. These researchers, using old court records and secondary sources, asserted that female juvenile delinquents often have received more severe punishment than males, although males usually have been charged with more serious crimes. They concluded that the harsh discriminatory treatment of female delinquents during the Progressive Era resulted from racial prejudice, new theories of adolescence, and Progressive Era movements to purify society.[143]

Socialist Feminism

Socialist feminists, in contrast to other feminists, give neither class nor gender the higher priority. Instead, socialist feminists view both class and gender relations as equal, as they interact with and co-reproduce each other in society. To understand class, socialist feminists argue, it is necessary to recognize how class is structured by gender; and to understand gender requires that one see how it is structured by class. Crime results from the interaction of these relationships, because it is the powerful who have more legitimate and illegitimate opportunities to commit crime. Low female crime rates, then, are related to women's powerless position in society.[144]

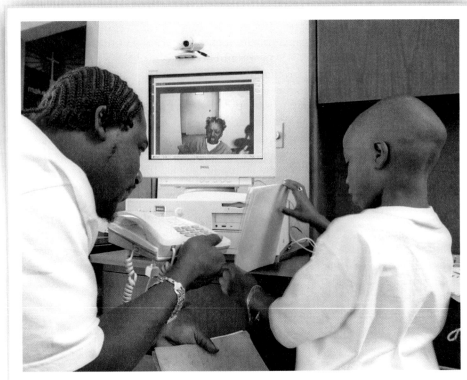

A young boy and his father talk through a camera-equipped speakerphone to the boy's mother, who is in prison hundreds of miles away. The boy is showing his recent drawings to his mother. The program is part of a virtual visitation pilot project run by the Florida Department of Corrections in an effort to strengthen mother–child bonds. ■ **With increasing numbers of women being sent to prison, many children grow up without a mother at home. What can be done to address this issue?**

Marxist Feminism

Marxist feminists argue that, as private property evolved, males dominated all social institutions. Consequently, gender and class inequalities result from property relations and the capitalist mode of production.[145] Sheila Balkan, Ron Berger, and Janet Schmidt further contended that the foundation for a theory of woman's criminality rests in a capitalist mode of production. Sexism, they said, is the result of capitalist relations that structure women's and juveniles' power status and types of involvement in crime. Accordingly, nonviolent female crimes such as shoplifting and prostitution reflect such conditions.[146]

Eleanor M. Miller's *Street Woman,* which is based on intensive interviews with sixty-four Milwaukee prostitutes, contended that prostitution evolves out of the profound social and economic problems confronting adolescent females, especially young women of color.[147] For African American women, constituting over half of Miller's sample, movement into prostitution occurred as a consequence of exposure to deviant street networks. Generally recruited by older African American males with long criminal records, these women organized themselves into "pseudo families" and engaged chiefly, though not exclusively, in prostitution. These women viewed prostitution as an alternative to boring and low-paying jobs and as a means to relieve the burdens of pregnancy and single motherhood. (The young women interviewed had a total of eighty-one children.) Although they were attracted by the excitement and money involved in prostitution, they soon learned that the life was not nearly as glamorous or remunerative as they had anticipated.[148]

For whites, Miller found, street prostitution was not so much a hustle into which one drifted as it was a survival strategy. For this group there was often a direct link between prostitution and difficulties with parents, runaway behavior, and contact with the juvenile justice system. Interviewees described family lives that were characterized by disorganization, extremely high levels of violence, and abuse. But running away from these chaotic settings resulted in the girls' arrest and lengthy detention as status offenders.[149]

Radical Feminism

Radical feminists view masculine power and privilege as the root cause of all social inequality. The most important relations in any society, according to radical feminists, are found in patriarchy, which includes masculine control of labor power and the sexuality of women.[150] Alison M. Jaggar and Paula Rothenberg, two radical feminists, stated that women were the first oppressed group in history, that women's oppression is so widespread that it exists in virtually every known society, and so deep that it is the hardest form of oppression to eradicate.[151] Radical feminists, especially, focus on sexual violence toward women.[152]

> " Radical feminists view masculine power and privilege as the root cause of all social relations and inequality. "

Third-Wave Feminism

Third-wave feminists, who are also called women-of-color feminists, womanists, and critical race feminists, object to white feminists defining "women's issues" from their own standpoint without including women of color and third-world concerns, and to antiracist theory presuming that racial and ethnic minority women's experiences are the same as those of their male counterparts. These feminist theories focus on the significant roles that sexism, racism, class bias, sexual orientation, age, and other forms of socially structured inequality have in women's lives. They introduced the concept of *intersectionalities* to understand the interlocking sites of oppression and to examine how the categories of race, ethnicity, class, gender, sexuality, and age in intersecting systems of domination rely on each other to function. Third-wave feminism helps clarify not only those behaviors of women defined as criminal but also the many crimes against women. This approach makes clear the need to understand issues of social justice in evaluating the criminalization of women.[153] Furthermore, this form of feminist theory seeks ways for men and women to work together to eliminate racism, sexism, and class privilege.[154] In the following quote, bell hooks attacks the anti-male stance of radical feminists:

> They were not eager to call attention to the fact that men do not share a common social status; that patriarchy does not negate the existence of class and race privilege or exploitation; that all men do not benefit equally from sexism. They did not want to acknowledge that bourgeois white women, though often victimized by sexism, have more power and privilege, are less likely to be exploited or oppressed, than poor, uneducated, non-white males.[155]

Postmodern Feminism   Postmodern feminists criticize other feminists for assuming that women are a "clearly defined and uncontroversially given interest group."[156] Positivist feminists, as well as other modernists, claim that the truth can be determined providing that all agree on responsible ways of going about it. Postmodern feminists question whether any knowledge is knowable and reject the idea that there is a universal definition of justice true for all people all of the time.[157]

A Feminist Theory of Delinquency

The **feminist theory of delinquency,** an expression of radical feminism, contends that girls' victimization and the relationship between that experience and girls' crime have been systematically ignored. Chesney-Lind, one of the main proponents of this position, stated that it has long been understood that a major reason for girls' presence

feminist theory of delinquency
A theory that adolescent females' victimization at home causes them to become delinquent and that this fact has been systematically ignored.

in juvenile courts is their parents' insistence on their arrest. Researchers and those who work with female status offenders, are discovering today that a substantial number are victims of both physical and sexual abuse.[158]

Chesney-Lind proposed that a feminist perspective on the causes of female delinquency includes the following propositions: First, girls are frequently the victims of violence and sexual abuse (estimates are that three-quarters of sexual-abuse victims are girls); but, unlike those of boys, girls' victimization and their response to that victimization are shaped by their status as young women. Second, their victimizers (usually males) have the ability to invoke official agencies of social control to keep daughters at home and vulnerable. Third, as girls run away from abusive homes characterized by sexual abuse and parental neglect, they are forced into the life of an escaped convict. Unable to enroll in school or take a job to support themselves because they fear detection, female runaways are forced to engage in panhandling, petty theft, and sometimes prostitution to survive. Finally, it is no accident that girls on the run from abusive homes or on the streets because of impoverished homes become involved in criminal activities that exploit their sexuality. Because U.S. society has defined physically "perfect" young women as desirable, girls on the streets, who have little else of value to trade, are encouraged to utilize this resource. Not surprisingly, the criminal subculture also views them from this perspective.[159] In Voices Across the Profession 7.1, Chesney-Lind expands on this notion of the feminist theory of delinquency.

Voices
Across the Profession 7.1

Interview with Meda Chesney-Lind

The question now is whether the theories of delinquent behavior can be used to understand female crime, delinquency, and victimization. Will the "add women and stir" approach be sufficient to rescue traditional delinquency theories? My research convinces me that it will not work. Gender stratification or the patriarchal context within which both male and female delinquency is lodged has been totally neglected by conventional delinquency theory. This omission means that a total rethinking of delinquency as a social problem is necessary.

The exclusion of girls from delinquency theory might lead one to conclude that girls are almost never delinquent and that they have far fewer problems than boys. Some might even suspect that the juvenile justice system treats the few girls who find their way into it more gently than it does the boys. Both of these assumptions are wrong.

Current work on female delinquency is uncovering the special pains that girls

growing up in male-dominated society face. The price one pays for being born female is upped when it is combined with poverty and minority status, but it is always colored by gender. Consequently, sexual abuse is a major theme in girls' lives, and many girls on the run are running away from abusive and violent homes. They run to streets that are themselves sexist, and they are often forced to survive as women—to sell themselves as commodities. All of this is shaped by their gender as well as by their class and their color.

You might ask, How about the system's response to girls' delinquency? First, there has been almost no concern about girls' victimization. Instead, large numbers of girls are brought into juvenile courts across America for noncriminal status offenses—running away from home, curfew, truancy, et cetera. Traditionally, no one in the juvenile justice system asked these girls why they were in conflict with their parents; no

one looked for reasons why girls might run away from home. They simply tried to force them to return home or sentenced them to training schools. The juvenile justice system, then, has neglected girls' victimization, and it has acted to enforce parental authority over girls, even when the parents were abusive. Clearly, the patterns described above require an explanation that places girls' delinquent behavior in the context of their lives as girls in a male-dominated society—a feminist model of delinquency if you will. That's what I'm working on these days.

■ Is it as hard for girls to grow up in male-dominated society as Chesney-Lind suggests? What do you think of her feminist theory of delinquency?

Source: Reprinted with permission from Meda Chesney-Lind. Meda Chesney-Lind is professor of sociology at the University of Hawaii at Manoa. Her articles have appeared in criminal justice journals and edited criminal justice volumes, and she is widely acknowledged as one of the top authorities on female delinquency.[160]

Considerable research supports the frequent victimization of adolescent females. Mimi Silbert and Ayala M. Pines found that 60 percent of the street prostitutes they interviewed had been sexually abused as juveniles.[161] R. J. Phelps and colleagues, in a survey of 192 female youths in the Wisconsin juvenile justice system, discovered that 79 percent of these youths (most of whom were in the system for petty larceny and status offenses) had been subjected to physical abuse that resulted in some form of injury.[162] Chesney-Lind's investigation of the backgrounds of adult women in prison underscored the links between their victimization as children and their later criminal careers. Interviews revealed that virtually all these women were victims of physical and/or sexual abuse as youngsters; more than 60 percent had been sexually abused, and about half had been raped.[163]

Gender Bias and the Processing of Female Delinquents

The underlying theme of this chapter is that adolescent females grow up in a culture that facilitates domination and control by males.[164] In this patriarchal society, troublesome adolescent females are seen through lenses of discrimination, exploitation, and oppression.[165] Sexism, classism, and racism affect the processing of the female delinquent in the juvenile justice system.

Gender Relations

Gender oppression affects adolescent females in several ways. First, adolescent females face discriminatory treatment because of society's disapproval of sexual activity by adolescent girls. Etta A. Anderson provides evidence that this widely held social attitude has resulted in their discriminatory treatment by the juvenile justice system.[166] Marvin D. Krohn, James P. Curry, and Shirley Nelson-Kilger's analysis of 10,000 police contacts in a midwestern city over a thirty-year period found that adolescent females who were suspected of status offenses were more likely than their male counterparts to be referred to juvenile court for such offenses during all three decades.[167] Christy A. Visher's examination of 785 police–suspect encounters revealed that younger females received harsher punishment than older females. She noted that "police officers adopt a more paternalistic and harsher attitude toward younger females to deter any further violation or inappropriate sex-role behavior."[168] Chesney-Lind further found that police in Honolulu, Hawaii, were likely to arrest females for sexual activity and to ignore the same behavior among males.[169]

Jean Strauss observed that juvenile court judges commonly place adolescent females in confinement for even minor offenses because they assume that these females have engaged in sexual activity and believe that they deserve punishment.[170] Yona Cohn, in her study of the disposition recommendations of juvenile probation officers, found that females constituted only one-sixth of her sample of youths in a metropolitan court, yet they constituted one-fifth of the youths sentenced to institutional care. She attributed this uneven distribution to the fact that female adolescents frequently "violate" the sexual norms of the middle-class probation officers.[171] Furthermore, Kristine Olson Rogers's study of a training school for girls in Connecticut found the treatment staff greatly concerned with residents' sexual history and habits.[172] Both Rogers and Chesney-Lind also comment on the practices, common among juvenile courts and detention homes, of forcing females to undergo pelvic examinations and extensively questioning female juveniles about their sexual activities, regardless of the offenses with which they are being charged.[173]

Laurie Schaffner further observed that female adolescents' sexual behavior, orientation, and histories often bring them to the attention of juvenile authorities. However, for many of these girls, rather than being the problem, much of their delinquent behavior actually is their misguided solution to larger life dilemmas. They are taught to be sexy and frequently solve nonsexual problems, such as family and educational troubles, with sexually related romantic solutions. In examining the sexual solutions that female adolescents devise, Schaffner found from her examination of policies and practices in runaway shelters, psychiatric facilities, and juvenile detention facilities across the United States that much of the state's response is ultimately a criminalization of young women's survival strategies. Schaffner went on to conclude that "girls' troubles with the law often take on sexual overtones as the state participates in a gendered sexualizing and criminalizing of female attention, concerns, bodies, desires, and actions."[174]

Second, Rosemary C. Sarri concluded that juvenile law has long penalized females. She claimed that although the law may not be discriminatory on its face, the attitudes and ideologies of juvenile justice practitioners administering it may result in violations of the equal protection clause of the Fourteenth Amendment, by leading practitioners to commit females to longer sentences than males under the guise of "protecting" the female juvenile.[175] She added that "females have a greater probability of being detained and held for longer periods than males, even though the overwhelming majority of females are charged with status offenses."[176]

Randall G. Shelden and John Horvath further found that adolescent females who were reported to court for status offenses were more likely than their male counterparts to receive formal processing or a court hearing.[177] C. R. Mann's research on runaway youths revealed that adolescent females were more likely than adolescent males to be detained and to receive harsh sentences.[178] Chesney-Lind also concluded that adolescent females are more likely than adolescent males to be held for long periods of time in detention centers.[179]

Randall R. Beger and Harry Hoffman's examination of detention orders by an Illinois juvenile court for technical probation violations found that females are confined in detention longer than males for disobeying probation rules.[180] Probation staff interviews revealed that both personal and contextual factors accounted for the gender-based disparity in the application of detention. Five basic factors were cited as responsible for this disparity: (1) Probation officers perceived female offenders to be more difficult to work with than males; (2) female offenders generally had more severe family dysfunctions than males; (3) conflicts with parents were an issue, because parents reacted more negatively to minor deviations by daughters; (4) community-based resources were inadequate; and (5) more females than males had had multiple social service interventions before probation.[181]

Robert Terry, in a study of 9,000 youths apprehended by police in a Midwestern city, found that females were more likely to be referred to the juvenile court than males and, if referred, were more likely to receive an institutional sentence.[182] Rogers found that females as a group had longer stays in confinement in Connecticut than those of males.[183] Clemens Bartollas and Christopher M. Sieverdes, in a study of institutionalized youths in North Carolina, found that 80 percent of the confined females had committed status offenses and that they had longer institutional stays than the males.[184]

Third, the oppressive treatment of adolescent females is hidden in a couple of ways in the juvenile justice system. Following the decriminalization of status offenders in 1979, Anne Rankin Mahoney and Carol Fenster reported that many girls appeared in court for criminal-type offenses that had previously been classified as status offenses. They suggested that juvenile justice officials might have redefined these girls to make them eligible for the kinds of protectionist sanctions that have been traditionally applied.[185]

Another expression of the gender bias found in this "hidden justice" is that certain provisions of the Juvenile Justice and Delinquency Prevention Act provide that status offenders found in contempt of court for violating a valid court order may be placed in secure detention facilities. This permits juvenile judges to use their contempt power to incarcerate repeat status offenders. If a runaway girl, for example, has been ordered by the court to remain at home but chooses to run away again, she may be found in contempt of court—a criminal-type offense. There is reason to believe that

A teenage shoplifter slips makeup into her friend's purse. Middle-class white youths are likely to receive a milder response to their offending than would lower-class or African American youths. Female offenders, of whatever race, are likely to experience harsher treatment for minor offenses that are sexual in nature. ■ **What aspects of contemporary society produce such varied responses? Are such responses fair?**

juvenile judges apply their contempt power differentially more often to female status offenders than to their male counterparts.[186]

Finally, the early studies, especially, found that police officers, intake personnel, and judges supported a sexual double standard. Female status offenders, as previously indicated, were more likely than their male counterparts to be petitioned to formal court proceedings, to be placed in preadjudicatory detention confinements, and to be incarcerated in juvenile institutions. At the same time, males who committed delinquent acts frequently received harsher treatment than their female counterparts. Consistent with what is known as the "chivalry" or "paternalism" thesis, police were less likely to arrest females suspected of property or person crimes. If arrested, female delinquents were less likely than male delinquents to be formally charged with criminal offenses; and if charged, they were less likely than males to be incarcerated for their offenses.[187]

On balance, some evidence does exist that the discriminatory treatment of female status offenders may be declining since passage of the Juvenile Justice and Delinquency Prevention Act of 1974 and its various revisions. No longer do many states send status offenders to training school with delinquents. But the long tradition of sexism in juvenile justice will be difficult to change. Due process safeguards for female delinquents and status offenders must be established to ensure them greater social justice in the juvenile justice system. The intrusion of extralegal factors into the decision-making process in the juvenile court has led to discrimination against the adolescent female that must become a relic of the past.

The Influence of Class

As part of the female delinquent's "multiple marginality," class oppression is another form of exploitation experienced by this young person.[188] In many ways, powerful and serious problems of childhood and adolescence related to poverty set the stage for the young person's entry into homelessness, unemployment, drug use, survival sex and prostitution, and ultimately even more serious delinquent and criminal acts. Even those adolescents coming from middle-class homes may be thrust into situations of economic survival if they choose to run away from abusive environments.

Traditional theories also fail to address the life situations of girls on the economic and political margins, because researchers typically fail to examine or talk with these girls. For example, almost all urban females identified by police as gang members have been drawn from low-income groups.[189] Lee Bowker and Malcolm Klein's examination of data on girls in gangs in Los Angeles stated the importance of classism as well as racism:

> We conclude that the overwhelming impact of racism, sexism, poverty and limited opportunity structures is likely to be so important in determining the gang membership and juvenile delinquency of women and girls in urban ghettos that personality variables, relations with parents and problems associated with heterosexual behavior play a relatively minor role in determining gang membership and juvenile delinquency.[190]

Class becomes important in shaping the lives of adolescent females in a number of other ways. Lower-class adolescent females tend to confront higher risk levels than middle- and upper-class adolescent females. They are more likely to have unsatisfactory experiences at school, to lack educational goals beyond high school, to experience higher rates of physical and sexual abuse, to deal with pregnancy and motherhood, to be involved in drug and alcohol dependency, to confront the risk of HIV/AIDS, and to lack supportive networks at home.[191] Although not all adolescent females at risk end up in the juvenile justice system, the likelihood of such a placement is greater for lower-class girls.

Racial Discrimination

Young women of color, as well as other minority girls, often grow up in contexts very different from those of their white counterparts. Signithia Fordham's article, "Those Loud Black Girls," showed that young African American women resisted accepting the Anglo norm of femininity by being loud or asserting themselves through their voices. Yet this behavior led to negative school experiences, and it did not take long for these juvenile females to discover that it was the quiet ones who did well in school. Some of this population decided to "pass for white" or to adopt more acceptable norms of femininity in order to be successful in the school experience. Others refused to adopt this survival strategy, and their tool for liberation contributed to isolating or alienating them from school success.[192]

Because racism and poverty often go hand in hand, these girls are forced by their minority status and poverty to deal early and on a regular basis with problems of abuse, drugs, and violence.[193] They also are likely to be attracted to gang membership.[194] H. C. Covey, Scott Menard, and R. Franzese summarized the effect of ethnicity on gang membership:

> Racial differences in the frequency of gang formation such as the relative scarcity of non-Hispanic, white, ethnic gangs may be explainable in terms of the smaller proportion of the non-Hispanic European American population that live in neighborhoods characterized by high rates of poverty, welfare dependency, single-parent households, and other symptoms that characterize social disorganization.[195]

Minority girls' strategies for coping with the problems of abuse, drugs, violence, and gang membership, as Chesney-Lind has noted, "tend to place them outside the conventional expectations of white girls," and it also increases the likelihood that they will come to the attention of the juvenile justice system.[196]

There is also the belief that girls of color enjoy the benefits of chivalry much less than white girls do. Middle-class white girls—especially those who have committed minor offenses, not sexual ones—may be given greater latitude by the police, court intake officers, and juvenile court judges than their minority counterparts who have committed similar offenses. As with male minority offenders, female minority offenders are likely to be viewed as more dangerous to society and more likely to require long-term institutionalization.

The Whole Is Greater Than the Sum of Its Parts

An examination of the experience of African American women reveals the geometric effects of multiple forms of oppressions involving gender, class and race.[197] Diane Lewis has noted that because feminist theories of women's inequality "focused exclusively upon the effects of sexism, they have been of limited applicability to minority women subjected to the constraints of both racism and sexism."[198] Lewis further noted that "black women . . . tended to see racism as a more powerful cause of their subordinate position than sexism and to view the women's liberation movement with considerable mistrust."[199]

The Combahee River Collective's 1977 statement about African American feminism was an important historical contribution to the understanding of multiple simultaneous forms of discrimination. The group stated that it was committed to challenging all forms of "racial, sexual, heterosexual, and class oppression."[200]

Daly summarized this argument by saying that "unless you consider all the key relations of inequality—class, race, gender (and also age and sexuality)—you have considered none." She added that "unless you consider the inseparability of these relations in the life of one person, you do not understand what we are saying."[201] Spelman conceptualized the independence and multiple nature of gender, class, and race by saying that "how one form of oppression is experienced is influenced by and influences how another form is experienced."[202]

This suggests that gender, class, and race are interlocking forms of oppression and that the whole is greater than the parts. Thus, female delinquents, like adult women, suffer the consequences of multiple oppressions as they face processing by the justice system.[203]

Gender Across the Life Course

Jean Bottcher, in a study that targeted brothers and sisters of incarcerated teenagers, conceptualized gender as social practices and used these practices as the unit of analysis. Her study revealed six social factors that intertwined with delinquent activities, limiting female delinquency while at the same time enabling and rewarding male delinquency. These factors included male dominance, differences in routine daily activities, variations in both sexual interests and transition to adulthood, and an ideology that defined both crime as male activity and child care as female activity.

Longitudinal studies reveal that delinquent careers differ by gender. Male careers tend to begin earlier and to extend longer into the adult years. Studies of youth gangs show that female members are more likely than male members to leave the gang if they have a child. Conventional life patterns—especially marriage, parenting, and work—draw both males and females away from gangs and delinquency, but do so more completely and quickly for females.[204]

> " Longitudinal studies reveal that delinquent careers differ by gender. "

Amy C. D'Unger, Kenneth C. Land, and Patricia L. McCall, in a follow-up of the second Philadelphia cohort study, found both life-course-persistent and adolescence-limited delinquency (see Terrie Moffit's classification scheme in Chapters 2 and 3) among the males, with a high and low category for each group. Among the females in this study, there were comparable adolescence-limited groups, although with lower overall offending levels. The high-rate adolescence-limited female offenders did share marked similarities with low-rate chronic male offenders. However, the chronic or persistent category of offender was less prominent among the females.[205]

Rebecca S. Katz, using waves 1 and 7 of the National Longitudinal Study of Youth, found that much as in other studies, childhood victimization, sexual discrim-

Exhibit 7.2

Gender Differences in the Dunedin Longitudinal Study

In *Sex Differences in Antisocial Behaviour*, Terrie E. Moffitt and colleagues report on the findings of the Dunedin Longitudinal Study, which followed 1,000 males and females from age three to age twenty-one. The basic findings indicate that young people develop antisocial behavior for two reasons. One form of antisocial behavior may be understood as a disorder with neurodevelopmental origins—a disorder that, like hyperactivity, autism, and dyslexia, shows a strong male preponderance, early childhood onset, subsequent persistence, and low prevalence in the population. Extreme gender differences are apparent in this form of antisocial behavior. The other form represents the bulk of antisocial behavior, especially by females. This behavior is best understood as a social phenomenon originating in the context of social relationships, with onset in adolescence and high prevalence across the population. Gender differences in antisocial behaviors, according to this book, are negligible. Males and females' antisocial behaviors are particularly alike when alcohol and drugs are involved, near the time of female puberty, and when females are yoked with males in intimate relationships. Other important insights were:

- Increasing numbers of symptoms of conduct disorder predict increasingly poor young adult outcomes, regardless of gender.

- Antisocial behavior has disruptive effects on both females and males as they make the transition from adolescence to adulthood.
- The life-course-persistent antisocial female is extremely rare; approximately 1 in 100 females in a birth cohort seem to be on the life-course-persistent path.
- Females and males on the life-course-persistent path share similar risk factors of family adversity, poor discipline, cognitive deficits, hyperactivity, undercontrolled temperament, and rejection by peers.
- Almost all females who engage in antisocial behavior best fit the adolescence-limited type. Among adolescence-limited delinquency, the gender ratio is 1.5 males to 1 female.
- Males on the life-course-persistent path suffer from multiple poor outcomes as young adults, and youth on the adolescence-limited path also have some poor outcomes.

Why do you believe that this study found so few female life-course-persistent antisocial individuals? Why do females tend to be late-onset rather than early-onset offenders?

Source: Terrie E. Moffitt, Avshalom Caspi, Michael Rutter, and Phil A. Silva, *Sex Differences in Antisocial Behaviour* (Cambridge, England: Cambridge University Press, 2001).

ination, adult racial discrimination, and the experience of domestic violence largely explained women's involvement in crime and deviance. Katz found some support for revised strain theory as an explanation for female involvement in criminal behavior, but she concluded that female crime also may require a unique theoretical model that more directly takes into account females' social and emotional development in a racist and patriarchal society.[206] See Exhibit 7.2 for a discussion of gender differences in the Dunedin Longitudinal Study.

Alex R. Piquero, Robert Brame, and Terrie E. Moffitt, using data from the Cambridge Study of males and from the Dunedin, New Zealand, birth cohort, found that the vast majority of both males and females never experience a conviction, and for those who do, the number of convictions is quite small. They also found that boys, more than girls, tend to become involved in crime when measured by conviction experience, and once involved, boys exhibit more variations in conviction activity than do girls. The data further revealed that boys can be separated into low-, medium-, and high-frequency offender groups, whereas girls can be separated into low- and medium-frequency groups. Finally, their analysis found "that the process of continuity in criminal activity is formed by the end of adolescence similarly for both males and females," and that "there appear to be more similarities than differences across gender in how adolescent and adult patterns of offending are linked."[207]

There have been at least three studies that have examined the desistance process among women. I. Sommers, D. R. Baskin, and J. Fagan found that quality marriages led women to desist from crime, with some variation depending on the class and race of the women being studied.[208] A later study by Sommers and Baskin revealed that the desistance process was quite different for inner-city women of color. These women were more likely to desist as the result of receiving alcohol and drug treatment or because they grew tired or fearful of repeated imprisonments.[209] Finally, as discussed in Chapter 5, Peggy C. Giordano and colleagues followed up on a sample of serious adolescent female delinquents and found neither marital attachment nor job stability to be strongly related to female desistance. Instead, desisters underwent a cognitive shift, or transformation, in which they experienced successful "hooks for change." These hooks "facilitated the development of an alternative view of self that was seen as fundamentally incompatible with criminal behavior."[210]

CHAPTER
Summary

This chapter examines issues of gender as they relate to delinquency. Some of the most important points include:

- Female delinquency, like all other social behaviors, takes place in a world where gender shapes the lives of adolescents in powerful ways.

- Feminist theory, on which this chapter builds, starts with the assumption that adolescent females are socially positioned in society in ways that make them especially vulnerable to male victimization, including physical and sexual abuse and the negative effects of poverty.

- Feminist theory proposes that the meaning of gender and the nature of gender-related behavior depend heavily on the social context in which they are found.

- One area of agreement among feminists and nonfeminists is that delinquency theories are primarily focused on why males commit delinquent acts, and that not much attention has been given to the nature or causes of female delinquency.

- A major disagreement among theorists centers on whether separate perspectives are needed to explain female delinquency, with some writers charging that existing theories are inadequate to explain delinquency by females.

- Considerable evidence supports the position that female delinquency is produced by many of the same sociological factors as male delinquency. More behavioral variation exists within genders than between them.

- An argument can be made that the relationship between the sexual and physical victimization of adolescent females at home and later law-violating behavior has been ignored, and that new theoretical efforts are needed to deal with these experiences.

- Generally speaking, female delinquents are not treated more leniently by the juvenile justice system than are male delinquents when they commit status offenses, especially where disapproved sexual behavior is involved.

- Evidence shows that sexual offenses, incorrigibility, and running away from home do not make up the entire delinquent repertoire of girls; indeed, the offenses of male and female delinquents appear to be converging and are beginning to reflect similar patterns.

- Further examination of how gender, class, and race are interrelated will likely lead to additional insights into the problems facing female adolescents in the United States today.

CRITICAL THINKING
Questions

1. Has the study of female delinquency lagged behind the study of male delinquency? If so, why?
2. Why is society seemingly so sensitive to the sexual behavior of adolescent girls?
3. How do the delinquencies of males and females compare?
4. How has the social context affected the legal context of female delinquency?
5. Why is the relationship among gender, class, and race so important in understanding female delinquency?

WEB Interactivity

In 2004, the Office of Juvenile Justice and Delinquency Prevention awarded funding to the Girls Study Group project at the Research Triangle Institute International (RTI International) in North Carolina. As the group's website says, the Girls Study Group seeks to further understand female juvenile offending and to identify effective strategies to prevent and reduce female involvement in delinquency and violence. The Girls Study Group project center can be visited on the Web at **http:// girlsstudygroup.rti.org.**

The site's sections include *About Girls, About the Study,* and *About the Group.* Visit the *About the Study* section to learn about planned research activities, then write a description of the research and the four questions it is intended to answer. Submit your description to your instructor if asked to do so.

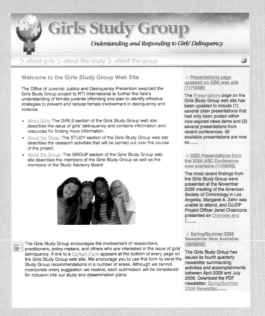

Source: From http://girlsstudygroup.rti.org/. Reprinted with permission from the Research Triangle Institute and the Department of Justice.

Notes

1. Meda Chesney-Lind, "Girls, Crime and Women's Place," *Crime and Delinquency* 35 (1988), pp. 5–29. See also Kathleen Daly and Meda Chesney-Lind, "Feminism and Criminology," *Justice Quarterly* 5 (1988), pp. 497–538.

2. Coramae Richey Mann, *Female Crime and Delinquency* (University Station: University of Alabama Press, 1984), pp. 262–263.

3. Dorie Klein, "The Etiology of Female Crime: A Review of the Literature," in *The Criminal Justice System and Women*, 2nd ed., edited by Barbara Raffel Price and Natalie J. Sokoloff (New York: McGraw-Hill, 1995), p. 31.

4. Carol Smart, *Women, Crime and Criminology: A Feminist Critique* (Boston: Routledge and Kegan Paul, 1976), p. 82.

5. Klein, "Afterword: Twenty Years Ago . . . Today," in *The Criminal Justice System and Women*, p. 47.

6. Ibid., p. 48.

7. Kathleen Daly and Meda Chesney-Lind, "Feminism and Criminology," *Justice Quarterly*, p. 498.

8. Office of Juvenile Justice and Delinquency Prevention, "Addressing Female Development in Treatment," *Juvenile Female Offenders: A Status of the States Report* (Washington, D.C.: U.S. Department of Justice, 1998), p. 1.

9. Paul Mazerolle, "Gender, General Strain, and Delinquency: An Empirical Examination," *Justice Quarterly* 15 (March 1998), p. 66.

10. Karen Heimer, "Gender, Race, and the Pathways to Delinquency: An Interactionist Perspective," in *Crime and Inequality*, edited by J. Hagan and R. Peterson (Stanford, Calif.: Stanford University Press, 1994), p. 164.

11. Jody Miller, *One of the Guys* (New York: Oxford University Press, 2001), pp. 3–4.

12. Kathleen Daly, "Looking Back, Looking Forward: The Promise of Feminist Transformation," in *The Criminal Justice System and Women*, p. 448.

13. Josephina Figueira-McDonough and Elaine Selo, "A Reformulation of the 'Equal Opportunity' Explanation of Fe-

male Delinquency," *Crime and Delinquency* 26 (1980), pp. 333–343; John Hagan, A. R. Gillis, and John Simpson, "The Class Structure of Gender and Delinquency: Toward a Power-Control Theory of Common Delinquent Behavior," *American Journal of Sociology* 90 (1985), pp. 1151–1178; and Douglas A. Smith and Raymond Paternoster, "The Gender Gap in Theories of Deviance: Issues and Evidence," *Journal of Research in Crime and Delinquency* 24 (1987), pp. 140–172.

14. Eileen Leonard, "Theoretical Criminology and Gender," in *The Criminal Justice System and Women*, pp. 55–70.

15. Meda Chesney-Lind, "Girls, Crime and Women's Place," *Crime and Delinquency* 35 (January 1989), pp. 5–29. For an update of this article, see Chesney-Lind, "Girls, Delinquency, and Juvenile Justice: Toward a Feminist Theory of Young Women's Crime," in *The Criminal Justice System and Women*, pp. 71–88.

16. Leonard, "Theoretical Criminology and Gender," in *The Criminal Justice System and Women*, p. 67.

17. Elizabeth V. Spelman, *Inessential Woman: Problems of Exclusion in Feminist Thought* (Boston: Beacon Press, 1989), p. 14.

18. Meda Chesney-Lind, *The Female Offender: Girls, Women, and Crime* (Thousand Oaks, Calif.: Sage Publications, 1974), p. 4.

19. Darrell Steffensmeier and Emilie Allen, "Gender and Crime: Toward a Gendered Theory of Female Delinquency," *Annual Review of Sociology* 22 (1996), pp. 459–487.

20. Kathleen Daly, "Gender, Crime, and Criminology," in *The Handbook of Crime and Punishment*, edited by Michael Tonry (New York: Oxford University Press, 1998), p. 100.

21. P. C. Giordano, J. A. Deines, and S. A. Cernkovich, "In and Out of Crime: A Life Course Perspective on Girls' Delinquency," in *Gender and Crime: Patterns in Victimization and Offending*, edited by Karen Heimer and Candace Kruttschnitt (New York: New York University Press, 2006), p. 18.

22. Ibid., p. 18.

23. Ibid., p. 36.

24. Daly and Chesney-Lind, "Feminism and Criminology," p. 515.

25. Jody Miller and Christopher W. Mullins, "Taking Stock: The Status of Feminist Theories in Criminology," in *The Status of Criminological Theory: Advances in Criminological Theory*, vol. 15, edited by F. Cullen, J. P. Wright, and K. Blevins, F. Adler and W. Laufer (series eds.) (New Brunswick, N.J.: 2006), p. 227.

26. D. Steffensmeier and J. Schwartz, "Trends in Female Criminality: Is Crime Still a Man's World?" in *The Criminal Justice System and Women: Offenders, Prisoners, Victims and Workers*, 3rd ed., edited by B. R. Price and N. J. Sokoloff (New York: McGraw-Hill, 2004), pp. 95–111.

27. Miller and Mullins, "Taking Stock: The Status of Feminist Theories in Criminology," p. 228.

28. Karen Heimer, Stazcy Wittrock, and Unal Haline, "The Crimes of Poverty: Economic Marginalization and the Gender Gap in Crime," *Gender and Crime: Patterns in Victimization and Offending*, p. 115.

29. Ibid., p. 121.

30. Ibid., p. 131.

31. Kathleen Daly, "Gender, Crime, and Criminology," in *The Handbook of Crime and Justice*, edited by Michael Tonry (New York: Oxford University Press, 1998), pp. 96–99.

32. Barrie Thorne, *Gender Play: Girls and Boys in School* (New Brunswick, N.J.: Rutgers University Press, 1993), p. 2.

33. Ibid., p. 157.

34. Mary Beyer, "Delinquent Girls: A Developmental Perspective," *Kentucky Children's Rights Journal* IX (Spring 2001), p. 17.

35. Ibid., p. 18.

36. Ibid., p. 19.

37. For most of the studies in this paragraph, see Jean Bottcher, "Social Practices of Gender: How Gender Relates to Delinquency in the Everyday Lives of High-Risk Youths," *Criminology* 39 (November 2001), p. 899.

38. Anne Campbell, "Female Participation in Gangs." In *The Modern Gang Reader*, edited by Malcolm W. Klein, Cheryl L. Maxson, and Jody Miller (Los Angeles: Roxbury, 1995).

39. John M. Hagedorn, *People and Folks*, 2nd ed. (Chicago: Lake View Press, 1998).

40. Jody Miller and Scott H. Decker, "Young Women and Gang Violence: Gender, Street Offending, and Violent Victimization in Gangs," *Justice Quarterly* 18 (March 2001), pp. 116–139.

41. Claire M. Renzetti and Daniel J. Curran, *Women, Men, and Society*, 2nd ed. (Boston: Allyn and Bacon, 1992).

42. Stephanie J. Funk, "Risk Assessment for Juveniles on Probation," *Criminal Justice and Behavior* 26 (March 1999), p. 49. For the importance of peer relationships with girls, see also Daniel P. Mears, Matthew Ploeger, and Mark Warr, "Explaining the Gender Gap in Delinquency: Peer Influence and Moral Evaluations of Behavior," *Journal of Research in Crime and Delinquency* 35 (August 1998), pp. 251–266.

43. Joanne Belknap and Karen Holsinger, "An Overview of Delinquent Girls: How Theory and Practice Failed and the Need for Innovative Changes," in *Female Offenders: Critical Perspectives and Effective Interventions*, edited by R. T. Zaplin (Gaithersburg, Md.: Aspen Publishers, 1998), p. 1.

44. Leslie Acoca and K. Dedel, *No Place to Hide: Understanding and Meeting the Needs of Girls in the California Juvenile Justice System* (San Francisco: National Council on Crime and Delinquency, 1998).

45. Ibid.

46. Acoca, "Investing in Girls: A 21st Century Strategy," *Juvenile Justice* (October 1999), p. 5.

47. Ibid., p. 6.

48. Ibid., p. 7.

49. Ibid., p. 8.

50. Ibid., p. 9.

51. Ibid., p. 10.

52. Paul Mazerolle, "Gender, General Strain, and Delinquency: An Empirical Examination," p. 66.

53. Cesare Lombroso, *The Female Offender* (New York: Appleton, 1920).

54. Ibid., p. 122.

55. Ibid., p. 151.

56. Ibid.

57. Ibid., p. 109.

58. Dorie Klein, "The Etiology of Female Crime: A Review of the Literature," *Issues in Criminology* 8 (Fall 1973), p. 9.

59. Lombroso, *The Female Offender,* pp. 150–152.

60. J. Cowie, B. Cowie, and E. Slater, *Delinquency in Girls* (London: Heinemann, 1968).

61. Ibid., p. 17.

62. T. C. N. Gibbens, "Female Offenders," *British Journal of Hospital Medicine* 6 (1971), pp. 279–286.

63. Cowie, Cowie, and Slater, *Delinquency in Girls.*

64. Ibid.

65. Anne Campbell, *Girl Delinquents* (New York: St. Martin's Press, 1981), p. 46.

66. Ibid., p. 48.

67. W. I. Thomas, *Sex and Society* (Boston: Little, Brown, 1907).

68. Ibid.

69. W. I. Thomas, *The Unadjusted Girl* (New York: Harper, 1923).

70. Campbell, *Girl Delinquents,* p. 52.

71. Thomas, *The Unadjusted Girl,* p. 109.

72. Mann, *Female Crime and Delinquency,* p. 79.

73. Sigmund Freud, *An Outline of Psychoanalysis,* translated by James Strachey (New York: Norton, 1949), p. 278.

74. Sigmund Freud, *New Introductory Lectures on Psychoanalysis* (New York: Norton, 1933), p. 183.

75. Peter Bols, "Preoedipal Factors in the Etiology of Female Delinquency," *Psychoanalytic Study of the Child* 12 (1957), p. 232.

76. Peter Bols, "Three Typical Constellations in Female Delinquency," in *Family Dynamics and Female Sexual Delinquency,* edited by Otto Pollak (Palo Alto, Calif.: Science and Behavior Books, 1969), pp. 99–110.

77. Herbert H. Herskovitz, "A Psychodynamic View of Sexual Promiscuity," in *Family Dynamics and Female Sexual Development,* p. 89.

78. Ibid.

79. Otto Pollak, *The Criminality of Women* (Philadelphia: University of Pennsylvania Press, 1950), p. 8.

80. Ibid., pp. 125–139.

81. Gisela Konopka, *The Adolescent Girl in Conflict* (Englewood Cliffs, N.J.: Prentice-Hall, 1966).

82. These key factors from Konopka's *The Adolescent Girl in Conflict* are listed in Peter C. Kratcoski and John E. Kratcoski, "Changing Patterns in the Delinquent Activities of Boys and Girls: A Self-Reported Delinquency Analysis," *Adolescence* 18 (Spring 1975), pp. 83–91.

83. Clyde Vedder and Dora Somerville, *The Delinquent Girl* (Springfield, Ill.: Charles C. Thomas, 1970).

84. Ruth Morris, "Attitudes towards Delinquency by Delinquents, Nondelinquents, and Their Friends," *British Journal of Criminology* 5 (1966), pp. 249–265.

85. Mary Gray Riege, "Parental Affection and Juvenile Delinquency in Girls," *British Journal of Criminology* (January 1972), pp. 55–73.

86. Emmy E. Werner and Ruth S. Smith, *Kauai's Children Come of Age* (Honolulu: University Press of Hawaii, 1977).

87. William Wattenberg and Frank Saunders, "Sex Differences among Juvenile Offenders," *Sociology and Social Research* 39 (1954), pp. 24–31.

88. Interviewed in May 1982.

89. Interviewed in May 1982.

90. Peggy C. Giordano and Stephen A. Cernkovich, "Changing Patterns of Female Delinquency" (research proposal submitted to the National Institute of Mental Health, February 28, 1979), p. 24.

91. Klein, "The Etiology of Female Crime: A Review of the Literature," in *The Criminal Justice System and Women,* p. 45.

92. Talcott Parsons, "Age and Sex in the Social Structure of the United States," *American Sociological Review* 7 (October 1942); James S. Coleman, *The Adolescent Society* (New York: Free Press, 1961); Ruth Rittenhouse, "A Theory and Comparison of Male and Female Delinquency" (Ph.D. dissertation, University of Michigan, Ann Arbor, 1963).

93. Susan K. Datesman, Frank R. Scarpitti, and Richard M. Stephenson, "Female Delinquency: An Application of Self and Opportunity Theories," *Journal of Research in Crime and Delinquency* 12 (1975), p. 120.

94. Jeffery O. Segrave and Douglas N. Hastad, "Evaluating Three Models of Delinquency Causation for Males and Females: Strain Theory, Subculture Theory, and Control Theory," *Sociological Focus* 18 (January 1985), p. 13.

95. Stephen A. Cernkovich and Peggy C. Giordano, "Delinquency, Opportunity, and Gender," *Journal of Criminal Law and Criminology* 70 (1979), p. 150.

96. Lisa Broidy and Robert Agnew, "Gender and Crime: A General Strain Theory Perspective," *Journal of Research in Crime and Delinquency* 34 (1997), pp. 275–306.

97. John P. Hoffman and S. Susan Su, "The Conditional Effects of Stress on Delinquency and Drug Use. A Strain Theory Assessment of Sex Differences," *Journal of Research in Crime and Delinquency* 34 (February 1997), pp. 46–78.

98. Mazzerolle, "Gender, General Strain, and Delinquency," pp. 66, 81.

99. Freda Adler, *Sisters in Crime* (New York: McGraw-Hill, 1975), p. 106.

100. Laura Crites, "Women Offenders: Myth vs. Reality," in *The Female Offender,* edited by Laura Crites (Lexington, Mass.: Lexington Books, 1976), pp. 36–39.

101. Darrell J. Steffensmeier, "Crime and the Contemporary Woman: An Analysis of Changing Levels of Property Crime," *Social Forces* 57 (1978), pp. 566–584.

102. Joseph G. Weis, "Liberation and Crime: The Invention of the New Female Criminal," *Crime and Social Justice* 6 (1976), pp. 17–27.

103. Giordano and Cernkovich, "On Complicating the Relationship between Liberation and Delinquency," p. 468.

104. Giordano and Cernkovich, "Changing Patterns of Female Delinquency," p. 25.

105. Peggy C. Giordano, "Girls, Guys and Gangs: The Changing Social Context of Female Delinquency," *Journal of Criminal Law and Criminology* 69 (1978), p. 127.

106. Travis Hirschi, *Causes of Delinquency* (Berkeley: University of California Press, 1969).

107. William E. Thornton Jr., Jennifer James, and William G. Doerner, *Delinquency and Justice* (Glenview, Ill.: Scott Foresman, 1982), p. 268.

108. Bobbi Jo Anderson, Malcolm D. Holmes, and Erik Ostresh, "Male and Female Delinquents' Attachments and the Effects of Attachments on Severity of Self-Reported Delinquency." Paper presented to the Annual Meeting of the

Academy of Criminal Justice Sciences, Albuquerque, New Mexico (March 1998).

109. Austin T. Turk, *Criminality and the Legal Order* (Chicago: Rand McNally, 1969), pp. 164–165.

110. Gary F. Jensen and Raymond Eve, "Sex Differences in Delinquency: An Examination of Popular Sociological Explanations," *Criminology* 13 (February 1976), pp. 427–448.

111. Teresa C. LaGrange and Robert A. Silverman, "Low Self-Control and Opportunity: Testing the General Theory of Crime as an Explanation for Gender Differences in Delinquency," *Criminology* 37 (1999), pp. 41–72.

112. Karen Heimer and Stacy De Coster, "The Gendering of Violent Behavior," *Criminology* 37 (1999), pp. 277–318.

113. Adler, *Sisters in Crime.*

114. F. T. Cullen, K. M. Golden, and J. B. Cullen, "Sex and Delinquency: A Partial Test of the Masculinity Hypothesis," *Criminology* 15 (1977), pp. 87–104.

115. William E. Thornton and Jennifer James, "Masculinity and Delinquency Revisited," *British Journal of Criminology* 19 (July 1979), pp. 225–241.

116. Stephen Norland and Neal Shover, "Gender Roles and Female Criminality: Some Critical Comments," *Criminology* 15 (1977), pp. 86–104.

117. Giordano and Cernkovich, "On Complicating the Relationship between Liberation and Delinquency," pp. 467–481.

118. Thornton and James, in "Masculinity and Delinquency Revisited," found limited support for the merger of social control theory and the masculinity hypothesis in explaining delinquency in girls, but perhaps other combinations would be more fruitful.

119. Segrave and Hastad, "Evaluating Three Models of Delinquency Causation for Males and Females"; R. E. Johnson, *Juvenile Delinquency and Its Origins: An Integrated Approach* (New York: Cambridge University Press, 1979).

120. Giordano, "Girls, Guys and Gangs," p. 132.

121. Ibid.

122. Daniel P. Mears, Matthew Ploeger, and Mark Warr, "Explaining the Gender Gap in Delinquency: Peer Influence and Moral Evaluations of Behavior," *Journal of Research in Crime and Delinquency* 35 (August 1998), pp. 251–266.

123. John Hagan, John Simpson, and A. R. Gillis, "Class in the Household: A Power-Control Theory of Gender and Delinquency," *American Journal of Sociology* 92 (January 1987), pp. 788–816; Hagan, Gillis, and Simpson, "The Class Structure of Gender and Delinquency," pp. 1151–1178.

124. Hagan et al., "Class in the Household," pp. 791–792.

125. Ibid., p. 793.

126. Ibid., pp. 813–814.

127. Simon I. Singer and Murray Levine, "Re-Examining Class in the Household and a Power-Control Theory of Gender and Delinquency." Paper presented at the Annual Meeting of the American Society of Criminology (November 1987), pp. 23–25.

128. Meda Chesney-Lind, "Girl's Crime and Woman's Place: Toward a Feminist Model of Female Delinquency." Paper presented at the Annual Meeting of the American Society of Criminology, Montreal, Canada (November 10–14, 1987), p. 16.

129. Dawn Jeglum Bartusch and Ross L. Matsueda, "Gender, Reflected Appraisals, and Labeling: A Cross-Group Test of an Interactionist Theory of Delinquency," *Social Forces* 75 (September 1996), p. 145.

130. Ibid.

131. Karen Heimer, "Gender, Interaction, and Delinquency: Testing a Theory of Differential Social Control," *Social Psychology Quarterly* 59 (1996), p. 57.

132. Mears et al., "Explaining the Gender Gap in Delinquency: Peer Influence and Moral Evaluations of Behavior," p. 251.

133. Ibid.

134. Giordano and Cernkovich, "Changing Patterns of Female Delinquency," pp. 24–28.

135. Chesney-Lind, "Girl's Crime and Woman's Place."

136. Sally S. Simpson, "Feminist Theory, Crime, and Justice," *Criminology* 27 (November 1989), p. 607.

137. Alison M. Jaggar and Paula Rothenberg, eds., *Feminist Frameworks* (New York: McGraw-Hill, 1984), pp. 83–84.

138. Piers Beirne and James Messerschmidt, *Criminology* (San Diego: Harcourt Brace Jovanovich, 1991), p. 518.

139. Figueira-McDonough and Selo, "A Reformulation of the Equal Opportunity Explanation of Female Delinquency," pp. 333–343.

140. Adler, *Sisters in Crime.*

141. J. H. Rollins, *Women's Mind, Women's Bodies: The Psychology of Women in a Biosocial Context* (Upper Saddle River, N.J.: Prentice-Hall, 1996), p. 3.

142. Ibid.

143. Steven Schlossman and Stephanie Wallach, "The Crime of Precocious Sexuality: Female Juvenile Delinquency in the Progressive Era," *Harvard Educational Review* 48 (February 1978), p. 65.

144. Kristine Olson Rogers, "For Her Own Protection . . . Conditions of Incarceration for Female Juvenile Offenders in the State of Connecticut," *Law and Society Review* 7 (1973), pp. 223–246.

145. Beirne and Messerschmidt, *Criminology.*

146. Sheila Balkan, Ronald Berger, and Janet Schmidt, *Crime and Deviance in America: A Critical Approach* (Monterey, Calif.: Wadsworth, 1980), p. 211.

147. Eleanor M. Miller, *Street Woman* (Philadelphia: Temple University Press, 1986).

148. Ibid.

149. Ibid.

150. Beirne and Messerschmidt, *Criminology,* p. 519.

151. Jaggar and Rothenberg, *Feminist Frameworks,* p. 86.

152. Beirne and Messerschmidt, *Criminology,* p. 519.

153. B. R. Price and N. J. Sokoloff, eds., *The Criminal Justice System and Women: Offenders, Victims, and Workers,* 3rd ed. (New York: McGraw-Hill, 2005), p. 3.

154. Rollins, *Women's Minds, Women's Bodies: The Psychology of Women in a Biosocial Context,* p. 5.

155. bell hooks, *Feminist Theory: From Margin to Center* (Boston: South Ends Books, 1984).

156. Smart, *Women, Crime, and Criminology,* p. 10.

157. P. H. Collins, *Black Feminist Thought* (New York: Routledge, Chapman, Hall, 1998).

158. Chesney-Lind, "Girl's Crime and Woman's Place," p. 17.

159. Ibid., p. 20.
160. This interview took place in 1988.
161. Mimi Silbert and Ayala M. Pines, "Entrance into Prostitution," *Youth and Society* 13 (1982), p. 476.
162. Cited in Chesney-Lind, "Girl's Crime and Woman's Place."
163. Ibid.
164. Spelman, *Inessential Woman*, p. 85.
165. Ibid., p. 51.
166. Etta A. Anderson, "The 'Chivalrous' Treatment of the Female Offender in the Arms of the Criminal Justice System: A Review of the Literature," *Social Problems* 23 (1976), pp. 350–357. See also Chesney-Lind, "Judicial Enforcement of the Female Sex Role: The Family Court and Female Delinquency," *Issues in Criminology* 8 (1973), pp. 57–59; and Kristine Olson Rogers, "For Her Own Protection," pp. 223–246.
167. Marvin D. Krohn, James P. Curry, and Shirley Nelson-Kilger, "Is Chivalry Dead?" *Criminology* 21 (1983), pp. 417–439.
168. Christy A. Visher, "Gender, Police Arrest Decisions, and Notions of Chivalry," *Criminology* 21 (1983), pp. 5–28.
169. Chesney-Lind, "Judicial Enforcement of the Female Sex Role."
170. Jean Strauss, "To Be Minor and Female: The Legal Rights of Women under Twenty-One, *Ms.* 1 (1972), p. 84.
171. Yona Cohn, "Criteria for Probation Officers' Recommendations to Juvenile Court," *Crime and Delinquency* 1 (1963), pp. 272–275.
172. Rogers, "For Her Own Protection."
173. Chesney-Lind, "Judicial Enforcement of the Female Sex Role"; Rogers, "For Her Own Protection."
174. Laurie Schaffner, "Female Juvenile Delinquency: Sexual Solutions and Gender Bias in Juvenile Justice." Paper presented at the Annual Meeting of the American Society of Criminology in Washington, D.C. (November 1998).
175. Rosemary C. Sarri, "Juvenile Law: How It Penalizes Females," in Crites, ed., *The Female Offender*, pp. 68–69.
176. Ibid., p. 76.
177. Randall G. Shelden and John Horvath, "Processing Offenders in a Juvenile Court: A Comparison of Males and Females." Paper presented at the Annual Meeting of the Western Society of Criminology, Newport Beach, Calif. (February–March, 1986).
178. Cited in Mann, *Female Crime and Delinquency.*
179. Meda Chesney-Lind, "Girls and Status Offenses: Is Juvenile Justice Still Sexist?" *Criminal Justice Abstracts* 20 (March 1988), p. 152.
180. Randall R. Beger and Harry Hoffman, "The Role of Gender in Detention Dispositioning of Juvenile Probation Violaters," *Journal of Crime and Justice* 21 (1998), p. 173.
181. Ibid., pp. 183–184.
182. Robert Terry, "Discrimination in the Police Handling of Juvenile Offenders by Social Control Agencies," *Journal of Research in Crime and Delinquency* 14 (1967), p. 218.
183. Rogers, "For Her Own Protection."
184. Clemens Bartollas and Christopher M. Sieverdes, "Games Juveniles Play: How They Get Their Way" (unpublished report, 1985).
185. Anne Rankin Mahoney and Carol Fenster, "Family Delinquents in a Suburban Court," in *Judge, Lawyer, Victim, Thief: Woman, Gender Roles and Criminal Justice*, edited by Nicole Hahn and Elizabeth Anne Stanko (Boston: Northeastern University Press, 1982).
186. Donna M. Bishop and Charles E. Frazier, "Gender Bias in Juvenile Justice Processing: Implications of the JJDP Act," *Journal of Criminal Law and Criminology* 82 (1992), p. 1167.
187. Ibid., p. 1164.
188. Chesney-Lind, *The Female Offender*, p. 4.
189. Ibid., p. 44.
190. Lee Bowker and Malcolm Klein, "The Etiology of Female Juvenile Delinquency and Gang Membership: A Test of Psychological and Social Structural Explanations," *Adolescence* 13 (1983), pp. 750–751.
191. For many of these findings, see Joy G. Dryfoos, *Adolescents at Risk: Prevalence and Prevention* (New York: Oxford University Press, 1990).
192. Signithia Fordham, " 'Those Loud Black Girls': (Black) Women, Silence and Gender 'Passing' in the Academy," in *Beyond Black and White: New Faces and Voices in U.S. Schools*, edited by Maxine Seller and Lois Weis (Albany: University of New York Press, 1997), pp. 81–111.
193. Chesney-Lind, *The Female Offender*, p. 23.
194. Finn-Aage Esbensen and L. Thomas Winfree, "Race and Gender Differences between Gang and Nongang Youths: Results from a Multisite Survey," *Justice Quarterly* 15 (September 1998), p. 510.
195. H. C. Covey, Scott Menard, and R. Franzese, *Juvenile Gangs*, 2nd ed. (Springfield, Ill.: Charles C. Thomas, 1997), p. 240.
196. Chesney-Lind, *The Female Offender*, p. 23.
197. Spelman, *Inessential Woman*, p. 123.
198. For this discussion on African American women I am indebted to Kathleen Daly, "Class–Race–Gender: Sloganeering in Search of Meaning," *Social Justice* 20 (1993), pp. 58. For Lewis's quote, see Diane K. Lewis, "A Response to Inequality: Black Women, Racism, and Sexism," *Signs: Journal of Women in Culture and Society* 3 (1977), p. 339.
199. Lewis, "A Response to Inequality," p. 339.
200. "The Combahee River Collective Statement," in *Capitalist Patriarchy and the Case for Socialist Feminism*, edited by Zilah Eisenstein (New York: Monthly Review Press, 1979), pp. 362–372.
201. Daly, "Class–Race–Gender," p. 58.
202. Spelman, *Inessential Woman*, p. 123.
203. Ibid.
204. Bottcher, "Social Practices of Gender: How Gender Relates to Delinquency in the Everyday Lives of High-Risk Youths," pp. 905–925.
205. Amy V. D'Unger, Kenneth C. Land, and Patricia L. McCall, "Sex Differences in Age Patterns of Delinquent/Criminal Careers: Results from Poisson Latent Class Analyses of the Philadelphia Cohort Study," *Journal of Quantitative Criminology* 18 (December 2002), pp. 371–373.
206. Rebecca S. Katz, "Explaining Girls' and Women's Crime and Desistance in the Context of Their Victimization Experiences," *Violence against Women* 6 (June 2000), pp. 652–655.
207. Alex R. Piquero, Robert Brame, and Terrie E. Moffitt, "Extending the Study of Continuity and Change: Gender Dif-

ferences in the Linkage Between Adolescent and Adult Offending," *Journal of Quantitative Criminology* 21 (June 2005), pp. 219–243.

208. I. Sommers, D. R. Baskin, and J. Fagan, "Getting Out of the Life: Crime Desistance by Female Street Offenders," *Deviant Behavior* 15 (1994), pp. 125–149.

209. I. Sommers and D. R. Baskin, "Situational or Generalized Violence in Drug Dealing Networks," *Journal of Drug Issues* 27 (1997), pp. 833–849.

210. Peggy C. Giordano, Stephen A. Cernkovich, and Jennifer L. Rudolph, "Gender, Crime, and Desistance: Toward a Theory of Cognitive Transformation," *American Journal of Sociology* 107 (January 2002), p. 1038.

8

The Family and Delinquency

> " The number of abused and neglected children has special significance for the juvenile justice system because many of these children end up in the system. "

—Federal Advisory Committee on Juvenile Justice

CHAPTER Objectives

AFTER READING THIS CHAPTER, YOU SHOULD BE ABLE TO ANSWER THE FOLLOWING QUESTIONS:

- How do problems in the family affect adolescents?
- What factors in the family are most likely to affect the likelihood of delinquent behavior?
- What are the main forms of child abuse and neglect?
- What is the relationship of child abuse and neglect to delinquency and status offenses?
- How does the child welfare or juvenile justice system handle charges of child abuse?

In 2004, Miami law enforcement officials said they were considering charges against an eleven-year-old girl whom they said sold heroin, sometimes in her nightgown, in a serene suburban neighborhood. The girl allegedly took orders from her thirty-six-year-old mother, Alison Davis, who was charged with six felonies and two misdemeanors after a police raid on their house, said Charles Blazek, a spokesperson for the City of South Miami. For months surveillance teams had watched the girl sell drugs to customers who arrived by car and on foot, said Basek.

"She did what her mother told her to do," he said of the girl. "Whether she knows it's wrong or not, we don't know."

Blazek said officers, who had observed the home since receiving a tip in October, had never encountered such a young dealer. Undercover officers who bought drugs from the girl two times before obtaining a warrant for the raid were shocked to learn that she was only eleven.

"She was a very obedient and very nice child," said Troy Davis, thirty-nine, who lives across the street from the girl's ramshackle white-and-yellow house, which stands out on a block of neatly kept homes and lawns. "She could not have known what she was doing."

After the girl was arrested and questioned at a juvenile detention center, she and her sister were released into the custody of the Florida Department of Children and Families and placed in foster care.

Adapted from Abby Goodenough, "Girl, 11, Sold Heroin for Mother, Police Say," *New York Times*, January 7, 2004. Copyright © 2004 by The New York Times Co. Reprinted with permission.

socialization

The process by which individuals come to internalize their culture; through this process an individual learns the norms, sanctions, and expectations of being a member of a particular society.

The family is the primary agent for the **socialization** of children. It is the first social group a child encounters and is the group with which most children have their most enduring relationships. The family gives a child his or her principal identity, even his or her name; teaches social roles, moral standards, and society's laws; and disciplines children who fail to comply with those norms and values. The family either provides for or neglects children's emotional, intellectual, and social needs; and, as suggested above, the neglect of these basic needs can have a profound effect on the shaping of a child's attitudes and values.

This chapter discusses adolescents and family problems; the relationship between the family and delinquency; and the types and impact of child abuse and neglect, both at the time of their occurrence and across the life course.

The Family and Delinquency

The importance criminologists have given the family as a contributing factor to delinquency has varied through the years. Karen Wilkinson classified the attention given to the family into three periods: 1900 to 1932, 1933 to 1949, and 1950 to 1972. In the first period the role of the family as a contributing factor to delinquent behavior was emphasized. A broken home was considered a major cause of delinquency, and a great deal of research was done to measure its influence. In the second period the family was minimized in comparison to the school, social class standing, and the influence of peers. In the third period there was revived interest in the family. Wilkinson attributed this to other variables studied as causes of delinquency that did not yield conclusive findings. Researchers in this post-1950 period also broadened their inquiry to encompass the nature of the relationship between parents and children, parental discipline and supervision, and family integration.[1]

In more recent decades the important role of the family in terms of understanding delinquent behavior is seen in the fact that most theories of delinquency rely heavily on the parent–child relationship and parent practices to explain delinquency.[2] The theoretical emphasis on family processes, in turn, is supported by findings that family relationships and parenting skills are directly or indirectly related to delinquent behavior.[3]

The structure-versus-function controversy has been one of the important and continuing debates on the relationship between family and delinquency. The structural perspective focuses on factors such as parental absence, family size, and birth order, whereas the functional or quality-of-life view argues for the significance of parent–child interaction, the degree of marital happiness, and the amount and type of discipline.[4]

Judith Rick Harris challenged beliefs about the role of the family with her provocative 1995 claim that parental behavior has few, if any, enduring effects on the development of children. She claims that a youth's conduct, including delinquency, is predominantly influenced by peers or group socialization. The media were struck by her central thesis that parenting does not affect children's behavior, and she was featured in a number of lead stories about her "truly revolutionary idea." Her 1998 book, *The Nurture Assumption: Why Children Turn Out the Way They Do*, which was written for the trade market, was widely reviewed.[5]

The Broken Home

Some empirical evidence supports the commonly accepted notion that delinquency results from a **broken home**.[6] In 1924, George B. Mangold declared, "The broken home is probably the single most important cause of delinquency."[7] Margaret Hodgkiss's 1933 study in Cook County (Chicago) also revealed a strong difference in the incidence of broken homes among delinquents compared to nondelinquents: 66.9 percent of delinquents and 44.8 percent of nondelinquents had broken homes.[8] Sheldon Glueck and Eleanor T. Glueck's classic study, which compared 500 delinquents and 500 nondelinquents, further reported strong evidence of the importance of broken homes: 60.4 percent of delinquents and 34.2 percent of nondelinquents came from broken homes.[9]

broken home
A family in which parents are divorced or are no longer living together.

Later studies, however, questioned the relationship between broken homes and delinquency. F. I. Nye's highly respected study of the family and research by R. A. Dentler and L. J. Monroe found no significant direct relationship between delinquency and family composition.[10] Lawrence Rosen recalculated statistical relationships for eleven different studies of broken homes and male delinquency conducted between 1932 and 1968 and discovered that virtually all the studies yielded only very weak positive relationships between broken homes and delinquency.[11] Both Patricia Van Voorhis and colleagues and Margaret Farnworth found that the effects of the broken home on most forms of delinquency were negligible.[12] James Q. Wilson and R. J. Herrnstein, in reviewing the research on delinquency and single-parent homes, concluded that findings had been inconclusive, inconsistent, and ambiguous.[13]

Other researchers have shed further light on this debate. Richard S. Sterne, Jackson Toby, and T. P. Monahan reported that the factor of broken homes affects adolescent females more than males.[14] Susan K. Datesman and Frank R. Scarpitti found that for adolescent females the relationship between broken homes and delinquency depends on the type of offense involved.[15] Ross L. Matsueda and Karen Heimer's study revealed that broken homes have a larger impact on delinquency among African Americans than on other racial groups.[16] Van Voorhis and colleagues found only a moderate relationship between broken homes and status offenses.[17] Joseph F. Rankin also reported that, except for running away and truancy, the relation between broken homes and delinquency is negligible.[18] But Marvin D. Free Jr.

A sixteenth-century inscription on a plaque on the wall of Venice's Pieta church discouraging parents from abandoning their unwanted babies in the *scaffetta*. ■ **What led some early writers to say that "the broken home is probably the single-most important cause of delinquency"? Do you agree?**

concluded that the connection between broken homes and delinquency is more evident for status offenses than it is for more serious offenses.[19]

Karen Wilkinson noted that research using self-report techniques has generally not shown the single-parent home to be a major factor in the cause of delinquency, whereas studies using official statistics have.[20] Some researchers maintain that divorce is more likely to predispose a child to delinquency than the death of a parent,[21] but Steven A. Cernkovich and Peggy C. Giordano's study failed to distinguish the effects of family factors across types of parental configurations.[22] Both Travis Hirschi and Martin Gold found the greatest rate of delinquency in families with stepfathers.[23] R. J. Chilton and G. E. Markle initially found that children living in broken homes are more frequently involved in status and delinquent offenses, but when they reclassified the families on the basis of income, they found that economics appeared to have more to do with the rate of referral to the juvenile court than did family composition.[24] Some research indicates that the juvenile justice system in some jurisdictions may be more likely to institute formal processing against children from broken homes.[25]

More recently, Cesar J. Rebellion, using a national probability sample of 1,725 adolescents, found that divorce or separation of parents early in a juvenile's life course may be related to delinquency more strongly than previous research has indicated. Rebellion also found that parents' remarriage during the juvenile's adolescence may be strongly associated with status offending. In addition, he found that association with deviant peers and attitudes favorable to delinquency account for the broken homes–delinquency relationship better than do other explanations.[26]

L. Edward Wells and Rankin's meta-analysis of fifty published studies dealing with broken homes and delinquency found that:

1. The prevalence of delinquency in broken homes is 10 to 15 percent higher than in intact homes.

2. The correlation between broken homes and juvenile delinquency is stronger for minor forms of juvenile misconduct (status offenses) and weakest for serious forms of criminal behavior (such as theft and interpersonal violence).

3. The type of family break seems to affect juvenile delinquency [because] the association with delinquency is slightly stronger for families broken by divorce or separation than by death of a parent.

4. There are no consistent or appreciable differences in the impact of broken homes between girls and boys or between black youths and white youths.

5. There are no consistent effects of the child's age at breakup on the negative effects of the separated family.

6. There is no consistent evidence of the often cited negative impact of stepparents on juvenile delinquency.[27]

Birth Order

Some evidence supports the significance of **birth order** in that delinquent behavior is more likely to be exhibited by middle children than by first or last children. The first child, according to this view, receives the undivided attention and affection of parents, and the last child benefits from the parents' experience in raising children as well as from the presence of other siblings, who serve as role models. The Gluecks, F. I. Nye, and William McCord, Joan McCord, and Irving Zola all reported that intermediate children were more likely to be delinquents.[28] Linda J. Waite and Lee A. Lillard found that children were initially stabilizing and later destabilizing in a marriage, because "firstborn children increase the stability of marriage through their preschool years," but "older children and children born before marriage significantly increase chances of disruption."[29]

birth order
The sequence of births in a family and a child's position in it, whether firstborn, middle child, or youngest.

Family Size

Research findings on **family size** generally reveal that large families have more delinquency than do small families. Hirschi explained the higher rate of delinquency with middle children as the result of family size rather than of birth position.[30] Rolf Loeber and Magda Stouthamer-Loeber suggested that a number of processes may explain why delinquency rates are greater in large families. First, parents in large families tend to have more difficulty disciplining and supervising their children than do parents with smaller families. Second, some parents with large families delegate child rearing to older siblings, who may not be equipped to execute this task. Third, large families frequently are more exposed to illegitimacy, poverty, and overcrowding.[31]

family size
The number of children in a family; a possible risk factor for delinquency.

Delinquent Siblings or Criminal Parents

Some evidence indicates that siblings learn delinquency from others in the family. The Gluecks reported that a much higher proportion of delinquents than nondelinquents had **delinquent siblings** and/or criminal mothers and fathers.[32] Joan McCord's follow-up of the Cambridge–Somerville (Massachusetts) Youth Study revealed that the sons of fathers who had serious criminal records were likely to be raised in poor families and experience bad child rearing, which increased their risk for an early first conviction.[33] David P. Farrington also found that the delinquency of siblings is a predictor of delinquency.[34] Janet L. Lauritsen further found that delinquency is predicted equally well "by the offending of an older sibling, the offending of a younger sibling, or by the average level of offending among all adolescents in the household."[35]

delinquent siblings
Brothers or sisters who are engaged in delinquent behaviors; an apparent factor in youngsters' involvement in delinquency.

Quality of Home Life

Studies have generally reported that poor quality of home life, measured by marital adjustment and harmony within the home, affects the rate of delinquent behavior among children more than whether or not the family is intact. Nye found the happi-

Web LIBRARY 8.1

Read the NIJ-sponsored publication *Communitywide Strategies to Reduce Child Abuse and Neglect: Lessons From the Safe Kids/Safe Streets Program* at **www.justicestudies.com/WebLibrary**.

A mother cries while holding her pregnant thirteen-year-old daughter. ■ **Why do children born to young mothers face greater risks?**

rejection by parents
Disapproval, repudiation, or other uncaring behavior directed by parents toward children.

Web PLACES 8.1

Visit the Center on Child Abuse and Neglect's website via **www.justicestudies.com/WebPlaces**.

supervision and discipline
The parental monitoring, guidance, and control of children's activities and behavior.

ness of the marriage to be the key to whether or not children become involved in delinquent behavior.[36] The Gluecks reported good marital relationships and strong family cohesiveness in homes of more nondelinquents than delinquents.[37] William McCord and colleagues and R. C. Audry further concluded that well-integrated and cohesive families produce fewer delinquents than do less-well-adjusted families.[38] Randy L. Lagrange and Helen R. White found that parental love, especially for youths in the middle of their adolescence, functions as a "psychological anchor" to conformity.[39] Paul Howes and Howard J. Markman's longitudinal study found that the quality of the parents' relationship before marriage as well as after a child is born is related to child functioning.[40] McCord's thirty-year follow-up study found that maternal behavior directly influenced delinquency and, subsequently, adult criminality, but that parental interaction with the family appeared "to have a more direct influence on the probability of adult criminal behavior."[41]

Family Rejection

Several studies have found a significant relationship between **rejection by parents** and delinquent behavior. S. Kirson Weinberg found that many parents of delinquents had rejected their children.[42] McCord, McCord, and A. Howard reported that some rejecting parents often exhibited aggressive behavior as well.[43] Loeber and Stouthamer-Loeber's review of the literature found that twelve of fifteen studies reported a significant relation between rejection and delinquency.[44] Although Nye found that the father's rejection is more often significantly related to delinquency than the mother's rejection,[45] a number of other studies concluded that rejection from mothers is more related to involvement with delinquency.[46]

McCord, McCord, and Zola reported that only a small percentage of delinquents had affectionate relationships with parents.[47] The Gluecks and Audry also found that parental affection is less apparent in the homes of delinquents than in those of nondelinquents.[48] W. L. Slocum and C. L. Stone further discovered that children from affectionate homes tend to be more conforming in behavior.[49] Richard E. Johnson found that young people report stronger ties to the mother, but it is the father–child bond that is more predictive of their involvement in crime, especially among boys.[50] Rosen's longitudinal study of African American and white boys residing in Philadelphia found that lower delinquency rates were reported for African American youths who had high father–son interaction and came from small families.[51] Rankin and Roger Kern found that children who are strongly attached to both parents have a lower probability of delinquency than do those who are attached to only one parent.[52]

Discipline in the Home

Inadequate **supervision and discipline** in the home have been commonly cited to explain delinquent behavior. Hirschi found that the rate of delinquency increased with the incidence of mothers employed outside the home. He attributed this finding to unemployed mothers' spending more time supervising their children's activities and behavior.[53] Nye found a slight causal relationship between the employment of the mother and delinquent behavior.[54] But the Gluecks' study failed to reveal a strong association between working mothers and delinquent behavior.[55] G. F. Jensen and R. Eve further found that the degree of supervision within the home was not a significant factor in the amount of delinquent activity of children.[56] Loeber and Stouthamer-Loeber concluded from their review of the literature that "the evidence suggests a stronger relation between lack of supervision and official delinquency than between lack of supervision and self-reported delinquency."[57]

Nye reported that strict, lax, and unfair discipline were all associated with high rates of delinquent behavior. He also found that the disciplinary role of the father was more closely related to delinquent behavior than was the disciplinary role of the mother.[58] More recently, Loeber and Stouthamer-Loeber, as well as James Snyder and Gerald Patterson, also concluded that both strict and punitive as well as lax and erratic disciplinary styles are related to delinquent behavior.[59] McCord, McCord, and Zola further found a relationship between inconsistent discipline and delinquent behavior.[60]

John Paul Wright and Francis T. Cullen, in using data from the National Longitudinal Survey of Youth, advanced the concept of "parental efficacy" as an adaptation of Robert Sampson and colleagues' "collective efficacy" (See Chapter 4). Wright and Cullen employed "parental efficacy" because they wanted to evaluate the relationship between parental controls and supports in reducing delinquency with children. They found that support and control are intertwined and that parental efficacy exerts substantive effects on reducing children's inappropriate behaviors.[61]

Ronald L. Simons and colleagues, using data from a sample of several hundred African American caregivers and their children, found that, over time, increases in collective efficacy within a community were associated with increases in authoritative parenting—which is defined as parents combining warmth and support with firm monitoring and control. Both authoritative parenting and collective efficacy, they added, served to deter both affiliation with deviant peers and involvement in delinquent behavior. The deterrent effect of authoritative parents was enhanced when it took place within a community with high collective efficacy.[62]

Family Factors and Delinquency

Conflicting findings make drawing conclusions about the relationship between delinquency and the family difficult, but the following observations have received wide support:

1. Family conflict and poor marital adjustment are more likely to lead to delinquency than is the structural breakup of the family.
2. Children who are intermediate in birth order and who are part of large families appear to be involved more frequently in delinquent behavior, but this is probably related more to parents' inability to provide for the emotional and financial needs of their children than to birth position or family size.
3. Children who have delinquent siblings or criminal parents may be more prone to delinquent behavior than those who do not.
4. Rejected children are more prone to delinquent behavior than those who have not been rejected. Children who have experienced severe rejection are probably more likely to become involved in delinquent behavior than those who have experienced a lesser degree of rejection.
5. Consistency of discipline within the family seems to be important in deterring delinquent behavior.
6. As the Gluecks predicted in 1950, lack of mother's supervision, father's and mother's erratic/harsh discipline, parental rejection, and parental attachment appear to be the most important predictors of serious and persistent delinquency.[63] John H. Laub and Robert J. Sampson's reanalysis of the Gluecks' data found that mother's supervision, parental attachment, and parental styles of discipline are the most important predictors of serious and persistent delinquency.[64] Similarly, Loeber and Stouthamer-Loeber's meta-analysis identified parent–child involvement and supervision, child–parent rejection and discipline practices, parental criminality and

> " Conflicting findings make drawing conclusions about the relationship between delinquency and the family difficult. "

deviant attitudes, and marital conflict and absence as the four dimensions of family functioning related to delinquency.[65]

7. The rate of delinquency appears to increase with the number of unfavorable factors in the home. That is, multiple risk factors within the family are associated with a higher probability of juvenile delinquency than are single factors.[66]

Transitions and Delinquency

Divorced and single-parent families, blended families, out-of-wedlock births, homelessness, unemployment, alcohol and drug abuse, and violence are some of the family problems that affect adolescents today. Adolescents experiencing such problems are at a high risk of becoming involved in socially unacceptable behaviors.

The high divorce rate in the United States translates into an increasing number of single-parent families. In 2004, 68 percent of children below the age of eighteen lived with two married parents. The percentage, which decreased from 1980 to 1994, has remained the same at 68 to 69 percent from 1994 to 2004.[67] Divorce has affected African American families more than white families. As many as 40 percent of white children and 75 percent of African American children will experience divorce or separation before they reach sixteen, and many of these children will experience multiple family disruptions over the course of their childhood.[68]

What needs to be addressed is the relationship between the impact of family transitions and problem behaviors, such as delinquency and drug use. An examination of the Rochester, Denver, and Pittsburgh studies reveals a consistent relationship between a greater number of family transitions and a higher level of drug use and delinquent behavior. The magnitude of the differences between juveniles with no family transitions and those with many family transitions was similar across the three cities.[69]

Poverty is a serious problem in the lives of children. Children living in female-headed families with no husband present continued to experience a higher poverty rate in 2002 than their counterparts in married-couple families: 40 percent compared with 9 percent. African American children had a poverty rate of 32 percent in 2002.[70] Economic hardship and lack of access to opportunity tend to undermine marital and parental functioning. Furthermore, adolescents who experience family transitions may have difficulty managing anger and other negative emotions that may contribute to their involvement with delinquency or drugs. See Figure 8.1 for percentages of children under eighteen living in poverty, by family type.

The majority of divorced parents remarry, and adolescents in these families must learn to adjust to a new parental figure. Blended families place stress on biological parents, stepparents, and children. In a typical blended family, the mother has custody of her children and the stepfather lives with his wife's children. His biological children, if any, usually visit the home on an occasional or regular basis. Few adolescents escape the experience of a blended family without feeling resentment, rejection, and confusion. Some stepparents even subject their stepchildren to emotional, physical, or sexual abuse.

Childbearing is a life experience that many female adolescents have. In some instances children are wanted and adolescent mothers are married; more often than not, however, pregnancy in adolescence leads to abortion or adoption. Between 1980 and 1994, the rate of childbearing by unmarried women rose sharply for women of all ages. In contrast, the birthrate for unmarried adolescent females has dropped considerably since 1994.[71] The rate for adolescent girls ages fifteen to seventeen in 2003 was 22 per 1,000—representing the lowest U.S. rate ever recorded for that age group. The decrease in adolescent births is especially notable among African American females ages fifteen to seventeen, where it has dropped by more than half between 1991 and 2003 (from 86 to 39 births per 1,000).[72]

Homelessness is a phenomenon that shapes the lives of an estimated 500,000 to 1.3 million young people each year. Many homeless youths leave their families after years of physical and sexual abuse, the addiction of a family member, strained interpersonal relations, and parental neglect. Homelessness, regardless of a child's age, is

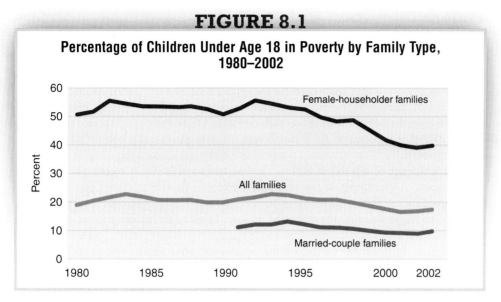

FIGURE 8.1

Percentage of Children Under Age 18 in Poverty by Family Type, 1980–2002

Source: Forum on Child and Family Service, *America's Children in Brief: Key National Indicators of Well-Being, 2004* (Washington, D.C.: Federal Interagency Forum on Child and Family Statistics, 2004), p. 6.

likely to expose him or her to settings permeated by substance abuse, promiscuity, pornography, prostitution, and crime.[73]

Unemployment also affects some family units in the United States. Between January 1994 and November 2004, the number of people sixteen years and older officially designated as unemployed declined from 6.6 to 5.4 percent.[74] The unemployment rate for African American men sixteen years and older declined from 12.1 percent in January 1994 to 10.5 percent in November 2004, and the rate for African American women declined from 11.5 to 9 percent. The bad news for African American families is that nearly 10 percent of this population is still experiencing unemployment and all its consequences.[75]

Adolescents whose family members have substance abuse problems also have their sad stories to tell. Neglect, abuse, and economic hardship are common factors in family settings where alcohol and substance abuse is ordinary behavior. Arrest data in *Crime in the United States 2005* reflect the nationwide scope of this problem in the general population: 1,846,351 arrests for drug abuse violations; 1,371,919 arrests for driving under the influence; and 597,838 arrests for liquor law violations.[76] But while the prevalence of substance abuse is unarguable, its actual impact on adolescents is not easily measurable, since it is simply not possible to display the impact on a "one abuse instance = one adverse impact on one or more adolescent(s)" basis. The impact is clearly visible, however, in the behaviors of the youths it affects.

Violence has long been a major characteristic of the problem family, and it is no stranger to family life today. Marital violence is a pervasive problem that affects nearly one-third of the married population. Numerous studies also show that some parents act out their aggression on their children.[77] Some families use physical violence for disciplinary purposes. Karen Heimer found that coercive discipline strategies teach youths to rely on force and coercion to resolve problems.[78]

The Mass Media and Delinquent Behavior

Part of the challenge of being a parent today is dealing effectively with the influence that the mass media has on children. For our purposes, the term *mass media* refers to the Internet, radio, television, commercial motion pictures, videos, CDs, music, and the press (newspapers, journals, and magazines).

Web PLACES 8.2

Visit the Child Welfare League of America's website via **www .justicestudies.com/ WebPlaces**.

Violent Television and Movies

Most people today watch a lot of television, and many seem to depend on media programming for their understandings of the surrounding world.[79] Consequently, criminologists have shown considerable interest in assessing the relationship between delinquent behavior and the exposure to violence viewed on television. Researchers in the area of delinquency generally conclude that TV violence is most likely to negatively impact the behavior of those children who are already predisposed toward violence, and that it seems to have much less influence on young people who are not so predisposed.[80]

The influence of television and motion pictures also extends to the phenomenon of *contagion.* An example of the contagion effect of motion pictures can be seen in the movie *Colors,* whose showing in theaters across America led gang members nationwide to begin wearing their groups' colors. Prior to seeing the movie, most gang members had not been wearing "colors."[81]

Walter B. Miller drew the following conclusion after examining the relationship between mass media content and the occurrence of gang violence:

> The influence of the media on the behavior of youth has long been a contentious issue. In recent years, increasing consensus has developed in support of the position that media images do have a significant influence, particularly on more susceptible youth.
>
> In the case of youth gangs, this contention would not be difficult to sustain. The lifestyle and subculture of gangs are sufficiently colorful and dramatic to provide a basis for well-developed media images. For example, the Bloods/Crips feud . . . caught the attention of media reporters in the early 1990s and was widely publicized. Gang images have served for many decades as a marketable media product—in movies, novels, news features, and television dramas.[82]

Violent Video Games

Video games involving violent scenarios, such as "Halo 2," "Grand Theft Auto," and "Asheron Call 2," are the focus of considerable controversy today. Some people accuse video game makers of promoting values that support violence. Not surprisingly,

Young children playing video games. Some people think that violent video games can lead to violent behavior. ■ **Do you agree?**

the software entertainment industry, with its annual $28 billion in sales paced by a nation's thirst for action, claims that their games are offered only for entertainment purposes.[83]

In August of 2005, members of the American Psychological Association (APA) adopted a resolution calling for less violence in video and computer games marketed to children. One APA panelist, Kevin M. Kieffer, reported research that shows playing violent video games tends to make children more aggressive and less prone to helping behaviors.[84] Craig A. Anderson, one of the pioneers of research in this area, adds, "There really isn't any room for doubt that aggressive game playing leads to aggressive behavior."[85]

In the fall of 2005, the Federal Trade Commission (FTC) launched an investigation into the system used for rating video games, particularly what some saw as undeservedly low ratings that made the violent and sexually themed game "Grand Theft Auto" available to teens. Around the same time, a group of bipartisan senators proposed that the National Institutes of Health oversee a comprehensive $90 million study on the effects of violent media, including video games, on children's development.[86]

Internet-Initiated Crimes

Internet access is easily available to nearly everyone in the United States today. The Web, however, has become a new frontier for innovative forms of cybercrime. One source of Internet-initiated crime is the supremacist and hate groups that target young people through the Web. In like manner, youthful perpetrators of violent crimes are sometimes influenced by information collected or contacts made on the Internet. Child sexual abuse, where initial contacts are made through the Web, now accounts for up to 4 percent of all arrests for sexual assaults against juveniles.[87] See Focus on Social Policy 8.1 for additional information on Internet-initiated sex crimes against minors.

Gangsta Rap

Gangsta rap is a form of hip-hop music that some believe negatively influences young people by devaluing human life, the family, religious institutions, schools, and the justice system.[88] Gangsta rap was pioneered by Ice T and other rappers influenced by Schooly D's hardcore rap. Gangsta rap portrays the lifestyles of inner-city gang members, and its lyrics relate stories of violence-filled lives. Guns play a prominent part in those lyrics, and are frequently depicted as a means for attaining manhood and status.

Today's gangsta rap devotees seem to consist predominantly of white young people.[89] The music is available to children via television (especially MTV), the Internet, radio (including satellite radio), and retail CDs and DVDs.

Gangsta rap's subject matter has created considerable controversy, with critics charging that the messages it espouses include misogyny, homophobia, racism, and materialism. Gangsta rappers usually defend themselves by pointing out that they are describing the reality of inner-city life and claim that when rapping, they are merely playing a character.[90]

In summary, today's parents must face the reality that their children's minds are being bombarded with extensive disturbing stimuli. Violence permeates movies and TV screens; video games are no less violent, and the most popular ones among teenagers are probably the most violent. Supremacist and hate groups are targeting young people through their websites. The Internet offers opportunities for the sexual abuse of vulnerable adolescent males and females. Finally, gangsta rap is filled with violence, appears to devalue human life, and contains lyrics proposing homophobia, misogyny, racism, and materialism.

Child Abuse and Neglect

Child abuse and neglect, like the other family problems addressed in this chapter, have a profound influence on shaping the behavior and attitudes of adolescents and

child abuse
The mistreatment of children by parents or caregivers. Physical abuse is intentional behavior directed toward a child by the parent or caregiver to cause pain, injury, or death. Emotional abuse involves a disregard of a child's psychological needs. Sexual abuse is any intentional and wrongful physical contact with a child that entails a sexual purpose or component. Such sexual abuse is termed *incest* when the perpetrator is a member of the child's family.

neglect
A disregard for the physical, emotional, or moral needs of children. Child neglect involves the failure of the parent or caregiver to provide nutritious food, adequate clothing and sleeping arrangements, essential medical care, sufficient supervision, access to education, and normal experiences that produce feelings of being loved, wanted, secure, and worthy.

FOCUS ON
Social Policy 8.1

Internet-Initiated Sex Crimes Against Minors

The goals of the *National Juvenile Online Victimization (N-JOV) Study* were to survey police agencies within the United States in order to document and enumerate arrests for Internet-related sex crimes committed against minors, and to describe the offenders' characteristics. One area studied was the availability of child pornography (CP) on the Internet. Key findings include:

- Law-enforcement agencies made an estimated 1,713 arrests for Internet-related crimes involving the possession of child pornography during the 12 months beginning July 1, 2000.
- Almost all of those arrested for CP possession were male; 91 percent were white, and 86 percent were older than age twenty-five. Only 3 percent were younger than age eighteen.
- Most arrestees had images of prepubescent children (83 percent) and images graphically depicting sexual penetration (80 percent).
- Approximately 1 in 5 arrested CP possessors (21 percent) had images depicting sexual violence involving children, such as bondage, rape, and torture.
- Thirty-nine percent of those arrested were in possession of at least one video containing moving images of child pornography.
- Fifty-three percent of the cases involving pornography came to the attention of the justice system as CP possession cases, 31 percent could be classified as cases of child sexual victimization, and 16 percent were cases involving Internet sexual solicitations of undercover investigators posing as children.
- CP possession cases originated at all levels of law enforcement, with 25 percent beginning in federal agencies, 11 percent in Internet Crimes Against Children (ICAC) Task Forces (which were not yet fully operational during the time frame covered by the study), 60 percent in other state and local agencies, and 3 percent in other agencies such as international law enforcement.

- Forty percent of arrested CP possessors were "dual offenders" who sexually victimized children and also possessed child pornography, with both crimes uncovered during the same investigation. An additional 15 percent were dual offenders who attempted to sexually victimize children by soliciting undercover investigators who posed online as minors.
- One in six investigations beginning with allegations or investigations of CP possession discovered dual offenders.
- In the overall N-JOV study, 39 percent of arrested offenders who met victims online, and 43 percent of offenders who solicited undercover investigators, were dual offenders.
- Almost all arrested CP possessors (96 percent) were convicted or plead guilty, and 59 percent were incarcerated.
- Victims in these crimes were primarily thirteen- through fifteen-year-old adolescent girls who met adult offenders (76 percent of such offenders were older than age twenty-five) in Internet chat rooms.
- The majority of offenders did not deceive victims about the fact that they were adults who were interested in sexual relationships.
- Most victims met and had sex with the adult offenders on more than one occasion. Half of the victims were described as feeling close bonds or being in love with the offenders.
- Almost all cases with male victims involved male offenders.
- Offenders used violence in 5 percent of the episodes recorded.

> ■ Why would an adolescent girl respond to an Internet solicitation and meet an adult who made it clear that he wanted to have a sexual relationship? Why would such a high percentage (half) develop a close relationship with the adult, with some of the victims describing themselves as "in love"? How are Internet-initiated sex crimes related to the failure of parents to assume responsibility for their children's well-being?

Source: Janis Wolak, David Finkelhor, and Kimberly J. Mitchell, *Child-Pornography Possessors Arrested in Internet-Related Crimes*: *Findings from the National Juvenile Online Victimization Study* (Washington, D.C.: National Center for Missing & Exploited Children), pp. vii–viii. See also Janis Wolak, David Finkelhor, and Kimberly J. Mitchell, "Internet-Initiated Sex Crimes Against Minors: Implications for Prevention Based on Findings from a National Study," *Journal of Adolescent Health* 35 (2004), p. 424.

adults.[91] Various categories of child abuse and neglect, also referred to as *child maltreatment*, are identified in Table 8.1. Kathleen M. Heide has found it helpful to distinguish among three types of neglect (physical, medical, and emotional) and four types of abuse (physical, sexual, verbal, and psychological).[92] According to Heide, the types of abuse and neglect are frequently interrelated; one type of child maltreatment often leads to another. For example, children who are sexually abused by parents become victims of neglect when their parents fail to seek medical attention for sexually transmitted diseases or resulting injuries.[93] Barbara Tatem Kelley, Terence

TABLE 8.1

Defining Child Maltreatment and Rating Its Severity

SUBTYPE OF MALTREATMENT	BRIEF DEFINITION	EXAMPLES OF LEAST AND MOST SEVERE CASES
PHYSICAL ABUSE	A caregiver inflicts a physical injury on a child by other than accidental means.	*Least*—Spanking results in minor bruises on arm. *Most*—Injuries require hospitalization, cause permanent disfigurement, or lead to a fatality.
SEXUAL ABUSE	Sexual contact or attempted sexual contact occurs between a caretaker or responsible adults and a child for the purposes of the caretakers' sexual gratification or financial benefit.	*Least*—A child is exposed to pornographic materials. *Most*—A caretaker uses force to make a child engage in sexual relations or prostitution.
PHYSICAL NEGLECT	A caretaker fails to exercise a minimum degree of care in meeting a child's physical needs.	*Least*—Food is not available for regular meals, clothing is too small, child is not kept clean. *Most*—A child suffers from severe malnutrition or severe dehydration due to gross inattention to his or her medical needs.
LACK OF SUPERVISION OR MORAL NEGLECT	A caretaker does not take adequate precautions (given a child's particular emotional and developmental needs) to ensure his or her safety in and out of the home.	*Least*—An eight-year-old is left alone for short periods of time (i.e., less than three hours) with no immediate source of danger in the environment. *Most*—A child is placed in a life-threatening situation without adequate supervision.
EMOTIONAL MALTREATMENT	Thwarting of a child's basic emotional needs (such as the need to feel safe and accepted) occurs persistently or at an extreme level.	*Least*—A caretaker often belittles or ridicules a child. *Most*—A caretaker uses extremely restrictive methods to bind a child or places a child in close confinement such as a closet or trunk for two or more hours.
EDUCATIONAL MALTREATMENT	A caretaker fails to ensure that a child receives adequate education.	*Least*—A caretaker allows a child to miss school up to 15 percent of the time when he or she is not ill and there is no family emergency. *Most*—A caretaker does not enroll a child in school or provide any educational instruction.
MORAL–LEGAL MALTREATMENT	A caretaker exposes a child to or involves a child in illegal or other activities that may foster delinquency or antisocial behavior.	*Least*—A child is permitted to be present for adult activities, such as drunken parties. *Most*—A caretaker causes a child to participate in felonies such as armed robbery.

Source: Adapted from Barbara Tatem Kelley et al., "In the Wake of Childhood Maltreatment," *Juvenile Justice Bulletin* (Washington, D.C.: U.S. Department of Justice, Office of Juvenile Justice and Delinquency Prevention, 1997), p. 4. Reprinted with permission from the U.S. Department of Justice.

P. Thornberry, and Carolyn A. Smith have defined seven types of child maltreatment: physical abuse, sexual abuse, physical neglect, lack of supervision, emotional maltreatment, educational maltreatment, and moral–legal maltreatment.[94] For the definitions and levels of severity of each type, see Table 8.1.

B. F. Steele's study of 200 juvenile first-time offenders found that between 70 and 80 percent had a history of neglect and abuse.[95] Joan McCord's longitudinal study of 253 males revealed that abused, neglected, and rejected children had significantly higher rates of delinquency than did nonabused children (10 percent, 15 percent, and 29 percent versus 7 percent, respectively). Her study also found that, as adults, half of the abused or neglected adolescent males had been convicted of serious crimes or had become alcoholics or mentally ill.[96] José Alfaro found that 50 percent of the children reported to area hospitals as abused children later were petitioned to the juvenile court.[97]

Cathy Spatz Widom's initial study of abuse and neglect found that 29 percent of those abused and neglected as children had a nontraffic criminal record as adults, compared with 21 percent of the control group.[98] Widom and Michael G. Maxfield's updated study, which followed 1,575 cases from childhood through adolescence and into

Web PLACES 8.3

Visit the National Center for Missing and Exploited Children's website via **www.justicestudies.com/ WebPlaces**.

Web PLACES 8.4

Visit the Child Welfare Information Gateway via **www .justicestudies.com/ WebPlaces**.

young adulthood, was able to examine the long-term consequences of abuse and neglect.[99] They found that:

1. Being abused or neglected as a child increased the likelihood of arrest as a juvenile by 59 percent, as an adult by 29 percent, and for a violent crime by 30 percent.
2. Maltreated children were younger at the time of their first arrest, committed nearly twice as many offenses, and were arrested more frequently.
3. Physically abused and neglected (versus sexually abused) children were the most likely to be arrested later for a violent crime.
4. Abused and neglected females also were at increased risk of arrest for violence as juveniles and adults.
5. White abused and neglected children were no more likely to be arrested for a violent crime than their nonabused and nonneglected white counterparts; in contrast, African American abused and neglected children showed significantly increased rates of violent arrests compared with African American children who were not maltreated.[100]

Thornberry and colleagues' ongoing study of delinquency examined direct child maltreatment as well as more general exposure to family violence. The 1994 study, which interviewed 1,000 seventh- and eighth-grade students and their caretakers every six months for four years, found that compared with youths who were not abused or neglected, these youths had higher rates of self-reported violence (70 percent versus 56 percent).[101]

However, Matthew T. Zingraff and colleagues found from their study in Mecklenburg County, North Carolina, that although child maltreatment is an important correlate of delinquency, "the maltreatment–delinquency relationship has been exaggerated in previous research."[102] Furthermore, Zingraff and colleagues challenged the simple and direct relationship between maltreatment and delinquency, which was widely used in the studies of the 1970s and 1980s, when they concluded that delinquency is only one of many possible social, social–psychological, and behavioral consequences of maltreatment. Finally, Zingraff and colleagues added that status offenders appear to be affected by maltreatment more than property and violent offenders are.[103]

Extent and Nature of Child Abuse and Neglect

C. H. Kempe first exposed child abuse as a major social problem with his groundbreaking 1962 essay on the battered child syndrome.[104] Kempe's research led to an avalanche of writing on neglect, physical abuse, and sexual abuse. The passage of legislation in all fifty states in the late 1960s requiring mandatory reporting of child abuse and neglect cases also focused attention on these problems. The passage by Congress of the Child Abuse and Prevention Act and the establishment of the National Center on Child Abuse in 1974 focused further attention on these problems. As an indication of the extent of maltreatment of children, the caregivers of an estimated 3,503,000 children were investigated for alleged abuse or neglect in the United States in 2004, and of that number an estimated 872,000 children were found to be victims.[105] Between the years 1990 to 2004, the rate of investigations increased from 35.1 per 1,000 children in 1990 to 47.8 children in 2004 (a 32.4 percent increase), whereas the rate of substantiated victimization decreased from 13.4 per 1,000 children in 1990 to 11.9 per 1,000 children in 2004 (an 11.2 percent decrease).[106]

Web PLACES 8.5

Visit the Child Exploitation and Obscenity Section of the U.S. Department of Justice's Criminal Division via **www .justicestudies.com/ WebPlaces**.

Victims of Child Maltreatment In 2004, more than 60 percent of child victims experienced neglect. Over 17 percent were physically abused, 10 percent were sexually abused, and 7 percent were psychologically maltreated. In addition, nearly 17 percent suffered "other" types of maltreatment.[107] See Figure 8.2 for victimization rates by maltreatment types.

Younger children make up the largest percentage of victims. Children age three or younger had the highest rate of victimization, at 16.1 per 1,000 children. Children

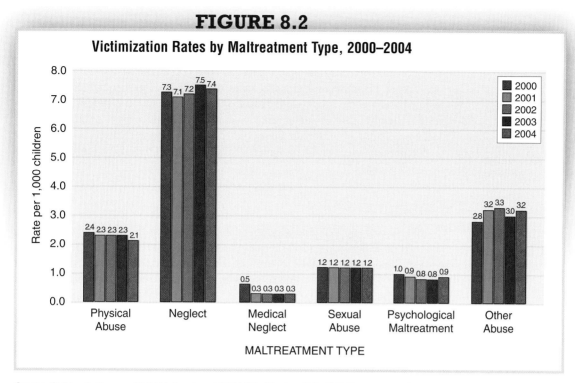

FIGURE 8.2

Victimization Rates by Maltreatment Type, 2000–2004

Source: Children's Bureau, *Child Maltreatment 2004* (Washington, D.C.: U.S. Department of Health and Human Services, 2004), p. 25.

age sixteen to seventeen had victimization rates of 6.1 per 1,000. Girls were slightly more likely to be victims than boys. African American children were victims of maltreatment at a rate of 19.9 per 1,000 children; the rate for Pacific Islanders was 17.6 per 1,000 children; for American Indians or Alaska Natives, 15.5 per 1,000 children; for whites, 10.7 for 1,000 children; for Hispanics, 10.4 percent 1,000 children; and for Asians, 2.9 for 1,000 children. Figure 8.3 shows the race and ethnicity of victims for the year 2004.[108]

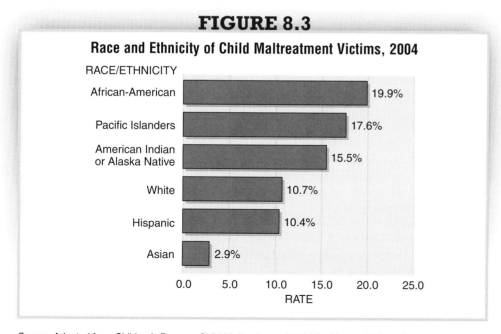

FIGURE 8.3

Race and Ethnicity of Child Maltreatment Victims, 2004

Source: Adapted from Children's Bureau, *Child Maltreatment 2004* (Washington, D.C.: U.S. Department of Health and Human Services, 2004), p. 26.

Perpetrators of Maltreatment   In 2004, nearly 84 percent of child victims were abused by parents acting alone or with another person. Mothers acted alone in maltreating approximately two-fifths of child victims. Fathers acted alone in maltreating 18.3 percent of victims. Another 18.3 percent suffered abuse at the hands of both mother and father. Nonparental abusers accounted for 10.1 percent of the total.[109]

Child fatalities are the most tragic result of maltreatment. In 2004, an estimated 1,490 children died because of neglect or abuse. More than four-fifths of children who were killed were younger than four years old. Nearly 12 percent were four to seven years old, 4.1 percent were eight to eleven years old, and 3.4 percent were twelve to seventeen years of age.[110]

See Focus on Social Policy 8.2 for additional information on children who are at risk of maltreatment.

Neglect   The word *neglect* generally refers to disregard for the physical, emotional, or moral needs of children or adolescents. The Children's Division of the American Humane Association established a comprehensive definition of neglect, stating that physical, emotional, and intellectual growth and welfare are jeopardized when a child can be described in the following terms:

1. Malnourished, ill-clad, dirty, without proper shelter or sleeping arrangement;
2. Without supervision, unattended;
3. Ill and lacking essential medical care;
4. Denied normal experiences that produce feelings of being loved, wanted, secure, and worthy (emotional neglect);
5. Failing to attend school regularly;
6. Exploited, overworked;
7. Emotionally disturbed due to constant friction in the home, marital discord, mentally ill parents; and/or
8. Exposed to unwholesome, demoralizing circumstances.[111]

Web PLACES 8.6

Visit the Institute on Violence, Abuse, and Trauma's website via **www.justicestudies.com/ WebPlaces**.

Defining neglect in legal or social terms, nevertheless, does not begin to capture an accurate picture of the neglected child. Such children must be seen if an observer is to realize the true hopelessness of their existence.[112] Newspapers frequently report the deaths of young children due to neglect or child abuse. As tragic as these cases are, however, Widom asked, "But what happens to the children who survive? The babies abandoned on streets or in hospitals, children left unattended for days without food in filthy roach-infested apartments, or children brutally abused?"[113]

In studying the case records of 180 families that had come to the attention of authorized agencies, Leontine Young separated them into cases of severe and moderate neglect and severe and moderate abuse. She defined severe neglect as occurring when parents fed their children inadequately and failed to keep their children clean, to furnish adequate clothing, and to provide proper medical care. Parents who were involved in moderate neglect usually fed their children, but their children were not kept clean, nor did they have adequate clothing or proper medical care.[114]

Norman A. Polansky and colleagues' studies of neglect in Georgia and North Carolina identified five types of mothers who are frequently guilty of child neglect. The apathetic–futile mother is emotionally numb to her children and neglects both their physical and emotional needs. The impulse-ridden mother is restless and craves excitement, movement, and change. She is unable to tolerate stress or frustration and is aggressive and defiant. Typically, she neglects her children by simply taking off on an escapade with a husband or a boyfriend and letting the children fend for themselves. The mentally retarded mother has difficulty providing adequate care for her children, especially if her IQ is below 60. If emotional problems are combined with mental deficiency, then severe neglect is even more likely. The mother in a reaction depression is preoccupied with the loss of a loved one or some other traumatic event. Her persistent feelings of despair and sadness can lead to physiological illness to the degree that she is unable to cope with her own reality, much less provide for her chil-

FOCUS ON
Social Policy 8.2

Children Who Are at Greater Risk of Victimization

The *Child Maltreatment 2004* survey identified several factors that influenced the determination that a child would officially be found to be a victim of maltreatment:

- Children with allegations of multiple types of maltreatment were nearly three times more likely to be determined by authorities to be maltreated than were children with allegations of physical abuse.
- Children reported to be victims of sexual abuse were about 71 percent more likely to be considered victims than children with allegations of physical abuse only.

- Children who were reported to be disabled were 68 percent more likely found to be a victim of maltreatment than children who were not disabled.
- Children who were reported by educational personnel were twice as likely to be considered maltreated as children reported by social and mental health personnel.
- Findings of victimization were inversely related to the ages of a child. Children who were younger than four years old were most likely determined to be maltreated compared to all other age groups.

> ■ Why do you think children whose cases are reported by educational personnel are more likely found to be maltreated than those reported by social and mental health personnel?

Source: Children's Bureau, *Child Maltreatment 2004* (Washington, D.C.: U.S. Department of Health and Human Services, 2004), p. 26.

---

dren. Finally, the borderline or psychotic mother, lost in her fantasies, may forget to feed the children or may even kill the children and herself in a psychotic outburst.[115]

Polansky and colleagues replicated their Appalachian study with an examination of neglect in Philadelphia. This study concluded that a general immaturity or high degree of infantilism was the strongest predictor of maternal neglect. The neglectful mother was likely to have been abused as a child, was isolated from informal helping networks, had a low rate of participation in formal organizations, had a lower IQ than the mothers used as controls, had more emotional pathology than the controls, and was "dirt" poor. The researchers also found that apathetic–futile and impulse-ridden mothers were far more common in the Philadelphia study than in the Appalachian study.[116]

Polansky and colleagues, based on the data from these two research projects, developed the Childhood Level of Living (CLL) scale. Originally designed to assess families with children between the ages of four and seven, the CLL has since been used for a wider range of ages. The scale presents nine descriptive categories; five assess physical care, and the other four assess cognitive, emotional, and psychological factors.[117] Realizing the limitations of the CLL scale, especially for issues of cultural diversity, a panel of child maltreatment experts in Ontario developed the Child Neglect Index (CNI). This scale assesses neglect in six areas: (1) supervision, (2) food and nutrition, (3) clothing and hygiene, (4) physical health care, (5) mental health care, and (6) developmental–educational care.[118]

Physical and Emotional Abuse   The term *physical abuse* refers to intentional behavior directed toward a child by the parents or caretaker to cause pain, injury, or death. Gelles and Claire Pedrick Cornell described a case in which a parent attempted to kill her child:

> Sue was a single parent who lived in a fourth-floor walk-up apartment. Her husband had left her three years earlier, and child support payments stopped within weeks of the final divorce decree. Poverty and illness were as much a part of Sue's home as the busy activity of her 4-year-old daughter Nancy. One cold gray March afternoon, Sue took Nancy out for a walk. Together they hiked up the steep pedestal of a suspension bridge that rose

up behind their apartment. At the top of the bridge, Sue hugged Nancy and then threw her off the bridge. She jumped a moment later.[119]

What was unusual about this case is that both Nancy and Sue survived. Plucked from the icy water by a fishing boat, mother and child were taken to different hospitals. When Nancy was released from the hospital six months later, she was placed out of the home. Sue's parental rights were terminated.[120]

Murray A. Straus has been one of the strongest proponents of defining corporal punishment as physical abuse. Straus examined the extent of physical abuse using data from a number of sources, notably the 3,300 children and 6,000 couples in the National Family Violence Survey. He found that 90 percent of U.S. citizens used physical punishment to correct misbehavior. He claimed that although physical punishment may produce conformity in the immediate situation, its long-run effect is to increase the probability of delinquency in adolescence and violent crime inside and outside the family.[121]

According to Straus, the most frequent forms of corporal punishment are slapping, spanking, hitting with certain objects (e.g., hairbrush, paddle, belt), grabbing, and shoving a child roughly. Straus pointed out that nearly every child has been hit by parents, that mothers hit children more than fathers do, that no relationship exists between parents' social class and corporal punishment, and that those parents who were hit as children are more likely to hit their own children.[122] Straus identifies what he considers to be several myths of corporal punishment:

1. Spanking works better than anything else.
2. Spanking is needed when everything else fails.
3. Spanking is harmless to the child.
4. Spanking a child one or two times won't cause any damage.
5. Spanking is something that parents can't stop without training or treatment.
6. Spanking is necessary or a child will be spoiled or run wild.
7. Spanking is something that parents rarely do or do only for serious problems.
8. Spanking no longer takes place by the time a child is a teenager.
9. Spanking is necessary or parents will verbally abuse their child.
10. Spanking is an inevitable part of child rearing; indeed, it is unrealistic to expect parents never to spank.[123]

One of the reasons that Straus and others are so opposed to corporal punishment is that they claim it legitimizes violence in children. They contend that it does this by weakening the bond to parent or teacher, by undermining faith in justice, by labeling children as "bad," by providing children with less opportunity to learn alternatives to violence, and by lowering self-esteem.[124]

Emotional abuse is more difficult to define than physical abuse because it involves a disregard for the psychological needs of a child or adolescent. Emotional abuse encompasses a lack of expressed love and affection as well as deliberate withholding of contact and approval. Emotional abuse may include a steady diet of putdowns, humiliation, labeling, name-calling, scapegoating, lying, demands for excessive responsibility, seductive behavior, ignoring, fear-inducing techniques, unrealistic expectations, and extreme inconsistency.[125] Randy, a sixteen-year-old boy, tells of emotional abuse he suffered:

> My father bought me a baby raccoon. I was really close to it, and it was really close to me. I could sleep with it, and it would snug up beside me. The raccoon wouldn't leave or nothing. A friend of mine got shots for it. My father got mad one night because I didn't vacuum the rug, and there were seven or eight dishes in the sink. He said "Go get me your raccoon." I said, "Dad, if you hurt my raccoon I'll hate you forever." He made me go get my raccoon, and he took a hammer and killed it. He hit it twice on the head and crushed its brains. I took it out and buried it.[126]

Nature of Abuse Some theorists argue that child abuse has five basic explanations: (1) structural factors such as lower socioeconomic class, large family size, or single parenting; (2) the mental illness of parents; (3) a parent's history of abuse as a child; (4) transitory situational factors, including such "triggers" as alcohol, drug use, or un-

Web PLACES 8.7

Visit the National Center for Children Exposed to Violence via **www.justicestudies.com/WebPlaces**.

emotional abuse

A disregard for the psychological needs of a child, including lack of expressed love, withholding of contact or approval, verbal abuse, unrealistic demands, threats, psychological cruelty, and so on.

employment; and (5) a particularly difficult, demanding, or problematic child. Stephanie Amedeo and John Gartrell's study of 218 abused children found that the characteristics of parents, including mental illness and having been abused themselves, have the greatest explanatory power of predicting abuse. Also, this study revealed that triggers or stressors, such as alcohol and drug use, perform as factors that precipitate abuse.[127]

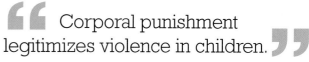
" Corporal punishment legitimizes violence in children. "

Blair and Rita Justice contended that eight models explain the causes of abuse: (1) the psychodynamic model, (2) the character trait or personality model, (3) the social learning model, (4) the family structure model, (5) the environmental stress model, (6) the social–psychological model, (7) the mental illness model, and (8) the psychosocial systems model.[128]

More recently, O. C. S. Tzeng and colleagues identified nine paradigms, each of which encompasses several theories or models:

1. The Individual Determinants Paradigm includes several theories dealing with the abnormal characteristics of the perpetrator.
2. The Sociocultural Determinants Paradigm covers social systems theory.
3. The Individual–Environment Interaction Paradigm involves theories considering the interaction between abusers and their environments.
4. The Offender Typology Paradigm fits abusers into specific categories.
5. The Family Systems Paradigm views the abusive family as a social system.
6. The Parent–Child Interaction Paradigm includes five theories outlining parental interaction with the child.
7. The Sociobiological Paradigm emphasizes the role played by genetic factors in human behavior.
8. The Learning Situational Paradigm applies learning theory to abusive situations, suggesting that abusive–violent behavior is learned.
9. The Ecological Paradigm brings together theories using the variables of the individual, the family, the community, and all cultural and societal factors to explain abuse.[129]

David G. Gil, in developing a classification of abusive families, found that seven situations accounted for 97.3 percent of the reported abuse cases:

1. Psychological rejection, leading to repeated abuse and battering.
2. Disciplinary measures taken in uncontrolled anger.
3. Male babysitter's acting out sadistic and sexual impulses in the mother's temporary absence, at times under the influence of alcohol.
4. Mentally or emotionally disturbed caretaker's causing mounting environmental stress.
5. Misconduct and persistent negative behavior of a child, leading to his or her own abuse.
6. Female babysitter's abusing child during the mother's temporary absence.
7. Quarrel between caretakers, at times when under the influence of alcohol.[130]

Research findings disagree concerning the age at which a child is most vulnerable to parental abuse. The National Incidence and Prevalence of Child Abuse and Neglect study found that the incidence of physical abuse increased with age.[131] Gil found that half the confirmed cases of abuse involved children over six years of age and that nearly one-fifth were teenagers.[132] Yet, while many adolescents may experience child abuse, the more serious cases still occur with infants and young children, who are more susceptible to injury. Indeed, according to some researchers, three months to three years of age is the most dangerous period in a child's life.[133] Teenagers are more physically durable, are able to protect themselves better, and can leave the home if parents become too abusive.

Child abuse also seems to be more prevalent in urban areas than in suburban or rural settings. Urban areas' having better resources to detect child abuse does not entirely explain why so many more cases are reported to urban police. Obviously, the congested populations and poverty of the city, which lead to other social problems, partly account for abuse being predominantly an urban problem.

The abusive situation is often characterized by one parent who is aggressive and one who is passive. The passive parent commonly defends the aggressive one, denies the realities of the family situation, and clings to the intact family and to the abusive partner. The passive parent behaves as though he or she is a prisoner in the relationship, condemned to a life sentence. This parent usually does not consider the option of separating from the aggressive partner because he or she is committed to the relationship, no matter how miserable the home situation may be.[134]

Child Sexual Abuse   Children and adolescents may be victimized by either nonfamilial sexual abuse or incestuous sexual abuse. **Child sexual abuse** is intentional and wrongful physical contact with a child that entails a sexual purpose or component. Oral–genital relations, the fondling of erogenous areas of the body, mutual masturbation, and intercourse are typical sexually abusive acts.[135]

Incest, according to the National Center on Child Abuse and Neglect, is "intrafamily sexual abuse which is perpetrated on a child by a member of that child's family group and includes not only sexual intercourse, but also any act designed to stimulate a child sexually or to use a child for sexual stimulation, either of the perpetrator or of another person."[136]

Nonfamilial sexual abusers may include any unrelated adult the child encounters outside the home (e.g., at school, church, recreational venues, etc.). Incestuous sexual abusers may include a parent, grandparent, stepparent, sibling, aunt, uncle, or other member of the child's extended family.

Linda Gordon's examination of incest from 1880 to 1930 found that incest appeared in 10 percent of case records of Boston child protection agencies. Ninety-eight percent of these cases were father–daughter incest and had a common pattern: the family relations made the girl victims into second wives. That is, these victims took over many of the functions and roles of mothers, including housework, sexual relations, and child care with their father. Despite their apparent acquiescence and obedience in these incestuous families, many of these girls actively sought escape from

Ronald Carroll McDonald (*left*), age seventy-one, of Lake Forest Park, Washington, pleads guilty in 1997 in a Seattle court to child rape and molestation charges. To many children, a photograph taken with McDonald was a Christmas tradition since he worked as Santa Claus in a local mall. ■ **Although cases involving sexual predators seem to appear in the news almost daily, national statistics show that the sexual abuse of children by their parents or guardians has declined significantly in the last decade or two. What might account for that decline?**

FIGURE 8.4

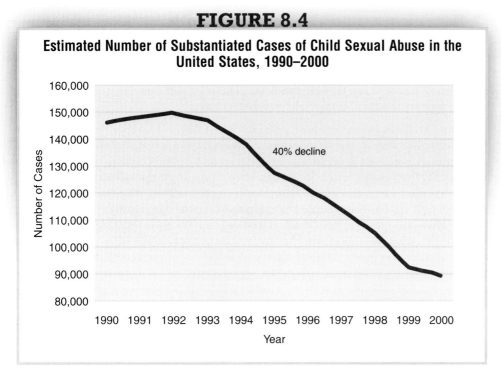

Estimated Number of Substantiated Cases of Child Sexual Abuse in the United States, 1990–2000

Source: David Finkelhor and Lisa M. Jones, *Explanations for the Decline in Child Sexual Abuse Cases* (Washington, D.C.: Office of Juvenile Justice and Delinquency Prevention, 2004), citing data from 1990–2000 National Child Abuse and Neglect Data System (NCANDS) reports (U.S. Department of Health and Human Services, 1992–2002).

their victimization and loitered on the streets, where their low self-esteem made them easily exploitable.[137]

In more recent times, the number of sexual abuse cases substantiated by child protective service agencies in the United States underwent a dramatic 40 percent reduction between 1992 and 2000. Opinion is divided as to why the estimated annual incidence dropped from 150,000 to 89,500 cases. See Figure 8.4 for substantiated cases of child sexual abuse in the United States from 1990 to 2000. The trend has occurred in the majority of states; of forty-nine states, thirty-nine experienced a total decline of 30 percent or more in substantiated cases of sexual abuse from their peak year to 2000.[138]

The decline in child sexual abuse, according to National Child Abuse and Neglect Data System (NCANDS) data, appears to account largely for a concurrent 15 percent decline in child maltreatment. Although neglect cases fluctuated during the 1990s with no overall decline, physical abuse has declined 30 percent since a peak in 1995. This decline in physical abuse is significant, but it is smaller and more recent than the decline in sexual abuse. In fact, the largest proportion of the decline in physical abuse (15 percent) occurred between 1998 and 1999, whereas the more gradual 40 percent decline in sexual abuse took place over an eight-year period.[139] Some explanations for this decline in sexual abuse are provided in Focus on Social Policy 8.3.

Incest reportedly occurs most frequently between a biological father or stepfather and a daughter, but it also may involve brother and sister, mother and son, and father and son.[140] Father–daughter incest usually is a devastating experience for the girl and sometimes has lifelong consequences. Stepfathers also sexually victimize stepdaughters, but biological fathers appear to be involved in more cases of sexual abuse than are stepfathers. Angela Browne and Finkelhor's review of the literature on sexual abuse revealed that abuse by fathers or stepfathers has a more negative impact than abuse by others. Experiences involving genital contact and force seem to result in more trauma for the victim.[141] The average incestuous relationship lasts about three and one-half to four years.[142] The completed act of intercourse is more likely to take place with adolescents than with younger children.

Helen, a sixteen-year-old, was sexually victimized by her father for three years. She had great difficulty getting anyone to believe that her father was committing incest. When the father was finally prosecuted, she made this statement:

> When I was thirteen, my father started coming into my room at night. He usually did it when he was drinking. He would force me to have sex with him. I told my mother. I told my teachers at school. But nobody would believe me.[143]

Some evidence exists that brother–sister incest takes place more frequently than father–daughter incest, but its long-term consequences are usually less damaging because it does not cross generational boundaries and often occurs as an extension of sex play.[144] But brother–sister incest can have damaging consequences for the sister if the act is discovered and she is blamed for being sexually involved with her brother. If the girl feels she has been seduced or exploited, then the damage may be even greater.

Mother–son incest is less common and only rarely reported, largely because of the strong stigmas and taboos attached to the idea of sex between boys and their mothers.[145] Mother–son incest usually begins with excessive physical contact, which eventually becomes sexually stimulating. "Don't leave me" or "don't grow up" messages are communicated to the son as the mother seeks ways to prolong physical contact with him, sleeping with him, bathing him, or dressing him.[146]

Father–son incest also is rarely reported, largely because it violates both the moral code against incest and the taboo against homosexuality. The stress of an incestuous relationship, as well as the threat to masculinity, often results in serious consequences for the boy when father–son incest does occur. Sons who are involved in father–son incest usually experience acute anxiety because they feel damaged, dirty, and worthless. They may cope by retreating into their own world and losing contact with reality.[147]

FOCUS ON Social Policy 8.3

The Decline in Child Sexual Abuse Cases

State child protection administrators frequently offer six explanations for why the 1990s saw a decline in substantiated cases of child sexual abuse:

- Increasing conservatism within child protective services (CPS). In this view, sexual abuse cases were declining in state caseloads because CPS agencies were adopting more conservative standards regarding "questionable" cases (e.g., allegations arising in divorces and custody disputes) or cases with weak initial evidence.
- Exclusion of cases that did not involve caretakers. In this view, CPS agencies were increasingly excluding from their jurisdiction sexual abuse cases in which the perpetrator was not a primary caretaker.
- Changes in CPS data collection methods or definitions. In this view, the decline was due to changes in the way CPS tabulated or counted its cases, such as a change from a three-tiered classification system (substantiated/indicated/unsubstantiated) to a two-tiered system (substantiated/unsubstantiated).
- Less reporting to CPS due to a sexual abuse backlash. In this view, negative publicity about sexual abuse cases and the potential liability of professionals made agencies more reluctant to report child sexual abuse.
- A diminishing reservoir of older cases. In this view, there was a reduction in the number of older but previously undisclosed cases available for new disclosures despite no true decline in new cases.
- A real decline in the incidence of sexual abuse. In this view, there was a reduction in the number of children actually being abused as a result of increased prevention efforts, more prosecution and incarceration of offenders, or other social or cultural changes.

No solid and convincing evidence exists for why sexual abuse cases declined in the 1990s. In all likelihood multiple factors were involved; still, based on the strength of current evidence, there probably was a true decline in the occurrence of sexual abuse.

■ What experiences have you had that would help you form an opinion as to whether there has been a significant decline in sexual abuse? Do you believe this apparent decline will continue in the future?

Source: David Finkelhor and Lisa M. Jones, *Explanations for the Decline in Child Sexual Abuse Cases* (Washington, D.C.: Office of Juvenile Justice and Delinquency Prevention, 2004).

The National Center on Child Abuse and Neglect has identified five factors that are usually present when father–daughter incest takes place: (1) the daughter's voluntary or forced assumption of the mother's role, (2) the parents' sexual incompatibility, (3) the father's reluctance to seek a partner outside the family unit, (4) the family's fear of disintegration, and (5) unconscious sanctioning by the mother.[148]

Justice and Justice have developed a classification that is helpful in understanding the behavior of fathers who commit incest.[149] They divide incestuous fathers into four groups: symbiotic personalities, psychopathic personalities, pedophilic personalities, and a small group of "others."

Symbiotic personalities, who make up 70 to 80 percent of the incestuous fathers, have strong unmet needs for warmth and for someone to whom they can be close. They hunger for a sense of belonging and intimacy. These fathers are out of touch with their needs and do not know how to meet them in healthy ways. These men, more than the others, look to the family to satisfy all their emotional needs. As relationships with their wives deteriorate, they turn to their daughters to satisfy their emotional and physical needs. They use a variety of rationalizations to justify their sexual abuse—for example, that physical intimacy is the highest form of love a father can show his daughter or that a father has exclusive property rights over the daughter and therefore can do whatever he wants. Alcohol is often used to loosen restraints on these fathers' behavior; after the sexual activity, they often blame the alcohol rather than themselves.

Psychopathic personalities seek stimulation and excitement through incestuous relationships. Sex is simply a vehicle to express the hostility they feel and to obtain the excitement they have felt deprived of in the past. The psychopath feels no guilt and has little capacity to love; he simply wants immediate gratification of his needs. Fortunately, this type of incestuous father is rare.

Pedophilic personalities are attracted to young children who show no signs of physical and sexual development. These extremely immature fathers have erotic cravings for children. They want sexual activity with someone who will not reject or belittle them. Only a small amount of incest is committed by these immature and inadequate personalities.

The Justices' "other" types include psychotic fathers and those who come from a subculture that permits incest. Psychotic fathers, who make up about 3 percent of incestuous fathers, experience hallucinations and delusions, and they are most often responsible for using force in incest. In some cultural groups it is normal for the oldest daughter to assume her mother's role, both in the kitchen and in bed. The youngest daughter also is often introduced to sex by her father or brothers. This group of fathers accounts for only a small fraction of the cases of incest, because culturally sanctioned incest has lost much of the acceptance it had in the past.

Abuse, Neglect, and Delinquency

An abused or neglected child is more likely to become involved in delinquency or status offenses. Neglect or abuse may have a negative impact on the emotional development of the child; it may lead to truancy and disruptive behavior in school, running away from home, or generate so much pain that alcohol and drugs are sometimes viewed as a needed escape. Neglect or abuse may cause so much self-rejection, especially in victims of incest, that these youths may vent their self-destructiveness through prostitution or may even commit suicide. Neglect or abuse may also create so much anger that abused youngsters later commit aggressive acts against others.

> An abused or neglected child is more likely to become involved in delinquency or status offenses.

Emotional Trauma of Child Abuse and Neglect   Victimized children have never received the love and nurturing necessary for healthy growth and development. They often feel abandoned and lack the security of being a part of a "real" family. They struggle, sometimes all their lives, to get the nurturing and the feeling of being cared for that they have never experienced.

Dirty children stand in front of run-down houses in a small Vermont town. Neglect is the most common form of child maltreatment today, and can involve a lack of food, clothing, medical care, and parental supervision. When neglect occurs, siblings may be left to care for one another as best they can. ■ **What social and economic factors might lead to an increased incidence of child neglect?**

Victims of child abuse and neglect often have low self-esteem, considerable guilt, high anxiety, mild to serious depression, and high internal conflict.[150] Physically, they may experience disturbances in sleeping patterns, weight loss or gain, or continual illnesses. They also tend to have poor social relationships.[151] Psychotherapists report a large number of child abuse victims among their clients.[152] They also note that women who were sexually abused as children often suffer from depression.[153]

Sometimes the emotional problems of abused children are so serious that they have difficulty functioning in family, social, or institutional settings. A social worker in a midwestern youth shelter described such youths:

> Some parents are really, really sick, but they don't see it. You can't get them to treatment. You get into some really messy situations. Their kids receive so little support that they feel so rejected and so mishandled that their only hope for survival into adulthood is to find someone in some institution or in some foster family that will make a commitment to them and will help them survive on their own. These kids need someone that will help them realize that what happened to them in their lives was not their fault and that they need to develop their own strengths so that they can feel good about themselves.[154]

Runaways   Teenagers who have been abused frequently run away from home.[155] One sexually abused girl explained: "I never thought about where I was running to—only what I was running from."[156] **Running away** becomes a way of coping with the pain of neglect, physical abuse, and sexual abuse. The youth often sees running away as the only way to manage an unmanageable problem. Parents sometimes tell a child to get out because they want to rid themselves of the problems that the abusive situation has created.

When abused adolescents are placed in foster homes, their running may not stop. They often choose to reject their new family rather than risk the possibility of being rejected again. Unfortunately, sometimes children are removed from abusive homes only to experience abuse all over again in a foster home.

running away

Leaving the custody and home of parents or guardians without permission and failing to return within a reasonable length of time. A status offense.

Disruptive and Truant Behavior in School   Several studies have found that abused and neglected children have greater difficulty in school than children who are not abused.[157] According to R. S. Kempe and C. H. Kempe, "Many of these children become academic and social failures almost immediately upon entering school."[158] Abused and neglected school-age children tend to have deficiencies in language development,[159] are more frequently placed in special education classes,[160] are more likely to be assigned to classes for children with disabilities,[161] have more learning problems,[162] are more disobedient and have a greater difficulty accepting authority,[163] and have more conflict with peers.[164]

Teachers who have worked with abused and neglected children add that these children have difficulty in concentrating, are aloof, have little or no confidence, frequently have emotional outbursts, lack internalized rules, and are often destructive of property.[165] Abused and neglected children are often labeled disruptive in the public school, are assigned to special learning classes, and are thus set up for failure.

Drug and Alcohol Abuse   In an effort to blot out their pain and isolation, many abused children turn to drug and alcohol abuse.[166] Widom found that abused and neglected adolescent females were at increased risk for drug offenses.[167] S. D. Peters found an association between sexual abuse and later alcohol abuse.[168] Richard Dembo and colleagues, in an examination of a sample of youths in a detention center, reported that sexual victimization had a direct effect on drug use, whereas physical abuse had an indirect and direct effect on drug use.[169] An adolescent female from an abusive home said, "Drugs became my great escape; there wasn't nothing I wouldn't try to get high."[170] Abused children often feel they have nothing to lose by taking drugs; they are concerned only with forgetting their insecurity, anxiety, and lack of confidence. A type of love and trust relationship that they have never had with people before sometimes develops through drugs. They can finally belong, experiencing closeness and security with peers who also take drugs.

Barbara L. Myers, former director of Christopher Street, Inc., and a victim of sexual abuse as an adolescent, told why she turned to drugs:

> I was eleven years old when I first discovered that drugs could make the terrible world around me disappear. . . . When I was on drugs, I felt high, happy, and in control of my life. When I was high, I had peers; I finally belonged somewhere—in a group with other kids who took drugs. Whatever the others were taking, I took twice as much or more. I wasn't aware like the rest of them; I got high without worrying about how much I could handle or what it would do to me. It made me feel big and powerful because I didn't care what happened to me.
>
> People said that taking too many drugs would burn out your brains. I used to think that I could become a vegetable if only I could succeed in burning out my brains. I wanted to be a vegetable. I used to picture myself as a head of lettuce. I used to look at mentally retarded people and think that they were so happy and didn't care about anything. I envied them because you could spit at them, and they would smile; they didn't seem to understand what hurt was.[171]

Sexual Behavior   A study of 535 young women who became pregnant as teenagers found that 66 percent had been sexually abused as children.[172] Considerable evidence shows that sexual abuse victims themselves often become involved in deviant sexual behavior. Promiscuity appears to be high among female sexual abuse victims.[173] Many female sexual abuse victims also become involved in prostitution,[174] and sexual abuse is frequently a part of the background of male prostitutes.[175]

It is not surprising that female sexual abuse victims are attracted to prostitution, because they have come to see themselves as shamed, marked, and good only for delivering sex. The self-destructive aspect of prostitution serves as another way of expressing rage for never having been loved and for having been sexually and/or physically abused. In prostitution, sexual abuse victims take control by making strangers pay for sex. Detachment has already been learned in childhood; therefore, it is relatively easy for them to disassociate themselves from brief sexual encounters.[176]

Violence and Abuse   The idea that violence begets violence is firmly entrenched in both the minds of professionals and those of the general public. There is considerable support for the finding that abused and neglected male victims are more likely to express their anger in ways that hurt others, whereas female victims of mistreatment are more likely to become self-destructive.[177] There is also substantial support for the finding that those who have been abused or neglected in the past are more likely to abuse or neglect their children than those who have not experienced abuse or neglect. For example, in reviewing the research on family violence, Gelles noted:

> One of the consistent conclusions of domestic violence research is that individuals who have experienced violent and abusive childhoods are more likely to grow up and become child and spouse abusers than individuals who have experienced little or no violence in their childhood.[178]

Several studies have found a positive relationship between abuse and neglect and later violent criminal acts. One study found that 85 percent of a group of teenagers who had committed murder unrelated to another crime had received severe corporal punishment as children.[179] Another investigation of crimes showed that in one-third of all homicides committed by adolescents in the state of New York, the delinquent had been either neglected or abused at home.[180] Thornberry, using data from the Rochester Youth Development Study, found that 69 percent of youths who were maltreated as children reported later involvement in violence, compared to 57 percent of those who were not maltreated.[181] Social World of the Delinquent 8.1 presents a possible link between abuse and children who kill their parents.

Child abuse appears in the backgrounds of many famous murderers; for example, Charles Manson was severely abused as a child. In 1976, this link between homicide and abuse was legally recognized when a jury acquitted a youth who had murdered five young women, deeming him "innocent by virtue of insanity" because he had multiple personalities created by the severe abuse he had received at home.[182]

However, other studies have reported that abused and nonabused delinquents did not differ in terms of violent behavior.[183] Jeffrey Fagan and colleagues found a low incidence of child abuse and parental violence among violent youthful offenders.[184] In a study of a North Carolina institutionalized population, Zingraff and Michael J. Belyea

SOCIAL WORLD of the Delinquent 8.1

Why Kids Kill Their Parents

Approximately three hundred parents are killed each year by their children. Kathleen M. Heide has contended that killing a parent is frequently "an act of desperation—the only way out of a family situation of abuse [the killer-child] can no longer endure." She claimed that there are three types of youths who kill their parents: (1) the severely abused child who is pushed beyond his or her limits, (2) the severely mentally ill child, and (3) the dangerously antisocial child. According to Heide's research, the severely abused child is the most frequently encountered type of offender.

She found that the characteristics of the severely abused child who kills one or both parents are:

- They are not violent.
- They are abused.
- Their parents are most likely substance abusers.
- They are isolated.
- They kill only when they feel there is no one to help them.
- They "block out" the murder, not revel in it.
- They see no other choice.
- They are sorry for what they did.

■ **If you were a social worker in a male institution and a severely abused juvenile on your caseload had killed his mother, how would you help him come to grips with what he had done? What would you do first, second, third, and so forth?**

Sources: Kathleen M. Heide, "Why Kids Kill," *Psychology Today* 25 (September–October 1992), pp. 62–77; Kathleen M. Heide, "Parents Who Get Killed and the Children Who Kill Them," *Journal of Interpersonal Violence* 8 (December 1993), pp. 531–544.

British medical student Brian Blackwell (*left*), age nineteen, pled guilty in 2005 to the murder of his father Sydney, (*right*), age seventy-two, and his mother Jacqueline, age sixty-one. The killings occurred at their home in Melling, England. ■ **A feature in this chapter says that some children kill their parents out of desperation. Might desperation have been the cause here? Why or why not?**

concluded that "abuse experienced as a child is neither a necessary nor sufficient condition for violent adult behavior."[185] Sara E. Gutierres and John W. Reich even reported that abused delinquents were less likely to engage in later aggressive acts.[186]

The Family and the Life Course

With the emergence of the life-course perspective, there has been increased empirical and theoretical interest in the role played by family relations both in fostering and in protecting against delinquent and drug involvements. Studies have documented the family-related risk factors that increase delinquency propensity. Researchers have most frequently explored the impact on delinquency of the informal social control exercised by parents and within families.[187]

Gottfredson and Hirschi's self-control theory argues that the principal cause of individuals' low self-control is ineffective parenting. Ineffective parents are those who fail to monitor their children, to recognize deviant behavior when it takes place, and to punish such deviance. They are likely to have children who are low in self-control and therefore are more delinquent.[188] Carter Hay's findings from a sample of urban high school students generally supported Gottfredson and Travis's position, linking ineffective parenting, low self-control in children, and higher rates of delinquency.[189]

Some research has examined the links between corporal punishment and adolescent delinquent behavior and drug use. Ronald L. Simons and colleagues found that when parents engage in severe forms of corporal punishment with the absence of parental involvement and warmth, children tend to feel angry and unjustly treated, resist parental authority, and are likely to become involved in delinquent behavior.[190] As mentioned earlier, Karen Heimer also found that families who use coercive discipline merely teach their children that force and violence are appropriate tactics for solving problems. Children thus learn definitions favorable to violence, which encourage them to be more prone to violent delinquent behavior.[191]

A Parent's Right to Know

In December, 2005, the U.S. Supreme Court heard arguments in *Ayotte v. Planned Parenthood*, a case concerning the right of parents to be notified on abortions given to minor children. The case is seen as a bellwether on the court's shifting majority on abortion as well as the future of parental notice and consent laws in 43 states.

Cases like *Ayotte* are produced by a collision of two powerful interests: The right of parents to participate in major medical and moral decisions affecting their minor children vs. the right of children to have abortions.

Pro-choice advocates have opposed parental notice and consent laws with unbridled passion that often seems more a matter of blind faith than reasoned principle. Recently, Becca Pawling, who heads a women's group in Portsmouth, N.H., explained that opposition is based on the simple fact that "any limitations put on [abortion] is heading backward in time."

Pawling's comment captures how abortion has become a zero-sum game for pro-choice groups: Every curb on abortion is seen as an equal loss for women's rights. It is a view that is not shared by most citizens, who see abortion in the context of other legitimate interests—not some absolute right that trumps all other rights.

Polls have consistently shown that a vast majority of Americans, including pro-choice citizens, favor either parental notice or consent for abortions performed on minors. In late 2005, a USA TODAY/CNN/Gallup Poll showed that 69% of citizens favored requiring minors to get parental consent. Polls routinely show that 75%–80% of citizens favor parental notice.

No Absolute Right

The absolutist view is equally at odds with our constitutional traditions. There are no absolute individual rights in our Constitution. The Framers forged a system protecting individual rights while recognizing legitimate countervailing interests of the state. In that balanced system, even such fundamental rights as the freedom of speech and free press, association and religion have been subject to some limitations.

For example, when states prohibit screaming "fire" in a crowded theater, they are not diminishing free speech. Such reckless conduct is not part of any reasonable definition of the right to free speech, just as the categorical exclusion of required parental participation is not part of any reasonable definition of the right to an abortion.

Pro-choice advocates would make abortion the only absolute right in our Constitution, even though it was not fully recognized by the Supreme Court until 1973. Conversely, parental rights have been recognized since the founding of our Republic but are routinely dismissed when they collide with the almighty right to an abortion.

As a pro-choice law professor, I was astonished to find myself on opposite sides with groups such as the ACLU when I helped draft Florida's parental notice amendment to its constitution. In Florida, a child could not get a tattoo or take an aspirin in school without parental consent, but any 12-year-old could walk into a clinic and demand an abortion without notifying her parents of a major medical procedure.

The amendment contained a requirement that any law would include a standard judicial bypass provision. Such bypass provisions allow courts to forgo parental notification for any number of reasons, including rape, incest, risk to the child, or where notification was not in the best interests of the child.

Hard-Core Minority

Pro-choice groups in Florida rallied against parental notice, even with a judicial bypass. As I sat in those hearings, I kept wondering whom these groups represent. Most pro-choice Americans favor parental involvement in abortions for minors. It is a hard-core minority that resists any and all limitations. Yet, those are the zealots that tend to give money and seek positions in advocacy organizations. The result is that both the pro-life and pro-choice movements tend to be led by the most extreme, not the most representative, voices of their respective constituencies.

The U.S. Supreme Court building in Washington, D.C. In 2005, the Court considered the right of parents to be notified when their minor children seek abortions. The case, *Ayotte v. Planned Parenthood*, centered on New Hampshire's Parental Notification Prior to Abortion Act. The Court did not issue a definitive ruling and sent the case back to lower courts for further consideration. ■ **Should parents be notified when their minor children seek abortions?**

Pro-choice groups generally cite anecdotal accounts of girls who are made pregnant by their fathers or have a history of abuse—ignoring the exceptions for such cases under bypass provisions. The fact is that most fathers are not incestuous rapists. Likewise, most parents are not unhinged throwbacks who simply cannot handle juvenile pregnancies. Indeed, parents know a lot more about their children than do abortion advocates or judges. They have the history and connection with their kids to help them get through the trauma of such a pregnancy. Even in the most caring families, though, children often try to hide misconduct rather than face recrimination or embarrassment. The law should not reinforce those inclinations by allowing minors to bar parental knowledge or consent.

What these groups fail to recognize is that the rights of speech, association and religion mean little if parents cannot teach and reinforce moral choices within their families. Family values and integrity are not the enemies of the right to privacy but the very things that privacy is meant to protect.

Source: Jonathan Turley, "A Parent's Right to Know," *USA Today*, December 6, 2005, p. A13. Copyright © 2005 by Jonathan Turley. Used by permission of the author.

There is some evidence that childhood maltreatment that does not persist into adolescence has minimal correlation with adolescent delinquency.[192] There is wide agreement, however, that the maltreatment of adolescents increases the risk of their antisocial behavior during their teen years.[193] The negative influence of severe maltreatment, such as sexual abuse by parents or caretakers, is commonly seen as carrying into adulthood and perhaps even throughout the life course. However, Peggy Giordano, Stephen A. Cernkovich, and Jennifer L. Rudolph's study of women across the life course is a reminder that female offenders who suffered extremely abusive childhoods can still have cognitive transformations as adults and can desist from criminal behaviors.[194]

Child Abuse and the Juvenile Justice System

The term *child protective services* usually refers to services that are provided by an agency authorized to act on behalf of a child when parents are unwilling or unable to do so. In all states, these agencies are required by law to conduct assessments or investigations of reports of child abuse and neglect and to offer treatment services to families where maltreatment has taken place or is likely to occur.[195]

Although the primary responsibility for responding to reports of abuse and neglect rests with state and local child protective service agencies, the prevention and treatment of child maltreatment can involve professionals from many organizations and disciplines. Jurisdictions do differ in their procedures, but community responses to child maltreatment generally include the following sequences of events:

Identification
- Individuals who are likely to identify abuse are often those in a position to observe families and children on a regular basis. These include educators, medical professionals, police officers, social service personnel, probation officers, day-care workers, and the clergy. Family members, friends, and neighbors also may be able to identify abuse.

Reporting
- Some individuals—educators, child care providers, medical and mental health professionals, social service providers, police officers, and clergy—often are required by law to report suspicions of abuse and neglect. Some states require such reporting by any person who has knowledge of abuse or neglect.
- Child protective services or law enforcement agencies generally receive the initial report of alleged abuse or neglect. This initial report may include the identity of the child and information about the alleged maltreatment, the parent or other caretaker of the child, the setting in which maltreatment took place, and the person making the report.

Intake and Investigation
- Protective service staff are required to determine whether the report constitutes an allegation of abuse or neglect and how urgently a response is needed. The initial investigation involves gathering and analyzing information about the child and family. Protective service agencies may work with law enforcement during this intake investigation.
- In some jurisdictions, a police officer always accompanies the social worker on the child abuse or neglect investigation to protect the social worker in case the parents become assaultive, to use legal authority to take the child out of an abusive home if necessary, to gather evidence and take pictures if admissible evidence is present, and to permit the social worker to focus on the family rather than being preoccupied with the legal investigation.
- Caseworkers usually respond to reports of abuse and neglect within two to three days. An immediate response is required if it is determined that the child is at imminent risk of injury or impairment. If the intake worker makes the decision that

the referral does not constitute an allegation of abuse or neglect, the case may be closed. If there is substantial risk of serious harm to the child or lack of supervision, state law allows the child to be removed from the home.

■ If the decision is to take the child out of the home, the juvenile court judge must be called for approval as soon as the social worker and police officer leave the house. If the child has been taken out of the home, a temporary removal hearing normally is held in the juvenile court within three to five days. At this hearing, the juvenile judge can decide to leave the child in the temporary placement—a foster home, youth shelter, or group home—or return the child to the parents.

■ Following the initial investigation, the protective service agency usually draws one of the following conclusions: (1) there is sufficient evidence to support or substantiate the allegation of maltreatment or risk of maltreatment; (2) there is insufficient evidence to support maltreatment; or (3) maltreatment or the risk of maltreatment appears to be present, although there is insufficient evidence to conclude or substantiate the allegation. When sufficient evidence does not exist, additional services may be provided if it is believed that there is risk of abuse or neglect in the future.

Assessment
■ Protective service staff are responsible for identifying the factors that contributed to the maltreatment and for addressing the most critical treatment needs.

Case Planning
■ Case plans are developed by protective services, other treatment providers, and the family to alter the conditions and/or behaviors that result in child abuse or neglect.

Treatment
■ Protective service and other treatment providers have the responsibility to implement a treatment plan for the family.

Evaluation of Family Progress
■ After implementing the treatment plan, protective services and other treatment providers evaluate and measure changes in family behavior and conditions that led to child maltreatment. They also assess changes in the risk of maltreatment and determine when services are no longer required.

Case Closure
■ Some cases are closed because the family resists intervention efforts and the child is seen as being at low risk of harm. Other cases are closed when it has been determined that the risk of abuse or neglect has been eliminated or reduced to the point that the family can protect the child from maltreatment without additional intervention.

■ If the determination is made that the family will not protect the child, the child may be removed from the home and placed in foster care. If the decision is made that a child cannot be returned home within a reasonable time, parental rights may be terminated so that permanent alternatives can be found for the child.

Involvement of Juvenile or Family Court
■ An adjudication (fact finding) hearing is held if a petition of abuse or neglect has been filed by the department of social services. Juvenile courts hear about 150,000 child abuse and neglect cases a year. Usually present at the adjudication hearing are the assistant district, state, or county attorney; the youth and his or her attorney; the parents and their attorney; the social worker assigned to the case; and the police officer who conducted the investigation. After the evidence has been presented, the juvenile court judge decides whether the petition charging neglect or abuse has been substantiated. If it has, a disposition hearing is set for about four weeks later.

■ States vary in the standard of proof needed to substantiate allegations of child abuse and neglect. Six states rely on the caseworker's judgment; eighteen states, on some credible evidence; eleven states, on credible evidence; and twelve states, on the preponderance of evidence. About 30 percent of all child abuse and neglect reports in the country are substantiated, which varies somewhat by type of maltreatment and by state.[196] For example, in Massachusetts, allegations were confirmed in 55 percent of investigations in 2002, whereas in New Hampshire, only 9 percent were substantiated.[197]

Termination of Parental Rights

■ In the most serious cases of child maltreatment, the state moves to terminate parental rights and to place a child for adoption. In 2000, parents of 64,000 children across the country had their parental rights terminated. However, not all terminations of parental rights resulted from child maltreatment; the overall rate of parental rights termination for substantiated child maltreatment cases is about 8 percent.[198]

Prosecution of Parents

■ The prosecution of parents in criminal court depends largely on the seriousness of the injury to the child and on the attitude of the district, state, or county attorney's office toward child abuse. The cases most likely to be prosecuted are those in which a child has been seriously injured or killed and those in which a father or stepfather has sexually abused a daughter or stepdaughter. The most common charges in prosecutions are simple assault, assault with intent to commit serious injury, and manslaughter or murder.

Reported cases of child abuse represent only the tip of the iceberg. Abuse and neglect cases among lower-class families are more likely to be reported than those among middle- or upper-class families. Procedures for dealing with abusive homes vary from one state to the next, as does their effectiveness. Moreover, much remains to be learned about dealing more effectively with abusive families, about creating the type of placements that will serve the best interests of the child, and about creating the kind of public policy that is necessary to reduce the amount of abuse and neglect in this nation.

To reduce the extent of child abuse and neglect in the United States, a number of strategies or interventions are needed. Widom recommends the following six principles: (1) "The earlier the intervention, the better"; (2) "Don't neglect neglected children"; (3) "One size does not fit all"—that is, "what works for one child in one context may not work for a different child in the same setting, the same child in another setting, or the same child in another period in his or her development"; (4) "Surveillance is a double-edged sword"—that is, intervention agents must be sensitive to the possibilities of differential treatment on the basis of race or ethnic background and take steps to avoid such practices; (5) "Interventions are not one-time efforts"; and (6) "Resources should be accessible."[199]

CHAPTER
Summary

As this chapter notes, the family is the most important social institution in the lives of most young children. This chapter also says that:

■ Studies of the relationship between the family and delinquency have generally concluded that the quality of life within the home is a more significant deterrent of delinquent behavior than the presence of both parents; that parental rejection is associated with delinquent behavior; and that inconsistent, lax, or severe discipline is associated with increased delinquency.

■ Similar research concludes that delinquent behavior among children increases proportionately with the number of problems within the family. Divorced and single-parent families, blended families, births to unmarried women, alcohol and drug abuse, poverty, and violence are problems that some families encounter.

- Adolescents are exposed to a variety of seemingly negative media influences, including violent movies, television shows, and video games; Internet pornography; and gangsta rap and other forms of music carrying violent themes.

- Research findings show at least a partial link between child abuse and neglect and delinquent behavior and status offenses.

- Children who have been neglected and abused may experience psychological problems, run away from home, become involved in truancy and disruptive behavior in school, and turn to drug and alcohol abuse.

- Some neglected and abused youngsters become involved in deviant sexual behavior and assume an aggressive stance toward others.

- In many cases of child maltreatment, authorities are reluctant to intervene unless severe physical injury, gross neglect, or sexual abuse can be demonstrated.

CRITICAL THINKING
Questions

1. What are the most serious problems facing the American family today? What are their effects on children?
2. What conditions within the family are more likely to result in delinquent behavior?
3. What is neglect? What are some examples of neglect within the home?
4. Define emotional and physical abuse. What are some examples of physical and emotional abuse within the home?
5. Define and discuss incest. What type of father is most likely to become involved in incest?
6. How are child abuse and neglect related to status offenses and delinquent behavior?

WEB
Interactivity

Visit the Prevent Child Abuse America website at **www.preventchildabuse.org** and click on the "Research" menu item on the site's home page. As the site notes, the National Center on Child Abuse Prevention Research was established in 1986 and charged with working to increase our nation's understanding of the complex causes of child maltreatment. It also strives to evaluate the effectiveness of prevention programs and to disseminate information needed to lessen maltreatment. Today, the center works in support of a national movement to improve child well-being through abuse prevention.

While viewing the Research page, make note of the various kinds of reports and fact sheets listed there. What categories do you see? What are some of the center's current projects? Submit your findings to your instructor if asked to do so.

Source: From www.preventchildabuse.org/index.shtml. Reprinted with permission from Prevent Child Abuse America.

Notes

1. Karen Wilkinson, "The Broken Family and Juvenile Delinquency: Scientific Explanation of Ideology," *Social Problems* 21 (June 1974), pp. 726–739.
2. Marvin D. Krohn, Susan B. Stern, Terence P. Thornberry, and Sung Joon Jang, "The Measurement of Family Process Variables: The Effect of Adolescent and Parent Perceptions of Family Life on Delinquent Behavior," *Journal of Quantitative Criminology* 8 (1992), p. 287. For these theories of delinquency, see Travis Hirschi, *Causes of Delinquency* (Berkeley: University of California Press, 1969); Marvin Krohn, "The Web of Conformity: A Network Approach to the Explanation of Delinquent Behavior," *Social Problems* 33 (1986), pp. 81–93; Gerald Patterson, *Coercive Family Process* (Eugene, Ore.: Castilia Press, 1982); and Terence Thornberry, "Toward an Interactional Theory of Delinquency," *Criminology* 25 (1987), pp. 863–892.

3. Krohn et al., "The Measurement of Family Process Variables," pp. 287–288. For studies supporting the proposition that family relationships and parenting skills are related to delinquency, see D. Elliott, D. Huizinga, and S. Ageton, *Explaining Delinquency and Drug Use* (Beverly Hills, Calif.: Sage, 1985); Walter R. Gove and R. Crutchfield, "The Family and Juvenile Delinquency," *Sociological Quarterly* 23 (1982), pp. 301–319; M. Krohn and J. Massey, "Social Control and Delinquent Behavior: An Examination of the Elements of the Social Bond," *Sociological Quarterly* 21 (1980), pp. 337–349; J. Laub and R. Sampson, "Unraveling Families and Delinquency: A Reanalysis of the Gluecks' Data," *Criminology* 26 (1988), pp. 355–380; R. Loeber and M. Stouthamer-Loeber, "Family Factors as Correlates and Predictors of Juvenile Conduct Problems and Delinquency," in *Crime and Justice: An Annual Review of Research,* edited by M. Tonry and N. Morris (Chicago: University of Chicago Press, 1986), pp. 29–149; W. J. McCord, J. McCord, and Irving Zola, *The Origins of Crime* (New York: Columbia University Press, 1959); F. I. Nye, *Family Relationships and Delinquency Behavior* (New York: John Wiley, 1958); G. R. Patterson and T. J. Dishion, "Contributions of Families and Peers to Delinquency," *Criminology* 23 (1985), pp. 63–79; M. D. Wiatrowski, D. B. Griswold, and M. K. Roberts, "Social Control and Delinquency," *American Sociological Review* 46 (1981), pp. 524–541.

4. Lawrence Rosen, "Family and Delinquency: Structure or Function," *Criminology* 23 (1985), p. 553.

5. John Paul Wright and Francis T. Cullen, "Parental Efficacy and Delinquent Behavior: Do Control and Support Matter?" *Criminology* 39 (August 2001), p. 677. See also Judith R. Harris, "Where Is the Child's Environment? A Group Socialization Theory of Development," *Psychological Review* 102 (1995), pp. 458–489; Judith R. Harris, *The Nurture Assumption: Why Children Turn Out the Way They Do.* (New York: The Free Press, 1998).

6. W. D. Morrison, *Juvenile Offenders* (London: T. Fisher Unwin, 1896), pp. 146–147; Sophonisba P. Breckenridge and Edith Abbott, *The Delinquent Child and the Home* (New York: Russell Sage Foundation, 1912), pp. 90–91; William Healy, *The Individual Delinquent* (Boston: Little, Brown, 1915), pp. 290–291; William Healy and Augusta Bronner, *Delinquents and Criminals: Their Making and Unmaking* (New York: Macmillan, 1926), p. 123; and Ernest H. Shideler, "Family Disintegration and the Delinquent Boy in the United States," *Journal of Criminal Law and Criminology* 8 (January 1918), pp. 709–732.

7. George B. Mangold, *Problems of Child Welfare,* rev. ed. (New York: Macmillan, 1924), p. 406.

8. Margaret Hodgkiss, "The Influence of Broken Homes and Working Mothers," *Smith College Studies in Social Work* 3 (March 1933), pp. 259–274.

9. Sheldon Glueck and Eleanor T. Glueck, *Unraveling Juvenile Delinquency* (Cambridge, Mass.: Harvard University Press for the Commonwealth Fund, 1950), p. 123.

10. Nye, *Family Relationships and Delinquent Behavior,* and R. A. Dentler and L. J. Monroe, "Social Correlates of Early Adolescent Theft," *American Sociological Review* 28 (1961), pp. 733–743.

11. Lawrence Rosen, "The Broken Home and Delinquency," in *The Sociology of Crime and Delinquency,* edited by M. E. Wolfgang et al. (New York: John Wiley and Sons, 1970), pp. 489–495.

12. Patricia Van Voorhis et al., "The Impact of Family Structure and Quality on Delinquency: A Comparative Assessment of Structural and Functional Factors," *Criminology* 26 (1988), p. 248; Margaret Farnworth, "Family Structure, Family Attributes, and Delinquency in a Sample of Low-Income, Minority Males and Females," *Journal of Youth and Adolescence* 13 (1984), p. 362.

13. J. Q. Wilson and R. J. Herrnstein, *Crime and Human Nature* (New York: Simon and Schuster, 1985).

14. Richard S. Sterne, *Delinquent Conduct and Broken Homes* (New Haven, Conn.: College and University Press, 1964), p. 65; J. Toby, "The Differential Impact of Family Disorganization," *American Sociological Review* 22 (1957), pp. 505–512; T. P. Monahan, "Family Status and the Delinquent Child: A Reappraisal and Some New Findings," *Social Forces* 35 (1957), pp. 250–258; and T. P. Monahan, "Broken Homes by Age of Delinquent Children," *Journal of Social Psychology* 51 (1960), pp. 387–397.

15. Susan K. Datesman and Frank R. Scarpitti, "Female Delinquency and Broken Homes: A Re-Assessment," *Criminology* 13 (May 1975), p. 51.

16. Ross L. Matsueda and Karen Heimer, "Race, Family Structure, and Delinquency: A Test of Differential Association and Social Control Theories," *American Sociological Review* 52 (1987), p. 836.

17. Van Voorhis, "The Impact of Family Structure and Quality on Delinquency," p. 248.

18. Joseph Rankin, "The Family Context of Delinquency," *Social Problems* 30 (1977), pp. 466–479, and L. Edward Wells and Joseph Rankin, "Broken Homes and Juvenile Delinquency: An Empirical Review," *Criminal Justice Abstracts* 17 (1985), pp. 249–272.

19. Marvin D. Free Jr., "Clarifying the Relationship between the Broken Home and Juvenile Delinquency: A Critique of the Current Literature," *Deviant Behavior* 12 (1991), pp. 109–167.

20. Karen Wilkinson, "The Broken Home and Delinquent Behavior: An Alternative Interpretation of Contradictory Findings," in *Understanding Crime: Current Theory and Research,* edited by T. Hirschi and M. Gottfredson (Beverly Hills, Calif.: Sage, 1980), pp. 21–42.

21. D. P. Farrington, *Further Analysis of a Longitudinal Survey of Crime and Delinquency* (Washington, D.C.: Final Report to the National Institute of Justice, 1983).

22. Steven A. Cernkovich and Peggy C. Giordano, "Family Relationships and Delinquency," *Criminology* 25 (1987), pp. 295–319.

23. Hirschi, *Causes of Delinquency,* and M. Gold, *Delinquent Behavior in an American City* (Monterey, Calif.: Brooks-Cole, 1970).

24. R. J. Chilton and G. E. Markle, "Family Disruption, Delinquent Conduct and the Effect of Subclassification," *American Sociological Review* 37 (February 1972), pp. 93–99.

25. R. E. Johnson, "Family Structure and Delinquency: General Patterns and Gender Differences," *Criminology* 24 (1986), pp. 65–80; H. Paguin et al., "Characteristics of Youngsters Referred to Family Court Intake and Factors Relating to Their Processing," in *Juvenile Justice,* edited by H. J. Rubin (Santa Monica, Calif.: Goodyear, 1982); C. R. Fenwick, "Juvenile

Court Intake Decision Making: The Importance of Family Affiliation," *Journal of Criminal Justice* 10 (1982), pp. 443–453.

26. Cesar J. Rebellion, "Reconsidering the Broken Homes/Delinquency Relationship and Exploring Its Mediating Mechanisms," *Criminology* 40 (February 2002), pp. 103–133.

27. L. Edward Wells and Joseph H. Rankin, "Families and Delinquency: A Meta-Analysis of the Impact of Broken Homes," *Social Problems* 38 (February 1991), pp. 87–88.

28. Glueck and Glueck, *Unraveling Juvenile Delinquency;* Nye, *Family Relationships and Delinquent Behavior;* and McCord, McCord, and Zola, *Origins of Crime.*

29. Linda J. Waite and Lee A. Lillard, "Children and Marriage Disruption," *American Journal of Sociology* 96 (January 1991), p. 930.

30. Hirschi, *Causes of Delinquency.*

31. Loeber and Stouthamer-Loeber, "Family Factors as Correlates and Predictors of Juvenile Conduct Problems and Delinquency," pp. 100–101.

32. Glueck and Glueck, *Unraveling Juvenile Delinquency.*

33. Joan McCord, "Crime in Moral and Social Contexts: The American Society of Criminology, 1989 Presidential Address," *Criminology* 28 (1990), p. 16.

34. David P. Farrington, "Environmental Stress, Delinquent Behavior, and Convictions," in *Stress and Anxiety,* edited by I. G. Sarason and C. D. Spielberger (Washington, D.C.: Hemisphere, 1979).

35. Janet L. Lauritsen, "Sibling Resemblance in Juvenile Delinquency: Findings from the National Youth Survey," *Criminology* 31 (August 1993), p. 387.

36. Nye, *Family Relationships and Delinquent Behavior,* pp. 47, 51.

37. Glueck and Glueck, *Unraveling Juvenile Delinquency.*

38. McCord, McCord, and Zola, *Origins of Crime,* and R. C. Audry, *Delinquency and Parental Pathology* (London: Methuen, 1960).

39. Randy L. Lagrange and Helen R. White, "Age Differences in Delinquency: A Test of Theory," *Criminology* 23 (1985), pp. 19–45.

40. Paul Howes and Howard J. Markman, "Marital Quality and Child Functioning: A Longitudinal Investigation," *Child Development* 60 (1989), p. 1044.

41. Joan McCord, "Family Relationships, Juvenile Delinquency, and Adult Criminality," *Criminology* 29 (August 1991), p. 397.

42. S. Kirson Weinberg, "Sociological Processes and Factors in Juvenile Delinquency," in *Juvenile Delinquency,* edited by Joseph S. Roucek (New York: Philosophical Library, 1958), p. 108.

43. Joan McCord, William McCord, and Alan Howard, "Family Interaction as Antecedent to the Direction of Male Aggressiveness," *Journal of Abnormal Social Psychology* 66 (1963), pp. 239–242.

44. Loeber and Stouthamer-Loeber, "Family Factors as Correlates and Predictors of Juvenile Conduct Problems and Delinquency," p. 55.

45. Nye, *Family Relationships and Delinquent Behavior,* p. 75.

46. John Bowlby, *Maternal Care and Mental Health* (Geneva: World Health Organization, 1951); Hirschi, *Causes of Delinquency;* M. J. Hindelang, "Causes of Delinquency: A Partial Replication," *Social Problems* 21 (Spring 1973), pp. 471–487; R. L. Austin, "Race, Father-Absence, and Female

Delinquency," *Criminology* 15 (February 1978), pp. 484–504.

47. McCord, McCord, and Zola, *Origins of Crime.*

48. Glueck and Glueck, *Unraveling Juvenile Delinquency,* and R. G. Audry, "Faulty Parental and Maternal Child Relationships, Affection, and Delinquency," *British Journal of Delinquency* 8 (1958), pp. 34–38.

49. W. L. Slocum and C. L. Stone, "Family Culture Patterns and Delinquent-Type Behavior," *Marriage and Family Living* 25 (1963), pp. 202–208.

50. Richard E. Johnson, "Attachments to Mother and Father as Distinct Factors in Female and Male Delinquent Behavior." Paper presented at the Annual Meeting of the American Society of Criminology Toronto, Canada (November 1982).

51. Rosen, "Family and Delinquency," p. 569.

52. Joseph H. Rankin and Roger Kern, "Parental Attachments and Delinquency," *Criminology* 32 (November 1994), pp. 495–515.

53. Hirschi, *Causes of Delinquency.*

54. Nye, *Family Relationships and Delinquent Behavior,* p. 59.

55. Glueck and Glueck, *Unraveling Juvenile Delinquency.*

56. G. F. Jensen and Raymond Eve, "Sex Differences in Delinquency: An Examination of Popular Sociological Explanations," *Criminology* 12 (1976), pp. 427–448.

57. Loeber and Stouthamer-Loeber, "Family Factors as Correlates and Predictors of Juvenile Conduct Problems and Delinquency," p. 43.

58. Nye, *Family Relationships and Delinquent Behavior.*

59. Loeber and Stouthamer-Loeber, "Family Factors as Correlates and Predictors of Juvenile Conduct Problems and Delinquency," p. 53; James Snyder and Gerald Patterson, "Family Interaction and Delinquent Behavior," in *Handbook of Juvenile Delinquency,* edited by H. C. Quay (New York: John Wiley and Sons, 1987), pp. 216–243.

60. McCord, McCord, and Zola, *Origins of Crime;* see also W. McCord and J. McCord, *Psychopathy and Delinquency* (New York: Grune and Stratton, 1956).

61. Wright and Cullen, "Parental Efficacy and Delinquent Behavior," p. 677.

62. Ronald L. Simons, Leslie Gordon Simons, Callie Harbin Burt, Gene H. Brody, and Carolyn Cutrona, "Collective Efficacy, Authoritative Parenting and Delinquency: A Longitudinal Test of a Model Integrating Community- and Family-Level Processes," *Criminology* (November 2005), pp. 989–1029.

63. Glueck and Glueck, *Unraveling Juvenile Delinquency.*

64. Laub and Sampson, "Unraveling Families and Delinquency," pp. 355–380, and Robert J. Sampson and John H. Laub, *Crime in the Making: Pathways and Turning Points through Life* (Cambridge, Mass.: Harvard University Press, 1993).

65. Loeber and Stouthamer-Loeber, "Family Factors as Correlates and Predictors of Juvenile Conduct Problems and Delinquency."

66. See Glueck and Glueck, *Unraveling Juvenile Delinquency,* pp. 91–92.

67. *America's Children in Brief: Key National Indicators of Well-Being 2005* (Washington, D.C.: Federal Interagency Forum on Child and Family Statistics, 2005), p. 1.

68. Terence P. Thornberry, Carolyn A. Smith, Craig Rivera, David Huizinga, and Magda Stouthamer-Loeber, "Family Disruption and Delinquency," *Juvenile Justice Bulletin* (September 1999), p. 1.

69. Ibid.

70. *America's Children in Brief: Key National Indicators of Well-Being 2004* (Washington, D.C.: Federal Interagency Forum on Child and Family Statistics, 2004), p. 4.

71. *America's Children in Brief: Key National Indicators of Well-Being 2005.*

72. Ibid.

73. National Coalition for the Homeless, *Homeless Youth: NCH Fact Sheet #13* (Washington, D.C.: National Coalition for the Homeless, 2006), p. 1.

74. U.S. Department of Labor, Bureau of Labor Statistics, www.bls.gov.

75. Ibid.

76. Federal Bureau of Investigation, *Crime in the United States 2005,* Table 29. www.fbi.gov:80/ucr/05cius/data/table_29.html.

77. Michael Hershorn and Alan Rosenbaum, "Children of Marital Violence: A Closer Look at the Unintended Victims," *American Journal of Orthopsychiatry* 55 (April 1985), p. 260. See also R. L. McNeely and Gloria Robinson-Simpson, "The Truth about Domestic Violence: A Falsely Framed Issue," *Social Work* 32 (November–December 1997), pp. 485–490.

78. Karen Heimer, "Socioeconomic Status: Subcultural Definitions and Violent Delinquency," *Social Forces* 75 (1997), pp. 799–833.

79. Comments made by Mike Carlie in the *Into the Abyss: A Personal Journey into the World of Street Gangs,* Chapter 12. See www.faculty.missouristate.edu/M/MichaelCarlie/what_I_learned_ about/media.htm.

80. This is the general consensus of the vast amount of research done on this topic.

81. See Walter B. Miller, *The Growth of Youth Gang Problems in the United States: 1970–98* (Washington, D.C.: U.S. Department of Justice; Office of Juvenile Justice and Delinquency Prevention, 2001).

82. Ibid.

83. *Experts Debate Effects of Violent Video Games,* September 26, 2005. See http://homepage.mac.com/iajukes/blogwavestudio/LH20050626175144/LHA2005092622.

84. Ibid.

85. Ibid.

86. Ibid.

87. CATTA, *Protecting Our Children Against Internet Perpetrators* (Sonoma State University: The California Institute on Human Services, 2006), p. 1.

88. Wikpedia, *Gangsta rap.* http://en.wikipedia.org/wiki/Gangsta_rap.

89. Ibid.

90. Ibid.

91. Matthew T. Zingraff and Michael J. Belyea, "Child Abuse and Violent Crime," in *The Dilemmas of Punishment,* edited by Kenneth C. Haas and Geoffrey P. Alpert (Prospect Heights, Ill.: Waveland Press, 1986), p. 51.

92. Kathleen M. Heide, "Evidence of Child Maltreatment among Adolescent Parricide Offenders," *International Journal of Offender Therapy and Comparative Criminology* 38 (1994), p. 151.

93. Ibid.

94. Barbara Tatem Kelley, Terence P. Thornberry, and Carolyn A. Smith, "In the Wake of Childhood Maltreatment," *Juvenile Justice Bulletin* (Washington, D.C.: U.S. Department of Justice, Office of Juvenile Justice and Delinquency Prevention, 1997), p. 4.

95. B. F. Steele, "Child Abuse: Its Impact on Society," *Journal of the Indiana State Medical Association* 68 (1975), pp. 191–194.

96. Joan McCord, "A Forty Year Perspective on Effects of Child Abuse and Neglect," *Child Abuse and Neglect* 7 (1983), p. 265.

97. José Alfaro, "Report of the Relationship between Child Abuse and Neglect and Later Socially Deviant Behavior," in *Exploring the Relationship between Child Abuse and Delinquency,* edited by R. J. Hunter and Y. E. Walker (Montclair, N.J.: Allanheld, Osmun, 1981), pp. 175–219.

98. Cathy Spatz Widom, "Child Abuse, Neglect, and Violent Criminal Behavior," *Criminology* 27 (1989), pp. 251–271. See also Cathy Spatz Widom, *The Cycle of Violence* (Washington, D.C.: National Institute of Justice, 1992), p. 3.

99. Cathy S. Widom and Michael G. Maxfield, "An Update on the 'Cycle of Violence'," *Research in Brief* (Washington, D.C.: National Institute of Justice, 2001).

100. Ibid. For other support for the relationship between abuse and neglect and later violent behavior, see Carlos E. Climent and Frank R. Erwin, "Historical Data on the Evaluation of Violent Subjects: A Hypothesis-Generating Study," *American Journal of Psychiatry* 27 (1972), pp. 621–624; Dorothy O. Lewis, Shelly S. Shanok, Jonathan H. Pincus, and Gilbert H. Glaser, "Violent Juvenile Delinquents: Psychiatric, Neurological, Psychological and Abuse Factors," *Journal of the American Academy of Child Psychiatry* 18 (1979), pp. 307–319; Mark Monane, "Physical Abuse in Psychiatrically Hospitalized Children and Adolescents," *Journal of the American Academy of Child Psychiatry* 23.

101. Terence Thornberry, "Violent Families and Youth Violence," *OJJDP Fact Sheet* (Washington, D.C.: Office of Juvenile Justice and Delinquency Prevention, 1994).

102. Matthew T. Zingraff, Jeffrey Leiter, Kristen A. Myers, and Matthew C. Johnson, "Child Maltreatment and Youthful Problem Behaviors," *Criminology* 31 (1993), p. 173.

103. Ibid., pp. 194, 196.

104. C. Henry Kempe et al., "The Battered-Child Syndrome," *Journal of the American Medical Association* 181 (July 1962), pp. 17–24.

105. Children Bureau, *Child Maltreatment 2004* (Washington, D.C.: U.S. Department of Health and Human Services, 2004), p. 24.

106. Ibid.

107. Ibid.

108. Ibid., pp. 25–26.

109. Ibid., p. 63.

110. Ibid.

111. *In the Interest of Children: A Century of Progress* (Denver: American Humane Association, Children's Division, 1966), p. 25.

112. Cynthia Crosson-Tower, *Understanding Child Abuse and Neglect* (Boston: Allyn and Bacon, 1999), p. 63.

113. Cathy Spatz Widom, "Child Victims: In Search of Opportunities for Breaking the Cycle of Violence." A speech made in the *Perspectives on Crime and Justice: 1996–1997 Lecture Series* 1 (November 1997), p. 75.

114. Leontine Young, *Wednesday's Children: A Study of Child Neglect and Abuse* (New York: McGraw-Hill, 1964).

115. Norman A. Polansky, Christine Deaix, and Shlomo A. Sharlin, *Child Neglect: Understanding and Reaching the Parent* (New York: Welfare League of America, 1972), pp. 21–52.

116. Norman A. Polansky et al., *Damaged Parents: An Anatomy of Child Neglect* (Chicago: University of Chicago Press, 1981), pp. 113–114.
117. Crosson-Tower, *Understanding Child Abuse and Neglect*, p. 64.
118. Ibid., p. 65. See also Nico Trocme, "Development and Preliminary Evaluation of the Ontario Child Neglect Index," *Child Maltreatment* 1 (1996), pp. 145–155.
119. Richard J. Gelles and Claire Pedrick Cornell, *Intimate Violence in Families*, 2nd ed. (Newbury Park, Calif.: Sage, 1985), p. 42.
120. Ibid.
121. Murray A. Straus, "Discipline and Deviance: Physical Punishment of Children and Violence and Other Crime in Adulthood," *Social Problems* 38 (May 1991), p. 133.
122. Murray A. Straus, *Beating the Devil Out of Them: Corporal Punishment in American Families* (New York: Lexington Books, 1994), pp. 5, 32, 54, 56, and 58.
123. Ibid., pp. 149–161.
124. Murray A. Straus, "Discipline and Deviance: Physical Punishment of Children and Violence and Other Crime in Adulthood," *Social Problems* 38 (May 1991), p. 148.
125. James Garbarino and Gwen Gilliam, *Understanding Abusive Families* (Lexington, Mass.: Heath, 1980), p. 68.
126. Interviewed in May 1981.
127. Stephanie Amedeo and John Gartrell, "An Empirical Examination of Five Theories of Physical Child Abuse." Paper presented at the Annual Meeting of the American Society of Criminology, Reno, Nevada (November 1989).
128. Blair Justice and Rita Justice, *The Abusive Family* (New York: Human Services Press, 1976).
129. O. C. S. Tzeng, Jay W. Jackson, and H. C. Karlson, *Theories of Child Abuse and Neglect* (New York: Praeger, 1991).
130. David G. Gil, *Violence against Children: Physical Abuse in the United States* (Cambridge, Mass.: Harvard University Press, 1970), pp. 130–132.
131. *Study Findings, National Incidence and Prevalence of Child Abuse and Neglect*, pp. 1–10.
132. Gil, *Violence against Children*.
133. Kempe et al., "Battered Child Syndrome," pp. 17–24; B. Fontana, *Somewhere a Child is Crying: Maltreatment—Causes and Prevention* (New York: Macmillan, 1973); R. Galdston, "Observations of Children Who Have Been Physically Abused by Their Parents," *American Journal of Psychiatry* 122 (1965), pp. 440–443.
134. Young, *Wednesday's Children*, p. 48.
135. Blair Justice and Rita Justice, *The Broken Taboo: Sex in the Family* (New York: Human Sciences Press, 1979), p. 25.
136. Ibid., p. 27.
137. Linda Gordon, "Incest and Resistance Patterns of Father–Daughter Incest, 1880–1930," *Social Problems* 33 (April 1986), p. 253.
138. David Finkelhor and Lisa M. Jones, *Explanations for the Decline in Child Sexual Abuse Cases* (Washington, D.C.: Office of Juvenile Justice and Delinquency Prevention, 2004).
139. Ibid.
140. For a more extensive discussion of the four types of incest possible within a family unit, see Crosson-Tower, *Understanding Child Abuse and Neglect*, pp. 155–162.
141. Angela Browne and David Finkelhor, "Impact of Child Abuse: A Review of the Research," *Psychological Bulletin* 99 (1986), p. 69.
142. K. C. Meiselman, *Incest: A Psychological Study of Causes and Effects with Treatment Recommendations* (San Francisco: Jossey-Bass, 1978); and Christine A. Curtois, *Adult Survivors of Child Sexual Abuse* (Milwaukee, Wisc.: Families International, 1993), p. 23.
143. Interviewed as part of a court case with which the author was involved.
144. Justice and Justice, *The Broken Taboo*, p. 192.
145. A. Nicholas Groth, "Patterns of Sexual Assault against Children and Adolescents," in *Sexual Assault of Children and Adolescents* (Lexington, Mass.: D.C. Heath, 1978), p. 17.
146. Justice and Justice, *The Broken Taboo*, p. 194.
147. Ibid., p. 196.
148. National Center on Child Abuse and Neglect, *Child Sexual Abuse*.
149. Justice and Justice, *The Broken Taboo*, pp. 59–91.
150. Eli H. Newberger and Richard Bourne, "The Medicalization and Legalization of Child Abuse," *American Journal of Orthopsychiatry* 48 (October 1977), pp. 593–607; and Straus, Gelles, and Steinmetz, *Behind Closed Doors*, pp. 181–182.
151. Garbarino and Gilliam, *Understanding Abusive Families*, pp. 173–176.
152. Judith Lewis Herman and Lisa Hirschman, "Father–Daughter Incest," *Signs* 2 (1977), pp. 1–22; and C. Swift, "Sexual Victimization of Children: An Urban Mental Health Center Survey," *Victimology* 2 (1977), pp. 322–327.
153. J. Henderson, "Incest: A Synthesis of Data," *Canadian Psychiatric Association Journal* 17 (1972), pp. 299–313; B. Molnar and P. Cameron, "Incest Syndromes: Observations in a General Hospital Psychiatric Unit," *Canadian Psychiatric Association Journal* 20 (1975), pp. 1–24; P. Sloane and F. Karpinsky, "Effects of Incest on Participants," *American Journal of Orthopsychiatry* 12 (1942), pp. 666–673; and Danya Glaser and Stephen Frosh, *Child Sexual Abuse*, 2nd ed. (Toronto, Canada: University of Toronto Press, 1993), p. 20.
154. Interviewed in May 1986.
155. Meda Chesney-Lind, "Girls' Crime and Women's Place: Toward a Feminist Model of Juvenile Delinquency." Paper presented at the Annual Meeting of the American Society of Criminology, Montreal, Canada (1987); M. Geller and L. Ford-Somma, *Caring for Delinquent Girls: An Examination of New Jersey's Correctional System* (Trenton, N.J.: New Jersey Law Enforcement Planning Academy, 1989).
156. "Incest: If You Think the Word Is Ugly, Take a Look at Its Effects" (Minneapolis: Christopher Street, 1979), p. 10.
157. For a review of these studies, see Diane D. Broadhurst, "The Effect of Child Abuse and Neglect in the School-Aged Child," in *The Maltreatment of the School-Aged Child*, edited by Richard Volpe, Margot Breton, and Judith Mitton (Lexington, Mass.: D.C. Heath, 1980), pp. 19–41.
158. R. S. Kempe and C. H. Kempe, *Child Abuse* (Cambridge, Mass.: Harvard University Press, 1978), p. 125.
159. Florance Blager and H. P. Martin, "Speech and Language of Abused Children," in *The Abused Child: A Multidisciplinary Approach in Development Issues and Psychological Problems*, edited by H. P. Martin (Cambridge, Mass.: Ballinger, 1976), p. 85.
160. D. F. Kline and J. Christiansen, *Educational and Psychological Problems of Abused Children* (Logan: Utah State University Department of Special Education, 1975), p. 107.
161. Martin, "Neurological Status of Abused Children," p. 77.
162. Ibid.

163. M. Halperin, *Helping Maltreated Children* (St. Louis: C. V. Mosby, 1979), p. 77.

164. Kline and Christiansen, *Educational and Psychological Problems,* p. 107.

165. Comments made by teachers interviewed in 1981.

166. T. Houten and M. Golembiewski, "A Study of Runaway Youth and Their Families" (Washington, D.C.: Youth Alternatives Project, 1976); J. Streit, "A Test and Procedure to Identify Secondary School Children Who Have a High Probability of Drug Abuse," *Dissertation Abstracts International* 34 (1974), pp. 10–13; and Glaser and Frosh, *Child Sexual Abuse,* p. 20.

167. Widom, "Child Abuse, Neglect, and Violent Criminal Behavior," pp. 265–266; see also Bergsmann, "The Forgotten Few: Juvenile Female Offenders," p. 74.

168. S. D. Peters, *The Relationship between Childhood Sexual Victimization and Adult Depression among Afro-American and White Women.* Unpublished doctoral dissertation, University of California, Los Angeles, 1984.

169. Richard Dembo, Max Dertke, Lawrence La Voie, Scott Borders, Mark Washburn, and James Schmeidler, "Physical Abuse, Sexual Victimization and Illicit Drug Use: A Structural Analysis among High Risk Adolescents," *Journal of Adolescence* 10 (1987), p. 13.

170. "Incest: If You Think the Word Is Ugly," p. 11.

171. Ibid., pp. 11–12.

172. Sarah Nordgren, "Experts Find Links between Teen Mothers, Sexual Abuse," *Waterloo Courier,* 11 September 1995, p. A1.

173. David Finkelhor, *Sexually Victimized Children* (New York: Free Press, 1979), p. 214.

174. J. James and J. Meyerding, "Early Sexual Experiences as a Factor in Prostitution," *Archives in Sexual Behavior* 7 (1977), pp. 31–42.

175. Justice and Justice, *Broken Taboo,* p. 197.

176. See "Incest: If You Think the Word Is Ugly," p. 13.

177. Widom, "Child Abuse, Neglect, and Violent Criminal Behavior," pp. 265–266.

178. Richard J. Gelles, "Violence in the Family: A Review of Research in the Seventies," *Journal of Marriage and the Family* (November 1980), pp. 873–885.

179. E. Tanay, "Psychiatric Study of Homicide," *American Journal of Psychiatry* 120 (1963), pp. 386–387.

180. Jose D. Alfaro, *Summary Report on the Relationship between Child Abuse and Neglect and Later Socially Deviant Behavior* (New York: Select Committee on Child Abuse, 1978).

181. Terence P. Thornberry, *Violent Families and Youth Violence* (Washington, D.C.: U.S. Department of Justice, 1994), p. 1.

182. Michael S. Wald, "State Intervention on Behalf of Neglected Children: A Search for Standards for Placement of Children in Foster Care, and Termination of Parental Rights," *Stanford Law Review* 26 (1976), pp. 626–627.

183. Peter C. Kratcoski, "Child Abuse and Violence against the Family," *Child Welfare* 61 (1982), pp. 435–444.

184. Jeffrey Fagan, Karen V. Hansen, and Michael Jang, "Profiles of Chronically Violent Delinquents: Empirical Test of an Integrated Theory," in *Evaluating Juvenile Justice,* edited by James Kleugel (Beverly Hills, Calif.: Sage, 1983).

185. Zingraff and Belyea, "Child Abuse and Violent Crime," p. 59.

186. Sara E. Gutierres and John W. Reich, "A Developmental Perspective on Runaway Behavior: Its Relationship to Child Abuse," *Child Welfare* 60 (1981), pp. 89–94.

187. Timothy O. Ireland, Carolyn A. Smith, and Terence P. Thornberry, "Developmental Issues in the Impact of Child Maltreatment on Later Delinquency and Drug Use," *Criminology* 40 (May 2002), pp. 360–363. See also Robert J. Sampson and John H. Laub, "Crime and Deviance in the Life Course," in *Life-Course Criminology,* edited by Alex Piquero and Paul Mazerolle (Belmont, Calif.: Wadsworth/Thompson Learning, 2001).

188. Michael R. Gottfredson and Travis Hirschi, *A General Theory of Crime* (Stanford, Calif.: Stanford University Press, 1990).

189. Carter Hay, "Parenting, Self-Control, and Delinquency: A Test of Self-Control Theory," *Criminology* 39 (August 2001), pp. 707–736.

190. Ronald L. Simons, Chyi-In Wu, Kuei-Hsui Lin, Leslie Gordon, and Rand D. Conger, "A Cross-Cultural Examination of the Link between Corporal Punishment and Adolescent Antisocial Behavior," *Criminology* 38 (January 2000), pp. 47–79.

191. Karen Heimer, "Socioeconomic Status, Subcultural Definitions, and Violent Delinquency," *Social Forces* 75 (1997), pp. 799–833.

192. Ireland, Smith, and Thornberry, "Developmental Issues in the Impact of Child Maltreatment on Later Delinquency and Drug Use," pp. 359–395.

193. Ibid., p. 363.

194. Peggy C. Giordano, Stephen A. Cernkovich, and Jennifer L. Rudolph, "Gender, Crime, and Delinquency: Toward a Theory of Cognitive Transformation," *American Journal of Sociology* 107 (January 2002), pp. 1000–1003.

195. The first part of the following section is modified from Howard N. Snyder and Melissa Sickmund, *Juvenile Offenders and Victims: 1999 National Report* (Washington, D.C.: Office of Juvenile Justice and Delinquency Prevention, 1999), pp. 43–44. See also David Finkelhor, Theodore P. Cross, and Elise N. Cantor, "How the Justice System Responds to Juvenile Victims: A Comprehensive Model, *Juvenile Justice Bulletin* (December 2005).

196. Finkelhor, Cross, and Cantor, "How the Justice System Responds to Juvenile Victims: A Comprehensive Model, *Juvenile Justice Bulletin* (December 2005), p. 5.

197. U. S. Department of Health and Human Services, Administration on Children, Youth and Families, *Child Maltreatment 2002: Reports from the States to the National Child Abuse and Neglect Data System* (Washington, D.C.: U.S. Government Printing Office, 2004.

198. Children's Bureau, *The Adoption and Foster Care Analysis Reporting System Preliminary Report* (Washington, D.C.: U.S. Department of Health and Human Services, Administration on Children, Youth and Families, 2001).

199. Widom, "Child Victims," pp. 81–85.

9

The School and Delinquency

Columbine

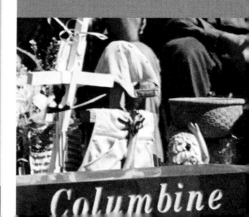

> If a child cannot go to school without fear of being raped, robbed, or even murdered, then nothing else the government does really matters. **"**
>
> —National Policy Forum

CHAPTER Objectives

AFTER READING THIS CHAPTER, YOU SHOULD BE ABLE TO ANSWER THE FOLLOWING QUESTIONS:

- How has education evolved over time in the United States?

- What is the relationship between delinquency and school failure?

- What theoretical perspectives related to the school experience best explain delinquency?

- What rights do school students have?

- How has the partnership between the school and the justice system changed?

- Which intervention strategies seem to be most promising in the school setting?

Columbine

On March 21, 2005, sixteen-year-old Jeffrey Weise went to his grandfather's house on Minnesota's Red Lake Indian Reservation and used a 22-caliber rifle to shoot and kill his fifty-eight-year-old grandfather, a tribal policeman. Weise also killed his grandfather's thirty-two-year-old girlfriend and stole his grandfather's police-issued handgun and a shotgun. He then drove to Red Lake Senior High School and shot dead an unarmed security guard at the school's main entrance before running inside and firing wildly at students and teachers. Weise chased down fleeing students, shooting some as they begged for their lives. School videotape shows him roaming through the school's hallways and classrooms, sometimes firing randomly. Four police officers responded to the incident and Weise fired several shots at them as they arrived at the school. When one of the officers returned fire, Weise went into a classroom and shot himself in the head. Five students, in addition to Weise, died, bringing the total number of people to die at his hand to nine.

The Red Lake school shooting was the deadliest school shooting in the United States since the 1999 Columbine High School shootings in Colorado, in which two students, Eric Harris and Dylan Klebold, shot and killed twelve students and a teacher before taking their own lives. Twenty-three other people were wounded at Columbine.[1]

Adapted from "U.S. School Gunman Stole Police Pistol, Vest," CNN, March 23, 2005.

> ❝ The public wants to know what is going on in the schools of this nation. ❞

The public wants to know what is going on in the schools of this nation. Experts are ready to render explanations for the school killings, which range from "merely an aberration," to lack of impulse control in children today, to the breakdown of the family, to the abundance of guns in the hands of young people, and to too much violence on television. What these killings certainly have done is focus attention on delinquency, especially violence, in school settings.[2]

In Social World of the Delinquent 9.1, Chris Geschke, a sophomore at Santana High School in Santee, California, tells what impact school shootings have on students.[3] Geschke was walking to his classroom in the San Diego suburb about 9:15 the morning of March 5, 2001. He passed by a bathroom, where inside a student senselessly began firing his weapon into a crowd of classmates. Before he was subdued by an off-duty police officer, the young shooter had killed two students and wounded thirteen others.

Chris saw several classmates who had been shot stagger out of the bathroom. He also saw a security guard race into the bathroom to try to subdue the crazed student. It later turned out that the security guard was wounded, but not fatally.

As Chris was running to his classroom, which was about ten feet from the bathroom, he spotted the shooter in hot pursuit of some students. The gunman shot three of Chris's classmates who were running behind Chris and fired countless rounds toward Chris.

That Chris was able to safely make it into the classroom and close the door was a miracle. Scores of bullets whizzed past his head. Seven bullet holes were later found on the outside walls of Chris's classroom.

On March 15, 2001, Chris wrote a poignant recollection for his English class of the tragic events he was involved in at his school on March 5. Appropriately enough, his essay was entitled "Scars on their Souls." (See Figure 9.1 for a time line of recent worldwide school shootings.)

"Scars on Their Souls," by Chris Geschke

"In the aftermath of the shooting at Santana High, one thing certainly rings true: bullets can do more than just physical damage.

"This is not to diminish the tragic consequences for fifteen families. Two are dead, thirteen others injured. Their blood is red, their pain cruel. Their loss cannot be measured by words, nor can their grief be consoled. The bullets surely did physical damage that can be seen with the eye. We saw arm, facial, leg, chest, and back wounds. But the invisible damage—the pain—inflicted on the heart—will never go away. In time, that invisible damage will evolve into painful or distant memories, maybe even fade into the back of the mind. But there will always be scars on their souls.

"There is no rational reason for this irrational act. The media has tried to find a motive. Experts and Ph.D.'s have pointed to a variety of reasons and social ills in attempts to justify their own theories.

"Talk show hosts have entertained thousands of callers, each with something to say and finding a new angle to say it. Was he bullied? Did bigger students abuse him? Did drugs cause this violent reaction? Was he a victim of a broken heart? Did the school not listen? Why didn't his friends do something? Where did the system fail?

"My question is, does it matter? Will an explanation bring back Brian Zuckor or Randy Gordon [two students who were killed]? Will a reason make things all better for 1,900 students, 300 faculty members and their families? Will a rational explanation help prevent my friends' mothers and fathers from worrying now every time they walk out the front door? Will an answer allow my mother to sleep peacefully again? Will a reason mean much to millions of other students at high schools just like Santana who watched us on TV and now worry the same thing could happen at their school?

"Their fear is real too. Again the invisible damage.

"I've learned a lot over the past couple of weeks. I've learned about my own mortality. I've learned about fate, and how easily one of those bullets could have hit me as I ran. I've retraced my steps in the past few days and felt the walls where the bullets hit. Bullets intended for me. I've learned that God was watching over me, and has an important purpose for my own life. I've learned that people hurt, inside and outside.

"But more importantly, I've learned that bullets cause invisible damage. And they leave scars on the soul."

> ■ Do you agree with Chris that the consequences of the shooting are more important to understand than the reasons why it happened? If you were a school counselor, what type of counseling would you give students who were victims of such a tragedy? What should we make of the fact that three weeks later another shooting took place at Granite Hills High School, another high school in the area?

Source: Reprinted with permission from Janet Christopulous.

Security personnel staff a booth at East Syracuse–Minoa High School in central New York State. Since the Columbine High School shootings in Colorado in 1999, and numerous other attacks that have occurred since, school security has been given high priority. ■ **What can be done to make schools safer still?**

FIGURE 9.1

A Time Line of Recent Worldwide School Shootings

October 3, 2006 **Nickel Mines, Pa.**	Carl Charles Roberts IV, 32, entered the one-room West Nickel Mines Amish School and shot 10 schoolgirls, ranging in age from 6 to 13 years old, then killed himself. Three of the girls died on-site; two died later in an area hospital.
September 29, 2006 **Cazenovia, Wis.**	A 15-year-old student shot and killed Weston School principal John Klang.
September 27, 2006 **Bailey, Colo.**	An adult male held six students hostage at Platte Canyon High School, then shot and killed Emily Keyes, 16, and himself.
September 13, 2006 **Montreal, Quebec Canada**	Kimveer Gill, 25, opened fire with a semiautomatic weapon at Dawson College, killing Anastasia De Sousa, 18, and wounding more than a dozen students and faculty before he killed himself.
August 24, 2006 **Essex, Vt.**	Christopher Williams, 27, looking for his ex-girlfriend at Essex Elementary School, shot two teachers, killing one and wounding another. Before going to the school, he had killed the ex-girlfriend's mother.
November 8, 2005 **Jacksboro, Tenn.**	A 15-year-old shot and killed an assistant principal at Campbell County High School and seriously wounded two other administrators.
March 21, 2005 **Red Lake, Minn.**	Jeffrey Weise, 16, killed his grandfather and his grandfather's girlfriend. He then drove to Red Lake High School where he killed a teacher, a security guard, five students, and finally himself, leaving a total of 10 dead.
September 28, 2004 **Carmen de Patagones, Argentina**	Three students killed and six wounded by a 15-year-old Argentinean student in a town 620 miles south of Buenos Aires.
September 24, 2003 **Cold Spring, Minn.**	Two students killed at Rocori High School by John Jason McLaughlin, 15.
April 24, 2003 **Red Lion, Pa.**	James Sheets, 14, killed Red Lion Area Junior High School principal Eugene Segro, then killed himself.
April 14, 2003 **New Orleans, La.**	One 15-year-old and three students wounded at John McDonogh High School by gunfire from four teenagers; none were students at the school. The motive was gang-related.
April 29, 2002 **Vlasenica, Bosnia-Herzegovina**	One teacher killed, one wounded by Dragoslav Petkovic, 17, who then killed himself.
April 26, 2002 **Erfurt, Germany**	Thirteen teachers, two students, and one policeman killed, ten wounded by Robert Steinhaeuser, 19, at the Johann Gutenberg secondary school. Steinhaeuser then killed himself.
February 19, 2002 **Freising, Germany**	Two killed in Eching by a man at the factory from which he had been fired. He then traveled to Freising and killed the headmaster of the technical school from which he had been expelled. He also wounded another teacher before killing himself.
January 15, 2002 **New York, N.Y.**	A teenager wounded two students at Martin Luther King Jr. High School.
November 12, 2001 **Caro, Mich.**	Chris Buschbacher, 17, took two hostages at the Caro Learning Center before killing himself.
March 30, 2001 **Gary, Ind.**	One student killed by Donald R. Burt Jr., a 17-year-old student who had been expelled from Lew Wallace High School.
March 22, 2001 **Granite Hills, Calif.**	One teacher and three students wounded by Jason Hoffman, 18, at Granite Hills High School. A policeman shot and wounded Hoffman.
March 7, 2001 **Williamsport, Pa.**	Elizabeth Catherine Bush, 14, wounded student Kimberly Marchese in the cafeteria of Bishop Neumann High School. Bush was depressed and frequently teased.
March 5, 2001 **Santee, Calif.**	Two killed and 13 wounded by Charles Andrew Williams, 15, firing from a bathroom at Santana High School.
January 18, 2001 **Jan, Sweden**	One student killed by two boys, ages 17 and 19.
January 17, 2001 **Baltimore, Md.**	One student shot and killed in front of Lake Clifton Eastern High School.
September 26, 2000 **New Orleans, La.**	Two students wounded with the same gun during a fight at Woodson Middle School.

FIGURE 9.1

(Continued)

May 26, 2000 **Lake Worth, Fla.**	Teacher Barry Grunow was shot and killed at Lake Worth Middle School by Nate Brazill, 13, with a .25-caliber semiautomatic pistol on the last day of classes.
March 10, 2000 **Savannah, Ga.**	Two students were killed by Darrell Ingram, 19, as they left a dance sponsored by Beach High School.
March 2000 **Branneburg, Germany**	One teacher killed by a 15-year-old student, who then shot himself. The shooter has been in a coma ever since.
February 29, 2000 **Mount Morris** **Twsp., Mich.**	Six-year-old Kayla Rolland shot dead at Buell Elementary School near Flint, Mich. The assailant was identified as a six-year-old boy with a .32-caliber handgun.
December 7, 1999 **Veghel, Netherlands**	One teacher and three students wounded by a 17-year-old student.
December 6, 1999 **Fort Gibson, Okla.**	Four students wounded as Seth Trickey, 13, opened fire with a 9mm semiautomatic handgun at Fort Gibson Middle School.
November 19, 1999 **Deming, N.M.**	Victor Cordova, Jr., 12, shot and killed Araceli Tena, 13, in the lobby of Deming Middle School.
May 20, 1999 **Conyers, Ga.**	Six students injured at Heritage High School by Thomas Solomon, 15, who was reportedly depressed after breaking up with his girlfriend.
April 28, 1999 **Tabler, Alberta, Canada**	One student killed, one wounded at W. R. Myers High School in first fatal high school shooting in Canada in 20 years. The suspect, a 14-year-old boy, had dropped out of school after he was severely ostracized by his classmates.
April 20, 1999 **Littleton, Colo.**	Twelve students and one teacher killed, 23 others wounded at Columbine High School in the nation's deadliest school shooting. Eric Harris, 18, and Dylan Klebold, 17, had plotted for a year to kill at least 500 and blow up their school. At the end of their hour-long rampage, they also killed themselves.
June 15, 1998 **Richmond, Va.**	One teacher and one guidance counselor wounded by a 14-year-old boy in the school hallway.
May 21, 1998 **Springfield, Ore.**	Two students killed, 22 others wounded in the cafeteria at Thurston High School by 15-year-old Kip Kinkel. Kinkel had been arrested and released a day earlier for bringing a gun to school. His parents were later found dead at home.
May 19, 1998 **Fayetteville, Tenn.**	One student killed in the parking lot at Lincoln County High School three days before he was to graduate. The victim was dating the ex-girlfriend of his killer, 18-year-old honor student Jacob Davis.
April 24, 1998 **Edinboro, Pa.**	One teacher, John Gillette, killed, two students wounded at a dance at James W. Parker Middle School. Andrew Wurst, 14, was charged.
March 24, 1998 **Jonesboro, Ark.**	Four students and one teacher killed, ten others wounded outside as Westside Middle School emptied during a false fire alarm. Mitchell Johnson, 13, and Andrew Golden, 11, shot at their classmates and teachers from the woods.
December 15, 1997 **Stamps, Ark.**	Two students wounded. Colt Todd, 14, was hiding in the woods when he shot the students as they stood in the parking lot.
December 1, 1997 **West Paducah, Ky.**	Three students killed, five wounded, by Michael Carneal, 14, as students participated in a prayer circle at Heath High School.
October 1, 1997 **Pearl, Miss.**	Two students killed and seven wounded by Luke Woodham, 16. Also accused of killing his mother, he and friends were said to be outcasts who worshiped Satan.
March 30, 1997 **Sanaa, Yemen**	Eight people (six students and two others) at two schools killed by Mohammad Ahman al-Naziri.
February 19, 1997 **Bethel, Alaska**	Principal and one student killed, two others wounded, by Evan Ramsey, 16.
March 13, 1996 **Dunblane, Scotland**	Sixteen children and one teacher killed at Dunblane Primary School by Thomas Hamilton, who then killed himself. Ten others wounded in attack.
February 2, 1996 **Moses Lake, Wash.**	Two students and one teacher killed, one other wounded, when 14-year-old Barry Loukaitis opened fire on his algebra class.

Note: Incidents listed all involve students (or former students) as the perpetrators.

Source: Adapted from www.infoplease.com/ipa/A0777958.html. Published by Infoplease/Fact Monster, Boston, MA. © 2006 by Pearson Education. Reprinted by permission of the publisher.

An Amish buggy passes a stone farmhouse in Lancaster County, Pennsylvania, on the day after thirty-two-year-old milk truck driver Charles Carl Roberts IV barricaded himself inside an Amish one-room schoolhouse in 2006, shot ten young girls, then killed himself. Five of the children died. ■ **How can the recent spate of school shootings be explained?**

There is no question that an examination of delinquency in the United States must take a long look at the school experience. J. Feldhusen, J. Thurston, and J. Benning's longitudinal study found school relationships and experiences to be the third most predictive factor in delinquency, exceeded only by family and peer group relationships.[4] Delbert S. Elliott and Harwin L. Voss found that "the school is the critical social context for the generation of delinquent behavior."[5] Arthur L. Stinchcombe found that failure in school leads to rebelliousness, which leads to more failure and negative behaviors.[6] More recently, Eugene Maguin and Rolf Loeber's meta-analysis found that "children with lower academic performance offended more frequently, committed more serious and violent offenses, and persisted in their offending."[7]

In sum, there is considerable evidence that the school has become an arena for learning delinquent behavior. This chapter will look at the evolution of education in the United States, at the nature of crime in the schools, at different aspects of the relationship between the school setting and delinquent behavior, and at interventions used by some schools to prevent and control delinquency within school settings.

▲ History of American Education

The U.S. Constitution says nothing about public schools, but by 1850 nearly all the northern states had enacted free-education laws. By 1918, education was both free and compulsory in nearly every state of the union. The commitment to public education arose largely from the growing need for a uniform approach to socialization of the diverse groups immigrating to this country. Joel H. Spring, a historian, writes of this movement:

> Education during the nineteenth century has been increasingly viewed as an instrument of social control to be used to solve the social problems of crime, poverty, and Americanization of the immigrant. The activities of public schools tended to replace the social training of other institutions, such as the family and church. One reason for the extension of school activities was the concern for the education of the great numbers of immigrants arriving from eastern and southern Europe. It was feared that without some form of Americanization immigrants would cause a rapid decay of American institutions.[8]

During most of the nineteenth century, U.S. schools were chaotic and violent places where teachers unsuccessfully attempted to maintain control over unmotivated, unruly, and unmanageable children through novel and sometimes brutal disciplinary methods.[9] For example, Horace Mann reported in the 1840s that in one school with 250 pupils he saw 328 separate floggings in one week of five school days, an average of over 65 floggings a day.[10]

Widespread dissatisfaction with the schools at the turn of the twentieth century was one of the factors leading to the Progressive education movement. Its founder, John Dewey, advocated reform in classroom methods and curricula so students would become more questioning, creative, and involved in the process of their own education. Dewey was much more concerned about individualism and personal growth than rigid socialization.[11]

The 1954 U.S. Supreme Court decision that ruled racial segregation in public schools unconstitutional was a pivotal event in the history of American education; it obligated the federal government to make certain integration in schools was achieved "within a reasonable time limit."[12] The busing of children to distant schools, which arose out of the Supreme Court decision and which has resulted in the shift from neighborhood schools, remains a hotly debated issue.

During the 1960s, open classrooms, in which the teacher served as a "resource person" who offered students many activities from which to choose, were instituted as an alternative to the earlier teacher-oriented classrooms. As was the case with the Progressive education movement, the open-classroom concept was accepted more widely in private schools than in public schools.

The baby boom of the 1950s resulted in increased enrollments and more formalized student–teacher contacts in public schools in the 1960s and early 1970s. Public education also became more expensive in the 1970s, because the increasing numbers of children in the classroom meant that more equipment had to be purchased (including expensive items such as computers, scientific equipment, and audiovisual aids). At the same time, teachers' unions took a firmer stance during contract talks, and many larger cities experienced teachers' strikes during this decade.

Since at least the mid-1980s, instead of optimism, dire warnings have been issued by all sides concerning the state of education. An expert on schools put it this way in 1984:

> American schools are in trouble. In fact, the problems of schooling are of such crippling proportions that many schools may not survive. It is possible that our entire public education system is nearing collapse. We will continue to have schools, no doubt, but the basis of their support and their relationship to families, communities and states could be quite different from what we have known.[13]

Web LIBRARY 9.1

Read the OJJDP Fact Sheet *Overcoming Barriers to School Reentry* at **www.justicestudies.com/WebLibrary**.

School Crime

Crime in the schools, especially public schools, is a serious problem now facing junior and senior high schools across the nation. This high crime rate expresses itself through **vandalism**, **violence**, drug-trafficking, and gangs. Vandalism and violence are examined in this section, and Chapters 10 and 11 will explore the difficulties that youth gangs and drugs bring to the school setting.

Vandalism and Violence

There are two major reasons why so much youth crime is taking place in our schools. First, while urban schools are frequently criticized for failing to provide safe, orderly environments, the communities around these schools suffer from serious levels of crime and disorder. Unsafe schools, in other words, are lodged within unsafe neighborhoods. The level of school crime and violence is also dependent on the community context because most of the student population are members of the community. For example, if a community has a large number of adolescent drug dealers, runners, and lookouts, youth gang leaders and followers, chronically disruptive youths, and

vandalism
Destroying or damaging, or attempting to destroy or damage, the property of another without the owner's consent, or destroying or damaging public property (except by burning).

violence
Forceful physical assault with or without weapons; includes many kinds of fighting, rape, other attacks, gang warfare, and so on.

juvenile property offenders, then local schools are likely to have high rates of youth crime. Similarly, schools with little violence or vandalism are usually lodged in supportive communities with low rates of criminal or delinquent behavior.[14]

Second, schools' authoritarian atmospheres and the likelihood of failure by many students, especially those with limited learning abilities, create bored, frustrated, dissatisfied, and alienated students. In one study, students consistently rated themselves as more bored in school than in any other setting.[15] The repressive methods of education, as Martin Gold has noted, make school one of the most difficult experiences for adolescents in American society.[16] Urie Bronfenbrenner adds that "the schools have become one of the most potent breeding grounds of alienation in American society."[17]

Craig Haney and Philip G. Zimbardo drew the following comparison between public high schools and prisons: High schools, like prisons, have stark, impersonal architecture and drab interiors; give arbitrary power to teachers to punish and humiliate the pupil whose behavior is unacceptable; have regimentation and many regulations, including movement in lines and at signals from bells; restrict movement within the building; and regulate personal appearance through dress codes. The impersonality of large classes also has taught students, like inmates, to lose themselves in the crowd.[18]

The need to establish a safe learning atmosphere is a serious issue in public education today, but the added security features of many public schools make them appear even more like prisons. Uniformed police are stationed in many schools; other schools have their own security staff. Students must submit to a metal detector search to enter some schools; electronically locked doors are becoming more common; and locker searches for drugs and weapons are everyday occurrences in many schools. Identification tags or photo ID badges for students and silent panic buttons for teachers are other means schools are using to regain control of the environment. Until it was ruled unconstitutional by the courts, a school in Boston even gave a drug test (urinalysis) to every student during the physical examination performed by the school physician at the start of each academic year.[19]

Web LIBRARY 9.2

Read the Bureau of Justice Statistics (BJS) publication *Indicators of School Crime and Safety* at **www.justicestudies.com/WebLibrary**.

School Violence in the 1970s   The pervasiveness of vandalism and violence in public schools came to public attention in the early to mid-1970s when the Senate Subcommittee to Investigate Juvenile Delinquency began an extensive examination of that phenomenon. Much of the material collected by the subcommittee appeared to show dramatic increases in overt acts of criminal violence and vandalism on the part of students. The public became alarmed, and demands were made for Congress and the executive branch of government to do something. Congress responded to the public's concern by mandating that the Department of Health, Education, and Welfare prepare a definitive report on the status of crime, violence, and vandalism in the nation's schools. That report, which was published in 1978 as *Violent Schools—Safe Schools: The Safe School Study Report to Congress,* took three years to complete and cost $2.4 million. Some of the significant findings of the Safe School Study were as follows:

- 1.3 percent of all high school pupils were attacked each month, and 42 percent of those had some injury.
- 36 percent of all assaults on twelve- to nineteen-year-olds occurred in school.
- 2 percent of all secondary-school pupils reported theft of valuable items in one month, and about 54 percent of this theft occurred in classrooms.[20]

School Violence in the 1980s   Violence became widely recognized in the 1980s as one of the critical problems facing schools in the United States. A new dimension of school violence was the threat of assault, murder, or rape of teachers. In a 1980 study of 575 inner-city teachers in Los Angeles, each teacher reported that his or her environment was extremely stressful and that violence and vandalism were out of control. They reported that violence directed toward them included threats of murder, threats of rape, actual physical assault and injury by students with and without weapons, as well as theft, arson, and other forms of vandalism of their personal property. Open-locker searches in their schools had revealed drugs, dynamite, knives, stilettos, ammunition, rifles, and handguns. Gang warfare caused a particularly volatile situation. Not surprisingly, most of these teachers had repeatedly petitioned their principals to transfer them to less violent schools.[21]

A football coach who took a job in a Los Angeles high school in the early 1980s gave a similar report about the violence of the school setting. He said: "On the first day the principal told new teachers that you don't have to worry about violence here. It didn't take me long to realize that whenever the three administrators walked on campus, they always walked in twos and had a walkie-talkie in their hands. They would never go out alone."[22]

Several 1980s surveys also documented the high rates of vandalism and violence in public schools. The National Crime Survey reported that although the school-age population had markedly declined since 1982, "the number of violent crimes in and around schools has remained high, ranging from a low of about 420,000 in 1982 and 1986, to a high of almost 465,000 in 1987."[23] This survey further revealed that nearly three million attempted or completed assaults, rapes, robberies, and thefts took place inside schools or on school property during 1987.[24]

A 1988 study on school violence that was part of the larger National Adolescent Student Health Survey (NASHS) dismissed the notion that violence in this nation's schools had gone down in the 1980s. Findings from the NASHS study, comprising surveys completed by eighth- and tenth-graders in 1987 in more than 200 public and private schools in twenty states, revealed:

Web **LIBRARY** 9.3

Read the NIJ-sponsored publication *Effectiveness of School-Based Violence Prevention Programs for Reducing Disruptive and Aggressive Behavior* at **www.justicestudies .com/WebLibrary**.

1. Over one-third of the 11,000 student respondents reported that they had been threatened with harm at school.
2. Nearly one-seventh of the students reported being robbed at school, and the same percentage said that they had been assaulted either at school or while riding on the school bus.
3. Almost one-half of the adolescent male respondents and one-quarter of the adolescent females had been in at least one fistfight that school year.
4. A weapon was involved in approximately one-third of the crimes against students.
5. More than one-fifth of the adolescent males surveyed admitted to carrying a knife to school at least once that year, and 7 percent carried one daily.[25]

The National Crime Victimization Survey (NCVS) interviewed 10,000 youths in 1989 in public and private schools and asked only about crimes that had occurred during the six months preceding the interview. This survey revealed that an estimated 9 percent of the students, ages twelve to nineteen, were crime victims in or around their school in the previous six-month period; 2 percent reported one or more violent crimes, and 7 percent reported at least one property crime.[26]

School Violence in the 1990s   Two surveys in the 1990s revealed that crime and safety continued to be a problem in schools in the United States. The National School Safety Center indicated in 1992 that violent crimes committed inside schools or on school campuses had risen markedly since 1987.[27] In a 1996 national random telephone survey of more than 1,300 public high school students, nearly half reported that violence and drugs were serious problems in their schools.[28]

Surveys in the 1990s also revealed that fear concerning personal safety and violence had become a serious concern for students and their parents. A 1993 national school survey conducted by the Centers for Disease Control and Prevention (CDC) found that of the 16,000 students in grades 9 through 12 responding to the questionnaire, fear for their own safety compelled as many as 4.4 percent to miss a day of school each month. Twenty-two percent of the students also felt fearful enough that they carried a weapon (e.g., a knife, club, gun) during the thirty days preceding the survey.[29] A 1994 national survey of parents of seventh- through twelfth-graders found that 40 percent of parents of high school students were "very or somewhat worried" about the safety of their child while in school or going to and coming from school.[30]

Surveys in the 1990s further found that students frequently witnessed acts of intimidation, violence, and drug transactions. For example, a 1995–1996 survey that took place in eleven high schools of the Los Angeles Unified School District reported a grim picture about the violence that students witnessed in the school setting. Of the 1,802 responding students, 49.1 percent had seen a weapon at school; 39.4 percent had experienced gang intimidation, especially on the way to and from school; 38.2 percent had seen a shooting going to or coming from school; and 13.5 percent had witnessed a shooting at school.[31]

School Crime Today   In 2005, the National Center for Education Statistics published its eighth annual report on school crime. This report, *Indicators of School Crime and Safety: 2005*, profiled school crime and safety and described the characteristics of the victims of these crimes (see Focus on Social Policy 9.1 for the report's basic findings).

In sum, it can be argued that schools are safer for children than other areas of their lives, because children experience higher rates of violence away from school than they experience when they are at school (including coming to or leaving school). In addition, as shown in Figure 9.2, there was some decline in violence from 1992 to

FIGURE 9.2

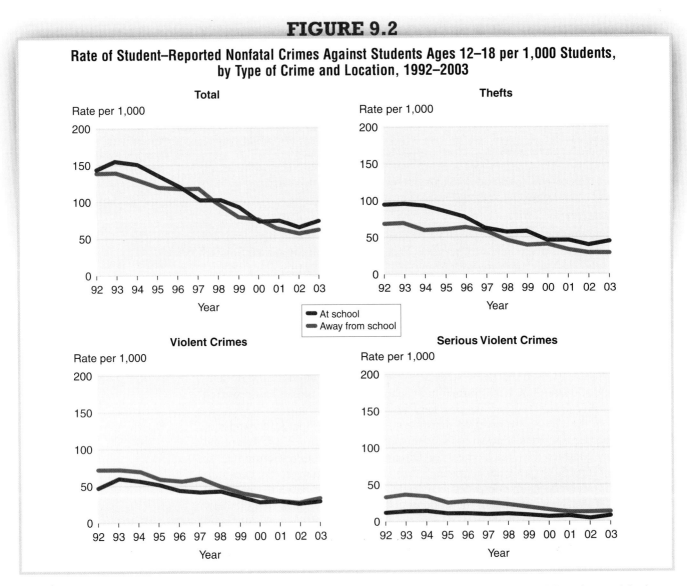

Rate of Student–Reported Nonfatal Crimes Against Students Ages 12–18 per 1,000 Students, by Type of Crime and Location, 1992–2003

Note: Serious violent crimes include rape, sexual assault, robbery, and aggravated assault. Violent crimes include serious violent crimes and simple assault. Total crimes include violent crimes and theft. "At school" includes inside the school building, on school property, or on the way to or from school.
Source: U.S. Department of Justice, Bureau of Justice Statistics, National Crime Victimization Survey (NCVS), 1992–2003.

FOCUS ON
Social Policy 9.1

Indicators of School Crime and Safety: 2005

Violent Deaths at School

- From July 1, 2001, through June 30, 2002, there were 17 homicides and 5 suicides of school-age youth (ages 5–19) at school. Combined, this figure translates into less than 1 homicide or suicide of a school-age youth at school per million students enrolled during the 2001–02 school year.

Nonfatal Student Victimization

- In 2003, students ages 12–18 were more likely to be victims of theft at school than away from school and were more likely to be victims of serious violence away from school than at school. That year, 45 thefts per 1,000 students occurred at school and 28 thefts per 1,000 students occurred away from school, while students reported being victims of serious violence at a rate of 12 crimes per 1,000 students away from school and 6 crimes per 1,000 students at school.

- In 2003, 5 percent of students ages 12–18 reported being victimized at school during the previous 6 months: 4 percent reported theft, and 1 percent reported violent victimization. Less than 1 percent of students reported serious violent victimization.

- In 2003, male students in grades 9–12 were more likely than female students to report being threatened or injured with a weapon on school property in the past year (12 vs. 6 percent).

Nonfatal Teacher Victimization

- Annually, from 1999 through 2003, teachers were the victims of approximately 183,000 total nonfatal crimes at school, including 119,000 thefts and 65,000 violent crimes. On average, these figures translate into an annual rate of 39 crimes per 1,000 teachers, including 25 thefts and 14 violent crimes (including 2 serious violent crimes) per 1,000 teachers.

- Annually, from 1999 through 2003, senior high school teachers were more likely than elementary school teachers to be victims of violent crimes and thefts (22 vs. 9 violent crimes and 36 vs. 20 thefts per 1,000 teachers).

- In 1999–2000, teachers in central city schools were more likely to have been threatened with injury or physically attacked during the previous 12 months than teachers in urban fringe or rural school. That is, 11 percent of teachers in central city schools had been threatened with injury by

students, compared with 8 percent each in urban fringe and rural schools had experienced such attacks.

School Environment

- In 1999–2000, 71 percent of public schools experienced one or more violent incidents and 36 percent of public schools reported violent incidents to the police. Twenty percent of public schools experienced one or more serious violent incidents, and 15 percent reported serious violent incidents to the police.

- In 1999–2000, 19 percent of public schools reported weekly student acts of disrespect for teachers, 13 percent reported student verbal abuse of teachers, 3 percent reported student racial tensions, and 3 percent reported widespread disorder in classroom. Nineteen percent of public schools reported undesirable gang activities, and 7 percent reported undesirable cult or extremist activities during the 1999–2000 school year.

- Middle schools were more likely than primary and secondary schools to report racial tensions, bullying, verbal abuse of teachers, and widespread disorder in classrooms in 1999–2000. For example, 43 percent of middle schools reported daily or weekly student bullying, compared with 26 percent of primary and 25 percent of secondary schools.

- In 2003, 21 percent of students ages 12–18 reported that street gangs were present at their school during the previous 6 months. Students in urban schools were the most likely to report the presence of street gangs at their school (31 percent), followed by suburban students and then rural students, who were the least likely to report them (18 and 12 percent, respectively).

- In 2003, 29 percent of students in grades 9–12 reported that someone had offered, sold, or given them an illegal drug on school property in the 12 months before the survey.

- In 2003, 12 percent of students ages 12–18 reported that someone at school had used hate-related words against them.

- In 2003, 7 percent of students ages 12–18 reported that they had been bullied (for example, picked on or made to do things they did not want to do) at school during the previous 6 months. Public school students were more likely to report being bullied than private school students (7 vs. 5 percent).

> ■ If violence in public schools is declining, why do so many teachers feel unsafe in the school setting? What can be done to make public schools even safer?

Source: J. E. DeVoe, K. Peter, M. Noonan, T. D. Snyder, and K. Baum, *Indicators of School Crime and Safety: 2005* (Washington, DC: U.S. Departments of Education and Justice, U.S. Government Printing Office, 2006), pp. iv–vi.

A teenage girl bullying another girl. Students report being more afraid of attacks at school than when away from school. ■ **What can be done to assuage such fears?**

2003. Yet students still experience high rates of disorders in some schools, especially public urban schools,[32] and they are more fearful of being attacked at school than away from school.[33] Some students avoid certain areas of their schools, and more students are faced with intimidation from bullies (see the discussion of reducing bullying later in this chapter). Weapons, gangs, and drugs in schools are further indicators of school disorder.[34]

Delinquency and School Failure

Lack of academic achievement, low social status at school, and dropping out are factors frequently cited as being related to involvement in delinquency. This section will look at each of these factors.

The 1967 report by the Task Force on Juvenile Delinquency concluded that boys who failed in school were seven times more likely to become delinquent than those who did not fail.[35] Anthony Meade showed that school failure was one of the best independent predictors of recidivism among first offenders appearing before juvenile court.[36] Albert K. Cohen was skeptical as to whether many youths can tolerate the censure and disparagement they receive at school:

> The contempt or indifference of others, particularly of those like schoolmates and teachers with whom we are constrained to associate with for long hours every day, is difficult, we suggest, to shrug off. It poses a problem with which one may conceivably attempt to cope in a variety of ways. One may make an active effort to change himself to conform with the expectations of others; one may attempt to justify or explain his inferiority. . . . One may tell himself he really doesn't care what these people think; one may react with anger and aggression. But the most probable response is simple, uncomplicated, honest indifference.[37]

LaMar T. Empey and Steven G. Lubeck's examination of delinquents and nondelinquents in Utah and Los Angeles found that both family variables (broken homes, relations with parents, and parental harmony) and school failure (especially grades in school) were highly associated with delinquency in both settings. Yet, when the two sets of conditions were simultaneously compared, the data clearly indicated that school (as measured by dropouts) had a stronger effect on delinquency.[38] Steven A. Cernkovich and Peggy C. Giordano conclude that school factors are no less important in understanding delinquency than other variables such as parental and peer attachments.[39] Allen E. Liska and Mark D. Reed suggest that parental attachment affects delinquency, which in turn affects school performance, which then affects parental attachment.[40]

Web PLACES 9.1

Visit the Anti-Bullying Network via **www.justicestudies.com/ WebPlaces**.

Achievement in School

Considerable evidence indicates that, whether measured by self-report or by official police data, both male and female delinquency is associated with poor **academic performance** at school.[41] Studies by E. B. Palmore, by J. F. Short and F. L. Strodtbeck, and by D. J. West found that delinquents' failure to perform, or achieve, in school is caused by either a lack of aptitude or lower intelligence.[42] Studies by Sheldon and Eleanor Glueck, by G. P. Liddle, and by N. W. Silberberg and M. C. Silberberg blamed delinquents' poor performance in school on deficient reading skills.[43] Travis Hirschi claims that the causal chain shown in Figure 9.3 may eventually lead to delinquent behavior.[44]

academic performance
Achievement in schoolwork as rated by grades and other assessment measures. Poor academic performance is a factor in delinquency.

Numerous researchers have pointed out that delinquents' lack of achievement in school is related to other factors besides academic skills. Several studies have found that delinquents are more rejecting of the student role than are nondelinquents.[45] For example, William E. Schafer and Kenneth Polk asserted, "There is considerable evidence that students who violate school standards pertaining to such things as smoking, truancy, tardiness, dress, classroom demeanor, relations with peers, and respect for authority are more likely to become delinquent than those who conform to such standards."[46] F. Ferracuti and S. Dinitz, Glueck and Glueck, and Donald West also found that delinquents tend to be more careless, lazy, inattentive, and "irresponsible" in school than nondelinquents.[47]

Delinquents' performance in school may be further affected by their relationships with classmates and teachers. Several studies have concluded that the relationship between school performance and delinquency is mediated by peer influence.[48] It would appear that the more problems adolescents have in school, the more likely they will turn to peers for support and acceptance. Conversely, the more adolescents have become affiliated with a delinquent subculture, the less receptive they tend to be to the process of academic education. A number of studies also have found that delinquent or delinquency-prone youngsters tend to be less popular and have poorer relations with classmates and peers in school than nondelinquents.[49]

" **Both male and female delinquency is associated with poor academic performance at school.** "

According to a 2001 report conducted by the Education Policy Center of the Urban Institute, the national graduation rate was 68 percent, with nearly one-third of all public high students failing to graduate. Significant racial and economic gaps exist between those who graduate and those who do not:

- Students from disadvantaged minority groups (American Indian, Hispanic American, African American) have little more than a fifty-fifty chance of finishing high school with a diploma.

FIGURE 9.3

Hirschi's Causal Chain

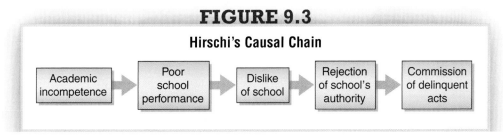

Academic incompetence → Poor school performance → Dislike of school → Rejection of school's authority → Commission of delinquent acts

Source: Adapted from Travis Hirschi, *Causes of Delinquency* (Berkeley: University of California Press, 1969), pp. 131–132, 156.

- By comparison, national graduation rates for whites and Asians are 75 and 77 percent, respectively.
- Males graduate from high school at a rate 8 percent lower than female students.
- Graduation rates for students attending school in high-poverty, racially segregated urban school districts lag from 15 to 18 percent behind those of their peers.
- A great deal of variation in graduation rates exists across regions of the nation as well as between the states.[50]

Several researchers relate lack of achievement to the absence of warm, supportive relations between teachers and students.[51] C. F. Cardinelli reported that schools tended to have more problems when teachers lacked genuine interest in students, and N. Goldman observed that good relationships among administrators, teachers, students, and even school custodians were associated with low levels of school vandalism.[52]

Maguin and Loeber did a meta-analysis of studies of academic performance and delinquency relationships and of intervention studies that were aimed at improving academic performance and reducing delinquency. As previously indicated, they found that children with lower academic performance committed more delinquent acts, committed more serious delinquent acts, and had a longer offending history than those with higher academic performance. This association was stronger for males than it was for females and for whites than it was for African Americans. Academic performance also predicted delinquent involvement independent of socioeconomic status.[53]

John Sampson and John Laub have demonstrated that high school can be a "turning point" in an individual's life course (see Chapter 2).[54] Richard Arum and Irenee R. Beattie assessed the effects of high school educational experiences on the likelihood of adult incarceration.[55] Using event history analysis and the National Longitudinal Survey of Youth data, they found that high school educational experiences have a lasting effect on an individual's risk of incarceration. This study offered specification of the high school context to identify how high school experiences can serve as a *defining moment* in an adolescent's life trajectory.[56]

In Canon City, Colorado, St. Scholastica Academy graduates hug each other before graduation at the Catholic boarding school for girls. ■ **Studies have shown that delinquents tend to perform poorly at school. What factors contribute to poor school performance?**

FOCUS ON
Social Policy 9.2

Public Schools in the Making of Black Masculinity

Ann Arnett Ferguson's book, *Bad Boys: Public Schools in the Making of Black Masculinity*, is an important resource for students of juvenile delinquency. According to Arnett there were two tracks for the student body of Rosa Parks Elementary School—a supposedly progressive school. Some children, mainly white, were tracked into futures as physicians, scientists, engineers, and attorneys. Other children, predominantly African American and male, were placed in a different tracking system that led to prison.

In Ferguson's words, her book "tells the story of the making of these bad boys, not by members of the criminal justice system on street corners, or in shopping malls, or video arcades, but in and by school, through punishment. It is an account of the power of institutions to create, shape, and regulate social identities."

African American boys made up only one-quarter of the student body, but they accounted for nearly half the number of students sent to the Punishing Room for minor and major misdeeds in 1991–1992. Three-quarters of youngsters suspended that year were boys, and four-fifths of these boys were African Americans. It became clear in the course of Arnett's study "that school labeling practices and the exercise of rules operated as part of a hidden curriculum to marginalize and isolate black male youths in disciplinary spaces and brand them as criminally inclined."

As Ferguson describes it, the troublemakers— those whom the school has labeled as the bad boys—use "the performance of masculinity through dramatic performances and disruptions in class, [and] through making a name through fighting, as a strategy for recouping a sense of self as creative, powerful, competent in the face of the tedium of the school's workday."

■ **Was what the author found in this progressive middle school in the West true of what minorities experienced in your school? How can education become more empowering of African Americans and other minority youths?**

Source: Ann Arnett Ferguson, *Bad Boys: Public Schools in the Making of Black Masculinity* (Ann Arbor: The University of Michigan Press, 2000), pp. 2, 223.

However, Richard B. Felson and Jeremy Staff, also using the National Education Longitudinal Survey, concluded that academic performance and delinquency have a spurious relationship. They estimated the effects of tenth-grade academic performance on delinquency in twelfth grade, and then controlled for the effects of social bonds and self-control. Surprisingly, they found that grades were not related to rates of delinquency. What did affect rates of delinquency were individual differences in self-control.[57]

Ann Arnett Ferguson spent three and a half years observing a classroom in a middle school in a western state. She found that the classroom experience was anything but positive for many African American children,[58] as discussed in Focus on Social Policy 9.2.

In short, most of the evidence points to three conclusions: Lack of achievement in school is directly related to delinquent behavior; most delinquents want to succeed in school; and the explanations for poor academic achievement are more complex than lack of general aptitude or intelligence.

Social Status

Albert K. Cohen's influential study of delinquent boys was one of the most comprehensive analyses ever undertaken of the role of the school in the development of delinquent subcultures. According to Cohen's theory, working-class boys, as discussed in Chapter 4, feel status deprivation when they become aware that they are unable to compete with middle-class youths in the school. Although avoiding contact with middle-class youths might solve the problem, working-class boys cannot do this, because they are forced to attend middle-class schools established on middle-class values. Consequently, they reject middle-class values and attitudes and form delinquent subcultures that provide them the status denied in school and elsewhere in society.[59] Jackson Toby's study, based on a variation of Cohen's thesis, contended that a lower-class background makes school success difficult because lower-class youths lack verbal skills and encouragement from home.[60] John C. Phillips proposed the steps by which low status in school can lead to deviant behavior; they are shown in Figure 9.4.[61]

FIGURE 9.4

Phillips's Steps Leading to Deviant Behavior

School status → [Negative] affect toward school → Involvement in an antischool subgroup → Deviant behavior

The proposed relationship between social class and delinquency in the school has been challenged. Cohen's argument that middle-class rewards, such as high grades, are of great importance to working-class boys has been particularly disputed. Polk and F. Lynn Richmond also found that any adolescent male who does poorly in school, regardless of class background, is more likely to become involved in delinquent behavior than one who performs well in school.[62] In another study, Polk found that controlling for social class did not alter the relationship between academic failure or success.[63] Palmore and Hammond reported a similar finding for African American and white youths.[64] Finally, George W. Nobit found that grade point average was associated with delinquency within socioeconomic classes.[65]

On balance, although the existence of a relationship between social class and delinquency in the school has mixed support, a relationship between school achievement and delinquency is much clearer.

Web **PLACES** 9.2

Visit Bullying.org via **www** **.justicestudies.com/** **WebPlaces**.

The School Dropout

The relationship between delinquent behavior and dropping out of school is a recurrent theme in the delinquency literature. An Elementary and Secondary Education Act (ESEA) Title II project in St. Paul, Minnesota, describes the student likely to become a **dropout** as follows:

A student trying on a school uniform as she prepares to return to school. ■ **Do private or church school students exhibit less delinquency than public school students?**

[The student likely to drop out is] one who is unable to function properly within the traditional classroom setting; who is generally recognized as an underachiever . . . who fails to establish goals regarding his future occupation; who has a record of tardiness as well as absenteeism; who lacks motivation, direction, and drive; who comes from a stressful family situation which appears to have a detrimental effect; who is hostile toward adults and authority figures; who has difficulty with community agencies and the law; who generally is not involved in any school activities; and, finally, who has had serious economic problems which threaten the completion of school.[66]

dropout

A young person of school age who, of his or her own volition, no longer attends school.

Joy Dryfoos found that getting poor grades and having to repeat a grade are excellent predictors of dropping out. Males are at higher risk of dropping out than females, and minority children are more likely to drop out than whites. Children whose families are on welfare have high dropout rates. Another significant antecedent of dropping out is early childbearing or marriage. Students who have been truant, suspended or expelled, or involved in other types of problem behaviors are high risks to drop out of school. Moreover, school quality affects dropout rates. Segregated schools, public vocational schools, large schools with large classes, and schools that emphasize tracking and testing have higher dropout rates.[67]

Wendy Schwartz analyzed information from the Educational Resource Information Center and determined the following:

- Students in large cities are twice as likely to leave school before graduating than nonurban youths.
- More than one in four Hispanic youths drop out; of those, nearly half leave by the eighth grade.
- Hispanics are twice as likely as African Americans to drop out of school.
- White and Asian youths are least likely to drop out.
- More than half of all students who drop out of school leave by the tenth grade, 20 percent by the eighth grade, and 3 percent by the fourth grade.
- In the last 20 years, the earnings level of dropouts doubled, while it nearly tripled for college graduates.
- Recent dropouts will learn $200,000 less than high school graduates, and over $800,000 less than college graduates, over the course of their lives.
- Dropouts comprise nearly half of all heads of households on welfare.
- Dropouts comprise nearly half of the nation's prison population.[68]

Elliott and Voss carried out a classic study of the school dropout, and their findings still hold true today. They studied 2,721 youths who entered the ninth grade in seven junior high schools in 1963 and followed them through their normal graduation year of 1967. Elliott and Voss discovered that the dropouts had much higher rates of police contact, officially recorded delinquent behavior, and self-reported delinquent behavior while in school than did those who graduated. The dropouts' delinquent behavior declined dramatically in the period immediately after they left school and then continued to decline. In contrast, the official delinquency and self-reported delinquency of the youths who remained in school gradually increased during these years.[69] Elliott and Voss's study is clearly supportive of strain theory. They found that the act of leaving school reduced school-related frustrations and alienation and thereby lowered the motivational stimulus for delinquency.[70]

Other researchers have found similar short-term results. S. K. Mukherjee, using data from the Philadelphia birth cohort of 1945, replicated Elliott and Voss's basic finding. For high school dropouts, more than two-thirds of those who had juvenile arrest records no longer committed delinquent offenses after they dropped out.[71] Marc Le Blanc and colleagues also found that delinquency declined for dropouts after they left high school.[72]

Studies that extended the follow-up period until participants were in their mid-twenties reported findings more consistent with a control perspective; that is, because dropping out of school represents a reduction in social control, it should result in increases in later criminal activity.[73] Polk and colleagues reported that during their early twenties, dropouts consistently had higher rates of criminality than did graduates.[74]

Starke R. Hathaway also followed dropouts and graduates in their mid-twenties and found that dropouts had consistently higher rates of criminal involvement.[75] Moreover, Jerald G. Bachman and Patrick M. O'Malley, in examining this relationship for a nationally representative sample of adolescents, found that through their early twenties, dropouts had higher rates of criminal activity than any other educational group.[76] Finally, Terence P. Thornberry, using a 10 percent sample of the Philadelphia cohort of 1945, discovered that "those who never graduated [the dropouts] had a considerably higher probability of becoming offenders than those who did graduate. This trend seemed particularly strong for minority subjects."[77]

G. Roger Jarjoura, in using data from the first two waves of the National Longitudinal Survey of Youth, explained some of the conflicting findings between dropping out of school and later offending behavior. He found that dropouts are not a homogeneous group. They vary by gender, race, and age; have different reasons for dropping out of school (personal, school related, or economic); and are dissimilar in prior misconduct (e.g., prior arrests, years sexually active, and suspensions from school). Examining these variables, adds Jarjoura, helps clarify why dropping out enhances delinquent involvement for some but not for others.[78]

Continuing research on this topic clearly reveals that the relationship between dropping out of school and delinquency is quite complex and multidimensional.[79] First, the relationship can be examined in terms of the short- and long-term benefits and consequences of dropping out of school and how they are related to delinquent behavior. Although there may be some short-term benefits, a number of negative long-term consequences result from dropping out of school. School dropouts have fewer job prospects, make lower salaries, are more often unemployed, are more likely to be welfare dependent, and experience more unstable marriages. They are prone to have other problem behaviors, such as delinquency, substance abuse, and early childbearing. Society ultimately suffers the consequences of students' dropping out because of lost revenue from diminished taxes and increased welfare expenditures. Table 9.1 lists some consequences of school failure and dropping out.[80]

The relationship between dropping out of school and delinquency can also be evaluated in terms of whether school or nonschool reasons were involved in a student's dropping out. Jeffrey Fagan and Edward Pabon found that nonschool reasons may have more significance for contributing to delinquent behavior than school-based factors.[81] In contrast, other studies reach the same conclusion as Elliot and Voss; that is, that school-based reasons for dropping out have the strongest connection with delinquency.[82] Furthermore, some research has found that the relationship between dropping out of school and delinquency is affected by a variety of personal, environmental, and economic conditions.[83] Accordingly, as Donald Shoemaker suggests, school dropouts' higher or lower rates of delinquency are "not necessarily explained by the frustrating experiences of lower-class youth in school, or by the lack of bonding with the school setting, or by any particular theoretical explanation of delinquency."[84]

Theoretical Perspectives on School and Delinquency

Most of the major theories of delinquency see the school as a factor contributing to delinquent behavior. Blocked opportunity theory, strain theory, cultural deviance theory, social control theory, labeling theory, the general theory of crime, integrated theory, life-course theory, and radical criminology, all make contributions to understanding delinquency in the school.

The majority of studies focusing on blocked opportunity have found that those most likely to commit delinquent acts are young people who do poorly in school or who believe that they have little chance of graduation. Observers says that when youthful offenders are unable to perform satisfactorily in school, they become disruptive, decide to drop out, or are suspended—all of which further reinforce involvement in deviant behavior.[85] Strain theorists contend that youngsters from certain

TABLE 9.1

Consequences of School Failure and Dropping Out

| EVENTS | CONSEQUENCES | |
	SHORT TERM	LONG TERM
Low achievement (poor grades)	Nonpromotion Difficulty getting admitted to college Truancy, absenteeism	Eventual drop out from school Low basic skills Low employability Lack of college degree
Nonpromotion (being left back)	Low self-esteem Low involvement in school activities Problem behavior Alienation	Eventual drop out from school
Dropping out	Unemployment	No entry to labor force Welfare dependency Low-level jobs
	Low wages	Low lifetime earnings Repeated job changes
	Depression and alienation	Later regrets Poor physical health Mental health problems
	Low basic skills	Illiteracy
	Delinquency	Criminal career, prison Marital instability Divorce
	Pregnancy	Early childbearing
	Abortion	Social costs: lost tax revenue, welfare expenditures

Sources: Adapted from Table 4.2 found in *Adolescents at Risk: Prevalence and Prevention* by Joy G. Dryfoos. Copyright © 1991 by Joy G. Dryfoos. Used by permission of Oxford University Press, Inc.; also draws on D. Kandel, V. Raveis, and P. Kandel, "Continuity in Discontinuities: Adjustment in Young Adulthood of Former School Absentees," *Youth and Society* 15 (1984), pp. 325–352; G. Berlin and A. Sum, *Toward a More Perfect Union: Basic Skills, Poor Families, and Our Economic Future* (New York: Ford Foundation, 1988), pp. 24–38; and E. Ginzberg, H. Berliner, and M. Ostow, *Young People at Risk: Is Prevention Possible?* (New York: Ford Foundation, 1988), pp. 105–121.

social classes are denied legitimate access to culturally determined goals and opportunities, and that the resulting frustration leads to either the use of illegitimate means to obtain society's goals, or the rejection of those goals. Strain theory views the school as a middle-class institution in which lower-class children are frequently unable to perform successfully. These youths then turn to delinquency to compensate for feelings of status frustration, failure, and low self-esteem.[86]

Cultural deviance theorists argue that children learn delinquent behavior through exposure to others and by mimicking or modeling others' actions. Children may come to view delinquency as acceptable because of their exposure to others whose definitions of such behavior are positive. Because schools tend to reflect the characteristics of the community of which they are a part, attending school in high-crime areas increases the likelihood of association with delinquent peers.[87]

Social control theorists believe that delinquency varies according to the strength of a juvenile's bond to the social order. The school is acknowledged as one of the major socializing institutions, providing youths with structure, incentives, expectations, and opportunities for social bonding. Accordingly, social control theorists posit that delinquency is likely to result when a strong bond to school does not develop.[88]

Labeling theorists argue that once students are defined as deviant, they adopt a deviant role in response to their lowered status. Early on, schools attach labels on the basis of achievement and behavior, and these labels may influence the subsequent

Black Youths Learn to Make the Right Moves

ATLANTA—DeKalb County is home to some of the nation's wealthiest African-American neighborhoods, a shining star in a city known as the Black Mecca. There are more than 98,000 students in DeKalb schools, but just 27 of them attend Project Destiny School. They are the toughest of the tough: This is where students come when they're kicked out of alternative schools.

On a recent afternoon, Orrin Hudson, a former Alabama state trooper, is teaching chess to 14 students in an after-school program. He uses the ancient game to instill a fundamental life lesson: They will win or lose because of choices they make—in real life and on the chess board.

Standing at a large, canvas chess board pinned to an easel, he runs his rap: "If you lose a game, you have only yourself to blame." But he's already lost half his audience. Students at one table in the cafeteria-style room are playing checkers, talking among themselves and ignoring Hudson. "Man, ain't nobody listening to you," a young man at another table mutters. Still another feigns sleep.

Hudson, 41, figures he has taught chess to 15,000 kids in Georgia, Alabama, Kentucky, Nevada and Washington state. He knows that what he's pushing won't save every child in the room. But he's hoping chess might rescue one—the way it did him. He's among a determined band of people and groups across the nation trying to combat a corrosive social problem: the loss of many young black males to prison, to poverty, to early deaths.

For many reasons—some of them not yet fully understood by sociologists and black families—African-American males drop out of high school and college in disproportionately high numbers. They have much higher unemployment rates—24.7% for youths ages 16–19, nearly twice the national average for this age group. Almost one-third of black men in their 20s are in prison or on probation or parole. Nationally, 60% of imprisoned youths 18 and younger are black—nearly four times their representation in the population.

A major part of the problem, conservatives and liberals agree, is that education, the great American equalizer and traditionally a nearly sacred value in black households, is often viewed with disdain by young men whose cultural landscape is shaped by rap music and its bling-bling, get-it-all-now emphasis. The situation is further complicated by public schools that quickly label black boys as discipline and behavior problems, fast-tracking many for special-education classes and suspending and expelling them into dead-end lives.

Black parents across the nation are struggling with this complex issue, which cuts across all socioeconomic lines. Even middle- and upper-class African-Americans fret that their children will squander the gains the parents have made.

"Even the most successful African-Americans in our communities have young people who will not pursue higher education and attainment," says Arlethia Perry-Johnson, who heads a Georgia effort to increase enrollment of black males on the state's 34 college and university campuses. "That becomes our own dirty laundry that we need to air."

Saying No to Bad Choices

The notion that chess can help people make better choices isn't new. In 1991, Maurice Ashley, the only black International Grand Master of chess, coached the Raging Rooks—a team of youths from Harlem and the Bronx—to a tie for first in the National Junior High School Chess Championship. Philadelphia educator Salome Thomas-EL started a chess program at Roberts Vaux Middle School in 1987 and inspired hundreds of children to attend magnet schools and college. Philadelphia plans to establish chess clubs at all 264 public schools.

Hudson heard the call years ago. By 1999, he already had been teaching chess to Birmingham school children for 13 years, having started because he believed the game could help instill character. That year, he says, he realized he needed to reach even more children. The catalyst: the May 24, 2000, armed robbery and execution-style murders of five employees at a Queens, N.Y., Wendy's restaurant that netted the gunmen just $2,400.

Hudson knew the two killers had ridden a series of bad choices to that eatery. "This was kids killing kids for money," he says. "I have a major problem with that. Our people don't value life. I looked at my life and I said, 'What do I know how to do? What has made a difference in my life? What has helped me?' "

The answer was chess. His brother had introduced him to the game as a teenager. His high school English teacher, who is white, had helped him refine his play, giving him a book on chess when he graduated from high school. Hudson learned to scrutinize every option, to plan ahead and to recognize patterns. Those skills helped propel him out of a public housing project in Birmingham, where he was the seventh of 13 children.

"Orrin's the best I've taught, by far," says Birmingham teacher James Edge, in

treatment of youths. When students are labeled as aggressive, difficult to manage, or slow learners at an early stage, they may be put into a slow track for the remainder of their schooling. According to labeling theorists, this differential treatment contributes to delinquent identities and behaviors.[89]

Some radical criminologists view the school as a means by which the privileged classes maintain power over the lower classes. Subjected to the controlling forces of the state, lower-class children are exploited as they experience powerlessness and alienation. They are more likely than middle- and upper-class children to be placed in the lowest tracks, to receive poor grades, to be suspended for disciplinary reasons, and to drop out of school. According to radical theorists, lower-class children are essentially being trained to accept menial roles in the social order.[90]

his 29th year. "Chess teaches you discipline, teaches you organization. Orrin wanted that. A lot of the kids I have now need that discipline."

After high school, Hudson spent six years as a state trooper and ran a car dealership. Along the way, he thought he could help youths find hope in the face of bleak prospects.

He knew a thing or two about long odds. In 1999, Hudson was the lowest-ranked player to enter the Birmingham City Chess Championship. He won, beating the highest-ranked player to become the first African-American city champion. He won the next year, too.

Hudson figured that what worked for him would work for others. He says a conversation with motivational self-help guru Tony Robbins inspired him: "He asked me what I would do if I only had six months to live."

In 2001, he founded Be Someone Inc., a non-profit group that teaches self-esteem, critical thinking and responsibility through the game of chess.

Since then, Hudson has taught the game at schools, libraries and recreation centers—wherever he's asked to give free lessons. Hudson, who is a paid motivational speaker, also offers paid chess lessons.

Hudson, who is married and has five children, pays for chess materials with grants and donations to Be Someone, which had $49,301 in income and $49,150 in expenses in 2002, according to the Georgia secretary of state.

Hudson no longer plays in chess tournaments. But he can teach the game. His students have won many awards in regional and state tournaments. "I teach them, 'Look, you can make one move in life—and never recover. You've got to always ask, 'Is this the best move I can make?' If you see a good move, look for a better move."

His efforts are drawing accolades. This year, he won a 2004 Martin Luther King Award for Community Service and a TBS Superstation Pathfinders Award for Education. "We were impressed by how dedicated he was to the kids," says Angela Thomas, coordinator of the King awards, which are given by Emory University here.

"Make a Smart Move"

Hudson's visit to the Project Destiny school is only his third. The non-profit, faith-based program was developed to prevent juvenile delinquency, reduce recidivism and teach families to be economically self-sufficient. "We take kids expelled for a semester to one year for everything from drugs to guns," director Rodney Mayfield says. "This is their last resort."

Despite their reticence, Hudson entices several kids to play against him. "I like this," says Ronald Jackson, 15. "Where we could be out doing something to get us in trouble, we're here doing something positive." What he says next shows he's been paying attention: "When you play chess, all your pieces have a clear purpose. Just like in life. You have to make sure you make the right move at the right time."

About 20 minutes after Hudson leaves Project Destiny, he walks into a roomful of third-, fourth- and fifth-graders at Charles R. Drew Charter School, part of a nationally recognized effort to revitalize East Lake Meadows, once one of the city's most treacherous public housing projects.

The students here, younger and less jaded than the group he's just left, practically cheer when Hudson enters. They cluster around him, clamoring to be his first victim. He sets the board up, then begins chanting as he explains how the

Orrin Hudson teaching a chess class at Charles R. Drew Charter School in Atlanta. ■ **What lesson does Hudson say the game teaches to young people?**

knight moves: "One, two, turn! In an L-shape! One, two, turn!"

He tells his rapt audience: "In life, you've got to position yourself to win. By coming to school early, by being ready to learn. You've got to make sure you make smart moves. If somebody says, 'Let's not go to school today. Let's play hooky,' you say, 'No, I'm not going to do that. I'm going to make a smart move.' "

Fourth-grader Kiera Anderson, 10, returns from her turn at the board with a big grin. "He's a great teacher," she says. "He breaks it down to the point where any age group can understand. I've learned a lot from him. I learned that you've got to work together as a team to do certain stuff you never knew you could do."

After an hour, Hudson instructs her and the 25 others to start cleaning up.

"I'm teaching them, 'You've got to think on your own, because the only thing that can save you is yourselves,' " he says, packing away dozens of chess pieces. "No one is coming to the rescue."

Source: Larry Copeland, "Black Youths Learn to Make the Right Moves," *USA Today*, June 16, 2004, p. A4. Copyright © 2004 by *USA Today*. Reprinted by permission.

In the general theory of crime, once self-control has formed in childhood, it affects adolescents in the choices they make in peer relations, school conduct and achievement, drug and alcohol use, and delinquent activities. Thus, students with self-control will be able to abstain from activities in school that would affect teachers' negative evaluations; from unwholesome peer relations in and out of school that would affect their desire to succeed, including gang participation; and from behaviors that would garner the attention of the police and juvenile justice system officials.[91]

Interactional theory, as developed by Thornberry and colleagues, is one integrated theory that can be applied to the school. It originally stated that attachment to parents and commitment to school are important buffers against delinquency. Thus, according to the theory, adolescents who are emotionally bonded to parents and who succeed at school are unlikely candidates for serious delinquency. Later versions of this theory have found that while weakened bonds to family and school do cause delinquency, delinquent behavior further reduces the strength of the bonds to family and school, thereby establishing a behavioral trajectory toward increasing delinquency.[92]

Another integrated theory related to the school is one developed by Wayne N. Welsh, Jack R. Greene, and Patricia H. Jenkins that draws on control theory, school climate theory, and social disorganization theory to examine the influence of individual, institutional, and community factors on misconduct in Philadelphia middle schools. One of the strong conclusions reached by these researchers is that the simplistic assumptions that bad communities typically produce "bad children" or "bad schools" is unwarranted.[93]

One study that related the school to a life-course perspective was undertaken by Zeng-yin Chen and Howard B. Kaplan. Using a longitudinal panel data set collected at three developmental stages (early adolescence, young adulthood, and middle adulthood), Chen and Kaplan investigated how early school failure influenced status attainment at midlife. They concluded that "early negative experiences set in motion a cascade of later disadvantages in the transition to adulthood, which, in turn, influences SES [socioeconomic status] attainment later in the life course."[94]

Students' Rights

The school's authority over students comes from two principal sources: the concept of *in loco parentis* and state-enabling statutes.[95] E. Edmund Reutter Jr. summarized *in loco parentis* as follows:

> The common law measure of the rights and duties of school authorities relative to pupils attending school is the *in loco parentis* concept. This doctrine holds that school authorities stand in the place of the parent while the child is at school. Thus, school personnel may establish rules for the educational welfare of the child and may inflict punishments for disobedience. The legal test is whether a reasonably knowledgeable and careful parent might so act. The doctrine is used not only to support rights of school authorities . . . but to establish their responsibilities concerning such matters as injuries that may befall students.[96]

State-enabling statutes authorize local school boards to establish reasonable rules and regulations for operating and keeping order in schools, which do not necessarily have to be in written form.[97] A classic statement on this type of authority was made in the 1966 case of *Burnside v. Byars*:

> The establishment of an educational program requires the formulation of rules and regulations necessary for the maintenance of an orderly program of classroom learning. In formulating regulations, including those pertaining to the discipline of schoolchildren, school officials have a wide latitude of discretion. But the school is always bound by the requirement that the rules and regulations must be reasonable. It is not for us to consider whether such rules are wise or expedient but merely whether they are a reasonable exercise of the power and discretion of the school authorities.[98]

The courts have become involved with schools in a number of important areas: procedural due process, freedom of expression, hair and dress codes, school searches, and safety.[99]

Procedural Due Process

Dixon v. Alabama State Board of Education (1961) was a major breakthrough for students' rights because the appeals court held for the first time that due process requires a student to receive notice and some opportunity for a hearing before being expelled for misconduct.[100]

In 1969, the U.S. Supreme Court issued its far-reaching decision in *Tinker v. Des Moines Independent School District,* declaring that students do not shed their constitutional rights of freedom of speech at the schoolhouse gate. The issue that was involved in this case was whether students had the right to wear black armbands to

in loco parentis
The principle according to which a guardian or an agency is given the rights, duties, and responsibilities of a parent in relation to a particular child or children.

protest the Vietnam war. The Court ruled that school authorities did not have the right to deny free speech, even the expression of an unpopular view, unless they had reason to believe that it would interfere with the school operations.[101] In the 1986 *Bethel School District No. 403 v. Fraser* case, the Court upheld a school system's right to suspend or discipline a student who uses profane or obscene language or gestures. The Court reasoned that the use of lewd and offensive speech undermined the basic educational mission of the school.[102] In a 1988 decision, *Hazelwood School District v. Kuhlmeier,* the Court ruled that the principal could censor articles having to do with pregnancy and parental divorce in a student publication. The Court's majority justified this censorship because such publications were perceived to be part of the educational curriculum of the school.[103]

In January 1975, the U.S. Supreme Court took up the problem of **due process rights** in the schools, stating in *Goss v. Lopez* that schools may not summarily suspend students, for even one day, without following fundamentally fair fact-finding procedures.[104] In suspensions of ten days or less, a student is entitled to oral or written notice of the charges, an explanation of the evidence, and an opportunity to be heard. The *Wood v. Strickland* ruling, issued a month after the *Goss* decision, found that school officials may be subject to suit and held financially liable for damages if they deliberately deprive a student of his or her clearly established constitutional rights.[105]

The issue of corporal punishment came before the U.S. Supreme Court in the 1975 *Baker v. Owen* and *Ingraham v. Wright* cases.[106] Although *Baker v. Owen* merely affirmed a lower court ruling, *Ingraham v. Wright* held that reasonable corporal punishment is not cruel and unusual punishment under the Eighth Amendment to the U.S. Constitution.[107]

Freedom of Expression

Several court cases have defined students' rights to freedom of religion and expression in schools. In *West Virginia State Board of Education v. Barnette*, the Supreme Court held that students could not be compelled to salute the flag if that action violated their religious rights.[108] In *Tinker*, the wearing of black armbands was declared symbolic speech and therefore within the protection of the First Amendment.[109]

Hair and Dress Codes

Court cases testing the power of school administrators to suspend students for violations of hair and dress codes were widespread in the late 1960s and early 1970s. In *Yoo v. Moynihan*, a student's right to style his or her hair was held to be under the definition of the constitutional right to privacy.[110] Then, in *Richards v. Thurston,* the Court ruled that a student's right to wear long hair derived from his interest in personal liberty.[111] In *Crossen v. Fatsi*, a dress code prohibiting "extreme style and fashion" was ruled unconstitutionally vague, unenforceable, and an invasion of the student's right to privacy.[112] Other decisions have held that schools cannot prohibit the wearing of slacks,[113] dungarees,[114] or hair "falling loosely about the shoulders."[115]

School Searches

The use of drugs and weapons is changing the nature of police–student relations in schools. In the 1990s, the police began to enforce the 1990 federal Gun-Free School Zones Act and increasingly, in communities across the nation, to enforce drug-free school zone laws. Drug-free zones usually include the school property along with the territory within a 1,000-foot radius of its perimeter. Alabama has the most aggressive law in this nation: Territory within three miles of a school is declared drug free.[116]

The use of drug-sniffing dogs, breathalyzers, hidden video cameras, and routine **school searches** of students' pockets, purses, school lockers, desks, and vehicles on school grounds, appears to be increasing as school officials struggle to regain control

> " Students do not shed their constitutional rights of freedom of speech at the schoolhouse gate. "

due process rights

Constitutional rights that are guaranteed to citizens—whether adult or juvenile—during their contacts with the police, their proceedings in court, and their interactions with the public schools.

school search

The process of searching students and their lockers to determine whether drugs, weapons, or other contraband are present.

over schools. In some cases school officials conduct their own searches; in other cases, the police are brought in to conduct the searches.

In the *New Jersey v. T.L.O.* decision (1985), the U.S. Supreme Court examined the issue of whether Fourth Amendment rights against unreasonable searches and seizures apply to the school setting.[117] On March 7, 1980, a teacher at Piscataway High in Middlesex County, New Jersey, discovered two adolescent females smoking in a bathroom. He reported this violation of school rules to the principal's office, and the two females were summoned to meet with the assistant vice principal. When one of the females, T.L.O., claimed that she had done no wrong, the assistant principal demanded to see her purse. On examining it, he found a pack of cigarettes and cigarette rolling papers, some marijuana, a pipe, a large amount of money, a list of students who owed T.L.O. money, and letters that implicated her in marijuana dealing. T.L.O. confessed later at the police station to dealing drugs on school grounds.[118]

The juvenile court found T.L.O. delinquent and sentenced her to a year's probation, but she appealed her case to the New Jersey Supreme Court on the grounds that the search of her purse was not justified under the circumstances of the case. When the New Jersey Supreme Court upheld her appeal, the state appealed to the U.S. Supreme Court, which ruled that school personnel have the right to search lockers, desks, and students as long as they believe that either the law or school rules have been violated. The legality of a search, the Court defined, need not be based on obtaining a warrant or on having probable cause that a crime has taken place. Rather, the legality of the search depends on its reasonableness, considering the scope of the search, the student's gender and age, and the student's behavior at the time.[119]

The significance of this decision is that the Supreme Court opened the door for greater security measures because it gave school officials and the police the right to search students who are suspected of violating school rules.[120] Of eighteen cases in the years from 1985 to 1991 that were decided by state appellate decisions applying the T.L.O. decision, school officials' intervention was upheld in fifteen.[121]

In its 1995 *Vernonia School District 47J v. Acton* decision, the U.S. Supreme Court extended schools' authority to search by legalizing a random drug-testing policy for student athletes. This decision suggests that schools may employ safe-school programs, such as drug-testing procedures, so long as the police satisfy the reasonableness test.[122]

In the 2002 *Board of Education of Independent School District No. 92 of Pottawatomie County v. Earls* decision, the U.S. Supreme Court reversed the judgment of the court of appeals and upheld the right of the school district to test students who participated in extracurricular activities. The Court found this to be a "reasonably effective means of addressing the School District's legitimate concerns in preventing, deterring, and detecting drug use by students."[123] The Court in *Pottawatomie* expanded the *Vernonia* decision by extending the drug testing of student athletes to the testing of students involved in extracurricular activities. This is an especially important issue, given the recent concern over steroid use on the part of professional, college, and high school athletes.

Safety

Court-imposed limitations on the school concerning the rules under which youths can be disciplined *(Tinker)* and the requirements for procedural due process relating to school administrators taking disciplinary action *(Goss, Ingraham,* and others) have made local school authorities increasingly wary of using tough methods to discipline students. Principals have become reluctant, for example, to suspend youths for acts such as acting insubordinate, wearing outlandish clothing, loitering in halls, and creating classroom disturbances; only a few decades earlier, such conduct would have drawn a quick notice of suspension. Increased judicial intervention in the academic area has contributed to (though not caused) an increase in unruly behavior, and thereby reduced the safety of students in the public schools.[124]

In sum, judicial intervention in the school over the past three decades has had both positive and negative impacts. Students' rights are less likely to be abused than in the past because the courts have made it clear that students retain specific constitutional rights in school settings. Meanwhile, school administrators who perceive themselves as handcuffed by court decisions have become reluctant to take firm and forceful action against disruptive students, and violence and delinquency in the schools have increased.

School and Justice System Partnerships

There is a growing trend toward increasing partnerships between schools and various agencies of the juvenile justice system.[125] Traditionally, school partnerships with juvenile justice agencies have centered on the use of police officers as informational sources, with their efforts aimed at prevention through education. Four well-known programs initiated through earlier police–school partnerships are Drug Abuse Resistance Education (D.A.R.E.), Police Athletic League (P.A.L.) programs, Gang Resistance Education and Training, and Law-Related Education. All are described in later chapters of this text. Police personnel who are involved with these programs use the school environment as a conduit for preventing youth crime through education and less intrusive intervention. Contemporary partnerships between schools and agents of the justice system are increasingly structured for student control and crime prevention, rather than education. This signals important changes in the social control mechanisms used in schools and with children.[126]

The U.S. Department of Education's report on *Violence and Discipline Problems in U.S. Public Schools 1996–1997* provided some preliminary indications on the extent of juvenile/criminal justice–public school collaboration. Taken from a national representative sample of elementary, middle, and secondary schools, this survey revealed that 97 percent of schools reported using some form of security measures. Of the surveyed schools, 84 percent reported that they had low security measures (no police officers or guards, no metal detectors, but controlled access to campus); 13 percent reported stringent to moderate security measures (full-time police officers or guards, metal detectors, and controlled access to campus). Of the schools with stronger security measures, 6 percent had police or other law enforcement personnel stationed for thirty hours or more at the school.[127] Despite the difficulty of gauging the extent of this collaboration, there did appear to be a growing number of schools using police officers, security personnel, or other security measures on a part-time basis (or more) to assist in maintaining school order, security, and control.[128]

The trends identified in the 1996–1997 report hold true today and the changing nature of the partnership between criminal and juvenile justice agencies and the schools is as significant as the quantity of official presence. An indicator of this changing nature is the shift in language used by schools. Officers are brought into the school to "fight campus crime," maintain "discipline," "combat victimization," and support "zero tolerance." Justice personnel in the school, formerly called resource officers and liaisons, now increasingly are called "Independent School District (ISD) Police," "security officers," "guards," and "gang intelligence officers." Yet changes in the partnership go beyond semantics. Criminal justice agencies in the school setting more frequently focus on identification and investigation, control of campus access, drug sweeps and drug testing, strip searches, surveillance, monitoring, and crowd control.[129]

Specialized Treatment and Rehabilitation (STAR) is Texas's application of the boot camp concept within the school setting. This program brings to the school the assistance of the juvenile court, juvenile correctional authorities, the police, and parents. See Focus on Social Policy 9.3 for a description and evaluation of STAR.

Promising Intervention Strategies

Several intervention strategies promise to benefit schools in the United States: improved quality of the school experience; reduced intimidation by bullies in the school setting; increased use of mentors for students who are encountering difficulties or experiencing problems; greater use of alternative schools for students who cannot adapt

FOCUS ON
Social Policy 9.3

Specialized Treatment and Rehabilitation (STAR)

The impetus for STAR grew out of the rise of disruptive behavior on school campuses, the increasing numbers of juveniles being placed in the Texas Department of Criminal Justice Institutional Division, and an interest in the development of a boot camp program for youth. With the collaboration of the Conroe Independent School District (CISD), the Executive Director of Juvenile Services in Montgomery County, Texas, and the Montgomery County Juvenile Court, STAR began operation in November 1993. The basic goal of the STAR program was to curb disruptive and delinquent behavior in the public school system and, at the same time, to reduce student movement in and out of the schools because of discipline problems.

STAR participants are not to exceed sixteen years of age at the time of sentence. STAR levels range from I to IV. Level I is a one-day "prevention" day for youths who have broken minor rules in school. Level II is for youths who have committed more serious school violations or violations that could result in detention. Level I and Level II youths are referred to STAR by their school principal, who reports school rule violations to STAR drill instructors. Level I and II involve short-term participation for youths referred for minor violations of school rules or lesser unlawful behaviors.

Level III and Level IV require longer terms of participation and are reserved for youths whose behaviors have brought them in contact with the juvenile justice system. Level III, for example, is a twelve-week deferred adjudication program to which youths are informally sentenced by the juvenile probation department with approval and oversight of the juvenile court. Level IV, the most restrictive level of STAR, is a twenty-four-week pro-gram to which the juvenile court judge sentences the youth who has been adjudicated as a delinquent.

The daily schedule of STAR is the same for all participants. Youths arrive at 5:30 A.M. and remain there for approximately two and one-half hours. This portion of the youth's day is made up of regimented quasi-military drilling and physical activities. At 8:00 A.M. the youths are taken to their regular schools, accompanied by STAR drill instructors who remain with them throughout the school day. At the end of the school day (3:30 P.M.), STAR youths are bused back to the STAR campus to endure an additional two hours—an hour of daily programming (e.g., reading, study time, and special presentations) and an hour of physical activities and cadence drills. The day ends at 5:45 P.M. Level III and Level IV have only Sundays away from STAR, using Saturdays to fulfill the terms of their community service sentences (e.g., cleaning buildings, picking up trash along the highways, and other needed community service).

A twelve-month follow-up evaluation of this program was done for the ninety-four Level III and Level IV participants who completed STAR in July 1997. (The evaluation excluded Level I and Level II because data were not collected for youths not under formal supervision of the probation department.) Survey responses obtained from STAR participants, their parents, and their teachers indicated that STAR was perceived as favorable in almost every area. However, results of the recidivism analysis revealed that STAR participants offended more times for more serious offenses in a six- and twelve-month postrelease follow-up when compared to Intensive Supervision Program (ISP) participants.

> ■ **What is your evaluation of such a boot camp experience in a public school? Do you think that it would have much effect on youth crime if such programs were established across the nation?**

Source: Chad Trulson, Ruth Triplett, and Clete Snell, "Social Control in a School Setting: Evaluating a School-Based Boot Camp," *Crime and Delinquency* 47 (October 2001), pp. 573–609.

to the traditional education setting; the development of a comprehensive approach to school success that includes home, school, church/synagogue, parents, and other institutions and persons who participate in school processes affecting students' lives; effective school-based violence prevention programs; and more effective transitions from correctional contexts to the school setting.

Improving the School Experience

Web LIBRARY 9.4

Read the Office of Community Oriented Policing Services (COPS) publication *Bullying in Schools* at **www.justicestudies.com/ WebLibrary**.

The quality of the school experience begins with good teaching. Good teachers can make students feel wanted and accepted and can encourage students to have more positive and successful experiences in the classroom. Gertrude Moskowitz and John L. Hayman, in a research project at three inner-city junior high schools in Philadelphia, found significant differences between effective and ineffective teachers. The best teachers expressed their feelings and enabled students to express their emotions. Good teachers combated student boredom and restlessness with timely topics, discussions, and open-ended questions. They smiled more than ineffective teachers did, and when they disciplined students, they did not raise their voices.[130]

Bill Mechlenburg contends that "private schools, even in the big city ghettos, are providing better education at one-half to one-third the cost of the public school system."[131] He, as well as others, believe that the major difference between public and private schools is the varying motivation underlying each. Public schools, according to this expert, are designed and run to satisfy the educational system's bureaucracy—not the parents.

In contrast, "the private schools' client/customer is the parents and everything is designed to satisfy them in order to attract students."[132] Mechlenburg claims that "the real solution to our education problem is to introduce parental choice and competition. Until this is done we're going to keep on just satisfying the educational establishment by allowing them to waste more money without getting performance in return."[133]

Furthermore, students have the right to be involved in the operation of the school. Youths too frequently see themselves as immersed in an educational system that is beyond their control and unresponsive to their needs. This perception, of course, does little to increase an adolescent's desire to maintain or create positive relationships with teachers, counselors, and administrators.[134]

Finally, safety is one of the most important prerequisites of effective involvement in the educational process. Unless students feel safe, they are unlikely to involve themselves very deeply in the school experience. To ensure safety, a critical problem in large urban schools, administrators must take firm action to reduce violence and delinquency.

> " Safety is one of the most important prerequisites of effective involvement in the educational process. "

Web LIBRARY 9.5

Read the OJJDP Fact Sheet *Addressing the Problem of Juvenile Bullying* at **www.justicestudies .com/WebLibrary**.

Web PLACES 9.3

Visit the School Safety section of the National Education Association's website via **www .justicestudies.com/ WebPlaces**.

Bullying and Intimidation

Bullying in school is a worldwide problem. Even though most of the research on bullying has taken place in Great Britain, Japan, and Scandinavian countries, it has been noted and discussed wherever formal schooling environments are found. Bullying consists of such direct behaviors as teasing, threatening, taunting, hitting, and stealing that have been initiated by one or more aggressive students against a weaker victim. In addition to such direct attacks, bullying may also be more indirect, and cause a student to be socially isolated through intentional exclusion. Boys typically are involved in more direct bullying methods, whereas girls utilize more subtle strategies, such as spreading rumors and enforcing social isolation. Whether the bullying is direct or indirect, its key component is the repeated physical or psychological intimidation that takes place which creates an ongoing pattern of harassment and abuse.[135] See Focus on Social Policy 9.4 for a description of the bullying problem and for information on intervention strategies that can reduce bullying in schools.

bullying
Hurtful, frightening, or menacing actions undertaken by one person to intimidate another (generally weaker) person, to gain that person's unwilling compliance, and/or to put him or her in fear.

Mentoring

Three million adults had formal, one-to-one mentoring relationships with young people in 2005, an increase of 19 percent since 2002.[136] Youth development experts generally agree that mentoring is a critical component in a child's social, emotional, and cognitive development. Mentoring has the potential of building a sense of industry and competency, boosting academic performance, and broadening horizons.[137]

School-based mentoring is one of the most promising types of youth mentoring taking place today and is experiencing rapid growth. According to a Big Brothers Big Sisters of America survey, the number of school-based matches grew from 27,000 in 1999 to 90,000 in 2002, an increase of 233 percent.[138] Still, school-based mentoring is impacting only a small percentage of all youths who could be helped. One of the findings of a 2002 survey is that of the 17.6 million young people who could

Web LIBRARY 9.6

Read the OJJDP publication *Juvenile Mentoring Program: A Progress Review* at **www .justicestudies.com/ WebLibrary**.

Web PLACES 9.4

Learn about bullying and what can done to prevent it from the National Youth Violence Prevention Resource Center's website via **www .justicestudies.com/ WebPlaces**.

Facts About Bullying and Possible Intervention Strategies

Facts About Bullying

- Between 15 to 30 percent of students in U.S. schools are bullies or victims.
- In a recent report by the American Medical Association of over 15,000 sixth- through tenth-graders, it was estimated that approximately 3.7 million youths engage in, and more than 3.2 million are victims of, moderate or serious bullying each year.
- Bullying is often blamed as an important factor in school-related deaths.
- Membership in either bully or victim groups is associated with dropping out of school, psychosocial adjustment problems, delinquent activity, and other long-term consequences.
- Physical bullying increases in elementary school, peaks in middle school, and declines in high school. Verbal abuse, on the other hand, tends to remain constant.
- Over two-thirds of students believe that schools respond poorly to bullying.
- Twenty-five percent of teachers see nothing wrong with bullying or putdowns and, as a result, intervene in only 4 percent of bullying incidents.

What Can Schools Do?

- *Early Intervention:* Researchers advocate intervening in elementary or middle school, or as early as preschool. Social skills training is highly recommended, along with counseling and systematic aggression interventions for students demonstrating bullying and victim behaviors.
- *Parent Training:* Parents must learn to reinforce their children's positive behavior patterns and must demonstrate appropriate interpersonal interactions.

- *Teacher Training:* Training can help teachers identify and respond to potentially damaging victimization, as well as implement positive feedback and modeling to address inappropriate social interaction. Support services personnel who work with administrators can be helpful in designing effective teacher training modules.
- *Attitude Change:* Researchers maintain that society must stop defending bullying behavior as part of growing up or by assuming the attitude that "kids will be kids." School personnel should never ignore bullying behaviors.
- *Positive School Environment:* Schools with easily understood rules of conduct, smaller class sizes, and fair discipline practices report less violence and bullying behaviors.

What Can Parents Do?

- *Contact* the school social worker, counselor, or school psychologist and ask for help concerning bullying or victimization concerns.
- *Provide positive feedback* to children for appropriate social behaviors that do not include aggression or bullying.
- *Use alternatives to physical punishment,* such as the removal of privileges, as consequences for bullying behavior.
- *Stop bullying behavior* as it takes place and work on more appropriate social skills.

■ As you think back to your own school experience, did you have any experience in being bullied? What did you feel at the time? If you were a bully instead of a victim, did you ever wonder why you were doing what you were doing? There tends to be a division between bullies and victims in the literature: How about those who are bullies at some times and victims at others times? How frequently do you think this takes place?

---

benefit from having a mentor, only 2.5 million were in a formal one-to-one mentoring relationship.[139]

Alternative Schools

disruptive behavior
Unacceptable conduct at school; may include defiance of authority, manipulation of teachers, inability or refusal to follow rules, fights with peers, destruction of property, use of drugs in school, and/or physical or verbal altercations with teachers.

Disruptive behavior is a very serious problem in many of this nation's classrooms. Such behavior takes many forms: defiance of authority, manipulation of teachers, inability or unwillingness to follow rules, fights with peers, destruction of property, use of drugs in school, and physical or verbal altercations with teachers. Disruptive students require teachers and counselors to spend a great deal of time trying to make such youngsters accountable for their conduct and teach them acceptable behavior. The unstructured periods of the school day—between classes, during lunch hours, and immediately after school hours—give disruptive students ample time to participate in a variety of unacceptable behaviors.

School administrators often suspend or expel students who cause trouble.[140] This policy of swift suspension stigmatizes troublemakers as failures and reinforces their negative behaviors. **Alternative schools** are deemed a much more satisfactory way of dealing with young people whom public schools cannot control or who are doing unsatisfactory work in a public school setting. The juvenile court sometimes requires disruptive students to attend an alternative school, but more frequently, students are referred by the public school system.

In 2000–2001, 39 percent of public school districts had alternative schools and programs. They served approximately 613,000 at-risk students in about 10,900 alternative schools and programs in the United States. Alternative schools and programs were found more frequently in large districts (those with 10,000 or more students) than small districts (those with fewer than 10,000 students), in urban districts than suburban or rural districts, and in southeastern districts more often than in districts in other regions of the nation.[141]

Alternative schools, which have smaller classrooms, usually deal with "turnovers" or acting-out behaviors by taking youths out of the classroom only until they have regained control over themselves. The ultimate goal of most alternative schools is to return students to the public school setting.

The DePaul University Alternative High School in Chicago was a noteworthy alternative school. Located in the Cabrini–Green community, then one of the most violent housing projects in the United States, this alternative school had a student body of more than 100 pupils. Faculty members either had doctorates in education or had many years' experience in working with disadvantaged youths. Most of the student body was made up of gang members or former gang members who were there to graduate from high school or to be prepared to pass their GEDs. The sessions took place from 6:00 to 9:00 P.M., permitting students to work during the day. Some pupils were in their late teens or early twenties; mothers were encouraged to bring their young children to school, and child care was provided. One indicator of the seriousness of the students was that there were no signs of antisocial behavior (graffiti, drugs, weapons, or physical altercations) in the school environment.[142]

alternative school
A facility that provides an alternative educational experience, usually in a different location, for youths who are not doing satisfactory work in the public school setting.

A police dog checks student lockers for contraband. In an attempt to provide a safe learning environment, some schools have adopted stringent security measures, leading some critics to compare today's public schools to prisons. ■ **Are such strict measures necessary?**

Many of the nearly 11,000 alternative schools and programs in existence today have noteworthy programs working to meet the needs of the students referred to them. One principal of an alternative high school, commenting on alternative schools throughout the nation, had this to say:

> We need to be proactive now. We've been reactive—reacting to the poverty, the abuse, and those things. It's time to be proactive and prevent these things from happening. Each of these kids has such a full plate. I respect them for the fact they can handle all these things that are happening to them and still get up in the morning and hope for something positive to happen. They really try hard. And I sometimes think they like for me to rap [pick] on them. They need and want the discipline.[143]

In summary, a major advantage of alternative school programs is that they deal more effectively with disruptive students than does the public school system. They also relieve the public schools of the disruptive behaviors these youths display in regular classrooms, and they tend to reduce absenteeism and dropout rates. Their success appears to be largely related to their individualized instruction; small student population; low student–adult ratio; goal-oriented classroom environment focused on work and learning; and caring, competent teachers.

Positive School–Community Relationships

"The legendary vision of the blackboard jungle," according to Stanley Cohen, has dominated social control policy in schools. Cohen adds that the desire for a safe and secure school has contributed to a "massive investment in hardware and preventive technology: video surveillance, ultrasonic detectors, hotline to the police, redesigning buildings into clusters of manageable space." Administrators stress such problems as bomb threats, arson, violence, drug pushing, and mass disruption. Cohen concludes that the relevant literature often reads "like a blueprint for converting the school into a closed-security prison."[144]

In contrast to efforts at reducing delinquency in the school by investing in hardware and preventive technology, an alternative intervention strategy is the development of a comprehensive, or multicomponent, approach that includes home, school, and other persons and institutions that participate in the social processes affecting the students' lives. Delinquency and the quality of the public school experience, then, must be analyzed within the larger context of school–community relationships.[145]

Gary Schwartz notes the example of Parsons Park, Illinois, in which the local schools served as "the cultural battleground of the community."[146] It was primarily through this neighborhood's educational system that ethnic traditions, family patterns, and other community standards were "woven into the fabric of local institutions." Yet the local high school in a second neighborhood in the same city was characterized as disorganized and "having little connection with the larger society's goals and values."[147] Schwartz concluded that it was no coincidence that the first area had a lower rate of juvenile delinquency and that the second had a heavy concentration of gang activity.

One way to achieve better school–community relationships is to allow representatives from various parts of the community to interact with students and to explain their roles in society. Another way is for the school to open its facilities for community events as well as to sponsor a wide range of activities designed to integrate families, the community, and students. Families and other community members also could take a larger part in the actual education of youths. For example, parents and elderly people could become volunteers or paid teacher aides. In addition, joint classes for parents and children could be conducted. Such classes, which could focus on family relations, community services, or politics, might also have an effect on parents' attitudes toward education and school.[148] Furthermore, community businesses could provide summer employment for high-risk youths who are still in school. Finally, Eugene Lang's 1981 promise to a sixth-grade East Harlem (New York City) class that he would subsidize their college study if they graduated from high school became "one of the country's most celebrated private-sector initiatives for disadvantaged youth."[149] Some 180 projects across twenty-seven states have implemented similar programs; 77 projects are currently active.[150]

School-Based Violence Prevention Programs

The real or perceived threat of school violence has influenced to a large degree the way principals manage, teachers teach, and students learn. In J. H. Price and S. A. Everett's national survey of secondary school principals, one-third indicated that they had already implemented some type of violence prevention or safe school program and another third said that they were planning to implement such a program.[151]

Some genuine prevention efforts have been sponsored by federal and state governments. At the federal level, the Safe and Drug-Free Schools and Communities Act of 1994 was a major initiative. This act provided $630 million in federal grants during 1995 to the states to implement violence and drug prevention programs in and around schools. State departments of education and local school districts also have developed guidelines and continue searching for effective violence prevention programs. However, by 1997, the programs implemented through the mid-1990s—including conflict resolution curricula, peer mediation, individual counseling, locker searches and sweeps, and metal detectors—either had not been thoroughly evaluated or had been found to be ineffective.[152]

Delbert S. Elliott, Beatrix A. Hamburg, and Kirk R. Williams's 1998 book *Violence in American Schools: A New Perspective* argues that "the most effective interventions [for reducing school violence] use a comprehensive, multidisciplinary approach and take into account differences in stages of individual development and involvement in overlapping social contexts, families, peer groups, schools, and neighborhoods."[153] The final chapter of the book uses the ecological, life-course, and developmental approaches as a framework for organizing the previous chapters' research findings and prevention recommendations and integrates the book's various perspectives through five themes:

> " The real or perceived threat of school violence has influenced to a large degree the way principals manage, teachers teach, and students learn. "

1. *The Interconnectedness of Family, Peer Group, School, and Neighborhood:* The interconnections among multiple social contexts result in the problems in one context's being swept into another. In view of the fact that many social institutions are losing ground, this deterioration "increasingly puts pressure on schools to compensate for other institutional failures."

2. *The Dynamic Interaction Between Individuals and Social Contexts in the Process of Development:* This theme relates "to the consequences of violence for schools and the functions of violence for individuals within their social settings." It is a reminder that "youth violence can have major consequences for the general climate of schools."

3. *Collaboration as a Requirement for Effective Prevention Efforts:* Key in this theme is the word *collaboration:* "The prevention of violence involves building relationships among representatives of all public and private sectors that touch on the lives of youth." Only through such collaboration can comprehensive prevention strategies be developed "that address multiple risk factors in the overlapping social contexts relevant to the developmental stages of youth."

4. *The Need for a Public Health Approach to Violence Prevention:* A "public health strategy should be used to assess the nature and extent of youth violence and to plan and carry out violence prevention programs." These activities involve such step-by-step procedures as "public health surveillance; risk and protective factor identification, intervention design, implementation, and program monitoring as well as short- and long-term outcome assessment; and dissemination of the results to inform public policy and promote effective prevention efforts."

5. *Effective Programs and Strategies for Preventing Violence:* This theme is "organized around three intervention strategies: systemic changes for schools, programs for individual youths, and public policy positions." Some intervention efforts may be crafted for individuals, such as anger management and conflict resolution training. Others "may be designed for system reform, such as improving family relations, the quality of the school climate, the prosocial orientation of peer groups, or improving the service capacity of community agencies."[154]

In sum, Elliott and colleagues provide a developmental and contextual framework for understanding school violence. In addition, this study includes a number of policy-driven recommendations for preventing violence in U.S. schools.

From Correctional Contexts to School Settings

A new priority in juvenile justice is an emphasis on the role of schools in the transition of juvenile offenders from institutional confinement to life in the community. Youthful offenders who are making the transition back to school are typically affected by the social and personal influences that contributed to the conduct that placed them under the jurisdiction of the juvenile court in the first place.[155]

An example of such a venture is found in Franklin Transitional High School in Kentucky, which has approximately forty students. Student-to-staff ratio is about two to one because the school employs twenty staff members. Students come directly from confinement to the school. A bridge coordinator team screens returning students. Students' length of stay at the school is based on individual needs. Although the goal is to prepare students for other educational placements, students actually can graduate from the transition school. The Institute of Families, a private agency, provides counseling services to students and their families.[156]

When an institutionalized delinquent returns to the public school setting there are potential problems. The needs of juvenile offenders, fellow students, teachers, and the community must all be considered.[157]

CHAPTER Summary

The costs of delinquency in schools can be measured in lost earning potential, reduction of a sense of safety in the school environment, and disruption of school activities. This chapter also points out that:

■ Delinquent behavior can be best understood as the product of complex socialization processes operating at many different levels within the school system.

■ A student's lack of school achievement appears to be directly related to the likelihood of delinquent behavior.

■ Court decisions have mandated provision of specific constitutional rights to students, such as free speech and due process, in the school environment.

■ Some school administrators perceive themselves as being handcuffed by court decisions and are reluctant to take firm and forceful action against disruptive students.

The school has long been acknowledged as important in the socialization of children, but public education is facing sharp criticism today. Critics charge that:

■ Public schools are failing to effectively educate and properly socialize American youths.

■ Since the 1970s, vandalism, violence, and drug trafficking have become serious problems in many schools.

■ High rates of school crime create unsafe conditions and an unwholesome environment for learning.

For schools to improve, a number of changes need to take place, including:

■ Elevating the quality of the school.

■ Reducing the effects of bullying.

■ Increasing the use of mentoring.

- Providing more effective alternative school experiences for disruptive students.

- Finding ways to renew urban schools.

- Developing more positive school–community relationships.

- Making schools safe from violence.

CRITICAL THINKING
Questions

1. What is the relationship between repressive education and delinquency?
2. What are the consequences of violence and vandalism in public schools?
3. What factors are most frequently cited as contributing to the link between schools and delinquency? Rank them in importance.
4. What kind of interventions are needed to reduce the amount of delinquency in public schools?
5. Do you think a program designed to reduce bullying in school would have any effect on school violence and victimization?

WEB
Interactivity

Visit the Stop Bullying Now site run by the U.S. Department of Health and Human Services at **http://stopbullyingnow.hrsa .gov**. How does the site define bullying? What does it say that victims of bullying should do?

View the twelve "Webisodes" on the Health Resources and Services Administration site (**www.hrsa.gov**) and identify your favorite. What message does it communicate? What seems special about it? Do you think that this site can be effective in combating bullying? Why or why not? Submit your answers to your instructor if asked to do so.

Source: From http://stopbullyingnow.hrsa.gov/index .asp?area=main. Reprinted with permission from the United States Department of Health and Human Services.

Notes

1. Greg Toppo, "Spate of Violence Raises Alarm," *USA Today,* Tuesday, October 21, 2003, p. 1D.
2. For one attempt to explain the homicides in school, see Shirley R. Holmes, "Homicide in School: A Preliminary Discussion," *Journal of Gang Research* 7 (Summer 2000), pp. 29–36. Editorials attempting to explain school homicides have included Patrick O'Neill, "Experts: Inner Chaos Fuels Kids Who Kill," *The Oregonian,* January 22, 1999; Gordon Witkin, Mike Tharp, Joanne M. Schrof, Thomas Toch, and Christy Scattarella, "Again in Springfield, a Familiar School Scene: Bloody Kids, Grieving Parents, a Teen Accused of Murder," *U.S. News On Line,* January 6, 1998; and Margaret Warner, "A Deadly Trend," *The NewsHour with Jim Lehrer On Line Focus,* May 22, 1998.
3. Janet Cristopulos, the aunt of Chris Geschke, provided this story.

4. John F. Feldhusen, John R. Thurston, and James J. Benning, "A Longitudinal Study of Delinquency and Other Aspects of Children's Behavior," *International Journal of Criminology and Penology* 1 (1973), pp. 341–351.

5. Delbert S. Elliott and Harwin Voss, *Delinquency and Dropout* (Lexington, Mass.: Lexington Books, 1974).

6. Arthur L. Stinchcombe, *Rebellion in a High School* (Chicago: Quadrangle Press, 1964), p. 158.

7. Eugene Maguin and Rolf Loeber, "Academic Performance and Delinquency," in *Crime and Justice: A Review of Research* 20, edited by Michael Tonry (Chicago and London: The University of Chicago Press, 1996), p. 145.

8. Joel H. Spring, *Education and the Rise of the Corporate State* (Boston: Beacon Press, 1972), p. 62.

9. Joan Newman and Graeme Newman, "Crime and Punishment in the Schooling Process: A Historical Analysis," in *Violence and Crime in the Schools*, edited by Keith Baker and Robert J. Rubel (Lexington, Mass.: Lexington Books, 1980), p. 11.

10. Horace Mann and the Reverend M. H. Smith, *Sequel to the So-Called Correspondence between the Rev. M. H. Smith and Horace Mann* (Boston: W. B. Fowle, 1847).

11. John Dewey, "My Pedagogic Creed" (1897), reprinted in *Teaching in American Culture*, edited by K. Gezi and J. Meyers (New York: Holt, Rinehart, and Winston, 1968).

12. *Brown v. Board of Education of Topeka, Kansas* (1954), 347 US 483.

13. John Goodlad, *A Place Called School* (New York: McGraw-Hill, 1984), p. 1.

14. Julius Menacker, Ward Weldon, and Emanuel Hurwitz, "Community Influences on School Crime and Violence," *Urban Education* 25 (1990), pp. 68, 77.

15. Mihaly Csikszentmihalyi, Reed Larson, and Suzanne Prescott, "The Ecology of Adolescent Activities and Experience," *Journal of Youth and Adolescence* 6 (1977), pp. 281–294.

16. Martin Gold, "School Experiences, Self-Esteem, and Delinquent Behavior: A Theory for Alternative Schools," *Crime and Delinquency* 24 (1978), pp. 294–295.

17. Urie Bronfenbrenner, "The Origins of Alienation," *Scientific American* 231 (1973), pp. 41–53.

18. Craig Haney and Philip G. Zimbardo, "The Blackboard Penitentiary—It's Tough to Tell a High School from a Prison," *Psychology Today* 9 (June 1975), p. 106.

19. Kathryn A. Buckner, "School Drug Tests: A Fourth Amendment Perspective," *University of Illinois Law Review* 5 (1987), pp. 275–310.

20. U.S. Department of Health, Education and Welfare, *Violent Schools–Safe Schools: The Safe School Study Report to Congress* (Washington, D.C.: U.S. Government Printing Office, 1977), p. 177.

21. Robert J. Rubel, "Extent, Perspectives, and Consequences of Violence and Vandalism in Public Schools," in *Violence and Crime in the Schools*, edited by Keith Baker and Robert J. Rubel (Lexington, Mass.: Lexington Books, 1980), p. 19.

22. Interviewed in July 1985.

23. J. R. Wetzel, "School Crime: Annual Statistical Snapshot," *School Safety* 8 (Winter 1989), p. 8.

24. Ibid.

25. Robert M. Regoli and John D. Hewitt, *Delinquency in Society: A Child-Centered Approach* (New York: McGraw-Hill, 1991), pp. 245–246.

26. Bureau of Justice Statistics, *School Crime: A National Crime Victimization Survey Report* (Washington, D.C.: U.S. Department of Justice, 1991), p. 1.

27. National School Safety Center, *Weapons in School* (Malibu, Calif.: Pepperdine University Press, 1992).

28. Jean Johnson, Steve Farkas, and Alie Bers, *Getting By: What American Teenagers Really Think about Their Schools* (New York: Public Agenda, 1997), p. 14.

29. Laura Kann, Charles W. Warren, William A. Harris, J. L. Collins, K. A. Douglas, M. E. Collins, Barbara I. Williams, James G. Ross, and Lloyd J. Kolbe, "Youth Risk Behavior Surveillance—United States, 1993," in CDC Surveillance Summaries, *Morbidity and Mortality Weekly Report* 44 (1995), p. 6.

30. Robert Leitman, Katherine Binns, and Akhil Unni, *The Metropolitan Life Survey of the American Teacher 1994, Violence in America's Public Schools: The Family Perspective* (New York: Louis Harris, 1994), p. 5.

31. Lena M. Chao, Allan Parachini, Fernando Hernandez, Michael J. Cody, and Daniel Cochece Davis, *From Words to Weapons: The Violence Surrounding Our Schools* (Los Angeles: ACLU Foundation of Southern California, 1997), pp. iii–iv.

32. For a discussion of school disorder, see Wayne N. Welsh, "Effects of Student and School Factors on Five Measures of School Disorder," *Justice Quarterly* 18 (December 2001), pp. 911–947.

33. This finding is from J. P. DeVoe, K. Kaufman, P. Ruddy, S. A. Miller, A. K. Planty, M. Snyder, T. D. Duhart, and M. R. Rand, *Indicators of School Crime and Safety: 2002* (Washington, D.C.: U.S. Departments of Education and Justice, 2002). For a discussion of students' fear, see Lynn A. Addington, "Students' Fear after Columbine: Findings from a Randomized Experiment," *Journal of Quantitative Criminology* 19 (December 2003), pp. 367–387.

34. For a discussion of weapons in school, see Pamela Wilcox and Richard R. Clayton, "A Multilevel Analysis of School-Based Weapons Possession," *Justice Quarterly* 18 (September 2001), pp. 510–539.

35. Task Force on Juvenile Delinquency, *Juvenile Delinquency and Youth Crime* (Washington, D.C.: U.S. Government Printing Office, 1967), p. 51.

36. Anthony Meade, "Seriousness of Delinquency, the Adjudicative Decision and Recidivism: A Conceptual Configuration Analysis," *Journal of Criminal Law and Criminology* 64 (December 1973), pp. 478–485.

37. Albert K. Cohen, *Delinquent Boys: The Culture of the Gang* (New York: Free Press, 1955), pp. 123–124.

38. LaMar T. Empey and Steven G. Lubeck, *Explaining Delinquency* (Lexington, Mass.: D.C. Heath, 1971).

39. Steven A. Cernkovich and Peggy C. Giordano, "School Bonding, Race, and Delinquency," *Criminology* 30 (1992), pp. 261–291.

40. Allen E. Liska and Mark D. Reed, "Ties to Conventional Institutions and Delinquency: Estimating Reciprocal Effects," *American Sociological Review* 50 (1985), pp. 547–560.

41. LaMar T. Empey and S. G. Lubeck, *Explaining Delinquency* (Lexington, Mass.: Lexington Books, 1971); M. Gold, *Status Forces in Delinquent Boys* (Ann Arbor, Mich.: Institute for Social Research, University of Michigan, 1963); Martin Gold and D. W. Mann, "Delinquency as Defense," *American Journal of Orthopsychiatry* 42 (1972), pp. 463–479; T. Hirschi,

Causes of Delinquency (Berkeley: University of California Press, 1969); H. B. Kaplan, "Sequel of Self-Derogation: Predicting from a General Theory of Deviant Behavior," *Youth and Society* 7 (1975), pp. 171–197; and A. L. Rhodes and A. J. Reiss Jr., "Apathy, Truancy, and Delinquency as Adaptations to School Failure," *Social Forces* 48 (1969), pp. 12–22.

42. E. B. Palmore, "Factors Associated with School Dropouts and Juvenile Delinquency among Lower-Class Children," in *Society and Education,* edited by R. J. Havighurst, B. L. Neugarten, and J. M. Falls (Boston: Allyn and Bacon, 1967); J. F. Short and F. L. Strodtbeck, *Group Process and Gang Delinquency* (Chicago: University of Chicago Press, 1965); and D. J. West, *Present Conduct and Future Delinquency* (New York: International Universities Press, 1969).

43. Sheldon Glueck and Eleanor Glueck, *Unraveling Juvenile Delinquency* (Cambridge, Mass.: Harvard University Press, 1950); G. P. Liddle, "Existing and Projected Research on Reading in Relationship to Delinquency," in *Role of the School in Prevention of Juvenile Delinquency,* edited by W. R. Carriker (Washington, D.C.: U.S. Government Printing Office, 1963); and N. W. Silberberg and M. C. Silberberg, "School Achievement and Delinquency," *Review of Educational Research* 41 (1971), pp. 17–31.

44. Hirschi, *Causes of Delinquency.*

45. M. L. Erickson, M. L. Scott, and L. T. Empey, *School Experience and Delinquency* (Provo, Utah: Brigham Young University, 1964); R. J. Havighurst et al., *Growing Up in River City* (New York: John Wiley and Sons, 1962); W. Healy and A. F. Bronner, *New Light on Delinquency and Its Treatment* (New Haven, Conn.: Yale University Press, 1963); and W. C. Kvaraceus, *Juvenile Delinquency and the School* (New York: World Book Company, 1945).

46. William E. Schafer and Kenneth Polk, "Delinquency and the Schools," in *Task Force Report: Juvenile Delinquency and Youth Crime* (Washington, D.C.: Government Printing Office, 1967), p. 233.

47. Franco Ferracuti and Simon Dinitz, "Cross-Cultural Aspects of Delinquent and Criminal Behavior," in *Aggression,* edited by S. H. Frazier (Baltimore: Williams and Williams, 1974); Glueck and Glueck, *Unraveling Juvenile Delinquency;* and West, *Present Conduct and Future Delinquency.*

48. J. David Hawkins and Denise M. Lishner, "Schooling and Delinquency," *Handbook on Crime and Delinquency Prevention* (Westport, Conn.: Greenwood Press, 1987), p. 181.

49. Glueck and Glueck, *Unraveling Juvenile Delinquency;* Ferracuti and Dinitz, "Cross-Cultural Aspects of Delinquent and Criminal Behavior"; Havighurst et al., *Growing Up in River City;* and West, *Present Conduct and Future Delinquency.*

50. Christopher B. Swanson, *Who Graduates? Who Doesn't? A Statistical Portrait of Public High School Graduation, Class of 2001* (Washington, D.C.: Urban Institute, 2004).

51. C. F. Cardinelli, "Relationship of Interaction of Selected Personality Characteristics of School Principal and Custodian with Sociological Variables to School Vandalism." Ph.D. dissertation, Michigan State University, 1969; Ferracutti and Dinitz, "Cross-Cultural Aspects of Delinquent and Criminal Behavior"; N. Goldman, "A Socio-Psychological Study of School Vandalism," *Crime and Delinquency* 7 (1961), pp. 221–230; M. J. Hindelang, "Causes of Delinquency: A Partial Replication and Extension," *Social Problems* 20

(1973), pp. 471–487; Hirschi, *Causes of Delinquency;* C. W. Thomas, G. A. Kreps, and R. J. Cage, "An Application of Compliance Theory to the Study of Juvenile Delinquency," *Sociology and Social Research* 61 (1977), pp. 156–175; and S. Vandenberg, "Student Alienation: Orientation toward and Perceptions of Aspects of Educational Social Structure," *Urban Education* 10 (1975), pp. 262–278.

52. Cardinelli, "Interaction of Selected Personality Characteristics," and Goldman, "A Socio-Psychological Study of School Vandalism."

53. Maguin and Loeber, "Academic Performance and Delinquency," p. 145.

54. Robert Sampson and John Laub, *Crime in the Making: Pathways and Turning Points through Life* (Cambridge, Mass.: Harvard University Press, 1993).

55. Richard Arum and Irenee R. Beattie, "High School Experience and the Risk of Adult Incarceration," *Criminology* 37 (August 1999), p. 515.

56. Ibid., p. 532.

57. Christopher B. Swanson, *Graduation Rates: Real Kids, Real Numbers* (Washington, D.C.: The Urban Institute Education Policy Center, 2004).

58. Ann Arnett Ferguson, *Bad Boys: Public Schools in the Making of Black Masculinity* (Ann Arbor: The University of Michigan Press, 2000). For other accounts with similar findings, see John D. Hull, "Do Teachers Punish According to Race," *Time,* April 4, 1994, pp. 30–31; Minnesota Department of Children, Families and Learning, *Student Suspension and Expulsion: Report to the Legislature* (St. Paul: Minnesota Department of Children, Families and Learning, 1996); Commission for Positive Change in the Oakland Public Schools, *Keeping Children in Schools: Sounding the Alarm on Suspensions* (Oakland, Calif.: The Commission, 1992).

59. Cohen, *Delinquent Boys.*

60. Jackson Toby, "Orientation to Education as a Factor in the School Maladjustment of Lower-Class Children," *Social Forces* 35 (1957), pp. 259–266.

61. John C. Phillips, "The Creation of Deviant Behavior in American High Schools," in *Violence and Crime in the Schools,* edited by Keith Baker and Robert J. Rubal (Lexington, Mass.: Lexington Books, 1980), p. 124.

62. Kenneth Polk and F. Lynn Richmond, "Those Who Fail," in *Schools and Delinquency,* p. 67.

63. Kenneth Polk, "Class, Strain, and Rebellion among Adolescents," *Social Problems* 17 (1969), pp. 214–224.

64. E. B. Palmore and P. E. Hammond, "Interacting Factors in Juvenile Delinquency," *American Sociological Review* 29 (1964), pp. 848–854.

65. George W. Nobit, "The Adolescent Experience and Delinquency: School versus Subcultural Effects," *Youth and Society* 8 (September 1976), pp. 27–44.

66. National Advisory Council on Supplementary Centers and Services, *Dropout Prevention* (Washington, D.C.: U.S. Government Printing Office, 1975), p. 2.

67. Joy G. Dryfoos, *Adolescents at Risk: Prevalence and Prevention* (New York: Oxford University Press, 1990), p. 89.

68. Wendy Schwartz, *After-School and Community Technology Programs for Low-Income Families* (Washington, D.C.: Educational Resource Information Center [ERIC] Clearinghouse on Urban Education, 2003).

69. Elliott and Voss, *Delinquency and Dropout,* pp. 127–128.

70. Ibid., p. 454.

71. S. K. Mukherjee, "A Typological Study of School Status and Delinquency." Unpublished doctoral dissertation, University of Pennsylvania, 1971.

72. Marc LeBlanc, Louise Biron, and Louison Pronovost, "Psycho-Social Development and Delinquency Evolution." Unpublished manuscript, University of Montreal, 1979.

73. Terence P. Thornberry, Melanie Moore, and R. L. Christensen, "The Effect of Dropping Out of High School on Subsequent Criminal Behavior," *Criminology* 23 (1985), pp. 7, 17.

74. Kenneth Polk et al., *Becoming Adult: An Analysis of Maturational Development from Age 16 to 30 of a Cohort of Young Men,* final report of the Marion County Youth Study (Eugene: University of Oregon, 1981), pp. 300–301.

75. Starke R. Hathaway et al., "Follow-up of the Later Careers and Lives of 1,000 Boys Who Dropped Out of High School," *Journal of Consulting and Clinical Psychology* 33 (1969), pp. 370–380.

76. Jerald G. Bachman and Patrick M. O'Malley, *Youth in Transition: Vol. VI. Adolescence to Adulthood: Change and Stability in the Lives of Young Men* (Ann Arbor: University of Michigan Press, 1978).

77. Thornberry et al., "The Effect of Dropping Out of High School on Subsequent Criminal Behavior," pp. 10–11.

78. G. Roger Jarjoura, "Does Dropping Out of School Enhance Delinquent Involvement? Results from a Large-Scale National Probability Sample," *Criminology* 31 (May 1993), pp. 149–171. For an examination of how disciplinary procedures produce dropouts, see Christine Bowditch, "Getting Rid of Troublemakers: High School Disciplinary Procedures and the Production of Dropouts," *Social Problems* 40 (November 1993), pp. 491–509.

79. Donald J. Shoemaker, *Theories of Delinquency: An Examination of Explanations of Delinquent Behavior,* 5th ed. (New York: Oxford University Press, 2005), p. 118.

80. Dryfoos, *Adolescents at Risk,* p. 89.

81. Jeffrey Fagan and Edward Pabon, "Contributions of Delinquency and Substance Abuse to School Dropouts among Inner-City Youth," 21 (1990), pp. 306–354.

82. Jarjoura, "Does Dropping Out of School Enhance Delinquent Involvement?" pp. 149–172.

83. Ibid.; Josefina Figueira-McDonough, "Residence, Dropping Out, and Delinquency Rates," *Deviant Behavior* 14 (1993), pp. 109–132; Timothy Hartnagel and Harvey Krahn, "High School Dropouts, Labor Market Success, and Criminal Behavior," *Youth and Society* 20 (1989), pp. 416–444; and Howard B. Kaplan and Xiaoro Liu, "A Longitudinal Analysis of Mediating Variables in the Drug Use–Dropping Out Relationship," *Criminology* 32 (1994), pp. 415–439.

84. Shoemaker, *Theories of Delinquency,* p. 110.

85. For this discussion, see LaMar T. Empey, Mark C. Stafford, and Carter H. Hay, *American Delinquency: Its Meaning and Construction* (Belmont, Calif.: Wadsworth, 1999), p. 195.

86. Albert K. Cohen, *Delinquent Boys: The Culture of the Gang* (Glencoe, Ill.: Free Press, 1955).

87. Walter B. Miller, "Lower-Class Culture as a Generating Milieu of Gang Delinquency," *Journal of Social Issues* 14 (1958), pp. 9–10.

88. Travis Hirschi, *Causes of Delinquency* (Berkeley: University of California Press, 1989).

89. Edwin M. Lemert, *Social Pathology* (New York: McGraw-Hall, 1951).

90. Mark Colvin and John Pauly, "A Critique of Criminology: Toward an Integrated Structural-Marxist Theory of Delinquency Production," *American Journal of Sociology* 89 (November 1983), pp. 513–551.

91. Michael R. Gottfredson and Travis Hirschi, *A General Theory of Crime* (Palo Alto, Calif.: Stanford University Press, 1990).

92. Terence P. Thornberry, "Toward and Interactional Theory of Delinquency," *Criminology* 25 (1987), pp. 862–891.

93. Wayne N. Welsh, Jack R. Greene, and Patricia H. Jenkins, "School Disorder: The Influence of Individual, Institutional, and Community Factors," *Criminology* 37 (February 1999), p. 73.

94. Zeng-yin Chen and Howard B. Kaplan, "School Failure in Early Adolescence and Status Attainment in Middle Adulthood: A Longitudinal Study, *Sociology of Education* 76 (April 2003), pp. 110–127.

95. Stephen Goldstein, "The Scope and Sources of School Board Authority to Regulate Student Conduct and Status: A Nonconstitutional Analysis," 117 *U. Pa. L. Rev.* 373, 1969.

96. E. Edmund Reutter Jr., *Legal Aspects of Control of Student Activities by Public School Authorities* (Topeka, Kans.: National Organization on Legal Problems of Education, 1970).

97. *Hanson v. Broothby,* 318 F. Supp. 1183 (D.Mass., 1970).

98. *Burnside v. Byars,* 363 F.2d 744 (5th Cir. 1966).

99. This section on the rights of students is derived in part from Robert J. Rubel and Arthur H. Goldsmith, "Reflections on the Rights of Students and the Rise of School Violence," in *Violence and Crime in the Schools,* pp. 73–77.

100. *Dixon v. Alabama State Board of Education,* 294 F.2d 150, 158 (5th Cir. 1961, cert. den., 368 U.S. 930).

101. *Tinker v. Des Moines Independent School District,* 383 U.S. 503.

102. *Bethel School District No. 403 v. Fraser,* 478 U.S. 675, 106 S. Ct. 3159, 92 L.Ed.2d 549 (1986).

103. *Hazelwood School District v. Kuhlmeier,* 488 U.S. 260, 108 S. Ct. 562, 98 L.Ed. 2d 592 (1988).

104. *Goss v. Lopez,* 419 U.S. 565.

105. *Wood v. Strickland,* 420 U.S. 308.

106. *Baker v. Owen,* 423 U.S. 907, affirming 395 F. Supp. 294 (1975); and *Ingraham v. Wright,* 430 U.S. 651 (1975).

107. 423 U.S. 907, affirming 395 F. Supp. 294 (1975).

108. *West Virginia State Board of Education v. Barnette,* 319 U.S. 624.

109. *Tinker.*

110. *Yoo v. Moynihan,* 20 Conn. Supp. 375 (1969).

111. *Richards v. Thurston,* 424 F.2d 1281 (1st Cir. 1970).

112. *Crossen v. Fatsi,* 309 F. Supp. 114 (1970).

113. *Scott v. Board of Education, U.F. School District #17, Hicksville,* 61 Misc. 2d 333, 305 N.Y.S. 2d 601 (1969).

114. *Bannister v. Paradix,* 316 F. Supp. 185 (1970).

115. *Richards v. Thurston.*

116. Ronald D. Stephens, "School-Based Interventions: Safety and Security," *The Gang Intervention Handbook,* edited by Arnold P. Goldstein and C. Ronald Huff (Champaign, Ill.: Research Press, 1993), p. 221.

117. *New Jersey v. T.L.O.,* 469 U.S. (1985).

118. Ibid.

119. Ibid.

120. For an extensive discussion of the relevant issues and court decisions related to the police in the schools, see Samuel M. Davis, *Rights of Juveniles: The Juvenile Justice System* (St. Paul, Minn: Thompson Publishing, 2003), Sections 3–19 to 3–34.3.

121. J. M. Sanchez, "Expelling the Fourth Amendment from American Schools: Students' Rights Six Years after T.L.O.," *Law and Education Journal* 21 (1992), pp. 381–413.

122. *Vernonia School District v. Acton*, 115 S. Ct. 2394 (1995).

123. *Board of Education of Independent School District No. 92 of Pottawatomie County et al. v. Earls et al.*, 536 U.S. 822 (2002).

124. Rubel and Goldsmith, "Reflections on the Rights of Students," pp. 98–99.

125. Sheila Heavihide, *Violence and Discipline Problems in U.S. Public Schools 1996–1997* (Washington, D.C.: U.S. Department of Education, 1998).

126. Ibid.

127. Ibid.

128. Ibid.

129. Ibid.

130. Gertrude Moskowitz and John L. Hayman, "Interaction Patterns of First-Year, Typical, and 'Best' Teachers in Inner-City Schools," *Journal of Education Research* 67 (1974), pp. 224–230.

131. Bill Mechlenburg, "I Can Assure You These Are Facts," in *Grandfather Education Report*, edited by Michael Hodges, pp. 2–3. http://mwhodges.home.att.net/education-b.htm

132. Ibid.

133. Ibid.

134. Paul C. Friday and John Halsey, "Pattern of Social Relationships and Youth Crime: Social Integration and Prevention," in *Youth Crime and Juvenile Justice*, edited by Paul C. Friday and V. L. Stewarts (New York: Praeger, 1977), pp. 150–151.

135. Ron Banks, *Bullying in Schools. ERIC Digest*, p. 2. www.ericddigests.org/1997-4bullying/bullying.htm

136. Mentor, *Mentoring in America 2005: A Snapshot of the Current State of Mentoring* (2005), p. ii. www.mentoring.org/program_staff/evaluation/2005_national_poll.php.

137. National Mentoring Center, *School-Based Mentoring*, p. 1. www.nerel.org/mentoring/topic_school.html

138. Carla Herrera, *School-Based Mentoring: A Closer Look* (Philadelphia: Public/Private Ventures, 2004).

139. Mentor, *Mentoring in America 2005*, p. 2.

140. *Public Alternative Schools for At-Risk Students*, Indicators 27 (2003), p. 1. http://165.224.221.98/programs/coe/2003/section4/indicator27.asp

141. Ibid.

142. One of the authors made a site visit to this school in December 1997. He interviewed a number of students as well as the director and other faculty. This alternative school was closed in 2001 when the Cabrini–Green housing units were torn down.

143. Interview of this principal is found in Mike Carlie, "Chapter 9: Schools," *Into the Abyss: A Personal Journey into the World of Street Gangs*. www.faculty.missouristate.edu/m/mkc096f/what_I_learned_about/schools.htm

144. Stanley Cohen, *Visions of Social Control: Crime, Punishment and Classification* (Cambridge, England: Polity Press, 1985), pp. 80–81.

145. Jacqueline R. Scherer, "School–Community Relations Network Strategies," in *Violence and Crime in the Schools*, p. 61.

146. Gary Schwartz, *Beyond Conformity or Rebellion* (Chicago: University of Chicago Press, 1987), p. 50.

147. Ibid., p. 22.

148. Friday and Halsey, "Patterns of Social Relationships and Youth Crime," pp. 150–151.

149. Marc Freedman, "No Simple Dream," *Public Private Ventures News* (Winter 1987), p. 2.

150. "I Have a Dream" Foundation. See www.ihad.org/aboutus.php.

151. J. H. Price and S. A. Everett, "A National Assessment of Secondary School Principals' Perceptions of Violence in the Schools," *Health Education and Behavior* 24 (1997), pp. 218–229.

152. Denise Gottfredson, "School-Based Crime Prevention," in *Preventing Crime: What Works, What Doesn't, What's Promising: A Report to the United States Congress*, edited by Lawrence W. Sherman and Denise Gottfredson (Washington, D.C.: U.S. Department of Justice, Office of Justice Programs, 1997), pp. 2–74; M. W. Lipset, "Juvenile Delinquency Treatment: A Meta-Analytic Inquiry into the Variability of Effects," in *Meta-Analysis for Explanation: A Casebook*, edited by T. D. Cook, H. Cooker, D. S. Cordray, H. Hartman, L. V. Hedges, R. J. Light, T. A. Louis, and F. Mosteller (New York: Russell Sage Foundation, 1992), pp. 83–127; Patrick Tolan and Nancy Guerra, *What Works in Reducing Adolescent Violence: An Empirical Review of the Field* (Boulder: University of Colorado, Center for the Study and Prevention of Violence, 1994); and D. W. Webster, "The Unconvincing Case for School-Based Conflict Resolution," *Health Affairs* 12 (1993), pp. 126–141.

153. Delbert S. Elliott, Beatrix A. Hamburg, and Kirk R. Williams, *Violence in American Schools: A New Perspective* (New York: Cambridge University Press, 1998), p. 1.

154. Delbert S. Elliott, Kirk R. Williams, and Beatrix Hamburg, "An Integrated Approach to Violence Prevention," in *Violence in American Schools*, pp. 379–384.

155. Ronald D. Stephens and June Lane Arnette, *From the Courthouse to the Schoolhouse: Making Successful Transitions* (Washington, D.C.: Office of Juvenile Justice and Delinquency Prevention, 2000), pp. 1–2.

156. Ibid., p. 8.

157. Ibid., p. 149.

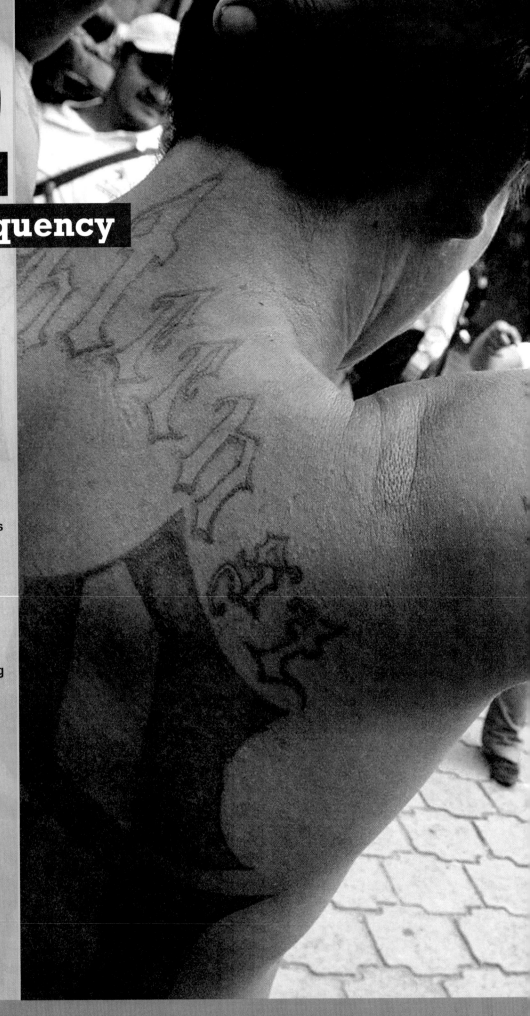

10
Gangs and Delinquency

> Gang members' mutual support of criminal activities, and possession of a value system which condones such behavior, distinguishes gang members and gangs from all other offenders and groups.
>
> —Michael K. Carlie, *Into the Abyss*

CHAPTER Objectives

AFTER READING THIS CHAPTER, YOU SHOULD BE ABLE TO ANSWER THE FOLLOWING QUESTIONS:

- What is the relationship between peer groups and gang activity?
- How have gangs evolved in the United States?
- What is the relationship between urban-based gangs and emerging gangs in smaller cities and communities?
- How extensive is gang activity in this country?
- How does gang activity affect communities?
- Why do youths join gangs?
- How can gangs be prevented and controlled?

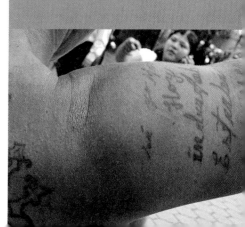

Introduction

Thirteen years ago, Walter Simon was shot eight times at the corner of Fillmore and Webster streets in San Francisco's violence-plagued Western Addition. Simon, a former gang member who survived the shooting, admits that he was not an innocent bystander—but had been targeted by members of a rival gang.

In June 2006, Simon and three other members of a San Francisco gang-prevention program told a gathering of 50 religious and community leaders about the realities of street life. The event was convened by District Attorney Kamala Harris after twenty-two-year-old Terrell Rollins, a witness in a gang-related homicide case, was shot to death by two gunmen. The men, believed to be gang members, were said to have been laughing as they murdered Rollins.

District Attorney Harris, an Indian-American woman, is the chief law enforcement officer for the city and county of San Francisco, and has a special interest in fighting gangs. "A lot of problems need to be fixed," Harris said after the meeting, which was closed to the media, "We all can do better."

Simon was in a gang before the shooting that put him in a wheelchair. Now thirty-one years old, he attends Contra Costa College in San Pablo, California, and is a member of the Omega Boys Club/Street Soldiers gang-intervention program, where at-risk youths receive counseling and have access to college scholarships.

Simon drew a distinction between "telling" about crime—which means being a responsible citizen—and "snitching," which he defined as someone in trouble naming others to escape harsher punishment. Simon doesn't have much use for "snitching," he said, but "telling" is vital to protect the community from violent criminals. "It could be fatal [to tell]," Simon said, "but if we don't stand for something, if we are not willing to die for what we believe in, what good is [sic] our lives?"

Joe Marshall, who co-founded the Omega Boys Clubs and who serves on the city's Police Commission, said he wants to reinforce the legacy of Rollins as a hero in the community. "Terrell was doing the right thing," he said. The conference, Marshall said, explored ways to make it safer to cooperate with police in solving crimes. "Everybody feels good about this," he said, "It was sorely needed."

Adapted from Jaxon Van Derbeken, "San Francisco: Former Gang Member Explains Street Reality to Community Leaders." *San Francisco Chronicle*, June 17, 2006. Copyright 2006 by *San Francisco Chronicle*. Reproduced with permission of *San Francisco Chronicle* in the format Other Book via Copyright Clearance Center.

Over the past thirty years, urban street gangs, armed with Israeli-made Uzis, Soviet AK-47s, diverted U.S. military M-16s, and other automatic weapons, have evolved into small criminal empires fighting for control of thriving narcotics, auto theft, prostitution, gun-running, and extortion operations. Illegal drugs form the backbone of most gang money-making criminal operations, with the manufacture and sale of **crack**, or rock cocaine, providing the bulk of the business. The crack trade, more than anything else, transformed street gangs into ghetto-based for-profit criminal organizations. Although most such gangs are led by adults, juveniles often play a central role in their day-to-day activities.[1]

As street gangs have become more businesslike, they have formed associations with other organized crime groups, including Mexican drug cartels, Asian criminal

crack
A generally less expensive but more potent form of cocaine.

groups, and Russian organized crime families. Gangs and their members are also becoming more sophisticated in their use of technology, including computers, cell phones, and the Internet. These new high-tech tools are frequently used to facilitate criminal activity and avoid detection by the police. Although some sources say that the number of gang members is in decline across the United States, some Hispanic gangs, such as *Mara Salvatrucha*, aka MS-13, are experiencing an influx of new members.[2] MS-13, one of the most violent gangs in the country, is highlighted in Social World of the Delinquent 10.1.

This chapter focuses on youths that are involved in gangs. Youth gangs have become a problem in many nations and are widespread in the United States in urban, suburban, and rural areas.

Peer Groups and Gangs

The increased focus on the individual in delinquency theory in the 1970s and 1980s provided a necessary balance to the previous overemphasis on group processes. But by the late 1980s, there was some concern that most theories of delinquency had become social-psychological rather than sociological, with the result that the group aspects of delinquent behavior had ceased to be examined and at times were virtually ignored.[3] A number of 1990s studies on the relationship between peers and delinquency revealed a renewed interest in group processes.[4]

Peer Groups and Delinquent Behavior

Inquiry into group delinquency has resulted in conflicting findings. Some self-report studies have found that most delinquent behavior occurs in groups. S. P. Breckinridge and E. Abbott's study found that most delinquent acts were committed with at least one other person.[5] Research by Clifford R. Shaw and Henry D. McKay showed that 82 percent of offenders committed their offenses in groups.[6] Maynard L. Erickson and Gary F. Jensen reported that regardless of their sex or whether they are in urban settings or small towns, juveniles tend to follow herd instincts when they violate the law. These authors did find that drug offenses have the highest group frequency and that status offenses—other than drinking and smoking—have the lowest.[7] Erickson reported in another study that between 37 and 42 percent of delinquent acts are committed by one person.[8] Paul Strasburg's study of violent delinquents in New York found that 69 percent of violent crimes were committed in a group of more than one person.[9] M. M. Craig and L. A. Budd, however, using a sample of youths in New York, found that only 38 percent of offenses were committed with companions.[10] Michael J. Hindelang further indicated that group delinquency may be overestimated.[11]

Elizabeth S. Piper, using the 1958 Philadelphia cohort data, investigated the relationships among the age of the offender, the type of offense, and the number of coparticipants. Piper found that, overall, 51 percent of offenses were committed in groups. Of these, 46 percent of nonviolent offenses and 68 percent of violent offenses were committed with others. At earlier ages, most offenses were committed by lone offenders; the peak in group offending was at ages thirteen and fourteen. An increasing tendency toward lone offending occurred later in the delinquent's career. Chronic offenders with five or more offenses, especially, were likely to have a greater mix of group and lone

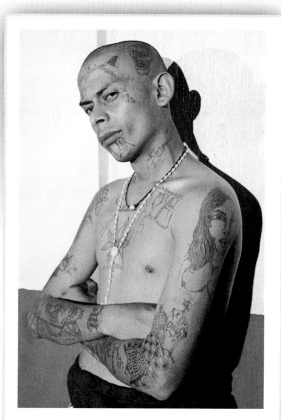

A *Mara Salvatrucha*, or MS-13, gang member displays his tattoos. MS-13 is one of the nation's most violent gangs. ■ **What are the attractions of gangs like MS-13 for their members?**

Mara Salvatrucha
MS-13

Mara is a Salvadoran word for "gang," and *Salvatrucha* means "Salvadoran guy."

Origin

Many Salvadoran refugees fled the U.S.-backed civil war against insurgents in El Salvador during the 1980s and relocated to the Rampart area of Los Angeles, California. Two stories exist as to how the gang formed. One version says that Salvadoran youths were accepted by the existing Hispanic gangs after they arrived in Los Angeles. Initially accepted because of the combat experience they had received during the civil war in El Salvador, the Salvadorans broke off on their own when differences arose and formed *Mara Salvatrucha* cliques. Another version says that after relocating to Los Angeles, the Salvadorian youths were targeted by the already established Hispanic gangs, and, for their own protection and the protection of their families, they formed the gang.

Cliques and Members

It is estimated that MS-13 has over 15,000 members and associates in at least 115 different cliques in 33 states and is experiencing a rapid growth. The areas with the greatest concentration are southern California with 20 different cliques and over 4,400 members and associates, and the northern Virginia/Metropolitan D.C. area, with 21 cliques and a total of more than 5,000 members and associates.

Sources also indicate a strong presence of *Mara Salvatrucha* in Alaska, Arkansas, Florida, Georgia, Illinois, Maryland, Michigan, Nevada, New Jersey, North Carolina, Oklahoma, Oregon, Rhode Island, Texas, and Utah. Foreign countries where they are known to exist include Canada, Guatemala, Honduras, Mexico, and El Salvador. Over 235,000 *Mara Salvatrucha* members are estimated to be active in Central America.

Identifiers

Mara Salvatrucha is also known as *Mara Salvatrucha* 13, MS-13, and MS XIII. Members consider the number 13 to be lucky,

and also believe that it demonstrates an alliance with southern California Hispanic gangs. The number 13 refers to the thirteenth letter of the alphabet, which is M. M is also synonymous with La Eme, or the Mexican Mafia. MS-13 members sometimes tattoo MS-related symbols on much of their body, even head to toe.

Operations

Members of this gang frequently use computers and other electronic technology. Dealers, lookouts, and carjackers carry wireless phones, pagers, radios, and police scanners. They also widely use the Internet, as they post photographs on their own websites, hailing their achievements against the police, taunting rivals, and speaking in bravado-soaked language to communicate with one another.

Recruitment of new members starts as early as elementary school. Hispanic children, especially those who are isolated from their peer groups, are targeted. Women are not formally accepted as MS-13 members, either in the United States or elsewhere, although females do provide services for gang members such as carrying weapons, acting as decoys, providing sex, and doing computer operations.

MS-13 in the United States replenishes its arsenal and narcotics stock from El Salvador, but its criminal activities within the United States go beyond smuggling contraband and gun-running. Activities also include human smuggling, hits for hire, theft, arson, and strong-arming businesses and individuals. MS-13 members are known for their violence and often do not hesitate to kill.

Methods that have been used to fight MS-13 are arrest, incarceration, and deportation. The most effective threat and deterrent seems to be deportation because deported members sometimes find themselves the targets of a vigilante group known as the Sombra Negra (Black Shadow).

■ Why do you think the MS-13 is such a violent gang? Why is it spreading so quickly throughout the United States? How do its connections to El Salvador strengthen the gang?

Source: Adapted from Robert Walker, "Mara Salvatrucha MS-13," *Gangs Or Us*, www.gangsorus.com/marasalvatrucha13.html.

---

offenses than nonchronic offenders. Another important finding of this study is a greater desistance rate among group offenders than among lone offenders, regardless of age at onset.[12]

Although there is general agreement that delinquency occurs most frequently within a group context, there is much less consensus about the nature and quality of delinquents' relationships with their friends or about the relationship between peers and delinquency. In terms of the quality of delinquents' relationships with their friends, Travis Hirschi believes that the causal significance of friendships has been overstated.

In referring to these relationships as "**cold and brittle**," he argues that "since delinquents are less strongly attached to conventional adults than nondelinquents they are less likely to be attached to each other. . . . The idea that delinquents have comparatively warm, intimate social relations with each other (or with anyone) is a romantic myth."[13]

Peggy C. Giordano and S. A. Cernkovich, in examining the relationships involved in delinquent groups, found that delinquents and nondelinquents have similar **friendship patterns.** This conclusion led them to question Hirschi's "cold and brittle" assumption, because Hirschi's position assumes social disability; "that is, that these kids are incapable of developing important and close friendships with each other and that they are just held together by the common quality of being losers." In contrast, these researchers believe that delinquents are able to develop good and close primary relationships.[14] Mark Warr's analysis of the National Youth Survey also found that delinquents are able to form close relationships with others. He stated that "delinquent friends tend to be 'sticky' friends (once acquired, they are not quickly lost)," but "recent rather than early friends have the greatest effect on delinquency."[15]

One of the stongest findings of criminology, according to Ross L. Matsueda and Kathleen Anderson, "is that delinquent behavior is correlated with delinquency of one's peers."[16] The process of examining this relationship between delinquency and peers has generated considerable debate. This debate has largely focused on the question of causal order. Do delinquents merely seek friends like themselves or do youths become delinquent because they associate with delinquent friends?

Robert Agnew's examination of data from the National Youth Survey found that when data indicate strong attachment to peers, longer periods of time spent with peers, and more extensive delinquent patterns, association with peers who engage in serious delinquent behavior has a strong positive effect on delinquency.[17] Warr and Stafford's analysis of data from the National Youth Survey reveals that peer attitudes tend to affect delinquency, but this effect is small compared with that of peers' behavior. The effect of peers' behavior, according to this study, remains strong even when the adolescent's own attitude and peers' attitudes are controlled.[18] D. S. Elliot and S. Menard's compelling research found that the acquisition of delinquent peers commonly preceded the onset of delinquency, which supports the notion of peer influence as a causal factor in delinquency.[19]

Merry Morash reported that adolescent females belong to less-delinquent groups, and this is a significant factor in accounting for their lower levels of delinquency. She contends that structural and situational constraints, as well as individual-level variables, explain why females end up in the least delinquent peer groups. Structural and situational factors, she suggests, may include the tendency of males to prefer to commit crime with other males, sex-typing of females by males as inappropriate colleagues and leaders, and a crime environment that emphasizes raw physical power. Moreover, gender-related characteristics of females, such as an aversion to aggression or greater empathy, may restrain females from joining peers who are prone to violent acts.[20]

> "'Delinquent behavior is correlated with delinquency of one's peers.'"

Some investigators contend that the relationship between delinquent behavior and delinquent peers is sequential or bidirectional.[21] Matsueda and Anderson found from their analysis of data from the National Youth Survey that "delinquent peer associations and delinquent behavior are reciprocally related, but the effect of delinquency on peer associations is larger than that of peer associations on delinquency."[22] Terence Thornberry and colleagues' examination of three waves of the Rochester Youth Development Study revealed that an interactional, rather than unidimensional, model better explains the relationship between peers and delinquency:

> Associating with delinquent peers leads to an increase in delinquency via the reinforcing environment of the peer network. Engaging in delinquency, in turn, leads to increases in associations with delinquent peers. Finally, delinquent beliefs exert lagged effects on peers and behavior, which tend in turn to "harden" the formation of delinquent beliefs.[23]

Web **LIBRARY** 10.1

Read the OJJDP publication *Co-Offending and Patterns of Juvenile Crime* at **www.justicestudies .com/WebLibrary**.

In 2005, Dana L. Haynie and D. Wayne Osgood, using social network data from the National Longitudinal Study of Adolescent Health, examined the contribution of peer relations to delinquency and discovered that adolescents do engage in higher rates of delinquency if they are in relationships with highly delinquent friends, and if they spend considerable amounts of time socializing with those friends. Haynie and Osgood found, however, that the influence of peers on delinquency is more limited than indicated by most previous studies. In addition, they found that peer influences are not necessarily more powerful than those of gender, age, school, or family.[24]

In another 2005 publication, Joan McCord and Kevin P. Conway's *Co-Offending and Patterns of Juvenile Crime*, a review of the literature reached the following conclusions:

- Offenders who are age thirteen and under are more likely to commit crimes in pairs and groups than are sixteen- and seventeen-year-old offenders (see Figure 10.1).
- About 40 percent of juvenile offenders commit most of their crimes with others.
- Co-offenders may learn through the influence of violent accomplices that violence can be an effective means of obtaining money or satisfying other desires.
- Youthful offenders are most at risk for subsequent crimes if they commit their crimes with accomplices.[25]

In sum, researchers generally agree that most delinquent behavior, especially more violent forms, is committed in groups, but they disagree on the quality of relationships within delinquent groups and on the influence of groups on delinquent behavior. There seems to be some agreement that the causal path is from peers to delinquent behavior and that more than a unidimensional model is needed. It would appear that an integrated approach, combining elements of control, strain, and subculture the-

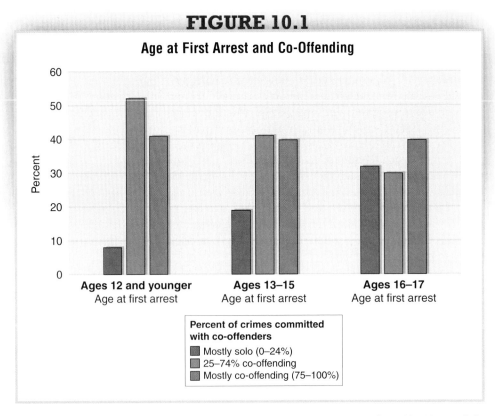

FIGURE 10.1

Age at First Arrest and Co-Offending

Source: Joan McCord and Kevin P. Conway, *Co-Offending and Patterns of Juvenile Crime* (Washington, D.C.: National Institute of Justice; Office of Justice Programs, 2005), p. 10. Reprinted with permission from the U.S. Department of Justice.

ory, can better account for delinquent behavior in groups than can any pure model alone. This integrated approach can also provide more clarity on several theoretical questions about groups and delinquency that are still being debated. For example, how do delinquent peers influence one another? What causes the initial attraction to delinquent groups? What do delinquents receive from these friendships that results in their continuing with them?[26]

The Development of Gangs in the United States

Gangs have existed in this nation for centuries. In the War of 1812, for example, Jean Laffite led his band of pioneers and smugglers against the British in support of Andrew Jackson. The Younger and James gangs, two infamous gangs of the Wild West, have long been folk heroes.[27] Youth gangs, as we know them, also originated in the early decades of this nation's history. Some evidence indicates that youth gangs may have existed as early as the American Revolution.[28] Others suggest that they first emerged in the Southwest following the Mexican Revolution in 1813.[29] Youth gangs seemed to have spread in New England in the early 1800s, primarily because of the shift from agrarian to industrial society. Youth gangs began to flourish in Chicago and other large cities in the nineteenth century as immigration and population shifts reached peak levels. In the nineteenth century, youth gangs were primarily Irish, Jewish, and Italian.[30] In the twentieth century, youth gangs changed rather significantly in nearly every decade.

> " Some evidence indicates that youth gangs may have existed as early as the American Revolution. "

Gangs and Play Activity: The 1920s Through the 1940s

Frederick Thrasher's 1927 study *The Gang: A Study of 1,313 Gangs in Chicago* was a pioneering and as yet unsurpassed work on gangs.[31] Thrasher viewed gangs as a normal part of growing up in ethnic neighborhoods. Adolescents who went to school together and played together in the neighborhood naturally developed a strong sense of identity that led to their forming close-knit groups. Thrasher saw these gangs, evolving from neighborhood play groups, as bonded together without any particular purpose or goal. They were largely transitory social groupings, typically with fewer than thirty members. They were generally organized in three concentric circles: a core composed of a leader and lieutenants, the rank-and-file membership, and a few occasional members. Finally, although each gang was different, the protection of turf was universally expected gang behavior.[32]

The *West Side Story* Era: The 1950s

From the late 1940s through the 1950s, teenage gangs became more established in urban areas, such as Boston, New York, and Philadelphia. In addition to the time they spent "hanging out," they partied together and, when necessary, they fought other gangs together. The musical *West Side Story,* later made into a movie, presented a picture of two 1950s New York youth gangs singing, dancing, and battling over turf. The Sharks, recent immigrants from Puerto Rico, defended their neighborhood while the Jets defended theirs; territorial lines were confined to neighborhood ethnic boundaries.

The 1950s gangs did not have the lethal weapons that today's gangs have, but they were very capable of violent behavior. One of the authors was hired to work with a white gang in Newark, New Jersey, in 1960–1961. The job became available because his predecessor, who had been on the job for two weeks, had a knife held to his chest, cutting his shirt and drawing a little blood. The predecessor was warned that bad things would happen if he did not quit. He chose to resign.

Millions of dollars in federal, state, and local money were spent on projects and programs designed to prevent and control the behavior of these fighting gangs. The detached workers program, one of the most widely funded efforts, sent professional workers into the community to work with gang youths. It proved to have little or no positive effect on reducing gangs' rates of delinquent behavior.[33]

Development of the Modern Gang: The 1960s

In the midst of a rapidly changing social and political climate in the 1960s, drugs influenced gang activity for the first time, "supergangs" emerged in several cities, and gangs became involved in social betterment programs and political activism.

Drugs led to reduced gang activity in some urban areas. When gangs began to reduce their activities or even to disappear from some urban areas in the mid- and late 1960s, some observers thought that the problem was coming to an end. New York City is one of the urban areas in which gang activity decreased significantly in the 1960s. The major reason offered for this apparent reduction of activity was the use of hard drugs. Lesser reasons included the civil rights movement, urban riots, the growth of militant organizations, the war in Vietnam, and an exodus from the ghettos.[34]

A leader of a large Bronx gang in New York City reflected on the lack of gangs in the 1960s: "You can't keep a brother interested in clicking [gang activities] if he's high or nodding."[35] A college student who was a heroin addict for several years in Spanish Harlem in New York City during the 1960s also blamed drugs for the lack of gang activity:

> My brother was a big gang member. But we did not go for that kind of thing. Man, we were on drugs. That was cool. We were too busy trying to score to fool around with gang activity. It was everybody for himself.[36]

The 1960s was also the decade in which the major supergangs developed. Some neighborhood gangs became larger and more powerful than other gangs in surrounding neighborhoods, and they forced these groups to become part of their gang organization. Eventually a few gangs would control an entire city. In the 1960s, the Crips, an African American supergang, began as a small clique in a section of south Los Angeles.[37] In Chicago the Vice Lords, Blackstone Rangers, and Gangster Disciples, all major supergangs today, also had their beginnings during that decade. See Social World of the Delinquent 10.2 for how the Gangster Disciples (GDs) developed at this time.

During the late 1960s the three Chicago supergangs became involved in social and political activism. The Vice Lords moved farther than any of the other Chicago street gangs toward programs of community betterment.[38] Their social action involvement began in the summer of 1967 when the Vice Lord leaders attended meetings at Western Electric and Sears, Roebuck. Operation Bootstrap, which resulted from these meetings, formed committees for education, recreation, and law, order, and justice. A grant from the Rockefeller Foundation in February 1967 enabled the Vice Lords to found a host of economic and social ventures. The Vice Lords also worked with Jesse Jackson on Operation Breadbasket and, in the summer of 1969, joined with the Coalition for United Community Action to protest the lack of African American employees on construction sites in African American neighborhoods.

In 1968, all three street gangs worked against the reelection of Mayor Richard Daley's Democratic machine, and this political activism brought increased strain to their relationship with the Democratic Party organization.[39] The interrelationships between the legal and political contexts became apparent on the streets of Chicago as street gangs experienced what they perceived as harassment from the police. As soon as he began a new term, Daley announced a crackdown on gang violence, and State's Attorney Edward Hanrahan followed by appraising the gang situation as the most serious crime problem in Chicago. The courts complied with this crackdown

Origins of the Gangster Disciples

Larry Hoover, the chief of the Gangster Disciples, speaks:

I remember how close I came to death when I was seventeen. It was the night I was standing near the front of the Sarah Harrison Lounge drinking Wild Irish Rose, and David Barksdale, who was the sole leader of the Disciples, and his main people confronted me. I don't know how they got into my neighborhood that fast. They had me surrounded. There were only two of us, and there must have been fifty of them.

As David and I faced each other, I noticed he held a beer can in his hand. The next thing I knew, his fist was in my face. The 180 pounds of muscular raw power sternly admonished, "You are not going with Charlie Atkins. You guys are going to be Disciples." I firmly stated, "I am not going to be a Disciple." Guns were made visible. I thought, I will do anything to get out of this alive, but that is not what I said. For some reason, they didn't shoot us. That still surprises me.

My 20 soldiers and I became members of the Double 6 King Cobras, a faction of the Cobrastones led by Charles Atkins. Charlie was tough, dangerous, and very lethal. His slight build didn't discourage him from quickly losing his temper. This be-

gan a three-year period from 1966 to 1969, where we were always fighting the Disciples. Out of the bloodbaths, two gangs emerged with tremendous power—the Blackstones and the Disciples.

Jeff Fort tried to make a deal with me to become a part of the Blackstone Nation. There were somewhere around 75 gang factions that made up the Nation. I did attend a few of their meetings, but he didn't offer to make me one of the Main 21. I remained bound to the Double 6 King Cobras until one night, David and his main leaders got out of their cars holding their hands in the air. This indicated there would be no shooting. They offered to form a treaty with us. We agreed to stop fighting the Disciples.

It wasn't long after that he asked me if we could merge and each have the same amount of power. We would share the power, two kings, coexisting in one land. Neither of us would be higher or more important. He would lead the Devil Disciples. I would conduct the Gangster Disciples. The merger left us 6,000 strong. It was then that I realized my sovereign power. I was a king, and I was only nineteen years old.

■ **What characterized the early days of the development of the supergangs? What else did you learn from these events in the life of a leader of a supergang?**

Source: Reprinted with permission from Linda Dippold Bartollas.

on gangs by increasing dramatically the number of gang members sent to prison in Illinois.[40]

Expansion, Violence, and Criminal Operations: The 1970s to the Present

In the 1970s and 1980s, as their leadership was assumed by adults, street gangs became responsible for an even bigger portion of muggings, robberies, extortions, and drug-trafficking operations in the United States. One city after another reported serious problems with gangs in the early 1970s. It became apparent that the gangs of the 1970s and early 1980s were both more violent than the gangs of the 1950s and more intent on making money from crime. Furthermore, they were systematic in their efforts to extort local merchants, engage in robberies, shake down students for money, intimidate local residents, and sell stolen goods.

Some gangs became so sophisticated that the police regarded their activities as organized crime. Those gangs kept attorneys on retainer. Some even printed up business cards to further their careers in extortion, and they sold the cards to businesses for "protection" and to warn away rivals.[41]

Although the gang has been the major concept used to examine collective youth crime in urban areas since the 1950s, little or no consensus exists as to what a gang actually is. Miller, as part of his nationwide examination of urban gangs, asked his

Larry Hoover, reputed leader of the Gangster Disciples street gang, is serving a life sentence in federal prison. A 1993 parole bid by Hoover was supported by several community leaders and politicians, including then-Chicago mayor Eugene Sawyer, who argued that Hoover was a peacemaker who could be a Pied Piper of reform for young people trapped in violence-racked neighborhoods. Hoover's bid for parole was turned down, however, and he was later convicted in federal courts of racketeering.

■ **Do you think that people like Hoover can serve as models of reform?**

respondents for a definition of a gang. In an analysis of 1,400 definitional elements provided by respondents, six major elements were cited most frequently: being organized, having identifiable leadership, identifying with a territory, associating continuously, having a specific purpose, and engaging in illegal activity.[42]

Through interviews, questionnaires, and visits to major cities, Miller came to the conclusion that gang members were committing as many as one-third of all violent juvenile crimes, terrorizing whole communities and keeping many urban schools in a state of siege. In Miller's study, justice system professionals reported problems with gangs in ten of the fifteen largest metropolitan areas. Respondents in Chicago, Detroit, New York, Philadelphia, Los Angeles, and San Francisco considered gang problems to be especially serious. Miller estimated that during the 1970s the number of gangs in these six cities ranged from 760 to 2,700 and included from 28,500 to 81,500 gang members.[43]

In a 1982 study Miller expanded the original six-city survey to twenty-six localities in the United States, including twenty-four of the largest cities and two counties. According to Miller's estimate, 2,300 youth gangs, with 100,000 members, were found in 300 cities. In addition to Boston, Chicago, Detroit, Los Angeles, New York, Philadelphia, and San Francisco, the list of cities reporting notable gang activity included Atlanta, Buffalo, Denver, Portland, and Salt Lake City. As in his earlier study, Miller concluded that law-violating youth groups accounted for a larger volume of less serious crimes, while gangs committed a smaller volume of more serious crimes. Furthermore, this study found that California's gang problems in both urban areas and smaller cities were particularly serious.[44]

Miller found that in the mid-1970s, the rate of murder by firearms or other weapons was higher than ever before; the five cities that had the most serious gang problems averaged at least 175 gang-related killings a year between 1972 and 1974. Forays by small bands, armed and often motorized, seemed to have replaced the classic "rumble."

The mid-1980s were a turning point for many ghetto-based street gangs, for crack cocaine had hit the streets. Urban street gangs competed with one another for the drug trade. Several Los Angeles gangs established direct connections to major Colombian smugglers, which ensured a continuous supply of top-quality cocaine. In some Chicago neighborhoods, heavily armed teams sold drugs openly on street corners, using gang "peewees" (youngsters) as police lookouts.

In 1988 and 1989 and through the early 1990s, an upsurge of youth gangs suddenly occurred throughout the United States. Some of these youth gangs used names of the national urban gangs, such as the Bloods and Crips from Los Angeles or the Gangster Disciples, Vice Lords, or Latin Kings from Chicago. Other gangs made up their own names, based on neighborhoods or images they wanted to depict to peers and the community. By the mid-1990s, nearly every city, many suburban areas, and even some rural areas across the United States experienced the reality of youths who considered themselves gang members.

The street gang traditionally has been a cultural by-product in the United States, but ganglike structures are now being reported in numerous cities worldwide. Cities in Asian/Pacific nations reporting gangs are Beijing, Hong Kong, Melbourne, Papua New Guinea, and Tokyo. European cities include Berlin, Frankfurt, London, Madrid, Manchester, and Zurich. There have also been indications that gang activity takes place in Canada, Russia, and South America.[45]

Cambodian gang members in California. Youth gangs appear to be spreading to our nation's smaller cities and towns. ■ **What accounts for this spread?**

The Nature and Extent of Gang Activity

According to the *2004 National Youth Gang Survey*, an estimated 760,000 gang members and 24,000 gangs were active in the United States in 2004. These estimates, although slightly higher than those from the National Youth Gang Surveys of 2002 and 2003, still reflect a decline in gang problems since 1996. (See Figure 10.2, which shows the percentage of law enforcement agencies reporting youth gang problems from 1996 to 2004.) In 2004, larger cities and suburban counties accounted for approximately 85 percent of the total number of gang members.[46]

Knowledge of the gang world requires an examination of the definition of gangs and the profile of gang members, and an understanding of gangs' intimidation of the school environment, of the structure and leadership of urban street gangs, of emerging gangs in small communities across the nation, of racial and ethnic backgrounds of gangs, and of female delinquent gangs.

Definitions of Gangs

Considerable disagreement still exists about what parameters define a **gang**. Researchers differ on questions such as:

- How many youths make up a gang?
- Must gang members commit crimes as a gang to be considered a gang?
- Must gangs have some semblance of organizational structure?
- Should motorcycle gangs, skinhead groups, and white supremacist groups be considered part of the youth gang problem?[47]

Thrasher's 1927 gang study was one of the first to attempt to define a youth gang:

A gang is an interstitial group originally formed spontaneously and then integrated through conflict. It is characterized by the following types of behavior: meeting face to face, milling, movement through space as a unit, conflict, and planning. The result of this collective behavior is the development of tradition, unreflective internal structure, esprit de corps, solidarity, morale, group awareness, and attachment to local territory.[48]

gang

A group of youths who are bound together by mutual interests, have identifiable leadership, and act in concert to achieve a specific purpose that generally includes the conduct of illegal activity.

FIGURE 10.2

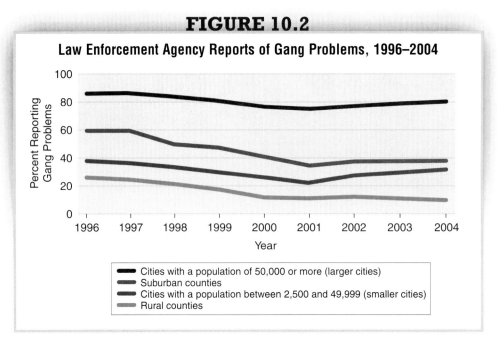

Law Enforcement Agency Reports of Gang Problems, 1996–2004

Cities with a population of 50,000 or more (larger cities)
Suburban counties
Cities with a population between 2,500 and 49,999 (smaller cities)
Rural counties

Note: For the random-sample groups, the observed variation in the percentage of agencies reporting gang problems from 2000 to 2004 is within the range attributable to sampling error; therefore, it does not represent a definitive change in the estimated number of jurisdictions with gang problems.
Source: Arlen Egley Jr. and Aline K. Mayor, *Highlights of the 2004 National Youth Gang Survey* (Washington, D.C.: Office of Juvenile Justice and Delinquency Prevention, 2006), p. 1. Reprinted with permission from the U.S. Department of Justice.

Miller's studies in the 1970s defined a gang more through its organizational characteristics and dynamics. A gang has "mutual interest," "identifiable leadership," and "well-developed lines of authority." Another organizational feature of the gang, according to Miller, is the desire to achieve a purpose, which usually includes "the conduct of illegal activity and control over a particular territory, facility, or type of enterprise."[49]

In a 2000 publication, Finn-Aage Esbensen concluded that the following elements should be present for a group to be classified a youth gang:

- The group needs to have more than two members.
- Group members must fall within a limited age range, usually acknowledged as ages twelve to twenty-four.
- Group members must take some steps to define their identity, such as naming the gang and/or using colors or symbols to claim gang affiliation.
- Youth gangs must have some permanence, such as association with a geographical area.
- Involvement in illegal activity is a central element of youth gangs.[50]

Thrasher does not specify that a gang's definition must include illegal activity, but Miller, Esbensen, and most other gang researchers do. Whereas Thrasher's definition focuses on group interaction and Miller's observes organizational characteristics and dynamics, Esbensen is interested in clarifying group demographics (age range, sense of identity, and permanence within a specific area). Combining all three definitions could provide a useful and comprehensive definition of a youth gang.

Profiles of Gang Members

The smaller the community, the more likely it is that gang members will be juveniles. Sample surveys of urban street gang members indicate that from 14 to 30 percent of adolescents join gangs at some point.[51] Nonetheless, the percentage of gang members who are juveniles has decreased over time. In 1996, half of all gang members

FIGURE 10.3

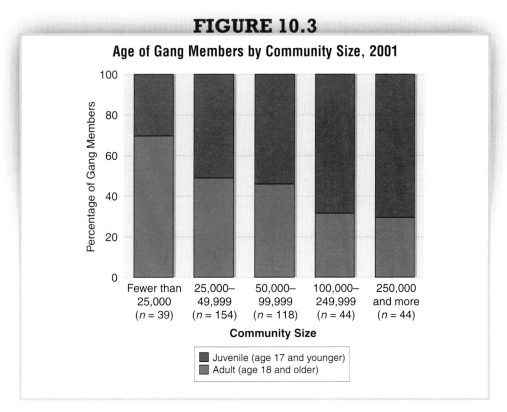

Age of Gang Members by Community Size, 2001

Source: Adapted from Arlen Egley Jr., James C. Howell, and Aline K. Major, *National Youth Gang Survey 1999–2001* (Washington, D.C.: Office of Juvenile Justice and Delinquency Prevention; U.S. Government Printing Office, 2006), p. 18. Reprinted with permission from the U.S. Department of Justice.

were reported to be age eighteen or older, but by 2001, this number had grown to 67 percent. Juvenile gang members make up 70 percent of all gang members in small communities—a statistic that steadily declines as community size increases. (See Figure 10.3.)[52]

Juveniles become involved as young as eight years of age, running errands and carrying weapons or messages. They are recruited as lookouts and street vendors and join an age-appropriate junior division of the gang. Gangs use younger and smaller members to deal cocaine out of cramped "rock houses" that are steel-reinforced fortresses. Gangs have long known that youngsters are invaluable because their age protects them against the harsher realities of the adult criminal justice system.[53]

Youth gang demographics include an average age of seventeen or eighteen years and a typical age range of twelve to twenty-four. More younger members recently have joined gangs, but the greatest increases in membership have still come from the older group. Adolescent males continue to outnumber adolescent females in gangs by a wide margin. Gangs vary in size depending on whether they are traditional or specialty gangs. Large, enduring traditional (territorial) gangs average about 180 members, whereas drug-trafficking gangs average only about 25 members. Some urban gangs (e.g., the supergangs of Chicago) number in thousands of members.[54]

Gang members have varying commitments to the gang. J. D. Vigil[55] and Vigil and J. M. Long[56] identified four basic types of gang involvement. First, *regulars* are strongly attached to the gang and have few interests outside of the gang. The regulars are the hard core, the inner clique who make key decisions, set standards, are the key recruiters, and enforce the sanctions against violators of group norms. Second, *peripheral members* are also strongly attached to the gang but participate less often

> **"The percentage of gang members who are juveniles has decreased over time."**

Web PLACES 10.1

Visit the National Youth Gang Center's website via **www .justicestudies.com/ WebPlaces**.

than the regulars because they have other interests besides the gang. Third, *temporary members* are marginally committed, joining the gang at a later age than the regulars and peripherals. They also tend to remain in the gang for only a short time. Fourth, *situational members* are very marginally attached and generally participate only in certain activities. They avoid the violent activities whenever possible.[57]

Ira Reiner identifies five different types of gang members based on their commitment to the gang.[58] The *at-risk* youths are not really gang members but are pre-gang juveniles who do not belong but have expressed some interest in gang participation. *Wannabes* are recruits who are usually in their preteen years and have begun to emulate gang members' dress and values. These young members sometimes only need an opportunity to prove that they are ready for gang membership. *Associates* make up the lowest level of gang membership. They are sometimes called Fringe, Li'l Homies, or soldiers, and it is not unusual for them to be assigned undesirable tasks or dangerous activities. *Hard core* are regarded as regular members or part of the inner clique. They spend most of their time engaging in gang-related activities and are the most gang-bound in terms of lifestyle. This group, according to Reiner, generally constitutes no more than 10 to 15 percent of gang membership. Finally, *veteranos /O.G.s* are made up of men in their twenties or even thirties who continue to be active in gang activities. In Chicano gangs, *veteranos* are regarded as elder statesmen who may be retired but still command respect; in African American gangs, O.G.s (original gangsters) are men who have earned respect and who are often expected to teach younger members the ways of the gang.[59]

Martín Sánchez Jankowski, who spent more than ten years studying thirty-seven gangs in Los Angeles, New York, and Boston, contends that certain characteristics distinguish those who belong to gangs from those who do not. What he refers to as *defiant individualism* has seven attributes: competitiveness, mistrust or wariness, self-reliance, social isolation, survival instinct, social Darwinist worldview, and a defiant air. According to Jankowski, while most members of lower-income communities display some of these traits, gang members typically display all of them. He argues that the very nature of these lower-income communities requires such traits if youth are to survive and prevail and that participation in gangs is a means or attempt to continue this spirit of defiant individualism.[60]

Why do young people join gangs? Willie Lloyd, legendary leader of a gang called the Almighty Unknown Vice Lords, tells why he became involved with gangs:

> I grew up on the streets of Chicago. When I was growing up, the Lords had a big impact on me. I never saw it as a gang, but a cohesive and unified principle on which a person could organize his life. Even as a kid of nine, I was intrigued by the Lords when I first saw them outside of the Central Park Theater. It was the first time I had ever witnessed so many black people moving so harmoniously together. They were motored by the same sense of purpose and they all wore similar dress and insignia. There were over a hundred guys, all in black, with capes and umbrellas. To my young eyes, it was the most beautiful expression I had ever seen. They all seemed so fearless, so proud, so much in control of their lives. Though I didn't know one of them at the time, I fell in love with all of them. In retrospect, I made up my mind the very first time I saw the Vice Lords to be a Vice Lord.[61]

Mike Carlie, in his national overview of youth gangs, expands on the question of why youths join gangs, asking instead why gangs form and what gangs offer to those who join them. (See Table 10.1.)

Types of Urban Gangs   Richard A. Cloward and Lloyd E. Ohlin's 1960 study identified criminal, conflict, and retreatist gangs (see Chapter 4),[62] and Lewis Yablonsky's research led him to conclude in 1962 that there were delinquent, violent, and social gangs.[63] Carl S. Taylor,[64] C. Ronald Huff,[65] and Jeffrey Fagan[66] found other types of gangs in the communities they studied in the 1980s.

Detroit urban gangs, according to Taylor, can be classified as scavenger, territorial, and corporate. Scavenger gangs have little sense of a common bond beyond their

TABLE 10.1

The Attraction of Gangs

WHY GANGS FORM	WHAT GANGS OFFER	WHY YOUTHS JOIN
Social discrimination or rejection.	Acceptance.	They are discriminated against and seek acceptance and a sense of belonging.
The absence of a family and its unconditional love, positive adult role models, and proper discipline.	A surrogate family.	Their need for a family, unconditional love, positive adult role models, and discipline.
Feelings of powerlessness.	Power.	To overcome their powerlessness.
Abuse, fear, and a lack of security.	Security.	To reduce feelings of fear and to feel secure.
Economic deprivation.	A means of earning money.	For economic gain.
School failure and delinquency.	An alternative to school.	Out of frustration.
Low self-esteem.	Opportunities to build high self-esteem.	To acquire high self-esteem.
The lack of acceptable rites of passage into adulthood.	A rite of passage to adulthood.	To accomplish the passage from childhood to adulthood.
The lack of legitimate free-time activities.	Activity.	To keep from being bored.
By building upon a pathological offender's needs.	A setting in which one can act out his or her aggression.	To vent their anger.
The influence of migrating gang members.	Any of the aforementioned.	Any of the aforementioned.
Mass media portrayals of gangs and gang members	Any of the aforementioned.	Any of the aforementioned.
Following in the footsteps of others.	Any of the aforementioned.	Tradition and acceptance.
Because they can.	Any of the aforementioned.	Any of the aforementioned.

Source: Mike Carlie, *Into the Abyss: A Personal Journal into the World of Street Gangs,* www.faculty.missouristate.edu/m/mkc096f/. Reprinted with permission from Michael K. Carlie.

own impulsive behavior. Without goals, purpose, and consistent leadership, these urban survivors prey on people who cannot defend themselves. Their crime can be classified as petty, senseless, and spontaneous.[67]

A territorial gang designates as a territory something that belongs exclusively to the gang. One fundamental objective of a territorial gang is to defend its territory from outsiders. In doing so, these gangs become rulers of the streets. A territorial gang defends its territory to protect its narcotic business.[68]

The organized/corporate gang has a strong leader or manager. The main focus of the organization is participation in illegal moneymaking ventures. Membership and promotion depend on a person's worth to the organization. Different divisions handle sales, distribution, marketing, and enforcement. Each member has a job to do, and part of that job is to work as a team member. Profit is the motivation to commit criminal acts. Although gang members have traditionally come from the lower class, some middle-class youths are attracted to these gangs.[69] Taylor concludes that "for the very first time in modern U.S. history, African Americans have moved into the mainstream of major crime. Corporate gangs in Detroit are part of organized crime in America."[70]

Huff's examination of gangs in Cleveland and Columbus identified three basic groups:

1. Informal hedonistic gangs, whose basic concern was to get high (usually on alcohol and/or marijuana and other drugs) and to have a good time. These gangs were involved in minor property crime more than in violent personal crime.
2. Instrumental gangs, whose focal concerns were more economic and who committed a high volume of property crimes for economic reasons. Most of these gang members used drugs, and some used crack cocaine. Some individual members of these gangs also sold drugs, but doing so was not an organized gang activity.
3. Predatory gangs committed robberies, street muggings, and other crimes of opportunity. Members of these gangs were more likely to use crack cocaine and to sell drugs to finance the purchase of more sophisticated weapons.[71]

Fagan's analysis of the crime–drug relationships in three cities identified four types of gangs. Type 1 was involved in a few delinquent activities and only in alcohol and marijuana use. This type of gang, according to Fagan, had low involvement in drug sales and appeared to be a social gang. Type 2 gangs were heavily involved in several types of drug sales, primarily to support their own drug use, and in one type of delinquency: vandalism. Although this type manifested several of the subcultural and organizational features of a gang, it still seemed to be more of a party gang. Type 3 gangs, representing the most frequent gang participation, included serious delinquents who had extensive involvements with both serious and nonserious offenses. Interestingly, this type of gang had less involvement than Type 2 gangs in both drug sales and the use of serious substances (cocaine, heroin, PCP, and amphetamines). Type 4 gangs had extensive involvement in both serious drug use and serious and nonserious offenses and had higher rates of drug sales. This cohesive and organized type, predicted Fagan, "is probably at the highest risk for becoming a more formal criminal organization."[72]

In probably the most comprehensive classification, Malcolm W. Klein and Cheryl L. Maxson distinguished among five types of street gangs: traditional, neotraditional, compressed, collective, and specialty, according to a series of dimensions—size, age range, subgroupings, duration, territoriality, and crime patterns.[73]

1 *The traditional gang:* Traditional gangs have typically been in existence for twenty or more years. They keep regenerating themselves. They contain fairly clear subgroups separated by age. O.G.s or *veteranos, seniors, juniors, midgets,* and other names are applied to these different aged-based groups. Traditional gangs tend to have a wide age range, sometimes including members from nine or ten years of age into their thirties or even older. They are usually large gangs, numbering 100 or even several hundred members.
2 *The neotraditional gang:* This gang resembles the traditional type but has not been in existence as long—probably no more than ten years. Its members may number fifty to one hundred or even into the hundreds. Often a neotraditional gang develops subgroups or cliques based on age or area, but sometimes it does not. Typically this gang looks as if it will evolve into a traditional gang in time.
3 *The compressed gang:* The compressed gang is small, usually fifty members or less, and has not formed subgroups. The age range tends to be more narrow—a difference of ten years or less between the youngest and the oldest member. Compressed gangs usually have been in existence for ten years or less. It is typically unclear whether a compressed gang will grow and solidify into a more traditional form or remain a less complex group.
4 *The collective gang:* The collective gang looks like the compressed form but is bigger and shows a wider age range—perhaps ten or more years between younger and older members. The gang may number under a hundred but is probably larger. It has not developed subgroups and usually has a ten- to fifteen-year history. The collective gang resembles a shapeless mass of adolescents and young adults that has not developed the distinguishing characteristics of other gangs.

5 *The specialty gang:* Unlike other gangs that engage in a variety of criminal offenses, this type of group narrowly focuses its activities on a few offenses. The group comes to be characterized by its criminal specialty. The specialty gang tends to be small—usually fifty or more members—and in most cases has no subgroups. It probably has a history of less than ten years but has developed a well-defined territory.[74]

A final typology is that of the supergangs known as **People** and **Folks**, the two main groups of Chicago gangs. Beginning in the Illinois prison system at the end of the 1970s, Chicago gangs began to align themselves into the People (represented by a five-point star) and the Folks (represented by a six-point star). As of 1998, thirty-one Chicago gangs now identified themselves as Folks, including the Gangster Disciples, Spanish Cobras, Imperial Gangsters, Latin Disciples, Latin Lovers, Braziers, Insane Popes, and Simon City Royals. The twenty-seven gangs identifying themselves as People included Vice Lords, El Rukns, Latin Kings, Future Stones, Gay Lords, Latin Lords, Bishops, and War Lords. There were also numerous factions within each major supergang.[75] For example, the Latin Kings had more than thirteen and the Vice Lords had eleven different factions.[76]

People and **Folks**
Two supergangs comprising the major Chicago street gangs.

Gangs in Schools

Schools have become fertile soil for violent youth gangs. G. David Curry and colleagues surveyed three St. Louis middle schools in 1996. Of the 533 respondents in the sample, 80, or 15 percent, reported either currently or formerly being a gang member. Of the 453 respondents who reported never having been a gang member, 260, or 57.4 percent, reported at least one kind of gang involvement. With regard to gender, 55.6 percent of the girls and 59.1 percent of the boys who were never gang members reported some degree of gang involvement. With regard to race, 60.1 percent of the African American youths and 37.5 percent of the white youths who were not gang members reported some degree of gang involvement. The authors' conclusion: The pervasive effect of gangs among middle school students in St. Louis was evident in the fact that the majority of nongang members reported some level of gang involvement.[77]

In other research, R. C. Huff and K. S. Trump studied youth gangs in Cleveland, Ohio; Denver, Colorado; and south Florida. They found that 50 percent of their respondents reported that members of their gangs had assaulted teachers, 70 percent admitted their gang had assaulted students, more than 80 percent said gang members took guns and knives to school, and more than 60 percent claimed gang members sold drugs at school.[78]

The violence perpetrated by gangs across the nation tends to vary from one school to the next, depending on the economic and social structure of the community, the gang tradition within that school, the gang's stage of development, and the extent of drug trafficking that is taking place. See Figure 10.4 for the percentages of students ages twelve through eighteen who reported that street gangs were present at school in 2001.

66 Schools have become fertile soil for violent youth gangs. 99

Gangs perpetrate school violence in a number of ways; for example, gang members are likely to bring concealed weapons into schools. George W. Knox, David Laske, and Edward Tromanhauser report that high school students who are gang members are significantly more likely than nongang members to carry a firearm to school for purposes of protection.[79] Joseph F. Sheley and James D. Wright also found higher rates of ownership and carrying of firearms among gang members than among nongang members.[80] Furthermore, Charles M. Callahan and Ira Rivara found that gang members were nearly three times as likely as nongang members to say firearm access was "easy."[81]

Gangs are also constantly recruiting new members, and nongang members are likely to be physically assaulted if they refuse to join. An African American male who grew up in Chicago, went to college on a football scholarship, and graduated from

FIGURE 10.4

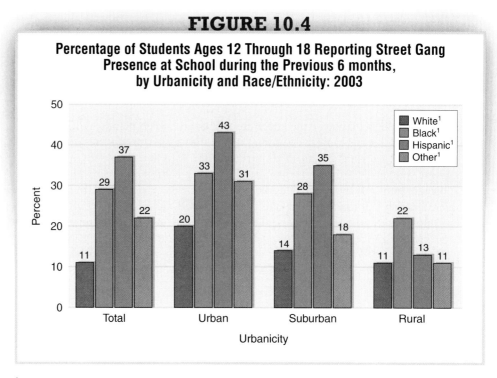

Percentage of Students Ages 12 Through 18 Reporting Street Gang Presence at School during the Previous 6 months, by Urbanicity and Race/Ethnicity: 2003

[1]Other includes Asians, Pacific Islanders, American Indians (including Alaska Natives), and students who indicated they were more than one race. For this report, non-Hispanic students who identified themselves as more than one race in 2003 (1 percent of all respondents) were included in the other category. Respondents who identified themselves as being of Hispanic origin are classified as Hispanic, regardless of their race.
Note: "At school" was defined as in the school building, on school property, on a school bus, or going to and from school.
Source: U.S. Department of Justice, Bureau of Justice Statistics, School Crime Supplement (SCS) to the National Crime Victimization Survey, 2003.

law school told how he avoided gang membership: "They were always on me to join a gang. The only way I kept from getting beaten up all the time was to run home from football practice and to run to school every morning. I kept moving all the time, but I kept out of the gangs."[82]

Moreover, because more than one gang is typically present in a high school, conflict among gangs takes place on a regular basis. This conflict may be based on competition over the drug market, or it may relate to individual gangs within the school that are seeking to expand their turf. Fights may erupt in the school hallways, in the cafeteria, or during dances. Warring gang youths sometimes start a mass riot; stabbings and shootings may occur during these altercations. The use of deadly weapons, of course, increases the likelihood of injuries or fatalities.

Finally, conflict among rival gangs in different schools also perpetrates violence. Fights commonly take place during athletic contests between competing schools. A drive-by shooting is the most serious violence that can erupt among rival gangs in the school setting. What usually occurs is that a gang youth is killed, and the victim's gang deems it necessary to retaliate. So before school, during lunch recess, or following school, a car speeds by, its occupants spraying bullets.[83]

A Portland, Oregon, high school head football coach told of an incident in which a group of Crips, dressed in blue, came speeding through the school's field-house parking lot. His team was standing by him when he shouted, "Slow it down, fellas." They did slow down, pulled out a semiautomatic weapon, and pointed it at the coach and his team. The coach hit the deck and ordered his team to drop for cover. The coach said, "I thought I had bought the farm. Fortunately, they didn't pull the trigger. In my 20 years of teaching, I have never been afraid until this year."[84]

Web PLACES 10.2

Visit the National Gang Crime Research Center's (NGCRC) website via **www.justicestudies .com/WebPlaces**.

Drugs and Gangs   Gangs in schools today have an economic base (drug dealing), which was not true in earlier years. By the 1980s, drug trafficking had become an attractive option, especially with the decline of economic opportunities for minority youths. Jeffrey Fagan's study of gang drug use and drug dealing in three urban communities found that:

> Drug use is widespread and normative among gangs, regardless of the city, the extent or nature of collective violence, or their organization or social processes. Serious and violent behavior occur among the majority of the gangs.[85]

Elizabeth Huffmaster McConnell and Elizabeth Peltz's examination of gang activity in an urban high school in Dallas found that drug distribution had become so extensive that the school required students to wear picture identification at all times in an attempt to control the number of "drug drops." School was an ideal setting for the distribution of drugs; mid-level distributors would come on campus, make their connections, and leave drugs with students who were street-level pushers. A single stop for the mid-level distributor resulted in contacts with multiple street-level pushers.[86]

Gangs have a number of techniques for selling drugs in schools. In some schools, gang members prop doors open with cigarette packs, then signal from windows to nonstudents waiting to enter the building.[87] Some gang members sell drugs in the bathrooms, in the lunchrooms, or in the parking lots. Daniel J. Monti's 1994 study of gangs and suburban schools tells how one school's lunchroom had Bloods tables and Crips tables.[88] Gangs also use younger children in their drug trafficking. The children first serve as lookouts. As they get older, they can become couriers (runners), who work as conduits between dealers and buyers.[89]

Urban Street Gangs

In urban settings, street gangs have become quasi-institutionalized and compete for status and authority within schools and other social institutions. Violence in schools and nearby neighborhoods has encouraged students to seek protection in gang membership. Youths hope that wearing the proper color and style of clothes and flashing the correct gang sign will keep them safe.

Urban gangs are sometimes able to effectively take control of schools. This control permits them to collect fees from other students for the privilege of attending school, traversing the corridors, and avoiding gang beatings. Fear and intimidation keep both students and faculty from reporting gang activities to authorities. Many urban schools have had to adopt extreme security measures to protect themselves from gang violence and drug trafficking.

Organizational Features of the Urban Gang   Jankowski contended that "one of the reasons that society does not understand gangs or the gang phenomenon very well is that there have not been enough systematic studies undertaken as to how the gang works as an organization." He suggested that the most important organizational features of urban gangs are structure, leadership, recruitment, initiation rites, role expectations and sanctions, and migration patterns.[90] Jankowski observed three types of gang organizational structure:

1. The *vertical/hierarchical type* divides leadership hierarchically into several levels. Authority and power are related to one's position in the line of command.
2. The *horizontal/commission type* is made up of several officeholders who share about equal authority over the members. The leaders share the duties, as well as the power and authority.

GANGS.COM: Crews Show Off Their Colors and Lifestyles on Web

SAN FRANCISCO—Street gangs have found new turf to defend: the Internet.

An underworld of Web sites created by gangs has sprung up to display their colors and symbols—and to warn off enemies, according to law enforcement agencies.

But some anti-gang forces have put pressure on the Internet companies that host these Web sites to shut them down, raising freedom-of-expression issues.

"There are thousands of gang-related Web sites," said Chuck Zeglin, a detective supervisor with the Los Angeles Police Department who has monitored the phenomenon. However, not all gang-related sites are connected to real gangs, he said.

"Only about 20 to 30 percent of them now—it is increasing—are run by active hard-core gang members," with the others being created by former gang members or people simply interested in gangs, Zeglin said. Kevin McGee, San Mateo's deputy district attorney, said he's found that many message postings on gang sites come from bored suburban teenagers, not gangsters.

According to Dr. Francine Garcia-Hallcom, who teaches about Latino gangs at California State University at Northridge, the Web sites serve a similar purpose to the graffiti tagging that gangs have done for years.

"Many of them have a bruised ego," Garcia-Hallcom said. "Publicity, more attention—that's kind of the purpose behind the whole [gang] thing."

That publicity is what makes these gang sites a threat to youths, according to the Chicago Crime Commission.

"It's just another risk for kids—they make [gangs] look attractive," said Thomas Kirkpatrick, president of the commission. "They have free e-mail, chat rooms. It's another recruiting avenue."

But Zeglin downplayed the Web sites' recruiting function.

"The gangs we deal with build their relationships on loyalty, trust and friendship, and there's no way of getting that on the Internet." But at the same time, Zeglin warns parents that the sites do promote the gangster mystique.

For example, a Web site for a Daly City gang displays photos of pit bull dogs, expensive cars and scantily clad women—all the trappings that can seduce some youths into the gangster life. The site also provides instructions for using household items such as padlocks and bottles as weapons.

Some Web sites include message boards where gangsters give one another props (respect) or dises (disrespect). There are even "Web rings," or networks of linked sites, devoted to gangs.

When the Chicago Crime Commission studied the Web sites of several Chicago-area gangs, they found to their surprise that many displayed corporate advertising, including banners for Amazon.com and computer seller Gateway. Last month, Kirkpatrick called on those companies and others to stop advertising on gang sites.

Amazon.com and Gateway had the ads removed as soon as reporters notified them. Spokeswoman Patty Smith said Amazon was not aware that its ads were appearing on a gang site because the company had purchased advertising in bulk from FreeYellow, the hosting service that provided one Chicago gang's free Web site.

The decision not to advertise on gang Web pages was an easy one for the advertisers—few companies want their brand name associated with gangs. But the decision posed a stickier problem for the free Web page services that hosted the sites, because these services face public scrutiny if they are seen as limiting their users' free expression.

In his report, Kirkpatrick asked that FreeYellow, the Express Page, AOL and Yahoo remove all gang pages from their servers. FreeYellow and the Express Page immediately did so, but an America Online-hosted gang site Kirkpatrick found is still active. And a Yahoo spokesman declined to say whether the company had shut down any gang sites

3. The *influential* model assigns no written duties or titles to the leadership positions. This type of system usually has two to four members who are considered leaders of the group. The authority of the influentials is based on charisma.[91]

The most conspicuous example of the vertical/hierarchical type of leadership is found in the Chicago-based gangs. The best known of these gangs—the Gangster Disciples, the Vice Lords, the Black Disciples, and the El Rukns—have leaders who command great respect among gang members. Jeff Fort of the El Rukns (formerly Blackstone Rangers and Black P. Stone Nation), David Barksdale of the Disciples, and Larry Hoover of the Gangster Disciples are the three most legendary leaders of past decades. Social World of the Delinquent 10.3 reveals some of the power that Jeff Fort had in the 1960s with the gang then called the Blackstone Rangers.

The Bloods and the Crips, the two most notorious Los Angeles gangs, are representative of the horizontal/commission type. They are confederations among hundreds of subgroups or sets. Sets are formed along neighborhood lines, and most sets have twenty to thirty members.[92]

Gangs regularly go on recruiting parties, and Jankowski points out that there are three basic recruitment strategies. In the "fraternity" type of recruitment, the gang presents itself as an organization that is the "in" thing to join. The "obligation" type involves members attempting to persuade potential members that it is their duty to

as a result of Kirkpatrick's request because the company does not comment on individual GeoCities sites.

Mark Feldman, a senior producer at Yahoo's publishing division, said that Yahoo's policies do not automatically exclude gang-related sites.

"We want to allow people to come to our site and build Web sites about those things that they are interested in, but we do that with the caveat that you can't cross certain boundaries," Feldman said. Hate speech and instructions for making bombs are against the rules, but gang sites that don't include those things might be acceptable, he said. Not all law enforcement officers want to see gang sites shut down.

When McGee, the deputy district attorney, first found a Web site created by a notorious Daly City gang, his first reaction was, "Oh, neat!"

The page laid out for him information that he had sought to verify for years: the gang's history, its structure, and the nicknames of its ringleaders and members.

"It gives us a window into the gang to see how it works and how they think," McGee said, browsing the site in his Redwood City office.

He called up a photo from the site, showing a teenager brandishing an Uzi.

"We have photo evidence that he has access to firearms," he said. "It's stuff that we can turn around and use in court."

In fact, since California law allows longer sentences for gang-related crimes, just appearing on this Web site could lead to three extra years in jail.

One part of the life that has not been seen much online is the crime. Zeglin recalls one Web site, www.killercop.com, that offered rewards for murdering Los Angeles police officers a few years ago. But since the LAPD had that site removed, Zeglin has not seen street gangs doing anything illegal online. Most gang members, even those with the basic skills required to set up a rudimentary Web site, don't have the know-how to carry out online fraud or hacking, Zeglin believes.

"I can't see them getting that sophisticated, to be serious hackers," Garcia-Hallcom, the professor, agreed.

There are a few so-called "cyber-gangs" that exist solely online. "If we get lots and lots of people like 200 and then we go out and make a big hit we'll be known to half the Web," read a page from one group.

Some local police officers who follow gangs were surprised to hear that gang members even have access to the Internet. But "Lista," a former gang member who volunteers as an online counselor for a site called GangStyle (www. gangstyle .com), believes that Web access is not out of reach for many gangsters these days.

"Most have jobs and can afford to purchase a computer and access the Internet from their own homes," Lista said. GangStyle is a site where gang members can go to chat with other gangsters—but without promoting the lifestyle or verbally attacking anyone.

"Others go to the library," she said, although she added that accessing gang-related sites from a library can be difficult because of the blocking software many libraries use.

Doug Jones, a teacher at the Community Computing Center in Bayview-Hunters Point, said gang members do not use computers at that free center. Using HTML skills to promote a gang online is a waste of ability, he said.

"If you could just focus that intelligence into something positive, just think about what they could really do," Jones said.

Rev. Roger Minassian, who runs Hope Now for Youth, a gang intervention program in Fresno, agrees that gang-banging online isn't much better than doing so on the street. So does detective Zeglin, who compared learning HTML to further a gang's reputation to learning how to hot-wire a car.

"You're learning electronics, but what are you going to use it for?" Zeglin asked.

Source: Carrie Kirby, "GANGS.COM: Crews Show Off Their Colors and Lifestyles on Web," *San Francisco Chronicle*, January 6, 2001. Copyright 2001 by *San Francisco Chronicle*. Reprinted with permission of *San Francisco Chronicle* in the format Other Book via Copyright Clearance Center.

join. The "coercive" type uses physical and/or psychological pressure on potential members and threatens that either he or his family will be attacked if he fails to join.[93] The recruitment of younger members is generally easy, because the life of a gang member looks very glamorous. With money from the sale of drugs, gang members are able to drive BMWs and Mercedes, flash big rolls of bills, and wear expensive jewelry. Recruitment begins early in the grade school years; adolescent males are most vulnerable in the junior high years.[94] But even if a youth has enough support systems at home to resist joining a gang, it is very difficult to live in a neighborhood that is controlled by a street gang and not join. A gang leader explained: "You had two choices in the neighborhood I grew up in—you could either be a gang member or a mama's boy. A mama's boy would come straight home from school, go up to his room and study, and that was it."[95]

Methods of initiation into gangs include some or all of the following:

- A new member may be *blessed-in* to a gang. Those who are blessed-in to a gang usually have older brothers, fathers, mothers, or other relatives who are already in the gang.
- A new male member more typically must be *jumped-in*, or fight other members. He may have to fight a specified number of gang members for a set period of time and demonstrate that he is able to take a beating and fight back. Or he may have

Jeff Fort and the Rise of the Blackstone Rangers

In 1959 a scrawny young boy by the name of Jeff Fort turned twelve years old in Woodlawn (Chicago) on the West Side. He and a few friends hung around the street corners, but nobody noticed. In the beginning they stole hubcaps and groceries, dividing the proceeds among themselves. The gang became the brightest light their young minds had ever dared to believe in, flickering through the darkness of the nights poisoned by danger, degradation, and despair. They were christened the Blackstone Rangers, and the light swelled brighter from its name alone.

Jeff Fort called twenty-one leaders to him, giving them responsibility and power, understanding intuitively that sharing his power would only make him stronger. They became known as the Main 21, but the gangs were well aware that they were the Enforcers. Bull, Mad Dog, Stone, Lefty, Thunder, Tom Tucker, Leto, Hutch, Bosco, Clark, Mickey Cogwell, Porgy, A.D., Old Man, Caboo, Moose, Dog, Crazy Paul, Bop Daddy, Cool Johnnie, and Sandman handled the problems that needed to be taken care of. The code dictated behavior. Punishment was meted out for not honoring the code. Everyone understood this. They could tell you to fight Louis, and out of sheer fear you would do it in a heartbeat.

Jeff and the Main 21 held meetings in the First Presbyterian Church at 6400 South Kimbark, where a large gymnasium held thousands of Blackstones. The Main 21 were seated in a semi-circle across the stage at the end of the gym. A microphone and podium were ready for the entrance of the awaited leader. He appeared out of nowhere, purposefully calm, controlled, loose, milking the crowd slowly, letting the heart rates increase steadily and build with the anticipation of what his next move would be.

He raised his fist, jerking it back hard, with power they all knew him to have. He yelled, "Blackstone," and together, as if one voice came from thousands of bodies, the thunderous roar resounded back: "Blackstone."

The spotlight circled the Main 21, then a second light appeared, dancing symmetrically with the first, increasing the rhythm, picking up a swaying motion that the bodies in the gym began to recognize and move to. A third spotlight flashed on, holding Jeff Fort in its sight, suggesting that the best was yet to come. It was.

Jeff, with his arms hanging loosely by his sides, began to feel the anticipation grow like a living thing. His breath quickening, nostrils flared, hair standing up on the back of his neck, his head slowly rotating back and forth across the crowd as if singling out each and every Stone in the audience, the piercing eyes held each one, looking directly at them.

In a deep, booming voice that sent static flying across the gym, he demanded, "Stones Run It!"

As if an electrical shock wave made its way through each nervous system, the brain registered a flight response translating to a simultaneous forward movement of thousands of bodies rising in a sea of exultation. There were thousands of voices singing praises to their master as they claimed, "Stones Run It!"

Jeff roared back, "Stones Run It!"

"Stones Run It!" they fired back.

Strangling the microphone, tap dancing to the energy bombarding off the four walls, Jeff screamed in a hoarse, rasping voice, "Blackstones!", moving the Main 21 into action as they deliberately made their way down the stage onto the auditorium floor among the Stones, fists pounding in and out of the air above them, as if forcing it to perform with them, directing the Stones to thunder over and over and over again, "Blackstones, Blackstones, Blackstones . . .!"

The Stones were literally everywhere in the late 1960s, incorporating other gangs into the nation like a confederacy under one flag. Known as America's most powerful gang, they reveled in the notoriety acquired as a nation of Stones. Members were arrested for crimes ranging from reckless conduct and resisting arrest to armed robbery and murder.

> ■ **Why do you think those who experienced this style of gang leadership responded with such enthusiasm? Why was Jeff Fort skillful in setting the stage for such a response?**

Source: Reprinted with permission from Linda Dippold Bartollas.

to stand in the middle of a circle and fight his way out, or run between lines of gang members as they administer a beating. Under such circumstances, he is expected to stay on his feet from one end of the line to the other.

■ A female is usually initiated into male-dominated gangs by providing sexual services for one or more gang members.

■ A new member in some gangs has been expected to play Russian roulette. Russian roulette involves loading a pistol's cylinder with one bullet, spinning the cylinder, closing it, then pointing the gun to one's head and pulling the trigger. If the player wins, they're in the gang. If they lose, well . . .

■ A new member is often expected to participate in illegal acts, such as committing thefts or larcenies.

■ A new member is frequently expected to assist in trafficking drugs.

■ A new member in some gangs is expected to participate in "walk-up" or "drive-by" shootings.

■ A new member is sometimes expected to commit a gang-assigned murder. Completing the procedure has sometimes been called a "blood-in," but is rarely part of initiation rites today.[96]

A street gang's clothing, colors, and hand signs are held sacred by gang members. In the world of gangs, warfare can be triggered by the way someone wears his hat, folds his arms, or moves his hands. Gang identity includes following codes for dress and behavior to make certain that the gang's name and symbol are scrawled in as many places as possible. Each gang has its own secret handshakes and hand signs, known as **representing**. Rival groups sometimes display the signs upside down as a gesture of contempt and challenge.[97]

Vigil, in his study of Hispanic gangs, reported that most of the time gang members make casual conversation and joke, drink beer or wine, play pickup games (baseball, basketball, football, and handball), and meet at the local barrio hangout. These gang youths speak a type of mixed Spanish–English slang; present a conservative appearance, with smartly combed-back hair; and affect a body language that is controlled, deliberate, and methodical.[98]

Fear is omnipresent in street life, Vigil added, particularly if one is unprotected, and it must be managed. The desired state is *locura,* a type of craziness or wildness. A person demonstrates this state of mind by displaying fearlessness, daring, and other unpredictable forms of destructive behavior, such as getting loco on drugs and alcohol. *Locura* also provides a sense of adventure and the emotional support gang camaraderie enhances.[99] As one gang member expressed it:

> I was born into my barrio. It was either get your ass kicked every day or join a gang and get your ass kicked occasionally by rival gangs. Besides, it was fun and I belonged.[100]

Gang migration is another important organizational feature of urban gangs. Gang migration can take place in at least three ways: (1) the establishment of satellite gangs in another location, (2) the relocation of gang members with their families, and (3) the expansion of drug markets.

Several studies in the 1980s were unable to document the establishment of satellite gangs in other locations.[101] In addition, chiefs of two of the largest Chicago supergangs, the Vice Lords and the Gangster Disciples, informed the author in the mid-1990s that their gangs did not have the desire or the organizational capacity to form nationwide satellite gangs. These gang chiefs even questioned how much control they had over gangs in other locations that use their gang name.[102] Maxson, Klein, and Cunningham, in surveying law enforcement agencies in over 1,100 cities nationwide, found that 713 reported some gang migration. The most typical pattern of this gang migration was the relocation of gang members with their families (39 percent). The next most typical pattern was the expansion of drug markets (20 percent).[103]

In recent decades more juveniles have remained with urban gangs into their adult years. The major reasons for this continuation of gang activity into the adult years are the changing structure of the economy, resulting in the loss of unskilled and semi-skilled jobs, and the opportunities to make money from the lucrative drug markets. Those juveniles who leave their urban gangs do it for many of the same reasons as other juveniles who mature out of committing delinquent behavior. Their leaving may involve the influence of a girlfriend, a move to another neighborhood or city, or the fear of arrest and incarceration in the adult system.[104]

representing
The use by criminal street gangs of secret handshakes and special hand signs.

locura
A state of mind said to be desirable in a Mexican American street gang; a type of craziness or wildness.

Web **PLACES** 10.3

Read Mike Carlie's *Into the Abyss: A Personal Journey Into the World of Street Gangs* at **www .justicestudies.com/ WebPlaces**.

Law-Violating Behaviors and Gang Activities   Despite the fluidity and diversity of gang roles and affiliation, it is commonly agreed that core members are involved in more serious delinquent acts than are situational or fringe members.[105]

In the mid-1980s a follow-up of a sample of Philadelphia Cohort I to the age of thirty by Wolfgang and colleagues provided insights into the influence of gangs on delinquency in Philadelphia. The researchers found that 17 percent of the whites belonged to gangs and were responsible for 33 percent of the offenses committed by whites; 44 percent of the nonwhites were gang members and were responsible for 60 percent of the offenses committed by nonwhites. Gang youths, who represented 29 percent of the total offender sample, were responsible for 50 percent of the offenses.[106]

This study also found that boys who belonged to gangs persisted in delinquent behavior nearly three years longer than did those who never joined. But when racial aspects were examined, it became clear that the persistence of delinquent behavior was traceable primarily to the nonwhite gang members. Moreover, Wolfgang and colleagues found that 81 percent of the boys (90 percent of the nonwhites and 60 percent of the whites) became delinquent after joining a gang. Another indicator of the relationship between gang membership and delinquency is that 90 percent of the whites committed no further offenses after leaving the gang; however, for nonwhites, no clear effect of leaving the gang was evident.[107]

In the 1990s, studies in Aurora, Colorado; Broward County, Florida; and Cleveland, Ohio, found some major differences between the behavior of gang members and that of other at-risk youths.[108] Individual gang members in these studies reported that they had stolen more cars, that they had participated in more drive-by shootings, that they were far more likely to own guns, that they owned guns of larger caliber, and that they were more involved in selling drugs than the sample of at-risk youths.[109] Of those youths selling drugs, "gang members reported doing so more frequently, having fewer customers, making more money from the sales, and relying more on out-of-state suppliers than nongang youths who sold drugs." This study added that "both gang members and at-risk youths reported that gangs do not control drug trafficking in their communities."[110]

Studies of large urban samples found that gang members are responsible for a large proportion of violent offenses. In Rochester, gang members made up 30 percent of the sample, but self-reported committing 68 percent of all adolescent violent offenses, or about seven times as many serious and violent acts as nongang youths.[111] Figure 10.5 reveals the differences between gang members and nonmembers in terms of delinquent acts in the Rochester Youth Development Study. In Seattle, gang members made up only 15 percent of the sample, yet self-reported committing 85 percent of adolescent robberies.[112] In Denver, gang members comprised 14 percent of the sample, and self-reported committing 89 percent of all serious violent adolescent offenses. Gang members committed about three times as many serious and violent offenses as nongang youth.[113]

A further study in Columbus, Ohio, analyzed the arrest records of eighty-three gang leaders in the years from 1980 to 1994. During these fifteen years, the eighty-three gang leaders accumulated 834 arrests, 37 percent of which were for violent crimes (ranging from domestic violence to murder). The researchers theorized that violent crimes tended to increase as the gangs began engaging in drug activity and may have been connected to the establishment of a drug market.[114]

> " The influence of gang membership on levels of youth violence is greater than the influence of other delinquent peers. "

Gang membership appears to contribute to the pattern of violent behavior. Studies in Rochester, Denver, and Seattle showed that the influence of gang membership on levels of youth violence is greater than the influence of other delinquent peers.[115] Youths commit more serious and violent acts while they belong to a gang than they do after they leave gang membership.[116] In addition, the effect of gang membership on a propensity toward violence seems to be long lasting. In all three sites, even though gang members' offense rates dropped after leaving the gang, the rates remained fairly high.[117]

FIGURE 10.5

Percentage of Delinquent Acts Attributable to Gang Members and Prevalence of Gang Membership in Rochester

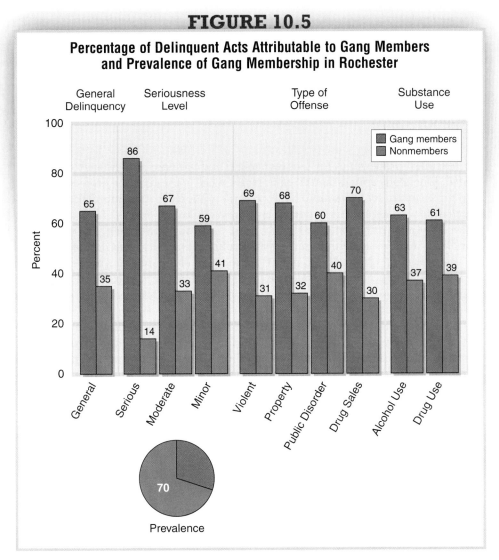

Source: Terence P. Thornberry and James H. Birch II, "Gang Members and Delinquent Behavior," *Juvenile Justice Bulletin* (Washington, D.C.: Office of Justice Programs, Office of Juvenile Justice and Delinquency Prevention, 1998), p. 3. Reprinted with permission from the U.S. Department of Justice.

In the *2004 National Youth Gang Survey*, a total of 173 cities with populations of 100,000 or more reported the number of homicides involving a gang member. In two cities, Los Angeles and Chicago, more than half of the combined nearly 1,000 homicides were considered to be gang-related. In the remaining 171 cities, approximately one-fourth of all the homicides were regarded as gang-related. In 2004, the number of gang homicides recorded in these cities was 11 percent higher than the previous eight-year average. More than 80 percent of agencies with gang problems in both smaller cities and rural counties recorded no gang homicides.[118]

Gang norms seem to contribute to the elevated rates of violence in youth gangs.[119] Most gangs have norms that support the expressive use of violence to settle disputes. The gang's sanctioning of violence is also dictated by a code of honor that stresses the importance of violence in demonstrating toughness and fighting ability and in establishing status in the gang. Levels of violence, as James C. Howell summarized it, do vary "from one city to another, from one community to another, from one gang to another, and even within cliques within the same gang."[120]

Scott H. Decker describes a seven-step process that accounts for the peaks and valleys in the levels of gang violence.[121] The process begins with a gang that is loosely organized and, according to Decker, moves through a sequence of phases:

1. Loose bonds to the gang.
2. Collective identification of threat from a rival gang (through rumors, symbolic shows of force, cruising, and mythic violence), reinforcing the centrality of violence that expands the number of participants and increases cohesion.
3. A mobilizing event that is possibly, but not necessarily, violent.
4. Escalation of activity.
5. Violent event.
6. Rapid de-escalation.
7. Retaliation.[122]

Juveniles' propensities for gun ownership and violence are known to be closely related. One study found that juvenile males who "own guns for protection rather than for sport are six times more likely to carry guns, eight times more likely to commit a crime with a gun, [and] four times more likely to sell drugs." This study added that these youths are "almost five times more likely to be in a gang, and three times more likely to commit serious and violent crimes than youth who do not own guns for protection."[123] In addition, gangs are more likely to recruit youths who own firearms, and gang members are more than twice as likely as those who do not belong to a gang to own a gun for protection, more likely to have peers who own guns for protection, and more likely to carry their guns outside their home.[124]

Other researchers have also discovered a "significant connection among gang involvement, gang violence, and firearms."[125] For example, one study based on the responses of 835 institutionalized male residents of six juvenile correctional facilities in four states found that "gang membership brought increases in most forms of gun-involved conduct." Indeed, 45 percent of the respondents in this study reported that gun theft is a regular gang activity, 68 percent indicated that their gang bought and sold guns on a regular basis, and 61 percent said that "driving around shooting at people you don't like" is a regular gang activity.[126]

In the *2005 National Gang Threat Assessment*, 45 percent of respondents reported use of technology in the commission of crimes. The most frequently reported use of technology involved cell phones with walkie-talkie or push-to-talk functions. Walkie-talkie cell phones enable gang members to alert one another to the presence of law enforcement officers or rival gang members. Gang members also use pay-as-you-go cell phones and call forwarding to insulate themselves from the police. In addition, gang members make use of police scanners, surveillance equipment, and equipment for detecting microphones or bugs to insulate their criminal activity and to impede police investigations.[127]

Gangs are making increased use of computers and the Internet. According to the *2005 National Gang Threat Assessment*, gangs are using computers to produce fraudulent checks and counterfeit currency and to develop and maintain databases of drug activity for the gang. Gangs use personal computers, laptops, and personal digital assistants to produce ledgers and maintain records of their criminal enterprises. In addition, some evidence exists that gangs are using the Internet to track court proceedings and to identify witnesses. Armed with publically available records of legal proceedings, gangs can identify and victimize witnesses. The Internet also is sometimes used for soliciting sexual acts—a form of Internet-supported prostitution. Finally, the Internet provides a venue for the sale of gang-related clothing, music, and other gang paraphernalia; gangs also are using the Internet to become more involved in the pirating of movies and music.[128]

A final dimension of law-violating behaviors of urban street gangs is the extent to which they are becoming organized crime groups. Scott Decker, Tim Bynum, and Deborah Weisel interviewed members of African American and Hispanic gangs in San Diego and Chicago and found that only the Gangster Disciples (GDs) in Chicago are assuming the attributes of organized crime groups.[129] Several commentaries have spelled out the organizational features of the GDs, including a chairman of the board, two boards of directors (one for the streets and one for prisons), governors who control drug trafficking on the streets, regents who supply the drugs, area coordinators who collect revenues from drug-selling spots, enforcers who punish those who violate the rules, and "shorties" who staff drug-selling spots and execute drug deals.[130]

It can be argued that aspects of organized crime groups are found in such drug-trafficking gangs as the Bloods and Crips in Los Angeles, the Miami Boys of south Florida, and the Jamaican Posses of New York and Florida. Beginning in the mid-1980s, these street gangs appeared to become criminal entrepreneurs in supplying illicit drugs. In a brief period of several years, many of these street gangs developed intrastate and interstate networks for the purpose of expanding their illegal drug market sales. The Crips and Bloods of Los Angeles have been the most active in drug trafficking across the United States. A study by the U.S. Congress concluded that during the latter part of the 1980s the Crips and Bloods controlled 30 percent of the crack cocaine market across the nation.[131] The Drug Enforcement Administration claimed in a 1988 report that Los Angeles street gangs were identified with drug sales in forty-six states.[132]

Web **LIBRARY** 10.2

Read the OJJDP Fact Sheet *Highlights of the 2002–2003 National Youth Gang Surveys* at **www.justicestudies.com/ WebLibrary**.

Gangs in Small Communities

Since the early 1990s, nearly every city, many suburban areas, and even some rural areas across the nation have experienced the reality of youths who consider themselves gang members. Thrasher's finding that no gangs he studied were alike appears to be true for these **emerging gangs** as well.[133] Curry and colleagues' 1992 national survey found that cities with emerging gangs reported that 90 percent of the gangs were made up of juveniles.[134]

Emerging gangs have been examined in Denver, Colorado; Kansas City, Missouri; Rochester, New York; and Seattle, Washington.[135] Esbensen and Huizinga found that about 3 percent of the Denver sample of 1,527 youths belonged to a gang during their four-year study. But by the fourth year, the percentage of youths who claimed gang membership increased to nearly 7 percent. Esbensen and Huizinga further found that male gang members were involved in levels of delinquent activity that were two or three times greater than those of nongang members. In addition to fights with other gangs, three-quarters of the gang members reported that they were involved in assaults, thefts, robberies, and drug sales.[136]

Mark S. Fleisher's street ethnography in Kansas City, Missouri, and Seattle, Washington, among teenage gang members found gang membership to be made up of "weak social ties formed among episodically homeless, socially rejected youth reared by deviant socializers."[137] Fleisher rejected the common assumption that gangs look on the set as family. Instead, he found that "these kids kill each other over 'respect,' fight for and kill one another in combat over girls or a gram or two of cocaine, and may severely beat or even kill a gang 'brother' in a violent ritual, known in some places as the 'SOS'—'Shoot-on-Sight' or 'Stomp-on-Sight.' "[138]

Thornberry and colleagues examined the relationship between gangs and delinquent behavior in Rochester, New York, from 1988 to 1991. They found some stability among gang members, because 21 percent were members in all three years. This research also revealed that gang members were much more heavily involved in street offenses while they were gang members than they were before or after their time with the gang.[139]

In the early 1990s, the rise of emerging gangs was being reported in many cities around the nation. Salem, Oregon, reported a 97 percent increase in the number of gang members and affiliates between October 1992 and April 1993. Davenport, Iowa, had 2,000 documented gang members and a gang-related shooting nearly each week. Des Moines, Iowa, had eighteen gangs with a total of 1,239 members. Peoria, Illinois, decided that its gang problem was so serious that it required the intervention of Chicago-based gang consultants to negotiate a truce between two rival gangs.[140] A statement from Rochester, Minnesota, is one to which many communities across the nation could relate:

> Gangs are a new element in the greater Rochester, Minnesota, area. In 1990, there were rumors. In 1991, there was substantiated evidence of gangs. In 1992, clear indicators

emerging gangs
Youth gangs that formed in the late 1980s and early 1990s in communities across the nation and that are continuing to evolve.

emerged that there were youth gangs with a stronghold in the community. In 1993, there have been regular reports of violence, fighting, and other gang related activities in the community.[141]

This nationwide expansion had begun in the late 1980s, and it appeared to be fueled in four different ways. First, in some communities it took place when ghetto-based drug-trafficking gangs sent ranking gang members to the community to persuade local youths to sell crack cocaine. Second, gang-related individuals operating on their own established drug-trafficking networks among community youths. Third, urban gang members whose families had moved to these communities were instrumental in developing local chapters of urban gangs. Fourth, youths in communities with little or no intervention from outsiders developed their own versions of gangs. The latter two types were less likely to become involved in drug trafficking than were the first two types.

Behind the first wave of nationwide gang expansion was urban gang leaders' knowledge that a lot of new markets were ripe for exploitation and that crack cocaine would command a high price in these new areas. To introduce the drug in these new markets, the representatives of most urban gangs promised the possibility of a gang satellite; that is, the emerging local gang would be connected by both name and organizational ties to the parent gang. However, urban gangs had neither the intent nor the resources to develop extensions of themselves in the emerging gang community. The promise of being a gang satellite was only a carrot to persuade local youths to sell crack cocaine for the urban gang. The development of drug-trafficking emerging gangs throughout the nation has seven possible stages, and the degree and seriousness of gang activity in a community depend on its stage of development.[142]

1. *Implementation:* The first stage begins when an adult gang member, usually a high-ranking officer, comes to a city that has no gangs. On arriving, this gang member goes to a low-income minority neighborhood where he recruits several juveniles to sell crack and be members of the new gang. The recruited juveniles are assured of a percentage of the money they make from the sale of crack. The exact percentage seems to vary from gang to gang but is typically about 10 percent.[143] The representative from the urban gang returns on a regular basis to supply drugs and pick up the money.

2. *Expansion and conflict:* In the second stage the adult who came to the community tells the recruited juveniles enough about his gang that they are able to identify with it. They start to wear the proper clothing, learn gang signs, and experience a sense of camaraderie, yet their primary motivation is still to make money from selling drugs. One midwestern youth claimed that he was making $40,000 a month selling crack for the Unknown Vice Lords when he was arrested and institutionalized.[144] Conflict inevitably arises as drug-trafficking gangs attempt to expand their markets, usually in the same neighborhoods. Fights may break out during school functions, at athletic events and shopping centers, and in parks and other common gathering places. Weapons may be used at this time, and the number of weapons increases dramatically in the community.

3. *Organization and consolidation:* In stage 3 youths identifying with a certain gang attempt to develop a group culture. The leadership is assumed by one or more members of the core group as well as by young adult males from the community. The increased visibility of the gang attracts a sizable number of "wannabes." The gang may be larger, but it is still relatively unorganized, consisting primarily of a group of males hanging around together. Recruitment is emphasized, and considerable pressure is put on young minority males to join the gang. One of these males noted, "If you are black, twelve or so, they really put pressure on you to join. It's hard not to."[145]

4. *Gang intimidation and community reaction:* Several events typically take place during stage 4. Some whites join the minority gangs, and other whites form gangs of their own. One youth represented the spirit of this white reaction when he said,

"The blacks ain't going to push us around."[146] Minority gangs are still more likely to wear their colors and to demonstrate gang affiliation. Drugs are also increasingly sold in the school environment, and gang control becomes a serious problem in the school. A high school teacher expressed her concern: "I've never had any trouble teaching in this school. Now, with these gang kids, I'm half afraid to come to school. It's becoming a very serious situation."[147] Gangs become more visible in shopping centers, and older people begin to experience some fear of shopping when gang youth are present. Equally disturbing, and much more serious in the long run, gangs become popular among children in middle school, and some allegiance is given to gangs among children as young as first and second grades.

5. *Expansion of drug markets:* Drugs are openly sold in junior and senior high schools, on street corners, and in shopping centers during the fifth stage. Crack houses are present in some minority neighborhoods. Extortion of students and victimization of both teachers and students take place frequently in the public schools. The gangs are led by adults who remain in the community, the organizational structure is more highly developed, and the number of gang members shows a significant increase. Outsiders have been present all along, but during this stage they seem to be continually coming into and going out of the community. Men in their mid-twenties roll into the community in expensive automobiles, wearing expensive clothes and jewelry, and flashing impressive rolls of money.

6. *Gang takeover:* Communities that permit the gangs to develop to stage 6 discover that gangs are clearly in control in minority neighborhoods, in the school, at school events, and in shopping centers. The criminal operations of gangs also become more varied and now include robberies, burglaries, aggravated assaults, and rapes. Drive-by shootings begin to occur on a regular basis, and citizens' fear of gangs increases dramatically. The police, whose gang units usually number several officers, typically express an inability to control drug trafficking and violence.

7. *Community deterioration:* The final stage is characterized by the deterioration of social institutions and the community itself because of gang control. Citizens move out of the city, stay away from shopping centers, and find safer schools for their children. When an emerging gang community arrives at this stage of deterioration, it is fully experiencing the gang problems of urban communities.

In sum, while a community's reaction greatly affects the seriousness of the problem, nongang and sometimes low-crime communities across the nation in the late 1980s and early 1990s began to experience the development of gangs. These emerging gangs developed along different trajectories, but the most toxic to a community was the process that would take hold when a ghetto-based drug-trafficking gang was able to persuade minority youths to sell crack cocaine for it and these youths, in turn, developed what they thought would be a satellite to the parent gang.

Racial and Ethnic Gangs

Hispanic, African American, Asian, white, and Native American gangs constitute the basic types of racial and ethnic gangs in the United States. Hispanic/Latino and African American gangs are generally more numerous and have more members than other racial/ethnic gangs. In 2001, due to the steady increase in the percentage of Hispanic/Latino members, these gangs approached nearly one-half of all reported gang members. (See Figure 10.6.)

Hispanic/Latino Gangs. Hispanic/Latino gangs are divided into Mexican American, or Chicano, Cuban, Puerto Rican, Dominican, Jamaican, and Central American members. According to the *2005 National Gang Threat Assessment,* law enforcement agencies across the nation reported that the most prominent Hispanic gangs in their jurisdictions were the Sur 13, Latin Kings, MS-13, 18th Street, Nortenos, and La Raza. More than 50 percent of reporting agencies indicated that Los Surenos

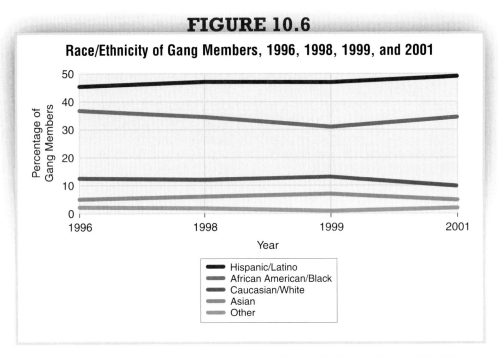

FIGURE 10.6

Race/Ethnicity of Gang Members, 1996, 1998, 1999, and 2001

Source: Arlen Egley Jr., James C. Howell, and Aline K. Major, *National Youth Gang Survey 1999–2001* (Washington, D.C.: Office of Juvenile Justice and Delinquency Prevention, U.S. Government Printing Office, 2006), p. 21.

(Sur 13) was present in their jurisdiction, and nearly 40 percent reported moderate to high Sur 13 gang activity. Indeed, Sur 13 was found to be present in 35 states.[148] Hispanic/Latino gang members frequently dress distinctively, display colors, communicate through graffiti, use monikers, and bear tattoos.[149]

African American Gangs   African American gangs have received more attention in this chapter than any other racial or ethnic group because most of the ghetto-based drug-trafficking gangs that have established networks across the nation are African American. For example, the Bloods and Crips from Los Angeles, the People and Folks from Chicago, and the Detroit gangs are all mostly African American. African American gangs usually identify themselves by adopting certain colors in addition to other identifiers, such as the hand signals shown in Figure 10.7.

Asian Gangs   There is a variety of Asian gangs in California, including Chinese, Vietnamese, Filipino, Japanese, and Korean groups. The Chinese gangs, especially, have spread to other major cities in this nation, and some of the other gangs also are active outside California. Asian gangs tend to be more organized and to have more of an identifiable leadership than is true of other street gangs. Ko-Lin Chin's examination of Chinese gangs found them to be involved in some of the nation's worst gang-related violence and heroin trafficking. Unlike other ethnic gangs, Chinese gangs are closely tied to the social and economic life of their rapidly developing and economically robust communities.[150] A study of Vietnamese youth gangs in southern California found that these youths experienced multiple marginality but that they attained the American dream by robbing Vietnamese families of large amounts of cash that such families keep at home.[151]

White Gangs   Until the closing decades of the twentieth century, most gangs were made up of white youths. Today, according to Reiner, white youths make up about 10 percent of the gang population in the United States.[152] The 2002 National Youth Gang Survey reported that 13 percent of the gang members were white.[153] However, student surveys generally reveal a much larger representation of white adolescents among gang members.[154] For example, a survey of nearly 6,000 eighth-graders in eleven sites showed that 25 percent of the whites said they were gang members.[155]

In the 1990s, the West Coast saw the solidifying of lower- and middle-class white youths into groups who referred to themselves as *stoners*. These groups frequently abused drugs and alcohol and listened to heavy metal rock music. Some members of the group practiced Satanism, including grave robbing, desecration of human remains, and sacrificing animals.[156] Stoner groups can be identified by their mode of dress: colored T-shirts with decals of their rock music heroes or bands, Levis, and tennis shoes. They may also wear metal-spiked wrist cuffs, collars, and belts, and satanic jewelry. The emerging white gangs across the nation have used many of the symbols of the stoner gangs, especially the heavy metal rock music and the satanic rituals, but they are not as likely to call attention to themselves with their dress. They may refer to themselves as neo-Nazi skinheads and are involved in a variety of hate crimes and drug trafficking.

Native American Gangs Interest also has been given to Navajo youth gangs.[157] In 1997, the Navajo Nation estimated that about sixty youth gangs existed in Navajo country. Gang values have encouraged such risky behaviors as heavy drinking and drug use, frequently leading to mortality from injuries and alcohol. A small percentage of Navajo male youths were involved in these groups, and at most 15 percent were affiliated, peripherally, with gangs. Many gang activities involved "hanging around," drinking, and vandalism, but gang members also robbed people, bootlegged alcohol, and sold marijuana.[158]

FIGURE 10.7
Gang Signs

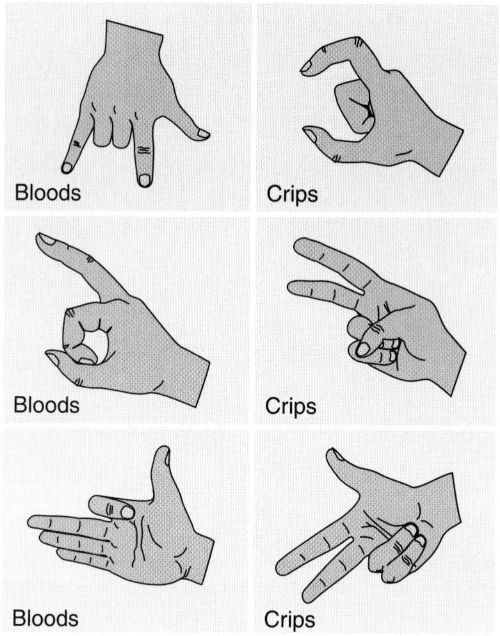

Source: Midwest Gang Investigators' Association, *Warning Signs for Parents* (n.d.).

Female Delinquent Gangs

Recent decades have brought increased awareness of adolescent girls who join gangs. Traditional sociologists once considered the female gang almost a contradiction in terms. In 1955, Albert K. Cohen argued that

> the gang, the vehicle of the delinquent subculture and one of its statistically most manageable earmarks, is a boy's gang. . . . If, however, female delinquents also have their subculture, it is a different one from that which we have described. The latter [the gang subculture] belongs to the male role.[159]

Thrasher's 1927 account of Chicago gangs also found them to be primarily male. He described the gangs that did include adolescent females as immoral rather than conflict gangs. Their chief activities included petting, illicit sex, necking, and mugging. They had names like the Lone Star Club, the Under the L gang, the Tulips, and the Night Riders. Using clandestine signals in the classroom, they arranged secret meetings in vacant lots.[160]

In 1984, Anne Campbell estimated that in New York City 10 percent of the membership of the 400 gangs was female. Female gang members ranged in age from fourteen to thirty. Some were married, and many had children.[161] A *CBS News* report estimated that in 1986 about 1,000 girls were involved in more than 100 female gangs in Chicago alone. These gangs, according to the report, were not sister organizations or auxiliaries to male gangs but independent female gangs. Like their male counterparts, these female gangs staked out their own turf, adopted distinctive colors and insignia, and had physical confrontations with rival gangs.[162]

In *Sisters in Crime* (1975), Freda Adler discussed female gangs in Philadelphia and in New York.[163] Miller and Ackley investigated two female gangs, the Molls and

Three Hispanic female 18th Street gang members strike a pose in South Central Los Angeles.
■ **What roles do girls play in street gangs?**

the Queens, in the inner-city district of an eastern seaport in the early 1970s. The gangs' illegal offenses included truancy, theft, drinking, property damage, sex offenses, and assault. Truancy took place about three times as frequently as the next most common offense, theft (largely shoplifting).[164] Peggy C. Giordano's 1978 examination of institutionalized adolescent females in Ohio revealed that 53.7 percent of the 108 institutionalized females had been part of a group that they called a gang, and 51.9 percent said their gang had a name. She noted that the names of these gangs (e.g., Outlaws, Cobras, Mojos, Loveless, Red Blood, White Knights, East Side Birds, Power) neither conveyed a particularly feminine image nor suggested a subordinate position to a male gang.[165]

Waln K. Brown, an ex–gang member himself, carried out a more comprehensive study of female participation in youth gangs in Philadelphia in 1970.[166] He suggested that female gang participation is usually limited to sexually integrated gangs. Girls' functions within these integrated gangs in Philadelphia included serving as participants in gang wars or individual and small-group combat fights and acting as spies to gain information about activities being planned by other gangs. Brown noted that most females joined Philadelphia gangs to be popular and to be "where the action is." But he did find one all-female African American gang. The Holy Whores were heavily involved in the subculture of violence, being accused of knifing and kicking pregnant females and of badly scarring and mutilating "cute" girls. "Getting a body" (knifing) was said to be an important part of their "rep."[167]

Lee Bowker and Malcolm W. Klein studied a group of African American gang females in Los Angeles in 1980 and reported they never planned a gang activity: The planning was done by the males, who usually excluded the females. But the female gang members would participate in violent crimes and drug-related gang activities.[168] J. C. Quicker studied Mexican American adolescent female gangs in east Los Angeles in 1983 and drew four conclusions about them. First, he found the gangs always had a connection to a male gang; indeed, they derived their name from their male counterparts. Second, adolescent females were not coerced into the gang but had to prove their loyalty and undergo an initiation procedure. Third, these females usually operated in a democratic manner. Finally, loyalty to the gang rivaled loyalty to the family, and most friends came from within the gang. The gang, according to Quicker, offered "warmth, friends, loyalty, and socialization" as it insulated its members from the harsh environment of the barrio.[169]

M. G. Harris's study of the Cholas, a Latina gang in California's San Fernando Valley in the 1980s, revealed that these adolescent females were becoming more independent of male gangs. In rejecting the traditional image of the Latina as wife and mother, the gang supported a more "macha" homegirl role. Gang affiliation also supported members in their estrangement from organized religion, as it substituted a form of familism that "provides a strong substitute for weak family and conventional school ties."[170]

Finn-Aage Esbensen, Elizabeth Piper Deschenes, and L. Thomas Winfree Jr. found from their analysis of the Denver Youth Survey that girl gang participants committed a wide variety of offenses and at only a slightly lower frequency than boys involved in gangs. Their findings also failed to support the notion that girls involved in gangs were mere sex objects and ancillary members. This study also showed that girls aged out of gangs before boys and that girls received more emotional fulfillment from their involvement with gang activity.[171]

Anne Campbell's 1984 examination of the relationships among adolescent females in three New York female gangs also revealed intense camaraderie and strong dependency among these gang members. But she still concluded that female gangs continued to exist as an adjunct to male gangs and that males dictated and controlled the females' activities. Campbell observed, "Girls are told how to dress, are allowed to fight, and are encouraged to be good mothers and faithful wives. Their principal source of suffering and joy is their men."[172]

Carl S. Taylor found in Detroit in 1993 that women were involved in many disparate gang types, ranging from compatriots to corporate. They were frequently represented in drug-trafficking gangs.[173] Fifteen-year-old Tracie responded, "Girls is in crews, gangs, money, shooting . . . they in it all! What makes you ask that question, is you from somewhere where the girls don't count?"[174] DeLores added, "Girls got guns for the same reason guys got 'em. . . . It's wild out here, you need to protect yourself. . . . It doesn't matter if it's selling crack, weed, or any kinda dope, business is business. Guns protect you and your business, right."[175]

David Lauderback, Joy Hansen, and Daniel Waldorf studied the Potrero Hill Posse, an African American girl group in San Francisco in 1992. After sharing the common experiences of being abandoned by the fathers of their children and being abused and controlled by other men, this group of girls began hanging around together. They found that selling crack and organized "boosting" (shoplifting) were among the few resources available for supporting themselves and their children.[176]

In 1993, Beth Bjerregaard and Carolyn Smith, using data from the Rochester Youth Development Study, found that involvement in gangs for both females and males was associated with increased levels of delinquency and substance abuse. For example, female gang members reported a serious delinquency prevalence of 66.8 percent, compared to 6.6 percent for nongang members. Although there was some similarity in the factors associated with gang membership for both males and females, lack of school success was a particularly important factor for female gang members.[177]

Joan Moore and John Hagedorn's 2001 summary of the research on female gangs reports that the majority of female gang members are involved in delinquent or criminal behaviors.[178] Delinquency rates of female gang members are lower than those of male gang members but higher than those of nongang females and males. Female gang members are likely to be involved in property crimes and status offenses, but they commit fewer violent crimes than their male counterparts. Female gang members are also heavily involved in drug dealing. For example, in Los Angeles County, drug offenses were the most frequent cause for the arrest of female gang members.[179] See Table 10.2 for gang-related charges for female arrestees in Chicago from 1993 to 1996.

Jody Miller, in several articles and in her 2001 book, *One of the Guys,* has contributed to what is known about gender dynamics in gangs.[180] From research conducted in St. Louis and Columbus, Ohio, Miller found that a female in a mixed-gender

TABLE 10.2

Gang-Related Charges for Female Arrestees in Chicago: 1993–1996

OFFENSE*	FEMALE ARRESTEES WITH GANG-RELATED CHARGE (%)			
	1993	1994	1995	1996
VIOLENT (TOTAL)	46.9	40.3	34.4	38.5
Homicide	0.2	0.1	0.0	0.1
Simple battery	17.6	16.1	14.1	14.9
Mob action	9.7	5.7	3.8	4.8
All other violent offenses	19.4	18.4	16.5	18.7
DRUG (TOTAL)	36.4	37.9	44.4	37.7
Cocaine possession	14.3	9.8	8.8	2.6
Crack possession	7.0	11.6	13.9	15.6
All other drug offenses	15.1	16.5	21.7	19.5
PROSTITUTION	0.8	1.5	4.1	9.8
PROPERTY	5.1	3.4	4.4	5.1
WEAPONS	3.7	4.3	2.5	2.8
LIQUOR	5.6	10.7	7.3	3.5
OTHER	2.2	1.7	2.7	2.3

Note: Percentages may not total 100 because of rounding. Total number (n) of cases per year: 1993, $n = 2,023$; 1994, $n = 2,029$; 1995, $n = 2,021$; 1996, $n = 2,193$.
*With the exception of vice offenses (drug, prostitution, and gambling), authorities define gang-related offenses as such by referring to the motive of the offender. Vice offenses are considered gang-related if they involve a known gang member. Almost all liquor offenses involve underage drinking.
Source: Joan Moore and John Hagedorn, "Female Gangs: A Focus on Research," *Juvenile Justice Bulletin* (Washington, D.C.: Office of Juvenile Justice and Delinquency Prevention, 2001), p. 5. These data were drawn from special tabulations provided to the authors by the Illinois Criminal Justice Information Authority (1998).

gang, an environment that supports gender hierarchies and the exploitation of young women, must learn to negotiate to survive in the gang milieu.[181] Gang involvement does expose young women to risks of victimization. Young women can choose to be "one of the guys" and expose themselves to higher risks of being arrested, injured, or even killed in conflcts with rival gangs. Or they can use gender to decrease their risk of being harmed by not participating in "masculine" activities such as fighting and committing crime. However, females who opt out of violence and crime are then viewed as lesser members and may expose themselves to greater risks of victimization within their gangs.[182]

In sum, most studies have found that girl gangs still serve as adjuncts to boy gangs. Yet an increasing number of important studies show that female gangs provide girls with the necessary skills to survive in their harsh communities while allowing them a temporary escape from the dismal future awaiting them.[183] What these studies reveal is that girls join gangs for the same basic reasons that boys do—and share with boys in their neighborhood the hopelessness and powerlessness of the urban underclass.[184]

> " Most studies have found that girl gangs still serve as adjuncts to boy gangs. "

Theories of Gang Formation

The classical theories about the origins of juvenile gangs and gang delinquency date from research done in the 1950s and were formulated by Herbert A. Bloch and Arthur Niederhoffer; Richard Cloward and Lloyd Ohlin; and Albert Cohen, Walter B. Miller, and Lewis Yablonsky.

Bloch and Niederhoffer's theory was based on the idea that joining a gang is part of the experience male adolescents need to grow up to adulthood. The basic function of the gang is thus to provide a substitute for the formalized puberty rites that are found in other societies.[185] Cloward and Ohlin's theory was based on the notion that lower-class boys interact with and gain support from other alienated individuals. These youngsters pursue illegitimate means to achieve the success they cannot gain through legitimate means.[186] Cohen's theory was that gang delinquency represents a subcultural and collective solution to the problem that faces lower-class boys of acquiring status when they find themselves evaluated according to middle-class values in the schools.[187] Miller held that there is a definite lower-class culture and that gang behavior is an expression of that culture. He saw gang leadership as based mainly on smartness and toughness, and viewed the gang as very cohesive and highly conforming to delinquent norms.[188] Finally, Yablonsky suggested that violent delinquent gangs arise out of certain conditions that are found in urban slums. These conditions encourage the development of the sociopathic personality in adolescents, and such sociopathic individuals become the core leadership of these gangs.[189]

These classical theories of gangs focused on sociological variables such as strain (Cloward and Ohlin), subcultural affiliation (Miller and Cohen), and social disorganization (Yablonsky). Cohen, Cloward and Ohlin, and Miller also stressed the importance of the peer group for gang membership.[190] Each of the five theories of gang formation has received both support and criticism, but research is needed into current expressions of gang activity, because the existing theories were based primarily on 1950s gangs.[191]

Other theories of gangs are associated with social disorganization theory.[192] This theory is based on the assumption that poor economic conditions cause social disorganization to the extent that there is a deficiency of social control. This lack of social control leads to gang formation and involvement because youths in low-income neighborhoods seek the social order and security that gangs offer.[193]

More recently, underclass theory has been widely used to explain the origins of gangs.[194] In the midst of big-city ghettos and barrios filled with poverty and deprivation, it is argued, gangs are a normal response to an abnormal social setting.[195] Part of the underclass's plight, according to Fagan, is being permanently excluded from participating in mainstream labor market occupations. Thus, members of the underclass are forced to rely on other economic alternatives, such as low-paying temporary jobs, part-time jobs, some form of welfare, or involvement in drug trafficking, prostitution, muggings, and extortions.[196] Hagedorn documented the loss of manufacturing jobs in Milwaukee during the 1980s. It resulted in an increasingly segmented labor force in which minorities were consigned low-wage or even part-time work, welfare, and the illegal economy.[197] Vigil added that people who join gangs are pushed into these groups by their condition of poverty and their status as minorities. Marginal to the wider society, their communities, and their families, they are subject to difficulties in all areas. This multiple marginality makes them the most likely candidates for gang membership, for in a real sense, they have little else going for them. Vigil added that this "dialectic of multiple marginality [also] applies to why females now are more active in gangs."[198]

Jankowski contended that gang violence and the defiant attitude of young men are connected with the competitive struggle in poor communities. Being a product of their environment, they adopt a "Hobbesian view of life in which violence is an integral part of the state of nature."[199] The operations and survival rate of gangs vary greatly but, according to Jankowski's theory, can be accounted for by the interaction of four elements:

> (1) inequality, and individual responses to reduce inequality; (2) the ability of the gang (both leadership and rank and file) to manage the desires and behavior of people with defiant individualist characters; (3) the degree to which a collective of individuals has been capable of developing a sophisticated organization to carry out its economic activities; and (4) the extent to which it has been able to establish ties to institutions belonging to the larger society.[200]

Moreover, Scott Decker and Barrik Van Winkle state that an explanation of why youths join gangs must be seen in the larger context of pulls and pushes. Pulls relate to the attractiveness and benefits that the gang is perceived to offer a youth. Benefits frequently cited are enhanced prestige or status among friends, excitement, and making money from drugs. These personal advantages make gang involvement appear to be a rational choice. The pushes of gang membership come from the social, economic, and cultural forces of the larger society. Youths' experiences in response to these forces may include needing protection from other gangs, seeking an identity to overcome feelings of marginality, being recruited or coerced into gangs, or growing up in a neighborhood in which gang membership is a tradition.[201]

Michael F. de Vries proposes that researchers need an integrated approach to understand why juveniles become involved with gangs. For African American youths, strain theory is "the heart of why African Americans find gang associations worthwhile." Gangs offer deprived African American youths opportunities to obtain status and financial gain that is denied to them in the larger culture. Asian immigrants, he argues, are also experiencing such strain. Although African Americans are more "likely to engage in illicit drug distribution to counteract their inherited inferior position in society, Asians are more apt to engage in home invasions, theft, and intimidation as their way of coping with a similar strain." According to de Vries, subcultural theory appears to be helpful in explaining Hispanic gangs. Largely spared from Anglo-American culture by their own traditions, "this subcultural group places a high degree of value on an individual's prowess (machismo), territorial identity, pride, and loyalty to their own group identity." Control theory, especially for middle-class whites, helps explain why these youths become involved in gang activity. Social bonds are coming under attack as the family unit is becoming weaker.[202]

Gangs Across the Life Course

The life-course perspective offers a number of insights on the study of gangs and their members. The most basic is that gang membership can be thought of as a trajectory. Some youngsters enter this trajectory and some do not. Those who enter it stay for varying lengths of time and become more or less involved in gang activities and behaviors. If gang membership is conceived as a trajectory with behavioral consequences, why some people enter it and some do not is an important consideration. The life-course perspective is a reminder that the origins of gang membership are found in several domains and are multidimensional, including childhood risk factors, the social structural position of the family, family relationships, and unfolding influences of adolescence. Moreover, the life-course orientation suggests that for many people gang membership may act as a turning point with the potential to alter or redirect basic life-course pathways. Finally, the life-course perspective suggests that duration of gang membership should intensify its consequences.[203]

Thornberry and colleagues contributed an important life-course orientation in their analysis of the gang behavior of Rochester youths as they aged into their young adult years. Following the sample in the Rochester Youth Development Study from age thirteen to age twenty-two, these researchers have been able to separate selection effects (the extent to which delinquents seek out the gang) from facilitation effects (the extent to which the gang fosters delinquent behavior in its members). They have done this analysis for a variety of illegal behaviors related to gang activity, delinquency, drug use, drug selling, violence, and gun carrying and use—and have found that gang membership seems to have a pronounced impact on facilitating all of these behaviors.[204]

Thornberry and colleagues also explored the longer-term consequences of joining a street gang. Does involvement in this strongly deviant form of adolescent social network exact a toll in the later life of the person? Or is gang membership merely a transitory adolescent phenomenon with few, if any, long-term consequences? The researchers concluded that "gang membership appears to have a pernicious impact on many aspects of life-course development. In addition, while the pattern of onset and duration of gang membership varies somewhat by gender, it has negative impacts on the life course of adolescent girls, as it does on adolescent boys."[205]

Preventing and Controlling Youth Gangs

Surveys of youth gangs across the nation reveal that the numbers of gangs and of gang members are decreasing slightly. Yet youth gangs are still a serious social problem. Gang involvements affect the quality of life for many youngsters and in most communities across the United States.

Even when gang youths are causing considerable problems at school and in the neighborhoods, communities across the nation have a tendency to deny that they have gangs.[206] Then, if a dramatic incident occurs—such as the killing of an innocent victim or a shoot-out in which one or more gang youths are killed—what began as denial becomes repression, or the collective phenomenon of making the gangs "invisible." Meanwhile, despite such efforts as establishing gang units in police departments (or increasing the size of existing units), and harassing gang members at every opportunity, gangs begin an inexorable process of intimidation and terror that ultimately touches all aspects of community life.

Another reason for seeking successful interventions is that gangs are destructive to their members. Gangs that originate as play groups frequently become involved in dangerous, even deadly, games. Joining a gang may be a normal rite of passage for a youth, but gangs minister poorly to such basic adolescent needs as preparation for marriage, employment, and adaptation to the adult world. Adolescent males who join gangs for protection are often exposed to dangers that most nongang youths are able to avoid. Adolescent females who join because they are attracted to male members are often sexually exploited. Gang members are more likely to both commit delinquent acts and to become victims of crime than are youths who do not join gangs.[207] Finally, joining a gang may provide status and esteem in the present, but gang membership frequently leads to incarceration in juvenile and/or adult facilities.

Web **LIBRARY** 10.3

Read the COPS publication *Solutions to Address Gang Crime* at **www.justicestudies.com/ WebLibrary**.

Irving Spergel and colleagues' 1989 report on forty-five cities with gang problems identified five strategies of intervention: (1) community organization, mobilization, and networking; (2) social intervention, focusing on individual behavioral and value change; (3) opportunities provision, emphasizing the improvement of basic education, training, and job openings for youths; (4) suppression, focusing on arrest, incarceration, monitoring, and supervision of gang members; and (5) organizational development and change, or the creation of special units and procedures.[208]

In examining the implementation of these strategies, Spergel and colleagues found that suppression was most frequently used (44 percent), followed by social intervention (31.5 percent), organizational development (10.9 percent), community organization (8.9 percent), and opportunities provision (4.8 percent).[209] Community organization was more likely to be used by programs in emerging gang cities, whereas social intervention and opportunity provision tended to be favored strategic approaches in cities with chronic gang problems. But only seventeen of the forty-five cities saw any evidence of improvement in the gang situation.[210]

Spergel and colleagues, in developing a model for predicting general effectiveness in intervention strategies, stated:

> A final set of analyses across all cities indicate that the primary strategies of community organization and provision of opportunity along with maximum participation by key community actors is predictive of successful efforts at reducing the gang problem.[211]

Spergel and colleagues expanded their approach into the Comprehensive Community-Wide Approach to Gang Prevention, Intervention, and Suppression Program. This model contains several program components for the design and mobilization of community efforts by school officials, employers, street outreach workers, police, judges, prosecutors, probation and parole officers, and corrections officers.[212] The Gang Violence Reduction Program, an early pilot of this model, was

Paroled Gang Members Find They Can't Return Home

CHICAGO—Shawn Betts apparently didn't realize it, but a police surveillance team had a video camera pointed at him the moment he stepped out of a state prison here last October.

Betts, a leader of a violent gang known as the 4 Corner Hustlers, was being watched because he had just signed an unusual parole agreement to secure his release after serving six years of a 12-year sentence for kidnapping: He promised not to return to the West Side turf controlled by his gang, with the understanding that police would be watching to make sure he didn't. Less than six hours after he left prison and ducked into a van with friends, Betts was back in custody.

That was because the surveillance team saw the 38-year-old felon make a brief detour into Indiana. The detour violated a separate part of Betts' parole—a violation that probably would have gone unnoticed if Betts hadn't agreed to the restrictions that led police to follow him.

The episode was a benchmark in a bold effort by Chicago to turn back the type of gang violence that has driven up violent crime rates here and elsewhere in recent years. During the past two years, Betts and four other gang figures have given up their rights to return to their home "turf" under one of the nation's most provocative strategies aimed at disrupting gang activity.

In a city where police say gangs typically are involved in about half the homicides each year, the new restrictions on parole coincided with a 25% decline in slayings last year.

Homicides have continued to decline this year in Chicago, although not as dramatically: As of July 29 there had been 258, five fewer than at the same time in 2004, the Chicago Police Department says.

Thomas Epach Jr., executive assistant to police Superintendent Philip Crane, says he can't be certain how much of the decline should be attributed to parole restrictions or to other anti-gang initiatives launched in troubled areas.

But Epach says the restrictions on even a small number of gang leaders—and the police surveillance attached to such agreements—have given authorities a better view of the activities of hundreds of key players among Chicago's estimated 68,000 gang members.

Crane says the restrictions also have allowed police to prevent violence that often has occurred after a gang leader is released from prison and he tries to re-establish his presence.

As a result, Epach says, police are working with the Illinois Prisoner Review Board, which oversees parole, to have more parolees agree to restrictions on their movements.

"It's hard to say which snowflake causes the avalanche," Epach says. "Our aim is simple. We're trying everything to take the catalysts for violence out of the equation."

Legality of Deals Questioned

The Chicago policy has raised a range of legal and law enforcement concerns, however.

Defense lawyers and civil rights advocates complain that parole restrictions on gang leaders violate the convicts' right to associate with their families and friends. They say the restrictions can make it particularly difficult for the felons to find work, which usually is another requirement of parole.

"The whole thing is 100% unconstitutional," says Sam Adam, a lawyer for Darren Jones, 34, a gang leader who accepted a non-negotiable release offer from the Illinois review board.

Jones agreed to stay away from his home turf on Chicago's West Side when he was freed from prison in January.

Adam says Jones—who wound up violating the agreement and is back in prison, serving the remaining 13 years of his original 25-year sentence for drug trafficking—had three children who lived in the area he was banned from visiting.

"How can you tell a man he can't go home and visit his kids?" Adam asks.

Chicago's policy hasn't been challenged in court, but Adam says he would have done so if Jones could have afforded it.

"I wish Darren had asked us to go forward," Adam says. "We had everything all lined up. We were ready to go."

Jorge Montes, chairman of the Illinois Prisoner Review Board, says the territorial restrictions are reserved for a small number of gang leaders who authorities suspect could pose a threat to public safety.

"I don't know if there is any direct correlation between this program and declining crime," Montes says. "But it makes perfect sense that inmates who are identified as kingpins should be watched very, very closely."

Still, Montes says it is "only a matter of time" before the policy is challenged in court.

Ed Yohnka, spokesman for the American Civil Liberties Union in Chicago, says a parolee's constitutional right to free association isn't all the policy jeopardizes.

"If you are cutting these people off from family, friends and opportunities for work, you might be setting them up for failure," he says.

Chicago police play down such concerns.

They say the restrictions hinder only a gang leader's ability to return to illegal activity.

In Jones' case, Epach says, police feared that the mandatory release would set off a violent turf battle if Jones sought to re-establish himself in the hierarchy of a gang known as the Traveling Vice Lords.

For roughly three months after his release from prison, police say, they watched Jones reconnect with old business partners as he ventured in and out of the prohibited territory.

They arrested him on alleged parole violations in March, soon after Jones—apparently concerned about police surveillance—bought a $300 radio frequency detector that can be used to check for bugging devices.

"If you're trying to get your life back together," Epach says, "you aren't going out to buy spy paraphernalia."

Chicago Suburb Wary

Chicago authorities are encouraged by the apparent success of the program, but their counterparts in nearby cities worry that the tactic will encourage released gang members to head to the suburbs.

Garnett Watson, police chief of neighboring Gary, Ind., says his city routinely feels the impact of anti-gang efforts in Chicago. It's too early to determine whether Chicago's parole initiative has triggered a significant migration of gang members to the city's Indiana suburbs, but Watson expects it.

"When Chicago sneezes, we catch a cold," Watson says.

Larry Ford, an assistant director with the federal Bureau of Alcohol, Tobacco, Firearms and Explosives, says years of battles involving urban police agencies and gangs already have driven some criminal groups to operate in the suburbs. "They are finding less competition for turf and less (police) scrutiny," Ford says.

Nationwide, there are an estimated 730,000 gang members associated with more than 21,000 groups, according to the National Youth Gang Center, an arm of the Justice Department.

The numbers have remained stable in recent years despite a decade-long decline in crime. But the percentage of cities reporting that gang problems were "getting worse" rose from 25% in 1999 to 37% in 2003, the center says.

During the same period, gang-related homicides increased about 50%, according to the most recent report by a coalition of urban police chiefs and prosecutors known as Fight Crime Invest in Kids.

Chicago's move against gang leaders comes as several cities—notably Los Angeles, San Antonio and El Paso—are using another tactic aimed at disrupting gangs: obtaining court orders to ban known gangsters from operating in designated sections of those cities.

Instead of targeting individual gang leaders, the cities are identifying troubled neighborhoods and enforcing strict rules of conduct in those areas that are aimed at making it more difficult for gang members to deal drugs or take part in other illegal activities.

For years, Los Angeles has sought court orders to limit the activities and movements of many of the city's estimated 40,000 gang members. The court orders do not prohibit certain known gang members from being in the designated areas, but the members are banned from associating with each other.

In a March 10 order aimed at combating Los Angeles' Grape Street Crips, at least 16 known gang members were prohibited from associating with other members, intimidating people in the neighborhood or acting as lookouts "by whistling, yelling or otherwise signaling" colleagues involved in drug trafficking or other illegal activity.

During the past four years, the city has ramped up its campaign dramatically, designating 16 new restricted zones, an increase of 243%. The strategy's effect on the crime rate is unclear, but the designation of every "safety zone" has been followed by a decline in violent crime of at least 6% in each area, says Jonathan Diamond, spokesman for City Attorney Rocky Delgadillo.

During his unsuccessful bid for re-election this year, Los Angeles Mayor James Hahn proposed designating the entire city—nearly 500 square miles—as a court-ordered safety zone. The plan remains under review by Delgadillo's office, but it has drawn criticism from legal analysts such as former Los Angeles district attorney Ira Reiner, who told the *Los Angeles Times* that it was "campaign talk and nothing else."

Safety Zones Expanded

The use of court orders in California was upheld in a 1997 ruling by the state Supreme Court in a case that involved an anti-gang effort in San Jose.

Courts have not always backed anti-gang strategies, however. In 1999, the U.S. Supreme Court scuttled a broad anti-loitering ordinance in Chicago that was aimed at sweeping gang members from the streets. Under that provision, opposed by the ACLU, police were able to make arrests if suspected gang members did not follow a police warning to move.

Until it was overturned, the anti-loitering ordinance appeared to give law enforcement a less-demanding alternative to court orders, which typically require police to carefully plot crimes committed in the designated zones and name gang members suspected in them.

Since the U.S. Supreme Court ruling, however, the use of court orders to establish "safety zones" has expanded. El Paso got its first court order in 2003. It established the troubled Downtown area known as the "Segundo Barrio" as

Members of the Miami Police Department's Gang Task Force monitor the crowd at Little Havan's annual *Calle Ocho* festival. ■ **What can the police do to combat the growing influence of street gangs?**

a target to rid the neighborhood of the Barrio Azteca gang.

The order identified 35 members of the gang by name and prohibited them from associating with each other in the zone. The order also established a curfew that made any of the members subject to arrest if they were found in the zone from 10 P.M. to 6 A.M.

El Paso police Sgt. Marylou Carrillo says that from April 2003, when the order took effect, to January 2005, the strategy contributed to a 33% decline in business burglaries, a 20% drop in robberies and a 12% decline in overall crime in the Downtown area. There also have been no homicides in the zone since the court action.

Carrillo says police are moving to extend the order through 2006.

"These residents for years have been terrorized," County Attorney Jose Rodriguez says. "Nobody in this town should live in fear."

Epach says the same principle applies in Chicago. The former prosecutor describes the territorial restrictions on released prisoners as part of a "big combo platter that appears to be working now" in reducing gang activity.

"We figure that watching and putting restrictions on one gang leader is the equivalent of watching 200 gang members," he says. "These people are at the top of the food chain. We can put a kind of embargo on violations by keeping the gang leaders unsettled."

Source: Kevin Johnson, "Paroled Gangsters Find They Can't Return Home," *USA Today*, August 9, 2005. Copyright © 2005 by *USA Today*. Reprinted by permission.

implemented in Chicago. After three years of program operations, the preliminary evaluation of this project was positive among the targeted group (lower levels of gang violence, few arrests for serious gang crimes, and hastened departures of youth from gang activities).[213]

The program was later implemented in five jurisdictions: Mesa, Arizona; Tucson, Arizona; Riverside, California; Bloomington, Illinois; and San Antonio, Texas.[214] These sites initially undertook the process of community mobilization as they identified or assessed the nature and extent of the gang problem. They then planned for program development and implementation in a problem-solving framework. It was not long thereafter that they began to implement appropriate interrelated strategies to target gang violence and its causes. At the same time, they continued to reassess the changing nature and extent of their gang problems. Their strategies consisted of a combination of community mobilization, social intervention and outreach, provision of social and economic opportunities for youth, suppression or social control, and organizational change and development.[215]

What these efforts by Spergel and colleagues demonstrate is that only an integrated, multidimensional, community-oriented effort is likely to have any long-term effect in preventing and controlling gangs in the United States. Such gang prevention, intervention, and control models must have several components: (1) The community must take responsibility for developing and implementing the model; (2) the model must take very seriously the structural hopelessness arising from the unmet needs of underclass children; (3) prevention programs, especially in the first six years of school, must be emphasized; (4) supporters must coordinate all the gang intervention efforts taking place in a community; and (5) sufficient financial resources must be available to implement the model.

CHAPTER
Summary

The relationship between gang membership and delinquency is clearly documented in the literature, with both incidence and persistence of delinquency being directly tied to a youth's gang involvement. This chapter also explains that:

- Young people derive meaning from and have their social needs met through contact with family members, peers, teachers, leaders and participants in churches, community organizations, and school activities.

- Some youngsters find little reason to become involved in law-violating activities, whereas others become involved with various forms of delinquent behavior— often through the negative influence of peers.

- Some delinquents, with frustrated needs and nowhere else to find hope, become attracted to gangs.

- For these youths, gangs become quasi-families and offer acceptance and status, as well as a sense of purpose and self-esteem.

- Youth gangs are widespread throughout the United States; even small towns and rural areas are contending with the problem of gangs.

- Although youth gangs are not a recent phenomenon, many of today's gangs seem especially violent, and more than a few are characterized by the widespread use of automatic and semiautomatic weapons.

- Although gangs have historically trafficked in illicit drugs, drug trafficking provides a central focus for many of today's gangs.

- Drug gangs, or those whose primary purpose involves trafficking in illegal drugs, are much more prevalent today than in the past.

- Youth gangs of the past often transformed into street gangs, particularly in urban areas, with control of the gang now in the hands of adults.

- In some urban areas, juveniles now constitute a minority of gang members.

- Many gang experts say that gangs thrive because of the poverty and lack of opportunity facing those who live in many of our nation's urban neighborhoods.

- The hopelessness of inner-city environments makes drug trafficking attractive and gang membership desirable for many young people, even in the face of a high possibility of being injured, killed, or imprisoned.

- Grassroots community groups have had some success in working with gang members, but gang reduction depends on providing children of the underclass with more positive options than they have today.

CRITICAL THINKING
Questions

1. Why are gangs so popular among young people?
2. How have street gangs changed through the years?
3. Discuss the seven possible stages of development that an emergent gang may go through. How does the gang's stage of development relate to the degree and seriousness of gang activity in the community?
4. Discuss the development of gangs in recent years in your community. At what stage are they? What gang activities are evident? If gangs have not yet developed in your community, analyze why this is so.
5. You have an opportunity to work with eight male gang members who are between fourteen and sixteen years of age. You have decided to design the twenty sessions around the theme of hopelessness. What would you do in these sessions to help instill more hope in the lives of these young men?
6. In your community or nearby communities, what activities are females involved in with male youth gangs? Are there any separate female gangs?
7. Why have adults taken over so many youth gangs? With adults in leadership roles, what roles are reserved for youths?
8. Why is denial such a favorite strategy of police chiefs, school superintendents, and public officials for dealing with gangs? How much has this strategy been used in the community where you live or in a situation you know of?
9. What do you think is the most effective way to break up street gangs?
10. Are there any ways in which gangs could have a positive impact on adolescents?
11. A particularly heinous crime has been committed by gang youths in your community. The community, which has been in a state of denial, is now alarmed. They invite you to speak to a group of concerned and leading citizens to develop a community-based plan to deal with gangs. What will you tell this group? What are the main steps in your plan?

WEB
Interactivity

Visit Professor Mike Carlie's website, *Into the Abyss: A Personal Journey Into the World of Street Gangs*, at **www.faculty .missouristate.edu/m/mkc096f**. The site, which is continuously updated, provides information on more than eighty gang-related topics, and contains a site map that allows visitors to easily jump to topics of interest.

View Part 8 of Chapter 4 ("Why Gangs Form") and identify the fourteen topics that Professor Carlie lists there. Rank those topics from 1 to 14 (with 1 being your first choice) to reflect your own beliefs as to why gangs come together. The first item in your list should be the one you think is the most important element leading to gang formation; the last should be the one you see as least important cause of gang formation.

(continued)

Source: From www.faculty.missouristate.edu/M/ MichaelCarlie/. Reprinted with permission from Michael K. Carlie.

Then read the summary of Part 8 ("Conclusion: Why Gangs Form") to see if you can identify Professor Carlie's personal belief as to the most significant cause(s) of gang formation. Which of the causes dis-cussed there do you think he believes is the most important? Explain your choices. Submit your answers to these questions to your instructor if asked to do so.

Notes

1. Robert Walker, "Mara Salvatrucha MS-13, *Gangs OR Us,* Web posted at www.gangsorus.com/marasalvatrucha13 .html. Accessed September 10, 2006

2. Ibid.

3. Robert J. Bursik Jr., "Social Disorganization and Theories of Crime and Delinquency: Problems and Prospects," *Criminology* 26 (November 1988), p. 523.

4. See Mark Warr and Mark Stafford, "The Influence of Delinquent Peers: What They Think or What They Do," *Criminology* 29 (November 1991), pp. 851–866; Robert Agnew, "The Interactive Effects of Peer Variables on Delinquency," *Criminology* 29 (February 1991), pp. 47–72; Mark Warr, "Age, Peers, and Delinquency," *Criminology* 31 (February 1993), pp. 17–40; and Terence P. Thornberry, Alan J. Lizotte, Marvin D. Krohn, Margaret Farnworth, and Sung Joon Jang, "Delinquent Peers, Beliefs, and Delinquent Behavior: A Longitudinal Test of Interactional Theory," *Criminology* 32 (February 1994), pp. 47–83.

5. S. P. Breckinridge and Edith Abbott, *The Delinquent Child and the Home* (New York: Russell Sage Foundation, 1917).

6. Clifford R. Shaw and Henry D. McKay, "The Juvenile Delinquent" in *Illinois Crime Survey* (Illinois Associations for Criminal Justice, 1931).

7. Maynard L. Erickson and Gary F. Jensen, "Delinquency Is Still Group Behavior: Toward Revitalizing the Group Premise in the Sociology of Deviance," *Journal of Criminal Law and Criminology* 68 (1977), pp. 388–395.

8. Maynard Erickson, "The Group Context of Delinquent Behavior," *Social Problems* 19 (1971), pp. 115–129.

9. Paul Strasburg, *Violent Delinquents* (New York: Monarch Press, 1978).

10. M. M. Craig and L. A. Budd, "The Juvenile Offender: Recidivism and Companions," *Crime and Delinquency* 13 (1967), pp. 344–351.

11. Michael J. Hindelang, "With a Little Help from Their Friends: Group Participation in Reported Delinquent Behavior," *British Journal of Criminology* 16 (1976), pp. 109–125.

12. Elizabeth S. Piper, "Violent Offenders: Lone Wolf or Wolfpack?" Paper presented at the Annual Meeting of the American Society of Criminology, San Diego, California (November 1985).

13. Hirschi, *Causes of Delinquency* (Berkeley, CA: University of California Press, 1969), p. 141.

14. Interview with Peggy Giordano conducted in 1984.

15. Warr, "Age, Peers, and Delinquency," pp. 17, 25.

16. Ross L. Matsueda and Kathleen Anderson, "The Dynamics of Delinquent Peers and Delinquent Behavior," *Criminology* 36 (1998), p. 270.

17. Agnew, "The Interactive Effects of Peer Variables on Delinquency," p. 47.

18. Warr and Stafford, "The Influence of Delinquent Peers," p. 851.

19. Delbert S. Elliott and Scott Menard, "Delinquent Friends and Delinquent Behavior: Temporal and Developmental Patterns," in *Delinquency and Crime: Current Theories,* edited by J. David Hawkins (Cambridge, England: Cambridge University Press, 1996).

20. Merry Morash, "Gender, Peer Group Experiences, and Seriousness of Delinquency," *Journal of Research in Crime and Delinquency* 25 (1986), pp. 43, 61.

21. Mark Warr, "Life-Course Transitions and Desistance from Crime," *Criminology* 36 (May 1998), p. 185.

22. Matsueda and Anderson, "The Dynamics of Delinquent Behavior and Delinquent Theory," p. 269.

23. Thornberry et al., "Delinquent Peers, Beliefs, and Delinquent Behavior," p. 47. For another study consistent with inter-actional theory, see Scott Menard and Delbert S. Elliott, "Delinquent Bonding, Moral Beliefs, and Illegal Behavior: A Three-Wave Panel Model," *Justice Quarterly* 11 (June 1994), pp. 174–188.

24. Dana L. Haynie and D. Wayne Osgood, "Reconsidering Peers and Delinquency: How Do Peers Matter?" *Social Forces* 84 (December 2005), pp. 1109–1130.

25. Joan McCord and Kevin P. Conway, "Co-Offending and Patterns of Juvenile Crime," *NIJ: Research in Brief* (Washington, D.C.: National Institute of Justice, 2005), pp. ii, 1.

26. Giordano's interview in Bartollas, *Juvenile Delinquency,* p. 354.

27. Carl S. Taylor, *Dangerous Society* (East Lansing: Michigan State University Press, 1990), pp. 2–3.

28. Luc Sante, *Low Life: Lures and Snares of Old New York* (New York: Vintage Books, 1991).

29. Robert Redfield, *Folk Culture of Yucatán* (Chicago: University of Chicago Press, 1941).

30. James C. Howell, *Youth Gangs: An Overview* (Washington, D.C.: Office of Justice Programs, Office of Juvenile Justice and Delinquency Prevention, 1998), p. 2; and Sante, *Low Life.*

31. Frederick Thrasher, *The Gang: A Study of 1,313 Gangs in Chicago* (Chicago: University of Chicago Press, 1927).

32. Ibid., p. 45.

33. See Walter B. Miller, "The Impact of a Total Community Delinquency Control Project," *Social Problems* 10 (Fall 1962), pp. 168–191.

34. Craig Collins, "Youth Gangs of the 70s," *Police Chief* 42 (September 1975), p. 50.

35. Ibid.

36. Student interviewed in March 1974.

37. John C. Quicker and Akil S. Batani-Khalfani, "Clique Succession among South Los Angeles Street Gangs, the Case of the Crips." Paper presented to the Annual Meeting of the American Society of Criminology, Reno, Nevada (November 1989).

38. See David Dawley, *A Nation of Lords: The Autobiography of the Vice Lords* (Garden City, N.Y.: Anchor Books, 1973).

39. James Jacobs, *Stateville: The Penitentiary in Mass Society* (Chicago: University of Chicago Press, 1977).

40. Ibid.

41. Paul Weingarten, "Mean Streets," *Chicago Tribune Magazine* 19 (September 1982), p. 12.

42. Walter B. Miller, "Gangs, Groups, and Serious Youth Crime," in *Critical Issues in Juvenile Delinquency*, pp. 120–121.

43. Walter B. Miller, *Violence by Youth Gangs and Youth Groups as a Crime Problem in Major American Cities* (Washington, D.C.: U.S. Government Printing Office, 1975). Much of the following material is derived from Chapter 15 of Miller's study.

44. Walter B. Miller, *Crime by Youth Gangs and Groups in the United States*. A report prepared for the National Institute of Juvenile Justice and Delinquency Prevention of the United States Department of Justice (February 1982).

45. Malcolm K. Klein, *Studies on Crime and Crime Prevention* (Stockholm, Sweden: Scandinavian University Press, 1993), p. 88.

46. Arlen Egley Jr. and Christina E. Ritz, *Highlights of the 2004 National Youth Gang Survey* (Washington, D.C.: Office of Juvenile Justice and Delinquency Prevention, 2006), p. 1.

47. Finn-Aage Esbensen, *Preventing Adolescent Gang Involvement: Juvenile Justice Bulletin* (Washington, D.C.: Office of Juvenile Justice and Delinquency Prevention, 2000), p. 2.

48. Thrasher, *The Gang*, p. 57.

49. Miller, "Gangs, Groups, and Serious Youth Crime," p. 121.

50. Esbensen, *Preventing Adolescent Gang Involvement*, pp. 2–3.

51. James C. Howell, *OJJDP Fact Sheet* (Washington, D.C.: Office of Juvenile Justice and Delinquency Prevention, 1997), p. 1.

52. Arlen Egley Jr., James C. Howell, and Aline K. Major, *National Youth Gang Survey 1999-2001* (Washington, D.C.: Office of Juvenile Justice and Delinquency Prevention, U.S. Government Printing Office, 2006), pp. 16–18.

53. For the role behavior of juveniles in gangs, see Mike Carlie, *Into the Abyss: A Personal Journal into the World of Street Gangs*, www.faculty.missouristate.edu/m/mkc096f/.

54. Howell, *Youth Gangs*, p. 2. See also Scott H. Decker and B. Van Winkle, *Life in the Gang: Family, Friends, and Violence* (New York: Cambridge University Press, 1996).

55. J. D. Vigil, "Cholos and Gangs: Culture Change and Street Youths in Los Angeles," in *Gangs in America*, edited by C. Ronald Huff (Newbury Park, Calif.: Sage, 1990).

56. J. D. Vigil and J. M. Long, "Emic and Etic Perspectives on Gang Culture: The Chicano Case," in *Gangs in America* (note 56).

57. Discussion of Vigil and Long's typology is based on Randall G. Shelden, Sharon K. Tracy, and William B. Brown, *Youth Gangs in American Society* (Belmont, Calif.: Wadsworth, 1997), pp. 69–70.

58. Ira Reiner, *Gangs, Crime and Violence in Los Angeles: Findings and Proposals from the District Attorney's Office* (Arlington, Va.: National Youth Gang Information Center, 1992), pp. 40–44.

59. Adapted from Shelden, Tracy, and Brown, *Youth Gangs in American Society*, pp. 70–71.

60. Martín Sánchez Jankowski, *Islands in the Street: Gangs and American Urban Society* (Berkeley: University of California Press, 1991). For a more up-to-date article by Sánchez-Jankowski, see "Gangs and Social Change," *Theoretical Criminology* 7 (2003), pp. 191–216.

61. Interviewed in 1982 at the Iowa State Penitentiary at Fort Madison, Iowa.

62. Richard A. Cloward and Lloyd E. Ohlin, *Delinquency and Opportunity: A Theory of Delinquent Gangs* (New York: Free Press, 1960).

63. Lewis Yablonsky, *The Violent Gang* (New York: Macmillan, 1962).

64. Taylor, *Dangerous Society*.

65. C. Ronald Huff, "Youth Gangs and Public Policy," *Crime and Delinquency* 35 (October 1989), pp. 524–537.

66. Jeffrey Fagan, "The Social Organization of Drug Use and Drug Dealing among Urban Gangs," *Criminology* 27 (1989), pp. 633–664.

67. Taylor, *Dangerous Society*, p. 4.

68. Ibid., p. 6.

69. Ibid., p. 7.

70. Carl S. Taylor, "Gang Imperialism," in *Gangs in America* (note 56), p. 113.

71. Huff, "Youth Gangs and Public Policy," pp. 528–529.

72. Fagan, "Drug Use and Drug Dealing among Gangs," pp. 649–651.

73. Malcolm W. Klein and Cheryl L. Maxson, *Gang Structure, Crime Patterns, and Police Responses*. Final Report to the National Institute of Justice (1996).

74. Ibid., pp. 4–6.

75. See L. J. Bobrowski, *Collecting, Organizing and Reporting Street Crime* (Chicago: Chicago Police Department, Special Function Group, 1988).

76. In a 1998 conversation, Willie Johnson, the leader of the Vice Lord Nation, reported that there are now eleven divisions of the Vice Lord Nation.

77. G. David Curry, Scott H. Decker, and Arlen Egley Jr., "Gang Involvement and Delinquency in a Middle School Population," *Justice Quarterly* 19 (June 2002), p. 283.

78. C. Ronald Huff and K. S. Trump, "Youth Violence and Gangs: School Safety Initiatives in Urban and Suburban School Districts," *Education and Urban Safety* 28 (1996), pp. 4492–4503. For the violence of youth gangs in schools, see also George W. Knox, *An Introduction to Gangs* (Berrien Springs, Mich.: Vande Vere Publishing, 1993); I. A.

Spergel, G. D. Curry, R. A. Ross, and R. Chance, *Survey of Youth Gang Problems and Programs in 45 Cities and 6 Sites* (Chicago: University of Chicago, School of Social Service Administration, 1989); and C. Ronald Huff, "Youth Gangs and Public Policy," *Crime and Delinquency* 35 (1989), pp. 524–537.

79. George W. Knox, David Laske, and Edward Tromanhauser, "Chicago Schools Revisited," *Bulletin of the Illinois Public Education Association* 16 (Spring 1992). For the relationship between gangs and weapons, see also Edward Tromanhauser, "The Relationship between Street Gang Membership and the Possession and Use of Firearms." Paper presented at the Annual Meeting of the American Society of Criminology, Boston, Massachusetts (November 1994).

80. Joseph F. Sheley and James D. Wright, "Gun Acquisition and Possession in Selected Juvenile Samples," *Research in Brief* (Washington, D.C.: National Institute of Justice, 1993).

81. Charles M. Callahan and Ira Rivara, "Urban High School Youth and Handguns: A School-Based Survey," *Journal of the American Medical Association* (June 1992).

82. Comment made in 1995 to one of the authors.

83. For more information on drive-by shootings, see William B. Sanders, *Gangbangs and Drive-Bys: Grounded Culture and Juvenile Gang Violence* (New York: Aldine de Gruyter, 1994).

84. Ronald D. Stephens, "School-Based Interventions: Safety and Security," in *The Gang Intervention Handbook*, edited by Arnold P. Goldstein and C. Ronald Huff (Champaign, Ill.: Research Press, 1993), pp. 222–223.

85. Jeffrey Fagan, "The Social Organization of Drug Use and Drug Dealing among Urban Gangs," *Criminology* 27 (1989), pp. 633–664.

86. Elizabeth Huffmaster McConnell and Elizabeth Peltz, "An Examination of Youth Gang Problems at Alpha High School." An unpublished paper (1989).

87. See "Dope Fiend Teaches Algebra at Austin High," *Austin Voice* 9 (March 1 and March 8, 1994), p. 1.

88. Daniel J. Monti, *Wannabe: Gangs in Suburbs and Schools* (Cambridge, England: Blackwell, 1994), p. 92.

89. Patricia Wen, "Boston Gangs: A Hard World," *Boston Globe*, Tuesday, May 10, 1988, p. 31. For a description of the various roles within gang drug trafficking, see Felix M. Padilla, *The Gang as an American Enterprise* (New Brunswick, N.J.: Rutgers University Press, 1992).

90. Janowski, *Islands in the Street.*

91. Ibid., pp. 64–66.

92. Joan Moore, Diego Vigil, and Robert Garcia, "Residence and Territoriality in Chicano Gangs," *Social Problems* 31 (December 1985), pp. 182–194.

93. Jankowski, *Islands in the Street,* pp. 49–50.

94. Knapp, "Embattled Youth," p. 13.

95. Gang leader interviewed in 1995.

96. Carlie, *Into the Abyss.*

97. Ibid.

98. James Diego Vigil, "The Gang Subculture and *Locura*: Variations in Acts and Actors." Paper presented at the Annual Meeting of the American Society of Criminology, San Diego, California (November 1985), pp. 5, 10.

99. Ibid., p. 13.

100. Quoted in Vigil, "The Gang Subculture and *Locura*," p. 6.

101. John M. Hagedorn, *People and Folks: Gangs, Crime and the Underclass in a Rustbelt City,* 2nd ed. (Chicago: Lake View Press, 1988); Huff, "Youth Gangs and Public Policy," pp. 524–537; and Dennis P. Rosenbaum and Jane A. Grant, *Gangs and Youth Problems in Evanston* (Chicago: Northwestern University, Center for Urban Affairs, 1983).

102. These conversations took place in 1994 and 1995 on prison visits to these gang leaders.

103. Cheryl Maxson, Malcolm W. Klein, and Lea C. Cunningham, "Street Gangs and Drug Sales." Report to the National Institute of Justice (1993). See also Cheryl L. Maxson, "Gang Members on the Move," *Juvenile Justice Bulletin* (Washington, D.C.: Office of Justice Programs, Office of Juvenile Justice and Delinquency Prevention, 1998).

104. See Reiner, *Gangs, Crime and Violence in Los Angeles.*

105. Jeffrey Fagan, "Social Processes of Delinquency and Drug Use among Urban Gangs," in *Gangs in America*, pp. 199–200. See also Fagan, "The Social Organization of Drug Use and Drug Dealing among Urban Gangs," pp. 633–669.

106. Marvin E. Wolfgang, Terence P. Thornberry, and Robert M. Figlio, *From Boy to Man: From Delinquency to Crime* (Chicago: University of Chicago Press, 1987), pp. 155–156.

107. Ibid., pp. 156–158.

108. See C. Ronald Huff, *Criminal Behavior of Gang Members and At-Risk Youths: Research Preview* (Washington, D.C.: National Institute of Research, 1998), p. 1.

109. Ibid., pp. 1–2.

110. C. Ronald Huff, *Comparing the Criminal Behavior of Youth Gangs and At-Risk Youths: Research in Brief* (Washington, D.C.: Office of Justice Programs, 1998), p. 1. See also Scott H. Decker and Barrik Van Winkle, " 'Slinging Dope': The Role of Gangs and Gang Members in Drug Sales," *Justice Quarterly* 11 (December 1994), pp. 583–603.

111. Terence P. Thornberry, "Membership in Youth Gangs and Involvement in Serious and Violent Offending," in *Serious and Violent Juvenile Offenders: Risk Factors and Successful Interventions*, edited by R. Loeber and D. P. Farrington (Thousand Oaks, Calif.: Sage Publications, 1998), pp. 147–166.

112. Sara R. Battin-Pearson, Terence P. Thornberry, J. David Hawkins, and Marvin D. Krohn, "Gang Membership, Delinquent Peers, and Delinquent Behavior," *Juvenile Justice Bulletin* (Washington, D.C.: Office of Justice Programs, Office of Juvenile Justice and Delinquency Prevention, 1998); and Sara R. Battin, Karl G. Hill, Robert D. Abbott, Richard F. Catalano, and J. David Hawkins, "The Contribution of Gang Membership to Delinquency beyond Delinquent Friends," *Criminology* 36 (February 1998), pp. 93–115.

113. David Huizinga, "Gangs and the Volume of Crime." Paper presented at the Annual Meeting of the Western Society of Criminology, Honolulu, Hawaii (1997).

114. Huff, *Criminal Behavior of Gang Members and At-Risk Youths,* p. 2.

115. Battin et al., "The Contribution of Gang Membership to Delinquency beyond Delinquent Friends," pp. 93–115; Huizinga, "The Volume of Crime by Gang and Nongang Members"; and Thornberry, "Membership in Youth Gangs and Involvement in Serious and Violent Offending," pp. 147–166.

116. Finn-Aage Esbensen and D. Huizinga, "Gangs, Drugs, and Delinquency in a Survey of Urban Youth," *Criminology* 31 (1993), pp. 565–589.

117. Howell, "Youth Gangs," p. 9.

118. Egley and Ritz, *Highlights of the 2004 National Youth Gang Survey.* For 1996, 1997, and 1998 gang homicides, see G. David Curry, Cheryl L. Maxson, and James C. Howell, "Youth Gang Homicides in the 1990s," *OJJDP Fact Sheet* (Washington, D.C.: Office of Juvenile Justice and Delinquency Prevention, 2001), p. 1. A real problem with homicide statistics is that it is difficult to know whether a given killing is gang motivated, gang affiliated, or nongang. See Richard Rosenfeld, Timothy M. Bray, and Arlen Egley Jr., "Facilitating Violence: A Comparison of Gang-Motivated, Gang-Affiliated, and Nongang Youth Homicides," *Journal of Quantitative Criminology* 15 (1999), pp. 495–516.

119. Howell, "Youth Gangs: An Overview."

120. Ibid.

121. Scott H. Decker, "Collective and Normative Features of Gang Violence," *Justice Quarterly* 13 (1996), p. 262.

122. Ibid.

123. Howell, "Youth Gangs: An Overview," p. 10. See Beth Bjerregaard and Alan J. Lizotte, "Gun Ownership and Gang Membership," *Journal of Criminal Law and Criminology* 86 (1995), pp. 37–53.

124. Bjerregaard and Lizotte, "Gun Ownership and Gang Membership," pp. 37–53.

125. Coordinating Council on Juvenile Justice and Delinquency Prevention, *Combating Violence and Delinquency: The National Juvenile Justice Action Plan* (Washington, D.C.: Office of Juvenile Justice and Delinquency Prevention, 1996), p. 35.

126. Joseph F. Sheley and James D. Wright, *Youth, Guns, and Violence in Urban America.* Paper presented at the National Conference on Prosecution Strategies against Armed Criminals and Gang Violence: Federal, State, and Local Coordination, San Diego, California (Washington, D.C.: National Institute of Justice, 1992).

127. *2005 National Gang Threat Assessment* (Washington, D.C.: Bureau of Justice Statistics, 2005), p. 3.

128. Ibid., p. 4. See also Carrie Kirby, "Crews Show Off Their Colors and Lifestyles on Web," *San Francisco Chronicle,* January 6, 2001.

129. Scott H. Decker, Tim Bynum, and Deborah Weisel, "A Tale of Two Cities: Gangs as Organized Crime Groups," *Justice Quarterly* 15 (September 1998), pp. 395–425.

130. James McCormick, "The 'Disciples' of Drugs—and Death," *Newsweek* (February 5, 1996), pp. 56–57; and I. A. Spergel, *The Youth Gang Problem* (New York: Oxford University Press, 1995).

131. General Accounting Office, *Nontraditional Organized Crime* (Washington, D.C.: U.S. Government Printing Office, 1989).

132. Drug Enforcement Administration, *Crack Availability and Trafficking in the United States* (Washington, D.C.: U.S. Department of Justice, 1998). For a discussion of gangs in organized crime, see *2005 National Gang Threat Assessment*, pp. 2–3.

133. Thrasher, *The Gang.*

134. Curry et al., "National Assessment of Law Enforcement Anti-Gang Information Resources."

135. For a review of studies of emergent gangs, see James C. Howell, "Recent Gang Research: Program and Policy Implications," *Crime and Delinquency* 40 (October 1994), pp. 495–515.

136. Esbensen and Huizinga, "Gangs, Drugs, and Delinquency in a Survey of Urban Youth," pp. 565–589.

137. Mark S. Fleisher, "Youth Gangs and Social Networks: Observations from a Long-Term Ethnographic Study." Paper presented to the Annual Meeting of the American Society of Criminology, Miami, Florida (November 1994), p. 1.

138. Ibid., p. 4.

139. Terence P. Thornberry, Marvin D. Krohn, Alan J. Lizotte, and Deborah Chard-Wierschem, "The Role of Juvenile Gangs in Facilitating Delinquent Behavior," *Journal of Research in Crime and Delinquency* 30 (1993), pp. 55–87.

140. "Youth Violence: Gangs on Main Street, USA," *Issues in Brief* (Winter 1993), pp. 3, 5. For the presence of gangs in rural communities, see L. Edward Wells and Ralph A. Weisheit, "Gang Problems in Nonmetropolitan Areas: A Longitudinal Assessment," *Justice Quarterly* 18 (December 2001), pp. 791–823; and Satasha L. Green, "Do Gangs Exist in Rural Areas and Small Cities: Perceptions of Law Enforcement Agencies," *Journal of Gang Research* 11 (Fall 2003), pp. 13–31.

141. "Youth Violence: Gangs on Main Street," p. 3.

142. This seven-stage development scheme was developed from conversations with a variety of individuals across the nation, ranging from gang leaders and gang members to police administrators, school officials, and newspaper reporters.

143. Gang youth were very reluctant to talk about the percentage.

144. Youth interviewed in August 1990.

145. Adolescent interviewed in February 1991.

146. Gang member interviewed in October 1989.

147. Comment made by a teacher to the author following a gang seminar he presented in March 1990.

148. *2005 National Gang Threat Assessment*, p. 7.

149. For an examination of Chicano gangs, see James Diego Vigil, *Barrio Gangs: Street Life and Identity in Southern California* (Austin: University of Texas Press, 1988), and Joan Moore, *Home Boys: Gangs, Drugs, and Prison in the Barrios of Los Angeles* (Philadelphia: Temple University Press, 1978).

150. See Ko-Lin Chin, "Chinese Gangs and Extortion," in *Gangs in America* (note 56), pp. 129–145.

151. James Diego Vigil and Steve Chong Yun, "Vietnamese Youth Gangs in Southern California," in *Gangs in America* (note 56), pp. 146–162.

152. Reiner, *Gangs, Crime and Violence in Los Angeles,* p. 114.

153. Arlen Egley Jr., *National Youth Gang Survey Trends from 1996 to 2000* (Washington, D.C.: Office of Juvenile Justice and Delinquency Prevention, 2002).

154. Howell, "Youth Gangs: An Overview," p. 2.

155. Finn-Aage Esbensen and D. W. Osgood, *National Evaluation of G.R.E.A.T.: Research in Brief* (Washington, D.C.: Office of Justice Programs, National Institute of Justice, 1997).

156. For an examination of the seriousness of the problem of Satanism among American youth, see Philip Jenkins and Daniel Maier-Katkin, "Satanism: Myth and Reality in a Contemporary Moral Panic." Revised paper presented at the American Society of Criminology, Baltimore, Maryland (November 1990).

157. See Eric Henderson, Stephen J. Kunitz, and Jerrold E. Levy, "The Origins of Navajo Youth Gangs, " *American Indian Culture and Research Journal* 23 (1999), pp. 243–264.

158. Ibid.

159. Albert K. Cohen, *Delinquent Boys: The Culture of the Gang* (Glencoe, Ill.: Free Press, 1955), pp. 46–48.

160. Thrasher, *The Gang*.

161. Anne Campbell, *The Girls in the Gang: A Report from New York City* (New York: Basic Blackwell, 1984), p. 5.

162. Found in Jack E. Bynum and William E. Thompson, *Juvenile Delinquency: A Sociological Approach* (Boston: Allyn and Bacon, 1989), p. 295.

163. Freda Adler, *Sisters in Crime: The Rise of the New Female Criminal* (New York: McGraw-Hill, 1975).

164. The Molls are discussed in W. B. Miller, "The Molls," *Society* 11 (1973), pp. 32–35, and the Queens in E. Ackley and B. Fliegel, "A Social Work Approach to Street Corner Girls," *Social Work* 5 (1960), pp. 29–31.

165. Peggy C. Giordano, "Girls, Guys and Gangs: The Changing Social Context of Female Delinquency," *Journal of Criminal Law and Criminology* 69 (1978), p. 130.

166. Waln K. Brown, "Black Female Gangs in Philadelphia," *International Journal of Offender Therapy and Comparative Criminology* 21 (1970), pp. 221–229.

167. Ibid., pp. 223–227.

168. Lee Bowker and M. W. Klein, "Female Participation in Delinquent Gang Motivation," *Adolescence* 15 (1980).

169. J. C. Quicker, *Home Girls: Characterizing Chicano Gangs* (San Pedro, Calif.: International University Press, 1983).

170. M. G. Harris, *Cholas: Latino Girls and Gangs* (New York: AMS Press, 1988), p. 172.

171. Finn-Aage Esbensen, Elizabeth Piper Deschenes, and L. Thomas Winfree Jr., "Differences between Gang Girls and Gang Boys: Results from a Multi-Site Survey." Paper presented to the Annual Meeting of the Academy of Criminal Justice Sciences in Albuquerque, New Mexico (1998), pp. 20–21.

172. Campbell, *The Girls in the Gang*; see also Anne Campbell, "Female Participation in Gangs," in *Gangs in America* (note 56), pp. 163–182.

173. Carl S. Taylor, *Girls, Gangs, Women and Drugs* (East Lansing: Michigan State University Press, 1993), p. 48.

174. Ibid., p. 95.

175. Ibid., pp. 102–103. For a study of female gang members in Fort Wayne, Indiana, and their trafficking of crack cocaine, see D. B. Kitchen, *Sisters in the Hood*. Ph.D. dissertation, Western Michigan University, 1995.

176. David Lauderback, Joy Hansen, and Daniel Waldorf, "Sisters Are Doin' It for Themselves: A Black Female Gang in San Francisco," *Gang Journal* 1 (1992), pp. 57–72.

177. Beth Bjerregaard and Carolyn Smith, "Gender Differences in Gang Participation, Delinquency, and Substance Abuse," *Journal of Quantitative Criminology* 9 (1993), pp. 347–348.

178. Joan Moore and John Hagedorn, "Female Gangs: A Focus on Research," *Juvenile Justice Bulletin* (Washington, D.C.: Office of Juvenile Justice and Delinquency Prevention, 2001).

179. Ibid.

180. Jody Miller, "Gender and Victimization Risk among Young Women in Gangs," *Journal of Research in Crime and Delinquency* 35 (November 1998), pp. 429–453; Jody Miller and Rod K. Brunson, "Gender Dynamics in Youth Gangs: A Comparison of Males' and Females' Accounts," *Justice Quarterly* 17 (September 2000), pp. 420–447; Jody Miller and Scott Decker, "Young Women and Gang Violence: Gender, Street Offending, and Violent Victimization in Gangs," *Justice Quarterly* 18 (March 2001), pp. 115–139; and Jody Miller, *One of the Guys: Girls, Gangs, and Gender* (New York: Oxford University Press, 2001).

181. Miller and Brunson, "Gender Dynamics in Youth Gangs," pp. 443–445.

182. Miller, "Gender and Victimization Risk," and Miller, *One of the Guys*.

183. Karen Joe and Meda Chesney-Lind, "Just Every Mother's Angel: An Analysis of Gender and Ethnic Variations in Youth Gang Membership." Paper presented at the Annual Meeting of the American Society of Criminology, Phoenix, Arizona (November 1993), p. 9.

184. Ibid.

185. H. A. Bloch and A. Niederhoffer, *The Gang: A Study in Adolescent Behavior* (New York: Philosophical Library, 1958).

186. Richard A. Cloward and Lloyd E. Ohlin, *Delinquency and Opportunity: A Theory of Delinquent Gangs* (Glencoe, Ill.: Free Press, 1960).

187. Cohen, *Delinquent Boys: The Culture of the Gang*.

188. Walter B. Miller, "Lower-Class Culture as a Generating Milieu of Gang Delinquency," *Journal of Social Issues* 14 (1958), pp. 5–19.

189. Lewis Yablonsky, *The Violent Gang* (New York: Macmillan, 1962).

190. Bjerregaard and Smith, "Gender Differences in Gang Participation, Delinquency, and Substance Use," p. 333.

191. See Patrick G. Jackson, "Theories and Findings about Youth Gangs," *Criminal Justice Abstracts* (June 1989), pp. 322–323.

192. See Gerald D. Suttles, *The Social Order of the Slum: Ethnicity and Territory in the Inner City* (Chicago: University of Chicago Press, 1968); and Thrasher, *The Gang*.

193. Jankowski, *Islands in the Street*, p. 22.

194. See William Julius Wilson, *The Truly Disadvantaged: The Inner City, the Underclass, and Public Policy* (Chicago: University of Chicago Press, 1987).

195. G. David Curry and Irving A. Spergel, "Gang Homicide, Delinquency, and Community," *Criminology* (1988), pp. 381–405.

196. J. E. Fagan, "Gangs, Drugs, and Neighborhood Change," in *Gangs in America*, 2nd ed., edited by C. R. Huff (Thousand Oaks, Calif.: Sage Publications, 1996), pp. 39–74.

197. Hagedorn, *People and Folks*.

198. J. D. Vigil, *Barrio Gangs: Street Life and Identity in Southern California* (Austin: University of Texas Press, 1988), p. 101.

199. Jankowski, *Islands in the Street*, p. 139.

200. Ibid.

201. Decker and Van Winkle, *Life in the Gang*, pp. 64–66.

202. Correspondence from Michael F. de Vries. See also R. E. Johnson, A. C. Marcos, and S. J. Bahr, "The Role of Peers in the Complex Etiology of Adolescent Drug Use," *Criminology* 25 (1987), pp. 323–340.

203. Terence P. Thornberry, Marvin D. Krohn, Alan J. Lizotte, and Carolyn A. Smith, *Gangs and Delinquency in Developmental Perspective* (Cambridge, England: Cambridge Press, 2003), pp. 6–7.

204. Ibid., pp. 3–4

205. Ibid., p. 3

206. See Huff, "Youth Gangs and Public Policy."
207. Short, "Gangs, Neighborhood, and Youth Crime," p. 3.
208. I. A. Spergel, G. D. Curry, R. A. Ross, and R. Chance, *Survey of Youth Gang Problems and Programs in 45 Cities and 6 Sites.* Tech. Report No. 2, National Youth Gang Suppression and Intervention Project (Chicago: University of Chicago, School of Social Service Administration, 1989), p. 211.
209. Ibid., p. 212.
210. Ibid., p. 216.
211. Ibid., p. 218.
212. Ibid.
213. Howell, "Youth Gangs: An Overview," p. 13.
214. Ibid., p. 14.
215. Terence P. Thornberry and James H. Burch II, "Gang Members and Delinquent Behavior," *Juvenile Justice Bulletin* (Washington, D.C.: Office of Justice Programs, Office of Juvenile Justice and Delinquency Prevention, 1997), p. 4.

11

Drugs and Delinquency

> For the foreseeable future, American youngsters will be aware of the psychoactive potential of many drugs and, in general, will have relatively easy access to them.
>
> —*Monitoring the Future* survey

CHAPTER Objectives

AFTER READING THIS CHAPTER, YOU SHOULD BE ABLE TO ANSWER THE FOLLOWING QUESTIONS:

- How are social attitudes related to drug use?

- How much drug use is there among adolescents in American society?

- What are the main types of drugs used by adolescents?

- What is the relationship between drug abuse and delinquency?

- What theoretical explanations best explain the onset of drug use?

- What can be done to prevent and control drug use among adolescents?

For almost a generation, members of the IRAK Crew have been the preeminent graffiti artists of New York City. Fans of one of the group's former members, Simon Curtis, still can't believe the odd series of events that led him to spend the last four years in prison. And although Curtis readily admits that he was living recklessly for a long time, drinking too much, taking drugs and spraying graffiti on the Lower East Side of New York, he didn't see incarceration in his future when he went to an art opening on the night of July 14, 2001.

The show, titled "The Life You Save May Be Your Own," after a Flannery O'Connor story, was held at a small, well-maintained gallery along a strip of paint-chipped warehouses in Brooklyn. It was a group show, and a young friend of Mr. Curtis's, a beautiful young photographer named Michelle Cortez, was among the artists whose work was on exhibit.

A good-size crowd turned out, and a loose, partylike atmosphere prevailed. As the evening wound down, Curtis found himself nearly alone inside the gallery and eyeing his favorite photo, a self-portrait of Ms. Cortez that showed her topless and wearing ripped stockings. He was feeling contented and mischievous and also a little drunk. It suddenly occurred to him that it would be funny to show up with the photo at Max Fish, a Lower East Side bar where Ms. Cortez had gone with friends. As a group of people stood outside smoking cigarettes in the sticky air, he reached up, plucked the photo from the wall and shuffled out.

It was a spur-of-the-moment act, a juvenile-type prank, but one that had far-reaching consequences. From the theft would spring a high-speed getaway, an alleged kidnapping and an assault on the gallery owner. Criminal charges and prison time would follow.

"I've run that night over in my head so many times," said Curtis, who was recently paroled, "I think about it way too much."

That night at the gallery wasn't Curtis's first crazy stint. He and the Irak Crew once descended on a house party and covered the host's apartment in graffiti. Another time, he appeared near catatonic and high on angel dust on a cable-access television show called *The Kid America Adventure Hour*. "That was a bad one," Curtis said.

Adapted from Steven Kurutz, "Unmerry Prankster," *New York Times*, May 22, 2005. Copyright © 2005 by The New York Times Co. Reprinted with permission.

At age thirty-one, Simon Curtis's reckless life—involving years pursuing drugs, alcohol, and dubious fame as a storied graffiti artist—caught up with him. Released from state prison at age thirty-five, life-course theory would suggest that he could make the best of his prison experience, see it as a turning point, and reorient his life. Should that not happen, he might continue abusing alcohol and drugs and become involved in additional destructive activities, which would likely mean that he'd suffer the consequences of those behavioral choices for the rest of his life.

Drug and alcohol use and juvenile delinquency have been identified as the most serious problem behaviors of adolescents.[1] The good news is that substance abuse among adolescents has dropped dramatically since the late 1970s. The bad news is that drug use has significantly increased among high-risk youths and is becoming commonly linked to juvenile lawbreaking. More juveniles are also selling drugs than ever before in the history of the United States. Furthermore, the spread of AIDS within populations of intravenous drug users and their sex partners adds to the gravity of the substance abuse problem.[2]

Young people usually prefer substances that are not too costly. Beer and marijuana meet this criterion better than hard drugs do. Availability and potency are also important in drug use, for the substances are generally used as a means to other ends, such as achieving excitement. For example, marijuana and alcohol are used at rock concerts, parties, dances, football games, and outings to add to the excitement that is already present in such activities and to produce excitement when it seems to be lacking. In addition to enhancing excitement, substances can promote exploring new social spheres, sexual relationships, and unfamiliar places. Users also ingest narcotic substances to escape to or retreat from the external world into a private inner self.

There is a difference between drug use and drug abuse. Drug use can be viewed as a continuum that begins with nonuse and includes experimental use, culturally endorsed use, recreational use, and compulsive use.[3] As an example of culturally endorsed use, peyote has been used sacramentally in the Native American church for centuries. Twenty-three states exempt this sacramental use of peyote from criminal penalties.[4]

Adolescent drug use becomes abuse only when the user becomes dysfunctional (e.g., is unable to attend or perform in school or to maintain social and family relationships; exhibits dangerous, reckless, or aggressive behavior; or endangers his or her health). The drug-dependent compulsive user's life usually revolves around obtaining, maintaining, and using a supply of drugs.[5] And as this chapter will show, drug use not only causes harm in itself but also is closely linked to delinquency.

Drug Use Among Adolescents

Society focuses on youths' use of harder drugs, although alcohol remains the drug of choice for most adolescents. Drug use among adolescents was extremely high during the late 1960s and into the 1970s, reaching epidemic proportions. Overall rates of illicit drug use appeared to peak sometime around 1979 and has leveled off since then.

An opium den in London's East End, circa 1880. The use of psychoactive drugs has a long history in our society, complicating efforts to identify the roots of modern-day drug abuse.
■ **Why do people use drugs?**

TABLE 11.1

Percentages of Students Reporting Use of Specific Drugs, by Type, 1999–2003

	1999	2001	2003
Lifetime marijuana	47.2%	42.4%	40.2%
Current marijuana	26.7	23.9	22.4
Lifetime cocaine	9.5	9.4	8.7
Current cocaine	4.0	4.2	4.1
Lifetime inhalant	14.6	14.7	12.1
Current inhalant	4.2	4.7	3.9
Lifetime heroin	2.4	3.1	3.3
Lifetime methamphetamine	9.1	9.8	7.6
Lifetime MDMA	na	na	11.1

Source: Centers for Disease Control and Prevention, *Youth Risk Behavior Surveillance–United States* (Washington, D.C.: Centers for Disease Control and Prevention, 2004), Table 11.2.

Web LIBRARY 11.1

Read the COPS publication *Underage Drinking* at **www.justicestudies.com/WebLibrary**.

Even with the leveling off that took place, rates of illicit drug use among youths remained high for some time. Then, in 2001, there was a significant downturn in drug-use levels.[6] And according to the 2003 Monitoring the Future study, illicit drug use by youths had declined further since 2001.[7]

This downward trend has been evident for marijuana, although its use rose dramatically in the early 1990s. According to the Centers for Disease Control and Prevention, the use of marijuana among high school students has declined since 1999. In 2003, of high school students surveyed nationally, 40.2 percent had used marijuana during their lifetime. This is a decline from 42.4 percent in 2001 and 47.2 percent in 1999.[8] A similar downward trend took place with cocaine, except that rates plateaued between 1979 and 1985 before starting to decline. Although cigarette use peaked in 1974, it did not begin declining significantly until about 1979. Finally, the highest rates of inhalant use were recorded in 1985, with slight reductions since that time. Table 11.1 reports the trends for several substances.

> *Alcohol remains the drug of choice for most adolescents.*

According to the 2002 National Survey on Drug Use and Health, 11.6 percent of juveniles aged twelve to seventeen reported current use of illicit drugs in 2002. In the same survey approximately 30 percent of juveniles reported having used an illicit drug at least once during their lifetime, and 22.2 percent reported having used an illicit drug within the past year. The major illicit drug this age group used was marijuana, with 8.2 percent of juveniles being current users.[9] The results of this survey were quite similar to those of the 2003 Monitoring the Future survey, which found that 24.1 percent of twelfth-graders reported using drugs during 2003. Table 11.2 reports the 2003 percentages of students reporting drug use in the past month, in the past year, and over their lifetimes.

TABLE 11.2

Percentages of High School Students Reporting Drug Use, 2003

STUDENT DRUG USE	EIGHTH GRADE	TENTH GRADE	TWELFTH GRADE
Past month use	9.7%	19.5%	24.1%
Past year use	16.1	32.0	39.3
Lifetime use	22.8	41.4	51.1

Source: Adapted from the University of Michigan's *Monitoring the Future* Program data from the *2003 In-School Surveys of 8th, 10th, and 12th Grade Students*, grant-funded by the National Institutes of Health. Current data available at www.monitoringthefuture.org/.

Recent studies have shown a marked decrease in gender differences among drug users. Female high school students are slightly more likely than high school males to smoke cigarettes and to use some illicit drugs, including amphetamines; they use alcohol and marijuana at about the same rates as male high school seniors. Nevertheless, male adolescents are much more likely to be involved in heavy, or binge, drinking than female adolescents.[10]

The rates of illicit drug use in 2002 were about the same for white, African American, and Hispanic/Latino youths. The highest use was found among those with two or more races—11.4 percent. American Indians/Alaska Natives had the second highest use (10.1 percent) followed by African Americans (9.7 percent); whites (8.8 percent); Hispanic/Latino (7.2 percent); and Asians (3.5 percent).[11]

Adolescents vary, of course, in terms of how frequently they use drugs and the type of drugs they use. The variables of age, gender, urban or rural setting, social class, and availability strongly affect the types of drugs used and have some effect on the frequency of drug use. Some users take drugs only at parties and on special occasions, some reserve them for weekends, and some use drugs every day.

Studies indicate that although fewer adolescents appear to be experimenting with drugs, those who use them tend to do so more frequently. Heavy users tend to be males, whites, and youths who do not plan to attend college. Substance abuse is more common on the East and West Coasts. In schools, low achievers abuse drugs more than do high achievers.[12]

In sum, although drug use among adolescents peaked during the late 1970s, rates of illicit drug use in this nation remain high, especially among high-risk youths.

Types of Drugs

The licit and illicit drugs used by adolescents, in decreasing order of frequency, are alcohol, tobacco, marijuana, cocaine, methamphetamine, inhalants, sedatives, stimulants (amphetamines and hallucinogens), steroids, prescription drugs, and heroin. The licit drugs are those that are permitted to users who are of age (eighteen and older for tobacco and twenty-one and older for alcohol). The illicit drugs are those that are forbidden by law. Exceptions would be drugs prescribed by a physician or marijuana in jurisdictions that permit the use of this drug. A number of illicit drugs take control of adolescents' lives when they become addicted. **Drug addiction**, according to James A. Inciardi, is "a craving for a particular drug, accompanied by physical dependence, which motivates continuing usage, resulting in tolerance to the drug's effects and a complex of identifiable symptoms appearing when it is suddenly withdrawn."[13] (See Figure 11.1.)

> " Although drug use among adolescents peaked during the late 1970s, rates of illicit drug use remain high. "

drug addiction
The excessive use of a drug, which is frequently characterized by physical and/or psychological dependence.

Alcohol and Tobacco

The reaction to Prohibition fostered the view of alcohol use as acceptable behavior that should be free from legal controls. The public did not perceive alcohol as a dangerous drug then nor does it now. What makes **alcohol** so dangerous is that it relaxes inhibitions, and adolescents participate in risky behavior while under its influence. Adolescents' alcohol use can be linked to property destruction, fights, academic failure, occupation problems, and conflict with law enforcement officials.[14] Youths who are under the influence of alcohol may commit delinquent acts that they otherwise would not.

The seriousness of alcohol use among adolescents can be seen in 2005 data from the National Institutes of Health. According to NIH, in that year 11 percent of eighth-graders, 21 percent of tenth-graders, and 28 percent of twelfth-graders reported having five or more drinks in a row at least once in the past two weeks (Figure 11.2). The percentage of heavy drinking by race and ethnicity remained stable from previ-

alcohol
A drug made through a fermentation process that relaxes inhibitions.

FIGURE 11.1

Drugs: What's in a Name?

Drug names have been a source of confusion for many who have attempted to understand the drug problem. One drug may have a dozen or more names. Drugs may be identified by brand name, generic name, street name, or psychoactive category.

Brand Name
The name that a manufacturer gives a chemical substance is its brand name. Brand names are registered and are frequently associated with trademarks. This brand name identifies a drug in the pharmaceutical marketplace and may not be used by other manufacturers. Psychoactive substances without any known medical application or experimental use are not produced by legitimate companies and, as a result, have no brand name.

Generic Name
The generic name is the chemical or other identifying name of a drug. Generic names are frequently used by physicians when they write prescriptions because generic drugs are usually less costly than brand-name drugs. Generic names are further used in most drug-abuse legislation at the federal and state levels to specify controlled substances. Generic names are sometimes applicable to the psychoactive chemical substances in drugs and not to the drugs themselves. For example, marijuana has the chemical tetrahydrocannabinol, or THC, as the active substance.

Street Name
Street names are slang terms. Many of them originated with the 1960s pop culture, and others continue to be produced in modern-day subculture. The street names for marijuana, cocaine, methamphetamine, and heroin are found in this chapter.

Psychoactive Category
Psychoactive drugs are categorized according to their effects on the human mind. Stimulants, narcotics, depressants, and hallucinogens are typical psychoactive categories.

An Example
PCP and angel dust are street names for a veterinary anesthetic marketed under the brand name Sernylan. Sernylan contains the psychoactive chemical phencyclidine, which is classified as a depressant under the Controlled Substance Act.

Source: Schmalleger, Frank. *Criminal Justice Today*, 9th Edition, © 2007, p. 634. Reprinted by permission of Pearson Education, Inc. Upper Sadle River, NJ.

ous surveys, showing that heavy drinking is more prevalent among white and Hispanic students than among African American youths.[15]

Television programs depicting the abuse of alcohol by adolescents, TV commercials aimed at adolescents saying that "it is not cool" to drink, and talk shows dealing with underage drinking are all expressions of this growing public concern. The organization Mothers Against Drunk Driving (MADD) has taken a strong stand against both teenage and adult drinking. The roots of MADD go back to 1980, when a thirteen-year-old California youth was killed by a hit-and-run driver. The child's mother, stunned that the operator of the automobile was not only drunk at the time but also out on bail for his third drunk-driving offense, launched MADD and initiated a nationwide campaign against driving under the influence.

The use of cigarettes by adolescents is also a national public health concern. Due largely to efforts designed to steer young people away from the use of tobacco, cigarette smoking has declined sharply among American adolescents since the mid-1990s. Between the mid-1990s and 2005, daily cigarette usage declined from 10 to 4 percent among eighth-graders, from 18 to 8 percent among tenth-graders, and from 25 to 14 percent among twelfth-graders. Moreover, the proportion of students who start to smoke has been falling sharply since the 1990s.[16] In 2005, 4 percent of eighth-graders, 8 percent of tenth-graders, and 14 percent of twelfth-graders reported that they had smoked cigarettes in the past 30 days (see Figure 11.3).

Tobacco use is often neglected in a discussion of drugs because nicotine is not considered a mind-altering drug. Yet there is considerable evidence that tobacco users

Web PLACES 11.1

Visit the Mothers Against Drunk Driving website via **www.justicestudies.com/WebPlaces**.

FIGURE 11.2

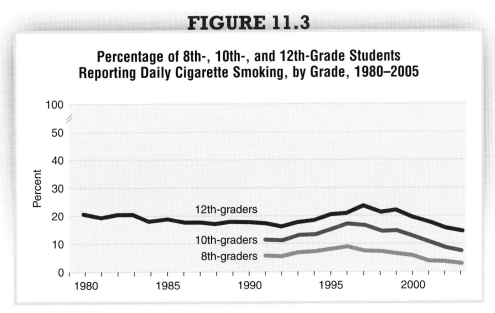

Percentage of 8th-, 10th-, and 12th-Grade Students Reporting Consumption of Five or More Alcoholic Beverages in a Row in the Past Two Weeks, by Grade, 1980–2005

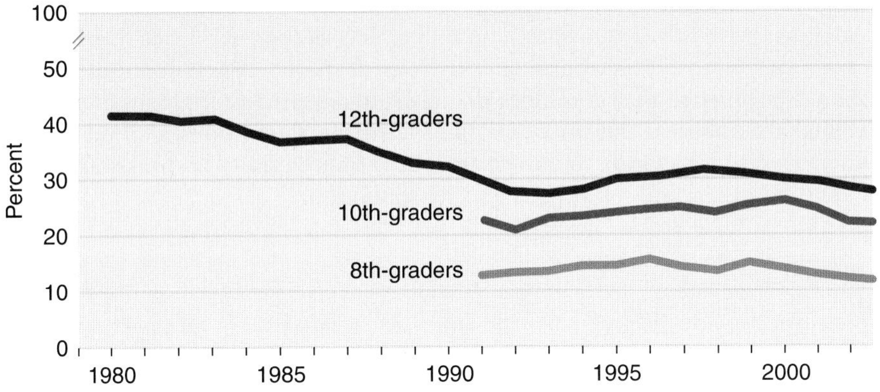

Note: Data were first collected in 1975 for twelfth-graders and in 1991 for eighth- and tenth-graders.
Source: Adapted from the University of Michigan's *Monitoring the Future* Program, grant-funded by the National Institutes of Health. Current data available at www.monitoringthefuture.org/.

FIGURE 11.3

Percentage of 8th-, 10th-, and 12th-Grade Students Reporting Daily Cigarette Smoking, by Grade, 1980–2005

Note: Data were first collected in 1975 for twelfth-graders and in 1991 for eighth- and tenth-graders.

Source: Adapted from the University of Michigan's *Monitoring the Future* Program, grant-funded by the National Institutes of Health. Current data available at www.monitoringthefuture.org/.

suffer severe health consequences from prolonged use and subject others to the same consequences. A 2000 analysis quantified the major factors contributing to death in the United States and found that tobacco contributed to 435,000 deaths annually, whereas alcohol contributed to 85,000 deaths, and all illicit drugs combined contributed to 20,000 deaths.[17]

Marijuana

Marijuana, made from dried hemp leaves and buds, is the most frequently used illicit drug. An interesting indicator of the popularity of marijuana is the number of street

Web **PLACES** 11.2

Visit the National Clearinghouse for Alcohol and Drug Information's website via **www.justicestudies .com/WebPlaces**.

marijuana
The most frequently used illicit drug; usually smoked, it consists of dried hemp leaves and buds.

terms that have been used to designate the substance. The many names given to it include *A-bomb, Acapulco Gold, African black, aunt mary, baby, ashes, bammy, birdwood, California red, Colombian gold, dope, giggleweed, golden leaf, grass, hay, joints, Mexican brown, Mexican green, Panama gold, pot, reefer, reefer weed, shit, seaweed, stinkweed, Texas tea,* and *weed.*[18]

Heated debates about the hazards of using marijuana have waged for some time. Research in the 1980s documented more ill effects of long-term marijuana use than had been suggested before. For example, several studies concluded that marijuana smoking is a practice that combines the hazardous features of alcohol and tobacco as well as a number of pitfalls of its own. Disturbing questions also remain about marijuana's effect on vital systems of the body, on immunity and resistance, on the brain and mind, and on sex organs and reproduction.[19]

Cocaine

cocaine

A coca extract that creates mood elevation, elation, grandiose feelings, and feelings of heightened physical prowess.

Cocaine, the powder derivative of the South American coca plant, is replacing other illegal drugs in popularity. Street names for cocaine include *coke, lady snow, nose candy, toot,* and *Super Fly.* The major source of cocaine is Colombia, and its distribution is a major diplomatic issue in many Central and South American countries.

Cocaine is so expensive ($360 a gram on the streets according to the U.S. Office of Drug Control Policy) that it is generally used in very sparing quantities. At one time cocaine was believed to be less addicting than other illegal hard drugs. But users crave the extreme mood elevation, elation, and grandiose feelings and heightened physical prowess that cocaine induces, and when these begin to wane, a corresponding deep depression is experienced. Users are strongly motivated to use the drug again to restore the euphoria.

Snorting (inhaling) is the most common method of using cocaine; freebasing (smoking) cocaine became popular in the 1980s. Freebase cocaine is derived from a chemical process in which the purified cocaine is crystallized. The crystals are crushed and smoked in a special heated glass pipe. Smoking freebase cocaine provides a quicker, more potent rush and a more powerful high than regular cocaine gives. Intravenous cocaine use also occurs, producing a powerful high, usually within fifteen to twenty seconds. A related method is *speedballing,* or the intravenous use of cocaine in combination with another drug. Speedballing intensifies the euphoric effect, but can be quite dangerous.[20]

A less expensive, more potent version of cocaine achieved great popularity in the 1980s and 1990s. Called crack, this dangerous substance has generated great concern among law enforcement and health professionals. Crack apparently arrived in inner-city neighborhoods in Los Angeles, Miami, and New York between 1981 and 1983,[21] then spread through the nation. It is known by users as *hard white, white, flavor, bricks, boulders, eight-ball* (large rocks), *doo-wap* (two rocks), and *crumbs.* Crack is most typically smoked in special glass pipes or makeshift smoking devices. It is also smoked with marijuana in cigarettes, which are called *geek joints, pin joints,* or *lace joints.* A *shotgun,* which is secondary smoke exhaled from one crack user into the mouth of another, also provides the desired high.[22] Crack is frequently smoked in "crack houses," which may be abandoned buildings or the homes of crack dealers or users.

The addiction to crack by adolescent boys and young men can lead to abusive treatment of others; denial of responsibilities to family, school, and work; and increased rates of delinquent and criminal behavior. In addition to high rates of prostitution, other consequences of the addiction of adolescent girls and adult women to crack are widespread child abuse and child neglect and the toxic effects of crack during pregnancy.[23] The use of crack during pregnancy contributes to the premature separation of the placenta from the uterus, which results in stillbirths and premature infants. Infants who survive cocaine use *in utero* suffer withdrawal symptoms at birth and are at greater risk of stroke and respiratory ailments.[24] There is also a greater risk of sudden infant death syndrome (SIDS) among cocaine-exposed infants. Such infants have a 17 percent incidence of SIDS, compared with 1.6 percent in the gen-

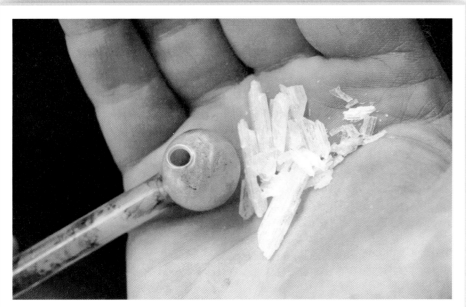

Methamphetamine crystals and a crack pipe. ■ **How much drug use is there among adolescents in American society today?**

eral population.[25] Furthermore, cocaine-exposed infants are more likely to experience emotional disorders, learning disabilities, and sensorimotor problems.[26]

Methamphetamine

Methamphetamine is a synthetic drug otherwise known by its street names: *meth, crank, ice, chalk, glass,* and *crystal meth* (to name just a few). It is a highly addictive stimulant. Meth can be snorted, smoked, or injected. Its effects last up to eight hours (with an initial rush at the beginning and a less intense high for the duration). This drug makes a user feel awake, aware, and happy, but also agitated and paranoid.

According to the 2004 National Survey on Drug Use and Health, 11.7 million Americans over the age of twelve have used methamphetamine in their lifetime, which represents 4.9 percent of the population age twelve and older. More than 583,000 (0.2 percent) reported using the drug in the past month. (See Table 11.3 for the percentage of students reporting the use of methamphetamine in 2004 and 2005.)[27]

The use of methamphetamine is growing. It originally was concentrated in California (especially in the San Diego area) but has widely spread to other states in the West and to states in the South and the Midwest. Social World of the Delinquent 11.1 describes a user's experiences with meth.

TABLE 11.3

Percent of Students Reporting Methamphetamine Use, 2004–2005

	8TH GRADE		10TH GRADE		12TH GRADE	
	2004	2005	2004	2005	2004	2005
Past month	0.6%	0.7%	1.3%	1.1%	1.4%	0.9%
Past year	1.5	1.8	3.0	2.9	3.4	2.9
Lifetime	2.5	3.1	5.3	4.1	6.2	4.5

Source: U.S. Department of Health and Human Services, *National Survey on Drug Use and Health* (Washington, D.C.: U.S. Department of Health and Human Services, 2005).

A Risky Process

A former meth user remembers:

Let me tell you about a drug I was addicted to for a long time. I even sold and manufactured this drug.

Cooking and Dealing Meth

Meth is made of common household products. Anyone can make it. It's really simple. You can buy the ingredients at Wal-Mart, hardware stores, and gas stations. When my boyfriend and I were cooking we tried to play it smart, though. We'd buy ingredients from different people in different states in order to not get caught, because the authorities pay attention to who made large purchases of the ingredients for the drug and would track you down. It is even worse now. If you go to Wal-Mart in my hometown, for example, and buy three things of drain cleaner or two packages of lithium batteries, your picture gets automatically taken at the register, and it is likely that the store will call the police on you.

The cooking process is complicated by the fact that you sometimes have to rely on a handful of people to assemble all the ingredients. And everyone wants a cut of the profit. One person might go to a farmer's field and steal anhydrous out of his tanks, another might buy ephedrine pills, and another might get the batteries or drain cleaner. If you do this all yourself, you increase the likelihood that you will get caught. Police are getting smarter all the time; they have even started setting up and monitoring anhydrous tanks on local farms.

Although it is made out of common household ingredients and is easy to cook, meth is very dangerous to make. I know people who have been burned and people who have had it blow up in their faces. It is really a risky process. You have to cover your face so that you don't breathe any of the materials. If you leave your face uncovered, you won't be happy (you will feel pain every time you breathe in). You also have to be careful what it touches. If any gets on your clothes, for example, it will burn holes right through your shirt, pants, shoes, or whatever fabric it comes into contact with.

Meth also stinks like mad when it is being made. That is why the Midwest and West are prime places for manufacturing the drug. With so many abandoned farmhouses, empty barns, and trailers and with so much land, it is much easier to find a safe place to cook. It would be virtually impossible to cook meth in New England because there is very little open space. If you were stupid and tried to cook it in a hotel or in your kitchen (as many

have done), your neighbors would smell it, you would call attention to yourself, and it is likely that you would be busted.

As simple as it is, not just anyone can cook meth. You have to learn how. Most cookers learn by being "taken in" by another cooker/dealer. It usually works like this: You start using, you use more frequently, and you get to know the person you buy from. If the person you buy from is also a cooker and you can earn their trust or become their friend, they might show you how to cook. Once someone like that takes you under their wing, you are "in," you are part of the inner circle. Being "taken in" is a very delicate process because meth makes people so paranoid. I remember thinking helicopters were following me, people were on my roof, and other crazy shit. And I always thought my friends were narcs. Everyone who used, cooked, or sold was constantly accusing each other of being narcs. This often led to violence in the ranks of the users—people getting jumped, beaten, stolen from, or threatened with guns or other violence.

Once you're in, though, once you're dealing, you don't want to be out. You have everyone's respect, everyone wants to talk to you, everyone wants what you have, everyone looks up to you, and you are making a lot of money. Add all of this to the physical addiction of the drug, and you might be able to begin to understand why people get "sucked in" once they are part of this lifestyle. This is what made it so hard for me to "leave the field." I was addicted to the drug and addicted to the money I was making. But when my best friend got busted cooking at age twenty (it was his first time getting in trouble *ever*) and got sent to prison for ninety-one years, I did not have to think twice. I have been sober and out of the "scene" for years.

Meth and the "Drug Problem"

No one can deny that meth is a very serious problem in the Midwest. Kids here are into it. From what I've seen and according to national drug-use data, more people are using meth and the users are getting younger and younger. Anyone from upper-class kids to kids from the "other side of the tracks" is using it. Jocks, cheerleaders, debate team members, and drama club kids are just as likely to use it as a high school dropout is. Meth is increasingly popular. It is not as popular as marijuana yet, but it is just as easy to get. It is everywhere. It is just as easy to get meth as it is to buy pot or to find someone to buy you alcohol underage, if you know the right people.

■ **Why do you think meth has become so popular among adolescents? Do you believe that giving a twenty-year-old first-time offender a ninety-one year sentence for manufacturing this drug is excessive? What does it mean that such a sentence would be given by the courts?**

Source: A college student provided this narrative.

Inhalants

Many types of **inhalants** are used by adolescents, but what these drugs have in common is that youths have to inhale the vapors to receive the high that they seek. One frequently used inhalant is butyl nitrite, commonly called *RUSH*, which is packaged in small bottles and can often be found in adult bookstores, as well as on the street. Other inhalants that are easier for young drug users to obtain are chlorohydrocarbons and hydrocarbons—which can be inhaled directly from gasoline, paint thinner, glue, or aerosol cans.

The use of these drugs brings about a feeling of excitement that is often followed by a disorientation accompanied by slurred speech and a feeling of sleepiness. The use of inhalants can also be followed by mild to severe headaches and/or nosebleeds. Chronic use of some inhalants is associated with neurological damage and injury to the liver and kidneys.[28]

Sedatives

Like inhalants, many different forms of **sedatives,** or barbiturates, are used by young people. The common factor among all barbiturates is that they are taken orally and that they affect the user by depressing the nervous system and inducing a drowsy condition. On the street, barbiturates are known by the color of their capsule. Seconal pills are known as *reds;* Amytals are called *blue devils;* and Tuinals are known as *rainbows.* Another popular sedative is methaqualone, which is known as *Quaaludes* or *Ludes* on the street.

Adolescents often abuse prescription drugs. Benzodiazepines (minor tranquilizers or sedatives) are among the most widely prescribed of all drugs. Valium, Librium, and Equanil are commonly prescribed for anxiety or sleep disorders; to obtain them, some adolescents simply raid their parents' medicine cabinets. Adolescents can also get these prescription drugs from older teens or young adults, or by purchasing them through Internet-based sources. The National Association of Boards of Pharmacy has identified about 200 websites that dispense prescription drugs but do not offer online prescribing services. According to a recent *Chicago Tribune* article that was cited by the American Medical Association, at least 400 websites both dispense and offer a prescribing service, and half of these sites are located in foreign countries.[29] Some adolescents have broken into pharmacies and stolen the drugs they want. Others obtain them through online trades in illicit clearinghouses called "pharms."

Web **LIBRARY** 11.2

Read the OJJDP Fact Sheet *Substance Abuse: The Nation's Number One Health Problem* at **www.justicestudies.com/WebLibrary**.

Amphetamines

Amphetamines were first made in Germany in the 1880s, but it was not until the Second World War that they were used by Americans. All the military branches issued Benzedrine, Dexedrine, and other types of amphetamines to relieve fatigue and anxiety, especially in battle conditions. Amphetamines became more readily available after the war and were widely used by students studying for examinations, by truck drivers who had to stay alert for extended periods of time, by people attempting to lose weight, and by people seeking relief from nasal congestion. Street names for the amphetamines that were ingested at the time included *bennies, black beauties, King Kong pills, pinks,* and *purple hearts.*[30]

In the late 1980s and early 1990s, MDMA and methamphetamine arrived on the U.S. drug scene. We have already discussed methamphetamine. MDMA, which was used by psychiatrists and other therapists because of its therapeutic benefits, had become a Schedule I drug by 1986, which meant that its manufacture, distribution, and sale violated federal law. It still maintained some popularity among undergraduate populations across the nation. In the 1990s, **Ecstasy,** the common name for MDMA, became popular on college campuses and with adolescents and was widely used at

FOCUS ON
Social Policy 11.1

Club Drugs

The term "club drugs" is a general term used for certain illicit substances, primarily synthetic, that are usually found at nightclubs, bars, and raves (all-night dance parties). Substances that are often used as club drugs include, but are not limited to, MDMA (Ecstasy), GHB (gamma hydroxybutyrate), Rohypnol, Ketamine, and methamphetamine.

Web PLACES 11.3

Visit Clubdrugs.org via
**www.justicestudies.com/
WebPlaces**.

To some, club drugs seem harmless; in reality, however, these substances can cause serious psychological and physical problems, including death. The raves where these drugs are used are sometimes promoted as alcohol-free events, which gives parents a false sense of security that their children will be safe attending such parties. But the effects of club drugs include the following:

• MDMA can cause a user's blood pressure and heart rate to increase to dangerous levels, and can lead to kidney failure. It can also cause severe hyperthermia from the combination of the drug's stimulant effect with the often hot, crowded atmosphere of a rave.

• MDMA users may suffer long-term brain injury. Research has shown that MDMA can cause damage to the parts of the brain that are critical to thought and memory.

• GHB and Rohypnol are central nervous system depressants that cause muscle relaxation, loss of consciousness, and an inability to remember what happened during the hours after the user ingests the drug. GHB and Rohypnol are often connected with drug-facilitated sexual assault, rape, and robbery.

• Ketamine is an animal anesthetic that, when used by humans, can cause impaired motor function, high blood pressure, amnesia, seizures, and respiratory depression.

• Methamphetamine, or meth, is a powerfully addictive stimulant that dramatically affects the central nervous system. Increased energy and alertness, decreased appetite, convulsions, high body temperature, shaking, stroke, and cardiac arrhythmia are all symptomatic of meth abuse.

■ **Have you ever been to parties where club drugs were available? How do you explain their popularity?**

Source: In the Spotlight: Club Drugs: Summary (Washington, D.C.: National Criminal Justice Reference Service, 2004), pp. 1–2.

---

club drug

A synthetic psychoactive substance often found at nightclubs, bars, "raves," and dance parties. Club drugs include MDMA (Ecstasy), ketamine, methamphetamine (meth), GBL, PCP, GHB, and Rohypnol.

parties. Ecstasy is usually ingested orally in tablet or capsule form, is sometimes snorted, and occasionally smoked. MDMA is reported to produce profound pleasurable effects, such as acute euphoria and positive changes in attitude and self-confidence.[31] Ecstasy and various other substances are sometimes called **club drugs** (see Focus on Social Policy 11.1).

Hallucinogens

A parade of hallucinogens has been available over the years to adolescents interested in embracing mind-expanding experiences. Leading the parade in the 1960s was D-lysergic acid diethylamide, popularly known as LSD. Public antagonism arose in the late 1960s against LSD and other psychedelic substances, and its use dramatically declined in the 1970s.

PCP, or phencyclidine, a nervous system excitant that has analgesic, anesthetic, and hallucinogenic properties, was introduced in the late 1960s and became popular during the 1970s. First marketed as the PeaCe Pill, PCP was also known as *angel dust, animal tank, aurora borealis, buzz, devil dust, DOA, dummy dust, elephant, elephant juice, goon, THC,* and *rocket fuel.* Concern over PCP mounted during the 1970s, as its dangerousness became apparent.[32] In 1987, for example, hospital emergency rooms reported 8,000 incidents involving PCP, sometimes in combination with other drugs.[33] Use of PCP declined during the 1980s, with national samples of high school seniors who had used PCP at least once dropping from 13 percent in 1979 to less than 3 percent by 1990.[34]

Anabolic Steroids

Currently, 100 different types of anabolic steroids have been developed, and each requires a prescription to be used legally in the United States. Street terms include *Arnolds, Gym Candy, Juice, Pampers, Stackers,* and *Weight Trainers.* Anabolic steroids can be taken orally, injected intramuscularly, or rubbed on the skin in the form of creams or gels. Steroids are often used in patterns called *cycling,* which involves taking multiple doses of the drugs over a period of time, stopping for a period, and then starting again. Users also often combine several different types of steroids in a process known as *stacking.* The reason for this, according to users, is that they believe the steroids will interact to produce a greater effect on muscle size than would happen using each drug individually.[35] A further method of steroid use is *pyramiding,* a process in which users slowly escalate steroid use, reaching a peak amount at mid-cycle and gradually lowering the dose toward the end of the cycle.[36]

The results from the *2005 Monitoring the Future* study, which surveyed students in eighth, tenth, and twelfth grades, showed that 1.7 percent of eighth-graders, 2.0 percent of tenth-graders, and 2.6 percent of twelfth-graders reported using steroids at least once in their lifetime (see Table 11.4). In terms of the difficulty of obtaining steroids, 18.1. percent of eighth-graders, 29.7 percent of tenth-graders, and 39.7 percent of twelfth-graders surveyed indicated that steroids were "fairly easy" or "very easy" to obtain.[37]

Anabolic steroid abuse has been associated with a wide range of adverse effects ranging from those that are physically unattractive, such as breast development in men and acne, to others that are life threatening. Although most of the effects are reversible if the abuser quits taking the drug, some can be permanent. In addition to its physical effects, anabolic steroids can cause increased irritability and aggression.[38] Furthermore, other health consequences occurring in both males and females using steroids include heart attacks, liver cancer, and elevated cholesterol levels. Finally, those who inject steroids run the risk of contracting or transmitting blood-borne diseases, including HIV.[39]

A teenager holds Special K (Ketamine) at a rave in Baltimore. Ketamine is a rapid-acting general anesthetic whose effects are similar to those of PCP. People who use it report feeling detached or disconnected from their surroundings. ■ **What other kinds of drugs are popular with young people today?**

Heroin

Opium, which is derived from certain species of poppy, is the source of heroin, morphine, paregoric, and codeine, some of which are still used medically. **Heroin,** a refined form of morphine, was introduced about the turn of the twentieth century. Its street names include *horse, shit, smack, H, harry, henry, boy, brown,* and *black tar.*[40]

heroin
A refined form of morphine that was introduced around the beginning of the twentieth century.

TABLE 11.4

Reported Steroid Use by Grade Level

	8th GRADE	10th GRADE	12th GRADE
Past month	0.5%	0.6%	0.9%
Past year	1.1	1.3	1.5
Lifetime	1.7	2.0	2.6

Source: Adapted from the University of Michigan's *Monitoring the Future* Program, grant-funded by the National Institutes of Health. Current data available at www.monitoringthefuture.org/.

Chronic heroin use, unlike the use of most other drugs, appears to produce relatively minor direct or permanent physiological damage. Nevertheless, street heroin users typically neglect themselves and, as a result, report such disorders as heart and lung abnormalities, scarred veins, weight loss, malnutrition, endocarditis (a disease of the heart valves), stroke, gynecological problems, hepatitis, local skin infections, and abscesses.[41] The danger of heroin overdose has for several decades marked heroin as a very dangerous drug. For example, the Drug Abuse Warning Network found that more than 20,000 heroin overdoses resulted in emergency room treatment each year, and that 3,000 resulted in a stop at the morgue.[42]

Table 11.5 provides a summary of the short- and long-term consequences of using alcohol and other drugs in adolescence. Although individuals differ in their reac-

TABLE 11.5

Consequences of Substance Abuse During Adolescence

SUBSTANCE	CONSEQUENCES	
	SHORT TERM	LONG TERM
CIGARETTES[a]		
Occasional use	Vulnerability to other drugs	Excess morbidity, mortality
Frequent use	Bad breath	Excess morbidity, mortality
	Respiratory problems	
ALCOHOL		
Occasional use	None	None
Frequent use	Drunk driving, leading to accidents, arrests, mortality	Alcoholism
	Impaired functioning in school	Cirrhosis of liver
	Family problems	Stomach cancer
	Depression	
	Accidental death (e.g., by drowning)	
MARIJUANA[b]		
Occasional use	Vulnerability to other drugs	Inconclusive
Frequent use	Impaired psychological functioning	Respiratory problems
	Impaired driving ability	Possible adverse reproductive effects
	Loss of short-term memory	Decrease in motivation
COCAINE[a,c]		
	Physical symptoms, such as dry mouth, sweats, headache, nosebleeds, and nasal passage irritation	Drug dependence
		Rhinitis, ulcerated nasal septum
		Hepatitis
	Loss of sleep	Psychological effects: depression, anxiety
	Chronic fatigue	Convulsions
	Feelings of depression	Social and financial problems
	Suicidal ideation	
MULTIPLE SUBSTANCE USE[a]		
	Dysfunction	Drug dependence
	Dropping out of school	Chronic depression, fatigue
	Suspension from school	Truncated education
	Motor vehicle accidents	Reduced job stability
	Illegal activities	Marital instability
		Crime

[a]Adapted from M. Newcomb and P. Bentler, *Consequences of Adolescent Drug Use: Impact on the Lives of Young Adults* (Newbury Park, Calif.: Sage, 1988), pp. 219–222.

[b]R. Peterson, "Marijuana Overview," in *Correlation and Consequences of Marijuana Use* (National Institute on Drug Abuse, *Research Issues* 34, 1984), pp. 1–19.

[c]Based on findings from a study reported by D. Chitwood, "Patterns and Consequences of Cocaine Use," in *Cocaine Use in America: Epidemiologic and Clinical Perspectives*, edited by N. Kozel and E. Adams (National Institute on Drug Abuse, USDHHS, NIDA Research Monograph, 61, 1985), pp. 111–129.

Source: Adapted from Joy G. Dryfoos, *Adolescents at Risk: Prevalence and Prevention* (New York: Oxford University Press, 1990), p. 48.

tions to drugs, especially people who have sensitivities and allergies to small amounts of substances, it is obvious that the more drugs are used and the greater the frequency of use, the more serious the damage will be.[43]

Drug Use and Delinquency

An issue that has long been debated is whether drugs cause delinquency or delinquency leads to drug use, or whether some other factors precede both delinquency and the onset of drug use.[44] Considerable research has found that delinquency tends to precede the use of drugs.[45] Other research suggests that what might appear to be a causal association is in fact a product of shared antecedents.[46] It is possible that a common factor, or syndrome, exists that underlies both delinquent behavior and drug use; this common factor may explain the frequency and type of drug use.[47]

As previously discussed, a number of researchers have found that substance abuse is just one of an interrelated and overlapping group of adolescent problem behaviors, including delinquency, teen pregnancy, school failure, and dropping out of school.[48] Substance abuse, then, is one of the problem behaviors developed by adolescents during their early life course. John M. Wallace Jr. and Jerald G. Bachman summarized what is involved, using Richard and Shirley L. Jessor's "problem behavior" model:

> " Considerable research has found that delinquency tends to precede the use of drugs. "

The basic theoretical structure of much present research can be subsumed under the "problem behavior" model posited by the Jessors. The Jessors' model is a comprehensive framework comprised of antecedent background variables and three systems of social-psychological and behavioral variables—the personality system, the perceived environment system, and the behavior system. The variables in the three primary systems interrelate to produce within the individual a greater or lesser proneness to become involved in problem behaviors. More specifically, the theory hypothesizes that young people who are less invested in traditional versus deviant behaviors, who are more strongly tied to peers than to parents, who are alienated from society, who have low self-esteem, and who hold unconventional beliefs, values, and attitudes are prone to become involved in problem behavior. The Jessors and their colleagues used their longitudinal dataset to test the theoretical model and found it to be quite successful in explaining adolescent problems—particularly drug use.[49]

Web **PLACES** 11.4

Visit the Office of National Drug Control Policy's website via **www .justicestudies.com/ WebPlaces**.

In the early 1990s, longitudinal studies of high-risk youths in Denver, Pittsburgh, and Rochester also provided evidence of the overlap of substance abuse with other problem behaviors.[50] These three longitudinal studies found that substance abuse was significantly related to delinquency in youths, regardless of race. Delinquent girls were at higher risk for drug use than were delinquent boys. Delinquency was further related to early sexual activity or pregnancy.[51] These studies concluded that "targeting delinquency and substance abuse simultaneously in intervention and prevention programs will more likely enhance the effectiveness of such programs in each problem area than will programs that focus uniquely on either substance abuse or delinquency."[52]

Other research has indicated large racial–ethnic differences in adolescent drug use, with the highest use among Native Americans, somewhat lower use among white and Hispanic youths, and lowest use among African American and Asian youths.[53] In contrast, Delbert S. Elliott, David Huizinga, and Scott Menard's analysis of the National Youth Survey found no association between social class, race, and substance abuse. Although lower-class youths and African Americans did have higher prevalence rates of serious delinquent behavior, whites had higher prevalence rates of minor delinquent acts and of alcohol, marijuana, and polydrug use. Urban residents had higher rates of marijuana and polydrug use and were also more at risk of

Web **PLACES** 11.5

Visit the Underage Drinking Enforcement Training Center's website via **www.justicestudies .com/WebPlaces**.

Prescription Drugs Find Place in Teen Culture

When a teenager in Jan Sigerson's office mentioned a "pharm party," Sigerson thought the youth was talking about a keg party out on a farm.

"Pharm," it turned out, was short for pharmaceuticals, such as the powerful painkillers Vicodin and OxyContin. Sigerson, program director for Journeys, a teen drug treatment program in Omaha, soon learned that area youths were organizing parties to down fistfuls of prescription drugs. Since then, several more youths at Journeys have mentioned that they attended pharm parties, Sigerson says.

"When you start to see a pattern, you know it's becoming pretty widespread," she says. "I expect it to get worse before it gets better."

Drug counselors across the USA are beginning to hear about similar pill-popping parties, which are part of a rapidly developing underground culture that surrounds the rising abuse of prescription drugs by teens and young adults.

It's a culture with its own lingo: Bowls and baggies of random pills often are called "trail mix," and on Internet chat sites, collecting pills from the family medicine cabinet is called "pharming."

Carol Falkowski, director of research communications for the Hazelden Foundation, says young abusers of prescription drugs also have begun using the Internet to share "recipes" for getting high. Some websites are so simplistic, she says, that they refer to pills by color, rather than their brand names, content or potency.

That, Falkowski says, could help explain why emergency rooms are reporting that teens and young adults increasingly are showing up overdosed on bizarre and potentially lethal combinations of pills.

Overdoses of prescription and over-the-counter drugs accounted for about one-quarter of the 1.3 million drug-related emergency room admissions in 2004, the federal Substance Abuse and Mental Health Services Administration reported recently.

The abuse of prescription and over-the-counter drugs—which barely registered a blip in drug-use surveys a decade ago—is escalating at what Falkowski and other analysts say is an alarming rate.

In a 2005 survey by the Partnership for a Drug-Free America, 19% of U.S. teenagers—roughly 4.5 million youths—reported having taken prescription painkillers such as Vicodin or OxyContin or stimulants such as Ritalin or Adderall to get high.

Vicodin has been particularly popular in recent years; a study by the University of Michigan in 2005 found that nearly 10% of 12th-graders had used it in the previous year. About 5.5% said they had used OxyContin. Both drugs are now more popular among high school seniors than Ecstasy and cocaine.

Marijuana is still the most popular drug by far; about one-third of the 12th-graders surveyed said they had used it in the previous year.

Falkowski, whose foundation is a treatment center based in Center City, Minn., says prescription pills have become popular among youths because they are easy to get and represent a more socially acceptable way of getting high than taking street drugs.

Some kids, she says, are self-medicating undiagnosed depression or anxiety, while others are using stimulants to try to get an edge on tests and studying.

Falkowski says prescription drugs are familiar mood-altering substances for a generation that grew up as prescriptions soared for Ritalin and other stimulants to treat maladies such as attention-deficit disorder. "Five million kids take prescription drugs every day for behavior disorders," she says.

"It's not unusual for kids to share pills with their friends. There have been inci-

Paul Michaud, a former OxyContin addict, says the painkiller made him feel like nothing could faze him. ■ **What makes drugs like OxyContin difficult to control?**

dents where kids bring a Ziploc baggie full of pills to school and share them with other kids."

Pharm parties, she says, are "simply everyone pooling whatever pills they have together and having a good time on a Saturday night. Kids . . . don't think about the consequences."

Lisa Cappiello, 39, of Brooklyn, N.Y., says that seemed to be the case with her son, Eddie. She says she knew that he had tried marijuana at 15 and sneaked beers at school.

But it wasn't until after he graduated from high school and took a year off before college that Cappiello realized the extent of her son's drug use—and the hold prescription drugs had on him.

"In what seemed like the blink of an eye, it went from marijuana and an occasional beer to so much Xanax that [one day] my husband had to pick him up when he fell asleep on a street corner waiting for some friends," she said. "He hid his drug use from me so well."

The next day, Eddie Cappiello admitted to his parents that he had taken 15 pills of Xanax, a brand name for ben-

becoming sellers.[54] Wallace and Bachman also found that controlling for background and lifestyle reduced or eliminated many of the racial–ethnic differences in drug use. Their data further revealed that several lifestyle factors, including time spent in peer-oriented activities, educational values and behaviors, and religious commitment, were strongly related to patterns of drug use and helped to explain the subgroup differences.[55]

Since the early 1990s, consensus has been increasing on the findings that explain the onset and continuing use of illicit drugs. First, there is widespread agreement that

zodiazepine that acts as a sedative. He told his parents Xanax helped him deal with anxiety and depression.

Eddie rejected professional help and vowed to stop taking pills, his mother says. He was clean for 10 months, she says, before he was hospitalized in July 2005 after overdosing.

Two months later, he entered a 28-day treatment program. After he was discharged, he stayed clean for about two months—then relapsed into weekend binging: 40 to 50 pills and a quart of Jack Daniels, sometimes by himself, sometimes with friends, Lisa Cappiello says.

Eddie Cappiello, 22, died in his bed on February 17, 2006, after overdosing on a mix of pharmaceuticals. He left behind a girlfriend and two young children.

A toxicology report said he had 134 milligrams of Xanax—the equivalent of 67 pills—and an opioid derivative in his system, his mother says. . . .

In recent months, federal anti-drug officials have acknowledged that they didn't anticipate the quick escalation of prescription-drug abuse. Most government-sponsored drug prevention programs focus on marijuana, tobacco, alcohol and methamphetamine.

"We were taken by surprise when we started to see a high instance of abuse of prescription drugs," says Nora Volkow, director of the National Institute of Drug Abuse (NIDA), which is collecting information about how teens perceive, get and use prescription drugs so it can try to craft an effective prevention campaign.

In a 2005 bulletin, NIDA called the increase in pharmaceutical drug abuse among teens "disturbing" and said pharm parties were a "troubling trend."

The increasing availability of prescription drugs is a big reason for the rise in their abuse, Volkow and other drug specialists say.

Pharmaceutical companies' production of two often-abused prescription drugs—hydrocodone and oxycodone, the active ingredients in drugs such as Vicodin and OxyContin—has risen dramatically as the drugs' popularity for le-

gitimate uses has increased. Drug companies made 29 million doses of oxycodone in 2004, up from 15 million four years earlier. Hydrocodone doses rose from 14 million in 2000 to 24 million in 2004.

The 2005 Partnership survey found that more than three in five teens can easily get prescription painkillers from their parents' medicine cabinets. And as Falkowski says, the rising number of youths being treated with stimulants has made it easier for kids to use such drugs illicitly. About 3% of children are treated with a stimulant such as Adderall or Ritalin, up from less than 1% in 1987.

Almost all of the 13 youths at Phoenix House's intensive outpatient treatment program on New York City's Upper West Side have dabbled in prescription drugs, director Tessa Vining says.

"There's definitely easy access," she says. "Maybe a parent had some surgery and took one or two painkillers from a bottle of 10, and the rest are just hanging out in the medicine cabinet."

After her son died, Cappiello says she wondered how kids in her area were getting pills. She says she learned from police that one local dealer got Xanax from his mother, who had been given a prescription for the drug. Instead of taking the pills, she gave them to her son to sell for $2 to $3 each.

Paul Michaud, 18, of Boston, says he got his first taste of OxyContin pills—he calls them OCs—from a friend during his freshman year in high school.

Until then, Michaud says, he had smoked marijuana daily and taken a Percocet pill occasionally. Michaud's father had recently died of cancer, and Michaud says he was depressed and feeling like an outsider at school. The prescription painkiller made him feel like nothing could faze him, he recalls.

"The first time I did it, I was hooked," says Michaud, who is four months into a yearlong drug treatment program at Phoenix House in Springfield, Mass. He says he quickly became a daily

OxyContin user, breaking apart the time-release capsules, crushing pills and snorting the powder from five 80-milligram pills a day.

"They're not very hard to get. I could find OCs easier than I could find pot," Michaud says. "There were plenty of people who sold them," including some dealers who got pills illicitly by mail order.

To try to reduce the supply of prescription drugs on the black market, authorities have shut down several "pill mills"—where doctors prescribe inordinate amounts of narcotics—as well as Internet pharmacies that ship drugs with little medical consultation, says Catherine Harnett, chief of demand reduction for the Drug Enforcement Administration (DEA).

Last September, DEA agents arrested 18 people allegedly responsible for 4,600 such pharmacies.

A tricky part of the prescription-drug problem, Harnett says, is addressing the perception among youths that pills are safe because they are "medicine." Many teens don't equate taking such pills with using drugs such as heroin or cocaine, she says.

"If you start with pills, it seems fairly sanitary and legitimate," she says. "Kids have been lulled into believing that good medicine can be used recreationally. . . ."

Michaud says he didn't equate his OxyContin addiction with hard-core drug abuse. "Where I come from, OC is a rich boys' drug," he says. "I thought, heroin abuse, that's pretty low. I'd never stick a needle in my arm."

However, Michaud says he eventually switched to heroin. "I sniffed it and a week later, I was shooting," he says. "I thought I wasn't like other people doing heroin. I wasn't that low. Come to figure out, it all leads to the same place."

there is a sequential pattern of involvement in drug use during adolescence.[56] Denise B. Kandel and colleagues, using cross-sectional research and longitudinal data, proposed a developmental model for drug-use involvement. According to this model, alcohol use follows a pattern of minor delinquency and exposure to friends and parents who drink. The use of marijuana follows participation in minor delinquency and adoption of beliefs and values that are consistent with those held by peers but opposed to parental standards. Finally, an adolescent's use proceeds to other illicit drugs if relationships with parents are poor and there is increased exposure to peers who use a variety of illegal drugs.[57]

Second, in examining drug use, it is important to identify in which of three major groups users belong. Some youths or adults experiment once or twice and then discontinue drug use. Others continue drug use into young adulthood, but drug use does not interfere with their lives in any major ways. Those in a third group become addicted or dependent on drugs, and their entire lifestyle is likely to be designed around acquiring drugs daily. Members of this third group also frequently commit crimes to maintain their drug supply.

Third, a number of risk factors appear to be related to delinquency and drug use. Early factors consist of perinatal difficulties, minor physical abnormalities, and brain damage. Later developmental risk factors are found in the family environment, including a family history of alcoholism, poor family management practices, and family conflict. Other risk factors are early antisocial behavior and academic failure. Community risk factors include living in economically deprived areas and disorganized neighborhoods. According to J. David Hawkins, Richard F. Catalano, and Devon D. Brewer, the more of these risk factors a child has, the more likely it is that he or she will become involved in drug abuse.[58]

There is little debate that youths who use hard drugs are more likely to engage in chronic delinquent behavior.[59] Elliott and Huizinga found that nearly 50 percent of serious juvenile offenders were also multiple drug users. Eighty-two percent of these offenders reported use, beyond experimentation, of at least one illicit drug. Incident rates of alcohol use among serious offenders were four to nine times those of nonoffenders, and rates of marijuana use among serious offenders were fourteen times those of nonoffenders.[60] Jeffrey Fagan and colleagues' survey of inner-city youths also found that heavy substance use was more prevalent and frequent among serious delinquents, but the type of substance used was more strongly associated with delinquency than was the frequency of drug use.[61]

David M. Altschuler and Paul J. Brounstein's examination of drug use and drug trafficking among inner-city adolescent males in Washington, D.C., found that use and sale of drugs affected the frequency and seriousness of delinquent behavior. The heaviest users were significantly more likely than nonusers to commit property offenses; those who trafficked in drugs were significantly more likely to commit crimes against persons than youths who did not sell drugs; and adolescents who both used and sold drugs were the most likely to commit offenses against property and persons.[62]

Web LIBRARY 11.3

Read the OJJDP Fact Sheet *Assessing Alcohol, Drug, and Mental Disorders in Juvenile Detainees* at **www .justicestudies.com/ WebLibrary**.

Drug-Trafficking Juveniles

Drug-trafficking juveniles can be divided into several groups. There are those who occasionally sell small amounts of drugs, usually to support their own drug appetites, but they commit few if any delinquent acts. They are most likely to sell marijuana to friends and classmates and usually will avoid coming to the attention of the police or the juvenile justice system. Another group of drug-trafficking juveniles sells drugs frequently, and may get their drugs from adult suppliers. They sell drugs in public places, such as on street corners, and are more likely to be arrested by the police and to be referred to the juvenile court. This group typically sells drugs independently of any gang affiliation, especially in suburban settings.[63] A third group, especially in urban settings, sells drugs as part of their gang affiliation. Unlike the first two groups, drug trafficking within this group is controlled by adults, and participants in this group often end up in training schools or adult prisons. A student on academic scholarship in college told about his role in a gang's drug-trafficking operation:

> I must have been ten or eleven, and I was told to show up on this street corner. When I got there, they gave me a gun and told me to keep watch. If anyone came around, they told me to shoot them. They were taking care of business inside the crack house.

A street corner drug deal goes down. ■ **The text says that drug-trafficking juveniles can be divided into several groups. What are those groups?**

Fortunately, nobody came around because I would have shot them. It surely would have changed my life.[64]

Our understanding of juveniles and drug trafficking is heightened by Felix M. Padilla's 1992 book *The Gang as an American Enterprise*[65] and Daniel J. Monti's 1994 work *Wannabe Gangs in Suburbs and Schools*.[66] Padilla studied a Hispanic drug-dealing gang in Chicago. He found that this drug enterprise had an occupational hierarchy, in which the cocaine and marijuana suppliers or distributors were on top, followed by "older guys," chiefs, and "mainheads." The street-level dealers, or main-heads, were juveniles who barely made a survival income and who usually had to supplement their drug income through stealing. Yet they never quite got ahead, because they would inevitably be arrested and the distributor would have his attorney bail them out. It would then take them months to repay the distributor.[67]

Monti's examination of gangs in suburbs and schools focused on juveniles' selling drugs. He found that the gangs, especially the Gangster Disciples, had real control in the suburban schools he studied. The Crips and Bloods were also represented in these schools. The drugs that were sold included marijuana, different types of pills, and some crack cocaine. The girls' involvement in drug trafficking typically consisted of holding drugs for boys, usually their boyfriends, when the boys thought they might be searched by the police or school officials. According to Monti, the youths who sold drugs kept the profits for themselves and did not pool the money with the gang. He also depicted drug dealing as a lucrative and exciting trade.[68] The chief effect of the so-called war on drugs has always been to make trafficking highly profitable. One interviewed youth commented:

A third teenager from yet another gang was more deeply involved in drug dealing and gave no indication of leaving the trade. "It's an everyday thing now," he said. [In one week] I made twenty-five hundred. At the first of the month you can make like ten thousand, because everybody gets their [welfare] checks then. They come to you and spend their whole check on it."[69]

Web **LIBRARY** 11.4

Read the National Drug Intelligence Center's *National Drug Threat Assessment* at **www .justicestudies.com/ WebLibrary**.

Principal Reports That Drug-Testing Students Works

High school principal Chris Steffner says she's seen many efforts to keep teens from using drugs: education programs, "Just Say No" campaigns, scary speeches from people who were caught driving drunk.

"None of those things have any lasting impact," she says. "Peer pressure is so strong."

That's why, Steffner says, she's a cheerleader for random drug testing of students. She tells other principals about the testing program she helped oversee for the past two years at Hackettstown High School, a 700-student campus in northern New Jersey.

During the program's first year, 10% of Hackettstown's students were tested randomly from a pool of students who took part in after-school activities or who drove to school. One student tested positive, she says. Last year, 25% of the students were screened. No one tested positive.

The results show testing deters teen drug use, Steffner says: "It works in the workplace and it works in the military. Why wouldn't it work in a school?"

At a time when drug testing is expanding in schools, precisely how well it works in reducing drug use among middle and high school students is a much-debated topic. Surveys by the University of Michigan indicate that teens' use of most drugs is stable or down slightly this year. Analysts are trying to find out whether testing might lower the numbers further.

To Reduce Use: More Schools Test for Drugs

The number of schools screening students for street drugs such as cocaine and marijuana—and for performance enhancers such as steroids—has jumped since the U.S. Supreme Court ruled in 2002 that testing athletes and those involved in competitive extracurricular activities did not violate their privacy rights.

However, only about 2% of the nation's 28,000 middle and high schools have testing policies. Meanwhile, drug education programs are everywhere, and many other factors—from teens' whims to the economy—have been cited as affecting drug use rates.

Little research has been done on testing's impact on student drug use because it's difficult and expensive to study, says Lloyd Johnston of the Monitoring the Future study at the University of Michigan, which surveys 50,000 students a year. And yet, concern about student drug use—including recent increases in the use of prescription drugs and steroids—has led hundreds of systems to embrace testing.

The Supreme Court said a school system's duty to provide a safe, drug-free environment outweighs students' expectations of privacy. Now, Hackettstown and a few other systems—such as the one in Hagerstown, Ind.—are using the court's standard to justify expanding random testing beyond students who are in sports or other competitive after-school activities. It's unclear whether such plans will draw new legal challenges.

The Bush administration was a key player in expanding student drug testing. The White House asked Congress to boost federal grants for testing programs by 45% in 2007, to $15 million. . . .

Even so, many systems have resisted testing because of its cost and questions about its necessity. Privacy laws in several states also pose legal hurdles, despite the Supreme Court's stance on testing.

Bush "elevated it to a level of prominence, so some schools are going to start doing it," says Graham Boyd of the ACLU's Drug Law Reform Project. But "most school administrators want programs that work and don't want to needlessly invade students' privacy."

The ACLU argues that testing destroys trust between students and schools and discourages teens from joining after-school activities. The group also questions testing's effectiveness. Research is inconclusive.

Chris Steffner, principal of Hackettstown High School in New Jersey, says D.A.R.E. programs and "Just Say No" slogans aren't as effective as random drug testing of students. ■ **What evidence does she offer?**

In a 2003 study, Johnston and a colleague suggested drug usage rates at schools with no testing were about the same as those of schools that had testing. In 2005, a Ball State University survey found declines in drug use at 58% of 54 Indiana high schools that had testing.

Such reports have inspired a few systems to expand drug testing to virtually all students.

The Nettle Creek school district in Hagerstown, Ind., will launch a program this fall involving most secondary school students: not just athletes and club members, but also those who drive to school or want to attend school dances. Superintendent Joe Backmeyer says the goal is to protect students' privacy and minimize embarrassment. Students will be chosen randomly by number and a saliva sample will be taken, instead of the more common urine testing. Counseling will be provided for those testing positive.

Source: Donna Leinwand, "Principal: Drug-Testing Students Works," *USA Today*, July 12, 2006. Copyright © by *USA Today*. Reprinted by permission.

Drug Use Across the Life Course

Two basic pathways are possible for substance-abusing youths. They may restrict themselves to substance abuse and not become involved in other delinquent activities. These offenders may desist from substance abuse during their adolescent years, or they may continue to use drugs as adults. Alternatively, substance-abusing youths may also participate in other delinquent activities. These youths, too, may desist from one or both types of activity during adolescence or continue to be involved in one or both as adults.

There is some evidence that about two-thirds of substance-abusing youths continue to use drugs after reaching adulthood, but about half desist from other forms of criminality. Researchers in the 1980s found that abusers who persisted in both crime and substance abuse as adults typically came from poor families, did poorly in school, used multiple types of drugs, were chronic offenders, and had an early onset of both drug use and delinquent behavior.[70]

Marvin D. Krohn, Alan J. Lizotte, and Cynthia M. Perez, in their 1997 analysis of the Rochester data, found that the use of alcohol and drugs in early adolescence increases a youngster's risk of becoming pregnant or impregnating someone, becoming a teenage parent, dropping out of school, and prematurely living independently from parents or guardians. In turn, the process of experiencing these early transitions increases the chances that individuals will use alcohol and drugs when they become young adults.

Thus, Krohn and colleagues are suggesting that the cumulative impact of experiencing various precocious, or early, transitions may be detrimental to the successful movement, or transition, to adult status and adult roles.[71] And it is not surprising that an early or unsuccessful transition in one arena will have implications for other trajectories.[72] Off-time and out-of-order transitions can be especially disruptive, because the individual may not be prepared for the added responsibilities and obligations that frequently accompany these transitions. Precocious transitions can further lead to problematic consequences because of the increased economic burdens and reduced economic prospects facing those who experience them. For example, teenage parenthood can disrupt the order of transitions by leading youth to enter full-time employment before completing high school, which can derail career development. The person who leaves school before graduation may not have any choice but an unskilled, low-paying job, which in turn produces job instability and ongoing economic disadvantages.[73]

Gary M. McClelland, Linda A. Teplin, and Karen M. Abram highlight several generalizations about drug use and adolescent development that are widely recognized and accepted:

- Substance use commonly follows a sequence from tobacco and alcohol to marijuana and then to more dangerous substances.
- Substance use and abuse that begins in early adolescence is associated with more serious delinquency and longer deviant careers, antisocial personality disorders in later life, and more numerous risky behaviors.
- Substance abuse is associated with poor academic performance.
- More severe substance abuse and dependence are associated with serious criminal offenses in general.
- Substance use and abuse are associated with higher rates of psychiatric disorders and with disorders of greater severity.[74]

Drug addicts, like those with a history of delinquency and criminality, sometimes have a turning point, or change, when they walk away from drug use. Those who were deeply entrenched in the drug world as adolescents and continue this activity in their adult years find it particularly difficult to give up drugs. Those who are able to stay with the straight life typically have had a religious experience or have had an extremely positive experience in a therapeutic community for drug addicts.[75] See Across

Web PLACES 11.6

Visit the Drug Enforcement Administration's (DEA) website via **www.justicestudies.com/ WebPlaces**.

Overcoming Chemical Dependency

A former addict tells his story:

My dad was an African American. During his prime years, he was rated as one of the ten best baseball players in the country. He was always on the road; I didn't get to see him much. He finally stopped traveling when I was in the eighth grade, but all that did was put him in the nightclub business. He didn't take much interest in my life. I can count the number of extracurricular activities he went to; he would show up late or not at all. He would say that he would pick me up from school, but he wouldn't. The animosity I had for my dad continued up until the day he passed.

My mom is white. She was divorced and had two children from her first marriage. She married my father while he was in prison. He was in prison for writing bad checks. She stayed married to him for as long as she could, and then they divorced. I saw so little of my dad that I was raised in a white society. But when I stepped out of that door, I was a black man. I had quite a time adjusting to the two societies. There were a lot of days I had to fight to get home from school.

I can remember one time when I was eight or nine and I was laying on the bed and crying. I couldn't understand why people would treat me the way they did. My mom really couldn't explain it because she was a white female trying to educate a black young boy about racism within both the white community and the black community.

I felt a lot of pressure as a kid. Due to the fact that my dad owned clubs, I had access to alcohol. I didn't start drinking un-til I was fifteen or sixteen. But when I did start drinking, I really drank. I also began to smoke marijuana.

I went away to college on an academic scholarship. I didn't like school and only drank and smoked more pot. My alcohol intake was soaring, and my smoking was also increasing. I joined the military and for five years drank a lot of alcohol.

I got out of the military, got married, and had three children. My drug and alcohol use increased dramatically from 1985 to 1990. When crack came around, I got into that. I was what you call a weekend crack addict. That lasted until one day I went to a college football game with a cousin of mine. I cashed my check. And that weekend I smoked my whole paycheck up.

I didn't know what to tell my wife. I committed myself to an inpatient treatment program. I went in on a Monday, and as I was walking down the hall on a Thursday after Recreation, this warm feeling came over my body. I had to hold on to the wall because I almost lost my balance. It was like it was washed out of me. And since that day to the day right now, I haven't had a drink. I haven't smoked marijuana. I haven't done cocaine. I haven't smoked cigarettes.

Unfortunately, my wife had had it with me. She divorced me, but I have spent a lot of time with my children. I want to be a good father, something my father was not to me.

I do not define myself as an alcoholic. I do not consider myself to be a drug addict. I am a chemically dependent person. When I go to the doctor, I tell him not to prescribe anything that will ever be addictive to me.

■ **What does this person mean when he says that he is chemically dependent? Is this person a classic addictive personality type? If someone is an addictive personality, what is the danger when the person quits using one chemical? How can people defend themselves against this danger?**

Source: Interviewed in May of 2004.

---

the Life Course 11.1 for one person's account of how he walked away from his addiction to alcohol and drugs after several decades of dependency.

Kandel and colleagues reported that significant status changes, including marriage and parenthood, were correlated with the cessation of marijuana smoking among users in their mid- to late twenties.[76] L. A. Goodman and W. H. Kruskal found that reasons for cessation involved the imposition of both internal control and external controls.[77] L. Thomas Winfree Jr., Christine S. Sellers, and Dennis L. Clason examined the reasons for adolescents' cessation of and abstention from substance use and found that social learning variables clearly distinguished abstainers from current users, but they were less able to distinguish former users from current users or former users from abstainers.[78]

One reason many drug addicts relapse is that they do not find the straight life sufficiently exciting, fulfilling, or satisfying. A former adolescent drug addict had given speeches in the community about how close she had come to being sentenced to the penitentiary; about the numerous burglaries she had committed; and about the damage that chemicals had done to her body, to her relationship with her parents, and to her reputation. Yet she returned to chemicals, and she gave the following explanation of why she failed:

> I found that living without drugs wasn't that good. All my friends do drugs; you have no social life without drugs. My boyfriend even went back to drugs. The night I saw him shoot up coke, I was devastated. I had to do something. I went to a friend's house and smoked some grass. I decided then that I was going to smoke pot, but I wasn't going back to chemicals. But it wasn't long before I went back to chemicals. It is really a good high, but I'm hooked on them now. I couldn't wait all day yesterday until we broke some crystal [took meth] last night.[79]

Explaining the Onset of Drug Abuse

As previously suggested, some adolescents never use drugs, others use drugs from time to time on an experimental or recreational basis, and still others go through a period of experimentation with substance use and become committed to continuous use. This latter group is physically and/or emotionally addicted to the continued use of drugs.

There are at least two issues that can help us understand juveniles who use drugs. The first is determining whether it is the onset of drug use, the escalation of drug use, the addiction to drug use, or the cessation of drug use that is being addressed. We might ask: Why do some juveniles never try drugs? Why do some juveniles experiment with drugs from time to time but do not become addicted? Why do other adolescents go from the beginning stages of drug use to more serious stages? Why do still other juveniles become addicted to drugs? Why are some of those who become addicted able to quit, whereas other addicts seem unable or unwilling to terminate drug use?

The second issue is that there is no single comprehensive picture of what causes adolescents' use of drugs. Simons, Conger, and Whitbeck make this point when they say that "while research has established a number of correlates of drug use, no theoretical model has been developed which specifies the causal ordering of these associations and explicates their relationship to each other."[80] Or to express this another way, we might be aware of many of the reasons why juveniles become involved in drug use, but we do not know how all of the pieces of the puzzle fit together.[81]

This section will address only adolescents' initial use of drugs, and it will focus on theories that attempt to explain substance use among adolescents.

Cognitive-Affective Theories

A number of theories have focused on how perceptions about the costs and benefits of drug use contribute to adolescents' decisions to experiment with these substances. Such models share two assumptions: (1) the decision to use substances rests in substance-specific expectations and perceptions held by adolescents and (2) the effects of all other variables (e.g., adolescents' personality traits or their involvement with peers who use substances) are mediated through substance-specific cognitions, evaluations, and decisions.[82] The *theory of reasoned action*, which holds that the most important determinant of a person's behavior is behavioral intent, is the most encompassing of these cost-benefit/decision-making models.[83]

Addictive Personality Theories

Another explanation for the onset and continued use of drugs says that the typical addict has an addiction-prone personality and suffers from some deep-rooted personality disorder or emotional problems. Isidor Chein and colleagues' celebrated study, *The Road to H*, contends that youthful heroin addicts suffer from such personality disorders as "weak ego functioning," "defective superego," and "inadequate masculine identification." A young male with an addiction-prone personality, according to these authors, is unable "to enter into prolonged, close, friendly relations with either peers or adults," has "difficulties in assuming a masculine role," is frequently overcome by a sense of futility, expectation of failure, and general depression," is "easily frustrated and made anxious," and finds "frustrations and anxiety intolerable."[84]

Stress Relief Theories

The desire to "get high" is common in adolescent peer culture. Getting high is seen as a way to relieve stress, depression, or the boredom of everyday life. The desire to drink alcohol and get high is very much related to the desire to feel good, to be comfortable in social situations, and to gain acceptance in peer culture. This explanation for the appeal of substance abuse says that stress relief provides a sought-after high or peak experience.

Anthropologist Philippe Bourgois puts it this way: "Substance abuse in general and crack in particular offers the equivalent of a born-again metamorphosis. Instantaneously," he says, "the user is transformed from an unemployed, depressed high school dropout, despised by the world—and secretly convinced that his failure is due to his own inherent stupidity and disorganization," to a person who has found life's purpose. "There is a rush of heart-palpitating pleasure," says Bourgois, "followed by a jaw-gnashing crash and wide-eyed alertness that provides his life with concrete purpose: Get more crack—fast."[85]

Social Learning Theories

Drug use by peers is consistently found to be the strongest predictor of an individual's involvement in drug use. The argument can be made that drug use begins and continues primarily because juveniles or adults have contact with peers who use drugs and who provide both role models and social support for using drugs. Peer influence, not surprisingly, is especially important during adolescence. Peers appear to influence initial marijuana use but seem to be less important for those starting the use of alcohol or hard drugs. Once peers persuade a person to begin using drugs, then a pattern of use is established that may eventually lead to addiction and continued use.[86]

Social learning theory says that an adolescent's involvement in substance abuse has three sequential effects, beginning with the observation and imitation of substance-specific behaviors; continuing with social reinforcement, such as encouragement and support for drug use; and culminating in a juvenile's expectation of positive social and physiological consequences from continued drug use. The anticipated consequences might be primarily social in nature during experimental use (such as the acceptance or rejection by peers) and might become largely physiological in nature during subsequent stages (taking the form of positive or negative physiological reactions to the substances themselves). Social learning theory essentially says that an adolescent who anticipates that using substances will produce more personal benefits than costs will be at risk for continued use.[87]

Social Control Theories

Travis Hirschi's social control theory and Hawkins and Weis's social development model both assume that emotional attachments to peers who use substances is a primary cause of substance abuse. Unlike social learning theories, however, these two approaches pay specific attention to weak conventional bonds to society and to the institutions and individuals who might otherwise discourage deviant behavior.[88] Hirschi asserts that the deviant impulses that most adolescents share are held in check or controlled by strong bonds to conventional society, families, schools, and religions. However, adolescents who do not have such controlling influences will not feel compelled to adhere to convention or to engage in socially acceptable behaviors.[89]

The social development model proposes that adolescents become attached to substance-using peers if they feel uncommitted to conventional society or to positive role models. Unlike Hirschi's social control model that focuses largely on social systems, the social development model focuses more on individuals, their social development, and their social interactions. This focus shifts developmentally, with parents dominating the preschool years, teachers dominating preadolescent years, and peers dominating behaviors during adolescence.[90]

Social Disorganization Theories

Social disorganization theories explain the onset and escalation of adolescents' drug use by claiming that a bleak economic environment for certain disenfranchised groups has created a generation of young adults in urban inner cities who regularly experience doubt, hopelessness, and uncertainty. According to this perspective, the hopelessness of the poor leads them to seek relief. Hence, drug and alcohol abuse provide an immediate fix for hopelessness but, in the long run, creates other problems.[91]

Integrated Theories

Delbert S. Elliott and colleagues offer a model that expands traditional strain, social control, and social learning theories into a single perspective that accounts for delinquent behavior and drug use.[92] They describe the mechanisms by which neighborhood disorganization, attachment to families, and social values contribute to involvement with drugs.[93] This model was initially created to explain the causes of delinquency, but it was later more fully developed to explain adolescents' drug-using behavior.[94]

Web **PLACES** 11.7

Visit the National Drug Intelligence Center's website via **www .justicestudies.com/ WebPlaces**.

Simons and colleagues expanded Ackers' social learning theory and attempted to "explain why adolescents join substance-using peer groups."[95] They did this through their multistage social learning model that integrates social learning process and several intrapersonal characteristics, including low self-esteem, emotional distress (e.g., anxiety, tension, and depressed affect), inadequate coping skills (e.g., using distraction or denial-avoidance), social interaction skills (e.g., uncompromising, unempathic, overly assertive, and impolite), and a personal value system that emphasizes present-orientation over long-term conventional goals concerning families, education, and religion.[96]

The attempt to explain a social phenomenon with a single theory has a long history in sociology, but, like delinquency theory, substance abuse theory owes its origins to several theoretical perspectives. For some individuals, drugs are an escape from the dreariness and toxicity of their home environments. For others, substance abuse is an attempt to escape from emotionally crippling problems. For still others, substance abuse arises rather normally, as part of peer influences. Integrated or interactionist models combining the effects of strain, control, and social learning theories probably make the most sense in explaining why adolescents start using alcohol and drugs.[97]

■Solving the Drug Problem

Prevention programs, treatment interventions, strict enforcement, and harm reduction are all possible means of controlling drug use among adolescents. Where prevention and treatment appear to be the most effective means of controlling drug abuse, there is abundant evidence that deterrence tactics, such as the federal war on drugs (involving mostly strict enforcement), have been largely ineffective with both juveniles and adults.

Prevention

The 1990s saw dramatic developments in drug-prevention programs. The Center for the Study and Prevention of Violence at the University of Colorado began an initiative called Blueprints for Violence Prevention, in which researchers evaluated 600 programs designed to prevent violence and drug abuse and to treat youths with problem behaviors.[98] The investigators were able to identify eleven model programs and twenty-one promising programs. Some of the more noteworthy are (1) Life Skills Training (LST), which is designed to prevent or reduce the use of "gateway" drugs such as tobacco, alcohol, and marijuana;[99] (2) the Midwestern Prevention Project (MPP), a comprehensive three- to five-year community-based prevention program targeting gateway use of alcohol, tobacco, and marijuana;[100] and (3) the Project Toward No Drug Abuse (PROJECT TND), which targets high school youths who are at risk for drug abuse. (See Chapter 12 for a wider description of these programs.)[101] Significantly, Blueprints for Violence Prevention reported that both model programs and promising programs had positive outcome assessments when evaluated over a period of several years.[102]

Police departments across the country conduct at least three substance abuse prevention programs in schools: D.A.R.E. (Drug Abuse Resistance Education), SPECDA, and Project Alert. The D.A.R.E. program is a widely replicated effort to prevent substance abuse, although Chapter 14 notes that recent evaluations of D.A.R.E. are less than encouraging. Yet, as the most popular school-based drug ed-

" There is abundant evidence that deterrence tactics, such as the federal war on drugs have been largely ineffective with both juveniles and adults. "

Web **LIBRARY** 11.5

Read the federal *General Counterdrug Intelligence Plan* at **www.justicestudies.com/ WebLibrary**.

Teen representatives of Drug Free Youth in Town are introduced at a Miami, Florida, workshop. ■ **How can the success of drug prevention programs be measured?**

ucation program in the United States, D.A.R.E. operates in about 70 percent of our nation's school districts, reaching 25 million students. It has also been adopted in forty-four other countries.[103] New York City's Project SPECDA (School Program to Educate and Control Drug Abuse), a collaborate project of the city's police department and board of education, is another highly praised drug prevention program.[104] Project Alert, a program originating in middle schools in California and Oregon, appears to have had some success in teaching students to avoid drugs and to resist peer pressure to use tobacco and alcohol.[105]

Effective programs need to incorporate early childhood and family interventions, school-based interventions, and comprehensive and communitywide efforts. The important dimension of drug-prevention interventions, as is continually emphasized throughout this text, is a multidimensional approach centering on the family, school, and community.

Treatment/Intervention

Treatment for drug abusers takes place in psychiatric and hospital settings for youngsters whose parents can afford it or who have third-party insurance benefits. Other youngsters, especially those substance abusers who have committed minor forms of delinquency, receive treatment in privately administered placements, which vary tremendously in the quality of program design and implementation. Substance abusers who are involved in serious forms of delinquency will likely be placed in county or state facilities whose basic organizational goals are custodial- and security-oriented. These youths generally receive some exposure to substance-abuse counseling, especially in group contexts.

Web LIBRARY 11.6

Read Key Findings from the University of Michigan's *Monitoring the Future* survey at **www.justicestudies.com/WebLibrary**.

Substance-abusing youths with typical multiple problems may be more malleable than adult offenders, but there is little evidence that the majority of substance-abuse programs are any more successful than those for adult substance abusers. Élan in Maine; Rocky Mountain in Colorado; Provo Canyon in Utah; and Cascade, Cedu, and Hilltop in California are privately administered therapeutic schools or emotional growth programs that may be better than the average substance-abuse program for juveniles.[106]

Élan, a therapeutic community for juveniles in Poland Springs, Maine, is a treatment program for adolescents with emotional, behavioral, or adjustment problems. This coeducational and residential program serves juveniles in grades 8 through 12. Joe Ricci, a former drug addict and one of the success stories of Daytop (a therapeutic community for drug addicts) in New York City and Dr. Gerald Davidson, a psychiatrist, started Élan in 1971.[107]

The program involves intense peer pressure, guilt admittance, and often humiliating punishments. It also stresses personal responsibility, honesty, self-control, and patience. Staff claim that the therapy is not as intense or encapsulated in negativity as it was in the past. Élan has grown into a finely tuned million-dollar operation. The 160 residents stay an average of 27 months and the annual fees for a 12-month stay are $49,071. A high percentage of those who are admitted to this program graduate or receive "diplomas." Of this number, according to an in-house evaluation, about 80 percent stay out of trouble. Supporters think that Élan is an exemplary therapeutic experience for youths; foes, including some former residents, regard it as coercive and brutal.[108]

The philosophy of Élan, like that of similar therapeutic experiences for juveniles, is perhaps correct—that substance abusers need a confrontational environment with intense pressure from peers and staff to change. It may well be that the 60 to 70 percent who stay at Élan to complete the two-year program are ready to change or to desist from drugs and negative behaviors and that this explains their high success rate. But privately administered programs such as Élan do not have enough places available for all the juveniles who need such a therapeutic experience.

Drug courts are another recent treatment innovation for those who have a history of drug use (see Chapter 12). To address alcohol and drug problems, treatment

Web LIBRARY 11.7

Read the Office of National Drug Control Policy's *National Drug Control Strategy 2006* at **www.justicestudies.com/WebLibrary**.

services in drug courts have been based on formal theories of drug dependence and abuse. They also attempt to employ the best therapeutic tools and to provide participants with the opportunities needed to build cognitive skills. Research findings generally show that drug courts can reduce recidivism and promote other positive outcomes, but research has been unable to uncover which court processes affect which outcomes and for what types of offenders.[109]

The balanced and restorative justice model, discussed further in Chapter 13, has been used as a form of treatment intervention with drug and alcohol-abusing adolescents. It forms the guiding philosophy in twelve states, and builds on restorative justice conferencing that takes place in informal settings where voluntary and negotiative encounters include victim, offender, and their relevant communities.[110] Restorative justice conferencing can also use more coerced restorative obligations, such as restitution or community service imposed by formal proceedings. What makes these processes and obligations "restorative," rather than rehabilitative or retributive, is the restorative intent underlying their imposition.[111]

Drug and alcohol abuse interventions have also been developed in a number of community-based and institutional settings. Some training schools, for example, conduct group sessions for those with histories of drug use. A social worker, for example, may conduct ongoing drug and alcohol abuse groups, and members from outside groups, such as Alcoholic Anonymous (AA) or Narcotics Anonymous (NA), may come into the institution and hold sessions.

Strict Enforcement

The War on Drugs has not been won with juveniles any more than it has with adults. A disastrous consequence of this "war" is that increasing numbers of minority youths who were involved in using or selling crack cocaine have been brought into the justice system for extended periods of time. Some have even argued that the war on drugs has been a factor contributing to the spread of youth gangs.[112] Strict enforcement, however, has seemed to make a difference in several ways:

- The destruction of overseas drug-producing crops has probably had some impact on the availability of drugs in the United States, raising prices and making some drugs harder to find.
- Heavy penalties associated with the sale of illicit drugs appear to have been at least somewhat effective in deterring both juvenile and adult offenders.
- Law enforcement's targeting of dealers has had some success in getting those offenders off the streets.
- The policing of the sale of tobacco products, especially cigarettes, at convenience stores and other places has made it more difficult for minors to purchase or obtain tobacco products.
- The strict enforcement of no-drug zones around schools has discouraged or at least reduced the number of persons trafficking drugs to school-aged children.
- Strict enforcement of adolescent drug trafficking at school and in neighborhoods may have reduced the availability of drugs to young people.

Harm Reduction

Harm reduction is an approach designed to reduce the harm done to youths by drug use and by the severe penalties resulting from drug use and sales. A number of harm-reduction strategies have been employed, including:

- Programs under which health professionals administer drugs to addicts as part of a treatment and detoxification regime.

- Drug treatment facilities that are available for those drug addicts wishing to enter treatment.
- Needle exchange programs intended to slow the transmission of HIV and that provide educational resources about how HIV is contracted and spread.

Juvenile drug users generally find a wide availability of treatment programs and facilities. Treatment programs are usually more readily available to middle- and upper-class youths than to lower-class youths, partially because wealthier parents can afford to pay for the care of their dependent children. The legalized administration of drugs to addicts and needle exchange programs are more typically found when working with adult drug users than with juveniles.

CHAPTER
Summary

This chapter has discussed drug and alcohol use by adolescents. Some of the key points of the chapter are as follows:

- Drug and alcohol abuse is one form of problem behavior, and its onset, duration, and termination are determined by the dynamics of the interplay between the environment and particular young people, which varies over developmental periods.

- The good news is that the trend of drug use appears to have declined significantly from the late 1970s, with perhaps slight increases since the early 1990s.

- It is also good news that the use of cigarettes has declined among American adolescents.

- The bad news is that alcohol abuse remains high among American adolescents and shows no signs of decreasing.

- The data seem to show that high-risk children are becoming increasingly involved in substance abuse.

- Although the use of crack cocaine may be declining across the nation, it remains the drug of choice for many disadvantaged youths.

- It is disconcerting that teenagers have increased their use of marijuana in the past decade.

- Recent increasing use of methamphetamine by adolescents may also be viewed as a matter of social concern.

- A number of theories examine why juveniles use drugs, but integrated theories appear to be the most adequate forms of explanation.

- Early prevention efforts in schools and in other social contexts appear to be making headway with low-risk children.

- The fact that substance abuse is usually one of several problems for high-risk youths makes it more difficult to achieve substantial success through therapeutic interventions.

CRITICAL THINKING
Questions

1. Why is drug use so popular in American society?
2. Why does the typical drug user use drugs up to a certain point and then go no further? At the same time, why do other youths who seem to be as committed to this stopping point continue using drugs?
3. What caused the use of marijuana to rise in the mid-1990s?
4. Why would a youth pursue only the drug pathway rather than the delinquency/drug pathway?
5. Why do college students drink as much as they do? How is their drinking related to the subject matter of this chapter?

Visit the National Criminal Justice Reference Service (NCJRS) on the Web at **www.ncjrs.gov**. Once there, click on Juvenile Justice in the left-hand menu and review the topics listed under that heading (i.e., Child Protection/Health; Corrections/Detention; Delinquency Prevention, etc.). Choose a topic that interests you from among those listed and create an overview of the resources it contains. Your overview should list resources by type (i.e., publications, links, etc.) and provide some details on the specific kinds of resources available. Which of the listed publications did you find the most useful? Which of the related links are the most interesting? Why? Submit your answers to these questions to your instructor if asked to do so.

Source: From www.ncjrs.gov. Reprinted with permission from the U.S. Department of Justice.

Notes

1. Matthew G. Muters and Christina Bethke were extremely helpful in doing the literature review and in drafting materials for this chapter.
2. Rand Drug Policy Research Center, *Newsletter* (June 1995), p. 1.
3. Howard Abadinsky, *Drugs: An Introduction,* 4th ed. (Belmont, Calif.: Wadsworth/Thompson Learning, 2001), p. 4.
4. In 1990, the U.S. Supreme Court ruled 6–3 in an Oregon case that states can prohibit the use of peyote by members of the Native American church. But Congress enacted a statute providing a defense for those who use the substance "with good faith practice of a religious belief."
5. Abadinsky, *Drugs: An Introduction,* p. 4.
6. *Juveniles and Drugs* (Washington, D.C.: Office of National Drug Control Policy, 2004).
7. L. D. Johnston, P. M. O'Malley, J. G. Bachman, and J. E. Schulenberg, *Monitoring the Future National Results on Adolescent Drug Use: Overview of Key Findings* (Bethesda, Md.: National Institute on Drug Abuse, 2004).
8. Centers for Disease Control and Prevention, *Youth Risk Behavior Surveillance—United States* (Washington, D.C.: Centers for Disease Control and Prevention, 2004).
9. Office of National Drug Control Policy, *National Drug Control Strategy* (Washington, D.C.: Office of National Drug Control Policy, 2003).
10. United States Department of Health and Human Services, 2002 *National Survey on Drug Abuse* (Washington, D.C.: U.S. Department of Health and Human Services, 2003).
11. Ibid.
12. U.S. Department of Health and Human Services, *2002 National Survey on Drug Abuse.*
13. James A. Inciardi, *The War on Drugs, II* (Mountain View, Calif.: Mayfield, 1992), p. 62.
14. Public Health Service, *Healthy People 2000: National Health Promotion and Disease Prevention Objectives—Full Report with Commentary* (Washington, D.C.: DHHS Publication, 1991).
15. National Institutes of Health, National Institute on Drug Abuse, *Monitoring the Future* (Washington, DC: U.S. Government Printing Office, 2005).
16. Ibid.
17. Ali H. Mokdad, James S. Marks, Donna F. Stroup, Julie L. Gerberding, "Actual Causes of Death in the United States, 2000," *Journal of the American Medical Association* (March 10, 2004), Vol. 291, No. 10, pp. 1238, 1241.
18. For many other names, see Inciardi, *The War on Drugs II,* p. 44.
19. For a review of these studies, see Joseph M. Rey, Andres Martin, and Peter Krabman, "Is the Party Over? Cannabis and Juvenile Psychiatric Disorder: The Past Ten Years," *Journal of the American Academy of Child and Adolescent Psychiatry* 43 (October 2004), pp. 1194–1208.
20. Inciardi, *The War on Drugs II,* p. 94.
21. Gordon Witkin, "The Men Who Created Crack," *U.S. News and World Report* (August 29, 1991), pp. 44–53. See also Malcolm W. Klein, Cheryl L. Maxson, and Lea C. Cunningham, "'Crack,' Street Gangs, and Violence," *Criminology* 29 (November 1991), pp. 623–650.
22. Inciardi, *The War on Drugs II,* p. 116.

23. Ibid.

24. Ibid., p. 93.

25. "Cocaine Abuse," *NIDA Capsules* (November 1989), p. 2.

26. James N. Hall, "Impact of Mother's Cocaine Use," *Street Pharmacologist* 11 (October 1987), p. 1.

27. United States Department of Health and Human Services, *2005 National Household Survey on Drug Abuse.*

28. T. M. McSherry, "Program Experiences with the Solvent Abuser in Philadelphia," in *Epidemiology of Inhalant Abuse: An Update,* edited by R. A. Crider and B. A. Rouse (Washington, D.C.: National Institute on Drug Abuse Research Monograph 85, 1989), pp. 106–120.

29. U. S. Food and Drug Administration, *Frequently Asked Questions,* www.fed.gov/oc/buyonline/faqs.html.

30. Inciardi, *The War on Drugs II,* p. 39.

31. Abadinsky, *Drugs: An Introduction,* pp. 143–144.

32. *Drug Enforcement Report* (January 3, 1990), p. 7.

33. Substance Abuse Health Service Administration, *Preliminary Estimates from the 1997 National Household Survey on Drug Abuse,* p. 3.

34. University of Michigan News and Information Services (January 24, 1991).

35. National Institute on Drug Abuse, *Infofax: Steroids* (Anabolic-Androgenic, 1999).

36. Ibid.

37. National Institute on Drug Abuse, *Monitoring the Future: National Results on Adolescent Drug Use: Overview of Key Findings,* 2006.

38. National Institute on Drug Abuse, *Research Report: Anabolic Steroid Abuse,* April 2000.

39. *Ibid.*

40. Inciardi, *The War on Drugs II,* p. 63.

41. For an overview of medical complications associated with heroin addiction, see Jerome J. Platt, *Heroin Addiction: Theory, Research, and Treatment* (Malabar, Fla.: Robert E. Krieger, 1986), pp. 80–102.

42. National Institute on Drug Abuse, *Annual Data, Data From the Drug Abuse Warning Network, Annual Trend Data.*

43. Dryfoos, *Adolescents at Risk,* pp. 48–49.

44. David M. Altschuler and Paul J. Brounstein, "Patterns of Drug Use, Drug Trafficking, and Other Delinquency among Inner-City Adolescent Males in Washington, D.C.," *Criminology* 29 (1991), p. 590.

45. Lloyd D. Johnson et al., "Drugs and Delinquency: A Search for Causal Connections," in *Longitudinal Research on Drug Use: Empirical Finds and Methodological Issues,* edited by Denise B. Kandel, Ronald C. Kessler, and Rebecca Z. Margulies (Washington, D.C.: Hemisphere, 1978), pp. 137–156; J. C. Friedman and A. S. Friedman, "Drug Use and Delinquency among Lower Class, Court Adjudicated Adolescent Boys," in *Drug Use in America* 1 (Washington, D.C.: National Commission on Marijuana and Drug Abuse: Government Printing Office, 1973); J. A. Inciardi, "Heroin Use and Street Crime," *Crime and Delinquency* 25 (1979), pp. 335–346; L. N. Robins and G. E. Murphy, "Drug Use in a Normal Population of Young Negro Men," *American Journal of Public Health* 57 (1967), pp. 1580–1596.

46. Altschuler and Brounstein, "Patterns of Drug Use, Drug Trafficking, and Other Delinquency among Inner-City Adolescent Males in Washington, D.C.," p. 590; Richard Jessor and Shirley L. Jessor, *Problem Behavior and Psychosocial Development: A Longitudinal Study of Youth* (New York: Academic Press, 1977); R. L. Akers, "Delinquent Behavior, Drugs and Alcohol: What Is the Relationship?" *Today's Delinquent* 3 (1984), pp. 19–47; D. S. Elliott and D. Huizinga, *The Relationship between Delinquent Behavior and ADM Problems* (Boulder, Colo.: Behavior Research Institute, 1985); Delbert S. Elliott, David Huizinga, and Scott Menard, *Multiple Problem Youth: Delinquency, Substance Use, and Mental Health Problems* (New York: Springer-Verlag, 1989).

47. See Marc Le Blanc and Nathalie Kaspy, "Trajectories of Delinquency and Problem Behavior: Comparison of Social and Personal Control Characteristics of Adjudicated Boys on Synchronous and Nonsynchronous Paths," *Journal of Quantitative Criminology* 14 (1998), pp. 181– 214, and Helene Raskin White, "Marijuana Use and Delinquency: A Test of the 'Independent Cause' Hypothesis," *Journal of Drug Issues* (1991), pp. 231–256.

48. Jessor and Jessor, *Problem Behavior and Psychosocial Development;* Denise B. Kandel, "Epidemiological and Psychosocial Perspectives on Adolescent Drug Use," *Journal of American Academic Clinical Psychiatry* 21 (1982), pp. 328–347; and Lee N. Robins and Katherine S. Ratcliff, "Risk Factors in the Continuation of Childhood Antisocial Behavior into Adulthood," *Internal Journal of Mental Health* 7 (1979), pp. 96–116.

49. John M. Wallace Jr. and Jerald G. Bachman, "Explaining Racial/Ethnic Differences in Adolescent Drug Use: The Impact of Background and Lifestyle," *Social Problems* 38 (August 1991), p. 334. See also Jessor and Jessor, *Problem Behavior and Psychosocial Development,* and Richard Jessor, "Problem Behavior Theory, Psychosocial Development, and Adolescent Problem Drinking," *British Journal of Addiction* 82 (1987), pp. 331–342.

50. David Huizinga, Rolf Loeber, and Terence Thornberry, *Urban Delinquency and Substance Abuse Initial Findings: Research Summary* (Washington, D.C.: U.S. Department of Justice; Office of Juvenile Justice and Delinquency Prevention, 1994).

51. Peter W. Greenwood, "Substance Abuse Problems among High-Risk Youth and Potential Interventions," *Crime and Delinquency* 38 (October 1992), p. 447.

52. Quoted in Greenwood, "Substance Abuse Problems among High-Risk Youth."

53. Wallace and Bachman, "Explaining Racial/Ethnic Differences in Adolescent Drug Use," p. 333.

54. Elliott, Huizinga, and Menard, *Multiple Problem Youth.*

55. Wallace and Bachman, "Explaining Racial/Ethnic Differences in Adolescent Drug Use," p. 333.

56. Bureau of Justice Statistics, *Drugs, Crime, and the Justice System* (Washington, D.C.: Government Printing Office, 1993), p. 23.

57. Denise B. Kandel, Ronald C. Kessler, and Rebecca Z. Margulies, eds., *Longitudinal Research on Drug Use: Empirical Findings and Methodological Issues* (Washington, D.C.: Hemisphere, 1978).

58. J. David Hawkins, Richard F. Catalano, and Devon D. Brewer, "Preventing Serious, Violent, and Chronic Juvenile Offending," in *A Sourcebook: Serious, Violent and Chronic Juvenile Offenders,* edited by James C. Howell, Barry Krisberg, J. David Hawkins, and John J. Wilson (Thousand Oaks, Calif.: Sage, 1995), pp. 48–49.

59. Delbert S. Elliott, David Huizinga, and Suzanne S. Ageton, *Explaining Delinquency and Drug Use* (Beverly Hills, Calif.: Sage, 1985).

60. D. S. Elliott and D. Huizinga, "The Relationship between Delinquent Behavior and ADM Problem Behaviors." Paper prepared for the ADAMHA/OJJDP State of the Art Research Conference on Juvenile Offenders with Serious Drug/Alcohol and Mental Health Problems, Bethesda, Maryland (April 17–18, 1984).

61. Fagan, Weis, and Cheng, "Delinquency and Substance Use among Inner-City Students," p. 351.

62. Altschuler and Brounstein, "Patterns of Drug Use, Drug Trafficking and Other Delinquency among Inner-City Adolescent Males in Washington, D.C.," p. 587.

63. Klein, Maxson, and Cunningham, "'Crack,' Street Gangs, and Violence," p. 623.

64. Interviewed in April 1995.

65. Felix M. Padilla, *The Gang as an American Enterprise* (New Brunswick, N.J.: Rutgers University Press, 1992).

66. Daniel J. Monti, *Wannabe Gangs in Suburbs and Schools* (Cambridge, England: Blackwell, 1994).

67. Ibid.

68. Ibid., pp. 76, 90.

69. Ibid., p. 55.

70. Marcia Chaiken and Bruce Johnson, *Characteristics of Different Types of Drug-Involved Youth* (Washington, D.C.: National Institute of Justice, 1988), p. 14.

71. Marvin S. Krohn, Alan J. Lizotte, and Cynthia M. Perez, "The Interrelationships between Substance Use and Precocious Transitions to Adult Status," *Journal of Health and Social Behavior* 38 (March 1997), p. 88.

72. Glen H. Elder Jr., "Time, Human Agency, and Social Change: Perspectives on the Life Course," *Social Psychology Quarterly* 57 (1994), pp. 4–15.

73. Krohn, Lizotte, and Perez, "The Interrelationships between Substance Use and Precocious Transitions to Adult Status," p. 88.

74. Gary M. McClelland, Linda A. Teplin, and Karen M. Abram, *Detention and Prevalence of Substance Use among Juvenile Detainees,* (Washington, D.C.: Office of Juvenile Justice and Delinquency Prevention, 2004), p. 1; see the report for the citations supporting each generalization.

75. The author has interviewed a number of adult former drug addicts and staff of therapeutic communities, and these explanations were typically given for why a drug addict went straight and stayed clean.

76. See D. B. Kandel and J. A. Logan, "Patterns of Drug Use from Adolescence to Young Adulthood: Periods of Risk for Initiation, Continued Use, and Discontinuation," *American Public Health* 74 (1984), pp. 660–666.

77. L. A. Goodman and W. H. Kruskal, *Measures of Association for Cross Classification* (New York: Springer-Verlag, 1979).

78. L. Thomas Winfree Jr., Christine S. Sellers, and Dennis L. Clason, "Social Learning and Adolescent Deviance Abstention: Toward Understanding the Reasons for Initiating, Quitting, and Avoiding Drugs," *Journal of Quantitative Criminology* 9 (1993), p. 101.

79. Interviewed in July 1983.

80. R. L. Simons, R. D. Conger, and L. B. Whitbeck, "A Multistage Social Learning Model of the Influence of Family and Peers Upon Adolescent Substance Abuse," *Journal of Drug Issues* 18 (1988), pp. 293–315.

81. John Petraitis, Brian R. Flay, and Todd Q. Miller, "Reviewing Theories of Adolescent Substance Use: Organizing Pieces in the Puzzle," *Psychological Bulletin* 117 (1995), pp. 67–86.

82. Ibid., p. 68.

83. I. Ajken and M. Fishbein, *Understanding Attitudes and Predicting Social Behavior* (Englewood Cliffs, N.J.: Prentice-Hall, 1980).

84. Isidor Chein, Donald L. Gerard, Robert S. Lee, and Eva Rosenfeld, *The Road to H: Narcotics, Juvenile Delinquency and Social Policy* (New York: Basic Books, 1964), p. 14.

85. Philippe Bourgois, "Just Another Night on Crack Street," *New York Times* (November 12, 1989), pp. 52–53, 60–65, 94.

86. For the positive relationship between peers and drug use, see T. J. Dishion and R. Loeber, "Adolescent Marijuana and Alcohol Use: The Role of Parents and Peers Revisited," *American Journal of Drug and Alcohol Abuse* 11 (1985), pp. 11–25; Elliott, Huizinga, and Ageton, *Explaining Delinquency and Drug Use;* Terence P. Thornberry, Margaret Farnworth, Marvin D. Krohn, and Alan J. Lizotte, "Peer Influence and Initiation to Drug Use," Working Paper No. 2 (National Department of Justice, n.d.); and D. B. Kandel, "Adolescent Marijuana Use: Role of Parents and Peers," *Science* 181 (1973), pp. 1067–1081. However, for research that found no predominant effects of peer pressure on substance use, see Mark D. Reed and Pamela Wilcox Roundtree, "Peer Pressure and Adolescent Substance Use," *Journal of Quantitative Criminology* 13 (1997), pp. 143–180.

87. Petraitis, Flay, and Miller, "Reviewing Theories of Adolescent Substance Use," p. 70.

88. Travis Hirschi, *Causes of Delinquency* (Berkeley, Calif.: University of California, 1969); and J. D. Hawkins and J. G. Weis, "The Social Development Model: An Integrated Approach to Delinquency Prevention," *Journal of Primary Prevention* 6 (1985), pp. 73–97.

89. Hirschi, *Causes of Delinquency.*

90. J. D. Hawkins, R. F. Catalano, and J. Y. Miller, "Risk and Protective Factors for Alcohol and Other Drug Problems in Adolescence and Early Adulthood," *Psychological Bulletin* 112 (1992), pp. 64–105.

91. Radical theorists have made this a theme of their research on poor adolescents, especially minority ones. See Chapter 6.

92. D. S. Elliott, D. Huizinga, and S. S. Ageton, *Explaining Delinquency and Drug Use* (Beverly Hills, Calif.: Sage, 1985).

93. D. S. Elliott, D. Huizinga, and S. Menard, *Multiple Problem Youth: Delinquency, Substance Abuse Mental Health Problems* (New York: Springer-Verlag, 1989).

94. Ibid.

95. Simons, Conger, and Whitbeck, "A Multistage Social Learning Model of the Influence of Family and Peers Upon Adolescent Substance Abuse," pp. 293–315.

96. Ibid.

97. Greenwood, "Substance Abuse Problems among High-Risk Youth," p. 449. For the reciprocal relationships that interactional theory posits among drug use, association with drug-using peers, and beliefs about drug use, see Marvin D. Krohn, Alan J. Lizotte, Terence P. Thornberry, Carolyn Smith, and

David McDowall, "Reciprocal Causal Relationships among Drug Use, Peers, and Beliefs: A Five-Wave Panel Model," *Journal of Drug Issues* 26 (1996), pp. 405–428.

98. Sharon Mihalic, Katherine Irwin, Abigail Fagan, Diane Ballard, and Delbert Elliott, *Blueprint for Violence Prevention* (Washington, D.C.: Office of Juvenile Justice and Delinquency Prevention, 2004), p. 55.

99. G. Botvin, S. Mihalic, and J. K. Grotpeter, "Life Skills Training," in *Blueprint for Violence Prevention: Book 5*, edited by D. S. Elliott (Boulder: University of Colorado, Institute of Behavioral Sciences, Center for the Study and Prevention of Violence, 1998).

100. Mihalic, Irwin, Fagan, Ballard, and Elliott, *Blueprint for Violence Prevention*, pp. 31–33.

101. Ibid., pp. 47–48.

102. Ibid.

103. National Institute of Justice, *The D.A.R.E. Program: A Review of Prevalence, User Satisfaction, and Effectiveness* (Washington, D.C.: U.S. Department of Justice, 1994).

104. William DeJong, *Arresting the Demand for Drugs: Police and School Partnership to Prevent Drug Abuse* (Washington, D.C.: National Institute of Justice, 1987), p. 5.

105. Phyllis Ellickson, Robert Bell, and K. McGuigan, "Preventing Adolescent Drug Use: Long-Term Results of a Junior High Program," *American Journal of Public Health* 83 (1993), pp. 856–861.

106. Deanna Atkinson, an administrator in the Élan program, suggested this list of noteworthy programs in a September 1995 telephone conversation.

107. For this information on Élan, see its web page: www.elanschool.com.

108. Ibid. There are also several statements from former residents testifying to the brutal methods used at Élan and its negative effects on them.

109. *Drug Courts: The Second Decade* (Washington, D.C.: National Institute of Justice, 2006), p. iii.

110. Gordon Bazemore and Lode Walgrave, "Restorative Juvenile Justice: In Search of Fundamentals and an Outline for Systemic Reform," in *Restorative Juvenile Justice: Repairing the Harm of Youth Crime*, edited by Gordon Bazemore and Lode Walgrave (Monsey, N.Y.: Criminal Justice Press, 1999), p. 45.

111. Ibid.

112. Thomas J. Dishion, Deborah Capaldi, Kathleen M. Spracklen, and Li Fuzhong, "Peer Ecology of Male Adolescent Drug Use," *Development and Psychopathology* 7 (1995), p. 803.

Preventing and Controlling Delinquency

Part Four of the text provides an overview of the issues involved in preventing and controlling delinquency. Chapter 12 points out that the most desired outcome is the prevention of youth crime. Failing prevention, diversion from formal handling by the juvenile justice system is frequently seen as a desirable alternative for juveniles who break the law. Diversion is likely to be ineffective, however, for adolescents who, for one reason or another, continue to violate the law.

Chapter 13 provides an overview of the juvenile justice process and describes the system of agencies and officials who play important roles in the handling of juvenile offenders. The chapter begins with a description of the historical development of the juvenile justice system, then outlines the present structure and functions of today's system. It also explores perspectives on correcting youthful offenders, including the increasingly popular restorative justice model. Racial inequalities within the system, the impact on the system of the Juvenile Justice and Delinquency Prevention Act of 1974, and the influence of graduated sanctions are all explored.

Chapter 14 looks at the pivotal role that the police play in responding to juvenile crime and in marshalling efforts to prevent it. Police discretion in the handling of juvenile offenders is an especially significant element that may determine the kinds of dispositions that juveniles receive. The chapter also discusses the rights that juvenile offenders have when taken into custody.

Chapter 15 focuses on the role of the 108-year-old juvenile court, including how expectations facing the court have changed. The various stages of juvenile court proceedings and the changing sentencing structure of juvenile court are also explored. The chapter concludes with a discussion of an especially important recent U.S. Supreme Court decision preventing the execution of offenders who commit any crime, no matter how serious, under the age of eighteen.

Chapter 16, this section's final chapter, explores juvenile corrections, including probation, community-based treatment programs, short- and long-term juvenile confinement, and aftercare. Underlying this chapter is the important question: What do we do about those youths who have committed a serious or violent crime or who continue to violate the law?

12

Prevention, Diversion, and Treatment

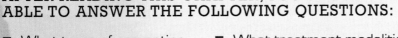

> " The principle of diversion means that juveniles will be diverted from the juvenile court into a system or organization that theoretically should be more responsible to the needs of today's youth than the present juvenile court system. "
>
> —Prof. Thomas A. Johnson

CHAPTER Objectives

AFTER READING THIS CHAPTER, YOU SHOULD BE ABLE TO ANSWER THE FOLLOWING QUESTIONS:

- What types of prevention programs are likely to work with high-risk youngsters?

- What are the advantages and disadvantages of diversionary programs?

- What treatment modalities are most widely used with juvenile delinquents?

- What are the ingredients of effective programs?

407

At age fifteen, Karl was a school dropout with a small-time drug habit who was hanging out on Portland, Oregon, streets with friends who supported themselves by shoplifting. When Karl was picked up by police for possession of marijuana, he would normally have been taken to the Multnomah County Juvenile Detention Center—Portland's juvenile jail.

But two years ago, using money from a small federal grant, the county started a program under which Karl and other teenagers like him, who would otherwise have been charged with minor offenses and formally processed by the juvenile justice system, are now taken to a privately run center where they receive a clinical assessment, drug treatment, and the chance to remake their lives.

Karl, whose last name cannot be made public because he is a juvenile, has become drug free and, officials say, is about to earn his high school equivalency degree. Since the program began, the number of young people taken to juvenile jail has fallen 73 percent, said Joanne Fuller, the director of the county Department of Community Justice.

But the Portland program, known as New Avenues for Youth, is in danger of being eliminated because of $250 million in proposed cuts in juvenile justice programs in the federal budget for next year, along with a $400 million cut in afterschool programs for at-risk children. "If the cuts go through, all our work goes away," Ms. Fuller said.

Adapted from Fox Butterfield, "Lifeline for Troubled Oregon Teenagers Is Imperiled by Planned U.S. Cuts," *New York Times*, March 9, 2003. Copyright © 2003 by The New York Times Co. Reprinted with permission.

Saul Alinsky, a community organizer, used to tell a story about social change. In this story, a man is walking by the riverside when he notices a body floating downstream. A fisherman also notices the body, leaps into the stream, pulls the body ashore, and gives mouth-to-mouth resuscitation, saving the person's life. The same thing happens a few minutes later, and then again and again. When yet another body floats by, the fisherman this time completely ignores the drowning man and starts running upstream along the bank. The observer asks the fisherman why he is not trying to rescue the drowning body. "This time," replies the fisherman, "I'm going upstream to find out who the hell is pushing those poor folks into the water."[1]

This story has an important message for students of delinquency: As long as we do nothing about original causes, we will just be pulling out bodies, mopping up the casualties. But Alinsky gave a twist to his story. While the fisherman was busy running up the bank to find the ultimate source of the problem, Alinsky asked, who was going to help those who continued to float down the river?

The study of delinquency, then, includes not only finding broad answers to the problem of youth crime but also helping youths in trouble who continue to founder in life. Accordingly, as part of our examination of the broad questions about youth crime, this chapter discusses both the prevention and treatment of delinquency.

Prevention and treatment interventions largely take place in community programs, which depend on adequate funding to provide needed services. Effective programs typically have involved and committed staff who can establish rapport, provide mentoring, reinforce positive behaviors, and offer encouragement and guidance to struggling young people.

The Justice Policy Institute of the Center on Juvenile and Criminal Justice of the Northwestern University School of Law profiled twenty-five individuals who were petitioned into juvenile court as hard-core delinquents when they were young, and

SOCIAL WORLD of the Delinquent 12.1

The Derrick Thomas Story

Tears streamed down his face as his mother cradled fourteen-year-old Derrick Thomas, already over six feet tall, in her arms. After years of beating the system, of committing crimes and not getting caught, of conning adults with his engaging smile and winning personality, Thomas's number had finally come up. He was going to juvenile jail.

Placed on home confinement while awaiting trial on a burglary charge, his first juvenile court referral, Thomas repeatedly left the house. His pretrial services officer had reached her breaking point. She pulled Thomas out of class and summoned him and his mother to her office to break the bad news. For the next thirty days, Thomas would be locked up.

At the time, "getting locked up seemed like the worst thing that could happen to me," says Thomas, who went on to become a ten-time All-Pro linebacker for the Kansas City Chiefs and one of the National Football League's all-time sack leaders. But getting involved in the juvenile justice system actually turned out to be "one of the most important breaks I ever got."

Through the court, Thomas would meet several people who helped him turn his life around. His juvenile court experiences led him to set up his own foundation for troubled inner-city youths and inspired him to use his life to make a difference on behalf of other troubled youths.

In public speaking engagements, Thomas told audiences the same thing he said in testimony before the United States Congress and the Missouri General Assembly, words that are a fitting epilogue to this profile: "I come to you today to say you can make a difference and to tell you that there are any number of success stories in the juvenile justice system, just like mine," he said.

■ Derrick Thomas died on February 8, 2000, from complications following an automobile accident. Was he right in his belief that we can make a difference in the lives of troubled youngsters? Why are some individuals so much more effective than others in making a difference in the lives of others?

Source: Office of Juvenile Justice and Delinquency Prevention, "Second Chances: Giving Kids a Chance to Make a Better Choice," in *Juvenile Justice Bulletin* (Washington, D.C.: U.S. Department of Justice, 2000), pp. 21–23. Reprinted with permission from the U.S. Department of Justice.

---

who turned their lives around. The book, *Second Chances—100 Years of the Children's Court: Giving Kids a Chance to Make a Better Choice,* profiles these twenty-five. One of them was Derrick Thomas, whose story is in Social World of the Delinquent 12.1.

Delinquency Prevention

The prevention of youth crime is certainly a desirable goal. An emphasis on prevention was written into federal law in the Juvenile Delinquency Prevention Act of 1972, the Juvenile Justice and Delinquency Prevention Act of 1974, and the Juvenile Justice Amendments of 1977 and 1980.[2] Despite this federal emphasis, prevention has been largely ignored in the study of delinquency. Yet there is evidence that the declining but still disturbing levels of teenage violent behavior and use of firearms, the continuing problems with drugs and alcohol, and the emergence of nationwide gangs still call for the development and evaluation of delinquency prevention programs.

Three different levels of **delinquency prevention** have been identified. **Primary prevention** is focused on modifying conditions in the physical and social environment that lead to delinquency. **Secondary prevention** is intervention in the lives of juveniles or groups identified as being in circumstances that dispose them toward delinquency. Secondary prevention also takes place in diversionary programs, in which youngsters in trouble are diverted from formal juvenile justice programs. **Tertiary prevention** is directed at the prevention of recidivism,[3] and takes place in traditional rehabilitation programs.

delinquency prevention
Organized efforts to forestall or prevent the development of delinquent behaviors.

primary prevention
Efforts to reduce delinquency by modifying conditions in the physical and social environments that lead to juvenile crime.

secondary prevention
Intervention in the lives of juveniles or groups who have been identified as being in circumstances that dispose them toward delinquency.

tertiary prevention
Programs directed at the prevention of recidivism among youthful offenders.

A police officer presents a delinquency prevention program to children in a Los Angeles classroom. ■ **What would a successful delinquency prevention program consist of?**

A History of Well-Meant Interventions

Delinquency prevention has a sad history. The highway of delinquency prevention is paved with punctured panaceas.[4] A member of the Subcommittee on Human Resources of the Committee on Education and Labor put it this way: "The public is looking for an inexpensive panacea. . . . These periodic panaceas for delinquents come along every 2 to 3 years in my experience. The harm they do is to divert the attention of the public from any long-term comprehensive program of helping youth, working to strengthen school systems, communities, job opportunities, housing and recreational programs."[5]

One reason for society's seeking of panaceas, or all-purpose remedies, is the human tendency to seek easy answers to complex problems.[6] Another reason is the frustration and sense of futility in a continuous, losing battle with juvenile crime that makes policymakers eager to discover a solution. Furthermore, the receptivity toward panaceas stems from a cultural belief in prevention—as exemplified by the expression "An ounce of prevention is worth a pound of cure."

Prevention panaceas have ranged from biological and psychological interventions to group therapy, gang intervention, recreational activities, job training and employment, community organization, and even structured reorganization of the entire society. The most widely known models of delinquency prevention are the Cambridge–Somerville Youth Study in Massachusetts; the New York City Youth Board; Mobilization for Youth in New York City; Boston's Midcity Project; Walter C. Reckless and Simon Dinitz's self-concept studies in Columbus, Ohio; the Chicago Area Projects; and La Playa de Ponce in Puerto Rico. For a description of the Chicago Area Projects, see Exhibit 12.1.

A number of studies in the 1970s examined the effectiveness of delinquency prevention programs. Michael C. Dixon and William W. Wright concluded from their examination of these programs that "few studies show significant results."[7] Richard J. Lundman, Paul T. McFarlane, and Frank Scarpitti drew the same pessimistic conclusion in 1976: "It appears unlikely that any of these [delinquency prevention] projects prevented delinquent behavior."[8] Lundman and Scarpitti collaborated on a later study of delinquency prevention and, adding fifteen projects to the twenty-five previously studied, concluded in 1978 that "a review of forty past or continuing attempts

Web LIBRARY 12.1

Read the OJJDP publication *Blueprints for Violence Prevention* at **www.justicestudies .com/WebLibrary**.

Exhibit 12.1

The Chicago Area Project

The Chicago Area Project (CAP) is a program that Clifford Shaw and his colleagues (see Chapter 4) initiated in the 1930s. Shaw's group sought to discover by actual demonstration and measurement a procedure for the prevention of delinquency and the treatment of delinquents. In 1932, the first projects were set up in three white, ethnically homogeneous neighborhoods: South Chicago, the Near West Side, and the Near North Side. The Near North and Near West area projects were located directly north and directly west of the Loop, Chicago's central business district. Both were areas with high delinquency rates. The third project was carried out in Russell Square on Chicago's southeast side. Russell Square was a heavily industrialized area consisting primarily of steel mills and railroad operations, but it had a lower delinquency rate than the other two neighborhoods. Eighteen area projects were eventually established in Chicago, and included several African American Southside neighborhoods. The concept of the area projects also spread to several other Illinois cities.

Shaw and his colleagues had lost confidence in official agencies' ability to deal adequately with the needs of youths, so they recruited local leaders to intervene with neighborhood youths. The CAP organizers believed that instead of throwing youths so quickly to the justice system, the community should intervene on their behalf. In the sixty-year existence of the CAP, community citizens have shown up in the juvenile court to speak on behalf of youths in trouble and have organized social and recreational programs for youths. They also have given special attention to local youths who are having difficulties at home or school or with the law.

Some critics contend that the CAP has been ineffective in coping with delinquency in its most serious forms in the areas of the city with the highest crime rates. The CAP has also been criticized because this program fails to attack the political and economic sources of power. Jon Snodgrass added that the CAP's neglect of the realities of Chicago politics and economics essentially made this project a conservative response to the radical changes that are needed in disorganized communities.

Although this latter structural limitation of the CAP is difficult to refute, it still has served as an exemplary model of what grass-roots organizations in the community can achieve in preventing juvenile delinquency. Steven Schlossman and colleagues summarized the effectiveness of the CAP by saying, "All of our data consistently suggest that the CAP has long been effective in organizing local communities and reducing juvenile delinquency."

■ **Why do you think this approach has generated so much enthusiasm through the years? How serious a flaw is it that the CAP has ignored the political and economic sources of power?**

Sources: See Steven Schlossman, Gail Aellman, and Richard Shavelson, *Delinquency Prevention in South Chicago: A Fifty-Year Assessment of the Chicago Area Project* (Santa Monica, Calif.: Rand, 1984); and Jon Snodgrass, "Clifford Shaw and Henry D. McKay," in *Delinquency, Crime and Society,* edited by James Short Jr. (Chicago: University of Chicago Press, 1976), p. 16.

at the prevention of juvenile delinquency leads to the nearly inescapable conclusion that none of these projects has successfully prevented delinquency."[9] These researchers even went on to say that given the poor history of past attempts at delinquency prevention, there was little reason to expect any greater success with any efforts.[10]

Prevention programs have received a number of other criticisms besides those dealing with their ineffectiveness. They are accused of widening the nets of social control over children, because they have resulted in sweeping more children to some program, agency, or system. Critics also charge that prevention programs are far too expensive. As part of its national evaluation of delinquency prevention, the U.S. Justice Department spent more than $20 million to provide intervention and services to 20,000 juveniles in sixty-eight cities. A further criticism is that prevention programs offer only piecemeal solutions to the profound problems that lead to juvenile crime. Finally, the rights of children, critics say, are sometimes compromised in prevention interventions.[11]

In the 1990s, the Office of Juvenile Justice and Delinquency Prevention (OJJDP) began targeting the prevention of serious and violent juvenile offending. It was recognized that these serious and violent juvenile offenders are responsible for a disproportionate number of crimes and that reducing chronic juvenile delinquency is a critical challenge facing society.[12] A multifaceted, coordinated approach toward these youths was identified, with prevention as a crit-

> " Prevention programs offer only piecemeal solutions to the profound problems that lead to juvenile crime. "

ical first step.[13] Pilot programs were established in a number of sites across the United States in the final few years of the twentieth century. The promise and problems of this new focus on prevention will be evaluated in this chapter.

Promising Prevention Programs

The juvenile justice system has traditionally focused on youths after they have had initial contact with law enforcement authorities. The last twenty years, however, has witnessed the emergence of a proactive approach to preventing juvenile crime. This new approach has sometimes been termed the "public health model of crime prevention."[14]

This public health model, which grew out of disease prevention efforts of a century ago, focuses on reducing risk and increasing opportunities for success. With its proactive emphasis on the prevention of social problems, the public health approach offers an appealing alternative to a reactive focus on rehabilitation or punishment. The public health approach employs the following four-step procedure to identify issues that need attention and to develop solutions: (1) define the nature of the problem using scientific methods or data; (2) identify potential causes using analyses of risk and protective factors associated with the problem; (3) design, develop, and evaluate interventions; and (4) disseminate successful models as part of education and outreach.[15]

Some researchers have recently begun advocating a shift in the prevention field intended to concentrate exclusively on building resiliency rather than on trying to reduce risks.[16] They contend that an emphasis on risks focuses primarily on deficits, whereas a prevention strategy can produce more significant outcomes by concentrating instead on building strengths. Research has shown, however, that delinquency prevention programs focusing too heavily on improving resiliency without addressing the source of the risks are largely unsuccessful.[17] The Model Program Guide of the Office of Juvenile Justice and Delinquency Prevention argues that the design of effective prevention programs and strategies needs to consider the interrelationships between reducing risk factors and building resiliency. See Focus on Social Policy 12.1 for an introduction to the OJJDP guide.

> "Some researchers have recently begun advocating a shift in the prevention field intended to concentrate exclusively on building resiliency rather than on trying to reduce risks."

The Blueprints for Violence Prevention, developed by the Center for the Study and Prevention of Violence at the University of Colorado–Boulder and supported by the Office of Juvenile Justice and Delinquency Prevention, identified eleven model programs and twenty-one promising violence and drug-abuse prevention programs that have received rigorous evaluation.[18] Table 12.1 presents a complete list of the model and promising programs the researchers identified; the following discussion will briefly describe the eleven model programs.

Big Brothers Big Sisters of America (BBBSA)   With a network of more than 500 local agencies throughout the United States that maintain more than 145,000 one-to-one relationships between youths and volunteer adults, Big Brothers Big Sisters of America (BBBSA) operates as the best known and largest mentoring program in the nation. The program serves youths ages six to eighteen, a significant number of whom are from single-parent and disadvantaged households. Mentors meet with their matches for three to five hours at least three times a month and participate in a variety of activities. The supervision of the match relationship is one of the program's hallmarks.[19] An eighteen-month evaluation found that, compared with a control group waiting for a match, youths in this mentoring program were 46 percent less likely to start using drugs, 27 percent less likely to start drinking, and 32 percent less likely to hit or assault someone. They also were less likely to skip school and more likely to have improved family relationships.[20]

FOCUS ON
Social Policy 12.1

OJJDP Model Programs Guide

The Office of Juvenile Justice and Delinquency Prevention's Model Programs Guide (MPG) is designed to assist practitioners and communities in implementing evidence-based prevention and intervention programs that can make a difference in the lives of children and communities. The MPG database of evidence covers the entire continuum of youth services from prevention through sanctions to reentry. The MPG can be used to assist juvenile justice practitioners, administrators, and researchers to enhance accountability, ensure public safety, and reduce recidivism. The MPG is an easy-to-use tool that offers the first and only database of scientifically proven programs across the spectrum of youth services.

The prevention programs presented are:

Academic Skills Enhancement
Afterschool/Recreation
Alternative School
Classroom Curricula
Cognitive Behavioral Treatment

Community and Policy-Oriented Policing
Community Awareness/Mobilization
Drug, Alcohol Therapy/Education
Family Therapy
Gang Prevention
Leadership and Youth Development
Mentoring
Parent Training
School/Classroom Enhancement
Truancy Prevention
Vocational/Job Training
Wraparound/Case Management

The MPG contains summary information (program description, evaluation design, research findings, references, and contact information) on evidence-based delinquency prevention and intervention programs. Programs are categorized into exemplary, effective, and promising, based on a set of methodological criteria and the strength of the findings.

■ **Why is a program guide that includes treatment and prevention programs by state a potentially helpful resource for both policymakers and practitioners?**

Source: Adapted from *OJJDP Model Programs Guide.* Web available at www.dsgonline.com/mpg2.5/mpg_index.htm. Reprinted with permission from the U.S. Department of Justice.

Bully Prevention Program   This model program aims to restructure the social environment of primary and secondary schools in order to provide fewer opportunities for bullying and to reduce the peer approval and support that reward bullying behavior. Adults in the school setting are seen as the driving force of this program; the program seeks to ensure that adults in the school are aware of bullying problems and are actively involved in their prevention. Classroom-level intervention involves the creation of class rules regarding bullying behavior and regular meetings in class to discuss issues as well as rule infractions.[21] This program has proved effective in large samples evaluated in Norway and South Carolina. In rural South Carolina, for example, children in thirty-nine schools in grades 4 through 6 reported that they experienced a 25 percent decrease in the frequency at which they felt bullied by other children.[22]

Functional Family Therapy (FFT)   This is a short-term, family-based prevention and intervention program that has been successfully applied in a variety of contexts to treat high-risk youths and their families from various backgrounds. Specifically designed to help underserved and at-risk youth ages eleven to eighteen, this multisystemic clinical program provides twelve one-hour **family therapy** sessions spread over three months. More difficult cases may receive up to thirty hours of therapy.[23] The success of this program has been demonstrated and replicated for more than twenty-five years. Evaluations using controlled follow-up periods of one, three, and five years have demonstrated significant and long-term reductions in the reoffending of youths, ranging from 25 percent to 60 percent.[24]

family therapy
A counseling technique that involves treating all members of a family; a widely used method of dealing with a delinquent's socially unacceptable behavior.

Incredible Years: Parent, Teacher, and Child Training Series   The Incredible Years model program has a comprehensive set of curricula designed to

TABLE 12.1

Model and Promising Programs and Age Groups of Targeted Juveniles

BLUEPRINTS PROGRAM	AGE GROUP				
	PREGNANCY/ INFANCY	EARLY CHILDHOOD	ELEMENTARY SCHOOL	JUNIOR HIGH SCHOOL	HIGH SCHOOL
Model Programs					
Big Brothers Big Sisters of America (BBBSA)			X	X	X
Bullying Prevention Program			X	X	
Functional Family Therapy (FFT)				X	X
Incredible Years		X	X		
Life Skills Training (LST)				X	
Midwestern Prevention Project (MPP)				X	
Multidimensional Treatment Foster Care (MTFC)				X	X
Multisystemic Therapy (MST)				X	X
Nurse–Family Partnership	X				
Project Toward No Drug Abuse (Project TND)					X
Promoting Alternative Thinking Strategies (PATHS)			X		
Promising Programs					
Athletes Training and Learning to Avoid Steroids					X
Brief Strategic Family Therapy			X	X	X
CASASTART			X	X	
Fast Track			X		
Good Behavior Game			X		
Guiding Good Choices			X	X	
High/Scope Perry Preschool		X			
Houston Child Development Center	X	X			
I Can Problem Solve		X	X		
Intensive Protective Supervision				X	X
Linking the Interests of Families and Teachers			X		
Preventive Intervention				X	
Preventive Treatment Program			X		
Project Northland				X	
Promoting Action through Holistic Education				X	X
School Transitional Environmental Program				X	X
Seattle Social Development Project			X	X	
Strengthening Families Program: Parents and Children 10–14			X	X	
Student Training through Urban Strategies				X	X
Syracuse Family Development Program	X	X			
Yale Child Welfare Project	X	X			

Source: Table 1.1 in Sharon Mihalic et al., *Blueprints for Violence Prevention* (Washington, D.C.: Office of Juvenile Justice and Delinquency Prevention, 2004). Reprinted with permission from the U.S. Department of Justice.

Web LIBRARY 12.2

Read the OJJDP publication *YouthBuild U.S.A.* at **www .justicestudies.com/ WebLibrary**.

promote social competence and to prevent, reduce, and treat conduct problems in young children. The target population of this program is children aged two to eight who exhibit or are at risk for conduct problems. In the parent, teacher, and child training programs, trained facilitators use videotaped scenes to encourage problem solving and sharing of ideas. The parent program teaches parents interactive play and reinforcement skills, logical and natural consequences, and problem-solving strategies. The teacher training component is designed to strengthen teachers' skills in classroom management. The child training component emphasizes building empathy with others, developing emotional competency, managing anger, solving interpersonal difficulties, and succeeding at school.[25] All three series of this program have received positive evaluations as meeting their original goals.[26]

Life Skills Training (LST) Consisting of a three-year intervention curriculum designed to prevent or reduce use of "gateway" drugs such as tobacco, alcohol, and marijuana, LST's lessons emphasize social resistance skills training to help students identify pressures to use drugs. This intervention is meant to be implemented in school classrooms by teachers but also has been taught successfully by health professionals and peer leaders. LST targets all middle/junior high school students, using an initial fifteen-lesson intervention in grade 6 or 7 and booster sessions over the following two years (ten sessions in year two and five sessions in year three). Lessons average forty-five minutes in length and use a variety of techniques. Components of the program are designed to teach youths personal self-management skills, social skills, and negative attitudes toward the use of drugs.[27] Using outcomes from more than a dozen studies, evaluators have found LST to reduce tobacco, alcohol, and marijuana use by 50 to 75 percent in intervention students compared to control students.[28]

Midwestern Prevention Project (MPP) This project includes school normative environment change as one of the components of a comprehensive three- to five-year community-based prevention program that targets gateway use of alcohol, tobacco, and marijuana. A central component of the program is the school-based intervention, which is designed as a primary prevention program. The program begins in either sixth or seventh grade and includes ten to thirteen classroom sessions taught by teachers trained in the curriculum. Five booster sessions are offered in the second year of the program. A parent component follows the school sessions and is designed to develop family norms (shared standards of behavior) that discourage drug use. The community component takes place during the last stages of the prevention effort and involves the support of community leaders.[29] Researchers followed students from eight schools who were randomly assigned to treatment or control groups for three years and found that the program brought net reductions of up to 40 percent in adolescent smoking and marijuana use, with results maintained through high school graduation.[30]

Web **PLACES** 12.1

Visit AfterSchool.gov via **www.justicestudies.com/ WebPlaces**.

Multidimensional Treatment Foster Care (MTFC) For adolescents who have had problems with chronic antisocial behavior, delinquency, and emotional disturbance, MTFC has been a cost-effective alternative to group or residential treatment, confinement, or hospitalization. This intervention provides short-term (generally about seven months), highly structured therapeutic care in foster families. Its goal is to decrease negative behaviors, including delinquency, and to increase youths' participation in appropriate prosocial activities, including school, hobbies, and sports. The program recruits, trains, and supervises foster families and provides youngsters with weekly skilled and focused therapy. Youth also participate in a structured daily behavioral management program implemented in the foster home. Counseling is further provided for the youngsters' biological (or foster) families in either an individual or a group format.[31] Evaluations of MTFC demonstrated that youths who participated in the program had significantly fewer arrests (an average of 2.6 offenses versus 5.4 offenses) and spent fewer days in lockup than youths placed in other community-based programs.[32]

Multisystemic Therapy (MST) Multisystemic Therapy provides cost-effective community-based clinical treatment to chronic and violent juvenile offenders who are at high risk of out-of-home placement. MST specifically targets the multiple factors contributing to antisocial behavior. The overarching goal of the intervention is to help parents understand and help their children overcome their behavior problems. MST uses strengths in each youth's social network to promote positive change in his or her behavior. Typically working in the home, at school, and in other community locations, therapists (who have low caseloads of four to six families) are available twenty-four hours a day, seven days a week. Treatment usually lasts about four months, which includes about sixty hours of therapist–family contact.[33] Program evaluations have revealed 25 to 70 percent reductions in long-term rates of rearrest and 47 to 64 percent reductions in out-of-home placements. These and other positive results were maintained for nearly four years after treatment ended.[34]

Nurse–Family Partnership Formerly called Prenatal and Infancy Home Visitation by Nurses, this model program sends nurses to the homes of lower-income, unmarried mothers, beginning during pregnancy and continuing for two years following the birth of the child. Tested with both white and African American families in rural and urban settings, this program is designed to help women improve their prenatal health and the outcomes of pregnancy by encouraging good health habits, giving mothers the skills they need to care for their infants and toddlers, and improving women's own personal development.[35] Follow-up showed that this program's positive outcomes had long-term effects for both mothers and children. During the first fifteen years after delivery of their first child, unmarried women who received nurse visits had 31 percent fewer subsequent births, longer intervals between births, fewer months on welfare, 44 percent fewer behavioral problems due to alcohol and drug abuse, 69 percent fewer arrests, and 81 percent fewer criminal convictions than those in the control group. Adolescents whose mother had received nurse home visits more than a decade earlier were 60 percent less likely to have run away, 56 percent less likely to have been arrested, and 80 percent less likely to have been convicted of a criminal violation than adolescents whose mothers had not received visits.[36]

Project Toward No Drug Abuse (Project TND) Project TND targets high school youths (ages fourteen to nineteen) who are at risk for drug abuse. Over a four- or five-week period, twelve classroom-based lessons offer students cognitive motivation enhancement activities, information about the social and health consequences of drug use, correction of cognitive misperceptions, help with stress management, instruction in active listening, and training in self-control to counteract risk factors for drug abuse.[37] At a one-year follow-up, participants in forty-two schools revealed reduced usage of cigarettes, alcohol, marijuana, and hard drugs.[38]

Promoting Alternative Thinking Strategies (PATHS) A comprehensive program for promoting social and emotional competencies, PATHS focuses on the understanding, expression, and regulation of emotions. The year-long curriculum is designed to be used by teachers and counselors with entire classrooms of children in kindergarten through fifth grade. Lessons include such topics as identifying and labeling feelings, assessing the intensity of feelings, expressing feelings, managing feelings, and delaying gratification. The basic outcome goals are to provide youths with tools to achieve academically and to enhance both the classroom atmosphere and the learning process.[39] Evaluations of this program have found positive behavioral changes related to peer aggression, hyperactivity, and conduct problems.[40]

These prevention programs are promising in their diversity and range of offerings. They work to prevent delinquency through family-, school-, peer-group-, and community-based interventions.

Programs That Work

Joy Dryfoos's 1990s analysis of the 100 most successful delinquency prevention programs tried through the 1980s identified the following common program components:

- High-risk children are attached to a responsible adult who is responsive to that child's needs. Techniques typically include individual counseling and small group meetings, individual tutoring and mentoring, and case management.
- A number of different kinds of programs and services are in place in a communitywide, multiagency, collaborative approach. Partners in the communitywide network include schools, businesses, community health and social agencies, church groups, police, courts, and universities.

Serena Williams visits with children at a Boys and Girls Club in Los Angeles. ■ **How do young people benefit from having role models like Ms. Williams?**

- In successful programs, an emphasis is placed on early identification and intervention, in which children and families are reached in the early stages of development of problem behaviors. As demonstrated in data on pregnancy, school achievement, substance abuse, and delinquency prevention, early identification and intervention have both short- and long-term benefits.

- The more successful programs located outside the school generally provide needed though controversial services, such as family planning and overnight shelter for homeless and runaway youths. These programs appeal to youngsters "turned off" by the school system. They also have the advantage of being able to offer weekend and summer programs.

- Many successful programs feature professional or nonprofessional staff who require training to implement the program. For example, Life Skills Training, school-based management, cooperative learning, and team teaching require extensive in-service training and ongoing supervision.

- Personal and social skills training are also found in many of these programs. This approach involves teaching youths about their own risky behavior, providing them with coping skills, and helping them make healthy decisions about the future.

- Several of the successful approaches use older peers to influence or help younger children, either in social skills training or as tutors. The training and supervision by the peer mentors appear to be important aspects of this component.[41]

In sum, the two program components that appeared to have the widest application were (1) providing individual attention to high-risk youngsters and (2) developing broad communitywide interventions.

Web **PLACES** 12.2

Visit the National Mentoring Partnership website via **www .justicestudies.com/ WebPlaces**.

Web **PLACES** 12.3

Visit the National Youth Violence Prevention Resource Center's website via **www. justicestudies .com/WebPlaces**.

Comprehensive Delinquency Prevention

Another prevention strategy emerged in the 1990s. Based on research spearheaded and funded by the Office of Juvenile Justice and Delinquency Prevention, a consensus developed that the most effective strategy for juvenile corrections is to focus comprehensive prevention and diversion emphases on high-risk juveniles who commit violent behaviors. These juveniles, the ones that officials are quick to dump into the adult system, commit the more serious and most frequent delinquent acts. At the same time that the seriousness of their behaviors was affecting changes in juvenile codes across the nation, research was beginning to find that these high-risk youths can be impacted by well-equipped and well-implemented prevention and treatment programs.[42]

Such programs are based on the assumption that the juvenile justice system does not see most serious offenders until it is too late to intervene effectively.[43] This strategy also presumes that if we want to reduce the overall violence in American society, it is necessary to successfully intervene in the lives of high-risk youthful offenders, who commit about 75 percent of all violent juvenile offenses.[44]

The general characteristics of these comprehensive programs is that they address key areas of risk in youths' lives, seek to strengthen the personal and institutional factors contributing to healthy adolescent development, provide adequate support and supervision, and offer youths a long-term stake in the community.[45] It is emphasized that these prevention programs for high-risk youths must be integrated with local police, child welfare, social service, school, and family preservation programs. Comprehensive approaches to delinquency prevention and intervention require strong collaborative efforts between the juvenile justice system and other service provision systems, including health, mental health, child welfare, and education. An important component of a community's comprehensive plan is to develop mechanisms that effectively link these service providers at the program level.[46]

> " Comprehensive approaches to delinquency prevention require strong collaborative efforts. "

The comprehensive or multisystemic aspects of these programs are designed to deal simultaneously with many aspects of youths' lives. The intent is that they are intensive, often involving weekly or even daily contacts with at-risk youths. They build on youths' strengths, rather than focusing on their deficiencies. These programs operate mostly, though not exclusively, outside the formal justice system, under a variety of public, nonprofit, or university auspices. Finally, they combine accountability and sanctions with increasingly intensive rehabilitation and treatment services. This is achieved through a system of graduated sanctions, in which an integrated approach is used to stop the penetration of youthful offenders into the system.[47] See Figure 12.1 for an overview of this comprehensive prevention strategy.

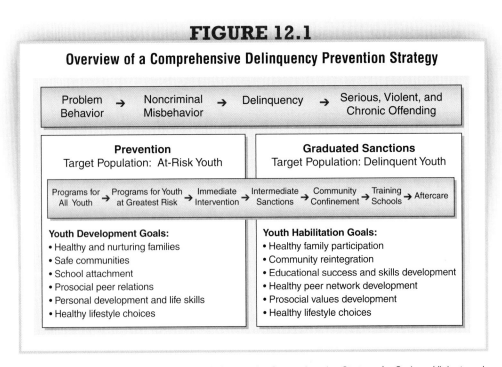

FIGURE 12.1

Overview of a Comprehensive Delinquency Prevention Strategy

Problem Behavior → Noncriminal Misbehavior → Delinquency → Serious, Violent, and Chronic Offending

Prevention
Target Population: At-Risk Youth

Graduated Sanctions
Target Population: Delinquent Youth

Programs for All Youth → Programs for Youth at Greatest Risk → Immediate Intervention → Intermediate Sanctions → Community Confinement → Training Schools → Aftercare

Youth Development Goals:
• Healthy and nurturing families
• Safe communities
• School attachment
• Prosocial peer relations
• Personal development and life skills
• Healthy lifestyle choices

Youth Habilitation Goals:
• Healthy family participation
• Community reintegration
• Educational success and skills development
• Healthy peer network development
• Prosocial values development
• Healthy lifestyle choices

Source: Mark A. Matese and John A. Tuell, *Update on the Comprehensive Strategy for Serious, Violent, and Chronic Juvenile Offenders* (Washington, D.C.: Office of Justice Programs; Office of Juvenile Justice and Delinquency Prevention, 1998), p. 1. Reprinted with permission from the U.S. Department of Justice.

In 1996, three communities—Lee and Duval Counties in Florida, and San Diego County in California—collaborated with the Office of Juvenile Justice and Delinquency Prevention to apply the processes and principles set forth in the OJJDP's *Comprehensive Strategy* statement. Initial evaluations of the three pilot projects reported that each of the three sites had benefited significantly from the comprehensive planning process.[48] The following were among the accomplishments identified in a 2000 report:

- Enhanced communitywide understanding of prevention services and sanctions options for juveniles.
- Expanded networking capacity and better coordination among agencies and service providers.
- Institution of performance measurement systems.
- Hiring of staff to spearhead ongoing Comprehensive Strategy planning and implementation efforts.
- Development of comprehensive five-year strategic action plans.[49]

How Diversion Works

The emphasis on **diversion programs** for youthful offenders began in 1967 when the President's Commission on Law Enforcement and Administration of Justice recommended the establishment of alternatives to the juvenile justice system.[50] This recommendation was based on the labeling perspective and Edwin Sutherland's differential association theory (see Chapters 5 and 6). The National Strategy for Youth Development and Delinquency Prevention tied labeling theory to diversion in identifying three processes that block juveniles from satisfactory maturation and weaken their ties to societal norms: the entrapment of negative labeling; limited access to acceptable social norms; and the resulting process of reflection, alienation, and estrangement.[51] Sutherland's differential association theory provided another justification for diversion, because it holds that individuals learn delinquent behavior from "significant others." Policymakers began to be concerned about placing status offenders and minor offenders with serious offenders because the former would learn delinquent motives, techniques, and rationalization from the latter.[52]

diversion programs

Dispositional alternatives for youthful offenders that exist outside of the formal juvenile justice system.

Traditional Forms of Diversion

Early proponents of diversion programs also claimed that these interventions offered numerous other advantages that would lead to a more effective and humane justice process. These included the reduction of caseloads, a more efficient administration of the juvenile justice system, and provision of therapeutic environments in which children and parents could resolve family conflicts.[53]

Diversion can come either from the police and the courts or from agencies outside the juvenile justice system (such as drop-in centers, alternative schools, social and mental health clinics, and youth service bureaus). With diversion initiated by the courts or police, the justice subsystems retain control over youthful offenders. But even with diversion outside the formal jurisdiction of the justice system, youthful offenders are usually referred back to the juvenile court if they do not participate in these programs.

Web PLACES 12.4

Visit the National Center for Mental Health and Juvenile Justice's website via **www.justicestudies.com/WebPlaces**.

The most positive characteristic of traditional diversionary programs is that they minimize the penetration of youthful offenders into the justice system.[54] Yet empirical studies of diversion generally have not demonstrated that doing something (treatment or services) is necessarily better than doing nothing. Researchers warn that the overlooked negative consequences of diversion challenge the viability of this concept.[55] Some of these negative effects include widening the net of juvenile justice by increasing the number of youths under the control of the system, increasing the size of the system (budget and staff), creating new legal entities, altering traditional programs, ignoring clients' due process rights or constitutional safeguards, and labeling minor offenders.[56]

In sum, excited by the original vision of diversion, reformers promised that it would bring far-reaching, positive changes in juvenile justice. But the problem does not rest with the original vision: It is in the business of implementation that things have gone wrong—goals are displaced, and vested interests operate. Administrators of these programs too often made the wrong decisions about the wrong young people at the wrong time.[57]

New Forms of Diversion

Web PLACES 12.5

Visit the National Youth Court Center's website via **www .justicestudies.com/ WebPlaces**.

In the 1990s, a new form of diversion developed in the United States. Expressions of this new form included community courts, alternative dispute resolution, gun courts, teen courts, and drug courts. Community courts offer a less bureaucratic and more timely response to offenses against the community. An offender tried in community court typically will be required to complete a restorative contract, including restitution payments. Alternative dispute resolution, such as family group conferences and restorative justice conferences, involve carefully structured meetings among offenders, victims, their families, and other members of the community. Gun courts provide intensive behavioral and attitudinal interventions that are designed to affect juveniles' orientation to weapons and increase their awareness of the reality of weapon injuries. Teen courts, which are also known as peer juries or youth courts, represent voluntary, nonjudicial alternatives for juveniles charged with minor law violations. Finally, drug courts offer such legal incentives as deferred prosecution for drug defendants willing to participate in drug treatment.[58] Teen courts, drug courts, and juvenile mediation programs are described in greater detail.

teen courts

Voluntary nonjudicial forums, also known as youth courts, that keep minor offenders out of the formal justice system.

Teen Courts   Also known as youth courts, **teen courts** have become a widely used intervention for young, usually first-time offenders. In 1998, a national evaluation of teen courts was conducted; a total of 335 teen court programs responded, which was more than 70 percent of the programs contacted.[59]

More than two-thirds of the court programs surveyed indicated that they had existed for less than five years; 20 percent had been operating for less than one year. Most teen courts have relatively small caseloads: 48 percent of programs surveyed revealed that they received fewer than 100 referrals per year. Survey authors also indicate that teen courts in the United States handled about 100,000 cases in 2002.[60]

Four possible case-processing models can be used by teen courts:

Web LIBRARY 12.3

Read the OJJDP publication *Juvenile Drug Court Programs* at **www.justicestudies.com/ WebLibrary**.

- *Adult judge:* An adult serves as judge and rules on legal terminology and courtroom procedure. Youths serve as attorneys, jurors, clerks, bailiffs, and so forth.
- *Youth judge:* This is similar to the adult judge model, but a youth serves as judge.
- *Tribunal:* Youth attorneys present the case to a panel of three youth judges, who decide the appropriate disposition for the defendant. A jury is not used.
- *Peer jury:* This model does not use youth attorneys: The case is presented to a youth jury by a youth or adult. The youth jury then questions the defendant directly.[61]

Most teen courts surveyed indicated that they used only one case-processing model; 47 percent used the adult judge model, 12 percent used the peer jury model, 10 percent used the tribunal model, and 9 percent used the youth judge model. The remaining 22 percent used more than one case-processing model. (See Table 12.2.)[62]

Teen courts usually handle first-time offenders who are charged with such offenses as theft, misdemeanor assault, disorderly conduct, and possession of alcohol. The majority (87 percent) of teen courts reported that they rarely or never accept juveniles with prior arrest records. Community service was most frequently used as a disposition in teen court cases. Other dispositions that were used included victim apology letters (86 percent), apology essays (79 percent), teen court jury duty (75 percent), drug/alcohol classes (59 percent), and monetary restitution (34 percent). The number of teen courts in the United States grew from only 50 in 1991 to 400 to 500 by 1998; and estimates put the number of teen courts in the United States at 800 in 2002.[63]

TABLE 12.2

Teen Court Case-Processing Models

The most popular teen court model is an adult judge with youth attorneys.

TEEN COURT MODEL	PERCENT OF U.S. TEEN COURTS USING EACH MODEL		
	USED EXCLUSIVELY	USED IN SOME CASES	TOTAL
Adult Judge	47%	17%	64%
Youth Judge	9	5	14
Tribunal	10	2	12
Peer Jury	12	14	26

Source: Jeffrey Butts et al., "Teen Courts in the United States: A Profile of Current Programs," *OJJDP Fact Sheet* (Washington, D.C.: Office of Juvenile Justice and Delinquency Prevention, 1999), p. 2. Reprinted with permission from the U.S. Department of Justice.

The Juvenile Drug Court Movement   By 2003, approximately 300 **juvenile drug courts** had opened and another 100 were being planned. The juvenile drug court movement is part of the adult drug court movement that has been stimulated by Title V of the Violent Crime Control and Law Enforcement Act of 1994. This act authorizes the U.S. attorney general to make grants to states, state and local courts, units of local government, and Indian tribal governments to establish drug courts.[64]

A number of strategies are common to juvenile drug courts compared with traditional juvenile courts:

- Much earlier and much more comprehensive intake assessments.
- Much greater focus on the functioning of the juvenile and the family throughout the juvenile court system.
- Much closer integration of the information obtained during the assessment process as it relates to the juvenile and the family.
- Much greater coordination among the court, the treatment community, the school system, and other community agencies in responding to the needs of the juvenile and the court.
- Much more active and continuous judicial supervision of the juvenile's case and treatment process.
- Increased use of immediate sanctions for noncompliance and incentives for progress for both the juvenile and the family.[65]

In 1997, six states operated juvenile drug courts, with the greatest activity in California (two programs) and Florida (four programs). For example, the Escambia County Juvenile Drug Court (Pensacola, Florida) began operations in April 1996. It is a twelve-month, three-phase approach to treating substance use and abuse. Phase I lasts about two months, Phase II lasts four months, and Phase III lasts six months. The drug court judge supervises treatment of up to forty offenders by reviewing reports from treatment personnel to determine the need for either positive or negative incentives to encourage participation and involvement.[66]

In 2000, using Braithwaite's theory of reintegrative shaming as an interpretative framework, Terance D. Miethe, Hong Lu, and Erin Reese studied a drug court and found that the risks of recidivism for drug court participants were significantly higher than for comparable offenders processed in conventional courts. Field observation, as well as a more detailed examination of daily practices, helped explain these unexpected findings: It emerged that the drug court is actually more stigmatizing than the conventional court process and is not reintegrative enough in its orientation toward punishment.[67] It remains to be seen whether such discouraging findings will affect the popularity of the juvenile court movement.

juvenile drug courts

Special courts designed for nonviolent youthful offenders with substance abuse problems who require integrated sanctions and services such as mandatory drug testing, substance abuse treatment, supervised release, and aftercare.

The staff of the Lewiston, Maine, Family Treatment Drug Court. The court's motto is "Focusing on the safety and welfare of children while expanding services to families with substance abuse." The court works to serves those families whose children are at risk of abuse or neglect due to parental abuse of drugs or alcohol. ■ **How are drug courts different from other courts?**

Juvenile Mediation Program   The purpose of a juvenile mediation program is to bring all involved parties together to resolve differences without court involvement. Various types of juvenile mediation programs can be found across the nation. In 2005, there were twenty California courts with juvenile dependency mediation programs, eleven juvenile conflict resolution programs in Massachusetts, five juvenile mediation programs in West Virginia, and the juvenile mediation program in Cook County whose model is influencing the establishment of other programs in Illinois.[68]

The Juvenile Mediation Program in Cook County began in 1992 and offers mediation to the juvenile and the victim by the State's Attorney before the case has been heard by a court. If the parties accept mediation, their case is referred to the Center for Conflict Resolution (CCR). In 2003, the CCR mediated eighty-four cases referred by the State's Attorney's Office. The model for this program appears to be influencing other communities. For example, in 2002 the Sangamon County (Illinois) juvenile mediation program was launched.[69]

The juvenile mediation program that serves Brooke, Hancock, Marshall, Ohio, Tyler, and Wetzel counties in West Virginia works with school-age children and adolescents who are ages six to eighteen and their families or guardians. First established in 1997 in Brooke County, it has since spread to the other five counties.

The program is designed to last no more than ninety days and is terminated under one of the following conditions: (1) Juveniles successfully complete the required contractual agreement in ninety days; (2) juveniles fail to meet the required agreement and are referred to the probation department for formal proceedings; or (3) the mediator recommends dismissal prior to disposition. As of September 30, 2000, the rate of successful contract resolutions was 93 percent, or 625 of the first 670 participants. As of July 1, 2001, all 625 juveniles had remained free of delinquent and status offenses.[70]

The Treatment Debate

When prevention or diversionary interventions fail to be effective, it is necessary to turn to rehabilitative interventions, commonly called corrections. Correctional treatment can be thought of as any means taken to correct an offender's character, habits, attitudes, or behavior patterns so as to overcome his or her delinquent propensities.[71] Correctional treatment came under growing criticism in the late 1960s and early 1970s.

In 1966, reporting on the results of 100 empirical evaluations of treatment, Walter C. Bailey concluded that there seemed to be little evidence that correctional treatment was effective.[72] In 1971, James Robison and Gerald Smith added that "there is no evidence to support any program's claim to superior rehabilitative strategy."[73] In 1974, the late Robert Martinson startled both correctional personnel and the public with the pronouncement that "with few and isolated exceptions, the rehabilitative efforts that have been reported so far have had no appreciable effect on recidivism."[74] The media quickly simplified Martinson's statement into the idea that **"nothing works"** in correctional treatment. In 1975, Douglas Lipton, Robert Martinson, and Judith Wilks published *The Effectiveness of Correctional Treatment*, which critically evaluated the effectiveness of treatment programs.[75] In that same year, Martinson announced on *60 Minutes* that "there is no evidence that correctional rehabilitation reduces recidivism."[76] A spirited debate on the "nothing works" thesis has continued to rage since the late 1970s.

Ted Palmer, a correctional researcher in California, challenged Lipton and his colleagues' research by tabulating eighty-two studies mentioned in the book and showing that thirty-nine of them, or 48 percent, had positive or partly positive results on recidivism.[77] Palmer used Martinson's own words to reject the "nothing works" thesis:

> These programs seem to work best when they are new, when their subjects are amenable to treatment in the first place, and when the counselors are not only trained people, but "good people" as well.[78]

"nothing works"
The claim that correctional treatment is ineffective in reducing recidivism of correctional clients.

A teenage boy works with a counselor. Studies seem to show that recidivism among delinquents can be prevented when treatment programs target people who are amenable to treatment. ■ **How might amenable subjects be identified?**

An Integrated Approach to Assessment and Treatment

Washington, Texas, and Colorado have already developed an integrated comprehensive treatment model, and California is in the process of developing one. These programs are basing their treatment philosophy and interventions on cognitive-behavior treatment. The particulars of these interventions may differ, but the concepts behind these treatment models are more or less the same. The Washington State Juvenile Rehabilitation Administration is the agency with the most fully documented model. This rehabilitative model conceptually unites evidence-based programs in a coherent and clearly articulated way. Open-ended, it can embrace any evidence-based intervention consistent with a cognitive-behavior model; the model has training materials and an implementation plan that can be modified over time to tailor it to the specific or changing needs it faces.

In its Integrated Treatment Model, the Division of Juvenile Justice in California provides the central guiding vision uniting screening, assessment, case planning, treatment, transition, and aftercare. These concepts are used across all parts of the agency, including the core treatment program, special treatment programs, academic and vocational education, work, recreation, mental health, and parole. Its principles are transparent, effective, recognizable, and universal. Everyone is a treatment provider; administrators, line staff, treatment providers, and support staff are receive training in the model. This not only struc-

tures the environment to help promote success in changing behavior, but also creates a common treatment vocabulary for all parts of the agency.

A central feature of the Integrated Treatment Model is the use of behavioral analysis in treatment planning. Behavioral analysis has a long history as a research and assessment tool in psychology. It examines the links in the behavior chain, which are:

- Pre-existing risk factors
- Cues
- Emotions
- Cognitive distortions ("thinking errors")
- Behavioral responses
- Outcomes that reinforce the behavior

Figure 12.2 illustrates the links in the behavior chain.

The advantages of an integrated treatment model, especially those possessing the clarity of a single modality as these models have, are that all parts of the system are working together to achieve a positive outcome for youngsters involved in the system, and this integrated approach increases the likelihood of identifying the problems behavior(s) and the interventions that should have the best results.

> ■ Has juvenile corrections in your state developed an integrated approach? If not, you might consider making recommendations to the agency responsible for juvenile corrections in the state in which you live.

Source: Christopher Murray, Chris Baird, Ned Loughran, Fred Mills, and John Platt, *Safety and Welfare Plan; Implementing Reform in California* (Sacramento: California Department of Corrections and Rehabilitation, Division of Juvenile Justice, 2006), pp. 42, 43, and 47.

FIGURE 12.2

Links in the Behavior Chain as Seen by the Integrated Treatment Model

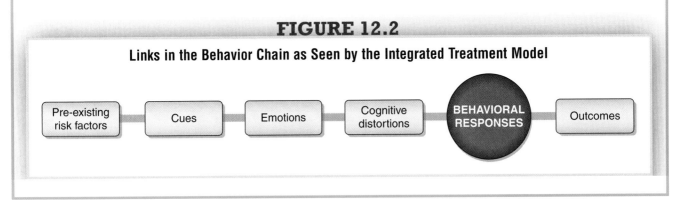

Paul Gendreau and Robert R. Ross reviewed the literature published between 1973 and 1978 and found that 86 percent of the ninety-five intervention programs studied reported success.[79] According to Gendreau and Ross, this success rate was "convincing evidence that some treatment programs, when they are applied with integrity by competent practitioners in appropriate target populations, can be effective in preventing crime or reducing recidivism."[80] In the late 1970s, Martinson conceded that "contrary to [his] previous position, some treatment programs *do* have an appreciable effect on recidivism. Some programs are indeed beneficial."[81] But, despite Martinson's recantation of his "nothing works" thesis and Palmer's and Gendreau and Ross's defense of correctional treatment, the general mood regarding offender rehabilitation in the late 1970s and early 1980s was one of pessimism and discouragement.

In the late 1980s, Gendreau and Ross reviewed the offender rehabilitation literature for the period between 1981 and 1987 and again found that the number and variety of successful reported attempts at reducing delinquent behavior disproved the "nothing works" hypothesis.[82] Moreover, the rehabilitative evidence in the 1980s grew at a much greater rate than it did during the 1970s and inspired several strategies for developing more effective programs.[83]

Several meta-analyses evaluating the effectiveness of correctional treatment have been done. The statistical tool of meta-analysis has been developed to enable reviewers to combine findings from different experiments. In meta-analysis, the "aggregation and side-by-side analysis of large numbers of experimental studies" is undertaken.[84] One of the advantages of meta-analysis is that it can "incorporate adjustments for the fact that studies vary considerably in the degree of rigor of their experimental design."[85] In summarizing the findings of six meta-analyses, James McGuire and Phillip Priestly concluded that in taking all of the meta-analyses together, "the net effect of treatment is, on an average, a reduction in recidivism rates of between 10 percent and 12 percent."[86]

One positive area of innovation in correctional treatment is that a number of states, including California, Colorado, Texas, and Washington, have either implemented an integrated approach to assessment and treatment or are in the process of developing one. See Focus on Social Policy 12.2 for a description of how these states have used an integrated approach to refocus their rehabilitative efforts.

Frequently Used Treatment Modalities

Various treatment modalities are used widely in community-based corrections and have been established in nearly every training school in the United States. Psychotherapy, transactional analysis, reality therapy, behavior modification, family therapy, guided group interaction, and positive peer culture are the traditional treatment modalities most commonly used in juvenile justice. Drug and alcohol abuse interventions and cognitive-behavior therapies also are used increasingly.

Psychotherapy

Various adaptations of Freudian **psychotherapy** have been used by psychiatrists, clinical psychologists, and psychiatric social workers since the early twentieth century. Either in a one-to-one relationship with a therapist or in a group context, juvenile offenders are encouraged to talk about past conflicts that cause them to express emotional problems through aggressive or antisocial behavior. The insight that offenders gain from this individual or group psychotherapy supposedly helps them resolve the conflicts and unconscious needs that drive them to crime. As a final step of psychotherapy, youthful offenders become responsible for their own behavior.

Within the community, psychotherapy has been used recently much more with middle- and upper-class youthful offenders than with lower-class youngsters. Middle- and upper-class youths who abuse drugs or alcohol or who have conflicts at home are likely to be referred for psychotherapy. Other than in a few private settings, little psychotherapy takes place in institutional contexts. The few psychiatrists and clinical psychologists available in these settings spend most of their time doing intake evaluations for classification purposes and crisis intervention with acting-out youths. Crisis intervention generally consists of one interview in which the therapist recommends a treatment plan for the resident's cottage; psychiatrists may also prescribe medication to calm a youth.

psychotherapy

A treatment method in which various adaptations of Freudian therapy are used by psychiatrists, clinical psychologists, and psychiatric social workers to encourage delinquents to talk about past conflicts that cause them to express emotional problems through aggressive or antisocial behavior.

Homeboy Industries Goes Gang-Busters

LOS ANGELES—On the mean streets from East L.A. to South-Central L.A., gang members are leaving the thug life and trying to make it in a 60-person business called Homeboy Industries.

They come from the region's most notorious gangs and housing projects. But they've chosen to leave their crews and take up honest, blue-collar trades that often resurrect their lives. Their slogans: "Jobs, Not Jails" and "Nothing Stops a Bullet Like a Job."

"When I got that first paycheck, damn, it made me feel good," says Gabriel Flores, 25, a former gang member who works at Homeboy Industries' silk-screen business. "I didn't go steal a car or sell drugs for money. I worked for it."

The Rev. Gregory Boyle, a Jesuit priest known to homies as *G-Dog* or "Father Greg," began Homeboy Industries in 1992 as a job-training program to salvage the futures of gang members.

Many had long arrest and prison records, and nearly all had no work skills. But Boyle and Homeboy Industries officials have counseled and found jobs for several thousand youths from 500 Los Angeles gangs—many of them enemies on the streets. Law enforcement officials have criticized Homeboy Industries for going too easy on gang members. But the non-profit and Boyle also have been praised by first lady Laura Bush, and they have gained national media attention.

Now Homeboy Industries—funded mostly by local and federal grants and foundation gifts—hopes to become more independent by growing its several small businesses, including its moneymaking silk-screen and merchandising operation.

"Two years ago, we were just a little non-profit," says Michael Baca, the operations manager. "But now we're a $3 million organization with businesses and investors—people interested in helping us with our mission."

To that end, Homeboy Industries—with the help of its board, business consultants and actors Angelica Huston and Martin Sheen—has embarked on corporate-style goals, including:

- **A new office project.** Homeboy Industries hopes to break ground this fall on

A former gang member displays tattoos of the "Florencia" gang on his neck, outside the offices of Homeboy Industries in East Los Angeles. Homeboy Industries works to find jobs and provide other services to help gang members leave gangs. ■ **How can jobs help people leave gangs?**

a two-story office-and-retail building on a blighted lot between downtown and Chinatown here. So far, Homeboy Industries has raised $4 million of the $10 million needed to build and operate the development, which it will own and use for its businesses.

- **Business and financial planning.** Homeboy Industries is developing long-term business strategies, yet to be disclosed, while Chief Financial Officer Bruce Palmore gets its finances in order. Accounting had been divided among Homeboy Industries' different businesses; now he's consolidating the books and keeping closer track of income and spending.

- **Small businesses.** Homeboy Industries' popular silk-screening business sells wholesale clothing and other goods with the "Homeboy Industries" logo. The only profitable Homeboy Industries business, it's growing at a double-digit pace, with corporate and non-profit customers nationwide.

The Homegirl Café and catering service, run by manager and cook Patricia Zarate, opened early this year and will expand in the coming months.

On a recent weekday, the café was

jammed after a review in the *Los Angeles Times* raved about its "light, fresh Mexican food," including tofu enchiladas, fish and chili soups, and salads.

Homeboy Industries' landscaping and maintenance business landed a major contract with the Metropolitan Transportation Agency, which runs the Metro light-rail line here.

Lastly, the non-profit plans to reopen its bakery, which burned down a few years ago. Former gang members are training at the *Mi Vida*-My Life bakery in Lynwood, and they'll soon market Homeboy Industries breads, muffins and cakes to cafes and stores.

"Right now, Homeboy Industries is subsidizing these businesses," Baca says. "We want these businesses to turn a profit, so they can subsidize Homeboy Industries."

The national attention won't hurt. Homeboy Industries has been featured on CBS News' *60 Minutes* and other media outlets. Boyle also is the subject of a book, *G-Dog and the Homeboys*, by Celeste Fremon.

In April, 2005, Laura Bush—publicizing a three-year, $150-million campaign by the White House to combat street gangs—visited the silk-screen business and praised the former gang members for their hard work.

At Homeboy Industries, young men learn how to control their anger and to treat women respectfully. They learn basic responsibilities, from getting to work on time to answering the telephone professionally. Thousands have had their tattoos removed by laser devices at Homeboy Industries' offices.

Even then, some youths make little or no progress. "It's a little like triage in an emergency room," Boyle says. "The main thing they learn here is resilience: how to cope with whatever the world throws at them without flipping out."

It's hard to imagine the white-bearded, 50-year-old Boyle, with his gentle voice and demeanor, mixing it up with gang members. But he frequently counsels and gives sermons to violent felons in prison.

On a recent June day, the Homeboy Industries office near downtown here is full of tattooed teens and young adults seeking help.

Boyle—who was diagnosed two years ago with leukemia, now in remission—juggles a media interview, phone calls and staff questions as calmly as saying grace before dinner.

A hands-off "CEO," he focuses on his spiritual mission and fundraising for the non-profit, while his managers run the day-to-day job program, counseling, small businesses and finances.

Raised in the Los Angeles suburbs, Boyle, a third-generation Irish-American, landed in East L.A. as a young pastor at Dolores Mission Church 20 years ago. His job-referral program there grew quickly, and his trustworthy reputation spread among gang members.

Today, Boyle calls Homeboy Industries "a bastion of unconditional love" for gang members. The non-profit places 300 youths a year in construction, clerical, textile, health care and other jobs, says Norma Robles Gillette, a former human resources manager at Neutrogena who is Homeboy Industries' job-development supervisor.

Job counselors coach the youths, helping them write their résumés, prepare for job interviews and fit into the business culture.

"We've seen a lot of really smart, talented kids who have been able to succeed in the work world," Robles Gillette says.

Some, such as Grace Nieto, discover hidden skills. Nieto grew up in a Boyle Heights housing project and was the girl-friend of a gang member in her youth. Homeboy Industries found her a job as a production assistant in Hollywood. Today, she jets throughout the country as a freelance production manager of TV commercials.

"Their job program is amazing," Nieto says. "If it wasn't for them, a lot of people—including myself—would never have had their lives changed."

Homeboy Industries executives also laud their wholesale silk-screen operation as a model for their other businesses. The outfit makes T-shirts, sweatshirts, caps, mugs and other goods, and it plans to launch an online business soon.

"We like to say that we were raised in public housing projects, but we're building our business without government assistance," says Ruben Rodriguez, who heads the silk-screen division. He started the business with his wife, Christina, in their garage 10 years ago.

Business is so hot that annual revenue grows 15% to 20% and may hit a record $1 million this year, Rodriguez says. Big customers include Pixar, Power 106 FM radio and universities nationwide. "These kids need jobs, stability in their lives and the tools of education to survive in society," says David Adams, a Homeboy Industries director and chairman of Marcus Adams Capital. "If we can train people and get these businesses to break even, we could move this problem forward."

But even with the new business approach, the homeboys know they're not far from their violent roots. Last year, two men with Homeboy Industries' graffiti-removal service were gunned down and killed.

According to the Los Angeles Police Department, 25-year-old Arturo Casas was shot in a pickup as he waited at a busy intersection one block from Homeboy Industries. Miguel Gomez, 34, was shot several times as he removed graffiti from a commercial building a short drive from Homeboy Industries.

Casas' killing was gang-related, while Gomez's death involved drugs, says LAPD homicide Detective Rick Peterson. The fact that the men worked for Homeboy Industries did not make them targets, he says. Police have identified suspects, but made no arrests, Peterson says.

Peterson praises the program for its "good heart"—especially its work with kids not fully involved in gangs. But he doubts that Homeboy Industries is helping hard-core gangsters. Some of the Homeboy Industries youths still deal drugs, sell guns and take part in drive-by shootings, he says.

"These are people with no loyalty to anything other than their gangs," Peterson says. "If they really want to change, they'd stop acting and dressing like gang members and start improving their lives."

Baca at Homeboy Industries says youths are reprimanded or fired if they commit crimes or come to work drunk or high. "We deal with everyone who is looking for help," Baca says. "In Father Greg's eyes, everyone is created equal."

Former gang member Flores says Homeboy Industries changed his life. As a teenager, Flores, known as "BooBoo," joined the Cypress Park gang in a Latino neighborhood north of downtown Los Angeles.

Over the years, police had arrested Flores on charges of vandalism, gun possession, drug possession and resisting an officer with violence, according to Flores and California Department of Corrections records. He was sentenced to several years in state prison and is working for Homeboy Industries while on parole, according to Flores and Homeboy Industries officials.

Flores met Boyle in jail after hearing that the priest "was cool" and would listen to his problems without judging him. Eventually, the clergyman offered Flores a job at Homeboy Industries' silk-screening business, making $6 an hour. After eight years on the job, Flores is ready for a change. He plans to earn his high school diploma, attend trade school, land a higher-paying job, then buy a house.

"I'm grateful for what Homeboy has done for me, but I don't want to be doing this for the rest of my life," Flores says. "I have goals now."

Source: Edward Iwata, "Homeboy Industries Goes Gang-Busters," *USA Today,* July 12, 2005, p. 1B. Copyright © 2005 by *USA Today.* Reprinted by permission.

Transactional Analysis

transactional analysis (TA)

A therapy, based on interpreting and evaluating personal relationships, that has proved to be of immediate value to many delinquents. Using catchy language, TA promises delinquents who feel "not OK" that several easy steps can be taken to make them "OK."

Transactional analysis (TA) focuses on interpreting and evaluating interpersonal relationships. This treatment modality tries to teach youthful lawbreakers to relate to others in an adult, mature way.[87]

In applying this modality, the TA leader usually first does a script analysis, which is an attempt to understand how the "tapes" of the past are influencing the behavior of the juvenile in the present. This concept of script analysis is based on the premise that human memory acts as a three-track tape that records the events individuals experienced during their first years of life, the meaning attached to those events, and the emotions they experienced when these events occurred. Each person replays his or her tape when similar situations are encountered later in life. The consequence of negative script replay is that many individuals become "losers," failing to attain their goals and becoming involved in self-defeating behavior. The TA leader seeks to discover the youth's script by diagnosing his or her voice, vocabulary, demeanor, gestures, and answers to questions. TA is based on the belief that persons can change their scripts, and the function of the TA leader is to help individuals make this change. For example, if a mother has told her daughter that she will never succeed at anything and if this has become a self-fulfilling prophecy, the therapist tries to communicate to the daughter that she can succeed in achieving her goals.[88]

One of the hoped-for outcomes of the life-script interview is that offenders will be willing to negotiate a treatment contract; that is, the youths will state how they wish to change. This treatment contract normally has both short- and long-range goals, project group goals, academic goals, and social behavior goals. Once goals are set, the youth is considered to be in treatment. Throughout the treatment period these goals and progress toward them are constantly reviewed by staff. Social World of the Delinquent 12.2 relates the success of TA with one youthful offender.

Reality Therapy

reality therapy

A treatment modality based on the principle that individuals must accept responsibility for their behavior.

Reality therapy, a very popular treatment modality, was developed by two Los Angeles psychiatrists, William Glasser and G. L. Harrington. This modality assumes that irresponsible behavior arises when persons are unable to fulfill their basic needs. According to this approach, the basic human needs are relatedness and respect, and one satisfies these needs by doing what is realistic, responsible, and right.[89]

The three Rs of reality therapy are reality, responsibility, and right-and-wrong. In using this approach with older delinquent girls at the Ventura School in California, Glasser always made each adolescent face the reality of her behavior in the present; he refused to accept any excuse for irresponsible behavior; and he expected the girls to maintain a satisfactory standard of behavior.[90]

> " Reality therapy assumes that irresponsible behavior arises when persons are unable to fulfill their basic needs. "

There are several advantages in using this modality with juveniles. The first is that paraprofessionals can play a major role in working with clients, because the basic tenets are easily learned. Second, paraprofessionals are much more attracted to the basic assumptions of reality therapy than to other treatment modalities. For example, they like its emphasis on responsibility, its negation of extenuating circumstances, and its focus on the present. Third, it seems to be easier to achieve consistent treatment with this modality.

Behavior Modification

behavior modification

A psychological treatment method that rewards appropriate behavior positively, immediately, and systematically and assumes that rewards increase the occurrence of desired behavior.

Behavior modification therapy applies instrumental learning theory to problems of human behavior. It is based on the assumption that all behavior is under the control of its consequences in the external environment. If a behavior is reinforced immediately and systematically in a positive way, the frequency and rate of that behavior should increase, but if a behavior does not receive a positive reinforcement, the frequency should decrease. Attention, praise, money, food, and privileges are positive reinforcers; threats, confinement, punishment, and ridicule are negative reinforcers. Positive reinforcers produce the more effective and enduring behavior changes. A wide variety of techniques reinforce positive and extinguish negative behavior. They include systematic desensitization, extinction of undesirable responses, training in assertiveness, counterconditioning, conditioning against avoidance responses, and the use of tokens. Behavior modification uses environmental contingencies to alter the offender's response.[91]

One of the great strengths of behavior modification therapy is that it appears to have a greater impact on the sociopathic offender than other treatment modalities. A major reason for this is that behavior modification techniques can immediately reinforce target behaviors. Behavior modification also appears to have a greater impact on manipulating youths than more traditional therapies. Furthermore, behavior modification is specific and is often effective in short-term intervention. Finally, behavior modification is one of the more flexible of the treatment modalities.[92]

Critics of behavior modification have leveled several major criticisms against it. One of the most frequent attacks states that treating only the offender's overt symptoms is too superficial to be effective. Many critics also charge that this treatment method is not lasting. Humanists believe that the human being is too unique and complicated to be treated only according to his or her overt behavior. Another criticism states that the principles of behavior modification require considerable consistency and continuity, if not sophistication, which is atypical of correctional treatment. Finally, critics feel that it is very difficult to apply behavior modification to youths who do not manifest overt behavioral problems.

Guided Group Interaction

Guided group interaction (GGI) is an appropriate design for residential treatment settings. It has been used in at least eleven states: Florida, Georgia, Illinois, Kentucky,

guided group interaction (GGI)
Interaction that, whether it occurs in the community or in an institution, places youthful offenders in an intensive group environment under the direction of an adult leader. The guided group interaction process substitutes a whole new structure of beliefs, values, and behaviors for the values of delinquent peer subcultures.

Treatment modalities such as reality therapy, behavior modification, and positive peer culture can help young people turn their lives around. ■ **Which of the treatment strategies discussed in this chapter do you think would be most effective at dealing with the problems of young people today? Why?**

Maryland, Michigan, Minnesota, New Hampshire, New Jersey, South Dakota, and West Virginia. Since the 1950s, when this modality was first used, it has been based on the assumption that peers could confront other peers and force them to face the reality of their behavior more effectively than could staff.

The GGI approach is characterized by giving residents responsibility for decision making. The adult leader constantly refers the decision making back to the group. When informed that a fellow group member planned to run away, for example, one staff member retorted: "So what do you want me to do? He's your buddy; he's part of your group. You can talk to him if you have to; but it's up to all of you to help one another."[93]

Youthful offenders usually go through several stages in becoming involved in guided group interaction. Youths initially are guarded in their responses, but as their defenses begin to weaken, they learn to give up their games and defenses because of the encouragement received from peers and the group leader. In the second stage, the residents' interpersonal problems are brought into the open. They are encouraged to talk about themselves and to have their values scrutinized and challenged by the group. In the third stage, the offenders begin to examine the difficulties they have had with their environment. The group members, who begin to develop real trust among themselves, probe the problems of institutional and street living. The fourth stage is that in which the offenders feel secure and accept reeducation. When they see that their problems are not unique and that dealing with them is possible, they feel less antagonistic toward the group and become more receptive to what is said. In the final stage, the residents set up an outline of a plan for change. Using his or her own self-evaluation, as well as that of the group, each youth makes a conscious decision about the way he or she wants to behave in the future.[94]

A strength of GGI is its determination to circumvent the values of the delinquent-peer subculture. This modality, in urging residents to be honest and open with each other, attempts to move group participants to a more positive, prosocial stance.

Another advantage is that it represents a comprehensive strategy for dealing with troubled youths. It is, in effect, a total system for mitigating the impact of a delinquent subculture. A third advantage is that GGI has gained acceptance on the state level. Also important is the fact that GGI can be led by line staff, thereby increasing staff involvement in the treatment process. A final advantage is that responsibility is given to offenders; thus, in interacting with peers, offenders become aware of their problems and are directed toward their resolution.

Positive Peer Culture

The concept of **positive peer culture** (PPC) generated considerable excitement in juvenile corrections in the 1970s. Developed by Harry Vorrath and associates as an outgrowth of guided group interaction, PPC has been implemented in all of the juvenile state institutions in West Virginia, Michigan, and Missouri.[95]

Vorrath believes that PPC "is a total system for building positive youth subcultures."[96] The main philosophy of PPC is to "turn around" the negative peer culture and to mobilize the power of the peer group in a positive way. PPC does this by teaching group members to care for one another: Caring is defined as wanting what is best for a person. Vorrath believes that once caring becomes "fashionable" and is accepted by the group, "hurting goes out of style."[97]

Positive peer culture involves the same stages as GGI, but it places more emphasis on positive behavior. Group members learn to speak of positive behaviors as "great," "intelligent," "independent," "improving," and "winning." In contrast, negative behavior is described as "childish," "unintelligent," "helpless," "destructive," "copping out," and "losing."

positive peer culture
A group treatment modality that (like its parent model, guided group interaction) aims to build a positive youth subculture; it encompasses a strategy that extends to all aspects of daily life.

Rational Emotive Therapy

From their research with the criminally insane at St. Elizabeth Hospital in Washington, D.C., Samuel Yochelson and Stanton E. Samenow concluded that there is a criminal personality that incorporates some fifty-two errors in thinking.[98] The basic rationale of **rational emotive therapy** is to identify the errors characteristic of a youthful offender's thinking. These errors include the blaming of others, the attempt to control or manipulate, the inability to empathize, the desire to play a victim role, the failure to accept obligations, and the attempt to lie or confuse.[99]

The therapist attempts to determine the sequence of thoughts, feelings, events, and other factors that make up the "offense syndrome" and then get the offender to "own" his or her behaviors. Once the offender owns the behaviors, he or she is taught how to intervene in the illegal behavior when it first starts to bring it under control. After a prolonged period of treatment, the offender is moved into residential aftercare, joins a support group, and is given continued access to treatment.[100]

This is a cognitive restructuring strategy that is specifically targeted at the dysfunctional cognitive patterns of offenders. These patterns are thinking errors that support, excuse, and even reinforce criminal behavior. This approach presumes that the use of such errors releases inhibitions toward committing a crime, which "frees" one to behave in a criminal or delinquent manner. The job of the counselor is to correct these thinking errors, and the task of the facility is to provide an environment in which such errors can be corrected by treatment and custody staff and also by residents in group sessions or day-to-day institutional living.[101]

In the 1980s, this notion that offenders have certain personality characteristics leading to basic errors in thinking became popular as society's need to control and reform serious habitual offenders increased. During the 1980s, the Ohio Department of Rehabilitation and Correction used this approach in some of its institutions and Paint Creek Youth Center also incorporated Yochelson and Samenow's principles into

rational emotive therapy
A cognitive restructuring strategy that seeks to identify delinquents' thinking errors (blaming others, trying to control or manipulate, failing to empathize, wanting to play the victim, etc.) and then to help young offenders "own" and control their behaviors.

the facility's token economy or point system. During the 1990s, rational emotive therapy was widely adopted throughout the nation.

Drug and Alcohol Abuse Interventions

Drug and alcohol abuse by juveniles, as well as their drug trafficking in the community, constitutes a serious social problem today. A director of guidance in a training school acknowledged the seriousness of the problem when he said, "Rarely do we get a boy who doesn't have some history of drug or alcohol abuse in his background."[102]

Drug and alcohol abuse interventions are increasingly being developed in community-based and institutional settings to assist those who need help with these problems. Training schools are conducting these groups in several ways. Institutionalized juveniles assessed to have a problem with alcohol and/or drugs are placed in a separate cottage or in a chemical abuse group. Specialized staff are hired to work in these cottages or lead these groups. Also, in some training schools, the social worker or another cottage staff member conducts ongoing drug and alcohol abuse groups. Furthermore, outside groups, such as Alcoholics Anonymous (AA) or Narcotics Anonymous (NA) come into the institution and hold group sessions for interested residents.

In view of the extensiveness of the problem of drug use and trafficking among juvenile offenders, too few programs are being offered in juvenile placements. The programs that are offered tend to be relatively unsophisticated, lacking adequate theoretical design, treatment integrity, and evaluation follow-up. Unquestionably, effective drug and alcohol abuse programs represent one of the most important challenges of juvenile justice today.

What Works

The frequent criticism that offender rehabilitation is defective in theory and a disaster in practice has been true on too many occasions. Enforced offender rehabilitation has sometimes resulted in making delinquents worse rather than better. Program designs often have given little consideration to what a particular program can realistically accomplish with a particular group of offenders, and frequently have relied on a single cure for a variety of complex problems. In addition, programs generally have lacked integrity, because they have not delivered the services they claimed with sufficient strength to accomplish the goals of treatment. Furthermore, the research on offender rehabilitation generally has been inadequate, with many projects and reports on rehabilitation almost totally lacking in well-developed research designs.[103]

Still, some progress has been made. Various meta-analyses and literature reviews from the 1980s indicated that treatment programs had somewhat more positive results in reducing recidivism than earlier studies had revealed.[104] The integrated treatment interventions recently developed in four states, based on cognitive behavioral modalities, are also promising indications of an improved quality of treatment in juvenile justice.

> " The frequent criticism that offender rehabilitation is defective in theory and a disaster in practice has been true on too many occasions. "

The challenge of correctional treatment is to discover what works for which offenders in which contexts. In other words, correctional treatment could be more effective if amenable offenders were offered appropriate treatments by matched workers in environments conducive to producing positive effects.[105]

To match up individual offenders with the treatments most likely to benefit them will be no easy task. Only through well-planned and soundly executed research will the necessary information be gained. Back in the 1970s, the Panel of Rehabilitative Techniques recommended the use of the "template-matching technique."[106] This technique creates a set of descriptors, or a "template," of the kinds of people who are most likely to benefit from a particular treatment according to the theory or basic assumptions underlying it.[107] Because of the scarcity of treatment resources, matching programs to those offenders most likely to profit from them is only sensible.

CHAPTER Summary

This chapter points out that the prevention of youth crime is the top priority of juvenile justice agencies. Failing prevention, diversion from formal handling by the juvenile justice system is frequently seen as a desirable alternative for juveniles who break the law. Treatment, the third topic with which this chapter concerns itself, offers hope for youths caught up in the system. It is also important to know that:

- Three different levels of delinquency prevention programs have been identified in this chapter: primary, secondary, and tertiary.

- Primary prevention is focused on modifying general conditions in the physical and social environment that lead to delinquency.

- Secondary prevention programs target particular juveniles who have been identified as living in circumstances that dispose them toward delinquency.

- Tertiary prevention efforts are directed at the root causes of recidivism, and usually work through traditional rehabilitation programs.

- A number of promising delinquency prevention programs were developed in the late nineteenth and early twentieth centuries.

- For prevention programs to have a continuing impact on youth crime in the United States, it will be necessary to modify the underlying social, economic, and political conditions in American society that lead to crime.

- Until those modifications are made, primary and secondary delinquency prevention programs will merely chip away at the tip of the iceberg rather than deal with the root of the delinquency problem.

- Diversion consists of programs sponsored by the police, the juvenile court, and agencies outside the justice system, which aim to help juveniles avoid formal processing by the justice system.

- Drug courts and teen courts are promising forms of diversion that were developed in the late twentieth century and that continue to function effectively today.

- Large training schools are among the least promising environments for effective treatment programs.

- Even in community-based programs, a lack of resources, overworked staff, clients' history of failure, and drug and alcohol addictions among clients result in far more failures than successes.

- Nonetheless, some delinquents do profit from treatment in community-based and institutional settings.

- In short, effective programs, wherever they are found, must provide a meaningful sense of purpose for problem juveniles so that they can go on to live crime-free lives.

CRITICAL THINKING Questions

1. Why have delinquency prevention programs been so popular in the United States?
2. Do you believe that prevention programs will have any effect on high-risk offenders? If they were to prove effective, how would that change youth crime in this nation?
3. Why are diversionary programs sometimes seen as being coercive?
4. Which treatment modality is the most promising for use in correctional institutions? Why?
5. Why has treatment traditionally had so little effect on reducing recidivism? What will have an impact on reducing the likelihood of future youthful offenders' becoming involved in crime?

Visit Homeboy Industries on the Web at **www.homeboy-industries.org**. As the site's homepage says, the mission of Homeboy Industries is to assist at-risk and former gang-involved youths to become contributing members of the community through a variety of services. Free programs—including counseling, education, tattoo removal, job training, and job placement—work to enable young people to redirect their lives and provide them with hope for the future.

Review the programs and services Homeboy Industries offers. Which program or service do you think would be most effective at preventing young people from becoming delinquent? Why?

Which program or service do you think would be most effective at preventing reoffending? Why?

Which program or service do you think would be most effective at helping gang members begin new lives? Why?

How might differing personal situations impact the effectiveness of the programs and services offered by Homeboy Industries?

Submit your answers to these questions to your instructor if asked to do so.

Source: From www.homeboy-industries.org/. Reprinted with permission from Jobs For A Future/Homeboy Industries, Los Angeles.

Notes

1. Stanley Cohen, *Visions of Social Control: Crime, Punishment and Classification* (Cambridge, England: Policy Press, 1985), p. 236.
2. J. David Hawkins et al., *Reports of the National Juvenile Justice Assessment Centers: A Typology of Cause-Focused Strategies of Delinquency Prevention* (Washington, D.C.: U.S. Government Printing Office, 1980), p. 1.
3. For development of these levels of prevention, see Steven P. Lab, *Crime Prevention: Approaches, Practices and Evaluations* (Cincinnati: Anderson, 2000), pp. 19–22.
4. James O. Finckenauer, *Scared Straight! and the Panacea Phenomenon* (Englewood Cliffs, N.J.: Prentice-Hall, 1982), p. 4.
5. U.S. Congress, House, Subcommittee on Human Resources of the Committee on Education and Labor, *Hearings, Oversight on Scared Straight!*, 96th Cong., 1st Sess., 4 June 1979, p. 305.
6. Finckenauer, *Scared Straight!*, p. 4.
7. Cited in Finckenauer, *Scared Straight!*, p. 35.
8. Richard J. Lundman, Paul T. McFarlane, and Frank R. Scarpitti, "Delinquency Prevention: A Description and Assessment of Projects Reported in the Professional Literature," *Crime and Delinquency* 22 (July 1976), p. 307.
9. Richard J. Lundman and Frank R. Scarpitti, "Delinquency Prevention: Recommendations for Future Projects," *Crime and Delinquency* 24 (April 1978), p. 207.
10. Ibid.
11. Richard J. Lundman, *Prevention and Control of Juvenile Delinquency,* 3rd ed. (New York: Oxford University Press, 2001).
12. Gail Wasserman, Laurie S. Miller, and Lynn Cothern, "Prevention of Serious and Violent Juvenile Offending," *Juvenile Justice Bulletin* (April 2000), p. 1.
13. Office of Juvenile Justice and Delinquency Prevention, *Guide for Implementing the Comprehensive Strategy for Serious, Violent, and Chronic Juvenile Offenders* (Washington, D.C.: U.S. Department of Justice, 1995), p. 17.
14. *OJJDP Model Program Guide*, p. 1. See www/dsgonline .com/mpg2.5/prevention.htm.
15. Ibid.
16. B. Bernard, "Fostering Resiliency in Kids: Protective Facts in the family, School, and Community" (Portland, Ore: Northwest Regional Educational Laboratory, 1991); and P. Benson, *All Kids Are Our Kids: What Communities Must Do to Raise Caring and Responsible Children and Adolescents,* 2nd ed. (Hoboken, N.J.: Jossey-Bass, 2006).

17. J. Pollard, J. D. Hawkins, and M. Arthur, "Risk and Protection: Are Both Necessary to Understand Diverse Behavioral outcomes in Adolescence?" *Social Work Research* 23 (1999), pp. 145–158.

18. Sharon Mihalic, Katherine Irwin, Abigail Fagan, Diane Ballard, and Delbert Elliott, *Successful Implementation: Lessons from Blueprints* (Washington, D.C.: Office of Juvenile Justice and Delinquency Prevention, 2004), p. 1.

19. Sharon Mihalic, Katherine Irwin, Abigail Fagan, Diane Ballard, and Delbert Elliott, *Blueprints for Violence Prevention* (Washington, D.C.: Office of Juvenile Justice and Delinquency Prevention, 2004), p. 55.

20. D. E. McGill, S. Mihalic, and J. K. Grotpeter, "Big Brothers Big Sisters of America," in *Blueprints for Violence Prevention: Book 2,* edited by D. S. Elliott (Boulder: University of Colorado, Institute of Behavioral Science, Center for the Study and Prevention of Violence, 1997).

21. Mihalic, Irwin, Fagan, Ballard, and Elliott, *Blueprints for Violence Prevention,* pp. 30–31.

22. M. A. Pentz, S. Mihalic, and J. K. Grotpeter, "The Midwestern Prevention Project," in *Blueprints for Violence Prevention: Book 1,* edited by D. S. Elliott (Boulder: University of Colorado, Institute of Behavioral Science, Center for the Study and Prevention of Violence, 1997).

23. Mihalic, Irwin, Fagan, Ballard, and Elliott, *Blueprints for Violence Prevention,* pp. 26–27.

24. J. F. Alexander et al., "Functional Family Therapy," in *Blueprints for Violence Prevention: Book 3,* edited by D. S. Elliott (Boulder: University of Colorado, Institute of Behavioral Science, Center for the Study and Prevention of Violence, 2000).

25. Mihalic, Irwin, Fagan, Ballard, and Elliott, *Blueprints for Violence Prevention,* pp. 22–23.

26. C. Webster-Stratton et al., "The Incredible Years: Parent, Teacher and Child Training Series," in *Blueprints for Violence Prevention: Book 11,* edited by D. S. Elliott (Boulder: University of Colorado, Institute of Behavioral Science, Center for the Study and Prevention of Violence, 2001).

27. Mihalic, Irwin, Fagan, Ballard, and Elliott, *Blueprints for Violence Prevention,* p. 47.

28. G. Botvin, S. Mihalic, and J. K. Grotpeter, "Life Skills Training," in *Blueprints for Violence Prevention: Book 5,* edited by D. S. Elliott (Boulder: University of Colorado, Institute of Behavioral Science, Center for the Study and Prevention of Violence, 1998).

29. Mihalic, Irwin, Fagan, Ballard, and Elliott, *Blueprints for Violence Prevention,* pp. 31–33.

30. Pentz, Mihalic, and Grotpeter, "The Midwestern Prevention Project."

31. Mihalic, Irwin, Fagan, Ballard, and Elliott, *Blueprints for Violence Prevention,* pp. 56–58.

32. P. Chamberlain and S. Mihalic, "Multidimensional Treatment Foster Care," in *Blueprints for Violence Prevention: Book 8,* edited by D. S. Elliott (Boulder: University of Colorado, Institute of Behavioral Science, Center for the Study and Prevention of Violence, 1998).

33. Mihalic, Irwin, Fagan, Ballard, and Elliott, *Blueprints for Violence Prevention,* pp. 27–28.

34. S. W. Henggeler et al., "Multisystemic Therapy," in *Blueprints for Violence Prevention: Book 6,* edited by D. S. Elliott (Boulder: University of Colorado, Institute of Be-

havioral Science, Center for the Study and Prevention of Violence, 2001).

35. Mihalic, Irwin, Fagan, Ballard, and Elliott, *Blueprints for Violence Prevention,* pp. 18–20.

36. D. Olds et al., "Prenatal and Infancy Home Visitation by Nurses," in *Blueprints for Violence Prevention: Book 7,* edited by D. S. Elliott (Boulder: University of Colorado, Institute of Behavioral Science, Center for the Study and Prevention of Violence, 1998).

37. Mihalic, Irwin, Fagan, Ballard, and Elliott, *Blueprints for Violence Prevention,* pp. 47–48.

38. Ibid., p. 48.

39. Ibid., p. 46.

40. M. Greenberg, M. Kusche, and S. Mihalic, "Promoting Alternative Thinking Strategies," in *Blueprints for Violence Prevention: Book 2,* edited by D. S. Elliott (Boulder: University of Colorado, Institute of Behavioral Science, Center for the Study and Prevention of Violence, 1998).

41. Joy G. Dryfoos, *Adolescents at Risk: Prevalence and Prevention* (New York: Oxford University Press, 1990), pp. 228–233.

42. James C. Howell, ed., *Guide for Implementing the Comprehensive Strategy for Serious, Violent, and Chronic Juvenile Offenders* (Washington, D.C.: Office of Juvenile Justice and Delinquency Prevention, 1995), p. 10.

43. Ibid., p. 3.

44. Ibid., p. 5.

45. Ibid.

46. Ibid., pp. 9–10.

47. Ibid., p. 11.

48. Kathleen Coolbaugh and Cynthia J. Hansel, "The Comprehensive Strategy: Lessons Learned from the Pilot Sites," *Juvenile Justice Bulletin* (2000), p. 1.

49. Ibid., p. 10.

50. President's Commission on Law Enforcement and Administration of Justice, *Task Force Report on Juvenile Delinquency and Youth Crime* (Washington, D.C.: U.S. Government Printing Office, 1967), p. 2.

51. Youth Development and Delinquency Prevention Administration, *The Challenge of Youth Service Bureaus* (Washington, D.C.: U.S. Government Printing Office, 1973).

52. Edwin H. Sutherland and Donald R. Cressey, *Criminology,* 9th ed. (Philadelphia: J. B. Lippincott, 1974).

53. Andrew Rutherford and Robert McDermott, *National Evaluation Program Phase I Report: Juvenile Diversion* (Washington, D.C.: U.S. Government Printing Office, 1976), pp. 2–3.

54. Arnold Binder and Gilbert Geis, "Ad Populum Argumentation in Criminology: Juvenile Diversion as Rhetoric," *Crime and Delinquency* 30 (1984), pp. 309–333.

55. Rutherford and McDermott, *Juvenile Diversion,* p. 5; see also Lloyd E. Ohlin, "The Future of Juvenile Justice Policy and Research," *Crime and Delinquency* (July 1983), pp. 463–472; Thomas Blomberg, "Diversion and Accelerated Social Control," *Journal of Criminal Law and Criminology* 68 (1977), pp. 274–282; and Charles E. Frazier, "Official Intervention, Diversion from the Juvenile Justice System, and Dynamics of Human Services Work: Effects of a Reform Goal Based on Labeling Theory," *Crime and Delinquency* 32 (April 1986), pp. 157–186.

56. Rutherford and McDermott, *Juvenile Diversion;* Dennis B. Anderson and Donald F. Schoen, "Diversion Programs: Ef-

fects of Stigmatization on Juvenile/Status Offenders," *Juvenile and Family Court Journal* 36 (Summer 1985), pp. 13–25.

57. Stanley Cohen, *Visions of Social Control*, p. 93.

58. Jeffrey A. Butts and Adele V. Harrell, *Delinquents or Criminals: Policy Options for Young Offenders* (Washington, D.C.: Urban Institute, 1988), p. 9.

59. Survey results are found in Jeffrey Butts, Dean Hoffman, and Jancen Buck "Teen Courts in the United States: A Profile of Current Programs," *OJJDP Fact Sheet* (Washington, D.C.: Office of Juvenile Justice and Delinquency Prevention, 1999). See also Jeffrey A. Butts and Jancen Buck, *Teen Courts: A Focus on Research: Juvenile Justice Bulletin* (Washington, D.C.: Office of Juvenile Justice and Delinquency Prevention, 2000).

60. Jeffrey A. Butts, Janeen Buck, and Mark B. Coggeshall, *The Impact of Teen Courts on Young Offenders* (Washington, D.C.: The Urban Institute, 2002).

61. T. M. Godwin, *Peer Justice and Youth Empowerment: An Implementation Guide for Teen Court Programs* (Lexington, Ky.: American Probation and Parole Association, 1998).

62. Butts, Hoffman, and Buck, "Teen Courts in the United States," From which the data in this section are derived.

63. Butts et al., *The Impact of Teen Courts on Young Offenders*, p. 2.

64. Jeffrey Butts and John Roman, *Juvenile Drug Courts and Teen Substance Abuse* (Alameda County, Calif.: Urban Institute Press, 2004).

65. Marilyn Roberts, Jennifer Brophy, and Caroline Cooper, *The Juvenile Drug Court Movement* (Washington, D.C.: Office of Juvenile Justice and Delinquency Prevention, 1997).

66. Ibid., pp. 1–2.

67. Terance D. Miethe, Hong Lu, and Erin Reese, "Reintegrative Shaming and Recidivism Risks in Drug Court: Explanations for Some Unexpected Findings," *Crime and Delinquency* 46 (October 2000), pp. 522–541

68. For description of the California programs, see www.courtinfo.ca.gov/programs/cfcc/programs/description/juvmed.htm; for listing of Massachusetts programs, see www.mass.gov/courts/admin/legal/redbook25.html. For description of the program in Cook County, see www.caadrs.org/adr/CCRjuvenile.htm.

69. For information on the Juvenile Mediation program in Cook County, see www.caadrs.org/adr/CCRjuvenile.htm.

70. Robert R. Smith and Victor S. Lombardo, "Evaluation Report of the Juvenile Mediation Program," *Corrections Compendium* (Laurel, Md.: American Correctional Association, 2001), p. 1.

71. Andrew von Hirsch, ed., *Doing Justice: The Choice of Punishments* (New York: Hill and Wang, 1970), p. 11.

72. Walter C. Bailey, "Correctional Outcome: An Evaluation of 100 Reports," *Journal of Criminal Law, Criminology, and Police Science* 57 (June 1957), pp. 153–160.

73. J. Robison and G. Smith, "The Effectiveness of Correctional Programs," *Crime and Delinquency* 17 (1971), pp. 67–70.

74. Robert Martinson, "What Works?—Questions and Answers about Prison Reform," *Public Interest* 35 (Spring 1974), pp. 22–54.

75. Douglas Lipton, Robert Martinson, and Judith Wilks, *The Effectiveness of Correctional Treatment* (New York: Praeger, 1975).

76. CBS Television Network. Excerpted from *60 Minutes* segment, "It Doesn't Work" (August 24, 1975).

77. Ted Palmer, "Martinson Revisited," *Journal of Research in Crime and Delinquency* 12 (July 1975), pp. 133–152.

78. Ibid., p. 137.

79. Paul Gendreau and Robert Ross, "Effective Correctional Treatment: Bibliotherapy for Cynics," *Crime and Delinquency* 27 (October 1979), pp. 463–489.

80. Robert R. Ross and Paul Gendreau, eds., *Effective Correctional Treatment* (Toronto: Butterworth, 1980), p. viii.

81. Robert Martinson, "New Findings, New Views: A Note of Caution Regarding Sentencing Reform," *Hofstra Law Review* 7 (Winter 1979), p. 244.

82. Paul Gendreau and Robert R. Ross, "Revivification of Rehabilitative Evidence," *Justice Quarterly* 4 (September 1987), pp. 349–407.

83. Ibid. For a review of the meta-analyses of correctional treatment in the 1980s, see Ted Palmer, *The Re-Emergence of Correctional Intervention* (Newbury Park, Calif.: Sage Publications, 1992), pp. 50–76.

84. James McGuire and Philip Priestley, "Reviewing 'What Works': Past, Present, and Future," in *What Works: Reducing Reoffending—Guidelines from Research and Practice*, edited by James McGuire (New York: John Wiley & Sons, 1995), pp. 7–8.

85. Ibid.

86. Ibid.

87. Eric Berne, *Transactional Analysis in Psychotherapy* (New York: Grove Press), p. 355.

88. Thomas A. Harris, *I'm OK—You're OK* (New York: Harper and Row, 1967), pp. 37–53.

89. William Glasser, *Reality Therapy* (New York: Harper and Row, 1965), p. xii.

90. Ibid., excerpts from pp. 44–45.

91. J. L. Bernard and Russell Eisenman, "Verbal Conditioning in Sociopaths with Spiral and Monetary Reinforcement," *Journal of Personality and Social Psychology* 6 (1976), pp. 203–206.

92. Ralph Schwitzgebel and David A. Kolb, "Inducing Behavior Change in Adolescent Delinquents," *Behaviour Research and Therapy* 1 (1964), pp. 297–304.

93. See Dennis A. Romig, *Justice for Our Children: An Examination of Juvenile Delinquent Rehabilitation Programs* (Lexington, Mass.: D. C. Heath, 1978), pp. 20–21.

94. Ibid., p. 87.

95. Ibid., pp. 92–93.

96. Interview with Harry Vorrath quoted in Oliver J. Keller Jr. and Benedict S. Alper, *Halfway Houses: Community Centered Correction and Treatment* (Lexington, Mass.: D. C. Heath, 1970), p. 55.

97. Robert J. Wicks, *Correctional Psychology: Themes and Problems in Correcting the Offender* (San Francisco: Canfield Press, 1974), pp. 50–51.

98. Samuel Yochelson and Stanton E. Samenow, *The Criminal Personality*, 2 vols. (New York: J. Aronson, 1976, 1977).

99. David Berenson, *Ohio Department of Youth Services Sex Offender Project: Preliminary Report on a Treatment Program for Adolescent Sex Offenders* (Columbus, Ohio: Department of Youth Services, 1989).

100. Ibid., pp. 6–8.

101. David Lester and Patricia Van Voorhis, "Cognitive Therapies," in *Correctional Counseling and Rehabilitation,* 3rd ed., edited by Patricia Van Voorhis, Michael Braswell, and David Lester (Cincinnati: Anderson Publishing, 1997), p. 172.

102. Interviewed in August 1996.

103. Lee Sechrest, Susan O. White, and Elizabeth D. Brown, eds., *The Rehabilitation of Criminal Offenders* (Washington, D.C.: National Academy of Sciences, 1979), and Susan Martin, Lee Sechrest, and Robin Redner, eds., *Rehabilitation of Criminal Offenders: Directions for Research* (Washington, D.C.: National Academy of Sciences, 1981).

104. For an examination of the various meta-analyses, see Palmer, *The Re-Emergence of Intervention,* pp. 48–76. See also Izzo and Ross, "Meta-Analyses of Rehabilitation Programs for Juvenile Delinquents," pp. 134–142.

105. Sechrest, White, and Brown, eds., *The Rehabilitation of Criminal Offenders,* pp. 35–37.

106. Ibid.

107. Ibid.

13

The Juvenile Justice Process

CHAPTER
Outline

> The current [juvenile justice] system, a relic from a more innocent time, teaches youthful offenders that crime pays and that they are totally immune and insulated from responsibility.
>
> —National Policy Forum

CHAPTER

AFTER READING THIS CHAPTER, YOU SHOULD BE ABLE TO ANSWER THE FOLLOWING QUESTIONS:

- What is the juvenile justice process?
- What are the stages in the juvenile justice process?
- In what ways are the juvenile and adult justice systems the same?
- In what ways are they different?
- Why is understanding the violent juvenile the key to effective interventions with juvenile offenders?
- Why is minority over-representation such a serious issue for the juvenile justice system?
- How do graduated sanctions work?
- What will the juvenile justice system look like in the future?

KEY
Terms

adjudicatory hearing, p. 451
adjustment model, p. 452
aftercare, p. 444
balanced and restorative model, p. 454
child savers p. 442
commitment, p. 451
cottage system, p. 445
crime control model, p. 455
detention, p. 451
dispositional hearing, p. 451
disproportionate minority confinement, p. 463
just deserts, p. 454
justice as fairness, p. 454
justice model, p. 453
juvenile court officer, p. 451
medical model, p. 452
minor, p. 451
petition, p. 451
petitioner, p. 451
probation, p. 444
recidivism, p. 449
rehabilitation model, p. 452
reintegration model, p. 453
residential programs, p. 444
respondent, p. 451
taking into custody, p. 451
training school, p. 445

439

On May 31, 2006, Lionel Tate, the Florida teenager who made headlines as the youngest child in modern times to be sentenced to life imprisonment, accepted a plea bargain and was ordered back to prison to serve up to 30 years in prison for the armed robbery of a Domino's Pizza deliveryman. Tate's life sentence, imposed in 2001, followed his transfer to adult criminal court and first-degree murder conviction for the 1999 stomping death of a six-year-old playmate, Tiffany Eunick. Tate, who was twelve years old and 166 lbs. when he killed the 46-lb. girl, claimed that he had been practicing wrestling moves he had seen on TV. Eunick, however, suffered horrendous injuries—including a lacerated liver, skull fracture, and broken ribs—causing the sentencing judge to remark, "The acts of Lionel Tate were not the playful acts of a child, [but] were cold, callous, and indescribably cruel."

Public outcry against Tate's lengthy sentence led a state appeals court to release him, citing Tate's questionable ability to have understood the criminal proceedings against him. The court ordered Tate to serve one year of house arrest and another ten years on probation. Soon after his release, however, Tate was found carrying a knife outside of his home, and was arrested for violating the terms of his probation. A judge extended his probation to fifteen years, telling him that another violation would return him to prison. Tate's downfall came on May 24, 2005, after the pizza deliveryman who had been robbed led police to the house where the incident occurred and identified the then eighteen-year-old Tate as the robber.

This vignette draws on editorials in the *Miami Herald*, material appearing on CNN.com, the Fourth District Court of Appeals decision of December 2003, and "Law Center: Young Killer Faces Armed Robbery Charge," *CNN*, May 24, 2005.

(Left:) Lionel Tate, age thirteen, looks at his mother, Kathleen Grossett-Tate, prior to opening statements in his 2001 Florida murder trial. Tate was tried as an adult and convicted of first-degree murder in the death of six-year-old Tiffany Eunick, whom he said he accidentally killed while imitating professional wrestling moves. *(Middle:)* Tate, age sixteen, and his mother stand outside the Broward County Courthouse after a plea bargain set him free after nearly three years in prison. *(Right:)* Tate, dressed in prison stripes, leaves the courtroom following a 2006 sentencing hearing for his conviction on gun-related charges and probation violations. Tate, who received a thirty-year prison sentence on those charges, is scheduled to be tried for holding up a pizza deliveryman at gun-point.

■ **Do you think he should get another chance?**

Society has long considered how best to process and treat juvenile offenders and how to determine at what age a person is able to form the mental intent necessary for the commission of a crime. Some observers suggest children are too immature to form the "evilness" required to plan and commit certain acts of violence and therefore deserve compassion. Elizabeth S. Scott, a professor of law, and Thomas Grisso, a professor of psychiatry, use a developmental lens to support "a presumption of youthful diminished responsibility for younger and mid-adolescents."[1] Marty Beyer, a child psychotherapist who has done extensive work with violent youthful offenders, argues even more forcefully that juveniles developmentally have less maturity, competency, and culpability than adults (see Juvenile Law 13.1).[2]

However, in support of the "get tough with juveniles" position, the argument is frequently made that society has some fifteen-, sixteen-, and seventeen-year-old youthful offenders who function on adult levels. Traditional treatment, this position adds, does not hold much promise in dealing with these kids. Fordham University Professor Ernest van den Haag charged that the only thing that seems to have an impact on these juveniles is to take them off the streets and put them in jail or training school. He claimed that we are too soft on juvenile crime and advocated severe punishment that would make the decision to commit a crime an "irrational" choice for the juvenile. Van den Haag's concerns about the ineffectiveness of society's means of preventing, correcting, and controlling juvenile crime are shared by many.

The juvenile justice system is responsible for controlling and correcting the behavior of law-violating juveniles. The system's inability to accomplish its basic mission has resulted in massive criticism from all sides. Indeed, both liberals and conservatives want to reduce the scope of the juvenile court's responsibilities. Conservatives want to refer serious youthful offenders to the adult court, while some liberals recommend divesting the juvenile court of its jurisdiction over status offenders.

Juvenile Law 13.1

Interview with Marty Beyer

Marty Beyer writes:

The offense is often the primary basis for determining intention and competency of children under eighteen in adult or juvenile court. But the capacity of juveniles to plan or to stop an action is affected by how far they have progressed developmentally. They need a developmental assessment to examine the unique interweaving of immaturity, disabilities, and trauma (and the different developmental pressures on girls) in order to understand the delinquent act, the young person's capacity to waive rights or cooperate with counsel, and his or her amenability to treatment.

The fact is that adolescents think differently from adults. Even late in their teens young people can have immature thought processes, including:

- First, not anticipating: Adolescents often do not plan or do not follow their plan and get caught up in an unanticipated event.
- Second, fear: Fear interferes with the adolescent's ability to make choices, particularly if they have been mistreated in the past.
- Third, minimizing danger: Risk-taking typical of adolescents reduces their use of mature cognitive strategies because they seldom consider the worst possible outcomes of their actions.
- Fourth, having only one choice: In situations where adults see several choices, adolescents may believe they have only one option.

■ Do you agree with Dr. Beyer that adolescents typically lack the cognitive development of adults? Does society then need a juvenile system separate from the adult system to treat juveniles? How about juveniles who commit a violent crime?

Source: Statement that Dr. Beyer sent to the authors in January 2002.

> **The [juvenile justice] system's inability to accomplish its basic mission has resulted in massive criticism from all sides.**

Another proposal is to abolish the juvenile court. Barry C. Feld, a widely published law professor in juvenile law and procedures, argues that it makes no sense to maintain a separate court because there are no practical or operational differences between the juvenile and adult courts. "Is there any reason," he questions, "to maintain a separate court whose only distinctions are procedures under which no adult would agree to be tried?"[3] He charges that, regardless of constitutional and legislative reforms since the mid-1970s, "the juvenile court remains essentially unreformed."[4] He suggests that the adult court "could provide children with all the procedural guarantees already available to adult defendants and additional enhanced protections because of the children's vulnerability and immaturity."[5]

▣ Development of the Juvenile Justice System

This chapter examines juvenile justice through the lenses of the past, the present, and the future. Beginning with the development of juvenile justice in the United States, its structures, functions, and issues are discussed, and future possibilities are suggested.

Origins of the Juvenile Court

During the final decades of the nineteenth century, the Progressive reformers viewed childhood as a period of dependency and exclusion from the adult world. To institutionalize childhood, they enacted a number of "child-saving" laws, including compulsory school attendance and child labor laws. The creation of the juvenile court was another means to achieve unparalleled age segregation of children. There were a number of contextual factors that influenced the creation of the juvenile court.[6]

Sociocultural Context   Three social conditions that characterized the last thirty years of the nineteenth century led to the founding of the juvenile court. First, many citizens were incensed by the treatment of children during this period, especially the jailing of children with adults. Jails were considered highly injurious to youthful offenders because of the deleterious effects of their association with adult criminals. Disenchantment of urban dwellers also became widespread. The population of Chicago tripled between 1880 and 1890, mostly by immigration, creating such problems as filth, poverty, the rise of crime, and corruption in city government. Furthermore, the higher status given middle-class women made them interested in exerting their newfound influence to improve the lives of children. In fact, child saving became an avocation for some middle-class women who wanted to do something outside the home.[7]

These pressures for social change took place in the midst of a wave of optimism that swept through U.S. society during the Progressive Era, the period from 1890 to 1920. The emerging social sciences assured reformers that their problems with delinquents could be solved through positivism, which held that youths were not responsible for their behavior and needed treatment rather than punishment. For example, the judge and scientific experts could work together in a separate court to discover a child's problem and to provide the cure.

Middle-class religious humanitarianism was another societal pressure for change. Such writers as Charles Dickens and Mary Carpenter challenged Christians to rescue children from degrading slums. The importance of religious humanitarianism is evident in the fact that many of the well-known **child savers** were ministers and most of the child-saving institutions were private charities supported, at least in part, by mainline religious denominations.

child savers

A name given to an organized group of progressive social reformers of the late nineteenth and early twentieth centuries who promoted numerous laws aimed at protecting children and institutionalizing an idealized image of childhood innocence.

Legal Context   The first juvenile court was founded in Cook County (Chicago), Illinois, in 1899, when the Illinois legislature passed the Juvenile Court Act. The *parens patriae* doctrine provided a legal catalyst for the creation of the juvenile court, furnishing a rationale for the use of informal procedures for dealing with juveniles and for expanding state power over children. *Parens patriae* was also used to justify the juvenile court's authority to determine the causes of delinquent behavior and to make decisions on the disposition of cases. The kindly parent, the state, could thus justify relying on psychological and medical examinations rather than on trial by evidence. Once the *parens patriae* rationale was applied to juvenile proceedings, the institution of the juvenile court followed.

> " The first juvenile court was founded in Cook County (Chicago) Illinois, in 1899, when the Illinois legislature passed the Juvenile Court Act. "

Political Context   In *The Child Savers*, Anthony Platt discussed the political context of the origin of the juvenile court. He claimed that the juvenile court was established in Chicago and later elsewhere because it satisfied several middle-class interest groups. He saw the juvenile court as an expression of middle-class values and of the philosophy of conservative political groups. In denying that the juvenile court was revolutionary, Platt charged:

> The child-saving movement was not so much a break with the past as an affirmation of faith in traditional institutions. Parental authority, education at home, and the virtues of rural life were emphasized because they were in decline at this time. The child-saving movement was, in part, a crusade which, through emphasizing the dependence of the social order on the proper socialization of children, implicitly elevated the nuclear family and, more especially, the role of women as stalwarts of the family. The child savers were prohibitionists, in a general sense, who believed that social progress depended on efficient law enforcement, strict supervision of children's leisure and recreation, and the regulation of illicit pleasures. What seemingly began as a movement to humanize the lives of adolescents soon developed into a program of moral absolutism through which youths were to be saved from movies, pornography, cigarettes, alcohol, and anything else which might possibly rob them of their innocence.[8]

Economic Context   Platt contended that the behaviors the child savers deemed worthy of penalty—such as engaging in sex, roaming the streets, drinking, fighting, frequenting dance halls, and staying out late at night—were found primarily among lower-class children. Therefore, juvenile justice from its inception, he argued, reflected class favoritism that resulted in the frequent processing of poor children through the system while middle- and upper-class children were more likely to be excused.[9]

The children of the poor were a particular problem to the child savers because the juvenile court emerged in the wake of unprecedented industrial and urban development in the United States. This process was closely connected with large-scale immigration to urban centers of people who had different backgrounds from the indigenous population. These immigrants brought new social problems to Chicago and other urban centers, and the child savers were determined to "rescue" the immigrant children and to protect them from their families.[10]

Emergence of Community-Based Corrections

The first application of community-based corrections for juveniles grew out of juvenile aftercare, or parole, used to supervise juveniles after their institutionalization. Such programs are nearly as old as juvenile correctional institutions. By the 1820s, superintendents of houses of refuge had the authority to release juveniles when they saw fit. Some juveniles were returned directly to their families, and others were placed in the community as indentured servants and apprentices who could reenter the community as free citizens once they finished their terms of service. This system became formalized only in the 1840s, when states set up inspection procedures to monitor the supervision of those with whom youths were placed.

Juvenile **aftercare** was influenced by the development of adult parole in the late 1870s. Zebulon Brockway, the first superintendent of Elmira Reformatory in New York State, permitted parole for carefully selected prisoners. When they left the institution, parolees were instructed to report to a guardian on arrival, to write immediately to the superintendent, and to report to the guardian on the first of each month.

Juvenile aftercare programs spread throughout the United States in the early decades of the twentieth century and took on many of the features of adult parole. Juveniles were supervised in the community by aftercare officers, whose jobs were similar to those of parole officers in the adult system. The parole board did not become a part of juvenile corrections, for in more than two-thirds of the states, institutional staffs continued to decide when youths would return to the community.

Probation as an alternative to institutional placements for juveniles arose from the effort of John Augustus, a Boston cobbler, in the 1840s and 1850s. Augustus, who is called "the father of probation," spent considerable time in the courtroom and in 1841 persuaded a judge to permit him to supervise an offender in the community rather than sentencing the offender to an institution. Over the next two decades, Augustus worked with nearly 2,000 individuals, including both adult and juvenile offenders. As the first probation officer, Augustus initiated several services still used in probation today: investigation and screening, supervision, educational and employment services, and the provision of aid and assistance.[11]

Expansion and Retrenchment in the Twentieth Century   In the twentieth century, probation services spread to every state and were administered by both state and local authorities. The use of volunteer probation workers had disappeared by the turn of the century, only to return in the 1950s. Probation became more treatment oriented: Early in the century the medical treatment model was used; later, in the 1960s and 1970s, probation officers became brokers who delivered services to clients. The upgrading of standards and training also was emphasized in the 1960s and 1970s.

Residential programs, the third type of community-based juvenile corrections to appear, had their origins in the Highfields Project, a short-term guided-group-interaction program. Known officially as the New Jersey Experimental Project for the Treatment of Youthful Offenders, this project was established in 1950 on the former estate of Colonel and Mrs. Charles Lindbergh. The Highfields Project housed adjudicated youths who worked during the day at the nearby New Jersey Neuro-Psychiatric Institute and met in two guided-group-interaction units five evenings a week at the Highfields facility. Similar programs were initiated in the 1960s at South Fields in Louisville, Kentucky; Essexfields in Newark, New Jersey; Pinehills in Provo, Utah; the New Jersey centers at Oxford and Farmingdale for boys and at Turrell for girls; and the START centers established by the New York City Division for Youth.

In the late 1980s and 1990s, a decline in federal funding, along with the get-tough mood of society, meant the closing of some residential and day treatment programs. Although probation remained the most widely used judicial disposition, both probation and aftercare services were charged to enforce a more hard-line policy with juvenile offenders. See Table 13.1 for a time line of the most important events in the evolution of community-based corrections for juveniles.

> " Juvenile aftercare was influenced by the development of adult parole in the late 1870s. "

The Development of Juvenile Institutions

Before the end of the eighteenth century, the family was commonly believed to be the source or cause of deviancy, and, therefore, the idea emerged that perhaps the well-adjusted family could provide the model for a correctional institution for children. The house of refuge, the first juvenile institution, reflected the family model wholeheartedly; it was designed to bring order, discipline, and care of the family into in-

TABLE 13.1

Time Line of Community-Based Corrections for Juveniles in the United States

DATE	EVENT
1820s	Superintendents of houses of refuge had the power to release juveniles from the institution
1840s	States set up inspection procedures to monitor the supervision of those with whom juveniles were placed
1841	John Augustus began to supervise juvenile and adult offenders in Boston
1869	Commonwealth of Massachusetts established a visiting probation agent system which supervised youthful offenders
1890	Probation was established statewide in Massachusetts
1950	Highfields Project was established
1980s to Present	Retrenchment in community-based corrections

stitutional life. The institution was to become the home; the peers, the siblings; and the staff, the parents.[12]

The New York House of Refuge, which opened on January 1, 1825, with six girls and three boys, is usually acknowledged as the first house of refuge. Several similar institutions already existed in England and Europe.[13] Over the next decade or so, Boston, Philadelphia, Bangor, Richmond, Mobile, Cincinnati, and Chicago followed suit in establishing houses of refuge for males. Twenty-three schools were chartered in the 1830s and another thirty in the 1840s. Some houses of refuge were established by private philanthropists, some by the state government or legislature, and some jointly by public authorities and private organizations. The vast majority of the houses of refuge were for males. The average capacity was 210; the capacity ranged from 90 at Lancaster, Massachusetts, to 1,000 at the New York House of Refuge for Boys.[14]

> Before the end of the eighteenth century, the family was commonly believed to be the source or cause of deviancy.

The development of the **cottage system** and the construction of these juvenile institutions outside cities were two reforms of the mid-nineteenth century. The cottage system was introduced in 1854 and quickly spread throughout the nation. This new system housed smaller groups of youths in separate buildings, usually no more than twenty to forty youths per cottage. Early cottages were log cabins; later cottages were built from brick or stone. Now called **training schools** or industrial schools, these juvenile facilities were usually constructed outside cities so that youths would be reformed through exposure to the simpler rural way of life. It was presumed that residents would learn responsibility and new skills as they worked the fields and took care of the livestock. Their work would enable the institution, in turn, to provide its own food and perhaps even realize a profit.

cottage system
A widely used treatment practice that places small groups of training school residents into cottages.

training school
A correctional facility for long-term placement of juvenile delinquents; may be public (run by a state department of corrections or youth commission) or private.

Twentieth-Century Changes Several significant changes occurred in juvenile institutionalization during the first several decades of the twentieth century. One change was that reformers advocated treatment on several fronts. Case studies were used to prescribe treatment plans for residents; reception units were developed to diagnose and classify new admissions; individual therapies, such as psychotherapy and behavior modification, were used; and group therapies, such as guided group interaction, became popular means of transforming the inmate subculture. Institutional programs also became more diverse. Confined juveniles could graduate from state-accredited high school programs; home furloughs and work-release programs were permitted in many training schools to include printing, barbering, welding, and automobile repair. Furthermore, the types of juvenile correctional facilities increased

TABLE 13.2

Time Line of Juvenile Institutionalization

DATE	EVENT
1825	New York House of Refuge was opened.
1854	Cottage system was introduced.
1850s and 1860s	Juvenile facilities were called training schools or industrial schools.
1880–1899	The public became disillusioned, realizing that training schools were primarily custodial institutions.
1900–1950	Training schools underwent a period of reform, especially with the introduction of varied forms of treatment.
1960s and 1970s	Training schools came under great criticism.
Late 1970S	Training schools underwent another period of reform.
Late 1980s to Today	Training schools became overcrowded, grew more violent, and confined increased numbers of minority youths.

to include ranches and forestry camps, as well as the traditional prisonlike training schools. Finally, several experimental forms of training schools developed that offered the promise of changing juvenile corrections.

In spite of the improvements in many reform schools, as well as the truly experimental efforts in a few, the story of the twentieth-century training school is one of scaled-down prisons for juveniles.[15] In the 1960s and 1970s, reformers began to accuse training schools of being violent, inhumane, and criminogenic.[16]

Widespread criticism of training schools, various court decisions, and pressure groups in state legislatures led to a number of reforms in the mid- and late 1970s. These innovations included no longer confining status offenders with delinquents in training schools, an increase in staff training programs, the growing acceptance of grievance procedures for residents, and the establishment of coeducational facilities.

In the late 1980s and 1990s, a number of disturbing changes took place in juvenile institutionalization. Training schools became overcrowded and more violent. Members of minorities made up a greater proportion of the population of juvenile correctional institutions, especially for drug offenses. Status offenders and juveniles who had committed nonserious delinquent acts continued to be committed to private training schools, but private placements also began to admit youngsters who had committed serious delinquent offenses. More youths were transferred to adult court for violent crimes and received long-term prison sentences. (See Table 13.2 for a time line of juvenile institutionalization.)

> " Widespread criticism of training schools, various court decisions, and pressure groups in state legislatures led to a number of reforms in the mid- and late 1970s. "

The Juvenile Justice System Today

Like most systems, private or public, the juvenile justice system is concerned first with maintaining its equilibrium and surviving. The system is able to survive by maintaining internal harmony while simultaneously managing environmental inputs. The police and the juvenile court, juvenile probation, residential and day treatment programs, detention facilities, long-term juvenile institutions, and aftercare are all closely interrelated, so changes in one organization have definite consequences elsewhere within the system.

Structures and Functions

The juvenile justice system is made up of three basic subsystems. These subsystems—the police, the juvenile court, and corrections—consist of between 10,000 and 20,000 public and private agencies, with annual budgets totaling hundreds of millions of dollars. Many of the 40,000 police departments across the nation have juvenile divisions, and over 3,000 juvenile courts and about 1,000 juvenile correctional facilities exist in the United States.[17] Of the 50,000 employees in the juvenile justice system, more than 30,000 are employed in juvenile correctional facilities, 6,500 are juvenile probation officers, and the remainder are aftercare (parole) officers and staff who work in residential programs. In addition, several thousand more employees work in diversion programs and private juvenile correctional systems.[18]

The functions of the three subsystems differ somewhat. The basic work of the police is law enforcement and maintaining order. The function of maintaining order, which occupies most of police officers' time, involves such responsibilities as settling family disputes, providing emergency ambulance service, directing traffic, furnishing information to citizens, preventing suicides, giving shelter to drunks, and checking the homes of families on vacation. The law-enforcement function requires that the police deter crime, make arrests, obtain confessions, collect evidence for strong cases that can result in convictions, and increase crime clearance rates. The police must also deal with juvenile lawbreaking and provide services juveniles need.

The juvenile courts are responsible for disposing of cases referred to them by intake divisions of probation departments (see Chapter 15), supervising juvenile probation, making detention decisions, dealing with cases of child neglect and dependency cases, and monitoring the performance of youths who have been adjudicated delinquent or status offenders. The *parens patriae* philosophy of the juvenile court charges the court with treating rather than punishing youngsters appearing before juvenile judges. But the treatment arm of the juvenile court goes only so far, and youths who commit serious crimes or persist in juvenile lawbreaking may be sent to training schools or transferred to the adult court.

The corrections system is charged with the care of youthful offenders sentenced by the courts. Juvenile probation, the most widely used judicial disposition, supervises offenders released to probation by the courts, ensuring that they comply with the conditions of probation imposed by the courts and desist from delinquent behavior in the community. Day treatment and residential programs (see Chapter 16) are charged with preparing youths for their return to the community, with preventing unlawful behavior in the program or in the community, and with providing humane care for youths directed to the programs. Long-term juvenile correctional institutions have similar responsibilities, but the officials of these programs also are charged with deciding when each youth is ready to be released to the community. Officials of long-term institutions must also ensure that residents receive their constitutional and due process rights. Aftercare officers, the final group in the juvenile justice system, have the responsibility of supervising youths released from long-term juvenile correctional institutions. Like probation officers, aftercare officers are expected to make certain that youthful offenders fulfill the terms of their aftercare agreements and avoid delinquent behavior.

Dr. Jerome G. Miller, circa 1972. In the early 1970s, Miller undertook a radical social experiment, closing down virtually all Massachusetts training schools and dispersing delinquent children to community-based programs. ■ **What would be the consequence of such an action today?**

Web LIBRARY 13.1

Read Chapter 4 of the OJJDP publication *Juvenile Offenders and Victims: 2006 National Report* at **www.justicestudies.com/WebLibrary**.

Web LIBRARY 13.2

Read the OJJDP publication *How the Justice System Responds to Juvenile Victims: A Comprehensive Model* at **www.justicestudies.com/WebLibrary**.

Web PLACES 13.1

View the OJJDP PowerPoint presentation "Juvenile Justice System Structure and Process," at **www.justicestudies.com/WebPlaces**.

Stages in the Juvenile Justice Process

The means by which juvenile offenders are processed by juvenile justice agencies are examined throughout this text. The variations in the juvenile justice systems across

Juvenile court judge Jeanne Meurer of Austin, Texas, gazes intently at a young defendant represented by a public defender during a detention hearing. ■ **How does the juvenile justice system differ from the adult criminal justice system?**

the nation make it difficult to describe this process, but Figure 13.1 is a flowchart of the juvenile justice system and the criminal justice system that shows what these systems have in common. The process begins when the youth is referred to the juvenile court. Some jurisdictions permit a variety of agents to refer the juvenile, whereas in others the police alone are charged with this responsibility. The more common procedure is that the youth whose alleged offense has already been investigated is taken into custody by the police who have made the decision to refer the juvenile to the juvenile court.

The intake officer, usually a probation officer (see Chapter 16), must decide whether the juvenile should remain in the community or be placed in a shelter or detention facility. As indicated in Figure 13.1, the intake officer has a variety of options in determining what to do with youths, but in more serious cases, the juvenile generally receives a petition to appear before the juvenile court.

The juvenile court judge, or the referee in many jurisdictions, hears the cases of juveniles referred to the court. If the juvenile is to be transferred to the adult court, this must be done before any juvenile proceedings take place. Otherwise, an adjudicatory hearing, the primary purpose of which is to determine whether the juvenile is guilty of the delinquent acts alleged in the petition, takes place. The court hears evidence on these allegations. *In re Gault* (see Chapter 15) usually is interpreted to guarantee to juveniles the right to representation by counsel, freedom from self-incrimination, and the right to confront and cross-examine witnesses. Some states also give juveniles the right to a jury trial.

A disposition hearing takes place when a juvenile has been found delinquent in the adjudicatory stage. Most juvenile court codes now require that the adjudicatory and disposition hearings be held at different times. The number of dispositions juvenile judges have available to them varies from one jurisdiction to the next. In addition to the standard disposition of warning and release, placement on juvenile probation, or adjudication to the department of youth services or corrections, some judges can place juveniles in a publicly or privately administered day treatment or residential program. Some jurisdictions even grant juvenile judges the authority to send a juvenile to a particular correctional facility.

FIGURE 13.1

The Stages of Delinquency Case Processing in the Juvenile Justice System

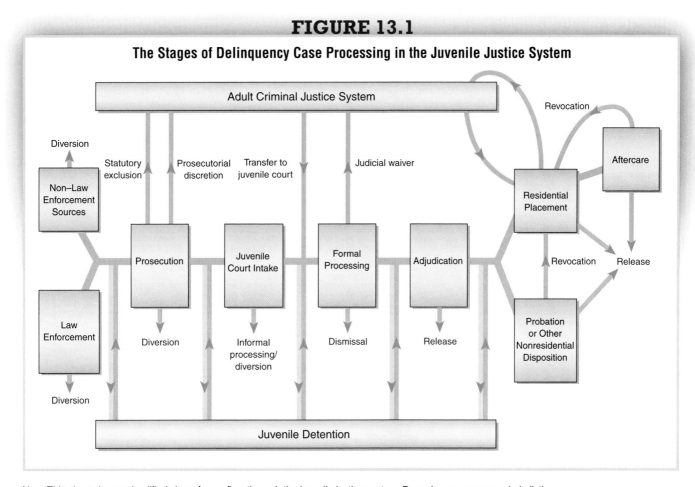

Note: This chart gives a simplified view of case flow through the juvenile justice system. Procedures vary among jurisdictions.
Source: Adapted from Howard N. Snyder and Melissa Sickmund, *Juvenile Offenders and Victims: 2006 National Report* (Washington, D.C.: Office of Juvenile Justice and Delinquency Prevention, 2006), p. 205. Reprinted with permission from the U.S. Department of Justice.

The juvenile adjudicated to a training school is generally treated somewhat differently in small states than in large states. In small states with one training school for males and (usually) one for females, a youth adjudicated to a training school usually is sent directly to the appropriate school. But large states that have several facilities for males and perhaps more than one for females may send the youth to a classification, or diagnostic, center to determine the proper institutional placement. Training school residents currently are not confined as long as they were in the past, and frequently are released within a year. Institutional release takes place in a variety of ways, but the juvenile released from the training school is generally placed on aftercare status. To be released from this supervision, the juvenile must fulfill the rules of aftercare and must avoid unlawful behavior.

Recidivism

Early cohort studies certainly did not present a favorable picture of the effect of the juvenile justice process on juvenile delinquents. The Philadelphia studies found that the probability of becoming an adult offender increased dramatically for individuals with a record of juvenile delinquency. The Philadelphia, Racine, and Columbus cohort studies found that stricter punishments by the juvenile justice system were likely to encourage rather than to eliminate **recidivism,** or further delinquent behavior.[19] The Racine cohort studies found that an increase in frequency and seriousness of misbehavior typically occurred in the periods following the administration of sanctions by the justice system and that those who had police contacts as juveniles were more

recidivism
The repetition of delinquent behavior by a youth who has been released from probation status or from training school.

likely to have police contacts as adults.[20] The Columbus cohort study further found that the impact of institutional treatment was basically negative. In fact, after institutionalization, the length of time between arrests decreased dramatically.[21] These studies found that the probabilities of continuing with juvenile crime and going on to adult crime increased for individuals who were brought to the attention of the juvenile justice system. See Social World of the Delinquent 13.1, which tells the story of Lee Boyd Malvo, who, along with John Allen Muhammad, became the notorious D.C.-area Beltway snipers in 2002.

> " The probability of continuing with juvenile crime and of going on to adult crime increased for individuals who were brought to the attention of the juvenile justice system. "

A cohort study conducted in the late 1990s in Maricopa County Juvenile Court (Phoenix, Arizona) found a somewhat more favorable picture of youths' contact with the juvenile justice system. Records captured the complete juvenile court careers of more than 150,000 youths who were born between 1962 and 1977. It was found that 54 percent of males and 73 percent of females who entered the juvenile justice system never returned on a new referral. Recidivism was much higher for males than females, with 19 percent of males but only 5 percent of females accruing four or more arrests. Because there was a standing policy in this county that all youths arrested be referred to the juvenile court for screening, this study provides a complete history of local youths' official contact with the juvenile justice system.[22]

SOCIAL WORLD
of the Delinquent 13.1

Lee Boyd Malvo

Lee Boyd Malvo (alias John Lee Malvo or Malik Malvo) was born in Kingston, Jamaica, on February 18, 1985, to Leslie Malvo, a bricklayer, and Una James, a seamstress.

Malvo's parents never married and separated when he was a toddler. The father rarely saw his son after that. Ms. James often traveled to find work, and Lee was left for long periods of time in the care of relatives and friends.

Malvo and his mother left Jamaica when he was about fourteen years of age and moved to the island of Antigua. In 2000, while they were in Antigua, they met John Allen Muhammad (born John Allen Williams). The mother claimed that she was not intimate with Muhammad, but that she and her son formed a strong bond with him. She reported that her son had spent most of his life seeking a father figure.

Ms. James eventually left Antigua for Fort Myers, Florida, traveling on false documents and living there illegally. She left Lee with Muhammad, and her son was supposed to join her a few months later.

In 2001, Malvo joined his mother for a brief period in Florida, before moving to Bellingham, Washington, where he and Muhammad lived in a homeless shelter. The two would spend their evenings in a local coffee shop playing chess. Malvo enrolled in high school, falsely listing Muhammad as his father. Classmates said that he was good in school, polite, well-

dressed, and willing to state his opinions, but he did not make any friends.

While in the Tacoma, Washington, area, Malvo shoplifted a Bushmaster XM-15 rifle from Bull's Eye Shooter Supply, a retail gun dealer. About this time, Lee converted to Islam.

The pair left Bellingham in the summer of 2002 and turned up in Baton Rouge, Louisiana, where one of Muhammad's ex-wives lived. Months later, Malvo was arrested along with Muhammad and charged with participating in the infamous D.C.-area sniper shootings that took place during three weeks in October 2002 and claimed the lives of ten people.

Malvo was charged with murder, but his defense team claimed that he was a defenseless young person who had been brainwashed by Muhammad. Although Malvo pleaded not guilty by reason of insanity, a Virginia court convicted him of two capital crimes and the unlawful use of a firearm. Five days later, on December 23, 2003, the jury recommended a sentence of life in prison without the possibility of parole. On March 10, 2004, a judge formally imposed that sentence.

■ **Do you agree with the sentencing decision of the Virginia court? Do you think that the possibility of an adult brainwashing an adolescent is a sufficient mitigation defense? How would you ascertain that an adolescent was brainwashed? Are there degrees of brainwashing?**

Source: This article is licensed under the GNU Free Documentation License. It uses material from the Wikipedia article, "Lee Boyd Malvo." Adapted from http://en.wikipedia.org/wiki/Lee_Boyd_Malvo. For copyright information, please see the full license on page 614.

In *Shared Beginnings, Divergent Lives*, John H. Laub and Robert J. Sampson report on interview respondents who identified the time they spent at the Lyman School for Boys, a training school in Massachusetts, as a turning point in their lives. For some men the school provided a setting in which they could acquire the discipline and structure that had been absent from their lives. Others saw their Lyman School experience as a deterrent that would keep them away from crime in the future. For some men the school provided an environment for learning important lessons about life. Others credited Lyman School, and military service, with offering needed boundaries and strictness. Yet still others defined the Lyman School as a horrible experience for them.[23]

In recent decades, training schools had far more critics than supporters. Although the old argument that juvenile institutions are "schools of crime" is much too simplistic, there is convincing evidence that the recidivism rates are very high among those who have been confined in training schools. A 1989 review demonstrated that the rearrest rates of juveniles in several jurisdictions that rely heavily on institutions ranged from a low of 51 percent to a high of 70 percent.[24] An analysis of youths released from state correctional and private facilities in Minnesota in 1985 and 1991 found that 53 to 77 percent continued their criminal careers into adulthood.[25] Peter Greenwood and Franklin Zimring add that most state training schools "fail to reform . . . [and] make no appreciable reductions in the very high recidivism rates, on the order of 70 to 80 percent, that are expected for chronic offenders."[26]

William P. Evans, Randall Brown, and Eric Killian analyzed two 2001 surveys administered to 197 youths in two Nevada juvenile detention facilities and found that the youths who possessed high levels of decision-making competence scored higher on a postdetention success scale.[27] This study is a reminder that human agency is involved in juveniles' outcomes—affecting whether juveniles use an experience as a positive or a negative transition in their lives. It is also reasonable to conclude that youths with higher decision-making abilities would find more reason to desist from crime.

Comparison of the Juvenile and Adult Justice Systems

There is much similarity between the juvenile and adult justice systems. Both are made up of three basic subsystems (police, court, and corrections) and numerous interrelated agencies. The flow of justice in both is supposed to progress from law violation to police apprehension, judicial process, judicial disposition, and rehabilitation in correctional agencies. The basic vocabulary is the same in the juvenile and adult systems; even when the vocabulary differs, the intent remains the same. (See Table 13.3.)

TABLE 13.3

Juvenile and Adult Justice System Terms

A JUVENILE'S:	IS AN ADULT'S:
Adjudicatory hearing	Trial
Aftercare	Parole
Commitment	Sentence to confinement
Detention	Holding in jail
Dispositional hearing	Sentencing hearing
Juvenile court officer	Probation officer
Offender	Defendant
Petition	Indictment
Petitioner	Prosecutor
Respondent	Defense attorney
Being taken into custody	Arrest

adjudicatory hearing
The stage of juvenile court proceedings that usually includes the child's plea, the presentation of evidence by the prosecution and by the defense, cross-examination of witnesses, and a finding by the judge as to whether the allegations in the petition can be sustained.

commitment
A determination made by a juvenile judge at the disposition stage of a juvenile court proceeding that a juvenile is to be sent to a juvenile correctional institution.

detention
The temporary restraint of a juvenile in a secure facility, usually because he or she is acknowledged to be dangerous either to self or to others.

dispositional hearing
The stage of the juvenile court proceedings in which the juvenile judge decides the most appropriate placement for a juvenile who has been adjudicated a delinquent, a status offender, or a dependent child.

juvenile court officer
A probation officer who serves juveniles (the term is used in some but not all probation departments).

minor
A person who is under the age of legal consent.

petition
A document filed in juvenile court alleging that a juvenile is a delinquent and asking that the court assume jurisdiction over the juvenile or asking that an alleged delinquent be waived to criminal court for prosecution as an adult.

petitioner
In the juvenile justice system, an intake officer (prosecutor) who seeks court jurisdiction over a youthful offender.

respondent
The defense attorney in the juvenile court system.

taking into custody
The process of arresting a juvenile for socially unacceptable or unlawful behavior.

Exhibit 13.1

Similarities and Differences Between the Juvenile and Adult Justice Systems

Similarities

- Police officers use discretion with both juvenile and adult offenders.
- Juvenile and adult offenders receive *Miranda* warnings and other constitutional rights at time of arrest.
- Juveniles and adults can be placed in pretrial facilities.
- The juvenile court and the adult court use proof beyond a reasonable doubt as the standard for evidence.
- Plea bargaining may be used with both juvenile and adult offenders.
- Convicted juvenile and adult offenders may be sentenced to probation services, residential programs, or institutional facilities.
- Boot camps are used with juvenile and adult offenders.
- Released institutional juvenile and adult offenders may be assigned to supervision in the community.

Differences

- Juveniles can be arrested for acts that would not be criminal if they were adults (status offenses).
- Age determines the jurisdiction of the juvenile court; age does not affect the jurisdiction of the adult court.
- Parents are deeply involved in the juvenile process but not in the adult process.
- Juvenile court proceedings are more informal, while adult court proceedings are formal and open to the public.
- Juvenile court proceedings, unlike adult proceedings, are not considered criminal. Juvenile records are generally sealed when the age of majority (usually sixteen or seventeen) is reached. Adult records are permanent.
- Juvenile courts cannot sentence juveniles to jail or prison; only adult courts may issue such sentences.

■ How much harm would it do juveniles if juvenile proceedings were abolished and juveniles would be handled in adult court? What would the advantages be to juvenile offenders to be handled with adult proceedings and procedures?

Both juvenile and adult systems are under fire to get tough on crime, especially on offenders who commit violent crimes. Both must deal with case overloads and institutional overcrowding; both must operate on fiscal shoestrings; and both face the ongoing problems of staff recruitment, training, and burnout. Exhibit 13.1 further describes the common ground and differences between the juvenile and adult justice systems.

Basic Correctional Models

rehabilitation model
A correctional model whose goal is to change an offender's character, attitudes, or behavior so as to diminish his or her delinquent propensities. The medical, adjustment, and reintegration models are variants of this model because they are all committed to changing the offender.

medical model
A correctional model whose proponents believe that delinquency is caused by factors that can be identified, isolated, treated, and cured— much like a disease.

adjustment model
A rehabilitative correctional approach that emphasizes helping delinquents demonstrate responsible behavior.

To correct the behavior of the juvenile delinquent, there have traditionally been four basic correctional models applicable to the juvenile justice system: (1) the rehabilitation model; (2) the justice model; (3) the balanced and restorative model, and (4) the crime control model. An emerging model in juvenile justice is based more on a balanced approach between treatment and punishment; this balanced approach is much more focused on punishment and accountability than has been the case in juvenile justice in the past.

The Rehabilitation Model   The goal of the **rehabilitation model** is to change an offender's character, attitudes, or behavior patterns to diminish his or her propensities for youth crime.[28] The three variations of the medical model—the adjustment model, and the reintegration model—all are expressions of rehabilitative philosophy.

The **medical model,** the first treatment model to be developed from the rehabilitative philosophy, contends that delinquency is caused by factors that can be identified, isolated, treated, and cured. Its proponents believe that delinquents should be treated as though they had a disease. Punishment should be avoided, because it does nothing to solve delinquents' problems and only reinforces the negative self-image these troubled youths have.

The **adjustment model** was developed in the late 1960s and 1970s, when some proponents of rehabilitation became dissatisfied with the medical model. According to the adjustment model, delinquents need treatment to help them deal with the prob-

DELINQUENCY in America 13.1

Report: Many Youths at Detention Centers Are Mentally Ill

WASHINGTON—The nation's juvenile detention centers have become warehouses for mentally ill youths, including many who have not committed any crimes, a recent report by Congress concludes.

The youths are sent to the detention centers because they are unable to get mental health services in their communities, according to the study by the Democratic staff of the House Government Reform Committee.

"This misuse of detention centers as holding areas for mental health treatment is unfair to youth, undermines their health, disrupts the function of detention centers and is costly," the study said.

Rep. Henry Waxman, D-Calif., requested the study along with Sen. Susan Collins, R-Maine.

Collins, chairman of the Senate Governmental Affairs Committee, held a hearing on the issue in 2004. She is sponsoring legislation to make mental heath services more widely available.

"It's a tragedy that we are incarcerating children because they are sick," Collins said.

The study surveyed 698 juvenile detention facilities across the nation. Seventy-five percent—or 524—of the detention centers responded, from every state except New Hampshire.

Among the study's findings:

• In 33 states, mentally ill youths were held in detention centers with no charges against them because there was no place else for them to go.
• In one recent six month period, 15,000 detained youths were waiting to obtain mental health services.
• Every day, about 2,000 youths remain locked up because mental health services are not available for them. That accounts for 7% of all youths held in juvenile detention.
• One detention center reported holding a 7-year-old who was waiting for mental health services. The center was one of 117 facilities that detained children 10 and younger.

"It is a terrible miscarriage of justice to detain or incarcerate children in order that they might be able to have a chance of getting any mental health services," Ernestine Gray, chief judge of the Orleans Parish Juvenile Court in New Orleans, testified. "Our detention facilities should not be used as substitute mental hospitals."

Leonard Dixon, director of the juvenile detention facility in Wayne County, Mich., said the problems are serious and widespread. He testified that 56% of youths admitted to his facility in the past

A recent report by Congress found that the nation's juvenile detention centers have become warehouses for mentally ill youths. ■ **Why are those children locked up?**

year needed or received mental health services.

Dixon said most facilities don't have the resources to provide treatment or services for mentally ill youths.

Others testified that mentally ill children are sent to juvenile detention centers because parents don't have access to services in schools and insurance often doesn't pay for mental health treatment.

Source: Pamela Brogan, "Many Youths at Detention Centers Are Mentally Ill, Report Finds," *USA Today*, July 8, 2004, p. 10A. Copyright © 2004 by *USA Today*. Reprinted by permission.

lems that led them to crime. The emphasis is placed on delinquents' responsibility at the present time. Youthful offenders cannot change the facts of their emotional and social deprivations of the past, but they can demonstrate responsible behavior in the present and avoid using past problems as an excuse for delinquent behavior. The various therapies used are not based on punishment, because punishment is seen as only increasing delinquents' alienation and behavior problems.

A basic assumption of the third rehabilitative approach, the **reintegration model,** is that delinquents' problems must be solved in the community where they began. This model also assumes that society has a responsibility for helping law violators reintegrate themselves back into community life. The reintegration model recommends community-based corrections for all but hard-core offenders, offers those hard-core offenders who must be institutionalized a wide variety of reentry programs, and provides the necessary services so that delinquents can restore family ties and obtain employment and education.[29] Supporters of the reintegration model established a wide variety of community-based programs in the 1970s, including diversion programs, residential and day treatment programs, and programs to treat drug abusers.

reintegration model

A perspective that holds that offenders' problems must be solved in the community in which they occur and that community-based organizations can help offenders readjust to community life.

The Justice Model The **justice model** holds to the belief that punishment should be the basic purpose of the juvenile justice system. Among the variants of the justice model for youth crime are those proposed by David Fogel, by the Report of the Committee for the Study of Incarceration, and by the Report of the Twentieth Century Fund.[30]

justice model

A contemporary model of imprisonment based on the principle of just deserts.

Web LIBRARY 13.3

Read the OJJDP Juvenile Justice Bulletin *Restorative Justice Conferences as an Early Response to Young Offenders* at **www .justicestudies.com/ WebLibrary**.

The concept of **just deserts** is the pivotal philosophical basis of the justice model. According to Fogel's model of **justice as fairness**, offenders are volitional and responsible human beings, and therefore they deserve to be punished if they violate the law. The punishment shows that the delinquent is blameworthy for his or her conduct. The decisions concerning delinquents should be based not on their needs but on the penalties that they deserve for their acts.[31] Punishment is not intended to achieve social benefits or advantages, such as deterrence or rehabilitation; rather, the only reason to punish an offender is because he or she deserves it. However, the punishment given an offender must be proportionate to the seriousness of the crime.

The Balanced and Restorative Model   Building on research and practical experience dating back to the early 1980s, the **balanced and restorative model** is an integrated effort to reconcile the interests of victims, offenders, and the community through programs and supervision practices. (For the background and philosophy of this model, see Focus on Social Policy 13.1.) "Balanced" refers to system-level decision making by administrators to "ensure accountability to crime victims, to increase competency in offenders, and to enhance community safety."[32] (See Figure 13.2.)

These three goals are summarized in accountability, competency, and community protection. *Accountability* refers to a sanctioning process in which offenders must accept responsibility for their offenses and the harm caused to victims, and make restitution to victims, assuming that community members are satisfied with the outcome. *Competency* refers to the rehabilitation of offenders. That is, when offenders improve their educational, vocational, emotional, social, and other skills, they can become responsible adults and live successfully in the community. *Community protection* refers to the ability of citizens to prevent crime, resolve conflict, and feel safe because offenders have matured into responsible citizens. Subsequently, the overall mission of the balanced and restorative model is to develop a community-oriented approach to the control of offenders rather than relying solely on punishment.[33]

The juvenile justice system, in implementing the balanced and restorative model, uses many of the same principles as the justice model to develop effective systems for the supervision of juvenile offenders in the community.[34]

FOCUS ON
Social Policy 13.1

Restorative Philosophy

A restorative philosophy has been a major development in criminological thinking, being grounded in traditions of justice from the ancient Arab, Greek, and Roman civilizations. The purpose of restorative justice is to restore or "make whole" victims, offenders, and communities through the participation of a plurality of stakeholders. Restorative justice is seen as an alternative to either rehabilitation or retribution in juvenile justice. Its appeal to liberals is a less punitive juvenile justice system. Its appeal to conservatives is an emphasis on victim empowerment, on empowering families, and on fiscal savings because of the parsimonious use of punishment.

In adult justice, restorative justice is found in victim–offender mediation, victim notification, victim input in sentencing, victim input in plea bargaining, family group conferences, healing circles, restorative probation, reparation boards on the Vermont model, and Chinese Bang Jiao programs.

Restorative justice is increasingly found in juvenile justice approaches such as restorative probation, antibullying programs in school, conflict resolution in school, teen courts, drug courts, healing circles, victim mediation, victim notification, and victim input in juvenile court dispositional matters.

■ **In what type of case is restorative justice more likely to be used? In what cases would it be rarely used?**

Source: John Braithwaite, "Restorative Justice: Assessing Optimistic and Pessimistic Accounts," in *Crime and Justice: A Review of Research* 25, edited by Michael Tonry (Chicago and London: The University of Chicago Press, 1999), pp. 1, 4.

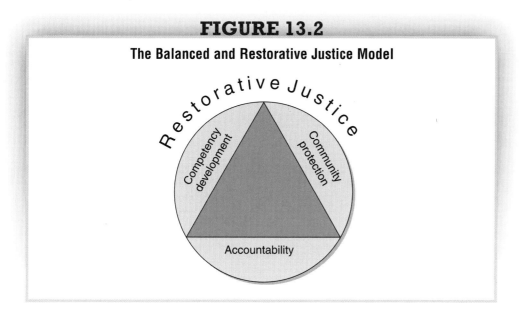

FIGURE 13.2

The Balanced and Restorative Justice Model

Restorative Justice

Competency development

Community protection

Accountability

Source: Gordon Bazemore and Mark S. Umbreit, *Balanced and Restorative Justice* (Washington, D.C.: Office of Juvenile Justice and Delinquency Prevention, 1994), p. 1. Reprinted with permission from the U.S. Department of Justice.

The Crime Control Model   The public has become increasingly intolerant of serious youth crime and is more and more receptive to the **crime control model,** which emphasizes punishment as the remedy for juvenile misbehavior. The crime control model is grounded on its adherents' conviction that the first priority of justice should be the protection of the life and property of the innocent. Supporters of the crime control model, which is based on the classical school of criminology (examined in

crime control model

A correctional model supporting discipline and punishment as the most effective means of deterring youth crime.

A neighborhood restorative justice coordinator conducts an intake interview with a new program client. The juvenile offender was referred to the program by a judge. ■ **What are the goals of the balanced and restorative model of corrections?**

CHAPTER 13 | The Juvenile Justice Process   **455**

TABLE 13.4

Comparison of Key Elements of the Rehabilitation, Justice, Balanced and Restorative, and Crime Control Models

ELEMENTS	MODELS			
	REHABILITATION	JUSTICE	BALANCED AND RESTORATIVE	CRIME CONTROL
Theory of why delinquents offend	Behavior is caused or determined; based on positivism	Free will; based on the classical school	Free will; based on the classical school	Free will; based on the classical school
Purpose of sentencing	Change in behavior or attitude	Doing justice	Community protection	Restoration of law and order
Type of sentencing advocated	Indeterminate	Determinate	Determinate	Determinate
View of treatment	Goal of correctional process	Voluntary but necessary in a humane system	Voluntary but necessary in a humane system	Ineffective and actually coddles offenders
Crime control strategy	Use therapeutic intervention to eliminate factors causing crime	Provide fairness for victims, for offenders, and for practitioners in the system	Make juvenile offenders accountable for their behavior	Declare war on youth crime by instituting "get tough" policies

Source: Reprinted with permission from Clemens Bartollas.

Chapter 3), charge that punishment is the preferred correctional model because it both protects society and deters crime. Youthful offenders are taught not to commit further crimes, while noncriminal youths receive a demonstration of what happens to a person who breaks the law.[35]

Comparison of the Four Models   The rehabilitation model is more concerned that juvenile delinquents receive therapy than that they be institutionalized. The crime control model, on the other hand, is a punishment model that contends juveniles must pay for their crimes. Those who back the crime control model also claim that punishment has social value for both offenders (deterrence) and society (protection). The justice model strongly advocates that procedural safeguards and fairness be granted to juveniles who have broken the law, yet proponents of this model also firmly hold that juveniles should be punished according to the severity of their crimes. The balanced and restorative model is an accountability model that is focused on recognizing the needs of victims, on giving proper attention to the protection of society, and on providing competency development for juveniles entering the system. Table 13.4 compares the four models.

▪Emerging Approaches to Handling Youthful Offenders

There is wide support for using the crime control model with the "serious and violent juvenile" offender. For example, from 1992 through 1997, legislatures in forty-seven states and the District of Columbia enacted laws that made their juvenile justice systems more punitive.[36] See Table 13.5. Many states added to the purpose clauses of their juvenile codes such phrases as "provide effective deterrents"; "hold youths accountable for criminal behavior"; "balance attention to youthful offenders, victims, and the community"; and "impose punishments consistent with the seriousness of the crime."[37]

Web **PLACES** 13.2

Visit the American Bar Association's Juvenile Justice Committee online via **www.justicestudies .com/WebPlaces**.

TABLE 13.5

Changes in State Juvenile Justice Systems in the 1990s

From 1992 through 1997, legislatures in forty-seven states and the District of Columbia enacted laws that made their juvenile justice systems more punitive.

STATE	CHANGES IN LAW OR COURT RULE*			STATE	CHANGES IN LAW OR COURT RULE*		
Alabama	T		C	Montana	T	S	C
Alaska	T		C	Nebraska			
Arizona	T	S	C	Nevada	T		C
Arkansas	T	S	C	New Hampshire	T	S	C
California	T		C	New Jersey		S	C
Colorado	T	S	C	New Mexico	T	S	C
Connecticut	T	S	C	New York			
Delaware	T	S	C	North Carolina	T		C
District of Columbia	T	S		North Dakota	T		C
Florida	T	S	C	Ohio	T	S	C
Georgia	T	S	C	Oklahoma	T	S	C
Hawaii	T		C	Oregon	T	S	C
Idaho	T	S	C	Pennsylvania	T		C
Illinois	T	S	C	Rhode Island	T	S	C
Indiana	T	S	C	South Carolina	T		C
Iowa	T	S	C	South Dakota	T		
Kansas	T	S	C	Tennessee	T	S	C
Kentucky	T	S	C	Texas	T	S	C
Louisiana	T	S	C	Utah	T		C
Maine			C	Vermont			
Maryland	T		C	Virginia	T	S	C
Massachusetts	T	S	C	Washington	T		C
Michigan		S	C	West Virginia	T		C
Minnesota	T	S	C	Wisconsin	T	S	C
Mississippi	T		C	Wyoming	T		C
Missouri	T	S	C				

*T = Transfer provisions, S = Sentencing authority, C = Confidentiality
Source: Howard N. Snyder and Melissa Sickmund, *Juvenile Offenders and Victims: 1999 National Report* (Washington, D.C.: Office of Juvenile Justice and Delinquency Prevention, 1999), p. 89. Reprinted with permission from the U.S. Department of Justice.

Yet in Table 13.6 it can be seen that in 1997 about as many states were emphasizing prevention/diversion/treatment philosophical goals as were advocating punishment philosophical goals. At the same time, nearly twice as many states placed importance on both sets of goals in their juvenile codes. The trend toward a balanced and restorative approach also was seen in the late 1990s. By the end of the 1997 legislative session, seventeen states had adopted the language of the balanced and restorative justice philosophy, emphasizing offender accountability, public safety, and competency development.[38]

Race and Juvenile Justice

One of the most disturbing issues facing the juvenile justice system today is the long-standing and pronounced disparities in the processing of white and minority youths. Northeastern University's Donna Bishop concludes: "Despite decades of research, there is no clear consensus on why minority youths enter and penetrate the juvenile justice system at such disproportionate rates."[39] According to Bishop, two explanations have been given: "The first is that minority overrepresentation reflects race and ethnic differences in the incidence, seriousness, and persistence of delinquent involvement (the 'differential offending' hypothesis)" and "the second is that overrepresentation is attributable to inequities—intended or unintended—in juvenile justice practice (the 'differential treatment' hypothesis)."[40]

TABLE 13.6

Philosophical Goals Stated in Juvenile Code Purpose Clauses

Some Juvenile Codes Emphasize Prevention and Treatment Goals, Some Stress Punishment, and Others Seek a Balanced Approach

PREVENTION/DIVERSION/ TREATMENT	PUNISHMENT	BOTH PREVENTION/DIVERSION/ TREATMENT AND PUNISHMENT	
Arizona*	Arkansas	Alabama	New Hampshire
District of Columbia	Georgia	Alaska	New Jersey
Kentucky	Hawaii	California	New Mexico
Massachusetts	Illinois	Colorado	New York
North Carolina	Iowa	Connecticut	North Dakota
Ohio	Louisiana	Delaware	Oklahoma
South Carolina	Michigan	Florida	Oregon
Vermont	Missouri	Idaho	Pennsylvania
West Virginia	Rhode Island	Indiana	Tennessee
		Kansas	Texas
		Maryland	Utah
		Maine	Virginia
		Minnesota	Washington
		Mississippi	Wisconsin
		Montana	Wyoming
		Nebraska	
		Nevada	

- Most states seek to protect the interests of the child, the family, the community, or some combination of the three.
- In seventeen states the purpose clause incorporates the language of the balanced and restorative justice philosophy, emphasizing offender accountability, public safety, and competency development.
- Purpose clauses also address court issues such as fairness, speedy trials, and even coordination of services. In nearly all states the code also includes protections of the child's constitutional and statutory rights.

* Arizona's statutes and court rules did not contain a purpose clause; however, the issue is addressed in case law.

Source: Author's adaptation of Torbet and Szymanski's *State Legislative Responses to Violent Juvenile Crime: 1996–97 Update.* Office of Juvenile Justice and Delinquency Prevention, "1999 National Report Series," *Juvenile Justice Bulletin* (Washington, D.C.: U.S. Department of Justice, 1999), p. 3. Reprinted with permission from the U.S. Department of Justice.

University of Missouri–St. Louis Professor Janet L. Lauritsen, in examining what is known about racial and ethnic differences in juvenile offending, offers the following conclusions that have wide support in the literature:

■ Rates of juvenile homicide are higher for minorities than rates for white youthful offenders. Similarly, variations exist in rates of lethal violence between minority groups.

■ Official data suggest disproportionate involvement in nonlethal violence on the part of African American youths. When arrest data are restricted to specific forms of nonlethal violence, African American youths appear to be disproportionately involved in robbery, aggravated assault, and rape.

■ Juvenile property crime data show that African American youths are slightly more involved in such offenses than white youths, although the level of involvement varies by type of property crime.

■ Arrest data show that white youths are disproportionately involved in alcohol offenses, and that American Indian youths are slightly more likely than African American or Asian American youths to be arrested for these crimes.

■ African American youths are disproportionately arrested for drug abuse violations and illicit drug use, but self-report data from juveniles on their own drug involvement do not confirm the differences between African American and white youths suggested by arrest data. In fact, white youths are somewhat more likely to report using marijuana, selling any drug, and selling marijuana.

DELINQUENCY International 13.1

A Cross-National Study of the Effects of Juvenile Justice Processing in Denver, Colorado, and Bremen, Germany

Differences between the juvenile justice systems of Denver, Colorado, and Bremen, Germany, include a more lenient, diversion-oriented system in Bremen and a more severe and punishment-oriented system in Denver. In Bremen arrest (commonly referred to as a "ticket") cannot legally occur until a youth is fourteen years old, and juvenile law can be and commonly is applied to those eighteen to twenty. In contrast, the age of responsibility in Denver is ten, and adult processing begins at age eighteen.

In Bremen, for adolescents aged fourteen to seventeen, more than 90 percent of cases referred to the prosecutor conclude with dismissal or diversion from court, often communicated by means of a letter to the offender. In Denver offenders may be ticketed or taken into cus-

tody; arrested offenders are most often referred to juvenile court and receive intermediate-level sanctions. Confinement is very rare in Bremen but is used in approximately 10 to 20 percent of Denver cases.

The effects of such system differences on juvenile offending rates are small. At both sites arrest had little effect on subsequent delinquency. When there was an effect, arrest resulted in sustaining or increasing the level of delinquent behavior. Also, the study findings indicated that the severity of the sanction applied had little influence on later delinquency and crime. It was particularly true in Bremen that when an effect was observed, more severe sanctions resulted in persistence or increases in subsequent delinquency/criminal involvement.

■ Do you believe that the U.S. juvenile justice system is too severe in how it handles juvenile offenders? What would happen if juvenile justice in this nation became as lenient as the system in Bremen, Germany? Why is it that arrests and other sanctions do not have more of a deterrent effect on youths, either in this nation or in Bremen, Germany?

Source: David Huizinga, Karl Schumann, Breate Ehret, and Amanda Elliott, *The Effect of Juvenile Justice System Processing on Subsequent Delinquent and Criminal Behavior: A Cross-National Study* (Washington, D.C.: The National Institute of Justice, 2003).

■ Weapons violations arrest data indicate that African American youths are disproportionately likely to be arrested for weapons possession or use.[41]

■ Although the most commonly occurring crimes exhibit few group differences, the less frequent and serious crimes of violence show generally higher levels of African American and Latino American involvement.[42] (See Table 13.7.)

Lauritsen concludes that this kind of empirical evidence suggests that the relationship between race and ethnicity and juvenile involvement in delinquency is complex and contingent on the type of offense. In contrast, Bishop suggests that minority overrepresentation in the juvenile justice system is attributable to inequities in system practices rather than differences in the incidence, serious, or persistence of offending.

Minorities are overrepresented among youths held in secure detention, petitioned to juvenile court, and adjudicated delinquents. Among those who are adjudicated delinquents, minorities are more often committed to the "deep end" of the juvenile system. That is, when confined, they are more likely to be housed in large public institutions rather then in privately run specialized treatment facilities or group homes. Furthermore, prosecutors and judges seem quicker to relinquish jurisdiction over minorities, transferring them to criminal court for prosecution and punishment.[43] See Focus on Social Policy 13.2 for insight into the relationship between race and juvenile justice system processing.

Web PLACES 13.3

Visit the Coalition for Juvenile Justice's website via **www .justicestudies.com/ WebPlaces**.

The Juvenile Justice and Delinquency Prevention Act of 1974

In the Juvenile Delinquency Prevention and Control Act of 1968, Congress recommended that children charged with status offenses be handled outside the juvenile court system. Congress subsequently passed the Juvenile Justice and Delinquency

TABLE 13.7

Summary of Racial and Ethnic Differences in Juvenile Offending by Crime Type

PATTERN FOUND IN ARREST DATA	SOURCE OF CONFIRMATION
Lethal violence: • Black youth most disproportionately involved • Latino youth disproportionately involved in some cities • American Indian youth disproportionately involved	Witness reports, case evidence
Nonlethal violence: • Black youth disproportionately involved	Victim reports, self-reports, parent and teacher reports
Property crime: • White youth more involved for some offenses • Black youth more involved for some offenses • Overall, minimal differences across groups	Self-reports
Alcohol violations: • White youth disproportionately involved • American Indian youth disproportionately involved	Self-reports (for white youth); no sufficient data for American Indian youth
Drug abuse violations: • Black youth disproportionately involved	Self-report data contrary to arrest data; white youth report higher levels in self-report data
Weapons violations: • Black youth disproportionately involved	Self-reports (also show higher prevalence for Hispanic youth)

Source: Janet L. Lauritsen, "Racial and Ethnic Differences in Judicial Offending," *Our Children, Their Children: Confronting Racial and Ethnic Differences in American Juvenile Justice*," edited by Darnell F. Hawkins and Kimberly Kempf-Leonard (Chicago: The University of Chicago Press, 2005), p. 96. Reprinted by permission.

Prevention Act of 1974 (JJDPA), which required the deinstitutionalization of status offenders and nonoffenders, and the separation of juvenile delinquents from adult offenders as a condition for state participation in the Formula Grant Programs. In 1980, an amendment to the 1974 Act required that juveniles be removed from adult jail and lockup facilities. The 1992 amendment to the Act required that states determine the existence and extent of "disproportionate confinement of minority youth." Where disproportionate minority confinement is a problem, the state must demonstrate efforts to reduce it. The Act was further modified in 1996, especially in terms of contacts of juveniles with adults in correctional facilities.[44] Reauthorized in late 2002, the JJDPA took effect in its latest amended form in October 2003. The mandates from 1968, 1974, and 1980, for the most part, stayed the same. The 1992 disproportionate minority confinement (DMC) mandate was changed to emphasize efforts to reduce minority contact with the system. The revised Act encourages programs geared toward delinquency prevention as well as multiprong approaches to DMC.[45]

Let's look more closely at the key mandates of the JJDPA.

Deinstitutionalization of Status Offenders

Before the 1974 Act was implemented, one of the critical issues of juvenile corrections was the difficulty that status offenders and noncriminal youths had when

FOCUS ON
Social Policy 13.2

The Politics of Race and Juvenile Justice

In his 1999 book *Race and the Transformation of Juvenile Justice* and in a 2003 article entitled "The Politics of Race and Juvenile Justice: The 'Due Process Revolution' and the Conservative Reaction," Barry Feld analyzes the social structural and political context of juvenile justice reforms in the late twentieth century.

During the 1960s, social structural changes in the United States motivated the Supreme Court under Chief Justice Earl Warren to reassess juvenile justice and criminal practices. In response to broader concerns about civil rights and racial discrimination, the Court's decisions on school desegregation, juvenile justice, and criminal procedures all reflected a fundamental shift in constitutional jurisprudence to protect individual rights and the rights of racial minorities.

The second phase of juvenile justice legal changes, Feld writes, "emerged in response to the *In re Gault* decision and culminated in 'get tough' law reforms that now fall disproportionately on minority offenders.... From the 1970s to the 1990s, conservative Republican politicians pursued a 'southern strategy,' used crime as a code word for race for electoral advantage, and advocated harsher policies that have affected juvenile justice throughout the nation."

Feld then argues that two other factors contributed to "get tough" policies. The first was the crack cocaine epidemic of the 1980s as well as the gun violence and rash of youth homicides that took place during that decade with the deindustrialization of the urban core and the emergence of the black underclass. The second factor was media coverage "that disproportionately put a black face on young criminals and reinforced the white public's fear and racial animus."

"By the early 1990s," Feld contends, "the words *youth crime* had become code for 'crimes committed by African American juveniles.'" Juvenile justice policies became particularly punitive toward juveniles who were charged with drug offenses and violent crimes—offense categories to which African Americans youths contributed disproportionately.

This punitive direction was reflected in the fact that in the late 1980s and early 1990s, nearly every state "enacted laws either to simplify the transfer of youths to criminal courts or to require juvenile court judges to impose determinate or mandatory minimum sentences on those who remained with a more punitive juvenile system."

■ What is your reaction to arguments by Feld (and others) that the "get tough" strategy tends to single out African American youthful offenders? Why has this strategy been able to avoid being defined as a racist position? Is there anything that the juvenile justice system can do to avoid such disproportionate confinement of African American and other minority youths?

Sources: Barry C. Feld, *Bad Kids: Race and the Transformation of the Juvenile Court* (New York: Oxford University Press, 1999), and Barry C. Feld, "The Politics of Race and Juvenile Justice: The 'Due Process Revolution' and the Conservative Reaction," *Justice Quarterly* 20 (December 2003), pp. 766, 777–778, 793.

they were placed in institutions with juvenile delinquents. Status offenders and noncriminal youths frequently stayed longer in these institutions because they often had more difficulty complying with rules and limits than most delinquent youth.[46] A more disturbing issue was that status offenders and noncriminal youths frequently were victimized by delinquent youths in institutional contexts. Clemens Bartollas, Stuart J. Miller, and Simon Dinitz document the plight of these youths in attempting to survive with aggressive delinquents. On too many occasions, they became the cottage's scapegoats and were victimized in every conceivable way. As one institutionalized status offender put it to Bartollas one day, "I don't belong here. These guys are animals."[47]

Although it can be argued that status offenders still are placed in private training schools with delinquents, few are placed in public correctional facilities (see Chapter 16). There is also an attempt to keep status offenders separate from juvenile delinquents in community residential programs. For example, status offenders are typically placed in youth shelters, but delinquents are confined in juvenile detention centers.

> " Status offenders and noncriminal youths frequently were victimized by delinquent youths in institutional contexts. "

Youthful offenders at the Los Angeles County Youth Authority's Camp Karl Holton. As this book points out, minorities are overrepresented among youths held in secure detention.

■ **What are the reasons for such overrepresentation?**

Removal of Juveniles from Jails and Lockups

Another way that the JJDPA has affected juvenile corrections is that few juveniles are confined presently in jails with adults. Before the JJDPA was enacted in 1974, between 500,000 and 1,000,000 youths were confined in jails each year.[48] In 2000, the estimated daily population of juveniles in jail was 7,600.[49]

The reason so many youths remain confined in county jails and police lockups is that many juvenile court jurisdictions in the United States simply have no alternatives available. For example, juveniles who are transferred to adult court to await criminal trial make up an increasingly large category of juveniles confined in adult jails.

Total jail removal remains a distant goal; forty-four states continue to resist full compliance with the jail-removal mandate. Two arguments have been made to explain this failure to comply with the JJDPA mandate. Some claim that the resistance is attributable to the failure of federal officials to push harder for compliance. Others argue that states lack the necessary resources and alternatives to implement the jail-removal mandate.[50]

Some states, however, have taken a strong stand against the jailing of juveniles. In Utah, legislation was passed that makes jailing a juvenile a misdemeanor.[51] In 1986, California adopted the strongest law in the nation prohibiting the confinement of children in jails and lockups for adults. What was so encouraging about SB 1637, which became effective on January 1, 1987, was that California had been jailing about 20 percent of the U.S. incarcerated juveniles.[52] Also, since 1984, Illinois, Missouri, North Carolina, Tennessee, and Virginia have enacted legislation prohibiting the jailing of juveniles or restricting the number of admissions.[53]

Disproportionate Minority Confinement

Carl E. Pope and William H. Feyerherm's highly regarded assessment of the issue of discrimination against minorities reveals that two-thirds of the studies they examined found "both direct and indirect race effects or a mixed pattern (being present at some stages and not at others)."[54] They add that selection bias can take place at any stage and that small racial differences may accumulate and become more pronounced as minority youths are processed into the juvenile justice system.[55]

The Coalition for Juvenile Justice (then the National Coalition of State Juvenile Justice Advisory Groups) brought national attention to the problem of **disproportionate minority confinement** in their 1988 annual report to Congress. In that same year, Congress responded to evidence of disproportionate confinement of minority juveniles in secure facilities by amending the Juvenile Justice and Delinquency Prevention Act of 1974 to provide that states must determine whether the proportion of minorities in confinement exceeded their proportion in the population of the state. If there was overrepresentation, states must demonstrate efforts to reduce it.[56]

During the 1992 reauthorization of the JJDPA, Congress substantially strengthened the effort to address disproportionate confinement of minority youth in secure facilities. Elimination of disproportionate minority confinement was elevated to the status of a "core requirement" alongside deinstitutionalization of status offenders, removal of juveniles from adult jails and lockups, and separation of youthful offenders from adults in secure institutions. The 2002 reauthorization of the JJDPA also changed the disproportionate minority confinement (DMC) mandate to reduce minority contact with the system. See Table 13.8 for a summary of state compliance with DMC core requirements, as of December 2002.

Michael J. Leiber's 2003 book, *The Contexts of Juvenile Justice Decision Making*, examines four jurisdictions in Iowa and reveals the presence of race effects that were not accounted for by legal and relevant extralegal factors. Race effects began at the intake stage in all four jurisdictions. Interviews with juvenile court personnel, as well as an analysis of community and historical factors, provided insights into the contexts of court decision making and the roles played by race in this decision making. The race effects vary in other stages of juvenile justice processing, sometimes involving both more severe and more lenient outcomes in the same jurisdiction. Leiber's study found that although decision making is more complex than often suggested by previous research, the cumulative effect is still the disproportionate confinement of minorities, especially African Americans, in the juvenile justice system.[57]

Web PLACES 13.4

Learn more about Disproportionate Minority Contact (DMC) from the Juvenile Justice Evaluation Center online via **www.justicestudies.com/WebPlaces**.

Graduated Sanctions

In adult corrections, increased attention has been given to intermediate sanctions, and in recent decades these intermediate sanctions have included a system of graduated sanctions, ranging from fines, day reporting centers, drug courts, and intensive probation to residential placements.

This same movement has gained some momentum in juvenile justice, but in juvenile justice the system of graduated sanctions is focused on serious, violent, and chronic juvenile offenders. These offenders are moved along a continuum through a well-structured system that addresses both their needs and the safety of the community. At each level, juvenile offenders are subject to more severe sanctions if they continue in their delinquency offenses.[58]

Core Principles of Graduated Sanctions

According to John J. Wilson and James C. Howell, a model graduated system combines the treatment and rehabilitation of youth with fair, humane, reasonable, and appropriate sanctions. It offers a continuum of care that consists of diverse programs. Included in this continuum are immediate sanctions within the community both for first-time nonviolent offenders and for more serious offenders, secure care programs for the most violent offenders, and aftercare programs that provide high levels of both social control and treatment services.[59]

Each of the graduated sanctions is intended to consist of gradations, or sublevels, that together with appropriate services constitute an integrated approach. This approach is designed to stop the youthful offender's further penetration into the

TABLE 13.8

Summary of State Compliance with the DMC Core Requirement

The following summary of state compliance with the DMC core requirement, pursuant to Section 31.303(j) of the JJDP Formula Grants Regulation (28 C.F.R. Part 31), is based on FY 2002 Formula Grant applications as of December 2002.

- In addition to completing the identification and assessment phases in earlier years, three states continue to monitor their DMC trends each year, update their assessment studies, implement intervention strategies to address identified factors that contribute to DMC, and conduct evaluations of their DMC efforts:

Colorado	Pennsylvania	Washington

- The District of Columbia and twenty states have completed the identification and assessment phases, are implementing the intervention phase, and also have submitted updated DMC data, demonstrating ongoing monitoring efforts:

Alaska[*]	Idaho	New York
Arkansas	Minnesota	North Dakota
California[*]	Mississippi	Oklahoma
Connecticut	Missouri	Oregon
Delaware[†]	Montana	South Carolina[‡]
District of Columbia	Nevada	Tennessee[*]
Georgia	New Jersey	Virginia

- Four states have completed the identification and assessment phases, are implementing the intervention phase, and plan to update DMC identification data and/or assessment studies:

Indiana	Michigan	New Mexico[‡]
Kansas		

- One state has completed the identification phase, is implementing the intervention phase, and conducting a formal assessment study:

  Alabama

- Four states have completed the identification phase, are implementing the intervention phase, and plan to conduct formal assessments:

Louisiana	Ohio	West Virginia
North Carolina		

- Eleven states have completed the identification and assessment phases and are implementing the intervention phase:

Arizona	Iowa	Texas
Florida	Maryland	Utah
Hawaii	Massachusetts[‡]	Wisconsin
Illinois	Nebraska	

- One state became a participating state in the Formula Grants Program in 1999. It has completed the identification phase and is conducting an assessment study:

  Kentucky[‡]

- Two states in which the minority juvenile population recently exceeded 12 percent of the total juvenile population, which requires them now to comply with the DMC requirement, have partially completed the identification phase:

  Maine
  Vermont

- Four territories have completed the identification phase, which revealed that minority juveniles were not being disproportionately detained:

  American Samoa
  Guam
  Northern Marianas
  Virgin Islands

- One territory has been exempted by the U.S. Census Bureau from reporting racial statistics and, therefore, is exempt from complying with the DMC requirement:

  Puerto Rico

- Two states are under a draw down restriction of 25 percent of the FY 2002 Formula Grant allocation pending submission of required information:

  New Hampshire
  Rhode Island

- Two states did not participate in the FY 2002 Formula Grants Program:

  South Dakota
  Wyoming

[*]Began to receive invensive DMC technical assistance in January 2002 to further enhance DMC efforts.
[†]Received intensive DMC technical assistance from November 2000 to July 2001 to further enhance DMC efforts.
[‡]Received intensive DMC technical assistance since November 2000 to further enhance DMC efforts.
Source: Heidi M. Hsia, *Disproportionate Minority Confinement: 2002 Update* (Washington, D.C.: Office of Juvenile Justice and Delinquency Prevention, 2004), pp. 10–11. Reprinted with permission from the U.S. Department of Justice.

juvenile system by inducing law-abiding behavior as early as possible through the combination of treatment sanctions and appropriate interventions. The family must be involved at each level in the continuum. Aftercare must be actively involved in supporting the family and in reintegrating the youth into the community. Programs will need to use risk and needs assessments to determine the placement that is appropriate for the offender. The effectiveness of interventions depends on their being swift, certain, and consistent, and the incorporation of increased sanctions that include the possible loss of freedom. As the severity of sanctions are increased, so must the intensity of treatment be increased. These sanctions could ultimately mean confinement in a secure setting, ranging from a secure community-based facility to a public or private training school, camp, or ranch. The programs that are most effective for hard-to-handle youths address key areas of risk in their lives, provide adequate support and supervision, and offer youths a long-term stake in the community.[60]

In 2005, OJJDP authors cited research indicating that "many incarcerated youth can be managed effectively in well-structured community-based programs."[61] Consequently OJJDP has sponsored the implementation of small, community-based, or regional facilities to provide secure economical confinement for a population of serious, violent, and/or chronic juvenile offenders. Federal funding now provides states that are considering new facilities with an opportunity to replace large traditional training schools with smaller regional or commu-

> " The effectiveness of interventions depends on their being swift, certain, and consistent. "

nity-based facilities that are part of a continuum of sanctions and services supported by local justice systems and communities. According to Shelley Zavick, president of the International Partnership for Youth/Justice Solutions Group, "Such facilities are more likely to be rooted in local values, engender community support and involvement, and reflect the needs of local jurisdiction. Equally important, these smaller facilities can target programming and operations to be responsive to the specific treatment and supervision needs of the youth in their care."[62]

Trends for the Future

The present problems of youth violence, as well as a growing cohort of older juveniles in the future, will surely place pressure on the juvenile justice system and its policy makers to address several important issues. How these issues are resolved will greatly influence how the juvenile justice system will function in the future.

- *Issue:* There is increased dissatisfaction with the juvenile justice system. Some even question whether the juvenile justice system, as we have known it, will survive.
  First Trend: It is likely that the adult justice system will become more involved with older juveniles than it currently is and that the structure of the juvenile justice system will change in rather significant ways. But it is very unlikely that this nation will soon abandon its century-long experiment with a separate system for juveniles.
- *Issue:* There is a concern that a projected increase in the juvenile population in the next twenty years will make greater demands on the juvenile justice system.
  Second Trend: The U.S. Bureau of the Census estimates that juveniles under the age of eighteen will increase 14 percent between 2000 and 2025—about one-half of 1 percent per year. By 2050, it is estimated that the juvenile population will be 36 percent larger than it was in 2000.[63]
- *Issue:* Many of these juveniles will come from impoverished homes headed by single mothers. Concern exists that this may mean more minorities in the juvenile justice system.
  Third Trend: In 2002, African American juveniles and Hispanic American juveniles were more than three times as likely to live in poverty, as were non-Hispanic white juveniles. Since juvenile poverty appears to be associated with juvenile crime, it is likely that minority juveniles will continue to be the focus of social control.[64]
- *Issue:* With the increased population of poor juveniles, the rate of juvenile violence, including homicides, may again grow, as it did in the late 1980s and early 1990s.
  Fourth Trend: It is hoped that new laws will improve law enforcement's ability to keep guns out of the hands of juveniles. Hence, these rates are unlikely to attain the levels of the late 1980s and early 1990s.

Web LIBRARY 13.4

Read the OJJDP publication *Juveniles Facing Criminal Sanctions: Three States That Changed the Rules* at **www.justicestudies.com/WebLibrary**.

Web LIBRARY 13.5

Read the NIJ article *Brick by Brick: Dismantling the Border Between Juvenile and Adult Justice* at **www.justicestudies.com/WebLibrary**.

■ *Issue:* The widespread feeling among many in the U.S. population today is that there are more troubled teenagers than in the past.

Fifth Trend: The field of adolescent psychiatry will be more frequently called on to treat troubled youths, but it will be the children of the economically advantaged who will benefit the most, as they are the ones who will receive the benefits of private hospitals and treatment centers.

■ *Issue:* Some argue that stiffer penalties could be a deterrent to juveniles who might otherwise kill.

Sixth Trend: The 2005 *Roper v. Simmons* decision, discussed in more detail in Chapter 15, means that the death penalty debate for juveniles under the age of eighteen is resolved—at least for now—and it is unlikely that any changes will take place in the near future.[65]

■ *Issue:* Gangs are perceived as a serious social problem, but there is a lack of agreement about what to do to reduce the threat of gang violence.

Seventh Trend: After a number of years of expansion, the growth of youth gangs stalled in the final years of the twentieth century. Gangs will not disappear, however; they provide too much of a support system for those who lack other support systems. Youth gangs are increasingly becoming a minority problem, and this is likely to increase in the decades to come. It is unlikely that the future will provide any greater insight on what to do about gangs.

■ *Issue:* The use of drugs by adolescents remains an issue in American society.

Eighth Trend: The drug choices of juveniles may well change in the future, but no evidence exists that drug use will be less of a problem in the future than it is today. There is currently a movement away from juveniles' use of crack cocaine to the use of methamphetamines.

■ *Issue:* Many adolescents consume alcohol to excess.

Ninth Trend: Given peer pressures, juveniles will likely continue to drink, and the use of alcohol will continue to be a problem.

■ *Issue:* Debate has focused for some time on the disparity of juvenile court sentencing, especially between jurisdictions.

Tenth Trend: The current tendency to create uniformity and reduce discretion in juvenile sentencing procedures is likely to continue.

■ *Issue:* State legislatures are increasingly passing laws intended to deter juvenile crime.

Eleventh Trend: Serious juvenile offenders will likely continue to be removed from the jurisdiction of the juvenile court, and additional mechanisms for the direct referral of serious juvenile criminals to adult criminal court will be created.

■ *Issue:* Debate is ongoing over the proper role of private programs in juvenile justice processing.

Twelfth Trend: Private programs will continue to be an important component of juvenile corrections.

■ *Issue:* There has been increased support and enthusiasm for the use of restorative justice in juvenile justice processing.

Thirteenth Trend: Restorative justice programs will continue to spread throughout the United States.

■ *Issue:* The debate goes on between those who want to deinstitutionalize and those who want to increase the use of long-term confinement for serious juvenile offenders

Fourteenth Trend: Given the high costs of lengthy institutionalization, the deinstitutionalization movement is likely to continue to expand.

■ *Issue:* Racial and ethnic inequities in the juvenile justice system are a serious contemporary concern.

Fifteenth Trend: In spite of legislation such as the Juvenile Justice and Delinquency Prevention Act, intended to reduce disproportionate minority confinement, DMC will likely remain an ongoing problem, and juvenile institutions will continue to be "dumping grounds" for poor and minority problem children.

CHAPTER
Summary

The juvenile justice system is responsible for controlling and correcting the behavior of law-violating juveniles. Of special note are the following points:

■ It can be argued that the juvenile justice system has improved since the mid-1970s, but the improvements hardly seem to have scratched the surface in terms of designing a justice system that will effectively deal with juvenile delinquency in the United States.

■ The problem of continued serious juvenile delinquency in the United States challenges the juvenile justice system to mobilize a coordinated and effective approach to dealing with youth crime.

■ Racial and ethnic inequities represent one of the most serious issues facing the juvenile justice system today.

■ Conflicting philosophies and strategies for dealing with youth crime, and a fragmented juvenile justice system that varies from one jurisdiction to another, make it nearly impossible for the juvenile justice process to handle delinquency cases effectively.

■ The restorative and balanced justice model is rapidly gaining acceptance in more and more jurisdictions as a promising modality that should be employed in the fight against juvenile crime.

■ Efforts to coordinate a continuum of increasing sanctions for violent and chronic youthful offenders offer hope and represent positive directions for the juvenile justice system.

CRITICAL THINKING
Questions

1. The juvenile justice system has devised four ways to deal with delinquency: the rehabilitation model, the justice model, the balanced and restorative model, and the crime control model. Which do you think works best? Why? Why is the balanced and restorative model gaining such popularity nationwide?

2. After reading this chapter, do you feel encouraged or discouraged about the ability of society to deal effectively with delinquency? Why?

3. Evaluate current approaches to working with violent and chronic juvenile offenders. Are these strategies likely to have much of an impact? Justify your answer.

4. Does society really need a juvenile justice system that is separate from the adult system used with criminals? Be able to debate your explanation.

WEB
Interactivity

Read the article "Juvenile Delinquency" on Wikipedia (**http://en .wikipedia.org/wiki/Juvenile_delinquency**). Wikipedia is an open source online encyclopedia built and maintained by a community of knowledge workers and users just like you. Anyone can contribute to Wikipedia articles, adding information and improving the accuracy of the encyclopedia's content.

Review Wikipedia's juvenile delinquency article and determine what might be added to it to make it more informative. Look specifically for information (either in this article or elsewhere on Wikipedia) on the juvenile justice system and think about what you might be able to add.

Armed with your ideas, work with your classmates to enhance the Wikipedia entries on juvenile delinquency and on the juvenile justice system. Submit your work to your instructor if asked to do so.

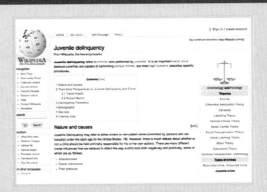

Source: From http://en.wikipedia.org/wiki/Juvenile_ delinquency. For copyright information, please see the full license on page 614.

Notes

1. Elizabeth S. Scott and Thomas Grisso, "The Evolution of Adolescence: A Developmental Perspective on Juvenile Justice Reform," *The Journal of Criminal Law & Criminology* 88 (1988), p. 88.
2. Marty Beyer, "Immaturity, Culpability & Competency in Juveniles: A Study of 17 Cases," *Criminal Justice* (Summer 2000), pp. 26–35.
3. Barry C. Feld, "The Transformation of the Juvenile Court," *Minnesota Law Review* 75 (February 1991), p. 578.
4. Ibid., p. 723.
5. Ibid., pp. 723–724.
6. Barry C. Feld, *Bad Kids: Race and the Transformation of Juvenile Court* (New York: Oxford University Press, 1999), p. 64.
7. Frederic L. Faust and Paul J. Brantingham, eds., *Juvenile Justice Philosophy* (St. Paul, Minn.: West Publishing, 1974), pp. 569–575.
8. Anthony M. Platt, *The Child Savers*, 2nd ed. (Chicago: University of Chicago Press, 1977).
9. Ibid. See also Sanford J. Fox, "Juvenile Justice Reform: An Historic Perspective," *Stanford Law Review* 22 (1970), p. 1187, and Douglas Rendleman, "*Parens Patriae:* From Chancery to the Juvenile Court," *South Carolina Law Review* 28 (1971), p. 205, for interpretations similar to Platt's.
10. David Shichor, "Historical and Current Trends in American Juvenile Justice," *Juvenile and Family Court Journal* 34 (August 1983), p. 61.
11. John Augustus, *First Probation Officer* (Montclair, N.J.: Patterson-Smith Company, 1972), pp. 4–5.
12. David J. Rothman, *The Discovery of the Asylum* (Boston: Little, Brown & Company, 1971), pp. 53–54.
13. Steven Schlossman, "Delinquent Children: The Juvenile Reform School," in *The Oxford History of the Prison*, edited by Norval Morris and David J. Rothman (New York: Oxford University Press, 1995), p. 365.
14. Rothman, *The Discovery of the Asylum*, p. 65.
15. Schlossman, "Delinquent Children," p. 348.
16. See Howard Polsky, *Cottage Six: The Social System of Delinquent Boys in Residential Treatment* (New York: Russell Sage Foundation, 1963); Clemens Bartollas, Stuart J. Miller, and Simon Dinitz, *Juvenile Victimization: The Institutional Paradox* (New York: Halsted Press, 1976); Barry C. Feld, *Neutralizing Inmate Violence: The Juvenile Offender in Institutions* (Cambridge, Mass.: Ballinger, 1977); and Kenneth Wooden, *Weeping in the Playtime of Others: America's Incarcerated Children* (New York: McGraw-Hill, 1976).
17. For specific numbers of staff in juvenile corrections, see Timothy J. Flanagan and Kathleen Maguire, *Sourcebook of Criminal Justice Statistics—1999* (Washington, D.C.: U.S. Government Printing Office, 2000).
18. Ibid.
19. Marvin E. Wolfgang, Robert M. Figlio, and Thorsten Sellin, *Delinquency in a Birth Cohort* (Chicago: University of Chicago Press, 1972), pp. 91, 131.
20. Lyle W. Shannon, *Assessing the Relationships of Adult Criminal Careers to Juvenile Careers: A Summary* (Washington, D.C.: U.S. Government Printing Office, 1982), pp. 14–15.
21. Donna Martin Hamparian et al., *The Violent Few: A Study of Dangerous Juvenile Offenders* (Lexington, Mass.: Lexington Books, 1980), p. xvii.
22. Howard N. Snyder and Melissa Sickmund, *Juvenile Offenders and Victims: 1999 National Report* (Washington, D.C.: Office of Juvenile Justice and Delinquency Prevention, 1999), p. 80.
23. John H. Laub and Robert J. Sampson, *Shared Beginnings, Divergent Lives: Delinquent Boys to Age 70* (Cambridge, Mass.: Harvard University Press, 2003), pp. 128–131.
24. Barry Krisberg, James Austin, and Patrick Steele, *Unlocking Juvenile Corrections: Evaluating the Massachusetts Department of Youth Services* (San Francisco: The National Council on Crime and Delinquency, 1989), pp. 26–32.
25. Minnesota Legislative Auditor, *Residential Facilities for Juvenile Offenders* (St. Paul: State of Minnesota, 1995), pp. 71–73.
26. Peter Greenwood and Franklin Zimring, *One More Chance: The Pursuit of Promising Intervention Strategies for Chronic Juvenile Offenders* (Santa Monica, Calif.: Rand Corp., 1985), p. 40.
27. William P. Evans, Randall Brown, and Eric Killian, "Decision Making and Perceived Postdetention Success among Incarcerated Youth," *Crime and Delinquency* 48 (October 2002), p. 553.
28. Andrew von Hirsch, *Doing Justice: The Choice of Punishments* (New York: Hill & Wang, 1976), p. 12.
29. President's Commission on Law Enforcement and Administration of Justice, *Task Force Report: Corrections* (Washington, D.C.: U. S. Government Printing Office, 1967).
30. David Fogel, ". . . We Are the Living Proof: The Justice Model for Corrections* (Cincinnati: Anderson Publishing Company, 1975); Andrew von Hirsch, *Doing Justice: The Choice of Punishments;* and Twentieth Century Fund Task Force on Sentencing Policy toward Young Offenders, *Confronting Youth Crime* (New York: Holmes and Meier, 1978).
31. Fogel, "We Are the Living Proof."
32. D. W. Ness, "Restorative Justice," in *Criminal Justice, Restitution, and Reconciliation,* edited by Burt Galaway and Joe Hudson (Monsey, N.J.: Willow Tree Press, 1990); H. Zehr, *Retributive Justice, Restorative Justice* (Akron, Pa.: Mennonite Central Committee, 1985); and H. Zehr, *Changing Lenses* (Scottsdale, Pa.: Herald Press, 1990).
33. G. Bazemore, "What's 'New' about the Balanced Approach?" *Juvenile and Family Court Journal* (1997), pp. 2, 3.
34. Ibid.
35. See James Q. Wilson, *Thinking about Crime,* rev. ed. (New York: Basic Books, 1983), and Ernest van den Haag, *Punishing Criminals: Concerning a Very Old and Painful Question* (New York: Hill and Wang, 1976).
36. Snyder and Sickmund, *Juvenile Offenders and Victims,* p. 89.
37. Ibid.
38. Ibid.

39. Donna M. Bishop, "The Role of Race and Ethnicity in Juvenile Justice Processing," in *Our Children, Their Children: Confronting Racial and Ethnic* Differences *in American Juvenile Justice*," edited by Darnell F. Hawkins and Kimberly Kempf-Leonard (Chicago: The University of Chicago Press, 2005), p. 23.

40. Ibid.

41. Janet L. Lauritsen, "Racial and Ethnic Differences in Judicial Offending," *Our Children, Their Children: Confronting Racial and Ethnic* Differences *in American Juvenile Justice*, pp. 91–95.

42. Ibid., p. 99.

43. Bishop, "The Role of Race and Ethnicity in Juvenile Justice Processing," p. 23.

44. Snyder and Sickmund, *Juvenile Offenders and Victims*, p. 89.

45. Michael J. Leiber, a consultant for the OJJDP, provided this information in the winter of 2004.

46. Paul Lerman, "Child Convicts," *Transaction* 8 (July/August, 1971), pp. 35–42; and Clemens Bartollas, Stuart J. Miller, and Simon Dinitz, *Juvenile Victimization: The Institutional Paradox* (New York: Halsted Press, 1976), pp. 151–168.

47. Bartollas, Miller, and Dinitz, *Juvenile Victimization*.

48. The estimated number of youths confined in jails during the 1970s ranged from 900,000 (Children's Defense Fund) to 100,000 (National Council on Crime and Delinquency). See also Rosemary C. Sarri, "Gender Issues in Juvenile Justice," *Crime and Delinquency* 29 (1983), p. 390.

49. Melissa Sickmund, *Juveniles in Corrections: National Report Series Bulletin* (Washington, D.C.: Office of Juvenile Justice and Delinquency Prevention, 2004), p. 1.

50. James Austin, Kelly Dedel Johnson, and Maria Gregorious, *Juveniles in Adult Prisons and Jails: A National Assessment* (Washington, D.C.: Institute on Crime, Justice and Corrections at the George Washington University and National Council on Crime and Delinquency, 2000), p. x.

51. Ira M. Schwartz, Linda Harris, and Laurie Levi, "The Jailing of Juveniles in Minnesota: A Case Study," *Crime and Delinquency* 34 (April 1988), p. 146.

52. David Steinhart, "California's Legislature Ends the Jailing of Children: The Story of a Policy Reversal," *Crime and Delinquency* 34 (1988), pp. 169–170.

53. David Steinhart and Barry Krisberg, "Children in Jail," *State Legislatures* 13 (1987), pp. 12–16.

54. Carl E. Pope and William Feyerherm, *Minorities and the Juvenile Justice System* (Washington, D.C.: Office of Juvenile Justice and Delinquency Prevention, 1995), pp. 2–3.

55. Ibid. See Donna M. Bishop and Charles E. Frazier, *A Study of Race and Juvenile Processing in Florida*. A report submitted to the Florida Supreme Court Racial and Ethnic Bias Study Commission, 1990. See also Carl E. Pope, Rick Ovell, and Heidi M. Hsia, *Disproportionate Minority Confinement: A Review of the Research Literature from 1989 through 2001* (Washington, D.C.: Office of Juvenile Justice and Delinquency Prevention, 2002).

56. Snyder and Sickmund, *Juvenile Offenders and Victims*, p. 192.

57. Michael J. Leiber, *The Contexts of Juvenile Justice Decision Making* (Albany: State University of New York, 2003), pp. 148, 153–155.

58. Krisberg et al., *Guide for Implementing the Comprehensive Strategy for Serious, Violent, and Chronic Juvenile Offenders* (Washington, D.C.: Office of Juvenile Justice and Delinquency Prevention, 1995).p. 133.

59. Ibid.

60. Ibid., pp. 12–13.

61. Shelley Zavlek, *Planning Community-Based Facilities for Violent Juvenile Offenders as Part of a System of Graduated Sanctions* (Washington, D.C.: Office of Juvenile Justice and Delinquency Prevention, 2005), p. 5.

62. Ibid.

63. Howard N. Snyder and Melissa Sickmund, *Juvenile Offenders and Victims: 2006* (Washington, D.C.: Office of Juvenile Justice and Delinquency Prevention, 2006), p. 2.

64. Ibid., p. 7.

65. *Roper v. Simmons*, 543 U.S. 551 (2005).

14

The Police and the Juvenile

> "The vast majority of youth are good citizens who have never been arrested for any type of crime."

**—Shay Bilchik, President,
Child Welfare League of America**

KEY Terms

arrest, p. 484

citation, p. 482

fingerprinting, p. 487

gang unit, p. 499

juvenile officer, p. 474

Miranda v. Arizona, p. 486

police discretion, p. 477

police interrogation, p. 486

pretrial identification practices, p. 488

search and seizure, p. 485

station adjustment, p. 482

CHAPTER Objectives

AFTER READING THIS CHAPTER, YOU SHOULD BE ABLE TO ANSWER THE FOLLOWING QUESTIONS:

- What has been the history of police–juvenile relations?

- How have the attitudes of juveniles toward the police changed?

- How are juvenile offenders processed?

- What are the legal rights of juveniles in encounters with police?

- What kinds of efforts do the police make to deter delinquency?

- How does community policing impact juveniles?

471

In June 2006, a $41,000 reward was offered for information leading to the arrest of individuals involved in the shootings of eighteen young African Americans in a number of incidents spanning six weeks in Miami-Dade County (Florida).

In setting the amount of the reward, county commissioners had added $40,000 to Crime Stoppers' standard $1,000 reward. Police were hoping the increased reward might lead them to some of those involved in the rash of violence plaguing the county. The incidents that motivated the commissioners' action included the following:

■ *April 23, 2006*: James "J. T." Anderson, sixteen, died as the result of a drive-by shooting. His family says the real target may have been a friend who had gotten into a fight at school. No arrests have been made.

■ *April 24, 2006*: Walter King, nineteen, was gunned down during what police called an "ongoing neighborhood" dispute. A seventeen-year-old was also wounded. A man named Willie James Pinson has been arrested and charged with the shooting.

■ *April 25, 2006*: Young Jessica Dixon was shot to death in front of a market where she had gone to buy groceries. Police said she was an innocent bystander in an argument between two men. Police arrested Cory D. Harris, twenty-seven, a previously convicted armed robber, in connection with the shooting.

■ *April 29, 2006*: Recent high school graduate Sharika Wilson, nineteen, was buying milk for her baby when she and a man were gunned down in Opa-locka. Police said she was an unintended target.

■ *May 23, 2006*: Police say Antwan Grace, who has since been arrested, shot and killed college-bound Jeffrey Johnson, seventeen, in an argument over tricked-out cars. Johnson, the third member of his class at Carol City High School to be shot and killed in 2006, would have graduated *summa cum laude*.

■ *May 24, 2006*: Eighteen-month-old Zykarious Cadillon and fifty-two-year-old Sam Gorgalis were shot in Miami's desperately poor Little River neighborhood. Zykarious, who had been playing in his front yard, died. Gorgalis survived. Police have no suspects and neighbors are keeping quite about the shooting.

■ *May 26, 2006*: Recent high school graduate Kennetha Jordon, eighteen, was killed while driving in Opa-locka. A suspect, Kion Mathis, was arrested on murder charges the next day.

■ *May 26, 2006*: Two people were shot, neither one fatally. Police have no suspects.

■ *May 30, 2006*: Former high school wrestler Robert Phillips, seventeen, was shot and killed in northwest Miami-Dade. No arrests have been made.

■ *June 5, 2006*: Luckson Branel, Edwin Terma, and Lamar Atron Kelly were all killed. Miami police are searching for suspects. One person survived the ambush, believed to have been carried out by a Haitian gang.

■ *June 10, 2006*: Toddler Ashanti Simpson was caught in cross-fire from a domestic argument outside her house. The two-year-old was critically wounded.

The United States is a free and democratic society, and law enforcement officials must respect the rights and freedom guaranteed to all citizens under the Constitution. Democratic systems of government strive to maintain a delicate balance between individual rights and collective needs. Traditionally, the balance has been weighted in favor of individual rights. Some claim that criminal activity, such as the murders cited above, is made all too easy by the relative lack of restrictions on personal freedoms that characterize American society. Consequently, "get tough" strategies for dealing with crime have become increasingly popular in recent years. Such strategies are fed by the growing belief that intensified law enforcement efforts are the only workable remedy for the crime problems we face today—including the threat of increasingly serious juvenile crime. Juvenile crime represents one of the most demanding and frustrating areas of police work. A common complaint of police officers is that arrested juvenile offenders are back on the streets before the officers have had a chance to complete the necessary paperwork. Also, with the rise of youth gangs and with increased numbers of juveniles carrying weapons, policing juveniles is much more dangerous than it used to be. Finally, police departments give little status to those dealing with youth crime because they regard arresting a juvenile as a poor "bust."

> " The United States is a free and democratic society, and law enforcement officials must respect the rights and freedom guaranteed to all citizens under the Constitution. "

Policing juveniles is similar in some ways to policing adults, yet in other ways it is quite different. It is similar in that both juveniles and adults have constitutional protections; that juveniles can be as hostile to the police as adults can be; that armed juveniles, of course, are as dangerous as armed adults; that both juveniles and adults are involved in gangs, some of which traffic drugs; and that alcohol and drugs affect the functioning of both juveniles and adults. A major difference is the belief that juveniles are more salvageable than adults. Few would argue with the widely held tenet that juveniles are more likely than adults to experience a turning point where they can walk away from crime.

> " In a real sense, the police officer becomes an on-the-spot prosecutor, judge, and correctional system when dealing with a juvenile offender. "

Accordingly, the importance of police–juvenile relations cannot be minimized. The police are usually the first contact a youth has with the juvenile justice system. As the doorway into the system, the police officer can use his or her broad discretion to either detour youths or involve them in the system. In a real sense, the police officer becomes an on-the-spot prosecutor, judge, and correctional system when dealing with a juvenile offender.

The History of Police–Juvenile Relations

In the seventeenth and eighteenth centuries, American colonists and immigrants installed in the small colonial towns such informal methods of control as the "mutual pledge," the "watch and ward," and the constable system. These informal methods of control by the family, the church, and the community were sufficient until the expansion of towns in the late eighteenth and nineteenth centuries resulted in increased disorder and crime. To deal with their crime problem, New York, Boston, and Philadelphia created police forces in the 1830s and 1840s; by the 1870s, all major cities had full-time police forces. At that time, however, the police were drawn from the least educated segments of society, were ill treated, and were poorly paid. Furthermore, they often became instruments of political corruption, used for personal gain and political advantage.

In the late nineteenth century, law-violating juveniles received various kinds of treatment from officers walking the beat. Juveniles might receive the same treatment as adult offenders, or they might be treated as erring children and receive only slaps on the wrist. Juvenile offenders were sometimes taken to the parish priest for admonition and spiritual instruction.

In the first third of the twentieth century, the New York City, Portland, Oregon, and Washington, D.C., police departments began to address the problem of juvenile crime. The New York City Police Department began a program in 1914 that, with prevention as its goal, helped juveniles develop relationships with local police. This idea of prevention became so popular that 90 percent of the nation's cities had instituted some type of juvenile program by 1924.[1] The Police Athletic League (PAL) was launched in the 1920s, and by the 1930s most large departments had either assigned welfare officers to difficult districts, initiated employment bureaus for youthful males, assigned officers to juvenile courts, or set up special squads to deal with juvenile crime.[2]

In the 1930s, August Vollmer introduced the concept of a youth bureau in the Berkeley, California, police department, emphasizing the importance of crime prevention by the police. Youth bureaus were soon established in other urban departments as the need arose for **juvenile officers**—police specialists in juvenile law enforcement. These specialized units were variously called *crime prevention bureaus, juvenile bureaus, youth aid bureaus, juvenile control bureaus,* and *juvenile divisions.*

juvenile officer

In some police departments, a police officer who has received specialized training so as to be able to work effectively with juveniles.

Contemporary Developments in Police–Juvenile Relations

The role of the juvenile officer developed further after World War II, and it was formalized when a group of juvenile officers organized the Central States Juvenile Officers Association in 1955 and the International Juvenile Officers Association in 1957. Through their participation in regional, national, and international associations, juvenile officers expended considerable effort in developing the duties, standards, procedures, and training necessary for dealing with juvenile lawbreakers. As defined by the officers themselves, the basic responsibility of the juvenile officer was to be helpful, rather than punitive, in handling youthful offenders.

In the 1960s, a number of police programs designed to improve relations with juveniles and to reduce delinquency were developed throughout the United States. Police officers came into the public schools to interact with grade school and high school students and to discuss some aspects of the law with them. The PAL programs were expanded to cover leadership training, full- and part-time employment opportunities, moral training, and extensive recreational programs (see Exhibit 14.1). To prevent and control delinquency, the police also became involved in truancy prevention programs, drug abuse rehabilitation, and the actual supervision of youthful offenders.

The degree of involvement in juvenile work varied among different police departments during the 1970s. Although some departments became even more actively involved in juvenile work, the trend in the late 1970s and early 1980s was for police departments to move away from deep involvement in juvenile work. Budgetary constraints, as well as the administrative problems caused by specialization, caused many police departments to drop their juvenile divisions or to limit their jurisdiction to dependent, neglected, and abused children. Detective divisions in these departments generally assumed responsibility for juvenile and adult criminal investigations.

In the 1980s and 1990s, the proliferation of substance abuse among young people resulted in the movement of the police back into the schools. This trend in juvenile–police relations was more concerned with preventing the use of drugs than with diverting drug users from the juvenile justice system. The widely used Drug Abuse Resistance Education (D.A.R.E.) program, which will be evaluated later in this chapter, demonstrated this trend in police–juvenile work.

In addition to the drug prevention programs of the 1980s, the police in the 1990s were called on to provide security and safety in the school, to enforce drug-free school zone laws and the Gun-Free School Zones Act, and to conduct various school attendance programs. Needless to say, the explosion of drug-trafficking gangs across the

Web PLACES 14.1

Visit New York City's Police Athletic League via **www.justicestudies .com/WebPlaces**.

Police Athletic League (PAL)

PAL started with a literal bang—a rock through a window.

A gang of New York toughs, harassing storekeepers and generally making life miserable in their neighborhood, threw the rock that eventually pioneered this new approach to the problem of juvenile delinquency.

Lieutenant Ed W. Flynn of the New York City Police Department's Crime Prevention Bureau was on duty that fateful day more than 100 years ago. To him it was another day of kids getting in trouble. But it was more than that.

Lieutenant Flynn liked kids. He wondered at the uselessness of always punishing them. He wondered why they couldn't be reached before they were in trouble.

He made it a point to search out the gang's ringleader. They talked, Flynn looking for the reasons behind the kids' antisocial behavior, the ringleader pouring out the frustrations of the ghetto, telling the cop, "Man, we ain't got no place to play . . . nothin' to do. The cops are always hasslin' us. We can't even play baseball."

Flynn thought about that. A staunch baseball fan himself, he began to wonder: "Why should the police chase kids for doing what was normal? Why not help those kids form a team? Give them a place to play under police supervision. Be a friend instead of an enemy."

Flynn found a playground where the group could play under the eyes of friendly policemen.

The team was an instant success. Before the year was out, there were close to a dozen such teams in the city. In 1910, Captain John Sweeney, commanding officer of a lower-side police precinct in New York City, began the Police Athletic League, or PAL. In 1937 PAL dedicated its first indoor youth center, and in 1941 it became incorporated under the laws of the state of New York.

That was the birth of PAL.

At present, PAL in New York City provides programming for 65,000 children, including:

- Seventeen full-time youth centers and seventy-one part-time centers operating from October through May.
- Summer day camps.
- Educational programs (computer training, illustrated art and poetry contests, homework help and remedial reading, and many others).
- Employment training and placement.
- Sports and precinct programs (17,000 teams in basketball, baseball, flag football, and soccer).
- Child care (five Head Start centers and four day care centers).

PAL has become the largest juvenile crime prevention program in the United States, with over three million youth members. The National PAL encompasses more than 500 cities, townships, and counties.

■ Why have the police in so many jurisdictions responded so enthusiastically to PAL? Why don't we hear more about PAL? Is it as good and as positive for juveniles as it appears to be?

Sources: New Mexico Police Athletic League, www.nmpal.com and New York City Police Athletic League, www.palnyc.org (2003).

nation and the greater accessibility of firearms among adolescents have made it much more difficult to provide safety for students and school personnel and to ensure the enforcement of the law.

■ Juveniles' Attitudes Toward the Police

The subject of juveniles' attitudes toward the police received considerable attention in the 1970s, less attention in the 1980s, and more attention in the 1990s. Robert Portune's 1971 study of almost 1,000 junior high students in Cincinnati found that whites had more favorable attitudes toward the police than African Americans, that girls had more favorable attitudes than boys, and that students from middle- and upper-class families had more positive attitudes than those from lower-class families. He also found that hostility toward the law and police increased progressively during grades seven through nine.[3]

Several studies have reported that juveniles who have had contact with the police have more negative attitudes toward police than do those who have not had contact. L. Thomas Winfree Jr. and Curt T. Griffiths's 1977 study of students in seventeen high schools found that, to a considerable degree, juveniles' attitudes toward the police are shaped by contacts with police officers. Negative contacts, according to Winfree and Griffiths, influence juvenile attitudes more than do the factors of gender, race, residence, or socioeconomic status and appear to be twice as important as positive contact in determining juvenile attitudes toward police officers.[4]

William T. Rusinko and his colleagues, in examining about 1,200 ninth-grade students in three junior high schools in Lansing, Michigan, in 1978, explored the importance of police contact in shaping juveniles' attitudes toward the police. They found that positive police contacts by the white youths in their study clearly neutralized their encounters with police that had negative connotations. But these researchers found that positive police contact did not reduce the tendency for African American youths to be less positive in their opinions of police. The findings agree with several other studies that show the development of a culturally accepted view of police among African Americans independent of their arrest experience.[5]

> " Juveniles who have had contact with the police have more negative attitudes toward police than do those who have not had contact. "

Scott H. Decker, in a 1981 review of the literature on attitudes toward the police, concluded that youths had more negative attitudes toward the police than did older citizens and that race, the quality of police services, and previous experiences with the police also affected citizens' attitudes.[6] In 1990, however, James R. Davis found, in a very small sample of New Yorkers younger than age twenty, that attitudes toward the police were not statistically related to age.[7]

Komanduri S. Murty, Julian B. Roebuck, and Joann D. Smith found in a 1990 Atlanta study that "older, married, white-collar, educated, and employed respondents reported a more positive image of the police than their counterparts—younger, single, blue-collar, low-educated, unemployed/underemployed respondents."[8] Murty and colleagues offered support for previous findings that younger African American males are particularly hostile toward the police. These researchers demonstrated that the chances that respondents will have negative attitudes toward the police also vary, in descending order, with residence in high-crime tracts, single marital status, negative contacts with the police, and blue-collar occupations.[9]

Michael J. Leiber, Mahesh K. Nalla, and Margaret Farnworth's 1998 study challenges the traditional argument that juveniles' interactions with the police are the primary or sole determinant of youths' attitudes toward the police. Instead, according to these authors, juveniles' "attitudes toward authority and agents of social control develop in a larger sociocultural context, and global attitudes toward police affect youths' assessment of specific police contacts." Using a sample of Iowa youths who were accused of delinquency or adjudicated as delinquent, these researchers found that social background variables (particularly minority status) and subcultural preferences (particularly commitment to delinquent norms) affected youths' attitudes toward the police both directly and indirectly (through police–juvenile interactions).[10]

Data from the Monitoring the Future survey of high school seniors from the mid-1980s through the mid-1990s indicate that high school seniors' attitudes toward the police became more negative during those decades across all subsets of the sample. For example, in response to a question about their attitudes toward the police and law enforcement agencies, the percentages of youths responding "good" and "very good" tended to decline throughout the 1980s and into the early 1990s across the categories of gender, race, and geographic region. However, these

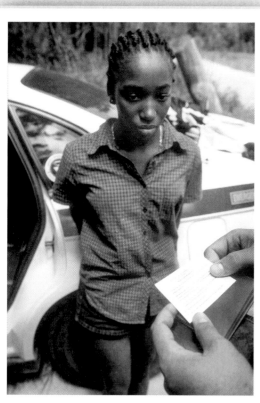

An officer reading the *Miranda* rights to a handcuffed juvenile following an arrest for drug possession. Respect for and deference to police officers may result in leniency, but youths who are disrespectful, hostile, or abusive toward police officers are more likely to end up in juvenile court. ■ **Should police officers be allowed to exercise such discretion?**

general downward trends showed some improvement in later years. The Monitoring the Future Project data for 2001 revealed that some 33.2 percent of high school seniors (up from 26.6 percent in 1996) responded either "good" or "very good." If the 33.7 percent of "fair" responses in 2001 were added to the "good" and "very good" categories, roughly 67 percent of high school seniors could be considered to have a positive attitude toward the police.[11]

Youthful offenders, as anyone who has worked with this population can testify, are the most negative toward the police. Many juveniles claim that they have experienced police harassment on a regular basis and police brutality at least occasionally. They often charge that police "run them off" the streets without justification, that police stop and arrest them without probable cause, and that police are quick to put their hands on them.

To sum up: As Leiber and colleagues point out, juveniles' attitudes toward the police are formed in a larger sociocultural context. Most youths appear to have positive attitudes toward the police. Younger juveniles have more positive attitudes than older ones; whites are usually more positive than African Americans; girls are more positive than boys; and middle- and upper-class youngsters tend to be more positive than lower-class ones. The more deeply committed a juvenile is to crime, the more hostile he or she is toward the police. But the findings about the influence of contacts with the police are mixed. Some researchers have found that the more contacts a juvenile has with the police, the more negative he or she feels about the police. Others have concluded that for white youths, positive contacts tend to neutralize the effect of negative contacts. Finally, a recent survey of high school seniors reveals that the attitudes of juveniles toward the police today seem to be more positive than they were during the 1980s and 1990s.

The Processing of Juvenile Offenders

When responding to juvenile lawbreakers, police are influenced by a variety of individual, sociocultural, and organizational factors. They can choose a more or less restrictive response to an individual offender. In Exhibit 14.2, Ann Miller, an FBI Special Agent and former municipal police officer, explains some of her reasoning in terms of how juvenile offenders should be handled.

Factors That Influence Police Discretion

Police discretion can be defined as the choice a police officer makes between two or more possible means of handling a situation. Discretion is important, for the police actually act as a court of first instance in initially categorizing a juvenile. The police officer thus becomes a legal and social traffic director who can use his or her wide discretion to detour juveniles from the justice system or involve them in it.

Police discretion has come under attack because many believe the police abuse their broad discretion. But most police contact with juveniles is impersonal and nonofficial and consists simply of orders to "Get off the corner," "Break it up," or "Go home." Studies generally estimate that only 10 to 20 percent of police–juvenile encounters become official contacts.[12] For example, David Bordua's 1967 study of the Detroit police reported only 5,282 official contacts out of 106,000 encounters.[13] In 2004, Stephanie M. Myers reported on data collected for the Project on Policing Neighborhoods (POPN), a study of police in Indianapolis, Indiana, and St. Petersburg, Florida. She found that 84 (13 percent) of the 654 juvenile suspects were arrested.[14]

police discretion
A police officer's ability to choose from among a number of alternative dispositions when handling a situation.

> " Police discretion has come under attack because many believe the police abuse their broad discretion. "

The point can also be made that the juvenile justice system could not function without police discretion. Urban courts, especially, are overloaded. Probation officers' caseloads are entirely too high. Many juvenile correctional institutions are jammed to

Decisions Police Officers Face

FBI Special Agent and former police detective Ann Miller describes how she decides on a course of action in an incident involving a juvenile:

Let us take an incident: A juvenile male is involved in some form of criminal mischief. He causes a little damage to a house (for example, egging, spray-painting, etc.), and his basic intention was not to do any major damage, but primarily as a prank.

How I would handle this depends on several factors: How much damage was done, what kind of damage, the juvenile's intent, and how the victim feels. If the damage is minor and the victim does not want to press charges but still wants some type of restitution, the juvenile may be asked to come back and clean up the damage and/or pay for the damage him-

self. Along with that is the juvenile's intent and attitude. Was it just a prank and the juvenile is apologetic for it, or does he have the attitude that he won't go back and clean it up and does not feel remorseful for the damage? Finally, how much support does the juvenile have at home? Are the parents supportive of the police and victim, and will they hold the juvenile accountable for his actions? Or is there no support at home? If the attitude of the juvenile is poor and if the juvenile is not going to be held accountable for the damage by his parents, then I would most likely have to handle it in a more formal way with charges.

> Do you feel that Special Agent Miller's statement is a reasonable one? What are some of the advantages of not being arrested and processed through the juvenile system?

Source: Interviewed in September 2001.

capacity. If police were to increase by two to three times the number of youths they referred to the system, the resulting backlog of cases would be unmanageable.

The police officer's disposition of the juvenile offender is mainly determined by nine factors: (1) the offense, (2) citizen complainants, (3) gender, (4) race, (5) socioeconomic status, (6) individual characteristics of the juvenile, (7) nature of the interaction between the police officer and the juvenile, (8) departmental policy, and (9) external pressures (see Table 14.1).

The Offense   The most important factor determining the disposition of the misbehaving juvenile is the seriousness of the offense. Donald J. Black and Albert J. Reiss Jr. point out that the great bulk of police encounters with juveniles pertain to matters of minor legal significance, but the probability of arrest increases with the legal seriousness of the alleged offense.[15]

TABLE 14.1

Factors That Influence Disposition

Individual Factors
Personality characteristics of the juvenile
Personality characteristics of the police officer
Interaction between the police officer and the juvenile

Sociocultural Factors
Citizen complaints
Gender of the juvenile
Race/ethnicity of the juvenile
Socioeconomic status of the juvenile
The influence of cultural norms in the community and values of the wider society on both juveniles and
   police officers
External pressures in the community to arrest certain types of juvenile offenders

Organizational Factors
Nature of the offense
Departmental policy

Citizen Complainants   A number of studies have found that the presence of a citizen or the complaint of a citizen is an important determining factor in the disposition of an incident involving a juvenile.[16] If a citizen initiates a complaint, remains present, and wishes the arrest of a juvenile, the chances are that the juvenile will be arrested and processed.[17] If the potential arrest situation results from police patrol, the chances are much greater that the youth will be warned and released.

Gender   Traditionally, girls have been less likely than boys to be arrested and referred to the juvenile court for criminal offenses, but there is some evidence of the erosion of police "chivalry" in the face of youthful female criminality.[18] Yet, as Chapter 7 noted, girls are far more likely to be referred to the court if they violate traditional role expectations for girls through behaviors such as running away from home, failing to obey parents, or being sexually promiscuous.[19] In short, the police tend to reflect the views of complaining parents (i.e., that girls should be chaste and should be protected from immoral behavior).

Race   Studies differ on the importance of race in determining juvenile disposition. On the one hand, several studies (after results were corrected to account for offense seriousness and prior record) have found that the police are more inclined to arrest minority juveniles.[20] The strongest evidence showing race as a determining factor is found in the Philadelphia cohort study. Marvin Wolfgang and his colleagues concluded in 1972 "that the most significant factor related to a boy not being remediated by the police, but being processed to the full extent of the juvenile justice system, is his being nonwhite."[21]

A white police officer questions a handcuffed African American juvenile. ■ **What constitutes racial profiling? Is racial profiling ever justified?**

However, several other studies failed to find much evidence of racial bias. It is difficult to appraise the importance of race in the disposition of cases involving juveniles, because African Americans and members of other minority groups appear to be involved in serious crimes more often than whites. Nonetheless, it does seem that racial bias makes minority juveniles special targets of the police.[22] See Focus on Social Policy 14.1 for a discussion of racial profiling and the police.

Socioeconomic Status   Substantiating the effect of class on the disposition of cases involving juveniles is difficult because most studies examine race and socioeconomic status together. But lower-class youngsters, according to many critics of the juvenile justice system, receive different "justice" than middle- or upper-class youths. What the critics mean by this is that lower-class youths are dragged into the net of the system for the same offenses for which white middle- and upper-class juveniles often are sent home. Patrol and juvenile police officers generally agree that there is more concern about "saving" middle- and upper-class juveniles than lower-class ones; but they justify this use of discretion by saying that the problematic behavior of middle- and upper-class children is more likely to be corrected, because their parents can afford psychotherapy and other such resources.

Individual Factors   Such individual factors as prior arrest record, previous offenses, age, peer relationships, family situation, and conduct of parents also have a bearing on how the police officer handles each juvenile.[23] A juvenile who is older and has committed several previous offenses is likely to be referred to the juvenile court. Merry Morash found that fitting the common image of a delinquent and dangerous person increases a youth's chances of arrest.[24] The family of the juvenile is also an

FOCUS ON
Social Policy 14.1

Racial Profiling and the Police

Minority motorists, especially African Americans, have long complained that the police, especially in suburban areas, stop them for no legitimate reason but solely because they are African Americans—a practice known as racial profiling. Furthermore, during such stops, African Americans may be subjected to detailed questioning and searches and given little or no explanation of why they were stopped. This phenomenon has achieved such notoriety among African Americans that it is called "driving while black."

The use of race as a key factor in police decisions to stop and interrogate citizens has received attention from the mass media, civil rights groups, and political leaders. In 1999, President Clinton condemned racial profiling and directed federal agencies to collect information on the race of individuals they stop and interrogate. More recently, President George W. Bush has labeled profiling as "wrong" and argued that it must end. Congressional hearings on racial profiling have been held, and several states are considering or have passed legislation that would require law enforcement agencies to collect demographic data on persons they stop. More than 80 percent of U.S. citizens said in a 1999 Gallup poll that they "disapproved" of racial profiling. Profiling has been blamed for ills ranging from increased friction between the police and minority communities to overall reduced confidence in and cooperation with the police.

A Bureau of Justice Statistics survey of police–public contact found that in 1999 African Americans were somewhat more likely than Hispanics and whites to report being stopped by the police. African Americans who had been stopped were more likely than whites to report that they had been ticketed, handcuffed, arrested, or searched by police officers; they also were more likely to say that officers had threatened or used force against them. In this survey African Americans also were much less likely than whites or Hispanics to feel that the physical search or the vehicle search was legitimate.

Ronald Weitzer and Steven A. Tuch analyzed recent national survey data on citizens' views of racial profiling. The researchers found that both race and personal experience are strong predictors of attitudes toward profiling. They also found that African Americans' social class affects their view of the prevalence and acceptability of this practice. Yet there is evidence that even middle-class African Americans feel they have experienced racial profiling when they drive through predominantly white areas.

The importance of this finding is that regardless of the reality, the perception of racial profiling reinforces the feeling in the African American "collective consciousness" that the police serve an oppressive function. Police can do much to dispel beliefs that stops are racially motivated by offering more information to justify stops. Officers who are polite, listen to individuals they stop, and explain their actions also are likely to receive cooperation from citizens.

■ **Is it racial profiling when a police officer tells a group of African American juveniles hanging around a corner to scatter and go home? Does your answer change if the police officer believes that these particular juveniles are members of a criminal gang? Is it unacceptable for a police officer to stop a new BMW full of African American juveniles who, in the judgment of the officer, are involved in drug trafficking?**

Sources: Tom R. Tyler and Cheryl J. Wakslak, "Profiling and Police Legitimacy: Procedural Justice, Attributions of Motive, and Acceptance of Police Authority," *Criminology* 42 (May 2004), pp. 253–281; Ronald Weitzer and Steven A. Tuch, "Perceptions of Racial Profiling: Race, Class, and Personal Experience," *Criminology* 40 (May 2002), pp. 435–456; and Albert J. Meehan and Michael C. Ponder, "Race and Place: The Ecology of Racial Profiling African American Motorists," *Justice Quarterly* 19 (September 2002), pp. 399–430.

---

important variable. An assistant police chief who had spent several years working as a juvenile officer put it this way:

> Most juvenile problems derive from the parents. You've got to get the parents involved to be successful. You've some parents who are concerned, and you can tell they'll take things by the handle when they're dealing with the problem. Other parents simply don't care. If you want to make any headway in this work, it is necessary to stay on top of the family.[25]

Police–Juvenile Interaction   Three studies found that a juvenile's deference to a police officer is influential in determining disposition. In 1964, Irving Piliavin and Scott Briar discovered that if a youth is polite and respectful, the chances for informal disposition are greatly increased. But if the juvenile is hostile, police will probably judge him or her to be in need of juvenile court intervention.[26] Carl Werthman and Piliavin found in 1967 that the hostility and scorn that African American gang members displayed toward the police resulted in a high rate of court referral.[27] Richard J. Lundman,

Richard E. Sykes, and John P. Clark's 1980 replication of Black and Reiss's study concluded that in encounters in which no evidence links a juvenile to an offense, the demeanor of the juvenile is the most important determinant of whether or not formal action is taken.[28]

> " A juvenile's deference to a police officer is influential in determining disposition. "

In the 1990s, the relationship between demeanor and arrest of adult offenders stirred up considerable controversy among criminologists. David A. Klinger's 1994 and 1996 studies of police behavior in Dade County, Florida, spearheaded this debate in challenging the long-standing belief that police officers are more likely to arrest citizens who do not show them an acceptable level of deference. His basic argument was that demeanor had been measured improperly and had not been controlled adequately for other important variables.[29] Robert E. Worden and Robin L. Shepard's 1996 reanalysis of data collected for the Police Services Study, however, supported the original finding of the importance of disrespectful or hostile demeanor toward the police in influencing the likelihood of arrest.[30]

The police officer's personality also shapes the nature of police–juvenile interaction. An officer who "just plain doesn't like kids" is more prone to hassle juveniles than one who is concerned; and when a juvenile reacts to this harassment with profanity or aggressive behavior, the officer may decide an official contact is necessary. An officer who loses his or her cool may likewise become involved in a confrontation requiring an official contact.

Departmental Policy   Police departments vary in their policies on handling misbehaving juveniles. In his 1970 study of forty-six departments in southern California, Malcolm Klein found that some departments referred four out of five to the juvenile court, whereas others warned and released virtually all juvenile contacts.[31] Nathan Goldman's 1969 study of four Pennsylvania communities reported that the proportion of juvenile arrests varied from 9 percent in one community to a high of 71 percent in another.[32] James Q. Wilson found in 1968 that the more professional police departments had higher numbers of juveniles referred to the juvenile court, because they used discretion less than the departments that were not as professional.[33]

External Pressures   The attitudes of the press and the public, the status of the complainant or victim, and the philosophy and available resources of referral agencies usually influence the disposition of juvenile lawbreakers. The press can do much to encourage a get-tough policy with youthful offenders; for example, a series of newspaper articles on violent youth crime or gang activity can alarm the public and put pressure on police departments to get youthful thugs off the streets. In addition, the higher the socioeconomic status of the complainant or victim, the more likely that a juvenile will be arrested and processed for a crime. On the other hand, when police officers believe that the juvenile court is too permissive to juvenile crime, this "wrist-slapping" may discourage them from arresting youthful offenders.[34] Finally, the police officer who has available such community resources as a youth services bureau frequently responds to juvenile encounters differently than the officer who has no available community resources.

In sum, sufficient studies have been done to provide an outline of an empirical portrait of the policing of juveniles. Of the nine factors influencing police officers' dispositions of juveniles, the seriousness of the offense and complaints by citizens appear to be more important than the other seven factors. Yet individual characteristics of the juvenile, as well as departmental policy and external pressures in the community, also are highly influential in determining how police–juvenile encounters are handled.

Informal and Formal Dispositions

A patrol officer or juvenile officer has at least five options when investigating a complaint against a juvenile or arriving at the scene of law-violating behavior: warning

FIGURE 14.1

Juvenile Dispositional Alternatives Available to the Police

Possible Outcomes of Police–Juvenile Encounters

1. Warning and release to the juvenile community

2. Station adjustment and release

3. Referral and release to diversion agency

4. Referral to juvenile court intake without detention

5. Detention and referral to juvenile court intake

station adjustment

One of several disposition options available to a police officer whereby a juvenile is taken to the police station following a complaint, the contact is recorded, and the juvenile is given an official reprimand and then released to his or her parents or guardians.

citation

A summons to appear in juvenile court.

and releasing the juvenile to the community; making a station adjustment; referring the juvenile to a diversionary agency; issuing a citation and referring him or her to the juvenile court; and taking him or her to a detention facility (see Figure 14.1). In general, police choices among these options have tended to hold steady since the late 1990s.

Warning and Release   The least severe sanction is applied when the patrol officer decides merely to question and release the youth. Commonly, this occurs when a juvenile is caught committing a minor offense. The patrol officer usually gives an informal reprimand to the youth on the street or takes the juvenile in for a longer interview at the police station. In 1997, about 25 percent of juveniles were handled informally within the department and released.[35]

Until the 1970s, a patrol officer often warned a juvenile by saying something like "This better not happen again, or I'll beat your ass the next time I catch you." It was not unheard of for a patrol officer to bring out a paddle and to give the erring juvenile two or three whacks. Now it would be very unwise for a patrol officer to strike a juvenile under any circumstances because of the potential liability that the officer might face if the juvenile's parents decided to sue.

Station Adjustment   The juvenile can be taken to the station, where the contact will be recorded, be given an official reprimand, and then be released to the parents. In a **station adjustment** the first thing the department does when the juvenile is brought to the station is to contact the parents. In some police departments, juveniles can be placed under police supervision, to remain under supervision until released from probation.[36]

Referral to a Diversion Agency   The juvenile can be released and referred to a diversion agency. In some jurisdictions, the police operate their own diversion program; more typically, juveniles are referred to agencies such as Big Brothers or Big Sisters, a runaway center, or a mental health agency. In 1997, about 1 percent were referred to diversion programs.[37]

Citation and Referral to the Juvenile Court   The police officer can issue a **citation** and refer the youth to the juvenile court. The intake counselor of the juvenile court, who is usually a probation officer, then decides whether or not a formal petition should be filed and the youth should appear before the juvenile judge. The juvenile is returned to the family with this disposition.

In 2002, more than four-fifths of the delinquency cases handed in juvenile court were referred by law enforcement agencies. Property delinquency cases were referred by law enforcement most often, followed by delinquency person and drugs cases. A smaller proportion of public order cases were referred to juvenile court by law enforcement, primarily because this offense category contains cases involving contempt of court and probation violations that are most frequently referred by probation or court personnel.[38] Table 14.2 gives the percent of delinquency cases referred to juvenile court by police agencies in 2002.

Detention   Finally, the police officer can issue a citation, refer the youth to the juvenile court, and take him or her to a detention center. An intake worker at the detention center then decides whether the child should be returned to the parents or left at the detention center. A juvenile is left in detention when he or she is thought to be dangerous to self or others in the community or has no care in the home. A few communities have shelter care facilities that are available for status offenders. In communities that lack detention facilities, juveniles must be taken to the county jail or the police lockup, both of which are inappropriate places for juveniles. Taking youths out of their own homes and placing them in detention facilities clearly must be a last resort.

Police Attitudes Toward Youth Crime

The police overall have more positive attitudes toward youthful offenders today than in the past, but three occupational determinants of the police work against even more positive attitudes toward youth crime.[39] First, the police see themselves as skilled in their ability to apprehend criminals, but the leniency of juvenile court codes makes them believe that nothing will happen to apprehended youths unless the offense is serious.[40] The police, in large cities especially, think that youth crime is out of control because of the permissiveness of the juvenile justice system. In 1977, Edward M. Davis, who was then chief of police for Los Angeles, predicted some grim consequences of this permissiveness:

> As the juvenile justice system continues to operate under present constraints, we know that it is building an army of criminals who will prey on our communities. The benign neglect that we have shown has made children with special problems into adult monsters that will be with us forever. If improvements to this system don't come, it will ensure a generation of criminals who will make the current batch look like kids on a Sunday school picnic.[41]

The dangers in their jobs also require the police to be alert to assailants who indicate trouble or danger; therefore, experienced police officers know that they must be guarded in a police–juvenile encounter, because juveniles' unpredictability and resistance make their arrests difficult.[42] The hard-core offender represents the greatest danger to the police officer. Violent gang members, for example, have few qualms about killing police officers.[43] This is especially true for adult street gang members, but it is increasingly true for juveniles who are members of street and youth gangs. See the interview with Loren A. Evenrud later in this chapter for more details on the increased dangers in juvenile work today for the police officer.

Furthermore, the police must always defend the authority of their position, which requires them to quash any verbal or physical abuse from either teenagers or adults.[44] Juvenile offenders, especially those who have had prior contact with the system, are likely to challenge the authority of the police officer. They usually know how far they can push the officer, and they are quite cognizant of their rights. Juveniles are even more likely to challenge the authority of the police officer when they are with peers; therefore, new officers are advised to avoid talking with a youthful offender in front of his or her peers.[45]

Patrol officers are particularly reluctant to engage in a police–juvenile encounter; their first reaction is to call out juvenile police officers or detectives who work with juveniles to get this "mess" off their hands. But juvenile officers and

TABLE 14.2

Percentages of Delinquency Cases Referred by Law Enforcement, 2000

MOST SERIOUS OFFENSE	PERCENT
Delinquency	82%
Person	87%
Property	91%
Drugs	90%
Public order	61%

Source: Howard N. Snyder and Melissa Sickmund, *Juvenile Offenders and Victims: 2006 National Report* (Washington, D.C.: National Center for Juvenile Justice, Office of Juvenile Justice and Delinquency Prevention, 2006), p. 157. Reprinted with permission from the U.S. Department of Justice.

" The police overall have more positive attitudes toward youthful offenders today than in the past. "

DELINQUENCY International 14.1

Juvenile Justice and the Police in Canada, Australia, England, and China

Police–juvenile relations in Canada and Australia have much in common with police–juvenile relations in the United States. In Canada, for example, the police must follow strict procedures in investigating cases. If the police ask any questions of a juvenile that prompt a self-incriminating response, the information gained is inadmissible in court unless the youth has been warned about the right to remain silent, the right to have defense counsel, and the right to contact counsel or other adults before questioning. Equally important, the juvenile must sign a written waiver that acknowledges the voluntary nature of his or her statement.

Australia's state and territory police forces must adhere to special rules governing the arrest, interrogation, pretrial detention, fingerprinting, and photographing of youthful suspects. All jurisdictions also place controls on the use of the power of arrest, although there is still wide variation throughout Australia with regard to arresting juveniles. The presence of an adult witness, normally a parent or a guardian, is required if police are to interview a youthful suspect.

In England the police cautioning process serves as a means of diverting juveniles from the formal justice system. Based on the notion of what is proper and improper for young people, this process begins when a juvenile is brought to a police station. The offense is investigated by a station officer, whose job is to make certain that the charge is supported by credible evidence. The parents or guardians are asked to appear at the police station, and it is likely that the juvenile will be released to their custody. The case is referred to the juvenile bureau, and an officer from that bureau visits the home to interview the juvenile with the parents present. On the basis of all the information collected, the chief inspector in charge of the bureau decides whether to prosecute the juvenile in court, to issue a formal caution, or to take no further action.

Another distinctive approach to police–juvenile relations is found in China. Police work in Chinese society is conducted quite informally and is primarily oriented toward crime prevention and services. In a cultural tradition much different from that found in the United States, it is not unusual for police officers to casually visit families in which juveniles

have been involved in disruptive behaviors in the past. The police also work closely with neighborhood committees and schools. At the first sign of a behavioral problem, an informally organized coalition—consisting of parents, teachers, police officers, and neighborhood committee volunteers—deals with the problematic behavior. Chinese police officers usually devote 90 to 95 percent of their time and resources to serving the community's various social and human needs.

> ■ What is your reaction to how police officers deal with disruptive behavior in China? Would anything of this nature work in the United States?

Sources: Raymond R. Corrado and Alan Markwart, "Canada"; John Seymour, "Australia"; William Wakefield and J. David Hirschel, "England"; and Xin Ren, "People's Republic of China," all in *International Handbook on Juvenile Justice*, edited by Donald J. Shoemaker (Westport, Conn.: Greenwood Press, 1996).

detectives who work with juveniles on a day-to-day basis are more service oriented than patrol officers. The police officers who run such programs as D.A.R.E. and SPECDA (both discussed later in this chapter) in the public schools, who are involved in the Police Athletic League, and who interact with juveniles in other prevention programs usually feel quite positive about police–juvenile interactions. As previously stated, the positive attitudes that some juvenile officers and detectives have toward youthful offenders enable them sometimes to develop remarkable rapport with offenders.

■The Legal Rights of Juveniles

arrest

The process of taking a person into custody for an alleged violation of the law. Juveniles who are under arrest have nearly all the due process safeguards accorded to adults.

The rights of juveniles in custody have changed dramatically since the days when the "third degree" was given at the station. Although some departments have lagged behind others in granting due process rights to juveniles under **arrest,** the majority of them now comply with court decisions concerning the rights of juveniles. Yet because few juvenile cases are appealed, police practices by which juveniles are denied their due process rights are usually known only at the local level.[46]

Police officers take information from handcuffed gang members in Phoenix, Arizona.

■ **What rights do juvenile offenders have when facing processing by the juvenile justice system?**

Search and Seizure

The Fourth Amendment to the Constitution of the United States protects citizens from unauthorized **search and seizure.** In 1961, the Supreme Court decision in *Mapp v. Ohio* affirmed Fourth Amendment rights for adults. This decision stated that evidence gathered in an unreasonable search and seizure—that is, evidence seized without probable cause and without a proper search warrant—was inadmissible in court.[47] In *State v. Lowry* (1967), the Supreme Court applied the Fourth Amendment ban against unreasonable searches and seizures to juveniles:

> Is it not more outrageous for the police to treat children more harshly than adult offenders, especially when such is violative of due process and fair treatment? Can a court countenance a system, where, as here, an adult may suppress evidence with the usual effect of having the charges dropped for lack of proof, and, on the other hand, a juvenile can be institutionalized—lose the most sacred possession a human being has, his freedom—for "rehabilitative" purposes because the Fourth Amendment right is unavailable to him?[48]

Juveniles thus must be presented with a valid search warrant unless they have waived that right, have consented to have their person or property searched, or have been apprehended in the act. When these conditions have not been met, courts have overturned rulings against juveniles. For example, a 1966 District of Columbia ruling suppressed evidence seized when the police entered a juvenile's apartment without a warrant at 5:00 A.M. to arrest him. The court held that "the Fourth Amendment to the United States Constitution is a protection designed to secure the homes and persons of young and old alike against unauthorized police searches and seizures."[49]

In another case, a Houston police officer stopped a car being driven without lights and issued the driver, a youth, a traffic ticket for that offense as well as for driving without a driver's license. The youth was taken to a police station because the officer had some questions about the automobile's ownership. Five hours after the initial contact, another police officer searched the youth without his consent and without

search and seizure
Police procedures used in the investigation of crimes for the purpose of gathering evidence.

a search warrant and discovered fifty milligrams of marijuana. For this possession of marijuana the youth was committed to the Texas Youth Council. An appellate court released the youth from training school, finding that a search some five hours after the original arrest for driving without lights "can hardly be justified as incidental to the arrest for a traffic offense."[50]

Interrogation Practices

The Fourteenth Amendment of the Constitution affirms that police must adhere to standards of fairness and due process in obtaining confessions. Current standards also require that the courts must take into consideration the totality of circumstances under which a confession was made in determining the appropriateness of the confession.

The Supreme Court decision *Haley v. Ohio* is an early example of **police interrogation** excesses. In the *Haley* case, a fifteen-year-old youth was arrested at his home five days after a store robbery in which the owner was shot. Five or six police officers questioned the boy for about five hours; he then confessed after being shown what were alleged to be the confessions of two other youths. No parent or attorney was present during the questioning. The Supreme Court invalidated the confession, stating:

> The age of the petitioner, the hours when he was grilled, the duration of his quizzing, the fact that he had no friend or counsel to advise him, the callous attitude of the police toward his rights combine to convince us that this confession was wrung from a child by means which the law should not sanction. Neither man nor child can be allowed to stand condemned by methods which flout constitutional requirements of due process of law."[51]

The Supreme Court also ruled in *Brown v. Mississippi* that police may not use force to obtain confessions.[52] In this case, police used physical force to extract a confession. Other confessions have been ruled invalid because the accused was too tired; was questioned too long; and/or was not permitted to talk with spouse, friends, or lawyer either while being interrogated or until he or she confessed.[53]

Juveniles taken into custody are entitled to the rights stated in the 1966 *Miranda v. Arizona* decision. This Supreme Court decision prohibits the use of a confession in court unless the individual was advised of his or her rights before interrogation, especially of the right to remain silent, the right to have an attorney present during questioning, and the right to be assigned an attorney by the state if the individual could not afford one.[54] *In re Gault* (see Chapter 15) made the right against self-incrimination and the right to counsel applicable to juveniles.[55] But the *Gault* decision failed to clarify whether or not a juvenile could waive the protection of the *Miranda* rules; it also failed to specify what is necessary for a juvenile to waive his or her *Miranda* rights intelligently and knowingly. For example, is a juvenile's ability to waive *Miranda* rights impaired if the youth is under the influence of drugs or alcohol or in a state of shock?

The 1979 *Fare v. Michael C.* decision applied the "totality of the circumstances" approach to the interrogation of juveniles. The circumstances behind this case were that Michael C. was implicated in a murder that took place during a robbery. The police arrested the sixteen-year-old youth and brought him to the station. After he was advised of his *Miranda* rights, he requested to see his probation officer. When this request was denied, he proceeded to talk to the police officer, implicating himself in the murder. The Supreme Court ruled in this case that Michael appeared to understand his rights, and that when his request to talk with his probation officer was denied, he expressed his willingness to waive his rights and continue the interrogation.[56]

Thomas Grisso studied juveniles interrogated by the St. Louis police in 1981 and found that virtually all of them had waived their *Miranda* rights. He then questioned whether juveniles were even "capable of providing a meaningful waiver of the rights to avoid self-incrimination and to obtain legal counsel."[57] After surveying a sample of juveniles, Grisso found that almost everyone younger than fourteen and half the

police interrogation
The process of interviewing a person who has been arrested with the express purpose of obtaining a confession.

Miranda v. Arizona
The landmark 1966 U.S. Supreme Court ruling that suspects taken into police custody must, before any questioning can take place, be informed that they have the right to remain silent, that anything they say may be used against them, and that they have the right to legal counsel.

juveniles in the fifteen- to sixteen-year-old age bracket had less than adequate understanding of what their *Miranda* rights entailed.

Several court cases have held that the minority status of a juvenile is not an absolute bar to a valid confession. A California case upheld the confession of two juveniles from Spanish-speaking families. Although both had been arrested before, one had an IQ of sixty-five to seventy-one, with a mental age of ten years and two months.[58] Similarly, a North Carolina court of appeals approved the confession of a twelve-year-old youth who was charged with shooting out a window in a camper truck.[59] Moreover, a Maryland appellate court approved the confession of a sixteen-year-old youth who was a school dropout and had an eighth-grade education. He was charged with fire-bombing and burning a store and a school during a racial confrontation.[60]

To protect juveniles against police interrogation excesses, many jurisdictions have a statutory requirement that a parent, someone acting *in loco parentis* for the child, or counsel for the child must be present at police interrogation in order for a confession to be admissible. In *Commonwealth v. Guyton* (1989), the Massachusetts court held that no other minor, not even a relative, can act as an interested adult.[61] Other courts have ruled that the interested adult may be a child's relative.[62] Some states attempt to protect the juvenile by requiring that the youth be taken to the juvenile detention center or to the juvenile court if not returned immediately to the parents' custody. They obviously prefer that police interrogation take place within juvenile facilities rather than at a police station.

Fingerprinting

Fingerprinting, along with other pretrial identification practices, has traditionally been highly controversial in juvenile corrections. Some juvenile court statutes require that a judge approve the taking of fingerprints of juveniles, control access to fingerprint records, and provide for fingerprint destruction under certain circumstances.[63] In many other jurisdictions, the police department determines policy; some police departments routinely fingerprint all juveniles taken into custody and suspected of serious wrongdoing. The Juvenile Justice and Delinquency Prevention Act of 1974 recommended that fingerprints be taken only with the consent of the judge, that juvenile fingerprints not be recorded in the criminal section of the fingerprint registry, and that they be destroyed after their purpose has been served.

A 1969 Supreme Court decision that reversed a Mississippi ruling is the most important case dealing with juvenile fingerprints. In this case, a rape victim had described her assailant only as an African American youth. The only leads at the outset of the police investigation were finger and palm prints found on the sill and borders of the window of the victim's home. Without warrants the police took at least twenty-four African American youths to police headquarters, where they were questioned, fingerprinted, and then released without charge. A fourteen-year-old youth who had performed yard work for the victim was brought to headquarters the day after the offense, questioned, fingerprinted, and released. He was interrogated on several additional occasions over the next four days; several times he was shown to the victim in her hospital room, but she did not identify the youth as her assailant. The police then drove the youth ninety miles to another city, where he was confined overnight in jail. The next day the youth signed a confession statement and was returned to the jail in his community. He was fingerprinted a second time and his fingerprints, along with those of twenty-three other African American youths, were sent to the FBI for comparison with the latent prints taken from the window. The FBI reported that the youth's prints matched those taken from the window. The Supreme Court found that the fingerprint evidence used at the trial was the second set and rejected this evidence because the police had not complied with procedures required in the Fourth Amendment:

> The detention at police headquarters of petitioner and the other young Negroes was not authorized by a judicial officer; petitioner was unnecessarily required to undergo two fingerprinting sessions; and petitioner was not merely fingerprinted during the [first] detention but also subjected to interrogation.[64]

fingerprinting
A pretrial identification procedure used with both juveniles and adults following arrest.

Yet, during the late 1980s and 1990s, fingerprinting of juvenile offenders took place frequently across the United States. At the end of 1997, forty-six states and the District of Columbia allowed law enforcement agencies to fingerprint juveniles who had been arrested for felonies or had reached a certain age.[65]

Pretrial Identification Practices

pretrial identification practices
Procedures such as fingerprinting, photographing, and placing juveniles in lineups for the purpose of identification prior to formal court appearance.

Among other **pretrial identification practices,** both photographing and placing juveniles in lineups are highly controversial. Another recent practice is to notify the school district regarding juveniles who have been convicted of serious or violent crimes. The Juvenile Justice and Delinquency Prevention Act recommended that a photograph not be taken without the written consent of the juvenile judge and that the name or picture of any juvenile offender not be made public by the media.

An important case in terms of these pretrial identification practices took place in California. A rape victim was shown pictures of a young male taken by the police in another matter. She could not make positive identification, but a few days later she was asked to come to the probation office at a time when this young male was present. This time she did identify him as her assailant. She was also certain of his identification as her assailant at the detention hearing some six weeks later. But the California appellate court held the one-on-one identification attempts to be constitutionally defective: "The practice of showing suspects singly to persons for the purpose of identification has been widely condemned." The judgment was upheld, however, on the basis that the victim's identification of the young male at trial was based on her observation of him during the rape, rather than during the three identification attempts.[66]

Another important case was *United States v. Wade* (1967), in which the Supreme Court ruled that the accused has a right to have counsel present at postindictment-lineup procedures.[67] In *Kirby v. Illinois* (1972), the Court went on to add that the defendant's right of counsel at postindictment lineup procedures goes into effect as soon as the complaint or the indictment has been issued.[68] In the *In re Holley* decision (1970), a juvenile accused of rape had his conviction reversed by the appellate court because of the lack of counsel during the lineup identification procedure.[69]

At the end of 1997, forty-five states and the District of Columbia had statutes permitting photographing of juveniles under certain circumstances for criminal history record purposes. Juvenile codes in forty-two states allowed names, and sometimes even pictures and court records, of juveniles who were involved in delinquency proceedings to be released to the media.[70] Since 1997, still more states have permitted similar pretrial identification practices.

▮Prevention and Deterrence of Delinquency

Now we move to the final section of this chapter which examines what police can do about preventing and deterring juvenile crime. Juvenile delinquency poses a difficult problem for police officers who must deal with a wide range of behaviors, from drug-trafficking street gangs to status and runaway offenders. That more juveniles own handguns and are exhibiting violent behavior are two of the major challenges facing the police today. The interview with Sergeant Loren A. Evenrud of the Minneapolis Park Police, Minneapolis, Minnesota, describes these and other challenges facing the police (Focus on Social Policy 14.2).

Police–juvenile relations today take place in the larger context of community policing. By the early 1990s, community-oriented policing (COP), according to Vincent J. Webb and Nanette Graham, had become "contemporary American policy."[71] A 1992 survey of the twenty-five largest police departments in the nation revealed that 78 percent reported practicing community policing, 13 percent planned

FOCUS ON
Social Policy 14.2

Interview with Loren A. Evenrud

Question: How has policing with juveniles changed since the mid-1980s?

Dr. Evenrud: The most obvious change is the dramatic increase in violence among the juvenile population. The availability of firearms has increased dramatically; therefore police can no longer confront juvenile violators in traditional ways. Front-line law enforcement professionals today are often forced to apply the highest level of the "use of force continuum" in daily street contacts. For example, officers are forced to conduct a "felony stop" on juveniles reported to be in possession of firearms. This means in the real world that the juvenile will be placed in a prone position at gunpoint in the street or in a park until police can neutralize the situation. This recent phenomenon has placed considerable stress on citizens, not to mention individual police officers who are trying to bring the rule of law to the community.

Question: What has been the impact of street gangs on policing in the community?

Dr. Evenrud: It is abundantly clear that gangs today have collectively learned how to manipulate the community as well as the criminal justice system. It is also well known that gang members transport negative, antisocial behaviors from the prison culture to our local communities. Gang-connected males today are tougher and are prone to use threats and intimidation to achieve status and property. With no legitimate means of support, these adult gang-connected males have effectively learned to manipulate politicians and responsible community members. As a result, gangs have become stronger and more entrenched, with more adult males assuming leadership roles without ever meeting even the most basic educational, ethical, and social standards. The gang phenomenon is really about men running kids, and little will change until the issue of the negative adult male role model is addressed. Fundamentally, gangs today are philosophically opposed to the rule of law, which is clearly essential in a healthy society.

Gangs have also changed. Unlike gangs in the early 1900s, when a young person hung out for a time with a local street gang for protection, the typical gang member today is a career criminal who survives by victimizing others. The reality is that gang youth are not growing out of gangs as in the past. Gangs today feature adult leaders who, in essence, call all the shots. The gang organizational structure has been proven to produce money and status; therefore, gang-connected youth are hard-pressed to follow a legitimate career path. Obviously, this decision is also impacted by other economic and societal factors.

Police are now faced with criminal street gangs that span the ethnic and social spectrum. Along with African American, Asian American, Anglo American, Hispanic American, Native American, and even Somalian American gangs, communities in the upper Midwest have been faced with motorcycle gangs and clusters of Neo-Nazi youth who have adopted the philosophies and practices of white supremacist/extremist groups who base their ideology on hate. Occasionally, these hate groups mobilize white youth to challenge openly persons of color in public and private settings. It is appropriate to view any group that threatens the social order in the community as a threat group. Gang organizations or "nations" of any type victimize and polarize communities across the nation.

From a police perspective, it is critical that all helping professionals share in the monitoring of threat groups. It is no secret that the code of silence is very difficult to penetrate and crime victims must have support from all agency professionals. In essence, there must be a melding of aggressive law enforcement with effective gang prevention programs.

◼ **Why is the police role with gangs so difficult? What insights does Sergeant Evenrud provide about gangs?**

Source: Reprinted with permission from Loren A. Evenrud. Minneapolis Police Park Sergeant Loren A. Evenrud received his Ph.D. in Educational Policy and Administration from the University of Minnesota in 1987 and is a widely acknowledged authority on street gangs. He has also published numerous articles on gangs in local, state, and national publications.

to adopt a community policing program for the near future, and only 9 percent had no plans for a community policing program.[72] It is no wonder that the 1994 crime bill provided nearly $9 billion in federal funds to be expended over the next twelve years to support community policing and related initiatives.

This new police paradigm has focused on developing a cooperative relationship between police officers and communities. Law enforcement officers are quite cognizant that fear of crime makes people reluctant to participate in their neighborhoods; the result is that citizens cede control to criminals. COP attempts to empower citizens by helping them regain ownership and pride in their neighborhoods, thereby fostering a greater feeling of well-being, increased interest in community affairs and events, and a greater willingness to participate in efforts to reduce crime. By encouraging community building, COP endeavors to enhance the preventive capacity of neighborhood institutions. COP also attempts to empower police officers: It expands officers' discretion and encourages them to solve problems creatively, in ways that do not necessarily involve arrest.[73]

Community-oriented policing appears to be especially useful in juvenile justice for a number of reasons. It moves police officers from anonymity in the patrol car to *direct* engagement with a community, thus giving them more immediate information about neighborhood problems and insights into their solutions. COP frees officers from an emergency response system and permits them to engage more directly in proactive crime prevention. In addition, COP makes police operations more visible to the public, which increases police accountability to the public; decentralizes operations, which allows officers greater familiarity with the workings and needs of various neighborhoods; encourages officers to view *citizens as partners,* which improves relations between the public and the police; and moves decision making and discretion to those who best know the community's problems and expectations.[74]

> " Community-oriented policing appears to be especially useful in juvenile justice. "

Three ways police departments are attempting to implement community-based policing in the prevention and deterrence of youth crime are community-based, school-based, and gang-based interventions.

Community-Based Interventions

Community relations is a major focus of police officers who work with juveniles. They must cultivate good relations with school administrators and teachers, with the staffs of community agencies, with the staffs of local youth organizations and youth shelters, with the juvenile court, and with merchants and employees at popular juvenile hangouts. Of course, juvenile police officers also must develop good relations with parents of youthful offenders as well as with the offenders themselves. The officer who has earned the respect of the youths of the community will be aware of what is happening in the community and will be called on for assistance by youths in trouble. Special Agent Ann Miller (see Exhibit 14.2) gives an example of good community relations:

> The most challenging task of working with juveniles is to get them to realize the importance of the decisions they make. Lots of juveniles have an attitude in which they think they are untouchable and nothing will happen to them.
>
> I don't think juveniles respond to me differently than they would to a male police officer. The bottom line is the type of rapport you build with juveniles. If you are a jerk, juveniles will respond in negative ways. But if you treat juveniles with decency and respect, the chances are that they will respond to you in the same way.
>
> What I find exciting about working with juveniles is that you can have a positive effect on kids. Kids want to learn. The challenge is to be there and to encourage kids to make something positive happen even though they have had trouble in the past. There are some kids I've arrested three or four times before they are able to get some positive things going in their lives.[75]

One of the important challenges the police face today is finding missing children. The AMBER Alert System began in 1996 when Dallas-Fort Worth broadcasters teamed with local police departments to develop an early warning system to assist in finding abducted children, which they called the Dallas Amber Plan. AMBER, which stands for America's Missing: Broadcast Emergency Response, was named in memory of nine-year-old Amber Hagerman, who was kidnapped and brutally murdered while riding her bicycle in Arlington, Texas, in 1996. Other states and communities soon set up their own alert plans, and the AMBER Alert network was adopted nationwide.[76] Focus on Social Policy 14.3 describes AMBER alerts.

Sex Crimes Break the Lock on Juvenile Records

Laws meant to protect the public by listing sex offenders on Internet registries are colliding with laws intended to shield the identities of children who get into trouble.

Amie Zyla, 18, of Waukesha, Wis., has successfully promoted the idea that the public's right to know of a sex offender living nearby trumps a juvenile's right to keep court records secret. Last year, she persuaded her state's legislators to let police notify neighbors about the presence of a juvenile sex offender they consider a public risk.

This year, she went national. Congress is finishing work on a bill she promoted that could include juveniles on a federal registry being created. It would make failure to register a felony.

Zyla began her campaign when Joshua Wade, who was sent to a juvenile home for sexually assaulting her when she was 8 and he was 14, was arrested again for assaulting children. The community-notification law could have prevented him from molesting again, Zyla says.

"If they're a juvenile and they've done it, people should know about it," she says. "Josh got out and he did it all over again." He has been sentenced to 25 years in prison.

Changes like Wisconsin's are at odds with a long-standing practice of giving juvenile offenders a clean slate when they become adults.

"Let Me Go On with My Life"

Leah DuBuc, 22, a Michigan college student, says sexual experimentation when she was 10 has tarred her as a criminal for the 25 years she must stay on the state's registry.

DuBuc says she and her stepbrothers, ages 8 and 5, "flashed" each other and play-acted sex while clothed. She pleaded guilty at 12 to charges of criminal sexual conduct in the first and second degree and spent 18 months in a residential treatment program. In court proceedings, she said she engaged in sexual activity with both boys. However, she says she lied in court to get away from her stepmother.

"It was stupid child's play," she says, "and now I'm on the list until I'm 37."

Since her name was added to the state registry three years ago when she turned 18, DuBuc has found angry messages taped to her dorm room door and pinging into her e-mail inbox. She has been turned down for jobs at fast-food restaurants and internships for a degree in social work by employers she says saw her on the registry.

It's illegal for DuBuc to attend her 9-year-old half-brother's hockey games or her 10-year-old half-sister's dance recital because sex offenders aren't allowed into school buildings. She petitioned to be put on a non-public registry limited to police use but was denied because, the court said, she was more than five years older than one victim. She says the court's math is wrong.

She notes that she leads Bible study, has taught English in Japan and volunteers at a homeless shelter. "Look at everything I've done," she says. "Let me go on with my life."

Some states list juveniles on public registries, some wait until they turn 18, and some never list them. Some list an offender for life; others specify a period of years, depending on the crime.

Some states have recently reconsidered putting juveniles on sex offender registries. In May, three changed their laws:

- Vermont no longer applies sex offender laws to people ages 15–18 who engage in consensual sex, joining other states with "Romeo and Juliet laws" that keep such teens off offender registries.
- Kansas gave juvenile court judges the discretion to keep juveniles off the public registry.
- In Missouri, a teenager convicted of consensual sex with another teen can appeal to be removed from the non-public police registry. Missouri does not put juveniles on its public registry.

Federal Bill Would Mandate Inclusion

The proposed federal law would require states to put juveniles on public registries after sex offenses are handled in juvenile court.

The House version of the proposal would list on a national Internet registry, for a minimum of 20 years, youths whose crimes have been handled in juvenile court. The Senate version would not list juveniles. Senate and House negotiators will work out the differences before a final vote.

Wisconsin Governor Jim Doyle shakes hands with Amie Zyla in May 2005 after signing a law to let police notify people about juvenile sex offenders living nearby. Zyla had lobbied for the measure.
■ **Should juvenile sex offenders be publicly identified?**

"We have to remember whose interest we need to put first. We put the interest of victims and potential victims first," says Rep. Mark Green, R-Wis., a co-sponsor of the House bill.

If treated, juvenile sex offenders are far less likely to commit another offense, says Mark Chaffin, research director at the National Center on Sexual Behavior of Youth at the University of Oklahoma. The rate at which juveniles repeat sex offenses ranges from 5% to 15%, compared with 20% to 25% for adult sex offenders, he says.

Putting juveniles on public registries tars them for life, opponents of the practice say.

"The whole logic of a juvenile system is that your behavior at 8, 9, 10 or even 13 or 14 should not stigmatize you for life," Chaffin says.

When an adolescent assaults a grade-schooler, "They're both children," says Morna Murray, director of youth development for the Children's Defense Fund, which opposes the House bill. "And both of them need to be protected."

Source: "Sex Crimes Break the Lock on Juvenile Records," *USA Today*, July 10, 2006, p. 5A. Copyright © 2006 by *USA Today*. Reprinted by permission.

FOCUS ON
Social Policy 14.3

AMBER Alert

The following material, which describes the AMBER Alert system in a question-answer format, comes from the federal Office of Justice Programs.

How does Project AMBER work?

Once law enforcement has determined that a child has been abducted and the abduction meets the AMBER Alert criteria, law enforcement notifies broadcasters and state transportation officials. AMBER Alerts interrupt regular programming and are broadcast on radio and television and appear on highway signs. AMBER Alerts can also be issued on lottery tickets, to wireless devices such as mobile phones, and over the Internet. Through the coordination of local, state, and regional plans, the Department of Justice (DOJ) is working toward the creation of a seamless national network.

How effective has it been?

AMBER Alert has been very effective. The programs have helped save the lives of 200 children nationwide.

Over 84 percent of those recoveries have occurred since October 2002, when President George W. Bush called for the appointment of an AMBER Alert Coordinator at the first-ever White House Conference on Missing, Exploited and Runaway Children.

AMBER Alerts serve as deterrents to those who would prey on children. Program data have shown that some perpetrators release the abducted child after hearing the AMBER Alert on the radio or seeing it on television.

Now that all 50 states have AMBER Alert plans, how does this help children and families?

The establishment of AMBER Alert plans in all 50 states marks an important milestone in the efforts to prevent child abductions. No matter where a child is abducted, communities and law enforcement work together to recover missing children quickly and safely. The numbers of recovered children speak for themselves. In 2001, only two children were recovered via AMBER Alert; in 2004, that number rose to seventy-one. Interstate expansion has had a marked impact in saving children's lives.

An AMBER Alert sign informs motorists of a child abduction incident in Orange County, California. ■ How does the AMBER Alert system work?

What are the criteria for issuing AMBER Alerts?

Each state AMBER Alert plan has its own criteria for issuing alert notices. The PROTECT Act, passed in 2003, which established the role of AMBER Alert Coordinator within the Department of Justice, calls for the Department of Justice to issue minimum standards or guidelines for AMBER Alerts that states can adopt voluntarily. The Department's Guidance on Criteria for Issuing AMBER Alerts follows:

- Law enforcement must confirm that an abduction has taken place.
- The child is at risk of serious injury or death.
- There is sufficient descriptive information of the child and the captor or captor's vehicle to issue an Alert.
- The child must be seventeen years old or younger.
- It is recommended that immediate entry of AMBER Alert data be entered into the FBI National Crime Information Center. Text information describing the circumstances surrounding the abduction of the child should be entered, and the case flagged as Child Abduction.

Most states' guidelines adhere closely to the DOJ's recommended guidelines.

> ■ What is the significance of the AMBER Alert program for local communities and for the nation? How do local media and national law enforcement networks serve as a deterrent to those who might otherwise abduct children?

Source: Adapted from www.amberalert.gov/faqs.html. Reprinted with permission from the U.S. Department of Justice.

A police officer talks to a preschool class about home safety in Port Angeles, Washington. Establishing good community relations is crucial for police officers who work with juveniles.

■ **What are these children likely to remember from this experience?**

The police are called on to intercede in a variety of juvenile problems. In the 1990s, they were charged with enforcing the curfew ordinances that more and more communities across the nation were passing. Juvenile arrests for curfew law violations increased very dramatically from 1993 to 1996. Although it is unlikely that many more youths were violating curfew in 1996 than in 1993, communities apparently decided that keeping juveniles off the streets would reduce juvenile violence.[77]

Juvenile drug abuse arrest rates climbed 77 percent between 1993 and 1997. Self-report studies, as previously discussed, do not reflect a large change in drug use among adolescents at this period. In view of the fact that the increase in drug abuse arrests was attributable to arrests for marijuana possession, what seems to have taken place is that communities have become more concerned about marijuana use among youth and that the police have responded to this concern by arresting more youth for this offense.[78]

Communities have further turned to the police to prevent hate crimes committed by teenagers against minority groups—Jews, other ethnic groups, and homosexuals. Most hate crimes appear to be committed by offenders under the age of twenty. This is not surprising when it is remembered that films, music, and humor often target young people as the primary audience for a culture of hate.[79]

In 1983, when research indicated that a small proportion of offenders commit most of the serious and violent juvenile crimes, the Office of Juvenile Justice and Delinquency Prevention introduced the Serious Habitual Offender/Drug Involved (SHODI) Programs, funding five demonstration sites.[80] SHODI concentrated on monitoring the behavior of known juvenile offenders. A key to these programs was giving police access to delinquents' arrest records so they could be checked by computer any time a youth was stopped for questioning. Once a youth is identified as a delinquent (based on certain guidelines, such as four arrests for four serious crimes within a year), police officers keep a closer watch on this youth.[81] The Serious Habitual Offender Comprehensive Action Program (SHOCAP) grew out of these initial efforts. SHOCAP seeks to improve public safety by involving those who work in law enforcement, prosecution, probation, corrections, education, and social services in a

Unruly Students Facing Arrest, Not Detention

TOLEDO, Ohio—The 14-year-old girl arrived at school here on Oct. 17 wearing a low-cut midriff top under an unbuttoned sweater. It was a clear violation of the dress code, and school officials gave her a bowling shirt to put on. She refused. Her mother came to the school with an oversize T-shirt. She refused to wear that, too.

"It was real ugly," said the girl, whose mother did not want her to be identified.

It was a standoff. So the city police officer assigned to the school handcuffed the girl, put her in a police car and took her to the detention center at the Lucas County juvenile courthouse. She was booked on a misdemeanor charge and placed in a holding cell for several hours, until her mother, a 34-year-old vending machine technician, got off work and picked her up.

She was one of more than two dozen students in Toledo who were arrested in school in October for offenses like being loud and disruptive, cursing at school officials, shouting at classmates and violating the dress code. They had all violated the city's safe school ordinance.

In cities and suburbs around the country, schools are increasingly sending students into the juvenile justice system for the sort of adolescent misbehavior that used to be handled by school administrators. In Toledo and many other places, the juvenile detention center has become an extension of the principal's office.

School officials say they have little choice. "The goal is not to put kids out, but to maintain classrooms free of disruptions that make it impossible for teachers to teach and kids to learn," said Jane Bruss, the spokeswoman for the Toledo public schools. "Would we like more alternatives? Yes, but everything has a cost associated with it."

Others, however, say the trend has gone too far.

"We're demonizing children," said James Ray, the administrative judge for the Lucas County juvenile court, who is concerned about the rise in school-related

cases. There were 1,727 such cases in Lucas County in 2002, up from 1,237 in 2000.

Fred Whitman, the court's intake officer, said that only a handful of cases—perhaps 2 percent—were for serious incidents like assaulting a teacher or taking a gun to school. The vast majority, he said, involved unruly students.

In Ohio, Virginia, Kentucky and Florida, juvenile court judges are complaining that their courtrooms are at risk of being overwhelmed by student misconduct cases that should be handled in the schools.

Although few statistics are available, anecdotal evidence suggests that such cases are on the rise.

"Everybody agreed—no matter what side of the system they're from—that they are seeing increasing numbers of kids coming to court for school-based offenses," said Andy Block, who assisted in a 2001 study of Virginia's juvenile justice system by the American Bar Association's Juvenile Defender Center. "All the professionals in the court system were very resentful of this. They felt they were being handed problems and students that the schools were better equipped to address."

According to an analysis of school arrest data by the Advancement Project, a civil rights advocacy group in Washington, there were 2,345 juvenile arrests in 2001 in public schools in Miami-Dade County, Fla., nearly three times as many as in 1999. Sixty percent, the project said, were for "simple assaults"—fights that did not involve weapons—and "miscellaneous" charges, including disorderly conduct.

Many of the court cases around the country involve special-education students whose behavior is often related to their disabilities, Mr. Block and others say.

In an elementary school in northeastern Pennsylvania, an 8-year-old boy in a special-education class was charged with disorderly conduct this fall for his

A woman pointedly disapproves of at her teen daughter's choice of clothes. ■ **What is the purpose of school dress codes? Are they fair?**

behavior in a time-out room: urinating on the floor, throwing his shoes at the ceiling and telling a teacher, "Kids rule."

"Teachers and school administrators know now that they can shift these kids into juvenile court," said Marsha Levick, legal director for the Juvenile Law Center of Philadelphia, which is representing the boy and has asked that the charges be dismissed. "The culture has shifted. Juvenile court is seen as an antidote for all sorts of behavior that in the past resulted in time out or suspension."

Experts say the growing criminalization of student misbehavior can be traced to the broad zero-tolerance policies states and local districts began enacting in the mid-1990s in response to a sharp increase in the number of juveniles committing homicides with guns, and to a series of school shootings.

While the juvenile homicide rate has since fallen, and many studies have found that school violence is rare, the public perception of schools—and students—as dangerous remains. Experts say zero-tolerance policies have created an atmosphere in which relatively minor student misconduct often leads to suspensions, expulsions and arrests.

"The idea that you try to find out why somebody did something or give a person a second chance or try to solve a problem in a way that's not punitive—that's become almost quaint now," said Laurence Steinberg, a professor of psychology at Temple University and the director of the MacArthur Foundation Research Network on Adolescent Development and Juvenile Justice.

What has also changed, Dr. Steinberg said, is that principals are less able to depend on parents to enforce the discipline schools mete out. "I think in the past the threat of getting in touch with a kid's parents was often enough to get a kid to start behaving," he said. "Now, kids feel parents will fight on their behalf."

In addition, Dr. Steinberg said, schools—particularly urban schools with large numbers of poor children—have been forced to reduce or eliminate mental health services. "In the past a lot of these kids would have been referred to specialists within the school or the school district. The juvenile justice system has become the dumping ground for poor minority kids with mental health and special-education problems."

The Toledo City Council passed the safe school ordinance in 1968 in response to concerns that schools had become dangerous. The ordinance allows for the filing of misdemeanor charges against students for anything from disrupting a class to assaulting a teacher. Juvenile court officials say relatively few students were charged with violating the ordinance before 1995, when Toledo police officers were assigned to secondary schools.

In 1993, only 314 charges were filed, according to Dan Pompa, the administrator for the Lucas County juvenile court. By 1997, he said, the number had more than tripled, to 1,111.

Arrests in the past year or so include two middle school boys whose crime was turning off the lights in the girls' bathroom and an 11-year-old girl who was arrested for "hiding out in the school and not going to class," according to the police report, which also noted, "The suspect continuously does not listen in class and disrupts the learning process of other students."

The girl's mother, who declined to be named, said, "I told them if she didn't want to go to school, put her in the detention center." The police took her daughter there in handcuffs, in the back of a police car.

Of the school district's 35,000 students, 47 percent are black, 43 percent white and 7 percent Hispanic. According to Mr. Pompa's figures, minorities account for about 65 percent of the safe school violations.

These higher rates are "something we would certainly want to keep an eye on," said Eugene Sanders, Toledo's schools superintendent.

Ms. Bruss, the schools spokeswoman, said it was the school district's policy that students be charged with violating the ordinance only as a last resort. In addition, she said, most of those cases involve students with long histories of offenses.

Craig Cotner, chief academic officer for the Toledo public schools, said he believed part of the problem was that schools were being called upon to educate a far wider range of students than before. Thirty years ago, he said, students who were not performing well were counseled to drop out, and they easily found jobs at auto plants and other factories.

"For students who did not fit the mold—whatever mold that may be—there were many more options," Mr. Cotner said. "In some cases, those students who found it impossible to sit for five hours in a classroom could function very well in a labor environment." Today, he said, those students, with far fewer options, remain in school, but the school district has fewer resources to handle difficult students.

With a $15 million budget deficit last year, the district laid off 10 percent of the teaching force, or 231 teachers. Class size increased. With a $16 million deficit this year, more cuts must be made, Mr. Cotner said.

In addition, he said, a significant percentage of the district's resources must be used to fulfill federal mandates like the No Child Left Behind law, with its emphasis on accountability and testing.

Judge Ray of the county juvenile court says he sympathizes with school officials. "The schools have been called upon to fix everything that hasn't been working up to this point," he said. However, he said, juvenile court is not the appropriate place to solve adolescent problems.

Judge Ray has Mr. Whitman, the court's intake officer, and other court officers handle minor nonviolent offenses, offering counseling and referrals to the proper programs.

Mr. Whitman, 50, said he believed that no young person should ever be written off. "If a kid's not doing well, I think we need to sit down and find out what we can do to help him or her out," he said.

Mr. Whitman talked at length with the 14-year-old girl who had worn the midriff top and with her mother. "She didn't come across as a major problem at all," he said. "She knew the shirt was inappropriate. She just wanted to show off a certain image at the school. Probably she just copped an attitude. I expect that from a lot of girls."

An official of the girl's school said he could not discuss her case. He referred a reporter to the principal, who did not return calls to his office.

The girl's mother, who declined to be named, said she had not objected to the decision to arrest her daughter. "She wants to push authority to the hilt," she said.

The girl said of her encounter with school officials and the police: "I don't like to get yelled at for stupid stuff. So I talk back."

Source: Sara Rimer, "Unruly Students Facing Arrest, Not Detention," *New York Times*, January 4, 2004. Copyright © 2004 by The New York Times Co. Reprinted by permission.

cooperative process to manage juvenile justice cases. The program provides the structure for focusing attention on serious habitual offenders and enhances the quality and relevance of information that is exchanged through active interagency collaboration. SHOCAP has become a vital component of the comprehensive strategy's graduated sanctions system. With increased interagency cooperation and information sharing, SHOCAP reduces duplicate services.[82]

The control of gun-related violence in the youth population is one of the most serious problems facing the police in deterring youth crime. A justice department report issued in 2000 said that from 1980 to 1997, three out of four homicides involving juveniles age twelve or older were committed with a firearm, and that homicides among juveniles aged fifteen to seventeen were more likely to involve a firearm than were homicides committed by adults.[83]

Some communities have pursued a number of strategies to get the guns out of the hands of juveniles. The Kansas City (Missouri) Gun Experiment was one of the more innovative efforts. A working group made up of the Department of Justice (DOJ), the U.S. Attorney's Office, and the Kansas City Police Department decided to focus police efforts in high-crime neighborhoods by routinely stopping traffic violators and curfew violators. During these stops, police looked for any infraction that would give them the legal authority to search a car or pedestrian for illegal guns. Special gun-intercept teams proved to be ten times more cost effective than regular police patrols.[84]

Programs adopted by other communities in the 1990s include seizing firearms from juvenile offenders in school and ensuring that firearms information is submitted to the federal Alcohol, Tobacco, and Firearms agency for tracing; developing appropriate intervention programs for youth who bring guns to school; developing a broad-based, multidisciplinary strategy to inform juveniles about the dangers of using firearms; preventing youths from illegally possessing firearms; rigorously enforcing firearms laws as they relate to juveniles; and reviewing and revising existing state firearms statutes as needed in light of the Youth Handgun Safety Act and Department of Justice's Model Code so as to eliminate illegal handgun possession and use by juveniles.[85]

In many larger cities, police departments form juvenile units to handle youth crime. A 2000 survey of law enforcement agencies (those with 100 or more sworn officers) reported that a large proportion of these agencies had special units targeting juvenile justice concerns (see Table 14.3).[86]

TABLE 14.3

Special Units Targeting Juvenile Justice Concerns

TYPE OF SPECIAL UNIT	TYPE OF AGENCY	
	LOCAL POLICE	STATE
Drug education in schools	70%	30%
Juvenile crime	62	10
Gangs	45	18
Child abuse	46	8
Domestic violence	45	10
Missing children	48	31
Youth outreach	33	6

Source: Office of Juvenile Justice and Delinquency Prevention, *Juvenile Offenders and Victims: 2006 National Report* (Washington, D.C.: U.S. Government Printing Office, 2006), p. 153. Reprinted with permission from the U.S. Department of Justice.

School-Based Interventions

Developing effective delinquency prevention programs in the school is one of the most important challenges facing the police at the present time. Community predelinquent programs have included courses in high school, junior high school, and elementary school settings addressing school safety, community relations, drug and alcohol abuse, city government, court procedures, bicycle safety, and juvenile delinquency. The Officer Friendly Program and McGruff "Take a Bite Out of Crime," were established throughout the nation to develop better relations with younger children.

More recently, popular prevention programs have included G.R.E.A.T. (Gang Resistance Education and Training) and LRE (Law-Related Education). As of June 1997 more than 2,400 officers from forty-seven states and the District of Columbia had completed G.R.E.A.T. training. The program is now found in school curricula in all fifty states and the District of Columbia.[87] A 1995 evaluation, based on a cross-sectional survey of 5,935 eighth-graders from forty-two schools where G.R.E.A.T. was taught, found that students who completed these lessons reported more prosocial behaviors and attitudes than their peers who did not finish the program or who failed to participate in the first place.[88] In a 1999 evaluation, Finn-Aage Esbensen and colleagues found that students who had completed the G.R.E.A.T. curriculum four years before did not show levels of gang or delinquency involvement significantly different from those of a control group. This evaluation also revealed that students who had finished the curriculum continued to have more prosocial attitudes than those who had not.[89]

Law-Related Education is designed to teach students the fundamental principles and skills needed to become responsible citizens in a constitutional democracy.[90] A 1985 national curriculum survey reported that LRE has been added to the curriculum in more than half of the forty-six states involved in the study.[91] One of the few studies evaluating LRE programs found that, when properly conducted, these programs can reduce tendencies toward delinquent behavior and improve a range of attitudes related to responsible citizenship. Successful students, this study found, were also less likely to associate with delinquent peers and to use violence as a means of resolving conflict.[92]

Today, the need for substance abuse prevention programs demands creativity and involvement on the part of the police. The D.A.R.E. program, discussed in Focus on Social Policy 14.4, is a widely replicated effort by the police to prevent substance abuse. New York City's Project SPECDA (School Program to Educate and Control Drug Abuse), which is a collaborative project of the city's police department and board of education, is another highly praised drug prevention program. In this project, a sixteen-session curriculum, with the units split evenly between fifth and six grades, imparts basic information about the risks and effects of drug use, makes students aware of the social pressures that cause drug use, and teaches acceptable methods of resisting peer pressure to experiment with drugs.[93]

In addition to drug prevention programs, the police respond to incidents ranging from student fights and assaults to drug and weapon possession. Officers also regularly drive by schools during night and weekend patrol to prevent vandalism and burglary to school property. In addition, the police are responsible for providing security and safety to the school. In some schools, this requires conducting searches of students as they come into the school, monitoring the halls, doing conflict mediation when necessary, and protecting students as they come to and go home from school. The police are frequently called on to assist the school in searching for weapons and drugs on school property and are charged to enforce drug-free school zone laws and the federal Gun-Free School Zones Act. The police are also expected to enforce school attendance programs in a few school districts across the nation.

The federal Office of Community-Oriented Policing Services (COPS) has awarded almost $715 million to more than 2,900 law enforcement agencies to fund more than 6,300 school resource officers (SROs) through the COPS in Schools (CIS) program.

Web LIBRARY 14.1

Read the OJJDP Juvenile Justice Bulletin *Effective Intervention for Serious Juvenile Offenders* at **www.justicestudies.com/ WebLibrary**.

FOCUS ON
Social Policy 14.4

Project D.A.R.E.

Project D.A.R.E. is designed to equip elementary school children with skills for resisting peer pressure to experiment with tobacco, drugs, and alcohol. Developed in 1983 as a cooperative effort by the Los Angeles Police Department and the Los Angeles Unified School District, this program uses uniformed law enforcement officers to teach a formal curriculum to students in the classroom. Using a core curriculum consisting of seventeen hour-long weekly lessons, D.A.R.E. gives special attention to fifth- and sixth-graders to prepare them for entry into junior high and high school, where they are most likely to encounter pressure to use drugs. Since it was founded, D.A.R.E. has expanded to encompass programs for middle and high school students, gang prevention, conflict resolution, parent education, and after-school recreation and learning. As the most popular school-based drug education program in the United States, it is administered in about 70 percent of this nation's school districts, reaching 25 million, and has been adopted in forty-four other countries.

Several evaluations done in the 1980s and early 1990s were positive about the effectiveness of the D.A.R.E. program. However, D.A.R.E. began to be more critically evaluated in the mid-1990s. A 1994 meta-analysis of D.A.R.E. programs by the Research Triangle Institute in North Carolina raised questions about the effectiveness of D.A.R.E. and other substance abuse programs. It found that these programs were most effective in increasing students' knowledge about substance abuse and enhancing their social skills, but the effect of these programs was more modest on attitudes toward drugs and the police and on improving self-esteem. This evaluation further found that D.A.R.E.'s short-term effects on substance abuse by fifth- and sixth-graders were small. Dennis P. Rosenbaum and Gordon S. Hanson's 1994 longitudinal evaluation was also critical of D.A.R.E.'s effectiveness. In this randomized experiment conducted with 1,584 students in the year following exposure to the program, Rosenbaum and Hanson found that "D.A.R.E. had no statistically significant main effects on drug use behaviors and had few effects on attitudes or beliefs about drugs."

In their ten-year follow-up of D.A.R.E., Donald Lynam and colleagues reported one of the most critical evaluations of this program. They followed a cohort of sixth-grade children who attended thirty-one schools; twenty-three of the schools received D.A.R.E. instruction, and eight schools did not. The researchers assessed participants yearly through the tenth grade and then again when they were twenty years old. Lynam and colleagues found that D.A.R.E. had no effect on students' drug use at any time through the tenth grade. The tenth-year follow-up also revealed no difference between those who received the instruction and those who did not in the use of cigarettes, alcohol, marijuana, or other drugs when the participants were twenty. Also disturbing to supporters was the finding that those who received D.A.R.E. instruction had slightly lower levels of self-esteem at twenty than the control group.

In view of these negative findings, D.A.R.E. began testing a new curriculum in 2001. Focused on seventh-graders rather than on fifth-graders, the new curriculum is designed to help students test their assumptions about drug use. A booster program is added in ninth grade. Police officers act more as coaches than as lecturers and seek to challenge the social norm of drug use in discussion groups. The program has students do role-playing in an effort to improve their decision-making skills. The new curriculum is undergoing assessment in 80 high schools and 167 middle schools—half the schools are using the earlier curriculum, and the other half are using D.A.R.E.'s new curriculum.

▓ **Why do you believe that the program evaluations of D.A.R.E. have not been more positive? If D.A.R.E. turns out not to be effective in preventing drug and alcohol abuse, what do you think would be effective with middle and junior high youths?**

Sources: National Institute of Justice, *The D.A.R.E. Program: A Review of Prevalence. User Satisfaction, and Effectiveness* (Washington, D.C.: U.S. Department of Justice, 1994), p. 1; Dennis P. Rosenbaum and Gordon S. Hanson, "Assessing the Effects of School-Based Education: A Six-Year Multilevel Analysis of Project D.A.R.E.," *Journal of Research in Crime and Delinquency* 35 (November 1998), pp. 381–412; Donald R. Lynam et al., "Project D.A.R.E.: No Effects at 10-Year Follow-Up," *Journal of Consulting and Clinical Psychology* 67 (1999), pp. 590–593; and Kate Zernike, "Antidrug Program Says It Will Adopt a New Strategy," *New York Times*, 15 February 2001, p. 1.

In addition, COPS has appropriated nearly $21 million to train COPS-funded SROs and school administrators in partnering schools or school districts to work more collaboratively through the CIS program. An SRO in a school can serve in a variety of ways; he or she may function not only as a law enforcement officer, but as a problem solver, LRE educator, and community liaison. SROs also teach classes in crime prevention, substance abuse awareness, and gang resistance; monitor and assist troubled students through mentoring programs; and promote social and personal responsibility by encouraging student participation in community service activities. Moreover, these officers help schools develop policies to address delinquent activity and school safety.[94]

Gang-Based Interventions

As discussed in Chapter 10, the number of street gangs rose dramatically across the nation beginning in the late 1980s. The characteristics of these gangs vary widely from one city to another. Some of the gangs are simply groups of adolescents who hang around together and who seldom get into any serious trouble. Other gangs engage in extensive drug activity, and some have become involved in violent drive-by shootings in which innocent citizens have been killed.

Drugs and violence have made gangs a problem for the police. Indeed, police officers caught a group of Los Angeles Crips conducting a drug sales seminar in St. Louis, Missouri.[95] Once a community becomes aware of the seriousness of the gang problem, usually after a violent gang incident has taken place, then pressure is typically put on the police to solve the problem. Police departments have frequently responded to this pressure by setting up one of three types of intervention units to work with gangs.[96]

> " The number of street gangs rose dramatically across the nation beginning in the late 1980s. "

The Youth Service Program is one such unit. This departmental unit is formed to deal with a specific gang problem and is not a permanent unit within the police department. Officers continue to perform their regular duties and are not exclusively concerned with gang problems. The gang detail is a second type of unit. The officers in these units generally are pulled from detective units or juvenile units. The gang detail differs from the Youth Service Bureau in that its officers are assigned solely to gang problems and do not routinely work on other assignments. The **gang unit** is the third type of unit. The members of these permanent units see themselves as specialists who are working on gang problems. For example, many gang units will develop extensive intelligence networks with gang members in the community.[97]

gang unit
A specialized unit established by some police departments to address the problem of gangs.

In 1999, a Law Enforcement and Management Administrative Services (LEMAS) survey reported that among large departments with 100 or more sworn officers, special gang units existed in 56 percent of all municipal police agencies, 50 percent of all sheriffs' agencies, 43 percent of all county police departments, and 20 percent of all state law enforcement departments. Based on these findings, there are an estimated 360 police gang units in the United States. It is significant that 85 percent of specialized gang units have been established since 1990.[98]

The 1995 federally funded Office of Community-Oriented Policing Services (COPS) Anti-Gang Initiative selected fifteen cities to participate in an antigang project. The most complete evaluations of these antigang interventions have been done in Chicago, Dallas, Detroit, and St. Louis.[99] Most of these programs were heavily weighted toward the suppression and prosecution end of the policing continuum, although a couple of programs (Chicago and Dallas) gave some lip service to prevention and long-term strategies aimed at minimizing youth gang involvement.[100]

The focus of the antigang initiative of the Dallas Police Department was to combat violent crime. The grant period lasted from June 1, 1996, through May 31, 1997, and the study focused on the effect of three suppression tactics: saturation patrol, aggressive curfew, and truancy enforcement. The findings indicated that aggressive curfew and truancy enforcement led to significant reductions in gang violence, whereas simple saturation patrol had little effect.[101]

Web LIBRARY 14.2

Read the NIJ-sponsored publication *Children in an Adult World: Prosecuting Adolescents in Criminal and Juvenile Jurisdictions* at **www.justicestudies.com/ WebLibrary**.

CHAPTER Summary

This chapter has focused on the relationship between the police and juveniles in U.S. society. Policing juveniles is similar in some ways to policing adults, yet in other ways it is quite different. It is important to note that:

- Because the police usually represent the first contact a juvenile has with the justice system, effective police–juvenile relations are vitally important.

- In the late nineteenth and early twentieth centuries, the policing of juveniles came to be viewed differently than the policing of adults.

- This change, which coincided with reforms in the community-based and institutional care of delinquents, emphasized the importance of delinquency prevention.

- Specialized police units were soon created in many of our country's large cities and charged with delinquency prevention and the apprehension of juveniles who broke the law.

- In the late 1970s and early 1980s, budgetary constraints led to reduced police involvement in delinquency prevention and in diversionary programs for juveniles.

- By the late 1980s and early 1990s, however, a rise in juvenile violence, growing juvenile drug abuse, and the proliferation of youth gangs again led to an expanded police emphasis on delinquency prevention and to an examination of the problems faced by juveniles.

- Juveniles today generally demonstrate a better attitude toward the police than in the past, and police officers today are typically more positive about the handling of juveniles, showing that efforts to enhance police–juvenile relations have been at least partly successful.

- The most important elements in understanding police–juvenile relations today may be the public's expectation that the police should address the problems of juvenile crime and prevent youth crime in rich and poor communities alike.

- Today's police have wide discretion toward juvenile lawbreakers, and several studies have found that 80 to 90 percent of police–juvenile encounters result in diversion from official processing by the juvenile justice system.

- Although a number of factors influence how police officers respond to juvenile offenders, the most important element influencing police discretion and disposition of the juvenile offender is the nature of the offense committed.

- Over time, juveniles have been granted a number of significant due process rights by the courts, and those rights have placed increased requirements on the police for the proper handling of juveniles.

- Of special concern today is the need for the police to deal with the problem of violent youth crime—a challenge made all the more difficult by the fact that many juveniles possess handguns, gangs are widespread, juvenile drug abuse remains at significant levels, and some juveniles have become involved in hate crimes.

CRITICAL Thinking Questions

1. Why do the attitudes of minority and white youths toward the police tend to differ? Why would youthful offenders feel differently toward the police than nonoffenders? Have your experiences with the police made a difference in how you feel about the police?

2. Summarize the rights of a juvenile taken into custody.

3. What is your evaluation of D.A.R.E.? Did you participate in a D.A.R.E. program in high school? If so, did it make a difference in your using or not using drugs?

4. Why is the police role in working with juveniles more difficult today than it was in the past?

Visit New York City's Police Athletic League homepage on the Web at **www.palnyc.org**. How did the PAL form? What is its purpose? What programs does it sponsor? What are some of the upcoming events that the PAL is planning to host? Do you believe that groups like the PAL can make a significant difference in the lives of children? Why or why not? Submit your answers to your instructor if asked to do so.

Source: From www.palnyc.org/index.asp. Reprinted with permission.

Notes

1. Robert M. Fogelson, *Big-City Police* (Cambridge, Mass.: Harvard University Press, 1977), pp. 86–87.
2. Ibid.
3. Robert Portune, *Changing Adolescent Attitudes toward Police* (Cincinnati: W. H. Anderson Company, 1971).
4. L. Thomas Winfree Jr. and Curt T. Griffiths, "Adolescents' Attitudes toward the Police: A Survey of High School Students," in *Juvenile Delinquency: Little Brother Grows Up* (Beverly Hills, Calif.: Sage Publications, 1977), pp. 79–99.
5. William T. Risinko, W. Johnson Knowlton, and Carlton A. Hornung, "The Importance of Police Contact in the Formulation of Youths' Attitudes toward Police," *Journal of Criminal Justice* 6 (1978), p. 65; J. P. Clark and E. P. Wenninger, "The Attitudes of Juveniles toward the Legal Institution," *Journal of Criminal Law, Criminology and Police Science* 55 (1964), pp. 482-489; D. C. Gibbons, *Delinquent Behavior* (Englewood Cliffs, N.J.: Prentice-Hall, 1976); and V. I. Cizanckas and C. W. Purviance, "Changing Attitudes of Black Youths," *Police Chief* 40 (1973), p. 42.
6. Scott H. Decker, "Citizen Attitudes toward the Police: A Review of Past Findings and Suggestions for Future Policy," *Journal of Police Science and Administration* 9 (1981), pp. 80–87.
7. James R. Davis, "A Comparison of Attitudes toward the New York City Police," *Journal of Police Science and Administration* 17 (1990), pp. 233–242.
8. Komanduri S. Murty, Julian B. Roebuck, and Joann D. Smith, "The Image of Police in Black Atlanta Communities," *Journal of Police Science and Administration* 17 (1990), pp. 250–257.
9. Ibid., p. 256.
10. Michael J. Leiber, Mahesh K. Nalla, and Margaret Farnworth, "Explaining Juveniles' Attitudes toward the Police," *Justice Quarterly* 15 (March 1998), pp. 151–174.
11. Data for 2001 are from Lloyd D. Johnston, Jerald G. Bachman, and Patrick M. O'Malley, *Monitoring the Future Project Questionnaires Responses: High School Seniors* (Ann Arbor: Institute for Social Research, Survey Research Center, University of Michigan).
12. James Q. Wilson, "Dilemmas of Police Administration," *Police Administration Review* 28 (September–October 1968).
13. David J. Bordua, "Recent Trends: Deviant Behavior and Social Control," *Annals* 359 (January 1967), pp. 149–163.
14. Stephanie M. Myers, *Police Encounters with Juvenile Suspects: Explaining the Use of Authority and Provision of Support* (Washington, D.C.: National Institute of Justice, 2004).
15. Donald J. Black and Albert J. Reiss Jr., "Police Control of Juveniles," *American Sociological Review* 35 (February 1979), pp. 63–77.
16. Robert M. Terry, "Discrimination in the Handling of Juvenile Offenders by Social Control Agencies," *Journal of Research in Crime and Delinquency* 4 (July 1967), pp. 218–230; Nathan Goldman, *The Differential Selection of Juvenile Offenders for Court Appearance* (New York: National Council on Crime and Delinquency 1963), pp. 35–47; Black and Reiss, "Police Control of Juveniles," pp. 63–77; and Irving Piliavin and Scott Briar, "Police Encounters with Juveniles," *American Journal of Sociology* 70 (September 1964), pp. 206–214.
17. Terry, "Handling of Juvenile Offenders"; Black and Weiss, "Police Control of Juveniles"; and Robert M. Emerson, *Judging Delinquents: Context and Process in Juvenile Court* (Chicago: Aldine, 1969), p. 42.
18. Gail Armstrong, "Females under the Law—Protected but Unequal," *Crime and Delinquency* 23 (April 1977), pp. 109–120; Meda Chesney-Lind, "Judicial Paternalism and the Female Status Offender," *Crime and Delinquency* 23

(April 1977), pp. 121–130; and Meda Chesney-Lind, "Girls and Status Offenses: Is Juvenile Justice Still Sexist?" *Criminal Justice Abstracts* (March 1988), p. 144–165.

19. Meda Chesney-Lind, "Juvenile Delinquency: The Sexualization of Female Crime," *Psychology Today* 8 (July 1974), pp. 43–46, and I. Richard Perleman, "Antisocial Behavior of the Minor in the United States," in *Society, Delinquency, and Delinquent Behavior,* edited by Harwin L. Voss (Boston: Little, Brown & Company, 1970).

20. Theodore N. Ferdinand and Elmer C. Luchterhand, "Inner-City Youths, the Police, the Juvenile Court, and Justice," *Social Problems* 17 (Spring 1970), pp. 510–527; Goldman, *Differential Selection for Juvenile Offenders;* and Piliavin and Briar, "Police Encounters with Juveniles."

21. Marvin E. Wolfgang, Robert M. Figlio, and Thorsten Sellin, *Delinquency in a Birth Cohort* (Chicago: University of Chicago Press, 1972), p. 252.

22. Philip W. Harris, "Race and Juvenile Justice: Examining the Impact of Structural and Policy Changes on Racial Disproportionality." Paper presented at the 39th Annual Meeting of The American Society of Criminology, Montreal, Quebec, Canada (November 13, 1987).

23. James T. Carey et al., *The Handling of Juveniles from Offense to Disposition* (Washington, D.C.: U.S. Government Printing Office, 1976), p. 419; A. W. McEachern and Riva Bauzer, "Factors Related to Disposition in Juvenile–Police Contacts," in *Juvenile Gangs in Context,* edited by Malcolm W. Klein (Englewood Cliffs, N.J.: Prentice-Hall, 1967), pp. 148–160; Thorsten Sellin and Marvin E. Wolfgang, *The Measurement of Delinquency* (New York: John Wiley & Sons, 1964), pp. 95–105; and Ferdinand and Luchterhand, "Inner-City Youths," pp. 510–527.

24. Merry Morash, "Establishment of Juvenile Police Record," *Criminology* 22 (February 1984), pp. 97–111.

25. Interviewed in August 1980.

26. Piliavin and Briar, "Police Encounters with Juveniles," pp. 206–214.

27. Werthman and Piliavin, "Gang Members and Police," in *The Police,* edited by David J. Bordua (New York: Wiley, 1967), p. 70.

28. Richard J. Lundman, Richard E. Sykes, and John P. Clark, "Police Control of Juveniles: A Replication," in *Police Behavior: A Sociological Perspective,* edited by Richard J. Lundman (New York: Oxford University Press, 1980), pp. 147–148.

29. David A. Klinger, "Demeanor or Crime? Why 'Hostile' Citizens Are More Likely to Be Arrested," *Criminology* 32 (1994), pp. 475–493, and David A. Klinger, "More on Demeanor and Arrest in Dade County," *Criminology* 34 (1996), pp. 61–82.

30. Robert E. Worden and Robin L. Shepard, "Demeanor, Crime, and Police Behavior: A Reexamination of the Police Services Study Data," *Criminology* 34 (1996), pp. 83–105.

31. Malcolm W. Klein, "Police Processing of Juvenile Offenders: Toward the Development of Juvenile System Rates," in Los Angeles County Sub-Regional Board, California Council on Juvenile Justice, Part III, 1970.

32. Nathan Goldman, "The Differential Selection of Juvenile Offenders for Court Appearance," in *Crime and the Legal Process,* edited by William Chambliss (New York: McGraw-Hill, 1969).

33. Wilson, "Dilemmas of Police Administration," p. 19.

34. Donald J. Black, "Production of Crime Rates," *American Sociological Review* 35 (August 1970), pp. 733–748; Joseph W. Eaton and Kenneth Polk, *Measuring Delinquency* (Pittsburgh: University of Pittsburgh Press, 1961); Lyle W. Shannon, "Types and Patterns of Delinquency Referral in a Middle-Sized City," *British Journal of Criminology* 10 (July 1963), pp. 206–214; and Norman L. Weiner and Charles V. Willie, "Decisions by Juvenile Officers," *American Journal of Sociology* 76 (September 1971), pp 199–210.

35. Howard N. Snyder and Melissa Sickmund, *Juvenile Offenders and Victims: 1999 National Report* (Washington, D.C.: National Center for Juvenile Justice, 1999), p. 139.

36. Ibid.

37. Ibid.

38. A. Stahl, T. Finnegan, and W. Kang, *Easy Access to Juvenile Court Statistics: 1995–2000* (Washington, D.C.: National Center for Juvenile Justice, 2002).

39. Jerome Skolnick, *Justice without Trial,* 3rd ed. (New York: Macmillan, 1994).

40. Ibid.

41. Edward M. Davis, "Juvenile Justice Since the Gault Decision," *Police Chief* 44 (1977), p. 8.

42. Skolnick, *Justice without Trial.*

43. Interviewed homicide detectives are quick to say that juveniles who murder are more hard and less feeling than they were in the past.

44. Skolnick, *Justice without Trial.*

45. This advice that the police officer hears in the academy and from his or her training officer applies to everyone who works with gang youth.

46. The following section is based on H. Ted Rubin, *Juvenile Justice: Police Practice and Law* (Santa Monica, Calif.: Goodyear, 1979), pp. 75–82.

47. *Mapp v. Ohio,* 367 U.S. 643 (1961).

48. *State v. Lowry* 230 A.2d 907 (1967).

49. *In re Two Brothers and a Case of Liquor,* Juvenile Court of the District of Columbia, 1966, reported in *Washington Law Reporter* 95 (1967), p. 113.

50. Ronald D. Stephens, "School-Based Interventions: Safety and Security," *The Gang Intervention Handbook,* edited by Arnold P. Goldstein and C. Ronald Huff (Champaign, Ill.: Research Press, 1993), p. 221.

51. *Haley v. Ohio,* 332 U.S. 596 (1948).

52. *Brown v. Mississippi,* 399 F.2d 467 (5th Circ. 1968).

53. Davis, *Rights of Juveniles,* Section 3-45.

54. *Miranda v. Arizona,* 384 U.S. 436 (1966).

55. *In re Gault,* 387 U.S. (1967).

56. *Fare v. Michael C.,* 442 U.S. 23, 99 S. Ct. 2560 (1979).

57. T. Grisso, *Juveniles' Waiver of Rights: Legal and Psychological Competence* (New York: Plenum Press, 1981).

58. *People v. Lara,* 62 Cal. Reporter 586 (1967), cert. denied 392 U.S. 945 (1968).

59. *In re Mellot,* 217 S.E. 2d 745 (C.A.N. Ca. 1975).

60. *In re Dennis P. Fletcher,* 248 A. 2d. 364 (Md. 1968), cert. denied 396 U.S. 852 (1969).

61. *Commonwealth v. Guyton,* 405 Mass. 497 (1989).

62. *Commonwealth v. McNeil,* 399 Mass. 71 (1987).

63. Elyce Z. Ferster and Thomas F. Courtless, "The Beginning of Juvenile Justice, Police Practices, and the Juvenile Offender," *Vanderbilt Law Review* 22 (April 1969), pp. 598–601.

64. *Davis v. Mississippi,* 394 U.S. 721 (1969).

65. Snyder and Sickmund, *Juvenile Offenders and Victims*, p. 101.
66. *In re Carl T.*, 81 Cal. Reporter 655 (2nd. C.A. 1969).
67. *United States v. Wade*, 388 U.S. 218, 87 S. Ct. 1926 (1967).
68. *Kirby v. Illinois*, 406 U.S. 682, 92 S. Ct. 1877 (1972).
69. *In re Holley*, 107 R.I. 615, 268 A.2d 723 (1970).
70. Snyder and Sickmund, *Juvenile Offenders and Victims*, p. 101.
71. Vincent J. Webb and Nanette Graham, "Citizen Ratings of the Importance of Selected Police Duties." Paper presented at the Annual Meeting of the American Society of Criminology (November 7–12, 1994), p. 7.
72. Peter Kratcoski and Duane Dukes, *Issues in Community Policing* (Cincinnati: Anderson Publishing, 1994), p. 38.
73. Gorden Bazemore and Scott Senjo, "Police Encounters with Juveniles Revisited: An Exploratory Study of Themes and Styles in Community Policing," in *Essential Readings in Juvenile Justice*, edited by David L. Parry (Upper Saddle River, N.J.: Prentice-Hall, 2004), pp. 180–181.
74. U.S. Department of Justice, "Community Policing," *National Institute of Justice Journal* 225 (1992), pp. 1–32.
75. Interviewed in September 2001.
76. Source: Office of Justice Programs, *America's Missing: Broadcast Emergency Response: Frequently Asked Questions on AMBER Alert*, www.amberalert.gov/faqs.html.
77. Snyder and Sickmund, *Juvenile Offenders and Victims*, p. 132.
78. Howard N. Snyder and Melissa Sickmund, *Juvenile Offenders and Victims: 2006 National Report* (Washington, D.C.: National Center for Juvenile Justice, Office of Juvenile Justice and Delinquency Prevention, 2006), p. 144.
79. See Mark S. Hamm, *American Skinheads: The Criminology and Control of Hate Crime* (Westport, Conn.: Praeger Publishers, 1993), pp. 63–64.
80. See Wolfgang Pindur and Donna K. Wells, "Chronic Serious Juvenile Offenders," *Juvenile and Family Court Journal* 37 (1986), pp. 27–30.
81. "Kids, Crime and Punishment," NBC-TV News Special, 26 July 1987.
82. For this discussion of SHOCAP, see www.ncjrs.org/txtfiles/shocap.txt.
83. *DOJ Study Links Juvenile Homicide Rate to Gun Access Laws*. See http://archives.cnn.com/2000/US/03/07/gun.study.
84. Lawrence W. Sherman, J. W. Shaw, and D. P. Rogan, *The Kansas City Gun Experiment: Research in Brief* (Washington, D.C.: National Institute of Justice, U.S. Department of Justice, 1995).
85. Coordinating Council on Juvenile Justice and Delinquency Prevention, *Combating Violence and Delinquency: National Juvenile Justice Action Plan*, (Washington, D.C.: Juvenile Justice and Delinquency Prevention 1996), p. 46.
86. Snyder and Sickmund, *Juvenile Offenders and Victims*, p. 152.
87. Finn-Aage Esbensen and D. Wayne Osgood, *National Evaluation of G.R.E.A.T.* (Washington, D.C.: National Institute of Justice, Office of Justice Programs, 1997), p. 1.
88. Ibid.
89. Finn-Aage Esbensen and D. Wayne Osgood, "Gang Resistance Education and Training (G.R.E.A.T.): Results from the National Evaluation," *Journal of Research in Crime and Delinquency* 36 (1999), pp. 194–225.
90. Norman D. Wright, "From Risk to Resiliency: The Role of Law-Related Education." Paper printed in an Institute on Law and Civil Education pamphlet (Des Moines, Iowa), June 20–21, 1995.
91. Carole L. Hahn, "The Status of the Social Studies in Public School in the United States: Another Look," *Social Education* 49 (1985), pp. 220–223.
92. Judith Warrent Little and Frances Haley, *Implementing Effective LRE Programs* (Boulder, Colo.: Social Science Education Consortium, 1982).
93. William DeJong, *Arresting the Demand for Drugs: Police and School Partnership to Prevent Drug Abuse* (Washington, D.C.: National Institute of Justice, 1987), p. 5.
94. *COPS in Schools: The COPS Commitment to School Safety* (Washington, D.C.: Office of Community-Oriented Policing Services, n.d.). For how police resource officers spend their time, see Richard Lawrence, "The Role of Police–School Liaison Officers in School Crime Prevention." Paper presented at the Annual Meeting of the Academy of Criminal Justice Sciences, Albuquerque, New Mexico (March 11, 1998).
95. Ronald D. Stephens, "School-Based Interventions: Safety and Security," *The Gang Intervention Handbook*, edited by Arnold P. Goldstein and C. Ronald Huff (Champaign, Ill.: Research Press, 1993), p. 219.
96. Jerome A. Needle and William Vaughn Stapelton, "Police Handling of Youth Gangs," in *Reports of the National Juvenile Justice Assessment Centers* (Washington, D.C.: U.S. Department of Justice, 1983).
97. Ibid.
98. Charles M. Katz, "The Establishment of a Police Gang Unit: An Examination of Organizational and Environmental Factors," *Criminology* (February 2001), pp. 37–38.
99. Scott H. Decker, *Policing Gangs and Youth Violence* (Belmont, Calif.: Thomson Learning, 2003), p. xi. For an examination of some of these sites, see Charles M. Katz and Vincent J. Webb, *Police to Response to Gangs: A Multi-Site Study* (Washington, D.C.: National Institute of Justice, 2003).
100. Jack R. Greene, "Gangs, Community Policing, and Problem Solving," in *Policing Gangs and Youth Violence* (note 101), p. 6.
101. Eric J. Fritsch, Tory J. Caeti, and Robert W. Taylor, "Gang Suppression through Saturation Patrol, Aggressive Curfew, and Truancy Enforcement: A Quasi-Experimental Test of the Dallas Anti-Gang Initiative," *Crime and Delinquency* 45 (January 1999), pp. 122–139.

15

The Juvenile
Court

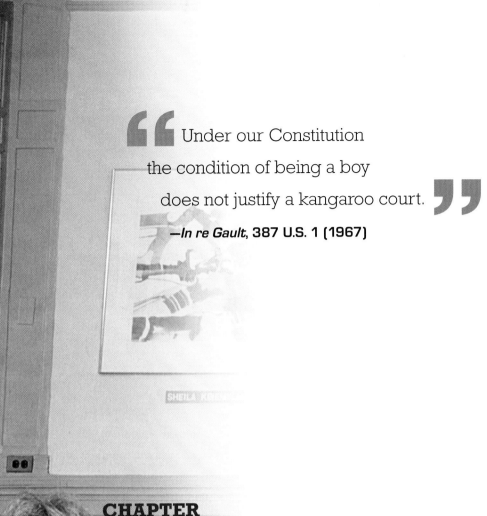

> "Under our Constitution the condition of being a boy does not justify a kangaroo court."
>
> —*In re Gault*, 387 U.S. 1 (1967)

CHAPTER
Objectives

AFTER READING THIS CHAPTER, YOU SHOULD BE ABLE TO ANSWER THE FOLLOWING QUESTIONS:

- How did the juvenile court begin?

- What pretrial procedures are involved in juvenile court proceedings?

- How is a trial conducted in juvenile court?

- What are the various forms of sentencing available to a juvenile court judge?

- What can be done to improve the juvenile court?

In 2005, the U.S. Supreme Court ruled in the case of *Roper v. Simmons*[1] that the Eighth Amendment to the U.S. Constitution, through its "cruel and unusual punishments" clause, prohibits the execution of juvenile offenders who were younger than eighteen years old when their crimes were committed. The death penalty, concluded the Justices, "is a disproportionate punishment for juveniles."

The *Simmons* case began in 1993, when the body of Shirley Crook was found in the Meramec River in St. Louis County, Missouri, bound with electric cable and leather straps. Shirley's assailant, seventeen-year-old Christopher Simmons, was arrested the next day at his school and charged with the crime. He confessed after two hours of police questioning.

The background for the killing was set when Simmons told two friends that he wanted to murder someone. In chilling, callous terms he talked about his plan, discussing it with Charles Benjamin and John Tessmer, then aged fifteen and sixteen. Simmons told the two that he wanted to commit burglary and murder by breaking and entering, tying up a victim, and then throwing the victim off a bridge. Simmons assured his friends they could "get away with it" because they were minors.

The three teenagers met at 2:00 A.M. on the night of the murder, but Tessmer left before the other two set out. Simmons and Benjamin entered the home of the victim after reaching through an open window and unlocking the back door. Simmons turned on a hallway light. Awakened, Mrs. Crook called out, "Who's there?" In response, Simmons entered Mrs. Crook's bedroom, where he recognized her from a previous car accident involving them both. Simmons later admitted this confirmed his resolve to murder her. Using duct tape to cover her eyes and mouth and bind her hands, the two perpetrators put Mrs. Crook into her minivan and drove to a state park. They reinforced the bindings, covered her head with a towel, and walked her to a railroad trestle spanning the river. There they tied her hands and feet together with electrical wire, wrapped her entire head in duct tape and threw her from the bridge, drowning her in the waters below.

The description that you've just read is taken directly from the opinion issued by the Court in the *Simmons* case. Although Simmons was tried in adult court, many considered him to be a child victim because he was the product of a dysfunctional family and suffered severe physical and psychological abuse at the hands of his alcoholic stepfather. Defense attorneys argued that his family life was characterized by intergenerational psychiatric disorders, and that Simmons was himself predisposed to mental illness. Psychiatrists who were consulted said that Simmons exhibited personal characteristics associated with low self-esteem, impulsivity, loneliness, hopelessness and depression.

Although the *Simmons* case set a precedent in making juveniles immune for execution for the crimes they commit, no matter how serious, it is significant for yet another reason. In the face of calls by many for reform of the juvenile court and for the imposition of adult punishments on juvenile offenders, the case reinforces the line separating juveniles from adults. In so doing, it seemed to echo the sentiments of Judge Gustav L. Schramm, who, as first juvenile court judge of Allegheny County (Pittsburgh), Pennsylvania, made clear the duties of juvenile court when he said:

> Neither umpire nor arbiter, [the juvenile judge] is the one person who represents his community as *parens patriae*, who may act with the parents, or when necessary even in place of them, to bring about behavior more desirable. As a judge in a juvenile court, he does not administer criminal law.

> The child before him is not a defendant. There is no conviction, no sentence. There is no lifelong stigma of a criminal record. In a juvenile court the judge administers equity; and the child, still immature and unable to take his place as an adult before the law, is the recipient of consideration, of guidance and of correction. The stake is no less than the saving of human being at a time more favorable than any in an uncertain future.[2]

Judge Schramm claimed, as do other advocates of the **juvenile court**, that the informal setting of juvenile court and the parental demeanor of the judge enable wayward youths to be saved or rescued from possible lives of crime. Indeed, during the first half of the twentieth century the juvenile court, a unique contribution to the world of jurisprudence, was widely praised for its attempt to redeem wayward youths.[3]

juvenile court
Any court that has jurisdiction over matters involving juveniles.

Critics eventually challenged these idealistic views of the juvenile court. They claimed that the juvenile court had not succeeded in rehabilitating youthful offenders, in bringing justice and compassion to them, or even in providing them with their due process rights.[4] Some investigators even accused the juvenile court of doing great harm to the juveniles who appeared before it.[5]

Today, three different positions have emerged concerning the role of the juvenile court. One position continues to support the *parens patriae* philosophy, or the state as parent, and holds to "the best interest of the child" standard for decision making. According to Judge Leonard P. Edwards, implicit in this standard is the position that "children are different from adults, that they have developmental needs which they cannot satisfy without assistance and that care and supervision are critical to their upbringing."[6] Edwards makes this telling statement, "If children were no different from adults, the juvenile court would be unnecessary."[7] This position contends that the juvenile court is superior to the criminal court because the juvenile court offers the rehabilitation of offenders, the protection of children, and the flexibility to provide the needed individualized justice for children in their formative years.[8] The concept of individualized justice is actually the hallmark of the juvenile court:

> Individualized justice for children is the legitimate goal of the juvenile justice system. The court must, within the bounds of state and constitutional law, tailor its response to the peculiar needs of the child and family, with goals of (1) rehabilitating the child; (2) reuniting the family; and (3) protecting the public safety.[9]

A second position proposes that the justice model (see Chapter 13) replace the *parens patriae* philosophy as the basis of juvenile court procedures. In the 1980s, proposed procedural changes such as decriminalization of status offenses, determinate sentencing, mandatory sentencing, and opening up juvenile proceedings and records struck at the very heart and core of traditional juvenile court proceedings.[10] The wide acceptance of these recommendations, as Barry C. Feld noted in 1991, was seen in the fact that "about one-third of the states now use the present offense and prior record [in the juvenile court] to regulate at least some sentencing decisions through determinate or mandatory minimum sentencing statutes or correctional administrative guidelines."[11] The proposed Model Juvenile Justice Code, which attracted considerable attention, also was based on the principles of the justice model.[12] The 1994 revisions in Minnesota's juvenile code showed how one state was influenced by the justice model in the remodeling of its juvenile code.[13]

A third position advocates that the juvenile court be abolished.[14] For example, Proposition 102 amended the Arizona Constitution in 1996 so that juvenile courts no longer have "exclusive" or "original" jurisdiction for offenders under eighteen years of age.[15] Feld is one of the most articulate spokespeople for this position. Feld argues that an integrated criminal court with a youth discount (juveniles would receive lesser sentences than adults for similar violations of the law) would provide

Abolish the Juvenile Court?

Barry Feld writes:

[Since the mid-1970s] judicial decisions, legislative amendments, and administrative changes have transformed the juvenile court from a nominally rehabilitative social welfare agency into a scaled-down, second-class criminal court for young people. The reforms have converted the historical ideal of the juvenile court as a social welfare institution into a penal system that provides young offenders with neither therapy nor justice. The substantive and procedural convergence between juvenile and criminal courts eliminates virtually all the conceptual and operational differences in strategies of criminal social control for youths and adults. No compelling reasons exist to maintain, separate from an adult criminal court, a punitive juvenile court whose only remaining distinctions are its persisting procedural deficiencies. Rather, states should abolish juvenile courts' delinquency jurisdictions and formally recognize youthfulness as a mitigating factor in the sentencing of younger criminal offenders. Such a policy would provide younger offenders with substantive protections comparable to those afforded by juvenile courts, assure greater procedural regularity in the determination of guilt, and avoid the disjunctions in social control caused by maintaining two duplicative and inconsistent criminal justice systems.

■ **How do you feel about abolishing the juvenile court? What would be the disadvantages of such a move across the United States?**

Source: Barry C. Feld, "Abolish the Juvenile Court: Youthfulness, Criminal Responsibility, and Sentencing Policy," *Journal of Criminal Law and Criminology* 88 (Fall 1997), p. 68.

---

youthful offenders with greater protections and justice than they currently receive in the juvenile justice system and with more proportional and humane consequences than judges currently inflict on them as adults in the criminal justice system.[16] He contends that "a statutory sentencing policy that integrates youthfulness and limited opportunities to learn self-control with principles of proportionality and reduced culpability would provide" youthful offenders with categorical fractional reductions of sentences given to adults.[17] This categorical approach is what Feld means by an explicit "youth discount" at sentencing. For example, a fourteen-year-old delinquent might receive 25 to 33 percent of the adult penalty; a sixteen-year-old, 50 to 66 percent; and an eighteen-year-old adult, the full penalty.[18] In a 1997 article, "Abolish the Juvenile Court," Feld made his point even stronger (see Juvenile Law 15.1). Although the juvenile court would likely survive the implementation of the justice model, perhaps in a much altered form, the success of this movement would sound the death knell of the juvenile court.[19]

In sum, significant changes are clearly sweeping through the almost 110-year old corridors of the juvenile court. As we approach the completion of the first decade of the twenty-first century, what is actually taking place is that all three positions are represented. For minor offenses, as well as for status offenses in most states, the "best interest of the child" position is the guiding standard of juvenile court decision making. For offenders who commit more serious delinquent acts, the principles of the justice model are increasingly used in adjudicatory and disposition hearings. Repetitive or violent youthful offenders are commonly transferred quickly to the adult court and handled as adults. Perhaps the question is not whether the traditional juvenile court will change but whether the court will survive.

■ The Changing Juvenile Court

The concept of the juvenile court, whose history was discussed in Chapter 13, was rapidly accepted across the nation. Thirty-one states had instituted juvenile courts by 1905, and by 1928, only two states did not have a juvenile court statute. In Cook

County, the amendments that followed the original act brought the neglected, the dependent, and the delinquent together under one roof. The "delinquent" category comprised both status offenders and actual violators of criminal law.

Juvenile courts throughout the nation were patterned on the Chicago court. Children in trouble were offered informal and noncriminal hearings. Their records generally were kept confidential, and the hearings were not open to the public. Children were detained separately from adults. Reformers then proposed that the noncriminal aspects of the proceedings be echoed in the physical surroundings of the court:

> The courtroom should be not a courtroom at all; just a room, with a table and two chairs, where the judge and the child, the probation officer and the parents, as occasion arises, come into close contact, and where in a more or less informal way the whole matter may be talked over.[20]

Reformers further advocated that the juvenile judge sit at a desk rather than on a bench and that he occasionally "put his arm around [the delinquent's] shoulder and draw the lad to him."[21] But the sympathetic judge was instructed not to lose any of his judicial dignity. The goals of the court were defined as investigation, diagnosis, and the prescription of treatment. Lawyers were deemed unnecessary, because these civil proceedings were not adversary trials but informal hearings in which the best interests of the children were the chief concern.

In short, the juvenile court was founded on several basic ideals: that the court should function as a social clinic designed to serve the best interests of children in trouble; that children who were brought before the court should be given the same care, supervision, and discipline as would be provided by a good parent; that the aim of the court is to help, to restore, to guide, and to forgive; that children should not be treated as criminals; and that the rights to shelter, protection, and proper guardianship are the only rights of children.[22]

Changes in Legal Norms

In the twentieth century the group known as the **constitutionalists,** one of the most formidable foes of the juvenile court, contended that the juvenile court was unconstitutional because under its system the principles of a fair trial and individual rights were denied. The constitutionalists were particularly concerned that the children appearing before the court have procedural rights as well as the rights to shelter, protection, and guardianship. They also believed that dependent and neglected children are different from children who break the law and therefore must be dealt with through separate judicial proceedings; that diagnostic and treatment technologies are not sufficiently developed to ensure that the delinquent can be treated and cured of his or her misbehavior; and that the state must justify interference with a youth's life when his or her freedom is at stake.[23] Their recommendations included modifications of juvenile court procedures by the adoption of separate methods for dealing with dependent and neglected children and those who are accused of criminal behavior; by the use of informal adjustments to avoid official court actions as frequently as possible; and by the provision of rigorous procedural safeguards and rights for children appearing before the court at the adjudicatory stage.[24]

A series of decisions by the U.S. Supreme Court in the 1960s and 1970s demonstrated the influence of the constitutionalists on juvenile justice. As Figure 15.1 shows, the five most important cases were *Kent v. United States* (1966), *In re Gault* (1967), *In re Winship* (1970), *McKeiver v. Pennsylvania* (1971), and *Breed v. Jones* (1975).

Kent v. United States (1966)
This is the first decision in which the U.S. Supreme Court dealt with a juvenile court case, concerned the matter of **transfer.** Juvenile Law 15.2 presents the facts of this case. The juvenile judge did not rule on the motions of Kent's counsel. He held no hearings, nor did he confer with Kent, Kent's mother, or Kent's counsel. The judge instead entered an order saying that after full investigation

constitutionalists
The name given to a group of twentieth-century reformers who advocated that juveniles deserve due process protections when they appear before the juvenile court.

Kent v. United States
A 1966 U.S. Supreme Court decision on the matter of transfer; the first decision in which the Supreme Court dealt with a juvenile court case.

In re Gault
A 1967 U.S. Supreme Court case that brought due process and constitutional procedures into juvenile courts.

In re Winship
A 1970 case in which the U.S. Supreme Court decided that juveniles are entitled to proof beyond a reasonable doubt during adjudication proceedings.

McKeiver v. Pennsylvania
A 1971 U.S. Supreme Court case that denied juveniles the right to trial by jury.

Breed v. Jones
A 1975 double jeopardy case in which the U.S. Supreme Court ruled that a juvenile court cannot adjudicate a case and then transfer the case over to the criminal court for adult processing of the same offense.

transfer
The process of certifying a youth over to adult criminal court; takes place by judicial waiver and legislative waiver.

FIGURE 15.1

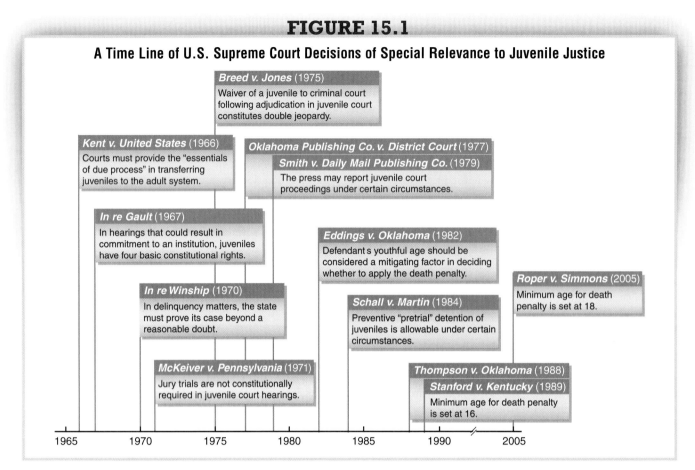

A Time Line of U.S. Supreme Court Decisions of Special Relevance to Juvenile Justice

Breed v. Jones (1975)
Waiver of a juvenile to criminal court following adjudication in juvenile court constitutes double jeopardy.

Kent v. United States (1966)
Courts must provide the "essentials of due process" in transferring juveniles to the adult system.

Oklahoma Publishing Co. v. District Court (1977)
Smith v. Daily Mail Publishing Co. (1979)
The press may report juvenile court proceedings under certain circumstances.

In re Gault (1967)
In hearings that could result in commitment to an institution, juveniles have four basic constitutional rights.

Eddings v. Oklahoma (1982)
Defendants youthful age should be considered a mitigating factor in deciding whether to apply the death penalty.

Roper v. Simmons (2005)
Minimum age for death penalty is set at 18.

In re Winship (1970)
In delinquency matters, the state must prove its case beyond a reasonable doubt.

Schall v. Martin (1984)
Preventive "pretrial" detention of juveniles is allowable under certain circumstances.

McKeiver v. Pennsylvania (1971)
Jury trials are not constitutionally required in juvenile court hearings.

Thompson v. Oklahoma (1988)
Stanford v. Kentucky (1989)
Minimum age for death penalty is set at 16.

1965　1970　1975　1980　1985　1990　2005

Source: Adapted from Office of Juvenile Justice and Delinquency Prevention, *Juvenile Offenders and Victims: 2006 National Report* (Washington, D.C.: OJJDP, 2006), p. 101. Reprinted with permission from the U.S. Department of Justice.

he was transferring jurisdiction to the adult criminal court. He made no findings and entered no reasons for the waiver.

On appeal, the U.S. Supreme Court held that the juvenile court proceedings were defective. The Court held that during a transfer hearing, Kent should have been afforded an evidential hearing; that he should have been present when the court decided to waive jurisdiction; that his attorney should have been permitted to examine

Juvenile Law 15.2

Kent v. United States

Morris A. Kent Jr., a sixteen-year-old youth living in Washington, D.C., was on juvenile probation and was charged with three counts each of housebreaking and robbery and two counts of rape. His mother retained an attorney who had Kent examined by two psychiatrists and a psychologist. The attorney then filed a motion for a hearing on the question of waiver, together with a psychiatrist's affidavit that certified that Kent was "a victim of

severe psychopathology," and recommended hospitalization for psychiatric observation. Counsel contended that psychiatric treatment would make Kent a suitable subject for juvenile court rehabilitation. His counsel also moved for access to juvenile court probation records.

■ **What did Supreme Court Justice Fortas mean when he said that "there may be grounds for concern that the child receives the worst of both worlds?" Do you agree with his criticism of the juvenile court?**

Source: Kent v. United States, 383 U.S. 541, 86 S. Ct. 1045, 16 L. Ed. 2d 84 (1966).

DELINQUENCY in America 15.1

In Family Court, Child Defendant's Welfare Takes Priority

There is no jury, no media gallery, no victim impact statement, no public eye at all in the Family Court trial of a child accused of killing someone, as a 9-year-old Brooklyn girl was yesterday in a juvenile petition.

The process is not called a trial at all, but a fact-finding. And juvenile court judges issue dispositions, never sentences.

On paper at least, the language of juvenile justice in New York reflects a gentler application of criminal law than the one used in the adult model. It is a system informed in part by the principles of child welfare and in part by the 19th-century prison-reform ethic of rehabilitation over punishment.

"The overarching goal of the process is to protect the child's welfare," said Laurence Busching, chief of the Family Court division of the City Law Department. In the adult world, Mr. Busching's agency would fill the role as prosecutor of the 9-year-old defendant (known in the juvenile system as the respondent), who is accused of fatally stabbing her 11-year-old friend on Monday afternoon during a quarrel over a ball.

"The standard the court uses is to meet the needs and best interests of the child while considering the needs and protection of the community," Mr. Busching said. Depending on the finding of facts in her case, the 9-year-old will probably face no more than 18 months in a detention center, though a judge could seek to hold her for longer, even until her 18th birthday, he said. New York excludes children under 13 from being prosecuted as adults, no matter the crime.

But in 23 other states, including Florida and Pennsylvania, there is no such age barrier in homicide cases. "A child of 6 can be charged with murder

as an adult" in those states, though no such case has gone to trial, said Marsha Levick, legal director of the Juvenile Law Center, a Philadelphia-based organization that advocates for children in the court system.

Ms. Levick helped direct the legal appeal for Lionel Tate, a 12-year-old Florida boy initially sentenced as an adult to life in prison for the 1999 killing of a 6-year-old playmate, Tiffany Eunick. She recently filed a friend-of-the-court brief in a United States Supreme Court case, *Roper* v. *Simmons*, weighing the issue of the death penalty for juveniles, which the court ultimately ruled unconstitutional.

In her brief to the Supreme Court, Ms. Levick presented evidence compiled by Laurence Steinberg, a psychologist and psychology professor at Temple University, indicating that the human brain may not reach full maturity until well past puberty. "New research on brain maturation shows there is continued development—in regions of the brain important for impulse control and foreseeing the consequences of one's actions—into the early and mid-20's," Professor Steinberg said in a telephone interview.

In response to a significant rise in juvenile crime from 1987 to 1994, much of it attributed to the crack epidemic, most states in the country, including New York, New Jersey and Connecticut, amended juvenile court laws to make it easier to prosecute children as adults, especially in cases of violent crime. But while many of those laws took effect in 1996 or later, juvenile crime rates began declining in 1994 and have continued to fall, Ms. Levick said.

Studies show that sparing the rod often spares the child. "There is growing

The Family Court building in the Bronx, New York.

■ **What does this text mean when it says that "the language of juvenile justice reflects a gentler application of criminal law than the one used in the adult court"?**

evidence that kids who are sentenced as adults come out worse than they would have if they are sentenced as juveniles," Professor Steinberg said. All states require schooling for juveniles serving time in detention centers, and most also provide psychiatric counseling and treatment, he said. In adult prisons, services are far more stinted, and the environment often brutalizing.

Leslie Acoca, a therapist based in Oakland, Calif., and the director of a health study focusing on girls in the juvenile court system, said a vast majority had experienced domestic violence, sexual abuse, substance abuse or combinations of those.

In a study of 1,000 California girls in juvenile detention, 88 percent suffered one or more serious physical or mental disorder, Ms. Acoca said.

Source: Paul Vitello, "In Family Court, Child Defendant's Welfare Takes Priority," *New York Times*, June 1, 2005. Copyright © 2005 by The New York Times Co. Reprinted with permission.

the social worker's investigation of the youth, which the court used in deciding to waive jurisdiction; and that the judge should have recorded a statement of reasons for the transfer. Justice Abe Fortas, in the decision, stated:

> There is evidence, in fact, that there may be grounds for concern that the child receives the worst of both worlds; that he gets neither the protection accorded to adults nor the solicitous care and regenerative treatment postulated for children.[25]

The Court decided that withholding Kent's record essentially meant a denial of counsel. The Court also held that a juvenile has a right to be represented by counsel, that a youth charged with a felony has a right to a hearing, and that this hearing must "measure up to the essentials of due process and fair treatment." Finally, a juvenile's attorney must have access to his or her social or probation records.[26]

Juvenile Law 15.3

In re Gault

Gerald Gault, a fifteen-year-old Arizona boy, and a friend, Ronald Lewis, were taken into custody on June 8, 1964, on a verbal complaint made by a neighbor. The neighbor had accused the boys of making lewd and indecent remarks to her over the phone. Gault's parents were not notified that he had been taken into custody; he was not advised of his right to counsel; he was not advised that he could remain silent; and no notice of charges was made either to Gerald or his parents. Additionally, the com-

plainant was not present at either of the hearings. In spite of considerable confusion about whether or not Gerald had made the alleged phone call, what he had said over the phone, and what he had said to the judge during the course of the two hearings, Judge McGhee committed him to the State Industrial School "for the period of his minority (that is, until twenty-one) unless sooner discharged by due process of law."

■ **What due process rights did this case grant juveniles? What due process rights did juveniles still lack after this decision?**

Source: In re Gault, 387 U.S. 1, 18 L. Ed. 2d 527, 87 S. Ct. 1428 (1967).

Web LIBRARY 15.1

Read Chapter 6 of the OJJDP publication *Juvenile Offenders and Victims: 2006 National Report* at **www.justicestudies.com/ WebLibrary**.

Web PLACES 15.1

View the OJJDP PowerPoint presentation "Juvenile Offenders in Court" at **www.justicestudies .com/WebPlaces**.

***In re Gault* (1967)** In May 1967, the U.S. Supreme Court reversed the conviction of a minor in *In re Gault*. This influential and far-reaching decision represented a new dawn in juvenile court history because, in effect, it brought the light of constitutional procedure into juvenile courts. No longer could due process and procedural safeguards be kept out of the adjudication proceedings. Juvenile Law 15.3 gives the facts of this case.

In *Gault*, the U.S. Supreme Court overruled the Arizona Supreme Court for its dismissal of a writ of habeas corpus. This writ had sought Gerald Gault's release from a training school.[27] Justice Fortas, for the Court majority, ruled on four of the six issues raised in the appeal:

1. Notice, to comply with due process requirements, must be given sufficiently in advance of scheduled court proceedings so that reasonable opportunity to prepare will be afforded, and it must "set forth the alleged misconduct with particularity."
2. The due process clause of the Fourteenth Amendment requires that in respect of proceedings to determine delinquency which may result in commitment to an institution in which the juvenile's freedom is curtailed, the child and his parent must be notified of the child's right to be represented by counsel retained by them, or if they are unable to afford counsel, that counsel will be appointed to represent the child.
3. The constitutional privilege against self-incrimination is applicable in the case of juveniles as it is with respect to adults.
4. No reason is suggested or appears for a different role in respect of sworn testimony in juvenile courts than in adult tribunals. Absent a valid confession adequate to support the determination of the Juvenile Court, confrontation and sworn testimony by witnesses available for cross-examination are essential for a finding of "delinquency" and an order committing Gerald to a state institution for a maximum of six years.[28]

Justice Fortas, in delivering the Court's opinion, recalled other cases that had provided juveniles with due process of law. In both *Haley v. Ohio* (1948) and *Gallegos v. Colorado* (1962), the Supreme Court had prohibited the use of confessions coerced from juveniles, and in *Kent* the Court had given the juvenile the right to be represented by counsel.[29] Justice Fortas concluded his review of legal precedent with the sweeping statement that juveniles have those fundamental rights that are incorporated in the due process clause of the Fourteenth Amendment to the U.S. Constitution.

The *In re Gault* decision affirmed that a juvenile has the right to due process safeguards in proceedings in which a finding of delinquency can lead to institutional confinement. The decision also established that a juvenile has the right to notice of the charges, right to counsel, right to confrontation and cross-examination, and privilege against self-incrimination. But the Court did not rule that juveniles have the right to a transcript of the proceedings or the right to appellate review.

In choosing not to rule on these two latter rights, the Court clearly did not want to turn the informal juvenile hearing into an adversary trial. The cautiousness of this decision was underlined by a footnote stating that the decision did not apply to preadjudication or postadjudication treatment of juveniles.

***In re Winship* (1970)**   In *Winship* the Supreme Court decided that juveniles are entitled to proof **beyond a reasonable doubt** during the adjudication proceedings.[30] Juvenile Law 15.4 presents the facts of this case. In ruling that the "preponderance of evidence" is not a sufficient basis for a decision when youths are charged with acts that would be criminal if committed by adults, the *Winship* decision not only expanded *Gault* but also reflected other concerns of the Justices. The Court desired both to protect juveniles at adjudicatory hearings and to maintain the confidentiality, informality, flexibility, and speed of the juvenile process in the prejudicial and postadjudicative states. The Court obviously did not want to bring too much rigidity and impersonality to the juvenile hearing.

> **beyond a reasonable doubt**
> A legal standard establishing the degree of proof needed for a juvenile to be adjudicated a delinquent by the juvenile court during the adjudicatory stage of the court's proceedings.

***McKeiver v. Pennsylvania* (1971)**   During the 1969 through 1971 sessions, the Supreme Court heard three cases together (*McKeiver v. Pennsylvania, In re Terry,* and *In re Barbara Burrus*) concerning whether the due process clause of the Fourteenth Amendment guaranteeing the right to a jury trial applies to the adjudication of a juvenile court delinquency case.[31] The decision, which was issued in *McKeiver v. Pennsylvania,* denied the right of juveniles to have jury trials. Juvenile Law 15.5 summarizes the facts of these three cases.

> " In *Winship* the Supreme Court decided that juveniles are entitled to proof beyond a reasonable doubt during the adjudication proceedings. "

The Supreme Court gave the following reasons for its ruling:

1. Not all rights that are constitutionally assured for the adult are to be given to the juvenile.
2. The jury trial, if required for juveniles, may make the juvenile proceedings into a fully adversary process and will put an end to what has been the idealistic prospect of an intimate, informal protecting proceeding.
3. A jury trial is not a necessary part even of every criminal process that is fair and equitable.
4. The jury trial, if injected into the juvenile court system, could bring with it the traditional delay, the formality, and the clamor of the adversary system.

Juvenile Law 15.4

In re Winship

The *Winship* case involved a New York boy who was sent to a state training school at the age of twelve for taking $112 from a woman's purse. The commitment was based on a New York statute that permitted juvenile court decisions on the basis of

a "preponderance of evidence," a standard that is much less strict than "beyond a reasonable doubt."

> ■ What is the actual difference between "preponderance of evidence" and "proof beyond a reasonable doubt"? What was the importance of this difference in this case?

Source: In re Winship, 397 U.S. 358, 90 S. Ct. 1968, 25 L. Ed. 2d 368 (1970).

Juvenile Law 15.5

McKeiver v. Pennsylvania

McKeiver v. Pennsylvania

Joseph McKeiver, age sixteen, was charged with robbery, larceny, and receiving stolen goods, all of which were felonies under Pennsylvania law. This youth was found delinquent at an adjudication hearing and was placed on probation after his request for a jury trial was denied.

In re Terry

Edward Terry, age fifteen, was charged with assault and battery on a police officer, misdemeanors under Pennsylvania law. His counsel's request for a jury trial was denied, and he was adjudicated a delinquent on the charges.

In re Barbara Burrus

Barbara Burrus and approximately forty-five other youths, ranging in ages from eleven to fifteen years, were the subjects of juvenile court summonses in Hyde County, North Carolina. The charges arose out of a series of demonstrations in the county in late 1968 by African American adults and children protesting school assignments and a school consolidation plan. These youths were charged with willfully impeding traffic. The several cases were consolidated into groups for hearing before the district judge, sitting as a juvenile court. A request for a jury trial in each case was denied. Each juvenile was found delinquent and placed on probation.

■ **Some states now permit jury trial for juveniles. How can they grant a jury trial with this Supreme Court decision?**

Source: McKeiver v. Pennsylvania, 403 U.S. 528, 535 (1971); In re Terry, 215 Pa. Super 762 (1970); and In re Barbara Burrus, 275 N.C. 517, 169 S.E.2d 879 (1969).

5. There is nothing to prevent an individual juvenile judge from using an advisory jury when he or she feels the need. For that matter, there is nothing to prevent individual states from adopting jury trials.[32]

A number of states do permit jury trials for juveniles, but most adhere to the constitutional standard set by the Supreme Court. Surveys of states report that juveniles choose jury trials in only about 1 to 3 percent of cases.[33] The significance of the

Teenage sniper Lee Boyd Malvo, shown here flanked by police officers as he is brought into a Maryland courtroom. ■ **Did Malvo deserve to be treated as an adult for purposes of the law?**

Juvenile Law 15.6

Breed v. Jones

In 1971 the juvenile court in California filed a petition against Jones, who was then seventeen, alleging that he had committed an offense that, if committed by an adult, would have constituted robbery. Jones was detained pending a hearing. At the hearing, the juvenile judge took testimony, found that the allegations were true, and sustained the petition. At the disposi-

tional hearing, Jones was found unfit for treatment in the juvenile court, and it was ordered that he be prosecuted as an adult offender. At a subsequent preliminary hearing, Jones was held for criminal trial. An information hearing was held against him for robbery, and he was tried and found guilty. Counsel objected that Jones was being subjected to double jeopardy, but the defendant was committed to the California Youth Authority.

■ **What is double jeopardy? Why is it important for juveniles and adults in the legal process?**

Source: Breed v. Jones, 421 U.S. 519, 95 S. Ct. 1779 (1975).

McKeiver decision is that the Court indicated an unwillingness to apply further procedural safeguards to juvenile proceedings, especially during the preadjudicatory and postadjudicatory treatment of juveniles.

Breed v. Jones (1975)   The question of transfer to an adult court, first considered in the *Kent* case, was taken up again in the *Breed v. Jones* decision.[34] This case raised the issue of **double jeopardy,** questioning whether a juvenile could be prosecuted as an adult after an adjudicatory hearing in the juvenile court. The increased use of transfers, or the binding over of juveniles to the adult court, makes this decision particularly significant today (see Juvenile Law 15.6).

> **double jeopardy**
> A common law and constitutional prohibition against a second trial for the same offense.

The U.S. Supreme Court ruled that Breed's case did constitute double jeopardy: A juvenile court cannot adjudicate a case and then transfer the case over to the criminal court for adult processing on the same offense. The significance of *Breed* is that prosecutors must determine which youthful offenders they want to transfer to the adult court before juvenile court adjudication; otherwise, the opportunity to transfer, or certify, those youths is lost.[35]

Today, as is indicated in more detail later in this chapter, nearly every state has defined the specific requirements for transfer proceedings in its juvenile code. At present, when a transfer hearing is conducted in the juvenile court, due process law usually requires (1) a legitimate transfer hearing, (2) sufficient notice to the juvenile's family and defense attorney, (3) the right to counsel, and (4) a statement of the court order regarding transfer.

▮Juvenile Court Actors

Judges, referees, prosecutors (or petitioners), and defense attorneys (or respondents) are the main participants in the juvenile court process. Their roles have changed significantly since the groundbreaking cases of the 1960s and 1970s.

Judges

The juvenile court judge, the ultimate decision maker, is the most important person in the juvenile court. The most traditional role of the juvenile court judge is to decide the legal issues in the cases that appear before the court. The judge must make a determination, according to Edwards, "whether certain facts are true, whether a child should be removed from a parent, what types of services should be offered to the family, and whether the child should be returned to the family and the community or placed permanently in another setting."[36]

The juvenile court judge also has the following role responsibilities:

1. To set standards within the community and the criminal and juvenile justice system related to juvenile justice.
2. To make certain that juveniles appearing before the court receive the legal and constitutional rights to which they are entitled.
3. To ensure that the systems that detect, investigate, resolve, and bring cases to court are working fairly and efficiently.
4. To make certain that adequate numbers of attorneys of satisfactory quality are available to represent juveniles in court.
5. To know how cases that do not reach the juvenile court are being resolved.
6. To monitor the progress of the child, the family, and the supervising agency to make certain that each complies with the terms of the court's orders.
7. To be an advocate within the community on behalf of children and their families.
8. In some communities, to serve as the administrator of the juvenile probation department and court staff.[37]

More specifically, juvenile judges rule on various pretrial motions such as arrest, search and seizure, interrogation, and lineup identification; make decisions about the continued use of or the need for detention of youths before juvenile court hearings; make decisions about plea-bargaining agreements; settle questions of evidence and procedure and guide the questioning of witnesses; hold dispositional hearings or approve the contract presented and decide on the necessary treatment; handle waiver (transfer) proceedings; and handle appeals where allowed by statute.[38]

> " The juvenile court judge, the ultimate decision maker, is the most important person in the juvenile court. "

Significant changes, however, are occurring in the funding process and in the administration of the juvenile court. In some jurisdictions, separately organized juvenile courts are being recast as juvenile divisions of a multi-jurisdictional trial court. The central responsibility for budget preparation and presentation then is shared by the trial court administrator and the presiding judge of the trial court. State legislatures also are assuming more responsibility for funding trial courts; this trend will probably continue, because it is seen as leading to a more uniform system of justice. Furthermore, some state legislatures are transferring the responsibility for administering juvenile probation and detention services from the judiciary to the state executive branch. Finally, more judges are taking the bench through appointment rather than through a victory in a public election; they have very different relationships with local funding authorities than elected judges have.

> " David Matza, addressing the abuse of power in the juvenile court, refers to the justice of some judges as kadi justice. "

Juvenile court judges not only have important and difficult jobs but also wield considerable power. Power, of course, sometimes corrupts, and occasionally a judge becomes a despot or dictator in the court. David Matza, addressing the abuse of power in the juvenile court, refers to the justice of some judges as "**kadi justice.**"[39] The *kadi* is a Muslim judge who sits in the marketplace and makes decisions without any apparent reference to rules or norms; he seems to make a completely free evaluation of the merits of each case. The "justice" dispensed by some juvenile judges has caused considerable criticism of the juvenile court.

Yet the majority of juvenile judges rise to the challenge and do extremely competent jobs. Procedural safeguards and due process rights for juveniles are scrupulously observed in their courts. These judges are always seeking better means of detention and reserve the use of correctional institutions as a last resort. They are very committed, work long hours, and sometimes pass up promotions to more highly paid judgeships with greater prestige. Such judges usually improve the quality of juvenile justice in their jurisdictions.

kadi justice

A judicial approach similar to that of a Muslim judge who sits in the marketplace and makes decisions without any apparent reference to established or traditional rules and norms.

Referees

Many juvenile courts employ the services of a **referee**. Characterized as "the arm of the court," a referee is called a *commissioner* in the State of Washington and a *master* in Maryland. California has both referees and commissioners. A number of states, such as Florida and Iowa, use only judges in the juvenile court; in other states, referees, masters, and commissioners are the primary hearing officers. Referees may or may not be members of the bar, but their basic responsibility is to assist judges in processing youths through the courts. They hear cases at the fact-finding stage and sometimes in detention hearings, but if a judicial disposition is necessary, it is usually left to a juvenile judge.

Prosecutors

The **prosecutor,** or petitioner, is expected to protect society while ensuring that children who would harm society are provided their basic constitutional rights. Almost two-thirds of prosecutors' offices handling juvenile cases transferred at least one juvenile case to criminal court in 1994.[40]

In larger courts, prosecutors are typically involved at every stage of the proceedings, from intake and detention through disposition and review. The prosecutor is particularly involved before the adjudication stage, because witnesses must be interviewed, police investigations must be checked out, and court rules and case decisions must be researched. The prosecutor also plays a role in detention decisions and represents the local or state government in all pretrial motions, probable cause hearings, and consent decrees. The prosecutor further represents the state or county at transfer hearings, at the adjudication hearing, and at the disposition of the case. In some urban courts, the prosecutor may frequently be involved in **plea bargaining** with the defense counsel. Prosecutors in some states are even permitted to initiate appeals for the limited purpose of clarifying a given law or procedure. Furthermore, the prosecutor represents the state or county on appeals and in habeas corpus proceedings. Some critics argue that the prosecutor in the juvenile court has come to dominate juvenile court proceedings.[41]

Defense Attorneys

The number of juveniles represented by counsel, or respondents, has been gradually increasing since the early 1960s. Juveniles in more serious cases are especially likely to be represented by counsel.[42] Yet Feld found that nearly half the juveniles who appeared before the juvenile courts for delinquency and status offense referrals in Minnesota, Nebraska, and North Dakota were not represented by counsel. Equally serious, he found that many of the juveniles who were placed out of their homes in these states did not have counsel.[43]

Feld added in a 1999 publication that "waiver of counsel is the most common explanation why so many youths appear without counsel."[44] Even though more juveniles now are being represented by counsel, considerable confusion still exists among defense attorneys concerning their proper role in the courtroom, and many questions have been raised about their effectiveness in court. Defense counsels have at least three roles to choose from: (1) assist the court with its responsibilities to children, (2) serve as a legal advocate for the child, and (3) be a guardian or parent surrogate to the child.[45]

Public defenders frequently do a more adequate job of representing youths than do private and court-appointed attorneys, particularly when the same public defender must appear in juvenile court day after day. Court-appointed private counsel, particularly those who need the work to supplement slim private practices, can be more easily swayed to the court's wishes.[46]

Some evidence exists that children who have counsel may get more severe dispositions than those without counsel.[47] For example, studies reported in 1980 and

referee
A juvenile justice worker who may or may not be a member of the bar. In many juvenile courts referees assist judges in processing youths through the juvenile court system.

prosecutor
The representative of the state in court proceedings. Also called *county's attorney, district attorney,* or *state attorney.*

plea bargaining
A court process in which the defense counsel and the prosecution agree that the defendant will plead guilty, usually in exchange for a reduction of charges or a lessened sentence.

1981 that juveniles with counsel were more likely to receive an institutional disposition than those without counsel.[48] When it exists, there are two possible explanations for this positive relationship between counsel and punitive dispositions: First, the juvenile judge is punishing youths who choose to be represented by counsel. Second, the youths who have committed the more serious crimes are the ones requesting counsel, and they are the ones most likely to be adjudicated to training school or transferred to the adult court. Although the former may have been true in the past, the latter is typically true today.

Web **LIBRARY** 15.2

Read the OJJDP publication *Juvenile Court Statistics 2000* at **www.justicestudies.com/WebLibrary**.

Pretrial Procedures

The types of cases that are under the jurisdiction of the juvenile court vary widely among and even within states, but they generally include those involving delinquency, neglect, and dependency. In 2002, juvenile courts handled 51.5 delinquency cases for every 1,000 juveniles who appeared before it. Figure 15.2 shows that delinquency case rates generally increase with age. Juvenile courts also may deal with cases involving adoption, termination of parental rights, appointment of guardians for minors, custody, contributing to delinquency or neglect, and nonsupport.

Pretrial procedures in the juvenile justice system include the detention hearing, the intake procedure, and the transfer procedure, all of which take place before the adjudication stage of juvenile court proceedings.

The Detention Hearing

Legislative acts that govern the juvenile court normally require that the police either take a child to an intake officer of the court or a detention facility, or release the child

FIGURE 15.2

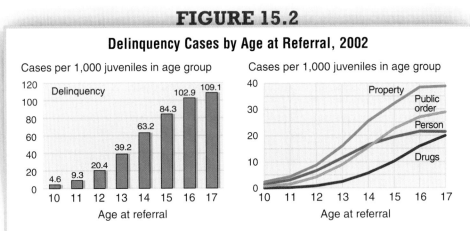

Delinquency Cases by Age at Referral, 2002

- In 2002, the delinquency case rate for 16-year-olds was 1.6 times the rate for 14-year-olds and the rate for 14-year-olds was 3.1 times the rate for 12-year-olds.

- The increase in rates between ages 13 and 17 was sharpest for drug offenses; the rate for drug offenses for 17-year-old juveniles was 8 times the rate for 13-year-olds.

- The growth in age-specific case rates was less dramatic for person offense cases. Person offense rates increased steadily through age 16 then dropped off at age 17, unlike rates for other offenses that increased through age 17. The person case rate for 17-year-olds was 84% higher than the rate for 13-year-olds.

Source: Adapted from Howard N. Snyder and Melissa Sickmund, *Juvenile Offenders and Victims: 2006 National Report* (Washington, D.C.: Office of Juvenile Justice and Delinquency Prevention, 2006), p. 166. Reprinted with permission from the U.S. Department of Justice.

DELINQUENCY International 15.1

Juvenile Court Systems in Australia, Canada, England, Japan, and South Africa

The United States is not alone in re-thinking its handling of law-violating juveniles.

Australia

All six Australian states and the two territories abandoned the "welfare model" of juvenile justice during the 1970s and 1980s, adopting an alternative "justice model" that emphasizes deterrence and accountability while diverting most non-criminal offenses. In 1995 South Australia shifted to a "restorative justice" model (see Chapter 13), and other Australian states are monitoring developments there.

Canada

With the "Young Offenders Act" of 1984, inspired by calls for tougher crime control as well as demands for increased protection of juvenile rights, the Canadian government basically abolished the concept of *parens patriae*. The 1984 law introduced proportional sentencing for young offenders and extended the youth justice system to include sixteen- and seventeen-year-olds once handled in adult court. The law failed to stop public criticism; calls for reform resumed immediately, and have continued to this day.

England

In 1992 the British system replaced all juvenile courts with "youth courts" that focus on offender accountability. Youth court jurisdiction was extended to include seventeen-year-olds previously tried in adult court. In 1997, the British Home Office expressed dissatisfaction with inefficiency in the youth court system and called for returning all seventeen-year-olds (or "near adults") to the jurisdiction of criminal courts. However, the present youth courts continue to have jurisdictions over nearly all seventeen-year-old offenders.

Japan

In Japan separate family courts have original jurisdiction over all crimes by youth under the age of twenty, although family court judges may refer youths ages sixteen to nineteen to the Public Prosecutor for trial as adults. Pressures for reform erupted in the 1990s after several highly publicized acts of juvenile violence. Critics called for more youths under age sixteen to be eligible for trial as adults, but this has not yet taken place.

South Africa

The South African Law Commission has considered several options for the first national juvenile justice system:

1. Completely separate, district-level juvenile courts with jurisdiction to try all juvenile cases
2. Specialized district-level juvenile courts with the capacity to refer serious cases to regional or high courts
3. No separate juvenile courts, but special rules and procedures in any court where an accused person under eighteen appears
4. Special courts that operate chiefly as a mechanism to refer juvenile matters to other community-based forums, such as family group conferences or sentencing circles.

> ■ Why do you feel that other nations, like the United States, are tending to "get tough" on youth crime? Do any of the structural changes described here seem to offer more promise than the juvenile court system currently in place in the United States?

Source: Jeffrey A. Butts and Adele V. Harrell, *Delinquents or Criminals? Policy Options for Young Offenders* (Washington, D.C.: Urban Institute, 1998), p. 13. Reprinted by permission of the Urban Institute.

---

to his or her parents. At **detention hearings** the criteria for detention are based on the need to protect the child and to ensure public safety. The decision to detain must be made within a short period of time, usually forty-eight to seventy-two hours, excluding weekends and holidays. Urban courts, which have intake units on duty twenty-four hours a day for detention hearings, frequently act within a few hours.[49]

In some states, intake officers of the juvenile court, rather than juvenile judges, conduct detention hearings. Such a procedure represents a progressive move, because having the same judge preside over both the detention hearing and the adjudication hearing is a poor practice. Some states still require that the juvenile judge be responsible for the policies and operations of the detention facility. Juvenile judges also are usually required to decide, to preclude inappropriate or overly long detention, whether a child who was admitted to detention a few days earlier must remain locked up.

In 2002, the offense profile of detained delinquency cases was as follows: drug law violations, 12 percent; public order cases, 25 percent; person cases, 24 percent; and property cases, 39 percent.[50] Juveniles who are held in detention may be assigned to one of several different types of placements. The **detention center** (detention hall

detention hearing

A hearing, usually conducted by an intake officer of the juvenile court, during which the decision is made as to whether a juvenile will be released to his or her parents or guardians or be detained in a detention facility.

detention center

A facility that provides custodial care for juveniles during juvenile court proceedings. Also called *juvenile halls* and *detention homes*, detention centers were established at the end of the nineteenth century as an alternative to jails for juveniles.

or detention home) physically restricts youths for a short period. **Shelter care** is physically nonrestrictive and is available for those who have no homes or who require juvenile court intervention. A third type of placement is the **jail** or police lockup. A fourth is **home detention.** In-home detention restricts a juvenile to his or her home and is supervised, normally by a paraprofessional staff member. Finally, **attention homes** offer services and staff support in a nonrestrictive setting. See Juvenile Law 15.7 for a discussion of detention facilities in the United States.

Five states have legislated a hearing on probable cause for detained youths, and appellate cases in other states have moved in the direction of mandating a probable cause hearing to justify further detention. Courts in Georgia and Alaska have ruled that a child is entitled to counsel at a detention hearing and to free counsel if the child is indigent. The supreme courts of California and Alaska and an appellate court in Pennsylvania all have overturned cases in which no reason or inadequate reason was stated for continuing detention. Finally, courts in the District of Columbia, Baltimore, and Nevada have ruled that a juvenile who is in detention is entitled to humane care. The appeals court in the District of Columbia stated that there is a statutory obligation to provide a juvenile with care "as nearly as possible equivalent to that which should have been given him by his parents."[51]

Steven Schlossman's detailed account of the history of Milwaukee's juvenile court found that judges and probation officers frequently relied on detention to make juveniles cooperative.[52] Although Charles E. Frazier and Donna M. Bishop's study of detention found no evidence that detention status greatly affected the severity of judicial dispositions, it did find that juveniles who were male, white, and older were more disadvantaged by detention than were those who were female, nonwhite, and younger.[53]

Court decisions have differed concerning **bail** for a juvenile. Decisions have found that juveniles have a constitutional right to bail; that juvenile act procedures, when applied in a manner consistent with due process, provide an adequate substitute for bail; or that juveniles do not have a constitutional right to bail. Nine states (Arkansas, Colorado, Connecticut, Georgia, Massachusetts, Nebraska, Oklahoma, South

A teenage defendant (*right*) and his court-appointed defender stand before a juvenile court judge in Orange, California. ■ **What is the role of juvenile defense counsel?**

Juvenile Law 15.7

Detention Facilities

Detention centers are administered by state agencies, city or county government, welfare departments, juvenile courts, or private vendors, but the majority of detention facilities are administered by the county. In 1997, of forty-four states responding to a survey conducted by the National Council on Crime and Delinquency, 73 percent operated detention facilities at the county level; 36 percent at the state level; 30 percent under multiple jurisdictions; 16 percent had court-administered or -operated detention facilities; and 11 percent contracted with private vendors to provide detention services.. . .

The traditional model of detention for youths was woefully inadequate. A grim-looking detention facility usually was attached to the building that housed the administrative offices and hearing rooms of the juvenile court. Locked outer doors and high fences or walls prevented escapes. The lack of programming made it clear that these facilities were intended merely to be holding centers. A former resident, interviewed in May 1981, described her experience in a traditional detention home:

> It [the facility] sucks. It was the worst place I've ever been in. They're [the staff] cruel. They used to give work details for punishment. For an entire hour, I scrubbed the kitchen floor with a toothbrush. They can get away with this, and it is not against the law. The place is falling apart. They are just not very caring people. They didn't do much for me except scare me.

Fortunately, the nationwide movement to develop standards for detention as well as more innovative detention programs resulted in marked improvement in the overall quality of detention facilities and programs [in the 1980s and 1990s]. The bureau of detention standards, in those states that have such oversight units, usually inspects detention centers once a year; this inspection ensures better-quality detention practices.

Attention homes, which were initiated in Boulder, Colorado,

by the juvenile court to improve the detention process for children, have spread to other jurisdictions. The stated purpose of the attention homes program is to give youths *attention* rather than *detention*. Problem resolution is the focus of the program, and professional services are provided to residents on a contractual basis. These nonsecured facilities have no fences, locked doors, or other physical restraints. They also are characterized by more extensive programming and by more intensive involvement between residents and staff than is typical in other facilities.

Home detention, a nonresidential approach to detention, was first used in St. Louis, Newport News, Norfolk, and Washington, D.C., and now is used throughout the United States. The in-home detention program is commonly within the organizational structure of the juvenile court and is administered by the community services unit of the probation department. An in-home detention coordinator typically meets with the intake officer, a field probation officer, and sometimes a juvenile officer before the detention hearing to decide whether a youth is an appropriate candidate for in-home detention. Some jurisdictions use a release risk evaluation to decide whether in-home detention for a particular youth should be recommended to the juvenile judge. Youths who are placed on in-home detention are required to remain at home twenty-four hours a day; the in-home detention worker visits the youth and family seven days a week and also makes random phone calls throughout the day to make certain that the juvenile is at home. As will be discussed in Chapter 16, electronic monitoring is starting to be used as part of home-detention programs.

■ **What are the detention facilities like in your jurisdiction? Are you familiar with attention homes or home detention programs?**

Source: Adapted from Kelly Dedel, "National Profile of the Organization of State Juvenile Correctional Systems," *Crime and Delinquency* 44 (October 1998), p. 514. Copyright © 1998 by Sage Publications. Reprinted by permission of Sage Publications, Inc.

Dakota, and West Virginia) have enacted laws granting juveniles the right to bail. On the other hand, Hawaii, Kentucky, Oregon, and Utah deny juveniles the right to bail.

Alida V. Merlo and William D. Bennett's examination of bail in Massachusetts in 1988 revealed that bail was a factor in 72 percent of the cases statewide. The trend in Massachusetts at the time was for higher bail: Detention admissions receiving from $101 to $500 bail were up 16 percent, $501 to $1,000 bail were up 70 percent, and over $1,000 bail up 48 percent. These statewide developments, the researchers concluded, suggested that juvenile judges might be starting to use bail as a means of ensuring the youth's detention and thus that judges, without actually using the term, might be engaging in the practice of preventive detention.[54]

The U.S. Supreme Court decision in the *Schall v. Martin* (1984) case represents an example of a fundamental change that seems to be occurring in detention practices.[55] The plaintiffs originally filed a lawsuit in federal district court claiming that the New York Family Court Act was unconstitutional because it allowed for the preventive detention of juveniles:

> The District Court struck down the statute as permitting detention without due process and ordered the release of all class members. The Court of Appeals affirmed, holding . . . the statute is administered not for preventive purposes, but to impose punishment for unadjudicated criminal acts, and that therefore the statute is unconstitutional.[56]

The Supreme Court, however, reversed the decision of the appeals court. Justice William H. Rehnquist, in writing the opinion for the majority, declared that the "preventive detention under the statute serves the legitimate state objective held in common with every State, of protecting both the juvenile and the society from the hazards of pretrial crime."[57] Some experts believe that the Court's ruling may encourage a significant expansion of preventive, or secure, detention for juveniles.

The constitutionality of preventive detention may have been confirmed by the Supreme Court in *Schall,* but this policy still raises several controversial issues. First, there is the technical difficulty of accurately predicting which offenders should be detained to prevent their commission of further offenses before trial. Second, the detainee considers preventive detention as punitive confinement, regardless of the stated purpose of the practice. Finally, there are issues of the propriety of incarceration before the determination of guilt and of the procedural safeguards that must accompany such a practice. Indeed, evaluations of the detention process indicate that the majority of juveniles who are preventively detained are not charged with serious offenses.[58]

> " The constitutionality of preventive detention . . . still raises several controversial issues. "

The Intake Process

Intake essentially is a preliminary screening process to determine whether a court should take action—and, if so, what action—or whether the matter should be referred elsewhere. Larger courts usually handle this function through a specialized intake unit. Probation officers or other officers of the court screen incoming cases in smaller courts.[59]

Between 1985 and 2002, the formal processing of property, person, public order, and drug offense violations increased. In the United States in 2002, 58 percent of all delinquency cases were formally processed. Drug offense cases were more likely than other offense cases to be handled formally, and property offense cases were the least likely to be petitioned for formal handling.[60]

Intake procedures follow **complaints** to authorities against children. Juvenile law varies from state to state regarding who is permitted to sign such a complaint. Typically, most complaints are filed by the police, although they may be initiated and signed by a victim or by the youth's parents. In some states, parents, victims, probation staff, social service staff, neighbors, or anyone else may go directly to the court to file a complaint. Complaints also may be brought by school officials and truant officers.

After the intake officer receives the complaint, he or she must first decide whether the court has statutory jurisdiction. If the statutory guides are unclear, the intake officer should seek the advice of the prosecuting attorney. Once legal jurisdiction is established, the second step is to conduct a preliminary interview and investigation to determine whether the case should be adjudicated nonjudicially or petitioned to the court. This evaluation procedure varies from jurisdiction to jurisdiction, principally because so many juvenile courts have failed to provide written guidelines. Therefore the intake officer usually has broad and largely unregulated discretion in making the intake decision.

Options for the Disposal of Cases   The intake unit, especially in larger urban courts, may have up to five options for the disposal of cases: (1) outright dismissal of the complaint, (2) informal adjustment (chiefly diversion to a nonjudicial agency), (3) informal probation, (4) consent decree, and (5) filing of a petition.

Outright dismissal of the complaint takes place when legal jurisdiction does not exist or when the case is so weak that the intake officer questions the feasibility of petitioning the youth to the juvenile court. **Informal adjustment** means that the intake officer requires restitution from the youth (see Chapter 16), warns him or her, and then dismisses the case or diverts the youth to a social agency. The diversion agency supervises such referrals and generally reports to the intake unit on the youth's progress; status offenders and juveniles charged with minor offenses typically are dealt with under this option.

Informal probation, which has been under increased criticism since the 1970s, involves the casual supervision of a youth by a volunteer or probation officer who reserves judgment on the need for filing a petition until the intake officer (or other designated person) sees how the youth fares during the informal probation period. See Juvenile Law 15.8 for more information on informal sanctions.

A **consent decree** is a formal agreement between the child and the court in which the child is placed under the court's supervision without a formal finding of delinquency. Consent decrees provide an intermediate step between informal handling and probation. The consent decree is used less often than the other options that are currently open to the intake officer. The consent decree, it should be noted, comes after the petition but before the adjudication hearing.

If none of these options is satisfactory, the intake officer can choose to file a petition. Unfortunately, the broad discretionary power given intake workers has often been abused. For example, Duran Bell Jr. and Kevin Lang's study of intake in Los Angeles County revealed the importance of extralegal factors, especially cooperative behavior, in reducing the length of detention and the effect of age in increasing the length of detention.[61]

Research is needed to determine which approach to intake will result in the greatest services to youth and the least misuse of discretion. But until a systematic examination of the intake process is done, the principles of fairness and of doing the least harm possible to the youth should guide the intake screening process.

informal adjustment
An attempt to handle a youthful offender outside of the formal structures of the juvenile justice system.

informal probation
An arrangement in which, instead of being adjudicated as a delinquent and placed on probation, a youth is informally assigned to the supervision of a probation officer.

consent decree
A formal agreement between a juvenile and the court in which the juvenile is placed under the court's supervision without a formal finding of delinquency.

Juvenile Law 15.8

Informal Sanctions

Informal processing is considered when decision makers (police, intake workers, probation officers, prosecutors, or other screening officers) believe that accountability and rehabilitation can be achieved without the use of formal court intervention.

Informal sanctions are voluntary and, consequently, the court cannot force a juvenile to comply with an informal disposition. If the court decides to handle the matter informally (in lieu of formal prosecution), a youthful offender agrees to comply with one or more sanctions such as voluntary probation supervision, community service, and/or victim restitution. In some jurisdictions, before juveniles are offered informal sanctions, they must agree that they committed the alleged act.

When informally handled, the case is usually held open pending the successful completion of the informal disposition. Upon successful completion of these arrangements, the charges against the offender are dismissed. But if the offender does not fulfill the court's conditions for informal handling, the case is likely to be reopened and formally prosecuted.

Informal handling is less common than in the past but is still used in a large number of cases. According to *Juvenile Court Statistics 2001–2002*, 42 percent of delinquency cases disposed in 2002 were handled informally, compared with more than half in 1987.

> ■ **What is your opinion of informal sanctions? What do you see as their strengths and weaknesses?**

Source: Howard N. Snyder and Melissa Sickmund, *Juvenile Offenders and Victims: 2006 National Report* (Washington, D.C.: National Center for Juvenile Justice, 2006).

The Transfer Procedure

All state legislatures have passed laws permitting juveniles to be transferred to **adult court,** but the waiver of juveniles to adult court is taking place less frequently than it has in the past. Juvenile courts waived fewer cases in 2002 than in 1985, and 2001 saw the fewest waivers of any years since 1985.[62] Some states have implemented transfer procedures by lowering the age of judicial waiver; some by excluding certain offenses from juvenile court jurisdiction; and others by passing legislation aimed at transfer of serious juvenile offenders. Indeed, between 1992 and 1995, forty-one states passed laws that facilitated trying juveniles in adult court.[63]

Every state currently has some provision for transferring juvenile offenders to adult criminal courts. Vermont (age ten), Montana (age twelve), and Georgia, Illinois, and Mississippi (age thirteen) transfer children at very young ages; more states transfer children at fourteen than at any other age; and seven states transfer children at either fifteen or sixteen years of age.

Several states grant prosecutors, rather than juvenile court judges, the nonreviewable discretionary power to determine the court before which juveniles will be required to appear. For example, in the early 1980s the state of Florida expanded the discretionary power of prosecutors in dealing with juveniles who are sixteen or older.[64] Table 15.1 indicates which states allow prosecutors to try juveniles in either juvenile or criminal court.

Fifteen states exclude murder from juvenile court jurisdiction. Ten states exclude rape, eight exclude armed robbery or robbery, six exclude kidnapping, and three exclude burglary. Eleven states use a combination of offense categories.[65]

Judicial waiver and legislative waiver are the two basic mechanisms (also called *remand, certification,* and *waiver of jurisdiction*) for transferring juvenile offenders

TABLE 15.1

States That Permit Prosecutorial Discretion

STATE	MINIMUM AGE FOR CONCURRENT JURISDICTION	CONCURRENT JURISDICTION OFFENSE AND MINIMUM AGE CRITERIA, 2004							
		ANY CRIMINAL OFFENSE	CERTAIN FELONIES	CAPITAL CRIMES	MURDER	CERTAIN PERSON OFFENSES	CERTAIN PROPERTY OFFENSES	CERTAIN DRUG OFFENSES	CERTAIN WEAPON OFFENSES
Arizona	14		14						
Arkansas	14		16	14	14	14			
California	14		14	14	14	14	14	14	
Colorado	14		14		14	14	14		
Dist. of Columbia	16				16	16	16		
Florida	NS	16	16	NS	14	14	14		14
Georgia	NS			NS					
Louisiana	15				15	15	15	15	
Michigan	14		14		14	14	14	14	
Montana	12				12	12	16	16	16
Nebraska	NS	16	NS						
Oklahoma	15		16		15	15	15	16	15
Vermont	16	16							
Virginia	14				14	14			
Wyoming	13		14		14	14	14		

Note: Ages in the minimum age column may not apply to all offense restrictions, but represent the youngest possible age at which a juvenile's case may be directly filed in criminal court. "NS" indicates that in at least one of the offense restrictions indicated, no minimum age is specified.

In states with concurrent jurisdiction, the prosecutor has discretion to file certain cases in either criminal court or juvenile court.

Source: Howard N. Snyder and Melissa Sickmund, *Juvenile Offenders and Victims: 2006 National Report* (Washington, D.C.: U.S. Department of Justice, Office of Juvenile Justice and Delinquency Prevention, 2006), p. 113. Reprinted with permission from the U.S. Department of Justice.

to the adult criminal justice system. Judicial waiver, the most common, takes place after a judicial hearing on a juvenile's amenability to treatment or his or her threat to public safety.[66]

Judicial waiver, as previously discussed in regard to the *Kent v. United States* and *Breed v. Jones* decisions, contains certain procedural safeguards for youthful offenders. The criteria that are used to determine the **binding over** (transfer) decision typically include the age and maturity of the child; the seriousness of the referral incident; the child's past record; the child's relationship with parents, school, and community; whether the child is considered dangerous; and whether court officials believe that the child may be helped by juvenile court services. Most juvenile court judges appear to be influenced primarily by prior record and the seriousness of the present offense.

Legislative waiver is accomplished in five ways. The first occurs when legislatures simply exclude certain offenses from juvenile court jurisdiction. Any juvenile, then, who commits a specified offense automatically goes before the adult court. The second lowers the age over which the juvenile court has jurisdiction. For example, if a state's age of juvenile court juris-

Scott Dyleski, age sixteen, appears behind a protective glass barrier in Judge David Flinn's courtroom in Martinez, California, on October 27, 2005. Dyleski was charged as an adult with first-degree murder in the death of Pamela Vitale, the wife of well-known attorney Daniel Horowitz. Convicted in 2006, he was sentenced to life in prison without possibility of parole. ■ **Are such lengthy sentences appropriate for juvenile offenders who commit crimes like Dyleski's?**

diction is eighteen, the legislature may lower the age to sixteen. The third form of legislative waiver specifies that juveniles of specific ages who commit specific crimes are to be tried by adult court. This method of legislative waiver focuses as much on the offense as it does on the age of the offender. The fourth method of legislative waiver involves statutes that simply state that anyone who commits a specific crime may be tried in adult court. This approach is attractive to those who believe that any youth who violates the law should receive an appropriate punishment. The fifth method is for state legislatures to give both the juvenile and the adult courts concurrent jurisdiction over all children who are under the jurisdictional age of the juvenile court.

Statutes mandating that the decision to prosecute a juvenile as an adult be made on the basis of the seriousness of the offense charged are inconsistent with the rehabilitative philosophy of the juvenile court. Legislative waiver also is problematic because it usually has a rationale of incapacitation of chronic offenders through longer sentences than those provided by the juvenile process.[67]

Reverse waiver and **blended sentencing** must also be considered in discussing waiver. In reverse waiver, some state laws permit youths who are over the maximum age of jurisdiction to be sent back to the juvenile court if the adult court believes the case is more appropriate for juvenile court jurisdiction. For a reverse waiver, defense counsel and prosecutors attempt to make their case for their desired action. Some evidence and testimony are allowed, and arguments are presented. When each side has had a chance to present its case and to rebut the opponents' arguments, the judge makes the decision.[68]

In blended sentencing, some states permit juvenile court judges at the disposition hearing to impose both an adult and a juvenile sentence concurrently. In these cases, the juvenile is given both sentences, but is ordered first to fulfill the requirements of the juvenile disposition. If the juvenile meets the requirements of this disposition satisfac-

adult court
Criminal courts that hear the cases of adults charged with crimes, and to which juveniles who are accused of having committed serious offenses can be waived (transferred). In some states, adult criminal courts have jurisdiction over juveniles who are accused of committing certain specified offenses.

judicial waiver
The procedure of relinquishing the processing of a particular juvenile case to adult criminal court; also known as *certifying* or *binding over to the adult court.*

binding over
The process of transferring (also called *certifying*) juveniles to adult criminal court. Binding over takes place after a judicial hearing on a juvenile's amenability to treatment or his or her threat to public safety.

legislative waiver
Legislative action that narrows juvenile court jurisdiction, excluding from juvenile courts those youths charged with certain offenses.

reverse waiver
Provisions that permit a juvenile who is being prosecuted as an adult in criminal court to petition to have the case transferred to juvenile court for adjudication or disposition.

blended sentencing
The imposition of juvenile and/or adult correctional sanctions on serious and violent juvenile offenders who have been adjudicated in juvenile court or convicted in criminal court.

torily, then the adult disposition is suspended. If the juvenile does not fulfill the conditions of the juvenile disposition, then he or she is required to serve the adult sentence. In some states, the juvenile may be ordered to abide by the requirements of the juvenile disposition until reaching the age of majority; at this point, the juvenile begins serving the adult sentence minus the time already spent under juvenile court supervision.[69]

In sum, although waivers are still relatively infrequent, they remain an important issue in juvenile justice. Significantly, juveniles waived to adult court are not always the most serious or violent offenders. Donna Bishop and colleagues' examination of 583 prosecutorial waivers of sixteen- and seventeen-year-old youths in Florida from 1981 to 1984 revealed that most transferred juveniles were property and low-risk offenders.[70] Examinations of waivers have found that little consensus exists as to which criteria should be used in making waiver decisions.[71] Furthermore, although remanded youths are receiving severe penalties, waiver generally does not result in more severe penalties for juvenile offenders than they would have received in juvenile court. Several states have attempted to develop a process that might identify juveniles unfit for retention in juvenile court. Using such criteria as age, offense, and prior record, for example, Minnesota has codified transfer procedures to be followed by judges and prosecutors. An evaluation undertaken by Lee Ann Osburn and Peter A. Rose, however, concluded that Minnesota's procedures were inadequate for making effective transfer decisions.[72] With adult courts' massive caseload and their limited judicial experience in sentencing juveniles, little evidence exists that adult judges know what to do with juveniles who appear before them.[73]

The Juvenile Trial

The trial stage of juvenile court proceedings is divided into the adjudicatory hearing, the disposition hearing, and judicial alternatives.

The Adjudicatory Hearing

adjudication

The court process wherein a judge determines if the juvenile appearing before the court committed the act with which he or she is charged. The term *adjudicated* is analogous to *convicted* in the adult criminal justice system and indicates that the court concluded that the juvenile committed the act.

jury trial

Court proceeding in which a panel of the defendant's peers evaluate evidence and render a verdict. The U.S. Supreme Court has held that juveniles do not have a constitutional right to a jury trial, but several jurisdictions permit juveniles to choose a jury trial.

Adjudication is the fact-finding stage of the court's proceedings. The adjudicatory hearing usually includes the following steps: the child's plea, the presentation of evidence by the prosecution and by the defense, cross-examination of witnesses, and the judge's finding. The number of cases in which the juvenile was adjudicated delinquent rose steadily from 1985 to 2002, except for property cases[74] (see Figure 15.3).

The steps followed in the adjudicatory hearing serve as protections to ensure that youths are provided with proof beyond a reasonable doubt when they are charged with an act that would constitute a crime if it had been committed by an adult, and that the judge follows the rules of evidence and dismisses hearsay from the proceedings. Hearsay is dismissed because it can be unreliable or unfair, inasmuch as it cannot be held up for cross-examination. The evidence must be relevant and must contribute to the belief or disbelief of the act in question.

Prosecutors in most juvenile courts begin the adjudication proceedings by presenting the state's case. The arresting officer and witnesses at the scene of the crime testify, and any other evidence that has been legally obtained is introduced. The defense attorney then cross-examines the witnesses. Defense counsel also has the opportunity at this time to introduce evidence that is favorable to his or her client, and the youth may testify in his or her own behalf. The prosecutor then cross-examines the defense witnesses. The prosecution and the defense present summaries of the case to the judge, who reaches a finding or a verdict.

Ten states provide for a **jury trial** for juveniles, but jury trials are seldom demanded. Statutory provisions often close juvenile hearings to the general public, although this decision varies from one jurisdiction to the next. The right to a speedy trial has been provided by state court decisions and by statutes that limit the amount of time that can elapse between the filing of a complaint and the actual hearing.[75]

In sum, the typical adjudication hearing has come a long way since the *In re Gault* decision. Although some judges and defense attorneys are exemplary in the support

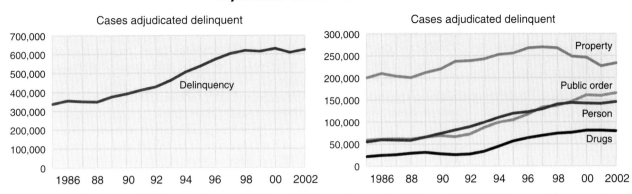

FIGURE 15.3

Adjudicated Cases in Juvenile Court

Cases adjudicated delinquent

Cases adjudicated delinquent

The number of cases in which the youth was adjudicated delinquent rose steadily from 1985 to 2002; except for property cases, the offense-specific trends followed the same pattern.

The number of cases in which the youth was adjudicated delinquent increased for all offense categories between 1985 and 2002 (person 162%, property 16%, drugs 257%, and public order 180%).

Only property offenses had a decline in adjudicated cases in recent years—down 13% between 1997 and 2002.

Source: Adapted from Howard N. Snyder and Melissa Sickmund, *Juvenile Offenders and Victims: 2006 National Report* (Washington, D.C.: Office of Juvenile Justice and Delinquency Prevention, 2006), p. 173. Reprinted with permission from the U.S. Department of Justice.

they give to the due process protection of juveniles during this stage of the court's proceedings, other judges and defense attorneys fall short in living up to either the spirit or the letter of post-*Gault* juvenile law. This is particularly true of defense attorneys who lack knowledge of juvenile court procedures or the juvenile law itself. Significantly, largely because of the changing standards for transfer to the adult court, the prosecutor has become a prominent figure at these proceedings.

> " Adjudication is the fact-finding stage of the court's proceedings. "

The Disposition Hearing

Once a child has been found delinquent at the adjudicatory stage, some juvenile court codes still permit judges to proceed immediately to the disposition (sentencing) hearing. But the present trend is to hold **bifurcated hearings,** or split adjudicatory and dispositional hearings, because a split hearing gives the probation officer appointed to the case an opportunity to prepare a social study investigation of the youth.

The disposition stage of the court's proceedings normally is quite different from the fact-finding stage, especially when it is held at a different time. The traditional purpose has been to administer individualized justice and to set in motion the rehabilitation of the delinquent; therefore the judge is not limited by constitutional safeguards as much as he or she was at the adjudication hearing. Rules of evidence are relaxed, parties and witnesses are not always sworn in, and hearsay testimony may be considered.[76] The starting point of the disposition hearing is usually the written social study of the child prepared by the probation officer. This report examines such factors as school attendance and grades, family structure and support, degree of maturity and sense of responsibility, relationships with peers, participation in community activities, and attitudes toward authority figures. In this final stage of the proceedings, juveniles are permitted to have legal counsel, and the *Kent* decision ensures the right of counsel to challenge the facts of the social study.

In 2002, residential placement or formal probation was ordered in 85 percent of cases in which the juvenile was adjudicated delinquent. The number of out-of-home placements rose 44 percent between 1985 and 2002, from 104,400 to 144,000. In

bifurcated hearing

Split adjudication and disposition hearings, which are the present trend of the juvenile court.

comparison, those who received formal probation as the most severe disposition following adjudication more than doubled from 1985 to 2002, from 189,000 to 385,400. Once adjudicated, females were less likely than males, and white juveniles were less likely than African American juveniles or juveniles of other races, to be ordered to residential placement.[77]

The factors that influence judicial decision making at the dispositional stage can be separated into formal and informal factors. The three most important formal factors are (1) the recommendation of the probation officer and the information contained in the social study investigation, (2) the seriousness of the delinquent behavior and previous contacts with the court, and (3) the options available. The recommendation of the probation officer in the social study report is usually followed by the juvenile judge. The seriousness of the delinquent behavior and the previous contacts with the court probably have the greatest impact on judicial decision making at this stage. Terence Thornberry confirmed that seriousness of the current offense and the number of previous offenses have the greatest impact.[78] Bortner's examination of disposition decision making in a large midwestern county revealed that age, prior referrals, and the detention decision surfaced as the most important influences.[79] Studies of the juvenile courts in Colorado, Pennsylvania, and Tennessee also indicated that prior decisions by juvenile court personnel were related more strongly to disposition than any other factor.[80] Finally, the juvenile judge is influenced by the options that are available. The most desirable placement may not be available in that jurisdiction, or the desired placement may have no space for the youth. Judge Forest Eastman reflected on this reality when he said:

> It is frustrating for a juvenile judge not to have the treatment or treatment programs that are absolutely necessary. You may at times know or think you know what needs to be done, but you can't find anyone who provides that kind of service for this type of kid.[81]

The informal factors that sometimes influence judicial decision making at the disposition stage are the values and philosophy of the judge; the social and racial background of the youth, as well as his or her demeanor; the presence or absence of a defense counsel; and potential political repercussions of the delinquent acts. In terms of the values and philosophy of the judge, some judges work from a legal model, some from an educational model, and some from a medical model. The model that a particular judge emphasizes will, of course, affect his or her handling of juvenile delinquents.[82]

Ruth D. Peterson found that racial, ethnic, gender, and age factors affected the disposition of older adolescents in New York state courts. Race and ethnicity did not significantly influence disposition decisions in New York City, but outside the city, minority youths tended to become targets of stereotypes and to receive harsh treatment.[83] Barry Krisberg and colleagues were even more critical of the disposition decisions for minority youths, especially disproportionate incarceration of these youths in juvenile facilities. In 1986, they warned:

> In a society committed to pluralism and social justice the growing numbers of incarcerated minority youth is a harbinger of future social turmoil. This problem must be placed at the top of our national agenda to reform the juvenile justice system.[84]

In sum, the process of judicial decision making at the disposition stage is influenced by a variety of formal and informal factors. The more informal factors intrude on the decision-making process, the more problematic the decisions are likely to be.

Judicial Alternatives

The alternatives that are available to different juvenile courts vary significantly. Large urban courts have all or most of the following alternatives at their disposal, but rural courts may have only a few. Several of the alternatives listed here are discussed in detail in Chapter 16.

1. *Dismissal* is certainly the most desired disposition for juveniles. The fact-finding stage may have shown the youth to be guilty, but the judge can decide, for a variety of reasons, to dismiss the case.

Web **LIBRARY** 15.3

Read the OJJDP publication *Juvenile Drug Court Programs* at **www.justicestudies.com/ WebLibrary**.

2. *Restitution* also is usually very desirable. Youths may be required to work off their debt with a few hours each week, but their lives are not seriously interrupted.

3. Outpatient *psychiatric therapy*, whether in the court clinic, the community mental health clinic, or with a private therapist, is a treatment-oriented decision and is often reserved for middle-class youths to keep them from being sent to "unfitting" placements.

4. *Probation*, the most widely used disposition, seems to be a popular decision with delinquents and a good treatment alternative for the court. Probation is sometimes set for a specific length of time, usually a maximum of two years. The judge can direct the probation officer to involve the youth in special programs, such as alternative schools, speech therapy, or learning disability programs.

5. *Foster home placements* are more restrictive, inasmuch as youths are removed from their natural homes. These placements are used most frequently for status offenders and dependent, neglected children.

6. *Day treatment programs* are a popular alternative with juveniles because the youths who are assigned to these programs return home in the evening. But these programs are few in number and are available in only a few states.

7. The option of *community-based residential programs*, such as group homes and halfway houses, is available to many judges. These residential facilities may be located in the community or in a nearby community, but they are not as desirable as community-based day programs, because youths are taken from their homes to live in these facilities.

8. *Institutionalization in a mental hospital* may be seen as appropriate for a child's needs. This placement requires a psychiatric evaluation, after which the doctor may recommend that the court initiate proceedings for commitment to a mental hospital.

9. *County or city institutions* are available to a few judges across the nation. Placement in these facilities may be deemed appropriate for a youth who needs more security than probation offers but who does not require long-term placement in the state training school.

10. *State or private training schools* are usually reserved for youths who have committed serious crimes or for whom everything else has failed. In some states, state training schools include minimum-security (forestry camps, farms, and ranches), medium-security, and maximum-security institutions.

11. *Adult facilities* or *youthful offender facilities* are used as alternatives in a few states if the youth has committed a serious offense and is seen as too hard-core for juvenile correctional institutions.

The Right to Appeal

Juveniles do not yet have a constitutional right to **appeal** their cases to a higher judiciary. Nevertheless, practically all states grant them the right to appeal by statute. The states are following the lead of the U.S. Supreme Court, which pointed out in *Gault* that juveniles should have the same absolute right to appeal as do adults under the equal protection clause of the Constitution. Since that ruling, most state legislatures have passed laws granting juveniles the right to appeal. State courts have also ruled that state statutes granting the right to appeal for juveniles must be applied uniformly to all juveniles. This decision effectively undermines the past practice in which some courts gave judges the discretion to determine which juvenile cases could be appealed. The common practice today is to give juveniles the same rights to appeal that adults have.[85]

The right to appeal is limited for the most part to juveniles and their parents. States may appeal in some circumstances; but this right is seldom exercised, and few cases have come before the courts. Another issue of appeal concerns the type of orders that may be appealed. Although states generally permit the appeal of final orders, what is "final" varies from state to state. Most state statutes call for the case to be appealed to an appellate court, but a few states call for a completely new trial. Other common

Web **PLACES** 15.2

Learn about the Juvenile Detention Alternatives Initiative from the Annie E. Casey Foundation via **www.justicestudies.com/WebPlaces**.

Web **PLACES** 15.3

Visit the National Institute of Mental Health's Child and Adolescent Mental Health Center's website via **www.justicestudies.com/WebPlaces**.

Web **LIBRARY** 15.4

Read the OJJDP Juvenile Justice Bulletin *Alternatives to the Secure Detention and Confinement of Juvenile Offenders* at **www.justicestudies.com/WebLibrary**.

appeal
The review of juvenile court proceedings by a higher court. Although no constitutional right of appeal exists for juveniles, the right of adjudicated juveniles to appeal has been established by statute in some states.

appellate review

Review of the decision of a juvenile court proceeding by a higher court. Decisions by appellate courts, including the U.S. Supreme Court, have greatly affected the development of juvenile court law and precedent.

determinate sentencing

A model of sentencing that provides fixed terms of sentences for criminal offenses. Terms are generally set by the legislature rather than determined by judicial discretion.

indeterminate sentencing

In juvenile justice, a sentencing model that encourages rehabilitation through the use of general and relatively unspecific sentences. Under the model, a juvenile judge has wide discretion and can commit a juvenile to the department of corrections or youth authority until correctional staff make the decision to release the juvenile. This type of sentencing is used with juveniles in most jurisdictions other than those that have mandatory or determinate sentencing.

Juvenile Justice Standards Project

A project jointly sponsored by the Institute of Judicial Administration and the American Bar Association that proposes that juveniles' sentences be based on the seriousness of the offense committed rather than on the "needs" of the child.

> One of the first efforts at reform was the Juvenile Justice Standards Project . . . launched in 1971.

felony

A criminal offense punishable by death or by incarceration in a state or federal correctional institution, usually for one year or more.

statutory rights of juveniles at appeal are the right to a transcript of the case and the right to counsel.[86]

Organizational factors limit the use of **appellate review** of juvenile court decisions. Many juveniles lack counsel at trial who can make a record and obtain a transcript. Even more juveniles lack access to appellate counsel. In addition, juvenile public defenders' caseloads frequently preclude the luxury of filing appeals. Many public defenders neither authorize their clients to file appeals nor advise their clients of the possibility of an appeal. The only study that compared rates of appeals by criminal defendants and juvenile delinquents found that convicted adults appealed more than ten times as often as did juveniles.[87]

Juvenile Sentencing Structures

Determinate sentencing (fixed sentences for specified offenses) is a new form of sentencing in juvenile justice and is replacing in some jurisdictions the traditional form, **indeterminate sentencing** (sentencing at the judge's discretion). In addition, increasing numbers of juvenile courts are using a blended form of sentencing.

Criticism of the decision making of the juvenile court has increased since the 1970s. Early on, the criticism focused on the arbitrary nature of the decision making that violated the due process rights of juveniles; more recently, this criticism has been based on the belief that the juvenile court is too "soft" on crime. This latter criticism, especially, has led to a number of attempts to change sentencing and other juvenile procedures.

One of the first efforts at reform was the **Juvenile Justice Standards Project,** jointly sponsored by the Institute of Judicial Administration and the American Bar Association. Officially launched in 1971 by a national planning committee under the chairmanship of Judge Irvin R. Kaufman, the project proposed comprehensive guidelines for juvenile offenders that would base sentences on the seriousness of the crime rather than on the needs of the youth. The guidelines represented radical philosophical changes and still are used by proponents to attempt to standardize the handling of juvenile lawbreakers.

The belief that disparity in juvenile sentencing must end was one of the fundamental thrusts of the recommended standards. To accomplish this goal, the commission attempted to limit the discretion of juvenile judges and to make them accountable for their decisions, which would then be subject to judicial review. Also important in the standards was the provision that certain court procedures would be open to the public, although the names of juveniles still would remain confidential.

At the beginning of the twenty-first century, juvenile court judges remain quite concerned about these proposed standards. Their basic concern is that these standards attack the underlying philosophy and structure of the juvenile court. Judges also are concerned about how these standards would limit their authority. They see the influence of the hard-liners behind this movement toward standardization and feel that the needs of children will be neglected in the long run. They also challenge the idea that it is possible, much less feasible, to treat all children alike.

Nevertheless, the adoption of the standards has been taking place across the nation. New York State was the first to act on them through the Juvenile Justice Reform Act of 1976, which went into effect on February 1, 1977. The act orders a determinate sentence of five years for Class A **felonies,** which include murder, first-degree kidnapping, and first-degree arson. The initial term can be extended by at least one year. The juvenile, according to the act, should be placed in a residential facility after the first year. Then, if approved by the director of the division, the confined youth can be placed in a nonresidential program for the remainder of the five-year term. But the youth must remain under intensive supervision for the entire five-year term.

In 1977, the state of Washington also created a determinate sentencing system for juveniles in line with the recommendations of the Juvenile Justice Standards Project. Moreover, in the 1980s, a number of states stiffened juvenile court penalties for serious juvenile offenders, either by mandating minimum terms of incarceration (Colorado, Kentucky, and Idaho) or by enacting a comprehensive system of sentencing guidelines (Arizona, Georgia, and Minnesota).[88]

In 1995, the Texas legislature introduced such get-tough changes in the juvenile justice system as lowering the age at which waiver could occur to fourteen years for capital, first-degree, and aggravated controlled substance felony offenses and greatly expanding the determinate sentence statute that was first enacted in 1987. Under determinate sentences, any juvenile, regardless of age, can be sentenced for up to forty years in the Texas Youth Commission, with possible transfer to the Texas Department of Corrections. Finally, prosecutors can choose to pursue determinate sentence proceedings rather than delinquency proceedings, but they first must obtain grand jury approval.[89]

Daniel P. Mears and Samuel F. Field's examination of the determinate sentencing statute for Texas found the increased proceduralization and criminalization of juvenile courts did not eliminate consideration of age, gender, or race/ethnicity in sentencing decisions.[90]

In the 1990s, nearly every state enacted **mandatory sentencing** for violent and repetitive juvenile offenders. The development of graduated, or accountability-based, sanctions was another means that states used in the 1990s to ensure that juveniles who are adjudicated delinquent receive an appropriate disposition by the juvenile court. Several states have created a "blended" sentencing structure for cases involving repeat and

mandatory sentencing
The requirement that individuals who commit certain offenses be sentenced to a specified length of confinement if found guilty or adjudicated delinquent.

These photos, provided by the Texas Department of Criminal Justice, show eight of the twelve executed Texas inmates who were under age eighteen when they committed their crimes. From left: Charles Rumbaugh, Joseph Cannon, Curtis Harris, Jay Pinkerton, Robert Carter, Johnny Garrett, Ruben Cantu, and Gerald Mitchell. In 2005, a closely divided U.S. Supreme Court ruled that it is unconstitutional to execute killers who committed their crimes as juveniles. ■ **What reason did the Court give for its decision?**

serious juvenile offenders. Blended sentences are a mechanism for holding those juveniles accountable for their offenses. This expanded sentencing authority allows criminal and juvenile courts to impose either juvenile or adult sentences, or at times both, in cases involving juveniles.[91] See Figure 15.4 for blended sentencing options.

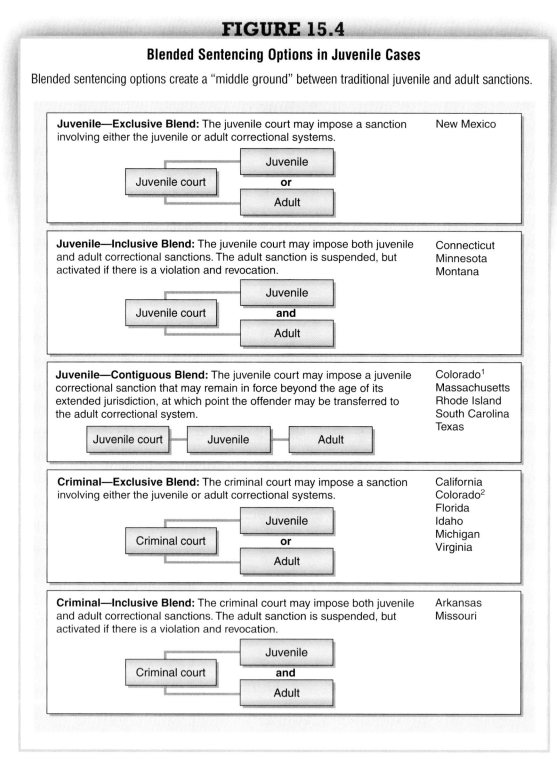

FIGURE 15.4

Blended Sentencing Options in Juvenile Cases

Blended sentencing options create a "middle ground" between traditional juvenile and adult sanctions.

Juvenile—Exclusive Blend: The juvenile court may impose a sanction involving either the juvenile or adult correctional systems.

New Mexico

Juvenile court → Juvenile **or** Adult

Juvenile—Inclusive Blend: The juvenile court may impose both juvenile and adult correctional sanctions. The adult sanction is suspended, but activated if there is a violation and revocation.

Connecticut
Minnesota
Montana

Juvenile court → Juvenile **and** Adult

Juvenile—Contiguous Blend: The juvenile court may impose a juvenile correctional sanction that may remain in force beyond the age of its extended jurisdiction, at which point the offender may be transferred to the adult correctional system.

Colorado[1]
Massachusetts
Rhode Island
South Carolina
Texas

Juvenile court — Juvenile — Adult

Criminal—Exclusive Blend: The criminal court may impose a sanction involving either the juvenile or adult correctional systems.

California
Colorado[2]
Florida
Idaho
Michigan
Virginia

Criminal court → Juvenile **or** Adult

Criminal—Inclusive Blend: The criminal court may impose both juvenile and adult correctional sanctions. The adult sanction is suspended, but activated if there is a violation and revocation.

Arkansas
Missouri

Criminal court → Juvenile **and** Adult

Note: Blends apply to a subset of juveniles specified by state statute.
[1]Applies to those designated as "aggravated juvenile offenders."
[2]Applies to those designated as "youthful offenders."
Source: Adapted from Office of Juvenile Justice and Delinquency Prevention, *1999 National Report Series* (Washington, D.C.: U.S. Department of Justice, 1999), p. 19. Reprinted with permission from the U.S. Department of Justice.

The Death Penalty and Juveniles

The most severe sentence possible is capital punishment, and it has been the topic of considerable debate. In June 1989, in the case of *Stanford v. Kentucky*, the U.S. Supreme Court ruled that no one below the age of sixteen could be executed for a criminal offense.[92]

Some, who believed that juveniles are mollycoddled by the juvenile court, applauded the decision because it still allowed for the possible execution of some sixteen- and seventeen-year-old offenders. Others, however, objected to the decision, arguing that the death penalty should play no role in a "civilized" society, and that youthful offenders, who are still in their formative years, should be rehabilitated.

Victor L. Strieb, dean and professor of law at Ohio Northern University, has traced the development of the current debate over capital punishment for juveniles.[93] The constitutionality of the death penalty, notes Strieb, was decided in 1967 in the case of *Gregg v. Georgia*.[94] In *Gregg*, the Court ruled that the death penalty did not violate the Eighth Amendment's prohibition against cruel and unusual punishment. The Court did stipulate, however, that before lower courts cold impose the death penalty, any special characteristics of the offender, such as his or her age, as well as the circumstances of the crime, should be considered.[95] In later decisions considering statutes in Ohio and other states, the Court ruled that mitigating circumstances had to be considered as well. Accordingly, states that permit the death penalty must statutorily require that mitigating circumstances be considered.[96]

Strieb points out that historically, few juveniles have ever been executed for their crimes. According to Streib, the United States has put approximately 366 juveniles to death since the seventeenth century. These juveniles account for less than 2 percent of the total 20,000 executions in the United States that have been carried out since that time.[97] The first juvenile execution occurred in 1642 in Plymouth Colony, Massachusetts, when sixteen-year-old Thomas Graunger was put to death for sodomizing a horse and a cow.[98]

Fourteen states have never executed juveniles, but Georgia leads all states with forty-one juvenile executions, followed by North Carolina and Ohio, with nineteen each. Table 15.2 lists the executions of juvenile offenders from January 1, 1973, through June 30, 2004.

Of the thirty-eight states that permitted capital punishment, twenty-five allowed for those who were under the age of eighteen when they committed the crime. In 1982, in the case of *Eddings v. Oklahoma*, the Supreme Court was able to avoid directly addressing the constitutionality of the juvenile death penalty by ruling that "the chronological age of a minor is itself a relevant mitigating factor of great weight."[99] Monty Lee Eddings was sixteen when he shot and killed an Oklahoma State Highway Patrol officer, but his execution sentence was reversed in 1982 because of his age.[100] In 1988, the Court heard the case of *Thompson v. Oklahoma*.[101] Wayne Thompson was fifteen when he was arrested along with his half brother—then age twenty-seven—and two other older men, for the shooting and stabbing death of Charles Keene, Thompson's former brother-in-law. The Court ruled by a five-to-three vote that "the Eighth and Fourteenth Amendments prohibit the execution of a person who was under sixteen years of age at the time of his or her offense."[102]

The Court finally upheld the constitutionality of the death penalty with juveniles in two 1989 cases. In the case of *Stanford v. Kentucky*, Kevin Stanford, a seventeen-year-old African American youth, repeatedly raped and sodomized his victim during a robbery. He then drove her to a secluded area, where he shot her point-blank in the face and the back of the head. A jury convicted Stanford of first-degree murder, first-degree sodomy, first-degree robbery, and receiving stolen property. Stanford was sentenced to death on September 28, 1998.[103] In *Wilkins v. Missouri*, sixteen-year-old Heath A. Wilkins stabbed Nancy Allen Moore to death as she worked behind the counter of a convenience store on July 27, 1985. The jury found that Wilkins was guilty of first-degree murder, armed criminal action, and carrying a concealed weapon. During the sentencing hearing, both the prosecution and Wilkins himself urged the

Ruling by High Court: Teen Killers Can't Be Executed

WASHINGTON—A divided U.S. Supreme Court ruled Tuesday that convicted killers who were younger than 18 at the time of their crimes cannot be executed, in part because there is a "national consensus" among states that such executions are wrong.

By a 5-4 vote, the justices said the Eighth Amendment's prohibition of cruel and unusual punishment bans the execution of juvenile offenders. The decision, announced by Justice Anthony Kennedy during a dramatic court session that revealed the tension among the justices over the issue, invalidates laws in 20 states. It lifts the death sentences of 70 juvenile offenders nationwide; they probably will be resentenced to life in prison.

The decision comes three years after the court banned executions of mentally retarded inmates. The rulings reflect the prevailing view of today's court: that capital punishment should be reserved for the "worst offenders" and that the mentally retarded and juveniles cannot reliably be classified that way.

Kennedy, writing for the majority, said juvenile criminals lack maturity and are particularly susceptible to peer pressure. "The age of 18 is the point where society draws the line for many purposes between childhood and adulthood," he said. "It is . . . the age at which the line for death eligibility ought to rest."

The decision reversed a 1989 ruling in which the court allowed executions of killers who committed their crimes at age 16 or 17. Kennedy noted that of the 38 states with the death penalty, 18 exempt juvenile offenders from executions. When the court ruled 16 years ago, about a dozen states had such exemptions.

Since the Supreme Court reinstated the death penalty in 1976, 22 inmates have been executed for crimes they did as juveniles. Thirteen were in Texas, which executes more inmates than any other state. During the past decade, only Texas, Oklahoma and Virginia have carried out executions for juvenile crimes.

The case involved a Missouri man, Christopher Simmons, who was 17 when he abducted a woman from her home, bound and gagged her, and threw her into a river to drown in 1993. His death sentence was reversed by Missouri's Supreme Court; the U.S. justices backed that ruling.

The USA has been virtually alone in the world in sanctioning a juvenile death penalty, and Simmons' case drew attention from international human rights groups such as Amnesty International, which praised the ruling. Kennedy noted that "the stark reality is that the United States is the only country in the world" that sanctioned executions for juvenile crimes.

That drew an angry response from Justice Antonin Scalia, who read parts of his dissent from the bench. "The basic premise—that American law should conform to the laws of the rest of the world—ought to be rejected out of hand," he said in his written opinion.

Officials in states with juvenile offenders on death row said they were reviewing the opinion. Alabama Attorney General Troy King, whose office had urged the justices to keep the juvenile death penalty, said he was disappointed "on behalf of victims."

Alabama has 13 death row inmates who were juveniles when they committed their crimes, second to Texas' 28. Many of the inmates have been on death

Christopher Simmons, shown in this 2003 photo provided by the Missouri Department of Corrections, was the plaintiff in the 2005 U.S. Supreme Court case of *Roper v. Simmons*, in which the Court held it unconstitutional to execute killers who were juveniles when they committed their crimes. Simmons bound a woman with duct tape and threw her off a bridge when he was seventeen years old. ■ **Do you agree with the Court's ruling?**

row for several years because of lengthy appeals and other factors. In Alabama, for example, Timothy Charles Davis was convicted in 1980 of killing a woman when he was 17; he is now 43.

Kennedy usually joins the court's conservative wing, and in 1989 he voted for executions of juvenile offenders. He became the key vote this time by siding with liberals John Paul Stevens, David Souter, Ruth Bader Ginsburg and Stephen Breyer. Dissenting were Scalia, Chief Justice William Rehnquist, Sandra Day O'Connor and Clarence Thomas.

Source: Joan Biskupic, "Teen Killers Can't be Executed," *USA Today*, March 2, 2005, p. 1A. Copyright © 2006 by *USA Today*. Reprinted by permission.

court to apply the death penalty. The aggravating circumstances in the case led the court to the decision that the death penalty was in fact appropriate and Wilkins was sentenced to die. The Missouri Supreme Court later upheld this decision.[104] Yet in 1995, in keeping with the pattern of most juvenile death decisions, the *Wilkins* decision was reversed.[105]

The important *Atkins v. Virginia* decision by the Supreme Court on June 20, 2002, held that executions of mentally retarded criminals are cruel and unusual punishments, and as such are prohibited by the Eighth Amendment to the U.S. Constitution.[106] At the time, *Atkins* applied equally to adults and juveniles facing the possibility of capital punishment.

TABLE 15.2

Executions of Juvenile Offenders, January 1, 1973, Through February 28, 2005

NAME	DATE OF EXECUTION	PLACE OF EXECUTION	RACE AND SEX OF OFFENDER/VICTIM	AGE AT CRIME	AGE AT EXECUTION
Charles Rumbaugh	9/11/1985	Texas	WM/WM	17	28
J. Terry Roach	1/10/1986	South Carolina	WM/WM, WF	17	25
Jay Pinkerton	5/15/1986	Texas	WM/WF, WF	17	24
Dalton Prejean	5/18/1990	Louisiana	BM/WM	17	30
Johnny Garrett	2/11/1992	Texas	WM/WF	17	28
Curtis Harris	7/1/1993	Texas	BM/WM	17	31
Frederick Lashley	7/28/1993	Missouri	BM/BF	17	29
Ruben Cantu	8/24/1993	Texas	LM/LM	17	26
Chris Burger	12/7/1993	Georgia	WM/WM	17	33
Joseph John Cannon	4/22/1998	Texas	WM/WF	17	38
Robert A. Carter	5/18/1998	Texas	BM/LF	17	34
Dwayne D. Wright	10/14/1998	Virginia	BM/BF	17	26
Sean R. Sellers	2/4/1999	Oklahoma	WM/WM,WM,WF	16	29
Christopher Thomas	1/10/2000	Virginia	WM/WF	17	26
Steve E. Roach	1/19/2000	Virginia	WM/WF	17	23
Glen C. McGinnis	1/25/2000	Texas	BM/WF	17	27
Gary L. Graham	6/22/2000	Texas	BM/WM	17	36
Gerald L. Mitchell	10/22/2001	Texas	BM/WM	17	33
Napoleon Beazley	5/28/2002	Texas	BM/WM	17	25
T. J. Jones	8/8/2002	Texas	BM/WM	17	25
Toronto Patterson	8/28/2002	Texas	BM/BF	17	24
Scott A. Hain	4/3/2003	Oklahoma	WM/WM,WF	17	32

Source: Victor L. Streib, *The Juvenile Death Penalty Today: Death Sentences and Executions for Juvenile Crimes, January 1, 1973–February 28, 2005*, p. 4. Report available online at www.law.onu.edu/faculty/streib. Reprinted by permission of Victor L. Streib.

As the opening story in this chapter showed, all debate over the possible use of capital punishment as a sanction for juveniles ended with the 2005 case of *Roper v. Simmons*, when the Court held that executing those who commit their crimes as juveniles is neither consistent with the constitution, nor in keeping with the standards of a civilized society.[107]

CHAPTER
Summary

This chapter has examined the juvenile court. Key points are as follows:

- The juvenile court concept, as originally formulated, was built on the idea of *parens patriae*, or of the state acting as substitute parent in keeping with the best interests of the child.

- Another ideal underlying the juvenile court concept is that children are malleable and that their personalities are not yet fully formed—offering the opportunity for reformation and rehabilitation.

- The classic purposes of the juvenile court have today come under scrutiny as policymakers, facing public outcry over what some see as an increasingly violent and dangerous juvenile population, have been forced to rethink the proper role of the court.

- The resolution of the current debate, whatever its outcome, will have long-term repercussions for American juvenile justice.

- Beginning in the 1960s, important U.S. Supreme Court decisions accorded juveniles a significant number of due process rights. As a consequence, the typical juvenile court hearing today has many of the trappings of an adult criminal trial.

■ Noteworthy decisions of the 1970s show that the Court has been unwilling to transform the activities of the juvenile court completely into an adversarial battleground like proceedings in adult criminal court.

■ The pretrial procedures of the juvenile court consist of the detention hearing, the intake process, and the transfer procedure.

■ The adjudicatory hearing is the fact-finding stage in juvenile court. The judge, the defense attorney, and the prosecutor are typically present at the adjudicatory hearing, especially in larger jurisdictions; witnesses are cross-examined and proof beyond a reasonable doubt must be established.

■ Once a child is found delinquent, the judge then determines the most fitting disposition. Available judicial alternatives may range from dismissal to placement in a state or private training school.

■ Juvenile court sentencing structures have expanded in many jurisdictions; having gone beyond the indeterminate sentence model, they today include various forms of determinate sentencing.

■ The 2005 U.S. Supreme Court case of *Roper v. Simmons* precludes execution of anyone who commits a crime while under the age of eighteen.

CRITICAL THINKING
Questions

1. Define the main types of waiver to adult court.
2. Why is waiver such a controversial matter in juvenile justice?
3. Do you believe that plea bargaining should be more widely used in juvenile court?
4. Do you think the structure of the juvenile court should be changed? Why or why not?

5. Should there be less variation in juvenile court procedures from jurisdiction to jurisdiction? Why or why not?
6. How should the juvenile justice system deal with status offenders?
7. How should juveniles who commit serious crimes be handled?

WEB
Interactivity

Visit the National Council of Juvenile and Family Court Judges (NCJFCJ) on the Web at **www.ncjfcj.org**. As the site says, the NCJFCJ was begun in 1937 by a group of judges dedicated to improving the effectiveness of the nation's juvenile courts. The organization has been headquartered on the University of Nevada campus in Reno since 1969, and provides cutting-edge training, wide-ranging technical assistance, and research to help the nation's juvenile court judges and staff. The NCJFCJ consistently works to improve courts and systems practices and to raise awareness of the core issues that touch the lives of many of our nation's children and their families. Some of its most significant initiatives include:

■ The Child Victims Act Model Courts Project
■ The Juvenile Sanctions Division
■ The Resource Center on Domestic Violence
■ The National Center for Juvenile Justice

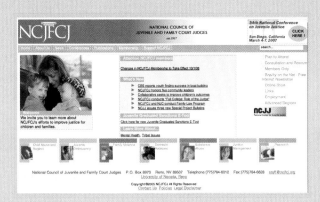

Source: From www.ncjfcj.org/. Reprinted with permission from the National Council of Juvenile and Family Court Judges.

Research these initiatives by using information provided on the NCJFCJ website and describe each in your own words. Submit your findings to your instructor if asked to do so.

Notes

1. *Roper v. Simmons*, 543 U.S. 551 (2005).
2. Gustav L. Schramm, "The Judge Meets the Boy and His Family," *National Probation Association 1945 Yearbook*, pp. 182–194.
3. G. Larry Mays, "Transferring Juveniles to Adult Courts: Legal Guidelines and Constraints." Paper presented at the Annual Meeting of the American Society of Criminology, Reno, Nevada (November 1989), p. 1.
4. Barry Krisberg, *The Juvenile Court: Reclaiming the Vision* (San Francisco: National Council on Crime and Delinquency, 1988); Arnold Binder, "The Juvenile Court: The U.S. Constitution, and When the Twain Shall Meet," *Journal of Criminal Justice* 12 (1982), pp. 355–366; and Charles E. Springer, *Justice for Children* (Washington, D.C.: U.S. Department of Justice, 1986).
5. Lisa Aversa Richette, *The Throwaway Children* (New York: J. B. Lippincott, 1969); Patrick Murphy, *Our Kindly Parent—The State* (New York: Viking Press, 1974); Howard James, *Children in Trouble: A National Scandal* (New York: Pocket Books, 1971); and William Ayers, *A Kind and Just Parent* (Boston: Beacon Press, 1997).
6. Leonard P. Edwards, "The Juvenile Court and the Role of the Juvenile Court Judge," *National Council of Juvenile and Family Court Judges* 43 (1992), p. 4.
7. Ibid.
8. Ibid.
9. Cited in Edwards, "The Juvenile Court and the Role of the Juvenile Court Judge."
10. Dean J. Champion, "Teenage Felons and Waiver Hearings: Some Recent Trends, 1980–1988," *Crime and Delinquency* 35 (October 1985), p. 578.
11. Barry C. Feld, "The Transformation of the Juvenile Court," *Minnesota Law Review* 75 (February 1991), p. 711.
12. Drafted by the American Legislative Exchange Council and Rose Institute of State and Local Government at Claremont McKenna College, Claremont, CA.
13. For an extensive discussion of these sweeping changes in Minnesota's juvenile code, see Barry C. Feld, "Violent Youth and Public Policy: A Case Study of Juvenile Justice Law Reform," *Minnesota Law Review* 79 (May 1995), pp. 965–1128.
14. See Feld, "The Transformation of the Juvenile Court," pp. 691–725; Barry C. Feld, "Criminalizing Juvenile Justice: Rules of Procedure for Juvenile Court," *Minnesota Law Review* 69 (1984), pp. 141–164; and Janet E. Ainsworth, "Re-Imagining Childhood and Reconstructing the Legal Order: The Case for Abolishing the Juvenile Court," in *Child, Parent, and State*, edited by S. Randall Humm, Beate Anna Ort, Martin Mazen Anbari, Wendy S. Lader, and William Scott Biel (Philadelphia: Temple University Press, 1994), pp. 561–595.
15. Jeffrey A. Butts and Adele V. Harrell, *Delinquents or Criminals: Policy Options for Young Offenders* (Washington, D.C.: The Urban Institute, 1998), p. 1.
16. Barry C. Feld, *Bad Kids: Race and the Transformation of Juvenile Court* (New York: Oxford University Press, 1999), p. 324.
17. Ibid., p. 317.
18. Ibid.
19. For a biting criticism of this proposal to abolish the juvenile court, see Mark I. Soler, "Re-Imagining the Juvenile Court," in *Child, Parent, and State*, pp. 596–624.
20. Anthony M. Platt, *The Child Saver*, 2nd ed. (Chicago: University of Chicago Press, 1977), p. 144.
21. Ibid.
22. Frederic L. Faust and Paul J. Brantingham, eds., *Juvenile Justice Philosophy* (St. Paul, Minn.: West Publishing, 1974), pp. 568, 569.
23. Ibid., pp. 574–575.
24. Ibid.
25. *Kent v. United States*, 383 U.S. 541, 86 S. Ct. 1045, 16 L.Ed. 2d 84 (1966).
26. Ibid.
27. *In re Gault*, 387 U.S. 1, 18 L.Ed. 2d 527, 87 S. Ct. 1428 (1967).
28. Ibid.
29. *Haley v. Ohio*, 332 U.S. 596 (1948); and *Gallegos v. Colorado*, 370 U.S. 49, 82 S. Ct. 1209 (1962).
30. *In re Winship*, 397 U.S. 358, 90 S. Ct. 1968, 25 L.Ed. 2d 368 (1970).
31. *McKeiver v. Pennsylvania*, 403 U.S. 528, 535 (1971), and *In re Barbara Burrus*, 275 N.C. 517, 169 S.E. 2d 879 (1969).
32. *McKeiver v. Pennsylvania*.
33. Feld, "Violent Youth and Public Policy," pp. 965–1128.
34. *Breed v. Jones*, 421 U.S. 519, 95 S. Ct. 1779 (1975).
35. H. Ted Rubin, *Juvenile Justice: Policy, Practice, and Law* (Santa Monica, Calif.: Goodyear Publishing, 1979), p. 177.
36. Edwards, "The Juvenile Court and the Role of the Juvenile Court Judge," p. 25.
37. Ibid., pp. 25–28. For a more expansive list of the juvenile judge's role responsibilities, see Rule 24 of the California Judicial Council.
38. Forest Eastman, "Procedures and Due Process," *Juvenile and Family Court Journal* 35 (1983). For a more extensive examination of the juvenile judge's role, see Ted H. Rubin, *Behind the Black Robes: Judges and the Court* (Beverly Hills, Calif.: Sage, 1985).
39. David Matza, *Delinquency and Drift* (New York: John Wiley and Sons, 1964), p. 118.
40. Carol J. DeFrances, *Juveniles Prosecuted in State Criminal Courts: National Survey of Prosecutors, 1994* (Washington, D.C.: Office of Juvenile Justice and Delinquency Prevention, 1997), p. 1.
41. For other examinations of the prosecutor's role in the juvenile court, see John H. Laub and Bruce K. MacMurray, "Increasing the Prosecutor's Role in Juvenile Court: Expectation and Realities," *Justice System Journal* 12 (1987), pp. 196–209, and Charles W. Thomas and Shay Bilchik, "Prosecuting Juveniles in Criminal Courts: A Legal and Empirical Analysis," *Journal of Criminal Law and Criminology* 76 (Northwestern University, School of Law, 1985), pp. 439–479.
42. See Floyd Feeney, "Defense Counsel for Delinquents: Does Quality Matter?" Paper presented at the Annual Meeting of the American Society of Criminology, Montreal, Canada (November 1987).
43. Feld, "Criminalizing Juvenile Justice," pp. 191, 199.
44. Feld, *Bad Kids*, p. 128
45. H. Ted Rubin, *Juvenile Justice*, p. 177.

46. Ibid.
47. See Charles Thomas and Ineke Marshall, "The Effect of Legal Representation on Juvenile Court Disposition." Paper presented at the Southern Sociological Society (1981). Also S. H. Clarke and G. G. Koch, "Juvenile Court: Therapy or Crime Control and Do Lawyers Make a Difference?" *Law and Society Review* 14 (1980), pp. 263–308.
48. Thomas and Marshall, "The Effect of Legal Representation on Juvenile Court Disposition."
49. Brenda R. McCarthy, "An Analysis of Detention," *Juvenile and Family Court Journal* 36 (1985), pp. 49–50. For other discussions of detention, see Lydia Rosner, "Juvenile Secure Detention," *Journal of Offender Counseling, Services, and Rehabilitation* 12 (1988), pp. 77–93, and Charles E. Frazier and Donna M. Bishop, "The Pretrial Detention of Juveniles and Its Impact on Case Disposition," *Journal of Criminal Law and Criminology* 76 (1985), pp. 1132–1152.
50. Howard N. Snyder and Melissa Sickmund, *Juvenile Offenders and Victims: 2006 National Report* (Washington, D.C.: National Center for Juvenile Justice; Office of Juvenile Justice and Delinquency Prevention, 2006), p. 166.
51. *Creek v. Stone*, 379 F.2d 106 (D.C. Cir. 1967).
52. Steven L. Schlossman, *Love and the American Delinquent: The Theory and Practice of "Progressive" Juvenile Justice, 1825–1920* (Chicago: University of Chicago Press, 1977).
53. Frazier and Bishop, "The Pretrial Detention of Juveniles and Its Impact on Case Dispositions," p. 1151.
54. Alida V. Merlo and William D. Bennett, "Criteria for Juvenile Detention: Who Gets Detained?" Paper presented at the Annual Meeting of the American Society of Criminology, Reno, Nevada (November 1989), p. 8.
55. *Schall v. Martin* (1984), *United States Law Review* 52 (47), pp. 4681–4696.
56. Ibid., p. 4681.
57. Ibid.
58. Feld, "Criminalizing Juvenile Justice," pp. 191, 199.
59. Duran Bell Jr. and Kevin Lang, "The Intake Dispositions of Juvenile Offenders," *Journal of Research on Crime and Delinquency* 22 (1985), pp. 309–328. See also Randall G. Sheldon and John A. Horvath, "Intake Processing in a Juvenile Court: A Comparison of Legal and Nonlegal Variables," *Juvenile and Family Court Journal* 38 (1987), pp. 13–19.
60. Snyder and Sickmund, *Juvenile Offenders and Victims: 2006 National Report*, p. 171.
61. Bell and Lang, "The Intake Dispositions of Juvenile Offenders," p. 324.
62. Snyder and Sickmund, *Juvenile Offenders and Victims: 2006 National Report*, p. 187.
63. Emily Gaarder and Joanne Belknap, "Tenuous Borders: Girls Transferred to Adult Court," *Criminology* (August 2002), p. 481.
64. Thomas and Bilchik, "Prosecuting Juveniles in Criminal Courts," pp. 439–479.
65. Barry C. Feld, "The Juvenile Court Meets the Principle of the Offense: Legislative Changes in Juvenile Waiver Statutes," *Journal of Criminal Law and Criminology* 78 (1987), pp. 512–514.
66. Barry C. Feld, "Legislative Policies toward the Serious Juvenile Offender," *Crime and Delinquency* 27 (October 1981), p. 500.
67. Ibid., pp. 501–502.
68. Samuel M. Davis, *Rights of Juveniles: The Juvenile Justice System*, 2nd ed. (New York: Clark Boardman Company, 1986), Section 4-2; see also Melissa Sickmund, *How Juveniles Get to Juvenile Court* (Washington, D.C.: Juvenile Justice Bulletin, 1994).
69. Davis, *Rights of Juveniles*, pp. 24–26.
70. Donna Bishop, Charles E. Frazier, and John C. Henretta, "Prosecutorial Waiver: Case Study of a Questionable Reform," *Crime and Delinquency* 35 (1989), pp. 179–201.
71. Marcy R. Podkopacz and Barry C. Feld, "The End of the Line: An Empirical Study of Judicial Waiver," *Journal of Criminal Law and Criminology* 86 (1996), pp. 449–492.
72. Lee Ann Osburn and Peter A Rose, "Prosecuting Juveniles as Adults: The Question for 'Objective' Decisions," *Criminology* 22 (1984), pp. 187–202.
73. Donna M. Bishop, Charles E. Frazier, Lonn Lanza-Kaduce, and Lawrence Winner, "The Transfer of Juveniles to Criminal Court: Does It Make a Difference?" *Crime and Delinquency* 42 (1996), pp. 171–191.
74. Snyder and Sickmund, *Juvenile Offenders and Victims: 2006 National Report,* p. 173.
75. For example, in the Laws of Pennsylvania, Act No. 333 (Section 18a) requires a hearing date within ten days after the filing of a petition.
76. Rubin, *Juvenile Justice*, p. 137.
77. Snyder and Sickmund, *Juvenile Offenders and Victims: 2006 National Report,* pp. 174–175.
78. Terence P. Thornberry, "Sentencing Disparities in the Juvenile Justice System," *Journal of Criminal Law and Criminology* 70 (Summer 1979), pp. 164–171.
79. M. A. Bortner, *Inside a Juvenile Court: The Tarnished Idea of Individualized Justice* (New York: New York University Press, 1982).
80. Lawrence Cohen, "Delinquency Dispositions: An Empirical Analysis of Processing Decisions in Three Juvenile Courts," *Analytic Report 9* (Washington, D.C.: U.S. Government Printing Office, 1975), p. 51.
81. Interviewed in 1981.
82. Rubin, *Juvenile Justice,* pp. 139–140. See also Joseph B. Sanborn, "Factors Perceived to Affect Delinquent Dispositions in Juvenile Court: Putting the Sentencing Decision into Context," *Crime and Delinquency* 42 (January 1996), pp. 99–113.
83. Ruth D. Peterson, "Youthful Offender Designations and Sentencing in the New York Criminal Courts," *Social Problems* 35 (April 1988), pp. 125–126. See also Christina De Jong and Kenneth C. Jackson, "Putting Race into Context: Race, Juvenile Justice Processing, and Urbanization, *Justice Quarterly* 15 (September 1998), pp. 487–504; and Barry C. Feld, "Social Structure, Race, and the Transformation of the Juvenile Court." Paper presented to the Annual Meeting of the American Society of Criminology, Washington, D.C. (November 1998).
84. Barry Krisberg et al. *The Incarceration of Minority Youth* (Minneapolis, Minn.: University of Minnesota, Hubert H. Humphrey Institute of Public Affairs, 1986).
85. Samuel M. Davis, *Rights of Juveniles: The Juvenile Justice System.*
86. Ibid., pp. 634–637.
87. Feld, *Bad Kids,* p. 136.
88. Martin L. Forst, Bruce A. Fisher, and Robert B. Coates, "Indeterminate and Determinate Sentencing of Juvenile

Delinquents: A National Survey of Approaches to Commitment and Release Decision-Making," *Juvenile and Family Court Journal* 36 (Summer 1985), p. 1.

89. Daniel P. Mears and Samuel H. Field, "Theorizing Sanctioning in a Criminalized Juvenile Court," *Criminology* 38 (November 2000), pp. 985–986.

90. Ibid., p. 983.

91. Feld, "Violent Youth and Public Policy: Minnesota Juvenile Justice Task Force and 1994 Legislative Reform." Paper presented at the annual meeting of the American Society of Criminology, Miami, Florida (1994), p. 4. See also Feld, "Violent Youth and Public Policy: A Case Study of Juvenile Justice Law Reform," *Minnesota Law Review* 79 (May 1995), pp. 965–1128.

92. This decision was rendered in two cases. One was *Stanford v. Kentucky*, 492 U.S. 361 (1989). See Linda Breenhouse, "Death Sentences Against Retarded and Young Upheld," *New York Times*, June 27, 1989, pp. A1, A18.

93. Much of this information in the history of the death penalty comes from Victor L. Strieb, *Death Penalty for Juveniles* (Bloomington, Ind.: Indiana University Press, 1987), pp. 21–40.

94. *Gregg v. Georgia*, 48 U.S. (1976).

95. Ibid.

96. *Lockett v. Ohio*, 438 U.S. 536 (1978).

97. Victor L. Streib, *The Juvenile Death Penalty Today: Death Sentences and Executions for Juvenile Crimes, January 1, 1973–June 30, 2004* (Updated July 1, 2004), p. 4. Report available on the Web at www.law.onu.edu/faculty/streib.

98. Ibid.

99. *Eddings v. Oklahoma*, 102 S. Ct. (1982).

100. Ibid.

101. *Thompson v. Oklahoma*, 102 S. Ct. (1988).

102. Ibid.

103. *Stanford v. Kentucky*, 492 U.S. 361 (1989).

104. Ibid.

105. "Capital Punishment for Minors," *Journal of Juvenile Law* (1994), pp. 150–167.

106. *Atkins v. Virginia* (2002).

107. *Roper v. Simmons*, No. 093-633 (2005).

16
Juvenile Corrections

> ❝Our society is fearful of our kids. I think we don't know how to set limits on them. They begin to behave in severely outrageous ways, and nobody stops them.❞
>
> —David York, cofounder of Toughlove International

CHAPTER Objectives

AFTER READING THIS CHAPTER, YOU SHOULD BE ABLE TO ANSWER THE FOLLOWING QUESTIONS:

- What types of experience do juveniles have in various institutional placements?

- Why do some juveniles benefit more from institutionalization than others? How effective are institutions at correcting juvenile crime?

- What rights do juveniles have while confined?

- What can be done to improve juvenile correctional institutions in the United States?

541

On August 1, 2005, Connecticut Governor M. Jodi Rell stood inside the troubled Connecticut Juvenile Training School in Middletown and declared it a $57 million failure that had to be shut down.

"It was intended to give young men the tools that they needed to succeed when they returned home, to strengthen the connections to home, to family and to community and to help them succeed in school and in life," the governor said. "But," she continued, "it became apparent all too soon that it simply wasn't working, and it simply wasn't happening here. There was too little programming and little opportunity, and too much of a prison-like atmosphere, and far too much recidivism."

What Governor Rell did not say was that the school had also become a symbol of the folly and corruption that eventually put her predecessor, former-Governor John G. Rowland, in federal prison. The scandal that led then-Governor Rowland to resign in 2004 and later to plead guilty to a conspiracy charge, was made sensational with tales of free vacations and home renovations that he received for favors he doled out. Central to the scandal were connections between the former governor and the contractor who gave him many of those gifts, William A. Tomasso. Tomasso's companies built the juvenile center in a "fast-track" process, pushed through with the help of Governor Rowland—even though criminologists and some lawmakers had warned that the school was not in keeping with current trends in juvenile justice and was destined to be out-of-date even before it was built.

Juvenile justice experts have been saying for years that the school, designed to hold 240 boys under 16 who have been convicted of largely nonviolent crimes, is out of step with evolving approaches to juvenile rehabilitation. They say that the state should have smaller, less restrictive facilities with a heavy emphasis on educational programs designed to prepare youths for life after confinement.

Mrs. Rell said her decision to close the school was based on the conclusions of a report she commissioned from the Department of Children and Families. "This is not a political issue, and please don't make it one," she said. "We need to do what is best for these boys."

Often echoing the 13-page report, the governor proposed phasing out the school by 2008 and replacing it with three smaller facilities, called Treatment and Reintegration Education Centers. Two would house 36 to 45 boys each, and a third would hold about 12 girls. The report also recommends creating 16 places in "therapeutic group homes" and adding 7 places to "therapeutic foster care homes."

The training school, behind barbed wire on a slope beside the Connecticut Valley Hospital, will probably be converted for use by the department of public safety or homeland security, the governor said, but it will not become a prison.

This chapter examines juvenile corrections, including corrections in both the community and in long-term institutions. The basic forms of **community-based corrections** are probation, day treatment and residential programs, and aftercare. These services are alternatives to institutional placements and keep juvenile delinquents out of training schools, jails, and adult prisons. This chapter also focuses on long-term juvenile

FIGURE 16.1

Long-Term Institutional Placement Alternatives for Juveniles

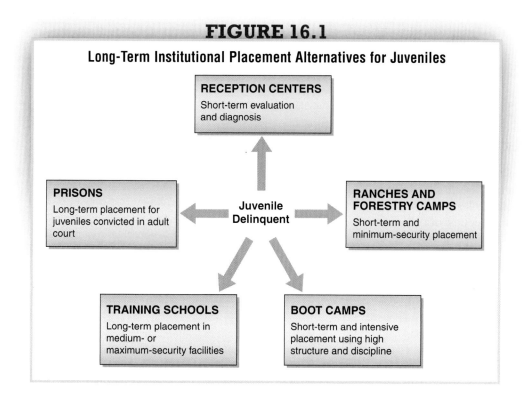

RECEPTION CENTERS
Short-term evaluation and diagnosis

PRISONS
Long-term placement for juveniles convicted in adult court

Juvenile Delinquent

RANCHES AND FORESTRY CAMPS
Short-term and minimum-security placement

TRAINING SCHOOLS
Long-term placement in medium- or maximum-security facilities

BOOT CAMPS
Short-term and intensive placement using high structure and discipline

institutional placements, which include reception or diagnostic centers, ranches and forestry camps, boot camps, and training schools. Juveniles may also be sent to adult prisons. Figure 16.1 gives thumbnail descriptions of these various types of long-term institutional placement alternatives for juveniles. Finally, this chapter looks at how the juvenile justice system may change in the future (see Focus on Social Policy 16.1).

Probation

Probation permits juvenile offenders to remain in the community under the supervision of a probation officer, subject to certain conditions imposed by the court. Probation, which many consider to be the brightest hope of corrections, has several different connotations in the juvenile justice system. It is a legal system in which an adjudicated delinquent can be placed, an alternative to institutionalization, and a subsystem of the juvenile justice system.

The *Desktop Guide to Good Juvenile Probation Practice*, a recent publication of the National Center for Juvenile Justice, says that "good juvenile probation practice is mission-driven, performance-based, and outcome-focused."[1] Mission-driven means that "the work of juvenile probation must be directed at clearly articulated and widely shared goals" that must guide everyday procedures, budget allocations, and staff assignments.[2] Performance-based means it should move from general goals to specific objectives, and designate "concrete activities that are calculated to achieve its goals and hold itself responsible for performing them."[3] Outcome-focused means it "systematically measures the tangible results of its interventions, compares those results to its goals, and makes itself publicly accountable for any differences."[4]

The Operation of Probation Services

Intake, investigation, and supervision, the basic functions of probation services, take place in an increasingly get-tough approach to juvenile crime. In intake, the initial decision is made about what to do with the law-violating juvenile. Preparation of the social history report, which assists the juvenile judge at the disposition stage of the

community-based corrections
Corrections programs that include probation, residential and day treatment programs, and parole (aftercare). The nature of the linkages between community programs and their social environments is the most distinguishing feature of community-based corrections. As frequency, duration, and quality of community relationships increase, the programs become more community based.

probation
A court sentence under which the juvenile's freedom in the community is continued or only briefly interrupted, but the person is subject to supervision by a probation officer and the conditions imposed by the court.

Web PLACES 16.1

View the OJJDP PowerPoint presentation "Juvenile Offenders in Correctional Facilities" at **www.justicestudies.com/WebPlaces**.

FOCUS ON
Social Policy 16.1

Is the System Broken?

Changes are coming in juvenile justice, and some states, like California, are bound to lead the charge toward reforming the system. This box contains some of the summary statements contained in a 2006 report commissioned by California's Division of Juvenile Justice when it sought guidance on how to go about reforming the state's juvenile correctional institutions.

The Division of Juvenile Justice has many good people working for it—hard working, dedicated, and well meaning. The current leadership is professional, knowledgeable, and committed to reform. But if reform is to happen, they will need help. For this is not a system that needs tinkering around the edges, this is a system that is broken almost everywhere you look. It is a system with:

- High levels of violence and fear in its institutions
- Unsafe conditions for both residents and staff
- Antiquated facilities unsuited for any mission
- An adult corrections mentality with an adult/juvenile mix
- Management by crisis with little time to make changes
- Frequent lockdowns to manage violence with subsequent program reductions
- Time added for infractions that extends average lengths of stay more than eight months

- Lengths of stay that are almost triple the average for the nation
- Hours on end when many youths have nothing to do
- Vocational classrooms that are idle or running at half speed
- Capitulation to gang culture with youths housed by gang affiliation
- Low levels of staffing amidst huge living units
- Abysmal achievement despite enormous outlays for education
- Information systems incapable of adequately supporting management
- Little partnership with counties and a fragmented system
- Poor re-entry planning and too few services in parole
- Enormous costs with little to show for it

It is not just reform that is needed. Everything needs to be fixed.

■ Juvenile institutions in California have long been acknowledged as models for the rest of the nation. Why is it, then, that juvenile institutionalization in California appears to have ended up in such dismal shape? Does this report blame staff commitment, performance, or loyalty? If not, what do you think are the underlying problems plaguing this state's juvenile correctional system?

Source: Adapted from Christopher Murray, Chris Baird, Ned Loughran, Fred Mills, and John Platt, *Safety and Welfare Plan: Implementing Reform in California* (Sacramento: California Department of Corrections and Rehabilitation: Division of Juvenile Justice, 2006), p. 1.

court proceedings, is the most important process during investigation. The supervisory function is divided into managing a caseload, providing treatment services, and maintaining surveillance.

probation officer
An officer of the court who is expected to provide social history investigations, to supervise individuals who have been placed on probation, to maintain case files, to advise probationers on the conditions of their sentences, to perform any other probationary services that a judge may request, and to inform the court when persons on probation have violated the terms of that probation.

Intake The intake officer is usually a **probation officer,** although larger probation departments may have separate intake units in which intake officers are not probation officers. Regardless of the organizational structure, the intake officer is the chief decision maker for juveniles prior to the juvenile court proceedings. The intake officer has two important decisions to make: what to do with the case and whether to detain the youth until a detention hearing can be scheduled.

The intake officer is commonly faced with one of the following situations: Parents bring a child in on their own, parents bring a child in because of a letter requesting their presence, or a police officer brings in a child who has been apprehended on suspicion of committing an unlawful act. Parents who walk in with their child typically complain, "My kid won't obey," "My kid won't do the chores," "My kid won't come home at night," or "My kid is running around with the wrong crowd." They want someone in authority to say, "You're going to get punished unless you clean up your act." After interviewing both youth and parents, sometimes separately, the intake officer might make a contract with the child and parents, by which each agrees to an acceptable compromise solution, or the intake officer might decide to refer the youth to a diversion agency.[5]

Police and probation officers talk with young members of the Crips street gang outside of a Los Angeles high school. A recent publication discussed in this text says that "good juvenile probation practice is mission-driven, performance-based, and outcome-focused."
■ **What does that mean?**

Parents whose child has been apprehended by the police for a criminal act are commonly instructed by letter to bring their child to the intake unit at a particular time. The intake officer must conduct a preliminary investigation at this time and, on the basis of the findings, decide what to do about the petition. Ordinarily, the child is not retained in a detention facility but is released to the parents.

Police officers also frequently bring juveniles who have been apprehended committing an unlawful act to the intake unit. As part of the preliminary investigation, the intake officer must get in touch with the parents and make an immediate decision about the need for detention. The child is detained if he or she is judged dangerous to self or others or lacks supervision in the home.

Investigation   Investigation requires that probation officers prepare a **social history report** on a youth ruled delinquent to aid the judge in making the correct disposition. If a juvenile court uses a bifurcated hearing (separate adjudicatory and disposition stages), the judge orders a social history when a juvenile is found delinquent at the adjudicatory or fact-finding stage. But if the court combines the adjudicatory and disposition stages, the social history must be completed before a juvenile appears in front of the judge, who waits until the youth has been found delinquent to read the report.

The probation officer usually has thirty to sixty days to write this report. He or she will review the youth's arrest record, reports of the current offense, any available psychiatric or psychological evaluations, and any information from social agencies; interview the youth and the parents, usually at least once in the home; and may also interview the arresting officer, school administrators or teachers, neighborhood religious leaders, and peers who know of or were involved in the alleged offense. Peers often volunteer information, saying to the probation officer, "I hear you're Fred's PO. I want you to know that he's a real crazy and did the crime," or "John is a real loser. Let me tell you some of the other shit he's done."

social history report
A written report of a juvenile's social background that probation officers prepare for a juvenile judge to assist the court in making a disposition of a youth who has been ruled delinquent.

Supervision   When a juvenile judge sentences a youth to probation, the probation officer generally takes the youth aside and explains the meaning of probation. The probationer is informed of how frequently he or she will report to the probation officer and of the importance of complying with the conditions of probation. See Juvenile Law 16.1 for some of the probation rules for one juvenile probation office.

The length of time a youth must spend on probation varies from state to state. In some states, the maximum length is until the juvenile reaches the age of majority, normally sixteen or eighteen but sometimes twenty-one years of age. Other states limit the length of time a juvenile or adult can spend on probation: in Illinois it is limited to five years; in New York, to two years; in Washington, D.C., to one year; and in California, to six months.

The supervisory function is divided into casework management, treatment, and surveillance. Effective casework management requires that a probation officer keep an up-to-date casework file, carry out periodic reviews, decide how each client is to be handled, and divide probationers into several categories—depending on their needs

Juvenile Law 16.1

Probation Rules

1. Obey all federal, state, and local laws.
2. Must contact Juvenile Court Officer by the next working day if taken into custody for questioning on a new law violation(s).
3. No possession or usage of alcohol or drugs, unless prescribed by a doctor.
4. Obey parent(s) rules, including assigned household chores.
5. Attend all scheduled appointments with Juvenile Court Officer, assigned Tracker, and/or Volunteer Juvenile Court Officer.
6. Continued involvement in a school program; includes supervision and monitoring by Juvenile Court School Liaison.
7. Obey curfew regulations.
8. Participate in family therapy until successfully discharged, if deemed appropriate.
9. Participate in individual counseling until successfully discharged, if deemed appropriate.
10. Make reasonable restitution as agreed upon in the Restitution Contract.
11. Complete _____ hours of Community Service Work Project.
12. Participate in tutoring, if appropriate.
13. Write a letter of apology to the victim(s) for your actions.
14. No use of verbal/physical violence nor intimidation.
15. Participate in outpatient substance evaluation and cooperate with recommended counseling; pay service fee to insure completion of evaluation.

16. Attend AA/NA meetings weekly, if deemed appropriate.
17. May not frequent establishments nor residences where controlled substances/alcohol are served, nor associate with individuals involved.
18. May not leave the county without permission from Juvenile Court Officer.
19. May not use or possess weapons of any kind.
20. Actively seek and maintain employment.

Failure to comply with the above rules will result in one, or a combination, of the following consequences/ recommendations to the court:

1. Grounding.
2. Tightening of curfew hours.
3. Assignment of Community Service Work Project hours.
4. Tracking and Monitoring.
5. Supervision by Juvenile Court School Liaison/participation/completion in School Violence Program.
6. Day Treatment Program.
7. Additional appointments with Juvenile Court Officer.
8. Assignment of two hours of Community Service Work Project for each hour, or part of an hour, of unauthorized school absence.
9. Forty-eight-hour detention hold.
10. Return to Court for modification of last Court Order.

■ **As a juvenile, would you have found the above rules restrictive? Are they too restrictive? What would you add or omit?**

Source: Adapted from materials provided by Juvenile Court Services of Black Hawk County (Waterloo, Iowa) in October of 2001.

and the risk they present to the community. Those with more serious needs and who present a greater risk to the community are required to report to their probation officer more frequently.

Surveillance requires that the probation officer make certain that probationers comply with the conditions of probation and that they do not break the law. The probation officer has a number of opportunities to observe the behavior of probationers in the office, at home, and perhaps at school, and will also visit the probationer's parents. If a probationer's behavior is unacceptable, the probation officer is likely to receive reports from school or from law enforcement agencies.

The importance of surveillance was underscored in the mid-1970s when, with the emphasis on law and order, probation services were accused of failing to protect society. If a youth does not comply with the conditions of probation or commits another delinquent act, the probation officer must inform the judge by filing a notice of violation. If the violation is serious enough, the probation officer must recommend that probation be revoked. Thus the probation officer has a law enforcement role as well as a treatment role. In Exhibit 16.1, probation officers reveal the questions that they consider in making decisions. The answers to these questions clearly place the probation officer in an enforcement role.

surveillance

The observation of probationers by probation officers, intended to ensure that probationers comply with the conditions of probation and that they do not break the law.

Risk Control and Crime Reduction

The current emphasis in juvenile probation, as in adult probation, is on risk control and crime reduction approaches, including restitution and community service, intensive supervision, house arrest, and electronic monitoring.

Exhibit 16.1

Decisions Facing Probation Officers

To make the decision of whether to revoke probation, modify the conditions of probation, or place a juvenile outside the home, probation officers consider such questions as:

1. Is the juvenile a danger to self or others?
2. Is the juvenile exceeding the limits in the home, community, and school?
3. Is the family amenable to services?
4. How can the scarce resources be used wisely with this juvenile?
5. What are other consequences that can be imposed without court intervention (e.g., community service)?

To make the decision on what to do with a juvenile on Informal Adjustment Agreement who is not following home rules, violating curfew, dropping dirty U. A.s [urine analysis], or failing to attend the Second Chance Program, probation officers consider such questions as:

1. Does the juvenile show any remorse for his or her actions?
2. Does the juvenile want to change or make an adjustment to the Contract?

3. Have all other options been utilized?
4. Is the charge worth sending to the court to get compliance? (Is simple misdemeanor worthy of the expense of court action?)

To answer the question of what to do with a juvenile who is already adjudicated delinquent with the charge of Possession with Intent to Deliver a Controlled Substance and who continues to use/drop dirty U. A., probation officers consider such questions as:

1. Does use of evaluation/treatment help?
2. Does a 48-hour lock-up work? (Take away freedom)
3. Have we tried all other services and consequences?
4. Would it be fair to modify the court order with a mittimus withheld to placement or commitment to Training School in Eldora?

■ **What questions do you think would have the most influence on probation officers in these three scenarios? Why?**

Source: Materials provided by Juvenile Court Services of Black Hawk County (Waterloo, Iowa) in October 2001.

restitution

Court-ordered repayment to the victim; often used together with community service as a condition of juvenile probation.

Web **LIBRARY** 16.1

Read Chapter 7 of the OJJDP publication *Juvenile Offenders and Victims: 2006 National Report* at **www.justicestudies.com/ WebLibrary**.

Web **PLACES** 16.2

Visit the National Association for Juvenile Correctional Agencies' website via **www.justicestudies .com/WebPlaces**.

The main goals of **restitution** and community service programs are to hold youthful offenders responsible for their crimes. Over the past thirty years, restitution programs and community service orders have had significant growth. Much of this growth has resulted from the Office of Juvenile Justice and Delinquency Prevention. In 1977, OJJDP launched a major resitution initiative by spending $30 million to fund the use of restitution in eighty-five juvenile courts throughout the United States. OJJDP followed this initiative with the National Restitution Training Program in 1983 and the Restitution Education, Specialized Training, and Technical Assistance (RESTTA) Project in 1985. These initiatives are directly responsible for most of the growth of restitution programs.[6] Figure 16.2 shows the growth of restitution programs through the early 1990s.

Three broad types of restitution can be ordered by the juvenile court: straight financial restitution, community service, and direct service to victims. Community service is the most common, probably because it is the easiest to administer. Direct service takes place less frequently, largely because of victim reluctance to have contact with offenders. However, the three program types frequently blend together. For example, a local jurisdiction may organize work crews and even enter into recycling, janitorial, and other service contacts with public or private agencies in order to provide youthful offenders with jobs so that they can pay restitution. The most common goals of restitution programs are holding juveniles accountable, providing reparation to victims, treating and rehabilitating juveniles, and punishing juvenile offenders.[7]

When it comes to making restitution and community service work, probation officers are key players, and in many jurisdictions it is up to a juvenile probation officer to do some or all of the following:[8]

- Determine participation eligibility.
- Calculate appropriate amounts of restitution to be made.
- Assess the offender's ability to pay.
- Determine payment/work schedules.
- Monitor performance.
- Close the case.

FIGURE 16.2

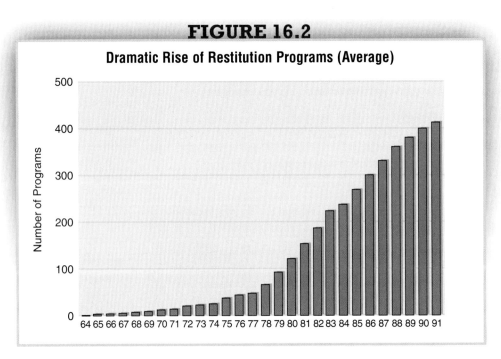

Dramatic Rise of Restitution Programs (Average)

Source: Peter R. Schneider and Matthew C. Finkelstein, *New Trends in Restitution Programming: Results from the 1991 RESTITTA Survey* (Washington, D.C.: Office of Juvenile Justice and Delinquency Prevention, 2000), p. 15. Reprinted with permission from the U.S. Department of Justice.

Young offenders paint fences as part of their sentence to community service. ■ **What are the responsibilities of juvenile probation officers who work with offenders sentenced to community service?**

A 1991 survey found that most of the juveniles referred to programs strictly for juveniles are diverted out of the formal justice system. Some restitution programs accept both juveniles and adults. This survey also revealed the racial breakdown of participants in these programs (see Figure 16.3).[9] Community service programs are more widely used than are financial restitution programs, because many juveniles lack the means to pay financial restitution. Some probation offices have a full-time restitution officer who administers such programs, and other offices divide restitution into formal and informal programs.

With community work restitution, juveniles are generally ordered to perform a certain number of work hours at a private nonprofit or government agency. Some

FIGURE 16.3

Racial Breakdown of Restitution Programs (Average)

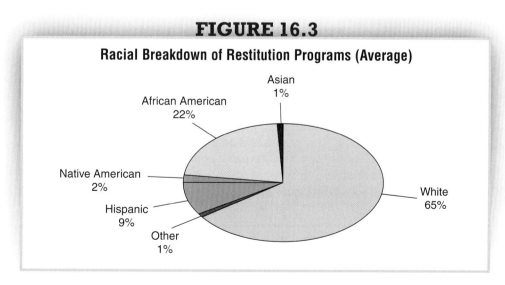

- Asian 1%
- African American 22%
- Native American 2%
- Hispanic 9%
- Other 1%
- White 65%

Source: Peter R. Schneider and Matthew C. Finkelstein, *New Trends in Restitution Programming: Results from the 1991 RESTITTA Survey* (Washington, D.C.: Office of Juvenile Justice and Delinquency Prevention, 2000), p. 13. Reprinted with permission from the U.S. Department of Justice.

large probation departments have established up to 100 sites where this service may be performed. Sites typically include public libraries, parks, nursing homes, animal shelters, community centers, day-care centers, youth agencies, YMCAs and YWCAs, and the local streets. Some restitution programs involve supervised work crews; in these situations, juveniles go to a site and work under the supervision of an adult.

community service project
Court-required restitution in which a juvenile spends a certain number of hours working in a community project.

Youthful offenders in Hennepin County (Minneapolis), Minnesota, find themselves very quickly dispatched by the juvenile judge to the Saturday work squads for **community service projects.** A first-time property offender will usually be given a sentence of forty hours. Each Saturday morning, youths who are assigned to the work squad are required to be at the downtown meeting place at 8:00. The coordinator of the program, who is on the staff of the probation department, then assigns each to a specific work detail; these include recycling bottles and cans, visiting with patients at a nursing home, doing janitorial work, cleaning bus stops, planting trees or removing barbed wire fences at a city park, and working at a park reserve. This program sends out five trucks each Saturday with ten youths and two staff members in each truck.[10]

Intensive Supervision   In the 1980s and 1990s, as probation continued to be criticized as a lenient measure that allowed offenders to escape punishment, intensive supervision programs (ISPs) became more widely used in juvenile probation. Georgia, New Jersey, Oregon, and Pennsylvania are experimenting with statewide programs for juveniles.[11] But more and more juvenile judges, especially in metropolitan juvenile courts, are placing high-risk juveniles on small caseloads and assigning them more frequent contact with a probation officer than would be true of traditional probation.

The Juvenile Court Judges' Commission in the Commonwealth of Pennsylvania developed an intensive probation project because of its concern with increased commitments to training schools. In addition to investing $1,868,014 to support intensive probation and aftercare programs, the Commission also provides program guidelines and monitoring to each county that is willing to set up an intensive probation program. By the end of 1989, thirty-two counties had established intensive probation programs that featured such standards as providing a caseload size of no more than fifteen high-risk delinquents for each intensive probation officer, requiring a minimum of three face-to-face contacts per week with each of these youths and a minimum of one contact per week with the family and/or guardian, and establishing intensive probation services for a minimum of six months and a maximum of twelve months.[12]

Intensive supervision programs are widely used in adult corrections and have received considerable praise for their effectiveness in keeping high-risk offenders out of long-term confinement. However, two national reviews of ISPs in juvenile probation discovered that "neither the possible effectiveness nor the possible ineffectiveness of these programs had been carefully examined. As a result, their status in this regard, including their impact on recidivism, was essentially unknown."[13]

Some criminologists have sought to develop an Integrated Social Control (ISC) model of intensive supervision addressing the major causal factors identified in delinquency theory and research. This proposed model integrates the central components of strain, control, and social learning theories. It contends that the combined forces of inadequate socialization, strains between educational and occupational aspirations and expectations, and social disorganization in the neighborhood lead to weak bonding to conventional values and activities in the family, community, and school. Weak bonding, in turn, can lead youths to delinquent behavior through negative peer influence. Figure 16.4 shows a diagram of this model.[14]

House Arrest and Remote Location Monitoring   House arrest is a sentence imposed by the court whereby youths are ordered to remain confined in their own homes for the length of their sentence. They may be allowed to leave their homes for medical reasons, school, employment, and approved religious services. They may also

FIGURE 16.4

Integrated Strain–Control Paradigm

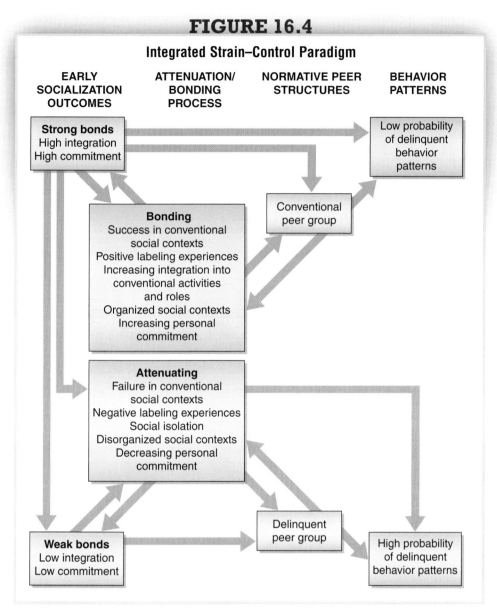

| EARLY SOCIALIZATION OUTCOMES | ATTENUATION/ BONDING PROCESS | NORMATIVE PEER STRUCTURES | BEHAVIOR PATTERNS |

Strong bonds
High integration
High commitment

Bonding
Success in conventional social contexts
Positive labeling experiences
Increasing integration into conventional activities and roles
Organized social contexts
Increasing personal commitment

Attenuating
Failure in conventional social contexts
Negative labeling experiences
Social isolation
Disorganized social contexts
Decreasing personal commitment

Weak bonds
Low integration
Low commitment

Conventional peer group

Delinquent peer group

Low probability of delinquent behavior patterns

High probability of delinquent behavior patterns

Source: Barry Krisberg et al., *Juvenile Intensive Supervision: Planning Guide* (Washington, D.C.: Office of Juvenile Justice and Delinquency Prevention, 1994), p. 7. Reprinted with permission from the U.S. Department of Justice.

be required to perform community service. Electronic monitoring equipment may or may not be used to monitor juveniles' presence in a residence where they are required to remain.

Remote location monitoring was inspired by a New Mexico district court judge's reading of a comic strip in which the character Spiderman was tracked by a transmitter affixed to his wrist. The judge approached an engineer, who designed an electronic bracelet to emit a signal picked up by a receiver placed in a home telephone. The bracelet was designed so that if the offender moved more than 150 feet from the home telephone, the transmission signal would be broken, alerting the authorities that the offender had fled his or her home.[15]

Today's electronic monitoring (EM) equipment receives information about monitored offenders and transmits the information to a computer at the monitoring agency. Electronic monitoring methods include:

- Continuous signaling devices, which use a transmitter attached to the probationer that emits a continuous radio signal.

remote location monitoring
The use of electronic equipment to verify that an offender is at home or in a community correctional center during specified hours, or to track his or her whereabouts. Also called *electronic monitoring*.

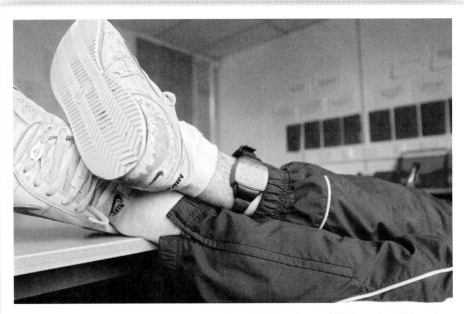

A youthful offender's remote location monitoring ankle bracelet. ■ **What are the different kinds of electronic monitoring that can be employed in the supervision of juvenile offenders?**

■ Programmed contact devices, which call the juvenile probationer at scheduled or random times and use various technologies to determine the identity of the person who answers (voice verification or a device worn by the probationer that is inserted into a verifier box attached to the phone, or a digital camera for visual verification).

■ Global positioning systems, in which the juvenile probationer wears a transmitter that communicates signals to a satellite and back to a computer monitor, pinpointing the offender's whereabouts at all times.

■ Remote alcohol testing devices, which may be used alone or with other devices listed above. The probationer is required to blow into a device (alcosensor), which transmits results to a computer that records the amount of alcohol in the offender's blood. Such devices may also be attached to automobile ignition systems in order to prevent an offender who has been drinking from driving.[16]

In 1997, an estimated 89,095 adults—3.5 percent of all probationers—were on electronic monitoring surveillance. Nearly every state has adults on electronic surveillance, although the courts in some states limited the use of EM by banning certain types of monitoring equipment and allowing monitoring only by consent.[17] The use of EM in juvenile justice has been gradually gaining acceptance. For example, according to a November 1988 survey, only eleven juvenile programs used EM.[18] Today, EM programs are widely used in juvenile justice programs throughout the United States. Electronic monitoring programs:

■ increase the number of juveniles safely released into existing home confinement programs;

■ reduce the number of juveniles returned to juvenile detention for violating home confinement restrictions;

■ reduce the number of field contacts required of home confinement officers;

■ provide a reasonably safe alternative to confinement for lower-risk offenders;

■ provide for early reunification of children with their families; and

■ allow juveniles to return to school.[19]

Electronic monitoring tends to be more effective when used as a tool in conjunction with other programs, rather than when operating alone as a supervision program. Yet there seems to be no consistent findings that successful completion of EM programs leads to a decrease in recidivism.[20]

The Community Volunteer

As stated earlier, probation was initially staffed with volunteers. Professional staff did not begin appearing until the turn of the twentieth century. But in the 1950s, Judge Keith J. Leenhouts initiated a court-sponsored volunteer program in Royal Oak, Michigan, that sparked the rebirth of the volunteer movement. Today, over two thousand court-sponsored **volunteer programs** are in operation, using volunteers to assist probation officers in a variety of ways. The use of volunteers has become one of the most valuable ways to help offenders adjust to community life.

The National Information Center on Volunteers in Court has identified several areas in which **community volunteers** can work effectively with juvenile offenders. A volunteer can provide a one-to-one support relationship for the youth with a trustworthy adult; can function as a child advocate with teachers, employers, and the police; can be a good role model; can set limits and teach prosocial values; can teach skills or academic subjects; and can help the youth develop a realistic response to the environment.

In addition to these areas of direct contact, volunteers can assist in administrative work. They can help recruit, train, and supervise other volunteers; serve as consultants to the regular staff; become advisers to the court, especially in the policymaking area; develop good public relations with the community; and contribute money, materials, or facilities.

Volunteers can improve the morale of the regular probation staff because they are usually positive and enthusiastic about the services they are providing. Since many volunteers are professionals (physicians, psychiatrists, psychologists, and dentists), they can provide services that the probation department may not have the financial resources to obtain. Finally, their contributions can reduce the caseload of the regular staff.

Several criticisms have been leveled at volunteer programs. Critics say that volunteers sometimes create more work than they return in service. Volunteers cannot handle serious problems and sometimes can harm their clients. Parents may resist the volunteer as an untrained worker. But proper screening, training, and supervision can do much to ensure a high quality of probation services from volunteers.

volunteer programs
The use of unpaid adult community members to assist probation officers in a variety of ways.

community volunteer
An individual who donates his or her time to work with delinquents in the community.

> " Today, over two thousand court-sponsored volunteer programs are in operation. "

Web LIBRARY 16.2
Read the OJJDP National Report Series publication *Juveniles in Corrections* at **www .justicestudies.com/ WebLibrary**.

Web PLACES 16.3
Read the OJJDP Model Programs Guide via **www.justicestudies .com/WebPlaces**.

Residential and Day Treatment Programs

Residential and day treatment programs are usually reserved for juvenile probationers who are having difficulty dealing with the looseness of probation supervision. In day treatment programs, juveniles attend morning and afternoon program sessions and return home in the evening. In residential programs, which are usually group homes or foster care placements, delinquents are taken away from the supervision of parents and are assigned twenty-four hours a day to their new placement. Some group homes are like the halfway houses used in adult corrections and serve as a placement for juveniles on aftercare status who have nowhere else to go.

Types of Residential and Day Treatment Programs

Group homes, day treatment programs, and wilderness programs are the main types of community-based programs. Group homes are a residential placement to which juveniles are adjudicated, either while on probation or when released from a training school. Day treatment programs are nonresidential programs that juveniles attend during the day, returning home in the evening. Wilderness programs, sometimes called "survival programs," take place in such settings as the mountains, the woods, the sea, and the desert. The intent of these survival programs is to improve youths' self-confidence and sense of self-reliance.

Group Homes Such terms as *group residence, halfway house, group home,* and *attention home* are used in various parts of the United States to identify a small facility serving about thirteen to twenty-five youths. **Group homes** fulfill several purposes: They provide an alternative to institutionalization; they serve as a short-term community placement, wherein probation and aftercare officers can deal with youths' community problems; and they serve as a "halfway-in" setting for youths having difficulty adjusting to probation and as a "halfway-out" placement for delinquents who are returning to the community but lack an adequate home placement.

Intake criteria, treatment goals, length of stay, target population services, services offered, physical facilities, location in reference to the rest of the city, and house rules of group homes throughout the United States are extremely diverse. Some homes are treatment oriented, using a modality such as guided group interaction (GGI) to generate a supportive environment among residents and staff. In GGI, residents are expected to support, confront, and be honest with one another so that they can help each other deal with their problems.[21]

The Silverlake Experiment was set up in Los Angeles County in the mid-1960s, in a large family residence in a middle-class neighborhood, to provide group living for male youths between the ages of fifteen and eighteen. Only twenty residents at a time lived in the group home, and all participated in daily group meetings.[22]

A well-developed **group home model** is the **teaching family group model,** which was developed in 1967 with the establishment of the Achievement Place group home in Lawerence, Kansas. The teaching family group model has been used in more than forty homes in twelve states.[23] The Criswell House in Tallahassee, Florida, established in 1958, housed twenty-five youths on probation and parole and used guided group interaction. In the 1970s, Florida developed a network of nine group homes modeled on Criswell House.[24] The Dare Program in Massachusetts is another widely used model. Established in 1964, this program had ten specialized programs and thirteen community residences, including nine group homes, four **foster care** programs, two residential schools, shelter care programs, and a high-security intensive care facility.[25]

Founded in 1968, the House of Umoja (HOU) was officially organized in 1970 as a youth development agency. On discovering that one of her six sons had joined a gang, Sister Falaska and her husband, David Fattah, took the bold step of inviting the gang to become a part of the family. Sister Falaska saw possible solutions to the violence of gangs in "the strength of the family, tribal concepts, and African value systems." She and her husband created an African-style extended family in which members of the gangs could find alternative values to those of their street-life culture. Residents are required to be drug-free and are encouraged to maintain good grades. Since its establishment, 3,000 adolescents belonging to 73 different street gangs have passed through the HOU doors. The success of the Umoja concept has led to its duplication in Bridgeport, Connecticut, and Portland, Oregon. The principles of this residential program are part of the National Center for Neighborhood Enterprise's highly successful Violence-Free Zone initiative that has been instituted in five cities.[26]

Unfortunately, such exciting programs as the House of Umoja or the Achievement Place are not typical of group homes across the nation. In too many group homes, beds (vacancies) are hard to find, and group homes may even have long waiting lists. Residents also typically have longer stays than they would have in training schools, and this raises real questions about whether group homes are a less punitive placement than juvenile institutions.

Day Treatment Programs Nonresidential **day treatment programs** multiplied nationwide during the early 1970s. Their popularity can be traced to the advantages they offer community-based corrections: They are more economical because they do not provide living and sleeping quarters, they make parental participation easier, they

---

group home

A placement for youths who have been adjudicated by the court—called a *group residence, halfway house,* or *attention home*—that serves a group of about thirteen to twenty-five youths as an alternative to institutionalization.

group home model

A form of community-based residential program that has had some success with youthful offenders.

teaching family group model

A community-based residential program that has had some success with delinquent youths.

foster care

A home setting for juveniles who are lawfully removed from their birth parents' homes.

day treatment programs

Court-mandated, community-based corrections programs that juveniles attend in the morning and afternoon. They return home in the evening.

A staff member talks with a future program participant at the Center for Young Women's Development in San Francisco. The Center reaches over 3,500 young women each year through street-based outreach efforts. Its staff is comprised entirely of women under the age of twenty-five. ■ **What kinds of services are likely to be of greatest interest to marginalized young women?**

require fewer staff members, and they are less coercive and punishment-oriented than residential placements.

Nonresidential programs usually serve male juveniles, although California operates two such programs for girls as well as several coeducational programs. These nonresidential programs have been used widely by the California Community Treatment Project. The New York Division for Youth has also established several nonresidential programs, called STAY. The STAY programs also expose youths to a guided-group-interaction experience.

Another nonresidential program is conducted by the Associated Marine Institutes (AMI). Twenty-five of their forty schools and institutes are nonresidential. Funded by state and private donations, this privately operated program tailors its institutes to the geographical strengths of each community, using the ocean, wilderness, rivers, and lakes to stimulate productive behavior in juvenile delinquents. In the nonresidential programs that include both males and females, the fourteen- to eighteen-year-old trainees live at home or in foster homes. Youths are referred to this program either by the courts or by the Division of Youth Services (see Exhibit 16.2).[27]

For the Marine Institutes, which constitute most of AMI's schools, the contract that the youth signs on entering the program sets individual goals for the training period in a dozen categories, including diving, ship-handling skills, ocean science, lifesaving, first aid, and such electives as photography and marine maintenance. The major incentive for youths is the opportunity to earn official certification as scuba divers. Other incentives that are designed to maintain enthusiasm include sew-on patches; certificates awarded for short-term achievement in first aid, ship-handling skills, and diving; trophies for trainee of the month; and field trips, such as a cruise to the Bahamas or the Florida Keys.[28]

Project New Pride is a day treatment program that offers services to juveniles in Denver, Colorado, who have committed serious offenses. Most of the youngsters involved in the project are African Americans or Mexican Americans. This program

Web LIBRARY 16.3

Read the OJJDP National Report Series publication *Juvenile Residential Facility Census* at **www.justicestudies.com/ WebLibrary**.

Programs of the Associated Marine Institutes

Since 1969, the Associated Marine Institutes have been working with juvenile delinquents. Over the years, new institutes were started throughout the United States and in the Cayman Islands.

AMI's main objective is to develop attitudes in the youths it serves which will help them meet their responsibilities, develop employable skills, increase self-confidence, and encourage further education. After attending the program, each youth is placed in a school, a job, or the armed forces. Aftercare coordinators monitor youths for three years after they graduate to offer assistance.

In September of 1993, Attorney General Janet Reno and President Bill Clinton visited the Pinellas Marine Institute in St. Petersurg, Florida, one of AMI's forty schools. In a nationally televised program where he announced his crime bill, the president said, "These programs are giving young people a chance to take their future back, a chance to understand that there is good inside them."

One of the ingredients of AMI's programs is a strong commitment to meaningful work. AMI looks upon work as one of the most beneficial forms of therapy and teaches that nothing worthwhile is achieved without hard work.

Academic success is also emphasized. The intent of the AMI programs is to motivate students and to give them the right tools and opportunities so that they can succeed in school. Indeed, the goal of the AMI teaching staff is to prepare youths to take their GED exam and then attend vocational school, community college, or a four-year college.

A further important ingredient of this program is modeling. AMI staff support the belief that what they do is more important than what they say. Their philosophy on modeling is: Tell me, I'll forget. Show me, I may remember. Involve me, I'll be committed.

■ **What are the advantages that the Associated Marine Institutes have over other community-based programs for juveniles? Is the emphasis given to aftercare in this program one that should be pursued more by other programs?**

Source: The Associated Marine Institutes.

offers intensive services for youths during the first three months and then continues with treatment geared to the juveniles' needs and interests for a nine-month follow-up period. Academic education, counseling, employment, and cultural education are the four main areas of service. For academic education, youths are assigned to either the New Pride Alternative School or the Learning Disabilities Center. The purpose of the counseling is to enhance self-image and to help the youth cope with the environment. Job preparation is emphasized through a job-skills workshop and on-the-job training. The purpose of cultural education is to expose participants to a range of experiences and activities in the Denver area.[29]

Project New Pride has established four primary goals in working with its difficult clientele: (1) reduction of recidivism, (2) job placement, (3) school reintegration, and (4) remediation of academic and learning disabilities. The project has had some success in achieving the first three of these goals, but less success in educational remediation. The popularity of this project has been demonstrated by its replication in Boston; Chicago; Fresno, California; Haddonfield, New Jersey; Kansas City, Missouri; Los Angeles; Pensacola, Florida; Providence, Rhode Island; San Francisco; and Washington, D.C.[30]

The better-known programs, such as AMI and Project New Pride, continue to thrive, but with the decline of federal funding sources in the late 1970s and early 1980s, many day treatment programs had to close their doors. There is no question that these programs play a much smaller role in community-based corrections than they did in the 1970s.

Outward Bound

A wilderness-type survival program that is popular in many states as an alternative to the institutionalization of juveniles.

Wilderness Programs Outward Bound is the most widely used wilderness program. Its main goal is to use the "overcoming of a seemingly impossible task" to gain self-reliance, to prove one's worth, and to define one's personhood.[31] The first Outward Bound program in the United States was established in Colorado in 1962.

Today, Outward Bound offers 750 wilderness courses serving adults, teens, and youths. Courses include rock climbing, kayaking, dogsledding, sailing, rappelling, backpacking, and more. Over 10,000 students participate in wilderness courses. Outward Bound also offers multi-year partnerships with 125 schools across the United States, and it encourages over 30,000 students and 4,000 teachers to reach high levels of achievement and to discover their potential. Outward Bound also has urban programs in New York, Boston, Philadelphia, Baltimore, and Atlanta.[32]

> " The first Outward Bound program in the United States was established in Colorado in 1962. "

Arthur Conquest, a former delinquent who became an Outward Bound instructor, tells why he thinks this learning experience works for delinquents:

> But I think in the end, and I don't just mean the end of the course, but when the kids have to deal with life—they'll have whatever it takes to go to the wall. That's what an Outward Bound course for these kids is for—when things get tough, you've got to really believe in yourself, persevere, go to that wall, and do all the things you're capable of doing.[33]

VisionQuest, another survival program, was started by Robert Ledger Burton and Sten Rogers in 1973 in Tucson, Arizona. This program seeks to provide adjudicated youths the opportunity to succeed in challenges, to see a new future for themselves, and to give them skills to accomplish their goals and reach their highest potential. Other key components of the VisionQuest approach include the emphasis on staff as parents rather than counselors, the use of rigorous outdoor activity, the use of living history to connect youths to their heritage and culture, and the blending of military influences with education and treatment. The Madalyn Rite of Passage, located in Donegal Township in western Pennsylvania, is one of the many VisionQuest programs that span the United States. This program opened in 2004 and is a community-based group home for adolescent girls that combines treatment with career-focused vocational education.[34]

Web LIBRARY 16.4

Read the OJJDP Juvenile Justice Bulletin *Psychiatric Disorders of Youth in Detention* at **www.justicestudies.com/WebLibrary**.

Types of Institutional Placement

Youthful offenders who do not adequately adjust to community-based programs or who commit another offenses while under community supervision may be adjudicated to a private or public institutional placement. Public institutional facilities are sometimes administered by the county, but the vast majority are under state control. Reception centers, ranches, forestry camps, boot camps, and training schools are the main forms that juvenile correctional institutions take. Recently, however, it should also be noted that juveniles have increasingly been sent to adult prisons. Private facilities play a significant role in the long-term custody of juveniles. In fact, although there are more than twice as many privately operated juvenile facilities as publicly operated ones, private facilities hold less than half as many youths as do public facilities.[35]

In 2003, 307 juvenile offenders were in custody for every 100,000 juveniles in the United States. Nationwide, the total number of youthful offenders in residential placement facilities rose 41 percent from 1991 to 1999, but then declined 10 percent from 1999 to 2003. The result was an overall increase of 27 percent between 1991 and 2003. The number of status offenders in juvenile facilities peaked in 1995 but declined 36 percent between 1995 and 2003.[36]

In terms of the most serious offense leading to confinement, 38 percent of confined juveniles were being held for person offenses in 2003, 31 percent for property offenses, and 12 percent for technical offenses. Public order offenses ranked fourth, at 10 percent, and drug offenses—perhaps a little surprisingly—ranked last among all the types of offenses on which statistics were kept; they made up only 9 percent of all committed juvenile offenders.[37]

There were 14,590 female juvenile offenders were held in custody throughout the country in 2003, which accounted for 15 percent of all offenders in custody. The

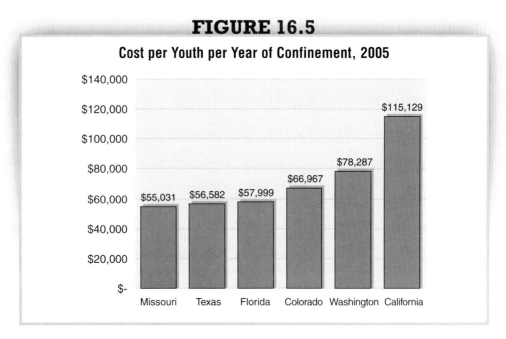

FIGURE 16.5

Cost per Youth per Year of Confinement, 2005

Missouri $55,031 · Texas $56,582 · Florida $57,999 · Colorado $66,967 · Washington $78,287 · California $115,129

Source: Christopher Murray, Chris Baird, Ned Loughran, Fred Mills, and John Platt, *Safety and Welfare Plan: Implementing Reform in California* (Sacramento: California Department of Corrections and Rehabilitation, Division of Juvenile Justice, 2006), p. 5.

proportion of females increased from 13 percent in 1991 to 15 percent in 2003. The female proportion was greater among status offenders (40 percent) than among delinquents (14 percent), and for detained (18 percent) than for committed (12 percent) delinquents.[38] In 2003, more than 59,000 minority offenders were in residential placement in juvenile facilities in the United States, which was 61 percent of the custody population nationwide. Of the 96,655 in placement in 2003, 37,347 were white, 36,740 were African American, 18,422 were Hispanic/Latino, 1,771 were American Indian, 1,462 were Asian, and 913 were of other or mixed races.[39]

The 2006 report, *Implementing Reform in California*, reveals the skyrocketing cost of juvenile institutional care. It costs California $115,129 per year to institutionalize each juvenile resident (Figure 16.5). California's 2004's average length of stay was 25.9 months—nearly three times as long as the average of nineteen states that participated in a nationwide survey (Figure 16.6). It should be noted, however, that juvenile offenders in California may be kept in institutional care until they are twenty-four years old—something that has contributed significantly to the average length of stay for those sentenced to juvenile facilities in California.[40]

Reception and Diagnostic Centers

reception and diagnostic centers

Facilities where juveniles who have been committed to correctional institutions frequently are first sent; these centers diagnose youths' problems and develop individualized treatment plans.

The purpose of **reception and diagnostic centers,** which are managed and operated by either public or private agencies, is to determine which treatment plan suits each adjudicated youth and which training school is the best placement. The evaluation of each resident used to take four to six weeks, but the process has been condensed today to an average length of thirty-four days. Evaluations are normally done by a psychiatrist, a clinical psychologist, a social worker, academic staff, and a chaplain. Each youth undergoes a psychiatric evaluation and a battery of psychological tests to measure intelligence, attitude, maturity, and emotional problems, and a social case study is completed. During this orientation period, the academic staff determines the proper school placement and attempts to identify any debilitating learning problems. Physical and dental examinations also typically are given to the youth at this time and child care workers in living units evaluate institutional adjustment and peer

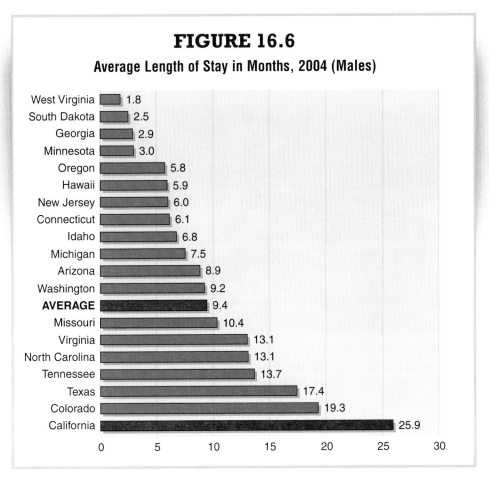

FIGURE 16.6
Average Length of Stay in Months, 2004 (Males)

West Virginia	1.8
South Dakota	2.5
Georgia	2.9
Minnesota	3.0
Oregon	5.8
Hawaii	5.9
New Jersey	6.0
Connecticut	6.1
Idaho	6.8
Michigan	7.5
Arizona	8.9
Washington	9.2
AVERAGE	9.4
Missouri	10.4
Virginia	13.1
North Carolina	13.1
Tennessee	13.7
Texas	17.4
Colorado	19.3
California	25.9

Source: Christopher Murray, Chris Baird, Ned Loughran, Fred Mills, and John Platt, *Safety and Welfare Plan: Implementing Reform in California* (Sacramento: California Department of Corrections and Rehabilitation, Division of Juvenile Justice, 2006), p. 2.

relationships. When all the reports have been prepared, a case conference is held on each resident to summarize that youth's needs and attitudes and recommend the best institutional placement.

In large youth commissions or departments of youth services, the recommendation must be approved by an institutional coordinator. Upon approval, the youth is transferred to the selected institution, accompanied by the diagnostic report. Because many training schools have their own orientation programs, however, it is not unusual for the report to receive little attention and for the youth to undergo nearly the same process again in the training school cottage.

Ranches and Forestry Camps

Minimum-security institutions, such as **ranches** and forestry camps, are typically reserved for youths who have committed minor crimes and for those who have been committed to the youth authority or private corrections for the first time. **Forestry camps** are popular in a number of states. Residents usually do conservation work in a state park, including cleaning up, cutting grass and weeds, and general maintenance. Treatment programs usually consist of group therapy, individual contacts with social workers and the child care staff, and one or two home visits a month. Residents also may be taken to a nearby town on a regular basis to make purchases and to attend community events. Escapes are a constant problem because of the nonsecure nature of these facilities.

ranches
Public and private juvenile correctional institutions that, like forestry camps, are usually less secure than training schools and have a more normalizing atmosphere.

forestry camps
Correctional facilities where residents usually do conservation work in state parks, including cleaning up, cutting grass and weeds, and general maintenance.

A resident in the Hennepin County School spending time with horses. Riding horses and canoeing are two of the activities that make this placement very different from most institutional settings. ■ **How do such activities further the treatment goals of institutions that employ them?**

Horseback riding is a popular recreational activity on ranches, but work details usually consist of taking care of the livestock, working in the garden, and performing general maintenance duties. Guided group interaction is the most widely used treatment, and as part of a "continuum of care," one or two home visits a month help residents reintegrate themselves into community living.

Residents are generally much more positive about a placement at a forestry camp or ranch than about placement at a training school. They like both the more relaxed approach to security and the more frequent community contact. Residents also respond to the generally shorter stays at these minimum-security institutions, and, given the looser atmosphere of these settings, it is not surprising that they have better relations with staff members here than in training schools. Yet some youths who are homesick or are victimized by peers cannot handle these settings and repeatedly run away until they are transferred to more secure institutions. For a description of the Hennepin County Home School, see Exhibit 16.3.

Boot Camps

Boot camps for youthful offenders, like those for adult offenders, developed in the mid-1980s and 1990s. Emphasizing military discipline, physical training, and regimented activity for periods typically ranging from 30 to 120 days, these programs endeavor to shock juvenile delinquents out of committing further crimes.

The rationale for juvenile boot camps is consistent with the juvenile justice system's historical emphasis on rehabilitation, usually incorporating explicit assumptions about the needs of delinquent youths and providing remedial, counseling, and after-care programs to address these needs.[41] All the programs employ military customs and courtesies, including uniformed drill instructors, a platoon structure, and summary punishment of participants, including group punishment under some circumstances. Although there are differences in emphases, with Denver creating the most militaristic environment, juvenile boot camp programs have generally discovered that they must tailor their environment to participants' maturity levels.[42]

Web LIBRARY 16.5

Read the OJJDP Juvenile Justice Bulletin *Planning Community-Based Facilities for Violent Juvenile Offenders as Part of a System of Graduated Sanctions* at **www .justicestudies.com/ WebLibrary**.

boot camp

A military-style facility used as an alternative to prison in order to deal with prison crowding and public demands for severe punishment.

Exhibit 16.3

Hennepin County Home School

The Hennepin County Home School (HCHS) is a state-licensed residential institution for juvenile males and females between the ages of thirteen and eighteen who have been committed by the Hennepin County Juvenile Court. This innovative facility, which combines features of camps and ranches, is located on a beautiful 167-acre wooded lake site in Minnetonka, Minnesota, approximately seventeen miles from downtown Minneapolis. The campus includes seven twenty-four-bed residential cottages, a school facility with a full gymnasium, an administration and services building with a sixteen-bed secure internal support unit, a new sixteen-bed transitional living unit (TLU), a horse barn and arena, and playfields. Hennepin County Home School is licensed for 168 open and 16 secure beds.

The Adolescent Male Treatment Program (Cottages 5, 6, and 7) is a corrective treatment program with development specialization for residents who have committed major property offenses and crimes against persons. The length of commitment is determined by the juvenile court and ranges from ten to thirteen months, including a forty-five-day transition and a two-month furlough component, during which time the juvenile returns to the community at the conclusion of his institutional stay. The Female Offender Program (Cottage 2) is a corrective treatment program for property and person offenders. The length of the commitment is determined by the juvenile court and ranges from ten to thirteen months with a specialized forty-five-day transition and a minimum two-month furlough. The Juvenile Sex Offender Program (Cottage 3) is a corrective treatment program for boys who have committed sexual offenses. The length of the commitment is indeterminate, with a furlough option after twelve months. The Beta Program (Cottage 1) is for less serious offenders. The length of stay is three to six weeks, and the focus of the program's activities is on work for repayment of court-ordered restitution and public service projects.

One of the exciting new programs is the Intensive Aftercare Program (IAP). Residents are offered a continuum of services to meet their full range of needs, including successful community reintegration and aftercare. This continuum-of-care model reflects the Intensive Community-Based Aftercare Model developed by the Office of Juvenile Justice and Delinquency Prevention (OJJDP). The County School's IAP model includes six interwined phases: assessment, case planning, institutional treatment, prerelease, transition, and community reintegration.

Superintendent Theresa E. Wise had this to say about (HCHS):

> The value of Hennepin County Home School is that we provide a safe and secure environment where the youth has an opportunity to look at himself or herself. Some youth are afraid at home and school, and we want them to be and feel safe here. This institution believes that a safe and secure environment helps youth internalize change. We are also concerned about the whole youth, and, therefore, we attempt to partner with the external community and work with families.

■ **What does the photograph of the resident and the horses suggest about this school? How does this facility seem to be different from the average public or private training school? Why is the continuum-of-care model such an important program?**

Source: Information received in brochures, other materials developed by the Hennepin County Home School, and the website page of the school. Interview conducted in 2006.

Boot camps for juveniles are generally reserved for midrange offenders, those who have failed with lesser sanctions such as probation but who are not yet hardened delinquents. The shock aspect of the boot camp experience includes incarceration as the environment within which the program takes place.[43] These programs typically focus on youths in their mid- to late teens and exclude sex offenders, armed robbers, and violent offenders. Yet only a few programs limit themselves to nonviolent youths who have committed their first serious offense or are being confined for the first time. For example, the Orleans Parish program accepts anyone who is sentenced by the juvenile judge.[44]

> " The rationale for juvenile boot camps is consistent with the juvenile justice system's historical emphasis on rehabilitation. "

As of 1999, ten states had implemented about fifty boot camps, which housed about 4,500 juvenile offenders nationwide. The oldest program was established in Orleans Parish, Louisiana, in 1985. Three of the newer programs—located in Cleveland, Denver, and Mobile—are funded through the Office of Juvenile Justice and Delinquency Prevention, which launched a three-site study of boot camps for youthful offenders in 1991.

The guidelines of these three experimental programs identified six key components to maximize their effectiveness: education, job training and placement, community service, substance abuse counseling and treatment, health and mental health care, individualized and continuous case management, and intensive aftercare services. A 1994 evaluation of the three sites found that they were unable to implement the program guidelines fully. Each program "experienced considerable instability and staff turnover" and was unable to "implement and sustain stable, well-developed aftercare services."[45]

Boot camps for juveniles include some type of work detail; most allocate more than half the day to educational and counseling activities, and most also include some form of drug and alcohol counseling. In addition, most boot camp programs assign graduates to a period of intensive community supervision.[46]

A fair assessment may be that the quality of boot camps depends largely on how much they tailor their programs to participants' maturity levels and how effective they are in implementing and sustaining effective aftercare services. In 2000, Doris McKenzie and colleagues completed a study of twenty-six juvenile boot camps, comparing them with traditional facilities (the experiences of 2,668 juveniles in twenty-six boot camps were compared to those of 1,848 juveniles in twenty-two traditional facilities).[47] They found that overall, juveniles in boot camps perceived their environments as more positive or therapeutic, less hostile or dangerous, and more structured than juveniles in traditional facilities perceived their environments. Moreover, this study revealed that over time, youths in boot camps became less antisocial and less depressed than youths in traditional facilities.[48]

Other follow-ups on juvenile boot camps have almost all found recidivism rates of boot camps to be slightly higher or about the same as those of traditional juvenile facilities.[49] Charges of abuse in boot camps have been made in Arizona, Maryland, South Dakota, and Georgia. In the summer of 1999, a fourteen-year-old girl in South Dakota died from dehydration during a long-distance run.[50] On July 1, 2001, Anthony Haynes, a fourteen-year-old boy from Arizona, died at a boot camp where troubled juveniles were allegedly kicked and forced to eat mud. In this camp, the reg-

Web LIBRARY 16.6

Read the NIJ Publication *National Study Comparing the Environments of Boot Camps with Traditional Facilities for Juvenile Offenders* at **www.justicestudies.com/ WebLibrary**.

Web PLACES 16.4

Visit the National Juvenile Detention Association's website via **www .justicestudies.com/ WebPlaces**.

Residents do early-morning physical training at the Summit Shock Camp in Schoharie, New York. The facility, a military-style boot camp for first-time juvenile offenders who have been convicted of felonies, is supposed to shock residents into conforming their behavior to the requirements of the law. ■ **How successful have such programs been?**

imen includes forced marches, in-your-face discipline, and a daily diet of an apple, a carrot, and a bowl of beans.[51]

The combined disappointing recidivism results, as well as the charges of abuse, have prompted Georgia, Maryland, Arizona, and South Dakota to shut down or reevaluate the get-tough-with-juveniles approach popularized in the early 1990s. Arizona removed fifty juveniles from the boot camp in which Haynes died. Maryland shut down one boot camp and suspended the military regimens at its other two facilities after reports of systematic assaults. In Maryland, the charges of abuse led to the ouster of the state's top five juvenile justice officials.[52]

" Gangs dominate daily life in bulging dormitories, in crowded cafeterias, and on the recreational fields. "

Panaceas die hard in juvenile corrections, and this highly acclaimed approach of the 1980s and 1990s will continue to be used across the nation. However, criticisms of boot camps and disappointing recidivism data probably will result in fewer new programs being established and in greater scrutiny of existing programs.

Public and Private Training Schools

Some training schools look like prisons. Others resemble college campuses, and still others have a homelike atmosphere. Yet, regardless of what they look like, training schools are used more today than they were in the 1970s and 1980s.

Youth gangs are becoming a serious problem in some training schools. In California Youth Authority facilities, for example, gangs dominate daily life in bulging dormitories, in crowded cafeterias, and on the recreational fields.[53] In Steve Lerner's 1986 study on violence at Preston, he concluded that "the open dorms at the Youth Authority have become so vicious with the increasingly dense overcrowding that many inmates feel they have to join a gang in order to purchase protection."[54] The gang organization that is present in the California Youth Authority is relatively absent in training schools elsewhere, but gang members are increasingly being sentenced to public training schools in other states.

L. Thomas Winfree Jr. and G. Larry Mays's 1994 study of three juvenile institutions in New Mexico revealed that up to 33 percent of those confined were gang members or had pro-gang attitudes.[55] The National Gang Crime Research Center's 1995 report on a national survey of 1,015 gang members stated that two juvenile correctional institutions in Ohio confined 268 gang youths, and a juvenile facility in Michigan confined 61 gang youths.[56] In addition, in the early 1990s the Maclaren Training School in Portland, Oregon; the Ethan Allen School in Wales, Wisconsin; and the School for Boys in Eldora, Iowa, found it necessary to develop treatment programs for their increasingly expanding numbers of gang members.[57]

M. A. Bortner and Linda M. Williams's 1997 study of "Unit Four" reveals the promise and the reality of what took place in a "model" juvenile training school program in Arizona. Created because of a class action suit against Arizona's juvenile correction system, this model program generated much excitement; but it failed, partly because of the presence of gang youth who were involved in the program over the period of its evaluation.[58]

The larger states, such as California, Illinois, Michigan, and New York, have several training schools each.[59] Smaller states commonly have one training school for boys and another for girls. Massachusetts and Vermont have no training schools. Coeducational institutions gained some acceptance in the 1970s, when several states opened one or more coeducational campuses, but that trend seems to have passed.

The physical structure of training schools ranges from the homelike atmosphere of small cottages, to open dormitories that provide little privacy, to fortresslike facilities that have individual cells and fences. The level of security is usually higher for public than for private facilities, because a larger proportion of the public facilities are detention centers designed to control residents' movement through staff monitoring and physical restrictions, such as fences.[60]

Web LIBRARY 16.7

Read the NIJ Research in Brief *Resources for Juvenile Detention Reform* at **www.justicestudies .com/WebLibrary**.

DELINQUENCY in America 16.1

Dismal California Prisons Hold Juvenile Offenders

WHITTIER, Calif.—The mission of the California Youth Authority, which runs the state's 10 juvenile prisons, housing 4,600 inmates, is to educate and rehabilitate offenders sentenced by juvenile courts. But state officials and outside experts brought in to study the system say it fails in its most basic tasks, because of antiquated facilities, undertrained employees and violence endemic within the walls.

Youths with psychological problems are ignored or overmedicated, classes are arbitrarily canceled, and inmates or whole institutions are locked down for days or weeks at a time because of recurring gang violence, according to the independent experts, retained by the state after it was sued two years ago in a class action brought on inmates' behalf.

Two wards committed suicide at one prison last month, and dozens more try to kill themselves every year, officials and parents of wards say. Conditions in many of the institutions were described by the experts as "deplorable," with blood, mucus and dried feces on the walls of many high-security cells.

Youths in solitary confinement are often fed what officials call "blender meals," in which a bologna sandwich, an apple and milk are pulverized and fed to the inmate by straw through a slit in the cell door.

The system's mental health programs are in "complete disarray," the experts found.

"The vast majority of youths who have mental health needs," one report said, "are made worse instead of improved by the correctional environment."

There are more than 4,000 serious assaults by wards on other wards each year throughout the California juvenile prison system, an average of more than 10 a day, according to Dr. Barry Krisberg, a nationally recognized criminologist who was among the experts reviewing the Youth Authority.

"These levels of ward-on-ward and ward-on-staff assaults are unprecedented in juvenile corrections across the nation," Dr. Krisberg wrote in a damning report released this month.

He said corrections leaders elsewhere were "astounded" to hear of the prevalence of violence in California juvenile prisons. Guards instigate fights among wards, he found, and fail to protect those who are singled out for rapes or beatings by other inmates.

"It is abundantly clear from a range of data that I collected as part of this review," Dr. Krisberg wrote, "that the Youth Authority is a very dangerous place and that neither staff nor wards feel safe in its facilities."

He also noted that California was the only state that used small cages, known as secure program areas, or SPAs, to isolate prisoners from one another and from members of the staff during instruction or counseling, a practice one prison pastor called "demonic."

State officials newly appointed to run the Youth Authority do not dispute most of the findings. They have promised quick action to remedy them, starting with the elimination of the security cages, which are in use in several of the juvenile prisons.

State Senator Gloria Romero, a Democrat who heads a special legislative committee overseeing the state's adult and juvenile prison networks, called conditions in the Youth Authority "barbaric" and "inhumane."

Senator Romero said that while the latest accounts were shocking, there was

Programs and Services   The programs that public and private training schools offer are superior to those of other juvenile institutions. The medical and dental services that residents receive tend to be very good. Most larger training schools have a full-time nurse on duty during the day and a physician who visits one or more days a week. Although institutionalized delinquents frequently complain about the medical and dental care they receive, most youths still receive far better care than they did before they were confined.

According to research that one of the authors has conducted in six states, the educational program is usually accredited by the state and is able to grant high school diplomas. The majority of training schools also offer classes to prepare residents for the general educational development (GED) high school equivalency certificate examinations. College preparation classes are sometimes provided in some training schools, but this seems to have been more true in the past than at present. Additionally, basic skills education classes are usually available in reading, writing, and mathematics, and special education and literacy or remedial reading are also provided in most training schools. Classes tend to be small, and students are permitted to progress at a rate that fits their needs.[61]

The vocational training provided by training schools usually depends on the size of the school. Larger training schools for boys may offer courses such as computer repair; auto shop/engine repair; small appliance repair; carpentry/building trades; printing, electrical, and welding trades; and forestry/agriculture. Schools for girls may offer courses in cosmetology, computer training, secretarial trades, and food services.

little new in them. She said that investigations and lawsuits over the last decade had uncovered similar abuses and that little had been done beyond hiring more guards and pouring vast sums of money into the system. The state now spends $115,000 a year on each imprisoned young offender, . . . and yet recidivism approaches 90 percent. "On all counts," she said of the system, "it's been a failure."

Karapet Darakchyan, an 18-year-old car thief, has been in the juvenile prison system for three years. For more than four months—he has not counted the days—he has been confined to the high-security lockup at the Fred C. Nelles Youth Correctional Facility here in Whittier, a result of an assault on a guard last fall.

Mr. Darakchyan, a former member of the notorious White Fence gang in East Los Angeles and a young man with an admitted "anger problem," spends 23 hours a day in a 4-by-8-foot cell. Other than for showers, he leaves the cell only to receive instruction or counseling, during which he is confined inside a steel mesh cage barely big enough to stand or turn around in.

Mr. Darakchyan, who was led from his cell in handcuffs for a brief interview, offered no specific complaints about his treatment at Nelles. "It's not a good place to be," he said matter-of-factly. "It's a jail. You've got to deal with it."

Asked whether he was receiving any useful treatment or training, he just shook his head.

The crisis in the Youth Authority, and similar problems in the vastly larger adult prison system, pose serious managerial and political challenges for Gov. Arnold Schwarzenegger. He has said he is "gravely concerned" about the California prison system, which costs $6 billion a year, and has already replaced the directors of youth and adult corrections. He has also proposed reductions in spending on prisons and wants to revamp the parole system to reduce the prison population, which now exceeds 160,000.

Mr. Schwarzenegger has vowed to renegotiate a contract that provides large raises over the next three years for prison guards. The guards' union, the California Correctional Peace Officers Association, which negotiated that contract with the governor's predecessor, Gray Davis, has been a heavy contributor to political campaigns and until now considered politically untouchable.

Walter Allen III, the new director of the Youth Authority, said that the reports so critical of the system were "substantially correct" and that he had ordered his staff to prepare remedies and a timetable for achieving them. He also said he had retained Dr. Krisberg to advise him and would work to set-

tle the class-action lawsuit against his agency.

Laura Talkington of Fresno, whose 19-year-old son, David, has been held in Youth Authority prisons since he was convicted of arson four years ago, makes no excuses for his crime. But she is furious at the state for the treatment he has received, which has included beatings by the staff and fellow inmates. Attention deficit disorder has been diagnosed, she said, but he has received no treatment for it, or remedial education.

"There is no rehabilitation," Mrs. Talkington said. "There is only punishment and a lot of abuse."

Sara Norman, a staff lawyer with the Prison Law Office, one of the groups that brought the suit against the Youth Authority, said inmate advocates were seeking the appointment of a special master to ensure a top-to-bottom overhaul of juvenile corrections in California.

"The system is completely out of control," she said. "We don't want another blue-ribbon commission. The panel of experts' findings are right there. The system needs to be fixed now."

Source: Adapted from John M. Broder, "Dismal California Prisons Hold Juvenile Offenders," *New York Times,* February 15, 2004. Copyright © 2004 by The New York Times Co. Reprinted with permission.

Generally speaking, vocational training is often not helpful in finding employment. Some released residents have difficulty being admitted to labor unions, and some may not come away with a sufficient skill set. Nonetheless, a few residents do leave the institution and find excellent jobs with the skills they have acquired.[62]

The rehabilitation of juvenile delinquents remains the avowed purpose of most training schools. In the twentieth century, seemingly every conceivable method was used in the effort to rehabilitate residents so they would refrain from unlawful behavior. The treatment technologies that are still in use include classification systems, treatment modalities, skill development, and prerelease programs. The most widely used treatment modalities are transactional analysis, reality therapy, psychotherapy, behavior modification, guided group interaction, positive peer culture, and drug and alcohol treatment. Rational therapy, sometimes called the "errors-in-thinking modality" or Cognitive Thinking Skills Program (CTSP), is a relatively recent treatment modality in juvenile corrections that has been implemented in a number of private and public training schools across the nation.

> " The rehabilitation of juvenile delinquents remains the avowed purpose of most training schools. "

In their 2000 meta-analysis of eighty-three studies on interventions with institutionalized offenders, Mark W. Lipsey, David B. Wilson, and Lynn Cothern, found that seventy-four involved youthful offenders in the custody of juvenile justice institutions and nine involved residential institutions that were administered by mental health or private agencies. All juveniles in these placements had committed serious delinquencies

TABLE 16.1

A Comparison of Treatment Types in Order of Effectiveness

NONINSTITUTIONALIZED OFFENDER TREATMENTS	INSTITUTIONALIZED OFFENDER TREATMENTS
Positive effects, consistent evidence	
Individual counseling	Interpersonal skills
Interpersonal skills	Teaching family homes
Behavioral programs	
Positive effects, less consistent evidence	
Multiple services	Behavioral programs
Restitution, probation/parole	Community residential
	Multiple services
Mixed but generally positive effects, inconsistent evidence	
Employment-related training	Individual counseling
Academic programs	Guided group counseling
Advocacy/casework	Group counseling
Family counseling	
Group counseling	
Weak or no effects, inconsistent evidence	
Reduced caseload, probation/parole	Employment-related training
	Drug abstinence
	Wilderness/challenge
Weak or no effects, consistent evidence	
Wilderness/challenge	Milieu therapy
Early release, probation/parole	
Deterrence programs	
Vocational programs	

Source: Mark W. Lipsey et al., *Effective Intervention for Serious Juvenile Offenders* (Washington, D.C.: Office of Juvenile Justice and Delinquency Prevention, 2000), p. 5. Reprinted with permission from the U.S. Department of Justice.

that warranted confinement or close supervision in an institutional setting.[63] Table 16.1 compares treatment types in order of effectiveness with both noninstitutionalized and institutionalized offenders.

One of the serious shortcomings of programming in many training schools is the lack of attention given to the needs of the adjudicated female offenders. The 1992 Amendment to the 1974 Juvenile Justice and Delinquency Prevention Act addressed the issue of gender bias, requiring states to analyze the need, types, and delivery of gender-specific services. As an example of gender bias treatment, a comparative study of 348 violent juvenile females and a similar number of males reported in 1992 that half the males were admitted to rehabilitative or alternative programs, but only 29.5 percent of females received treatment in any form.[64]

Recreation has always been emphasized in training schools. Male residents are usually offered such competitive sports as softball, volleyball, flag football, basketball, and sometimes even boxing or wrestling. Cottages may compete against each other, and the institution may have a team that competes against other institutional teams. Other popular recreational activities include attending weekly movies; building model cars; participating in talent shows, dramatics, and choir; decorating the cottage during holidays; and playing Ping-Pong, pool, and chess. Some training schools offer sailing or canoeing for residents, some have swimming pools, and some sponsor dances with residents of nearby training schools.

Religious instruction and services are always provided in state training schools. A full-time Protestant chaplain and a part-time Roman Catholic chaplain are available in most schools. Unlike adult prisons, Muslims, Buddhists, Native Americans, or Jewish religious leaders generally are not available. Religious services that are offered include Sunday Mass and morning worship, confession, baptism, instruction for church membership, choir, and religious counseling. Usually few residents respond to these religious services—unless attendance is compulsory, and then residents respond with considerable resistance.

The punishment of misbehaving residents varies from school to school. Fortunately, blatant staff brutality has disappeared from most schools. Adult correctional systems have had enough problems with the federal courts that state governments do not want confinement conditions in their juvenile institutions to be declared unconstitutional. The amount of time residents spend in solitary confinement, or maximum isolation, is also generally less than it was in the 1980s. The use of force and mechanical restraints in training schools increased in the 1990s. Training schools began to use handcuffs, anklets, security belts, four-point ties, and straitjackets.[65] Increasing numbers of staff seemed to believe that restraints are needed to control residents.[66] The danger is that improperly applied mechanical restraints that are applied for excessively long periods of time can result in serious physical injury or emotional trauma to a juvenile.

Evaluation of Private versus Public Training Schools   One of the debates that has raged for years concerns the comparison of private and public training schools. Privately administered training schools are usually better known to the public than are state institutions, because private institutions' soliciting of funds has kept them in the public eye. Proponents of private institutions claim that they are more effective than public training schools; they have a limited intake policy, which allows them to choose whom they want to admit, and they can be more flexible and innovative.

A real problem of evaluating **private juvenile placements** is that few studies have examined the accuracy of these claims or the effects of institutional life on residents. Peter W. Greenwood, Susan Turner, and Kathy Rosenblatt's 1989 evaluation of the Paint Creek Youth Center (PCYC) in southern Ohio is probably the most positive evaluation of a private institutional placement for juveniles.[67] Their evaluation claimed that this program is different from the traditional training school because it is small (thirty-three beds); because it features a comprehensive and integrated therapeutic approach that emphasizes accountability, social learning, and positive peer culture; and because it has been able to implement family therapy and intensive aftercare services.[68]

Examining a group of youths who supposedly were randomly assigned to PCYC; to Training Institution, Central Ohio (TICO); or to other Department of Youth Services (DYS) institutions, Greenwood and colleagues found that the experimentals (those who had been assigned to PCYC) were less likely to have been recommitted to a correctional institution on new charges than were the controls (who had been assigned to TICO and other DYS facilities).[69]

Glen Mills is an impressive private residential school for court-adjudicated male delinquents between fifteen and eighteen years of age. Founded in 1826 as the Philadelphia House of Refuge, Glen Mills has provided services continuously for more than 175 years. Situated on nearly 800 acres in Delaware County, Pennsylvania, it has been at its present location for over 100 years. Exhibit 16.4 describes the programs and facilities of Glen Mills.

David Shichor and Clemens Bartollas's 1990 examination of the patterns of public and private juvenile placements in one of the larger probation departments in southern California revealed that relatively few differences were apparent between juveniles who were sent to private and public placements. Although youths who were placed in private facilities had more personal problems and those in public institutions appeared to be somewhat more delinquent, the two populations did not vary markedly. Several other claims made by advocates of private placements also were

private juvenile placements
Training schools that operate under private auspices; the county or state generally pays the school a per diem rate for the care of youths committed to these facilities.

Exhibit 16.4

Glen Mills School

Glen Mills, located near Philadelphia, provides services to more than 1,000 students. In the impressive facilities of this training school, students have access to fifteen different vocations, contemporary educational amenities, and five state-of-the-art athletic facilities. There is also a library, a learning center, a computer lab, and a biology lab. The class of 1999 demonstrates the quality of the school's education program: 75 students earned a Glen Mills High School diploma; 294 earned a G.E.D.; 235 took the ACT exam (with 155 scoring above 17 and 91 scoring 20 or above); and 70 enrolled in college.

Athletic programs at Glen Mills include JV football, varsity football, cross-country, golf, soccer, basketball, wrestling, indoor and outdoor track, swimming, bowling, baseball, volleyball, tennis, and lacrosse. Facilities used for these sports consist of a natatorium, Hayes Recreation Center, Harrison Gymnasium, a campus field house, and a stadium locker room and weight room.

Staff widely uses the confrontation process at Glen Mills, both in and outside of the guided group interaction (GGI) treatment groups. Yet physical and emotional abuse of residents is not permitted by either staff members or other residents. In a book-length evaluation of Glen Mills, the authors conclude by saying:

Glen Mills is a world apart. . . . Where undeveloped potential flourishes in the rich soil of staff encouragement, competent and individualized instruction, varied programs, excellent facilities, and positive peer pressure. Where status and self-esteem can never be secured in service to Aggression and Manipulation, the twin gods of the delinquent subculture, but rather are built with every step, however modest, toward self-improvement. Where students take pride in and accept responsibility for themselves and the community. Where boredom yields to a full daily schedule of educational and recreational activities rather than to that staple of the institutional environment, the television set. Where staff and students regard one another as allies. Where all are entitled to the basics of respect, safety, good food, and clean living quarters, and no reward is beyond the reach of a student willing to invest talents he possesses on his own and his peers' behalf.

But at the same time that staff give students respect and expect students to accept responsibility for themselves and not to harm each other, staff "take no nonsense" from students. In spite of the sizable number of students, staff are definitely in control. Cosimo D. (Sam) Ferrainola has served as executive director of the school since 1975.

> ■ **How does Glen Mills seem to be different from most training schools? What are the dangers of a confrontational approach? Do you believe it is possible to overcome the negative effects of the delinquent peer culture? Would you like to work in such an institution?**

Sources: Interviews with Glen Mills Schools staff in 2001; the pamphlet, "Glen Mills Schools: Service to Youth Since 1826"; and Grant R. Grissom and William L. Dubnov, *Locks and Bars: Reforming Our Reform Schools* (Westport, Conn.: Praeger, 1989), p. 212.

---

not documented by this study, especially the claims that private placements provide more professional and treatment services to juveniles than do public placements and that private placements have lower staff/client ratios than do public placements. Furthermore, this study found that hard-core delinquents in private placements were not separated from those who had committed more minor offenses.[70]

A fair assessment of private placements is that, with some glaring exceptions, private training schools are usually more flexible and innovative than state facilities. The smaller size of private training schools is somewhat balanced by the fact that one-half of them still house 100 or more residents, numbers that are too large for effective work with institutionalized juveniles. Perhaps the old adage is right after all: The best institutions are private ones, and the worst juvenile institutional placements are also private ones.

Training School Life

residential social system
The social hierarchy that is established by residents in an institution.

The nature of the **residential social system** (the social hierarchy established by inmates) is an important factor in the quality of life in a training school. The many empirical studies on the residential social system have consistently challenged the efficacy of juvenile institutionalization. Too many of these studies present a frightening picture of what a juvenile experiences during confinement. These studies also have found that there are more similarities than differences in residential life in single-sex and coeducational institutions.

The Glen Mills School, which has been at its present location in Concordville, Pennsylvania, for over 100 years, is the oldest existing residential school for court-adjudicated male delinquents in the country. ■ **Why aren't there more facilities like Glen Mills?**

Training Schools for Boys

With few exceptions, studies of training schools for boys reflect an inmate society in which the strong take advantage of the weak. In their 1959 study of the State Industrial School for Boys in Golden, Colorado, Gordon E. Barker and W. Thomas Adams found two types of residential leaders: One held power through brute force and the other ruled through charisma. According to these researchers, residents were involved in an unending battle for dominance and control.[71]

"With few exceptions, studies of training schools for boys reflect an inmate society in which the strong take advantage of the weak."

In the early 1960s, Howard W. Polsky studied a cottage in a residential treatment center in New York supported by the Jewish Board of Guardians and devoted to individual psychoanalytic treatment of emotionally disturbed children. The staff in Cottage 6 were unable to keep residential leaders from exploiting peers. The social hierarchy the researchers identified in this cottage had the following pecking order: leaders, their associates, "con artists," "quiet types," "busboys," and "scapegoats." The tougher the youth, the higher he ranked in the social order. Polsky also found that boys in higher classes in the hierarchy used ranking, scapegoating, aggression, "threat-gestures," and deviant skills and activities to keep lower-status boys in place. Those at the bottom of the status hierarchy found life so debilitating that most of them ended up in mental hospitals.[72]

Sethard Fisher, who studied a small training school in California, identified victimization and patronage as two of the major behaviors taking place. He defined *victimization* as "a predatory practice whereby inmates of superior strength and knowledge of inmate lore prey on weaker and less knowledgeable inmates."[73] *Patronage* referred to youths' building "protective and ingratiating relationships with others more advantageously situated on the prestige ladder." Fisher also saw victimization as being made up of physical attack, agitation, and exploitation; *agitation* was a form of verbal harassment, and *exploitation* was "a process whereby an inmate will attempt to coerce another by means of threat and duress."[74]

Clemens Bartollas, Stuart J. Miller, and Simon Dinitz's *Juvenile Victimization: The Institutional Paradox,* published in 1976, examined the culture that end-of-the-line delinquents established in a maximum-security institution in Columbus, Ohio (TICO). In this "jungle"—as residents frequently called the training school—dominant youths exploited submissive ones in every way possible. Ninety percent of the 150 residents were involved in this exploitation matrix; 19 percent were exploiters who were never themselves exploited, 34 percent were exploiters and victims at different times, 21 percent were occasionally victims and never exploiters, 17 percent were chronic victims, and 10 percent were neither victims nor exploiters.[75]

Bartollas and colleagues drew this conclusion about the lawless environment of this training school:

> The training school receives the worst of the labeled—the losers, the unwanted, the outsiders. These young men consider themselves to be among the toughest, most masculine and virile of their counterparts and they have the societal credentials to prove it. Yet, in much the same way that they themselves are processed, they create, import, and maintain a system which is as brutalizing as the one through which they passed. If anything, the internal environment and the organization and the interaction at TICO are less fair, less just, less humane, and less decent than the worst aspects of the criminal justice system on the outside. Brute force, manipulation, and institutional sophistication carry the day, and set the standards which ultimately prevail. Remove the staff, and a feudal structure will emerge which will make the dark ages seem very enlightened.[76]

In a fifteen-year follow-up evaluation of this training school, Miller, Bartollas, and Dinitz found that the negative youth culture described in the 1976 study still thrived and that the strong still victimized the weak. Staff members were more disillusioned than they were at the time of the first study. They also were more fearful of victimization from residents.[77]

Training Schools for Girls and Coeducational Institutions

Until 1960, studies about confined juvenile girls were as numerous as those about incarcerated adult females. The early studies found that girls in training school became involved in varying degrees of lesbian alliances and pseudo-family relationships. Since 1970, only two major studies have been done on the female's adjustment to training school: Rose Giallombardo's *The Social World of Imprisoned Girls* and Alice Propper's *Prison Homosexuality: Myth and Reality.*[78]

Giallombardo examined three **training schools for girls** in various parts of the United States and found that a kinship system existed, with some variation, in each of the training schools. Pseudo-family membership organization was pervasive in all three institutions, whether called the "racket," the "sillies," or "chick business." It embraced 84 percent of the girls at the eastern institution, 83 percent at the central, and 94 percent at the western. Some of the social roles identified were "true butches," "true fems," "trust-to-be butches," "trust-to-be fems," "jive time butches," "jive time fems," "straights," "squealers," "pimps," "foxes," "cops," and "popcorns."[79]

The "parents," the leaders of these families, had considerable authority vested in their role. One resident explained the deference to the "parents": "The mother and the father—they're the ones that have the say. If they say, 'Don't go to school,' you say you have cramps, a backache, a stomachache, anything, but you don't go."[80]

Propper's *Prison Homosexuality* examined three coeducational and four girls' training schools scattered through the East, Midwest, and South, of which five were public and two were private Catholic training schools. Residents reported homosexual behavior involving from 6 to 29 percent of the inmates in the various institutions. Propper found that the best indicator of homosexual participation during a juvenile's present term of institutionalization was previous homosexuality. Only 12 percent of those who had never had a homosexual experience before entering the institution admitted engaging in homosexuality, compared with 71 percent of those with previous

training school for girls

Correctional facility for long-term placement of adjudicated female juvenile delinquents.

homosexual experience. In contrast to previously held assumptions, Propper found very little overlap between pseudo-family roles and homosexual behavior. Participation in homosexuality and make-believe families was just as prevalent in co-educational as in single-sex institutions, and homosexuality was as prevalent in treatment-oriented as in custody-oriented facilities. She also reported that residents sometimes continued homosexual experiences when they were released, even when their first experience was as the unhappy victim of a homosexual rape.[81]

Christopher M. Sieverdes and Bartollas's study of six coeducational institutions in a southeastern state drew the following conclusions: Females adhered more strongly to inmate groups and peer relationships than did males; felt more victimized by peers than did males; did not harass or manipulate staff as much as males did; and were more satisfied with institutional life than were males.[82] Unlike Propper's study, these researchers found that pseudo-families existed among girls, but they were based much less on homosexual alliances than were those in all-girls training schools.[83] Status offenders, who made up 70 percent of the girls and 30 percent of the boys, were the worst victims in these training schools and had the most difficulty adjusting to institutional life.[84] White males and females experienced high rates of personal intimidation and victimization by African American and American Indian youths.[85]

The Rights of Confined Juveniles

The rights of institutionalized juveniles have been examined by the federal courts and addressed in the Civil Rights of Institutionalized Persons Act (CRIPA). CRIPA gives the Civil Rights Division of the U.S. Department of Justice (DOJ) the power to bring actions against state or local governments for violating the civil rights of institutionalized persons.

The Courts

The courts long paid less attention to juvenile institutions than to adult prisons, because juvenile facilities were assumed to be more humane and to infringe less on the constitutional rights of offenders. Yet deteriorating conditions in juvenile correctional facilities, including overcrowded living conditions, frequent assaults among residents and against staff, and the growing presence of gang youths, led to a wave of litigation in the latter decades of the twentieth century. The courts have mandated two major rights: the right to treatment and the right to be free from cruel and unusual punishment.

Right to Treatment   Several court decisions have held that a juvenile has a **right to treatment** when he or she is committed to a juvenile institution. The *White v. Reid* (1954) decision held that juveniles could not be kept in facilities that did not provide for their rehabilitation.[86] The *Inmates of the Boy's Training School v. Affeck* (1972) decision also held that juveniles have a right to treatment because rehabilitation is the true purpose of the juvenile court.[87] The Indiana Seventh Circuit's decision in *Nelson v. Heyne* (1973) agreed with the district court that residents of the Indiana Boys' School had a right to rehabilitative treatment.[88]

In the *Morales v. Thurman* decision (1973), the U.S. District Court for the Eastern District of Texas issued the most extensive order ever justified by a child's right to treatment.[89] The court held that the state of Texas had to follow a number of criteria to ensure that proper treatment would be provided to confined juveniles. Among these criteria were minimum standards for assessing and testing children committed to the state; minimum standards for assessing educational skills and handicaps and for providing programs aimed at advancing a child's education; minimum standards for delivering vocational education and medical and psychiatric care; and minimum standards for providing a humane institutional environment. But the order was vacated by the Fifth Circuit Appeals Court on the grounds that a three-judge court

right to treatment
The entitlement of a juvenile who has been committed to a training school to receive any needed services (i.e., therapy, education, etc.).

should have been convened to hear the case. The U.S. Supreme Court, however, reversed the Court of Appeals and remanded the case. The order of the District Court has withstood the assault against it and ultimately prevailed.[90]

Right to Be Free from Cruel and Unusual Punishment   Considerable case law has also been established ensuring confined juveniles the right to be free from **cruel and unusual punishment**. The *Pena v. New York State Division for Youth* decision (1976) held that the use of isolation, hand restraints, and tranquilizing drugs at Goshen Annex Center was punitive and antitherapeutic and therefore violated the Fourteenth Amendment right to treatment and the Eighth Amendment right to protection against cruel and unusual punishment.[91] The Court in *Inmates of the Boys' Training School* condemned such practices as solitary confinement and strip cells, and the lack of educational opportunities, and established a number of minimum standards for youths who were confined at the training school.[92]

In *Morales,* the court found numerous instances of physical brutality and abuse, including hazing by staff and inmates, staff-administered beatings and tear gassings, homosexual attacks, extensive use of solitary confinement, and minimal clinical services.[93] In *Morgan v. Sproat* (1977), the court found youths confined in padded cells with no windows or furnishings and only flush holes for toilets, and denied access to all services or programs except a Bible.[94] In *State v. Werner* (1978), the court found that residents were locked in solitary confinement, beaten, kicked, slapped, and sprayed with mace by staff members; required to scrub floors with a toothbrush; and subjected to such punishments as standing and sitting for prolonged periods without changing position.[95] Federal courts have also held that extended periods of solitary confinement and the use of Thorazine and other medications for the purpose of control represent cruel and unusual punishment.[96] In a 1995 case, *Alexander v. Boyd and South Carolina Department of Juvenile Justice,* the district court ruled that the use of gas in three training schools to punish juveniles for disciplinary infractions violated the juveniles' due process rights. In its decision, the court noted that the use of gas irritates the mucous membranes of those who are exposed to it and causes instant pain and spasms in the eyelids, breathing problems, and coughing fits.[97]

Access to the Courts[98]   In *Morgan,* the Federal District Court for the Southern District of Mississippi held that juveniles committed to training schools have a constitutional right of access to the courts.[99] In *Germany v. Vance* (1989), the first Circuit Court of Appeals held that the stigma of violating the law, being arrested, and being incarcerated is similar for juveniles and adults and therefore juveniles have a constitutional right to court access like that enjoyed by adults.[100] Finally, in *John L. v. Adams* (1992), the Sixth Circuit Court of Appeals held that juveniles have a constitutional right of access to the courts, finding that, for purposes of access, no substantial legal differences could be found between an incarcerated juvenile and an incarcerated adult.[101]

CRIPA and Juvenile Correctional Facilities

Through November 1997, the Civil Rights Division had investigated 300 institutions under CRIPA. Seventy-three of these institutions, or about 25 percent, were juvenile detention and correctional facilities. The Civil Rights Division was monitoring conditions in thirty-four juvenile correctional facilities through consent decrees in Kentucky, New Jersey, and Puerto Rico. The consent decree filed in Kentucky included all thirteen juvenile facilities in the state; the decree in New Jersey was with one facility, and the decree in Puerto Rico with twenty facilities.[102]

The decree in Kentucky requires the state "to take a number of steps to protect juveniles from abuse, mistreatment, and injury; to ensure adequate medical and mental health care; and to provide adequate educational, vocational, and aftercare services."[103] The consent degree in Puerto Rico addressed life-threatening conditions

---

cruel and unusual punishment

A guarantee provided by the Eighth Amendment to the U.S. Constitution against inhumane punishments. Accordingly, juveniles in correctional custody must not be treated with unnecessary harshness.

including "juveniles committing and attempting suicide without staff intervention or treatment, widespread infection control problems caused by rats and other vermin, and defective plumbing that forced juveniles to drink from their toilet bowls."[104]

Juvenile Aftercare

Release is the prime goal of a confined youth. The days, weeks, months, and sometimes years spent in confinement are occupied by thoughts and fantasies of release or even escape. The entire juvenile justice system is focused on release. Staff are responsible for guiding residents throughout their confinement. Punishment, education and vocational training, and rehabilitative techniques are used in an effort to guarantee that a resident's return to the community will be permanent and positive.

Parole, or **juvenile aftercare**, as it is usually called, is concerned with the release of a youth from an institution when he or she can best benefit from release and can make an optimal adjustment to community living. In 1994, thirty-six state agencies reported that 57,359 juveniles were released from institutional care. The average length of stay for juveniles released was 9.8 months. The recidivism rates for eighteen agencies averaged 36.5 percent (the follow-up periods used to estimate recidivism for eighteen of these nineteen agencies averaged 3.7 years).[105]

Once a youth is adjudicated to a state training school, the state normally retains jurisdiction until his or her release. The authority to make the decision about when to release a youth from training school is usually given to institutional staff, although a number of states give other agencies and boards the authority to parole juveniles. Often the cottage staff will review the progress of each youth at designated intervals, and, when the staff recommends release, the recommendation is reviewed by a board made up of staff from throughout the institution. If this board concurs, the recommendation must be approved by an institutional coordinator at the youth authority or youth commission.

Cottage staffs usually consider several factors in recommending a youth for release. The juvenile's overall institutional adjustment—including performance in school, participation in recreation, and relationships with peers in the cottage—is reviewed. The youth's attitude is also evaluated; personality conflicts with staff, especially those in the cottage, will usually be interpreted as the result of a poor attitude. The probability of community success is considered: A youth's willingness and ability to set realistic goals are frequently seen as evidence of readiness to return to the community. Finally, reports on the juvenile's performance on the cottage work detail and on personal hygiene generally must be positive before the staff will recommend release.

juvenile aftercare
The supervision of juveniles who are released from correctional institutions so that they can make an optimal adjustment to community living.

The Administration and Operation of Aftercare Services

Aftercare is the responsibility of the state and is administered by the executive branch in forty-four states. In four states, aftercare is under the organization of the probation department and is administered by probation officers. In three states, other means of organizing and administering aftercare are used.[106]

Early release from training school because of overcrowded conditions has complicated the decision-making process for institutional release. In six states, a parole board appointed by the governor considers early release for institutionalized juveniles.[107] Michael D. Norman's study of the Utah Youth Parole Authority found that the early-release criteria were primarily related to institutional behavior, rather than prospects for successful reintegration into the community.[108]

The Nokomis Challenge Program was launched by the Michigan Department of Social Services in 1989. It combines three months of residential and wilderness experience in a remote wilderness camp with nine months of intensive community-based aftercare. It is designed for low- and medium-risk youths convicted of a felony offense who would otherwise be given a fourteen- to sixteen-month placement in a residential facility. The basic focus of the Nokomis program is on relapse prevention. A 1996 evaluation found, however, that only about 40 percent of the youths in this study successfully completed the twelve-month program. This evaluation also revealed "that the Nokomis youth failed at a faster rate than graduates of regular residential programs, in spite of the fact that they were receiving intensive aftercare following their release."[109]

Another aftercare program that perhaps has been more successful is at the Florida Environmental Institute (FEI). This program, which is also known as "The Last Chance Ranch," targets the state's most serious and violent juvenile offenders. Located in a remote area of Florida's Everglades, FEI offers a residential phase as well as a nonresidential aftercare program. Its strong emphasis on education, hard work, social bonding, and aftercare has resulted in positive results among participants. The 30 percent recidivism rates of youths who have gone through the program are substantially less than the 50 to 70 percent rates of traditional training school programs.[110]

An **interstate compact** is sometimes initiated when a youth has no acceptable home placement within his or her own state. The institutional social worker usually contacts the appropriate agency in another state where the youth has a possible placement and submits an interstate compact for the transfer of the youth to that state after release from training school. The state of original jurisdiction retains authority over the youth and is kept advised of the juvenile's status.

The aftercare or probation officer (probation officers in many jurisdictions have aftercare youths as part of their caseloads) who is responsible for the case sometimes corresponds with or may even visit the institutionalized youth in training school. In many states, a youth cannot be released until the aftercare officer approves the home placement plan submitted by the institutional home worker. This usually involves a visit to the home by the officer to make certain that the home is a good placement. At other times, the aftercare officer must locate an alternate placement, such as a foster home, group home, or **halfway house.**

Part of the problem in juvenile aftercare is that youthful offenders usually are sent back to the same communities (and same families) and exposed again to the same problems they could not handle earlier. Most of their friends are still around, and it is not long before a friend suggests that they commit another crime. If the returnee is determined, he or she may be able to say, "Hey, get out of my face; I don't want to hear that business." But if the young person cannot find a job—and jobs are scarce for delinquent youths, who frequently are school dropouts—or feels under financial pressure, it becomes harder and harder not to return to crime.

Most youths on aftercare status are placed on supervision in the community for a year or more after release. The aftercare officer, who is expected to monitor the behavior of youths under supervision, provides each youth with a list of rules. These rules usually resemble those given to adult parolees and pertain to such matters as obeying parents, maintaining a satisfactory adjustment at school or at work, being home at a certain time every night, avoiding contact with other delinquents, avoiding the use or possession of any narcotic, and reporting to the aftercare officer as requested.

Risk Control and Crime Reduction

The current emphasis in aftercare is on short-term behavior control. The Office of Juvenile Justice and Delinquency Prevention has developed an intensive aftercare program that incorporates the principles of preparing youths for release to the community, facilitating youth–community interaction and involvement, and monitoring youths' reintegration into the community.[111]

Similar to juvenile probation, intensive supervision programs are being increasingly used. As of 1992, there were over eighty aftercare intensive supervision programs in the United States.[112] The intensive program in thirty counties in Pennsylvania and

interstate compact
Procedures for transferring a youth on probation or aftercare/parole from one state to another.

halfway house
A residential setting for adjudicated delinquents, usually those who need a period of readjustment to the community following institutional confinement.

the Violent Juvenile Offender Research and Development Programs in Boston, Detroit, Memphis, and Newark have been particularly noteworthy. New York has also developed an intensive supervision program for juveniles on parole.

In 1988, the Juvenile Court Judges' Commission of Pennsylvania implemented pilot intensive aftercare programs in Philadelphia and Allegheny Counties for youths who would be classified as habitually serious and violent offenders.[113] The sample in Philadelphia consisted of ninety juveniles who were released from the Bensalem Youth Development Center between December 1988 and January 1990. Placed in a caseload of no more than twelve and supervised by probation officers, about 50 percent of the juveniles assigned to intensive aftercare were rearrested, compared to 64 percent of the control subjects, with equal seriousness of new offenses for both groups.[114] By the end of 1989, thirty counties in Pennsylvania had established intensive aftercare programs.[115]

Lifeskills '95 is an intensive aftercare treatment program in California that is designed to assist high-risk and chronic juvenile offenders who are released from secure confinement.[116] The basic paradigm of this intensive aftercare program uses a series of lifestyle and life skill treatment modalities in an integrated educational approach to healthy decision making.[117] Don A. Josi and Dale K. Sechrest's 1995 study of this treatment intervention compared the parole performances of a control group and an experimental group of California Youth Authority offenders. They found that in the first ninety days those in the control group were about twice as likely as the experimental group to be unemployed, to lack the resources to gain or maintain employment, and to have been arrested.[118]

There has also been a concern to develop an integrated theoretical framework for guiding intensive supervision of chronic juvenile offenders. Based largely on combinations of social control, strain, and social learning theories, this Intensive Aftercare Program (IAP) model focuses on the reintegrative process.[119] Figure 16.7 shows the

Web LIBRARY 16.8

Read the OJJDP Juvenile Justice Bulletin *Aftercare Services* at **www.justicestudies.com/ WebLibrary**.

A fifteen-year-old juvenile in separate housing for juveniles in an Orange County, Florida, jail. The color of the teenager's ID bracelet identifies him as a maximum-security, high-risk inmate. ■ **Why should juveniles be separated from adults when confined?**

FIGURE 16.7

An Intervention Model for Juvenile Intensive Aftercare

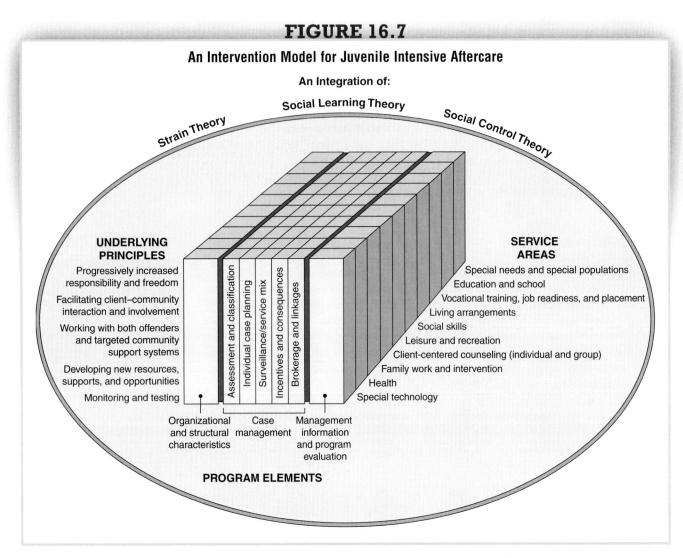

Source: David Altschuler et al., *Reintegration, Supervised Release, and Intensive Aftercare* (Washington, D.C.: Office of Juvenile Justice and Delinquency Prevention, 1999). Reprinted with permission from the U.S. Department of Justice.

program elements of this model. Underlying assumptions of this model are that chronic and serious delinquency is related to weak controls produced by social disorganization, inadequate socialization, and strain; that strain is produced by social disorganization independent of weak controls; and that peer group influences intervene as a social force between youths with weak bonds and/or strain on the one hand and delinquent behaviors on the other.[120]

This IAP model was initially implemented in Clark County (Las Vegas), Nevada; Denver, Arapaho, Douglas, and Jefferson Counties and metropolitan Denver, Colorado; Essex, Newark, and Camden Counties, New Jersey; and the city of Norfolk, Virginia. The participation of the New Jersey counties ended in 1997, but the other three programs have carried through on preparing high-risk offenders for progressively increased responsibility and freedom in the community. The well-developed transition components that begin shortly after a youth is adjudicated to an institution and continue through the early months of community adjustment are particularly striking about these programs (see Table 16.2 for these transition components). The results of the first five years of implementation (1995–2000) reveal a dramatically improved level of communication and coordination between institutional and aftercare staff as well as the ability to involve parolees in community services almost immediately after institutional release.[121]

TABLE 16.2

Transition Components of Intensive Aftercare Programming

TRANSITION COMPONENT	INTENSIVE AFTERCARE PROGRAMMING SITE		
	COLORADO	NEVADA	VIRGINIA
EARLY PAROLE PLANNING	Initial plan complete at 30 days after institutional placement: final plan complete at 60 days prior to release.	Initial plan complete at 30 days after institutional placement; final plan complete 30 days prior to furlough.	Initial plan complete 30 days after institutional placement; final plan complete 30 days prior to release.
MULTIPLE PERSPECTIVES INCORPORATED IN PLAN	Case manager, institutional staff, youth, parents and community providers all routinely involved.	Parole officer; institutional community liaison, institutional staff, and youth; parent participation limited.	Parole officer, institutional case manager, youth, interagency "Community Assessment Team," and parent.
PAROLE OFFICER VISITS TO INSTITUTION	One to two times per week; routine.	Once per month; routine since spring 1997.	One to two times per month; routine.
TREATMENT BEGUN IN INSTITUTION AND CONTINUED IN COMMUNITY	Via community providers. Includes multifamily counseling, life skills training, individual counseling, and vocational skills training; done routinely.	Via an institution–community liaison and parole officers. Includes life skills and drug/alcohol curriculums; done routinely until liaison vacancy.	Via one provider at Hanover only. Drug/alcohol treatment; sporadic use; state policy discourages contract services by community providers for institutionalized youth.
YOUTH PRE-RELEASE VISITS TO COMMUNITY	Supervised day trips to community programs, beginning 60 days prior to release.	Not allowed.	Not allowed.
PRE-PAROLE FURLOUGH	Overnight/weekend home passes, beginning 30 days prior to release.	Thirty-day conditional release to community, prior to official parole.	Not allowed.
TRANSITIONAL RESIDENCE	Not part of the design, but occurs for some youth.	Not part of the design.	Two group homes in Norfolk; 30- to 60-day length of stay; used for most youth.
TRANSITIONAL DAY PROGRAMMING	Two day-treatment programs in Denver; used for almost all youth during the first few months after release.	One day-treatment supervision/treatment program; used for most youth.	Day treatment used for youth who do not go to group homes.
PHASED SUPERVISION LEVELS ON PAROLE	Informal system: contact once per week during the first few months, down to once per month later.	Four-phase system: contact four times per week during furlough; three times per week next 90 days; two times per week next 60–90 days; once per week next 30–60 days.	Four-phase system: group home; contact five to seven times per week next 60 days; three to five times per week next 60 days; three times per week last 30 days.

Source: Richard G. Wiebush, Betsie McNulty, and Thao Le, *Implementation of the Intensive Community-Based Aftercare Program* (Washington, D.C.: Office of Juvenile Justice and Delinquency Prevention, 2000), p. 2.

Yet in-house detention and electronic monitoring programs still have not received the attention that they deserve in juvenile aftercare.[122] Juvenile aftercare also emphasizes drug and alcohol urinalyses (sometimes called "drug drops") and continues to use boot camp programs as a means of releasing juveniles early from training schools.

In both traditional and intensive aftercare, if the rules are violated or a law is broken, a youth may be returned to a training school. Although guidelines for the **revocation of aftercare** for juveniles have not been formulated by court decisions, revocation of a youth's aftercare status is no longer based solely on the testimony of the aftercare officer, who could be influenced by personality clashes or prejudice toward the client. Today, most jurisdictions have formal procedures for the revocation of aftercare. The aftercare officer may initially investigate the charge and, if the find-

revocation of aftercare
Cancellation of parole and return of the offender to an institution; takes effect if a juvenile on aftercare commits another offense or violates the conditions of parole.

DELINQUENCY International 16.1

Long-Term Juvenile Placements

An examination of juvenile institutions in other nations reveals that these facilities are of many different forms, are committed to diverse philosophies, and are situated in varying systemic structures. The major difference between juvenile institutions in the United States, where the focus is on confinement, and elsewhere is that rehabilitation continues to be the guiding force of the institutionalization of juveniles in many other societies. For example, in China, the rehabilitation of the juvenile is the responsibility of the juvenile justice system, and "the three words, 'education, persuasion, and rescue,' exemplify the overriding principle for Chinese juvenile institutions." Another example of a rehabilitative emphasis is that judges in Germany sometimes visit offenders in juvenile prisons. It is not surprising, then,

that in Germany "the stated purpose of incarceration is to educate the convicted [juvenile] to live a law-abiding and responsible life."

Yet there are far more similarities than differences among juvenile institutions in the United States and other countries. In situations analogous to the disproportionate commitment of minority youth in this nation, there is some question about whether Native American youth in Canada and aboriginal offenders in Australia are disproportionately sent to juvenile facilities. In Russia the institutional "colonies" housing juveniles who have been convicted of crimes reveal an inmate subcultural system that, as in the Ohio training school examined by Bartollas and colleagues, has a "prisonization" effect on residents.

■ Are there any reasons why rehabilitation is used more in other cultures than it is in our culture? Do you believe that there is a relationship between the reduced use of rehabilitation on serious offenders and the disproportionate commitment of minority youths?

Sources: Xin Ewn, "People's Republic of China"; Raymond R. Corrado and Alan Markwart, "Canada"; Nancy Travis Wolfe, "Germany"; John Seymour, "Australia"; and James O. Finckenauer, "Russia," in *International Handbook on Juvenile Justice*, edited by Donald J. Shoemaker (Westport, Conn.: Greenwood Press, 1996), pp. 72, 136–137, 14, 49, and 281–282.

ing is that the youth did commit the offense, will report the parole violation to the supervisor. The supervisor may review the case and make the decision, or a revocation committee may examine the violation. The aftercare officer may be required to submit a written recommendation for revocation but is not allowed to testify, and the youth is permitted to speak in self-defense.

Juveniles who end up in prison have usually been transferred to the adult court and been given a prison sentence. They soon discover that adult correctional institutions are a world apart from nearly all training schools. Prisons are much larger, some containing several thousand inmates, and can cover acres of ground. Life on the inside is typically austere, crowded, and dangerous. The violent and exploitative relationships that are found in adult correctional institutions make this disposition a hard one for juveniles. They are particularly vulnerable to sexual victimization and physical assault.[123]

Some variations on the practice of confining juveniles in adult institutions exist among the states. In some jurisdictions, judges have no alternative but to place juveniles in adult institutions if the law requires it. Judges in some states, under special circumstances, can place youths in either juvenile or adult institutions, whereas judges in some other states can refer juveniles back to juvenile court, but they are then transferred to adult institutions when they come of age.[124]

In October of 2000, Indiana stopped sending juveniles convicted of adult crimes into the general prison population. Those with lesser offenses are now held at the medium-security Plainfield Correctional Facility or at the minimum-security Medaryville Correctional Facility. But Indiana juveniles who commit violent or serious offenses are sent to Wabash Valley, a maximum-security facility.[125]

In 2002, an estimated 4,100 new court commitments involving juveniles younger than age eighteen were sent to adult state prison. Between 1985 and 2002, the annual number of new court commitments to state prisons involving juveniles younger than age eighteen increased 22 percent; new commitments overall increased 114 percent.[126]

In one recent study, Kelly Dedel Johnson, director of One in 37 Research, Inc., in Portland, Oregon, found that thirteen states permit the transfer of juveniles to adult facilities: California, Colorado, Hawaii, Indiana, Kentucky, Massachusetts, New Jersey, New York, Rhode Island, South Carolina, Texas, Washington, and Wisconsin. The court has authority to make such transfers in one-third of these states; the commitment agency has authority in one-third; and the transfer decision is a joint agreement between two authorities (e.g., agency and court or juvenile and adult agency) in one-third. The reason for such transfers include the age of the offender, seriousness of the offense, failure to benefit from the program, and poor institutional adjustment. A violent attack on a staff member by an older resident with a serious committing offense, for example, would be the type of case most likely leading to a transfer from a juvenile facility to an adult prison.[127]

CHAPTER Summary

This chapter examines juvenile corrections, including probation, community-based treatment, and institutionalization. Among the most important issues discussed in this chapter are the following:

- Today, more delinquents are treated in the community than are adjudicated to training schools, because juvenile judges remain supportive of the least-restrictive or soft-line approach for minor offenders.

- Community-based corrections includes probation, residential and day treatment programs, and aftercare.

- Clients placed on probation or in aftercare are more likely to participate in intensive supervision programs than in the past.

- Youths who have failed on probation or who have committed serious crimes are likely to be sent to a private or public juvenile correctional placement.

- Long-term juvenile institutions consist of camps, ranches, boot camps, and training schools.

- Although the proportion of juveniles who are sent to long-term facilities is small, these institutions of last resort are an integral part of society's efforts to exercise control over juveniles who break the law.

- Training schools tend to be quite expensive, but the length of time residents spend there, the programs that are offered, and the nature of the peer subcultures within them tend to vary from state to state and even from training school to training school.

- Aftercare, or parole as it is called in some states, has much in common with probation. Indeed, in some jurisdictions, the same officer is responsible for both a probation and aftercare caseload.

- Juveniles who are transferred to adult court may be sentenced to spend time in an adult prison.

CRITICAL THINKING Questions

1. What are the job responsibilities of a probation officer?
2. What are the differences between probation and aftercare services?
3. What are the main types of residential and nonresidential programs for juvenile delinquents?
4. Of the programs discussed in this chapter, which do you believe is the most effective for helping offenders reintegrate into the community?
5. What specific strategies can juvenile corrections departments pursue to enlist greater support from the community for community programs?
6. What experiences is a juvenile likely to have in each type of correctional institution discussed in this chapter?
7. Compare private and state training schools. How do they differ?
8. Evaluate the quality of life in training schools. How can it be improved?
9. How effective are community-based corrections programs? What can be done to improve the effectiveness of community-based corrections?
10. Evaluate the effectiveness of training schools. What can be done to make training schools more effective?

WEB Interactivity

Visit **www.myCJspace.com**, the website community for criminal justice professionals, students, and instructors. MyCJspace.com allows you to create your own profile, communicate with others with similar interests, check out employment options in the justice field, and search the Web for criminal justice-specific information and sites.

Create a profile on myCJspace.com describing your professional interests, and search for others with similar interests. You need not reveal your actual identity in your profile, but can choose to do so later if you decide to use the site for a job search. How might this site be useful to those seeking a career in the juvenile justice field? Submit your answer to your instructor if asked to do so.

Source: Reprinted with permission from Frank Schmalleger.

Notes

1. Patrick Griffin and Patricia Torbet, eds., *Desktop Guide to Good Juvenile Probation Practice* (Washington, D.C.: National Center for Juvenile Justice, 2002), p. 2.
2. Ibid.
3. Ibid.
4. Ibid.
5. Larry Grubb, juvenile probation officer in Sangamon County, Illinois, was extremely helpful in shaping this section on the functions of probation.
6. OJJDP Model Program Guide, *Restitution/Community Service.* www.dsgonline.com/mpg_non_flash/restitution?community?service.htm.
7. Griffin and Torbet, *Desktop Guide to Good Juvenile Probation Practice*, p. 85.
8. Ibid., pp. 85–86.
9. The results of a 1991 survey found in Peter R. Schneider and Matthew C. Finkelstein, *New Trends in Restitution Programming: Results from the 1991 RESTTA Survey* (Washington, D.C.: Office of Juvenile Justice and Delinquency Prevention, 1996).
10. Information gained during an on-site visit and updated in a phone call to a staff member in September 2001.
11. See James Byrne, ed., *Federal Probation* 50 (1986), and Emily Walker, "The Community Intensive Treatment for Youth Program: A Specialized Community-Based Program for High-Risk Youth in Alabama," *Law and Psychology Review* 13 (1989), pp. 175–199.
12. Cecil Marshall and Keith Snyder, "Intensive and Aftercare Probation Services in Pennsylvania." Paper presented to the Annual Meeting of the American Society of Criminology, Baltimore, Maryland (November 7, 1990), p. 3.
13. Ted Palmer, *The Re-Emergence of Correctional Intervention* (Newbury Park, Calif.: Sage, 1992), p. 82.
14. Barry Krisberg et al., *Juvenile Intensive Supervision Planning Guide* (Washington, D.C.: Office of Juvenile Justice and Delinquency Prevention, 1994), p. 7.
15. Richard A. Ball, Ronald Huff, and J. Robert Lilly, *House Arrest and Correctional Policy: Doing Time at Home* (Newbury Park, Calif.: Sage, 1988), pp. 35–36.
16. Griffin and Torbet, eds., *Desktop Guide to Good Juvenile Probation Practice*, p. 79.
17. TDCJ-Community Justice Assistance Division, *Electronic Monitoring: Agency Brief* (Austin: Texas Department of Criminal Justice, 1997), p. 1.
18. Joseph B. Vaughn, "A Survey of Juvenile Electronic Monitoring and Home Confinement Program," *Juvenile and Family Court Journal* 40 (1989), pp. 4, 22.
19. TDCJ-Community Justice Assistance Division, *Electronic Monitoring: Agency Brief*, p. 1.
20. Ibid.
21. Oliver J. Keller Jr. and Benedict S. Alper, *Halfway Houses: Community-Centered Correction and Treatment* (Lexington, Mass.: D. C. Heath, 1970).
22. LaMar T. Empey and Steven G. Lubeck, *The Silverlake Experiment: Testing Delinquency Theory and Community Intervention.* (Chicago: Aldine, 1971).
23. D. L. Fixsen, E. L. Phillllips, and M. M. Wolf, "The Teaching Family Model of Group Home Treatment," in *Closing Correctional Institutions*, edited by Yitzak Bakal (Lexington, Mass.: D. C. Heath, 1973).
24. Ronald H. Bailey, "Florida," *Corrections Magazine* 1 (September 1974), p. 66.

25. Information from Dynamic Action Resistance Enterprise (DARE), Jamaica Plain, Mass.

26. House of Umoja, www.volunteersolutions.org/volunteerway/org/1236595.html.

27. Information on Associated Marine Institutes supplied in a phone conversation with Ms. Magie Valdès in 1996.

28. Ibid. See also Ronald H. Bailey, "Can Delinquents Be Saved by the Sea?" *Corrections Magazine* 1 (September 1974), pp. 77–84.

29. S. E. Laurence and B. R. West, *National Evaluation of the New Pride Replication Program: Final Report,* Vol. 1 (Lafayette, Calif.: Pacific Institute for Research and Evaluation, 1985).

30. Ibid.

31. Refer to Joshua L. Miner and Joe Boldt, *Outward Bound USA: Learning through Experience* (New York: William Morrow, 1981). For other examinations of Outward Bound–type programs, see Steven Flagg Scott, "Outward Bound: An Adjunct to the Treatment of Juvenile Delinquents: Florida's STEP Program," *New England Journal on Criminal and Civil Confinement* 11 (1985), pp. 420–436, and Thomas C. Castellano and Irina R. Soderstrom, "Wilderness Challenges and Recidivism: A Program Evaluation." Paper presented to the Annual Meeting of the American Society of Criminology, Baltimore, Maryland (November 1990).

32. *Outward Bound USA,* www.outwardbound.org/outreach.html.

33. Miner and Boldt, *Outward Bound USA,* pp. 327–328.

34. *VisionQuest Changes Lives,* accessed online at www.vq.com/overview.htm.

35. Howard N. Snyder and Melissa Sickmund, *Juvenile Offenders and Victims: 2006 National Report* (Washington, D.C.: National Center for Juvenile Justice; Office of Justice Programs, 2006), p. 195.

36. Ibid., p. 200.

37. Ibid., p. 203.

38. Ibid., p. 206.

39. Ibid., p. 211.

40. Murray, Baird, Loughran, Mills, and Platt, *Safety and Welfare Plan: Implementing Reform in California,* p. 2.

41. Jean Bottcher, "Evaluating the Youth Authority's Boot Camp: The First Five Months." Paper delivered to Western Society of Criminology, Monterey, California (February 1993); Institute for Criminological Research and American Institute for Research, *Boot Camp for Juvenile Offenders: Constructive Intervention and Early Support—Implementation Evaluation Final Report* (New Brunswick, N.J.: Rutgers University, 1992).

42. Roberta C. Cronin, *Boot Camps for Adult and Juvenile Offenders: Overview and Update* (A Final Summary Report Presented to the National Institute of Justice, 1994), p. 37.

43. Anthony W. Salerno, "Boot Camps: A Critique and a Proposed Alternative," *Journal of Offender Rehabilitation* 20 (1994), p. 149.

44. Ibid., p. 37.

45. Michael Peters, David Thomas, Christopher Zamberlan, and Caliber Associates, *Boot Camps for Juvenile Offenders: Program Summary* (Washington, D.C.: Office of Juvenile Justice and Delinquency Prevention, 1997), p. 3, 25.

46. Ibid.

47. Doris Layton MacKenzie, David B. Wilson, Gaylene Styve Armstrong, and Angela R. Gover, "The Impact of Boot Camps and Traditional Institutions on Juvenile Residents: Perceptions, Adjustment, and Change," *Journal of Research in Crime and Delinquency* 38 (August 2000), pp. 279–313.

48. Ibid. See also Gaylene Styve Armstrong and Doris Layton MacKenzie, "Private versus Public Juvenile Correctional Facilities: Do Differences in Environmental Quality Exist?" *Crime and Delinquency* 49 (October 2003), pp. 542–563.

49. MacKenzie et al., "The Impact of Boot Camps and Traditional Institutions on Juvenile Residents," p. 279.

50. Alexandra Marks, "States Fall Out of (Tough) Love with Boot Camps," *The Christian Science Monitor,* December 27, 1999, p. 1.

51. Associated Press, "Teen Dies at Boot Camp for Troubled Kids," *Milwaukee Times,* 4 July 2001. For an article that suggests that what takes place at boot camps may be considered cruel and unusual and give rise to costly inmate litigation, see Faith E. Lutze and David C. Brody, "Mental Abuse as Cruel and Unusual Punishment: Do Boot Camp Prisons Violate the Eighth Amendment?," *Crime and Delinquency* 45 (April 1999), pp. 242–255.

52. Marks, "States Fall Out of (Tough) Love with Boot Camps," p. 1.

53. Steve Lerner, *Bodily Harm: The Pattern of Fear and Violence at the California Youth Authority* (Bolinas, Calif.: Common Knowledge Press, 1986).

54. Ibid., p. 12.

55. See L. Thomas Winfree Jr. and G. Larry Mays, "Family and Peer Influences on Gang Involvement: A Comparison of Institutionalized and Free-World Youths in a Southeastern State." Paper presented to the Annual Meeting of the American Society of Criminology in Boston, Massachusetts (November 1994), and L. Thomas Winfree Jr., G. Larry Mays, and Teresa Vigil-Backstrom, "Youth Gangs and Incarcerated Delinquents: Exploring the Ties between Gang Membership, Delinquency and Social Learning Theory," *Justice Quarterly* 11 (June 1994), pp. 229–256.

56. Task Force Report of the National Gang Crime Research Center, "The Economics of Gang Life." Paper presented at the Annual Meeting of the Academy of Criminal Justice Sciences, Boston, Massachusetts (March 1995), p. 24.

57. Catherine H. Conley, *Street Gangs: Current Knowledge and Strategies* (Washington, D.C.: U.S. Department of Justice, 1993), p. 55.

58. M. A. Bortner and Linda M. Williams, *Youth in Prison: We the People of Unit Four* (New York: Routledge, 1997), pp. 54–60.

59. For the diverse forms of state juvenile institutionalization, see Kelly Dedel, "National Profile of the Organization of Juvenile Correctional Systems," p. 509.

60. Bradford Smith, "Children in Custody: 20-Year Trends in Juvenile Detention, Correctional, and Shelter Facilities," *Crime and Delinquency* 44 (October 1998), p. 531.

61. Bartollas has conducted research of juvenile institutions in Illinois, Iowa, Minnesota, North Carolina, Ohio, and South Carolina.

62. Ibid.

63. Mark W. Lipsey, David B. Wilson, and Lynn Cothern, *Effective Intervention for Serious Juvenile Offenders: Juvenile*

Justice Bulletin (Washington, D.C.: Office of Juvenile Justice and Delinquency Prevention, 2000), p. 5.

64. Randall G. Sheldon and Sharon Tracey, "Violent Female Juvenile Offenders: An Ignored Minority with the Juvenile Justice System," *Juvenile and Family Court Journal* 43 (1992), pp. 33–40.

65. Bartollas's examination of training schools in six states led him to these conclusions. Also, he worked in one Ohio training school for four years.

66. Ibid.

67. Peter W. Greenwood, Susan Turner, and Kathy Rosenblatt, *Evaluation of Paint Creek Youth Center: Preliminary Results* (Santa Monica, Calif.: Rand, 1989).

68. Ibid., p. 3.

69. Ibid., p. 58.

70. David Shichor and Clemens Bartollas, "Private and Public Placements: Is There a Difference?" *Crime and Delinquency* 36 (April 1990), pp. 289–299.

71. Gordon E. Barker and W. Thomas Adams, "The Social Structure of a Correctional Institution," *Journal of Criminal Law, Criminology and Police Science* 49 (1959), pp. 417–499.

72. Polsky, *Cottage Six*, pp. 69–88.

73. Sethard Fisher, "Social Organization in a Correction Residence," *Pacific Sociological Review* 5 (Fall 1961), p. 89.

74. Ibid., pp. 89–90.

75. Bartollas, Miller, and Dinitz, *Juvenile Victimization*, pp. 131–150.

76. Ibid., p. 271.

77. Stuart J. Miller, Clemens Bartollas, and Simon Dinitz, *Juvenile Victimization Revisited: A Fifteen-Year Follow-Up at TICO* (unpublished manuscript).

78. Rose Giallombardo, *The Social World of Imprisoned Girls: A Comparative Study of Institutions for Juvenile Delinquents* (New York: John Wiley & Sons, 1974), and Alice Propper, *Prison Homosexuality: Myth and Reality* (Lexington, Mass.: D. C. Heath & Company, 1981).

79. Giallombardo, *The Social World of Imprisoned Girls*, pp. 145–211.

80. Ibid., p. 210.

81. Propper, *Prison Homosexuality*.

82. Christopher M. Sieverdes and Clemens Bartollas, "Institutional Adjustment among Female Delinquents," in *Administrative Issues in Criminal Justice*, edited by Alvin W. Cohn and Ben Ward (Beverly Hills, Calif.: Sage Publications, 1981), pp. 91–103.

83. Ibid.

84. Clemens Bartollas and Christopher M. Sieverdes, "The Victimized White in a Juvenile Correctional System," *Crime and Delinquency* 34 (October 1981), pp. 534–543.

85. Ibid., p. 540.

86. *White v. Reid*, 125 F. Supp. (D.D.C. 1954).

87. *Inmates of the Boys' Training School v. Affeck*, 346 F. Supp. 1354 (D. R. I. 1972).

88. *Nelson v. Heyne*, 355 F. Supp. 451 (N. D. Ind. 1973).

89. *Morales v. Turman*, 364 F. Supp. 166 (E. D. Tex. 1973); *Morales v. Turman*, No. 74-3436, U.S. Court of Appeals for the Fifth Circuit, 562 F.2d 993; 1977 U.S. App. LEXIS 10794, November 11, 1977. As Corrected; Petition for Rehearing and Rearing En Banc denied December 16, 1977; *Morales v. Turman*, Civil Action No. 1948, United States District Court for the Eastern District of Texas, Sherman Division, 569 F. Supp. 332; 1983 U.S. Dist LEXIS 15935; 37 Fed. R. Serv. 2d (Callaghan) 1294, June 28, 1983.

90. Adrienne Volnik, "Right to Treatment: Case Development in Juvenile Law," *Justice System Journal* 3 (Spring 1973), pp. 303–304.

91. *Pena v. New York State Division for Youth*, 419 F. Supp. 203 (S. D. N. Y. 1976).

92. 346 F. Supp. 1354 (D. R. I. 1972), p. 1343.

93. *Morales v. Turman*.

94. *Morgan v. Sproat*, 432 F. Supp. 1130 (S. D. Miss. 1977).

95. *State v. Werner*, 242 S.E. 2d 907 (W.Va. 1978).

96. See *Lollis v. New York State Dept. of Social Services*, 322 F. Supp. 473 (S. D. N. Y. 1970); *U.S. ex. rel. Stewart v. Coughlin*, No. C. 1793 (N. D. 111, November 22, 1971).

97. *Alexander v. Boys and South Carolina Department of Juvenile Justice*, 876 F. Supp. 773 (1995).

98. This section on access to the courts is adapted from Rolando V. del Carmen and Chad R. Trulson, *Juvenile Justice: The System, Process, and the Law* (Belmont, Calif.: Thompson, 2006), pp. 376–377.

99. *Morgan v. Sproat*, 432 F. Supp. 1130, 1136 (S.D. Miss. 1997).

100. *Germany v. Vance*, 868 F.2d 9 (1st Cir. 1989).

101. *John L. v. Adams*, 969 f.2d 228 (6th Cir. 1992).

102. Patricia Puritz and Mary Ann Scali, *Beyond the Walls: Improving Conditions of Confinement for Youth in Custody: Report* (Washington, D.C.: Office of Juvenile Justice and Delinquency Prevention, 1998), pp. 4–5.

103. Ibid., p. 5.

104. Ibid.

105. George M. Camp and Camille Graham Camp, *The Corrections Yearbook, 1995* (South Salem, N.Y.: Criminal Justice Institute, 1995), p. 16.

106. Patricia McFall Torbet, *Organization and Administration of Juvenile Services: Probation, Aftercare, and State Delinquent Institutions* (Pittsburgh: National Center for Juvenile Justice, 1988), p. 23.

107. Dean J. Champion, *The Juvenile Justice System: Delinquency, Processing, and the Law* (New York: Macmillan, 1992), p. 446.

108. Michael D. Norman, "Discretionary Justice: Decision-Making in a State Juvenile Parole Board," *Juvenile and Family Court Journal* 37 (1986), pp. 19–25.

109. Elizabeth Piper Deschenes, Peter W. Greenwood, and Grant Marshall, *The Nokomis Challenge Program Evaluation* (Santa Monica, Calif.: Rand, 1996).

110. J. D. Howell et al., eds., *Sourcebook on Serious, Violent, and Chronic Juvenile Offenders* (Thousand Oaks, Calif.: Sage Publications, 1995).

111. D. M. Altschuler and T. L. Armstrong, *Intensive Aftercare for High-Risk Juveniles: A Community Care Model* (Washington, D.C.: Office of Juvenile Justice and Delinquency Prevention, 1994).

112. Palmer, *The Re-Emergence of Correctional Intervention*, p. 86.

113. Henry Sontheimer, Lynne Goodstein, and Michael Kovacevic, *Philadelphia Intensive Aftercare Probation Evaluation Project* (Pittsburgh: Center for Juvenile Justice Training and Research, 1990), p. 3. See also Lynne Goodstein and Henry Sontheimer, "The Implementation of an Intensive Aftercare Program for Serious Juvenile Offenders:

A Case Study," *Criminal Justice and Behavior* 24 (September 1997), pp. 332–359.

114. Sontheimer et al., *Philadelphia Intensive Aftercare Project*, p. x.

115. Marshall and Snyder, "Intensive and Aftercare Probation Services in Pennsylvania," p. 4. For a description of two other programs, see Peter W. Greenwood, Elizabeth Piper Deschenes, and Helen Giglio, *Research Design and Program Description for the Skillman Intensive Aftercare Experiment* (Santa Monica, Calif.: Rand Corp., 1989).

116. Don A. Josi and Dale K. Sechrest, "A Pragmatic Approach to Parole Aftercare Evaluation of a Community Reintegration Program for High-Risk Youthful Offenders," *Justice Quarterly* 16 (March 1999), p. 66.

117. William Degnan, *Lifeskills Post-Parole Treatment Program* (Sanger, Calif.: Operation, New Hope, 1994).

118. Josi and Sechrest, "A Pragmatic Approach to Parole Aftercare Evaluation of a Community Reintegration Program for High-Risk Youthful Offenders," p. 66.

119. David M. Altschuler and Troy L. Armstrong, *Intensive Aftercare for High-Risk Juveniles: Policies and Procedures* (Washington, D.C.: Office of Juvenile Justice and Delinquency Prevention, 1994), p. 3.

120. For more extensive examination of these intensive aftercare programs, see Betsie McNulty, Richard Wiebush, and Thao Le, "Intensive Aftercare Programs for Serious Juvenile Offenders: Preliminary Results of Process and Outcome Evaluation." Paper presented to the Annual Meeting of the American Society of Criminology, Washington, D.C. (November 1998).

121. Richard G. Wiebush, Betsie McNulty, and Thao Le, *Implementation of the Intensive Community-Based Aftercare Program* (Washington, D.C.: Office of Juvenile Justice and Delinquency Prevention, 2000), p. 17.

122. For an example of a house detention component of an aftercare program, see W. H. Barton and Jeffrey A. Butts, "Visible Options: Intensive Supervision Program for Juvenile Delinquents," *Crime and Delinquency* (1990), pp. 238–256.

123. Melissa Sickmund, *Juveniles in Corrections: National Report Series Bulletin* (Washington, D.C.: Office of Juvenile Justice and Delinquency Prevention, 2004), p. 1.

124. Donna Hamparian et al., "Youth in Adult Court: Between Two Worlds," *Major Issues in Juvenile Justice Information and Training* (Columbus, Ohio: Academy for Contemporary Problems, 1981).

125. Vic Rychaert, "15 Youths Doing Time with State's Meanest," *Indianapolis Star,* 30 April 2001, A1.

126. Snyder and Sickmund, *Juvenile Offenders and Victims: 2006 National Report*, p. 237.

127. Dedel, "National Profile of the Organization of State Juvenile Corrections Systems," p. 515.

Glossary

This glossary incorporates selected terms adapted from the FBI's *Uniform Crime Reporting Handbook,* the *Juvenile Court Statistics* report series, and the Census of Juveniles in Residential Placement. The National Center for Juvenile Justice's *State Juvenile Justice Profiles* was also influential in determining the content of selected definitions.

academic performance Achievement in schoolwork as rated by grades and other assessment measures. Poor academic performance is a factor in delinquency.

adjudication The court process wherein a judge determines if the juvenile appearing before the court committed the act with which he or she is charged. The term *adjudicated* is analogous to *convicted* in the adult criminal justice system and indicates that the court concluded that the juvenile committed the act.

adjudicatory hearing The stage of juvenile court proceedings that usually includes the child's plea, the presentation of evidence by the prosecution and by the defense, cross-examination of witnesses, and a finding by the judge as to whether the allegations in the petition can be sustained.

adjustment model A rehabilitative correctional approach that emphasizes helping delinquents demonstrate responsible behavior.

adolescence The life interval between childhood and adulthood; usually the period between the ages of twelve and eighteen years.

adult court Criminal courts that hear the cases of adults charged with crimes, and to which juveniles who are accused of having committed serious offenses can be waived (transferred). In some states, adult criminal courts have jurisdiction over juveniles who are accused of committing certain specified offenses.

aftercare The supervision of juveniles who are released from correctional institutions so that they can make an optimal adjustment to community living. Also, the status of a juvenile conditionally released from a treatment or confinement facility and placed under supervision in the community.

age of onset The age at which a child begins to commit delinquent acts; an important dimension of delinquency.

alcohol A drug made through a fermentation process that relaxes inhibitions; adolescents tend to participate in risky behavior while under its influence.

alternative school A facility that provides an alternative educational experience, usually in a different location, for youths who are not doing satisfactory work in the public school setting.

amphetamines Stimulant drugs that occur in a variety of forms and are frequently used by adolescents.

appeal The review of juvenile court proceedings by a higher court. Although no constitutional right of appeal exists for juveniles, the right of adjudicated juveniles to appeal has been established by statute in some states.

appellate review Review of the decision of a juvenile court proceeding by a higher court. Decisions by appellate courts, including the U.S. Supreme Court, have greatly affected the development of juvenile court law and precedent.

arrest The process of taking a person into custody for an alleged violation of the law. Juveniles who are under arrest have nearly all the due process safeguards accorded to adults.

attention deficit hyperactivity disorder (ADHD) A cognitive disorder of childhood that can include inattention, distractibility, excessive activity, restlessness, noisiness, impulsiveness, and so on.

attention home An innovative form of detention facility, found in several locations across the nation, that is characterized by an open setting.

autonomic nervous system The system of nerves that govern reflexes, glands, the iris of the eye, and activities of interior organs that are not subject to voluntary control.

bail The money or property pledged to the court or actually deposited with the court to effect the release of a person from legal custody. Juveniles do not have a constitutional right to bail as do adults.

balanced and restorative model An integrative correctional model that seeks to reconcile the interests of victims, offenders, and the community through programs and supervision practices.

behavior modification A psychological treatment method that rewards appropriate behavior positively, immediately, and systematically and assumes that rewards increase the occurrence of desired behavior.

beyond a reasonable doubt A legal standard establishing the degree of proof needed for a juvenile to be adjudicated a delinquent by the juvenile court during the adjudicatory stage of the court's proceedings.

bifurcated hearing Split adjudication and disposition hearings, which are the present trend of the juvenile court.

binding over The process of transferring (also called *certifying*) juveniles to adult criminal court. Binding over takes place after a judicial hearing on a juvenile's amenability to treatment or his or her threat to public safety.

biological positivism The belief that juveniles' biological characteristics and limitations drive them to delinquent behavior.

birth order The sequence of births in a family and a child's position in it, whether firstborn, middle child, or youngest.

blended sentencing The imposition of juvenile and/or adult correctional sanctions on serious and violent juvenile offenders who have been adjudicated in juvenile court or convicted in criminal court.

blocked opportunity Limited or nonexistent chances of success; according to strain theory, a key factor in delinquency.

body-type theory Theory developed by William Sheldon, Sheldon Glueck, and Eleanor Glueck, and others, who proposed that youths with the mesomorphic (bony, muscular, and athletic) body type are more likely to be delinquent than are those with the endormorphic (soft, round, and fat) and ectomorphic (tall, thin, and fragile) body types.

boot camp A military-style facility used as an alternative to prison in order to deal with prison crowding and public demands for severe punishment.

born criminal According to Cesare Lombroso, an individual who is atavistic, or reverts to an earlier evolutionary level and is unabler to conform his or her behavior to the requirements of modern society; thus, an individual who is innately criminal.

Breed v. Jones A 1975 double jeopardy case in which the U.S. Supreme Court ruled that a juvenile court cannot adjudicate a case and then transfer the case over to the criminal court for adult processing of the same offense.

broken home A family in which parents are divorced or are no longer living together.

brother–sister incest Sexual activity that occurs between brother and sister.

bullying Hurtful, frightening, or menacing actions undertaken by one person to intimidate another (generally weaker) person, to gain that person's unwilling compliance, and/or to put him or her in fear.

capitalism An economic system in which private individuals or corporations own and control capital (wealth and the means of production) and in which competitive free markets control prices, production, and the distribution of goods.

child abuse The mistreatment of children by parents or caregivers. Physical abuse is intentional behavior directed toward a child by the parent or caregiver to cause pain, injury, or death. Emotional abuse involves a disregard of a child's psychological needs. Also see **child sexual abuse.**

child savers A name given to an organized group of progressive social reformers of the late nineteenth and early twentieth centuries who promoted numerous laws aimed at protecting children and institutionalizing an idealized image of childhood innocence.

child sexual abuse Any intentional and wrongful physical contact with a child that entails a sexual purpose or component. Such sexual abuse is termed *incest* when the perpetrator is a member of the child's family.

chivalry factor The idea that the justice system treats adolescent females and women more leniently because of their gender. Although the chivalry factor might have played a role in justice system processing in the past, most people believe that it no longer applies to American justice today.

chronic youthful offender A juvenile who engages repeatedly in delinquent behavior. The Philadelphia cohort studies defined chronic offenders as youths who had committed five or more delinquent offenses. Other studies use this term to refer to a youth involved in serious and repetitive offenses.

citation A summons to appear in juvenile court.

clearance by arrest The solution of a crime by arrest of a perpetrator who has confessed or who has been implicated by witnesses or evidence. Clearances can also occur by exceptional means, as when a suspected perpetrator dies prior to arrest.

club drug A synthetic psychoactive substance often found at nightclubs, bars, "raves," and dance parties. Club drugs include MDMA (Ecstasy), ketamine, methamphetamine (meth), GBL, PCP, GHB, and Rohypnol.

cocaine A coca extract that creates mood elevation, elation, grandiose feelings, and feelings of heightened physical prowess.

cohort A generational group as defined in demographics, in statistics, or for the purpose of social research.

cohort study Research that usually includes all individuals who were born in a specific year in a particular city or county and follows them through part or all of their lives.

"cold and brittle" According to Travis Hirschi, the nature of interpersonal relationships among delinquents, specifically delinquents in gangs.

commitment A determination made by a juvenile judge at the disposition stage of a juvenile court proceeding that a juvenile is to be sent to a juvenile correctional institution.

commitment to delinquency David Matza's term for the attachment that a delinquent juvenile has to a deviant identity and values.

commitment to the social bond In Travis Hirschi's theory of social control, the attachment that a juvenile has to conventional institutions and activities.

committed juveniles those whose cases have been adjudicated and disposed in juvenile court and those who have been convicted and sentenced in criminal court.

community-based corrections Corrections programs that include probation, residential and day treatment programs, and parole (aftercare). The nature of the linkages between community programs and their social environments is the most distinguishing feature of community-based corrections. As frequency, duration, and quality of community relationships increase, the programs become more community-based.

community service project Court-required restitution in which a juvenile spends a certain number of hours working in a community project.

community volunteer An individual who donates his or her time to work with delinquents in the community.

complaint A charge made to an intake officer of the juvenile court that an offense has been committed.

conduct norms The rules of a group governing the ways its members should act under particular conditions; the violation of these rules arouses a group reaction.

conflict theory A perspective which holds that delinquency can be explained by socioeconomic class, by power and authority relationships, and by group and cultural differences.

consensual model A model of society that views the social order as a persistent stable structure that is well integrated and that is based on a consensus of values.

consent decree A formal agreement between a juvenile and the court in which the juvenile is placed under the court's supervision without a formal finding of delinquency.

constitutionalists The name given to a group of twentieth-century reformers who advocated that juveniles deserve due process protections when they appear before the juvenile court.

containment theory Walter C. Reckless's theoretical perspective that strong inner containment and reinforcing external containment provide insulation against delinquent and criminal behavior.

control theory Any of several theoretical approaches that maintain that human beings must be held in check, or somehow be controlled, if delinquent tendencies are to be repressed.

cottage system A widely used treatment practice that places small groups of training school residents into cottages.

crack A generally less expensive but more potent form of cocaine.

crime control model A correctional model supported by James Q. Wilson, Ernest van den Haag, and others, who believe that discipline and punishment are the most effective means of deterring youth crime.

criminal opportunity theory A theory claiming that criminals tend to be attracted to targets that offer a high payoff with little risk of legal consequences.

criminal street gang A formal or informal group or association of three or more individuals, who commit two or more gang crimes in two or more separate criminal episodes.

critical criminologists Social scientific thinkers who combine Marxist theory with the insights of later theorists, such as Sigmund Freud.

cruel and unusual punishment A guarantee provided by the Eighth Amendment to the U.S. Constitution against inhumane punishments. Accordingly, juveniles in correctional custody must not be treated with unnecessary harshness.

cultural deviance theory A theory promoted by Clifford R. Shaw, Henry D. McKay, and Walter B. Miller, who view delinquent behavior as an expression of conformity to cultural values and norms that are in opposition to those of the larger U.S. society.

culturally defined goals In Robert K. Merton's version of strain theory, the set of purposes and interests a culture defines as legitimate objectives for individuals.

cultural transmission theory An approach which holds that areas of concentrated crime maintain their high rates over a long period, even when the composition of the population changes rapidly, because delinquent "values" become cultural norms and are passed from one generation to the next.

culture conflict theory A perspective proposed by Thorsten Sellin and others which includes the idea that delinquency or crime arises because individuals are members of a subculture that has conduct norms which are in conflict with those of the wider society.

curfew violation Violation of an ordinance forbidding persons below a certain age from being in public places during set hours. A status offense.

day treatment programs Court-mandated, community-based corrections programs that juveniles attend in the morning and afternoon. They return home in the evening.

deinstitutionalization The process of closing long-term institutions and moving residents to community-based corrections facilities. *Deincarceration* is another term used to describe this process.

Deinstitutionalization of Status Offenders Project (DSO) A project that evaluated the effects of deinstitutionalization of status offenders in eight states and prompted a national evaluation.

delinquency prevention Organized efforts to forestall or prevent the development of delinquent behaviors. See also *primary prevention, secondary prevention,* and *tertiary prevention.*

delinquent act An act committed by a juvenile for which an adult could be prosecuted in a criminal court, but when committed by a juvenile is within the jurisdiction of the juvenile court. Delinquent acts include crimes against persons, crimes against property, drug offenses, and crimes against public order, when juveniles commit such acts.

delinquent siblings Brothers or sisters who are engaged in delinquent behaviors; an apparent factor in youngsters' involvement in delinquency.

desistance The termination of a delinquent career or behavior.

detention The temporary restraint of a juvenile in a secure facility, usually because he or she is acknowledged to be dangerous either to self or to others.

detention center A facility that provides custodial care for juveniles during juvenile court proceedings. Also called juvenile halls and detention homes, detention centers were established at the end of the nineteenth century as an alternative to jails for juveniles.

detention hearing A hearing, usually conducted by an intake officer of the juvenile court, during which the decision is made as to whether a juvenile will be released to his or her parents or guardians or be detained in a detention facility.

determinate sentencing A model of sentencing that provides fixed terms of sentences for criminal offenses. Terms are generally set by the legislature rather than determined by judicial discretion.

determinism A philosophical position that suggests that individuals are driven into delinquent or criminal behavior by biological or psychological traits that are beyond their control.

differential association theory Edward H. Sutherland's view that delinquency is learned from others; and that delinquent behavior is to be expected of individuals who have internalized a preponderance of definitions that are favorable to law violations.

differential identification theory A modification of differential association theory offered by Daniel Glaser.

differential opportunity structure Differences in economic and occupational opportunities open to members of different socioeconomic classes.

disorderly conduct Unlawful interruption of the peace, quiet, or order of a community, including offenses called disturbing the peace, vagrancy, loitering, unlawful assembly, and riot.

dispositional hearing The stage of the juvenile court proceedings in which the juvenile judge decides the most appropriate placement for a juvenile who has been adjudicated a delinquent, a status offender, or a dependent child.

disproportionate minority confinement The court-ordered confinement, in juvenile institutions, of members of minority groups in numbers disproportionate to their representation in the general population.

disruptive behavior Unacceptable conduct at school; may include defiance of authority, manipulation of teachers, inability or refusal to follow rules, fights with peers, destruction of property, use of drugs in school, and/or physical or verbal altercations with teachers.

diversion The act of officially stopping or suspending a case prior to court adjudication and referring the juvenile to a community education, treatment, or work program in lieu of adjudication or incarceration. Successful completion of a diversion program results in the dismissal or withdrawal of formal charges.

diversion programs Dispositional alternatives for youthful offenders that exist outside of the formal juvenile justice system.

double jeopardy A common law and constitutional prohibition against a second trial for the same offense. The U.S. Supreme Court's *Breed v. Jones* decision (1975) ruled that juveniles cannot be tried in juvenile court and then be referred to the adult court, as that would constitute double jeopardy. The Fifth Amendment to the U.S. Constitution holds that no person may be twice put in jeopardy of life or limb for the same offense.

drift theory David Matza's theoretical perspective that juveniles neutralize the moral hold of society and drift into delinquent behavior.

dropout A young person of school age who, of his or her own volition, no longer attends school.

drug addiction The excessive use of a drug, which is frequently characterized by physical and/or psychological dependence.

drug and alcohol abuse interventions Treatment modalities in which drug-abusing juveniles are usually treated in a group context.

due process rights Constitutional rights that are guaranteed to citizens—whether adult or juvenile—during their contacts with the police, their proceedings in court, and their interactions with the public school.

Ecstasy A form of amphetamine that began to be used by adolescents in the United States in the 1980s and 1990s, and is now rather widespread.

electronic monitoring See *remote location monitoring*.

emerging gangs Youth gangs that formed in the late 1980s and early 1990s in communities across the nation and that are continuing to evolve.

emotional abuse In the field of adolescence, a disregard for the psychological needs of a child, including lack of expressed love, withholding of contact or approval, verbal abuse, unrealistic demands, threats, psychological cruelty, and so on.

emotionality An aspect of temperament; it can range from a near absence of emotional response to intense, out-of-control emotional reactions.

escalation of offenses An increase in the frequency and severity of an individual's offenses; an important dimension of delinquency.

family size The number of children in a family; a possible risk factor for delinquency.

family therapy A counseling technique that involves treating all members of a family; a widely used method of dealing with a delinquent's socially unacceptable behavior.

father–daughter incest Sexual activity between father and daughter. Also refers to incest by stepfathers or the boyfriend(s) of the mother.

father–son incest Sexual activity between father and son. Also refers to incest by stepfathers or the boyfriend(s) of the mother.

felicific calculus A method for determining the sum total of pleasure and pain produced by an act, Also, the assumption that human beings strive to obtain a favorable balance of pleasure and pain.

felony A criminal offense punishable by death or by incarceration in a state or federal correctional institution, usually for one year or more.

feminist theory of delinquency An argument made by Meda Chesney-Lind and others that adolescent females' victimization at home causes them to become delinquent and that this fact has been systematically ignored.

financial restitution See *restitution*.

fingerprinting A pretrial identification procedure used with both juveniles and adults following arrest.

focal concerns of the lower class As proposed by Walter B. Miller, values or focal concerns (toughness, smartness, excitement, fate, and autonomy) of lower-class youths that differ from those of middle-class youths.

forestry camps Correctional facilities where residents usually do conservation work in state parks, including cleaning up, cutting grass and weeds, and general maintenance.

foster care A home setting for juveniles who are lawfully removed from their birth parents' homes.

free will The ability to make rational choices among possible actions, and to select one over the others. Proponents of the classical school of criminology, as well as advocates of crime control or the justice model, believe that juveniles have free will and thus can be held responsible for their behavior.

friendship patterns The nature of peer relationships that exist within a teenage culture.

gang A group of youths who are bound together by mutual interests, have identifiable leadership, and act in concert to achieve a specific purpose that generally includes the conduct of illegal activity.

gang unit A specialized unit established by some police departments to address the problem of gangs.

gender The personal traits, social positions, and values and beliefs that members of a society attach to being male or female.

gender roles Societal definitions of what constitutes masculine and feminine behavior.

group home A placement for youths who have been adjudicated by the court—called a *group residence, halfway house,* or *attention home*—that serves a group of about thirteen to twenty-five youths as an alternative to institutionalization.

group home model A form of community-based residential program that has had some success with youthful offenders. See also *group home.*

guided group interaction (GGI) Interaction that, whether it occurs in the community or in an institution, places youthful offenders in an intensive group environment under the direction of an adult leader. The guided group interaction process substitutes a whole new structure of beliefs, values, and behaviors for the values of delinquent peer subcultures.

halfway house A residential setting for adjudicated delinquents, usually those who need a period of readjustment to the community following institutional confinement.

heroin A refined form of morphine that was introduced around the beginning of the twentieth century.

hidden delinquency Unobserved or unreported delinquency.

home detention House arrest. A form of detention that is used in some jurisdictions in which an adjudicated juvenile remains at home under the supervision of juvenile probation officers.

houses of refuge Institutions that were designed by eighteenth- and nineteenth-century reformers to provide an orderly, disciplined environment similar to that of the "ideal" Puritan family.

human agency The active role juveniles take in their lives; the fact that juveniles are not merely subject to social and structural constraints but make choices and decisions based on the alternatives that they see before them.

incest Intrafamily sexual abuse which is perpetrated on a child by a member of that child's family group and includes not only sexual intercourse but also any act designed to stimulate a child sexually, or to use a child for sexual stimulation, either of the perpetrator or of another person.

incidence of delinquency The frequency with which delinquent behavior takes place.

incorrigible (*ungovernable* or *incorrigibility*) Being beyond the control of parents, guardians, or custodians.

indeterminate sentencing In juvenile justice, a sentencing model that encourages rehabilitation through the use of general and relatively unspecific sentences. Under the model, a juvenile judge has wide discretion and can commit a juvenile to the department of corrections or youth authority until correctional staff make the decision to release the juvenile. This type of sentencing is used with juveniles in most jurisdictions other than those that have mandatory or determinate sentencing.

index offenses The most serious offenses reported in the FBI's Uniform Crime Reporting Program, including murder and nonnegligent manslaughter, forcible rape, robbery, aggravated assault, burglary, larceny-theft, motor vehicle theft, and arson.

informal adjustment An attempt to handle a youthful offender outside of the formal structures of the juvenile justice system.

informal probation An arrangement in which, instead of being adjudicated as a delinquent and placed on probation, a youth is informally assigned to the supervision of a probation officer.

inhalants Volatile liquids that give off a vapor, which is inhaled to produce short-term excitement and euphoria followed by a period of disorientation.

in loco parentis The principle according to which a guardian or an agency is given the rights, duties, and responsibilities of a parent in relation to a particular child or children.

In re Gault A 1967 U.S. Supreme Court case that brought due process and constitutional procedures into juvenile courts.

In re Winship A 1970 case in which the U.S. Supreme Court decided that juveniles are entitled to proof beyond a reasonable doubt during adjudication proceedings.

institutionalized means In Robert K. Merton's theory, culturally sanctioned methods of attaining individual goals.

instrumental Marxists A group whose members view the entire apparatus of crime control as a tool or instrument of the ruling class.

instrumental theory A perspective developed by Herman Schwendinger and Julia Siegel Schwendinger, which holds that the most important variable predicting delinquency in teenagers is their status position relative to that of their peers.

intake The first stage of juvenile court proceedings, in which the decision is made whether to divert the juvenile being referred or to file a formal petition in juvenile court.

intake decision The decision made by a juvenile court intake officer that results in a case either being handled informally at the intake level or being petitioned and scheduled for an adjudicatory or waiver hearing.

interstate compact Procedures for transferring a youth on probation or aftercare/parole from one state to another.

jail A police lockup or county holding facility for adult offenders. Jails have few services to offer juveniles.

judicial decision The decision made in response to a petition that asks the court to adjudicate or waive the youth. This decision is generally made by a juvenile court judge or referee.

judicial disposition Definite action taken or treatment plan decided on or initiated regarding a particular case after the judicial decision is made. For the *Juvenile Court Statistics* report series, case dispositions are coded into the following categories: 1.) Waived to criminal court (Cases that were transferred to criminal court as the result of a waiver hearing in juvenile court.); 2.) Placement (Cases in which youth were placed in a residential facility for delinquents or were otherwise removed from their homes and placed elsewhere.); 3.) Probation (Cases in which youth were placed on informal/voluntary or formal/court-ordered probation or supervision.); 4.) Dismissed (Cases dismissed—including those warned, counseled, and released—with no further action anticipated.); 5. Miscellaneous (A variety of actions not included above. This category includes fines, restitution and community services, referrals outside the court for services with minimal or no further court involvement anticipated, and dispositions coded as "other" by the reporting courts.

judicial waiver The procedure of relinquishing the processing of a particular juvenile case to adult criminal court; also known as *certifying* or *binding over to the adult court.*

jury trial Court proceeding in which a panel of the defendant's peers evaluate evidence and render a verdict. The U.S. Supreme Court has held that juveniles do not have a constitutional right to a jury trial, but several jurisdictions permit juveniles to choose a jury trial.

just deserts A pivotal philosophical underpinning of the justice model which holds that juveniles deserve to be punished if they violate the law, and that the punishment must be proportionate to the seriousness of the offense or the social harm caused.

justice as fairness David Fogel's justice model, which advocates that it is necessary to be fair, reasonable, humane, and constitutional in the implementation of justice.

justice model A justice systems model based on the belief that individuals have free will and are responsible for their decisions and thus deserve to be punished if they violate the law, and that the punishment they receive should be proportionate to the offense or the harm done.

juvenile A youth at or below the upper age of juvenile court jurisdiction in a particular state.

juvenile aftercare See *aftercare.*

juvenile court Any court that has jurisdiction over matters involving juveniles.

juvenile court officer A probation officer who serves juveniles; the term is used in some but not all probation departments.

juvenile court statistics Data about youth who appear before the juvenile court, compiled annually by the National Center for Juvenile Justice.

juvenile delinquency An act committed by a minor that violates the penal code of the government with authority over the area in which the act occurs.

juvenile drug courts Special courts designed for nonviolent youthful offenders with substance abuse problems who require integrated sanctions and services such as mandatory drug testing, substance abuse treatment, supervised release, and aftercare.

Juvenile Justice and Delinquency Prevention Act of 1974 A federal law that established a juvenile justice office within the Law Enforcement Assistance Administration to provide funds for the prevention and control of youth crime.

Juvenile Justice Standards Project A project jointly sponsored by the Institute of Judicial Administration and the American Bar Association that proposes that juveniles' sentences be based on the seriousness of the offense committed rather than on the "needs" of the child.

juvenile officer In some police departments, a police officer who has received specialized training so as to be able to work effectively with juveniles.

juvenile petition See *petition.*

kadi justice A judicial approach similar to that of a Muslim judge who sits in the marketplace and makes decisions without any apparent reference to established or traditional rules and norms.

Kent v. United States A 1966 U.S. Supreme Court decision on the matter of transfer; the first decision in which the Supreme Court dealt with a juvenile court case.

labeling theory The view that society creates the delinquent by labeling those who are apprehended as "different" from other youth, when in reality they are different primarily because they have been "tagged" with a deviant label.

Law Enforcement Assistance Administration (LEAA) A unit in the U.S. Department of Justice established by the Omnibus Crime Control and Safe Streets Act of 1968 to administer grants and provide guidance for crime prevention projects. Until funding ended for LEAA in the late 1970s, its grants permitted the expansion of community-based programs throughout the nation.

learning disabilities (LD) Disorders in one or more of the basic psychological processes involved in understanding or using spoken or written language. Some support exists for a theorized link between juvenile delinquency and learning disabilities.

least-restrictive model A model based on the assumption that a juvenile's penetration into the justice system should be minimized as much as possible.

legislative waiver Legislative action that narrows juvenile court jurisdiction, excluding from juvenile courts those youths charged with certain offenses.

life-course perspective A sociological framework suggesting that four key factors determine the shape of the life course: location in time and place, linked lives, human agency, and timing of lives.

locura A state of mind said to be desirable in a Mexican American street gang; a type of craziness or wildness.

mandatory sentencing The requirement that individuals who commit certain offenses be sentenced to a specified length of confinement if found guilty or adjudicated delinquent.

mandatory waiver A provision that requires juvenile courts to waive cases under certain circumstances.

marijuana The most frequently used illicit drug; usually smoked, it consists of dried hemp leaves and buds.

masculinity hypothesis The idea that as girls become more boylike and acquire more "masculine" traits, they become more delinquent.

McKeiver v. Pennsylvania A 1971 U.S. Supreme Court case that denied juveniles the right to trial by jury.

medical model A correctional model whose proponents believe that delinquency is caused by factors that can be identified, isolated, treated, and cured—much like a disease.

minor A person who is under the age of legal consent.

Miranda v. Arizona The landmark 1966 U.S. Supreme Court ruling that suspects taken into police custody must, before any questioning can take place, be informed that they have the right to remain silent, that anything they say may be used against them, and that they have the right to legal counsel.

mother–son incest Sexual activity that occurs between a

mother and her son. Also refers to incest by stepmothers or the girlfriend(s) of the father.

neglect A disregard for the physical, emotional, or moral needs of children. Child neglect involves the failure of the parent or caregiver to provide nutritious food, adequate clothing and sleeping arrangements, essential medical care, sufficient supervision, access to education, and normal experiences that produce feelings of being loved, wanted, secure, and worthy.

neutralization theory Gresham M. Sykes and David Matza's theory examining how youngsters attempt to justify or rationalize their responsibility for delinquent acts.

norms The guidelines individuals follow in their relations with one another; shared standards of desirable behavior.

"nothing works" The claim made by Robert Martinson and his colleagues in the mid-1970s that correctional treatment is ineffective in reducing recidivism of correctional clients.

offenses against the family and children Nonsupport, neglect, desertion, or abuse of children or other family members.

Office of Juvenile Justice and Delinquency Prevention (OJJDP) Federal agency established with the passage of the 1974 Juvenile Justice and Delinquency Prevention Act.

onset of delinquency See *age of onset.*

opportunity theory Richard A. Cloward and Lloyd E. Ohlin's perspective which holds that gang members turn to delinquency because of a sense of injustice about the lack of legitimate opportunities open to them.

orthomolecular imbalances Chemical imbalances in the body, resulting from poor nutrition, allergies, and exposure to lead and certain other substances, which are said to lead to delinquency.

Outward Bound A wilderness-type survival program that is popular in many states as an alternative to the institutionalization of juveniles.

parens patriae A medieval English doctrine that sanctioned the right of the Crown to intervene in natural family relations whenever a child's welfare was threatened. The philosophy of the juvenile court is based on this legal concept.

peer group influence The impact of the values and behaviors of fellow age-group members on teenagers' involvement in delinquency.

People and Folks Two supergangs comprising the major Chicago street gangs.

petition A document filed in juvenile court alleging that a juvenile is a delinquent and asking that the court assume jurisdiction over the juvenile or asking that an alleged delinquent be waived to criminal court for prosecution as an adult.

petitioner In the juvenile justice system, an intake officer (prosecutor) who seeks court jurisdiction over a youthful offender.

placement facility type Identifies whether a juvenile placement facility is publicly or privately owned/operated. Public facilities are those operated by state or local government agencies in which the employees working daily in the facilities and directly with the residents are state or local government employees. Private facilities are those operated by private nonprofit or for-profit corporations or organizations in which the employees working daily in the facili-

ties and directly with the residents are employees of the private corporation or organization.

placement status Identifies categories of juveniles held in residential placement facilities, usually according to one of the following: (1) Committed (includes juveniles in placement in the facility as part of a court-ordered disposition); (2) Detained (includes juveniles held while awaiting an adjudication hearing in juvenile court; juveniles held after adjudication while awaiting disposition or placement elsewhere; and juveniles awaiting transfer to, or a hearing or trial in, adult criminal court); and (3) Diversion (includes juveniles sent to the facility in lieu of adjudication as part of a diversion agreement.)

plea bargaining A court process in which the defense counsel and the prosecution agree that the defendant will plead guilty, usually in exchange for a reduction of charges or a lessened sentence.

police discretion A police officer's ability to choose from among a number of alternative dispositions when handling a situation.

police interrogation The process of interviewing a person who has been arrested with the express purpose of obtaining a confession.

positive peer culture A group treatment modality that (like its parent model, guided group interaction) aims to build a positive youth subculture; it encompasses a strategy that extends to all aspects of daily life.

positivism The view that, just as laws operate in the medical, biological, and physical sciences, laws govern human behavior; and that these law can be understood and used. According to positivism, the causes of human behavior, once discovered, can be modified to eliminate many of society's problems, including delinquency. Positivism has been the guiding philosophical perspective in juvenile justice since the juvenile court was established at the beginning of the twentieth century.

power-control thesis The view of John Hagan and his associates that the relationship between gender and delinquency is linked to issues of power and control.

pretrial identification practices Procedures such as fingerprinting, photographing, and placing juveniles in lineups for the purpose of identification prior to formal court appearance.

prevalence of delinquency The percentage of the juvenile population who are involved in delinquent behavior.

primary deviation According to labeling theory, the initial act of deviance that causes a person to be labeled a deviant.

primary prevention Efforts to reduce delinquency by modifying conditions in the physical and social environments that lead to juvenile crime.

private juvenile placements Training schools that operate under private auspices; the county or state generally pays the school a per diem rate for the care of youths committed to these facilities.

probation A court sentence under which the juvenile's freedom in the community is continued or only briefly interrupted, but the person is subject to supervision by a probation officer and the conditions imposed by the court.

probation officer An officer of the court who is expected to provide social history investigations, to supervise individuals who have been placed on probation, to maintain case files, to advise probationers on the conditions of their sentences, to perform any other probationary services that a judge may request, and to inform the court when persons on probation have violated the terms of that probation.

process of becoming deviant In labeling theory, the concept that the process of acquiring a delinquent identity takes place in a number of steps.

Progressive Era The period from around 1890 to 1920, when a wave of optimism swept through American society and led to the acceptance of positivism. The emerging social sciences assured reformers that through positivism society's problems could be solved.

prosecutor The representative of the state in court proceedings. Also called *county's attorney, district attorney,* or *state attorney.*

psychoanalytic theory Sigmund Freud's insights, which have helped shape the handling of juvenile delinquents. They include these axioms: (1) the personality is made up of three components—id, ego, and superego; (2) all normal children pass through three psychosexual stages of development—oral, anal, and phallic; and (3) a person's personality traits are developed in early childhood.

psychopath or sociopath A youth with a personality disorder; a hard-core juvenile criminal. The claim is made that the psychopath or sociopath is the unwanted, rejected child who grows up but remains an undomesticated child and never develops trust in or loyalty to another person.

psychotherapy A treatment method in which various adaptations of Freudian therapy are used by psychiatrists, clinical psychologists, and psychiatric social workers to encourage delinquents to talk about past conflicts that cause them to express emotional problems through aggressive or antisocial behavior.

radical criminology A perspective that holds that the causes of crime are rooted in social conditions that empower the wealthy and the politically well organized but disenfranchise the less fortunate.

radical nonintervention Edwin Schur's proposed policy toward delinquents, which advises that authorities should "leave the kids alone whenever possible."

ranches Public and private juvenile correctional institutions that, like forestry camps, are usually less secure than training schools and have a more normalizing atmosphere.

rational emotive therapy A cognitive restructuring strategy that seeks to identify delinquents' thinking errors (blaming others, trying to control or manipulate, failing to empathize, wanting to play the victim, etc.) and then to help young offenders "own" and control their behaviors.

reaction formation Psychological strategy for dealing with frustration by becoming hostile toward an unattainable object.

reality therapy A treatment modality developed by William Glasser and G. L. Harrington based on the principle that individuals must accept responsibility for their behavior.

reception and diagnostic centers Facilities where juveniles who have been committed to correctional institutions frequently are first sent; these centers diagnose youths' problems and develop individualized treatment plans.

recidivism The repetition of delinquent behavior by a youth who has been released from probation status or from a training school.

referee A juvenile justice worker who may or may not be a member of the bar. In many juvenile courts, referees assist judges in processing youths through the juvenile court system.

rehabilitation model A correctional model whose goal is to change an offender's character, attitudes, or behavior so as to diminish his or her delinquent propensities. The medical, adjustment, and reintegration models are variants of this model because they are all committed to changing the offender.

reinforcement theory A perspective that holds that behavior is governed by its consequences, especially rewards and punishments that follow from it.

reintegration model A perspective that holds that offenders' problems must be solved in the community in which they occur and that community-based organizations can help offenders readjust to community life.

rejection by parents Disapproval, repudiation, or other uncaring behavior directed by parents toward children; it can be a factor in delinquency.

reliability The extent to which a questionnaire or interview yields the same answers from the same juveniles when they are questioned two or more times.

remote location monitoring The use of electronic equipment to verify that an offender is at home or in a community correctional center during specified hours, or to track his or her whereabouts. Also called *electronic monitoring.*

representing The use by criminal street gangs of secret handshakes and special hand signs.

residential programs Programs conducted for the rehabilitation of youthful offenders within community-based and institutional settings.

residential social system The social hierarchy that is established by residents in an institution.

respondent The defense attorney in the juvenile court system.

restitution Court-ordered repayment to the victim; often used together with community service as a condition of juvenile probation.

reverse waiver Provisions that permit a juvenile who is being prosecuted as an adult in criminal court to petition to have the case transferred to juvenile court for adjudication or disposition.

revocation of aftercare Cancellation of parole and return of the offender to an institution; takes effect if a juvenile on aftercare commits another offense or violates the conditions of parole.

right to treatment The entitlement of a juvenile who has been committed to a training school to receive any needed services (i.e., therapy, education, etc.).

routine activities approach Lawrence E. Cohen and Marcus Felson's contention that crime rate trends and cycles are related to the nature of everyday patterns of social interaction that characterize the society in which they occur.

running away Leaving the custody and home of parents or guardians without permission and failing to return within a reasonable length of time. A status offense.

school search The process of searching students and their lockers to determine whether drugs, weapons, or other contraband are present.

search and seizure Police procedures used in the investigation of crimes for the purpose of gathering evidence. Juveniles, like adults, have constitutional safeguards to protect them against unauthorized police searches and seizures. Before police can search a person or location, the Constitution usually requires a lawfully obtained search warrant.

secondary deviation According to labeling theory, deviance that is a consequence of societal reaction to an initial delinquent act.

secondary prevention Intervention in the lives of juveniles or groups who have been identified as being in circumstances that dispose them toward delinquency.

sedatives Drugs that are taken orally and affect the user by depressing the nervous system, causing drowsiness.

self-report studies Studies of juvenile crime based on surveys in which youths report on their own delinquent acts.

sex-role socialization The process by which boys and girls internalize their culture's norms, sanctions, and expectations for members of their gender.

shelter care Facilities that are used primarily to provide short-term care for status offenders and for dependent or neglected children.

social capital theory James S. Coleman's perspective which holds that lower-class youths may become delinquent because they lack "social capital," or resources that reside in the social structure, including norms, networks, and relationships.

social contract An unstated or explicit agreement between a people and their government as to the rights and obligations of each.

social control theory A perspective advocated by Travis Hirschi and others, who propose that delinquent acts result when a juvenile's bond to society is weak or broken.

social development model A perepective based on the integration of social control and cultural learning theories which proposes that the development of attachments to parents will lead to attachments to school and a commitment to education as well as a belief in and commitment to conventional behavior and the law.

social disorganization theory An approach developed by Shaw, McKay, and others who argue that juvenile delinquency results when social control among the traditional primary groups, such as the family and the neighborhood, breaks down because of social disarray within the community.

social history report A written report of a juvenile's social background that probation officers prepare for a juvenile judge to assist the court in making a disposition of a youth who has been ruled delinquent.

social injustice According to many conflict-oriented criminologists, unfairness in the juvenile justice system resulting from the fact that poor youth tend to be disproportionately represented, female status offenders are subjected to sexist treatment, and racial minorities are dealt with more harshly than whites.

social interactionist theories Theoretical perspectives that derive their explanatory power from the give and take that continuously occurs between social groups, or between individuals and society.

socialization The process by which individuals come to internalize their culture; through this process an individual learns the norms, sanctions, and expectations of being a member of a particular society.

social process theories Theoretical approaches to delinquency that examine the interactions between individuals and their environments, especially those that might influence them to become involved in delinquent behavior.

social reaction theories Theories that focus on the role that social and economic groups and institutions have in producing delinquent behavior.

social structure The relatively stable formal and informal arrangements that characterize a society, including its economic arrangements, social institutions, and values and norms.

sociobiology An expression of biological positivism that stresses the interaction between biological factors within an individual and the influence of the person's particular environment. Also, the systematic study of the biological basis of all social behavior.

sociopath See *psychopath*.

soft determinism David Matza's view that delinquents are neither wholly free nor wholly constrained in their choice of actions. Matza claimed that the concept of soft determinism offers the best resolution of the debate between advocates of free will and positivists.

soft-line approach The lenient treatment of those youths who pose little threat to the social order.

specialization Repeated involvement of a juvenile in one type of delinquency during the course of his or her offending.

state training school See *training school*.

station adjustment One of several disposition options available to a police officer whereby a juvenile is taken to the police station following a complaint, the contact is recorded, and the juvenile is given an official reprimand and then released to his or her parents or guardians.

status frustration The stress that individuals experience when they cannot attain their goals because of their socioeconomic class.

status offender A juvenile who commits a minor act that is considered illegal only because he or she is underage. Various terms used to refer to status offenders include MINS (minors in need of supervision), CHINS (children in need of supervision), CHINA (children in need of assistance), PINS (persons in need of supervision), FINS (families in need of supervision), and JINS (juveniles in need of supervision).

status offense A nondelinquent/noncriminal offense; an offense that is illegal for underage persons, but not for adults.

Status offenses include curfew violations, incorrigibility, running away, truancy, and underage drinking.

strain theory A theory which proposes that the pressure exerted on youths who cannot attain cultural success goals by the social structure will push them to engage in nonconforming behavior.

structural Marxists A group which argues that the form taken by the legal system in a society can work to reinforce capitalist social relations.

supervision and discipline The parental monitoring, guidance, and control of children's activities and behavior. Unfair and inconsistent supervision and discipline often are associated with delinquency.

surveillance The observation of probationers by probation officers, intended to ensure that probationers comply with the conditions of probation and that they do not break the law.

symbolic interactionist theory A perspective in social psychology that analyzes the process of interaction among human beings at the symbolic level, and which has influenced the development of several social process theories of delinquent behavior.

taking into custody The process of arresting a juvenile for socially unacceptable or unlawful behavior.

teaching family group model A community-based residential program that has had some success with delinquent youths.

teen courts Voluntary nonjudicial forums, also known as youth courts, that keep minor offenders out of the formal justice system.

tertiary prevention Programs directed at the prevention of recidivism among youthful offenders.

theory of differential oppression Robert M. Regoli and John D. Hewitt's view that, in the United States, authority is unjustly used against children, who must adapt to adults' ideas of what constitutes "good children".

training school A correctional facility for the long-term placement of adjudicated juvenile delinquents; may be public (run by a state department of corrections or youth commission) or private.

training school for girls Correctional facility for long-term placement of female juvenile delinquents.

trait-based personality models Theories that attribute delinquent behavior to an individual's basic, inborn personal characteristics.

transactional analysis (TA) A therapy, based on interpreting and evaluating personal relationships, that has proved to be of immediate value to many delinquents. Using catchy language, TA promises delinquents who feel "not OK" that several easy steps can be taken to make them "OK."

transfer The process of certifying a youth over to adult criminal court; takes place by judicial waiver and legislative waiver.

truancy A violation of a compulsory school attendance law. A status offense.

turning point A gradual or dramatic change in the trajectory of an individual's life course.

underage drinking Possession, use, or consumption of alcohol by a minor. A status offense.

Uniform Crime Reports The Federal Bureau of Investigation's annual statistical reports of crimes committed in the United States.

upper age of juvenile court jurisdiction The oldest age at which a juvenile court has original jurisdiction over an individual for law-violating behavior. It must be noted that within most states there are exceptions to the age criteria that place or permit youth at or below the state's upper age of jurisdiction to be under the original jurisdiction of the adult criminal court. For example, in most states if a youth of a certain age is charged with one of a defined list of what are commonly labeled "excluded offenses," the case must originate in the adult criminal court. In addition, in a number of states, the district attorney is given the discretion of filing certain cases either in the juvenile court or in the criminal court. Therefore, while the upper age of jurisdiction is commonly recognized in all states, there are numerous exceptions to age criteria.

utilitarianism A doctrine which holds that the useful is the good, and that the aim of social or political action should be the greatest good for the greatest number.

validity The extent to which a research instrument measures what it says it measures. For example, skeptics question the validity of self-report studies, asking how researchers can be certain that juveniles are being truthful when they fill out self-report questionnaires.

vandalism Destroying or damaging, or attempting to destroy or damage, the property of another without the owner's consent, or destroying or damaging public property (except by burning).

victimization studies Ongoing surveys of crime victims in the United States conducted by the Bureau of Justice Statistics to determine the extent of crime.

violence Forceful physical assault with or without weapons; includes many kinds of fighting, rape, other attacks, gang warfare, and so on.

volunteer programs The use of unpaid adult community members to assist probation officers in a variety of ways.

youth population at risk For delinquency and status offense matters, this is the number of children from age ten through the upper age of juvenile court jurisdiction. In all states, the upper age of jurisdiction is defined by statute. In most states, individuals are considered adults when they reach their eighteenth birthday. Therefore, for these states, the delinquency and status offense youth population at risk would be the number of children ten through seventeen years of age living within the geographical area served by the court.

youth service bureaus (YSBs) Agencies outside the juvenile justice system that were designed to divert children and youths from the justice system by (1) mobilizing community resources to solve youth problems, (2) strengthening existing youth resources and developing new ones, and (3) promoting positive programs to remedy delinquency-generating conditions in the environment.

youth shelter See *shelter care*.

Name Index

Subject Index

Photo Credits

The following license agreement applies *only* to the following Wikipedia material:

Web Interactivity on p. 179: http://en.wikipedia.org/wiki/Differential_association; "Lee Boyd Malvo" in Social World of the Delinquent 13.2 on p. 450: http://en.wikipedia.org/wiki/Lee_Boyd_Malvo; and Web Interactivity on p. 467: http://en.wikipedia.org/wiki/Juvenile_delinquency.

Wikipedia: Text of the GNU Free Documentation License

From Wikipedia, the free encyclopedia

Version 1.2, November 2002

Copyright © 2000, 2001, 2002 Free Software Foundation, Inc.
51 Franklin St, Fifth Floor, Boston, MA 02110-1301 USA
Everyone is permitted to copy and distribute verbatim copies
of this license document, but changing it is not allowed.

0. PREAMBLE

The purpose of this License is to make a manual, textbook, or other functional and useful document "free" in the sense of freedom: to assure everyone the effective freedom to copy and redistribute it, with or without modifying it, either commercially or noncommercially. Secondarily, this License preserves for the author and publisher a way to get credit for their work, while not being considered responsible for modifications made by others.

This License is a kind of "copyleft", which means that derivative works of the document must themselves be free in the same sense. It complements the GNU General Public License, which is a copyleft license designed for free software.

We have designed this License in order to use it for manuals for free software, because free software needs free documentation: a free program should come with manuals providing the same freedoms that the software does. But this License is not limited to software manuals; it can be used for any textual work, regardless of subject matter or whether it is published as a printed book. We recommend this License principally for works whose purpose is instruction or reference.

1. APPLICABILITY AND DEFINITIONS

This License applies to any manual or other work, in any medium, that contains a notice placed by the copyright holder saying it can be distributed under the terms of this License. Such a notice grants a world-wide, royalty-free license, unlimited in duration, to use that work under the conditions stated herein. The "Document", below, refers to any such manual or work. Any member of the public is a licensee, and is addressed as "you". You accept the license if you copy, modify or distribute the work in a way requiring permission under copyright law.

A "Modified Version" of the Document means any work containing the Document or a portion of it, either copied verbatim, or with modifications and/or translated into another language.

A "Secondary Section" is a named appendix or a front-matter section of the Document that deals exclusively with the relationship of the publishers or authors of the Document to the Document's overall subject (or to related matters) and contains nothing that could fall directly within that overall subject. (Thus, if the Document is in part a textbook of mathematics, a Secondary Section may not explain any mathematics.) The relationship could be a matter of historical connection with the subject or with related matters, or of legal, commercial, philosophical, ethical or political position regarding them.

The "Invariant Sections" are certain Secondary Sections whose titles are designated, as being those of Invariant Sections, in the notice that says that the Document is released under this License. If a section does not fit the above definition of Secondary then it is not allowed to be designated as Invariant. The Document may contain zero Invariant Sections. If the Document does not identify any Invariant Sections then there are none.

The "Cover Texts" are certain short passages of text that are listed, as Front-Cover Texts or Back-Cover Texts, in the notice that says that the Document is released under this License. A Front-Cover Text may be at most 5 words, and a Back-Cover Text may be at most 25 words.

A "Transparent" copy of the Document means a machine-readable copy, represented in a format whose specification is available to the general public, that is suitable for revising the document straightforwardly with generic text editors or (for images composed of pixels) generic paint programs or (for drawings) some widely available drawing editor, and that is suitable for input to text formatters or for automatic translation to a variety of formats suitable for input to text formatters. A copy made in an otherwise Transparent file format whose markup, or absence of markup, has been arranged to thwart or discourage subsequent modification by readers is not Transparent. An image format is not Transparent if used for any substantial amount of text. A copy that is not "Transparent" is called "Opaque".

Examples of suitable formats for Transparent copies include plain ASCII without markup, Texinfo input format, LaTeX input format, SGML or XML using a publicly available DTD, and standard-conforming simple HTML, PostScript or PDF designed for human modification. Examples of transparent image formats include PNG, XCF and JPG. Opaque formats include proprietary formats that can be read and edited only by proprietary word processors, SGML or XML for which the DTD and/or processing tools are not generally available, and the machine-generated HTML, PostScript or PDF produced by some word processors for output purposes only.

The "Title Page" means, for a printed book, the title page itself, plus such following pages as are needed to hold, legibly, the material this License requires to appear in the title page. For works in formats which do not have any title page as such, "Title Page" means the text near the most prominent appearance of the work's title, preceding the beginning of the body of the text.

A section "Entitled XYZ" means a named subunit of the Document whose title either is precisely XYZ or contains XYZ in parentheses following text that translates XYZ in another language. (Here XYZ stands for a specific section name mentioned below, such as "Acknowledgements", "Dedications", "Endorsements", or "History".) To "Preserve the Title" of such a section when you modify the Document means that it remains a section "Entitled XYZ" according to this definition.

The Document may include Warranty Disclaimers next to the notice which states that this License applies to the Document. These Warranty Disclaimers are considered to be included by reference in this License, but only as regards disclaiming warranties: any other implication that these Warranty Disclaimers may have is void and has no effect on the meaning of this License.

2. VERBATIM COPYING

You may copy and distribute the Document in any medium, either commercially or noncommercially, provided that this License, the copyright notices, and the license notice saying this License applies to the Document are reproduced in all copies, and that you add no other conditions whatsoever to those of this License. You may not use technical measures to obstruct or control the reading or further copying of the copies you make or distribute. However, you may accept compensation in exchange for copies. If you distribute a large enough number of copies you must also follow the conditions in section 3.

You may also lend copies, under the same conditions stated above, and you may publicly display copies.

3. COPYING IN QUANTITY

If you publish printed copies (or copies in media that commonly have printed covers) of the Document, numbering more than 100, and the Document's license notice requires Cover Texts, you must enclose the copies in covers that carry, clearly and legibly, all these Cover Texts: Front-Cover Texts on the front cover, and Back-Cover Texts on the back cover. Both covers must also clearly and legibly identify you as the publisher of these copies. The front cover must present the full title with all words of the title equally prominent and visible. You may add other material on the covers in addition. Copying with changes limited to the covers, as long as they preserve the title of the Document and satisfy these conditions, can be treated as verbatim copying in other respects.

If the required texts for either cover are too voluminous to fit legibly, you should put the first ones listed (as many as fit reasonably) on the actual cover, and continue the rest onto adjacent pages.

If you publish or distribute Opaque copies of the Document numbering more than 100, you must either include a machine-readable Transparent copy along with each Opaque copy, or state in or with each Opaque copy a computer-network location from which the general network-using public has access to download using public-standard network protocols a complete Transparent copy of the Document, free of added material. If you use the latter option, you must take reasonably prudent steps, when you begin distribution of Opaque copies in quantity, to ensure that this Transparent copy will remain thus accessible at the stated location until at least one year after the last time you distribute an Opaque copy (directly or through your agents or retailers) of that edition to the public.

It is requested, but not required, that you contact the authors of the Document well before redistributing any large number of copies, to give them a chance to provide you with an updated version of the Document.

4. MODIFICATIONS

You may copy and distribute a Modified Version of the Document under the conditions of sections 2 and 3 above, provided that you release the Modified Version under precisely this License, with the Modified Version filling the role of the Document, thus licensing distribution and modification of the Modified Version to whoever possesses a copy of it. In addition, you must do these things in the Modified Version:

- **A.** Use in the Title Page (and on the covers, if any) a title distinct from that of the Document, and from those of previous versions (which should, if there were any, be listed in the History section of the Document). You may use the same title as a previous version if the original publisher of that version gives permission.
- **B.** List on the Title Page, as authors, one or more persons or entities responsible for authorship of the modifications in the Modified Version, together with at least five of the principal authors of the Document (all of its principal authors, if it has fewer than five), unless they release you from this requirement.
- **C.** State on the Title page the name of the publisher of the Modified Version, as the publisher.
- **D.** Preserve all the copyright notices of the Document.
- **E.** Add an appropriate copyright notice for your modifications adjacent to the other copyright notices.
- **F.** Include, immediately after the copyright notices, a license notice giving the public permission to use the Modified Version under the terms of this License, in the form shown in the Addendum below.
- **G.** Preserve in that license notice the full lists of Invariant Sections and required Cover Texts given in the Document's license notice.
- **H.** Include an unaltered copy of this License.
- **I.** Preserve the section Entitled "History", Preserve its Title, and add to it an item stating at least the title, year, new authors, and publisher of the Modified Version as given on the Title Page. If there is no section Entitled "History" in the Document, create one stating the title, year, authors, and publisher of the Document as given on its Title Page, then add an item describing the Modified Version as stated in the previous sentence.
- **J.** Preserve the network location, if any, given in the Document for public access to a Transparent copy of the Document, and likewise the network locations given in the Document for previous versions it was based on. These may be placed in the "History" section. You may omit a network location for a work that was published at least four years before the Document itself, or if the original publisher of the version it refers to gives permission.
- **K.** For any section Entitled "Acknowledgements" or "Dedications", Preserve the Title of the section, and preserve in the section all the substance and tone of each of the contributor acknowledgements and/or dedications given therein.
- **L.** Preserve all the Invariant Sections of the Document, unaltered in their text and in their titles. Section numbers or the equivalent are not considered part of the section titles.
- **M.** Delete any section Entitled "Endorsements". Such a section may not be included in the Modified Version.
- **N.** Do not retitle any existing section to be Entitled "Endorsements" or to conflict in title with any Invariant Section.
- **O.** Preserve any Warranty Disclaimers.

If the Modified Version includes new front-matter sections or appendices that qualify as Secondary Sections and contain no material copied from the Document, you may at your option designate some or all of these sections as invariant. To do this, add their titles to the list of Invariant Sections in the Modified Version's license notice. These titles must be distinct from any other section titles.

You may add a section Entitled "Endorsements", provided it contains nothing but endorsements of your Modified Version by various parties—for example, statements of peer review or that the text has been approved by an organization as the authoritative definition of a standard.

You may add a passage of up to five words as a Front-Cover Text, and a passage of up to 25 words as a Back-Cover Text, to the end of the list of Cover Texts in the Modified Version. Only one passage of Front-Cover Text and one of Back-Cover Text may be added by (or through arrangements made by) any one entity. If the Document already includes a cover text for the same cover, previously added by you or by arrangement made by the same entity you are acting on behalf of, you may not add another; but you may replace the old one, on explicit permission from the previous publisher that added the old one.

The author(s) and publisher(s) of the Document do not by this License give permission to use their names for publicity for or to assert or imply endorsement of any Modified Version.

5. COMBINING DOCUMENTS

You may combine the Document with other documents released under this License, under the terms defined in section 4 above for modified versions, provided that you include in the combination all of the Invariant Sections of all of the original documents, unmodified, and list them all as Invariant Sections of your combined work in its license notice, and that you preserve all their Warranty Disclaimers.

The combined work need only contain one copy of this License, and multiple identical Invariant Sections may be replaced with a single copy. If there are multiple Invariant Sections with the same name but different contents, make the title of each such section unique by adding at the end of it, in parentheses, the name of the original author or publisher of that section if known, or else a unique number. Make the same adjustment to the section titles in the list of Invariant Sections in the license notice of the combined work.

In the combination, you must combine any sections Entitled "History" in the various original documents, forming one section Entitled "History"; likewise combine any sections Entitled "Acknowledgements", and any sections Entitled "Dedications". You must delete all sections Entitled "Endorsements."

6. COLLECTIONS OF DOCUMENTS

You may make a collection consisting of the Document and other documents released under this License, and replace the individual copies of this License in the various documents with a single copy that is included in the collection, provided that you follow the rules of this License for verbatim copying of each of the documents in all other respects.

You may extract a single document from such a collection, and distribute it individually under this License, provided you insert a copy of this License into the extracted document, and follow this License in all other respects regarding verbatim copying of that document.

7. AGGREGATION WITH INDEPENDENT WORKS

A compilation of the Document or its derivatives with other separate and independent documents or works, in or on a volume of a storage or distribution medium, is called an "aggregate" if the copyright resulting from the compilation is not used to limit the legal rights of the compilation's users beyond what the individual works permit. When the Document is included in an aggregate, this License does not apply to the other works in the aggregate which are not themselves derivative works of the Document.

If the Cover Text requirement of section 3 is applicable to these copies of the Document, then if the Document is less than one half of the entire aggregate, the Document's Cover Texts may be placed on covers that bracket the Document within the aggregate, or the electronic equivalent of covers if the Document is in electronic form. Otherwise they must appear on printed covers that bracket the whole aggregate.

8. TRANSLATION

Translation is considered a kind of modification, so you may distribute translations of the Document under the terms of section 4. Replacing Invariant Sections with translations requires special permission from their copyright holders, but you may include translations of some or all Invariant Sections in addition to the original versions of these Invariant Sections. You may include a translation of this License, and all the license notices in the Document, and any Warranty Disclaimers, provided that you also include the original English version of this License and the original versions of those notices and disclaimers. In case of a disagreement between the translation and the original version of this License or a notice or disclaimer, the original version will prevail.

If a section in the Document is Entitled "Acknowledgements", "Dedications", or "History", the requirement (section 4) to Preserve its Title (section 1) will typically require changing the actual title.

9. TERMINATION

You may not copy, modify, sublicense, or distribute the Document except as expressly provided for under this License. Any other attempt to copy, modify, sublicense or distribute the Document is void, and will automatically terminate your rights under this License. However, parties who have received copies, or rights, from you under this License will not have their licenses terminated so long as such parties remain in full compliance.

10. FUTURE REVISIONS OF THIS LICENSE

The Free Software Foundation may publish new, revised versions of the GNU Free Documentation License from time to time. Such new versions will be similar in spirit to the present version, but may differ in detail to address new problems or concerns. See http://www.gnu.org/copyleft/.

Each version of the License is given a distinguishing version number. If the Document specifies that a particular numbered version of this License "or any later version" applies to it, you have the option of following the terms and conditions either of that specified version or of any later version that has been published (not as a draft) by the Free Software Foundation. If the Document does not specify a version number of this License, you may choose any version ever published (not as a draft) by the Free Software Foundation.